Florida

Nick Selby

Corinna Selby

LONELY PLANET PUBLICATIONS
Melbourne • Oakland • London • Paris

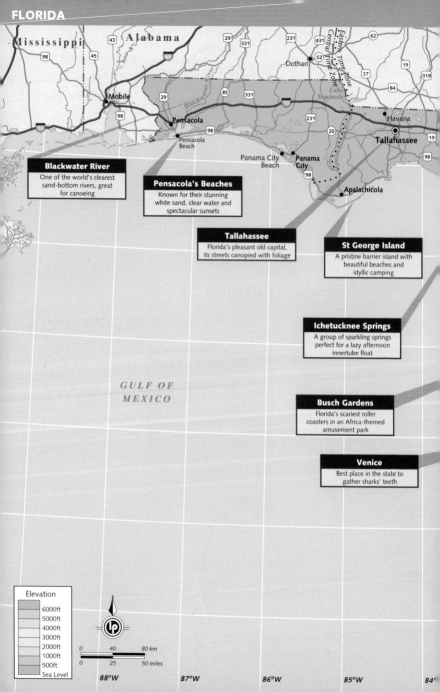

Blackwater River
One of the world's clearest sand-bottom rivers, great for canoeing

Pensacola's Beaches
Known for their stunning white sand, clear water and spectacular sunsets

Tallahassee
Florida's pleasant old capital, its streets canopied with foliage

St George Island
A pristine barrier island with beautiful beaches and idyllic camping

Ichetucknee Springs
A group of sparkling springs perfect for a lazy afternoon innertube float

Busch Gardens
Florida's scariest roller coasters in an Africa-themed amusement park

Venice
Best place in the state to gather sharks' teeth

Mississippi

Alabama

Dothan

Mobile

Pensacola

Pensacola Beach

Panama City Beach

Panama City

Apalachicola

Havana

Tallahassee

GULF OF MEXICO

Elevation
6000ft
5000ft
4000ft
3000ft
2000ft
1000ft
500ft
Sea Level

0   40   80 km
0   25   50 miles

88°W   87°W   86°W   85°W   84°

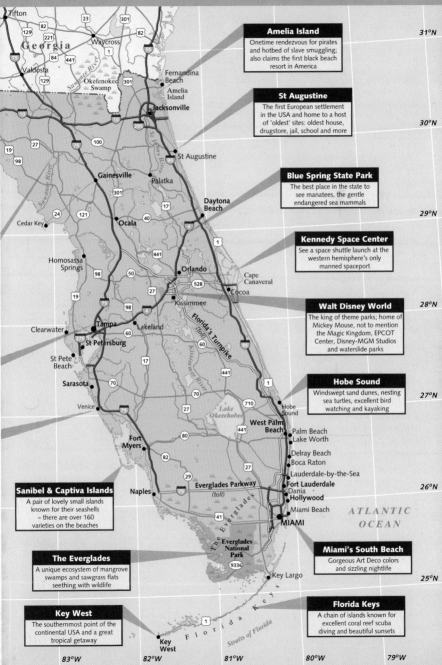

FLORIDA

Amelia Island
Onetime rendezvous for pirates and hotbed of slave smuggling; also claims the first black beach resort in America

St Augustine
The first European settlement in the USA and home to a host of 'oldest' sites: oldest house, drugstore, jail, school and more

Blue Spring State Park
The best place in the state to see manatees, the gentle endangered sea mammals

Kennedy Space Center
See a space shuttle launch at the western hemisphere's only manned spaceport

Walt Disney World
The king of theme parks; home of Mickey Mouse, not to mention the Magic Kingdom, EPCOT Center, Disney-MGM Studios and waterslide parks

Hobe Sound
Windswept sand dunes, nesting sea turtles, excellent bird watching and kayaking

Sanibel & Captiva Islands
A pair of lovely small islands known for their seashells – there are over 160 varieties on the beaches

Miami's South Beach
Gorgeous Art Deco colors and sizzling nightlife

The Everglades
A unique ecosystem of mangrove swamps and sawgrass flats seething with wildlife

Key West
The southernmost point of the continental USA and a great tropical getaway

Florida Keys
A chain of islands known for excellent coral reef scuba diving and beautiful sunsets

31°N
30°N
29°N
28°N
27°N
26°N
25°N

Georgia

Tifton
Waycross
Valdosta
Okefenokee Swamp
Fernandina Beach
Amelia Island
Jacksonville
St Augustine
Gainesville
Palatka
Daytona Beach
Cedar Key
Ocala
Homosassa Springs
Orlando
Cape Canaveral
Cocoa
Kissimmee
Clearwater
Tampa
Lakeland
St Petersburg
St Pete Beach
Sarasota
Venice
Florida's Turnpike
Kissimmee River
Hobe Sound
West Palm Beach
Palm Beach
Lake Worth
Delray Beach
Boca Raton
Lauderdale-by-the-Sea
Fort Lauderdale
Dania
Hollywood
Miami Beach
MIAMI
Fort Myers
Naples
Everglades Parkway (toll)
Lake Okeechobee
The Everglades
Everglades National Park
Key Largo
Key West
Florida Keys
Straits of Florida

ATLANTIC OCEAN

83°W   82°W   81°W   80°W   79°W

Florida
2nd edition – January 2000
First published – January 1997

Published by
Lonely Planet Publications Pty Ltd ABN 36 005 607 983
90 Maribyrnong St, Footscray, Victoria 3011, Australia

Lonely Planet Offices
Australia Locked Bag 1, Footscray, Victoria 3011
USA 150 Linden St, Oakland, CA 94607
UK 10a Spring Place, London NW5 3BH
France 1 rue du Dahomey, 75011 Paris

Photographs
Many of the images in this guide are available for licensing from
Lonely Planet Images.
w www.lonelyplanetimages.com

Front cover photograph
Manatees (Brandon D Cole)

ISBN 0 86442 745 X

text & maps © Lonely Planet Publications Pty Ltd 2000
photos © photographers as indicated 2000
climate charts compiled from information supplied by Patrick J Tyson,
© Patrick J Tyson, 2000

Printed by The Bookmaker International Ltd
Printed in China

SPACE COAST   409

NORTHEAST FLORIDA   427

SOUTHWEST FLORIDA   479

NORTHWEST FLORIDA & THE PANHANDLE   555

ACKNOWLEDGMENTS   605

INDEX   611

MAP LEGEND   624

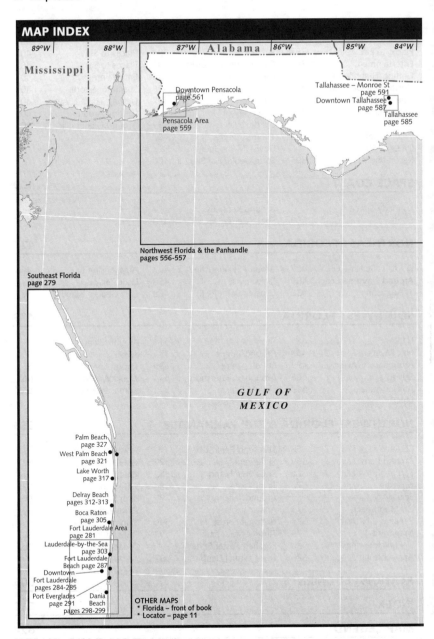

MAP INDEX

89°W   88°W   87°W   **Alabama**   86°W   85°W   84°W

Mississippi

Downtown Pensacola
page 561

Tallahassee – Monroe St
page 591

Downtown Tallahassee
page 587

Tallahassee
page 585

Pensacola Area
page 559

Northwest Florida & the Panhandle
pages 556-557

Southeast Florida
page 279

Palm Beach
page 327

West Palm Beach
page 321

Lake Worth
page 317

Delray Beach
pages 312-313

Boca Raton
page 305

Fort Lauderdale Area
page 281

Lauderdale-by-the-Sea
page 303

Fort Lauderdale
Beach page 287

Downtown
Fort Lauderdale
pages 284-285

Port Everglades
page 291

Dania
Beach
pages 298-299

**GULF OF
MEXICO**

OTHER MAPS
* Florida – front of book
* Locator – page 11

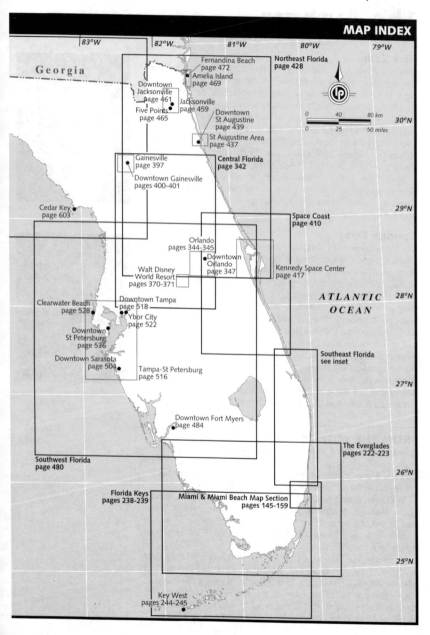

MAP INDEX

83°W 82°W 81°W 80°W 79°W

Georgia

Fernandina Beach
page 472

Amelia Island
page 469

Northeast Florida
page 428

0   40   80 km
0   25   50 miles

30°N

Downtown
Jacksonville
page 461

Jacksonville
page 459

Five Points
page 465

Downtown
St Augustine
page 439

St Augustine Area
page 437

Gainesville
page 397

Central Florida
page 342

Downtown Gainesville
pages 400-401

Cedar Key
page 603

29°N

Space Coast
page 410

Orlando
pages 344-345

Downtown
Orlando
page 347

Walt Disney
World Resort
pages 370-371

Kennedy Space Center
page 417

ATLANTIC
OCEAN

28°N

Clearwater Beach
page 528

Downtown Tampa
page 518

Ybor City
page 522

Downtown
St Petersburg
page 536

Downtown Sarasota
page 504

Tampa-St Petersburg
page 516

Southeast Florida
see inset

27°N

Downtown Fort Myers
page 484

The Everglades
pages 222-223

Southwest Florida
page 480

26°N

Florida Keys
pages 238-239

Miami & Miami Beach Map Section
pages 145-159

25°N

Key West
pages 244-245

The Authors

Nick Selby

Nick Selby was born and raised in New York City. Escaping from sound engineering (he recorded rap 'music' at Walker & Six Recording and Chung King in New York; connected *Mofo the Psychic Gorilla* for Penn & Teller's Broadway show; and worked hauling cables and 'mixing' 'music' on *As the World Turns* and *Guiding Light*, as well as sound for CBS Sports), Nick moved to Poland in 1990 and DJ'd at Radio Zet, Warsaw's first independent radio station. He moved to Russia in late 1991, where he wrote *The Visitor's Guide to the New St Petersburg*.

Since then, Nick has been traveling and working for Lonely Planet on a positively bizarre group of destinations including *Brazil*, *Germany*, *Russia*, *Texas* and *St Petersburg*. He and his wife, Corinna, now live in Munich, Germany.

Corinna Selby

Corinna Selby was born and raised in Munich. As soon as she could afford it, she set out traveling through Europe and spent a year in Portugal. After making more money back home, Corinna traveled to Southeast Asia, where she spent the next two years traveling. When she wasn't working as an English teacher in Tainan, Taiwan, as a sunglass merchant in Thailand or as an art merchant in Japan, she spent her time perfecting her suntan on the beaches of the Philippines and studying the local flora.

Corinna returned to Germany to get her degree in English and Spanish translations and to work for Munich's *Süddeutsche Zeitung*. After graduation, she traveled to Eastern Europe, Russia, Cuba, back through Asia, down to Australia, and up to the USA. She and Nick have settled in Europe, but who knows what's next.

Corinna is the co-author of Lonely Planet's *Miami* guide.

FROM THE AUTHORS

Thanks first to Peter and Lorraine and Maddie and Grace, John Noble and Susan Forsyth, and Marlies Arnold for rearranging their lives and homes to help us arrange ours so we could write this book. Thanks as well to Kate Hoffman and to Tom Brosnahan.

In Florida, thanks to Doug Luciani and the staff at Visit Florida, Lorna Meehan, Maran Hilgendorf and The Conservancy, Laura Hildebrand, Michelle Rose, Floyd and Susan Creamer, Roxanne Escobales, Jeanne Sullivan and the Miami CVB, CVB personnel throughout the state, and John Casey.

Thanks also to Duncan, Cathy and Phil, and Ada and Doug. And in Miami, thanks yet again to Eugene Patron and Joe Thomas and Melanie Morningstar. Thank you, Kees, for keeping Nick in one piece. Also thanks, as last time, to the mysterious Architect X for Deco assistance, the staff of Books & Books, and Les Standiford for literature information. And thanks, of course, to Angela Wilson.

This Book

The 1st edition of *Florida* was researched and written by Nick and Corinna Selby.

FROM THE PUBLISHER

This 2nd edition of *Florida* was whipped into shape by Lonely Planet's US left coast office. Suki Gear and Rebecca Northen edited the book, with help from Don Root. Brigitte Barta was the sage and helped keep the project rolling smoothly. Julie Connery, Karla Huebner, Kevin Anglin, Suki and Rebecca proofread. Ken DellaPenta maintained his status as our favorite indexer.

Cartographic wizards Ivy Feibelman and Sean Brandt created and fine-tuned all the maps, with help from Chris Gillis, Lori (Guphy) Gustafson, Darin Jensen, Monica Lepe and Kimberly Moses, and with guidance from Amy Dennis.

Layout and design was skillfully undertaken by Henia Miedzinski, with help from Ruth Askevold. Shelley Firth created the bright and lovely color pages. Rini Keagy designed the wet and wonderful cover. The illustrations were crafted by Shelley, Hugh D'Andrade, John Fadeff, Hayden Foell, Jennifer Steffey, Jim Swanson and Wendy Yanagihara. Margaret Livingston and Susan Rimerman did a fine job of shepherding the design crew and directing the layout process.

THANKS
Many thanks to the travelers who used the last edition and wrote to us with helpful hints, advice and interesting anecdotes. Your names appear in the back of this book.

Foreword

ABOUT LONELY PLANET GUIDEBOOKS

The story begins with a classic travel adventure: Tony and Maureen Wheeler's 1972 journey across Europe and Asia to Australia. Useful information about the overland trail did not exist at that time, so Tony and Maureen published the first Lonely Planet guidebook to meet a growing need.

From a kitchen table, then from a tiny office in Melbourne (Australia), Lonely Planet has become the largest independent travel publisher in the world, an international company with offices in Melbourne, Oakland (USA), London (UK) and Paris (France).

Today Lonely Planet guidebooks cover the globe. There is an ever-growing list of books, and there's information in a variety of forms and media. Some things haven't changed. The main aim is still to help make it possible for adventurous travelers to get out there – to explore and better understand the world.

At Lonely Planet we believe travelers can make a positive contribution to the countries they visit – if they respect their host communities and spend their money wisely. Since 1986 a percentage of the income from each book has been donated to aid projects and human-rights campaigns.

Updates Lonely Planet thoroughly updates each guidebook as often as possible. This usually means there are around two years between editions, although for more unusual or more stable destinations the gap can be longer. Check the imprint page (following the color map at the beginning of the book) for publication dates.

Between editions, up-to-date information is available in two free newsletters – the paper *Planet Talk* and email *Comet* (to subscribe, contact any Lonely Planet office) – and on our website at www.lonelyplanet.com. The *Upgrades* section of the website covers a number of important and volatile destinations and is regularly updated by Lonely Planet authors. *Scoop* covers news and current affairs relevant to travelers. And, lastly, the *Thorn Tree* bulletin board and *Postcards* section of the site carry unverified, but fascinating, reports from travelers.

Correspondence The process of creating new editions begins with the letters, postcards and emails received from travelers. This correspondence often includes suggestions, criticisms and comments about the current editions. Interesting excerpts are immediately passed on via newsletters and the website, and everything goes to our authors to be verified when they're researching on the road. We're keen to get more feedback from organizations or individuals who represent communities visited by travelers.

Lonely Planet gathers information for everyone who's curious about the planet – and especially for those who explore it firsthand. Through guidebooks, phrasebooks, activity guides, maps, literature, newsletters, image library, TV series and website, we act as an information exchange for a worldwide community of travelers.

Research Authors aim to gather sufficient practical information to enable travelers to make informed choices and to make the mechanics of a journey run smoothly. They also research historical and cultural background to help enrich the travel experience and allow travelers to understand and respond appropriately to cultural and environmental issues.

Authors don't stay in every hotel because that would mean spending a couple of months in each medium-size city and, no, they don't eat at every restaurant because that would mean stretching belts beyond capacity. They do visit hotels and restaurants to check standards and prices, but feedback based on readers' direct experiences can be very helpful.

Many of our authors work undercover; others aren't so secretive. None of them accept freebies in exchange for positive write-ups. And none of our guidebooks contain any advertising.

Production Authors submit their raw manuscripts and maps to offices in Australia, the USA, the UK or France. Editors and cartographers – all experienced travelers themselves – then begin the process of assembling the pieces. When the book finally hits the shops, some things are already out of date, we start getting feedback from readers and the process begins again....

WARNING & REQUEST

Things change – prices go up, schedules change, good places go bad and bad places go bankrupt – nothing stays the same. So, if you find things better or worse, recently opened or long since closed, please tell us and help make the next edition even more accurate and useful. We genuinely value all the feedback we receive. A well-traveled team reads and acknowledges every letter, postcard and email and ensures that every morsel of information finds its way to the appropriate authors, editors and cartographers for verification.

Everyone who writes to us will find their name listed in the next edition of the appropriate guidebook. They will also receive the latest issue of *Planet Talk*, our quarterly printed newsletter, or *Comet*, our monthly email newsletter. Subscriptions to both newsletters are free. The very best contributions will be rewarded with a free guidebook.

We may edit, reproduce and incorporate your comments in all Lonely Planet products, such as guidebooks, Web sites and digital products, so let us know if you don't want your comments reproduced or your name acknowledged.

Send all correspondence to the Lonely Planet office closest to you:

Australia: Locked Bag 1, Footscray, Victoria 3011
USA: 150 Linden St, Oakland, CA 94607
UK: 10a Spring Place, London NW5 3BH
France: 1 rue du Dahomey, 75011 Paris

Or email us at: talk2us@lonelyplanet.com.au

For news, views and updates, see our Web site: www.lonelyplanet.com

HOW TO USE A LONELY PLANET GUIDEBOOK

The best way to use a Lonely Planet guidebook is any way you choose. At Lonely Planet, we believe the most memorable travel experiences are often those that are unexpected, and the finest discoveries are those you make yourself. Guidebooks are not intended to be used as if they provided a detailed set of infallible instructions!

Contents All Lonely Planet guidebooks follow the same format. The Facts about the Country chapters or sections give background information ranging from history to weather. Facts for the Visitor gives practical information on issues like visas and health. Getting There & Away gives a brief starting point for researching travel to and from the destination. Getting Around gives an overview of the transport options available when you arrive.

The peculiar demands of each destination determine how subsequent chapters are broken up, but some things remain constant. We always start with background, then proceed to sights, places to stay, places to eat, entertainment, getting there and away, and getting around information – in that order.

Heading Hierarchy Lonely Planet headings are used in a strict hierarchical structure that can be visualized as a set of Russian dolls. Each heading (and its following text) is encompassed by any preceding heading that is higher on the hierarchical ladder.

Entry Points We do not assume guidebooks will be read from beginning to end, but that people will dip into them. The traditional entry points are the list of contents and the index. In addition, however, some books have a complete list of maps and an index map illustrating map coverage.

There may also be a color map that shows highlights. These highlights are dealt with in greater detail later in the book, along with planning questions and suggested itineraries. Each chapter covering a geographical region usually begins with a locator map and another list of highlights. Once you find something of interest in a list of highlights, turn to the index.

Maps Maps play a crucial role in Lonely Planet guidebooks and include a huge amount of information. A legend is printed on the back page. We seek to have complete consistency between maps and text, and to have every important place in the text captured on a map. Map key numbers usually start in the top left corner.

Although inclusion in a guidebook usually implies a recommendation, we cannot list every good place. Exclusion does not necessarily imply criticism. In fact, there are a number of reasons why we might exclude a place – sometimes it is simply inappropriate to encourage an influx of travelers.

2   Contents

Contents

Introduction

For a destination known throughout the world for its beaches and theme parks, the 'real' Florida astounds those who set out to find it. On just the other side of massive attractions such as Walt Disney World, Miami's South Beach and the Kennedy Space Center, some of the most beautiful, rugged, challenging and bizarre natural attractions in the USA await travelers.

And it's accessible. The real Florida is where you'll be if you stay on the turnpike one extra exit in any direction from Orlando, Miami, Tampa or any major city – off the beaten path in a state where a designated historic district can be as young as 50 years old or older than 400. You *can* get away from tourist traps in a state that was developed specifically for tourists, and be off on your own in the land of crackers, anglers and alligators, manatees and mangroves, sinkholes, springs and swamps.

The first European settlement in the New World was right here in St Augustine, founded by the Spanish in 1565, and over the next 300 years Florida found itself at the epicenter of a struggle for control of the New World. With British to the north and French to the west, the world's three superpowers skirmished constantly – and when America became a power of its own, it too joined the fight over the continent's tropical paradise.

In the end, Florida was ceded to the USA by a Spain that was taking beatings around the world, one of the last feathers in the cap of a now-creaky superpower has-been. It was Spain's fault, really, for not attempting to settle the area more aggressively. If the Spanish had gotten out and explored the

territory they'd lucked onto, they never would have let it go.

Florida's settlement was accomplished only after American money was offered by developers to lure enough workers to battle the state's desperately difficult terrain, and after the army had thoroughly dispossessed the Native Americans who had called the territory home. Throughout the late 19th and early 20th centuries, certain groups of these Indians gave US Army Indian fighters a run for their money – and to this day, the Seminole people have never officially surrendered.

The contrast between nature and development in Florida is shocking, but the horrifying construction of high-rise developments and water-sucking, sprawling golf courses is offset by easily accessible spots of such lush beauty you wouldn't be surprised if Ricardo Montalban popped out from behind a palm tree and handed you a piña colada in a hula glass.

The theme parks of central and southwest Florida set the worldwide standard and are the primary reason the state has become so popular with international travelers. And down on Miami's South Beach, arguably the world's hippest photo backdrop, the mix of communities – straight and gay, white and Latino, fabulous models and barrel-bellied central Europeans – gives the place a feeling of tolerance that is refreshing to anyone. Add great diving along the Keys' coral reefs; eco-tourism in the Everglades' mangrove swamps and sawgrass flats; rafting, tubing, boating and every other conceivable water sport in the Atlantic Ocean, Gulf of Mexico, and Florida's 30,000 rivers and lakes, and Florida is an easy place to promote.

Reports of violence and mayhem from the early 1990s, combined with a lack of information about the state's interior, scared visitors away for years. That was a mistake. With spring-fed rivers so clear you can easily make out details 60 feet under water, pristine state parks and wonderfully weird tourist attractions as goofy as anything Disney could dream up, the real Florida is truly where the action is. Goofy? You bet. Head for psychic fulfillment at Cassadaga, the nation's only township made up entirely of spiritualists. Or look into the rich history of a different type of fulfillment at one of the nation's only bordello museums in Yahoo Junction (that's right, *Yahoo Junction*). See an underwater performance of dancing mermaids and mermen at Weeki Watchee Springs (yes, *Weeki Watchee*). Watch residents of a state that saw about as much action as Wisconsin in the Civil War stage fantastically complex Civil War reenactments. And grab a bag of Bull's potato chips in the city of Spuds (uh-huh, *Spuds*).

So when your last nerve is trounced by a bright-faced French teenager in a fur suit urging you to 'have a Disney day' (they really say that), it's nice to know that even in the heart of Walt Disney World, the real Florida is as close as a 40-minute drive away.

Facts about Florida

HISTORY
Early Inhabitants

Discounting beguiling theories of direct transpacific crossings from Southeast Asia, historians now believe that, bar a few Vikings in the north, the pre-Hispanic inhabitants of the Americas arrived from Siberia in waves of migrations between about 60,000 and 8000 BC, crossing land now submerged beneath the Bering Strait. The earliest known human traces in the US date from about 50,000 BC.

These tribes were highly mobile and, once they crossed into Alaska, moved south to warmer climates.

While there was settlement throughout Florida, the highest concentration of groups was in the coastal areas, as it remains today. In the late Archaic period, about 3000 BC, populations were heaviest in the Panhandle, northeast and southwest portions of the state and around present-day Tampa. Shell middens (mounds) are evidence of settlements, created from the shells of snails, mussels and oysters in such riotous abundance one wonders how it was possible to eat that many shellfish. Seeing it for yourself is the only way to get a grasp on the quantities. See the Southwest Florida chapter for information on Mound Key, whose shell mounds reach heights of 30 feet and were dense enough to provide the foundation for an entire village.

By 600 to 500 BC, more defined cultures began to develop ceramic, shell and copper items; in the northeast of the state, the St John's River villages had sand burial mounds and highly developed village life that for the first time showed signs of dependence on agriculture – corn – as opposed to hunting.

Indian Peoples

Because little written history exists of the various groups of Florida natives, most information comes from the period after European settlement. But it seems clear that by the time the first Europeans arrived in the 16th century, several distinct groups of Indians had settled in the region.

The largest northern group were the Timucuan, described as being very tall (it is said that height was inbred, by mating the tallest males and females) and very beautiful. (If we can believe the illustrations by early Spanish explorers, the men were handsome and the women stunning – but they sure do look white, so these pictures must be taken with a grain of salt.)

The 20,000 or so Calusa were the largest group on the southwest part of the peninsula. There's tantalizing speculation as to the origin of the Calusa's hatred of the Spaniards, which suggests contact earlier than is recorded, but one thing is clear: the Calusa didn't much care for the Spanish and were highly demonstrative of their animosity.

Other groups included the Tequesta, who lived at the southern tip of the peninsula between the 10,000 Islands and present-day Miami; Ais and Jeaga, on the southeast coast; Tocobaga, on the Gulf Coast north of the Calusa; and the 25,000 Apalachee who occupied the eastern end of the Panhandle.

Spanish Exploration

Juan Ponce de León, an explorer who had sailed on Christopher Columbus' second voyage (1493) and had taken part in the Spanish siege of Puerto Rico (1506-7), sailed northwest from Spanish settlements in the Caribbean and wound up running smack into central Florida's Atlantic coastline in 1513, probably near present-day Cape Canaveral. In honor of Pascua Florida, the Easter Feast of Flowers, Ponce de León named this new land Florida.

Ponce de León didn't see anyone on the shore of what he thought was an island, but he claimed the land for Spain just in case and then tried to sail around it. After making his way around the Florida Keys, he ended up at San Carlos, near present-day

Who Were the Seminole?

The native group with the most name recognition in Florida, the Seminole, was not a single tribe, nor did it exist when the first Europeans landed in Florida. Instead, the Seminole began as a collection of breakaways from other Indian tribes as well as runaways – slaves and others.

The name Seminole is a tricky one: the Florida Department of State says it derives from the Spanish *cimarrone*, while most historical texts claim it was a Creek Indian word *sim-in-ole* or *sem-in-ole*; in any case, in both languages it means 'wild one' or 'runaway' or even 'one who camps at a distance,' and reflects the origins of the Seminole nation.

The Muskhogean Indians once existed all around the Gulf Coast of the present-day USA. A subgroup, the Creek Confederacy, settled in Georgia and Alabama and had gained in number and strength by the turn of the 19th century, when skirmishes with the ever-encroaching Americans escalated into mass killings on both sides. Andrew Jackson enlisted the help of the American-friendly Lower Creeks against the Upper Creeks in the Battle of Horseshoe Bend on March 27, 1814, and all but wiped them out. The surviving Red Sticks, a faction of the Upper Creeks, escaped south into still-Spanish Florida, where they were joined by other groups of Indians escaping similar treatment. The Seminole welcomed them, as well as runaway slaves, with open arms.

All these groups eventually became the Seminole and Miccosukee nations, and though technically in Spanish territory, they were far from safe from Andrew Jackson's purges. Partly in the interest of reclaiming escaped black slaves living among the Seminole, the Americans continued to pursue the Indians across the border. See Seminole Wars later in this chapter.

Tampa, where he was welcomed by the Calusa with arms – not open ones, just arms.

The Calusa attacked until he sailed away, but Ponce de León had discovered a good source of fresh water and, he presumed, a line on all the riches the area undoubtedly held. He returned to Spain, and on the way he discovered the arid keys west of Key West and named them *Las Tortugas* for the huge numbers of turtles there (see Dry Tortugas in the Florida Keys chapter).

King Ferdinand V named Ponce de León governor of Florida in 1514. Ponce de León was unable to return to the land until 1521, when he brought settlers, animals and missionaries back to San Carlos. You can guess what the Calusa did. Ponce de León died shortly thereafter in Cuba from a poison-arrow wound. But this did not discourage

the Spanish, who were convinced – based on their experiences in South America and the recent discoveries in Mexico – that Florida was a land of untold mineral wealth.

After Ponce de León's death, several other attempts were made by the Spanish to suss out just what it was that Florida (the area now encompassing much of the present-day southeastern USA) had to offer. Attempts were made by the feckless Pánfilo de Narváez, who blew it in 1528 and lost everything – four ships, 400 men (including himself) and 80 horses. Despite the disaster, much understanding about the land was gained from the diaries of Narváez's treasurer, Núñez Cabeza de Vaca, who survived among the Indians for eight years before rejoining his own people in Mexico City. Considerably more successful was the

4000-some-odd-mile expedition by Hernando de Soto in 1539. De Soto explored a huge area of the southeastern USA, and when he died in 1542, he was buried in the Mississippi River.

The French & British Sniff Around

Over the next 20 years, the Spanish were still unable to make a permanent settlement in Florida. Meanwhile, the British and French were sniffing around the region, looking for minerals and possible colonial lands.

Despite the Spanish claim on the region, the French arrived in 1562 under the command of Jean Ribault and established a colony on Parris Island, at the southern end of present-day South Carolina. It failed, and Ribault's deputy, René de Laudonnière, pushed on to establish Fort Caroline in 1564 on the St John's River near present-day Jacksonville.

Never one to let the French pull a fast one, Spain's King Philip II sent Pedro Menéndez de Avilés to stomp the French and establish a fort of his own. In 1565 Menéndez arrived at Cape Canaveral with about 1500 soldiers and settlers. They made their way north and established St Augustine, named for the day on which they arrived on the Florida coast, August 28, the Feast Day of Saint Augustine, Bishop of Hippo. St Augustine was established on September 4 – the USA's first permanent European settlement.

Menéndez and his troops headed north, where they were whupped by the French; the Spaniards retreated south to St Augustine. Soon after, the French, in an effort to fight *fuego* with *feu*, launched a fleet to take on the pesky Spaniards. But the French fell victim to one of Florida's famous coastal storms, and their fleet was destroyed. Menéndez, always optimistic, immediately forged north to the relatively unpopulated French fort and destroyed it. Menéndez executed all prisoners, as well as survivors from the French fleet washed ashore south of St Augustine. In all, almost 600 were butchered, giving the inlet its name: *matanzas*, or slaughter.

And so a full 50 years before the Pilgrims lurched up to Plymouth Rock, and 40 before even the establishment at Jamestown, Florida was finally settled for the Spanish by Menéndez.

Florida would become to North America what Poland is to Europe: the flattest piece of land between battling superpowers. Before it was ceded to the USA by Spain in 1821, the area was occupied by several armies – a total of eight flags have flown over Amelia Island.

A Good Christian Colony

In addition to chasing away Frenchmen and seeking to get rich, Menéndez also sought to convert the Indians to Christianity and generally show them what swell folks the Spanish were. His goal was to establish a territory-wide series of missions, forts and trade posts.

All did not go as planned. Missionaries were murdered, and Indian uprisings became as common as one would expect when a new force comes in and tells you everything you believe in is wrong, and in any case it belongs to them. To make matters worse, in 1568 a new bunch of Frenchmen showed up to avenge the deaths at Fort Caroline; they were assisted by turncoat Timucuans, who led them right into the fort.

Menéndez regained control of the situation in a method still common today: he threw money and people at it. He tidied up problems that were delaying his supply lines from Cuba, and offered highly attractive conditions to settlers, who came in droves. St Augustine became a bustling and wealthy trading town.

The French & British in North America

In the late 16th century, the French and British were both making overtures to settle the New World, or at least keep their hands in. In 1584, Elizabeth I granted Sir Walter Raleigh a charter to settle lands in North America. His colony, on Roanoke

Island in North Carolina's Outer Banks, is remembered today as the Lost Colony for the mysterious disappearance of its settlers.

Meanwhile, Spanish St Augustine was under constant pressure from the Brits: the city was attacked and burned by troops led by Sir Francis Drake in 1586. Later, in 1702, the British returned and attacked the city for 52 days, burning it down – but the Castillo de San Marcos fort held. (See St Augustine in the Northeast Florida chapter.)

The Jamestown, Virginia settlement of 1607 (which generally gets Anglocentric textbook honors for being the first European settlement in the New World, despite St Augustine) was a problem-plagued English colony. Half the party died during its first winter.

Meanwhile, the French were wondering how to get their hands on the Louisiana Territory, which they would claim in the late 17th century.

That's Dedication

When the first Europeans arrived in Florida, they could not have imagined a less welcoming place. Aside from hostile natives and the unforgiving heat, the land itself was swampy, overgrown and fraught with dangers. Early settlers had to contend with alligators, poisonous snakes, thick undergrowth and vegetation, and perhaps worst of all, biting insects in such prodigious quantities the explorers wondered if they had arrived in hell.

As settlers pushed southward in Florida, workers related stories about black clouds of mosquitoes swarming from sunrise to sunset. And the swamp-like conditions throughout the state, especially in the south, made reclaiming land a nightmare.

As we look at Florida today, with its winding ribbons of asphalt and urban sprawl, it's easy to forget just how recently much of the state was uninhabitable by any but the most dedicated backwoods travelers.

From Settlement to Colony

St Augustine grew, and life gained a degree of normalcy. Even the original missionary activities were starting to work, and Spain was forging relations with Indians throughout the territory. With a few notable exceptions near the turn of the 17th century, including rebellions by Guale and Ais Indians, Florida was humming right along. It was still a very dangerous place, fraught with the peril of Indian or European attacks, fires set either by invading armies or drunken card players, and a sense that it could all end at a moment's notice.

The population of St Augustine was mainly soldiers and traders, and the city limits at the time were far smaller than they are today. As the Indians and settlers began to pair off (and as prostitution became more common), the Indians found themselves looking at a slew of new diseases. These diseases would, over the next 100 years, finish what the early explorers had started and exterminate all but a smattering of Florida's once-thriving Indian population.

Superpower Shift

During the 17th century, the shape of the world superpowers was altered, with Spain losing control of many colonies and possessions and Britain and France gaining more power. While the British and French sent troops and explorers scurrying all over the new territories, the Spanish seemed perfectly content to maintain their itsy-bitsy settlements at St Augustine and Pensacola, at the western end of the state.

By the end of the 17th century, the Brits, who in the northeast had well-established colonies, were continually pressing the Spanish on the southern boundaries of the British territory. In 1670 a demarcation line was established on what are roughly the present-day borders of Georgia and South Carolina, but the line was taken more as a suggestion than a rule, and the Brits repeatedly ran raids into the Spanish territory – either overtly or covertly.

To the west, the French were quickly establishing colonies along the Mississippi River, trying to link up the South with their new Canadian territories. Alliances between the powers were formed as quickly as they were scrapped – and they were scrapped as soon as they were formed.

Throughout the 18th century, the very proximity of the British in Georgia, the French in Louisiana and the Spanish in Florida heightened tensions. By 1700 there were 12 British colonies, and the British were definitely setting their sights on Florida. In 1732 James Oglethorpe settled Savannah, Georgia, and after a trip to England for supplies and armaments, attacked St Augustine in 1740. That attack, which laid siege to the city for 27 days before Oglethorpe's troops ran out of supplies and were forced to retreat, led to the construction of tiny Fort Matanzas, at the southern end of St Augustine. While the Spanish repelled the attack again, their position had become one under constant pressure from the British.

French & Indian War

As pressure on Spain mounted, so too did the friction between the other two big boys in the fray, England and France. As they began feeling the urge to stretch their legs to the west and east respectively, hostilities broke out between the British and French in 1754. Known as the French & Indian War for the French alliance with Indian groups against the British, it was the first war between European powers fought outside of Europe.

Choosing the marginally lesser of two evils, the Spanish jumped in on the side of France in 1761, to which England replied, 'Fine, and by the way, we hope you liked Havana 'cause we just took it.' In the First Treaty of Paris (1763), ending the seven-year-long war, Spain was offered a swap of Cuba for Florida, and they jumped at the chance.

American Revolution

England tried to force the 13 colonies to float the cost of its war with France in the form of new taxes. As George Bush discovered, tax hikes aren't the best way to win votes in America; higher taxes – including tariffs on just about anything Americans held dear, a hated Stamp Act and taxes on iron goods – precipitated a break from England. America's rallying cry was 'No taxation without representation' (taxation imposed on the colonists while they had no ability to plead their own case to the Court of St James). Today, of course, content in their ample congressional representation, Americans happily chip in and pay all new taxes.

Officially declared in 1776, the American Revolution barely affected Florida, which remained avidly loyalist. Florida's governor at the time invited other loyalists to move down to the region.

But after just 20 years of British rule – during which Florida developed a social structure the Spanish had never succeeded in creating – the Second Treaty of Paris (1783, ending the Revolution) returned Florida to the hands of Spain.

US Expansion

The northernmost portion of the state was becoming quite alluring indeed to expansionist Americans toward the end of the 18th century; in 1795 some Georgian hotheads attacked the San Nicolás mission in present-day Jacksonville. They held it for several months before being beaten back to Georgia. And in 1800 Spain finally gave up the Louisiana Territory to Napoleon, who promptly gave it up to the Americans!

A little later, the strategic location of Amelia Island, northeast of Jacksonville, became key. In 1807-08 President Thomas Jefferson imposed his wildly unpopular Embargo Act, which banned the importation of French and British products, and prohibited slave importation – Amelia Island became black-market central.

As the superpowers – and the USA was fast on its way to becoming one, at least in this region – squared off for what was to become the War of 1812 (1812-15), the Spanish ended up allied with the British against the US and France. The War of 1812, aside from being a power struggle between the Americans and British, was an aggressive campaign of US expansion, north into Canada, westward across the plains and south into Florida.

The 1814 Battle of Horseshoe Bend, in Alabama, proved pivotal for Florida. There, notorious (and heroic to his compatriots) Indian-hunter Andrew Jackson (1767-1845) defeated the Creeks in an overwhelming massacre of a victory, and then took half of their huge territory for the US. The battle also gave him an excuse to chase fleeing Creeks into Spanish Florida under the guise of defense. In late 1817 Jackson instigated the First Seminole War; see below.

Osceola

As the US sent more and more troops into the region on Indian-hunting and Spanish-harassing missions, the pressure became too much for Spain. It had gradually lost its grip on the East Florida settlements – Amelia Island was a Sodom-like den of smuggling, piracy, prostitution and debauchery – and the Spanish government's inability to adequately supply and police the area led to its decision to cede the territory to the US in 1819.

But an itchy Spanish King Ferdinand VII began to waiver. After the US told the Spanish to give up and get out or face US troops, a renegotiated treaty was signed, specifying among other things that the US would assume Spanish debt in the region. The Spanish finally gave up control of Florida in 1821. The debts, by the way, were never repaid. And who do you think was made governor of the new American territory? Yep, Jackson himself.

Seminole Wars

The treaty signed in 1814 at the end of the Battle of Horseshoe Bend opened to white settlers some 20 million acres of land in the region owned by the Creeks. Tensions ran very high, and skirmishes periodically broke out; there were a total of three Seminole Wars.

Instigated by Andrew Jackson, the first began in 1817, when Indians in the Miccosukee settlement of Fowltown had the audacity to respond to an attack by whites, killing about 50, including some women and children. Enter Jackson, who late that year stormed through Florida with a force of 5000, destroying Seminole villages and, while he was at it, engaging in a totally unsanctioned attack on Pensacola. (He actually took it, but the US gave it back – see Pensacola in the Northwest Florida chapter.)

Jackson was elected president of the USA in 1828, and the extermination of the American Indian was accelerated by his Indian Removal Act of 1830. The Treaty of Moultrie Creek of 1823 and the Treaty of Payne's Landing of 1832 were both signed by *some* Seminole, who agreed to give up their Florida lands and move west to reservations, but the provisions of the treaties were flouted by both sides. When the US began moving troops in 1835 to enforce the Treaty of Payne's Landing, Osceola, a Seminole leader, planned an attack on an army detachment. Major Francis Dade and 108 of his men were ambushed by the Seminole as they marched between Tampa and Fort King – only three survived. The attack triggered the beginning of the Second Seminole War, which lasted seven years.

The war dragged on so long because it was fought guerrilla-style in swamps and hammocks by the Seminole, versus the traditional European tactics employed by US soldiers. Creek Indian warriors from Alabama were engaged to fight for the US, in exchange for promises of federal protection of their families while they were away fighting. (Not surprisingly, they returned to pillaged homes and were interned in camps and gradually forced west.)

Osceola was captured on October 27, 1837, as he approached US Major General Thomas Jesup, commander of the Florida troops, both traveling under white flags. Jesup snatched Osceola, who later died at Fort Moultrie in South Carolina.

By 1842, thousands of Seminole had been displaced, marched to reservations in the west by army troops. As the war wound down, the surviving Florida Seminole took refuge in the Everglades. Despite their relegation to the swamps, the Seminole weren't really left alone, and in 1853 they were actually outlawed – a law proclaiming Indians illegal in the state of Florida called for their removal to any place west of the Mississippi River.

In 1855, a party of surveyors were killed after they encroached on Seminole territory. The resulting backlash became the Third Seminole War, which ended after Chief Billy Bowlegs agreed to go west (he was paid) in 1858. He and about 100 Seminole did migrate, but about 200 or 300 refused to acknowledge the agreement and retreated into the Everglades. There was never a full treaty ending the war, and some Seminole today say they are technically still at war with the USA.

Statehood & the Civil War

With the Indians out of the way, Florida became the 27th state admitted to the Union on March 3, 1845, only to secede 16 years later with the onset of the Civil War: admitted to the Union as a slave-owning, agricultural state, Florida seceded from USA along with the Confederacy on January 10, 1861.

The US Civil War (1861-65) stemmed from a number of issues, but a few stand in the foreground. There was a profound debate over the moral and economic issues surrounding slavery. In the 19th century, public opinion against it – and in favor of 'free labor' – in the northern states and in England was quickly rising Compounding this issue were the distinct economic differences between the northern and southern states.

Northern states, while maintaining an agrarian base, were moving quickly over to manufacturing and industry. The South depended on selling raw materials, principally cotton, to manufacturing nations such as Britain, but the North was in favor of instituting trade tariffs to protect its fledgling industry.

Additionally, the introduction of new territories to the USA through westward expansion potentially introduced a tilt in the balance of power between free and slave states within the US Congress. That issue was underscored by the admittance of California in 1850 as a free state.

Florida's Role Aside from providing troops, Florida's role in the Civil War was mainly one of supplying the ever-growing food needs of the Confederate war machine. As Yossarian explained to Milo in *Catch-22*, troops just can't eat cotton (even when chocolate covered), and since cotton was the South's main crop, the Confederate army pressed Florida's citrus and cattle farmers into heavy overtime.

All did not go well. Cattle ranchers and packing plants were heavily overburdened.

A Tenuous Florida Connection

While Florida saw some action in the Civil War, none of it was crucial to the outcome of the war. But Florida's claim to fame was this: After shooting Abraham Lincoln (who was not from Florida) at Ford's Theatre in 1865, John Wilkes Booth (also not a Floridian) leapt from the President's box and broke his leg when landing on the stage. Also not from Florida was the good Dr Samuel Mudd, who patched up Booth's leg, enabling him to make his escape from Washington. *But*, poor Dr Mudd – who hadn't the foggiest idea what was going on when he fixed the assassin's leg – found himself arrested on charges of aiding and abetting the assassin; his ass was hauled – you guessed it – to Florida. Fort Jefferson in the Dry Tortugas, to be precise.

Mudd served out his sentence well, and was pardoned after he showed 'great courage and compassion' treating victims of a yellow fever outbreak at the fort in 1867.

Florida cattle were so valuable to the Confederates that the Union's attentions focused on Florida in an effort to cripple the South – the largest battle of the war held on Florida soil, at Olustee, began as a Union effort to cut off beef supplies.

Battles of the Civil War in Florida included the following:

Santa Rosa Island – October 9, 1861
1200 Union soldiers captured Fort Pickens at Pensacola.

St John's Bluff – October 1 to 3, 1862
A Union flotilla carrying about 1500 troops on ships steamed into the mouth of the St John's River. They were joined by infantry forces at Mt Pleasant Creek and then landed forces at Mayport. The Confederates got out of Dodge.

Fort Brooke – October 16 to 18, 1863
Under cover fire from two Union ships, the Union marched to the Hillsborough River and captured the *Scottish Chief* and *Kate Dale*.

Olustee – February 20, 1864
After a fine start sacking several Confederate encampments, Union General Truman Seymour's troops ran into the decidedly unimpressed Brigadier General Joseph Finegan and 5000 of his closest friends. Finegan broke the Union line but allowed the troops to retreat to Jacksonville in this, the largest battle in Florida.

Natural Bridge – March 6, 1865
Occurred near St Marks. Major General John Newton went after Confederate troops who had attacked at Cedar Keys and Fort Myers. The Union army advanced and tried to cross the river at Natural Bridge, but the Confederates (Home Guard as well as a 'Baby Corps' of adolescent boy cadets) held their position.

At the end of the war, Tallahassee was the only Confederate state capital that hadn't fallen to Federal troops.

Reconstruction

The Civil War was one of the bloodiest conflicts in the history of modern warfare, and wounds ran incredibly deep. From early on in the conflict until his assassination, President Abraham Lincoln (1809-65) had been putting together a framework for reconstruction of the Union – the 10% Plan. Under the plan, the Union would give federal recognition to states in which as few as 10% of the populace had taken oaths of loyalty to the USA – a plan designed to grant political viability to dependable groups (in the Union's opinion) as quickly as possible.

But with Lincoln's assassination, all bets were off and a political void opened; Florida was ruled by martial law under Union troops. Any semblance of a state government disappeared right after the war. Florida's governor, John Milton, blew his brains out, preferring death to Reconstruction, and the state was run by troops carrying out orders from Washington. In the confusion that followed, dozens of factions struggled for power – from labor organizers to the Ku Klux Klan, an organized gang of white supremacists who began a campaign of violence against blacks that continues to this day.

But as the federal government established and maintained order, the return to normalcy progressed. Farmers scrambled to reestablish their businesses, and Florida blacks, though freed technically from slavery, found themselves working for the same plantations as before, now as hired hands. As businessmen and former politicians struggled to re-create a state government, heated arguments arose at every level on the role of blacks in the state and the level of freedom and recognition they would receive. This was not contained to Florida: throughout the country, a consensus on how to reestablish state and local government, and on what platform, was proving far more difficult to achieve than had been expected.

President Andrew Johnson, a Southerner and former slave owner who succeeded Lincoln, devised a Reconstruction plan that compromised between Lincoln's 10% Plan and the more radical proposals that were filtering in from the South. While his Presidential Reconstruction granted many concessions, it was absolutely firm that the states' constitutions ratify the 13th Amendment, abolishing slavery, before readmittance.

The issue of contention was black suffrage, something the southern states were loathe to grant, but under the congressional

Reconstruction plan, martial law was eventually imposed to install it. When Florida was re-admitted to the Union in 1868, it had technically granted the vote to blacks, but the state's new constitution was carefully worded to ensure Florida did not get a 'negro government.' After Federal troops left, discriminatory laws were enacted – including one forbidding a black man to testify at a white man's trial – and a poll tax was imposed, which kept droves of black and poor white voters away from the voting booth.

The new Florida government began what in many ways continues to this day: an agenda of pro-business, pro-development activities to open up Florida's natural resources to exploitation at the expense of social programs, which have never been prevalent. While schools went underfunded and overcrowded, developers and tourists were enticed to the area – the former by unbelievably and criminally cheap land prices (25¢ an acre was not unheard of) and the latter by the hotels and resorts built by the former.

Development

At the end of the 18th century, real-estate developers were creating holiday resorts throughout the state. As Florida's agricultural trade – especially citrus and cattle – expanded, the need for railroads increased; as communications advanced, the ability to shuttle tourists to hitherto remote areas of the state became feasible.

The first trans-state railroad had been constructed just prior to the Civil War by David Yulee (the first Jewish member of the US Senate), but sadly it remained open for only about a month, running from Fernandina Beach to Cedar Key, before being rerouted north during the war. After the war, railroads popped up throughout the state, and much of Florida was finally connected to the Atlantic coast railroads and thus with the northern states for the first time.

Developer Henry Flagler (1830-1913), who made his money as a partner of John D Rockefeller in Standard Oil, was arguably the single most important force in the development of Florida as a holiday destination. Flagler, whose real-estate career began in Westchester County, New York, became convinced that the Atlantic coast of Florida was the perfect playground for the rich and famous, and by gum, he was the man to bring them there.

Flagler's first move toward that end was the purchase of existing railroad between Jacksonville and St Augustine, and from that created what would become the Florida East Coast (FEC) Railway, which would eventually traverse the entire length of the state's east coast from Jacksonville to Key West.

Flagler built resorts in each of the railway's main terminals, beginning in St Augustine, where he constructed the Ponce de León Hotel (now Flagler College) and helped spur a boom of resorts in the area. The railroad extended southward; Flagler had planned to make the southern terminus in Palm Beach, where he built an even more lavish resort, the Royal Poinciana Hotel, to which he added on the Palm Beach Inn (now known as The Breakers).

After a record freeze in 1895 that shocked tourists and stunned the fledgling Florida citrus industry, Flagler took Julia Tuttle (a major landowner in Miami) up on her offer to extend the FEC to Miami and eventually to Key West across Flagler's crown jewel, the Overseas Highway. The highway connected Key West to the mainland over a series of causeways, but it wasn't profitable and was destroyed by a hurricane in 1935. The foundations of the FEC's bridges were incorporated in the second incarnation of the Overseas Highway, the road that exists today, over the next several years.

Another major contributor to the development of South Florida was Addison Mizner (1872-1933). In the years just after WWI, he become a favorite architect of rich vacationers and homeowners in Palm Beach and especially Boca Raton, where Mizner developed most of his Mediterranean-style, pastel-colored mansions. Mizner was wiped out in the land bust of 1926.

Railroads in Florida

Railroads quite simply were the most important factor in the development of Florida, and as demand grew, several cropped up around the state. Most people associate railroads in Florida with Henry Flagler (depicted below), who owned the Florida East Coast (FEC) Railway, but Flagler was a latecomer.

Henry B Plant (1819-1899) was probably the biggest player in the railroad scene; his Plant Railroad System ran up the southwest coast and across the state, connecting with steamships between Tampa, Key West and Havana. By the time he sold his railroad empire in 1902, his system included or connected with a network including the East Florida Railway from Jacksonville to the St Mary's River, the Savannah, Florida & Western Line and the Louisville & Nashville line running across the Panhandle.

After the land bust in 1926, service throughout the state became less and less in demand and several lines folded. WWII breathed life into John Williams' Seaboard Air Line Railway for a while, but business stayed slow even after a merger of competing rail lines in the late 1960s. The beginning of the end was the arrival in 1971 of Amtrak, which gobbled up remaining companies, cut service and raised prices. The merger of the remaining lines, Seaboard Coast Line and the Chessie System, created the CSX Corporation in 1980.

Today railroad museums pop up here and there throughout the state, and if you do find a functional line – like the Seminole Gulf Railway in Fort Myers – it's probably only being run as a tourist attraction, for dinner and mystery rides, as opposed to transport.

Spanish-American War

The USA showed the world it was a power to be reckoned with during the 10-week Spanish-American War in 1898. As Cuba struggled for independence from Spanish rule, and as reports drifted back of Cuban farmers being gathered into prison camps, newspapers like William Randolph Hearst's *New York Journal* began a propaganda campaign of 'yellow journalism,' which successfully riled the American public.

The news stories ostensibly supported the 'humanitarian annexation' of Cuba, which perhaps not coincidentally would have been the culmination of the USA's Manifest Destiny – a doctrine that held that it was destined to control all of North America – and a happy windfall to US businessmen.

President William McKinley resisted intervention, but when the battleship *Maine* was destroyed in Havana harbor, McKinley declared war on Spain; Congress ratified the declaration on April 25. (Debate rages today about the *Maine*'s destruction. On the one hand, it's suspicious that all the ship's officers were ashore at the time of the detonation. On the other, new evidence that the explosion was an accident has recently surfaced.)

The main fighting took place in two theaters: the South Pacific and Cuba. After handy victories in Manila and Guam, US army and volunteer regiments landed in Cuba in late June, including the Rough Riders (who actually had to leave all their horses in Florida), led by Leonard Wood and Theodore Roosevelt. Bully.

As the military buildup began, many Florida towns – especially Tampa, Key West and Miami but also northern cities such as

Jacksonville – saw land-office business as people poured into the region and lined up to receive plots of homesteading land. As reports filtered back to the northern states about conditions in Florida, it was gaining a reputation as a paradisiacal location affordable to all: tourists came in droves. As a result of the military buildup and because it became the most important staging area for the fight in Cuba, South Florida experienced something of a mini-boom.

The Spanish-American War itself was something of a letdown to war buffs; the Spanish surrendered on July 17.

Social Conditions

Since the Civil War, tensions between black and white settlers in Florida had remained high, and blacks probably felt nervous when Federal troops withdrew from Florida. As the developers began to move into Florida, conditions for the poor grew worse with railroad and land barons practically buying the state outright. Government was rife with corruption, land deals were questionable, and social services were maintained at an appallingly low level.

But as farmers and workers began to organize, a distinct antideveloper mood began to slowly infiltrate the state's political system, and the organization and collective protests of farmers, blacks and women in conjunction with a strong populist movement resulted in the election of Napoleon Bonaparte Broward as governor in 1905.

Elected as a populist, antideveloper/pro-little-guy candidate, Broward actually followed through with many social programs, including child labor laws, an inspired education system, labor law reforms and new jobs. Unfortunately, his theories on how to create new jobs were the very cause of the destruction of the Everglades: it was he who initiated drainage and canals throughout the Everglades in an effort to expose mucklands necessary for growing sugar.

WWI & the Roaring '20s

Once again war became a boon to Florida: by the time the USA entered WWI in 1917, Florida had again been built up with a large naval presence at Key West, Pensacola, Tampa and Jacksonville. By the time the war was over, Florida had thousands of new permanent residents. The WWI boom, especially in Miami, lead the state into the '20s with great momentum.

At the imposition of Prohibition (the ban on sale or manufacturing of alcohol in the USA), Florida became a smuggler's haven, with lots of unguarded coastline, convenient proximity to Cuba and Puerto Rico, and an endless supply of imbibers not just on the beaches of Florida but in other states as well.

Miami especially never took much to Prohibition; Al Capone himself moved in to grab a piece of the action, and Miami Beach became one constant party, packing in the gamblers, drinkers and funsters.

The entire state was in the midst of an enormous boom the likes of which had never been seen in the USA on such a huge scale. Hundreds of thousands of people were migrating to Florida, and land prices soared. Railroads and roads were popping up everywhere, and cities were expanding at staggering rates.

Land Bust

In a manner similar to the stock markets of the '20s, margin buying of land was the ticket in Florida, where shysters could buy land with incredibly small down payments and shuck it onto settlers at huge profits. With such buying and construction, transport was ever more important, and several disasters were straining the limits of existing communications – among them a debilitating rail strike and a sunken supply ship in Miami harbor blocking the entrance to the Miami River and keeping other boats from dropping off their loads.

But the end came in a flash: a major hurricane hit South Florida in late 1926, wiping out construction, killing 400 and injuring thousands. In the aftermath, the hordes of people who thought they were getting the deal of a lifetime found the catch – deadly storms – and pulled out quickly, taking their money with them. Land prices plummeted and banks folded like books. And as if to hammer the nails in the coffin, the area was hit by another devastating hurricane and several smaller storms a little more than a year later.

Great Depression

Florida businesses pretty much followed the national trend during the Great Depression, after the stock market crash of 1929. As banks failed, businesses failed, and many of Florida's rich developers ran home with their tails between their legs. As Florida had already been in the midst of a state depression after the land bust, it was strongly affected by the depression and in need of more federal bail-outs than most other states.

Florida was a major supporter of Franklin Delano Roosevelt. When elected president, Roosevelt made his way to Miami to thank South Florida for its support. During that visit, in a speech at Bayfront Park, a deranged man named Guiseppe Zangora fired several shots at the president-elect. While FDR escaped unharmed, Chicago Mayor Anton Cernas, standing nearby, was critically injured.

In Roosevelt's first '100 Days,' he called an emergency session of Congress, the result of which was the creation of dozens of government agencies that had a profound effect on the state and the nation as a whole. As part of Roosevelt's New Deal, the Works Progress Administration (WPA) and the Civilian Conservation Corps (CCC) were created. The WPA sent armies of workers to construct buildings, roads, dams, trails and housing, while the CCC worked to restore state and national parks. Other federal programs included Social Security, which gives money to the elderly and infirm (memo to Republicans: if you don't like it, give yours back). It was the largest campaign of government-created jobs ever in the USA, and while critics at the time called it busywork, projects by both the WPA and CCC stand today, many as national landmarks.

WWII

The most effective means of jump-starting the American economy was, again, military. After the Japanese attack on Pearl Harbor, Hawaii, on December 7, 1941, the USA

began work on its war machine. What set the area abuzz and ensured Florida's role in national security was U-boat activity off the Florida coast. In early 1942, U-boats were sinking US freighters at an alarming rate.

Though it sounds cruel, a good war was just what the state needed. Almost overnight Florida was turned into one of the biggest war factories and training grounds in the Union: almost every US pilot who flew in WWII trained in Florida; the Army's anti-U-boat school was in Miami; Key West's naval base overflowed with sailors.

The area was also the beneficiary of increased demand for agricultural products, and Florida's farmers raked in the big bucks. During the war, Florida's citrus production was the highest in the nation.

1950s

As the war ended, soldiers and sailors who trained here returned to the region, and those with wartime jobs ended up settling. Once again, Florida experienced a boom initiated by war.

In the 1950s, Miami Beach had another boom, as it became known as the 'Cuba of America'; see the History section in the Miami chapter for details on gambling and gangsters.

In 1954, Leroy Collins became the first Southern governor to declare racial segregation 'morally wrong.'

Orange and cotton growing were becoming huge businesses in northern Florida, and as the aerospace industry moved into Florida near the end of the '50s, an entire 'Space Coast' was created to support the high-falutin' goals of the National Aeronautics & Space Administration (NASA) in its race to beat the Russkies into space – see the Space Coast chapter for a full history of the US space program.

Cuba & the Bay of Pigs

After the 1959 Cuban revolution, Miami and South Florida became flooded with many anti-Castro immigrants, who, in gathering to arrange a counterrevolutionary (CR) force, managed to establish a permanent Cuban community in Miami.

A group of exiles formed the 2506th Brigade, sanctioned by the US government, which provided help in the form of weapons and CIA training for the purpose of launching an attack on Cuba (memo to would-be Cuban dictators: enlist for your opponents the help of the CIA).

In April 1961, the CRs launched an attack on the beaches at Playa de Giron: the Bay of Pigs. But warning somehow leaked to the

Cuban Revolutions

Fidel Castro

While most people peg the influx of Cubans to the rise of Fidel Castro in 1959, Cubans have been flocking to Miami – and Florida in general – for more than a century. The first large wave of immigration was in 1868, when socialist-minded cigar workers fleeing the Ten Years' War made Key West sort of an 'enlightened-masses tobacco combine.'

Those enlightened masses, educated about the struggle in Cuba, began demanding more and more money and benefits at a time when the economy was in a downturn. Cigar-maker Vicente Martínez Ybor almost single-handedly squashed Key West's cigar industry by moving his factory to Tampa and steaming in Cuban laborers from Havana.

The move to Miami began during the Spanish-American War but took off after Cuban independence and really soared after regular aviation between Miami and Havana was established in the late 1920s.

From then until Castro's Revolution – despite intrigue and the murderous Batista regime – were the swinging days of the Cuban-American relationship. Gamblers and hot shots poured into Cuba on hourly flights from Miami, and wealthy Cubans poured right back at Miami to buy clothes and American products.

What ended this reign has played a key role in US attitudes towards Cuba and Cubans to this very day.

Most people agree that Fulgencio Batista, whose regime controlled Cuba for almost 30 years, was a horrible gangster who terrorized a nation. At the time, it seemed the best hope of losing him was to back his adversaries, a coalition headed by Fidel Castro that had been trying for years to oust Batista.

In late 1958, President Eisenhower announced an arms embargo against the Batista government, which was interpreted by many as tacit US support for Fidel Castro and his revolutionary coalition. Castro had made a formal promise to the coalition to hold free elections as soon as they took power.

Batista abdicated on January 1, 1959. There is some dispute as to just how forthcoming Castro was about his intentions, but over the next year and a half, Castro broke his promise of free elections, consolidated his power, and in a move that would set the tone of the next three decades, nationalized businesses – including major US-owned businesses – and property without compensation.

The US responded by canceling its Cuban sugar quota, and Castro, pressed for cash, turned to the Soviet Union. In the ultimate thumb-nose to the USA, which was reaching the height of its Cold War with the Soviets, Castro allied himself with Moscow.

Cubans – a *New York Times* correspondent says he heard about the impending attack weeks before it happened – and the pathetic, half-baked, poorly planned and badly executed attack was little more than an ambush.

And to add insult to injury, when the magnitude of the botch-up became clear, President Kennedy refused to send in air cover or naval support in the name of 'plausible deniability.' The first wave of CRs was left on the beach with their cheese in the wind – no reinforcements or supplies arrived. The CRs were all captured or killed (though all prisoners were released by Cuba about three months later).

Kennedy Versus Krushchev

Kennedy and the CIA both looked rather silly after the fiasco, and that is probably why Kennedy stood his ground so firmly during the event that brought the world to the brink of nuclear war: the Cuban Missile Crisis.

Smelling blood after the Bay of Pigs, the USSR's General Secretary Nikita Krushchev began secretly installing missile bases in Cuba. By some stroke of luck – or perhaps by accident – the CIA managed to take photographs of the proceedings, which were shown to Kennedy on October 16, 1962. The Kennedy administration debated what to do, and for almost a week after Kennedy saw the photos, the Soviet embassy denied the existence of the bases.

On October 22, Kennedy went on national television and announced that the USSR was installing missiles on Cuba, 90 miles south of Key West, and that this was a direct threat to the safety and security of the country. He announced a naval 'quarantine' of Cuba (a euphemism for a naval blockade, which would have been an act of war) and further, that any attack on the USA from Cuba would be regarded as an attack by the USSR.

Tensions mounted, and a flurry of letters passed between Washington and Moscow, beginning with 'Well, okay, we *do* have missiles, but they're there as a deterrent and not as an offensive threat' and culminating in two offers from the Soviets to end the stalemate.

The first, dated October 26, agreed to remove the missiles in exchange for a promise by the USA not to attack Cuba. The second, on October 27, tied the removal to the USA's removal of similar sites it had in Turkey.

Kennedy responded to the first offer publicly; it was announced that the USA would not invade Cuba, and the Soviets began removing their missiles. Several months later, and with markedly less fanfare, the US removed its missiles from Turkey.

Miami's Cuban population swelled as Cubans emigrated to the USA. A special immigration center was established to handle the overflow in Miami's Freedom Tower – the Ellis Island of the South.

During the mid-'60s, the 'freedom flights' running between Miami and Havana brought in large numbers of Cuban refugees, creating high tensions between blacks and Cubans.

1970s & the Mariel Boatlift

A major development in the 1970s was the introduction to Florida of something that would change the face of the state's tourism market forever: Walt Disney World. Around this massive entertainment center and resort spurted hundreds of thousands of tourist-related jobs in service industries. Hangers-on and imitators also moved in.

In the late 1970s, as Florida's economy began to recover from the oil crisis and recession, Fidel pulled a fast one and opened the floodgates, allowing anyone who wanted to leave Cuba access to the docks at Mariel. Before the ink was dry on the proclamation, the largest flotilla ever launched for nonmilitary purposes set sail (or paddle) in practically anything that would float to cover the 90 miles between Cuba and Florida. The Mariel Boatlift, as the largest of these would be called, brought 150,000 Cubans to Florida, including an estimated 25,000 prisoners and mental patients that Ol' Frisky Fidel had cleverly decided to foist off on the US. The resulting economic, logistical and infrastructural strain on South Florida only added to still-simmering racial tensions, which would explode on May 17, 1980 in

Liberty City, a Miami neighborhood – see the Miami chapter for information on the Liberty City Riots.

Also in the late 1970s, Florida distinguished itself by becoming the first state to reinstate the death penalty, and Tampa became the first place where a Led Zeppelin concert turned into a major riot. Music, then, must have really irritated Florida judges, and one of them rang in the 1980s by declaring a 2 Live Crew album 'obscene' and banning its sale within the state.

1980s

In the 1980s, Florida was gaining recognition as an economic powerhouse both in banking and drug dealing – which, despite an unsavory reputation, happened to be a major force in the rejuvenation of South Florida. Jacksonville was becoming an insurance capital, and tourism was playing an ever more important role statewide. Key West, rescued from bankruptcy after the Great Depression, was becoming an area as romantic to tourists as Paris, and terrorist activity targeting Americans abroad in the mid-'80s put Florida in the very enviable position of being America's holiday spot – 'nearby, easy to get to, no passports required and they talk good English like us.'

While technology began to boom throughout the country, the Space Coast and its support industries in the Central Florida corridor between the Kennedy Space Center and Orlando began to gain importance as simulation technology businesses set up shop. (See the Orlando section in the Central Florida chapter and the Space Coast chapter for more information.)

'Cocaine,' Robin Williams once said, 'is God's way of telling us we're making too damn much money,' and if ever a nation was making too much money it was America in the '80s. All that blow had to come from somewhere, and Miami's excellent Caribbean location made it a major source of America's incoming drugs. As pink-clad detectives made the whole thing look sexy on *Miami Vice* (see the Miami chapter), South Florida began looking more and more like an armed camp. I-95

and US Hwy 1 were patrolled by officers from an alphabet soup of agencies, empowered to stop pretty much anyone who fit 'drug runner profiles.' The Conch Republic was one form of public protest against this (see the Key West chapter), but more serious problems were developing in Miami and Ybor City, where drug use and displacement of the poor were becoming more and more of a problem.

By the late 1980s, Miami Beach had risen to international Fabulousness on a comet of big-name models and movie stars coming to the area to be 'seen,' and the rest of South Florida was riding its coattails.

But Florida entered the 1990s bumpily, with Hurricane Andrew – the most expensive storm ever to hit the USA – devastating South Florida in 1992 (see the Miami chapter). Coup and chaos in Haiti led to waves of refugees washing up on South Florida's shores, and upheaval in Cuba lead to several new waves of Cuban raft refugees as well. Florida leapt to the national spotlight in the abortion fight when, in 1993, Dr David Gunn was shot dead by Paul Hill outside a Pensacola abortion clinic.

Haitian Coup

In late September 1991, the Haitian military, led by Lieutenant General Raoul Cedras, overthrew the government of constitutionally elected President Jean-Bertrand Aristide. The US response was economic sanctions, to be removed only after the return of Aristide to power.

Under Cedras' leadership, Haitian armed forces, which at that time were given extreme legal and institutional autonomy, were responsible for law enforcement and 'public safety.' As human rights abuses – beatings, torture, executions and 'disappearances' – escalated, refugees began to flee to the relative (they thought) safety of the USA in anything that would float. Many refugees ended up in Little Haiti, and as many as possible were rounded up by the Immigration and Naturalization Service (INS) for deportation. Signs posted throughout Miami urged people 'Don't Be a Snitch,' meaning don't report Haitians to the police, but rather point them in the direction of Little Haiti.

For the next three years, media images of Haitians being rounded up by the US Coast Guard permeated local media: in the first seven months of 1992 alone, the UN High Commissioner for Refugees (UNHCR) said the US Coast Guard had intercepted and detained at Guantanamo Bay, Cuba, a total of 38,315 Haitians fleeing their country. Of those, only 11,617 were given the INS stamp of approval as 'potentially qualified for political asylum.'

As pressure mounted from Haitian groups in Miami, which pointed out the historical carte blanche given any Cuban who manages to wash up on US soil, the US Supreme Court upheld a detestable Bush-administration policy that allows the Coast Guard to return refugees it has intercepted on the high seas directly to their home country without the benefit of an asylum hearing. And that's what the Coast Guard did.

Through a series of maneuvers (including, some say, covert payment of a cool $1 million by the USA to Cedras), Aristide was returned to power. Cedras resigned and was granted political amnesty. For the second time in a century, the US sent troops to Haiti to restore democracy.

This event allowed the Clinton administration to say to the rest of the Haitians who were being held at Guantanamo Bay, in essence, 'Please go home now; you no longer have a claim of asylum as your country is again a model democracy.' As if to accentuate the divergent treatment of Haitians and Cubans, Clinton made that move the day after agreeing to allow some 20,000 Cubans at Guantanamo entry to the USA.

Cuban Affairs

With the fall of the Soviet Union in 1991, the USA's relationship with Cuba entered a new era. The loss of Soviet imports of fuel and purchases of sugar and tobacco crippled the Cuban economy, and the USA began work on a *coup de grâce*: further isolation of Cuba from the international community, which the US expected would lead to Castro's down-

fall. The USA, which many now say precipitated the fall of the Soviet Union in a spending, not arms, race, turned up the pressure on a broke Fidel Castro through a number of measures.

The looniest of these was Radio and TV Martí, a Reagan-era project lasting through to the Clinton administration. In 1985 Martí began wasting about $50,000 a day on broadcasts of American 'cultural offerings' – *Days of Our Lives, Kate & Allie, Cheers* and *Lifestyles of the Rich & Famous* – between 3 and 6 am from a blimp hovering off the Keys. Yes, a blimp.

In some of the finest of Cold War justifications, Martí was considered to be a high priority to show US determination – despite the fact that Cubans didn't know about it, didn't watch it, didn't have the equipment to watch it, and even if they had, the Cuban government jammed the broadcasts anyway. *The Nation* magazine said that less than 1% of Cubans had seen Martí.

On a far more serious note, the US in the early 1990s put a stop to instant acceptance of Cuban refugees in an effort to keep the simmering hotheads in Fidel's court rather than on the streets of Miami. As anti-Castro demonstrators continually stepped up pressure, and as Cuba sank deeper into debt and became more desperate for hard currency, the USA started its death watch, with pundits predicting the imminent fall of Castro.

February Shoot-Down

They would be disappointed, at least up through early 1999, by a Castro that kept fighting back. But Castro made things far more difficult for himself by authorizing the shooting-down of two American planes in February, 1995, flown by pilots of Brothers to the Rescue.

Brothers to the Rescue is a Miami-based group of pilots that patrol the waters of the Caribbean looking for refugee rafters. Part of a group of rabid anti-Castro, Miami-based Cubans who characterize their work as 'humanitarian aid,' BTTR claims to have been responsible for the rescue of thousands of rafters and boat people. It claims that

The Brothers, the CIA & the FBI

Many people in Miami, and several newspaper and Internet e-zine articles, say that Brothers to the Rescue is certainly a CIA-backed operation. But a CIA spokesperson we spoke with (less spooky than you'd think) called such claims 'errant nonsense' and said there was 'no truth whatsoever' in claims that the CIA backs BTTR, though he went on to say cryptically that it was 'entirely possible' there 'may have been some law enforcement connection' with the group and that we should maybe check with the FBI.

The FBI?

After a long tour through the FBI's infuriating phone system (with its easy-listening hold music), a spokesperson said the FBI doesn't engage in the support or nonsupport of any group, but then seemed to contradict that by saying the FBI could not comment on whether it has offered any support to Brothers to the Rescue. Maybe yes, maybe no.

Spook-backed or not, with rampant speculation in South Florida media and local gossip, BTTR has certainly found itself at the center of an international brouhaha of Ludlumesque proportions.

rafters are shot at by Cuban patrol boats and helicopters.

After BTTR planes skirted in and out of Cuban airspace as part of a flotilla and airborne demonstration, they were fired upon and downed by Cuban Air Force planes. The US government's outrage over the attack raised one of the biggest stinks since the Bay of Pigs.

The Helms-Burton Bill increased sanctions against Cuba, ending regular flights between Miami and Havana, and putting the ixnay on many business deals that had been in the works between US and Cuban companies. But provisions in the law that gave the US the right to sue and deny US entry to foreigners working or doing business in Cuba infuriated European leaders, and the bill was allowed to lapse into oblivion. As we write, while tensions remain high, a 1998 visit by the Pope and the American Democratic Party's interest in the Cuban swing vote in Miami have resulted in a slight thawing. Regular flights from Miami to Havana resumed in 1998, and it is thought by Cuba travel experts that easing of travel restrictions (actually, they are monetary restrictions; see the boxed text in the Getting There & Away chapter) on Americans may be in the cards.

Though foreign governments are doing nothing to stop their citizens from traveling and doing business with Cuba, it is clear from any visitor to Cuba (wanna be one? – see that same boxed text in the Getting There & Away chapter) that the situation there is dire. Miami's Cuban population is watching with great interest the events unfolding at the close of the century.

Crime Against Tourists

Another reason Florida's image didn't shine in the early '90s was a heavily publicized spree of foreign-tourist-related crimes in 1993. With several shootings and many robberies, the state was in a panic that it would lose its tourism market, which was fast becoming the state's most important industry. In May 1993, one of Great Britain's top tour companies quoted polls showing that Miami was perceived as the most dangerous destination in the world, followed by North Africa, Kenya and Turkey.

The state bounced back, helped by heightened security, ever-brighter tourist attractions and the creation of a Tourist Police Force. Attacks against tourists have been substantially reduced.

But South Florida's image as some sort of wild, wild west was brought to light again: on

July 15, 1997, fashion designer Gianni Versace was gunned down in front of his Miami Beach mansion. The publicity was instant and worldwide. (See the boxed text in the Miami chapter for more information.)

Florida Today

Miami and Orlando are still the powerhouse tourism draws, but other cities – notably Key West, Fort Lauderdale, Tampa, St Petersburg, St Augustine and Pensacola – have been seeing more business than ever.

Theme parks account for much of the draw to regions outside the southeast: while Disney is still decidedly king of the hill, tough competition from Universal Studios Florida, SeaWorld and Busch Gardens and smaller entries like Wet 'n' Wild and even Splendid China are packing them in. And more and more people are discovering just how accessible the state and national parks – such as the Everglades, Ichetucknee, Blue Spring, Jonathan Dickinson and Hobe Sound – can be.

While Florida's famed agriculture- and developer-friendly government still has a long way to go, the demand for more ecologically minded reforms has increased thanks to involvement from the federal government.

Some visitors are complaining that SoBe (South Beach) and Miami are getting overcrowded and that the boom is done. There may be some truth in that, but regions throughout the state are seeing renovation, renewal and a new lease on life.

GEOGRAPHY

Florida's terrain is mainly flat, with coastal lowlands, and slightly hilly in the center, though you won't find anything over 350 feet above sea level in Florida. The south-central portion of the state is all wetlands and reclaimed wetlands. As nature intended it, the sheet-flow ecosystem of water from the Kissimmee River fed Lake Okeechobee at the southeast center of the state, which then overflowed, feeding sheets of fresh water to the Everglades. But nature was overruled in South Florida, and the Kissimmee was dammed, diked, canaled and

diverted – see the Everglades chapter for more information.

The coasts are buttressed by natural barrier islands. The waterways between the barrier islands and the mainland were deepened and widened by the Army Corps of Engineers to create a sheltered inland route from Miami to Virginia: the Atlantic Intracoastal Waterway, one of the country's most important commercial and recreational waterways. A similar waterway, the Gulf Intracoastal Waterway, is found along the Gulf Coast.

The Panhandle refers to the handle-like strip of land jutting off to the northwest. The northern borders are Alabama and Georgia, and the state's other borders are the Atlantic Ocean and the Gulf of Mexico on the east and west, respectively.

Florida is the 22nd largest state in the USA: it's more than 600 miles from Miami to Pensacola. Key West is closer to Havana than Miami, and Tallahassee (the state capital) is 239 miles from Tampa, which is almost 200 miles from St Augustine.

GEOLOGY

On the face of it, geologically speaking, Florida's not much to jump up and down about. It's essentially an enormous arched slab of porous limestone. However, when the seas receded and exposed the Florida peninsula – recently enough that dinosaurs never made it here – the limestone caused some interesting things to happen.

First, the saltwater that saturated the limestone was forced out by fresh water from rainfall. Decaying plant matter washed into the ground by rainfall created a carbonic acid, which ate away at the limestone, forming tunnels and caverns and eventually entire underground freshwater systems of rivers and streams.

These systems are aquifers, and while there are several, the entire system is the Florida Aquifer, the source of the state's freshwater supply.

Weaknesses and cracks in the limestone, combined with the pressure of the circulating water, result in springs, of which Florida has hundreds, if not thousands. And those same weaknesses are responsible for sink-holes – amusing when they're not on your property – which occur when the carbonic acid eats away at a section of limestone that's not thin enough to become a spring. When enough stone is dissolved, entire sections of ground simply sink into, well, a hole. One of the best examples of a fascinating Florida sinkhole is the Devil's Millhopper just north of Gainesville.

CLIMATE

Florida's warm weather may have been the only reason anyone dreamed of inhabiting the place at all.

Ideal conditions in the south of the state exist between December and May, when temperatures average between 59° and 75°F (15° to 24°C), and average rainfall is a scant 2.01 inches. But in northern Florida, the winter months are cool and, in recent years, downright cold – not just Florida cold: northern Florida had several nights in 1996 with temperatures in the teens (°F).

Summer everywhere in the state can be summed up as very hot and humid with thunderstorms at 3 pm. June is the rainiest month, with an average of 9.33 inches, and temperatures average between 75° and 88°F (24° to 31°C). August is probably the hottest month, with average temperatures between 77° and 89°F (25° to 31°C), but with all these temperatures you have to take into account the heat index, a product of heat and humidity. It feels a *lot* hotter than 89°F when there's 90% humidity!

See the climate charts for more detailed information.

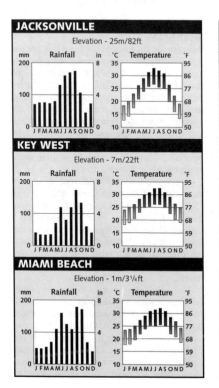

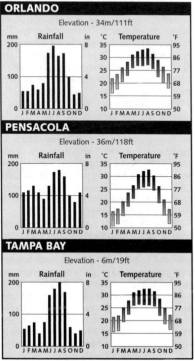

Florida Rain

There's a cats-and-dogs quality to Florida rain that will be unfamiliar to anyone who hasn't spent time in the tropics. And it comes on quickly. In summer, rainstorms are preceded by inhuman rises in humidity, closely followed by fantastically ominous clouds, which sweep in and reduce daylight to twilight in a matter of minutes. The rain – copious doses of fist-sized raindrops – has a ferocity that floods streets in minutes and causes drivers to pull over and cower. The thunder sounds as if the end of the world is upon us.

But the rains rarely last very long, and the weather – and the raindrops – are so warm that they can actually be refreshing. Afterward, cool breezes make it all seem worth it.

ECOLOGY & ENVIRONMENT

While this will sound grim, keep in mind that things are improving and that government is now taking an active role in limiting and repairing damage and managing land use.

The *Encyclopedia of Florida* says that Florida's state motto, 'In God We Trust,' was 'evidently taken from the inscription on American currency.' In that spirit lies the fundamental philosophy behind Florida's environmental and ecological policies. The destruction of vast tracts of Florida's natural balance was a direct result of the government's encouragement.

From the mid-1800s, when developers 'discovered' the paradise of South Florida, the state government supported irresponsible large-scale agricultural projects and real-estate development. The destruction of the Everglades began in an effort to create jobs, by controlling the flow of water from Lake Okeechobee and draining significant portions of wetlands to expose mucklands perfect for sugar farming.

While the Florida Aquifer has the capability to supply unbelievably large quantities of water, ground contamination from sources like pesticides, heavy metals, sewage and gasoline (leaking from underground storage tanks) has drastically affected the quality of Florida's drinking water in many areas of the state. Similarly, Florida's rivers, streams and lakes have been polluted to the extent that largemouth bass are inedible from several lakes. Mercury levels in the Everglades are startlingly high.

While beaches are relatively clean, the coast has seen high levels of bacteria at times. Health authorities monitor conditions and are rather good about letting people know when limits are exceeded.

FLORA
Mangroves

Mangroves are halophytes, trees that are tolerant to saltwater conditions. Located where the land meets the sea, they stabilize the shoreline and reduce inland flooding during storms, simply because they prevent sand and dirt from washing away. Silt builds up, forming more and more land; eventually the mangroves are strangled by the very land they've created and they die. Another special quality of mangroves is their seeds sprout while still on the tree.

There are about 50 different species of mangroves around the world, and three of them can be found in Florida. The red mangrove *(Rhizophora mangle)*, sometimes called walking tree, drops salt-filtering aerial prop roots, which make the plant look as if it's propped up on stilts. Their leaves are deep green on top and lighter green underneath.

The black mangrove *(Avicennia germinans)* has *pneumatophores* or 'breathing roots,' which grow upwards and take oxygen into the system. This kind of mangrove excretes salt through its leaves, which are dark green with white salt crystals on them.

The white mangrove *(Laguncularia racemosa)* does not have a root system like the

Islamorada Beach, Florida Keys

Hurricane Opal damage (1996)

Smallest post office in the USA, Ochopee

Portofino Towers, Miami Beach

Alligator wrestling, Miccosukee Cultural Center

NICK & CORINNA SELBY

LEE FOSTER

KEN LAFFAL

RICHARD CUMMINS

NIK WHEELER

ROBERT HOLMES
American alligators

ART WOLFE
Rare pink flamingo among mangroves

DOUG PERRINE
Loggerhead turtle

JAMES D WATT
Loggerhead turtle

TED LEVIN
Cottonmouth snake

CATHERINE GEHM
Sea grapes

TED LEVIN
Male red-bellied woodpecker

RICHARD P PERKINS
Hibiscus

other two and looks more like a run-of-the-mill tree. Its leaves are light green; they excrete salt through glands at their base.

Hammocks

Hammocks are tracts of forested land that rise above adjacent marshes, pineland, prairie or swamp. In South Florida, they're often tropical hardwood forests, usually very dense, with an understory of shade-loving plants. Common plant species include gumbo-limbo *(Bursera simaruba)*, pigeon plum *(Cocoloba diversifolia)*, soldierwood *(Colubrina elliptica)*, crabwood *(Psychotria undata)* and white stopper *(Eugenia axillaris)*, which is the bush that produces that skunk aroma you keep smelling all over South Florida.

Sea Oats

Sea oats *(Uniola paniculata)* get their name from the large plumes they produce, but they're far from oats. They're protected vegetation in Florida because they trap wind-blown sand and thereby stabilize sand dunes. It's illegal to pick or disturb them in any way.

Sea Grapes

Sea grapes *(Coccoloba uvifera)* are coastal landscape plants native to Florida that stand up to wind and saltwater. They have large, round leaves and produce a small, purple, edible fruit that braver people eat or make into jelly.

Pine Flatwoods

Pine flatwoods usually don't have very rich soil and are home to mainly slash pine and saw palmetto, though sometimes cabbage palms (see below) grow in these as well.

Spanish Moss

The most surprising thing about Spanish moss *(Tillandsia usneoides)*, the ubiquitous, armpit-hair-like frilly stuff attached to trees in the northern areas of the state, is that it's not a moss at all; it's an air plant and a member of the pineapple family. That's right, pineapple. Its seeds have tiny parachutes that carry them from tree to tree. In some areas of the state, notably Tallahassee and on St George Island, Spanish moss can get so thick and tangled that it jumps from treetop to treetop across roads, creating a 'canopy.'

Sawgrass

Sawgrass is the main vegetation in the Everglades but grows wherever it's wet. It's rough, firm, stiff and green; fine teethlike edges give it its name.

Strangler Figs

The rope-like roots you'll see growing on cypress trees or cabbage palms are the strangler fig *(Ficus aurea)*, whose seeds start growing as an air plant. As the strangler fig grows, it sends off roots, which wrap around the trunk of its host, eventually literally strangling and killing it.

Palms

Florida has many species of palms, which are tropical evergreen trees and shrubs with branchless trunks and fanned leaves in clumps at their top. The following are the most common palms you'll run into:

Cabbage palm *(Sabal palmetto)*
    Tall and sometimes bent at fantastic angles, as on Lincoln Road Mall in Miami Beach.

Coconut palm *(Cocos nucifera)*
    The classic desert-island fantasy, tall and gracefully curved, these do indeed produce coconuts. It's rare to find mature fruit in Florida, as landscapers hack them off as soon as they're large enough to hurt someone if the fruit should fall during a windstorm. If you do find one large enough (it's about the size and shape of an American football), hack off the top with a machete and use a straw to drink the juice. You'll sometimes see this offered from carts on the street in Miami's Little Havana.

King palm *(Archontophoenix alexandrae)*
    Native to Australia, this introduced ornamental is a knobby-trunked beast that can reach heights of up to 75 feet.

Royal palm *(Roystonea regia)*
    Native to South Florida and Cuba, these enormous and very straight-growing palms have a white trunk and very long foliage. They line Palm Beach's Royal Palm Way.

Sago palm *(Cycas revoluta)*
  Short-trunked with leaves spreading out like a Japanese fan, these introduced ornamentals look as if they're playing a game of cards.

Yellow butterfly/areca palm *(Chrysalidocarpus lutescens)*
  Another introduced ornamental, native to Asia, these grow in clumps of several plants, which look as if they're racing their siblings to attain maximum height. Look for curved trunks and lush leaves.

Flowering Plants

The following are some flowering plants and trees you're most likely to encounter in Florida (not necessarily native ones):

Allamanda – White or pink, trumpet-shaped flower; toxic

Bougainvillea – A vine with clusters of red, pink, white or orange flowers

Cassia – Also called golden or pink shower tree, depending on the color of the flowers, which appear before the leaves of the tree do

Cup of Gold – An 8- to 10-inch-diameter flower that opens white and turns bright yellow; toxic

Frangipani – An evergreen shrub with delicious-smelling white, pink or red flowers; instantly recognizable to anyone who's ever seen a movie or TV show featuring somebody getting off a plane in Hawaii

Hibiscus – A big, delicate, trumpet-shaped flower in red, white, yellow or pink; each flower blooms only for one day

Ixora – Red, sometimes white, clusters of starlike flowers; an evergreen perennial

Jacaranda – Purplish-blue bell-shaped flowers on a tree with fernlike leaves; one of our absolute favorites

Oleander – Pink, white, red or yellow flowers; a very toxic shrub

Royal Poinciana – Also called flame tree, with reddish-orange flowers; also a favorite of ours

Spider lily – You'll see many different kinds of lilies, but we particularly like the smell of this one; it's white and spider-like and toxic

Fruit Trees

Throughout Florida, you'll run into orange, grapefruit, lemon, lime and tangerine groves (see Economy later in the chapter). And when you wonder why all the fruit you see in Publix and Winn-Dixie supermarkets sucks,

it's because the good stuff is sent up north! There are also wild banana, mango and papaya trees almost everywhere you go. Most people are a little touchy about strangers walking up to their trees and snatching fruit, so ask first.

FAUNA
Crocodolians

Crocodilians are the world's largest living reptiles, and two species are native to the USA: the American alligator *(Alligator Mississippiensis)* and the American crocodile *(Crocodylus acutus)*. Crocodiles are very rare in Florida, so if you see a crocodilian here, it's probably an alligator. This can be considered a good thing by visitors: crocs are the more aggressive of the two.

Alligators The name derives from the Spanish *el lagarto*, the lizard. Alligators are carnivorous; hatchlings eat insects, frogs, small fish, snails and the like. As they grow, they move on to bigger game, but they're never above small snacks like a cricket or grasshopper. Alligators' jaws close on reflex: when open (the muscles to open their mouths are far weaker than those that close them), their closing mechanisms are triggered by anything touching the inside of their mouths.

When that something is edible, the alligator clamps down upon it, raises its head and gulps – swallowing prey small enough in one gulp, and crushing and tearing larger prey repeatedly until swallowable. Stories of alligators dragging prey underwater to drown it are hooey.

Appearance Alligators indeed look like long and scary lizards. Males grow to between 9 and 12 feet, females 6 to 8 feet; the largest found in Florida was a terrifying 17 1/2 feet. Alligators generally live to an age of 30 to 35 years in the wild, longer when raised in captivity.

Young alligators are black with bright stripes and blotches of yellow on their backs, and cream-colored bellies. As they grow older, they lose the stripes, but the stomach remains light-colored. It's said that Indians believed rubbing a gator's stomach would make it fall asleep – volunteers?

Alligators have a broad snout (the most obvious difference between alligators and crocodiles, which have narrow ones), and a socket in the upper jaw hides their fourth tooth (which is visible on crocs). There's nothing external to distinguish male and female alligators to the casual observer.

Alligators have large corneas, which enhance their night vision. They can see underwater, too: transparent, protective membranes cover their eyes when submerged.

Habitat Alligators are usually (but not exclusively) found in fresh water such as shallow lakes, marshes, swamps, rivers, creeks, ponds and man-made canals. American alligators are found primarily in Louisiana, Florida and southern Georgia. They're a common sight sunning themselves along Florida riverbanks, and occasionally you can catch a glimpse of the lazy reptiles swimming across rivers and streams.

Gators are warm-weather fans and will rarely feed when the temperature dips below 68°F; their metabolism slows considerably in cold weather. But gators are cold-blooded and can die when the temperature is more than 100°F. To cool themselves, alligators sit on riverbanks or in the shade with their mouths wide open, which dissipates heat.

In the Everglades, where deep, open water is limited, females live in ponds, venturing into open areas for breeding. Males prowl, and during mating season make house calls on many ponds, searching for female companionship. Nesting occurs in June and July, hatching in August.

In the winter dry season, alligators become a crucial factor in the survival of many species by digging 'gator holes' – artificial ponds. They dig with their mouth and legs, sweeping out mud and vegetation with lashes of their tails. As the hole fills with water, the gators keep it free of vegetation with further tail-lashing housekeeping. When the dry season comes, gator holes are often the only source of fresh water for many

Alligator Attacks

Generally speaking, alligators don't pose a threat to humans, and they attack from hunger, not maliciousness. But certain activities will cause alligators to become aggressive.

The most common mistake people make is feeding alligators, which is about as stupid as climbing a zoo fence to pet a cute tiger. When humans feed alligators, the gators naturally begin to associate humans with food – and if you're not holding out a cheeseburger, an alligator used to being fed by people might then consider making a snack of your arm. It is illegal in Florida to feed alligators.

Alligators – males and females – are also very protective of their young and will descend upon any threat to any young alligator, not just their own, with great vigor. Acts seen as threatening can be as inadvertent as coming between a parent and child, say, in a canoe. The chief warning that you've behaved offensively is a loud hissing sound – a call for assistance, answered by other gators with as much enthusiasm as cops to an 'officer down' radio call. Get away as fast as possible and do not look back until you are safe – in a bar.

other animals, and many come to hang out. Rent, however, can be expensive: some of the visitors become gator dinner.

Threats to Alligators While alligator eggs and infants are eaten by raccoons, otters and sometimes even other alligators, generally speaking, humankind is alligators' only natural enemy. Formerly abundant in the wild in Florida, an estimated 10 million alligators were killed from hunting and the draining of wetlands in the late 19th century until the Mason-Smith Act, which banned the sale of endangered species in 1969. Alligators had been considered endangered since the mid-1940s. Thanks to protection, the alligator population has recovered to such an extent it was reclassified as 'threatened' in 1985. It is still illegal to hunt or molest alligators in the wild, and strict penalties apply to violators.

Other threats to alligators include cars and loss of habitat.

Crocodiles The crocodile is classified as an endangered species. While there have never been as many crocs as alligators in Florida, there are only an estimated 400 to 500 left in the wild, and their numbers are not substantially increasing.

Crocodiles are more aggressive than alligators (though the American crocodile is not particularly aggressive) and will attack humans with relatively less provocation. They can be smaller than alligators but range in size from 3 to 15 feet; males are larger than females. Crocodiles nest on marl banks, porous sand or shell beaches.

American crocodiles prefer coastal, brackish and saltwater habitats (but they can live in fresh water). Their snouts are more tapered and triangular than those of alligators, and their fourth tooth is exposed. Their bodies are grayish-green, with a light-colored underside; young crocs have dark bands on their back and tail.

Adult crocodiles feed at night in the water. They eat fish, crabs, birds, turtles, snakes and small mammals. In daytime they rest in creeks or in dens, which they build within vegetation.

Nests – which you really don't want to approach, okay? – are found near deep water. Eggs are laid in April and May, and after hatching in July and August, mothers carry their newborns to the water in their mouths.

As with alligators, humans are their only natural enemies, though smaller crocs fall victim to the same attacks as smaller alligators.

Turtles

Florida turtles, both sea and land, are either threatened or endangered species, protected by state and federal law. The (relatively) most common sea turtle found in Florida is the loggerhead sea turtle *(Caretta caretta)* (threatened). Also seen, but far more rarely, are the green sea turtle *(Chelonia midas)* and, even more rarely, leatherbacks *(Dermochelys coriacea)*, the largest of the sea turtles. Both the green sea and leatherback turtle are endangered. Disturbing turtle nests or possession of live or dead turtles can result in fines or imprisonment.

Nesting Florida's beaches are a perfect nesting ground for sea turtles. Nesting occurs from May to September. Turtles swim ashore at night, preferably onto a wide beach, and pull themselves forward using their foreflippers to find a suitable (the drier the better) area for nesting. They hollow a pit with their front flippers, which helps them settle into the sand, and then dig a cylindrical cavity of about 20 inches with their rear flippers.

The turtle raises its hind flippers and releases two to three eggs at a time; she'll lay about 100 in all, each about the size of a ping-pong ball. The eggs have a leathery shell, which prevents them from breaking when they hit the sand. Using her front flippers, the turtle covers the eggs with sand and returns to the water. Sea turtles don't guard their nests, but loggerheads build four to five nests per season at intervals of 10 to 12 days.

The eggs fall victim to raccoons and other small animals that dig them up for food. Surviving to the hatching stage is really a matter of luck, and only one in 1000 turtles will reach maturity.

Hatching Hatching occurs after about 60 days. Baby turtles orient themselves by moonlight to find the water, and here is yet another instance of humankind's development leading to tragedy for nature: turtle hatchlings are frequently disoriented by the lights from the condominiums and hotels that line the beaches, and often walk off in the wrong direction.

Volunteers in Turtle Watch programs throughout the state (see especially the John D MacArthur State Park section in the Southeast Florida chapter and also the

Canaveral National Seashore section in the Space Coast chapter) stand by at hatching time and try to point the turtles in the right directions, employing any method they can – including flashlights and search lights – to get them into the sea.

Manatees

The Florida manatee *(Trichechus manatus)* is a subspecies of the West Indian manatee. Also called the sea cow, the Florida manatee is another endangered species. Once abundant throughout the tropical and subtropical Caribbean waters, only between 1500 and 2200 manatees are left in the wild today.

Manatees have large, plump, grayish-brown bodies with two small forelimbs and a tail shaped like a beaver's. They have a large, flexible upper lip that's covered with small whiskers. Manatees range in size from about 9 to 12 feet, and weigh between 1000 to 2500 pounds.

They are herbivores and consume 10 to 15% of their body weight daily. After 13 months of pregnancy, females give birth to only one calf – every two to five years. They have no natural enemies except humans.

Dolphins

The most common dolphin species in Florida is the bottle-nosed dolphin *(Tursiops truncatus)*, which isn't as shy as a common dolphin. It's very easy to see them throughout Florida, even in Biscayne Bay! If you're canoeing or kayaking in the Everglades and notice playful critters leaping out of the water alongside your boat, you may be looking at bottle-nosed dolphins or porpoises – look for the long snout (bottle-nosed) or no snout (porpoise).

Bubba: Manatees' Biggest Threat

Manatees are shy and utterly peaceful mammals, and humankind is their only natural threat. Pollution is a problem, but their biggest killers are boaters, and of those, the worst offenders are pleasure boaters. Manatees seek warm, shallow water and feed on vegetation. South Florida is surrounded by just such an environment, but, unfortunately for the manatees, it also has one of the highest concentrations of pleasure boats in the world.

Despite pleas from environmental groups, wildlife advocates and the local, state and federal governments, which have declared many areas Manatee Zones, some pleasure boaters routinely exceed speed limits and ignore simple practices that would help protect the species.

After grabbing a bite, manatees float up for air and often float just beneath the surface, chewing and hanging around. When speedboats zoom through the area, manatees are hit by the hulls and either knocked away or pushed under the boat, whose propeller then gashes the mammal repeatedly as the boat passes overhead. Few manatees get through life without propeller scars, which leave slices in their bodies similar to the diagonal slices on a loaf of French bread.

And yet some boaters don't see this as a problem. They consider manatees to be stupid ('cause so many git kilt') and, if you can believe this, a cause of reduced property values. 'Guy moves into a $4 million house down in the Grove,' said Norm, who runs a water-taxi service in Miami, 'and he wants to take his boat up to Miami to eat at Hard Rock. Then you say he can only go 5 mph to save a manatee? He'll move somewhere else.'

There are several organizations throughout the state that rescue and rehabilitate injured manatees, but they're fighting what would appear to be a losing battle. The two largest are SeaWorld in Orlando and Seaquarium in Miami. See the Central Florida and Miami chapters for more information.

To identify an individual bottle-nosed dolphin, look at its dorsal fin – when dolphins fight (and they do, so get those Flipper images out of your head), they take chunks out of their fins. Every dorsal fin is shaped differently.

Florida Panthers

The beautiful Florida panther *(Felis concolor coryi)* has been on the endangered species list since 1973. Only about 30 to 50 remain in the wild. The reasons for their decline are hunting, habitat loss and cars and trucks. Because they're so rare, inbreeding has lead to genetic defects.

In 1982, they became the official mammal of Florida. Panthers are large, light-brown, sleek and very elegant cats. They're solitary animals that grow to about 7 feet long, 4 feet high and weigh up to 150 pounds. They feed on deer, hogs, raccoons and sometimes even alligators. Three kittens is an average litter; the gestation period is about three months.

The few that are left are found primarily in South Florida, in the Everglades and Big Cypress parks. Sadly, the only opportunity most visitors will have to see one is in a zoo, or dead on a roadside.

Birds

Pelicans are large brown birds that live to an average age of 30 years. They weigh 5 to 8 pounds, and eat about half their body weight in fish daily. They're also positively prehistoric looking, resembling pterodactyls, and are hilarious – especially when they've grabbed a fish and are carrying it around in the sack beneath their chins.

Florida has several types of herons, long-necked wading birds who fold their necks over their backs in flight. Throughout the state, you'll see snowy egrets and great white herons, along with ibis and the pink and orange roseate spoonbill. You'll only see pink flamingoes in a zoo.

Bald eagles, our national symbol, are an endangered species; there are only about 600 pairs of them left in Florida. Adults have a white head and tail. The body is dark, and the eyes, bill and legs are yellow. They grow to about 3 feet high and can reach a

wingspan of 8 feet. They're visible in several Atlantic coast state parks, but you'll have to wait around for a while.

Wood storks, large wading birds with a dark featherless head, a stout bill, and a 5-foot wingspan, have been classified as endangered since 1985, when they were recognized as victims of wetlands draining.

Coral Reef

Florida's coral reef is the largest in North America and the third largest in the world. Corals belong to the phylum Cnidaria; they look like plants, but they're actually animals. Individual members of coral (polyps) attach themselves to reefs and form a coral colony by producing calcium carbonate. The sea fans and whips found here – the ones that make it all seem like plant life – are unique to coral reefs in this area.

Coral reefs are to the underwater world what sea oats (see earlier) are to sand dunes: their rigidity catches sand and protects the shoreline from erosion by violent seas or storms. Coral reefs have an ecological diversity equal to, if not greater than, an entire tropical rainforest and are home to thousands of varieties of plant and animal life, many with symbiotic relationships.

To exist, coral reefs require very stable warm temperatures and pure water, conditions threatened on several fronts. Storms and radical temperature shifts have both affected the area. According to the World

Meteorological Organization, the earth's average surface temperature in 1999 (58°F) was the highest since the 19th century. This heat is causing bleaching of the reefs in Indonesia and the Seychelles and is expected to occur in Florida and the Caribbean as well.

The purity of the water may have been threatened by a decline in fresh water in Florida Bay, a result of diverting water from the Everglades. In an effort to rebalance the salinity in Florida Bay, 'fresh' – that is, non-saline – water was pumped into the bay. But that water was full of agricultural runoff, including phosphates and nitrates, which disturbed the area's ecological balance.

All this, combined with humankind's meddling, is killing the coral in the Keys. It has already long since died in areas to the north. Some of the reef's enemies are boaters carelessly dropping anchor or running aground on coral, swimmers, divers and snorkelers standing on it or taking pieces of it, fishing and overfishing, and 'nutrient' – that's sewage to you and me – being pumped into South Florida water from the Florida Keys (where the sewage is only partially treated before being pumped directly into the ocean).

GOVERNMENT & POLITICS

With the exception of its long and proud history of open and seemingly encouraged graft, corruption and conflict of interest dating to Spanish explorers and pirates of all nationalities, the Florida state government is a miniature replica of the US federal government. (The US government at least has the decency to attempt to hush up such activities.) The US legislature is made up of the bicameral Congress – the Senate and the House of Representatives. The Senate has two senators from each of the 50 states, while the 435-member House has one or more members from each state, depending on the state's population. Florida, the USA's fourth-most-populous state, has 23 representatives.

The US judicial branch is headed by the Supreme Court, which has nine justices who are appointed for life by the President and

The Florida Lottery

Florida has no state income tax and relies heavily on tourists (who pay a hotel tax), consumers (who pay state sales tax) and lottery players to support itself. The Florida Lottery is an unbelievably crafty dodge that brings in hundreds of millions of dollars a year to the state by promising – and sometimes even delivering – huge payoffs. While we think lotteries unconscionably suck money from the poor, the Florida Lottery is too big to ignore.

All lottery games are variations of the centuries-old numbers racket, in which the player picks numbers and hopes to match them to those chosen at random (at least in official games) on live television by large-breasted women supervised by hulking thugs. You can buy tickets at supermarkets, liquor stores and even in video stores.

Some games include the following:

Lotto Choose six from 48 numbers. The weekly Lotto drawing has a minimum payoff of $7 million – and if no one wins it, the pot is increased weekly until someone does. When we were last in town, the payoff got up to almost $70 million, and folks drove in from neighboring southern states and from as far away as New York to buy tickets.

Fantasy 5 Pick five from 26 numbers from Monday to Friday; payoffs start at $20,000.

Scratching games Laminated cards you scratch to see if you've won. Prizes range from another ticket to a billion gezillion dollars. Win for Life is a scratch-off game that pays off winners at the rate of $1000 a week for the rest of their lives.

approved by the Senate. The executive branch consists of the President, elected to a four-year term, the 14-member Cabinet and various assistants.

The Florida legislature is also a bicameral body made up of a House of Representatives and a Senate. Bills are introduced by representatives and go through several subcommittees before being argued and amended on the floor of the House, which then passes them on to the Senate, which sends them through several subcommittees, and argues and amends them further. They're then sent back to the House for even *further* amendment, and, finally, to the Governor, who can sign a bill into law or veto it. About half of all bills die in the process.

The capital city is Tallahassee, in the northwest central section of the state, which was a geographical compromise reached when Florida had two capitals, St Augustine and Pensacola.

ECONOMY

Florida's economy relies heavily on tourism, its most lucrative and important business. Almost 49 million tourists visited Florida in 1998.

But Miami's status as gateway to Latin America has also made it a powerhouse in international business: more than 400 multinational companies have operations in Miami, and 150 have their Latin American headquarters here, including Sony, Toshiba, Apple, American Airlines, UPS, Eastman Kodak and Texaco.

Miami customs processes 40% of all US exports to Latin America and the Caribbean. The city is also establishing itself as an international banking center: more than 100 international banks call it home.

Other important economic activities in the state include sugar production; the $8-billion-a-year citrus industry, which produces much of the country's frozen concentrated orange juice, bottled juice, grapefruit sections and citrus salad; electronics, programming and simulation technology; space exploration and space-related industry.

Minerals are important to Florida's economy as well. In fact, Florida mines about a quarter of the world's phosphate. Other minerals include limestone, peat,

zircon, dolomite and sulfur. Oil and gas exploration continues in the Big Cypress National Preserve, but drilling is heavily restricted if not impossible. There is oil and gas drilling in about 20 fields in Florida.

POPULATION & PEOPLE

The latest figures estimate Florida's population is just about 14.7 million, up almost 700,000 since 1995, and from 11.9 million in 1990 and 9.5 million in 1980.

An astounding 45% of the population of Miami is foreign born: Cubans are the largest group, followed by Canadians, Haitians, Germans and Jamaicans.

Most of the population in the state is concentrated in coastal cities, and the largest of

Flocks of 'snowbirds' head to Florida in winter.

those are in the south: more than a quarter of the state's population lives south of Alligator Alley (Hwy 84/I-75).

There are two federally recognized Indian tribes in Florida with reservations: the Seminole Tribe of Florida (☎ 954-370-3900, www.seminoletribe.com), with reservations in Hollywood, Tampa, Big Cypress National Preserve and Brighton, near Lake Okeechobee; and the Miccosukee Tribe (☎ 305-223-8380), with a reservation on the Tamiami Trail. Of the direct descendants of the Florida Creek Indians (see the boxed text Who Were the Seminole? earlier in the chapter), there are today about 500 Miccosukee and 2500 Seminole, though the 1990 census claimed there were about 3600

Native Americans living in the state of Florida. That figure included the Panhandle, descendants of Creeks from Alabama and Georgia, and members of other tribes.

Gaming, usually bingo, is held on Indian reservations (the Miccosukee have a bingo hall along the Tamiami Trail, the Seminole at several sites), and cultural celebrations are held throughout the state throughout the year. Contact the tribes or check the Seminole tribe's great website for information about these.

Sadly, until recently, souvenir shops and airboat-ride franchises and the reprehensible alligator wrestling shows at the Miccosukee Cultural Center were the main form of contact travelers could make with Florida's Indians.

But in the last few years, the Seminole Tribe has been expanding its efforts to preserve and interpret the culture, language and customs of the Florida Seminole beyond the reservation. Their excellent website (see above) is a great starting point, and Lee Tiger, the Seminole Tribe's tourism coordinator (himself a Miccosukee), has been working closely with Visit Florida to build tours and excursions around Seminole traditions. The Ah-Tah-Thi-Ki Museum on the Big Cypress Reservation is one superb result of this work. See the Everglades chapter for more information.

EDUCATION

Florida's public grade schools and Florida's students fall short of the national average in many areas, notably in Scholastic Aptitude Tests (SATs), the criterion for college and university admissions in the USA. And the number of students who drop out before graduation is more than the national average. It's not surprising: Florida spends less than almost any other state on its education system, though it spends more than any other state on prison construction. As one local said, 'You can't blame the state for that; they're executing prisoners as quickly as they can!'

The US education system places children in classes (grades) based on age and performance from first to 12th grade. Generally speaking, normally progressing pupils are placed in a grade number five less than their age: 1st grade begins at age six, 12th grade at age 17, etc.

Florida has several state and private universities: the University of Florida in Gainesville, University of Miami, Florida International University in Miami and Florida State University in Tallahassee are the major players.

ARTS

Much of the state's arts – with the exception of local crafts, which can be found all over – emanate from South Florida, the vast majority from Miami. Over the past decade, Miami's gentrification and redevelopment have resulted in an explosion of artistic and cultural activity, and it's coming from all demographic sectors. Many artists who were formerly based in other areas of the country, notably the northeast, headed down there to take advantage of lower real-estate prices and the increase in quirky and affluent visitors.

The influx of foreigners to the area has resulted in a boom in Caribbean and South American art as well.

Literature

While inroads are being made in poetry and experimental fiction, the Miami literature scene remains primarily a hotbed of mystery, scandal and detective novels. But no list of Florida writers would be complete without mention of Florida's best known: Marjorie Kinnan Rawlings, Ernest Hemingway and Zora Neale Hurston.

Rawlings' books contain beautiful descriptions of rural Florida life. She's best known for *The Yearling*, the story of Jodie Baxter's love for a fawn that alienates the boy from his family, but Rawlings is also author of books including *Cross Creek*, which describes her home in a town near Gainesville, and *Jacob's Ladder*.

Ernest Hemingway, known as much (in Florida, anyway) for his drinking in Key West bars as for his distinctive style and riveting tales of moral dilemmas, lived in that city during one of his most fertile periods. It was there that he completed many of his best-loved works, including *A Farewell to Arms*. Key West is rife with Hemingway-obelia. See the Florida Keys chapter for more information.

Author of seven books, Zora Neale Hurston (1903-60) is best known for *Their Eyes Were Watching God*, her 1937 novel about an independent black woman in rural Florida. Hurston, born in Eatonville, also compiled southern black folklore. Also see the Central Florida chapter.

Poetry Of the poets emerging, most notable are Richard Blanco (*City of a Hundred Fires*), Jeffrey Knapp and Adrian Castro (mainly spoken-word performances), Campbell McGrath (*American Noise* and *Capitalism*), Michael Hettich (*Small Boat* and *Immaculate Bright Rooms*), John Balaban (*Blue Mountain* and *Words for My Daughter*) and Ricardo Pau-Llosa (*Cuba*).

Pick up *Latino Stuff Review* or *Mangrove*, both free journals of local poetry and literature available at Books & Books.

Suspense/Thriller South Florida has more than a dozen international superstar suspense/thriller writers, and more are appearing every day. Heavy hitters include Carl Hiassen, whose books (*Stormy Weather, Skin Tight, Native Tongue* and *Strip Tease*) offer snarling satire of South Florida and especially its tourists and developers. Hiassen's latest work, published by Ballantine Books, is *Team Rodent: How Disney Devours the World*, an eminently readable, if only 83-big-font-wide-spaced-pages-long rant against Mauschwitz and all who run it.

Not to be forgotten, of course, is Elmore Leonard, author of dozens of books including *Get Shorty, Swag, The Moonshine War, Gold Coast, The Switch* and *Maximum Bob*.

Other Miami stars include Pulitzer Prize-winning *Miami Herald* columnist Edna Buchanan (*Miami, It's Murder; Suitable for Framing; Nobody Lives Forever*); Paul Levine, whose attorney Jake Lassiter and his ex-coroner sidekick traipse through intricate psychological suspense in books such as *Mortal Sin, To Speak for the Dead* and *Night*

Vision; Les Standiford, author of the eco-thriller *Spill* and other novels starring building contractor John Deal in *Deal to Die For, Done Deal* and *Book Deal*.

Tampa-based Randy Wayne White writes richly detailed thrillers set on Sanibel Island, an enclave of weirdness on the Florida gulf coast; his hero, Doc Ford, stars in books including *North of Havana, Captiva* and *Sanibel Flats*.

Tom Corcoran's *The Mango Opera*, starring Key West-based freelance photographer Alex Rutledge, is a seriously good read of a first novel.

The quintessential grizzled Miami author is Charles Willeford, best known for *Miami Blue*, but author of almost two dozen other titles including *The Way We Die Now* and *Sideswipe*. Still others are James W Hall, whose Florida Keys-based mysteries include *Mean Hightide, Beginning Algebra, Buzz Cut* and *Hard Aground*; and Dan Wakefield, who wrote *Going All the Way* and *Starting Over*, in addition to *New York in the '50s*.

Fred D'Aguiar, a poet who teaches at the University of Miami, has just seen two new novels published, and brothers Robert and Brian Antony are novelists, very well known around the Miami literature scene.

Keep one eye on Lynn Barrett, whose collection of short stories is entitled *The Land of Go*, and the other eye on Cuban-born mystery writer Carolina Garcia-Aguilera, whose first book, *Bloody Waters*, has been very successful.

Naked Came the Manatee, a series by 13 of Miami's best-known writers including Les Standiford, Carl Hiassen, Dave Barry (see Humor, below), Paul Levine, Edna Buchanan, James W Hall, Vicky Hendricks, John Dufresne and Elmore Leonard in *Tropic* magazine, was expanded into book form. It's published by Putnam; proceeds are being donated to charity.

The last Friday of every month is Open Poetry Night at Books & Books (see the Miami chapter), and every November the Miami Book Fair is among the finest in the USA (see the Facts for the Visitor chapter). Books & Books runs a delightful series of events in South Florida throughout the year;

check its Website (www.booksandbooks .com) for a calendar of events.

The Butterfly Reading Series is held during the winter season upstairs at Tobacco Road (see Places to Eat in the Miami chapter) on Tuesday evenings at 8 pm.

Florida International University (FIU) publishes *Gulf Stream*, a national magazine of poetry and literature. The FIU Creative Writing Program, with Standiford as current director, has spawned several new literary up-and-comers, most notably Vicky Hendricks (the bordering-on-pornographic snuff-book *Miami Purity*) and Barbara Parker (*Suspicion of Innocence* – is that a great title or what?).

Humor Also incredibly well known is Dave Barry, the humorist whose columns are syndicated throughout the world. He's the author of books including *Dave Barry Is Not Making This Up*, *Dave Barry Turns 40*, *Dave Barry's Only Travel Guide You'll Ever Need*, *Dave Barry's Guide to Cyberspace* and *Dave Barry's Greatest Hits*.

Music & Theater

While classical music has a local hero in the innovative New World Symphony, and some local bands are gaining recognition, the biggest story in Florida is Latin- and Caribbean-influenced music, including salsa, reggae, merengue, mambo, rhumba, cha-cha and calypso. The big stars are Gloria Estefan, Celia Cruz, the androgynous Albita, Giolberto Santa Rosa, Willy Chirino and Jerry Rivera as well as dance bands like Los Van Van, who perform in all-night *bailable* dance concerts.

The best times to see ensemble Cuban bands – often with up to 20 musicians and singers – is during special celebrations, like the Calle Ocho Festival (see the Facts for the Visitor chapter).

And then there's classical. Every once in a while you hear of an idea so absolutely sensible and so totally reasonable that you kick yourself for not having thought it up yourself: Miami's New World Symphony is one of those. Established in 1987, the NWS is described as a 'learning and performing experience for gifted graduates of the most prestigious music schools.' It is a collection of the best and the brightest young (usually in their 20s) musicians in the country, spending about three years of postgraduate time performing with the symphony in concerts around the country and the world.

The members live in absolutely tiny rooms in a renovated Art Deco hotel near the Bass Museum and spend pretty much all their waking hours either talking about, rehearsing, jamming or otherwise being involved with the performance of music. The energy level in the dorms is enough to guarantee a good concert, so by the time these people get into the fantastically renovated Lincoln Theatre for a concert – whoa, Nelly, hold on to your hat. See the Miami chapter for further information.

Throughout the state, regional orchestras, such as the Florida Symphony and the Jacksonville Symphony, perform classical concerts regularly; performances and venues are listed throughout the book.

Dance

There are 46 nonprofit dance organizations registered with the Metro-Dade (Miami area) cultural-affairs council alone, and the state has thousands of dance-related businesses such as studios, schools and production companies. The mix of American, African, Cuban, Haitian, European and Latin American cultures is obvious in the productions you'll see throughout the state. The two biggest players in the state are the Miami City Ballet and the Miami-based Florida Dance Association, which holds and coordinates many performances throughout Florida.

Painting & Sculpture

In the mid-1980s, artists began to discover South Beach/Miami was a place where they could get much more space and live far cheaper than in other art centers like New York and Los Angeles. While there are small pockets of artists in other Florida cities, among them St Augustine and Ybor City in Tampa, the art scene in Florida is very Miami-centric.

The SoBe Boom was almost single-handedly responsible for the injections of cash that have fueled the art boom in South Beach. As recently as the early 1980s, Miami's art scene was virtually nonexistent, and today, though the lack of many major galleries or a truly world-class museum is still an issue, the arts market can definitely be described as established, if not thriving.

Real-estate developers encouraged the arts by incorporating local artists' projects in the designs of private and public spaces, such as the Margulies sculpture garden, which includes works by Richard Serra, Isamu Noguchi, Mark di Suivero and Jonathan Borofsky, now on long-term loan to the campus of Florida International University. The South Florida Art Center (an artist-run organization) bought and leased buildings to provide affordable studios and exhibition space in the mid-'80s, which significantly helped revitalize Lincoln Road. And the Museum of Contemporary Art (MOCA), designed by Charles Gwathmey, is an excellent example of a fusion of urban and cultural planning, placing a civic and cultural center within a residential and commercial area.

Established Miami artists today include Susan Banks, Carol Brown, Robert Thiele, Marilyn Gottlieb-Roberts, Sheila Friedman and Salvatore La Rosa. Transplants (artists well known in other markets who have made their homes in Miami) include Jack Pierson, Felix Gonzalez-Torres, Robert Juarez and Kenny Scharf.

Another major impact on Miami's art community has been the influence of Cuban and Latin American artists such as Felix Gonzalez-Torres, Jac Leirner, Ernesto Nero, Gabriel Orozco, Jorge Pardo, Jose Bedia (perhaps best known), Tomas Sanchez, Consuelo Castaneda, Teresita Fernandez, Maria Martinez-Canas and Wilfredo Lam.

Film

At the turn of the 19th century, before Hollywood was the shoe-in for world-film central, places like Jacksonville and even Hollywood, Florida, were cranking out films. These days, with Miami as hot as it is, filmmakers are flocking back to the area. In the last few years the Beach was featured in staggeringly successful films including *There's Something About Mary*, *Wild Things*, *The Bodyguard*, *Donnie Brasco*, *Ace Ventura: Pet Detective*, *True Lies*, *Get Shorty* and *Bird Cage*. There was also a string of stinkers including Eddie Murphy's *Holy Man*; Sly Stallone, Sharon Stone and James Woods in the unspeakably embarrassing *The Specialist*; proof that a wonderful novel can make the worst movie of the year with *Strip Tease*; and, for your dining and dancing pleasure, ladies and gentlemen, thespian Cindy Crawford as a tough-talkin', no-nonsense attorney in the unfathomable *Fair Game*.

From the beginnings of film, the area has been featured in some of America's most beloved classics, such as *The Cocoanuts* (the Marx Brothers' first feature); *Where the Sidewalk Ends*, filmed entirely at Miami Studios; *Citizen Kane*, which used the South Florida coastline as the setting for Xanadu, the largest pleasure palace in the world; *Key Largo* with Bogie and Bacall; *The Barefoot Mailman*; and three Bond films: *Dr No*, *Live & Let Die* and *Goldfinger*.

For a wonderful glimpse of Miami Beach in the worst of its recent troubles, rent a copy of *Black Sunday*, which features a car-and-foot chase through the South Beach of the early 1980s – as witnessed by thousands of octogenarians in beach chairs.

The glitzy and glamorous world of cocaine dealing and organized crime was explored in *Scarface*, a classic Miami movie starring Al Pacino.

Alec Baldwin played a delightful sicko in *Miami Blues*, based on the book by Charles Willeford, but by that time everyone in the world knew where Miami is, due to a television phenomenon: *Miami Vice*. If you watch the show today (it's available in many of the larger video-rental shops), you'll see the Beach at the turning point from Scuz-ball Alley to Fabulous beach spot. The series was filmed mainly in Miami Beach, but it's hilarious to see the way the action jumped to locations throughout the city. No film could possibly get away with that today, now that the layout of Miami is so universally recognizable.

The annual Miami International Film Festival, the Miami Beach Film Festival and the Miami Beach Film Society showcase the works of some of the area's rising talent as well as classics. (See the Special Events section in Facts for the Visitor, and the Entertainment section in the Miami chapter.)

Independent filmmaking is slowly making inroads, and foreign productions are streaming into the area.

Architecture

Florida's architecture can be referred to as 'prosaic,' but we'd rather call it 'spectacularly unspectacular.' With very few exceptions – notably Key West, Miami's Art Deco District, Ybor City in Tampa, and the historic districts in Pensacola and especially St Augustine – the architecture you'll run into is run-of-the-mill post-1950s urban sprawl. Buildings that don't look like shopping centers are probably condos – high-rise monsters that line the coasts.

There are several exceptions. The Spanish Colonial and Revival styles, predominant in St Augustine and Pensacola, resemble more the grand buildings of Mediterranean Spain, with archways, adobe, wood and terra-cotta tile, than the relatively stark version of Spanish Mission architecture found in the USA's Southwest. A perfect example, we hate to say it, is taste-bastion Donald Trump's Mar-a-Lago in Palm Beach.

Pockets of Victorian and Queen Anne pop up here and there, recognizable by their riotous colors and baubles, gingerbread towers, doo-dads and hoo-has. If you feel as if you've just walked into an expensive soap shop – or a B&B – it's probably a Victorian.

Cracker architecture, also called Florida Vernacular, is classic pioneer homesteading architecture with a twist: enormous sun porches. Early 'single pen' houses – simple boxes with porches – were later expanded by adding a wall that either straddled the

existing chimney (saddlebag) or was adjacent to the wall opposite the fireplace (double pen). Cracker homes run from quaint to enormous, and are wood inside and out.

While famous for three distinct architectural styles – Mediterranean, towering skyscrapers and Art Deco – Miami is made up mainly of boom-era construction with vibrant pockets of style here and there.

Of its three notable styles, Miami Beach is best known for its collection of Art Deco buildings. In the course of researching this book, we became convinced of only one thing: a group of architects discussing Art Deco will undoubtedly behave in the same manner as would a group of economists discussing...anything. Few agree on anything except the derivation of the term, a contraction of the title of the 1925 Parisian *Exposition Internationale des Arts Décoratifs et Industriels Modernes*, in which a strong emphasis was placed upon decorative arts.

The Exposition wasn't exactly the starting point; it was the dawn of a style that combined many forms – predominantly turn-of-the-19th century and pre-WWI European movements such as Art Nouveau, Arts & Crafts, the Vienna Secession and Italian Futurism, and the more geometric Modernism.

Today the term 'Art Deco' loosely refers to the product of the morphing of many styles in decorative and applied arts as well as architecture that occurred *essentially* between the 19-teens and 1940s. Deco can be broken into three distinct categories, European, Northeast/WPA and 'Tropical' Art Deco.

European Art Deco Art Deco in Europe, which was fairly short lived, had a lot to do with the Exposition itself. It was a play on classical Greek, Roman and Egyptian decorations, using more modern materials like sandstone, steel and frosted glass in an almost cubist manner – plain lines as opposed to the froufrou associated with architecture of the time. Good examples are the Au Palais de Chaillot, at the Trocadero in Paris, and Miami's main post office at 13th St and Washington Ave. It maintains the austerity of a government building while achieving a modern look.

Northeast/WPA This is a category that's almost absent on Miami Beach but is seen mainly in the northeastern USA as well as in any project associated with Roosevelt's Works Progress Administration (WPA). The style is characterized by heavy overtones of socialist ideals in concrete and granite, with lots of stainless steel and socialist frescos and big relief sculptures of workers – a perfect example is New York's Rockefeller Center. Northeast/WPA never caught on down here: there's no place for socialism in this bourgeois vacationland.

'Tropical' Art Deco The Deco of Miami Beach relied less on the implied meaning of decoration and more on simple geometric forms and colors, which worked well with the harsh sunlight to create interesting facades. It's important to note that the colors you now see are more garish than they originally were. Earlier, many of the buildings were white with only a color trim, and more pastels were used as opposed to the neon colors of today, which look very pretty but are essentially island color.

This branch of Deco – thrown up in boom-era construction – is often asymmetrical and inexpensively constructed of masonry and stucco with applied color. This is unlike the other two, richer styles of Deco, which relied on the color of the materials, like the pinkish hue of sandstone or the pink, brown or gray of granite. It's also interesting that the value of these buildings in Miami Beach is based more on the sheer number of protected historic buildings: individually, the inexpensively constructed houses would be worth far less.

SOCIETY & CONDUCT

'People in New York and Los Angeles,' said former *Miami Herald* columnist Eugene J Patron, 'have a lifestyle. Floridians have a life.' Northerners are often pleasantly surprised when interacting with Floridians (at least outside Miami), who tend to be more laid-back and friendly. Southern hospitality

is as good as its reputation, but one must remember that in Florida, the farther *north* you go, the farther *south* you get. The Panhandle may as well be Alabama, while Miami may as well be Newark, New Jersey.

Outside the major cities, especially in rural areas, Floridians tend to be more conservative; their politics and attitudes are old-fashioned and right wing. In rural areas, travelers should avoid behavior or dress that may be considered offensive – American flag T-shirts or pants are a definite no-no, as they're considered to be a desecration of the American flag. It's also not a good idea for women to wear revealing clothing or go braless. Gay and lesbian travelers in these areas should do their best to behave as 'straight' as possible. And all travelers should avoid public displays of affection.

Rednecks, who refer to themselves as just that, can be found in many areas of northern Florida, easily identified by their foul and racially derogatory language. It's best to leave them in peace to wallow in their ignorance. It is possible that travelers may hear remarks directed at Cubans, Jews, blacks, Asians and Native Americans, but racially motivated crimes are rare.

RELIGION
Western Religions
The area's residents are mostly Christians, but there are significant numbers of Jews here as well: many are transplants from the northeastern USA, but there are also a healthy number of Russian-Jewish and Cuban-Jewish immigrants. Many of the area's Jews are Reform, who do not adhere as strictly to the religious and social teachings of the Torah, as opposed to Conservative, more religious and ceremonial, and the extremely religious Orthodox.

The area is also home of the Florida branch of the Chabad Lubovitchers, a faction of Orthodox Judaism that proselytizes within the Jewish faith: if a long-haired, bearded man dressed in a black suit and white shirt and wearing a black hat or *yarmulke* asks you a) if you're Jewish and b) to step inside a recreational vehicle, you've just met a Lubovitcher.

Afro-Caribbean Religions

These religions include Santeria, a synchronism of the West African Yoruba religion with Catholicism. It was brought to Cuba by slaves who settled there and is primarily practiced in Cuba. Voodoo is Yoruba, as practiced by Haitians. Both of these religions practice animal sacrifice as a token of fidelity to the gods and spirits, and it's not uncommon to come upon animal remains at various places around the city, like along the Miami River, in parks and, strangely, near the Bass Museum.

Afro-Brazilian Religions

Afro-Brazilian religions, or cults, do not follow the ideas of major European or Asian religions; neither do they use doctrines to define good and evil. One of the things that was most shocking to Europeans in their first contact with the African images

and rituals was the cult of Exú. This entity was generally represented by combined human and animal images, complete with a horn and an erect penis. Seeking parallels between their own beliefs and African religions, European Catholics and Puritans identified Exú as Satan. For Africans, however, Exú represents the transition between the material and the spiritual worlds.

Candomblé, an African word denoting a dance in honor of the gods, is the most orthodox of the cults brought to Brazil from Africa by the Nago, Yoruba and Jeje peoples. In the ritual of Candomblé, Exú acts as a messenger between the gods and human beings. For example, everything related to money, love and protection against thieves comes under the watchful eye of Exú. Ultimately, Exú's responsibility is the temporal world.

LANGUAGE

'One of the nicest things about Miami,' goes an old joke, 'is how close it is to the USA.' Indeed, while English is the predominant language in the USA, Miami's proximity to countries that have generated mass refugee migrations has resulted in an above-average number of non-English-speaking, and some may say intentionally unassimilated, foreigners.

It's a somewhat unique situation in the USA. While pockets of foreigners have gravitated to other large cities, notably New York, Chicago and Los Angeles, there seems to be a higher degree of linguistic assimilation there than here, where as some put it, 'Them Cubans just won't talk English like everybody else.'

Visitors can get away with English only, but to do that is to essentially write off experiencing a huge chunk of Miami culture and life. While we've never had cause to speak the Creole patois, we found our Spanish indispensable when we lived here.

Spanish is the main language in almost every shop, café, coin laundry and restaurant in Little Havana, and in a surprising number of businesses elsewhere in the city.

The Voodoo Squad

Each weekday morning, members of the janitorial staff at the Metro-Dade Courthouse at 1351 NW 12th St In Miami patrol the grounds outside the building as part of the Voodoo Squad. According to an article in the *Miami Herald*, they're on the lookout for the remains of voodoo rituals performed by family members of those in custody in an effort to sway the outcome of trials.

Objects the janitors ecounter on a regular basis include dead goats, roosters, chickens and lizards with their mouths tied (though sometimes a cow tongue that's tied with twine is substituted), voodoo powder, corn kernels, cakes and eggs.

See the Facts for the Visitor chapter for Spanish menu information.

Spanish

Books Lonely Planet's *Latin American Spanish Phrasebook*, by Anna Cody, is comprehensive and compact. If you're planning on romancing some Latin types, the absolute finest resource is *Hot Spanish for Guys and Girls* and *Hot Spanish for Guys and Guys*, both published by BabelCom Books (New York) and both containing an amazing number of useful phrases from 'I'd like to hold your hand' to 'Lick around the edges.'

Pronunciation Spanish has five vowels: **a**, **e**, **i**, **o** and **u**. They are pronounced something like the highlighted letters of the following English words: f**a**ther, **e**nd, mar**i**ne, **o**r and tr**u**th. The stress is placed on the syllable with an accent over it (México = MEH-hiko) or the second to last syllable (hasta luego = AH-sta loo-EH-go).

Useful Words & Phrases

yes	*sí*
no	*no*
good/OK	*bueno*
bad	*malo*

Floridisms

The sheer size of the USA means that different regions have different accents and terminology to such an extent that people from different parts of the country have trouble communicating: a Bostonian asking for a 'tonic and a grinder' in New York would get a puzzled look, and then receive a glass of tonic water and a meat grinder instead of a cola and a large sandwich. Pick up a copy of Lonely Planet's *USA Phrasebook* for more – sometimes hilarious – information.

You'll hear generic southern vernacular as well as slang peculiar to Florida:

Anymore – In the South, 'anymore' refers to present as well as past tense, meaning both 'any longer' ('I don't love you anymore') *and* 'nowadays' ('We used to take US Hwy 1 but anymore we take I-95').

Bubba – Standard Key West catch-all greeting or reference ('Hey, Bubba, howzit goin?').

Chickee – Thatched hut, derived from Indian word for house. Pseudo-chickees are usually found in picnic areas in parks, but real chickees suitable for sleeping are found in the 10,000 Islands in the Everglades.

Conch – Native Key West resident; see the Key West chapter for information on the Conch Republic.

Cracker – Named for the sound of the cracking whips of cattle drivers, this is a term for white native Floridians whom you'd otherwise call rednecks. It can be pejorative if you need it to be.

CST – Cuban Standard Time; Miami excuse implying that Cubans are always late ('Sorry, I'm on CST').

Gorby – Derogative Key West term for tourists.

Parrothead – Jimmy Buffet fan.

Snowbird – Vacationing Northerner.

Touron – Derogative Key West term for tourists.

Y'all – Contraction of 'you all'; a generic reference to one or more ('Y'all ain't got no grits in Germany?').

YUCA – Cuban Yuppie – Young Urban Cuban American.

better	*mejor*	the train station	*la estación del ferrocarril*
best	*lo mejor*	bus	*gua gua* or *autobús**
more	*más*	train	*tren*
less	*menos*	taxi	*taxi*
very little	*poco* or *poquito*	toilet	*sanitario*

Greetings & Civilities

hello/hi	*hola*
good morning/day	*buenos días*
good evening/night	*buenas noches*
see you later	*hasta luego*
goodbye	*adiós*
pleased to meet you	*mucho gusto*
please	*por favor*
thank you	*gracias*
you're welcome	*de nada*
excuse me	*perdóneme*

*Gua gua is Latin American slang for *autobús*. The former is universally understood in Miami; the latter is not.

Numbers

0	*cero*
1	*un, uno* (m), *una* (f)
2	*dos*
3	*tres*
4	*cuatro*
5	*cinco*
6	*seis*
7	*siete*
8	*ocho*
9	*nueve*
10	*diez*
11	*once*
12	*doce*
13	*trece*
14	*catorce*
15	*quince*
16	*dieciséis*
17	*diecisiete*
18	*dieciocho*
19	*diecinueve*
20	*veinte*
30	*treinta*
40	*cuarenta*
50	*cincuenta*
100	*cien*
200	*doscientos*
500	*quinientos*
1000	*mil*
1,000,000	*millón*

Shopping

How much does it cost?	*¿Cuanto cuesta?*
I want...	*Quiero...*
What do you want?	*¿Qué quiere?*
Do you have...?	*¿Tiene…?*
Is/are there…?	*¿Hay…?*
I understand.	*Entiendo.*
I do not understand.	*No entiendo.*
Do you understand?	*¿Entiende usted?*
Please speak slowly.	*Por favor hable despacio.*

Getting Around

street	*calle*
avenue	*avenida*
corner (of)	*esquina (de)*
block	*cuadra*
to the left	*a la izquierda*
to the right	*a la derecha*
straight ahead	*adelante*
Where is…?	*¿Donde está…?*
the bus station	*el terminal de gua gua**

Facts for the Visitor

PLANNING
When to Go

See the Climate section in Facts about Florida for specifics on temperature and rainfall. While Florida used to be thought of as a winter destination, many areas in the northern reaches of the state, notably St Augustine, Gainesville, Tallahassee and the Panhandle, are booming summer destinations. And even in South Florida, the boundaries of the 'season' have been blurred by the stampede of models, photo and film shoots and huge numbers of people moving to the area, both from the US and abroad.

The advantage of coming during the early summer, despite the higher temperatures and increased rainfall, is you get more of the place to yourself. The hurricane season – from June 1 to November 30 – can be a perfectly pleasant time to visit, but you've got to be aware that one little hurricane can ruin a holiday. See the Dangers & Annoyances section for more information.

The Orlando area is a year-round destination, though there is heavy rainfall in summer. It is always crowded, especially during holidays, so reserve early if you plan to go there.

Miami and the southern part of the state are most visited in winter, when the weather is pleasantly warm and the humidity isn't too high, so be prepared for higher prices and larger crowds. In summer, humidity and mosquitoes can be a problem (especially in the Everglades), but the advantages are fewer people and cheaper prices. Also keep in mind that sometimes summertime is the only time to see certain things – turtles, for example, lay their eggs on Florida's beaches from May to August.

In the Panhandle and the northern part of the west and east coast, summer is considered high season. Winter gets quite cool, and the waters aren't really warm enough for swimming. But again, certain events happen only during winter – manatees, for example, seek the warm water springs throughout the

northern part of the state in winter, whereas in summer chances to see those fellows are slim outside South Florida.

What Kind of Trip?

This really depends on what you're after and how much time you have. If you're here for a short time, your trip will probably center around the Miami area, Orlando or Key West. But if you have time to explore, the most fascinating aspects of Florida – its surprising diversity and wonderful parks – have the opportunity to show themselves. Then you'll be able to take a trip out to the Panhandle area, go tubing on the Blackwater River or Itchetucknee Springs, see the majesty of southwest Florida and even take a jaunt or two to the Bahamas or Cuba.

It's easily possible to plan thematic trips through the state. From B&B holidays to hang gliding or biking treks to adventures in the Everglades, the information and tourism infrastructure in Florida is highly developed and easy to navigate.

Travel, including solo travel, is generally safe and easy going. But it's always easier with a car or motorcycle, and Florida is a good place to buy a used car (see the Getting Around chapter).

What to Bring

What to bring depends very much on where and when you go. Generally, if you come here in summer, you'll need light clothing (it rarely gets cool enough for a sweater), but you'll need to be prepared for sudden downpours. Keep in mind, this is a first-world destination, so anything you might forget is readily available. Here is a list of things we suggest you pack (some of these may only be seasonal).

In summer, bring a pair of light-weight long pants and a sweater to fend of mosquitoes and no-see-ums (see the Dangers & Annoyances section). If you plan on going north in winter, bring slightly heavier clothes.

A key item on the list at any time is sunscreen. Bring lots of this stuff (again, see the Dangers & Annoyances section), as well as good sunglasses and mosquito repellent (and/or a mosquito net with no-see-um netting). Swimming and snorkeling gear, a rainjacket or an umbrella (especially in summer), a day backpack for hiking trips or other excursions, solid shoes (if you're a

walking kind of person) and flip-flops or sandals (sometimes the sand on the beaches really heats up) will definitely make your trip more pleasant.

See the Outdoor Activities chapter for the equipment you'll need to bring for hiking, canoeing, kayaking or backpacking in the wilderness.

Florida is a very casual place for the most part. The minimal requirement is a pair of cut-off jeans and a bathing suit, with an optional set of in-line skates, but people wear just about anything they want. That casualness, however, is a tricky bugger: Cubans in the Miami area dress very fashionably for a night out, and for South Beach, Palm Beach, Boca Raton, Sarasota or Tampa nightlife, you'll want to dress to the nines.

Toiletries, hygiene and first-aid products are readily available, and Florida is an inexpensive place to buy clothes, so plan on leaving with more than you arrived with.

MAPS

Free maps to the state of Florida are easy to come by; the *Official Transportation Map of Florida* is a free road map that's probably better than most commercial maps covering the same area. It's available through Visit Florida (see State Tourist Offices below) and through some larger convention & visitors bureaus. Members of the American Automobile Association (AAA) can receive free Florida maps from their local AAA office.

For city maps, many convention & visitors bureaus and chambers of commerce will either hand them out or sell them cheaply, usually for $2.25 to $3.50. Those maps are probably created by the *Dolph Map Company*, which covers every major city in the state. Its maps usually sell for $2.95 in bookstores, gas stations and map shops – the ones the visitors bureaus and chambers sell have local advertising on the back.

Hikers and backpackers can purchase topographical maps from specialty map shops, such as A World of Maps (☎ 954-776-3679), 6820 N Florida Ave, Tampa, FL 33604; A Galaxy of Maps (☎ 954-267-9000), 5975 N Federal Hwy, Suite 107, Fort Lauderdale, FL 33308; or the Map & Globe

Store (☎ 904-385-8869), 537-E Scotty's Lane, Tallahassee, FL 32303.

You can also purchase topographical maps directly from the US Geological Survey (USGS; ☎ 703-648-4090), Map & Book Sales, Denver, CO 80225. The USGS is an agency of the federal Department of the Interior that publishes very detailed maps of the entire country at different scales up to 1:250,000. A list of maps is available upon request. Many camping stores and national park and national forest ranger stations sell USGS maps of their immediate area. Maps at 1:62,500, or approximately 1 inch=1 mile, are ideal for backcountry hiking and backpacking. Some private cartographers are producing updated versions of old USGS maps at 1:62,500.

Boaters, canoers and kayakers can buy the National Oceanic & Atmospheric Administration's Coast & Geodetic Survey maps directly from the Distribution Division N/CG33, National Ocean Service, 6501 Lafayette Ave, Riverdale, MD 30737.

For getting off the beaten path, DeLorme's *Florida Atlas & Gazetteer* (scale 1:150,000) is the best all-around source for really tiny roads, though it's useless for navigating in cities. It also has listings – some dated but others useful – of campgrounds, historic sites, parks, natural features and even scenic drives.

Two good map companies to contact for all kinds of maps are MapLink (☎ 805-692-6777, fax 805-692-6787, custserv@maplink.com), 30 S La Patera Lane, No 5, Santa Barbara, CA 93117, and Omni Resources (☎ 336-227-8300, 800-742-2677, custserv@omnimap.com), 1004 South Mebane St, PO Box 2096, Burlington, NC 27216.

TOURIST OFFICES
Local Tourist Offices

Many towns don't have tourist offices per se. Chambers of commerce, or, in larger cities, the convention & visitors bureau (sometimes called a visitors & convention bureau and abbreviated as CVB/VCB) can provide you with local information about what to see and do, make hotel reservations and generally point you in the right direction.

One handy and under-utilized service performed by CVB/VCBs is, if you're stuck in a place and don't know what to do with yourself, they can set up an itinerary for you. They'll try to tailor the itinerary to your needs (travel with kids, eco-tourism, organized tours, etc). But note that CVB/VCBs vary in usefulness from place to place. The address and telephone number of each chamber of commerce and/or other tourist offices are given in the Information headings under each town.

If you're in a town with unhelpful, useless or hateful chamber or CVB/VCB personnel, and you don't know whom to turn to for information, the next best bet is the research desk at the main branch of the public library. They can tell you about local organizations that specialize in whatever you're interested in. In this book, we list libraries as often as possible.

State Tourist Offices

Visit Florida (FLA USA; ☎ 888-735-2872, www.flausa.com), 661 E Jefferson St, Tallahassee, FL 32301, is the state's privatized tourism agency, and it does a very good job. Its Website is first rate, and Visit Florida will send you (upon request by mail, Web or phone) a shiny, colorful folder of information about the state. The brochures and vacation guide also include numbers of local convention & visitors bureaus and Tourist Development Councils. If you have a specific need or question, state tourist offices may be able to answer it or refer you to the appropriate office.

Visit Florida offices include the following:

Campbellton Welcome Center
(☎ 850-263-3510, fax 850-263-3510)
5885 Hwy 231, Campbellton, FL 32426,
3 miles north of Campbellton on Hwy 231

Capitol Welcome Center
(☎ 850-488-6167, fax 850-414-2560)
Florida Capitol Building (intersection of
Apalachee Parkway and Monroe St),
Plaza Level W, Tallahassee, FL 32399-2000

Coral Gables Welcome Center
(☎ 305-442-6926, fax 305-442-6929)
2701 Le Jeune Rd, Suite 406, Coral Gables,
FL 33134

Jennings Welcome Center
  (☎ 904-938-2981, fax 904-938-1292)
  Route 2, Box 20, Jennings, FL 32053,
  4 miles north of Jennings on I-75 S

Pensacola Welcome Center
  (☎ 850-944-0442, fax 850-944-3675)
  PO Box 17842, Pensacola, FL 32505,
  18 miles west of Pensacola on I-10 W

Yulee Welcome Center
  (☎ 904-225-9182, fax 904-225-0064)
  PO Box 339, Yulee, FL 32097,
  7 miles north of Yulee on I-95 S

Tourist Offices Abroad

International tourist offices for Florida include the following:

Brazil
  (☎ 011-283-4741, fax 011-251-0438)
  Alameda Ribeirão Prêto 01331-000,
  São Paulo, SP 01414-901

Canada
  (☎ 416-928-3139, fax 416-928-6841)
  121 Bloor St E, Suite 1003, Toronto,
  Ontario, M4W 3M5

Germany
  (☎ 69-131-0091, fax 69-131-0647)
  Schillerstrasse 10, 60313
  Frankfurt am Main

Japan
  (☎ 03-5276-0260, fax 03-5276-0264)
  Belvedere Kudan Building, No 204, 2-15-5,
  Fujimi, Chiyoda-ku, Tokyo 102-0071

UK
  (☎ 020-7630-7703, fax 020-7630-7703)
  Roebuck House, Palace St,
  London SW1E 5BA

VISAS & DOCUMENTS
Passport

All foreign visitors (other than Canadians) must bring a passport. All visitors should bring their driver's license and any health-insurance or travel-insurance cards.

If you could on the best of days be mistaken as under 30 years old, you'll need a passport or other picture ID with your age on it (to show you are over 21) to buy alcohol or gain admission to bars and clubs.

It's a good idea to make a photocopy of your passport and international ID to carry around instead of the original (though you can't use the photocopy to get into a bar).

There's nothing worse than losing your identity on a trip.

Canadians must have proper proof of Canadian citizenship, such as a citizenship card with photo ID or a passport. Most visitors also require a US visa.

Visas

Apart from Canadians, and those entering under the Visa Waiver Pilot Program (see below), all foreign visitors need to obtain a visa from a US consulate or embassy. In most countries, the process can be done by mail or through a travel agent.

Your passport should be valid for at least six months longer than your intended stay in the USA, and you'll need to submit a recent photo (37 x 37mm) with the application. Documents of financial stability and/or guarantees from a US resident are sometimes required, particularly for those from developing, eastern-European and former Soviet-bloc countries.

The most common visa is a Non-Immigrant Visitors Visa, B1 for business purposes, B2 for tourism or visiting friends and relatives. A visitor's visa is good for one or five years with multiple entries, and it specifically prohibits the visitor from taking paid employment in the USA. The validity period depends on what country you're from. The length of time you'll be allowed to stay in the USA is ultimately determined by US immigration authorities at the port of entry. If you're coming to the USA to work or study, you will probably need a different type of visa, and the company or institution you're going to should make the arrangements. Allow six months for processing the application.

Visa Waiver Pilot Program Citizens of certain countries may enter the USA without a US visa, for stays of 90 days or less, under the Visa Waiver Pilot Program. Currently these countries are Andorra, Argentina, Australia, Austria, Belgium, Brunei, Denmark, Finland, France, Germany, Iceland, Ireland, Italy, Japan, Liechtenstein, Luxembourg, Monaco, the Netherlands, New Zealand, Norway, San Marino, Spain,

Sweden, Switzerland and the UK. Under this program, you must have a roundtrip ticket that is nonrefundable in the USA, and you will not be allowed to extend your stay beyond 90 days. Check with the US embassy in your home country for any other requirements.

Visa Extensions Tourists are usually granted a three-month stay on first arrival. If you try to extend that time *after* the date stamped on your visa, it will usually lead to an unamusing conversation with an INS official who will assume you want to work illegally. So come prepared with concrete evidence that you've been traveling extensively and will continue to be a model tourist. Extensions are manhandled by the US Government Justice Department's Immigration & Naturalization Service (INS) at 7880 N Biscayne Blvd in Miami (☎ 305-536-5741), and at 400 W Bay St, Room G18 in Jacksonville (☎ 904-232-2624). Get there early, bring along a good long book, and pack a lunch.

Travel Insurance

No matter how you're traveling, make sure you take out travel insurance. This not only covers you for medical expenses and luggage theft or loss but also for cancellation or delays in your travel arrangements (you might fall seriously ill two days before departure, for example).

Everyone should be covered for the worst possible scenario, such as an accident that requires hospital treatment and a flight home. Coverage depends on your insurance and type of ticket, so ask both your insurer and your ticket-issuing agency to explain the finer points.

STA Travel offers a variety of insurance options at reasonable prices. Ticket loss is also covered by travel insurance. Make sure you have a separate record of all your ticket details – or better still, a photocopy of your ticket. Also make a copy of your policy, in case the original is lost.

Buy travel insurance as early as possible. If you buy it the week before you fly, you may find, for instance, that you're not

HIV & Entering the USA

Anyone entering the USA who is not a US citizen is subject to the authority of the Immigration & Naturalization Service (INS), who can keep someone from entering or staying in the USA by excluding or deporting them, meaning they have the power to prevent entrance or to return a visitor from whence they came. Being HIV-positive is not a grounds of deportation, but it is a grounds of exclusion, and the INS can refuse to admit HIV-positive visitors to the country.

Although the INS does not test people for HIV when they try to enter the USA, the form for the non-immigrant visa asks 'Have you ever been afflicted with a communicable disease of public health significance?'. The INS will try to exclude anyone who answers 'yes' to this question.

If you do have HIV but can prove to the consular officials you are the spouse, parent or child of a US citizen or legal resident (green-card holder), you are exempt from the exclusionary rule.

For legal immigration information and referrals to immigration advocates, visitors may contact the National Immigration Project of the National Lawyers Guild (☎ 617-227-9727), 14 Bacon St, Suite 506, Boston, MA 02108; and the Immigrant HIV Assistance Project, Bar Association of San Francisco (☎ 415-267-0795), 685 Market St, Suite 700, San Francisco, CA 94105.

covered for delays to your flight caused by strikes or other industrial actions that may have been in force before you took out the insurance.

If you're planning to travel a long time, the insurance may seem very expensive – but if you can't afford it, you certainly won't be able to afford a medical emergency in the USA.

Driver's License & Permits

Bring your driver's license if you intend to rent a car; visitors from some countries may find it wise to back up their national license with an International Driving Permit, available from their local auto club for a nominal fee. Note that your foreign driver's license *is* valid in the USA. An IDP is not a license but rather an official translation of yours (valid for one year, and you still need to carry your license), and while the major rental companies are used to seeing foreign licenses, local traffic police are more likely to accept an IDP as valid identification than an unfamiliar document from another country.

Automobile Association Cards

If you plan on doing a lot of driving in Florida, it would be beneficial to join your national automobile association. Just be sure it's cheaper to join your organization at home than spending the $55 it costs to join the American Automobile Association (AAA) for a year, including the one-time sign-up fee. Members of the AAA or an affiliated automobile club can get car-rental and sightseeing-admission discounts with membership cards.

More important, membership gives you access to AAA road service in case of an emergency, from locking your keys in the car to having major engine problems.

Hostelling International Card

About half the hostels in Florida are members of Hostelling International/American Youth Hostel (HI/AYH), which is affiliated with the International Youth Hostel Federation (IYHF). You can purchase membership on the spot when checking in, although it's advisable to purchase it before

you leave home. The advantage of having one of these cards is you'll get about a $2 to $3 discount off the nonmember rates. Surprisingly, though, some non-HI hostels, such as ones in Miami and St Petersburg, will also extend a discount to HI cardholders. Go figure.

Student & Youth Cards

If you're a student, get an international student ID (ISIC), or bring along a school or university ID card (not as good) to take advantage of the discounts available to students. You can get an ISIC from Council Travel offices around the world on proof of enrollment. The ISIC can get you substantial discounts at museums and tourist attractions and on some airfares.

Seniors' Cards

British Railways and the American Association of Retired People issue identification cards for seniors, usually people over 55. These are absolutely key in Florida, where almost all major attractions, most hotel chains and some smaller hotels offer seniors' discounts. Discounts can be substantial – up to 20% off on a room. You'll also save on some transport, including airfare.

Photocopies

It's a good idea to make photocopies of your most important documents – such as a driver's license, visa and data pages of your passport – to assist in replacement in the event of a loss. Leave one copy with someone at home and keep another with you, separate from the originals.

EMBASSIES & CONSULATES

As a tourist, it's important to know what your embassy – the embassy of the country of which you are a citizen – can and can't do.

Generally speaking, it won't be much help in emergencies if the trouble you're in is remotely your own fault. Remember that you are bound by the laws of the country you are in. Your embassy will not be sympathetic if you end up in jail after committing a crime locally, even if such actions are legal in your own country.

In genuine emergencies, you might get some assistance, but only if other channels have been exhausted. For example, if you need to get home urgently, a free ticket home is exceedingly unlikely – the embassy would expect you to have insurance. If you have all your money and documents stolen, it might assist in getting a new passport, but a loan for onward travel is definitely out of the question.

Embassies used to hold letters for travelers or have a small reading room with home newspapers, but these days the mail-holding service has been stopped and even newspapers tend to be out of date.

US Embassies

US diplomatic offices abroad include the following:

Australia
 (☎ 02-6270-5900)
 21 Moonah Place, Yarralumla ACT 2600

Austria
 (☎ 1-313-39)
 Boltzmanngasse 16, A-1091, Vienna

Belgium
 (☎ 2-513-38-30)
 Blvd du Régent 27, B-1000, Brussels

Canada
 (☎ 613-238-5335)
 100 Wellington St, Ottawa, Ontario 1P 5T1

Denmark
 (☎ 31-42-31-44)
 Dag Hammarskjolds Allé 24, Copenhagen

France
 (☎ 01 42 96 12 02)
 2 Rue Saint Florentin, 75001 Paris

Germany
 (☎ 228-33-91)
 Deichmanns Au 29, 53179 Bonn

Greece
 (☎ 1-721-2951)
 91 Vasilissis Sophias Blvd, 10160 Athens

India
 (☎ 11-60-0651)
 Shanti Path, Chanakyapuri 110021, New Delhi

Ireland
 (☎ 1-687-122)
 42 Elgin Rd, Ballsbridge, Dublin

Israel
 (☎ 3-517-4338)
 71 Hayarkon St, Tel Aviv

Italy
 (☎ 6-46-741)
 Via Vittorio Veneto 119a-121, Rome

Japan
 (☎ 3-224-5000)
 1-10-5 Akasaka Chome, Minato-ku, Tokyo

Korea
 (☎ 2-397-4114)
 82 Sejong-Ro, Chongro-ku, Seoul

Mexico
 (☎ 5-211-00-42)
 Paseo de la Reforma 305, Cuauhtémoc, 06500 Mexico City

Netherlands
 (☎ 70-310-92-09)
 Lange Voorhout 102, 2514 EJ, The Hague

New Zealand
 (☎ 4-722-068)
 29 Fitzherbert Terrace, Thorndon, Wellington

Norway
 (☎ 22-44-85-50)
 Drammensvein 18, Oslo

Russia
 (☎ 095-252-2451)
 Novinskiy Bulvar 19/23, Moscow

Singapore
 (☎ 338-0251)
 30 Hill St, Singapore 0617

South Africa
 (☎ 12-342-1048)
 877 Pretorius St, Box 9536, Pretoria 0001

Spain
 (☎ 1-577-4000)
 Calle Serrano 75, 28006 Madrid

Sweden
 (☎ 8-783-5300)
 Strandvagen 101, S-115 89 Stockholm

Switzerland
 (☎ 31-357-70-11)
 Jubilaumsstrasse 93, 3005 Berne

Thailand
 (☎ 2-252-5040)
 95 Wireless Rd, Bangkok

UK
 (☎ 020-7499-9000)
 5 Upper Grosvenor St, London W1

Foreign Consulates in Florida

All of the consular offices in the state are in the greater Miami area. Check the Miami white pages in the telephone book under Consulates for diplomatic representation in the city. Embassies are located in

Washington, DC, the US capital. Be patient: Miami is considered a cushy post by the always-hardworking diplomatic set, and some consular offices have ridiculously limited hours and act as if you're interfering with their day if you ask for things like help. Dress neatly and be polite. Most consulates are in Miami, but a few are in Coral Gables.

Consulates include the following:

Argentina
(☎ 305-373-1889)
800 Brickell Ave, Penthouse 1

Austria
(☎ 305-325-1561)
1454 NW 17th Ave, Suite 200

Bahamas
(☎ 305-373-6295)
25 SE 2nd Ave, Suite 818

Bolivia
(☎ 305-358-3450)
25 SE 2nd Ave, Suite 545

Brazil
(☎ 305-285-6200)
2601 S Bayshore Drive, Suite 800

Canada
(☎ 305-579-1600)
200 S Biscayne Blvd, Suite 1600

Chile
(☎ 305-373-8623)
1110 Brickell Ave, Suite 616

Colombia
(☎ 305-448-5558)
280 Aragon Ave, Coral Gables

Costa Rica
(☎ 305-871-7485)
1600 NW 42nd Ave, Suite 300

Dominican Republic
(☎ 305-358-3220)
1038 Brickell Ave

Ecuador
(☎ 305-539-8214)
1101 Brickell Ave, M 102

El Salvador
(☎ 305-371-8850)
300 Biscayne Blvd Way

France
(☎ 305-372-9798)
2S Biscayne Blvd, Suite 1710

Germany
(☎ 305-358-0290)
100 N Biscayne Blvd, Suite 2200

Guatemala
(☎ 305-443-4828)
300 Sevilla Ave, Suite 210, Coral Gables

Honduras
(☎ 305-447-8927)
300 Sevilla Ave, Suite 201, Coral Gables

Israel
(☎ 305-935-9400)
100 N Biscayne Blvd, Suite 1800

Italy
(☎ 305-374-6322)
1200 Brickell Ave

Jamaica
(☎ 305-374-8431)
25 SE 2nd Ave, Suite 842

Mexico
(☎ 305-716-4977)
1200 NW 78th Ave, Suite 200

Netherlands
(☎ 305-789-6646)
801 Brickell Ave, Suite 918

Nicaragua
(☎ 305-220-6900)
8370 W Flagler St, Suite 220

Paraguay
(☎ 305-573-5588)
2800 Biscayne Blvd, Suite 700

Peru
(☎ 305-374-1305)
444 Brickell Ave, Suite 135

Portugal
(☎ 305-444-6311)
1901 Ponce de León Blvd, Coral Gables

South Korea
(☎ 305-372-1555)
201 S Biscayne Blvd

Spain
(☎ 305-446-5511)
2655 Le Jeune Rd, Suite 203, Coral Gables

Switzerland
(☎ 305-274-4210)
7319 SW 97 Ave

UK
(☎ 305-374-1522)
1001 Brickell Bay Dr,
Suite 2800

Uruguay
(☎ 305-443-9764)
1077 Ponce de León Blvd, Suite B,
Coral Gables

Venezuela
(☎ 305-577-3834)
1101 Brickell Ave, Suite 901

Australian and New Zealand citizens may contact the British or Canadian consulates for emergency assistance, as neither country maintains consular offices in Miami.

CUSTOMS & IMMIGRATION

Most international flights land in either Miami or Orlando. You'll pass first through immigration – which checks your passport and visa – and if they're happy about *everything*, they'll pass you through to the next section, where you clear customs.

US Customs allows each person over the age of 21 to bring 1 liter of liquor and 200 cigarettes duty free into the USA. US citizens are allowed to import, duty free, $400 worth of gifts from abroad, while non-US citizens are allowed to bring in $100 worth. US law permits you to bring in, or take out, as much as $10,000 in American or foreign currency, traveler's checks or letters of credit without formality. Larger amounts of any or all of the above – there are no limits – must be declared to customs.

Due to Miami's infamous popularity as a drug-smuggling gateway, customs officers in Miami are known to be…let's call them *thorough* in their examination of backpackers and other travelers who may fit the profile of what they call a 'mule,' or someone ferrying narcotics. They may not be very polite, but you should be, and you should dress neatly and carry a large wad of cash or traveler's checks and credit cards – or show signs of prosperity lest they think you're here to work illegally.

Both customs and immigration officers have the right to drag you into a room for questioning, or worse; Corinna was once hauled into the back room in Miami. Her tip:

Be as polite as you can. I was detained, it turned out, to verify that my resident visa was still current, but no one told me that. They just said, 'Follow me.' The immigration officer in the holding area told me to 'sit down and shut up,' and when I asked why I was being detained, he told me that if I wanted to make things difficult for myself, I could keep asking questions. I left four hours later.

If you are taken back there, make certain a representative of your airline (who can call your relatives and get you information) knows you're there and who to tell of your predicament.

MONEY
Currency

The US dollar ($) is divided into 100 cents, with coins of one cent (penny), five cents (nickel), 10 cents (dime), 25 cents (quarter) and relatively rare 50 cents (half dollar). There are even rarer $1 coins in circulation; they're unpopular and used almost exclusively at post office stamp machines and toll booths as change. A new $1 coin, gold colored and featuring a design by American artist Glenda Goodacre, is in the works now.

Banknotes are called bills. Be sure to check the corners for amounts, as they're all the same size and color. Circulated bills come in denominations of $1, $2 (rare), $5, $10, $20, $50 and $100.

Note that the US has two types of $20, $50 and $100 notes. The new bill, featuring larger, off-center portraits, are worth exactly the same as the old ones. The older $100s, $50s and $20s will stay in circulation for the foreseeable future.

There are three straightforward ways to handle money in the US: cash, US-dollar traveler's checks and credit cards, with the proliferation of ATMs (Automated Teller Machines, see later in the chapter) facilitating the process.

Bucks, Sawbucks, Portraits & Yards

Americans have a lot of nicknames for their money, as they do for everything else. Some have interesting etymologies, like 'two bits,' a once-common name for a 25¢ piece or quarter (think of the jingle in old cartoons and movies *shave and a haircut/two bits*). It's named after the Spanish *bit*, worth at one time about 12.5¢. Some nicknames, like a 'portrait of Franklin,' are more obvious.

Other nicknames draw from dated exchange rates (like 'pound' for $5). Others draw from typically imaginative analogies – 'sawbuck' ($10) is so named because a Roman numeral 10 (X) resembles a sawbuck or sawhorse. And still others are colorful gangster lingo – 'G' is short for grand ($1000), 'C-note' for $100.

Things get murky when you look for the origin of the 'buck' (which is also short for 'sawbuck,' but that isn't the root of this slang). Some say that it's trapper terminology: skins were classified as 'buckskins' or 'bucks' and 'does,' the former being larger and therefore more valuable. Other stories say that priests were called 'bucks,' and they could always be counted on for a handout, but that sounds pretty silly – as do words like 'smacker,' 'clam,' 'simoleon' and 'yard.'

As with a lot of slang terms, we'll probably never really be sure about the origins.

Exchange Rates

These are particularly volatile, but *at press time* exchange rates were as follows:

country	unit		US dollars
Australia	A$1	=	$0.63
Canada	C$1	=	$0.67
euro	€1	=	$1.05
France	FF1	=	$0.16
Germany	DM1	=	$0.53
Hong Kong	HK$10	=	$1.30
Japan	Y100	=	$0.90
New Zealand	NZ$1	=	$0.51
UK	£1	=	$1.59

Daily exchange rates are listed in the *New York Times, Wall Street Journal* and *International Herald Tribune*. You can also get up-to-the-second exchange rates, if you're so inclined, on the Internet from sites such as Olsen & Associates' www.oanda.com/converter/classic.

Note that the exchange rates listed in newspapers and on the Web are those for chunks of currency; actual street exchange rates will always be lower (unless you bring in a suitcase full of cash).

Exchanging Money

Cash The best advice for people who need to exchange a foreign currency for US dollars is to do so at home, before you arrive. Exchange rates are generally poorer in the US than at home. For example, when banks in Munich are routinely charging DM1.68 for $1, banks in the US are charging as much as DM1.77 for $1.

If you must change money in the states, you're probably best off at a real bank, as opposed to an exchange office. Nations-Bank (☎ 305-350-6350) offers foreign exchange services in all its branches and has branches all through the state. Worse rates are available at some branches of SunTrust Bank (☎ 305-592-0800). Shop around if you have time.

Private exchange offices generally offer the least competitive rates and charge the highest commissions. There are also private exchange offices around town, such as drugstores and record stores.

Traveler's Checks Traveler's checks are virtually as good as cash in the USA; most establishments (not just banks) will accept them like cash. The major advantage of traveler's checks over cash is they can be replaced if lost or stolen. But changing traveler's checks denominated in a foreign currency (while much easier than it used to be) is rarely convenient or economical.

Get larger-denomination US$100 cheques, as you may be charged service fees when cashing them at banks.

ATMs You can often withdraw money straight from your bank account when traveling. Most ATMs in the area accept bank cards from the Plus and Cirrus systems, the two largest ATM networks in the USA, as well as Visa and MasterCard cards. Honor is another popular network. See below for some options of cards you can carry to make getting cash on the road easier.

The disadvantage of credit card cash advances is you are charged interest on the withdrawal, beginning immediately, until you pay it back.

Credit & Debit Cards Major credit cards are accepted at hotels, restaurants, gas stations, stores and car-rental agencies throughout the USA. In fact, you'll find it hard to perform certain transactions such as renting a car or purchasing tickets to performances without one.

Even if you loathe credit cards and prefer to rely on traveler's checks and ATMs, it's a good idea to carry one for emergencies. Banks in Australia, New Zealand and the UK are now selling Visa Travel Money, a prepaid Visa card similar to a telephone card: Your credit limit is the amount you buy the card with, and while it's not rechargeable, it's accepted like a regular Visa card. Banks charge a fee of 2% of the card's purchase price, so the card is more expensive than traveler's checks but more accessible.

If you're planning to rely primarily upon credit cards, it would be wise to have a Visa or MasterCard in your deck, since other cards aren't as widely accepted.

Places that accept Visa and MasterCard are also likely to accept debit cards. Unlike a credit card, a debit card deducts payment directly from the user's checking account. Instead of an interest rate, users are charged

a minimal fee for the transaction. Be sure to check with your bank to confirm that your debit card will be accepted in other states – debit cards from large commercial banks can often be used worldwide.

Carry copies of your credit card numbers separately from the cards. If you lose your credit cards or they get stolen, contact the company immediately. Following are toll-free numbers for the main credit card companies. Contact your bank if you lose your ATM card.

Visa	☎ 800-336-8472
MasterCard	☎ 800-826-2181
American Express	☎ 800-528-4800
Discover	☎ 800-347-2683
Diners Club	☎ 800-234-6377

International Transfers You can instruct your bank back home to send you a draft. Specify the city, bank and branch to which you want your money directed, or ask your home bank to tell you where a suitable one is, and make sure you get the details right. The procedure is easier if you've authorized someone back home to access your account.

Money sent by telegraphic transfer should reach you within a week. Transfers by SWIFT (Society of Worldwide Interbank Financial Transactions) are faster; ask the destination bank for its SWIFT address, usually a combination of letters and numbers. By mail, allow at least two weeks. When the money arrives, it will most likely be converted into local currency – you can take it as cash or buy traveler's checks.

You can also transfer money by American Express, Thomas Cook or Western Union, though the latter has fewer international offices.

Security

Be cautious – but not paranoid – about carrying money. If your hotel or hostel has a safe, keep your valuables and excess cash in it. It's best not to display large amounts of cash in public. A money belt worn under your clothes is a good place to carry excess currency when you're on the move or otherwise unable to stash it in a safe. Avoid carrying your wallet in a back pocket of your pants. This is a prime target for pickpockets, as are handbags and the outside pockets of day packs and fanny packs (bum bags). See Dangers & Annoyances later in this chapter.

Costs

You can really get away with the amount of luxury or penury you're striving to hit: youth hostels and cheap hotels abound, and there are good choices for every price range from backpacker to business traveler.

Getting here is sometimes stunningly cheap, especially from the UK or Germany, which are rife with package deals. It's also cheap from the US, especially if you take a Greyhound bus or drive here. See the Getting There & Away chapter for more information.

Florida rental cars tend to run cheaper than in most other states. Rates start at around $20 a day (see Getting Around for more information) or $100 a week, but you have to seek those out; an average rate can be figured at $25/$140.

Accommodation rates range widely in the state and, as with so many things here, depend a lot on when and where you go. Generally, you'll find the cheapest beds in the state in the Orlando/Kissimmee area, where competition is so fierce that motel rooms start at about $20. Youth hostels are the cheapest option if you're traveling alone (rates start at $13 for a bed in a dorm), and

hotel prices range anywhere from $25 to, well, anything really.

The cheaper-end restaurants usually have breakfast for about $1.50 to $4; lunch can be $3 to $5 and dinner $4 to $7. A Big Mac costs about $2. A beer in a supermarket is $1 (a six-pack $4 to $7, depending on the brand) and in a bar $2 to $3.50. A quart of milk in a supermarket will cost about $1.50, a loaf of bread anywhere from $1 to $2.50. Local phone calls are 35¢ at pay phones, and newspapers are 50¢ to $1 – note that sales tax is charged on newspapers in Florida. Out-of-town newspapers sell for as much as vendors can get: the *Süddeutsche Zeitung* costs about $3 in Miami; British papers like the *Sun* are about $2 (you won't find anything non-tabloid from the UK); and the Sunday *New York Times* is $4.

Tipping

This is a US institution that can, initially, be a little confusing to foreign visitors. Wait-staff at restaurants, bartenders, taxi drivers, bellhops, hotel maids and others are paid a mere stipend. Owners, and indeed American culture, expect that customers compensate these people directly: the tips are actually part of their salary.

So tipping is not really an option; the service has to be absolutely *appalling* before you should consider not tipping. In a bar or restaurant, a tip is customarily 15% of the bill (for a standard tip, double the tax and add a smidgen); a tip for outstanding service

---

Just Say 'No! No!' to Tipping Twice

There's an insidious plot afoot in many Miami-area restaurants: a 15% tip may be included in the bill. Of course, the staff may not go to heroic lengths to point this out to you – if you forget to check, and leave a cash tip as well, staff gets tipped twice. Unless you're feeling inordinately philanthropic, are a show-off or were *really* happy with the service, make absolutely certain that you're not tipping twice by examining the bill before you pay.

in a restaurant is 20%. You needn't tip at fast-food restaurants or self-serve cafeterias. Hotel maids should be tipped about $1.50 a day, unless they don't deserve it. Tip daily, as maids rotate shifts.

Add about 10% to taxi fares even if you think your driver should be institutionalized. Hotel porters who carry bags a long way expect $3 to $5 (or add it up at $1 per bag); smaller services (holding the taxi door open for you) might justify $1, but we don't think so. A tip for valet parking should be about $2, to be given when your car is returned to you.

Special Deals

The USA is probably the most promotion-oriented society on earth. Though the bargaining common in many other countries is not generally accepted in the US, you can work angles to cut costs. For example, at hotels in the off-season, casually and respectfully mentioning a competitor's rate may prompt a manager to lower the quoted rate. Artisans may consider a negotiated price for large purchases. Discount coupons are widely available - check circulars in Sunday papers, at supermarkets, tourist offices or chambers of commerce.

Taxes

In this book, we list base prices, onto which you must add the 6% state sales tax, unless otherwise indicated. In Miami, the consumer (value-added) tax is 6.5% (6% state and .5% local) on goods and services, with additional taxes of 5% on hotel accommodations (11.5% total tax on hotels). Rental cars in the state carry the 6% state sales tax plus local taxes and a Florida state-road surcharge of $2.05 a day. City taxes vary from city to city.

POST & COMMUNICATIONS
Postal Rates

Currently, rates for 1st-class mail within the USA are 33¢ for letters up to 1oz (28 grams; 22¢ for each additional ounce) and 20¢ for postcards.

International airmail rates are 60¢ for a half-ounce letter (to Canada/Mexico it's 46¢/40¢), $1 for a 1oz letter and 40¢ for each additional half ounce. International postcard and aerogramme rates are 50¢.

Parcels airmailed anywhere within the USA are $3.20 for 2lb or less, increasing by $1.10 per pound up to $6.50 for 5lb. For heavier items, rates differ according to the distance mailed. Books, periodicals and computer disks can be sent by a cheaper 4th-class rate.

Sending Mail

Mail within the USA generally takes two to three days, and mail to destinations within Florida from one to two days – except in St Augustine, where delivery time ranges from three days to never. Not to sound like a postal pamphlet, but it *does* help speed delivery to put the correct zip (postal) code on the envelope. If you know the address but not the zip code, you can find a list at the post office or on the Internet (www.usps .gov/ncsc).

Allow mail at least a week to reach Europe, and up to two weeks at peak times of the year like Christmas. If you have the correct postage, you can drop your mail into any official blue mailbox, which are found many places like shopping centers and street corners. Mail pickup times are written on the inside of the mailbox lid.

Receiving Mail

You can have mail sent to you care of General Delivery at any post office that has its own zip (postal) code. It's best to have your intended date of arrival (if the sender knows it) clearly marked on the envelope. Mail is usually held for 30 days before it's returned to sender; you might request that your correspondents write 'hold for arrival' on letters.

Miami Beach South
    13th St at Washington Ave
    General Delivery, Miami Beach, FL 33139

Orlando downtown
    46 E Robinson St
    General Delivery, Orlando, FL 32802

Alternatively, you can have mail sent to the local representative of American Express or

Thomas Cook, which provide mail service for their clients.

Telephone

All phone numbers within the USA consist of a three-digit area code followed by a seven-digit-local number. If you are calling locally, just dial the seven-digit number. To call long distance, dial 1 + the three-digit area code + the seven-digit number.

If you're calling from abroad, the international country code for the USA is 1.

The 800, 888 and 877 area codes are designated for toll-free numbers within the USA and sometimes from Canada as well. Some can be called from anywhere in the USA, others are only used within the state. Those that are state-specific are indicated in the text. Some long-distance carriers will allow you to call an 800, 888 or 877 number collect from overseas.

The 900 area code is designated for calls for which the caller pays a premium rate, usually only available from a private phone. They have a reputation for being sleazy operations – a smorgasbord of phone sex and psychic hotlines at $2.99 a minute.

Directory assistance can be reached locally by dialing either ☎ 411 or ☎ 555-1212; this is free from most pay phones but can cost as much as 50¢ from a private phone. For directory assistance outside your area code, dial 1 + the three-digit area code of the place you want to call + 555-1212. For example, to obtain directory assistance for a toll-free number, dial ☎ 1-800-555-1212. For all other out-of-state numbers, toll charges will apply on calls to directory assistance; from a pay phone, it's usually 75¢.

Pay Phones Local calls usually cost 35¢ at pay phones. Almost all hotels (especially the more expensive ones) add a service charge of 50¢ to $1 for each local – and sometimes even toll-free – call made from a room phone, and they also have hefty surcharges for long-distance calls, like 50% on top of their carrier's rates. Public pay phones, which can be found in most lobbies, are always cheaper. You can pump in quarters, use a phone card or make collect calls from pay phones.

Long-distance rates vary, depending on the destination and which telephone company you use. There are literally hundreds of long-distance companies in the US, and rates vary by several hundred percent – call the operator (☎ 0) for rate information. Don't ask the operator to put your call through, however, because operator-assisted calls are much more expensive than direct-dial calls. Generally, nighttime (11 pm to 8 am), all day Saturday and from 8 am to 5 pm Sunday are the cheapest times to call. Discounts also apply in the evenings from 5 to 11 pm daily. Daytime calls (Monday to Friday from 8 am to 5 pm) are full-price calls within the USA.

Phone Cards Phone debit cards enable purchasers to pay in advance, with access through an 800 number. You call the 800 number, enter your card number, and then enter the number you're calling. The service tells you how much time you have left on your card before the call is put through. In amounts of $5, $10, $20 and $50, these are available in airports, post offices, some hostels and other sources.

Bucking the Trend: Miami's Quasi-Unique Local Dial System

To make up for the huge numbers of cellular phone and fax numbers crowding the ☎ 305 area code, the local telephone powers-that-be initiated a new and slightly confusing system for local calling that's different from the system in many other cities in the US (though not unheard of by any means). If you are calling locally in Miami, you must dial 305 + the seven-digit number. Note that you leave off the preceding 1 before local calls – just 305.

Lonely Planet's eKno Communication Card is aimed specifically at independent travelers and provides budget international calls, a range of messaging services, free email and travel information – for local calls, you're usually better off with a local phone card. You can join eKno online at www.ekno.lonelyplanet.com, or by phone from the USA by dialing ☎ 1-800-707-0031. Once you have joined, to use eKno from the USA, dial ☎ 1-800-706-1333.

Check the eKno Website for joining and access numbers from other countries as well as updates on super budget local access numbers and new features.

International Calls To make an international call direct from the Miami area, dial 011 + country code + area code (dropping the leading 0) + number. Treat Canada as a domestic call. If calling from a pay phone, dial all those numbers before inserting coins; a recorded voice will tell you how much to pay after you dial the number. To obtain international operator assistance and rates, dial ☎ 00.

As a general rule, it's cheaper to make international calls at night, but this varies with the country you're calling. The exact cost for making an overseas call from a pay phone depends on the long-distance company and the country in question. For calls from a private phone to Australia and Europe, typically the cost should be about $1.50 for the first minute and $1 for each subsequent minute. Calls to other continents usually cost about twice that.

Collect & Country Direct You can call collect (reverse charge) from any phone. There is an increasing number of providers, but prices vary, so check before you dial. The main players (at the time of writing) are AT&T (☎ 800-225-5288, or 800-CALL-ATT) and MCI (☎ 800-265-5328, or 800-COLLECT). (During our research, MCI was always more expensive than AT&T.) You can also simply dial ☎ 0 and then the area code and number (omitting the 1 that normally precedes the area code, for example, 0+212+123-4567), but local tele-

---

Cheaper Collect Calls

Want to get your family really mad at you? Use MCI to call them collect in Australia.

Sometimes the savings of using Country Direct Service over AT&T and MCI are substantial. But long-distance carriers are always changing their rates, so be sure to check which is cheapest during your stay before you make the call. One other advantage of Country Direct Service is you can use your home-country's telephone company charge card. Australia's Telstra says that its cards are cheaper than collect calls.

Country Direct Service numbers are the following:

Australia	☎ 800-682-2878
Austria	☎ 800-624-0043
Belgium	☎ 800-472-0032
Denmark	☎ 800-762-0045
France	☎ 800-537-2623
Germany	☎ 800-292-0049
Greece	☎ 800-443-4437
Hong Kong	☎ 800-992-2323
Ireland	☎ 800-562-6262
Italy	☎ 800-543-7662
Japan	☎ 800-543-0051
Netherlands	☎ 800-432-0031
Norway	☎ 800-292-0047
New Zealand	☎ 800-248-0064
Portugal	☎ 800-822-2776
Singapore	☎ 800-822-6588
Spain	☎ 800-247-7246
Sweden	☎ 800-345-0046
Taiwan	☎ 800-626-0979
United Kingdom	☎ 800-445-5667

---

phone carriers are generally the most expensive option of all.

If you're calling a country outside the USA, it *may* pay to use that country's Country Direct Service number (see the chart), which will connect you with an operator in the country you want to call. To use

Key Biscayne with Biscayne Bay, Virginia Key and Miami in the background

South Pointe Park and Government Cut

Miami lifeguard station

Dining at Smith & Wollensky in South Beach

Moon over Miami

One of the many outdoor bars and cafés in South Beach

an American carrier to call overseas, you can't use services like CALL-ATT or 800 COLLECT – you need a live operator.

Fax

Fax machines are easy to find in the USA, at shipping outlets like Mail Boxes Etc, photocopy services and hotel business service centers, but be prepared to pay high prices (more than $1 a page within the US, $4 or more to Europe and elsewhere). Prices for incoming faxes are usually half the outgoing domestic rate – about 50¢ a page.

Telegram

Telegrams can be sent by Western Union (☎ 800-325-6000). You can charge telegrams to a credit card or be billed directly at your home address or hotel (Western Union doesn't exactly go around shouting this out). To be billed, you'll have to sound like a solid citizen; request it and insist even when the operator says you need a credit card.

Telegrams are delivered generally within five hours inside the USA; overseas deliveries are not under the control of Western Union, which immediately sends the message overseas for delivery by your local company.

Email & Internet Access

Email is quickly becoming the preferred method of communication; however, unless you have a laptop and modem that can be plugged into a telephone socket, it's sometimes difficult to get online. In this book we list Internet cafés or other sources of Internet access wherever possible.

A great deal for staying in touch while on the road is the free email account that many of the larger search engines and other Internet resources provide. Companies such as Hotmail (www.hotmail.com), Pobox (www.pobox.com) and Excite (www.mailexcite .com) will give you a free email account (for example, johnsmith@mailexcite.com), which you can access from any Web browser, like ones

at Internet cafés (see Internet Resources below) or libraries. To access your mail, point the browser at the provider's homepage, enter your user name and password, and download your mail. Remember to log off before you leave to avoid misuse of your account.

INTERNET RESOURCES

The World Wide Web is a rich resource for travelers. You can research your trip, hunt down bargain airfares, book hotels, check on weather conditions or chat with locals and other travelers about the best places to visit (or avoid).

There's no better place to start your Web explorations than the Lonely Planet Website (www.lonelyplanet.com). Here you'll find succinct summaries on traveling to most places on earth, postcards from other travelers and the Thorn Tree bulletin board, where you can ask questions before you go or dispense advice when you get back. You can also find travel news and updates to many of Lonely Planet's most popular guidebooks, and the subWWWay section links you to the most useful travel resources elsewhere on the Web. You can also visit the Lonely Planet Website on America Online (Keyword: lp).

There are Internet cafés in larger cities and even in smaller towns throughout Florida, where, for fees that range from free with purchase of coffee to $10 an hour, you can connect to the Web to surf the Internet or check your email. Increasingly, public libraries are getting computers and Internet connections and offering them to anyone, sometimes free, sometimes not.

Hotel business service centers may provide connections. Trendy restaurants and Internet cafés offer Internet service as well. Many Kinko's locations now offer Web access for about 20¢ a minute. CyberGate (☎ 305-954-428-4283, 800-638-4283, sales@ gate.net, www.gate.net) is Florida's largest commercial provider.

BOOKS

Most books are published in different editions by different publishers in different countries. As a result, a book might be a hardcover rarity in one country while it's readily available in paperback in another. Fortunately, bookstores and libraries can search by title or author, so your local bookstore or library is the best place to find out about the availability of the following recommendations.

Most of the books listed here are available locally, some nationally and internationally. One of the best publishers of books on Florida and its regions is Pineapple Press, PO Drawer 16008, Southside Station, Sarasota, FL 34239. See the Facts about Florida chapter for works by local writers. For more difficult-to-find books, we list the International Standard Book Number (ISBN) to assist you in a bookstore or library search.

Lonely Planet

Lonely Planet publishes guides to *Miami*, the *USA*, the neighboring states of the *Deep South*, Pisces diving & snorkeling guides to *Florida's East Coast* and *The Florida Keys* as well as guides to nearby destinations including *Eastern Caribbean*, *Cuba* and *Mexico*. LP also publishes a complete series of guides to Central and South America, including several French-language titles to those regions. Lonely Planet's *Travel with Children* is a parent must-read for preparation and strategy.

Guidebooks

One of our favorites is Frank Zoretich's *Cheap Thrills Florida – The Bottom Half* (Pineapple Press), written by an admittedly very stingy man and containing lots of cheap things to do around here. If you're coming with kids, don't miss the excellent *Places to Go with Children in Miami & South Florida* by Cheryl Lani Juárez and Deborah Ann Johnson (Chronicle Books), which is indispensable in keeping the little darlings calm and entertained. Chelle Koster Walton's excellent *Fun with the Family in Florida* is just what it sounds like.

If you're sailing or boating around the state, two books stand out: *A Gunkholer's Cruising Guide to Florida's West Coast* by Tom Lefenstey (ISBN 0-8200-0127-9) and *Florida Under Sail* by Janey and Gordon Groene (ISBN 1-56626-088-8).

Backcountry Travel

For getting out in nature, don't miss the late Marjory Stoneman Douglas' classic *The Everglades: River of Grass* (Pineapple Press), which should be required reading for those heading out into the Glades. Also check out Susan D Jewell's excellent *Exploring Wild South Florida* (Pineapple Press) and Allen de Hart's *Adventuring in Florida* (The Sierra Club). *The Green Guide, Florida* by Marty Klinkenbergh and Elizabeth Leach (ISBN 1-56626-025-6) is good on details and practicalities for travel in state parks and wilderness. If you are planning on canoeing, a fine investment is *The Canoe Handbook* by Slim Ray (ISBN 0-8117-3032-8), which has very good instructions and illustrations of canoeing techniques for one or more.

A Canoeing & Kayaking Guide to the Streams of Florida, by Elizabeth F Carter and John L Pearce (ISBN 0-89732-033-6), is well written and has lots of maps.

History

The best book on Florida history is *The New History of Florida* (University Press of Florida, ISBN 0-8130-1415-8), edited by Michael Gannon and written by Gannon and many experts in Florida history. The book is a concise and complete, beautifully written, flawlessly edited masterpiece of a good read – actually reading more like a novel than a history in many chapters. Another great read, though it's a bit more stilted, is *Adventures into the Unknown Interior of America* (ISBN 0-8263-0656-X), by Cabeza de Vaca and translated by Cyclone Cavey, describing the doomed expedition of Pánfilo de Narváez, the first European to explore Florida thoroughly (see the History section of Facts about Florida).

The standard work on the history of Florida, available in every Florida library, is the ever-so-dry *A History of Florida* by

Charlton W Tebeau (pronounced 'TEE-bow'); though it's patchy on pre-European history, many state-history texts are as well, and Tebeau's book has been the classic reference for years. For a breezier read than all of the above, Michael Gannon's *Florida: A Short History* (University Press, ISBN 0-8130-1168-X) is a good bet. There's a good, quick history in *The Florida Handbook* by Allen Morris (Peninsular Publication Company, ISBN 0-9616-0005-5).

Jonathan Dickinson's Journal (ISBN 0-912451-00-9) is the interesting story of Quaker trader Jonathan Dickinson's shipwreck in 1696 near Hobe Sound and his journey home. The *Ybor City Story*, translated by Eustasio Fernandez and Henry Beltran, is a good overall history of the development of Tampa.

Architecture

Deco Delights by Barbara Capitman, and *Miami: Architecture of the Tropics*, edited by Maurice Coulot and Jean François Legune, are two excellent books on Art Deco architecture.

Flora & Fauna

David W Nellis' *Seashore Plants of South Florida & the Caribbean* (Pineapple Press) is a gorgeous book, with color photos throughout and good descriptions. A more scholarly and complete – yet accessible – guide is Ralph W Tiner's *Field Guide to Coastal Wetland Plants of the Southeastern United States* (University of Massachusetts Press), which has well-organized descriptions and line drawings. It's probably best to get *The Audubon Society Book of Water Birds* by Les Line, Kimball L Garrett and Ken Kaufman from a library. It's a coffee-table-size book, large and heavy enough to kill someone, and published with the usual impeccable quality of an Abrams book – astounding photography and great information but expensive.

NEWSPAPERS & MAGAZINES

There is usually at least one place in every city, town and village that carries, besides the local papers, national papers like the *New York Times*, the *Wall Street Journal* and *USA Today*. If you can't find a newsstand that carries whatever you're looking for, try a supermarket like Publix or one of the larger hotels.

Most major western European newspapers are available at good newsstands. Speaking of newsstands, they're almost non-existent in Florida outside the big cities, having been replaced by steel boxes on street corners. We hate it, too.

The paper with the largest circulation in the state is the *Miami Herald*, the flagship of the Knight Ridder newspaper group. It's available in many cities around the state.

For excellent, unbiased and thoughtful coverage of international news, pick up a copy of the *Christian Science Monitor*. *Time* and *Newsweek* magazines are also available in supermarkets, bookstores and newsstands.

In cities around Florida, look for local tabloids, like Miami's *New Times* or Fort Lauderdale's *City Link*, which have features, hard-hitting investigative journalism, comics and, of course, totally perverted and thoroughly enjoyable personal and classified advertisements.

Spanish

The *Miami Herald* publishes *el Nuevo Herald*, an excellent Spanish daily (in fact, if you speak Spanish, you should look here first for coverage of Latin America). *El Diario Américas* is another good Spanish-language daily available throughout South Florida. See the Miami section for more information.

RADIO

All rental cars have radios. Most stations have a range of less than a hundred miles, so if you're driving, you may constantly have to change stations. In South Florida, Spanish-language broadcasts are common, and in major cities there's usually a good mix of rock, disco, Top 40, dance, adult contemporary and easy-listening, and usually there's at least one AM all-news station (at least in South Florida).

As we went to press, a new privately held statewide network of tourist-information radio stations was being set up. With ads one minute out of every ten, the station will provide information of interest specifically to travelers in the state, from traffic reports to pieces on attractions. The network is on AM radio, and highway signs will point out the frequency in each region.

National Public Radio (NPR) is an excellent source of balanced news coverage, with a more international approach than most US stations. Its news programs, *All Things Considered* and *Morning Edition*, are three-hour news programs in the evening and morning that take the time to cover stories in a way that commercial radio simply can't. On Saturday mornings, *Car Talk* deals with cars and car problems – it's a funny and very popular show, and great if you're driving. And on Sunday, *Prairie Home Companion* with Garrison Keillor is an excellent old-style variety show that casts a humorous, wry eye at the American culture.

In most Florida cities, you'll also have the opportunity to listen to hate and political radio, featuring fat blabbermouths, convicted felons and former high-school football coaches touting conservative political values. And Christian radio is big in the rural areas.

British news junkies and those who appreciate neatly clipped accents will appreciate broadcasts of the BBC news on short-wave. While there's generally news on the hour and half-hour throughout the day, pinning down exact frequencies or broadcast times is very difficult. Even the venerable Beeb can't give a straight answer:

The nature of short wave is extremely unpredictable. The schedules, and some of the frequencies, change twice a year (beginning of April and end of October for the USA) to take into account changes in propagation conditions and shifts in listening habits.

Sound like a cop out? Yeah, well, we don't see *you* bouncing signals off the ionosphere, now do we? You can get a complete program (sorry, programme) guide from the BBC by writing to PO Box 76, Bush House, Strand, London WC2B 4PH, or calling ☎ 020-7257-8165, fax 020-7257-8252.

TELEVISION

Because of the popularity of American television around the world, you'll find few surprises on TV. American television is a hodgepodge of talk shows, cop shows, dramas, melodramas, sit-coms, soap operas, game shows and commercials. Despite pressure from the US Congress to clean up what it considers to be inappropriate content or subject matter on daytime TV's talk shows (Geraldo has once again been accepted as a journalist), the genre is in no immediate danger, and American TV can still be an interesting place to spend an afternoon.

The five major broadcast television networks in the USA are ABC, CBS, Fox, NBC and PBS. Of them, Fox shows the most sensationalistic – but also the most groundbreaking – TV shows: it was Fox that syndicated *The Simpsons*, *Married with Children*, *The X-Files* and *King of the Hill*.

CBS, ABC and NBC all show a mix of quasi-current films, news and news-magazine shows, sit-coms and dramatic programming like *ER*. ABC, CBS and NBC broadcast national news at 6:30 pm eastern standard time (EST).

PBS, the Public Broadcasting System, shows mainly educational programs, classical music and theater presentations, foreign programs and films (usually uncensored) and excellent current affairs shows like *Newshour with Jim Lehrer*. And the best part of it all is, it's mostly viewer supported – there are no standard commercial interruptions but rather a list of corporate sponsors is read at the end of each program.

On local Florida TV stations, gore springs eternal: the local news motto is 'If it bleeds, it leads.' Local TV stations are cleaning up their acts in response to public outcry that news programs show too much violent video and concentrate on the negative, but most of the local news stuff is still as sensationalistic as a British daily newspaper.

Cable TV is available at almost every hotel, which gives you access to, at the very least, ESPN (sports), CNN and CNN Headline News, the Weather Channel and Comedy Central. Some offer premium channels like HBO and Showtime (feature films).

PHOTOGRAPHY & VIDEO
Film & Equipment
Print film is widely available at supermarkets and discount drugstores throughout the state. Color print film has a greater latitude than color slide film; this means that print film can handle a wider range of light and shadow than slide film. However, slide film, particularly the slower speeds (under 100 ASA), has much better resolution than print film. Like black & white film, the availability of slide film outside major cities is rare or is found at inflated prices. We found that for sharpness, vivid colors and ease of commercial developing, the two widely available slide films around are by Fujichrome: Velvia and Provia. Unlike Kodachrome, which is easy to screw up and must usually be sent out of house by developing places, these films are developed using the standard E-6 process, and it's virtually idiot-proof. And while Kodachrome when used and developed correctly is fine film, these are simply more user-friendly.

For certain subjects, like Indian petroglyphs, carry high-speed (400 ASA) film to avoid using a flash, which is not permitted at these sites.

Film can be damaged by excessive heat, so don't leave your camera and film in the car on a hot summer day, and avoid placing your camera on the dashboard while driving.

It's worth carrying a spare battery for your camera to avoid disappointment when your camera dies in the middle of nowhere. If you're buying a new camera for your trip, do so several weeks before you leave and practice using it.

Processing
Drugstores are a good place to get your film cheaply processed. If film is dropped off by noon, you can usually pick up photos the next day. A roll of 100 ASA, 35mm color film with 24 exposures will cost about $10 to get processed.

If you want your pictures right away, you can find one-hour processing services in the yellow pages under Photo Processing. The prices tend to creep up to the $13 to $15 scale, so be prepared to pay dearly. Many one-hour photo finishers operate in the larger cities, and a few can be found near tourist attractions.

Technical Tips
Many parts of Florida experience more than 220 days of sunshine annually, so there's plenty of light for photography. However, when the sun is high in the sky, photographs tend to emphasize shadows and wash out highlights. It's best to take photos during the early morning and the late afternoon when light is softer. This is especially true of landscape photography. Always protect camera lenses with a haze or ultraviolet (UV) filter. A polarized filter can dramatically emphasize cloud formations in mountain and plains landscapes.

Video Systems
The USA uses the National Television System Committee (NTSC) color TV standard, which is not compatible with other standards (PAL or SECAM) used in Africa, Europe, Asia and Australia unless converted.

Properly used, a video camera can give a fascinating record of your holiday. Often the most interesting things occur when you're actually intent on filming something else.

One good rule to follow for beginners is to try to shoot in long takes, and don't move the camera around too much. If your camera has a stabilizer, you can use it to obtain good footage while traveling on various means of transport, even on bumpy roads. Remember, you're traveling – don't let the video take over your life and turn your trip into a Cecil B De Mille production.

Finally, remember to follow the same rules as for still photography regarding people's sensitivities – having a video camera shoved in their face is probably even more annoying and offensive to locals than a still camera. Always ask permission first.

Airport Security
All passengers on flights have to pass their luggage through X-ray machines. Technology as it is today doesn't jeopardize lower-speed film, but it's best to carry film and

cameras with you and ask the X-ray inspector to check your camera and film visually.

TIME

Except for the western section of the Panhandle, the entire state is in US eastern time zone, three hours ahead of San Francisco and Los Angeles, and five hours behind GMT/UTC. West of the Apalachicola River, the Panhandle is in the US central time zone, one hour behind the rest of the state, two hours ahead of San Francisco and Los Angeles, and six hours behind GMT/UTC.

city	time
Auckland	6 am in summer, 4 am in winter
Beijing	1 am in winter, midnight in summer (when Beijing ignores daylight-saving time)
Berlin, Frankfurt, Munich	6 pm
London	5 pm
Los Angeles, San Francisco	9 am
Miami	12 pm
Panama City, Pensacola	11 am
Sydney	4 am in summer, 2 am in winter

ELECTRICITY

Electric current in the USA is 110-115 volts, 60 Hz AC. Outlets may be suited for flat two- or three-prong plugs. If your appliance is made for another electrical system, you will need a transformer or adapter; if you didn't bring one along, check Radio Shack or another consumer electronics store.

WEIGHTS & MEASURES

Americans continue to resist the imposition of the metric system. Distances are in feet, yards and miles: 3 feet equal 1 yard (.914 meters); 1760 yards or 5280 feet equal 1 mile. Dry weights are in ounces (oz), pounds (lb) and tons (16oz are 1 pound; 2000lb are 1 ton), but liquid measures differ from dry measures. One pint equals 16 fluid oz; 2 pints equal 1 quart, a common measure for liquids like milk, which is also sold in half gallons (2 quarts) and gallons (4 quarts). Gasoline is measured in US gallons, about 20% smaller than the imperial gallon and equivalent to 3.79 liters.

Temperatures are given in degrees Fahrenheit: from C° to F° multiply by 1.8 and add 32; from F° to C° subtract 32 and divide by 1.8. See the inside back cover of this book for more conversions.

LAUNDRY

There are coin laundries in almost every city in the state except Palm Beach. Generally, the cost is $1.25 to wash and either a flat rate (like $1.25) to dry or 25¢ for each five or 10 minutes in dryers.

Some laundries have attendants who will wash, dry and fold your clothes for an additional charge. To find a laundry, look under Laundries or Laundries – Self-Service in the yellow pages. Dry cleaners are also listed under Laundries or Cleaners.

RECYCLING

Traveling in a car seems to generate lots of cans and bottles. A nice thing to do is save these for recycling (hint, nudge, wink, poke); you'll find recycling centers in the larger towns. Materials accepted are usually plastic and glass bottles, aluminum and tin cans and newspapers. Some campgrounds and a few roadside rest areas also have recycling bins next to the trash bins, so look out for those.

These Backward Americans

Americans write short-format dates in the reverse order from the rest of the world, in month-day-year (not day-month-year). So 4/3/97 is April 3, not March 4.

Numbers above 999 are written with a comma, and a period (full stop) separates decimal places, such as 10,256.33.

American light switches are 'on' in the *up* position.

The 1st floor in the USA is the ground floor, the 2nd is the European 1st and so on.

And we drive on the right, as in *correct* side of the road.

Perhaps better than recycling is reducing your use of these products. Many gas stations and convenience stores sell large plastic insulated cups with lids, which are inexpensive and ideal for hot and cold drinks. You can usually save a few cents by using your cup to buy drinks.

Despite the appearance of many large cities, littering is frowned upon by most Americans. Travelers need to respect the places they are visiting even though it may seem some locals think it's OK to trash their territory. Some states have implemented anti-littering laws (which impose fines for violation) to curb the problem. When hiking and camping in the wilderness, take out everything you bring in – this includes *any* kind of garbage you may create.

TOILETS

The USA is one of the worst countries in the world when it comes to the availability of public toilets. Few cities have them, and when they do, toilets are usually near a beach or a public park and not in the middle of the city where you need them. The only alternative is to ask permission to use the restrooms in restaurants and hotels, and,

Johns, Commodes & Comfort Stations

NICK SELBY

For a country with a worldwide reputation for outspoken, sometimes coarse and even foul-mouthed language, it's an amazing phenomenon that very few Americans can bring themselves to utter the word for the porcelain appliance into which they empty their bowels and bladders.

In decades past, for ladies and gentlemen to refer to anything vaguely personal was to open themselves to scorn and embarrassment – even today, American television commercials hawk 'bathroom tissue,' not toilet paper.

So Americans don't have toilets. They have (and these are just a few of the euphemisms you will come across in your travels) a/the restroom, facilities, comfort station (?!?), commode, john, latrine, head, powder room, little girl's/boy's room, bathroom, way station and potty.

Even to natives, it can be confusing. As an old Southern legend has it, a woman of 'old-fashioned' values wanted to make certain the campsite in which she would vacation had a toilet on the premises. She tried writing her question in a letter to the management but kept coming up against that awful word, which she could not bring herself to commit to paper. She finally settled upon 'BC,' short for 'Bathroom Commode,' and wrote to the manager, 'Does your campground have a BC on the premises?'.

The manager couldn't figure out what on earth she meant, and after showing the letter around, he finally decided she must mean the local Baptist Church. He wrote back

Madam,
Unfortunately, the nearest BC is located 6 miles from the campsite. It is a lovely BC, with seating for 175 people, and on Sundays the organ sounds are quite spectacular. I haven't been able to go much lately, as my advancing age makes it difficult, but that's not for lack of desire. Perhaps when you arrive, we can go together...

less frequently, businesses. In cheaper restaurants, or ones near heavily trafficked areas, there may be a 'customers only' policy in place – a sign will usually say so at the front door. Fear not – even in these places a polite request of 'May I use your bathroom, please' will more often than not lead to permission. Gas stations and fast-food places almost always have public toilets, but the best revenge is using the ones in five-star restaurants and hotels. Something about that five-star toilet paper…

HEALTH

Florida is a typical first-world destination when it comes to health. For most foreign visitors, no immunizations are required for entry, though cholera and yellow fever vaccinations may be required of travelers from areas with a history of those diseases. There are no unexpected health dangers, excellent medical attention is readily available, and the only real health concern is that, as elsewhere in the USA, a collision with the medical system can cause severe injuries to your financial state.

Hospitals and medical centers, walk-in clinics and referral services are easily found throughout the state of Florida.

In a serious emergency, call ☎ 911 for an ambulance to take you to the nearest hospital's emergency room. But note that ER charges in the USA are stellar: Mount Sinai Hospital in Miami, a good hospital, charges a *minimum* ER fee of $276, and that's just the flagfall. There are additional charges for X rays, casting, medicines, analysis…*everything*, so the cost of a visit can easily top $1000. That's just slightly above average in Florida. The price of health care in US hospitals and clinics is so outrageously high that most foreign visitors can't believe it. But there it is: aspirin does indeed cost $7 a tablet in a US hospital.

The moral: don't get sick or hurt in the USA without insurance!

Predeparture Preparations

Make sure you're healthy before you start traveling. If you are embarking on a long trip, make sure your teeth are in good shape. If you wear glasses, take a spare pair and your prescription. You can get new spectacles made up quickly and competently for about $100, depending on the prescription and frame you choose. If you require a particular medication, take an adequate supply and bring a prescription. Certain medications that don't require a prescription at home (such as Clarityne, called Claritin in the US, and aspirin or paracetemol with codeine) require a prescription in the USA.

There are a number of excellent travel health sites on the Internet. From the Lonely Planet Website, there are links (at (www.lonelyplanet.com.au/weblinks/wlprep .htm) to the World Health Organization, the US Center for Disease Control and Prevention and Stanford University Travel Medicine Service.

Health Insurance A travel insurance policy to cover theft, lost tickets and medical problems is a good idea, especially in the USA, where some privately run hospitals will refuse care without evidence of insurance. (Public hospitals must treat everyone, though standards are lower and waits can carry on for hours before you're looked at, except in the most serious of cases.)

There are a wide variety of policies; your travel agent will have recommendations. International student travel policies handled by STA Travel and other student travel organizations are usually a good value. Some policies offer lower and higher medical-expenses options, and the higher one is chiefly for countries like the USA with extremely high medical costs. Check the fine print.

Some policies specifically exclude 'dangerous activities' like scuba diving, motorcycling and trekking. If these activities are on your agenda, avoid this sort of policy.

You may prefer a policy that pays doctors or hospitals directly, rather than requiring you to pay on the spot and claim later. If you have to claim later, keep *all* documentation. Some policies ask you to call back (reverse charges) to a center in your home country for an immediate assessment of your problem.

Facts for the Visitor – Health   73

Medical Kit

If you're going off the beaten path, it's wise to take a small, straightforward medical kit. The kit should include the following:

- Aspirin, acetaminophen or Panadol, for pain or fever
- Antihistamine (such as Benadryl), useful as a decongestant for colds; to ease the itch from allergies, insect bites or stings; or to help prevent motion sickness
- Kaolin preparation (Pepto-Bismol), Immodium or Lomotil, for stomach upsets
- Rehydration mixture, to treat severe diarrhea, which is particularly important if you're traveling with children
- Antiseptic, mercurochrome and antibiotic powder or similar 'dry' spray, for cuts and grazes
- Calamine lotion, to ease irritation from bites or stings
- Bandages, for minor injuries
- Scissors, tweezers and a thermometer (note that airlines prohibit mercury thermometers)
- Insect repellent, sunscreen lotion, lip balm and water purification tablets

Check whether the policy covers ambulance fees or an emergency flight home. If you have to stretch out, you will need two seats and somebody has to pay for them!

Food & Water

Care in what you eat and drink is the most important health rule; stomach upsets are the most common travel health problem (between 30% and 50% of travelers on a two-week stay experience this), but the majority of these upsets will be relatively minor. American standards of cleanliness in places serving food and drink are very high.

Bottled drinking water, both carbonated and noncarbonated, is widely available in the USA. You can get a gallon of filtered drinking water (bring your own jug) from dispensers at Publix and Winn-Dixie supermarkets for 25¢. Tap water in Florida is usually OK to drink (though it tastes lousy).

Everyday Health

Normal body temperature is 98.6°F or 37°C; more than 4°F or 2°C higher indicates a high fever. The normal adult pulse rate is 60 to 100 per minute (children 80 to 100, babies 100 to 140). You should know how to take a temperature and a pulse rate.

Respiration (breathing) rate is also an indicator of illness. Count the number of breaths per minute: between 12 and 20 is normal for adults and older children (up to 30 for younger children, 40 for babies). People with a high fever or serious respiratory illness (like pneumonia) breathe more quickly than normal. More than 40 shallow breaths a minute usually means pneumonia.

Travel & Climate-Related Problems

Motion Sickness Eat lightly before and during a trip to reduce the chances of motion sickness. If you are prone to motion sickness, try to find a place that minimizes disturbance, for example, near the wing on aircraft or near the center on buses. Fresh air helps. Commercial anti-motion-sickness preparations, which can cause drowsiness, must be taken before the trip commences; once you feel sick, it's too late. Ginger, a natural preventative, is available in capsule form from health-food stores.

Jet Lag People experience jet lag when traveling by air across more than three time zones (each time zone usually represents a one-hour time difference). It occurs because many of the functions of the human body are regulated by internal 24-hour cycles called circadian rhythms. When we travel long distances rapidly, our bodies take time to adjust to the 'new time' of our destination, and we may experience fatigue, disorientation, insomnia, anxiety, impaired concentration and loss of appetite. These effects will usually be gone within three days of arrival, but there are ways to minimize the impact of jet lag:

- Rest for a couple of days prior to departure; try to avoid late nights and last-minute dashes for traveler's checks or your passport.
- Try to select flight schedules that minimize sleep deprivation; arriving in the early evening means you can go to sleep soon after you arrive. For very long flights, try to organize a stopover.
- Avoid excessive eating (which bloats the stomach) and alcohol (which causes dehydration) during the flight. Instead, drink plenty of noncarbonated, nonalcoholic drinks such as fruit juice or water.
- Make yourself comfortable by wearing loose-fitting clothes and perhaps bringing an eye mask and ear plugs to help you sleep.

Sunburn Most doctors recommend sunscreen with a high sun protection factor (SPF) for easily burned areas like your shoulders, and areas not normally exposed to sun – especially if you'll be hanging out at Haulover Beach in Miami or other nude beaches throughout the state.

Heat Exhaustion Dehydration or salt deficiency can cause heat exhaustion. Take time to acclimatize to high temperatures, and make sure you get enough liquids. Salt deficiency is characterized by fatigue, lethargy, headaches, giddiness and muscle cramps. Salt tablets may help. Vomiting or diarrhea can also deplete your liquid and salt levels. Anhydrotic heat exhaustion, caused by the inability to sweat, is quite rare, but unlike the other forms of heat exhaustion, it is likely to strike people who have been in a hot climate for some time, rather than newcomers. Always carry – and use – a water bottle on long trips.

Heat Stroke Long, continuous periods of exposure to high temperatures can leave you vulnerable to this serious, sometimes fatal, condition, which occurs when the body's heat-regulating mechanism breaks down and body temperature rises to dangerous levels. Avoid excessive alcohol intake or strenuous activity when you first arrive in a hot climate.

Symptoms include feeling unwell, lack of perspiration and a high body temperature of 102° to 105°F (39° to 41°C). Hospitalization is essential for extreme cases, but meanwhile, get out of the sun, remove clothing, cover with a wet sheet or towel and fan continually.

Fungal Infections Fungal infections, which occur with greater frequency in hot weather, are most likely to occur on the scalp, between the toes or fingers (athlete's foot), in the groin (jock itch or crotch rot) and on the body (ringworm). You get ringworm (which is a fungal infection, not a worm) from infected animals or by walking on damp areas such as shower floors.

To prevent fungal infections, wear loose, comfortable clothes, avoid artificial fibers, wash frequently and dry carefully. If you do get an infection, wash the infected area daily with a disinfectant or medicated soap and water, and rinse and dry well. Apply an antifungal powder, and try to expose the infected area to air or sunlight as much as possible. Change underwear and towels frequently and wash them often in hot water.

Infectious Diseases

Diarrhea A change of water, food or climate can cause 'the runs,' diarrhea caused by contaminated food or water is more serious. It's unlikely in the USA but common in Mexico. Despite all your precautions, you may still get a mild bout of traveler's diarrhea from exotic food or drink. Dehydration is the main danger with any diarrhea, particularly for children, who can get dehydrated quite quickly. Fluid replacement remains the mainstay of management. Weak black tea with a little sugar, soda water or soft drinks diluted 50% with water are all good. With severe diarrhea, a rehydrating solution is necessary to replace minerals and salts. Such solutions, like Pedialyte, are available at pharmacies.

Hepatitis Hepatitis is a general term for inflammation of the liver. There are many causes of this condition: poor sanitation, contact with infected blood products, drugs, alcohol and contact with an infected person are but a few. The symptoms are fever, chills, headache, fatigue, and aches and pains, followed by loss of appetite, nausea, vomiting, abdominal pain, dark urine, light-colored feces and jaundiced skin. The whites of the eyes may also turn yellow.

Hepatitis A is the most common strain. You should seek medical advice, but there is not much you can do apart from resting, drinking lots of fluids, eating lightly and avoiding fatty foods. People who have had hepatitis should avoid alcohol for some time after the illness, as the liver needs time to recover. Viral hepatitis is an infection of the liver, which can have several unpleasant symptoms, or no symptoms at all, with the infected person not knowing they have the disease.

HIV/AIDS HIV, the Human Immunodeficiency Virus, develops into AIDS, Acquired Immune Deficiency Syndrome, which is a fatal disease. Any exposure to blood, blood products or body fluids may put the individual at risk. The disease is often transmitted through sexual contact or dirty needles – vaccinations, acupuncture, tattooing and body piercing can be potentially as dangerous as intravenous drug use.

Fear of HIV infection should never preclude treatment for serious medical conditions. One good resource for help and information is the US Center for Disease Control AIDS hotline (☎ 800-342-2437, 800-344-7432 in Spanish). AIDS support groups are listed in the front of phone books.

Cuts, Bites & Stings

Skin punctures can easily become infected in hot climates and heal slowly. Treat any cut with an antiseptic such as Betadine. Where possible, avoid bandages and Band-Aids, which can keep wounds wet.

Bee and wasp stings and nonpoisonous spider bites are usually painful but not dangerous. Calamine lotion will give relief, and ice packs will reduce the pain and swelling. Avoid bites by not using bare hands to turn over rocks or large pieces of wood (see also Treating Bites in Dangers & Annoyances).

Ticks are a parasitic arachnid that may be present in brush, forest and grasslands, where hikers often get them on their legs or in their boots. The adults suck blood from hosts by burying their heads into skin, but they are often found unattached and can simply be brushed off. However, if one has attached itself to you, pulling it off and leaving the head in the skin increases the likelihood of infection or disease, such as Rocky Mountain spotted fever or Lyme disease.

Always check your body for ticks after walking through a high-grass or thickly forested area. If you do find a tick on you, induce it to let go by rubbing on oil, alcohol or petroleum jelly, or press it with a very hot object like a match or a cigarette. The tick should back out and can then be disposed of. If you get sick in the next couple of weeks, consult a doctor.

WOMEN TRAVELERS

Women often face different situations when traveling than do men. If you are a woman traveler, especially a woman traveling alone, get in the habit of traveling with a little extra awareness of your surroundings.

Women must recognize the extra threat of rape, which is a problem not only in urban but also in rural areas. The best way to deal with the threat of rape is to avoid putting yourself in vulnerable situations. Conducting yourself in a common-sense manner will help you avoid most problems. It's said that shouting 'Fire!' may draw assistance more effectively than yelling 'Help!'

If despite all precautions you are assaulted, call the police. In any emergency, phoning ☎ 911 will connect you with the emergency operator for police, fire and ambulance services.

Men may interpret a woman drinking alone in a bar as a bid for male company, whether you intended it that way or not. If you don't want the company, most men will respect a firm but polite 'no thank you.'

Don't hitchhike alone, and don't pick up hitchhikers if driving alone. If you get stuck on a road and need help, it's a good idea to have a pre-made sign to signal for help. At night, avoid getting out of your car to flag down help; turn on your hazard lights and wait for the police to arrive. Be extra careful at night on public transit, and remember to check the times of the last bus or train before you go out at night.

The Associated Press reported in June 1996 that Rohypnol, a tasteless sedative 10 times more powerful than Valium, was being added to women's drinks in Florida bars by the men who bought them – the women were sedated and raped. Never accept drinks offered by strangers in bars.

To deal with potential dangers, many women protect themselves with a whistle, mace, cayenne pepper spray or some self-defense training. If you do decide to purchase a spray, contact a police station to find out about regulations and training classes. Laws regarding sprays vary from state to state, so be informed based on your destination. It's a federal felony to carry sprays on airplanes (because of their combustible design).

The headquarters for the National Organization for Women (NOW; ☎ 202-331-0066), at 1000 16th St NW, Suite 700, Washington, DC 20036, is a good resource for any woman-related information, and it can refer you to state and local chapters. Planned Parenthood (☎ 212-541-7800), 810 7th Ave, New York, NY 10019, can refer you to clinics throughout the country and offer advice on medical issues. Check the yellow pages under Women's Organizations & Services for local resources.

GAY & LESBIAN TRAVELERS

The biggest news in the Miami gay and lesbian scene was the passage in 1998 of a law barring discrimination of homosexuals in the workplace and housing. Miami had been, in the 1970s, one of the first municipalities in the USA to pass such legislation, which became the highly publicized target of a campaign by conservative witch Anita Bryant in 1977. The law was repealed then but was reenacted in 1998 after a close vote.

Miami Beach is a key spot for gay and lesbian tourism in the USA: gay and lesbian visitors account for nearly $100 million a year in revenues to the Miami area and are treated with the respect such financial clout brings with it.

Florida would appear to be a very gay-friendly destination, but outside the major cities, it's probably not wise to be as out as you can be in Miami, Fort Lauderdale, Key West or even Orlando. In rural areas especially, gay travelers may occasionally find hostility or open rudeness, but gay-bashing episodes are not common in Florida. Regardless, you should alway use caution in strange situations.

Outside South Beach and Key West, there are cities with gay and lesbian bars, clubs and community centers, but there aren't any 'gay neighborhoods' of the type one would find in New York and San Francisco.

In this book, we list gay and lesbian resources wherever possible. On the Internet, a very useful page is QueerAmerica (www.queeramerica.com), which lists gay and lesbian resources and community groups within specified area codes – enter your zip code and the Website will spit out as much as it knows. If we don't list something and it doesn't either, call the local public library's reference desk and ask them. They will usually be able to come up with something. Other good sources are college and university campuses.

Also on the Internet is PlanetOut (www.planetout.com), with hundreds of links to gay and lesbian travel resources and other information.

America Online (AOL) hosts the Gay & Lesbian Community Forum. This is also the online home of the National Gay/Lesbian Task Force (NGLTF), the Gay & Lesbian Alliance Against Defamation (GLAAD), Parents, Families and Friends of Lesbians and Gays (P-FLAG) and other regional, state and national organizations. Michelle Quirk, host of AOL's Gay & Lesbian Community Forum, can be contacted by email at quirk@aol.com.

National resource numbers include the National AIDS/HIV Hotline (☎ 800-342-2437), the National Gay/Lesbian Task Force (☎ 202-332-6483 in Washington, DC) and the Lambda Legal Defense Fund (☎ 212-995-8585 in New York City, 213-937-2727 in Los Angeles).

Books

The Out Pages, an excellent book filled with listings of gay-owned and gay-friendly businesses in Miami and South Florida, is available at many local bookshops and gay/lesbian-owned businesses. For information on those businesses, contact the SoBe Business Guild (☎ 305-234-7224). National guidebooks with sections on South Florida are *The Women's Traveler*, providing listings for lesbians, and *Damron's Address Book* for men, both published by the Damron Company (☎ 415-255-0404, 800-462-6654), PO Box 422458, San Francisco, CA 94142-2458. The *Gay Yellow Pages* (☎ 212-674-0120), PO Box 533, Village Station, NY 10014-0533, has a *Southern Edition*, covering areas from Washington, DC, south to the US Caribbean ($5).

DISABLED TRAVELERS

Travel within the USA is becoming easier for people with disabilities. Public buildings (including hotels, restaurants, theaters and museums) are now required by law to be wheelchair accessible and have special toilet facilities. Public transportation services (buses, trains and taxis) must be made accessible to all, including those in wheelchairs, and telephone companies are required to provide relay operators for the hearing impaired. Many banks now provide ATM instructions in braille, and you will find audible crossing signals as well as dropped curbs at busier roadway intersections.

Larger private and chain hotels (see Accommodations later in this chapter for listings) have suites for disabled guests. Main car-rental agencies offer hand-controlled models at no extra charge. All major airlines, Greyhound buses and Amtrak trains will allow service animals to accompany passengers and will frequently sell two-for-one packages to accommodate attendants of seriously disabled passengers. Airlines will also provide assistance for connecting, boarding and deplaning the flight – just ask for assistance when making your reservation. (Note that airlines must accept wheelchairs as checked baggage and have an onboard chair available, though some advance notice may be required on smaller aircraft.) Of course, the more populous the area, the greater the likelihood of facilities for the disabled, so it's important to call ahead to see what is available.

Be sure to contact local public transportation providers at least two weeks before you intend to be in town to arrange for Special Transportation Services (STS) if you'll require them.

Organizations

There are a number of organizations and tour providers around the world that specialize in the needs of disabled travelers. In Australia, try Independent Travellers (☎ 08-232-2555, fax 08-232-6877), 167 Gilles St, Adelaide, SA 5000; and in the UK, RADAR (☎ 020-7250-3222), 250 City Rd, London, or Mobility International (☎ 020-7403-5688). The following is a list of organizations within the USA:

Access: The Foundation for Accessibility
  by the Disabled
  (☎ 516-887-5798)
  PO Box 356, Malverne, NY 11565

Handicapped Travel Newsletter
  (☎/fax 903-677-1260)
  PO Drawer 269, Athens, TX 75751
  This is a nonprofit publication with good information on world travel and US government legislation (subscriptions are $10 annually).

Information Center for Individuals
  with Disabilities
  (☎ 617-727-5540, TTY 617-345-9743, 800-248-3737), Fort Point Place, 1st Floor, 27-43 Wormwood St, Boston, MA 02210

Mobility International USA
  (☎/TDD 503-343-1284,
  fax 503-343-6812, miusa.igc.apc.org)
  PO Box 3551, Eugene, OR 97403
  This organization advises disabled travelers on mobility issues and runs an exchange program.

Moss Rehabilitation Hospital's Travel
  Information Service
  (☎ 215-456-9600, TTY 215-456-9602)
  1200 W Tabor Rd, Philadelphia, PA 19141-3099

SATH Society for the Advancement of Travel
  for the Handicapped
  (☎ 212-447-7284)
  347 5th Ave, No 610, New York, NY 10016

Twin Peaks Press
(☎ 202-694-2462, 800-637-2256)
PO Box 129, Vancouver, WA 98666
This press offers several useful handbooks for disabled travelers, including *Travel for the Disabled* and the *Directory of Travel Agencies for the Disabled*.

SENIOR TRAVELERS

Though the age at which senior benefits kick in changes from place to place, travelers aged 50 and up (though more commonly 65 and up) can expect to receive cut rates at such places as hotels, museums and restaurants.

Some national advocacy groups that can help seniors in planning their travels are the American Association of Retired Persons (AARP; ☎ 202-434-2277, 800-424-3410), 601 E St NW, Washington, DC 20049 (for Americans 50 years or older); Elderhostel (☎ 617-426-8056), 75 Federal St, Boston, MA 02110-1941 (for people 55 and older, and their companions); and the National Council of Senior Citizens (☎ 202-347-8800), 1331 F St NW, Washington, DC 20004.

Grand Circle Travel (☎ 617-350-7500, fax 617-350-6206) offers escorted tours and travel information in a variety of formats and distributes a useful free booklet, *Going Abroad: 101 Tips for Mature Travelers*. Contact them at 347 Congress St, Boston, MA 02210.

Visitors to national parks and campgrounds can cut costs greatly by using the Golden Age Passport (see Golden Passports later in the chapter).

FLORIDA FOR CHILDREN

Florida is very kid-friendly – especially with all those beaches. (Watch out for the topless spots if that sort of thing bothers you.) There are museums specifically targeted to children's interests in many large cities and even in some smaller ones. Cities with outstanding children's museums (many focusing on science and technology) are Orlando (of course), Miami, Tampa, Fort Lauderdale, Sarasota, Boca Raton, St Augustine, Key West and West Palm Beach.

In this book we list, as often as possible, attractions kids might like as well as children's admission prices. There's almost never an extra charge for kids in hotels.

Some cities also have circuses and zoos, which are quite good. Lion Country Safari in West Palm Beach is definitely a fun stop.

Discovery Zone (☎ 800-282-4386) is a chain of indoor playgrounds that kids and parents absolutely adore. Kids like the ramps, ball rooms, rope ladders, swings, tunnels, slides and trampolines; adults like DZs because there are usually other kids there to entertain yours, and you can sit down, for god's sake. Admission to DZs is $5.99 per child (adults don't pay, but adults are also not admitted without a child), and it's open daily. DZ has branches in Clearwater, Fort Myers, Jacksonville, Kendall, Pembroke Pines, Pensacola, Sarasota and Tallahassee.

Many McDonald's, some Burger King and all Pollo Tropical restaurants have kids' play zones that do a good job of emulating DZ, and a kids' meal at many fast-food places is a very cheap admission to a good, safe playground. There are also public playgrounds in every city, especially along the beaches, and there are public toilets and water fountains at most of them.

Every sizable Florida city has a municipal swimming pool with organized programs and free swim periods. The Police Athletic League in many cities is a great source for weekend and after-school programs.

Pick up Lonely Planet's excellent *Travel with Children* by Maureen Wheeler (1995) for general information and encouragement.

Ask at your hotel about babysitters. If you really need a day (or week) of peace, there are a variety of cool programs that'll take the kids off your hands. The US Space Camp is a fantastic week-long educational program for kids interested in science and space exploration; see the Space Coast chapter under Titusville.

The nonprofit Newfound Harbor Marine Institute's Sea Camp programs are another fun, educational option for kids in the Florida Keys. Most science museums and even some art museums offer sleepover programs for kids, who can spend a night or a weekend within the museum, with staff running exciting camplike programs. And almost every state park has some sort of ranger-led program specifically for kids, although not every day. Campfire programs are a favorite, with rangers organizing storytelling for campers, but even the simplest of nature walks are very popular with kids.

And Disney's Discovery Island Kidventure provides childcare in the form of an afternoon eco-adventure on Disney's island zoological preserve; see Walt Disney World in the Central Florida chapter.

If you're stuck for ideas on what to do with the kids, contact the nearest convention & visitors bureau. They'll be more than happy to help you work out an itinerary.

USEFUL ORGANIZATIONS
American Automobile Association
AAA (☎ 800-374-1258), with offices in all major cities and many smaller towns, provides useful information, free maps and routine road services, like tire repair and towing (free within a limited radius), to its members. Members of its foreign affiliates, like the Automobile Association in Canada and the UK and ADAC in Germany, are entitled to the same services. For others, the basic membership fee is $45 per year with a one-time $10 sign-up fee, an excellent investment for the maps alone (even for nonmotorists). Its nationwide toll-free roadside assistance number is ☎ 800-222-4357.

National Park Service (NPS) & US Forest Service (USFS)
The NPS and USFS administer the use of parks and forests. National forests are less protected than parks, allowing commercial exploitation in some areas (usually logging or privately owned recreational facilities).

National parks most often surround spectacular natural features and cover hundreds of square miles. A full range of accommodations can be found in and around national parks; contact individual parks for more spe-

cific information. National park campground and reservations information can be obtained by calling ☎ 800-365-2267 or writing to the National Park Service Public Inquiry, Department of the Interior, 18th and C Sts NW, Washington, DC 20013.

Current information about national forests can be obtained from ranger stations, which are also listed in the text. National forest campground and reservation information can be obtained by calling ☎ 800-280-2267 or writing to the National Park Service at the address above. General information about federal lands is also available from the US Fish & Wildlife Service (☎ 404-679-7289), whose Georgia office fields Florida-related questions.

Golden Passports Golden Age Passports allow permanent US residents 62 years and older unlimited entry to all sites in the national park system, with discounts on camping (50%) and other fees. (There's a one-time $10 processing fee.)

Golden Access Passports offer the same benefits to US residents who are legally blind or permanently disabled.

Golden Eagle Passports cost $50 annually and offer the holder and accompanying guests free entry into national parks. You can apply in person for any of these at any national park or regional office of the USFS or NPS, or call ☎ 800-280-2267 for information and ordering.

DANGERS & ANNOYANCES
Crime
In 1992 and 1993, several highly publicized attacks on tourists in Miami made headlines all over the world. Since then, attacks against tourists have been considerably reduced. In fact, of the 8.7 million tourists who stayed in unincorporated Dade County in 1995, there were 134 reported robberies; in 1993, the 'really bad year,' there were 391 robberies. You'd still do well to use caution.

The cities of Florida generally have lower levels of violent crime than larger, better-known cities such as Washington, DC, New York and Los Angeles. Nevertheless, violent crime is certainly present, and you should take the usual precautions, especially in the cities.

Always lock cars and put valuables out of sight, whether leaving the car for a few minutes or longer, and whether you are in town or in the remote backcountry. Rent a car with a lockable trunk.

Be aware of your surroundings and of who may be watching you. Avoid walking on dimly lit streets at night, particularly if you are alone. Walk purposefully. Exercise particular caution in large parking lots or parking structures at night. Avoid unnecessary displays of money or jewelry. Split up your money and credit cards to avoid losing everything, and try to use ATM machines in well-trafficked areas.

In hotels, don't leave valuables lying around your room. Use safety deposit boxes, or at least place valuables in a locked bag. Don't open your door to strangers – check the peephole or call the front desk if unexpected people are trying to enter.

Highway Robbery & Carjacking

Official police cars have flashing blue *and* red lights; if any other vehicle attempts to pull you over using any other means, keep driving and get to a well-lit area like a gas station and call the police. And that's what you should do if someone rams your car from behind. Forget about stopping to exchange insurance information; just get to someplace safe and call the police. Don't stop for 'stranded' motorists.

Carjacking is a relatively new activity, in which someone approaches you at a stoplight, points a gun at you and orders you out of the vehicle, which they drive off in. Police say that resisting a gun-wielding person is not wise; just follow instructions and hope for the best.

Credit Card Scams

When you use phone credit cards of any sort, be aware of people watching you, especially in public places like airports. Thieves will memorize numbers and use them to make lots of international calls. Shield the telephone with your body when punching in

your credit card number. Don't give your credit card number aloud over the phone in public places – people can charge anything they want if they have your name, card number and expiration date. Destroy any carbons generated by a credit card sale.

Never, ever, *ever* give out personal information over the phone to someone who's called you. No legitimate company representative would ever call and ask for your social security number, credit card number and expiration date or other personal information.

Hotels customarily ask for a credit card imprint when you check in to cover incidental expenses. Make certain this is destroyed if not used.

Enter a $ sign before – and make certain there's a decimal point in – numbers written in the 'total' box on a credit card slip. We've heard reports of Japanese tourists being charged $1500 for a T-shirt instead of $15.

Hurricanes

A hurricane is a concentrated system of very strong thunderstorms with high circulation. The 74- to 160-mph winds created by a hurricane can extend for hundreds of miles around the eye (center) of a hurricane system. Floods and flash floods caused by the torrential rains it produces cause additional property damage, and perhaps most dangerous of all, hurricanes can cause a storm surge, forcing the level of the ocean to rise between 4 and 18 feet above normal. The 13- to 18-foot storm surge caused by a category-4 hurricane like Hurricane Andrew would have easily destroyed the entire city of Miami Beach – and the 9- to 12-foot surge caused by Hurricane Opal did destroy much of the coast of the Florida Panhandle in 1995.

Hurricane Georges (which few in Florida could pronounce, and many dubbed 'George') ripped through the state with a double whammy in 1998, first demolishing Cuba and passing mercifully quickly across Key West, but then following the west coast of Florida up to the Panhandle and once again battering Panama City Beach and Pensacola.

Floridians are very hurricane conscious: school children participate in hurricane evacuation drills and take preparedness classes, and all Floridians have committed to memory facts and statistics on meteorological phenomena matched perhaps only by San Franciscans' knowledge of plate-tectonics theory.

The Saffir/Simpson scale breaks hurricanes into five levels of intensity, based on the speed of circular wind intensity. Storms circulate counterclockwise in the northern hemisphere.

The following is some hurricane and storm terminology:

Tropical depression
  Formative stage of a storm. This is an organized cloud system with winds of less than 39 mph.

Tropical storm
  Strengthened tropical depression. This is an organized system of powerful thunderstorms with high circulation and wind speeds between 39 and 73 mph.

Category-1 hurricane
  Winds between 74 and 95 mph. This primarily affects plants, small piers and small boats, and can produce a storm surge of between 4 and 5 feet, flooding coastal roads. Note that a category-1 hurricane is still a hurricane and not to be treated lightly.

Category-2 hurricane
  Winds between 96 and 110 mph. This hurricane causes major damage to plants and uproots trees. Mobile homes, roofs, doors and windows are damaged or destroyed. It can cause a 6- to 8-foot storm surge.

Category-3 hurricane
  Winds between 111 and 130 mph. Large trees are uprooted and knocked over; signs, mobile homes and small buildings near the coast are destroyed; roofs, windows, doors and building structures are damaged. A 9- to 12-foot storm surge cuts off coastal escape routes three to five hours before the storm.

Category-4 hurricane
  Winds between 131 and 155 mph. Mobile homes, plants, trees and signs are ripped up and destroyed; roofs, windows and doors are damaged; buildings suffer major structural damage. A 13- to 18-foot storm surge cuts off coastal escape routes three to five hours before the storm.

Category-5 hurricane
  Winds above 155 mph. Buildings and roofs are destroyed. An 18-foot storm surge cuts off coastal escape routes three to five hours before the storm.

Every year during hurricane season (June 1 to November 30) storms form over the Atlantic Ocean and the Gulf of Mexico and gather strength – and some roll right over Florida. Some years – notably 1992, when Hurricane Andrew flattened the land, decimating the city of Homestead just south of Miami – are worse than others. In 1994, there was no major hurricane activity in the state.

Hurricanes are deadly. They can throw cars and trucks. And as anyone can attest who saw the carnage left behind in the city of Homestead after Hurricane Andrew, they can wipe out communities, leaving little more than flat land, felled trees and broken gas lines.

Hurricanes are generally sighted well in advance, giving people time to prepare. When a hurricane threatens, listen to radio and television news reports. Give credence only to forecasts attributed to the National Weather Center (shortwave radio listeners can tune to 162.55 MHz), and dismiss anything else as a rumor. You can also call the National Hurricane Center (☎ 305-229-4470, option 1) for hurricane tracking information. There are two distinct stages of alert:

Hurricane watch
  This is given when a hurricane *may* strike in the area within the next 36 to 48 hours.

Hurricane warning
  This is given when a hurricane is likely to strike the area.

If a hurricane warning is issued during your stay, you may be placed under an evacuation order. Hotels generally follow these orders and ask guests to leave. The Red Cross operates hurricane shelters, but they're just that – shelter. They do not provide food. You must bring your own food, first-aid kit, blanket or sleeping bag – and hey, bring a book. Ask your hotel or hostel for more information about the logistics of evacuation.

Plotting a Hurricane

Scientists and National Weather Center (NWC) meteorologists now closely observe tropical depressions over the ocean and gulf as they become tropical storms and are finally upgraded to hurricanes. But plotting a hurricane's path is a tricky biz – in fact, it can't really be done.

In 1995, Miami television and NWC meteorologists predicted that Hurricane Erin was headed for a touchdown right in the center of the city. Miami and Miami Beach neighborhoods were evacuated and shelters sent out pleas for volunteers and supplies. Local television news teams gleefully ran around looking for driving rain ('Well, Patricia, it isn't coming down quite yet, but it's looking *very* ominous indeed…'), waiting for something awful to happen, while a mild degree of panic set in among local residents who had not evacuated. And then…

Nothing.

At least, nothing in Miami, where it rained a little. That evening a startlingly clear, star-filled sky, combined with a gentle breeze across the bay, made conditions lovely for a stroll on the beach.

The storm had suddenly veered north, catching northern Florida residents totally by surprise – in fact, many South Florida residents who had listened to news reports and evacuated their homes actually drove into the eye of the storm!

As Erin continued over land, it socked the Florida Panhandle with a wallop that knocked out power, destroyed houses as if they were built from matchsticks, and caused millions of dollars in damage.

About a month later, the second half of the one-two punch slammed the Panhandle as Hurricane Opal came through and flattened almost all of Panama City Beach, ripping down condominiums, actually tearing up highways, houses and hotels. The city of Pensacola Beach was still under several feet of sand when we visited in the late fall of 1995. Three years later, as we write, the area is close to full recovery.

What this illustrates is the danger of becoming lulled into a false sense of security (or of panic) by mustachioed television personalities with complicated Doppler radar charts and satellite imagery. Hurricanes are much like the proverbial 800lb gorilla: they set down wherever, and whenever, they want.

If you're determined to sit out a hurricane warning, you will need the following:

- Flashlight
- As much fresh drinking water as possible (storms knock out water supply)
- Butane lighter and candles
- Canned food, peanut butter, powdered or UHT milk
- Cash (ATMs don't function)
- Portable, battery-powered radio

Stay in a closet or other windowless room. Cover yourself with a mattress to prevent injury from flying glass. Taping windows does not stop them from breaking, but it does reduce shatter. For a full list of tips on preparedness, check on page 29 in the Miami white pages.

Tornadoes

For a brief period after a hurricane, as if to add insult to injury, conditions become just ducky for a tornado. A tornado watch is generally issued as standard operating procedure after a hurricane, but actual twisters have popped up in Miami as recently as late 1995. There's not much you can do about a tornado except be aware of the situation and follow the instructions of local radio and television stations and police.

Ocean Dangers

Florida's Atlantic coastline isn't for the most part very rough, but there are a few areas of rough surf, rip tides (see below) and undertows. The entire coast is dangerous before and after storms, when it is inconceivably stupid to go in the water.

The most important thing to keep in the water is your calm. Even if you're stuck in what seems like a bad rip tide, you're just a few minutes away from an easy swim back to shore. We watched in horror as two panicked swimmers made the wrong choice – to fight a rip tide. That they lived through the experience was a miracle. Use your head: Human versus Ocean is no contest.

Rip Tides Rips, rip currents or rip tides are fast-flowing currents of water within the ocean, moving from shallow areas out to sea. They are most common in conditions of high surf, forming when water from incoming waves builds up near the shore – essentially, when the waves are coming in faster than they can flow back out.

The water then runs along the shoreline until it finds an escape route out to sea, usually through a channel or out along a point. Swimmers caught up in the current can be ripped out to deeper water. Here's where that Don't Panic thing comes in.

Though rips can be powerful, they usually dissipate 50 to 100 yards offshore. Anyone caught in one should either go with the flow until it loses power, or swim parallel to shore to slip out of it. Trying to swim against a rip current will exhaust the strongest of swimmers.

Undertows Undertows are common along steeply sloped beaches when large waves backwash directly into incoming surf. The outflowing water picks up speed as it flows down the slopes. When it hits an incoming wave, the water pulls under it, creating an undertow. Swimmers caught in an undertow can be pulled beneath the surface. Once

again, go with the current until you get beyond the wave.

Jellyfish Take a peek into the water before you plunge in to make certain it's not jellyfish territory. These gelatinous creatures with saclike bodies and stinging tentacles are fairly common on Florida's Atlantic coast. They're most often found drifting near the shore or washed up on the beach. The sting of a jellyfish varies from mild to severe, depending on the type of jellyfish. But unless you have an allergic reaction to jellyfish venom, the stings are not generally dangerous.

The Portuguese man-of-war is the worst type to encounter. Not technically a jellyfish, the man-of-war is a colonial hydrozoan, or a colony of coelenterates, rather than a solitary coelenterate like a true jellyfish.

Its body consists of a translucent, bluish bladderlike float, which generally grows to about 4 to 5 inches long. A man-of-war sting is very painful, similar to a bad bee sting, except you're likely to get stung more than once from clusters of their incredibly long tentacles, containing hundreds of stinging cells. Even touching a man-of-war a few hours after it's washed up on shore can result in burning stings.

If you do get stung, quickly remove the tentacles and apply vinegar or a meat tenderizer containing papain (derived from papaya), which neutralizes the toxins. For serious reactions, including chest pains or difficulty in breathing, seek medical attention.

Snakes

Five of Florida's native snakes are venomous. The first four are members of the *Crotalidae* family (pit vipers), which inject venom that destroys red blood cells and the walls of blood vessels. Coral snakes are in the family of *Elapidae*, producing venom that paralyzes the victim, whom they then begin to nibble. Before you freak out, we'd just like to point out that in all the time we've spent in Florida, we have never come across a poisonous snake.

The diamondback rattlesnake *(Crotalus adamanteus)* is the largest, most dangerous of the pit vipers. They can grow to 8 feet long. They have a big, heavy, brownish body, marked with dark (almost black) diamond shapes, set off by yellowish-white borders. Diamondbacks usually rattle before they attack.

The pygmy rattlesnake *(Sistrurus miliarius)* is much smaller (from 1½ to 2 feet). It's grayish-brown with round black and reddish-orange markings. It also rattles before an attack, but its rattle is so quiet, one can usually only hear it when it's very close. The pygmy rattlesnake's poison generally isn't fatal.

The copperhead snake *(Agkistrodon contortrix)* is only found in the northwestern section of Florida and is not very aggressive. It grows to about 4 feet and has an hourglass-shaped head. They too are grayish-brown with chestnut-colored bands; the head is more copper-toned.

The cottonmouth (sometimes also called water moccasin; *Agkistrodon piscivorus conanti)* is named for the white interior of its mouth. This olive-green to brown snake with a dark stripe from its eyes to jaws grows to about 5 feet and has a heavy body ending in a thin, pointy tail. They live near lakes and streams and are very venomous.

The coral snake *(Micrurus fulvius)*, a relative of the cobra, is small and deadly: its poison is the most potent of any North American snake. They are very pretty – their slim bodies have sections of black and red divided by thin orange-yellow stripes. They can easily be mistaken for the harmless scarlet king snake. To keep them apart, remember this little rhyme: Red on yellow, kill a fellow; red on black, venom lack. Fortunately for us, coral snakes are very shy and generally nocturnal.

Snake Bites In the unlikely event of a bite by a poisonous snake, the main thing to do is stay calm – that's easy for us to say. If you can get to a telephone, call ☎ 800-282-3171, which will connect you with the nearest Poison Information Center. If you can, find a ranger.

If you're alone, stave off panic with the knowledge that snake bites don't, no matter what you've seen in the movies, cause instantaneous death. But they are dangerous, and you need to keep a good, clear head on your shoulders.

Wrap the bitten limb as you would a sprained ankle (not too tightly), and then attach a splint to immobilize the limb. Get medical help as soon as possible, and if you can, bring along the dead snake for identification – but *do not* attempt to catch the snake if there's *any* chance of being bitten again. Sucking out the poison and attaching tourniquets has been widely discredited as treatment for snake bites, so do not apply ice, a tourniquet, elevate the limb or attempt to suck out the poison yourself. Instead, keep the affected area below the level of the heart and move it as little as possible. Do not ingest alcohol or any drugs. Antivenoms are available in hospitals.

Sharks

Shark attacks off Miami Beach happen a few times a year, and there are more sharks out there than you would like to think. But other than staying out of the water, there's not much one can do about it. So, like, don't go see *Jaws* right before you come, okay?

Alligators

It's pretty unlikely that you'll even see an alligator in cities, but it's been known to happen. Alligators generally only eat when they're hungry – not as a punitive measure – unless they're feeling attacked. Things alligators like: small animals or things that look like them, such as small children or people crouching down real small to snap a photo. Things alligators don't like: you.

Alligators are fairly common in suburban and rural lakes, and they move around but generally mind their own business. 'Nuisance alligators' – those that eat pets or livestock – become the bailiwick of the police (call ☎ 911 if you see an alligator in a city). Generally speaking, the best thing to do with an alligator is stay away from it completely.

Biting Insects

Florida has about 70 types of mosquitoes and other biting insects like deer flies and fleas. They're bloody annoying, but there are some steps you can take to minimize your chances of getting bitten. Most larger Florida cities have mosquito-control boards that supervise spraying to reduce the problem, but in low-lying cities like St Augustine, insects abound – especially in summer.

Prime biting hours are around sunrise and sunset. Cover up – wear long pants, socks and long-sleeved shirts. The better brands of insect repellent in the USA are OFF! and Cutter for city use and industrial-strength products like REI Jungle Juice or any repellent that contains a high percentage of DEET for more severe situations such as the Everglades or the backwoods. Another wonderful alternative is Avon Skin-So-Soft, a moisturizer that happens to be excellent at repelling mosquitoes.

Treating Bites One great thing about Florida is that aloe vera grows wild. If you've been bitten, grab an aloe vera leaf, break off a piece, squeeze out the juice and rub it on bites – great stuff. Calamine lotion, available at all drugstores, is what Nick's parents swore by, and he hated them for it! You get pink globs all over your skin and the itch stays anyway – but it must work for some people.

Tiger Balm, available in better drugstores and health-food shops, reduces itch and swelling from bites. Rub it on the bite and try to control yourself from scratching for about five minutes, when the itch should be gone. If that doesn't work for you, try cortisone cream, also available at all drugstores. Antihistamine tablets are also known to work.

Panhandlers & the Homeless
The waves of refugees from poor countries, in addition to the waves of refugees from the northeastern US, has resulted in a high percentage of homeless people and panhandlers in South Florida. This is a very touchy issue,

and all we'll do is toe the official Lonely Planet line: don't encourage them – it only helps make visitors an easy mark. If you're really concerned, you can volunteer at a homeless shelter or donate to homeless relief programs at local churches and synagogues.

EMERGENCY
Dial ☎ 911 for police, fire and ambulance emergencies – it's a free call from any phone. Check the inside front cover of the Miami white pages for a slew of emergency numbers.

If you're robbed, report the theft to police on the nonemergency numbers. You'll need a police report in order to make an insurance claim back home.

If your credit cards, debit cards or traveler's checks have been stolen, notify your bank or the relevant company as soon as possible. For refunds on lost or stolen traveler's checks (but not cards) call American Express (☎ 800-221-7282), MasterCard (☎ 800-223-9920), Thomas Cook (☎ 800-223-7373) or Visa (☎ 800-227-6811).

To report lost or stolen credit cards, call American Express (☎ 800-528-4800), Visa (☎ 800-336-8472), MasterCard (☎ 800-826-2181), Diners Club (☎ 800-234-6377) or Discover (☎ 800-347-2683).

Foreign visitors who have lost their passports should contact their country's consulate. Having a photocopy of the important pages of your passport will make replacement much easier.

LEGAL MATTERS
Florida law tends to be tougher than in most northern states when it comes to drug possession or use. It's less strict in the far south of the state than in the north. In Miami, the police are more tolerant than in, say, St Augustine, where someone arrested for carrying a pot pipe makes the newspaper. But the late 1990s have seen an increase in police raids on nightclubs, and dozens of people are arrested on minor drug charges each week. Consider that possession of any marijuana or speed (amphetamines) is a misdemeanor and technically punishable by up to one year in prison *and* a $1000 fine.

It's illegal to walk with an open alcoholic drink – including beer – on the street, unless you're on Panama City Beach. If you're driving, all liquor has to be unopened (not just sealed, but new and untouched) and, technically anyway, stored in the trunk of the car.

See below for more on the severe penalties for drinking and driving in Florida.

If you are stopped by the police for any reason, bear in mind that there is no system of paying fines on the spot. For traffic offenses, the police officer will explain your options to you. Attempting to pay the fine to the officer is frowned upon at best and may lead to a charge of bribery to compound your troubles. Should the officer decide you need to pay up front, he or she can take you directly to the magistrate instead of allowing you the usual 30-day period to pay the fine.

For those of you who missed every cop movie ever made: everyone arrested legally has (and is given) the right to remain silent, to make one phone call and to representation by an attorney. If you don't have a lawyer or family member to help you, call your embassy. The police will give you the number upon request. You are presumed innocent until proven guilty.

Note that police officers in Florida are allowed to search you if they have 'probable cause' – an intentionally vague condition that can almost be defined as 'if they want to.' The police will likely be able to search your car as well, under many different circumstances. There is no legal reason for you to speak to a police officer if you don't want to (although the officer may try to offer compelling reasons – like handcuffs – if they wish to speak with you and you ignore them).

Florida law upholds the death penalty for capital crimes.

Driving Laws

As we went to press, speed limits in the USA were in flux as the states were set free from federal regulation of the speed limit. Currently, Florida is determining new speed limits on its roads, but as we write, the maximum permissible speed is 70 mph on interstate highways and between 55 and 65 mph on state highways unless otherwise posted. You can drive about 5 mph over the limit without much likelihood of being pulled over by the police, but if you're doing 10 mph over the limit, you'll be caught sooner or later.

Speed limits on smaller highways are 55 mph or less, and in cities they can vary from 25 to 45 mph.

Watch for school zones, where speed limits can be as low as 15 mph during school hours – and these limits are strictly enforced: Nick once got a ticket for $127.28 (!) for going 24 mph in a school zone. Seat belts must be worn in most states, and motorcyclists must wear helmets.

Drinking & Driving

The USA is one of the least tolerant countries in the world when it comes to drunk driving, and the concept of 'drunk' is a fairly loose one: maximum permissible blood alcohol content in Florida is .08%.

While alcohol levels vary from person to person, generally speaking, if you have *one* beer, you're pushing the legal limit. If you're pulled over and an officer suspects you're drunk, you'll be given a 'field sobriety test.' If you fail, you'll be placed under arrest immediately. In the police station, you'll be offered a breath test. Refusal isn't admission of guilt, but if you think refusing helps, you're nuts – they'll undoubtedly find some charge on which to hold you even longer. If you fail a breath test, your license will be immediately suspended pending a hearing, and you'll be fined a minimum of $250 and maximum of $500 for a first offense. Depending on alcohol level and whether you've had an accident, this fine could easily reach $5000.

During festive holidays and special events, police road blocks are sometimes set up to check for, and hopefully deter, drunk drivers.

For information on other car-related topics, see the Getting Around chapter.

BUSINESS HOURS

Office hours in Florida are generally 9 am to 5 pm, though there can be a variance of half an hour or so. In large cities, a few supermarkets are open 24 hours a day. Shops are usually open from 9 or 10 am to 5 or 6 pm but are often open until 9 pm in shopping malls, except on Sundays, when hours are noon to 5 pm.

Post offices are open Monday to Friday from 8 am to 4 or 5:30 pm, and some are open Saturday from 8 am to 3 pm. Banks are usually open Monday to Friday from 9 or 10 am to 5 or 6 pm. A few banks are open Saturday from 9 am to 2 or 4 pm (hours are decided by the individual bank branches).

PUBLIC HOLIDAYS

National public holidays are celebrated throughout the USA. Banks, schools and government offices (including post offices) are closed, and transportation, museums and other services are on a Sunday schedule. Holidays falling on a Sunday are usually observed on the following Monday.

The following are the current national holidays:

New Year's Day	January 1
Martin Luther King Jr Day	3rd Monday in January
Presidents' Day	3rd Monday in February
Easter	a Sunday in April
Memorial Day	last Monday in May
Independence Day	July 4
Labor Day	1st Monday in September
Columbus Day	2nd Monday in October
Veterans' Day	November 11
Thanksgiving	4th Thursday in November
Christmas Day	December 25

CULTURAL EVENTS

The USA is always ready to call a day an event. Retailers remind the masses of coming events with huge advertising binges running for months before the actual day. Because of this tacky overexposure, some of these events are nicknamed 'Hallmark Holidays' (after the greeting-card manufacturer). In larger cities with diverse cultures, traditional holidays of other countries are also celebrated with as much, if not more, fanfare. Some of these are also public

holidays (see above) and therefore banks, schools and government buildings are closed.

January

Chinese New Year – Beginning at the end of January or the beginning of February, this event lasts two weeks. The first day is celebrated with parades, firecrackers, fireworks and lots of food.

February

Valentine's Day – February 14. No one knows why St Valentine is associated with romance in the USA, but this is the day of roses, sappy greeting cards and packed restaurants. Some people wear red and give out 'Be My Valentine' candies.

March

St Patrick's Day – March 17. The patron saint of Ireland is honored by all those who feel the Irish in their blood – and by those who want to feel Irish beer in their blood. Everyone wears green, stores sell green bread, bars serve green beer, and towns and cities put on frolicking parades of marching bands and community groups.

April

Easter – Observers of this holiday go to church and often paint eggs, which are usually hidden (by the 'Easter Bunny') for children to find. Chocolate eggs and bunnies are also eaten. Travel during this weekend is usually expensive and crowded. Incidentally, Good Friday is not a public holiday and often goes unnoticed.

Passover – This is celebrated either in March or April, depending on the Jewish calendar. Jewish families get together to partake in the traditional Seder dinner, which commemorates the exodus of Jews from their slavery in Egypt.

May

Cinco de Mayo – This event celebrates the day the Mexicans wiped out the French army in 1862. Now it's the day on which all Americans get to eat lots of Mexican food and drink margaritas.

Mother's Day – Held on the second Sunday of the month, the day is celebrated with lots of cards, flowers and busy restaurants.

June

Fathers Day – Held on the third Sunday of the month, it's the same idea, different parent.

July

Independence Day – On this day, often called the Fourth of July, flags are flown, barbecues abound, parades storm the streets of many towns, fireworks litter the air and ground – all to commemorate America's Declaration of Independence.

October

Halloween – October 31. Kids and adults both dress in costumes. In safer neighborhoods, children go door to door 'trick-or-treating' for candy, and adults go to parties and act out their alter egos. Miami and Orlando are especially good places to be on Halloween, as the gay communities hold impromptu parades with wild and lavish costumes.

November

Day of the Dead – November 2. Observed in areas with Mexican communities, this is a day for families to honor dead relatives. People make breads and sweets resembling skeletons, skulls and such.

Election Day – Held on the second Tuesday of the month, this is the chance for US citizens to perform their patriotic duty by voting. Shamefully, only about 45% of them do. Even more flags are flown than on the Fourth of July, and signs with corny photos of candidates decorate the land.

Thanksgiving – This is held on the last Thursday of the month. A day to give thanks, and ostensibly commemorating the short-lived cooperation between the original Pilgrims and Native Americans at the harvest, this most important family gathering is celebrated with a bounty of food and football games on TV. The following day is declared by retailers to be the biggest shopping day of the year, with everyone burning off pumpkin pie by running shopping relays through the malls. The day before Thanksgiving is often the heaviest travel day in the country.

December

Chanukah – This is an eight-day Jewish holiday commemorating the victory of the Maccabees over the armies of Syria. The date of Chanukah changes year to year, as it's tied to Kislev 25 to Tevet 2 in the Hebrew calendar, a nonlunar system.

Christmas – December 25. The day before is as much an event as Christmas itself, with church services, caroling in the streets, people cruising neighborhoods looking for the best light displays and stores full of procrastinators.

Kwanzaa – This seven-day celebration, held from December 26 to 31, is based on an African holiday that gives thanks to the harvest. Families join together for a feast and practice seven different principles corresponding to the seven days of celebration.

New Year's Eve – December 31. People celebrate with little tradition other than dressing up and drinking champagne, or staying home and watching the festivities on TV. The following day, people stay home to nurse their hangovers and watch college football.

SPECIAL EVENTS

There are special events all the time in Florida; the Florida Division of Tourism has a complete list, updated annually, and each city's CVB/VCB or chamber of commerce publishes a list of its own celebrations.

January

FedEx Orange Bowl (Miami; ☎ 305-371-4600) See December, below, for information on the New Year's Eve Orange Bowl Parade, a Miami tradition. The Orange Bowl football classic is a major college football game at Pro Player Stadium.

Florida Citrus Bowl Classic (Orlando; ☎ 407-849-2020) The Citrus Bowl is also a college football game; teams play at the Florida Citrus Bowl Stadium on or close to New Year's Day.

Indian River Native American Festival (New Smyrna Beach; ☎ 904-424-0860) Native American arts & crafts, storytelling and demonstrations are offered at this festival.

Hall of Fame Bowl (Tampa; ☎ 813-874-2695) This football match takes place in the Tampa Stadium on January 1.

Circus Festival (Sarasota; ☎ 941-352-8888) Performers, acrobats, magicians and artists get together here in Ringling Country during the first week of January at the Sarasota County Fairgrounds.

Sun 'n Fun EAA *Fly-In* (Lakeland; ☎ 941-644-2431) Pilots and flight buffs must check out this enormous aviation convention in early January.

Art Deco Weekend Festival (Miami; ☎ 305-672-2014) This is held the second week in January, and 1996 became the first year in recent memory when it didn't rain on the parade. Arts & crafts stalls line the east side of Ocean Drive;

there are food stalls and the usual block-party types. When it doesn't rain, it's great.

Martin Luther King Jr Festival (actually festivals) Martin Luther King's birthday is celebrated in different towns throughout the state, sometime in mid-January.

Miami River Blues Festival (☎ 305-374-1198) In late January along the Miami River, near Tobacco Road, you can hear plenty of blues music.

February, March & April

Miami Film Festival (☎ 305-374-2444) Held the first two weeks of February, this international film festival is at the Gusman Center for the Performing Arts.

Edison Festival of Lights (Fort Myers; ☎ 941-334-2550) During the first two weeks of February, this festival celebrates the famous inventor. Arts & crafts are sold, and at the end there is a parade of lights.

Speed Weeks (Daytona; ☎ 904-253-7223) This is a three-week auto race celebration beginning in early February, including Bike Week, leading up to Daytona 500 at the Daytona International Speedway.

Florida State Fair (Tampa; ☎ 800-345-3247) During the second week of February, fruits, vegetables and arts & crafts are sold at the Florida State Fairgrounds.

Carnaval Miami (☎ 305-644-8888) There are festivals and parties throughout this nine-day event at the beginning of March, including a Miss Carnaval contest, Carnaval Night concerts at the Orange Bowl, an in-line skating contest and jazz concerts at South Beach, a Latin drag queen show and a Calle Ocho cooking contest.

Calle Ocho Festival (Miami; ☎ 305-644-8888) The culmination of Carnaval Miami, the Calle Ocho Festival is a great time in Little Havana, with lots of concerts, giveaways and Cuban food on the second Sunday in March.

Bike Week (Daytona; ☎ 904-255-0981) During the first week in March, lawyers, Hells Angels, speed heads, accountants and other suits from all over the state saddle up and get together for this wild party, based around motorcycle races at the Daytona Speedway.

Sanibel Shell Fair (Sanibel Island, near Fort Myers; ☎ 941-472-2155) A tradition since 1937, this four-day celebration is all things shells, starting the first Thursday of March.

Sarasota Jazz Festival (☎ 941-366-1552) This is a weeklong jazz, blues and big band festival during the third week of March.

Underwater Music Festival (Big Pine Key; ☎ 800-872-3722) Held in late March, this is an underwater symphony staged for divers.

Festival of the States (St Petersburg; ☎ 813-898-3654) Taking place from late March into early April, this 70-year tradition offers competitions, music performances, an antique car show and the like.

Springtime Tallahassee (☎ 850-224-5012) Lasting about four weeks from March into April, this is one of the largest festivals in the state – those ubiquitous arts & crafts are sold, and there is a balloon rally and music entertainment.

Fort Lauderdale Seafood Festival (☎ 954-463-4431) One of Florida's uncountable seafood celebrations, the first week of April is a great opportunity to taste local fish, oysters, crabs and regional cooking in Fort Lauderdale.

Kissimmee Jazz Festival (☎ 407-846-6257) This music festival lasts for two days in mid-April at Kissimmee Lakefront.

May & June

Fun 'n' Sun Festival (Clearwater; ☎ 813-462-6531) Sport contests, musical events and lots of action on the beach and in town mark this festival, which starts after Easter and continues into May.

Conch Republic Celebration (Key West; ☎ 305-296-0123) The founders of this island nation are toasted in true Key West style; the event starts in April and lasts into May.

Fiesta of Five Flags (Pensacola; ☎ 850-433-6512) The arrival of the Spanish is celebrated the first week of June, complete with reenactments and Spanish food and music.

Cross & Sword (St Augustine; ☎ 904-471-1965) The story of the settlement of Florida is staged late June to early September in the amphitheater at Anastasia State Recreation Area.

International Orchids Fair (Kissimmee; ☎ 407-396-1881) All kinds of orchids are on display and for sale toward the end of June at A World of Orchids.

July, August & September

America's Birthday Bash (Miami; ☎ 305-358-7550) Held on the Fourth of July at Bayfront Park, this excellent fireworks and laser show with live music and celebrations draws crowds of more than 100,000.

Hemingway Days Festival (Key West; ☎ 305-294-4440) The best thing about this festival, held the last week in July, is the Hemingway look-alike contest, but there are also short-story competitions and more.

Space Week (Titusville; ☎ 407-452-2121 x235) This celebration of space exploration, on the last week of July, is a must for space junkies (like us).

Annual Miami Reggae Festival (☎ 305-891-2944) One of the largest reggae events in the country, this is held in the first week of August at Bayfront Park.

Shark's Tooth & Seafood Celebration (Venice Beach; ☎ 941-488-2236) Experience a fabulous shark's-tooth hunt and incredible seafood in mid-August at and around our favorite spot, Venice Airport.

Bon Festival (Delray Beach; ☎ 561-495-0233) This Japanese cultural celebration is at the excellent Morikami Gardens in mid-August, with folk music, food and dancing.

Festival Miami (☎ 305-284-3941) This annual concert series, at the Gusman Concert Hall at the University of Miami campus in Coral Gables, runs from mid-September to mid-October.

October & November

Fantasy Fest (Key West; ☎ 305-296-1817) One of many Florida Halloween celebrations, this is perhaps the most outrageous, with drag queens and other wacky entrants.

Biketoberfest (Daytona Beach; ☎ 800-854-1234) October offers another week of motorcycle celebration.

Fifth Avenue Oktoberfest (Naples; ☎ 941-435-3742) This German-themed beer festival in Naples is held erroneously in October (in Germany it's held in September).

Miami Book Fair (☎ 305-237-3258) Held in the second week of November, this international book fair is among the most important and well attended in the USA, with scores of nationally known writers joining hundreds of publishers and hundreds of thousands of visitors. The last three days of the eight-day fair is a street fair. If you're in town, you must check it out.

Lincolnville Festival (St Augustine; ☎ 904-829-8379) This festival features ethnic foods, live entertainment and arts & crafts shows during the first weekend in November.

December

Winterfest Boat Parade (Fort Lauderdale; ☎ 954-767-0686) This parade features almost a hundred decorated boats cruising up the Intracoastal Waterway in the beginning of December.

Grand Illuminations (St Augustine; ☎ 904-824-9550) The entire historic district is lit with tens of thousands of little lights from December until the first week in January – you'll feel as if you're in a fairy tale. There are also reenactments plus other shows and events.

Orange Bowl Parade (Miami; ☎ 305-371-4600) The annual New Year's Eve blowout is the enormous Orange Bowl Parade: floats, clowns (professional and unintentional), a folkloric dance competition, a queen and a whole lot of other stuff. It would seem that all of Miami turns out for the parade, which starts at Biscayne Boulevard and SE 2nd St and ends at Bayfront Park with a fireworks salute.

WORK

Foreigners are not allowed to work legally in the USA without the appropriate working visa, and recent legislative changes are specifically targeting illegal immigrants, which is what you will be if you try to work while on a tourist visa.

Miami and much of southeast Florida have been ground zero for large numbers of refugees from the Caribbean area, notably Haiti and Cuba, so INS checks are frequent. Local businesses are probably more concerned here than anywhere outside Southern California and Texas when it comes to verifying your legal status. See Visa Extensions in the Visas & Documents section for information about longer stays.

ACCOMMODATIONS
Reservations

The cheapest bottom-end motels may not accept reservations, but at least you can call and see if they have a room – even if they don't take reservations, they'll often hold a room for an hour or two.

Chain hotels will take reservations days or months ahead. Normally, you have to give a credit card number to hold the room. If you don't show and don't call to cancel, you will be charged the first night's rental. Cancellation policies vary. Some places let you cancel at no charge 24 hours or 72 hours in advance; others are less forgiving. Find out about cancellation penalties when you book.

Also make sure to let the hotel know if you plan on a late arrival – many places will rent your room if you haven't arrived or called by 6 pm. Chains often have a toll-free number (see Hotels below), but their central reservation system might not know about any local discounts.

Some places, especially B&Bs, won't accept credit cards and require a check as a deposit before they reserve a room for you.

Camping

While less convenient than in Europe, camping opportunities abound in Florida. There are three types of campsites available in the state: undeveloped, public and privately owned. Both privately owned and public campgrounds – usually located within or close to state parks – are clean and, generally speaking, very safe. Both usually have hot showers and sewage hookups for recreational vehicles (RVs). Your fellow campers will be an interesting mix of foreigners and rural Americans – American city dwellers tend to camp less than rural dwellers.

Undeveloped Campgrounds Undeveloped campgrounds are what they are anywhere in the world: backwoods areas in which camping is permitted, including riverbanks and fields within state or national parks or forests. Undeveloped campsites obviously have no running water, toilets or any other facilities, and generally accommodate only tent camping, not RVs or vans.

Camping in an undeveloped area, such as along the Florida National Scenic Trail, in the Everglades, Big Cypress National Preserve, Ocala National Forest or along rivers like the Blackwater River, whether from your car, canoe or just backpacking, entails basic responsibility. See the Outdoor Activities chapter for proper outdoor etiquette.

Public Campgrounds Although public campgrounds are more Spartan than their private counterparts (there are usually no swimming pools, laundry facilities or other niceties), they can nevertheless be the most fun. Not only are public campgrounds an inexpensive place to crash, but park rangers usually operate some sort of entertainment or educational programs at least once a week, such as campfire talks or organized nature walks. We give samples of ranger-led programs in the text, where available. Public campgrounds usually accommodate tents, RVs and vans.

These campgrounds usually have toilets, drinking water, fire pits (or charcoal grills) and picnic benches. Some don't have drinking water (it's always a good idea to have a few gallons of water with you out in the boonies). These basic campgrounds usually cost between $7 and $20 a night. More developed areas may have showers or RV hookups, costing several dollars more.

Costs given in the text for public campgrounds are per site. A site is normally for two people and one vehicle. If there are more of you, you'll need to pay more, and if there are more than six of you, you'll need two sites. Public campgrounds often have seven- or 14-night limits; the Everglades and Dry Tortugas have a 14-night-per-stay limit, up to 30 days per calendar year per person.

Private Campgrounds Privately owned campgrounds are the most expensive option and are usually located several miles from town. Most are designed with RVs in mind, but there is almost always a small section reserved for tenters. Fees are several dollars higher than in public campgrounds. The advantage to privately owned campgrounds are their amenities: usually a swimming pool, laundry, shuffleboard, restaurant, convenience store and bar, and in better ones, a lake with boating and fishing.

Kampgrounds of America (KOA) is a national network of private campgrounds, setting the standard for privately owned campgrounds in quality and price, with sites in or near most Florida cities. All KOA sites have a pool, laundry, restaurant, bar, games area (shuffleboard, volleyball and the like) as well as tent, RV/van sites and Kamping Kabins – small log cabins with air conditioning and sometimes full kitchens. Kamping Kabins come in one- and two-bedroom flavors and average about $30 a night throughout the state. Sites in KOA campgrounds average $17 to $22, with electricity, cable TV and sewage hookups costing several dollars more for RVs. The cost is higher in places like Miami and the Keys.

You can get a directory of KOA sites by calling or writing KOA (☎ 406-248-7444, www.koa.com), PO Box 30558, Billings, MT 59114-0558. Most KOA campsites have toll-free 800 numbers, and all accept reservations. We list other privately owned campsites in the text. Magazines and coupon books from welcome centers and tourist information booths will give listings as well.

Crew Houses

These are private guesthouses designed for those who work aboard ships and are waiting for the next gig. Crew houses are found mainly in Fort Lauderdale, the yachting capital of the East Coast, and generally charge around $100 per week. They're generally clean and comfortable, and are a great source of information and networking for crew. See the Getting There & Away chapter for more information.

Hostels

Hostels are not just for youth; rather, they're places where travelers of all ages can get a cheap bed and exchange travel tales and information on where to do what.

There are hostels in Key West, Florida City, Miami Beach, Clearwater, St Petersburg, Fort Lauderdale (though we don't recommend its HI offering; see that chapter for information), Orlando, Kissimmee, Indialantic (near the Kennedy Space Center), Daytona Beach (not under any circumstances recommended) and St Augustine. There's also a new hostel in the city of Ponce de León, north of Panama City Beach on the Panhandle.

About half of Florida's hostels are affiliated with Hostelling International/American Youth Hostels (HI/AYH). Affiliated hostels offer discounts to HI/AYH members and usually allow nonmembers to stay for a few dollars more.

It's important to note that while HI/AYH hostels all maintain that organization's standards, some private hostels meet or

---

Top Five Hostels

We strongly recommend the following hostels:

Floyd's Hostel & Crew House
Fort Lauderdale; non-HI. We like this one for safety, cleanliness and attitude almost as much as for value, which is phenomenal.

Clay Hotel & International Hostel
Miami Beach; HI member. The location is only surpassed by the setting: a Spanish Mediterranean villa once occupied by both Desi Arnaz and Al Capone. Great traveler information and atmosphere.

St Augustine Hostel
Non-HI. It has a perfect location and friendly and helpful staff, but it's under new ownership and may close.

Clearwater Beach International Hostel
The newest HI member. You'll find fantastic perks like canoes and bicycles, great staff, a good beach and a pool.

HI Orlando Resort
HI member. It's 4 miles from Disney World and has a pool, spotless rooms and very friendly staff. The downside is that you'll need a car.

---

exceed them. Don't pass on a place just because it is or is not an HI hostel: check out the rooms, and speak to travelers staying there before paying.

HI/AYH hostels expect you to rent or carry a sheet or sleeping bag to keep the beds clean. In all hostels, there are information and advertising boards, TV rooms and lounge areas. Most hostels have a common kitchen, available to everyone staying there. There's a common room where travelers can get together and hang out, and often there are coin-operated laundry facilities (about 50¢ for the dryer and $1 for the washing machine). Books and games are also often available.

Independent hostels may offer a discount to HI/AYH members. They often have a few private single/double rooms available, although bathroom facilities are still usually shared.

Dormitory beds cost about $11 to $15 a night. Private rooms – also available – are in the upper $20s for one or two people, sometimes more. Dorms generally have between four and eight single beds, mostly bunk beds, and are often segregated by sex (some have mixed rooms). You'll usually have to share a bathroom. Alcohol may be banned in some hostels.

Reservations are accepted and advised during the high season – there may be a limit of a three-night stay then. Get further information from HI/AYH (☎ 202-783-6161, fax 202-783-6171, hiayhserve@hiayh.org, www.hiayh.org), 733 15th St NW, Suite 840, Washington, DC 20005, or use its code-based reservation service at ☎ 800-909-4776. (You need the access code for the hostels to use this service, available from any HI/AYH office or listed in its handbook.)

B&Bs

Bed & breakfast inns in Florida really try hard, usually successfully, to provide personal attention, excellent rooms, great service and local advice, and on many occasions, the owners are absolutely lovely people. The B&B concept – spending a night or so in someone's house as opposed to a hotel – is a very nice one, and the several we stayed in were definitely worth the price. But defining B&Bs is tricky business, so we've resorted to this catchall, which we're sure you'll find accurate as you travel the state:

This charming (Victorian house/Key West mansion/Art Deco delight/Spanish Colonial villa/renovated turn-of-the-century hunting lodge) is run by a lovely (American/English/German/Uruguayan) (husband-and-wife team/gay couple) who make certain all the rooms, which feature (four-poster beds/sleek modern beds), coffeemakers, (TV and telephone/no TV or telephone) and (fireplaces/wood-burning stoves), are in shipshape.

The four (dogs/cats) that live here are named (Harris, Tudor, Rex and Fluffy/Calvin, Siamesey, Pirate and Tom), and breakfast is a (full, hot affair with pancakes, waffles, omelets and bacon/continental affair with freshly made muffins, breads and cakes, fruit) and coffee and tea. In the afternoon, there's (a free cocktail hour/free wine and beer). Out (front/back) there's a lovely (veranda/screened-in porch/sundeck), and there's (not) a pool and Jacuzzi. Room rates range from $69 to $179 a night.

Motels

Motels, a creation of the 1950s, are relatively inexpensive hotels designed for short stays by motorists (the name is a contraction of 'motor hotel') and travelers, and for trysts (usually by television evangelists).

A typical mid-range Florida motel is a one- or two-story building with a large parking lot often located just off a highway exit, near airports or along major roads. The entryway will smell like old coffee and have discount coupon and pamphlet racks against a wall.

Motels are usually about 10 years old, and some rooms show their age more than others. The more rundown ones might have old cigarette burns in the sink or a scruffy carpet, but they're usually clean enough. The better – not necessarily the more expensive – ones can be spotless.

Rooms have private bathrooms; towels, washcloths and soap are provided. There are either one or two double or queen-size beds, and there is almost always color cable TV. Some offer pay-per-view movies ($5.95 to $8.95 per movie), and many have free HBO or Showtime (see Television earlier in this chapter). All rooms have air conditioning.

Breakfast is rarely included – though many motels offer free coffee and donuts in the morning – and there are almost always soda and snack vending machines and free ice (wash that ice bucket before you fill it up).

Daily maid service is standard, and you should leave a tip if the service is good (see Tipping earlier in this chapter).

Budget These rooms, advertised as '$19.99,' are the cheesiest offering, and only to be explored by budget travelers. Mattresses are saggy, decor is preposterous, and the cleanliness is absolutely minimum – that means clean sheets and towels.

The cheapest national chain, and a noticeable step up in quality, is Motel 6 (☎ 800-466-8356). Rooms are small and very bland, but the beds are usually OK. Every room has a TV and phone (local calls are free), and most properties have a swimming pool. Rooms start in the $20s for a single in smaller towns, in the $30s in larger towns. They usually charge a flat $6 for each extra person.

Mid-Range Rooms from $29.95 to about $50 are actually perfectly pleasant: furniture and televisions are newer; there may be a clock radio, a fridge and a microwave; the decor is better (though where they bought that painting is beyond us); and carpets are newer. Several motel chains compete with one another at this price level. The main difference between these and Motel 6 rooms is the size – more space to spread out. Beds are always reliably firm, a 24-hour desk is often available and little extras like free coffee, a table, cable or rental movies, or a bathtub with your shower may be offered. If these sorts of things are worth an extra $10 or $15 a night, you'll be happy with the Super 8 Motel (☎ 800-800-8000), Days Inn (☎ 800-329-7466) or Econo Lodge (☎ 800-553-2666). Not all of these have pools, however – Super 8 Motels, especially, have many properties lacking a pool. Best Westerns (☎ 800-528-1234) in Florida vary greatly in quality.

Top End The larger and more expensive chains, charging in the $45 to $80 range, make a motel almost as nice as a hotel. There are clean and fresh rooms and lots of amenities, like better soap, shampoo, conditioner, in-room safes, more towels and more space. Usually a buffet continental breakfast is included, and cafes, restaurants or bars may be on the premises or adjacent to them. The swimming pool is often indoor, with a spa or exercise room also available. Very good are the Quality Suites (☎ 800-228-5151), Comfort Inns (☎ 800-228-5150) and Sleep Inns (☎ 800-627-5337). Rodeway Inns (☎ 800-228-2000) fall at the lower end of this category.

Hotels

As motels struggle to capture more of the business-travel market, the differences between motels and hotels is blurring, but hotels are still a different breed. Hotels are traditionally located within cities and try to offer better service than motels. This means there will be doormen, valet parking, room service, a copy of *USA Today* in the

Rack Rates

The 'rack rate' a hotel offers is the standard, person-walks-in-off-the-street price. It is not necessarily the final price, as all prices are negotiable in American hotels.

This is especially true in the larger, more expensive places. Sometimes a simple 'Do you have anything cheaper?' will result in an immediate price reduction. Sometimes, in chain hotels, it may help to walk to the telephone booth in the lobby and call that chain's toll-free reservation number and ask for specials. At other times, the toll-free line may quote you a price much higher than that particular hotel offers.

Always try both tactics whenever possible. For example, a room at a Marriott Residence Inn was listed with a rack rate of $129 a night on the toll-free number, but when we showed up at the desk and questioned the price, we were quoted $79 for the *same* room.

It's never bad form to negotiate in an American hotel, and the savings can be substantial if you do.

morning, laundry and dry cleaning, a pool and perhaps a health club, a business center and other niceties. The perks come at a price, to be sure: want a shirt washed? It's six bucks.

The basic hotel room differs little from the basic motel room except it's reasonable to expect newer, cleaner stuff in hotels. The surprising thing is that rooms at the really expensive hotels – the Hyatts and Sheratons of the state – are usually not any nicer than a high-quality motel room, and usually cost more than twice as much.

The exceptions are privately owned, smaller hotels in out-of-the-way places or unique settings, and larger hotels in larger cities, which have reduced their prices and increased their services to compete with better motels and resorts. And specialty hotels – like the Marlin, Casa Grande and La Voile Rouge in Miami Beach, the Breakers in Palm Beach and the Ritz-Carltons anywhere – offer decadence and a hotel experience that's worth it if you can afford it.

Chain-owned hotels in Florida include the following:

Hilton	☎ 800-445-8667
Holiday Inn	☎ 800-465-4329
Marriott	☎ 800-228-9280
Radisson	☎ 800-333-3333
Ritz-Carlton	☎ 800-241-3333
Sheraton	☎ 800-325-3535

There are, of course, nonchain establishments in all price ranges. Some of them are quirky historical hotels, full of turn-of-the-19th-century furniture. Others are privately run establishments that just don't want to be part of a chain. In smaller towns, complexes of cabins are available – these often come complete with a fireplace, kitchen and an outdoor area with trees and maybe a stream a few steps away.

Budget & Mid-Range The bottom end for hotels is about $70 a night throughout the state, usually at Holiday Inns and Marriotts. These offer basic amenities, room service, restaurants and nightclubs.

Top End Full-service hotels, with bellhops and doormen, restaurants and bars, exercise rooms and saunas, room service and concierges, are found in the main cities. Aimed at those with expense accounts, prices range from about $90 to $150 per room per night.

Resorts

Resorts in Florida are everything you want if you're looking for a place in which to spend your entire holiday without leaving the grounds. They offer good service and add-ons like golf, tennis, water sports, health clubs, several pools, game rooms, activities for kids and adults, restaurants, cafés, and sometimes even convenience stores and Pizza Huts. Resort prices are higher than hotel prices – count on at least $100 and usually about $200 a night for these places – and all the activities except those for kids usually cost extra.

FOOD

Florida's smorgasbord of multicultural cuisine can leave some visitors scratching their heads. The first thing that at least Europeans will find surprising is the unbelievable quantity of food you get at American restaurants. A plate of food in the states, especially in Florida, groans under its own weight. Two light eaters may do perfectly well to share one entrée – though some restaurants charge a 'sharing fee,' usually about $1 to $2.

Most important, you'll see dolphin on the menu in many restaurants throughout the state. This is dolphin *fish* – not the friendly and protected sea mammal. The other name for dolphin fish is mahi mahi.

Alligator tail is served in some restaurants; it's not from protected alligators but from those raised on federally licensed alligator farms. It's served mainly in boring deep-fried nuggets, which may as well be Chicken McNuggets, but it's also served marinated and grilled, which is gorgeous.

Florida cuisine is a mixture of American Southern, Cuban, Spanish, Caribbean, African and European foods, not to mention the bounteous gifts of the sea. There are also strong representations of French, Mexican and even English cuisine, along with Asian foods. Chinese food in Florida is generally poor, but Thai and Japanese are usually very good, sometimes excellent. Korean, Malaysian, Indonesian and Indian restaurants are very rare, and when you do find them they are very expensive. The most common foreign cuisine is Italian, which has been considerably Americanized to include dishes that never even existed in Italy (like veal parmigiani: breaded fried veal covered with melted mozzarella cheese and tomato sauce).

Highlights are the Jamaican jerk dishes – heavily spiced, marinated and grilled dishes usually of chicken but also beef and fish. Creole dishes, usually shrimp but also chicen, have a tomato-based sauce with peppers, garlic, onions and celery served on rice (shrimp in a sauce – you'll like it). Jambalaya is a tomatoey rice dish usually featuring ham or sausage, onions, garlic and peppers.

Gumbo is derived from the Bantu word for okra. Its only consistent property is that it's a stewlike substance served over rice. The stew is thickened first with browned flour and then with either okra (a slimy vegetable) or filé powder, made from sassafras leaves. You will find lots of variations on gumbo: the most popular is shrimp and crab, but look out for more exotic varieties like squirrel and oyster (!), duck and sausage, and z'herbes, a vegetarian version.

Note that Haitian and Cuban dishes sometimes use goat, which can be stringy.

Main Meals

See Fast Food below for chain restaurants serving breakfast, lunch and dinner throughout Florida.

Breakfast This meal in America is heavier than in many other countries, though Brits and the Irish will feel right at home tucking into eggs, toast, bacon, ham or sausage and fried potatoes. (Home fries are fried chunks of potato with onions and sometimes bell peppers; hash browns are shredded potatoes fried with any combination of stuff.) Europeans looking for their traditional breakfasts (cheeses, ham, salami and assorted breads) will have no luck here outside Orlando and Miami. We saw a traveler ask for a turkey sandwich in a deli at breakfast time, and when he inquired 15 minutes later why it was taking so long, he was told he'd have to wait because he 'ordered an unorthodox breakfast.'

'Continental breakfast' is a euphemism for anything from a donut and a cup of coffee (we can see the legions of French eating *that* on the Continent) to a European-like spread of cheese, bread, muffins and croissants, but usually no meats.

Many of the more upscale fast-food places, and some steak houses in Orlando, have all-you-can-eat breakfast buffets for around $9.95. Be suspicious of these, and calculate how much the same thing would cost at a Waffle House or a diner, where your meal would be made to order, would probably be cheaper, and your scrambled eggs wouldn't sit in a huge vat to be picked (and breathed) over by dozens of tourists before you get to them.

Lunch Traditionally, lunch is the least important meal in the USA. Many office workers have lunch at their desks, and most people simply grab something on the run – which is precisely why America has the best sandwiches in the world: we know how to eat on the go.

Sandwiches here are usually packed with stuff, including fresh vegetables, meats (like roast beef, ham and turkey), cheeses and condiments, and except for cheese, everything on top is free. Subway and Larry's Subs routinely offer sandwiches with any of the following at no extra charge: lettuce, tomato, onion, peppers, hot peppers, oil, vinegar, salt, pepper, mayonnaise, ketchup and mustard.

Many fine restaurants (and some not-so-fine ones) offer drastically reduced prices at lunchtime. You can get a meal at lunchtime for $5 that would cost $15 or more at dinner. Also in this category are early-bird dinners, offered from around 4 to 6 pm, which try to lure customers in for early trade by offering similar discounts.

Dinner The main, largest and most social meal of the day in the USA is dinner. Americans tend to eat at about 7 or 8 pm. It's the time when restaurants are the most expensive and the most crowded.

Fast Food
Burger places like McDonald's, Burger King, Wendy's and Checker's sell medium-size hamburgers, and toppings are usually free (at Wendy's you put them on yourself at a salad bar). Ketchup packets and other condiments are free.

In big cities, check prices. Sometimes fast food is more expensive than cheap local restaurants; this is especially true in Miami. But generally speaking, big fast-food places – primarily McDonald's, Burger King and Denny's (see below) – have the cheapest breakfasts by far.

Other fast-food chains in Florida include Taco Bell, with excellent and very cheap Mexican-style food, Subway (good, huge sandwiches), Larry's Sub Shops (even better sandwiches, though harder to find), KFC (Kentucky Fried Chicken) and more up-scale entries like Denny's (open 24 hours), Shoney's, Bennigans and Cracker Barrel for bland American food. Chilis has Southwestern-ish fare; Red Lobster has seafood; Pollo Tropical serves chicken with a Cuban twist; Boston Market and Kenny Rogers serve roasted chicken; and Waffle House has excellent breakfasts 24 hours a day.

Look in discount coupon booklets for coupons to fast-food places – usually two-for-one deals or reduced-price combination meals. Note that all fast-food places honor their competitor's coupons: a coupon for two Burger King Whoppers for the price of one will be happily accepted by McDonald's, which will give you two Big Macs. And this deal even extends to other kinds of fast-food places like KFC, where if you walk in with a coupon for a Whopper, fries and a drink, you can turn it into a three-piece chicken meal with fries and a drink. Poof!

Vegetarian
Vegetarianism is catching on in a big way in the USA, and non-meat-eaters will have an

Bagels

A bagel is a disk-shaped bread product made from heavy dough that has been boiled and then baked. The result is a substantial and chewy roll with a uniquely textured coating – the closest comparison would be a real Bavarian Brez'n, but that's not really it. Just eat one. Originally ethnic Jewish, the bagel has insinuated itself into the American menu and can now be bought in most big cities from coast to coast. They are usually offered in plain, sesame, poppy, onion, garlic, combinations of the previous and, more rarely, salt. They're available in any diner and in most restaurants that serve breakfast, but several bagel specialists have opened in the state.

easy time in the cities. In rural areas, though, it can be more difficult, with meat playing a key role in most Southern cooking. You may need to ask twice whether something contains meat – some crackers don't consider things like sausage seasoning, bacon bits or chicken to be meat! Salad bars are a good way to stave off hunger, and many restaurants serve large salads as main courses.

American
'Standard' American food is so influenced by the cuisines of other countries around the world that it's difficult to nail down other than the obvious: hamburgers. But modern American cooking can be summed up as combining American portions and home-grown foods with foreign sensibilities and techniques; there are many styles of American cooking that borrow heavily from French, Italian (which is probably the most popular foreign food in the USA), Asian and, to a lesser extent, Turkish and Greek cuisines.

Cuban
Cuban food is common in the southern section of the state but available throughout Florida. The most common Cuban foods

The Best of Florida Food

Last edition we got letters from people taking us to task for some of our opinions. So this time we decided instead of merely peppering the book with them, we'd go all out and state exactly what we think are the best of the best in Florida. Gotta problem with that? The addresses of our offices are listed on the last page of the book.

All-around dining value: Florida House Inn, Fernandina Island
Top-end restaurant value: Brass Pelican and Lafite, at the Registry Resort in Naples
Cinnamon bun: Theo's Restaurant, St Augustine
New England clam chowder: Marina Restaurant, Fernandina Island
Burrito: Burrito Brothers Taco Co, Gainesville (runner up: San Loco, Miami Beach)
Sushi: New Sushi Hana, Miami Beach
Barbecue sauce & chicken: Moses White & Sons Bar B Que, Ybor City (Tampa)
Turkey drumstick: Magic Kingdom, Walt Disney World
Steak: Joe Allen, Miami Beach
Milkshake: Beach Diner, Clearwater Beach
Martini: Raleigh Bar & Restaurant, Miami Beach

are pork, beef, rice, beans, eggs, tomatoes and lettuce, and rice, lemon and orange. *Yucca* (manioc or cassava) is a starchy root vegetable that can be boiled or baked. Garlic and onion, rather than spices and chile peppers, are used for seasoning. Another common seasoning in Floridian Cuban food is *mojo*, a garlic citrus sauce. Common accompaniments are rice *(arroz)*, black or red beans *(frijoles negro o rojo)*, yucca and, especially, *plantains* – a larger cousin to the banana, served fried. When done right, fried plantains are crispy outside and sweet and starchy inside. The darker the plantain, the sweeter the fruit.

Cuban Specialties The most common dish offered at Cuban restaurants is *carne asada* (roasted meat), usually *puerco asado* (roast pork) or *carne de cerdo* (pork). Other dishes include *bistec* (steak), *arroz con pollo* (chicken and rice), *ropa vieja* (literally 'old clothes' but actually shredded skirt steak stew served with rice and plantains) and *filete de pescado* (fish fillet).

Other seafood includes *calamar* (squid), *camarones* (shrimp), *jaiba* (small crab), *lan-gosta* (lobster), *mariscos* (shellfish) and *ostiones* (oysters).

Meat and poultry include *bistec* or *bistec de res* (beefsteak), *cabra* (goat), *cabrito* (kid, or small goat), *chorizo* (spicy pork sausage), *cordero* (lamb) and *jamón* (ham).

Sandwiches Cuban sandwiches available at *loncherias* (snack bars) are made by slicing Cuban bread loaves lengthwise, filling them with ingredients and toasting (and mushing) them in a *plancha*, a heated press. The biggies are the *Cubano* (pork or ham and cheese, sometimes with mustard and pickles, depending on how much you look like a *gringo*), *pan con lechón* (extra crispy-crunchy pork and *mojo*), *palomilla* (steak sandwich with fried onions) and *media noche* or 'midnight' (ham, cheese and roast pork on a roll).

Desserts Most desserts *(postres)* are small afterthoughts to a meal; they include *arroz con leche* (rice pudding), *crepa* (crêpe, a thin pancake), *flan* (custard, or crème caramel), *galletas* (cookies/biscuits), *gelatina* (jello), *helado* (ice cream) and *pastel* (pastry or cake). Watch out for that *tres leches* (which is literally 'three-milk' cake, actually a glucose-tolerance test disguised as a pudding).

Tea & Coffee The big players are *café con leche* (coffee with hot steamed milk or half-and-half), *café con crema* (coffee with cream, served separately), espresso served in thimble-size shots (also called 'zoom juice'), *té de manzanilla* (chamomile tea) and *té negro* (black tea).

Fruit & Vegetable Drinks Pure fresh juices *(jugos)* are popular all over Miami and are readily available: the fruit is often squeezed before your eyes. Every fruit and a few of the squeezable vegetables are used – ever tried pure beetroot juice?

Licuados are blends of fruit or juice with water and sugar. *Licuados con leche* use milk instead of water. Possible additions include raw egg, ice and flavorings such as vanilla or nutmeg.

Aguas frescas or *aguas de fruta* are made by mixing fruit juice or a syrup made from mashed grains or seeds with sugar and water. They are served chilled and are very refreshing.

Southern

Southern cuisine is heavy on fat and meats; typical specialties include biscuits – similar to scones – and mashed potatoes, collard greens (served with hot-pepper-infused vinegar) and black-eyed peas, all of which are prepared with chunks of pork or ham. Main courses include fried chicken, roasted ham, pork in any variety of ways (including that favorite light snack, pickled pigs' feet) and gravies with cornbread (a dry cakelike bread made from yellow cornmeal). If you're here on New Year's Day, have a plate of black-eyed peas for good luck in the coming year (every restaurant will be serving them); it's a Southern tradition.

Perhaps the biggest shock comes in the form of grits, a corn-derived white glop that's peculiar to the South. (Waitress to Corinna: 'Y'all ain't never trahd no *grits* before? Y'all ain't *got* no grits in Jermunee? Well, whadda y'all *eat* in Jermunee?') Treat grits as a hot cereal and add cream and sugar, or treat them as a side dish and add salt and pepper. Grits are served in lieu of potatoes at breakfast, and they're best when totally smooth and very hot.

Barbecue Barbecuing is a Southern tradition that has been entirely deconstructed in the hands of Australians, who can't even get the fire going and who depend on the women to cook while the men drink beer and give (faulty) instructions. Barbecue (purists say the proper pronunciation is 'bubbuh-kyu') consists mainly of seasoned pork, chicken and baby-back ribs cooked over an open flame – brutal, but, we have to admit, delicious. Barbecue is served with sweet-and-tangy sauce that has smoky overtones. The idea is that the meat is cooked and smoked simultaneously, so by the time it's done, the meat falls off the joints and bones. Whatever.

There are many places in Florida to experiment with this cuisine, and the best of them are in small towns with cheesy signs. One sure-fire way to tell if a restaurant is good is the number of police cars, fire trucks, ambulances and vehicles parked in front – if it's packed, it's good.

The best chain place we found in Florida – at least for ribs – is Sonny's, with branches all over northern Florida. Even if you don't partake, buy a bottle of Sonny's Sweet BBQ sauce to take with you, and put it on everything – we even use it on toast.

Seafood

Florida has more than 8000 miles of coastline, so it's no surprise seafood is on many menus. Most common are grouper, dolphin fish (mahi mahi), tuna, salmon and swordfish, all served grilled, deep fried or blackened – thrown into a white-hot frying pan filled with black pepper so the outside is burned to a crisp while the inside is cooked to medium. Incidentally, one sure-fire indicator of a town's sophistication is the availability of non-deep-fried foods – in some towns, everything, up to and perhaps including the check, is fried.

Stone crab

Another Florida favorite is stone crab, indigenous to South Florida and available in the winter only. Florida lobster doesn't hold a candle to Maine lobster, so if you like the latter, avoid the former. Many towns along the southwest and the Panhandle, especially the Apalachicola area, have 'raw bars,' where raw clams and oysters are served on the half shell. Be careful and make certain everything's fresh before digging in. (It is usually *very* fresh, but food poisoning isn't any fun, so look before you gulp.)

Supermarkets

To the first-time visitor, an American supermarket is as daunting and over-the-top as a visit to the set of *American Gladiators* would be to Mahatma Gandhi. Large enough to house a regulation football field, American supermarkets are one-stop shopping extravaganzas that stock everything you'd ever need in every room of the house plus the garage, the garden and in many cases the office. They sell everything from auto parts to garbage cans, electronics to pharmaceuticals, school supplies to contraceptives, and fresh produce, seafood, meats, wine and beer.

Most supermarkets have bakeries, but you can also choose from a hundred types of packaged breads. Some supermarkets also have full-service delicatessen counters, and fewer have full-service cafés or restaurants.

The biggest supermarket chains in the state are, in approximate order of size, Publix, Winn-Dixie and Hyde Park. There is free coffee at all Publix supermarkets, in the big stainless steel percolator near the entrance. Also note that machines selling cans of soda are almost always cheaper at supermarkets and outside K-Marts, where cans of cold soda sell for about 35¢.

DRINKS
Nonalcoholic Drinks

The soft drinks available in Florida are about the same as everywhere in the world. Smoothies are drinks made from yogurt and fresh fruits blended into a type of shake. A shake, or milkshake, is fast-blended ice cream, milk and flavoring, usually chocolate, vanilla or strawberry. The biggest surprise for many non-Latino foreign visitors is *guarapo*, or sugarcane juice. Cappuccino and European espresso are available in more upscale restaurants, but note that Starbuck's hasn't made any real inroads in Florida yet.

Alcoholic Drinks

The strictly enforced minimum drinking age in Florida is 21. Carry a driver's license or passport as proof of age to enter a bar, buy alcohol or order alcohol at a restaurant. Servers have the right to ask to see your ID and may refuse service without it – they're instructed to proof anyone who appears to be under 30. Minors are not allowed in bars and pubs, even to order nonalcoholic beverages. Unfortunately, this means most dance clubs are also off-limits to minors, although a few clubs have solved the under-age problem with a segregated drinking area. Minors are, however, welcome in the dining areas of restaurants where alcohol is served.

Beer and wine are sold in supermarkets in Florida, while harder stuff is sold in liquor stores. One shocking sight in Florida is the drive-through liquor stand, where customers pull through, order a bottle and zip away. There are several chain liquor stores in Florida, among them Walgreens (a pharmacy/liquor store) and regional chains like ABC.

Beer Commercially available American 'beer,' for lack of a better term, is weaker and sweeter than its equivalent around the world, perhaps to encourage drinking more of it. Indeed, the marketing of 'light' beer – with fewer calories than regular beer – stalled until marketers were able to convince the public that 'less filling' meant one could suck down many more beers on the same stomach.

Beer in the USA comes in cans and bottles. Bottles range from ponies (8oz) to standard 12oz, to long-neck (12oz as well, but the bottle neck is longer), to 32oz (1 quart) bottles. American beer also comes in 12oz and 16oz (1 pint) cans. Bottles and cans are generally sold in bundles of six (six-packs) or 12, or in 'cases' of 24.

The major brands are manufactured by Anheuser-Busch – Budweiser and Michelob – followed by Miller and its products, including Miller Genuine Draft and Lite. A six-pack of standard American beer sells for between $3 and $5 in supermarkets. You can visit the Anheuser-Busch Brewery in Jacksonville (see the Northeast Florida chapter) or sample the wares at the Anheuser-Busch Hospitality Center at SeaWorld in Orlando (see the Central Florida chapter).

Ice brew implies a 'cold filtration process,' but it adds up to beer with about 5.5% alcohol. Microbrewed beers are made by smaller companies with limited production. They can be excellent and taste much like their European counterparts. The biggest microbrews are Samuel Adams (Boston) and Anchor Steam (San Francisco). Both are gaining popularity so quickly that their 'micro' status will probably come under challenge. There are about a dozen microbrewers in Florida, and we try to mention them in the text where possible. Microbrews and ice brews cost between $5 and $8 a six-pack.

Wine Wine is also available in supermarkets, and foreign visitors will often find that wine from their home country is cheaper here – many Australian wines are about 20% less in Florida than at home. But while perfectly drinkable wine is available in supermarkets, connoisseurs will do far better in proper liquor stores, which sell a better range of higher-end wines from the USA and around the world.

ENTERTAINMENT
Clubs
Nightclubs in Florida are located in all larger cities. In almost all, you'll have to dress for the occasion – especially in Miami, where you'd better look as if you own the place or forget even getting in. In Miami Beach, competition is so fierce that nightclubs open and go out of business constantly.

In larger clubs, entry fees are between $10 and $12; in Orlando, admission to hootcha-terias (with loud music and cheap alcohol) like Church St Station and Pleasure Island is about $15 to $20, while local clubs charge less than average to try and draw people away from their huge competitors.

In most cities, bars turn into nightclub-ish places in the evenings, with live music of some sort, or contests.

Gay and lesbian nightclubs generally have live performances that range from drag shows, dating games and amateur nights to strippers.

Bars
Bars in Florida range from down-and-dirty to as chic as one could expect. The prices range accordingly.

Most American bartenders (except in the tonier places that spend money on automatic pourers) free-hand pour in a manner that would make British publicans blanch. A 'shot,' ostensibly 1oz, is often larger than that. American custom says that you tip the bartender for each drink – generally $1 – and that (except in very crowded nightclubs) you place your cash on the bar and leave it there while you drink.

'Happy hours,' usually a lot longer than an hour – sometimes all day – are periods in which drink prices are reduced, sometimes substantially. Deals are usually two or even three drinks for the price of one. 'Ladies' night,' a clever ploy to lure horny, thirsty males by using women (who drink free) as bait, is usually held once a week.

Performing Arts

The biggest center for music, dance and theater is Miami, though Fort Lauderdale, Tampa, Sarasota and the Palm Beaches are also noteworthy centers for performing arts. See the individual chapter sections for information on performing arts available.

Cinemas

Americans have been known to make a movie or two, and every Florida city has at least one chain theater. American movie houses have taken the as-many-as-possible approach, and the quaint one-movie cinema is practically extinct – look for five-, six-, nine-, 11- and up to 18-plex cinemas.

The best place to look for a cinema is in the nearest shopping mall. Prices are usually very cheap – from $2.50 to $4 in the afternoon before 4 pm and between $5 and $7 in the evening. Miami has several independent film outlets offering smaller budget, foreign or cult films, but outside Miami, expect only mass-appeal Hollywood films with few exceptions.

The main cinema chains in Florida are AMC and Cobb.

SPECTATOR SPORTS

Sports in the USA developed separately from the rest of the world, and baseball (with its clone, softball), football and basketball dominate the sports scene, both for spectators and participants. Football and basketball, in particular, are huge.

In professional basketball, the excellent Orlando Magic is still by far the most popular team in the state, while the Miami Heat have been slogging along for years in the NBA, playing competent if unspectacular hoops.

Florida has three NFL football teams: the winning Miami Dolphins, the greedy Tampa Bay Buccaneers and the Jacksonville Jaguars. If you've ever wondered whether it was true that the word fan derives from 'fanatic,' attend a Florida pro football game. And if you think that's bad, wait till you see the fanaticism associated with *college* football: the state has several good college teams, chief among them the University of Miami Hurricanes and the FSU Seminoles.

Baseball is so embedded in the country's psyche that – despite baseball's complex rules, the difficulty and expense of maintaining playing fields with an irregular configuration, and labor-management problems at the highest professional levels – the sport continues to flourish. Many of the most meaningful metaphors in American English and even political discourse – such as 'getting to first base' or the debased 'three strikes and you're out' – come from baseball. Softball, which requires less space than baseball, draws more participants, both men and women, than any other organized sport in the country.

Many professional baseball teams come to the warmth of South Florida for spring training, from March to April, and minor-league teams play here throughout the baseball season, from May to October. There are major-league baseball teams in Miami (Marlins) and St Petersburg (Devil Rays).

Jai alai, a fascinating and dangerous Spanish game in which teams hurl a *pelota* – a *very* hard ball – at more than 150 mph, can be seen (and bet on) in stadiums around the southern part of Florida.

Soccer has made limited inroads, mostly among immigrants, but it has failed as a spectator sport and is likely to remain a minor diversion for at least the next few years.

SHOPPING

Other than handicrafts and art in the major cities, there really isn't a big 'Florida product.' The main thing to buy here, especially if you're coming from Europe or even Australia, is clothing and consumer goods, all of which are cheaper than at home (see the boxed text).

Tourist-crap stands abound in major cities and in gas stations along highways. The big offerings are 'funny' T-shirts, lacquered alligator heads (they're real, culled from alligator farms) and other standard schlocky tourist stuff that can be found around the world.

Large Specialty Chain Stores

There are several large specialty retailers in the state. When we're shopping for something, we usually call the big shops first, as their prices give us a good idea for price comparison with other places. Check the ads in the local newspaper for special deals and sales. Many of these stores have more than one location in any given town, so call and ask for the location nearest you. The larger clothing specialty stores are listed below under Shopping Malls.

Car Max, a division of Circuit City, is a unique used-car dealership, based on flat, non-negotiable prices on late-model used cars. If you're looking for a good (or at least expensive) used car, call its corporate offices at ☎ 804-727-0427 for a list of shops around the country.

Circuit City sells a decent range of electronics, computers, appliances and other gizmotronics.

Eckerd is a chain of pharmacies around the state, some open 24 hours.

Incredible Universe has taken the PT Barnum approach to selling electronics – balloons for the kids, big bright colors and a veritable three-ring circus of bleeping things.

Sports Authority sells sporting goods; golf clubs; bicycles; running, hiking, climbing equipment; and a small selection of backpacks.

Walgreens is a chain of combination pharmacy/liquor stores throughout the area, so if you should ever need a pint of whiskey *and* a bandage, stop here.

Wal-Mart, *K-Mart* and *Sears* exist to be one-stop shopping centers for just about anything you'd need, from padlocks to plates, diapers to garbage disposals (pronounced 'dispose-all' in the South) and everything in between.

Cheaper in the States

While you won't find Vegemite anywhere (Publix does, however, stock Marmite and sometimes even Bovril), the USA has the best prices in the world on a slew of items – with the possible exception of Hong Kong. You'll get great deals on the following:

Cameras – We bought a good-quality new Minolta 400 series Maxxum for just about $350, including two lenses.

Camping equipment – All equipment costs less here.

CDs and musical instruments – The average price for a new CD release is between $12 and $14; musical instruments, especially items like DATs, ADAM and digital samplers, are in the same category as computers.

Computers – Though you may get hit with an import tax when you get home, the USA is definitely a great place for computers: take the price in UK£, switch the symbol to $ and you're about right. As we went to press, a 333 MHz Pentium II desktop with monitor could be yours for about $550.

Jeans – New blue jeans in the USA (like unwashed Levi's 501s) start as low as $24.

Running shoes – You can get a good pair of name-brand running shoes starting at $40.

Sunglasses – Ray Bans can be had for as low as $40.

Zippo lighters – These babies start at about $12.

Note that if you're buying electric or electronic appliances here (coffee grinders, telephones, tape recorders, CD players, etc), you may need a step-down transformer (not an adapter) to allow the thing to work in Europe or Australia. Check the power requirements on the back – if it says 120-240V, 50-60 Hz, you're set; you'll need only an adapter to change the shape of the plug. If it says 120V only, you'll need the transformer. If you're bringing electronics back to Japan, you'll always need a step-up transformer to turn the wimpy Japanese 100V current into something useful.

Shopping Malls

Massive shopping malls have so saturated the shopping scene it's difficult to find many items without entering one. And the insidious nature of the malls and the huge shops is that lower wages lead to higher employee turnover. In Sports Authority (see above), we complained to a manager that there wasn't one person who could tell us whether they had tents with no-see-um netting. 'Well,' he told us, 'we train them as best we can for the wage we pay them.'

The major shops in malls usually sell clothing (eg Neiman-Marcus, Saks Fifth Avenue, Gap, Burdines) and general merchandise (eg Sears, K-Mart, Wal-Mart, JC Penney), while all malls will have a food court (a collection of fast-food joints), a Sunglass Hut, shoe shops, some specialty jean and women's clothing shops, and bookstores.

Factory outlet malls sell old or overstocked items that manufacturers are, for some reason, trying to unload. It could be last season's gear, ugly as sin, damaged or 'irregular.' Most of the time the prices in a true factory outlet like Sawgrass Mills or Augustine Outlet Stores can be up to 70% lower than retail. Outlet malls are usually located several miles from a major city.

Thrift Shops

Thrift and second-hand shops can be found in most Florida cities. Most are affiliated with churches or relief organizations, to which items are donated. The organizations sell the donated items – usually very inexpensively – to raise money. The items range from books (usually about 50¢ apiece) to appliances to clothing. Clothing, while used, is always clean, and some absolutely fantastic vintage stuff can be had with a little digging.

The biggest are outlets of Goodwill, the Salvation Army and St Vincent de Paul. And of course, the best selection and the biggest scores are located in the more affluent neighborhoods, where donations are made more frequently and are of far higher quality than in other places.

It's unbelievable – a friend found a pair of Pucci original pants in amazing condition for $10 in a Palm Beach thrift shop. Also on offer at these places are cameras, movie cameras, film editors, bicycles and sometimes even cars. Check in the local yellow pages under Thrift Shops for listings.

Flea Markets

True flea markets are bazaars, usually held on weekends in huge parking lots, where merchants from all over the state get together to sell stuff. Prices are negotiable, and you should always bargain. In some cities, like Kissimmee, organized flea markets occur daily during the tourist season. Prices at these are higher.

Outdoor Activities

Florida is about the outdoors – from broiling on the beach to jumping out of a plane over it. With so much water, the opportunities for swimming, snorkeling, scuba diving, canoeing and kayaking are almost unparalleled.

The road traveler in Florida is faced with some of the world's most monotonous highways: endless ribbons of shimmering, straight blacktop lined on either side with such a uniform dark-green blur that it would appear that there's absolutely nothing on either side of you until you get to the next major city. But the truth is that just off the major roads lies an astonishing array of wilderness areas, thousands of rivers and lakes, and the opportunity to view subtropical flora and fauna unseen anywhere else in the continental USA.

Even just stopping off for a day of canoeing in a state park will give you a look at Florida that most visitors miss out on.

Though each pursuit has specialized gear shops (usually the best source for local information), Lauderdale Sports in Fort Lauderdale is probably the best overall sporting superstore in the south of the state, though the more poorly equipped (and staffed) Sports Authority has more stores around the state.

HIKING

There is perhaps no better way to appreciate the beauty of Florida – its beaches, parks and scenic trails, peaceful hammocks and marshes – than on foot and on the trail. Taking a few days' (or even a few hours') break away from the highway to explore the great outdoors can refresh road-weary travelers and give them a heightened appreciation of the scenery

that goes whizzing past day after day. Some travelers will experience one good hike and decide to plan the rest of their trip around wilderness or hiking areas.

Florida National Scenic Trail (FNST)

With more than 300 open and hikeable miles of trail out of a planned 1300, the FNST is maintained by the Florida Trail Association, an all-volunteer organization that maintains this and other trails throughout the state.

But the FNST is far from completed: there are significant gaps in south-central Florida and in the western Panhandle. But, when completed, the trail will run north from within Big Cypress National Preserve at the northern end of the Everglades National Park, around Lake Okeechobee, straight up through the central part of the state and through the Ocala National Forest, and then curve west, finally winding its way to the Gulf Island National Seashore near Pensacola.

Maintenance of the trail is unpredictable. In some sections it's terrible due to flooding and mud, but in others it's great. There are organized campsites only in certain sections, and the same can be said for water. When hiking the trail, you should bring everything you'll need to be entirely self-sufficient.

For information and a trail map, call the Florida Trail Association (☎ 352-378-8823, 800-343-1882), or write to PO Box 13708, Gainesville, FL 32604-1708.

National Parks

Unless you have a few days to get into the backcountry of a national park, or are visiting during nontourist season (between Memorial Day and Labor Day), expect the parks to be crowded.

Travelers with little hiking experience will appreciate well-marked, well-maintained trails in national parks, often with toilets at either end and interpretive displays along the way. The trails give access to the parks' natural features and usually show up on National Park Service (NPS) maps as nature trails or self-guided interpretive trails. These hikes are generally no longer than 2 miles.

Most national parks require overnight hikers to carry backcountry permits, available from visitors centers or ranger stations, which must be obtained 24 hours in advance and require you to follow a specific itinerary. While this system reduces the chance of people getting lost in the backcountry and limits the number of people using one area at any given time, it may detract from the sense of space and freedom hiking can give. In backcountry areas of the Everglades and Big Cypress, you'll have to have an interview with a ranger to determine if you're an experienced wilderness explorer or a misinformed yahoo. For more information, call the NPS at ☎ 800-365-2267, or check its Website, www.nps.gov.

Treading Lightly

Backcountry areas are composed of fragile environments and cannot support an inundation of human activity, especially insensitive and careless activity. A good suggestion is to treat the backcountry like you would your own backyard – minus the barbecue pit and those kids.

A new code of backcountry ethics is evolving to deal with the growing number of people in the wilderness. Most conservation organizations and hikers' manuals have their own set of backcountry codes, all of which outline the same important principles: minimizing the impact on the land, leaving no trace and taking nothing but photographs and memories. Above all, stay on the main trail, stay on the main trail and, lastly, even if it means walking through mud, *stay on the main trail*.

Wilderness Camping Camping in undeveloped areas is rewarding for its peacefulness but presents special concerns. Take care to ensure that the area you choose can comfortably support your presence and leave the surroundings in better condition

than on arrival. The following list of guidelines should help.

- Bury human waste in cat holes dug 6 to 8 inches deep. The salt and minerals in urine attract deer; use a tent-bottle (funnel attachments are available for women) if you are prone to middle-of-the-night calls by Mother Nature. Camouflage the cat hole when finished.

- Use soaps and detergents sparingly or not at all, and never allow these things to enter streams or lakes. When washing yourself (a backcountry luxury, not a necessity), lather up (with biodegradable soap) and rinse yourself off with cans of water as far away as possible from your water source. Scatter dishwater after removing all food particles.

- We recommend that you carry a lightweight stove for cooking and use a lantern instead of a campfire.

- If a fire is allowed and appropriate, dig a hole and build a fire in it. On islands or beach areas, build fires below the high-tide line. Gather sticks no thicker than an adult's wrist from the ground. Use only dead and down wood; do not twist branches off live or dead and standing trees. Pour wastewater from meals around the perimeter of the campfire to prevent the fire from spreading, and thoroughly douse it before leaving or going to bed.

- Designate cooking clothes to leave in the food bag, away from your tent.

- Burn cans to get rid of their odor, and then remove them from the ashes and pack them out.

- Pack out what you pack in, including all trash – yours *and* others'.

Safety

The major forces to be reckoned with while hiking and camping are the weather (which is uncontrollable) and your own frame of mind. Be prepared for unpredictable weather – you may go to bed under a clear sky and wake up in the midst of a thunderstorm the likes of which you haven't seen since you watched *Moby Dick*. Afternoon thunderstorms are very common in summer. Carry a rainjacket at all times. Backpackers should have a pack-liner (heavy-duty garbage bags work well), a full set of rain gear and food that does not require cooking. A positive attitude is helpful in any situation. If a hot shower, comfortable mattress and clean clothes are essential to your well-being, don't head out into the wilderness for five days – stick to day hikes (actually, in summer, you'll just have to wait until about half-past three for the hot shower, courtesy of one of Florida's spectacular thunderstorms).

Highest safety measures suggest never hiking alone, but solo travelers should not be discouraged, especially if they value solitude. The important thing is to always let someone know where you are going and how long you plan to be gone. Use sign-in boards at trailheads or ranger stations. Travelers looking for hiking companions can inquire or post notices at ranger stations, outdoors stores, campgrounds and youth hostels.

Fording rivers and streams is another potentially dangerous but often necessary part of being on the trail. In national parks and along maintained trails in national forests, bridges usually cross large bodies of water (this is not the case in designated wilderness areas, where bridges are taboo). Upon reaching a river, unclip all of your pack straps – your pack is expendable, you are not. Avoid crossing barefoot – you don't know where that bottom's been. Bring a pair of lightweight canvas sneakers or Teva-style sandals for crossing, or you'll be stuck sloshing around in wet boots for the rest of your hike.

Using a staff for balance is helpful, but don't rely on it to support all your weight. Don't enter water higher than mid-thigh; once higher than that, your body gives the current a large mass to work against.

If you get wet, wring your clothes out immediately, wipe off all the excess water on your body and hair and put on any dry clothes you (or your partner) might have.

People with little hiking or backpacking experience should not attempt to do too much, too soon, or they might end up being nonhikers for the wrong reasons. Know your limitations, know the route you are going to take and pace yourself accordingly. Remember, there is absolutely nothing wrong with turning back or not going as far as you had originally planned.

What to Bring

Equipment The following list is meant to be a general guideline for backpackers, not an 'if-I-have-everything-here-I'll-be-fine' guarantee. Know yourself and what special things you may need on the trail; consider the area and climatic conditions in which you will be traveling.

- Boots – light to medium weight are recommended for day hikes, while sturdy boots are necessary for extended trips with a heavy pack. Most importantly, they should be well broken in and have a good heel. Waterproof boots are preferable.
- Alternative footwear – thongs or sandals or running shoes for wearing around camp and canvas sneakers for crossing streams.
- Socks – frequent changes during the day reduce the chance of blisters, but are usually impractical and inconvenient.
- Subdued colors are usually recommended, but if hiking during hunting season, blaze orange is a necessity.
- Shorts, light shirt – for everyday wear; remember heavy cotton takes a long time to dry and is very cold when wet.
- Long-sleeve shirt – light cotton, wool or polypropylene. A button-down front makes layering easy and can be left open when the weather is hot and your arms need protection from the sun.
- Long pants – heavy denim jeans take forever to dry and hey, this is the subtropics. Sturdy cotton or canvas pants are good for trekking through brush, and cotton or nylon sweats are comfortable to wear around camp.
- Rain gear – light, breathable and waterproof is the ideal combination, but it doesn't exist no matter what those catalogs say. You need plastic, not GoreTex, for the kind of rains you'll get in Florida. We use Rainbird 2000 ponchos, which fold into their front pockets and crush down to very small sacks that are good for pillows. If nothing else is available, use heavy-duty trash bags to cover you and your packs.
- Hat – a cotton hat with a brim is good for sun protection.
- Bandanna or handkerchief – good for a runny nose, dirty face, unmanageable hair, picnic lunch and flag (especially a red one).
- Small towel – one which is indestructible and will dry quickly. Check in any sporting-goods store for camping towels.

- First-aid kit – should include, at the least, self-adhesive bandages and adhesive tape, disinfectant, antibiotic salve or cream, gauze, small scissors and tweezers. An ace-type bandage couldn't hurt either.

- Knife, fork, spoon and mug – a double-layer plastic mug with a lid is best. A mug acts as eating and drinking receptacle, mixing bowl and wash basin; the plastic handle protects you from getting burned. Bring an extra cup if you like to eat and drink simultaneously.

- Pots and pans – aluminum cook sets are best, but any sturdy 1-quart pot is sufficient. True gourmands who want more than pasta, soup and freeze-dried food will need a skillet or frying pan. A metal pot scrubber is helpful for removing stubborn oatmeal, especially when using cold water and no soap.

- Stove – lightweight and easy to operate is ideal. Most outdoors stores rent propane or butane stoves; test the stove before you head out, even cook a meal on it, to familiarize yourself with any quirks it may have.

- Water purifier – optional but really nice to have; water can also be purified by boiling for at least 10 minutes.

- Matches or lighter – waterproof matches are good, and having several lighters is smart.

- Candle or lantern – candles are easy to operate but do not stay lit when they are dropped or wet and can be hazardous inside a tent. Outdoors stores rent lanterns; test the lantern before you hit the trail.

- Flashlight – each person should have their own and be sure its batteries have plenty of life left in them. We like Petzl headlamps and Mag-Lites because they're both almost indestructible and have slots for spare bulbs.

- Sleeping bag – goose-down bags are warm and lightweight but worthless if they get wet; most outdoors stores rent synthetic bags.

- Sleeping pad – this is strictly a personal preference. We rarely use them, but a friend swears by ThermaRest pads, which fill up with air when unrolled and behave like an air mattress. Use a sweater or sleeping bag sack stuffed with clothes as a pillow.

- Tent – make sure it is waterproof, or has a waterproof cover, and has no-see-um – not just mosquito – netting, and know how to put it up *before* you reach camp. Remember that your packs will be sharing the tent with you.

- Camera and binoculars – don't forget extra film and waterproof film canisters (sealable plastic bags work well).

- Compass, GPS (see Global Positioning System boxed text) and maps – each person should have their own.

- Eyeglasses – contact-lens wearers should always bring a back-up set.

- Sundries – biodegradable toilet paper, small sealable plastic bags, insect repellent, sunscreen, lip balm, unscented moisturizing cream, moleskin for foot blisters, dental floss (burnable and good when there is no water for brushing), sunglasses, deck of cards, pen or pencil and paper or notebook, books and nature guides.

Food Keeping your energy up is important, but so is keeping your pack light. Backpackers tend to eat a substantial breakfast and dinner and snack heavily in between. There is no need to be excessive. If you pack loads of food, you'll probably use it all, but if you have just enough, you will probably not miss anything.

The following are some basic staples: packaged instant oatmeal, bread (the denser the better), rice or pasta, instant soup or ramen noodles, dehydrated meat (jerky), dried fruit, energy bars, chocolate, trail mix and peanut butter and honey or jam (in plastic jars or squeeze bottles). See Sea Kayaking later in this chapter for information on freeze-dried meals. Don't forget the wet-wipes, but be sure to dispose of them properly or pack them out.

Books

There are quite a few good how-to and where-to books on the market, usually found in outdoors stores, or bookstores' Sports & Recreation or Outdoors sections. Chris Townsend's *Backpacker's Handbook* (Ragged Mountain Press/McGraw Hill, 1997) is a beefy collection of tips for the trail. *How to Shit in the Woods* (Ten Speed Press, 1994) is Kathleen Meyer's explicit, comical and useful manual on toilet training in the wilderness.

Maps

A good map is essential for any hiking trip. NPS and US Forest Service (USFS) ranger stations usually stock topographical maps that cost $2 to $6. In the absence of a ranger station, try a stationery or hardware store.

Global Positioning System (GPS)

The GPS was developed by the US military. It involves 24 satellites operating in six orbital planes at an altitude of 12,500 miles, which put out coded signals to be received by small units on earth. With the magic of computer chips that can solve the several sets of simultaneous equations the readings produce, these instruments can determine their absolute location with surprising precision. In English, this little piece of gizmotronics tells you the following:

- where you are on earth (within about 50m to 100m)
- where you've been
- where you're going (bearing, distance from any specific destination)
- how fast you're going
- when you'll get there
- what your altitude is above sea level
- and, of course, the time

If you know where you want to be, you can enter the coordinates (latitude and longitude culled from, say, a good atlas or map) and the Garmin GPS will show you an electronic 'highway' (a graphical representation of a road going off into the horizon): if the 'road' bends left, you turn left at the same angle – the idea being that as long as you keep the electronic 'road' on the screen pointing straight, you're going toward your destination. We've now used it for practice in Germany, throughout Russia and in the Everglades, where it's an invaluable piece of gear.

An annoying feature, however, is that coverage changes depending on where you are – city readings are usually not very accurate and vertical readings are fantasy: While in the Alps, we once got a reading of 119 meters below sea level. Furthermore, they're not as easy as you'd hope. They have a terminology all their own and it takes a good while to get the hang of it.

As a guideline, a GPS will come in handy for traveling in remote areas without roads – if you're hiking, biking, canoeing, flying or parasailing. And if you'll be traveling anywhere off the beaten track in the Everglades, these gizmos are choice gear.

Just don't think that it can act as your *only* orienteering tool – unless you've spent a lot of money and/or had a lot of experience with it; bring along a good compass as well for critical measurements.

Longer hikes require two types of maps: US Geological Survey (USGS) Quadrangles and US Department of Agriculture-Forest Service maps. To order a map index and price list, contact the US Geological Survey, PO Box 25286, Denver, CO 80225. For general information on maps, see also the Facts for the Visitor chapter. For information regarding maps of specific forests, wilderness areas or national parks, see the appropriate geographic entry.

ROCK CLIMBING

In a state with no mountains, or even hills, to speak of, this heading may strike you as odd. Well, hell. There isn't any *real* rock climbing in the state, but the Eden Roc Resort in Miami Beach (☎ 305-531-0000; see the Places to Stay section in the Miami & Miami Beach chapter) has a 23-foot-high indoor rock-climbing complex. Contact the Eden Roc for information on its rock-climbing-only memberships.

BICYCLING

It's not as if there's a lot of excitement in Florida biking: the state's as flat as a pancake. That said, there are plenty of bicycle trails in and around cities and in city, county, state and national parks. Also, rail-trails – bicycle paths on the trackbeds of former railway lines – pop up here and there: in Tallahassee, Gainesville and along the southwest coast. In cities such as Miami Beach, Fernandina Beach on Amelia Island, St Augustine, Tallahassee, Pensacola and Pensacola Beach and Key West, a bike is a great way to get around, and rentals are readily available. Note that four bicyclists will pay more to enter a state park than will eight people in a car – generally admission for pedestrians and cyclists is $1 each.

Information

Members of the national League of American Bicyclists (LAB; ☎ 202-822-1333, fax 202-822-1334, www.bikeleague.org), 1612 K St NW, Suite 401, Washington, DC 20006, may transport their bikes free on selected airlines and obtain a list of hospitality homes in each state that offer simple accommodations to touring cyclists. The LAB also publishes an annual *Almanac* that lists contacts in each state, along with information about bicycle routes and special events. Bicycle tourists will also want to get a copy of the *Cyclosource Catalog*, listing books and maps, and *The Cyclist's Yellow Pages*, a trip-planning resource, both published by the Adventure Cycling Association (☎ 406-721-1776), 150 E Pine St, Missoula, MT 59802.

Laws & Regulations

Trail etiquette requires that cyclists yield to other users. Helmets should always be worn to reduce the risk of head injury, but they are not mandated by law. National parks, however, require that all riders under 18 years old wear a helmet.

HORSEBACK RIDING

Horseback riding is not as popular in Florida as in other areas of the country, and it tends to be expensive. Rates for recreational riding start around $18 per hour or $30 for two hours, though the hourly rate falls rapidly thereafter and full-day trips usually cost around $75 to $100 with a guide. Experienced riders may want to let the owners know, or else risk being saddled with an excessively docile stable nag. Horse country in Florida is just southwest of Gainesville, and riding is more popular in the central section of the state than in any other. See the sections on the Paynes Prairie State Preserve, Devil's Den and Disney in the Central Florida chapter.

CANOEING

Florida's covered with, and almost surrounded by, water – there are canoeing opportunities practically everywhere you go. The best opportunities for canoe adventures are in the Everglades, where the 99-mile Wilderness Waterway and trips around the 10,000 Islands offer fantastic opportunities for canoeists. There are also wonderful opportunities to canoe along the Steinhatchee River in northwest Florida, Itchetucknee Springs near Gainesville and throughout the southwestern section of the state.

For standard paddles of an hour or several, many state and county parks offer canoe rentals; private concessionaires operate in or near parks that don't. Generally speaking, the rentals are between $4 and $7 an hour, or $10 and $15 for four hours, and from $20 to $25 for a full day or 24 hours. Many of the trails are very easygoing paddles, and rangers are invariably helpful in letting you know how to see the most wildlife, and, if necessary, giving a paddling lesson.

What to Bring

The following are things you'll need to bring for individual backcountry canoe trips (obviously the overnight stuff is only if you plan to camp):

- good, sightable compass and GPS (optional)
- good flashlight (we like Petzl headlamps and Mini Maglite brands)
- nautical charts and tide chart
- tent with no-see-um – not just mosquito – netting

- sleeping bag
- one gallon of water per person per day, preferably in heavy-duty or army surplus water containers, not store-bought 1-gallon jugs
- as much food as you'll need plus an extra day's food per person
- a solid plastic sealable cooler, like a Coleman or Eskimo – *not* Styrofoam – for food storage
- portable cooking stove, pot and utensils
- Avon Skin-So-Soft or industrial-strength insect repellent like REI Jungle Juice
- sunscreen, sunglasses and a hat
- strong plastic garbage bags – Hefty-brand lawn bags are nice
- biodegradable toilet paper and a small spade to dig waste pit
- binoculars (to see route markers) and camera
- dry change of clothes for *when* you fall in the water
- good shoes or boots

Packing

If you'll be traveling in a canoe, the idea that you have to take as little as possible can take a back seat to the important stuff: a) being comfortable when you get where you're going; b) not cheating yourself on meals, which are very important; and c) having the right equipment to avoid getting yourself into trouble.

When we go we pack as much food and gear as we can into sealable coolers and use a trick encouraged by North American Canoe Tours in Everglades City: fill cleaned-out half-gallon milk jugs with water and freeze them; block ice lasts longer than cubes and as it melts you get cold drinking water. If you play your cards right and keep everything sealed tightly, you can make several of those last for two to three days.

One thing we skimp on is clothes: we know we're going to get wet, and pack as little as possible, but we always make certain to pack lightweight long pants, lightweight long-sleeve shirts and clean, dry socks and underwear. Keep these in the plastic garbage bags. Heavy-duty Ziploc-brand freezer bags are good for wallets and anything small that you don't want to get wet.

Speaking of things getting wet, expect that everything will, and be pleasantly surprised with whatever doesn't. That said, take preventative steps to protect the most important of your assets, which in approximate order are sleeping bag, tent, clothes and expensive electronics like your camera. Wrap these well in the heavy-duty garbage bags, remove the air from them, tie them off twice and place them in a backpack.

We tie everything – backpacks, coolers, water jugs – to each other in a daisy chain (that is, lines between each piece of gear, not tying everything together in a clump) and then tie one end of it to the inside of the canoe. In the unlikely event that you flip, it's nice to know you'll still have your stuff, and if you do flip, having all of your stuff safely tied, yet in the water, enables you to right the craft much faster.

SEA KAYAKING

This quiet, unobtrusive sport allows you to visit unexplored islands and stretches of coast and view marine life at close range. Sea kayaks, which hold one or two people, are larger and more stable than whitewater boats, making them safer and easier to navigate. They also have storage capacity so you can take them on overnight, or even week-long trips. Imagine paddling to a secluded beach on one of the Gulf Coast or Everglades islands and setting up camp for a week. One guy we met said he books passage on day cruises to the Bahamas and

takes his kayak and gear as carry-on. Once there he just paddles off into the sunset!

What to Bring

In terms of what you're bringing, kayaking is similar to hiking. There is enough room in one Sea Lion sea kayak for seven days' worth of supplies – if you're very good at packing.

You're going to want the same type of stuff that you'd want on a canoe trip, but the idea is to scale everything down. You'll be able to take smaller, 1-gallon bottles of water, or a collapsible water container, as you're able to seal the boat. Also, you can use the kayak's sealable hatch in place of the heavy and bulky plastic cooler, which saves on space. But you'll need to economize on size on things like your tent, stove and sleeping bag – actually, anywhere you can. The trick is to take only exactly what you need, and in the smallest form possible. So you're going to have to sacrifice them bananas: freeze-dried food is the order of the day for overnight trips.

If you've yet to sample it, you may be in for a shock: freeze-dried food, available from several companies, actually tastes a lot better than you'd expect (but it's not, like, *great* or anything). Companies like Natural High and Richmoore make a huge array of dishes. Some you dump into a pot of boiling water, with others you add the water directly to the bag. For side dishes, such as green beans or corn, expect to pay about $1.50 a bag. For a breakfast item such as – get this – a cheese omelet, it's about $2.50, and for a full dinner, which includes a main course and a side dish that's said to feed two but probably feeds only 1 1/2, expect to pay from $4.99 (for things such as beef stew and chicken teriyaki) to $5.99 (for more upscale stuff such as honey-lime chicken and whole-grain rice).

Lauderdale Sports (☎ 954-436-4186), 11249 Pines Blvd in Fort Lauderdale, is the best place we've found in South Florida to buy the stuff. (Actually, in terms of stock and knowledgeable staff, it's the best sports superstore in South Florida – better than Sports Authority.)

SURFING

The surfing in Florida isn't much to speak of compared to Costa Rica, California or Hawaii, but there is surfing along the entire Atlantic coast. The best places are north of Miami Beach but south of Fort Lauderdale, and then around the central Florida coast, where conditions are usually pretty decent, or very good if you're a longboarder. Count on 2- to 3-foot surf unless there's a storm, when it can get big. Daytona Beach, New Smyrna Beach and the area near the Space Coast are all great for surfing, as is the area from Flagler Beach up to St Augustine.

Surf shops may be loathe to rent out boards, because of insurance problems, but they will usually sell you a board and buy it back at the end of the day for about $15 less than you paid for it…Get it? Wink wink.

WINDSURFING

Though you can put in at any beach or public boat launch, there are few places that rent windsurfing equipment, making it necessary for serious boarders to bring their own. Beginners and casual boarders will find relatively calm conditions and rental facilities at Biscayne Bay, near Miami's Rickenbacker Causeway, and in resorts. Generally speaking, the best places for windsurfing are along the southeast and southwest coasts, though it's popular in the northeast as well; local weather forecasts give wind and surf conditions.

SCUBA DIVING & SNORKELING

To dive in Florida you need to have at least an Open Water I certificate, for which you'll need several open-water dives. You'll also need to work in the pool before even getting to the ocean. If you push yourself, and the weather and seas are right, you can certify in three days.

For information on dive courses and standards, contact the Professional Diving Instructors Corporation (PSIC; ☎ 717-342-9434), PO Box 3633, Scranton, PA 18505, or the National Association for Underwater Instruction (NAUI; ☎ 714-621-5801, 800-553-6284), PO Box 14650, Montclair, CA 91763. Note that medical-grade oxygen is now available in Florida without a prescription.

Quick one- to three-day certification courses can get you into shallow waters to see the underwater world for as little as $220, though you might want to buy your own snorkel, fins and various other gear and books, which can add up to a $400 to $500 total cost. Shallow diving is especially satisfying in places such as the Florida Keys, where the protected coral reefs house a rich marine environment close to the surface. Local dive shops are the best resources for equipment, guides and instructors. *Scuba Diving* and *Sport Diver* are widely available magazines dedicated entirely to underwater pursuits.

If you don't have the time, money or desire to dive deep, you can often rent a snorkel, mask and fins for under $10 an hour. In touristy spots such as South Beach, people set up equipment-rental stands along the beach. If you'll do it more than three times, it will pay off to invest $25 or so in an inexpensive mask and snorkel from a place such as Lauderdale Sports or Sports Authority.

FISHING

Saltwater fishing in Florida is an obsession, and every city along the coast has a marina packed with charter fishing boats. Freshwater fishing, or more specifically, bass fishing, inland on lakes throughout the state and especially near Orlando, is as much a Florida tradition as grits or speeding. There

are complex limits on catches in Florida; licenses are issued and fees and validity set on a county-by-county basis. Fishing boats are available at practically every marina in the state, but many seem to go out from the South Florida area – east or west. Charters run regularly from Miami Beach's marina, Fort Lauderdale's Bahia Mar, Key West, Naples, Marco Island and Dania.

SAILING

There are sailboats for charter at marinas throughout the state, with or without crew. Prices vary unbelievably, depending on the size of the boat, the season, the mood of the owner and your level of experience. Probably the best place to start is in Fort Lauderdale. See also the Getting There & Away chapter for suggestions on how to hook up with crew positions.

TENNIS

There are municipal tennis courts in almost every Florida city; check in the blue pages section of the telephone directory under Parks Department for local numbers. All resorts and many hotels have courts as well. You also may be able to get time on the courts at college or university campuses by asking.

GOLF

Golf courses can be found all over the state of Florida, and golfers say they're some of the best in the country. In many ways that's

Barracuda Danger

Do not eat barracuda in Florida no matter what size – they may carry ciguatera toxin (CTX), produced by microscopic algae. This is eaten by smaller fish and travels up the food chain and accumulates in larger fish, who pass it on to humans. It can cause severe illness, with symptoms including diarrhea, nausea, cramps, numbness of the mouth, chills, headaches, dizziness and convulsions. Don't believe local legends about the weight of the fish or cooking tests using a dime in the boiling water – this toxin can be deadly.

unfortunate. Golf courses waste colossal amounts of water for irrigation, and run-off from fertilizer poisons the very source of the state's freshwater supply: the Florida Aquifer. Golf courses also take up huge tracts of land, and environmentalists charge that the damage to local flora and fauna is unforgivable. The development in Florida associated with golf courses – condominiums and resorts – adds to the damage.

Golf courses are not listed in this book. There are many sources for information on golfing in Florida – practically every pamphlet that is handed out by CVB/VCBs (convention & visitors bureaus/visitors & convention bureaus) and chambers of commerce list all golf courses in the area.

HOT-AIR BALLOONING

Floating above the state in a wicker gondola has its attractions, given the scenery, but it's not cheap at the relatively few locations that offer it commercially. Most flights leave at dawn or at sunset and go 1000 to 2000 feet above the ground. They're available in southwest Florida but pop up almost everywhere; check in local airports, where people will know of balloonists in the area. A one-hour flight for two people typically costs $125 to $165.

SKYDIVING

If jumping out of a plane and falling at a speed of 150 mph before opening your chute 3000 feet above the ground sounds fun, then you should head to South Florida. There are skydiving companies that set up shop at airports around the state – just drive into any airport and ask at the information desk or tower.

At HGAA (see below) is Skydive Miami (☎ 305-759-3483), which will, in one day, get you trained and pushed out of the plane on your first jump for $129. If you saw the movie *Drop Zone* with Wesley Snipes, you've seen these folks in action. A former employee trained Snipes for the film, and most of the jumps – including the huge one allegedly over Washington, DC – were filmed here. It's open during daylight hours every day of the year, but call the day before.

FLYING
Gliding

Planes are fun, but they sure are noisy. Miami Gliders (☎ 304-271-6880), probably the best gliding school around, can get you up for an introductory lesson in a Super Blanick L-23 for $45. Or, if you're already a licensed pilot, you can get checked out in gliders after three hours of instruction and 10 solo flights.

Ultralight Aircraft

South Florida is an aviation center, and hundreds of small planes fill the skies each day. Ultralight aircraft, in fact, became so popular down here that Dade County built a field specifically for the tiny planes at Homestead General Aviation Airport (HGAA; ☎ 305-247-4883). Ultralights are small aircraft that are regulated but require no pilot's license to fly. Lessons cost about $75 an hour, and you'll need 10 to 12 hours of training before you can fly solo. Contact the Light Aircraft Flyers Association (☎ 305-460-3356) for information about lessons and upcoming events, or just show up at the field on the second Saturday of each month for their Fly-In and Social Day at HGAA, where there's barbecue breakfast and lunch, talk of flying and, if the weather's good, flying.

On the north side of Miami's Rickenbacker Causeway is Tony's Ultralight Adventures (☎ 305-361-6909), which offers sightseeing flights, lessons and rental of its two-seater ultralight seaplane. Your best chance here is to just show up. Either the phone isn't working or they just don't answer it, but they're there all right. They fly daily, and the plane's a nice one.

Single-Engine Planes

If you've got a pilot's license and a current medical certificate, you can stop into any decent airport and rent a plane to get yourself a bird's eye orientation to the area. The price for a single-engine plane such as a C-152 is usually between $50 and $60 an hour including fuel; a C-172 runs about $69 to $100. You'll need to bring your logbook, and go up first with the owner or an instructor for a checkride (at your expense), but this will give you a prime opportunity to ask about must-see attractions, local regulations, etc.

JET SKIING & MOTORBOATING

Jet skis and motorboats can kill manatees and fish, rip up sea plants and protected sea grass (also destroying the manatees' food supply), scare swimmers and annoy locals. They cause several deaths per year. Florida waters are very shallow and tricky to navigate. Many areas are protected Manatee Zones. You can rent these machines in various places around the state, but we wish you wouldn't.

Getting There & Away

AIR
Airports & Airlines

The state's two major international airports are Miami International Airport (MIA) and Orlando International Airport (MCO/ORL). But Fort Lauderdale's international terminal (FLL) has become a very popular place for inexpensive flights to land. If you have a really cheap deal to Miami, you may be landing in Fort Lauderdale, about 30 miles north.

Three other airports seeing increased international traffic are Tampa/St Petersburg (TPA), Daytona Beach (DAB) and Jacksonville (JAX), which are becoming important domestic hubs as well.

Most Florida cities have regional airports and offer connecting service to other US cities; these include Palm Beach (PBI, actually in West Palm Beach), Tallahassee (TLH), Gainesville (GNV), Fort Myers (RSW) and Pensacola (PNS).

In other locations, the airports are usually municipal and, while they support a small amount of commercial traffic, are geared more to private aviation. These can range from the sparkling new air strips at St Augustine to dirt strips.

With the exception of major tourist destinations like Miami, Fort Lauderdale, Palm Beach and Orlando, there is rarely public transportation between airports and downtown; you're at the mercy of car-rental agencies, taxis or, more rarely, shuttle services. In this book we list as many options as we've found and include average taxi fares.

Airlines are listed in the yellow pages under Airlines. Important offices in Miami include the following:

Air Canada
    ☎ 305-871-2828, 800-776-3000
Air France
    ☎ 305-374-2626, 800-237-2747
Alitalia
    ☎ 305-539-0593, 800-223-5730
American Airlines
    ☎ 800-433-7300

British Airways
    ☎ 305-526-7800, 800-247-9297
Carnival Airlines
    ☎ 305-891-0199, 800-437-2110
Continental Airlines
    ☎ 305-871-1400, 800-525-0280
Delta Air Lines
    ☎ 305-448-7000, 800-221-1212
Lufthansa
    ☎ 800-645-3880
Northwest Airlines
    ☎ 305-441-1096, 800-225-2525 domestic, 800-447-4747 international
Qantas Airways
    ☎ 800-227-4500
Tower Air
    ☎ 305-871-6431, 800-348-6937
TWA
    ☎ 305-371-7471, 800-221-2000
United Airlines
    ☎ 800-241-6522
US Airways
    ☎ 800-428-4322
Virgin Atlantic Airways
    ☎ 305-445-9940, 800-877-2537 in Florida, 800-862-8621 out of state

Buying Tickets

Numerous airlines fly to the USA, and a variety of fares are available. In addition to a straightforward roundtrip ticket, you can also get a Round-the-World ticket or a Visit USA pass (see Air Passes below). So rather than walking into the nearest travel agent or airline office and buying a ticket, it pays to shop around first. Consult reference books and check the travel sections of magazines like *Time Out* and *TNT* in the UK, or the Saturday editions of newspapers like the *Sydney Morning Herald* and *The Age* in Australia. Ads in these publications offer cheap fares, usually low-season fares on obscure airlines with conditions attached. But don't be surprised if agents are sold out.

The plane ticket will probably be the single-most expensive item in your budget, and buying it can be intimidating. Research the current state of the market and start shopping for a ticket early – some of the cheapest tickets must be bought months in advance, and some popular flights sell out quickly. Talk to other recent travelers – they may be able to stop you from making some obvious mistakes.

Note that high season in the USA is mid-June to mid-September (summer) and the two weeks around Christmas. The best rates for travel to and in the USA are offered November through March – except for major holidays, especially Thanksgiving (the third Thursday in November), which account for the heaviest travel days of the year.

Call travel agents for bargains. Airlines can supply information on routes and timetables; however, except during fare wars, they do not supply the cheapest tickets. Airlines often have competitive low-season student and senior citizens' fares. Before you buy, confirm the fare, the route, the dates and any restrictions on the ticket.

Cheap tickets are available in two distinct categories: official and unofficial. Official ones have a variety of names, including budget, advance-purchase, advance-purchase excursion (Apex) and super-Apex fares. Unofficial tickets are simply discounted tickets that the airlines release through selected travel agents (not through airline offices). The cheapest tickets are often nonrefundable and require an extra fee for changing your flight. (Many insurance policies will cover this loss if you have to change your flight in an emergency.) Return (roundtrip) tickets usually work out cheaper than two one-way fares – often *much* cheaper.

Use the fares quoted in this book as a guide only. They are approximate and based on the rates advertised by travel agents and airlines at press time. Quoted air fares do not necessarily constitute a recommendation for the carrier.

If traveling from the UK, you will probably find that the cheapest flights are being advertised by obscure bucket shops whose names haven't yet reached the telephone directory. Many such firms are honest and solvent, but there are a few rogues who will

take your money and disappear, to reopen elsewhere a month or two later under a new name. If you feel suspicious about a firm, don't give them all the money at once. Leave a deposit of 20% or so and pay the balance on receipt of the ticket. If they insist on cash in advance, go elsewhere. And once you have the ticket, call the airline to confirm you are booked on the flight.

You may decide to pay more than the rock-bottom fare by opting for the safety of a better-known travel agent. Established firms such as STA Travel, which has offices worldwide, Council Travel in the USA and Travel CUTS in Canada are valid alternatives, and they offer good prices to most destinations.

Once you have your ticket, write down its number, the flight number and other details, and keep the information somewhere separate. If the ticket is lost or stolen, this information will help you get a replacement.

Remember to buy travel insurance as early as possible.

Air Travel Glossary

Baggage Allowance This will be printed on your ticket and usually includes one 20kg item to go in the hold (checked luggage) plus one item of hand luggage.

Bucket Shops These are unbonded travel agencies specializing in discounted airline tickets.

Cancellation Penalties If you have to cancel or change a discounted ticket, there are often heavy penalties involved; sometimes you can take out insurance against these penalties. Some airlines impose penalties on regular tickets as well, particularly against 'no-show' passengers.

Check-In Airlines ask you to check in a certain time ahead of the flight departure (usually one to two hours on international flights). If you fail to check in on time and the flight is over-booked, the airline can cancel your booking and give your seat to somebody else.

Confirmation Having a ticket with the flight and date on it doesn't mean you have a seat until the agent has checked with the airline that your status is 'OK' or confirmed. Meanwhile you could just be 'on request.'

Courier Fares Businesses often need to send urgent documents or freight securely and quickly. Courier companies hire people to accompany the package through customs and, in return, offer a discount ticket that is sometimes a phenomenal bargain. In effect, what the companies do is ship their freight as your luggage on regular commercial flights. This is a legitimate operation, but there are two shortcomings – the short turnaround time of the ticket (usually not longer than a month) and the limitation on your luggage allowance. You may have to surrender all of your allowance and take only carry-on luggage.

ITX An ITX, or 'independent inclusive tour excursion,' is often available on tickets to popular holiday destinations. Officially, it's a package deal combined with hotel accommodations, but many agents will sell you one of these for the flight only and give you phony hotel vouchers in the unlikely event that you're challenged at the airport.

Lost Tickets If you lose your airline ticket, an airline will usually treat it like a traveler's check and, after inquiries, issue you another one. Legally, however, an airline is entitled to treat it like cash: if you lose it, it's gone forever. Take good care of your tickets.

MCO A 'miscellaneous charge order' is a voucher that looks like an airline ticket but carries no destination or date. It can be exchanged through any International Association of Travel

Getting Bumped

Airlines try to guarantee themselves consistently full planes by overbooking, assuming some passengers will not show up. When everyone who's booked actually does show up, some passengers can be 'bumped' off the full plane, but they are usually compensated for the inconven-

ience. Getting bumped can be a nuisance because you have to wait around for the next flight, but if you have a day's leeway, you can really take advantage of the system. On one occasion, Nick got bumped from an American Airlines flight and received $500 and a guaranteed seat on the next flight out, $1^3/_4$ hours later. Why,

Air Travel Glossary

Agents (IATA) airline for a ticket on a specific flight. It's a useful alternative to an onward ticket in those countries that demand one and is more flexible than an ordinary ticket if you're unsure of your route.

No-Shows These are passengers who fail to show up for their flight. Full-fare passengers who fail to turn up are sometimes entitled to travel on a later flight. The rest of the passengers are penalized (see Cancellation Penalties).

On Request This is an unconfirmed booking for a flight.

Onward Tickets An entry requirement for many countries is that you have a ticket out of the country. If you're unsure of your next move, the easiest solution is to buy the cheapest onward ticket to a neighboring country or a ticket from a reliable airline that can later be refunded if you do not use it.

Open Jaw Tickets These are return tickets on which you fly out to one place but return from another. If available, these can save you backtracking to your arrival point.

Overbooking Airlines hate to fly with empty seats and because every flight has some passengers who fail to show up, airlines often book more passengers than they have seats. Usually excess passengers make up for the no-shows, but occasionally somebody gets bumped. Guess who it is most likely to be? The passengers who check in late.

Point-to-Point Tickets These are discount tickets that can be bought on some routes in return for passengers waiving their rights to a stopover.

Reconfirmation At least 72 hours prior to departure time of an onward or return flight, you must contact the airline and 'reconfirm' that you intend to be on the flight. If you don't do this, the airline can delete your name from the passenger list and you could lose your seat.

Restrictions Discounted tickets often have various restrictions on them – such as advance payment, minimum and maximum periods you must be away (eg, a minimum of two weeks or a maximum of one year) and penalties for changing the tickets.

Travel Periods Ticket prices vary with the time of year. There is a low (off-peak) season and a high (peak) season, and often a low-shoulder season and a high-shoulder season as well. Usually the fare depends on your outward flight – if you depart in the high season and return in the low season, you pay the high-season fare.

that hourly rate is almost as much as Lonely Planet pays!

When you check in at the airline counter, ask if they will need volunteers to be bumped, and ask what the compensation will be. Depending on the desirability of the flight, this can range from a $200 voucher toward your next flight to a fully paid roundtrip ticket. Try to confirm a later flight so you don't get stuck in the airport on standby. If you have to spend the night, airlines frequently foot the hotel bill for their bumpees. All in all, it can be a great deal, and many people plan their trips with a day to spare, hoping to get a free ticket that will cover their next trip.

Be aware that, due to this same system, being just a little late for boarding can get you bumped with none of these benefits.

Flying Standby

When flying standby, call the airline a day or two before the flight and make a 'standby reservation.' This way you get priority over all the others who just appear and hope to get on the flight the same day.

Visit USA Passes

Almost all domestic carriers offer Visit USA passes to non-US citizens. The passes are actually a book of coupons – each coupon equals a flight. You have to book these outside of the USA and have a return flight out of the US. The following airlines are the most representative, but ask your travel agent about other airlines that offer the service.

Continental Airlines' Visit USA pass can be purchased in countries on both the Atlantic and Pacific sides. All travel must be completed within 60 days of the first flight into the US or 81 days after arrival in the US (if you arrive by some other means). You must have your trip planned before you purchase the coupons. If you decide to change destinations once in the USA, you will be fined $50. High-season prices are $407 for three flight coupons (minimum purchase), $518 for five and $1158 for 10 (maximum purchase). Low-season rates are $333/518/1407.

Northwest offers the same deal, but it lets you fly standby and make flight reservations beforehand.

American Airlines uses the same coupon structure and also sells the passes on Atlantic and Pacific sides. You must know your whole route and reserve your first flight (subsequent flights can be booked a day in advance), and you must stick to that schedule or be penalized $75 per change. If a coupon takes you only halfway to your destination, you will have to buy the remaining ticket at full price. A packet of 10 coupons costs $839.

Delta has two different systems for travelers coming across the Atlantic. Visit USA gives travelers a discount, but you need to have your itinerary mapped out. You get the cheapest fare between two places, but you don't get a set ticket price. The other option is Discover America, in which a traveler buys coupons good for standby travel anywhere in the continental USA. One flight equals one coupon. Only two transcontinental flights are allowed. Three coupons (minimum purchase) cost $419, four cost $519, five are $619 and 10 cost $1249. Children's fares are about $40 less – $379 for three coupons, etc. In order to purchase coupons, you must pay for the transatlantic flight in advance. These passes can be cheaper in conjunction with a Delta international flight that brings you to the USA. For Delta pass information in the UK, call ☎ 0800-414-767; elsewhere in Europe, call ☎ 44-181-566-8262.

Round-the-World Tickets

RTW tickets have become very popular in the last few years. They are often real bargains and can work out to be no more expensive, or even cheaper, than an ordinary return ticket. Prices start at about UK£675, A$2000/2500 (low/high) or US$1500.

The official airline RTW tickets are usually put together by a combination of two airlines and permit you to fly anywhere you want on their route systems as long as you do not backtrack. Other restrictions are that you must usually book the first sector in advance and cancellation penalties apply. There may be restrictions on the number of stops permitted, and tickets are usually valid from 90 days up to a year. An alternative type of RTW ticket is one put together by a travel agent using a combination of discounted tickets.

Although most airlines restrict the number of sectors that can be flown within the USA and Canada to four, and some airlines black out heavily traveled routes (like Honolulu to Tokyo), stopovers are otherwise generally unlimited. The majority of RTW tickets restrict you to three airlines.

From Australia, you can usually get a RTW ticket called the Global Explorer, which allows you a maximum of six flights and total of 28,000 miles, for US$3100 or A$3192 (high season).

One of the best places to get a RTW ticket is Germany, where, for example, you can book a RTW from Frankfurt to São Paulo or Buenos Aires, Lima, Miami and back to Frankfurt for US$1258.

Canadian Airlines offers numerous RTW combinations ranging from C$3100 to C$3600. Air Canada's base fare is C$3287, including two other carriers. As you add more, the price goes up.

Continental, TWA and Northwest also offer RTW fares.

Travelers with Special Needs

If you have special needs of any sort – a broken leg, dietary restrictions, dependence on a wheelchair, responsibility for a baby, fear of flying – you should let the airline know as soon as possible so they can make arrangements accordingly. You should remind them when you reconfirm your booking (at least 72 hours before departure) and again when you check in at the airport. It may also be worth calling different airlines before you make your booking to find out how they will handle your particular needs.

Airports and airlines can be surprisingly helpful, but they do need advance warning. Most international airports can provide escorts from check-in desk to plane where needed, and there should be ramps, elevators, accessible toilets and reachable phones. Aircraft toilets, on the other hand, are likely to present a problem; travelers should discuss this with the airline at an early stage and, if necessary, with their doctor.

Guide dogs for the blind will often have to travel in a specially pressurized baggage compartment with other animals, away from their owner, though smaller guide dogs may be admitted to the cabin. Guide dogs are not subject to quarantine as long as they have proof of vaccination against rabies.

Deaf travelers can request airport and inflight announcements in written form.

Children under two travel for 10% of the standard fare (or free on some airlines), as long as they don't occupy a seat. (They don't get a baggage allowance.) 'Skycots' should be provided by the airline if requested in advance; these will take a child weighing up to about 22 pounds. Children between two and 12 can usually occupy a seat for half to two-thirds of the full fare, and they do get a baggage allowance. Strollers can often be taken on as hand luggage.

Departure Tax

Airport departure taxes are normally included in the cost of tickets bought in the USA, although tickets purchased abroad may not have this included. There's an airport departure tax charged to all passengers bound for a foreign destination. However, this and the North American Free Trade Agreement (NAFTA) tax charged to passengers entering the USA from a foreign country are hidden taxes added to the purchase price of your airline ticket.

Within the USA

Scan the *New Times* and the *Miami Herald* for travel ads and news of discounted fares out of Miami. Good travel agents in Miami include Travel by Design (☎ 305-673-6336), 210 Washington Ave; Council Travel (☎ 305-670-9261, 800-226-8624), south of Coral Gables at 9100 S Dadeland Blvd; and Travel Now in Miami at 1455 Collins Ave (☎ 305-532-7273), and 14374 Biscayne Blvd (☎ 305-919-9000).

The *New York Times*, *Los Angeles Times*, *Chicago Tribune*, *San Francisco Examiner*, *San Jose Mercury News*, *Boston Herald* and many other major newspapers produce weekly travel sections that include numerous travel agents' advertisements. STA Travel (☎ 602-596-5151, 800-777-0112) and Council Travel have offices in major cities nationwide.

The magazine *Travel Unlimited*, PO Box 1058, Allston, MA 02134, publishes details of the cheapest air fares and courier possibilities.

The best deals to Miami by air are from New York metropolitan-area airports, but the New York-Miami route is the most crowded: reserve early as plane tickets sell out well in advance of the departure date. In addition to the big carriers, there are some itty-bitty airlines that compete on these routes. Of these, the best are Kiwi Airlines (☎ 800-538-5494) and Carnival Air, the aviation wing of the cruise giant, both of which occasionally offer fares between Miami and New York as low as $60 each way. On the major airlines, the lowest you can expect to pay is $150 advance purchase between New York and Miami, $300 from Los Angeles, $350 to $450 from San Francisco.

Bahamas

The main airlines running between Miami and the Bahamas are American and Gulfstream International. Typical roundtrip fares are $149 to Nassau and up to $275 roundtrip to the farther islands.

Travel by Design (☎ 305-673-6336, 800-358-7125) in Miami Beach specializes in this stuff, and it's a great source for information on getting around the Bahamas – from planes to mail boats.

Cuba

At the time of writing, charter flights between Miami and Cuba had just been resumed.

Anyone in Florida who wants to visit Cuba without the major hassle of obtaining US government permission can easily do so through the Bahamas. Cuban Airlines' Nassau-Havana flight operates three times a week, a useful connection for blockade runners – though watch for US Customs agents at the Nassau airport if you're an unlicensed American (see boxed text). Cuban tourist cards are sold at the airline desk in Nassau.

Elsewhere in the Caribbean

Miami is the Gateway to the Caribbean, and the vast majority of flights to Caribbean destinations are serviced by American Airlines, with daily service to many destinations, including San Juan, Puerto Rico; Santo Domingo, Dominican Republic; Montego Bay, Jamaica; St Martin and Barbados.

Prices change dramatically, and last-minute deals are always a possibility. In Miami, see a good discount travel agent like Travel by Design for the latest prices. Following are the lowest published roundtrip fares at press time – remember these may be far higher than you'll likely pay:

destination	price
Barbados	$390
Montego Bay	$260
San Jose, Puerto Rico	$481
Santo Domingo	$370
St Martin	$551

Canada

Travel CUTS has offices in all major cities. The Toronto *Globe & Mail* and *Vancouver Sun* carry travel agents' ads.

From Toronto, you can expect to pay a high-season/low-season roundtrip ticket price of C$250/350, and from Vancouver C$400/625.

Australia & New Zealand

There is no direct service from Australia or New Zealand to Miami; you'll have to change planes and/or carriers in Los Angeles, the US hub for Qantas and Air New Zealand. With long-range 747-400 aircraft, most services now overfly Hawaii, so at least the Pacific is covered in one mighty leap. Air New Zealand has the most comfortable coach seats in the sky.

From Auckland to Los Angeles, it takes 12 to 13 hours; from Sydney to Los Angeles $13^{1}/_{2}$ to $14^{1}/_{2}$ hours. Typical Apex roundtrip fares vary from A$2000 to A$2400 from the Australian east coast and NZ$2500 from Auckland.

In Australia and New Zealand, STA Travel and Flight Centres International are major dealers in cheap air fares; check the travel agents' ads in the yellow pages and call around. Qantas Airways flies to Los Angeles from Sydney, Melbourne (via Sydney or Auckland) and Cairns. United Airlines flies to San Francisco from Sydney and Melbourne (via Sydney) and also flies to Los Angeles.

Cuba: What's It All About?

Generally, travel to Cuba for Americans is heavily restricted to the point of being next to illegal. Americans who want to get a license to visit Cuba must fall into one of several categories:

- conference attendees
- researchers
- educational-program participants
- members of religious groups
- freelance journalists *on assignment*

If you can fit yourself into one of these categories, you may be able to get a license to visit Cuba from the Department of Treasury. There are daily flights from Nassau and Miami and several a day from Cancun, Mexico. Roundtrip air fares on Mexicana from Cancun and Nassau are $252, and allow a connection the same day from the US to Cuba. The fare is $299 from Miami.

Americans eligible for a US government license to visit Cuba should contact Marazul Tours Inc (☎ 201-319-9670, 800-223-5334, fax 201-319-9009, www.marazultours.com), Tower Plaza, 4100 Park Ave, Weehawken, NJ 07087, probably the best agency for US-Cuban travel. Marazul also books reservations throughout Cuba – its brochure is most informative.

Why on earth, you ask, is the license from the Treasury Department? Get this: it's not illegal for an American to travel to Cuba. What's illegal is for that American to spend *any* money at all there, or to allow any of his or her money to be given to a Cuban national by a third party (like, say, a Canadian or Bahamian travel agent for a Cuban hotel) without a license. In short, it's legal to travel to Cuba, but if you don't have a license and you buy a donut or a newspaper, or pay departure tax, let alone rent a hotel room, you're screwed if US customs gets hold of you.

The bad news: US customs has offices in Cancun and Nassau, and they are trained to look for Americans returning from Cuba. Around 400 people have been fined a total of $2 million in the last two years for just that. And new US regulations give US customs the right to assume you've spent money in Cuba if you've come from there. It's up to you to prove you didn't spend money (if you took a big lunch and slept on the beach, save your sandwich wrappers and don't wash your sleeping bag!).

All we can say is that the current political climate may make things easier, and with any luck at all these ridiculous restrictions on international travel will be lifted.

The UK

In the UK, some incredible deals can be had. For example, in January you can get a roundtrip air ticket from London for as low as £189, while in June and July the price goes as high as £450.

Good, reliable agents for cheap tickets in the UK are Trailfinders (☎ 020-7937-5400), 194 Kensington High St, London, W8 7RG; Council Travel (☎ 020-7437-7767), 28a Poland St, London, W1; and STA Travel (☎ 020-7937-9971), 86 Old Brompton Rd, London, SW7 3LQ.

The Globetrotters Club (BCM Roving, London WC1N 3XX) publishes a newsletter called *Globe*, which covers obscure destinations and can help you find traveling companions.

Continental Europe

Most major European airlines, including Air France, British Air, Finnair and Lufthansa, as well as others such as Aeroflot ('The Airline When There's Absolutely No Other Way'), have service to Miami. From Paris, the highest scheduled air fare hovers at about 3000FF. In June/January, other scheduled prices are f1450/1100 from Amsterdam, 4200/3690 mk from Helsinki, 80,000/65,000 ptas from Madrid, and DM1300/950 from Munich or Frankfurt.

In Amsterdam, NBBS, the Dutch Student Travel Service, is a popular travel agent. Kilroy Travels (☎ 020-524-5100), Singel 413 in Amsterdam, is a fine agency we've used on many occasions.

In Paris, Council Travel (☎ 01 44 55 55 44) is at 22 Rue des Pyramides, 75001. For great student fares, contact USIT Voyages (☎ 01 42 34 56 90) at 6 Rue de Vaugirard, 75006 Paris.

In Germany, an awesome travel discounter for students and nonstudents alike is Travel Overland, with offices in several cities. For the nearest one, contact the Munich office (☎ 089-272-76-30-0), Barerstrasse 73, 80799 München. Another good agency is Die Neue Reisewelle Berlin (☎ 305-030 323-1078).

South Africa

A reasonably easy-to-get discounted flight from Johannesburg to Miami would be approximately R5000/5800 in low/high season.

STA Travel (☎ 011-447-5551) has offices all over the country. Seriously helpful is the Jo'burg Student Union Building Branch at Wits University (☎ 011-716-3045).

Rennies Travel has a comprehensive network of agencies throughout South Africa. Its head office is in Johannesburg on the 11th floor of Safren House, 19 Ameshoff St, Braamfontein, Johannesburg (☎ 27-011-407-3211, fax 27-011-339-1247, rennies.internet@travel.rennies.co.za).

Asia

Hong Kong is the discount plane ticket capital of the region, but its bucket shops can be unreliable. Ask other travelers for advice before buying a ticket. STA Travel, which is dependable, has branches in Hong Kong, Tokyo, Singapore, Bangkok and Kuala Lumpur. Many if not most flights to the USA go via Honolulu, Hawaii.

United Airlines has three flights a day to Honolulu from Tokyo with connections to West Coast cities, where you can connect to Miami. Northwest and Japan Airlines also have daily flights to the USA's West Coast from Tokyo, and Northwest serves Dallas/Fort Worth (DFW) via Detroit. Japan Airlines also flies to Honolulu from Osaka, Nagoya, Fukuoka and Sapporo.

Central & South America

Miami is the main US/Latin American gateway, and Miami International Airport is served by all kinds of airlines. Deals are sometimes incredible – like $199 roundtrip to/from Caracas, which has been offered several times in the last couple of years.

Check with discount brokers in Latin America for the best deals, which come and go quickly. Generally speaking, the highest roundtrip tickets are $300 to $450 from San Jose, Costa Rica, $450 from Managua, Nicaragua and Guatemala City, Guatemala.

From Brazil, economy fares must often be purchased two weeks in advance and minimum stay restrictions apply. Varig offers a return ticket to Miami from Rio for around $850. Some of the cheapest flights from Brazil to Miami are charters from Manaus, which lies halfway between Rio and Miami. Air Bolivia also has a Miami-Manaus service for around $800.

From Caracas, Venezuela, count on prices of around $200 to $300 in June, $250 to $300 in January.

Baggage & Other Restrictions

On most domestic and international flights, you are limited to two checked bags, or three if you don't have carry-on luggage. There may be a charge if you bring more or if the size of the bags exceeds the airline's limits. On some international flights, the luggage allowance is based on weight, not number. Check with the individual airlines.

If your luggage is delayed upon arrival (which is rare), some airlines will give you a cash advance to purchase necessities. If sporting equipment is misplaced, the airline may pay for rentals. Should the luggage be lost, it is important to submit a claim. The airline doesn't have to pay the full amount of the claim; rather, they can estimate the value of your lost items. It may take them anywhere from six weeks to three months to process the claim and pay you.

Smoking You cannot smoke on any domestic flight within the USA. Many international flights are following suit. (Incidentally, the restriction applies to the passenger cabin and the lavatories but not the cockpit.) Most airports in Florida, and many in the USA, prohibit smoking (it's still allowed in Orlando's airport, however).

True smokers might consider joining a frequent flyer lounge (about $200 a year), which provide a place to smoke, even in airports that ban it. Other perks are free soft drinks, snacks, newspapers and magazines, TV and telephone/fax access and cheap alcoholic drinks.

Illegal Items The following items are illegal to take on a plane, either checked or as carry-on: aerosols of polishes, waxes, and so on; tear gas and pepper spray; camp stoves with fuel; and full divers' tanks. Matches should not be checked.

Arriving in the USA

Even if you are continuing immediately to another city, the first airport you land in is where you must carry out immigration and customs formalities. For example, if you're on a connecting flight from London to Orlando via Miami, you still have to take your bags through customs in Miami.

Passengers aboard the airplane are given standard immigration and customs forms to fill out. The cabin crew will help you fill them out if you have any questions, but the forms are straightforward. After the plane lands, you'll first go through immigration. There are two lines: one for US citizens and residents and the other for nonresidents. Immigration formalities are usually basic if you have all the necessary documents (passport and visa). Occasionally, you may be asked to show your ticket out of the country, but this doesn't happen very often.

After passing through immigration, you collect your baggage and then pass through customs. If you have nothing to declare, there is a good chance you can clear customs quickly and without a luggage search, but you can't rely on it. After passing through customs, you are officially in the country. If your flight is continuing to another city or you have a connecting flight, it is your responsibility to get your bags to the right place. Normally, there are airline counters just outside the customs area that will help you. Also see Customs & Immigration in the Facts for the Visitor chapter.

Leaving the USA

You should check in two hours early for international flights. All passengers will need to present photo identification on check-in.

During check-in procedures, you will be asked questions about whether you have packed your own bags, whether anyone else has had access to them since you packed them and whether you have received any parcels to carry. These questions are for security reasons.

LAND

Most travelers not arriving by air come by bus or private vehicle. Train is a little-used option.

Bus

Greyhound (☎ 800-231-2222, www.greyhound .com) is the main bus system in the USA, and it plays an important transportation role in Florida. As the only scheduled statewide bus service, Greyhound is the carless traveler's best friend, serving all major cities and many smaller ones. But bus travel can often be tiring, inconvenient and expensive, so look at all your options.

Greyhound serves places along its main routes only, and getting to places off those routes is impossible without a car. Buses tend to run infrequently and schedules are often inconvenient. Fares are relatively high: bargain air fares can undercut buses on long-distance routes; on shorter routes, renting a car can be cheaper. However, long-distance bus trips are often available at bargain prices by purchasing or reserving tickets three to seven days in advance. Then, once you've arrived at your far-flung destination, you can rent a car to get around.

Bus travel, of course, gives you the chance to see some of the countryside that travelers by air or private car might miss. Then again, bus travel can subject you to conversation with some of the inhabitants that travelers by air or private car might miss – perhaps a mixed blessing. Also, Greyhound stations are generally very sleazy places; solo travelers may feel uncomfortable in them. For these reasons, traveling by car is definitely recommended, if it's at all possible. However, in the text we give details of major bus routes in case you have the time or inclination to see the Greyhound side of travel.

Greyhound makes meal stops on long trips; you pay for your own simple food in inexpensive and unexciting cafés. Buses have on-board lavatories. Seats recline, ostensibly for sleeping, but a couple of days in a Greyhound seat is a memorable experience. Smoking is not permitted aboard buses.

In an effort to boost sagging ticket sales, Greyhound offers a series of incentive fares to a variety of locations around the country. These change frequently; as we went to press they had a $69-to-anywhere fare. Regular published Greyhound fares from Miami to some other major US destinations include the following:

destination	frequency	duration	price
Atlanta	10 per day	16-18 hrs	$79/146
New Orleans	6 per day	20 hrs	$69/132
New York City	8 per day	28 hrs	$89/139
Washington, DC	4 per day	23-24 hrs	$79/129

Note that these travel times can vary dramatically depending on the time of day you leave, the route you take and other factors. For example, the New York run can be as short as 23 hours.

AmeriPass AmeriPass is an unlimited travel pass available to anyone (not just non-US residents). It's available in seven-day ($199), 15-day ($299), 30-day ($409) and 60-day ($599) time periods, and unless you're going to be doing a whole lot of travel, it's probably not worth it.

Train

Amtrak (☎ 800-872-7245, www.amtrak.com) has been, since 1971, the US national railway system. It connects Florida with cities all over the continental USA and Canada, and two main routes serve Florida – the Silver Service from New York and the *Sunset Limited* train from Los Angeles.

The pricing structure is hugely complex and based on the date you're traveling – the date, not just the time of year, as the prices can change radically from one day to the next. You should always ask Amtrak if you can get a better deal by leaving a couple of days later or earlier. But generally speaking, in the winter months it's cheaper to go northbound and more expensive to travel southbound, and vice versa in spring. The cheapest period is usually summer.

On all Amtrak trains, each adult can bring one or two children ages two to 15 at half price. Seniors 62 and over get a 15% discount on tickets. There are two types of seating: airline-style seats and cabins. Cabins come in four flavors: single, double, family (sleeping two adults and two children under 12) and 1st-class singles or doubles (which include all meal service). Cabins always require a surcharge, and the surcharge changes depending on the date you're traveling.

Routes If you're coming to Florida by train from anywhere except Los Angeles, you will at some point have to connect with Amtrak's Silver Service: the *SilverMeteor* and *SilverStar* trains that run between New York City and Miami and Tampa.

The *SilverMeteor* runs directly to Miami via Orlando; the *SilverStar* splits after Orlando: half the train's cars head to Miami and the other to Tampa. Travel time from New York City to Miami is 27 hours, to Orlando 22 hours, to Tampa 28 hours. You can pick up the Silver Service at any spot on the route, which has stops in Washington, DC, Virginia, North Carolina, South Carolina, Georgia and Florida. The *SilverStar* leaves New York City's Penn Station at 10:10 am daily, the *SilverMeteor* at 4:05 pm.

The cheapest time to take the Silver Service is between April 1 and mid-June. Winter is the most expensive time to go.

On the route from Los Angeles, the *Sunset Limited* train runs three times a week (currently on Sunday, Tuesday and Friday), passing through Phoenix, Tucson and El Paso to New Orleans and across the Panhandle to Florida's east coast, where it turns south to Miami. Prices and peak times on this route differ from the Silver Service run, and depending on availability, a

roundtrip ticket on this route can cost less – sometimes significantly – than a one-way ticket. The peak season is July to December.

The other option is the *AutoTrain*, which runs between Lorton, Virginia (near Washington, DC) to Sanford, Florida (near Orlando). The trains leave both stations at 4:30 pm daily, arriving the following morning at 9 am.

On the *AutoTrain,* you pay for your passage, your cabin and your car separately.

Explore USA Tickets Some specials allow you to make Miami a stopover. The peak season is from June 17 to August 18. At the time of writing, a 30-day Explore USA ticket for the entire eastern portion of the USA was $158 off-peak and $208 in peak season, including unlimited (but scheduled) stopovers. But this is not a rail pass; it's a glorified roundtrip ticket, and you have to know exact dates and stops before you buy the ticket. Call Amtrak for more information.

Car & Motorcycle
Florida is served by three main interstate highways that connect it with Florida and the west: I-95 is the main East Coast interstate, extending from Miami to Maine; I-10 extends from Jacksonville west across the South all the way to Los Angeles; I-75 runs west from Miami across Alligator Alley and then north to Michigan.

Hitchhiking
Hitchhiking in the USA is dangerous, and it's therefore less common than in other countries. Lonely Planet, its attorneys, owners, management, editors, employees, successors and chattel (authors) do not recommend hitchhiking. And in Florida, chances are you won't get a lift anyway – odds of catching a lift here are as bad as in France. That said, if you do choose to hitch, the advice that follows should help to make your journey as fast, if not as safe, as possible.

Officially, hitching is not illegal, except on interstate highways, but it *is* frowned upon

A Free Car

Want a free car? Try Auto Driveaway of San Francisco (☎ 415-777-3740) or New York (☎ 212-967-2344). People who want their car moved from city A to city B leave the car with this organization and as long as you're willing to drive there at an average speed of 400 miles per day and pay for the gas (the first tank's free), the car's yours. To qualify, drivers (not passengers) must be 21 years old, have a valid driver's license and one other form of ID. Non-US citizens can use an international driver's license but must show a valid entry visa and passport as well. Auto Driveaway requires a $300 to $350 refundable cash or traveler's check deposit and a $10 nonrefundable registration fee.

by law enforcement, and you can expect to be hassled by them if they see you. As signs at the on-ramps will tell you, pedestrians are not allowed on major highways, so keep off the on-ramps and away from these signs. It helps to look neat and carry a neatly printed sign with your destination. Lots of baggage, two or more men, or groups of three of any sex slow you down substantially. Women should think very carefully about hitching – especially if alone, but even in groups. Let friends or family know where you're planning to go. (See Getting Around for more on hitchhiking.)

SEA

There are very few ways to hop aboard a tramp steamer these days. If you can get yourself to Fort Lauderdale, America's largest transatlantic yacht harbor, you may get your chance.

Yacht

Every year, hundreds of captains look for crew – professional or unpaid – to help them get their boats from here to wherever they're going. In May to June, they're taking them to Europe; in summer they're heading to New England, the Mediterranean and, less frequently but gaining in popularity, the West Coast of the USA and Alaska. At other times, boats could be heading just about anywhere. Boats leave for South American, Asian and Australasian destinations year round. Best of all, it's legal for foreigners to work on a boat that is leaving the USA.

Boats also leave from other marinas and ports, of course; check locally for more information.

Getting a slot on a boat is a very interesting way to get yourself transport and perhaps even some spending money for your destination. Many people have been getting around the world like this for years and don't see any reason to stop. Don't get it wrong – it's hard and serious work that requires concentration, dedication, common sense and the ability to work and live with others in close quarters. Those who do it say they wouldn't do anything else.

An experienced hand can pick up work at any time of the year within a week or two. In winter, the jobs go to the more experienced workers, but there's plenty of work for everyone. Inexperienced hands looking for volunteer work will also hook up in a week or two. Floyd from Floyd's Crew House (see below) says that consistently about 95% of those coming for work get it if they're serious.

Crew Information Sailing magazines are a good place to get an idea of trends and conditions. Try *Showboats*, *Cruising World* and *Sail* magazines, which run ads and classifieds. Blue Seas International runs the best job Website for crew anywhere (www.jobxchange.com/crewxchange), with postings on every type of vessel.

Crew placement agencies are located all over Fort Lauderdale, and they will, for a fee, match up crew and boat owners.

The best sources for information are crew houses in Fort Lauderdale, such as Floyd's Crew House (☎ 954-462-0631), essentially guesthouses populated primarily by people looking for work. Boat owners call crew houses when they have something up.

Agencies The premiere unofficial crew agency in Fort Lauderdale is the three-ring notebook at Smallwood's Yachtware (☎ 954-523-2282), 1001 SE 17th St at 10th Ave. Owners come here and write what their requirements are and wait for crew to get in touch. It's open Monday to Friday 7:30 am to 5:30 pm, Saturday 9 am to 3 pm, closed Sunday.

Official agencies charge between $25 and $35 for a listing. In Fort Lauderdale, agencies include Crew Unlimited (☎ 954-462-4624) at 2065 S Federal Hwy, Crew Finders (☎ 954-522-2739) at 4040 SE 17th St, the very friendly Hassel Free (☎ 954-763-1841) at 1635 S Miami Rd No 8, and Worldwide Yachting (☎ 954-467-9777) at 1053 SE 17th St.

Women on Crews The crew world is a tight one, and both Floyd at Floyd's Crew House and management at Smallwood's say they have not in many years heard of a woman being the subject of unwanted advances from boat owners. But as with all jobs, it's a possibility. Floyd says that most people can tell on the first interview the type of services the owner is going to want, and that it will become clear very quickly if services will include the personal kind. Interview carefully and ask around about the owner before taking on an assignment.

What to Bring Bring as little as possible – everything you'll need will be provided, except a toothbrush, toothpaste and a hairbrush. You'll of course need travel documents and, if necessary, visas for your destination country.

ORGANIZED TOURS

Tours of the USA are so numerous that it would be impossible to include a comprehensive listing here. For overseas visitors, the most reliable sources of information on the constantly changing offerings are major international travel agents such as Thomas Cook and American Express. Probably those of most interest to the general traveler are coach tours that visit the national parks and guest-ranch excursions. For those who have limited time, package tours can be an efficient and relatively inexpensive way to travel.

Trek America (☎ 973-983-1144, 800-221-0596, fax 973-983-8551, www.trekamerica .com), PO Box 189, Rockaway, NJ 07866, offers roundtrip camping tours to different areas of the country. In England, Trek America (☎ 01295-256-777, fax 01295-257-399) is at 4 Water Perry Court, Middleton Rd, Banbury, Oxon OX16 8QG. In Australia, contact Adventure World (☎ 9955-5000, fax 9954-5817), 75 Walker St, North Sydney, NSW 2060. These tours last from one to nine weeks and are designed for small, international groups (13 people maximum) of 18- to 38-year-olds. Tour prices vary with season, with July to September being the highest. Tours cost about $606 for a 10-day tour to $2570 for a nine-week tour of the entire country. Some side trips and cultural events are included in the price, and participants help with cooking and camp chores.

Similar deals are available from Suntrek (☎ 707-523-1800, 800-292-9696, fax 707-523-1911), Sun Plaza, 77 West Third St, Santa Rosa, CA 95401. Suntrek also has offices in Germany (☎ 089-480-28-31, fax 089-480-24-11), Sedanstrasse 21, 81667 Munich, and in Switzerland (☎ 01-387-78-78, fax 01-387-78-00), Bellerivestrasse 11, CH-8034, Zurich. Suntrek's tours are for the 'young at heart' and attract predominantly young international travelers, although there is no age limit. Prices range from a one-week trip, starting at $500 without flight or food but with ground transport, some activities and hotels, all the way up to around $5000 for its 13-week Around America treks – the latter is the highest price in the highest season.

Road Runner USA/Canada (☎ 800-873-5872), 1050 Hancock, Quincy, MA 02169, organizes one- and two-week treks. Planned in conjunction with Hostelling International, these treks take you to different parts of the USA and across the country. It also has offices in England (☎ 0892-512-700), at 64 Mt Pleasant Ave, Tunbridge Wells, Kent TN1 1QY. Prices run $449 for one week to $849 for two weeks.

AmeriCan Adventures (☎ 800-864-0335) offers seven- to 21-day trips to different parts of the USA, usually following a theme like Route 66 or Wild West. Prices range from $450 for seven days to $1200 for 21 days.

Specialized Tours

Elderhostel (☎ 617-426-8056), 75 Federal St, Boston, MA 02110, is a nonprofit organization offering educational programs for those 60 and above, and has programs throughout the USA.

Bicycling, hiking and walking, cross-country skiing, running and multisport tours are another possibility, with companies like Backroads (☎ 510-527-1555, 800-462-2848), 801 Cedar St, Berkeley, CA 94710.

Getting Around

AIR

Flying within Florida is convenient if you're trying to save time (it's more than 600 miles from Miami to Pensacola, so time is definitely a factor), but the cost is usually higher than that of driving. Most airlines that operate in Florida fly small commuter planes, so expect propellers!

There is service between all major cities in Florida. See individual city sections for specific information on routes and prices. The following are the main airlines operating within the state:

American Airlines	☎ 800-433-7300
Delta Air Lines	☎ 800-221-1212
Continental Airlines	☎ 800-525-0280
US Airways	☎ 800-428-4322
Northwest Airlines	☎ 800-225-2525
American Trans Air	☎ 800-435-9282
Air South	☎ 800-247-7688
Gulfstream International Airlines	☎ 800-992-8532

Charter Flights

You can charter a private flight at almost any airport in the state. Rates are negotiable, but count on $100 an hour flying time in small planes, up to $800 an hour in a King Air, and remember you have to pay the pilot for the return flight, not just for your one-way trip. In this book we list the airport telephone numbers for the major cities; in smaller cities, check in the blue section of the telephone directory under Municipal Airport or City Airport, or just drive out there and speak to the pilots.

BUS

Greyhound (☎ 800-231-2222, 01342-317-317 Greyhound International in the UK, www.greyhound.com) offers bus service between all major Florida cities. Individual city sections within this book often include the telephone number and address of the local Greyhound depot. For specific route and fare information, call Greyhound. The

following are some fares (one way/round-trip) and travel times between Miami and other Florida cities.

destination	duration	price
Cocoa Beach	5$\frac{1}{2}$ to 9$\frac{1}{4}$ hours	$39/78
Daytona Beach	6 to 7 hours	$29/56
Fort Lauderdale	$\frac{1}{2}$ hour to 1 hour	$5/8
Jacksonville	7 to 10 hours	$41/81
Orlando	5 to 11 hours	$32/63
St Augustine	7 to 9 hours	$41/81
Tampa	7 to 8 hours	$36/59
West Palm Beach	2 hours	$7/11

TRAIN
Amtrak

You can use Amtrak (☎ 800-272-7245, www .amtrak.com) for intra-Florida transport if you're heading to a destination on its routes (except between Miami and Palm Beach, which is covered by Tri-Rail – see below), but it's an expensive way to get around and you might actually do better to take a bus or perhaps fly. Special discount fares (which are offered only on a space-available basis) usually cost the same one way and roundtrip. And for destinations that require Amtrak connecting bus service, such as Daytona, Tampa, Clearwater and St Petersburg, the cost of the bus can be higher than a local taxi.

There are two trains a day on the Silver Service line from Miami up Florida's east coast, and on Sunday, Tuesday and Friday there's a third – the *Sunset Limited* – which heads up Florida's east coast and cuts west from Jacksonville.

Tri-Rail

A commuter rail system, Tri-Rail (☎ 954-728-8445, 800-874-7245 within Florida, TDD 800-273-7545) runs between three Florida counties: Dade, Broward and Palm Beach. The double-decker trains are a marvel of cleanliness and, at least for the time being, they're very cheap. However, for longer

Tri-Rail Rent-A-Cops

Europeans on Tri-Rail might be pleasantly reminded of home. As you wait for the train, you buy your ticket from Swiss-made ticket machines (the same ones used in U-Bahn stations throughout Germany). And when you board, it looks much the same as in Europe – basically it's the honor system, but if an inspector comes around and asks for your ticket and you don't have one, you're hit with a fine.

The key difference between Tri-Rail and metros in Europe is the ticket inspectors come around each and every time, and they're armed and provided hearts of stone by the Wackenhut Company, which hires them.

As you may suspect, I was hit with a ticket last time. I even had a tie on. But I really made an honest mistake – I accidentally pushed the button for a discount fare as opposed to a normal one. The amount of the discount was trifling, but when the Terminator asked for my ticket, she listened to neither rhyme nor reason nor pleas for mercy nor, finally, insults. ('This sucks,' I said. 'It's unfair. You know I made an honest mistake, and I think you're a mindless automaton with an inferiority complex.') She remained impassive.

The ticket was $50. Don't mess with Tri-Rail.

– Nick Selby

trips (such as to Palm Beach), it will take you about four times longer to take Tri-Rail than to drive.

Fares are calculated on a six-zone basis. Ticket costs are the following: $2/3.50 one way/roundtrip for one zone; $3/5 for two zones; $4/6.75 for three zones; $4.50/7.75 for four zones; $5/8.50 for five zones; and $5.50/9.25 for six zones . So the most you'll ever pay is for the ride between Miami International Airport and West Palm Beach, which is $5.50 one way, $9.25 roundtrip.

A transfer from Tri-Rail to Metrorail is free. From Metrobus, buy a 25¢ Tri-Rail transfer from the bus driver, and then trade the transfer at the Tri-Rail ticket booth for a $1.50 discount on your Tri-Rail ticket.

The new Tri-Rail station at Miami International Airport is now open. It's a one-zone ticket to ride Tri-Rail north to Metrorail, and Metrorail to downtown Miami.

The main connection between Miami city transportation and Tri-Rail is at the Tri-Rail/Metrorail Transfer Station, northwest of downtown at 2567 E 11th Ave, Hialeah.

Tri-Rail does some very neat marketing tricks; as we went to press, it was offering 'guided' tours from Miami to (on Monday) Lake Worth, and (on Thursday) Worth Ave in Palm Beach. The roundtrip cost is $3, including all bus transfers. A 'guide' rides with the group on the train, which leaves the Tri-Rail/Metrorail Transfer Station at 9:03 am, and answers questions about the destination. You get on a shuttle bus at the far end, which takes you to the destination and brings you back to the train about 2½ to three hours later.

There are Tri-Rail stations at the following: Miami Airport, Tri-Rail/Metrorail Transfer, Golden Glades, Hollywood, Fort Lauderdale Airport, Fort Lauderdale, Cypress Creek, Pompano Beach, Deerfield Beach, Boca Raton, Delray Beach, Boynton Beach, Lake Worth, Palm Beach Airport (actually West Palm International) and West Palm Beach.

CAR & MOTORCYCLE

By far the most convenient and popular way to get around Florida is by car – in fact, in many cities it's nearly impossible to get by without one. Even if you're in a small town like St Augustine, getting to a supermarket will undoubtedly require a car or an expensive taxi. Motorcycles are very popular in Florida, and with the exception of the rain in the summer, conditions are perfect: good flat roads and warm weather.

Overseas visitors: Unless you're coming here from Saudi Arabia or Indonesia, American gasoline prices are a gift from heaven. But remember to always use self-service gas pumps, as full-service ones cost 25¢ to 50¢ more per gallon.

Road Rules

Americans drive on the right (and yes, that also means *correct*) side of the road and pass on the left. Right turns on a red light are permitted after a full stop. At four-way stop signs, the car to your right has the right-of-way. Flashing yellow lights mean caution; flashing red lights are stop signs. Speed limits in the city are between 15 and 45 mph. Be especially careful in school zones, which are limited to 15 mph when the lights are flashing, and on causeways, which – no matter how fast cars actually travel – are limited to no more than 45 mph. Speeding tickets are outrageous: for example, if you're clocked at 50 mph in a 40-mph zone, the fine is about $127. Radar detectors are legal in Florida (hint nudge wink).

Florida police officers are merciless when it comes to speed-limit enforcement; see Legal Matters in the Facts for the Visitor chapter for more information on speed limits and what to do if you're pulled over.

All passengers in a car must wear seatbelts; the fine for not wearing a seatbelt can be as high as $150. All children under three must be in a child safety seat (the rental-car companies will rent you one for about $5 a day).

Parking

Always park in the shade if possible, and it may pay to invest in a windshield shade – even a cardboard one – to filter sunlight. Cars heat up to an unbelievable temperature very quickly.

Outside cities, park wherever you want, within reason. Parking in designated handicapped parking spaces or in front of a fire station, fire hydrant, taxi stand or police station is always illegal and your car may be towed. Believe it or not, in many cases it's also illegal to park in front of a church.

In cities, parking is often a challenge, especially in places like Miami, Miami Beach, Coral Gables, St Augustine, Ybor City in Tampa and Key West. In those places, look for metered parking or, if none is available, city or private parking lots. In city lots, parking is generally about 75¢ an hour; private lots can charge a lot more, especially during special events.

Valet parking is available at many finer restaurants and in front of hotels in Miami Beach and in Miami. It's usually at least $10.

There's always free parking in supermarkets and shopping malls, and parking is usually available for a small (about $2 to $5) fee at stadiums and theme parks.

Floridians are generally careful about not knocking over bikes parked on the street,

The US Highway System

There are five main categories of roads in Florida: Interstate highways are usually high-speed, multilane roads that cross several states; odd-numbered roads generally go north-south; even-numbered ones generally go east-west (in this book interstates are abbreviated as, for example, I-95 or I-4). US highways are smaller roads that nonetheless cross several states; they are lined with businesses and have stoplights (and are abbreviated in this book as, for example, US Hwy 1). State roads are about the same size as US highways, and county roads are smaller still (both are abbreviated simply as Hwy, such as Hwy 84). Finally, there are city streets.

Most roads in Florida are excellent for driving, motorcycling, bicycling or even in-line skating: flat, smooth, well maintained and well signed.

Note that bicyclists and wheelchair-bound travelers using the roads will often become angry at the distinct lack of shoulders on the roads.

Long Drive? Kinsey Milhone to the Rescue

On long drives, and there are lots of those in Florida, one of the best ways to pass the time once the conversation's all used up is listening to – believe it or not – books on tape. Almost all best-selling books are also released on tape, read by actors or sometimes even the authors themselves. We love mystery and suspense novels, such as Sue Grafton's Kinsey Milhone mysteries, for longer voyages. Books on tape generally run from two to five hours and take up four to six standard tape cassettes.

Cracker Barrel (sort of) rents books on tape, and the service is great. While it doesn't technically *rent* them, it does sell them – for about $40. When you return the tape – to any Cracker Barrel in the USA – it refunds your money minus a $2 per week per tape 'service fee.' Wink wink.

Cracker Barrel is a national chain of restaurants and 'general stores,' usually just off a major interstate highway: homey, hokey re-creations of old Western supply houses that have awful gravy and lots of candy, knick-knacks and Americana.

In Florida, Cracker Barrel has restaurants in Gainesville, Daytona Beach, Fort Myers, Fort Pierce, Kissimmee, Ocala, Orange Park, Orlando, Palm Coast, Pensacola, Stuart, Tallahassee and West Palm Beach.

but there aren't many motorcycle-only parking lots.

Towing

If your car is towed by the police, call the nearest police station and ask them which towing company they use. The tow will cost at least $50 plus the cost of the ticket to unimpound your car. It's not fun, and the location of the towing contractor is seldom convenient.

Theft

Car theft is a popular sport in Miami and throughout South Florida, where boats to the Caribbean are waiting to ship your car off to somewhere other than your garage. If you own a car, it may pay to invest in an antitheft device like the Club. But note that in Miami some car thieves have found a simple yet effective method of getting around the Club: they hacksaw through your steering wheel.

Obviously, don't tempt thieves by leaving your keys in the car or your doors unlocked, and remove valuables from plain sight before leaving your vehicle.

So if, despite all precautions, you come back and find your car gone, call the police on a nonemergency number to see if they had it towed. If it turns out your car was stolen, immediately call ☎ 911 and report the theft.

Breakdown

Most rental cars are covered for breakdown; see your rental agreement for a toll-free breakdown number. Depending on the company, someone will come rescue you soon or next to soon. If they can't get to you until the next day, ask if your motel costs can be covered. Even if they say no, keep the receipts for motel and food while you wait, and take the matter up with a manager when you return the car. You may get reimbursed, or at the very least get a coupon for a free rental next time.

If you break down in a privately owned vehicle, check in the yellow pages under Towing. If you're out on the road, get to a pay phone, call ☎ 411 for directory assistance and ask them for a towing company – if they argue with you and say they can't, ask for a supervisor and explain your situation.

They'll usually look up a company in the yellow pages for you. AAA members can call ☎ 800-222-4357, and a tow truck will be sent out quickly.

It may pay to rent or buy a cellular telephone, especially if you'll be traveling to remote areas. Most rental-car agencies rent phones for about $3 a day plus expensive air time (about $1.50 a minute).

Car Rental

All major car-rental companies in the USA have offices throughout Florida. Rates go up and down like the stock market, and it's always worth phoning around to see what's available. Booking ahead usually ensures the best rates – and booking ahead can mean calling the company's 800 number from the pay phone in the rental office. (Sometimes the head office can get you a better price than the branch office.) If you're a member of a frequent-flyer club, be sure to check whether the rental company has a deal with your airline.

Major car-rental companies in Florida include the following:

Alamo	☎ 800-327-9633
Avis	☎ 800-831-2847
Budget	☎ 800-527-0700
Dollar	☎ 800-800-4000
Enterprise	☎ 800-325-8007
Hertz	☎ 800-654-3131
Thrifty	☎ 800-367-2277

Rates In Florida, typically a small car costs $25 to $45 a day or $129 to $179 a week. On top of that there is a 6% state sales tax, $2.05 per day Florida road surcharge and $9 to $15 a day for each insurance option you take – plus local taxes. The Clay Hostel in Miami Beach has a special deal with Alamo; a discounted car is about $20 a day.

Generally speaking, the best deals come on weekly or weekend rental periods. At the time of writing, the lowest rates consistently seem to come from companies like Alamo, Budget, Enterprise and Value, and the highest from Avis and Hertz, though there are

always specials, and your best bet is to shop around carefully. The same car can vary in price from company to company by as much as $20 a day or $75 a week. Note, though, that Avis has more offices than any other company in Florida, and usually does not impose drop-off charges within the state; we have picked up cars in Pensacola and dropped them off in Tampa or Jacksonville or Miami at no extra charge. If you're planning on dropping off at a different location than the one you picked up from, make certain there won't be any penalty.

Most car-rental companies in Florida include unlimited mileage at no extra cost. Be sure to check whether you get unlimited mileage, as you can rack up hundreds of

---

Fill 'Er Up?

When you rent a car, the agent will no doubt cheerfully inquire whether you'd like to buy the fuel from them at a 'special discounted rate,' usually a few cents per gallon below street prices. Isn't that nice? They're so keen to provide this service because the amount of gas left in the tank when you return a rental car is a crucial profit center for car-rental companies. Unless you're the kind of person who can calculate *exactly* how far a tank will get you in a car you're not used to, and can run on fumes all the way back to the airport, this is a bad idea: there are no refunds on unused fuel.

If you bring the car back with the tank half full, congratulations: you've just paid *twice* the going street rate for gas.

If you don't buy gas from them, be certain to return the car with a full tank of fuel. If you let the company refill the car for you, the price is outrageous – generally $2.99 but sometimes as much as $3.99 a gallon. And, of course, filling stations near rental-car places are few and far between.

miles just in the city, and at 25¢ per mile, this could be an unhappy surprise.

Insurance Note that in Florida, liability insurance is not included in rental costs. Some credit cards cover Loss/Damage-Waiver (LDW, sometimes called CDW, or Collision/Damage Waiver), which means you won't have to pay if you damage the car itself. But liability insurance means you won't have to pay if you hit someone and they sue you. If you own a car and have insurance at home, your liability insurance may extend to coverage of rental cars, but be *absolutely* certain before driving on the roads in the litigious USA. If you aren't already covered, you should pay the extra money for liability and/or LDW insurance.

Motorcycle Rental

American Road Collection, 3970 NW 25th St in Miami (☎ 305-871-1040) and 3255 SE 6th Ave in Fort Lauderdale (☎ 954-561-1983), rents motorcycles. Its fleet includes many Harley-Davidsons, including White Glide, Fat Boy, Heritage Softtail, Road King and Road King Classic. Prices run from $109 to $189 a day depending on the day of the week (weekends are more expensive) and model. It also does multiday, weekly and monthly rates – for example, a Heritage Softtail runs approximately $1600 a month.

CruiseAmerica (☎ 800-327-7799) has several Florida locations and rents Honda and Harley-Davidson motorcycles from $69 to $109 per day, including unlimited mileage. It does not rent helmets (there's a helmet law in Florida). Renters must be over 21, have a valid motorcycle license and a credit card. CDW and liability insurance are each $12 per day.

RV Rental

Renting a recreational vehicle (RV) can make sense if you meet one of two conditions: a) you're as rich as Croesus or b) there are several of you. An RV can be a great way to get out into Florida. They're surprisingly roomy and flexible, and even the smaller ones can sleep four comfortably – as long as you're all close friends. If you're not, don't despair: many RV campsites are large enough to accommodate the RV and still leave room for a tent outside.

The downside is you'll need transport when you get where you're going – at an average highway gas consumption of between 8 and 10 miles per gallon, RVs are not exactly a good method of city transport. You can, of course, get a bicycle rack or, if you also have a car, a tow-hitch to bring that along, but note that it makes your already dismal gas mileage even worse.

CruiseAmerica (☎ 800-327-7799) is the largest and best known of the nationwide RV-rental firms. It has a huge variety of rentals available. The smallest – 22 to 24 feet with two double beds and a dinette that converts to a single bed, a bathroom with shower and a full kitchen – cost $804 a week in low season (from April to June and from August to mid-December) and $1032 in high season, including insurance and an electrical generator. A thousand miles are included; after that you're billed 29¢ a mile.

The Recreational Vehicle Rental Association (☎ 703-591-7130, 800-336-0355) publishes *Who's Who in RV Rentals*, a directory of rental agencies around the USA, Canada and Europe for $7.50, and *Rental Ventures*, which lists campgrounds that accommodate RVs ($3, or $2.50 when purchased with the directory). You can order by telephone, or send a check (payable to RVRA) for the purchase price of the publications you are looking for to RVRA, at

Age & Credit Requirements

Most car-rental agencies require that you be at least 25 years of age and have a major credit card in your own name. Some will let you compensate for the age thing by paying outrageous surcharges. But Jason Brome wrote from England to tell us he rented from Rent-A-Wreck in West Palm Beach, which let him get away with being under 25 for a mere $10 extra per day.

We called Rent-A-Wreck (☎ 561-802-4390 in West Palm Beach, 800-535-1391) and sure enough, that office will rent to people between the ages of 21 and 25 for an additional $10 a day. Jason said the price for the car was the same as everywhere else and that the car he got wasn't even a wreck but rather a new Dodge Neon with 4000 miles on the clock. (Rent-A-Wreck has offices throughout the USA, but each office individually sets its age policy.)

Renting without a credit card – if you can even accomplish it – will require a large cash deposit, and you'll have to work things out well in advance with the rental company. It's hard to do, and even if they let you rent without a credit card, you will be treated with great suspicion!

3930 University Drive, Suite 100, Fairfax, Virginia 22030.

Car & Motorcycle Purchase

One way to beat the high cost of renting a car is to buy a used vehicle on arrival and then sell it when you leave. If you go this route, it helps to either have a bit of the auto mechanic in you or to find a mechanic you can trust; you won't get much return value on a 'lemon' or a gas guzzler. Don't ask yourself, 'Do I feel lucky?' because even minor repairs could cost well over $100.

Any used-car owner who won't bring or let you take the car to a mechanic is hiding something. While you're there, tell the mechanic how much the seller wants for it, and if things look good, ask them to run an emissions test – it's no good finding out after you've bought it that the car won't pass state emissions levels. As a general idea of how much you'll spend on that, Shorty & Fred's Garage (☎ 305-672-1047) in Miami will check out a car for $48 and run an emissions test for $39.95.

Once you've bought the car, you must buy a rather costly auto insurance policy (generally $500 to $800 a year, depending on your age and driving record) and take the smog certificate and proof of insurance, along with the ownership title and bill of sale, to any office of the Department of Motor Vehicles (DMV). For full listings, check in the blue government section of the white pages under Florida State Department of Highway and Motor Vehicles.

It normally takes a full morning or afternoon to get your auto registration, waiting to speak with staff who, as one comedian put it, 'look as if they were raised in the trunk of a Buick.' Registration costs anywhere from 7 to 12% of the cost of the car.

As your departure from the USA approaches, you must set aside time to sell the car, which could require laying out additional money to place a classified ad in a newspaper.

If you don't object to a little wind, you might consider buying a motorcycle, which is cheaper than a car and tends to be easier to sell. But note that a) motorcycle insurance costs more, b) Nick's mother says motorcycles are too dangerous and c) helmets for yourself and any passengers are required by Florida law, which is strictly enforced.

BICYCLE

If you can stand the heat, Florida's not a bad place for cycling. Absolutely flat roads make it easy going, and biking is a convenient mode of transportation. Helmets are not required under Florida law, but they're a good idea, as are highly reflective everything-you-can-think-of. Florida drivers are not used to seeing bicyclists, and the more you can do to inform cars of your presence, the better chance you have of getting where you're going.

If you do get tired of biking, you can pack your bike. Most international airlines, and all flights within Florida, allow you to bring a bike at no extra charge as check-in luggage. They charge a fee (about $50) if it's in addition to your carry-on limit. Bike boxes usually cost $10 to $15 if you buy them from an airline, Greyhound or Amtrak. You'll have to remove the handlebars and pedals to box it, but you may also get away with bagging it. Greyhound and Amtrak charge $10 extra for your boxed bike, and Amtrak takes them only on trains that have baggage cars.

Many cities in Florida have outlets for bicycle rentals – at hostels, hotels, resorts or bike shops. Sports Authority, Sears, K-Mart, Wal-Mart and Lauderdale Sports all carry bicycle parts, so if you're in a town without a bike shop, there's still reason to hope.

Bicyclists are charged $1 each for admission to most state parks.

Especially in Miami Beach, where everyone we know (including us) has had a bicycle stolen, make certain to lock your bike. If you can remove the front tire and take it with you, do so. Also remove the seat if it has a quick-release height adjust. Use a sturdy U-type lock, not a chain and padlock.

Organizations

Members of the national League of American Bicyclists (LAB; ☎ 202-822-1333, fax 202-822-1334, www.bikeleague.org), 1612 K St NW, Suite 401, Washington, DC 20006, may transport their bikes free on selected airlines and obtain a list of hospitality homes in each state that offer simple accommodations to touring cyclists. The LAB also publishes an annual *Almanac,* listing contacts in each state, along with information about bicycle routes and special events. Bicyclists should also get a copy of the *Cyclosource Catalog,* listing books and maps, and *The Cyclist's Yellow Pages*, a trip-planning resource, both published by Adventure Cycling Association (☎ 406-721-1776), 150 E Pine St, Missoula, MT 59802.

State organizations include the Florida Bicycle Association, PO Box 16652, Tampa, FL 32687-6652, and the Office of the State Bicycle/Pedestrian Coordinator, Florida Department of Transportation (☎ 850-922-2935), 605 S Suwannee St, MS 82, Tallahassee, FL 32399-0450.

Bike Florida, sponsored by the Sunshine State Games Foundation (☎ 352-955-2120), is the best all-around source for information about bicycling in the state. They'll help you plan itineraries, assist with reservations for accommodations and counsel you on the realities of a bike trip through Florida. Write Bike Florida at 1408 NW 6th St, Gainesville, FL 32601.

HITCHHIKING

It is never entirely safe to hitchhike in any country in the world, and we don't recommend it. See Getting There & Away for more information.

Universities have ride-sharing programs, as well as bulletin boards, which can be a useful alternative, especially at the end of semesters and during school holidays. Check when you come for rides to or near where you're headed.

In Fort Lauderdale and in several of Florida's larger counties, there are share-a-ride programs designed to assist commuters. They can act, in a pinch, as the American equivalent of the German *Mitfahrzentrale –* a central source' that pairs up drivers and passengers. You'll have to chip in for gas and tolls, and it usually doesn't work for very long distances.

BOAT

The biggest news in waterborne transport in Florida is the Buquebus (say 'book-a-bus'), a high-speed ferry set to run between Key West and Fort Myers. If successful, the ferry service could seriously boost tourism in southwest Florida – see the Fort Myers section in the Southwest Florida chapter for more information.

There's also limited water-taxi service within Miami and Fort Lauderdale (see those chapters' Getting Around sections for more information).

Florida is a world center for two major types of boat transport: crewing aboard privately owned yachts and, of course, the fast-growing cruise ship industry. See the Getting There & Away chapter for information on crewing.

Cruise Ships

Port of Miami The largest cruise ship port in the world is the Port of Miami, serving more than three million passengers a year. You can find anything from day trips to top-end round-the-world voyages, with a whole spectrum in between, including the very common three-day Bahamas cruises and four-day to one-week trips to ports of call like San Juan, Puerto Rico; St Thomas; St John and St Martin. Ships leave from the Port of Miami Cruise Passenger Terminals on Dodge Island.

Rates change almost daily, and there are any number of discounts that apply – even quoted fares when you call are subject to discounts just for the asking...so ask. Port charges are not included in most of these prices.

Major cruise operators include the following:

Carnival Cruise Lines (☎ 800-327-9501)
The most popular line, offering three-night tours on the *Ecstasy* (fully repaired after a widely publicized onboard fire in 1997 – no one was seriously injured) from Friday to Monday to Nassau, Bahamas. An inside cabin (category four) is $372 per person; large suites (category 12) go from $792 per person. A four-night cruise (from Thursday to Monday) on the *Imagination* to Key West and Cozumel runs $442 per person for an inside cabin, $922 per person for a suite.

Discovery Cruise Line (☎ 800-937-4477)
Offers one-day, flush-it-all-away gambling cruises out of Fort Lauderdale to Freeport, the Bahamas. The cruises aboard the *Discovery Sun* leave Port Everglades daily at 7:45 am, arriving in Freeport at 1 pm. You depart Freeport at 5 pm, getting into Fort Lauderdale at 10:30 pm. The price, $179 per person (there are often discounts for auto-club members, seniors, etc), includes three all-you-can-eat buffet meals and entertainment. The casino opens 45 minutes after departure. Conveniently, there's a cash machine on board.

Norwegian Cruise Line (☎ 800-327-7030)
Three-night tours aboard the *Leeward* to the Bahamas running from $462 to $952 per person. Four-night voyages to Key West and Cancun, Mexico run from $622 to $1332 per person.

Royal Caribbean Cruise Line (☎ 800-327-6700)
Offers three-night Bahamas weekends on the *Sovereign of the Seas*, running from $412 to $1202 per person. A four-night cruise is $602 to $1552 per person; the seven-night Eastern Caribbean voyage aboard the *Grandeur of the Seas* is $1152 to $3502 per person.

Port Everglades The second-largest port after Miami, Port Everglades (☎ 954-523-0252), 18050 Eller Drive in Fort Lauderdale, offers a very similar range of cruises by the same companies and several others. The following cruise companies operate out of Port Everglades:

Celebrity Cruises	☎ 800-437-3111
Cunard Line	☎ 800-528-6273
Holland America Line	☎ 800-426-0327
Princess Cruises	☎ 800-421-0522
Royal Olympic Cruises	☎ 800-368-3888
SeaEscape	☎ 800-327-2005

Port Canaveral As the closest port to Orlando, Port Canaveral (☎ 407-783-7831) has been gaining popularity since Scandinavian World Cruises (☎ 954-474-3707) made its home base here in 1982. Since then, it's become one of the largest three- and four-night cruise ports in the world, and today it's a bustling cruise and cargo port with a great recreation area attached. When Disney Cruise Lines finally begin services (they've been delayed several times but should be up and running soon), the *Disney Magic* and the *Disney Wonder* will sail from here as well. Yes, the ship's horn plays '*When you wish upon a star...*'

Carnival Cruise Lines' *Fantasy* runs three- and four-night Nassau and Freeport, Bahamas, cruises every Monday and Friday; Premiere Cruise Lines' *Star/Ship Oceanic* runs to Nassau and Port Lucaya, Bahamas, on Monday and Friday; the *Star/Ship Atlantic* covers the same route on Thursday and Sunday.

Port of Palm Beach North of West Palm Beach, the Port of Palm Beach (☎ 561-842-4201) is a much smaller affair, with far fewer regularly scheduled sailings. Palm Beach Casino Lines (☎ 561-845-7447, 800-841-7447) offers six-hour gambling cruises 3 to 5 miles off the Atlantic Coast aboard the *Palm Beach Princess*, which also makes several weekly sailings to the Bahamas at 8:30 am, returning at midnight. You'll have about 3¹/₂ hours on the beaches over there, with gambling on the way there and back.

PUBLIC TRANSPORT

Local bus service is available only in larger cities; generally bus fare is between 75¢ and $1.25. Bus fare in Florida is paid as you board (you always board through the front doors), and usually exact change is required, though some buses take $1 bills. Transfers – slips of paper that will allow you to change buses – range from free to 25¢. Operating hours differ from city to city, but generally buses run from about 6 am to 10 pm.

Wheelchair-bound passengers should contact the local bus company to inquire about special transport services. Most buses in Florida are wheelchair accessible, though some bus companies offer individual transit services in addition to regular service for those with physical or mental disabilities. See the Facts for the Visitor chapter for information on organizations that assist with travel for the disabled.

Miami & Miami Beach

• **population 1.9 million**

It used to be called 'God's Waiting Room.' And even today, if you mention Miami Beach to someone who hasn't been there or read about it lately, they might be able to conjure up a blurry memory of octogenarians mingling poolside while Aunt Sadie implored them to wait half an hour before going into the water. But to the arbiters of Fabulousness, SoBe (the inevitable contraction of 'South Beach') has been the Fabulous Spot in the USA since the early 1990s.

The boom, which began in the late 1980s, brought renovation and the restoration of the city's Art Deco District. Overzealous developers were given a very short leash by local preservation groups, who made certain the Deco look wouldn't be demolished in favor of the high-rise monstrosities that line the beaches to the near north.

Today, Miami Beach is what you make of it: trendy or not, at the end of the day, it's a great stretch of white-sand beach lapped by clear blue water, on an island squarely between the Atlantic Ocean and downtown Miami, which sits only a causeway (and several lifestyle light years) to the west.

And the greater Miami area – Coral Gables, Miami, Coconut Grove and other cities – as well as unique and distinctive neighborhoods like Little Havana and Little Haiti, is a true melting pot.

HISTORY
The City's Beginnings

In 1895, a record freeze enveloped most of the north of Florida, where Henry Flagler's railroads were bringing thousands of rich and powerful Northerners to stay at his hotels and resorts. The freeze wiped out citrus crops and sent vacationers scurrying, and legend has it that Julia Tuttle (who owned large tracts of property here and had approached Flagler with the offer of partnership in exchange for the extension of his railroad to Miami, which he'd refused) went into her garden at Fort Dallas, snipped off

Highlights

• Explore miles of awesome beaches

• Experience the exotic aromas and tastes of the Fruit & Spice Park

• Splash in the Venetian Pool, the world's most beautiful public swimming pool

• Catch performances by the nation's brightest young musicians at the New World Symphony

• See the Holocaust Memorial, one of the most moving memorials we've ever seen

• Spend the day at Metrozoo, a 754-acre natural-habitat zoo

• Check out leaping killer whales and dolphins at Miami Seaquarium

• Stargaze and explore science at the Museum of Science & Space Transit Planetarium

• Browse the excellent exhibits at the Museum of Contemporary Art, Wolfsonian Foundation, and the Bass and Lowe Art Museums

• Go for cigars, 'zoom juice' and fiery Cuban music in Little Havana

• Eat mouth-watering cinnamon buns at Knauss Berry Farm

• Indulge in 12oz martinis at the Raleigh Bar & Restaurant

some flowers and sent them to Flagler, who then hightailed it down to Miami.

What he saw was a tropical paradise that was very warm indeed. Flagler and Tuttle came to terms, and Flagler announced the extension of his railroad. Thousands of people whose livelihoods had been wiped out by the big freeze, including citrus growers and service-industry workers like doctors and merchants, headed down to Miami in anticipation of the boom that was to come. Passenger-train service to Miami began April 22, 1896. In that year, the city of Miami incorporated and development kicked off. The wave peaked during WWI, when the US military established an aviation training facility here.

After WWI, the first full-fledged Miami boom (1923-25) was fueled not just by the area's idyllic beachfront location and perfect weather but also by gambling and the fact that Miami never really took to the idea of Prohibition. Though it was illegal, liquor flowed freely here throughout the entire Prohibition period.

But the boom was cut short by a devastating hurricane, which was immediately followed by statewide recession and a national depression.

In the mid-1930s, a mini-boom saw the construction of Miami Beach's famous Art Deco buildings, and this reasonably prosperous period continued until 1942, when a German U-boat sank an American tanker off Florida's coast. The ensuing freak-out created a full-scale conversion of South Florida into a massive military base, training facility and staging area.

Postwar Era & the 1950s

After WWII, many of Miami's trainee soldiers returned and settled; the city was maintaining its pre-war prosperity.

In the 1950s, Miami Beach had another boom, as the area began to be known as the 'Cuba of America.' Gamblers and gangsters, enticed by Miami's gambling, as well as its proximity to the fun, sun and fast times of Batista-run Cuba, moved in en masse. After the Castro coup in Cuba in 1959, Miami's Cuban population swelled. A special immigration center was established to handle the overflow in Miami's Freedom Tower – the Ellis Island of the South.

Racial Tensions

Blacks were relegated to an area north of downtown known as Colored Town, later Overtown. But in the 1950s, as the city grew, many were displaced to the federal housing projects at Liberty City, a misnomer if ever there was one.

In 1965, the two 'freedom flights' that ran every day between Miami and Havana disgorged more than 100,000 Cuban refugees. Sensing the tension that was building up between blacks and Cubans, Dr Martin Luther King Jr pleaded with the two sides not to let animosity lead to bloodshed.

But riots broke out, and skirmishes and acts of gang-style violence occurred. Not all were caused by Cuban-black tensions, however. In 1968, a riot broke out after two white police officers arrested a 17-year-old black male, stripped him naked and suspended him by his ankles from a bridge.

In 1970, the 'rotten meat' riot began when blacks picketed a white-owned shop they had accused of selling spoiled meat. Between 1970 and 1979, there were 13 other race-related violent confrontations.

The Mariel Boatlift (see the History section in Facts about Florida) brought

Julia Tuttle, the mother of Miami

150,000 Cubans to Florida. The resulting economic, logistical and infrastructural strain on South Florida only added to still-simmering racial tensions, which exploded on May 17, 1980, when four white police officers, tried on charges of beating a black suspect to death while in custody, were acquitted by an all-white jury. When the verdict was announced, severe race riots broke out all over Miami, lasting for three days. The Liberty City Riot resulted in 18 deaths, $80 million in property damage and 1100 arrests.

1980s

In the roaring 1980s, the area gained prominence as the major East Coast entry port for drug dealers, their products, and the unbelievable sums of money that went along with them. A plethora of businesses – some legitimate, some drug-financed fronts – and buildings sprung up all over Miami, and the downtown was completely remodeled. But it was still a city being reborn while in the grip of drug smugglers: shootouts were common, as were gangland slayings by cocaine cowboys.

The police, Coast Guard, Drug Enforcement Agency, Border Patrol and FBI were in a tizzy trying to keep track of it all.

And then it happened: *Miami Vice*.

The show – which starred Don Johnson and Philip Michael Thomas as Crockett and Tubbs, two outrageously expensively (and yet pastel) clad narcotics detectives driving around in a Ferrari Testarossa and million-dollar cigarette boats – was responsible for Miami Beach rising to international attention in the mid-1980s. The show's unique look, its slick soundtrack and music-video-style montages glamorized the rich life in South Florida. Before long, people were coming down to see it.

By the late 1980s, Miami Beach had risen to international Fabulousness. Celebrities were moving in, photo shoots from all over the world came here, and the Art Deco District, having been granted federal protection, was going through a renovation that turned the city into a showpiece of fashion and trendiness.

Miami Vice pushed the city into the limelight.

Miami Today

The area is riding the peak of a boom that's been going on for several years. Andrew barely affected the tourist industry, which is the city's economic backbone. And despite highly publicized crimes against tourists in 1993, Miami is now the third most popular city for international tourists after Los Angeles and New York.

The highly publicized murder in 1997 of fashion designer Gianni Versace stunned the celebrity world and once again brought negative media coverage to the area (see the boxed text later in this chapter). Yet the boom continues. Gentrification has made inroads, and South Beach has already gone from a funky, hip destination to a multi-national hot spot. Small, family-run shops and restaurants are out; Planet Hollywood, the Gap and Banana Republic are in.

What's Next?

How long the boom will last is debatable. On the one hand, more people than ever are coming to Miami. On the other, there are distinct murmurs among the European and

MIAMI

Hurricane Andrew

On August 24, 1992, Hurricane Andrew slammed down over Homestead with sustained 140-mph winds and gusts of up to 170 mph. By the time the hurricane passed, it was the costliest disaster to ever hit the USA.

Andrew Stats
- Deaths: 52
- Industry destroyed: tropical fruit, lime and nursery industries
- Property damage: $30 billion
- Evacuees: 300,000
- Residents who permanently left the area: 100,000
- Homes damaged: 77,000
- Homes destroyed: 8000
- Mobile homes damaged: 10,500
- Mobile homes destroyed: 8900
- Apartments damaged: 27,800
- Apartments destroyed: 10,700
- People left homeless: 175,000
- Top wind speed: clocked at 163 mph before the meter at the National Hurricane Center broke

(Sources: Florida Department of Community Affairs, Division of Emergency Management and *Wire*)

The damage could have been worse, but a) people had time to prepare and evacuate, and b) the hurricane – while a category-4 storm – was obliging enough to keep moving and not sit on the area. But had the storm been 20 miles farther north when it hit land (as was expected), the storm surge surely would have destroyed Miami Beach. See the Dangers & Annoyances section in the Facts for the Visitor chapter for complete hurricane information.

supermodel crowd that South Beach is imploding and getting – gasp – passé.

Locals are not worried. After the film, TV and European fashion shoots; the Stallones and Schwarzeneggers, the Sharon Stones and Madonnas, and the thousands of oh-so-trendy people who swarm the chic neon-emblazoned cafés and boutiques of SoBe leave, South Beach will still be here, and better than ever.

ORIENTATION
The city of Miami covers an enormous, sprawling area that's subdivided into neighborhoods and sections and is adjacent to several cities. Miami is on the mainland, while the city of Miami Beach is on a thin barrier island about 4 miles east, across Biscayne Bay. See Unsafe Areas, under Dangers & Annoyances (later in this chapter) for areas you may want to avoid.

Downtown Miami
Downtown is laid out with a fairly straightforward grid, with Flagler Ave as much the main drag as any. The downtown area is divided by the Miami River, crossed by the newly renovated Brickell Ave Bridge and continues on the south side of the river.

The north-south divider is Flagler St; the east-west divider is Miami Ave; prefixes are given to streets – N, W, S, E, NW, NE, SW, SE – based on that street's position relative to the intersection of Flagler St and Miami Ave.

Most avenues and streets are numbered: avenues begin at 1 and count upwards the farther east and west they are from Miami Ave, so E 1st Ave is one block east of Miami Ave, while W 42nd Ave is 42 blocks west of Miami Ave. Streets are numbered similarly, increasing in number progressively the farther north or south of Flagler St, so N 1st St is one block north of Flagler, etc.

Miami Beach
In this book, despite common practice, we break Miami Beach up into two distinct regions: South Beach (or SoBe) and northern Miami Beach.

Streets run east-west and avenues run north-south, but the avenues are named, not numbered, and there are no directional sectors like NW or SE.

Continued on page 160

Miami & Miami Beach Map Section

KEN LAFFAL

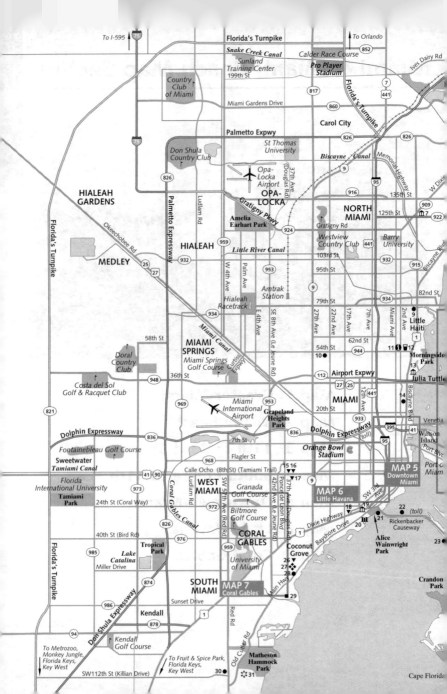

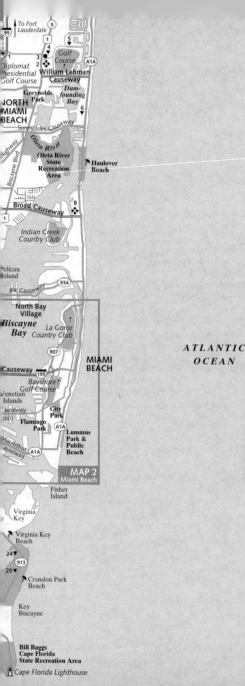

PLACES TO STAY
29 Coconut Grove B&B

PLACES TO EAT
1 JD's Pizza & Subs
4 Turn Bagel
5 Unicorn Village Market Waterfront Restaurant
6 Rascal House
15 Versailles
16 Hy Vong Vietnamese Restaurant
17 La Carreta (Little Havana Branch)
18 Daily Bread Marketplace
24 La Caretta (Rickenbacker Branch)
25 Hyde Park Market
26 Johnny Rockets
27 Cheesecake Factory

OTHER
2 Aventura Mall
3 Borders Books & Music
7 Museum of Contemporary Art (MOCA)
8 Bal Harbour Shops
9 Immigration & Naturalization Service
10 Black Archives Historical & Research Foundation of Southern Florida
11 Haitian Refugee Center
12 Churchill's Hideaway
13 The American Police Hall of Fame & Police Museum
14 Bacardi Imports Headquarters
19 Miami Museum of Science & Space Transit Planetarium
20 Vizcaya Museum & Gardens
21 Sailboards Miami
22 Tony's Ultralight Adventures
23 Miami Seaquarium
27 CocoWalk Shopping Center
28 Coconut Grove Playhouse
30 Parrot Jungle & Gardens
31 Fairchild Tropical Gardens

ATLANTIC
OCEAN

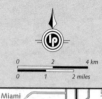

0   2   4 km
0   1   2 miles

Miami Quadrant Map

Florida's Turnpike

Palmetto Expwy

Palmetto Expwy

Miami Ave

NW NE

Dolphin Expwy

Flagler St

SW SE

968

1

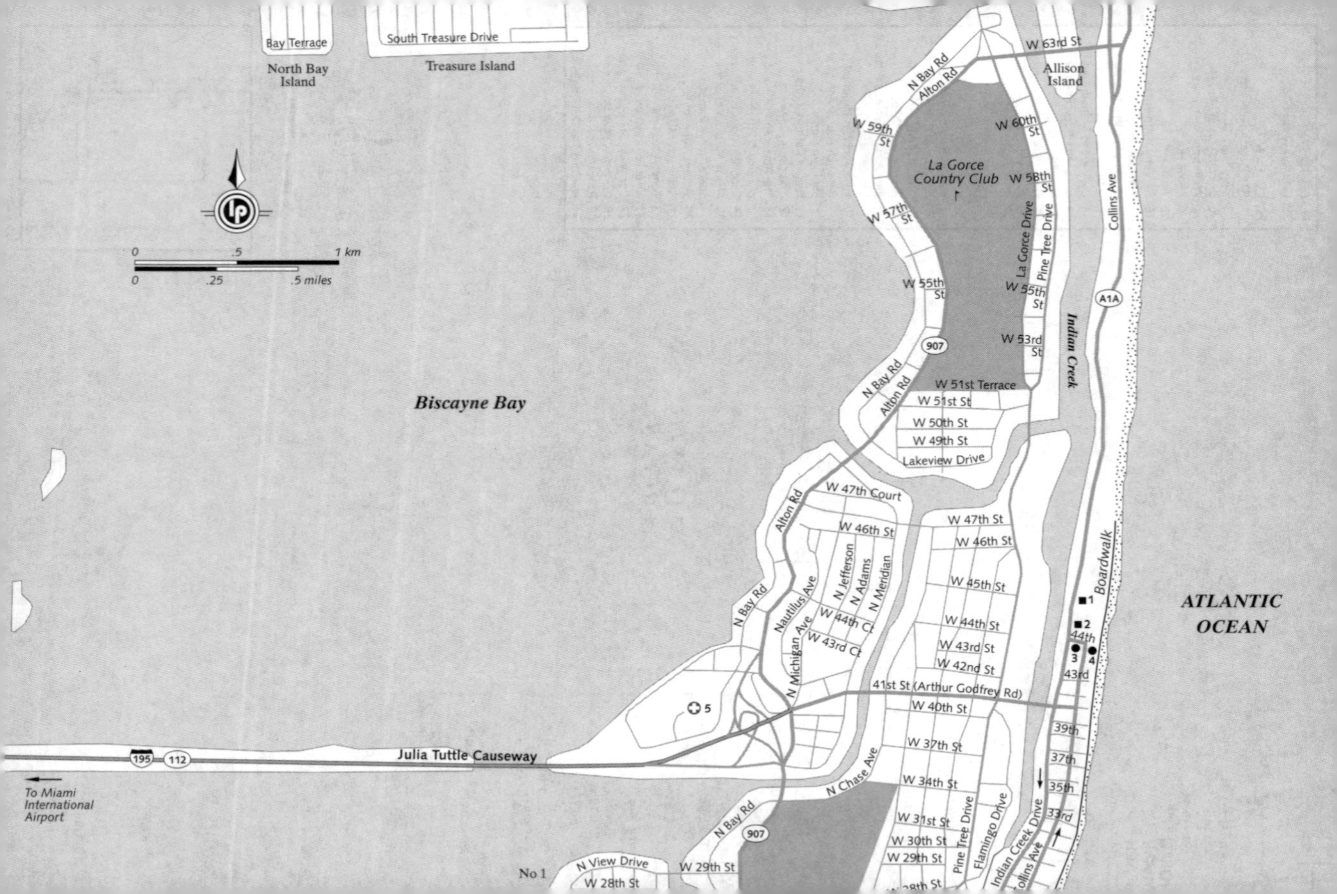

ATLANTIC OCEAN

Biscayne Bay

Indian Creek

La Gorce Country Club

Collins Ave
Boardwalk
A1A

Allison Island
Bay Terrace
North Bay Island
South Treasure Drive
Treasure Island

W 63rd St
W 60th St
W 59th St
W 58th St
W 57th St
W 56th St
W 55th St
W 53rd St
W 51st Terrace
W 51st St
W 50th St
W 49th St

N Bay Rd
Alton Rd
La Gorce Drive
Pine Tree Drive
Lakeview Drive
907

W 47th St
W 46th St
W 45th St
W 44th St
W 43rd St
W 42nd St
41st St (Arthur Godfrey Rd)
W 40th St
W 37th St
W 34th St
W 31st St
W 30th St
W 29th St

W 47th Court
W 46th St
N Jefferson Ave
N Adams
N Meridian
N Michigan Ave
Nautilus Ave
N Prairie Ave
W 44th Ct

Flamingo Drive
Pine Tree Drive
Indian Creek Drive
Collins Ave

N Bay Rd
Alton Rd
N Chase Ave
907

N View Drive
W 28th St

Julia Tuttle Causeway

195
112

To Miami International Airport

No 1

1 km
.5 miles
0 .25 .5

N

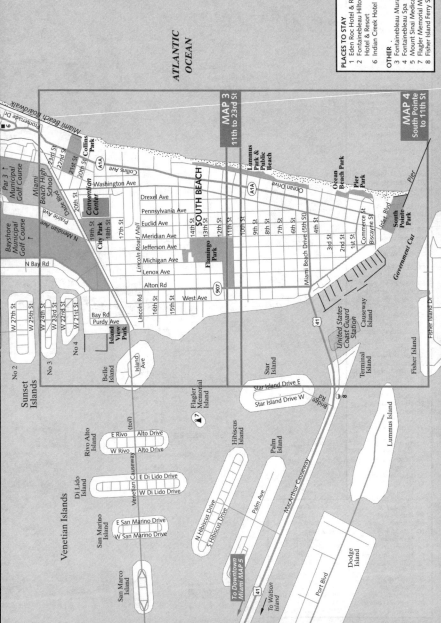

ATLANTIC OCEAN

PLACES TO STAY
1 Eden Roc Hotel & Resort
2 Fontainebleau Hilton Hotel & Resort
6 Indian Creek Hotel

OTHER
3 Fontainebleau Mural
4 Fontainebleau Spa
5 Mount Sinai Medical Center
7 Flagler Memorial Monument
8 Fisher Island Ferry Stop

MAP 3
11th to 23rd St

MAP 4
South Pointe to 11th St

Miami Beach Boardwalk
Promenade Dr

Miami Beach High School

Convention Center

City Park

Flamingo Park

Island View Park

Collins Park

SOUTH BEACH

Lummus Park & Public Beach

Ocean Beach Park

Pier Park

South Pointe Park

23rd St
22nd St
21st St
20th St
19th St
18th St
17th St

Collins Ave (A1A)
Washington Ave
Drexel Ave
Pennsylvania Ave
Euclid Ave
Meridian Ave
Jefferson Ave
Michigan Ave
Lenox Ave
Alton Rd

14th St
13th St
12th St
11th St
10th St
9th St
8th St
7th St
6th St
5th St
4th St
3rd St
2nd St
1st St

Ocean Drive (A1A)
Miami Beach Drive (5th St)
Commerce St
Biscayne St
Commerce St

Lincoln Road Mall

N Meridian Ave
Dade Blvd
Prairie Ave

Bayshore Municipal Golf Course

Par 3 Municipal Golf Course

N Bay Rd

Lincoln Rd
16th St
15th St
West Ave
Bay Rd
Purdy Ave
907

41

United States Coast Guard Station

Causeway Island

Terminal Island

Fisher Island

Fisher Island Dr

Government Cut

Pier

Inlet Blvd

W 27th St
W 25th St
W 24th St
W 23rd St
W 22nd St
W 21st St

Sunset Islands

No 2
No 3
No 4

Belle Island

Island Ave

Flagler Memorial Island

Star Island
Star Island Drive E
Star Island Drive W

Venetian Islands

Di Lido Island

Rivo Alto Island
E Rivo Alto Drive
W Rivo Alto Drive

E Di Lido Drive
W Di Lido Drive

San Marino Island
E San Marino Drive
W San Marino Drive

San Marco Island

Venetian Causeway (toll)

Hibiscus Island

Palm Island

N Hibiscus Drive
S Hibiscus Drive

Palm Ave

MacArthur Causeway

Lummus Island

Dodge Island

Port Blvd

bridge Rd

To Downtown Miami MAP 5

To Watson Island

41

MAP 3 11TH TO 23RD ST

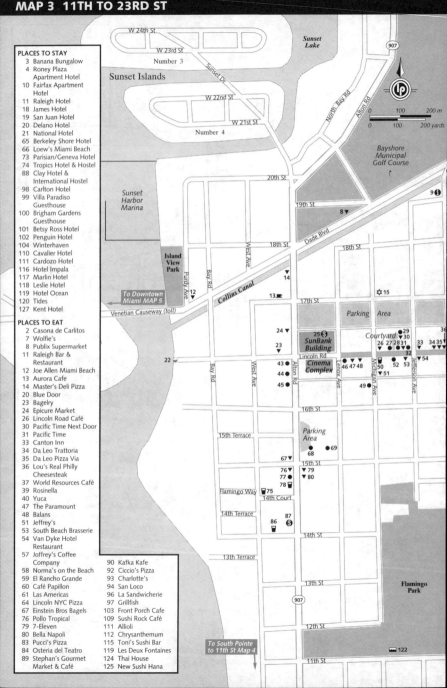

PLACES TO STAY

3 Banana Bungalow
4 Roney Plaza Apartment Hotel
10 Fairfax Apartment Hotel
11 Raleigh Hotel
18 James Hotel
19 San Juan Hotel
20 Delano Hotel
21 National Hotel
65 Berkeley Shore Hotel
66 Loew's Miami Beach
73 Parisian/Geneva Hotel
74 Tropics Hotel & Hostel
88 Clay Hotel & International Hostel
98 Carlton Hotel
99 Villa Paradiso Guesthouse
100 Brigham Gardens Guesthouse
101 Betsy Ross Hotel
102 Penguin Hotel
104 Winterhaven
110 Cavalier Hotel
111 Cardozo Hotel
116 Hotel Impala
117 Marlin Hotel
118 Leslie Hotel
119 Hotel Ocean
120 Tides
127 Kent Hotel

PLACES TO EAT

2 Casona de Carlitos
7 Wolfie's
8 Publix Supermarket
11 Raleigh Bar & Restaurant
12 Joe Allen Miami Beach
13 Aurora Cafe
14 Master's Deli Pizza
20 Blue Door
23 Bagelry
24 Epicure Market
26 Lincoln Road Café
30 Pacific Time Next Door
31 Pacific Time
33 Canton Inn
34 Da Leo Trattoria
35 Da Leo Pizza Via
36 Lou's Real Philly Cheesesteak
37 World Resources Café
39 Rosinella
40 Yuca
47 The Paramount
48 Balans
51 Jeffrey's
53 South Beach Brasserie
54 Van Dyke Hotel Restaurant
57 Joffrey's Coffee Company
58 Norma's on the Beach
59 El Rancho Grande
60 Café Papillon
61 Las Americas
64 Lincoln NYC Pizza
67 Einstein Bros Bagels
77 Pollo Tropical
79 7-Eleven
80 Bella Napoli
83 Pucci's Pizza
84 Osteria del Teatro
89 Stephan's Gourmet Market & Café

90 Kafka Kafe
92 Ciccio's Pizza
93 Charlotte's
94 San Loco
96 La Sandwicherie
97 Grillfish
103 Front Porch Cafe
109 Sushi Rock Café
111 Allioli
112 Chrysanthemum
115 Toni's Sushi Bar
119 Les Deux Fontaines
124 Thai House
125 New Sushi Hana

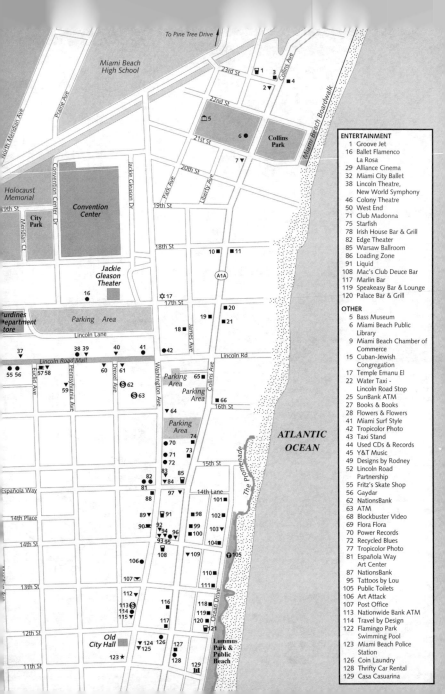

To Pine Tree Drive

Miami Beach High School

Holocaust Memorial

Convention Center

City Park

Jackie Gleason Theater

Burdines Department Store

Parking Area

Lincoln Lane

Lincoln Road Mall

Española Way

14th Place

14th St

13th St

12th St

11th St

Old City Hall

Lummus Park & Public Beach

ATLANTIC OCEAN

The Promenade

Collins Park

North Meridian Ave
Prairie Ave
Convention Center Dr
Meridian Ct
Euclid Ave
Pennsylvania Ave
Drexel Ave
Washington Ave
James Ave
Jackie Gleason Dr
Park Ave
Liberty Ave
Collins Ave
Ocean Drive
Miami Beach Boardwalk

23rd St
22nd St
21st St
20th St
19th St
18th St
17th St
16th St
15th St
14th Lane
14th St

Lincoln Rd

A1A

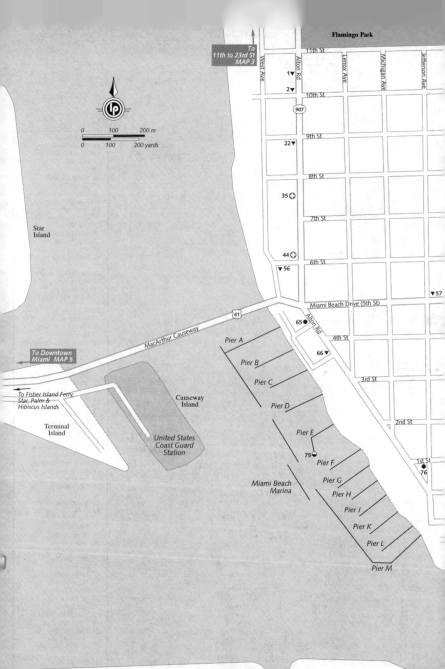

Flamingo Park

To
11th to 23rd St
MAP 3

11th St

West Ave
Alton Rd
Lenox Ave
Michigan Ave
Jefferson Ave

1 ▼
2 ▼

10th St

907

9th St

22 ▼

8th St

35 ✪

7th St

44 ✪

6th St

▼ 56

▼ 57

Miami Beach Drive (5th St)

65 ●

Alton Rd

4th St

66 ▼

3rd St

2nd St

1st St

76 ●

MacArthur Causeway

41

Star
Island

Pier A

Pier B

Pier C

Pier D

Pier E

Pier F

Pier G

Pier H

Pier J

Pier K

Pier L

Pier M

75 ●

Miami Beach
Marina

To Downtown
Miami MAP 5

To Fisher Island Ferry,
Star, Palm &
Hibiscus Islands

Terminal
Island

Causeway
Island

United States
Coast Guard
Station

0   100   200 m
0   100   200 yards

Fisher Island

ATLANTIC OCEAN

Lummus Park & Public Beach

The Promenade

Playground

Ocean Beach Park

Playground

Pier Park

South Pointe Park

Government Cut

Pier

Meridian Ave
Euclid Ave
Pennsylvania Ave
Washington Ave
Collins Ave
Ocean Drive
A1A
Commerce St
Biscayne St
Harley St
Inlet Blvd
Boardwalk

PLACES TO STAY
3 Kenmore Hotel
9 Essex House Hotel
14 Mermaid Guest House
15 Edison Hotel
16 Breakwater Hotel
17 Deco Walk Hotel
24 Miami Beach International
   Travelers Hostel
28 Lily Guesthouse
31 Casa Grande Hotel
40 Hideaway Suites
41 Colony Hotel
43 Avalon Hotel
53 Majestic Hotel
54 Park Central Hotel
55 Beach Paradise Hotel
71 Lord Balfour Hotel
79 Century Hotel

PLACES TO EAT
1 Mrs Mendoza's Tacos
   al Carbon
2 Wild Oats Community
   Market
4 11th St Diner
8 David's Café
11 Naked Earth
12 Astor Place Bar & Grill
19 Mango's Tropical Café
22 Dab Haus
23 Thai Toni's
29 Wish
30 Café Romano
32 Lario's on the Beach
34 News Cafe
39 Puerto Sagua
46 The Strand
52 Tutti's
56 7-Eleven
57 Tap Tap
60 Sports Café
61 Hyde Park Market
66 Monty's Seafood &
   Stone Crab Restaurant
67 China Grill
70 Pizza Rustica
78 Nemo Restaurant
80 Joe's Stone Crab
   Restaurant
83 Smith & Wollensky

ENTERTAINMENT
5 Twist
10 Clevelander Bar
36 Rose's Bar
42 Booking Table
45 Bash
47 Club Deep
48 Brandt's Break
77 Amnesia
81 Penrod's Beach Club

OTHER
6 Mars
7 Wolfsonian Foundation
13 Lee Ann Pharmacy
18 Sunglass Hut
20 Oceanfront Auditorium,
   Art Deco Welcome Center
21 Lifeguard Tower
25 LIB Color Labs
26 Betsey Johnson
27 Banana Republic
33 News Cafe Store
35 Stanley C Myers
   Community Health Center
37 Versace Jean Couture
38 A-X Armani Exchange
44 South Shore Hospital
49 Gap
50 Deco Denim
51 Urban Outfitters
58 Miami Beach Bicycle Center
59 Coin Laundry
62 Spec's Music
63 Fritz's Skate Shop
64 Public Toilets
65 Sea Kruz
68 X-Isle Surf Shop
69 The Paper Boy
72 Sanford L Ziff Jewish
   Museum of Florida
73 Library
74 Public Toilets
75 Water Taxi
76 Water Tower
82 Toilets; Soda, Water &
   Ice Machines
84 Observation Tower
85 Picnic Area

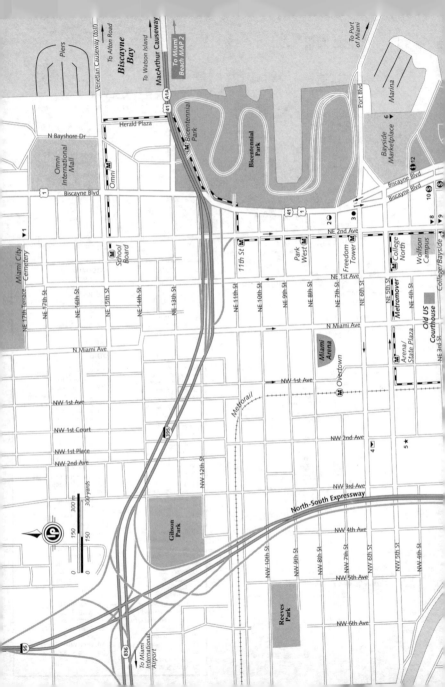

Biscayne Bay

Piers

To Alton Road
Venetian Causeway (toll)
To Watson Island
MacArthur Causeway
To Miami Beach MAP 2
41A

To Port of Miami
Port Blvd
Marina

N Bayshore Dr
Omni International Mall
Herald Plaza
Bicentennial Park
Bicentennial Park
Bayside Marketplace
6
12

Biscayne Blvd
Biscayne Blvd
1
Biscayne Blvd
Omni

Miami City Cemetery
1
School Board
11th St
Park West
Freedom Tower
NE 2nd Ave
2
3
College North
Wolfson Campus
8
9
10
S

NE 17th Terrace
NE 17th St
NE 16th St
NE 15th St
NE 14th St
NE 13th St
NE 11th St
NE 10th St
NE 9th St
NE 8th St
NE 7th St
NE 6th St
NE 1st Ave
N Miami Ave
NE 5th St
NE 4th St
Metromover
Old US Courthouse
NE 3rd St
College/Bayside

N Miami Ave
Miami Arena
Overtown
Arena/State Plaza

NW 1st Ave
NW 1st Ave
NW 1st Court
NW 1st Place
NW 2nd Ave
Metrorail
395
NW 2nd Ave
4
5

NW 12th St
NW 3rd Ave
North-South Expressway

Gibson Park
300 m
300 yards
150
150
0
0

NW 4th Ave
NW 10th St
NW 9th St
NW 8th St
NW 7th St
NW 6th St
NW 5th St
NW 4th St
NW 5th St

Reeves Park
NW 6th Ave

95
836
To Miami International Airport

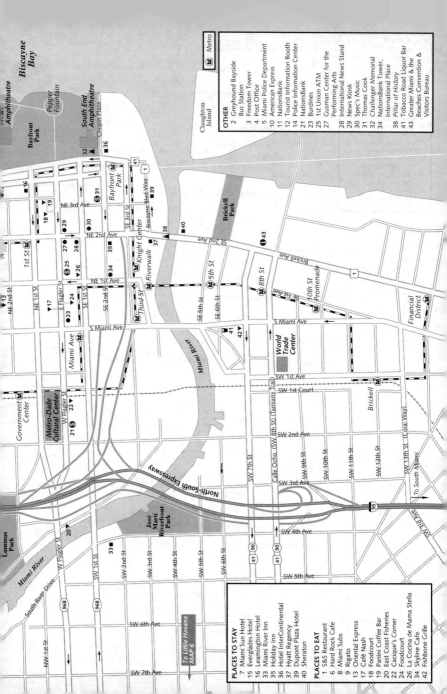

Biscayne Bay

Amphitheatre

Bayfront Park

Pepper Fountain

South End Amphitheatre

Chopin Plaza

Claughton Island

Brickell Park

Bayfront Park

Government Center

Metro-Dade Cultural Center

World Trade Center

Brickell

Financial District

José Martí Riverfront Park

Lummus Park

Miami River

North-South Expressway

Calle Ocho (SW 8th St) (Tamiami Trail)

Miami River (8th St) Trail

To Little Havana MAP 6

To South Miami

OTHER
2   Greyhound Bayside Bus Station
3   Freedom Tower
4   Post Office
5   Miami Police Department
10 American Express
11 NationsBank
12 Gusman Center for the Performing Arts
14 Tourist Information Booth
    Police Information Center
21 NationsBank
23 Burdines
25 1st Union ATM
27 Gusman Center for the Performing Arts
28 International News Stand
29 News Kiosk
30 Spec's Music
31 Thomas Cook
32 Challenger Memorial
34 NationsBank Tower, International Place
38 Pillar of History
41 Tobacco Road Liquor Bar
43 Greater Miami & the Beaches Convention & Visitors Bureau

Metro

PLACES TO STAY
7   Miami Sun Hotel
15 Everglades Hotel
16 Leamington Hotel
33 Miami River Inn
35 Holiday Inn
36 Hotel InterContinental
37 Hyatt Regency
39 Dupont Plaza Hotel
40 Sheraton

PLACES TO EAT
1   S&S Restaurant
6   Hard Rock Cafe
8   Miami Subs
9   Rigato
13 Café Nash
17 Oriental Express
18 Foodcourt
19 Panini Coffee Bar
20 East Coast Fisheries
22 Cacique's Corner
24 Foodcourt
26 La Cocina de Marma Stella
34 Skyline Cafe
42 Fishbone Grille

MAP 6 LITTLE HAVANA

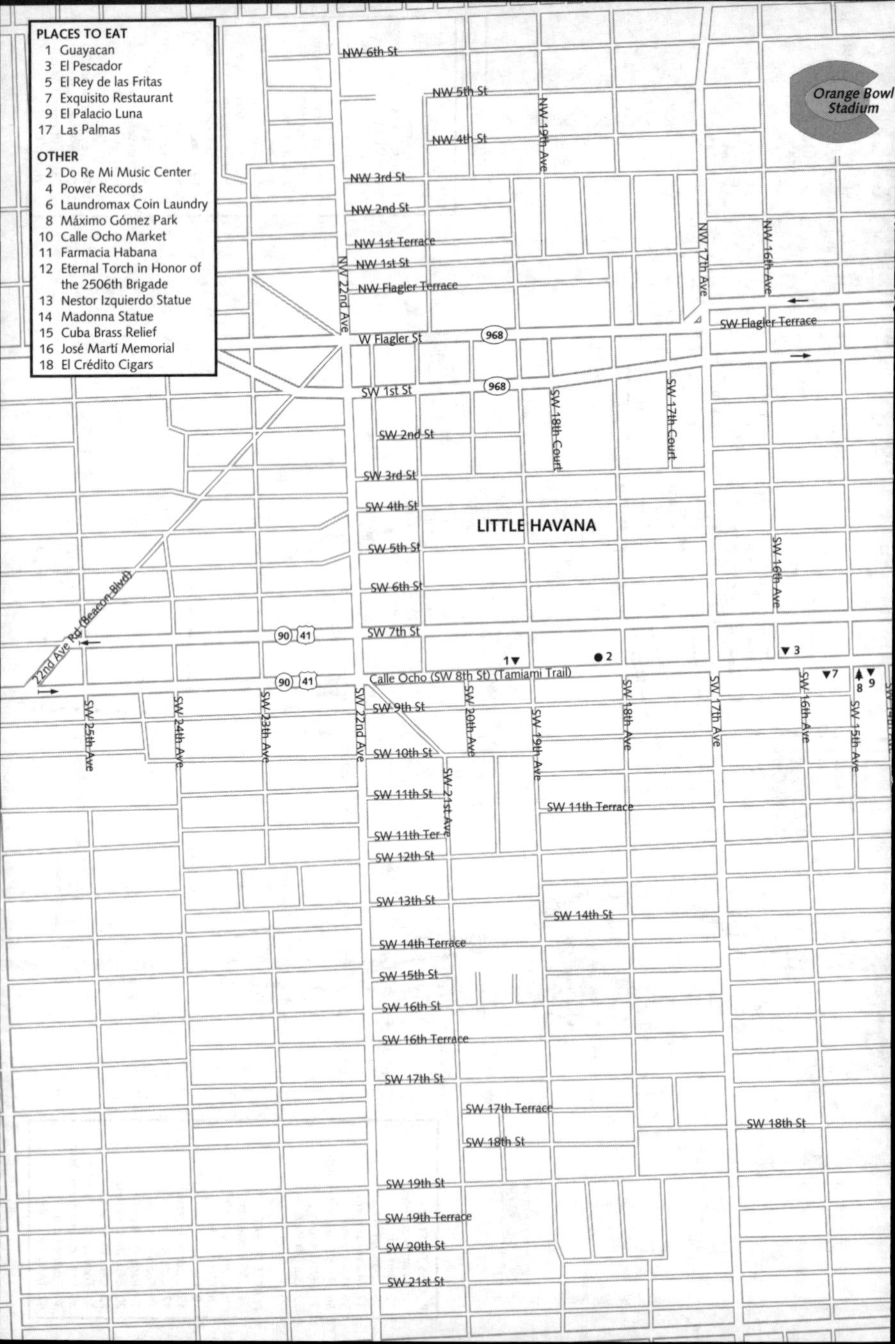

PLACES TO EAT
1 Guayacan
3 El Pescador
5 El Rey de las Fritas
7 Exquisito Restaurant
9 El Palacio Luna
17 Las Palmas

OTHER
2 Do Re Mi Music Center
4 Power Records
6 Laundromax Coin Laundry
8 Máximo Gómez Park
10 Calle Ocho Market
11 Farmacia Habana
12 Eternal Torch in Honor of the 2506th Brigade
13 Nestor Izquierdo Statue
14 Madonna Statue
15 Cuba Brass Relief
16 José Martí Memorial
18 El Crédito Cigars

Orange Bowl Stadium

NW 6th St
NW 5th St
NW 4th St
NW 3rd St
NW 2nd St
NW 1st Terrace
NW 1st St
NW Flagler Terrace
SW Flagler Terrace
W Flagler St
968
968
SW 1st St
SW 2nd St
SW 3rd St
SW 4th St
SW 5th St
SW 6th St
SW 7th St

NW 19th Ave
NW 17th Ave
NW 16th Ave
SW 18th Court
SW 17th Court
SW 16th Ave

LITTLE HAVANA

90 41
90 41

2nd Ave Rd (Beacon Blvd)

Calle Ocho (SW 8th St) (Tamiami Trail)
1▼   ● 2   ▼ 3   ▼ 7   ▲▼
                                          8 9

SW 9th St
SW 10th St
SW 11th St
SW 11th Ter
SW 12th St
SW 13th St
SW 14th Terrace
SW 15th St
SW 16th St
SW 16th Terrace
SW 17th St
SW 17th Terrace
SW 18th St
SW 19th St
SW 19th Terrace
SW 20th St
SW 21st St

SW 25th Ave
SW 24th Ave
SW 23rd Ave
SW 22nd Ave
SW 21st Ave
SW 20th Ave
SW 19th Ave
SW 18th Ave
SW 17th Ave
SW 16th Ave
SW 15th Ave

SW 11th Terrace
SW 14th St
SW 17th Terrace
SW 18th St

NW 6th St

NW 6th St

NW 5th St

NW 5th St

NW 4th St

NW 3rd St

Henderson Park

NW 2nd St

NW 1st St

Lummus Park

Miami River

95

NW 14th Ave

NW 12th Ave

NW 8th Ave

W Flagler St

968

SW 1st St

968

SW 2nd St

SW 3rd St

Riverside Park

José Martí Riverfront Park

933

SW 4th St

SW 5th St

To Downtown Miami Map 5

SW 8th Ave

SW 6th St

SW 14th Ave

SW 13th Ave

90 41

SW 7th St

90 41

Calle Ocho (SW 8th St) (Tamiami Trail)

● 4

▼ 5

● 6

SW 11th Ave

SW 10th Ave

SW 9th Court

SW 9th Ave

SW 8th Court

SW 8th Ave

SW 7th Ave

SW 6th Ave

SW 5th Ave

SW 9th St

▼● 18
17

SW 10th St

● 10 11
▲
● 12
13
14
15
16

SW 13th Court

SW 12th Court

SW 12th Ave

Cuban Memorial Blvd

SW 11th St

SW 15th Rd

SW 18th Terrace

SW 19th Rd

SW 12th St

SW 22nd Rd

SW 20th Rd

SW 21st Rd

SW 18th Rd

SW 13th St

SW 23rd Rd

SW 24th Rd

SW 14th St

SW 25th Rd

THE ROADS

North-South Expressway

SW 9th Ave

SW 26th Rd

SW 7th Ave

SW 8th Ave

SW 29th Rd

SW 4th Ave

0   200   400 m
0   200   400 yards

933

SW 30th Rd

SW 3rd Ave (Coral Way)

SW 31st Rd

Metrorail

95

1

To Coral Gables MAP 7

SW 2nd Ave

SW 1st Ave

S Miami Ave

Brickell Ave

MAP 7 CORAL GABLES

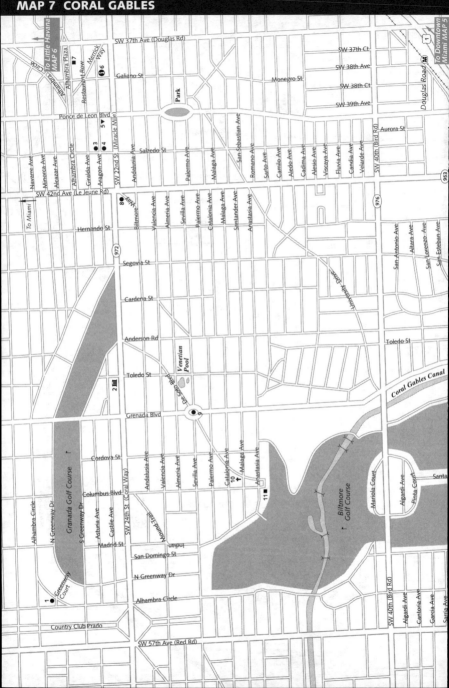

To Little Havana Map 6

Alhambra Circle

To Downtown Miami MAP 5

Douglas Road

SW 37th Ave (Douglas Rd)

SW 37th Ct

SW 38th Ave

SW 38th Ct

SW 39th Ave

Monegro St

Galiano St

Merrick Way

Alhambra Plaza

Restaurant Row 7

6

Park

953

Ponce de Leon Blvd

5

Miracle Mile

SW 22nd St

Salzedo St

Andalusia Ave

Palermo Ave

Malaga Ave

San Sebastian Ave

Romano Ave

Sarto Ave

Camilo Ave

Aledo Ave

Cadima Ave

Alesio Ave

Viscaya Ave

Fluvia Ave

Candia Ave

Velarde Ave

Aurora St

SW 40th (Bird Rd)

3

4

Giralda Ave

Aragon Ave

Alhambra Circle

Alcazar Ave

Minorca Ave

Navarre Ave

SW 42nd Ave (Le Jeune Rd)

976

8

Biltmore Way

Valencia Ave

Almeria Ave

Sevilla Ave

Palermo Ave

Catalonia Ave

Santander Ave

Anastasia Ave

San Antonio Ave

Altara Ave

San Lorenzo Ave

San Esteban Ave

To Miami

Hernando St

972

Segovia St

University Drive

Cardena St

Anderson Rd

Toledo St

Venetian Pool

De Soto Blvd

Toledo St

Coral Gables Canal

2

Grenada Blvd

9

Cordova St

Andalusia Ave

Valencia Ave

Almeria Ave

Sevilla Ave

Palermo Ave

Catalonia Ave

Malaga Ave

Anastasia Ave

10

11

Biltmore Golf Course

Mariola Court

Algardi Ave

Pinta Court

Santa

Columbus Blvd

SW 24th St (Coral Way)

Asturia Ave

Castle Ave

Madrid St

Mooring Trail

Granada Golf Course

Alhambra Circle

N Greenway Dr

S Greenway Dr

San Domingo St

N Greenway Dr

Alhambra Circle

1

Greenway Court

SW 40th (Bird Rd)

Algardi Ave

Cantoria Ave

Garcia Ave

Sarria Ave

Country Club Prado

SW 57th Ave (Red Rd)

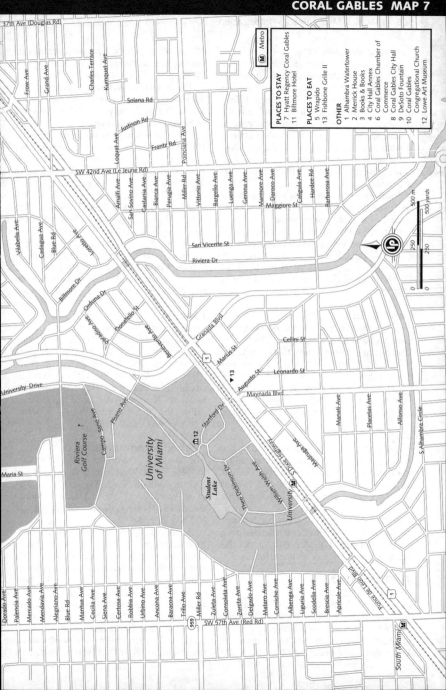

Ⓜ Metro

PLACES TO STAY
7 Hyatt Regency Coral Gables
11 Biltmore Hotel

PLACES TO EAT
5 Wrapido
13 Fishbone Grille II

OTHER
1 Alhambra Watertower
2 Merrick House
3 Books & Books
4 City Hall Annex
6 Coral Gables Chamber of Commerce
8 Coral Gables City Hall
9 DeSoto Fountain
10 Coral Gables Congregational Church
12 Lowe Art Museum

37th Ave (Douglas Rd)
Frow Ave
Grand Ave
Charles Terrace
Kumquat Ave
Solana Rd
Justison Rd
Loquat Ave
Frantz Rd
Poinciana Ave
SW 42nd Ave (Le Jeune Rd)
Amalfi Ave
San Sovino Ave
Castania Ave
Bianca Ave
Perugia Ave
Miller Rd
Vittorio Ave
Bargello Ave
Luenga Ave
Gerona Ave
Marmore Ave
Daroca Ave
Caligula Ave
Hardee Rd
Barbarosa Ave
Maggiore St
San Vicente St
Riviera Dr
Ylabella Ave
Cadagua Ave
Blue Rd
Loretto Ave
Biltmore Dr
Ordona Dr
Donatello St
Padua Ave
Bermenda Ave
Granada Blvd
Marius St
Cellini St
Leonardo St
Augusto St
Maynada Blvd
Manati Ave
Placetas Ave
Alfonso Ave
S Alhambra Circle
University Drive
Riviera Golf Course
Campo Sano Ave
Picano Ave
University of Miami
Maria St
Student Lake
Stanford Dr
Theo Dickinson Dr
William Walsh Ave
Dixie Highway
University
Mathusa Ave
Dorado Ave
Palencia Ave
Mercado Ave
Mendavia Ave
Alegriano Ave
Blue Rd
Mantua Ave
Cecilia Ave
Siena Ave
Certosa Ave
Robbia Ave
Urbino Ave
Ancona Ave
Baracoa Ave
Trillo Ave
Miller Rd
Zuleta Ave
Consolata Ave
Zoreta Ave
Delgado Ave
Mataro Ave
Corniche Ave
Albenga Ave
Liguria Ave
Scodella Ave
Brescia Ave
Apticale Ave
SW 57th Ave (Red Rd)
959
Ponce de Leon Blvd
South Miami

▶13
⛪12

500 m
500 yards
0 250
0 250

MIAMI

Continued from page 144

South Beach, on the widest section of the island, has a grid that mostly runs due north-south and east-west, except for curving bits of Alton Rd as well as Washington Ave, Collins Ave and Ocean Drive, which run at a 20° angle northeast to the main grid system.

Lincoln Rd is pedestrian-only between Washington Ave at the east and Lenox Ave at the west; the strip is called Lincoln Road Mall and seems to be perpetually under construction.

South Pointe is below 5th St at the southern tip of Miami Beach, directly across Government Cut from Fisher Island.

Northern Miami Beach is divided by narrow Indian Creek, which separates Collins Ave on the thin strip of land at the east from the residential districts at the west. The northern border of Miami Beach is 96th St.

Coral Gables

Coral Gables is essentially bordered by Calle Ocho at the north, Sunset Drive (SW 72nd St/Hwy 986) at the south, Le Jeune Rd (SW 42nd Ave/Hwy 953) at the east and Red Rd (SW 57th Ave/Hwy 959) at the west. US Hwy 1 slashes through at a 45° angle from northeast to southwest. Avenues here run east-west, while streets run north-south.

Maps

All car-rental companies are required by law to hand out decent city and area maps when you rent a car – Alamo's maps aren't bad at all. Rand McNally, AAA and Dolph Map Company make area maps of Miami. Freebies are usually not very good, as they're simplified to the point of being totally inaccurate. You can get somewhat usable free maps from the Greater Miami & the Beaches Convention & Visitors Bureau.

INFORMATION
Tourist Offices

The Greater Miami & the Beaches Convention & Visitors Bureau (☎ 305-539-3063, 800-283-2707, fax 305-539-3113, www.miamiandbeaches.com) is at 701 Brickell Ave, about a five-minute walk south of the

Miami River. The CVB also operates an information center at Bayside Marketplace (☎ 305-539-8070), 401 Biscayne Blvd.

The Art Deco Welcome Center (☎ 305-531-3484), 1001 Ocean Drive, run by the Miami Design Preservation League, has tons of Deco District information.

The Miami Beach Chamber of Commerce (☎ 305-672-1270, www.miamibeachchamber .com) has an office at 1920 Meridian Ave. It's open 9 am to 6 pm weekdays, 10 am to 4 pm Saturday.

The Black Archives Historical & Research Foundation of South Florida (☎ 305-636-2390), in Liberty City at 5400 NW 22nd Ave, Building B, has information about black culture and can arrange tours of Liberty City and other areas of the city.

The Coral Gables Chamber of Commerce (☎ 305-446-1557), 50 Aragon Ave, has that city's absolutely excellent tourist maps.

Money

NationsBank has branch offices all over Miami and Miami Beach. Some private exchange offices include American Express (☎ 305-358-7350) at 330 Biscayne Blvd, Thomas Cook (☎ 305-381-9252) at 80 N Biscayne Blvd, SunTrust Bank (☎ 305-591-6000) at 777 Brickell Ave and Lincoln Rd at Alton Rd, and Chequepoint (☎ 305-538-5348) at 865 Collins Ave.

Post & Communications

The two main post offices on the Beach are at 13th St at Washington Ave (General Delivery, Miami Beach, FL 33139) and 71st St at Versailles (General Delivery, Miami Beach, FL 33141). A downtown branch is at 500 NW 2nd Ave.

Anyone who's anyone in Miami has a cellular telephone, and you can rent one as easily as you buy a soda from a soda machine. That's right, there are cell-phone-rental *vending machines* in many airport car-rental offices. There are also cell-phone-rental places in larger hotels. You should make certain you only have to pay for air time (not equipment rental), and find out if there's a daily minimum – it's usually about three minutes. Note that air time on rentals is far more expensive than on normal cell phones. Count on about $1.25 to $2 a minute on local and incoming calls, and much more for long-distance outgoing calls.

Internet Resources
Kafka Kafe (☎ 673-9669), 1464 Washington Ave, is to date Miami Beach's only Internet café ($9 an hour for access), and the service when we visited was repellent.

Travel Agencies
Good travel agencies in the area include Travel by Design (☎ 305-673-6336), 210 Washington Ave; Council Travel (☎ 305-670-9261, 800-226-8624), south of Coral Gables at 9100 S Dadeland Blvd; and Travel Now at 1455 Collins Ave (☎ 305-532-7273) and at 14374 Biscayne Blvd in Miami (☎ 305-919-9000).

Bookstores
The best locally owned bookstores are the two branches of Books & Books, at 933 Lincoln Rd in Miami Beach (☎ 305-532-3222, www.booksandbooks.com) and at 296 Aragon Ave in Coral Gables (☎ 305-442-4408). The stores are host to visiting authors, discussions, poetry readings and, in Miami Beach, a café. There is an excellent selection of literature, fiction and Florida-related books.

Other than those bookstores, there is an excellent Borders (☎ 305-935-4712), 19925 Biscayne Blvd in Aventura, with a café and an enormous Florida selection.

Periodicals & Foreign Press
The News Cafe (☎ 305-538-6397), 800 Ocean Drive, has a separate 24-hour newsstand between the restaurant and the bar. It has a good selection of international (from countries considered to be fashionable) and domestic press, and some paperbacks.

You can get dailies from practically every Spanish-speaking country at a couple of places: in downtown Miami, try the newsstand that sets up just across the street from the Gusman Center for the Performing Arts at 174 E Flagler St, and the larger, more permanent one at SE 1st St and SE 2nd Ave.

Libraries
The Miami Public Library (☎ 305-375-2665, 305-375-5184), 101 W Flagler St, in the Metro-Dade Cultural Center, has an enormous Florida room containing thousands of books on all aspects of Florida life, history and travel, as well as a large video and audio-tape library.

A good branch of the library is in Miami Beach (☎ 305-535-4219) at 2100 Collins Ave, open Monday and Wednesday 10 am to 8 pm, Tuesday and Thursday to Saturday 10 am to 5:30 pm, closed Sunday.

Media
The *Miami Herald* is the city's major daily. The *New Times* has great coverage of local issues, along with superb listings of restaurants, a club/pub/bar/theater/cinema/special events calendar and reviews (available free around town).

Wire has up-to-date club listings and a club calendar. On Friday, the *Herald* features a pullout section called *Weekend*, which has movie and music reviews and listings, gallery information for Miami and surrounding areas, comedy and a whole lot of other stuff.

The *Miami Herald* publishes *el Nuevo Herald*, an excellent Spanish daily. *El Diario Américas* is another Spanish-language daily. Most major Western European newspapers are available at good newsstands.

National Public Radio (NPR) is at 91.3 FM.

Universities
The two major players in the area are the state-run Florida International University (FIU) and the University of Miami (UM).

FIU, a state university with a liberal arts core curriculum, is the larger of the two, with enrollment of more than 26,000 students. Its University Park campus is located on US Hwy 41 (west of Calle Ocho) between SW 107th Ave and Florida's Turnpike. The FIU North Campus is located off US Hwy 1 at NE 151st St.

Founded in 1925, UM's Coral Gables campus is on 260 acres. The university has a total enrollment of about 13,000 full- and part-time students.

MIAMI

Gay & Lesbian

In an emergency, call the Switchboard of Miami (☎ 305-358-4357). The South Beach Business Guild (☎ 305-534-3336, 888-893-5595), 1657 Drexel Ave, represents businesses that are owned by, or friendly to, gay men, lesbians and bisexuals.

twn is a local weekly newspaper focusing on gay and lesbian community issues.

Lips is a lesbian-oriented monthly newspaper with a very good calendar section; *Pride* is a biweekly gay listings magazine; *Hotspots* is much flashier and is packed with ads from nightclubs and straightforward classifieds for prostitutes. *Scoop* is *Hotspots*' main competitor. *She Times* is another monthly lesbian-oriented paper.

Gaydar (☎ 305-673-1690), 718 Lincoln Rd, rents videos and sells gay and lesbian literature as well as postcards, gifts, flags, magazines, condoms and leather. It's a good gay information source as well. *Lambda Passages* (☎ 305-754-6900), way north at 7545 Biscayne Blvd, sells gay and lesbian books and videos.

The club scene is ever changing (during the research for this book, four closed), so check the newspapers listed above for absolutely up-to-date information during your trip.

Photography

Of the many places to develop and buy film in the area, the best are on Miami Beach: Tropicolor Photo at 1442 Alton Rd (☎ 305-672-3729) and 1657 Washington Ave (☎ 305-538-1183), and LIB Color Labs (☎ 305-538-5600) at 851 Washington Ave.

Laundry

In Miami Beach, the folks at the coin laundry at 510 Washington Ave (☎ 305-534-4298) are very friendly; it's open daily 6 am to 2 am. Mark's Dry Cleaning (☎ 305-538-6275) is 'at the breezy corner of Alton Rd and 20th St.'

Medical Services

The Stanley C Myers Community Health Center (☎ 305-538-8835), 710 Alton Rd, is a public clinic that charges based on your income. You'll need to get there early (it's open Monday to Friday 7:30 am to 4:30 pm, closed Saturday and Sunday) as lines to this walk-in clinic are usually very long. You'll need to bring ID, and US citizens should bring proof of residence and income. If you're foreign born, bring your passport and I-94 card.

Check in the yellow pages under Physicians or Clinics to find a doctor, or call the Dade County Medical Association (☎ 305-324-8717) from 9 am to 5 pm Monday to Friday. Look in the yellow pages under Dentists to find one of those, or try 1-800-DENTIST (☎ 800-336-8478), a free referral service.

Planned Parenthood (☎ 305-285-5535) is at 1699 SW 27th Ave.

In a serious emergency, call ☎ 911 for an ambulance to take you to the nearest hospital's emergency room. Mount Sinai Medical Center (☎ 305-674-2121), 4300 Alton Rd, is considered the best in the area.

Dangers & Annoyances

If you encounter any problems with hotels, restaurants or businesses during your stay, you aren't powerless; you have options other than the police. For incidents that occur anywhere in Miami Beach, contact Michael Aller (☎ 305-673-7010, 305-886-4795 emergency beeper), Miami Beach's lovable Tourism and Convention coordinator.

Unsafe Areas There are a few areas considered by locals to be dangerous. Racism – overt or implied – may be responsible for some, like Liberty City, a predominantly black neighborhood in northwest Miami, and Little Haiti. We've never had any problems in either place, but in these and other reputedly 'bad' areas, you should avoid walking around alone late at night, use common sense and travel in groups. This is not, as one irascible *Herald* editor claimed, 'pooh-poohing' the danger. We're just saying that we never had problems and you should use common sense.

Any deserted area, like below 5th St in Miami Beach or the area near the Greyhound station in downtown Miami, is more dangerous at night, as are areas under causeways and bridges from Miami, where homeless people and some refugees have set up shantytowns.

If you're considering sex on the beach, realize it's not a very original idea: police patrol as do muggers.

Use caution when changing money – muggers have been known to hang around at exchange offices looking for victims.

Bad Service Service in some Miami Beach restaurants can be atrocious. Petulant and pouty wanna-be models of both sexes are employed at practically every Ocean Drive restaurant as 'hosts' and waitstaff. There's nothing much you can do about it, except keep your dignity and remember: real models don't have to hand you a menu.

MIAMI BEACH
• population 93,000

Most people come here for the beaches, clubs and bars, but there are other compelling attractions within Miami Beach that you should really try to see during your stay. And happily, these attractions are easy to access, so a day spent seeing what the Beach has to offer is one very well spent.

In addition to Cubans and a decidedly Latino flair, large numbers of Jews have settled here over the last 50 years. There is a Cuban-Jewish Congregation (☎ 305-534-7213), in a building that looks just like something out of Bedrock, at 1700 Michigan Ave.

South Beach
Art Deco Historic District The Deco District, one of the largest areas in the USA to be placed on the National Register of Historic Places, is in the very heart of South Beach. Its unique hotels and apartment buildings have now been renovated with a decidedly colorful flair, the facades painted with pastel pinks, blues and greens that make for a walk into the Roaring '20s, or a tour of the very best in American kitsch, depending on your views.

The listing on the Register protected the area from attempts by the city and developers to raze significant portions of what was

in the 1980s a crime-ridden collection of crumbling eyesores populated by drug-crazed lunatics, Cuban refugees and elderly residents.

The listing was fought for by Barbara Baer Capitman in 1976 after she heard plans by the city of Miami to raze several historic buildings in what became the Omni Mall. But Leonard Horowitz, one cofounder of the Miami Design Preservation League (MDPL), also played a pivotal role in putting South Beach back on the map by painting the then-drably painted Deco buildings in shocking colors like pinks, lavenders and turquoises.

The Deco District is bounded by Dade Blvd at the north, 6th St at the south, the Atlantic Ocean at the east and Lenox Court (half a block east of Alton Rd) at the west. It contains an estimated 800 buildings, and the best thing about them is scale in general: most are no taller than the palm trees. While the architecture is by no means uniform – you'll see examples of Streamline, Moderne and Mediterranean Revival as well as Art Deco – it all works well together, giving the entire district the feel of a small village.

Highlights in the Deco District include examples of Streamline, like the Avalon, Essex, Chesterfield, Carlyle, Leslie, Tides, Cardozo and Breakwater Hotels; Mediterranean, including most buildings along Española Way but especially the Clay Hotel & International Hostel, the Old City Hall at 1130 Washington Ave, the Wolfsonian Foundation building, Edison Hotel, Casa Casuarina (the late Versace's house), the Fernwood at 935 Pennsylvania Ave, and the Regal at the corner of 11th St and Pennsylvania Ave; Parc Vendome at 736 13th St; the Depression Moderne post office on Washington Ave; and the Neo-Classical Revival Betsy Ross Hotel. Another highlight is the Coral House at the corner of 9th St and Collins Ave.

South Pointe & Ocean Beach Historic District Because the boundaries of the Deco District only extended as far south as 6th St, the area from there to South Pointe at the island's southern tip was, as the

Gianni Versace

Gianni Versace (1947-97), born of a salesman and a seamstress in Reggio di Calabria, Italy, had moved to Milan and become a designer by the time he was 25. His collaboration with photographer Richard Avedon in 1975 marked the start of Versace as Fabulous and Famous. As his career skyrocketed, Versace designed gowns, dresses and costumes for a gaggle of celebrities including Elton John, the late Princess Diana and Elizabeth Hurley.

In the 1980s, his *Miami Vice* designs spawned an entire look, and celebrities were falling over themselves to buy any of the designer's playful, bawdy, revealing and sometimes demure offerings.

By the 1990s, Versace had propagated shops and studios around the world and had become Italy's leading ready-to-wear designer, while his more elaborate designs were catching ever more attention in Hollywood, Cannes, London, Paris and Milan.

His eye-catching creations simply oozed – and sometimes shouted at the top of their lungs – sex. Everyone who's seen it refers to the breast-pushing costume Versace created for model/actress Elizabeth Hurley as 'that dress,' and while Versace would tone things down for Diana and even Courtney Love, for the most part he flaunted his spirited, playful and sexy side to the hilt.

On July 15, 1997, Versace was shot and killed at the gate to his Miami Beach mansion, Casa Casuarina. Police named a suspect in the shooting several hours later: Andrew Cunanan, a 27-year-old wanted by the FBI in connection with a cross-country murder spree. Earlier, Cunanan was alleged to have killed two Minneapolis men, a Chicago millionaire and a cemetery worker from New Jersey. Police found Cunanan's abandoned red pickup truck near the

developers like to say, 'in play.' In February 1996, the city designated most of the area a historic district, but not before the developers managed to get many of their projects grandfathered in, meaning they were given variances because they were in the process of building when the regulations were passed.

So while construction will continue in the area, **South Pointe Park** is a wonderful place to spend a sunny afternoon. It has a nice playground, a fishing pier (from which kids – illegally – dive into Government Cut), a short boardwalk and an excellent stretch of beach that's less crowded during the week than the beaches to the near north (though on weekends it's positively overrun by Latino families – see Beaches below).

The graffitied Miami Beach logo on the pastel pink **water tower** at the intersection of Jefferson Ave and Alton Rd is classic 1980s Miami Beach.

At the southwest corner of 5th St and Collins Ave, **The Paper Boy** is a bronze sculpture by artist Glenna Goodacre, best known for her Vietnam Women's Memorial near the Vietnam Veterans Memorial in Washington, DC, as well as the image of Sacagawea on the face of the future $1 coin.

Ocean Drive A walk along Ocean Drive from north to south is a safari through the trendy. To the right are the hotels and sidewalk cafés that seem to spill into the street. Vehicular traffic is limited to vintage roadsters, '63 Mustangs and grandiose Harley-Davidsons.

Fashion plates will want to head immediately for the Miami Beach residence of the late Gianni Versace, **Casa Casuarina** (1930), at 1114 Ocean Drive, a flashy three-story Spanish-Mediterranean palace.

But the fashionably impaired needn't worry; despite the Drive's undeniable chic,

Gianni Versace

Versace murder scene and began the most widely publicized manhunt since the famous OJ Simpson car chase.

Miami Beach and the fashion world found themselves at the epicenter of international media attention, and millions watched live as police closed in on the houseboat where Cunanan had barricaded himself. He had already committed suicide.

There is speculation as to whether Cunanan and Versace had a relationship. Cunanan, described both as a 'prostitute' and a 'kept man,' had apparently boasted to friends that he knew the designer. Versace was involved in a long-term relationship when he died.

One thing is clear: the House of Versace fashion empire, which the designer ran with his brother Santo and sister Donatella, was one of the world's largest, with an estimated income of $2 billion a year. Versace was widely seen as being at the height of his career at the time of the murder, and he was mourned by the fashion world as a lost star. The company, which may be in the process of going public, remains under the control of his family.

it's definitely a come-as-you-are affair. The minimum requirements are a pair of cut-off blue jeans, a T-shirt and an optional pair of in-line skates.

Get your bearings while checking out the interior of one of the Beach's finest Deco treasures by heading to the **Park Central Hotel** – with its Vampire Lestat room as described in Anne Rice's *Tale of the Body Thief* – at 640 Ocean Drive. Take the elevator to the sundeck on the top floor and gaze out over the city. A good time to visit is around 4 pm, when the huge luxury cruise ships chug through Government Cut channel on their way to the Caribbean; the roof offers a stunning view of the ships against the Miami skyline and beach.

Washington Ave Other than the Wolfsonian Foundation and the clubs and restaurants, there's not much to see on Washington Ave. An exception, believe it or not, is the 1937 **post office** (☎ 305-599-1787), at 1300 Washington Ave, a Depression Moderne building with an enormous dome on the south corner.

At the corner of 17th St is the imposing **Temple Emanu El** synagogue (☎ 305-538-2503), which holds services Sunday to Thursday at 8 am and 5:30 pm, Friday at 8 am and 6:30 pm, and Saturday at 9 am and 6:30 pm. North of 17th St, on the west side of Washington Ave, is the **Miami Beach Convention Center**, home to huge auto and boat shows.

Lincoln Road Mall 'The Road' – a wide, pedestrian-only stretch of sidewalk – is the Beach's cultural epicenter, with galleries every hundred feet or so and sidewalk cafés filled with off-duty models trying to relax.

Highlights include the **Miami City Ballet** (where you can watch rehearsals through the picture window), the **Colony Theatre** and the **Lincoln Theatre** – a Deco delight that is home to the New World Symphony. See the Entertainment section for information on those venues.

Biweekly **gallery walks** take place on alternating Saturday nights (see Entertainment later in the chapter).

Every Sunday from November to March, there's a **farmers' market** on the Road between Euclid and Meridian Aves. If you have kids, note that the Lincoln Road Partnership arranges kids' activities during the farmer's market: meet at the fountain in front of World Resources Café (☎ 305-534-9095), 719 Lincoln Rd.

Free, golf-cart-drawn trams shuttle up and down the Road between Washington Ave and Alton Rd.

Española Way Originally designed as a 'Spanish village' in the early 1920s, Española Way (pronounced 'ess-pahn-YO-la') features the **Clay Hotel & International Hostel**, which has a special place in our hearts. It was formerly the home of none other than Desi Arnaz, who also had a club here, and Al Capone's S&H Gambling Syndicate, which had a casino in the middle wing (now rooms 128 to 138).

The most striking section is the short block between Washington and Drexel Aves, which is lined with – well, there's no other word but adorable – Spanish-style buildings. It was on this street that Desi himself started the rhumba phenomenon. Nothing like the rhumba…

Bass Museum The Bass Museum (☎ 305-673-7530), 2121 Park Ave, will be closed for renovation until February 2000, so call to confirm the following information.

The museum is a wonderful surprise, directly behind the Miami Beach Public Library, west of Collins Park. Selections from its permanent collection rotate through the galleries on the ground floor, while a widely varying array of visiting exhibitions rotate through other halls on the ground and 2nd floors. The star of the show here is the tapestry collection, to which the paintings play a definite second fiddle.

The South Gallery (to the left from the main entrance) contains *The Tournament* – said to be one of the finest examples of tapestry in an American museum.

The museum is open Tuesday to Saturday 10 am to 5 pm, Sunday 1 to 5 pm, closed Monday. On the second and fourth Wednesday of the month, the museum is open 1 to 9 pm. Admission is $5 for adults, $3 for senior citizens and students. For special exhibitions, admission is $7/5. On the second and fourth Wednesday of the month, admission is by donation only from 5 to 9 pm.

Wolfsonian Foundation In a foreboding Mediterranean-style building on the northeast corner of 10th St, the Wolfsonian Foundation (☎ 305-531-1001), 1001 Washington Ave, has a fascinating collection of American and European art. But works from this collection are meted out in rotating exhibitions held on the museum's 5th floor.

Admission to exhibitions is $5 for adults, $3.50 for seniors, students and youth six to 18, free for children under six. It's generally open Monday to Saturday 11 am to 6 pm, Sunday noon to 5 pm, closed Wednesday. On Thursday, admission is free from 6 pm to 9 pm, though donations are strongly encouraged.

Holocaust Memorial Created by Miami Beach Holocaust survivors and beautifully realized by sculptor Kenneth Treister, this is one of the most elaborate, exquisitely detailed and moving memorials we've ever seen. It's something all visitors to Miami Beach should visit, and admission is free.

There are five main areas, some of which contain more than one exhibit. Your first glimpse at the memorial, which is at the corner of Meridian Ave and Dade Blvd, opposite the Miami Beach Chamber of Commerce, is the *Sculpture of Love & Anguish*: an enormous arm cast in oxidized bronze bearing an Auschwitz tattooed number (the number is intentionally one that was never issued at the camp) rising from the depths – the last reach of a dying person. Scaling the arm are a terrifying series of bronze sculptures of concentration camp victims attempting to climb out of their hell.

The Lonely Hall, inscribed with the names of the major concentration camps, leads from the dome to the main plaza of the *Sculpture of Love & Anguish*, and only now does its force hit the visitor full on. While the figures climbing the arm are visible from over the wall, there's no indication of the level of detail on each character's face until you're inside. Surrounding the bronze arm is a terrifying gathering of statues, from *The Beginning* to the *Final Sculpture*.

As you exit through the dome again, turn right and walk past The Arbor of History, a colonnade of Jerusalem stone topped by vines. On the wall is a series of photographs etched in black granite. Beneath the photographs are captions by Professor Helen Fagin, the Memorial's historian, along with a summarized history of the Holocaust.

The memorial (☎ 305-538-1663) is open 9 am to 9 pm daily.

Sanford L Ziff Jewish Museum The Sanford L Ziff Jewish Museum of Florida (☎ 305-672-5044, www.jewishmuseum.com), 301 Washington Ave, is dedicated to exhibits on the history of Jews in Florida. Its mainstay is *MOSAIC: Jewish Life in Florida*, which features thousands of fascinating items from Russian samovar kettles to photographs, business cards, documents and other products of Jewish-owned or -run companies.

Their other star exhibit is the excellent *Birobidzhan: Zionist Utopia or Soviet Hoax?*, focusing on the autonomous Jewish region set up in Siberia in 1934 by the Soviet government under Joseph Stalin.

The museum is open Tuesday to Sunday 10 am to 5 pm, closed Monday. Admission is $5 for adults, $4 for senior citizens and students, or a flat fee of $10 per family; it's free on Saturday.

Middle & Northern Miami Beach

Once you pass 21st St on Collins Ave heading north, you're entering the world of 1950s and '60s Miami Beach – a series of monstrous high-rise hotels that line Collins Ave north of 20th St. With a few notable exceptions – like the lovingly restored **Indian Creek Hotel** at 2727 Indian Creek Drive – from there up to the city limits is a never-ending string of high-rise condominiums, hotels and apartment buildings.

As you approach the **Fontainebleau Hilton Resort & Towers**, just before Collins Ave makes its little jog to the left, you see what appears to be two magnificent pillars, through which the Fontainebleau pool is visible. As you get closer, you'll realize it's a spectacular *trompe-l'oeil* mural. The mural, designed by Richard Hass and painted over an eight-week period by Edwin Abreu, covers 13,016 sq feet of what was a big blank wall before 1986.

The **Eden Roc Hotel & Resort**, 4525 Collins Ave, is another notable 1950s-era resort.

Beaches

For a city beach, Miami Beach is one of the best around. The water is relatively clear and warm, the sand relatively white, and best of all, the beach is wide and certainly long enough to accommodate the throngs. The throngs, by the way, are generally rather considerate in that there's usually not a ton of litter or broken glass in the sand. Use caution when walking barefoot anyway.

The most crowded sections of the beach are, of course, in South Beach – from about 5th St to 21st St. Weekends are more crowded than weekdays, but except during special events, it's usually not too difficult to find a quiet spot. The beaches north of 21st St – especially the one at 53rd St, which has a playground and public toilets – are more family oriented.

For some reason, Latino families – predominantly Cuban – tend to congregate between 5th St and South Pointe. In this area, topless bathing is unwise and can be considered offensive.

The gay beach centers around 12th St, across from the Palace Bar & Grill. It's not as if there's sex going on; it's just a spot

MIAMI

where gay men happen to congregate. There's Fabulous volleyball Sunday afternoons at 4 pm, packed with fun and fun-loving locals.

Bathing nude is legal at Haulover Beach, north of Miami Beach. The area you're looking for is at the northern end of the park between the two northernmost parking lots. The area north of the lifeguard tower is predominantly gay; south of it is straight. There's no sex allowed on any of these beaches, and you will get arrested if you're seen trying to get to the bushes.

There's a **boardwalk** running from 21st St all the way north to 46th St, and another running for several blocks north of South Pointe Park.

The **Promenade** is a wavy ribbon of concrete at the beach's westernmost edge (just east of Ocean Drive) that runs from 5th St to almost 16th St. If you've ever looked at a fashion magazine, you've seen it: it's *the* photo-shoot site. (If you want to see a photo shoot, get here at 7 am and walk the length. Within 300 yards of your starting point you'll see a shoot.) All through the day and late into the night, this is where in-line skaters and roller skaters, bicyclists, skateboarders, dog walkers, yahoos, locals and tourists mill about and occasionally bump into each other.

BISCAYNE BAY

Between Miami and Miami Beach are about a dozen islands, some more exclusive than others, but all visible from the MacArthur and Julia Tuttle Causeways. We list them from east to west.

Port of Miami

Miami is the cruise capital of the world, and when the monstrous liners are docked at the Port of Miami waiting to fill up with people, it's a pretty amazing sight. You can't help but notice the ships as you look south from the MacArthur Causeway.

Flagler Memorial Monument

On a little island off the west coast of Miami Beach is a monument to Henry Flagler, one of Florida's pioneers. The monument is accessible only by private boat. If you have a private boat, there are mooring posts available around the island. The water is very shallow, more so at low tide, so be careful not to beach yourself!

Fisher Island

Carl Fisher, one of the Beach's pioneering developers, bought up this glorious little island and planned to die here – he even built a mausoleum. But after awhile he got bored with it, and when William K Vanderbilt II fell in love with the island, Fisher traded it for Vanderbilt's 250-foot yacht *and* its crew. Things were like that in those days.

Today, the island is a totally exclusive resort, accessible only by air and private ferry, and the condominiums that line the mile-long private beach range from $600,000 hovels to $6 million pads. Maybe that's why the sun still shines over the island when it's raining on Miami Beach.

You can stay here, at the Inn at the Fisher Island Club (see Places to Stay later in the chapter).

The island is usually open only to paying guests and residents, but you can arrange a tour if you're especially persistent. The *Eagle, Flamingo* and *Pelican* ferries leave from the Fisher Island ferry terminal off the MacArthur Causeway, just west of the Coast Guard Station, every 15 minutes around the clock.

Hibiscus, Palm & Star Islands

These islands are three little bastions of wealth – though far less exclusive than Fisher Island – just west of Miami Beach. There aren't too many famous people living there now (just very rich ones), though Star Island boasts Miami's favorite star, Gloria Estefan, whose estate is at the eastern end. Palm Island was for a short time infamous for its local resident Al Capone.

Star Island is the farthest east, accessed by the little bridge almost opposite the Fisher Island ferry terminal.

Watson Island

The island nearest to downtown Miami, just east of the mainland, is the grungiest of the lot. The north side of Watson Island holds the **Ichimura Miami-Japan Garden** (☎ 305-538-2121), given to the city in 1961 and featuring an octagonal Hakkaku-Do pavilion and a statue of Hotei, the Japanese god of prosperity. The garden is open Monday to Friday 8 am to 3 pm, Saturday 10 am to 4 pm, Sunday noon to 4 pm. Admission is free.

Watson Island is home to Pan Am Air Bridge Seaplanes (☎ 305-371-8628/9), formerly Chalk's, which runs shuttle services between Watson Island and Fort Lauderdale, Bimini and Paradise Island aboard 17-seat Grumman Mallard seaplanes.

This is also the place for **helicopter tours** of Miami and Miami Beach – the helipad here hums in high season. Action Helicopter Service (☎ 305-358-4723) offers jaunts out over South Beach, Fisher Island, the Port of Miami and Bayside Marketplace in 10 minutes (10 minutes!!) for $55 per person (two people minimum).

Parrot Jungle (described later in the chapter) has been planning a move to the island for a long time, and if that ever happens things will change considerably.

Pelican Island

On weekends, you can take a free ferry from the causeway west of North Bay Village (about 2 miles west of 71st St in Miami Beach) to little Pelican Island. It's just a pleasant place to have a picnic and look at the dozens of pelicans that congregate on and around the island.

DOWNTOWN MIAMI

Miami's downtown skyline is considered one of the nation's most beautiful, or at least most colorful. At night, the towering skyscrapers are lit in neon, and the most unmistakable symbol of downtown is the IM Pei-designed **NationsBank Tower** (1987) at 100 SE 2nd St. The building is illuminated every night. On special events, the lighting – on seven visible faces of the building – can be custom lit with a combination of seven colors per face. Other neon comes courtesy of the Metromover's rainbow-illuminated track (see boxed text).

For a downtown, Miami is not exactly the most exciting you'll encounter. Most of the streets are lined with shops selling electronics, luggage and clothing to Latin American visitors, and the place dies very quickly after 5 pm, when the office towers disgorge their yuppies.

Metro-Dade Cultural Center

The Mediterranean-style cultural center at 101 W Flagler St (Metromover stop: Government Center) is sort of a one-stop shopping center for culture. The 3.3-acre complex holds two museums and the city's excellent public library. A combination ticket for both the Historical Museum and Center for Fine Arts is $6 for adults, $3.50 for children.

Historical Museum of Southern Florida

This is one of our favorite museums, and it's excellent for kids. The Historical Museum (☎ 305-375-1492, www.historicalmuseum .org) has displays covering 10,000 years of Florida history. All the exhibits have excellent explanatory materials, all in English and Spanish. Count on spending more than an hour here.

Downstairs is a temporary exhibition hall, **La Plaza Theater**, which has new exhibitions every three to four months.

Admission is $4 for adults, $2 for children six to 12. On Monday the admission is waived – they still suggest the $4 donation, however. It's open Monday to Wednesday and Saturday from 10 am to 5 pm, Thursday to 9 pm, Sunday from noon to 5 pm.

Miami Art Museum of Miami-Dade County

This museum (☎ 305-375-3000), in Philip Johnson-designed digs, does rotating exhibitions of fine arts, concentrating on post-WWII International art.

Admission is $5 for adults, $2.50 for students and seniors, free to children under 12. It's open Tuesday, Wednesday and Friday 10 am to 5 pm, Thursday to 9 pm (free admission 6 to 9 pm), Saturday and Sunday noon to 5 pm, closed Monday.

Wolfson Campus

The Wolfson Campus of Miami-Dade Community College (☎ 305-237-3696), at 300 NE 2nd Ave (Metromover stop: College/Bayside), has two art galleries of rotating exhibitions: the Centre Gallery and the Frances Wolfson Gallery. Both are open Monday to Friday 10 am to 6 pm; admission is free.

Bayfront Park

A freight port during the first Miami boom in the 1920s, Bayfront Park (☎ 305-358-7550) is today a calm bit of green downtown, essentially between the Hotel InterContinental and Bayside Marketplace.

There are two performance venues here: the Amphitheater (home to Fourth of July and New Year's Eve festivities) and the smaller, 200-seat South End Amphitheater (the site of Bayfront Park After Dark, a free entertainment series). Bayfront Park also houses a monument to the astronauts killed in the 1986 explosion of the space shuttle *Challenger*.

Bayside Marketplace

Bayside Marketplace (☎ 305-577-3344), 401 Biscayne Blvd (it actually runs from NE 4th to NE 9th Sts), is a shopping mall that hordes of tourists just adore. It has a bunch of little tourist shops, some restaurants – including a Hard Rock Cafe – and the M/T *Celebration* (☎ 305-445-8456), which runs

Bay Ex-Cape sightseeing tours through Biscayne Bay, the Port of Miami and the Venetian Islands daily at 11 am and 1, 2, 5 and 7 pm. Bayside is home to free concerts every day of the year.

This is also the main stop for the Water Taxi, which runs shuttle service to many downtown hotels as well as to Miami Beach (see Getting Around later in the chapter).

Freedom Tower

At 600 Biscayne Blvd, Freedom Tower is famous for being the 'Ellis Island of the South': the immigration processing center for almost half a million Cuban refugees in the 1960s. The building, built in 1925, was for 32 years the home of the *Miami Daily News*. It was placed on the National Register of Historic Places in 1979. Today, despite renovation, it is abandoned and looms over Biscayne Bay near the entrances to the Port of Miami and Bayside Marketplace.

Old US Courthouse

The coquina headquarters of Miami's first major post office (1931) later became the Miami Courthouse. It was – in a kinder, gentler time – large enough to accommodate the needs of the US Government prosecutors.

As crime increased, the Feds outgrew the building and now occupy the nearby Federal Building. Today, the courthouse (☎ 305-523-5100), at 300 NE 1st Ave, is open to visitors. Stop here to get a look at Denman Fink's *Law Guides Florida Progress*, a mural depicting Florida in the 1930s, including a Cuba-bound Pan Am Clipper. The building is open Monday to Friday 9 am to 5 pm; the mural is in the main courtroom (2nd floor), which also boasts hardwood furnishings such as hewn-wood benches and beautiful arched windows.

Brickell Ave Bridge

The Brickell Avenue Bridge, which crosses the Miami River south of downtown, reopened after a $21 million renovation, which took several years. It's more beautiful than ever, but its claim to fame now is the 17-foot bronze statue by Cuban-born sculptor Manuel Carbonell of a Tequesta warrior and his family atop the towering *Pillar of History* column, at the center of the bridge's east side.

From downtown, take NE 2nd Ave south, which turns into SE 2nd Ave before the bridge and then becomes Brickell Ave, lined with office towers and hotels. There's nothing really to see in this area, with the possible exception of Tobacco Road, a small collection of bars that line S Miami Ave, including Tobacco Road Liquor Bar at 626 S Miami Ave (see Places to Eat and Entertainment later in the chapter).

Miami City Cemetery

The original cemetery of the city of Miami, at 1800 NE 2nd Ave, was established in July 1897, and you can still visit if that's the sort of thing you like to do. The 9000-plus-graves cemetery has separate white, black and Jewish sections. Julia Tuttle was the 13th burial, and she has a front and center gravesite. Luminaries include many mayors and politicians, alongside about 90 Confederate dead and veterans from all wars in the 20th century.

The cemetery is not in the friendliest part of town. The cemetery manager, Clyde Cates, suggests that if you want to visit, call him a day in advance and leave a message on his answering machine at ☎ 305-579-6938. Clyde will give visitors an informal tour.

Cates recommends only visiting during the day. Take Biscayne Blvd to NE 18th St and turn west to the cemetery, to avoid getting lost in the back streets. It's open Monday to Friday 7:30 am to 4 pm, and admission is free.

Bacardi Imports Headquarters

Visit the headquarters of Bacardi Imports (☎ 305-573-8511), in an intricately decorated building at 2100 Biscayne Blvd (the poorer cousin of the one in Havana). The building is also home to the small World of Bacardi Museum, dedicated to the history of the Bacardi family and the USA's most popular rum company, from 1838 to the present. It's filled with mementos and artifacts as well as artwork, paintings and sculptures by family

members, and the abortive attempt at a Macarena: a line dance celebrating the Cuba Libre – Bacardi and Coke – that went down like a lead balloon. It's open Monday to Friday 9 am to noon. Admission is free.

LITTLE HAVANA

After the Mariel Boatlift (see the History section in Facts about Florida), the section of town to which Cuban exiles had been gravitating for years exploded into a distinctly Cuban neighborhood, now known as Little Havana. The borders of Little Havana are arguable, but for the purposes of this book, they're *roughly* SW 13th St at the south, SW 3rd St at the north, SW 3rd Ave at the east and SW 37th Ave at the west. Note that while the Cuban influence is strongest in the southwest quadrant of the city, it's pervasive throughout Miami.

Spanish is the predominant language here, and you will absolutely run into people who speak no English; see the Language section in Facts about Florida for some key phrases, or pick up Lonely Planet's *Latin American Spanish Phrasebook*.

The heart of Little Havana is Calle Ocho (pronounced 'KAH-yeh AW-cho'), Spanish for SW 8th St (actually it's Spanish just for 8th St, but what the hell). The entire length of Calle Ocho is lined with Cuban shops, cafés, record stores, pharmacies, clothing stores and, most amusing, bridal shops, all teeming with action. Calle Ocho runs one way from west to east for most of the length of Little Havana.

But while the wall-of-sound-style speakers set up outside places like Power Records are blasting salsa and other Latin music into the street, Little Havana as a tourist attraction is an elusive bugger. The area is not concentrated like a Chinatown or a Harlem; it's actually not really a tourist attraction at all. It's just a Cuban neighborhood, so except during the occasional street fair or celebration, you shouldn't expect, like, Tito Puente and Celia Cruz leading a parade of colorfully attired, tight-trousered men and slinky, scantily clad women in a Carnaval or anything. More likely, you'll see old men playing dominos.

Which is exactly the attraction the area holds: it's real. It's not putting on airs for anyone, and it could not care less whether you see it or not. So you should definitely go.

The famous green sign reading *Republic Bank Welcomes You to Little Havana* is on Calle Ocho just east of where SW 22nd Ave shoots off to the northeast.

Calle Ocho

Cuban **botanicas** are scattered along Calle Ocho, selling Santería-related items such as perfumed waters named for properties you may desire, like 'Money' or 'Love me,' or the more esoteric 'Keep Dead Resting.'

And you'll want to stop for a guarapo, a café con leche or a thimbleful of zoom juice (espresso) and maybe a little pastry. See the Places to Eat section for proper restaurant listings, but for a quick something, try Karla Bakery at No 1842 (great-smelling and great-tasting pastries worth waiting in line for) or El Rey de las Fritas at No 1177.

Máximo Gómez Park

The scores of elderly Cuban men playing dominoes at this park, at the corner of SW 15th Ave, is an example of good government at work: this is a program for senior citizens run under the auspices of the Little Havana Development Authority. The park – named for Máximo Gómez y Baez, the Dominican-born chief of the Cuban Liberating Army, is open every day 9 am to 6 pm. It's a fascinating place to sit for a few minutes and watch the action, or join in yourself.

A couple of doors down (east) Calle Ocho is a little Cuban-Chinese restaurant with poor food but perfectly decent espresso (50¢) and café con leche (90¢) to bring out to the park.

El Crédito Cigars

Cigar smoking has really taken the USA by storm once again. Ernesto Curillo, the present owner of this very successful cigar factory (☎ 305-858-4162), 1106 Calle Ocho, is one of the leaders of the American cigar renaissance, according to an article in *Cigar Aficionado*.

You can stand in front of the picture window looking in at the dozen or so Cuban *tabaqueros* hand-rolling cigars, or go in to smell (it's very...shall we say, aromatic) and buy. They're really nice about letting people take photos, so ask if you want a photo. It's open Monday to Saturday 7:30 am to 6 pm, closed Sunday.

Cuban Memorial Blvd

For two blocks along SW 13th Ave south of Calle Ocho is a series of monuments to Cuban patriots and freedom fighters (read: anti-Castro Cubans).

The eternal flame at the corner of Calle Ocho is the **Eternal Torch in Honor of the 2506th Brigade**, for the counterrevolutionaries who died during the botched Bay of Pigs invasion (see the History section in Facts about Florida). Other monuments include the huge brass map of Cuba, 'Dedicated to the ideals of people who will never forget the pledge of making their Fatherland free,' as well as a bust of José Martí.

CORAL GABLES

Coral Gables is a lovely, if pricey, city that exudes opulence and comfort. A gaggle of architects and planners under the direction of George Merrick designed the city to be a 'model suburb,' with a decidedly Mediterranean theme, huge gateways, and wide, tree-lined streets.

Today, while exciting to multinational corporations and the diplomatic crowds that make their homes here, Coral Gables is a quiet place with a fledgling arts-and-culture scene.

Lowe Art Museum

Perhaps Miami's finest art museum, the Lowe (☎ 305-284-3535), at 1301 Stanford Drive (two blocks north of the University Metrorail station on the University of Miami campus), has one of the largest permanent collections of art in Dade County. It

MIAMI

houses more than 6000 pieces, including antiquities, Renaissance and Baroque art; 18th- through 20th-century European and American sculpture, Egyptian, Greek, and Roman antiquities and Asian, African, Pre-Columbian and Native American entries as well.

A recent renovation added 13,000 sq feet of exhibition space. In addition to the permanent collection, there are about 10 changing exhibitions every year.

Considered one of the USA's finest, the Alfred I Barton collection of Southwest Indian art comprises works from Pueblo, Navajo and Rio Grande weavings as well as a large sampling of Guatemalan textiles. The Samuel H Kress Collection of Renaissance and Baroque Art consists of paintings and sculpture from masters including Jordaens, Cranach the Elder, Isenbrandt and Tintoretto.

The Lowe's European collection includes works by Gauguin, Picasso and Monet. The Asian collection contains textiles, paintings, ceramics and stone work from throughout Asia, and a large Chinese ceramics exhibit spans from 3500 BC to the early 20th century. The Bischoff collection of Central and South American art contains almost 2500 items from Chile to Mexico in all media.

The museum is open Tuesday, Wednesday, Friday and Saturday 10 am to 5 pm, Thursday noon to 7 pm, Sunday noon to 5 pm, closed Monday. Admission is $5 for adults, $3 for seniors and students. Use the metered parking lots and get tokens (50¢) for them inside the gift shop.

Florida Museum of Hispanic & Latin American Art

The Florida Museum of Hispanic & Latin American Art (☎ 305-444-7060), 4006 Aurora St, is one of the few museums in the country dedicated solely to the culture of Hispanic and Latin Americans. It has 11 rotating exhibitions per year (the museum's closed in August). A great time to visit is during one of its free Opening Nights, held the first Friday of the month, featuring local, national and international artists, and, oh yes, free cocktails from 6 to 10 pm. After you reread that sentence, we'll continue. Nice, huh? Hours are Tuesday to Friday 11 am to 5 pm, Saturday 11 am to 4 pm. Admission is free.

Architectural Disneyland

George Merrick (1886-1942) envisioned what today would be called an 'Architectural Disneyland' filled with theme areas. His idea was to bring people into a place that felt 'old.' He created a Dutch South African Village (6612, 6700, 6704 and 6710 SW 42nd Ave and 6705 San Vicente St) modeled after 17th-century Dutch colonists' farmhouses; a tiny Chinese Village (one block between San Sovino Ave, Castania Ave, Maggiore St and Riviera Drive); a Florida Pioneer Village (4320, 4409, 4515, 1520 and 4620 Santa Maria St) that looks a lot more like New Hampshire than Miami; and the absolutely stunning French Normandy Village (on the block between SW 42nd Ave, Viscaya Court, Viscaya Ave and Alesio Ave).

Merrick lost the family fortune after the Great Depression, and the city of Coral Gables, which had been incorporated in 1925, went bankrupt. Eventually the city's finances were sorted out. Coral Gables grew with Miami, but it has always seemed to attract more money and less attention.

In fact, Coral Gables is one of the few places in metropolitan Miami that's lovely to walk in: the banyan trees that shelter the winding streets actually provide good relief from the sun, and it's relatively safe there.

Biltmore Hotel

From practically anywhere in Coral Gables, you can see the 315-foot-high tower of the Biltmore Hotel (☎ 305-445-1926), the city's crown jewel at 1200 Anastasia Ave. The historic landmark hotel, which opened in 1926, has a history that reads like an Agatha Christie novel on speed – a story of murder, intrigue, famous gangsters and detectives set against an Old World European-style backdrop.

Al Capone had a speakeasy here, in what's officially called the Everglades Suite but what everyone – even the hotel management privately – calls the Capone Suite. It was in that room that Fats Walsh, the owner of just one of the spirits said to haunt the hotel, was murdered.

The hotel's architecture is referred to as Mediterranean Revivalist. The tower is modeled after (but not a replica of) the Giralda bell tower at the Cathedral of Seville in Spain.

The Biltmore's pool – the largest hotel pool in the continental USA – deserves special mention. It may not have as stunning a setting as the Venetian Pool (see below), but it is one of the most beautiful in the world. There's a café out there, and you can sit poolside with an espresso.

Don't miss storyteller Linda Spitzer's Ghost Stories at the Biltmore (☎ 305-665-8829) every Thursday at 7 pm in front of the fireplace in the upper lobby. It's free, and you'll hear stories of ghosts, celebs who've stayed here, the construction of the hotel and lots more.

For more information on the Biltmore's health clubs, 10 tennis courts, Sunday brunches, Cigars under the Stars, or theater productions of the Gables Stage at the Biltmore (see the Entertainment section), contact the hotel.

Venetian Pool

After all that building taking place in the area, a large quarry was formed. Somebody came up with the brilliant idea of making the world's ugliest hole in the ground the world's most beautiful swimming pool – the Venetian Pool (☎ 305-460-5356), 2701 De Soto Blvd, just next to the DeSoto Fountain (also called the Granada Blvd Fountain), about two blocks south of Coral Way. It's listed on the National Register of Historic Places, and it's on our personal list of favorite places in Miami.

It's a fantastic spring-fed pool with caves, waterfalls and Venetian-style moorings. It's large enough to have a kiddie area and space for lap-swimming as well as room under the big waterfall to just romp around. Different sources come up with different figures, but we're settling on this: the pool holds 820,000 gallons of water. During the winter, the pool is drained and refilled every other night, in summer every night. (The water's recycled through a natural filtration process.)

This pool has horribly complicated opening hours that change four times a year; call them for specific hours. Sometimes the pool is closed on Monday, but it's open year round on Saturday and Sunday from 10 am to 4:30 pm.

Admission is $5 for adults, $4 for teens 13 to 17, $2 for kids; Coral Gables residents (with ID) pay $4/3/2. Token-operated lockers are available for $1.50. There are no refunds due to weather. Free parking is available.

City Hall

Coral Gables City Hall, 405 Biltmore Way at the intersection of Coral Way, is just a neat 1920s building. It has housed meetings of the city commission since February 29, 1928. The first commission was made up of Merrick, ET Purcell, Don Peabody, the city's first mayor – EE Dammers, and the interestingly named Wingfield Webster. Upstairs, there's a tiny display of Coral Gables public transport from the mid-20th century and rotating photography and art exhibits. And oh yes, look up at Denman Fink's *Four Seasons* ceiling painting in the tower, as well as his framed untitled painting of the underwater world on the 2nd-floor landing.

Merrick House

There's not much to see at the 1899 residence of the Merricks (☎ 305-460-5361),

907 Coral Way. In fact, the place is mostly used for meetings and receptions by local clubs. But it's a lovely house, and if the burly and friendly caretaker's around, he'll let you wander through for $2 for adults, 50¢ for kids Sunday and Wednesday 1 to 4 pm. The big draw is the well-maintained organic garden, which has some of the original fruit trees planted in the late 19th century, including king oranges, copperleaf and bamboo. There are good signs pointing the way here.

Watertower & Entrances
Still in restoration, the Alhambra Watertower (1931), where Greenway Court and Ferdinand St meet Alhambra Circle, looks for all the world like a lighthouse.

Merrick had planned a series of elaborate entry gates to the city, but the Great Depression bust dried up most of the planning. Worth noting are Country Club Prado (1927, at Calle Ocho and the Prado Country Club); the Douglas Entrance, *La Puerto del Sol* (1927, at Calle Ocho and Douglas Rd); and the Granada Entrance (Calle Ocho at Granada Blvd).

COCONUT GROVE
The site of the first major settlement in the Miami area, Coconut Grove was, for a time in the 1960s and '70s, a big-time bohemian hangout. The town has evolved – if that's the word – into a highly commercialized area. Its main attraction (other than the excellent Coconut Grove Playhouse, see the Entertainment section) is now the CocoWalk Shopping Center, a stylized shopping mall with some restaurants, shops and a cinema. There are a couple of attractions worth the trip, and a wonderful B&B (see Places to Stay). Just next to that B&B is the former home of Everglades champion Marjory Stoneman Douglas, which the city may soon turn into a museum.

Barnacle State Historic Site
Opposite the Playhouse, this 1891 pioneer residence (☎ 305-448-9445), 3485 Main Hwy, is owned by Ralph Monroe. It's open to the public Friday to Sunday (except Christmas), with guided tours at 10 and 11:30 am and

1 and 2:30 pm. During the week it's open to groups only. Admission is $1.

Coconut Grove Exhibition Center
This center, at 2700 S Bayshore Drive, is the sight of conventions and special events, such as the monthly Coconut Grove Cares antique and jewelry show (☎ 305-444-8454).

SOUTHEAST MIAMI
Miami Museum of Science & Space Transit Planetarium
What a total treat for kids – and we were pretty enthralled ourselves! The Miami Museum of Science (☎ 305-854-4247) & Space Transit Planetarium (☎ 305-854-2222) share a building at 3280 S Miami Ave, near the grounds of the Vizcaya Museum & Gardens (see below) and near the southern city limit. As you enter, the planetarium is to the left, the museum to the right. Before you go inside, take a look at the **ceiling painting** outside the main doors.

Both the museum and the planetarium are open daily 10 am to 6 pm (ticket sales end at 5 pm), closed Christmas and Thanksgiving.

On Friday and Saturday nights from 8:15 to 10 pm, access to the planetarium's telescopes costs $1 (for free stargazing Saturday nights, see Southern Cross Astronomical Society below).

A combination ticket for both attractions is $9 for adults, $7 for seniors and students, $5.50 for kids three to five, and half price for everyone after 4:30 pm.

Museum of Science This is one of the finest science museums in Florida – and Florida has some good ones – for hands-on and creatively fun exhibits. A few years ago the main focus was CyberCity, and many of its exhibits remained after the show closed. Among the draws: about 20 totally tweaked-out Macs and PCs with a T-1 connection to the Internet.

Tribal Spirits: Indians of the Americas has very realistic sculptures and interactive exhibits of North and South American Indian life and history. In Sports Challenge: Your Body at Play, you can go crazy (or tire out the little ones) on a climbing wall and an unintentionally demoralizing pitching speed tester (Nick used to pitch faster than 58 mph, honest).

There's also the museum's famous virtual-reality basketball game, in which you compete with very tall and very talented cyber-players.

Turbulent Landscapes celebrates tornadoes, hurricanes and other weather phenomena.

Space Transit Planetarium There are no major surprises here, though the free Friday and Saturday space lectures and cheap telescope-viewing sessions (free on the first Monday of each month from 8 to 10 pm) hold a special place in the budget traveler's heart. And star-nuts and tripsters will appreciate that the planetarium does movies, star shows and laser shows, including a daily *Star Trek: The Planetarium Experience* as well as a guide to the stars and planets in the sky this year.

On Friday and Saturday nights, the planetarium lets down its hair with three very cool laser-rock shows (additional fee of $6 for adults, $3 for seniors and students).

And weather permitting, on the first and third Friday of the month, *In the Miami Skies* is a free program looking at the skies over the city.

Southern Cross Astronomical Society

Every Saturday night, weather permitting, members of the Southern Cross Astronomical Society (☎ 305-661-1375) set up telescopes for free stargazing at 8 pm in the Old Cutler Hammock Nature Center, 79th Ave at SW 176th St. There are free astronomy lessons and just plain stargazing between 8 and 10 pm. They also hold special events throughout the year; call for more information.

Vizcaya Museum & Gardens

This opulent palace (☎ 305-250-9133), 3251 S Miami Ave, was built in 1916 by James Deering. It's an Italian Renaissance-style villa (used as the setting for the splendid

dinner party in *Ace Ventura: Pet Detective*) and filled with 15th- to 19th-century furniture and decorative arts. However, unless you're an early-20th-century-faux-Venetian-architecture or furniture buff, we can't for the life of us understand why you'd pay $10 for adults and $5 for children six to 12 ($1 AAA discount).

Okay, okay…there *are* undeniably stunning gardens, complete with beautiful fountains. Out back, a stone gondola in the center of the docking area acts as a breakwater, and there's a charming gazebo. The pool is to die for, and there are canals running everywhere. Several narrow trails run through the grounds as well.

Tours of the 1st floor, which are included in the price, are available from 10 am to 2 pm; they start every 15 to 20 minutes. All the rooms are roped off, though you can peek in.

Tickets can be bought daily from 9:30 am to 4:30 pm; once inside, you can stay in the house until 5 pm, the gardens until 5:30 pm.

Key Biscayne & Virginia Key

The Rickenbacker Causeway ($1 toll) links the mainland with Key Biscayne via Virginia Key.

Bill Baggs Cape Florida State Recreation Area The main attraction of Key Biscayne is this recreation area (☎ 305-361-5811), 1200 S Crandon Blvd. All of the 494-acre park's exotic plants – including about half a million Australian pines – were destroyed during Hurricane Andrew, but the park has now replaced most of them. There are walkways and boardwalks as well as nature trails and bike paths.

The 1845 **Cape Florida Lighthouse** (☎ 305-361-8779), at the park's southern end, has stairs leading to the top (kids under 8 are not allowed), where you'll find a 1st-order lens.

The scale of lighthouse lenses, since you asked, was developed by French physicist Augustin Jean Fresnel (1788-1827), who devised a beehive-like reflecting lens sized from 1st through 6th orders. The largest, 1st, is used on seacoasts, while 6th is used in harbors.

To access the recreation area and lighthouse, take the causeway to the very end and follow the signs. Admission is $4 per carload up to eight people; pedestrians and cyclists are $1 per person. The park is open daily 8 am to sundown.

Beaches Crandon Park and Hobie Beaches are public beaches on a 5-mile stretch of white sand on Key Biscayne.

Virginia Key Beach is a lovely city park with picnic tables, barbecue grills and relative peace and quiet. Parking is $2.

Biscayne Nature Center The Marjory Stoneman Douglas Biscayne Nature Center (☎ 305-642-9600) is a great place to bring the kids for hands-on demonstrations, nature talks and bike and boat trips (by reservation).

Miami Seaquarium While Lolita the killer whale is the advertised star of the show at this excellent 37-acre aquarium (☎ 305-361-5705, www.miamiseaquarium.com), 4400 Rickenbacker Causeway, we were far more impressed with what a genuine effort these great folks are making to preserve, protect and explain aquatic life. Case in point: their Manatee Presentation & Exhibit, where West Indian manatees are delivered after being injured by boat propellers. The manatees are nursed back to health and some are released. There are usually between five and eight manatees here: Juliet has been here since the late 1960s.

The shark presentations at Shark Channel are great for little kids if the sharks are hungry. Other shows include Splash of the Islands with Atlantic bottle-nosed dolphins, and Salty's Sea Scoundrels with Salty the Sea Lion.

The park is open daily 9:30 am to 6 pm, but tickets must be bought before 4:30 pm. Admission is $19.95 for adults, $18.95 for seniors, $15.95 for children three to nine. There's a AAA discount of 15%, and ISIC holders get $3 off.

Parking is $2. Wheelchairs and strollers can be rented for $4 (no deposit), and a kennel is available at no cost.

SOUTHWEST MIAMI
Equestrian Center
Kids go crazy over this center (☎ 305-226-7886) at Tropical Park (Bird Rd at the Palmetto Expressway), on the grounds of the Metro-Dade Police Stables. Each weekend you can watch purebred show, quarter and rodeo horses perform free of charge. The park is usually open 8 am to sunset, weather permitting.

Metrozoo
Miami's Metrozoo (☎ 305-251-0400, TDD 305-857-6680, 305-670-9099 sign-language interpreters five days in advance, www .metrodade.com/parks/metrozoo.htm), 12400 SW 152nd St, was one of the top 10 zoos in the USA before Hurricane Andrew, and it plans to reclaim the title. It will probably succeed: Metrozoo has a sprawling natural habitat with 900 animals from more than 200 species, including koalas and a pair of Komodo dragons!

There are nice waterfalls right outside the Metrozoo entrance; once inside, the picnic area is to your left. Animals have plenty of space to move around and there are no bars: instead, cleverly designed moats separate you from the animals. We loved the temple behind the white Bengal tigers. Signage is excellent.

For a great orientation tour, get on the Zoofari monorail for one complete circuit (don't let the safety announcements drive you insane). The monorail's four stops are (1) the amphitheater, (2) the Asian elephant, Wings of Asia and PAWS (the children's zoo, petting area, shows and rides section), (3) the pygmy hippo, and finally (4) the northernmost area of the zoo, home to colobus monkeys, a black rhinoceros and African elephants.

PAWS is wonderful: in the petting area, kids can play with pot-bellied pigs, sheep, ferrets, snakes (which are brought out by staff for the kids to touch), chickens, a monitor lizard and more.

The Ecology Theater offers shows at 11 am and 1 and 3 pm. Don't miss the constantly changing Wildlife Shows offered in the amphitheater daily at noon, 2 and 4:30 pm.

Another wonderful feature is the Behind the Scenes Tram Tour, a 45-minute ride around the public areas of the zoo as well as the veterinary hospital, brooder and hatchery building and quarantine pens. The tours cost $2; go to the admission booth for times and tickets.

Remember where you parked! Metrozoo's enormous parking lot is as confusing as those at major theme parks, so keep track of your car.

To get to Metrozoo, take Florida's Turnpike Extension to the Metrozoo exit at SW 152nd St. The zoo's open daily 9:30 am to 5:30 pm (you must buy tickets before 4 pm). Ticket prices including tax are $8 for adults, $4 for children three to 12. Wheelchair rentals are $6 ($10 deposit). Single/double strollers are $4/7 ($10 deposit). Video cameras can be rented for $6 an hour (two-hour minimum, $20 deposit and a driver's license or passport required); video tapes are $4.

Gold Coast Railroad Museum

Just near the entrance to Metrozoo is the Gold Coast Railroad Museum (☎ 305-253-0063), 12450 SW 152nd St. If you're at all interested in trains, it's worth checking out. The museum has more than 30 antique railway cars, including the *Ferdinand Magellan* Presidential car, used by US Presidents Roosevelt, Eisenhower, Truman and even Ronald Reagan (for whom the thing was outfitted with 3-inch-thick glass windows and armor plating). You have probably seen this train: it's the one in the photograph of newly elected president Harry Truman, which shows him standing at the rear holding a newspaper bearing the famous erroneous headline: 'Dewey Defeats Truman.'

The museum's open Friday to Sunday 11 am to 4 pm. Admission is $4 for adults, $1 for kids under 10 (kids under three are free), which includes a train ride lasting about 20 to 25 minutes (2 miles). Trains leave every hour on the hour between noon and 4 pm.

Weeks Air Museum

Air and history buffs will be delighted with this museum (☎ 305-233-5197), in the Tami-ami Airport at 14710 SW 128th St. Despite the damage it received from Hurricane Andrew, it's definitely open for business. What's nice about this, as compared to other air museums, is it's truly a history of aviation, not just military aviation, as is often the case. The staff is knowledgeable and dedicated – there's always someone out on the floor to answer questions.

The museum is open daily 10 am to 5 pm. Admission is $6.95 for adults, $5.95 for seniors, $4.95 for children 12 and under. From Miami, take Hwy 836 west to Florida's Turnpike, go south to exit 19 (120th St), then west on 120th St for about 2 miles to 137th Ave (Tamiami Airport). Turn left (south) and enter the airport, and then follow the signs.

Fairchild Tropical Gardens

The USA's largest tropical botanical garden, the Fairchild (☎ 305-667-1651), 10901 Old Cutler Rd, is 83 acres of lush greenery with lakes, streams, grottos and waterfalls. To call it a tourist attraction detracts from its purpose, which is the serious study of tropical flora by the garden's more than 6000 members.

The garden's absolutely excellent visitor pamphlet sets out three trails, with easy-to-follow self-guided walking tours. Signs inside the gardens are very clear. There's also a 40-minute tram orientation tour of the entire park. Plan on spending 30 minutes for the Palmetum Walk, 45 for the Upland Walk, and at least an hour for the Lowland Trail, which goes from the rainforest in the southeast of the park, up around the lakes and ends at Hammock Lake.

The gardens are open daily 9:30 am to 4:30 pm, closed Christmas. Admission is $8 for adults, free for members and children under 12. Take US Hwy 1 south to SW 42nd Ave (Le Jeune Rd), south to Cocoplum Circle, and drive south on Old Cutler Rd for 2 miles.

Parrot Jungle & Gardens

Don't be fooled. Parrot Jungle (☎ 305-666-7834, www.parrotjungle.com), 11000 SW 57th Ave, is more than just a parrot show.

The lush gardens, set in a hardwood hammock with more than 1200 varieties of exotic and tropical plants like heliconias and bromeliads, are home to alligators and crocodiles, orangutans, chimps, tortoises and the very-pink flamingoes from the intro sequence on *Miami Vice*. The parrot show is held five times a day; highlights include trained (as in bicycle riding and roller skating) parrots, macaws and cockatoos.

The park is open daily 9:30 am to 6 pm (tickets are on sale until 5 pm). Admission is $11.95 for adults, $10.95 for seniors over 62, $7.95 for children three to 10.

Take I-95 south to US Hwy 1, and go 5 miles south to SW 57th Ave; turn left and go 3 miles to SW 111th St. Parrot Jungle plans to move to Watson Island, which will make it more of a major player in the city's tourism market.

Fruit & Spice Park

The Preston B Bird & Mary Heinlein Fruit & Spice Park (☎ 305-247-5727), 24801 SW 187th Ave (Redland Rd), is the only public garden of its kind in the USA. It's a very romantic place to go with a date – a 20-acre public facility that shows more than 100 varieties of citrus fruits, 50 of bananas, 40 of grapes and a whole bunch of exotic tropical fruits, plants and spices. There's also a nice poisonous-plant area. Best of all, after walking through the paths smelling all that, you can buy exotic offerings at the Redland Gourmet & Fruit Store. We'd advise against the durian (which looks like a jackfruit, tastes like sugary fertilizer and smells like an aged corpse), but you can choose from pomello, rambutan, lychee, breadfruit, tamarind and seeds, spices, jellies and jams.

The park also offers an enormous range of classes and activities, from a Banana Workshop to tours of local commercial farms to Chainsaw Etiquette (we swear!) to Tropical Wine Making (all $15) to a Florida Keys Fruit Safari, which visits private gardens in the Florida Keys ($25).

The park is open daily 10 am to 5 pm. Admission to the park is just $1 for adults, 50¢ for kids. Tours of the park are given Saturday and Sunday at 1 and 3 pm; the cost for all tours is $1.50/1.

To get there, take US Hwy 1 to SW 248th St, go west, and turn left on SW 187th Ave; the park's on the left-hand side of the road. Stop for a heavenly cinnamon bun at Knauss Berry Farm (see Places to Eat later in the chapter).

Monkey Jungle

In 1933, an animal behaviorist named Joseph Du Mond released six monkeys into the 'wild.' Their descendants – now more than 60 of them – are the highlight of Monkey Jungle (☎ 305-235-1611), 14805 SW 216th St, which also features orangutans, chimpanzees and King, the lowland gorilla. The big show of the day is during the feedings, when the Java monkeys dive into the pool for fruit and treats.

To get there, take Florida's Turnpike Homestead Extension to exit 11 and head west for 5 miles. It's open daily 9:30 am to 5 pm. Admission is $13.50 for adults, $8 for children four to 12. While you're out here, you should go just a mile farther to Burr's Berry Farm for some of the world's best strawberries (see Places to Eat).

NORTHEAST MIAMI

With a few notable exceptions, Northeast Miami is an absolutely uninteresting industrial section of town, packed with warehouses and dust. It's not a very appealing place to head, unless you're after some specific sights.

American Police Hall of Fame & Police Museum

An American police officer is killed every 57 hours. This museum (☎ 305-573-0070), 3801 Biscayne Blvd, is dedicated to memorializing cops who have died in the line of duty – about 6000 as we went to press.

It's located in a boxy building with a highly visible and dramatic eye-catcher: a 1995 Chevy Caprice Classic police car on the side wall fronting Biscayne Blvd. While the museum has some fun items like the cop car from the movie *Blade Runner*, some interesting gangster memorabilia and a huge display of confiscated weapons, it's mainly a memorial. Each murdered officer's name, rank, city and state are engraved in the white Italian marble that makes up the main floor, where there's also an inter-denominational chapel.

Kids love the gore and descriptions of execution devices: you can have a seat in the gas chamber and the electric chair, but alas, you can only stand next to the guillotine ('please do not place your head beneath the blade'). You can work a crime scene as a detective, and there's a holding cell here as well.

The museum's open daily 10 am to 5:30 pm. Admission is $6 for adults, $4 for seniors, $3 for students and children.

Little Haiti

Haitians are the third-largest group of foreign-born residents in Florida after Cubans and (strangely) Canadians, and Little Haiti is the center of Haitian life in Miami. As with Little Havana, Little Haiti has absorbed waves of refugees during times of Haitian political strife (see History in Facts about Florida).

Little Haiti is a colorful neighborhood that is trying very hard, though with limited success, to make itself a tourist attraction. The **Haitian Refugee Center** (☎ 305-757-8538), 119 NE 54th St, is a community center dedicated to disseminating information about Haitian life in Haiti and in Miami. It is also a good resource for information about community events. Unfortunately, the opening of the Caribbean Marketplace, a combination tourist attraction and legitimate flea market at 5925-27 NE 2nd Ave, bombed. But with the growth of the nearby Miami Design District, the prospects are getting rosier all the time. The market is open Monday to Saturday 10 am to 9 pm, Sunday to 7 pm.

Haitian **botanicas** (which sell voodoo-related items) are worth visiting for beautiful bottles, beads and sequined banners with voodoo symbolism – while the banners may seem expensive ($100 to $200), they're far cheaper here in Little Haiti than at some art galleries around the USA, where the banners are selling as art.

There's also a pretty bitchin' live music venue here at Churchill's Hideaway (see the Entertainment section).

The Tap Tap, basically a colorfully painted group taxi mounted on a pick-up truck (the name is onomatopoeic: think of the sound of a third-world truck engine), is a free shuttle between NE 2nd Ave and 36th St to NE 2nd Ave and 59th St from Friday to Sunday.

Design District

Billed in the 1960s as 'The Square Mile of Style,' this area (in a neighborhood called Buena Vista) has been a center to the interior decoration and design industry for about 30 years – with showrooms like Country Floors, David and Dash, Lord Jay, EG Cody and Concept Casual. Since about 1993, the neighborhood has been going through something of a renaissance, as owners have ended their 'trade only' sales policy in favor of one that is 'courtesy to the trade and retail.'

People are pegging it as a 'new South Beach' because conditions are very similar to those just before the SoBe boom: higher rents in more fashionable neighborhoods are forcing creative people to move over. Already the area is home to artists and their studios and galleries, film companies, photographers and dancers – basically anyone who needs lots of space for not a lot of money.

To see the district in its best light, go over on the second Saturday of the month when all the studios and galleries stay open for a gallery walk of sorts. They do proper gallery walks as well, on the second Friday evening of the month.

Stop in at the Piccadilly Garden Lounge (see Places to Eat) for coffee and light meals in a lush little courtyard.

Museum of Contemporary Art (MOCA)

The Museum of Contemporary Art (☎ 305-893-6211), 770 NE 125th St, has moved to a brand-new and much larger space in the city of North Miami. The museum, which runs excellent rotating exhibitions of contemporary art by local, national and international artists, is also beginning a new permanent collection featuring the works of artists including Ian Hamilton Finlay, Quisqueya Henriques, Alex Katz, James Rosenquist and others.

To get to the MOCA, take I-95 to NE 125th St, and go east for 1¹/₂ miles. From Biscayne Blvd, take 123rd St west for 1 mile, and it will become 125th St. The museum is open Tuesday to Saturday 10 am to 5 pm (Thursday to 9 pm), Sunday noon to 5 pm, closed Monday. Admission is $4 for adults, $2 for students and seniors; children under 12, city of North Miami residents and MOCA members get in free

LIBERTY CITY & OVERTOWN

From the birth of Miami, blacks were only permitted to live in the northwest quarter of downtown called Colored Town. Later, the area's name was changed to Overtown because it was 'over the tracks.' Overtown has been pretty severly decimated by construction of freeways and bypasses. However, you can still check out a locally famous mural of prominent black Miamians on the side of the **Lyric Theatre**, at 819 NW 2nd Ave.

Liberty City, farther north and west, is a misnomer. Made infamous by the Liberty City Riots in 1980 (see the History section earlier in the chapter), the area is very poor and the crime rate is higher than in other areas of the city. And while plans exist to renovate the area by creating a village of cultural and tourist attractions, the prospects of that happening in the near future looked grim as we went to press.

In the 1950s, whites, fearing 'black encroachment' on their neighborhoods, actually went so far as to build a *wall* at the then-border of Liberty City – NW 12th Ave from NW 62nd to NW 67th Sts – to separate their neighborhoods. Part of the wall still stands, at NW 12th Ave between NW 63rd and 64th Sts.

For information on Liberty City, Overtown and other areas significant to black history, contact the exceedingly helpful Black Archives History & Research Center of South Florida (☎ 305-636-2390), at the Caleb Center at 5400 NW 22nd Ave. It's

open 9 am to 5 pm Monday to Friday (from 1 to 5 pm for specific research projects).

ACTIVITIES

See the Outdoor Activities chapter for information on skydiving and ultralight aircraft opportunities in the area.

Bicycling

Two Wheel Drive (☎ 305-534-2177), 1260 Washington Ave, rents bicycles for $5/15/45 an hour/day/week from Monday to Friday 10 am to 7 pm, Saturday to 6 pm, Sunday 11:30 am to 4 pm.

The Miami Beach Bicycle Center (☎ 305-674-0150), 601 5th St, rents bikes for $5/20/70. It's open Monday to Saturday 10 am to 7 pm, Sunday to 5 pm. All of these shops sell bicycles as well.

Bike and Skate Rentals, a booth on the beach at 14th St, rents tandem bicycles for $15 an hour or $35 for four hours.

Skating & Running

In-line skating is one of the most popular forms of transportation here. Everyone seems to have a pair of blades, and the streets are excellent for it. Be careful on Washington Ave, and remember there are very few shops that will allow you in with skates on around here. We usually tuck a pair of thong-type sandals in the back of our jeans to wear when we have to carry our skates. Running is also very popular, and the beach is a very good one for joggers as it's flat, wide and hard-packed.

Skate rental is easy but expensive: South Beach Rentals, a booth on the promenade around 8th St, rents skates for $8.50/23 (one hour/24 hours). Bike and Skate Rentals, the booth on the Beach at 14th St, rents skates for the same price. The most expensive option is Fritz's Skate Shop (☎ 305-532-1954), 726 Lincoln Rd. It's $8 an hour, but the $24 daily does not include a $15 overnight fee.

For rink skating – complete with laser shows, pulsating music and a bar – the answer is Hot Wheels Skating Center (☎ 305-595-3200), 12265 SW 112th St, where admission is $6.50 and skate rental is $2.

Surfing

In South Beach, the best surfing is just north of South Pointe Park, with 2- to 5-foot waves and a nice, sandy bottom. Unfortunately, it's usually closer to 2 than 5 (except, of course, before storms) and it can get a little mushy, so longboards are the way to go. The area is exceptionally crowded with swimmers and surfers on weekends, so getting a good ride can be a pain in the ass. Surfing is better north of the city, up near Haulover or anywhere north of about 70th St.

North of South Beach, Bird's Surf Shop (305-940-0929), 250 Sunny Isles Blvd, is a real surf shop that sells boards from its factories in California. It runs a recorded surf report at ☎ 305-947-7170.

The best-known place on the Beach, X-Isle Surf Shop (☎ 305-673-5900), 437 Washington Ave, more resembles a T-shirt shop, though they consider themselves to be experts in all areas of surfing knowledge. They rent BZ foam boards from around $45 a day (weekly rates are negotiable), and used boards sell for about $180 to $350; new ones go for $350 to how much you got? X-Isles is open Monday to Friday from 10 am to 7 pm, Saturday to 6 pm and Sunday from noon to 6 pm.

Diving

The diving off Miami Beach is crap, but South Beach Divers (☎ 305-531-6110), a five-star PADI dive center, runs regular diving excursions to the Key Largo area on Tuesday, Thursday and Saturday for $95 (minus mask, snorkel and fins). Got your own equipment? The boat trip alone is $39.

You can get certified with them for $249 in either two weekends or a four-day program including classes, books and all gear except mask, snorkel and fins. They also rent equipment to certified divers.

Kayaking & Canoeing

There is something absolutely magical about kayaking through the mangroves, and Haulover Beach and South Miami both offer this experience. The best thing is you don't need any lessons, and you can rent all the equipment you need very easily and cheaply.

We have used the Urban Trails Kayak Co (☎ 305-947-1302), on the bay side opposite Haulover Beach at 10800 Collins Ave, which rents one-person kayaks for $8 an hour, $20 for four hours or $25 for 24 hours, and two-person kayaks for $15/35/45 including paddles, lifejackets and instructions. There are 19 islands in the Intracoastal Waterway, many with barbecue facilities, and on some you can camp for nothing – Urban Trails can help you plan your trip. It's open daily, weather permitting, 9 am to 5 pm.

Sailboards Miami (☎ 305-361-7245) rents one-person kayaks for $13 an hour, two-person kayaks for $18 an hour. See the Windsurfing section below for the address and directions.

Canoeing around the 10,000 Islands, or on the Wilderness Waterway between Everglades City and Flamingo, is one of the most fascinating ways to see nature; see the Everglades chapter for complete information.

Windsurfing

The only place we found that rents sailboards was Sailboards Miami (☎ 305-361-7245), which rents short- and long-boards for $20 an hour ($38 for two hours) and holds two-hour 'guarantee-to-learn' windsurfing lessons for $49 for adults, $59 for kids. Private lessons are $30 per half hour, $50 an hour, including equipment. It's in the right place for it: Hobie Island, where the water is calm. Take the first right turn after the tollbooths for the Rickenbacker Causeway to Key Biscayne. It's open daily from

11 am to 7 pm in summer, from 9:30 am to 5 pm the rest of the year.

Swimming

The best pool in the area by anyone's standards is the Venetian Pool (see the Coral Gables section earlier), but you're here in Miami Beach, aren't you? Sitting poolside with a cool drink in your hand is a noble Miami tradition (maybe because of all the models in their skimpy bathing suits?) that's truly a great way to spend an afternoon – or at least part of one.

The excellent six-lane Flamingo Park Swimming Pool (☎ 305-673-7750), between Jefferson and Michigan Aves and 11th and 12th Sts (parking is adjacent to the pool), is open to the public. In winter, it's open Friday to Tuesday 9 am to 5:15 pm, and admission is free. In summer, there's adult lap swim every morning from 8:30 to 9:30 am, and the pool is open daily 8 am to 8 pm. Admission in summer is $1.25 for adults and 75¢ seniors and children.

The rest of the really good pools, unfortunately, are at hotels, and hotel pools are restricted to hotel guests. Now, we'd *never*, ever suggest breaking the policies of a hotel, so the following is clearly intended only to let you know what you're missing.

We have three favorite pools: the one at the Raleigh Hotel (☎ 305-534-6300), 1775 Collins Ave, is a class act all the way. Voted most beautiful pool in Florida by *Life* magazine in 1945, it's as curvaceous as a 1930s Hollywood vixen and open 24 hours. Walk through the hotel's very posh lobby and straight out to the back. There's a bar at the far end. (The bar inside makes the best martini on the Beach.)

Waterfalls, islands and exotic beautiful people make up the pool scene at the Fontainebleau Hilton, 4441 Collins Ave. Getting to the pool – if you're a hotel guest, of course – is much easier from the beach side than through the lobby, where security guards are everywhere.

The swimming pool at the fiercely fashionable Delano Hotel (☎ 305-672-2000), 1685 Collins Ave, is swank just like the hotel. In fact, it's so swank that classical and jazz music is piped in under the water, which you can only hear when you're submerged!

The two new stars are the pools at the National Hotel, 1677 Collins Ave, and the Loews, 1601 Collins Ave.

ORGANIZED TOURS

With more than 400 registered-historic-landmark buildings and about 800 buildings total, the Deco District always makes for an interesting walk. You can follow the boom phases of the Beach: beginning at 5th St in the 1930s to mid-Beach, the late '30s and early '40s, to the area north of 27th St, which begins the new era of '50s resort and luxury hotels, dotted with condominiums.

The Miami Design Preservation League (MDPL; ☎ 305-672-2014) runs 1½-hour walking tours of the Art Deco District every Saturday at 10:30 am and Thursday night at 6:30 pm. Reservations are not required, but you should show up about 15 minutes early. The tours leave from the Oceanfront Auditorium at 1001 Ocean Drive and cost $10 (no senior or student discounts). During February and March, the tours can get crowded, but during the rest of the year, there are usually crowds of 15 to 20 people.

Between September and late June every year, Dr Paul George (☎ 305-858-6021) does about 70 different walking tours as well as boat and train tours of Dade County in conjunction with the Historical Museum of South Florida. Tours are $10 for museum members, $15 for nonmembers. Dr George also offers private tours by appointment, though unless you're with a group, it's going to be very expensive: two-hour tours start at about $100. Write to him at 1345 SW 14th St, Miami, FL 33145.

For an interesting – if somewhat expensive – view of the city, you can take a spin over the city on an air tour from Action Helicopters (see Watson Island earlier in the chapter). Biscayne Helicopters (☎ 305-252-3883) does four-person helicopter tours of Miami for $650/hour (so a 15-minute flight, which is more than enough to see Miami

Beach and downtown Miami, would run you $41 per person).

PLACES TO STAY
Camping
This is not the best place for camping, but there are some interesting opportunities around. Urban Trails Kayak Co (☎ 305-947-1302), opposite Haulover Beach on the bay side (see the Activities section), rents kayaks. You can paddle to some of the 19 nearby islands and camp for nothing.

Kobe Trailer Park (☎ 305-893-5121, 11900 NE 16th Ave) is the closest you'll get to a commercial campsite in Miami Beach. Tent sites for two people, one tent or a motor home, are $20 a night without hookups, or $28 with hookups (electric, water and sewer) year round. The staff is friendly.

Miami-Homestead-Everglades KOA (☎ 800-562-7732, 20675 SW 162 Ave), at 200th St in Homestead, is the only KOA campsite in the area. Tent sites are $22, 'less' in low season.

Miami Beach
From budget to top dollar, the Beach has the greatest variety of places to stay in the area. But the information in this section is extremely volatile. From the start of our research to the finish, the prices we quote here rose by an average of $5 per night, and prices have risen dramatically since last edition. The only exception is the youth hostels, whose prices remained stable.

There are still places on the Beach where you can get away with paying less than $50 a night, but there are major differences in quality, and two hotels that cost the same don't necessarily give you the same thing. Shop around carefully before committing, and always check the rooms before you sign in. Even at the height of the high season, you've got a choice and don't let anyone convince you otherwise. Also note that true Deco style is compact by modern standards, so the more landmark Deco a hotel is, the smaller its rooms are likely to be.

Hostels Currently, there are four hostel-style places in town. The *Miami Beach*

International Travelers Hostel (☎ 305-534-0268, fax 305-534-5862, 236 9th St) has just a little less of everything than the competition, but that applies to prices as well – it's the cheapest bed in town, with dorm bunks at $12 for HI members, $14 for non-HI members (though they're not an HI hostel). Rooms are a tad worn. It also has basic private rooms for $36 for one or two people (no HI member discount) including tax. The hostel is a block and a half from the beach, just east of Washington Ave. You'll need to show an out-of-state university ID, HI card, US or foreign passport with a recent entry stamp, or an onward ticket, but these rules are only strictly enforced when the place is crowded. Visa and MasterCard are accepted.

Our new fave is the seriously fun *Banana Bungalow* (☎ 305-674-9660, 2360 Collins Ave) – now this is hostelling. A great pool, right on the canal, and more important, a great bar and a fun crowd of Americans, Europeans and Aussies. It's in a kitschy '50s building (the office was formerly a gas station) and dorm beds are $14 to $15; singles/doubles are $66 to $106.

Perhaps the most beautiful in the USA, the Beach's most established hostel is the HI-member *Clay Hotel & International Hostel* (☎ 305-534-2988, fax 305-673-0346, 1438 Washington Ave), at the corner of Española Way. Set in a 100-year-old Spanish-style villa (with some neat history: see the Española Way section above), the Clay has clean and comfortable dorm rooms with four bunk beds for $14 per night. It also has decent private rooms, all with TV, telephone and air conditioning: budget singles/doubles (with shared bath) are $42/47; standard rooms with private bath are $56/63; family rooms are $72; deluxe rooms are $63/68/77; and spacious VIP rooms, with balconies are $85 double and $97 family. Private rooms decrease by $5 in winter. All of the above prices are reduced by $1 for HI and ISIC cardholders. The hostel has an excellent kitchen, awesome garden, a message board and a small bookshop. It's a definite travelers' hangout and information exchange center. The staff is very friendly, if a little harassed due to sheer volume. The hostel accepts Visa and MasterCard but not American Express. The Moonlight Cafe downstairs offers breakfast from $2.99 to $8.99.

Perfectly located one block from the beach and sporting an Olympic-size swimming pool, a barbecue area and patio, and a full kitchen, the *Tropics Hotel & Hostel* (☎ 305-531-0361, fax 305-531-8676, 1550 Collins Ave) has dorm beds (four to a room) for $15 a night. The dorms are clean and have steel beds; attached bathrooms and lockers are available. The Tropic's private rooms ($50 a night) are also quite nice, some with great views of the pool and what's in it at the moment. Air conditioning works until 8 am. Visa and MasterCard are accepted; American Express is not.

Hotels – Budget Another good option in this price range is the *Carlton Hotel* (☎ 305-538-5741, 800-722-7586, fax 305-534-6855, 1433 Collins Ave), where you get a clean room (small bathroom) with telephone and a huge fridge from $45/50 a single/double in summer, $60/70 in winter. Rooms with kitchenettes are about $5 more. Each additional person is $10 a night, but you can get a discount for staying a week or longer. There is a swimming pool, free parking, free morning coffee and cake, and the staff is very friendly and helpful.

The *San Juan Hotel* (☎ 305-538-7531, fax 305-532-5704, 1680 Collins Ave) should be renovated by March 2000. When we visited, it didn't look very appealing, but its rooms were surprisingly clean and had small kitchens. Rooms are $49 to $59 a night but will go up substantially after renovation.

The *Berkeley Shore Hotel* (☎ 305-531-5731, 1610 Collins Ave) is a lovely Art Deco box with a très swirly facade. Staff is pleasant enough, if a bit grumpy at first. They're in the process of renovating the rooms, which currently are a bit worn but clean and cost $55 a day, $250 a week. The same management runs the cheerier *James Hotel* (☎ 305-531-1125, fax 305-538-4205, 1680 James Ave), about two blocks away. This hotel has clean and large rooms, though a friend of ours who stayed here said they didn't change the sheets as often as they could have. In both these hotels, the rooms have full kitchens, bathrooms, air conditioning, TVs, telephones and free parking. Rooms start at $80 (including tax) in the high season, $55 in low season.

Hotels – Mid-Range We like the *Winterhaven* (☎ 305-531-5571, 800-395-2322, fax 305-538-3337, 1400 Ocean Drive). It was about to be renovated at press time, but when we visited the rooms were sweet, with mosquito netting, ceiling fans and Mediterranean antique furnishings. Rooms are $60 to $95 in summer, $80 to $125 in winter (prices will go up after renovation).

Brigham Gardens Guesthouse (☎ 305-531-1331, fax 305-538-9898, 1411 Collins Ave) is a charming guesthouse set in a beautiful, lush green garden populated by tropical birds. The large and airy guest rooms (most with kitchens and bathrooms) have convertible futon sofas, and all the rooms have communicating doors. There's a barbecue area out back. Rooms are $60 to $110 a day in summer, $90 to $145 in winter, with a 10% discount for 7 nights or more year round. Pets are accepted! This place is very similar in style and personality to its friendly competitor next door, the *Villa Paradiso Guesthouse* (☎ 305-532-0616, fax 305-667-0074, 1415 Collins Ave), which charges $69/75 per night in summer and $119/125 in winter (weekly rates are discounted 10%).

The pleasant owners of the *Beach Paradise Hotel* (☎ 305-531-0021, 800-258-8886, fax 305-674-0206, 600 Ocean Drive) run a place with very clean and pleasant rooms, looking a lot more like LA than Miami. Prices are $60 to $150 in summer, $90 to $175 in winter (weekly rates are negotiable). There's free Showtime on TV and a nice lobby café; parking is available.

You'll appreciate the relative remoteness of the 1930s *Kenmore Hotel* (☎ 305-674-1930, fax 305-534-6591, 1050 Washington Ave), at the corner of 11th St. It's close enough to the scene and the beach but just across the demarcation point for screaming partiers on the west side of Washington. And, it's across the street from the police station. The hotel has a very distinctive Deco look, with a wavy concrete wall and figure-eight pool, a funky elevator, helpful and efficient staff, and well-worn (in a good way) rooms with heavy wooden furniture and Deco-tiled bathrooms. What's more, it's pretty cheap: rooms are $69 in summer, $99 in winter. It has more expensive deluxe rooms, and weekly rates are available as well.

Two friends from Germany stayed at and enjoyed the *Fairfax Apartment Hotel* (☎ 305-538-3837, 1776 Collins Ave), an old and slightly crumbling but clean and perfectly pleasant hotel with rooms from $70 to $95 in winter.

The *Parisian/Geneva Hotel* (☎ 305-538-7464, 1510 Collins Ave) has perfectly nice but not overly clean small rooms for $75, $85 for slightly larger ones, including breakfast.

The best deal on the Beach is *Hideaway Suites* (☎ 305-538-5955, 888-881-5955, fax 305-531-2464, 751 Collins Ave). Run by very friendly staff, the absolutely spotless apartments – in a little courtyard tucked away from the noise – feature a washer/dryer, coffee-maker and full kitchen, all for only $79/95 singles/doubles.

The cute little *Penguin Hotel* (☎ 305-534-9334, 800-235-3296, fax 305-672-6240, 1418 Ocean Drive) has pleasant, clean and large-ish rooms (fridges available free on request) and a nice staff. It has a little café and lounge downstairs. Rooms are $80 to $120 in summer, $115 to $165 in winter. All prices include continental breakfast.

Last edition we raved about the *Mermaid Guest House* (☎ 305-538-5324, fax 305-538-2822, 909 Collins Ave) and it pissed off lots of people. One couple got so ticked off with the hotel and our positive listing of it that they sicced *Condé Nast Traveler* on us. We visited again. It looked okay, though the woman managing the place was kind of bitchy and it wasn't nearly as clean as last time. So we say this: it's worth a look, but don't put any deposits down before you see the place and decide for yourself. Rooms are $85 to $95 in summer, $105 to $125 in winter. The rooftop apartment is $165 ($250 in winter).

The *Deco Walk Hotel* (☎ 305-531-5511, fax 305-531-5515, 928 Ocean Drive) is tucked a few feet back from the seafront and has nice – if slow and typically Cuban-Miami – service. Rooms are reasonably clean and large; singles/doubles right on the beach are $110/135, and rooms without a view (but still steps from the beach) are $85/110.

The *Lord Balfour Hotel* (☎ 305-673-0401, fax 305-531-9385, 350 Ocean Drive) is a newly renovated and super cool place with 66 rooms without kitchens but with very cold air conditioning. They will provide a refrigerator in the rooms on request at no extra charge. Rooms are $85 to $155.

Two hotels owned and operated by the same management company sit at the corner of Ocean Drive and 7th St. The northernmost one is the *Avalon Hotel* (☎ 305-538-0133, 800-933-3306, fax 305-534-0258, 700 Ocean Drive) in a gorgeous Streamline building (1941), and perhaps known more for its trademark white-and-yellow 1955 Lincoln convertible (parked out front) than for its rooms, which are very pleasant and clean. Rates run from $89 to $155 in summer, $110 to $195 in winter, including continental breakfast and (they say) no hidden service charges.

The *Majestic Hotel* (☎ 305-534-2995, 680 Ocean Drive), just south of 7th St, is similar in everything – decor, price and service – to the Avalon. But in a toss up, the Avalon would win.

The beautifully renovated *Betsy Ross Hotel* (☎ 305-531-3934, fax 305-531-5282, 1440 Ocean Drive) has a unique mix of Deco and colonial styles. The location at the end of the beachfront promenade gives it really nice ocean views, but the service is nowhere near what it could be. Rooms range from $85 to $160 in summer, $169 to $229 in winter.

The fabulously renovated *Indian Creek Hotel* (☎ 305-531-2727, 800-491-2772, fax 305-531-5651, 2727 Indian Creek Drive) is a delightfully serene place with excellent service and very friendly staff. When our family came to visit us in Miami, we put them up here. The spotless rooms have been painstakingly restored to their Deco glory. The hotel is far enough out of the madness 10 blocks south to be a restful retreat from the Fabulous, but close enough to be a two-minute drive (or 10-minute walk) from the action. The pool out back is really nice – we come here to recuperate. Rooms/suites are $90/150 in summer, $130/220 in winter.

Island Outpost, a management company that runs several local hotels, including the Marlin and Casa Grande, runs the **Cavalier Hotel** (☎ 305-534-2135, 1320 Ocean Drive). Service was a turnoff last time around but was great this time. Rooms are very nice, as are the prices, considering what you get. It's $95 to $155 for a standard room, $125 to $160 for a deluxe room, and oceanfront suites run from $240 to $255.

The **Colony Hotel** (☎ 305-673-0088, 800-226-5669, fax 305-532-0762, 736 Ocean Drive) is a Deco landmark, with friendly staff, interesting rooms with tiny TVs but nice touches like potpourri. Prices are $99 to $129 in summer, $190 to $225 in winter, including continental breakfast. There's free Showtime; parking is $16 a day; Discover cards are not accepted.

The charming **Lily Guesthouse** (☎ 305-535-9900, fax 305-535-0077, 835 Collins Ave) is very yellow, with friendly service and lots of flowers. The rooms (all of which have kitchens and new bathrooms) are impeccably done, bright and have very nice hardwood floors. Summer rates are $100 to $200; winter rates are $150 to $250.

The Deco-classic **Park Central Hotel** (☎ 305-538-1611, 800-727-5236, fax 305-534-7520, 640 Ocean Drive) is one of the consummate SoBe hot spots. Its pool is wonderful (if small), and its rooftop deck is a must-see even if you're not staying here. Rooms, which are also small, are $105 to $175 in summer, $165 to $215 in winter; suites are $225 to $305. The Vampire Lestat Room (No 419), while heavily booked, was available for $175 per night when we visited.

To get to the roof, walk in past the reception, take the elevator to the top floor and walk out to the right. Good times to go are at about 4 pm, when cruise ships chug out down Government Cut, or on any Friday or Saturday night for a great view of the Drive's action. There's a nice café downstairs in the lobby.

The lovingly restored **Essex House Hotel** (☎ 305-534-2700, 800-553-7739, fax 305-532-3827, 1001 Collins Ave), with its very cool lobby, is a friendly place with helpful staff and large rooms. If you're feeling flabby, you can use the South Beach Gym at 1020 Ocean Drive (in the Clevelander Hotel), where hotel guests get a $7 discount on day passes (you pay $8). Rooms are $109 to $385, with suites from $150 in summer, $250 in winter.

The **Century Hotel** (☎ 305-674-8855, fax 305-538-5733, 140 Ocean Drive) has the coolest logo of any hotel on the Beach – sort of a lizardy thing – and is a darned nice hotel far enough south to keep things quiet even on weekends. Rooms are $115 in summer, $190 in winter; suites are $215 in summer, $300 in winter.

Another Island Outpost property, the **Kent Hotel** (☎ 305-531-6771, 800-688-7678, fax 305-531-0720, 1131 Collins Ave) has most of the same perks as the other properties, though the rooms are somewhat smaller. In summer, rates are $120 to $275; in winter, they're $150 to $330. There are hammocks in the garden.

The Island Outpost-run **Leslie Hotel** (☎ 305-534-2135, 800-688-7678, fax 305-531-5543, 1244 Ocean Drive) has attentive and helpful staff, and baby-sitting services are available. It has many of the same perks as the Marlin (see below), including towels, flowers and TV/VCR, but the Leslie is ever-so-slightly less luxurious. The relatively simple and spotless rooms go for $125 to $350.

South Beach's **Roney Plaza Apartment Hotel** (☎ 305-531-8811, 2301 Collins Ave) is a hotel totally made up of efficiency apartments that cost $140 to $275 in summer, $160 to $290 in winter.

The **Edison Hotel** (☎ 305-531-2744, fax 305-534-4707, 960 Ocean Drive), with an entrance on 10th St, is a perfectly acceptable but rundown place with rooms from $145 and suites up to $495. Unfortunately, the 'oceanfront' rooms (the higher priced ones above) don't offer very good views – they are blocked by the auditorium across the street.

Hotels – Top End The *Eden Roc Resort* (☎ 305-531-0000, 800-327-8337, fax 305-531-6955, www.edenrocresort.com, 4525 Collins Ave) is gloriously renovated and giving the Fontainebleau Hilton (see below) a run for its money. With little extras like an indoor rock-climbing complex, an Olympic-size (if not as cool as the Fontainebleau's) pool, and its newly remodeled spa and health club, it's a great place to get away. Rates start at $175 for rooms and $285 for a deluxe room with ocean view in summer, $285/395 in winter.

The elegant, Mediterranean-style *Hotel Ocean* (☎ 305-672-2579, fax 305-672-7665, 1230-38 Ocean Drive) is a pleasure to write about. It's chic but not pompous, exclusive but not pretentious, and expensive but not really that expensive when you look at what you get. Twenty-two of its 27 rooms have an ocean view, and if you really want to treat yourself, the penthouse suite is almost sinfully luxurious, complete with rooftop terrace, a Jacuzzi and beautiful furniture. All the rooms have hair dryers. Its pricing scheme is straight out of Kafka (the writer, not the Internet café), but the least expensive ocean-view rooms are $199 to $255 single and double ($179 without views). Off-season, the same rooms are $180 to $225 and $169. The penthouse is $475 in summer, $515 in winter.

The *Raleigh Hotel* (☎ 305-534-6300, 800-848-1775, fax 305-538-8140, 1775 Collins Ave) is one of our favorite places – it's high-style, Deco South Beach luxury all the way, with an excellent bar, one of the best pools around, a fine restaurant and very nice and well-appointed rooms from $179 to $319 in summer, $289 to $419 in winter and suites all the way up to $1000.

Set back from the street, the *Casa Grande Hotel* (☎ 305-531-8800, 800-688-7678, fax 305-673-3669, 834 Ocean Drive) is a great deal for the admittedly high price; service is exquisite and rooms are beautiful, all with TV, VCR, CD/stereo, full kitchen, and tons of luxurious perks such as turn-down service each evening and chocolates or flowers on your pillow. All the furniture's Indonesian, and there are laundry and room services. In summer, studios are $180; one-

bedrooms are $225; one-bedrooms with ocean view are $300. In winter, the rates are $275/300/395. It also has two- and three-bedroom suites from $350 to $1500 a night. Valet parking is $10.

Tucked away and accessed through its lush courtyard, the *Hotel Impala* (☎ 305-673-2021, 800-646-7252, fax 305-673-5984, 1228 Collins Ave) is a European-style hotel with rooms that have an oversize bathtub, TV, VCR and stereo with CD player. The place is lovely, and the staff manages to create an atmosphere that's elegant but not arrogant. Rooms start at $185 in summer, $250 in winter; suites are $250 to $400, all including continental breakfast.

The *Fontainebleau Hilton Resort & Towers* (☎ 305-538-2000, 800-548-8886, fax 305-673-5351, 4441 Collins Ave) is probably the most recognizable landmark on the Beach. It opened in 1954 and was taken over by Hilton in 1978. Now it has three buildings surrounding its absolutely fantastic swimming pool (see Activities earlier in the chapter). It's a stylish act all the way, with every conceivable amenity including restaurants, bars, a grand ballroom, beachside cabanas, an activities program for kids, seven tennis courts, a business center, marina and a real shopping mall within the hotel. Room rates in summer run from $189 for a standard single to $234 for a deluxe double. In winter, rooms are $389 to $414. Rooms on the Towers Level, a separate building with keyed entry, concierge service and a bunch of other extras, run $269/289 single/double in summer, $439/459 in winter.

Singer Gloria Estefan's *Cardozo Hotel* (☎ 305-535-6500, 800-782-6500, fax 305-532-3563, 1300 Ocean Drive) looks a bit more expensive than it is: its large rooms (many with hardwood floors and all with TV/VCR and handmade furniture) are $195 (standard single), $225 (ocean-view or non-ocean-view king), and $400 to $1200 (suites) in winter. The same rooms are $150, $180 and $300 to $900 in summer.

For a special occasion, the Caribbean-style rooms at the landmark *Marlin Hotel* (☎ 305-604-5000, 800-688-7678, fax 305-673-9609, 1200 Collins Ave) are well worth the price tag of $195 to $350 June to September and $280 to $450 October to May, including continental breakfast. The service is superb, the place is astonishingly clean, the rooms are unique and the location is right in the thick of things. All rooms (actually they're suites) have a TV, VCR and stereo (with a CD collection), a small book collection, kitchen, bathrobes and beach towels, all-natural soaps and shampoos and evening turndown service. Look for the vintage pink Cadillac convertible outside. It has a rooftop patio for parties, but no pool.

The spanking-new and already controversial *Loews Miami Beach* (☎ 305-604-1601, fax 305-695-4490, www.loewshotels.com, 1601 Collins Ave) opened in late 1998. It looms at the northern end of Ocean Drive as sort of a towering monolith that architecturally nods its head to Deco. The hotel has 800 rooms and suites going for $209 to $439. There are several restaurants and bars, an oceanfront pool and lots of niceties.

The Art Deco-landmark *National Hotel* (☎ 305-532-2311, 800-327-8370, fax 305-534-1426, 1677 Collins Ave) is a completely renovated and now super chic Miami Beach resort. A nice location on the beach, a seriously great long and narrow pool, and a hokey tiki bar make it worth considering: from $215 to $280 in summer, $235 to $425 in winter.

You can also stay at the *Inn at the Fisher Island Club* (☎ 305-535-6020, 800-537-3708, fax 305-535-6003, 1 Fisher Island Drive) on exclusive Fisher Island (see this section earlier in the chapter). Room rates range from $315 to $1780 a night, and spa packages start at $3150 (double occupancy) for three nights, including (get this) two Swedish massages or aromatherapy treatments, one fitness assessment or seaweed body wrap, two island salt-glow or aromatherapy herbal wraps, a hydromassage or target massage, one deep-pore cleansing facial *and* one manicure.

Everything's chic and chi-chi at the *Tides* (☎ 305-604-5070, fax 305-605-5180, 1220 Ocean Drive), where service is cool but gracious and rooms – all of which face the ocean – are absolutely wonderful. They all

have nice features like VCRs and CD players as well as extra touches like telescopes for star (or whatever) gazing. Rooms run from $300 to $2000 in summer, $450 to $2000 in winter. The excellent swimming pool is open 24 hours.

To enter the fiercely fashionable *Delano Hotel* (☎ 305-672-2000, 800-555-5001, 1685 Collins Ave), you need to walk past two hyper-tanned beefcake doormen in white. Once inside, self-congratulatory staff will permit you to get one of their slick, sparse and minimally appointed rooms: from $370 for city view, $395 for partial ocean view and $450 for oceanfront rooms. The hotel hadn't yet set its new summer prices when we visited. This place is in demand, so reserve early. (Madonna had a birthday party here and used to own a piece of the Blue Door restaurant downstairs – see Places to Eat.)

The *Breakwater Hotel* (☎ 305-532-1220, 940 Ocean Drive) has our favorite beachfront sign, but we no longer recommend staying here.

Downtown Miami

Unless you're here on an expense account or with a rich friend who's paying, the city of Miami isn't really the best place. Accommodations are mainly the big chains, a couple of relatively cheap hotels, and flop houses that we don't recommend at all. The chain hotels here – Sheraton, Hyatt, Holiday Inn, Inter-Continental – offer no surprises whatsoever: they all have business centers, concierge service, expensive dry cleaning, restaurants and 'nightclubs,' where industrial-transmission-cog salesmen named Dieter and Hans-Joachim boogie the night away, waving fists with the thumbs-up sign up and down on the dance floor.

In terms of proximity to the action and just plain neighborhood ambiance, you will do far, far better staying on the Beach than in the city. But hey, if you're game, so are we.

There are two budget places we'd consider staying in downtown: the *Miami Sun Hotel* (☎ 305-375-0786, 800-322-0786, 226 NE 1st Ave) is clean and perfectly located for a downtown hotel, with rooms from $35 to $45 year round. The clean *Leamington Hotel*

(☎ 305-373-7783, fax 305-536-2208, 307 NE 1st St) has year-round prices of $40 to $50 and one of those old-fashioned elevators.

The **Miami River Inn** (☎ 305-325-0045, fax 305-325-9227, www.hotelguide.net/mia/ data/h100759.htm, 119 SW South River Drive) is a charming place right on the river between SW 1st and 2nd Sts. If we had to stay downtown and you were paying, this is where we'd stay. It has lovely rooms, six cats and excellent and friendly service. Rooms run from $69 to $129 in summer, $89 to $149 in winter.

The otherwise-unexciting **Dupont Plaza Hotel** (☎ 305-358-2541, 800-432-9076, fax 305-539-8034, 300 Biscayne Blvd Way), on the site of the groundbreaking of the original city of Miami, is the best deal in downtown if you're looking for a standard, steady-as-she-goes business hotel with friendly staff. Rooms go from $69 in summer, $99 in winter, including two buffet breakfasts.

Holiday Inn (☎ 305-374-3000, 800-465-4329, fax 305-374-5897, 200 SE 2nd Ave) has rack rates of $149, but typically you can book in for doubles at around $89 to $119. Watch for multinight and weekend specials.

The behemoth **Everglades Hotel** (☎ 305-379-5461, 800-327-5700, fax 305-577-8390, 244 Biscayne Blvd) looks like a three-star tourist hotel in post-embargo Havana: the lobby is suitably dark, the staff suitably morose, the decor suitably clunky. But the rooms are perfectly average, and with rates of $92 for singles or doubles (much better rates if you book through a travel agent), it's a worthwhile option in the heart of downtown.

The **Hyatt Regency** (☎ 305-358-1234, 400 SE 2nd Ave) downtown has rooms ranging from $149 to $189.

Another option is the **Sheraton** (☎ 305-373-6000, 800-325-3535, 495 Brickell Ave), which has rooms on its corporate floor from $234 and standard rooms priced from $175/185 single/double.

Coral Gables

The **Hyatt Regency Coral Gables** (☎ 305-441-1234, fax 305-441-0520, 50 Alhambra Plaza) is pricier than its downtown counterpart, with singles/doubles from $285/310. A better deal is its business-plan rooms, with a fax machine and access to the business center plus other perks, for $20 more. All the rooms are everything you'd expect from a Hyatt: we treated ourselves to a stay here and had a very nice time indeed, thank you very much.

The **Biltmore Hotel** (☎ 305-445-8066, 800-727-1926, fax 305-913-3158, 1200 Anastasia Ave) is a swank 1926 landmark (see Biltmore Hotel earlier in the chapter). High-season (mid-winter) singles/doubles are $319 (standard) to $469 (suite). In the lowest season (July to August), rates run $139 to $199. The infamous Capone Suite is priced according to demand – usually about $2450.

Coconut Grove

We recommend staying at the **Coconut Grove Bed & Breakfast** (☎ 305-856-4311, fax 305-860-8922, cocobandb@aol.com, 4286 Douglas Rd). The two-story house only has three rooms, but they're wonderfully decorated – as is the entire house – by the works of the owner, artist Annette Rawlings, whose pottery, textile and paintings have been shown throughout the world. This family has been in the Grove for decades and was actually among that legendary group of starving artists that set out to make names for themselves in the late '60s. Good for them. The rooms are $115 to $150 in summer, $135 to $175 in winter, including a spectacular homemade breakfast.

PLACES TO EAT
Miami Beach

Restaurants abound in South Beach, catering to absolutely every style and budget. You can get by incredibly cheaply if you stick to Cuban and fast food, and you may be in for some new taste treats. Try local favorites like *guarapo* (sugarcane juice), Cuban coffee (respectfully referred to by SoBe locals as zoom juice) and *café con leche* (strong coffee with milk). Don't expect some kind of chi-chi Seattle stuff: this is an over-sweetened (they put sugar in for you unless you specifically tell them not to) industrial-

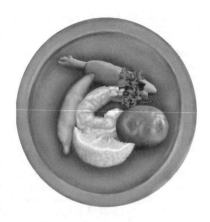

strength product, and Western palates may find it ghastly. But whatever you're in the mood for, you'll find it in South Beach.

Coffee Bars This is not Seattle, or even Atlanta, when it comes to the coffeehouse scene, and while many small local coffee bars on the Beach have fallen victim to Starbucks, there are a couple of alternatives to the reprehensible-to-Seattlites 'zoom juice' served at the Cuban places around town.

The *Aurora Cafe* (☎ 305-534-1744, 1205 17th St) has excellent espresso and cappuccino plus exotic coffees from around the world. It's a very slick yet unpretentious space and has a little library packed with lefty publications. It also does some food as well.

The 'Oh, look how hip we are with our intellectual name' *Kafka Kafe* (☎ 305-673-9669, 1464 Washington Ave) is to date the Beach's only Internet café, and the service when we visited was repellent. Nonetheless, it's got a nice atmosphere and coffee and tea.

Joffrey's Coffee Company (660 Lincoln Rd) is a chain coffee place that's newer than Starbucks, with still-unpretentious digs, friendly staff and nice little touches like doggie treats for customers who must leave the pooch outside.

Starbucks Coffee Company has come to town in a big way, with branches at 1451 Ocean Drive (☎ 305-674-0074), 749 Lincoln Rd (☎ 305-538-5906), 1570 Alton Rd (☎ 305-538-0958) and 200 Miracle Mile (☎ 305-443-6620) in Coral Gables.

Breakfast & Brunch This is the New York Jewish capital of the southern USA, and bagels are everywhere. (For a description of bagels, see Food in Facts for the Visitor.) They're available in any diner and in most restaurants that serve breakfast, but several bagel specialists have opened on the Beach. Most open early for breakfast (between 6:30 and 7:30 am), but all have fantastically confusing closing hours on different days. Suffice it to say they close in the early evening.

The chi-chiest entry is *Einstein Bros Bagels* (☎ 305-534-4003, 1500 Alton Rd), which has cream cheeses flavored with such exotic ingredients as scallions, sun-dried tomatoes and strawberries and other toppings like honey and whipped peanut butter. Any of the above on a bagel is $2 to $3; butter only is 90¢; a bottomless cup of coffee is $1.10.

But the *Bagelry* (☎ 305-531-9877, 1223 Lincoln Rd) is far less pretentious, with 45¢ bagels, 85¢ with butter and $3.70 with tuna salad. Most Beach restaurants serve brunch from around 10 am to about 3 pm on Saturday and Sunday.

Generally speaking, you can get a huge breakfast plus a bloody mary or mimosa for around $10 a person. *Monty's Seafood & Stone Crab Restaurant* (☎ 305-673-3344, 300 Alton Rd), in the marina, has a nice atmosphere – stylish, airy and bright, in addition to a great view of the boats – and offers a phenomenally large buffet brunch for $25 per person.

Fast Food There's nothing special about the fast food on the Beach, but the *Miami Subs* chain sells slightly up-market sandwiches and salads for less than $5, and extras like beer and cheap champagne.

South Beach also has a *Pollo Tropical*, doing very inexpensive and delicious grilled chicken. All Pollo Tropicals have playgrounds. Other than that, there are the usual offerings from McDonalds, Burger King,

MIAMI

Kentucky Fried Chicken (KFC), Taco Bell and Dunkin' Donuts.

Pizza Washington Ave is lined with pizzerias selling slices and pies, and pizza can be had all over South Beach. Most places are open late on weekends. Do your best to try some of the Beach's excellent home-grown product before resorting to the white-bread chains. For a real Italian-style pizza, head for the Sports Café (see Italian).

For delivery pizza, *Bella Napoli* (☎ 305-672-1558, 1443 Alton Rd) is the best on the Beach, selling large cheese (18-inch) pies for $8 (!) and large pies with garlic, mushrooms, peppers and onions for $13. There's a $1 delivery charge and a $5 minimum order on deliveries, or you can eat in the restaurant, though it's a bit threadbare. It's open Monday to Friday 11 am to 11 pm, Saturday and Sunday noon to 11 pm.

A worthy runner-up for either takeout or eat-in is *Pizza Rustica* (☎ 305-674-8244, 404 Washington Ave), which kicks ass and takes names in the Pizza Wars. Sicilian-style square slices topped with an exotic array of toppings (without going overboard) are a meal in themselves at $3 to $3.50. Both of these places have beer and wine.

Master's Deli Pizza (☎ 305-672-2763, 1720 Alton Rd), which bakes real New York-style pizzas, has large pies with two toppings for $9.99.

Slices at pizza stands run around $2, and most places do specials, like two slices and a Coke for $3. All stay open to at least 2 am for the Friday and Saturday night, zonked out of their brains, disco, oh-man-now-we-got-the-munchies crowd. Some of Washington Ave's better slice offerings include *Ciccio's Pizza* (☎ 305-534-7155, No 1405), *Pucci's Pizza* (☎ 305-673-8133, No 1447) and *Lincoln NYC Pizza* (☎ 305-672-2722, No 1595).

Da Leo Pizza Via (☎ 305-538-0803, 826 Lincoln Rd), run by the very good Da Leo Trattoria (see Italian), does traditional Italian-style pizzas priced from $7 to $11.

Hungry for white-bread, mass-produced stuff? *Pizza Hut* (☎ 305-672-1900), *Little*

Caesar's (☎ 305-531-4494) and *Dominos* (☎ 305-531-8211) all deliver.

Steak & Beef We had a total flesh fest at the magnificent *Joe Allen Miami Beach* (☎ 305-531-7007, 1787 Purdy Ave). They served up the best steak Nick's had in a year for about $20, and five of us ate, drank and got copiously merry for just about $150.

Now, we haven't eaten at the new *Smith & Wollensky* (☎ 305-673-2800, 1 Washington Ave), in the former South Pointe Brewery, but our friends tell us that Joe Allen is the better deal. However, S&W has one of the best locations on the Beach, reportedly good service (open daily noon to 2 am), and all main meat courses are $27. It's great to sit at the bar in the afternoon and look out into the channel.

Casona de Carlitos (☎ 305-534-7013, 2236 Collins Ave) may not be as good as a restaurant actually *in* Buenos Aires, but for a *parrillada* (Argentinean barbecued side of beef), you could do a whole lot worse than this one at $29.95 for two people – a deal that hasn't changed since our last edition, bless 'em! Argentinean food is heavy on the red meat – main courses average $20.

See the Downtown Miami for information on Porção and Brazilian steak houses.

American Despite its faux-frog name, baguettes and pretentious translations ('cornichons' = French pickles), *La Sandwicherie* (☎ 305-532-8934, 229 14th St) is as American as a sex scandal. Which means it has great – and great big – sandwiches. Create your own for $4 to $7, salads from $5 to $7. Beer and alcohol aren't served, but it does have fruit juices and sodas. It's a small sandwich bar with about four stools, located in the alley (which does smell a bit ripe now and then). The place is open noon to 5 pm every day, and it will deliver between noon and 3 pm.

The *News Cafe* (☎ 305-538-6397, 800 Ocean Drive) is an absolute South Beach landmark, and as much as we hate to admit it, it's worth spending an afternoon here. It's trendy enough to be painful, and it's open 24 hours. The salads are terrific, but its famous

Cigar-maker in Little Havana

Hot paella, served at the Calle Ocho Festival

Domino players at Máximo Gómez Park

Mural depicting Cuban culture in Little Havana

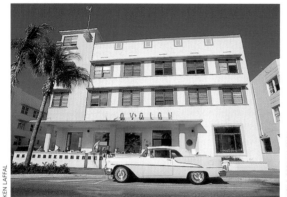

Hotel Avalon, in the Art Deco Historic District

Deco...

Fairmont Hotel, another Art Deco treasure

...Deco...

Fontainbleau *trompe-l'oeil* mural

...and more Deco

dish is the tomato bruschetta ($5.75), perfect with an iced tea while watching the skaters wiggle down Ocean Drive. Also try the plain omelet ($5) or pasta dishes from $8 to $10.25. They add a 15% tip to all checks, but if you're really unhappy with service, they'll remove it on request. There's a second branch (☎ 305-774-6397, 2901 Florida Ave) in Coconut Grove.

Lou's Real Philly Cheesesteak (805 Lincoln Rd) has some seriously good sandwiches from $6.75, and heaps of microbrews at $3.75 apiece.

At the corner of 11th and Washington is the ever-popular *11th St Diner* (☎ 305-534-6373, 1065 Washington), an original Art Deco diner trucked down from Wilkes-Barre, Pennsylvania, renovated and serving really good three-egg omelets ($4.25), sandwiches ($2.50 to $6.25), and American favorites such as fried chicken and meat loaf from $7.25 to $14.95. It's open 24 hours. Service is usually pretty slow – it's cheerful enough, though – and don't forget they include the tip in your check. There's an excellent mural in the smoking section.

The *Front Porch Cafe* (☎ 305-531-8300, 1418 Ocean Drive) has been around for eons by South Beach standards – since 1990 – so we're listing it (we left it out last time) for its atmosphere and its value as a quiet place to meet for a fashionable breakfast.

We disagreed about *Balans* (☎ 305-534-9191, 1022 Lincoln Rd), an all-too-chic British-owned bistro (cue: alarm bells) that tries to cover several cuisines, including American (clang), European (clang clang) and Asian (CLANG). But we think it's pretty good – a funky, modern yet comfortable atmosphere and friendly service. Breakfast specials go for $5 to $7.50, lunch specials around $8 for vegetarian and $10 for everyone else, and dinner main courses from $10 to $15.

Astor Place Bar & Grill (☎ 305-672-7217, 956 Washington Ave) does an interesting mix of American, Caribbean and European foods – friends recommended it to us.

The Strand (☎ 305-532-2340, 617 Washington Ave) is a posh place with many expensive items, with the exception of its special dinners, such as meatloaf for $6.75. Special deals are not offered every night, so call first.

Jeffrey's (☎ 305-673-0690, 1629 Michigan Ave), not to be confused with the coffee place Joffrey's, is romantic and good, with artwork, candles and Tiffany lamps. Appetizers ($7 to $10) include artichoke and shrimp, a chicken-salad plate and stuffed mushrooms; main courses ($15 to $20) include a nice vegetarian plate, crab cakes and veal cutlet.

The Delano Hotel's *Blue Door* (☎ 305-674-6400, 1685 Collins Ave) has very good service, and for a stuck-up place it's decidedly democratic about getting you a table. (Maybe it's a sign that the hotel's losing favor with the Fabulosos, or maybe it's because everyone simply assumes the place is outrageously expensive and thus difficult to get into.) The food is very good, with main courses hovering from $24 to $30, and don't miss out on the generous martinis and cosmopolitans.

The closest Miami Beach gets to a world-famous restaurant is *Joe's Stone Crab Restaurant* (☎ 305-673-0365, 227 Biscayne St). It's been around since 1913 and open only during stone-crab season from October 15 to May 15. There are seating politics (the restaurant's maitre d' was described by *Zagat* as 'the wealthiest man in Miami'), but the restaurant offers reliably excellent stone-crab and seafood dishes. At a price, to be sure: medium stone-crab claws (six per order) are $16.95, 'selects' (seven per order) are $21.95 and large (five per order) are $28.95. If your appetite is robust, you can easily polish off two orders per person. Other dishes are cheaper, like broiled swordfish steak ($16.95) or grouper ($13.95). There's also takeout service available, if you don't want to fight the crowds. And if you're feeling decadent in, say, Duluth, you can order an overnight air shipment of Joe's stone crabs to anywhere in the USA by calling them before 2 pm at ☎ 800-780-2722. The cost, including shipping, for a complete dinner for two (16 medium stone-crab claws plus fixings) is $84.95, or $116.95 for four. You can even order on the Internet at www.joesstonecrabs.com. Geez.

Cuban Especially at night, *Las Americas* (☎ 305-673-0560, 450 Lincoln Rd) is an interesting place for a sandwich (about $2.95), or go for breakfast (its greasy special has more than most and costs $3, though service is awful). In the evening, there's entertainment in the form of someone plinking on an old piano. It's open daily 8 am to 11 pm or midnight, depending on business.

The 24-hour café con leche market has been cornered by *David's Café* (☎ 305-534-8736, 1058 Collins Ave at 11th St). It offers not-awesome Cuban food in the $3 to $6 range and an OK breakfast for $2.50, but it's really here as an emergency stopgap when you're starving at 3:15 am and don't want pizza.

The majority of waiters at *Puerto Sagua* (☎ 305-673-1115, 700 Collins Ave) have been there for more than 30 years, serving up humongous portions of good Cuban food at reasonable prices: soup of the day is $4.50, *arroz con pollo* (rice with chicken) and *ropa vieja* (shredded beef) are $7.50, and its specialties like *filete de pargo grillet* (grilled red snapper) top off the menu at $13. Good breakfasts cost $4. It's open 7 am to 2 am daily and has probably the best Cuban café con leche on the Beach because they give you the elements (espresso and steamed milk) in separate cups and don't add the sugar. Breakfasts, though, can be a tad greasy.

Near the corner of Michigan Ave and just near Books & Books, the *Lincoln Road Café* (☎ 305-538-8066, 943 Lincoln Rd) is another long-time Cuban spot famous for its infuriatingly slow service and reliably decent food. It has sandwiches from $3 to $6 and very good poultry dishes from $6.95 to $8.95. For dessert, skip the sickeningly sweet *tres leches* (sugar and milkfat) in favor of its *arroz con leche* (rice pudding) for $2. It's open Monday to Saturday 8 am to 1 am, and Sunday 10 am to 5 pm. Sit outside and drink coffee during the gallery walks and save

yourself some cash over the trendy nearby competition.

Chicken Grill (☎ 305-672-7717, 1439 Alton Rd) does good if oily grilled chickens for $8 and a leg/thigh with rice and beans for $3.29. It has a window counter serving zoom juice and café con leche. The restaurant's open 8 am to 11 pm, closed Sunday.

Gloria Estefan's *Larios on the Beach* (☎ 305-532-9577, 820 Ocean Drive) deserves special mention in a category of its own. Fight through the crowds to get at the hostess (they don't pretentiously stand outside flagging people in) and apply for a table (no reservations accepted). The atmosphere is better than the food (which is good but not outstandingly so). Try the paella ($38 for two people, takes 45 minutes) or the less-expensive fish Creole ($8.25). Otherwise, two people can squeak out for $20 or so by getting three or four appetizers (like the huge Cuban sandwich for $4.35) and one drink each.

Yuca (☎ 305-532-9822, 501 Lincoln Rd) is the Beach's best Cuban Nouveau place (actually, it's the only one), with truly marvelous food and a chic European decor. Main courses, such as plantain-coated dolphin fish with tamarind tartar ($23) and baby-back ribs with spice guava sauce served with yucca shoestring fries and chipotle coleslaw ($29) are divine, and starters run from $6 to $16. All the prices come down 30% at lunchtime.

Mexican The battle of the burrito has come to South Beach, with two extremely worthy contenders and a couple of wanna-bes (including a Taco Bell at 1665 Washington Ave). After lengthy consideration, we've decided that *San Loco* (☎ 305-538-3009, 235 14th St), between Washington and Collins Aves, still has the best burrito in town, hands down. Lovely staff take care of you, serving up terrific and overstuffed burritos ($2.75 to $5.75), enchiladas ($3.50 to $5) and tacos ($1.50 to $4). San Loco doesn't throw bushels of cilantro at the food. It's open Sunday to Thursday 11 am to 5 am, Friday and Saturday to 6 am. Excellent salads are

$3.75 to $5.75, and beer and sodas are $1 to $2.75. No credit cards are accepted.

The somewhat awkwardly located *Mrs Mendoza's Tacos al Carbon* (☎ *305-535-0808, 1040 Alton Rd*) serves up even bigger burritos that have less garlic and heaps more cilantro for $3.99, tacos with chips and salsa for $2.99, guacamole and chips for $3.09, and rice and beans for $1.60. The atmosphere may seem more fast-food than San Loco, but they're not kidding about their salsa – when they say hot, it's head-blowing, ulcer-slammin' hot! It is open Monday to Thursday 11 am to 10 pm, Friday and Saturday to 11 pm, Sunday noon to 9 pm.

If you love cilantro, you'll love *El Rancho Grande* (☎ *305-673-0480, 1626 Pennsylvania Ave*), where they put cilantro in absolutely everything they serve. It's a comfortable and cozy sit-down and more formal affair than the previous two, but it has great lunch specials with main courses from $3.49 to $6 and fajitas from $7.99 to $9.99. All the food is served in terra-cotta dishware. Burritos come smothered with two types of melted cheese and sour cream, along with rice and beans and guacamole, but salads are a bit meager. Prices almost double at dinnertime. Margaritas are $3.50 a glass, $9 a half-pitcher or $17 a pitcher; other Mexican hootch is available as well.

Haitian & Caribbean Charming *Tap Tap* (☎ *305-672-2898, 819 5th St*) is an interesting place to have a drink – try Haitian Barbancourt rum, available in several grades – and their $4 pumpkin soup is awesome. There are unique Haitian handmade furniture and murals throughout the restaurant, and live music and other entertainment rotates through often – check the *New Times* for more information.

The tiny and tropical *Norma's on the Beach* (☎ *305-532-2809, 646 Lincoln Rd*) is only moderately priced at lunch – dinners become expensive. It offers good Jamaican specialties – lots of jerk seasoning – and dishes average $8 to $10 at lunch and $18 to $22 at dinner. Grab yourself a cold Red Stripe or Dragon Jamaican beer ($3.50) and be happy, mon.

Mango's Tropical Café (☎ *305-673-4422, 900 Ocean Drive*) has an incredible Haitian tropical mural that goes all around the room and over the bar. The specialty here is the Caribbean-style jerk chicken wings; an order of 10 is $5, 20 is $10. Also try Cassie's chef soup (chicken, shrimp and veggies with noodles) for $6.95.

Chinese A fine local hangout, *Charlotte's* (☎ *305-672-8338, 1403 Washington Ave*) has very good food. Our favorites are the curry shrimp ($8.95) and Singapore fried noodles ($8.95).

Canton Inn (☎ *305-673-2218, 843 Lincoln Rd*) is an old-fashioned kind of Chinese restaurant that feels as if you're walking back into the 1950s – especially the prices of the set lunch specials ($4.25 to $5.75) served Tuesday to Sunday 11:30 am to 3 pm. Dinner entrees average $8.

For $1, *Yeung's Chinese Restaurant* (☎ *305-672-1144, 954 41st St*) will deliver some pretty respectable food – though some dishes, like vegetable dumplings ($5.50) and shredded duck with Chinese veggies and rice noodles ($10.50) are better than others, such as the crispy chicken ($9.50).

Chrysanthemum (☎ *305-531-5656, 1248 Washington Ave*) is open for dinner only. It serves quite a variety of fish and seafood dishes, such as shrimp imperial (with cashew nuts and bamboo shoots) for $13 and crispy fish in lemon sauce for $11.80, but also orange-and-garlic frog legs for $14.95 and duck for $13.80. Low-calorie meals are indicated on the menu.

The *China Grill* (☎ *305-534-2211, 404 Washington Ave*) may be expensive, but it's the place to bring a date. (As one friend says, 'It will cost a packet, but you will get laid!') Service, though, is awful. Food is served family style (well, maybe *wealthy* family style) in large bowls intended to be shared. Menu items include grilled dry-aged Szechwan beef ($26.50 for one person, $46 for two), sizzling whole fish ($22/34), grilled rosemary scallops ($23) and wasabi-crusted grouper ($22). It's slightly – oh, slightly – cheaper at lunchtime, but the place comes highly recommended. For the cheapest and best deal offered, show up between 6 and 7 pm for the pre-event dinner for $24.96 per person, including an appetizer and two of five entrees (but not tax or tip).

Japanese Sushi's a happening thing in South Beach, and our favorite place for it is *New Sushi Hana* (☎ 305-604-0300, 1131 Washington Ave). The place is cavernous, but there are four traditional tatami tables in back, and service is usually very friendly (if rushed). There's free (and great) salad when you sit down. À la carte sushi is 95¢ to $3, *temaki* rolls (rice and fish and/or vegetables wrapped in seaweed) are $3.95 to $9.50, and sushi/roll combinations (big enough for two people to share) are $15.95 to $20.

Toni's Sushi Bar (☎ 305-673-9368, 1208 Washington Ave) is also very good (and it's certainly crowded); à la carte sushi is $1.50 to $2.50, sushi entrees run from $13 all the way up to the gigantic sushi-boat at $70. It also offers more expensive seafood dishes for $13 to $21.

We'd stay clear of the *Sushi Rock Café* (☎ 305-532-2133, 1351 Collins Ave) with sushi and OK service at slightly higher prices for sushi, slightly lower for combinations and temaki rolls. The music's awfully loud in the evenings and the last time we went it was terrible. But the place may pick back up – to be fair, we were there during the low season.

If you take all you can eat as a personal challenge, head directly for *Tokyo Club* (☎ 305-534-5358, 3425 Collins Ave) in the Hotel Versailles, for its all-you-can-eat sushi and teriyaki specials for $10.95: Tuesday to Saturday 5 pm to 4 am, Sunday to 11 pm (closed Monday). Not enough? It has an all-you-can-*drink* special (you read that right) for $12 for women and $16 for men on Friday and Saturday nights from 11 pm to 4 am. There is, of course, karaoke to wash down the booze.

Thai The *World Resources Café* (☎ 305-534-9095, 719 Lincoln Rd) does a Thai-based world cuisine menu, with appetizers ($4 to $6) and curries ($6 to $8) along with more expensive fare, but it has gone downhill since the last edition and may not last much longer.

Just next to the New Sushi Hana is the *Thai House* (☎ 305-531-4841, 1137 Washington Ave) with veggie dishes from $7 to $11, pad Thai noodles for $9 and higher-priced specialties.

Thai Toni's (☎ 305-538-8424, 890 Washington Ave) is renowned for its more expensive specialties. Service is arrogant and the place itself very chic. The Thai food, though, is indisputably good – especially the soups.

Pacific Time (☎ 305-534-5979, 915 Lincoln Rd) is still a favorite and serves consistently excellent Thai and other Pacific Rim food in a very elegant setting. It also does a lot of fundraising and community-minded projects, but service can get a tad snooty when it's busy, which is always.

For a more affordable and casual version of the same food, head next door and into the little alley to *Pacific Time Next Door* (☎ 305-534-2774, 927 Lincoln Rd) in the Stirling Building. It has super food (main courses from $12 to $24) and is open at 6 pm daily for dinner.

Pan-Asian *Nemo Restaurant* (☎ 305-532-4550, 100 Collins Ave) has a very interesting Pan-Asian menu with oyster-miso soup ($6), wok-charred salmon and sprout salad and, that old Asian standby, pan-roasted chicken with mashed potatoes and dried cranberry dressing, both for $16. Dress to kill and make reservations.

Jewish We left *Wolfie's* (☎ 305-538-6626, 2038 Collins Ave) out of the book last time because we thought it left lots to be desired. Then we got letters. We went back, and while for food we think you'll do better at the Rascal House or even S&S (see Northeast Miami later), Wolfie's is a classic Miami Beach haunt. Established in 1938, it's open 24 hours and is staffed by cantankerous schmoozers. Everything comes with a bowl of pickles on the table.

Italian The **Sports Café** (☎ 305-674-9700, 538 Washington Ave) is a local's favorite, and it's definitely our favorite. This unpretentious and comfortable café's unfortunate name disguises a family-run place that feels as if you've walked into a Roman café – not a slicked-up American version of a Roman café but a real one! When you sit down, they give you freshly baked bread with a spiced extra-virgin olive oil dipping plate. The homemade pastas are simply the best we've ever had in the USA and maybe even in Italy (and we like our pasta!); simple pasta dishes with basil-tomato sauce are $6.95, lasagna $7.25, and daily specials go for $7.25 to $8.95. Don't miss the crab ravioli in pink cream sauce topped with freshly ground Romano cheese and black pepper. Its pizza is made Euro style – smaller, thinner crust and a different method of layering the toppings – it's first rate. Can it get better? Yup. There's suave and attentive service, a good and inexpensive wine list and fish and chicken specials as well. Sports Café accepts Visa, MasterCard, traveler's checks and cash, and it's open 11 am to 1 am daily.

Because we like that place so much, we have no qualms about recommending a place the same family owns on Lincoln Rd: **Rosinella** (☎ 305-672-8777, 525 Lincoln Rd). Even though the family decided to sell out and get a chi-chi SoBe Lincoln Rd location, they couldn't bring themselves to charge too much or lower the standards of their cooking. This small and cozy place does wonderful organic and vegetarian soups (from $3 to $6), nice eggplant antipasto and main courses from $6.50 to $8.50, lasagna ($8.50) and the specialty of the house, gnocchi with tomato ($11) or gorgonzola ($12) sauces.

For a place with outside tables along Ocean Drive, **Café Romano** (☎ 305-672-8484, 900 Ocean Drive) is okay for drinks, but we're not so hot on the food. It has decent pizzas, sandwiches and snacks.

Another pleasant and inexpensive Italian place is **Tutti's** (☎ 305-535-0012, 635 Collins Ave), which cooks up excellent food at extremely reasonable prices: pasta with any sauce is $4.95, a side salad is only $1.50 extra,

and salads are $4 to $6. The atmosphere is Gen-X chic with pouty staff and counter service. Too much to handle? There are sidewalk seats as well, and there's a second entrance next door for takeout only.

Da Leo Trattoria (☎ 305-674-0350, 819 Lincoln Rd) is worth trying; tables spill outside in the evenings, and people seem both happy and well fed. Generous portions of pasta run $7 to $9, main courses $10 to $18.

Osteria del Teatro (☎ 305-538-7850, 1443 Washington Ave) has an expensive but very good Italian menu. If you get here before 7:30 pm, there's a fixed-price $19 dinner that's worth every penny.

Café Papillon (☎ 305-673-1139, 530 Lincoln Rd) is a good place to stop for lunch along the Road. Soup and half a large sandwich are $5.95, and Italian sandwiches (like tomato, mozzarella, basil and oil and vinegar) are about $5. There are newspapers on sticks, and a casual, if close, atmosphere.

Other European The **Dab Haus** (☎ 305-534-9557, 825 Alton Rd) has excellent German food such as bratwurst, currywurst and knoblauchwurst for $7, sauerbraten for $10, and pork and chicken schnitzel for $9. It also does crêpes – we like the mushrooms, potatoes, red cabbage and cheese. And don't miss the honey-garlic brie…mmm. (Also see Entertainment later in the chapter.)

Stephan's Gourmet Market & Café (☎ 305-674-1760, 1430 Washington Ave), just south of the Clay Hotel, is a market bursting with fresh and delicious Italian and European produce, cheeses, meats and spices, and its dining room upstairs has a special that's a very good deal on a date: dinner for two is $21.25 (including tax) for bread, an entree that changes nightly, salad and a bottle of wine. Try the penne with sautéed mushrooms in goat-cheese sauce.

The Paramount (☎ 305-535-8020, 1040 Lincoln Rd) is a local favorite, with imaginative food and reasonable prices. Appetizers, such as toasted yellow-pepper risotto cakes with pesto shrimp ($5.95), and main courses like lasagna ($9.95) and grilled tuna with caper lime butter ($13.95) are great.

For French cuisine, try **Les Deux Fontaines** (☎ 305-672-7878, 1030-38 Ocean Drive) in the Hotel Ocean. Open for lighter lunch fare and more substantial dinners, this patio restaurant sits above Ocean Drive – close enough to people-watch but far enough to keep the riffraff from your saumon au papilotte. It's a nice spot to have some tuna carpaccio ($8.50) and a glass of wine at lunch. At dinnertime, prices shoot upward, though like the hotel in which it's located, it's not as expensive as it looks or feels: main-dinner courses average about $15 per person without wine, tax or tip. There's a decent wine list (French and American).

Vegetarian The Beach is more veggie friendly than ever, with all but the most steadfastly carnivorous restaurants offering one or two vegetarian main courses and appetizers.

Grazing is the order of the day at the godsend **Wild Oats Community Market** (☎ 305-532-1707, 1020 Alton Rd), with a magnificent salad bar, and pre-made vegetarian, vegan, organic and even a couple of meat entries. Get the food at the deli counter and sit at the tables in front, where there's free spring water.

The Naked Earth (☎ 305-531-2171, 910 Pennsylvania Ave) is a good vegetarian restaurant and bakery that makes its own breads and soups, all for under $8. It offers live music Thursday to Saturday at 8 pm.

Another place for good vegetarian and organic soups and other fare is Rosinella (see Italian above).

Wish (☎ 305-531-2222, 801 Collins Ave), in The Hotel, is a splendid vegetarian place with scrumptious dinner main courses averaging $10 and highly innovative food that's even satisfying to carnivores. It's open for breakfast (7 am to noon) and dinner (6 pm to midnight).

Other Cuisines Michael Caine might own it, but **South Beach Brasserie** (☎ 305-534-5511, 910 Lincoln Rd) has service more out of *Alfie* than *Dirty Rotten Scoundrels*. We were incensed at the attitude of the waiter,

who ever so slowly brought forth plates of tired and uninspired food. But if you want to be seen, you might consider stopping in – it's as big as a ballroom.

The **Raleigh Bar & Restaurant** (☎ 305-534-1775, 1775 Collins Ave) is a gorgeous place to come before or after trying to gain access to its pool. Considering the FQ (Fabulous Quotient) of the place, it's rather reasonable and makes the best martini on the Beach ($12, but it's huge, dry and made with Bombay Saffire). For lunch, main courses such as roasted vegetables Provençal, tuna burger with ginger soy sauce or grilled jumbo shrimp gazpacho run from $8 to $15. Sunday brunch is a chi-chi affair (wild mushroom omelet with fresh herbs and goat cheese at $9.50) and dinner gets very expensive.

Grillfish (☎ 305-538-9908, 1444 Collins Ave), across from the Warsaw Ballroom, has a wonderful atmosphere – Greek? Mediterranean? 'Gay,' said the waiter. It's elegant, but tuxedos are forbidden. The mainly Italian seafood dishes are very good (grilled salmon and rainbow trout are $13), but chicken is also offered. Appetizers run from mussels at $4 to shrimp scampi at $6.25. The restaurant is open till 'eleven-ish, one-ish on the weekends.'

Still one of the Beach's hottest spots, the **Van Dyke Hotel Restaurant** (☎ 305-534-3600, 846 Lincoln Rd) serves adequate food in a very chic setting that's usually packed to the rafters and taking over half the sidewalk. Service is very friendly, and even efficient, and if you could just get rid of the models preening, posing and prodding each other, it would be a better place to eat. Burgers and chicken burgers are $6 to $9, an open roast beef sandwich is $8.75, and the house specialty is eggplant parmigiana. There's nightly jazz upstairs. Watch for that included tip.

Allioli (☎ 305-538-0553, 1300 Ocean Drive) is in the same building as the Cardozo Hotel (see Places to Stay earlier), both owned by Gloria Estefan. It provides a romantic, elegant atmosphere while serving Spanish food with Italian/Cuban influence. For lunch, roasted chicken with rice and vegetables is $9.50, *churrasco* (barbequed meat) $12.90, sandwiches $5.25 to $6.95. For dinner, you'll have to part with a little more: pastas are $10.50, paellas $14.95 to $18.95, meat and seafood $14.95 to $22.

Downtown Miami

Most places downtown cater to the 9-to-5ers and therefore close early; most are closed Sunday.

There are two good foodcourts offering a variety of Chinese, Mexican, Indian, pizza, sandwiches, etc, all for $1 to $6. The better of the two is at 243 E Flagler St – try the Brazilian *prata del dia*, a buffet-style feast for $5, and wash it down with an Antarctica beer or a Guarana and you'll think you're in Belo. There's another at 48 E Flagler St (upstairs).

A Cuban-run bagelry? Darn tootin'. Visit the ***Bagel Barn*** (☎ 305-373-0303, 30 NE 3rd Ave), run by one Titi Puente (no relation), for very good bagels. A coffee and bagel with cream cheese is $2.

Skyline Cafe (☎ 305-539-7097, 100 SE 2nd St), at the NationsBank Tower, is open for breakfast weekdays only 7:30 am to 11:30 am, with a $2.50 breakfast special, and for snacks and lunch Monday to Friday 11:30 am to 2:30 pm. You can get a decent lunch for about $7, and the view of downtown is pretty slick.

Seriously friendly service and some of the most authentic Brazilian mid-range food outside Brazil is at ***Le Ideal Cuban/ Brazilian*** (☎ 305-358-0881, 188 NE 3rd Ave), which does breakfast for $1.70 (two eggs and bacon), sandwiches around $2.50 and a nice *pechuga rellena* for $7. *Tudo bem!*

Café Nash (☎ 305-371-8871, 37 E Flagler St), inside the Seybold Building Arcade, is a fairly small place that's quite popular among the businesspeople downtown – it will probably have several locations when you read this. It is open for breakfast and lunch only. Omelets are $3.25 to $4.95, lots of different salads are $4 to $6, sandwiches are $2.95 to $6 and platters including two side orders are $6.25.

Rigato (☎ 305-358-5852, 212 NE 3rd St) does good Italian specials from about $3 to $6 and has a very pleasant little courtyard and friendly service.

La Cocina de Mama Stella (121 SE 1st St), next to the Royalton Hotel, is extremely small. There are maybe five tables outside, and the kitchen is more or less outside as well, but the food looks and smells fantastic, though the staff's English is extremely limited. Cuban dishes all cost $4.99.

Panini Coffee Bar (☎ 305-377-2888, 16 NE 3rd Ave) is an indoor/outdoor café, French-ish and trendy by downtown standards. It serves coffees and pastries (80¢ to $2.95) as well as sandwiches on wide French bread ($4.75 to $7.25), salads ($3.95 to $6.95) and soup by the cup/bowl ($2.50/3.15). It's open Monday to Friday 8 am to 6 pm, to 4 pm on Saturday.

Oriental Express (☎ 305-374-0177, 59 NE 2nd St) has a lunchtime buffet with dishes like veggie chow mein ($3.95), chicken or beef with broccoli ($4.85) and shrimp with tofu ($5.25). Everything comes with soup and rice.

Cacique's Corner (☎ 305-371-8317, 100 W Flagler St) is a classic Cuban place near the downtown bus center, library and federal building. Its fish soup ($4.95) is a meal in itself, a glorious mixture of squash, yucca, shrimp and chunks of fish – squeeze in as much fresh lime as you can. Mix that with the *bistec de pollo* with rice and beans and plaintains and two can roll out on their stomachs for under $10.

The inevitable ***Hard Rock Cafe*** (☎ 305-377-3110, 401 Biscayne Blvd), in Bayside Marketplace, is perhaps known more for the gigantic rotating electric guitar on its roof than for its food, which is perfectly fine (some is very good indeed) and not as expensive as we thought. Enormous and excellent sandwiches like the VLT (veggie, lettuce and tomato) are $6.99, smoked barbecue beef on a pretzel roll is $8.50 and full entrees range from $8.99 to $16.99. It's open 11 am to 2 am daily. Also in the Bayside Marketplace (actually near the flag entrance to it) is ***Las Tapas*** (☎ 305-372-2737), which is said to have excellent samplers of Latin foods.

Tobacco Road Liquor Bar (☎ 305-374-1198, 626 S Miami Ave) has been around for more than 80 years. Something of a Miami tradition, this place has Miami's first liquor license and was a speakeasy during Prohibition. It's primarily known as a blues spot, but it also cooks up good burgers with a variety of toppings from mundane (cheese) to strange (eggs) for $5 to $8, and offers homemade ice cream. It's open 11:30 am to 5 am daily.

Fishbone Grille (☎ 305-530-1915, 650 S Miami Ave) has fresh fish daily, which you can order grilled, blackened, sautéed, baked, Française or Oriental blackened. Prices change according to what's on the chalkboard. It has a very decent seafood gumbo ($3.95 to $4.95) and some interesting pizzas from $7.95 to $9.95. It also has a Coral Gables location – see that section.

You can watch the boats while you eat at *East Coast Fisheries* (☎ 305-372-1300, 360 W Flagler St), Miami's oldest fish restaurant, right on the Miami River. Entrees range from $8 to $20. It draws a very big lunch crowd and is popular for dinner.

Joe's Seafood Restaurant (☎ 305-374-5637, 200 NW North River Drive), also on the Miami River, has a deck where you can sit outside.

With all the business hotels downtown, you'd expect a couple of top-end offerings, but things aren't that rosy. *Porcão* (☎ 305-373-2777, 801 Brickell Ave) is a highly recommended Brazilian place with an elaborate *rodízio*, the traditional endless Brazilian feast of skewered, flame-broiled meat. There are several different cuts on offer – in Brazil, the tougher cuts come out first, but here waiters circulate with flaming skewers and describe exactly what's what. It has a spectacular deal for lunch Monday to Friday noon to 2:30 pm: unlimited buffet, choice of beef, fish or chicken and side dishes plus soft drinks for $12.95. Woo HOO!

Another good lunchtime deal is the buffet for $10 per person at the *Bayview Grille* (☎ 305-374-3900, 1633 N Bayshore Dr), in the Biscayne Bay Marriott Hotel opposite Omni Mall.

The *Capital Grille* (☎ 305-374-4500, 444 Brickell Ave) is a posh upmarket steak house. Steaks – big ones – hover in the $25 to $30 range.

Little Havana

Las Palmas (☎ 305-854-9549, 1128 Calle Ocho) gets top billing for its prices and for being open 24 hours. *Carne con papa* is $2.50, Cuban sandwiches are $3.50. *El Pescador* (☎ 305-649-8222, 1543 Calle Ocho) has very friendly service and excellent Cuban dishes for about $3.50, including rice, potatoes and bread.

When a place calls itself the King of Fries, you at least want to check it out. *El Rey de las Fritas* (☎ 305-858-4223, 1177 Calle Ocho) has grumpy service, but if your doctor told you that you need more cholesterol, this is the place to come for cheap fritas in several varieties, including with cheese for $2.25 and a *pan con bistec* for $3.75.

We really like the *Exquisito Restaurant* (☎ 305-643-0227, 1510 Calle Ocho) for cheap coffee, great atmosphere and excellent food; most dishes are less than $5.

El Palacio Luna (☎ 305-285-9088, 1444 Calle Ocho) is a neat Cuban-Chinese place, with everything under $6. Chow mein, curry and honey-garlic chicken are all good.

Hy Vong Vietnamese Restaurant (☎ 305-446-3674, 3458 Calle Ocho) continues to rock the Miami Vietnamese food world with consistently super food and service. One Lonely Planet staffer reported: 'It's just the best Vietnamese food I've ever had, and I love Vietnamese food. The best is the *bun*, thin-sliced meat with vermicelli, and squid salad marinated in lime juice and onions. Get there early: it looks like a dive, but the food is cheap and great, so it fills up fast.'

Don't expect the food at the very famous *Versailles* (☎ 305-444-0240, 3555 Calle Ocho) to match the gaudiness of the decor: that decor and the atmosphere are why you're here. The cavernous and unbelievably glitzy (in a 1980s *Scarface-Miami Vice* kind of way) restaurant is a Little Havana Cuban landmark, and you really should go out of your way to eat here during your trip. It can be great fun with a group of people and a pitcher of (weak) sangria ($10). Service is fine, but the food pushes hard at the average barrier: live with it. Try the *ropa vieja* or *palomilla* (Cuban steak) with fries or plantains ($8) or with white rice, black beans and plantains ($9); or *vaca frita*, shredded beef grilled with onions ($8.50). It is open Monday to Thursday 8 am to 2 am, Friday to 3:30 am, Saturday to 4:30 am, Sunday 9 am to 2 am.

Several other restaurants have been recommended to us on Calle Ocho: try *La Carreta* (☎ 305-444-7501, *No 3632*), a lot like Versailles but a little less glaring and in your face. *Guayacan* (☎ 305-649-2015, *No 1933*) is a Nicaraguan version of Versailles and about the same price as all the others. There's lots of glitz and flash here.

Many Cubans say the food at *Islas Canarias* (☎ 305-649-0440, *285 NW 27th Ave*) is the best in Miami. At any rate, the food is about the same price as, and much better than, Versailles'.

Coral Gables

Numero Uno on our list of places to eat in Coral Gables is the enormous new location of *Daily Bread Marketplace* (☎ 305-856-5893, *2400 SW 27th St*), which does superb lentil soup ($1.50), falafel and gyro sandwiches ($3.50) and lamb kebab ($4.50). It's also a Middle Eastern mini-supermarket selling olives, tahini and halvah, along with its own excellent brand of pita bread, plus baklava and other pastries. It is open Monday to Saturday 8 am to 8 pm (no falafel after 6 pm), Sunday 11 am to 4 pm.

There's drugstore chic and retro cheesiness at *Allen's Drug Store* (☎ 305-665-6964, *4000 Red Rd*), with inexpensive and reliably good burgers, diner specials and a cool jukebox. *Wrapido* (☎ 305-443-1884, *2334 Ponce de Leon Blvd*), which has a second location in south Miami (☎ 305-662-7999, *5812 Sunset Drive*), has seriously good wraps crammed with stuff for around $5 as well as decent soups. Happy hour for beer ($1 for domestic, $2 for imports) is from 4 to 7 pm daily. The place is a little full of itself, but it's good nonetheless.

Taisho (☎ 305-441-1217, *265 Aragon Ave*) is a serviceable restaurant with sushi and other Japanese specialties.

Redfish Grill (☎ 305-668-8788, *9610 Old Cutler Rd*), in peaceful (if mosquito-laden) Matheson Hammock Park, is a very cool place with a wonderful outdoor beachfront section, perfect for drinks and appetizers.

Just as much fun as the one in downtown Miami, and just as recommended for food, atmosphere and the inexpensive but excellent wine list is *Fishbone Grille II* (☎ 305-668-3033, *1450 S Dixie Hwy*), with appetizers from $3 to $6 and mains from $12 to $16.

Restaurant St Michel (☎ 305-446-6572, *162 Alcazar Ave*) is one of the most romantic restaurants in Miami. It's a four-star place on the ground floor of the Hotel St Michel. Destroyed by fire in 1995, the restaurant has come back, and everyone says the food is better than ever. Entrees range from $18 to $30, with dishes such as sautéed Florida Keys yellowtail and filet mignon with cabernet sauce and caramelized red onion marmalade along with chipotle mashed potatoes (whew), and Australian spring lamb. Desserts are excellent, and the place is absolutely charming.

There's a newly established and moderately priced 'restaurant row' on Giralda Ave between Ponce de Leon Blvd and Miller Ave with about a dozen places serving all kinds of food from Italian to French bistro. Offerings include the *Miss Saigon Bistro* (☎ 305-446-8006, *146 Giralda Ave*), a great family-run place with kitschy atmosphere and great Vietnamese food, main courses under $20 and specials around $15. It's open daily 11:30 am to 10 or 11 pm. *La Dorada* (☎ 305-446-2002, *177 Giralda Ave*) is a real treat for those looking for inventive presentation and fresh seafood, including dorada, the wonderful Mediterranean fish we go nuts over. (We only found one other place serving it, see Coconut Grove below.) Some main courses run from $13 to $15, but most of the fish dishes and the special sampler plate run around $25.

Coconut Grove

There are a couple of little places in Coco-Walk Shopping Center (3015 Grand Ave); we like the *Cheesecake Factory* (☎ 305-447-9898), which offers more than 40 kinds of cheesecake from $5 to $6 a slice – and it's worth $5 to $6. They also have burgers from $6.95 to $7.50 and pizzas (like roasted pepper, ricotta and sun-dried tomato or Thai chicken) from $8 to $10. They also whip up a mean Sunday brunch.

Franz, the former cook at Kaleidoscope (a 1970s Grove classic) opened his own restaurant, *Franz & Joseph's in the Grove* (☎ *305-448-2282, 3145 Commodore Plaza)*, and it's said to be excellent. They offer European-influenced American food: lunch specials are $11 or $12 (try the open-faced prime-rib sandwich for $11.95); for dinner, salads are around $6, the amazing asparagus soup $4.50; main courses run from $13 to $17. Try the lobster ravioli with saffron cream sauce ($17).

Johnny Rockets (☎ *305-444-1000, 3036 Grand Ave)*, right across the street from CocoWalk, is an excellent – if cramped – 1950s-style hamburger joint (they even use those old-fashioned Coca Cola glasses). Burgers and sandwiches run from $3 to $5; the No 12 cheeseburger (with red sauce, pickles, lettuce and tomato) is awesome, but get the red sauce on the side and give it a taste before you commit. They also do a good chicken breast sandwich. Johnny Rockets is open until 2 am on Friday and Saturday and delivers anywhere in Coconut Grove. There's another branch at the Dadeland Mall (see Shopping) and a third in South Beach.

Planet Hollywood Miami (☎ *305-445-7277, 3390 Mary St)*, fronted by a gaggle of action figure promoters like Sylvester Stallone, Arnold Schwarzenegger, Bruce Willis and Whoopi Goldberg, spends boatloads of cash on publicity. But the food prices – main courses from $9 to $15 – are a lot more reasonable than one would think. Entrees include penne pasta with fresh broccoli, cauliflower, zucchini, squash and peppers; carrots and onions over pasta in a pesto cream sauce; Thai shrimp; and generous portions of chicken or beef fajitas. It also offers Crunch Chicken (chicken breaded with Cap'n Crunch® cereal then deep fried – which might explain Arnold's puffy look). Reservations are recommended on weekends.

Le Bouchon du Grove (☎ *305-448-6060, 3430 Main Hwy)*, a bistro that *South Florida Magazine* called 'as French as de Gaulle,' is absolutely marvelous. It has a very friendly (if heavily accented) French staff and relaxed atmosphere. The restaurant has even reduced its prices to make it a reasonably inexpensive treat in the Grove. Expect a three-course dinner for two with wine to run $30 to $38. They do a very nice beef filet in peppercorn sauce ($20) and also serve the fish dorada ($19). Other specials include frog legs with garlic butter and some sort of 'whaht feesh' wrapped in a cabbage leaf, both at $17. Check out the Saturday and Sunday brunch from 8 am to 5:30 pm.

Rickenbacker Causeway & Key Biscayne

Peckish at the Seaquarium? There's a couple of options in the town of Key Biscayne, but most aren't what dreams are made of. Your best bet is to make a picnic lunch by packing a brown bag at the *Hyde Park Market* (☎ *305-361-5888, 724 Crandon Blvd)*, just south of W Wood Dr.

For quick, no-frills Cuban-style snacks, stop by *La Carreta* (12 Crandon Blvd)*, the Rickenbacker branch of the one on Calle Ocho (see Little Havana earlier), which offers uninspired but dependably filling and cheap food. Their big breakfast is $5, and Cuban sandwiches are $4.

Moving slightly upscale, the *Bayside Hut* (☎ *305-361-0808, 3501 Rickenbacker Causeway)* cooks up very fresh seafood for under $10. It has a tiki bar and is a nice place to sit and watch the ultralight seaplanes grapple with the Bernoulli principle.

Southwest Miami

The following two places are *way* west but absolutely worth the trip, especially if you're visiting Monkey Jungle or the Fruit & Spice Park.

Burr's Berry Farm (☎ *305-235-0513, 12741 SW 216th St)* in Goulds has simply the best strawberries in the USA. Not just strawberries, but huge, fist-sized, sumptuously sweet, breathtakingly fresh, unbelievably *sexually* satisfying strawberries. People come from miles around – a *lot* of miles (there's an air strip out back for well-known private pilot customers who fly here for these berries!) – and stand in the ever-present line to buy quarts ($7) or pints ($3.50). This place also makes the best strawberry shake we've ever tasted (about $2.50) and sells hot dogs ($1), jam ($4.50) and chili sauce and pickles ($3.75). It's open from December to May only, 9 am to 5:30 pm daily. The berry farm is 1 mile west of US Hwy 1 on Monkey Jungle Rd.

Farther out, **Knauss Berry Farm** (☎ 305-247-0668, 15980 SW 248th St), a couple of miles west of the Fruit & Spice Park, has similarly heavenly cinnamon rolls that create similarly long stagnant lines on Saturdays as people wait to grab them. It also has the same sort of strawberries, jams and jelly offerings as Burr's but with the addition of bread, cakes and brownies. Cinnamon rolls are 40¢, $2.25 for a half-dozen or $4.30 a dozen. It's open from mid-November to the last Saturday in April.

Northeast Miami

Step back into the past at **S&S Restaurant** (☎ 305-373-4291, 1757 NE 2nd Ave), a classic '40s-style diner with downright sassy service ('Keep yer shirt on, hon!'), great food (except for the crab cakes, which were execrable) and entrees all under $7, such as humongous burgers, baked macaroni and cheese, and more adventurous entries like shrimp Creole with two veggies and bread. It's a small horseshoe-shaped lunch counter that's always very crowded, and there's usually a wait of a few minutes for a seat. Lots of cops hang out here.

Another Miami tradition is the **Rascal House** (☎ 305-947-4581, 17190 Collins Ave at 172nd St) in north Miami Beach. While service here is just as snappy, and the atmosphere equally diner-ish (though it's much, much bigger than S&S), the Jewish food is uniformly great. Our favorite is the Lake Erie whitefish salad ($12), but we've been here several times and never had a bad or even not-great meal. Expect to wait in line; the line for the counter is usually shorter than that for proper tables. Sandwiches, like corned beef, tongue (yech!) or roast beef are generally $6 to $8, but some, such as liver-

wurst and salami, are around $5. Don't miss the grilled salmon for $4.

There's nothing much of note in Aventura except a shopping mall, an unreliable storage facility and three excellent places to eat, should you happen to be in the neighborhood. **JD's Pizza & Subs** (☎ 305-652-4455, 305-652-3387, 1620 NE 205 Terrace), just beneath the west side of the overpass of the Ives Dairy Rd entrance to I-95, doesn't look like much, but its pizza is absolutely divine – we stop here just for a slice ($2) whenever we can. Medium/large pizza pies are $10.28/12.19, and lasagna is around $6. There's no toilet, and service is from gruff, large Italian men. You sit at video-game tables. JD's has two other branches, both in the middle of nowhere: Miami Lakes off Palmetto (6828 NW 169th St), and Miami Springs (5683 NW 36th St).

In the Promenade Shops Mall sits one of the best diners, **Turn Bagel** (☎ 305-933-3354, 20475 Biscayne Blvd), a family-run place with uncommonly and frighteningly friendly service from uniformed waitresses who call people 'hon,' 'sweetie' and 'sugar.' Breakfast is the best time to come (they throw some free mini-Danish pastries on the table when you arrive) for eggs, potatoes and a bagel for $3. It also has lunch specials, such as a quarter-chicken with French fries for $4.99, from 11:30 am to 3 pm. Bagels to go are 45¢ each or $5 for a dozen.

The **Unicorn Village Market Waterfront Restaurant** (☎ 305-933-8829, 305-933-1543, 3565 NE 207th St) is in the waterways development northeast of the Aventura Mall. The restaurant serves healthy and delicious food, but it's not strictly vegetarian. At lunch, sandwiches run from $5.95 to $6.95, salads $4.75 to $7.95, and specials like Chinese chicken stir-fry or steamed veggie platter are $7.50. At dinner, veggie entrees range from $12 to $15, including spinach lasagna and angel-hair pasta in tomato sauce. The supermarket is a Babylon of fresh and organically grown vegetables and fruits, meats, cheeses, wines and natural products like vitamins and skin-care creams. Everything is good, prices aren't bad and service is excellent, though the place is less appealing since the opening of the excellent Wild Oats in South Beach (see Vegetarian under Miami Beach).

In the Design District, try *Piccadilly Garden Lounge* (☎ 305-573-8221, 35 NE 40th St) for coffee and light meals in a lush little courtyard. It does a very nice Caesar salad (for two) for $7, and beef dishes from $13.95 to $26.

We've had a couple of recommendations for the *Charcuterie Restaurant* (☎ 305-576-7877, 3612 NE 2nd Ave) as a lunch spot. It's open Monday to Friday 11:30 am to 3 pm.

ENTERTAINMENT

To call Miami Beach a trendy nightspot would be like calling New York a fairly large city. This is one of the most fashionable places in the country right now for clubs and nightspots. But nightlife around here is far more than clubs: the New World Symphony is an unexpected treat, and legitimate theater is very active in the area. There's an art scene here that has evolved from a couple of grungy studio-galleries into a driving force in the American art world.

Bars

There are perhaps more bars than street corners in Miami Beach, so we only list ones that we or our friends recommend. Remember to bring photo identification such as a driver's license, passport or national identity card, because if you look under 30, you will be asked for ID. The strictly enforced drinking age in Florida is 21.

Note that all the restaurants along Ocean Drive have outdoor seating, and unless it's very crowded – like on a weekend or holiday – you can usually sit in one of these places with a drink or two without ordering food. A few of our favorite places on the Drive are the *Clevelander's* oddly shaped bar in front of its pool at No 1020; the *Booking Table* at No 728 for its cheap appetizers and relatively friendly service; and the *Speakeasy Bar & Lounge*, a '20s-theme lounge at the Hotel Ocean at No 1230.

Watering Holes The oldest bar in Miami Beach is *Mac's Club Deuce Bar* (☎ 305-673-9537, 222 14th St), established in 1926. It's

definitely a prime local hangout, and it's easy to see why: there's no trendiness here, just a dark but friendly and welcoming room with a pool table and a jukebox, and no-nonsense service. It's open daily 8 am to 5 am. Bottled beers are around $3, well drinks $2.50 – what more could you want?

The *Marlin Bar* (☎ 305-673-8373, 1200 Collins Ave) rocks the martini world with the most incredible Bombay Saffire martinis – yeah, they're 12 bucks but they're worth every penny. It has a great atmosphere and good service, and there's live music occasionally.

Comfy *Irish House Bar & Grill* (☎ 305-534-5667, 1430 Alton Rd) is another local spot with a happy hour of varying specials Monday to Friday from 5 to 6:30 pm, two pool tables, some video games and a jukebox. Pitchers (depending on the brew) are $8 to $12.

Brandt's Break (☎ 305-532-4255, 619 Washington Ave) has come from a redneck pool hall to an all-around entertainment spot, with live bands, a mellow crowd, 12 beers on tap and 35 in bottles, plus dart boards and other games (including the seven pool tables). It's a fun place.

West End (☎ 305-538-9378, 942 Lincoln Rd) is a primarily gay but all-welcome place with a great happy hour from 8 am to 3 pm daily, and occasional specials like *three*-for-one drinks (!). It has three pool tables and is open daily 8 am to 5 am – check in *New Times* for its semi-regular drag shows with singers, drag magicians and dancers.

The aptly named *Lost Weekend* (☎ 305-672-1707, 218 Española Way) is a good neighborhood place with pool tables and ladies' night on Wednesday.

Theme Bars The Haitian restaurant and bar *Tap Tap* (☎ 305-672-2898, 819 5th St) also hosts art shows, is home to community meetings and is generally a cool and colorful place to hang out drinking Haitian Barbancourt rum ($5) or African Ngoma beer ($4). It's open Sunday to Thursday 11:30 am to 11 pm, Friday and Saturday to midnight. (Also see Places to Eat.)

Dab Haus (☎ 305-534-9557, 832 Alton Rd) has the best selection of German beers, wines and schnapps in the area. It has Dortmunder pils and Alt Tucher hefeweizen, dark hefeweizen and Kristall weizen, Königs pils and Hacker-Pschorr, all from $3.50 to $5, and wines by the glass from $4 to $7. It's also a darn serviceable German restaurant – see Places to Eat earlier.

Penrod's Beach Club (☎ 305-538-1111, 1 Ocean Drive) is kind of a beach-blanket-bimbo-theme place, with a pool and a semi-private stretch of beach with volleyball, dancing and nightly drink specials (like Wednesday margarita night, when 32oz drinks are $2 and buff dudes bray at bubble-breasted bleach-blonde bimbos). Penrod's has another stand at 14th St at Ocean Drive.

Microbreweries After the closure of the South Pointe Brewery, brewmaster Jeff Nelson moved on to **Miami Brewing Company** (☎ 305-888-6506, 9292 NW 101st St), from where the Hurricane Reef brand is made and distributed. They make a lager, pale ale, amber ale, honey nut brown ale and raspberry wheat beer.

Abbey Brewery (☎ 305-538-8110, 1115 16th St at Alton Rd) makes a really good selection of beers ($4.25 a pint).

Tobacco Road Liquor Bar (☎ 305-374-1198, 626 S Miami Ave) has entered the microbrew game and serves up several varieties of its own. (Also see Places to Eat.)

All the regional **Bennigan's**, a national chain serving blah food, microbrew their own beer, but that's grasping at straws, isn't it?

Live Music Listed earlier, **Brandt's Break** has live local bands and a Wednesday open-microphone night for local talent.

There's a cool variety of Latin music at **Studio 23** (☎ 305-538-1196, 247 23rd St), with both DJs and live music Thursday to Saturday.

Rose's Bar (☎ 305-532-0228, 754 Washington Ave) is one of the only places around where you can hear live local bands like Day by the River and Darwin's Waiting Room. It throws Monday night football parties during the season.

Over in Little Haiti, **Churchill's Hideaway** (☎ 305-757-1807, 5501 NE 2nd Ave) has

been around for 50 years. It's an English pub with satellite TV broadcasts of English football and rugby, eight draft beers, about 50 bottled beers and live rock music most nights. It's open Monday to Saturday 11 am to 3 am, Sunday noon to 3 am.

Clubs

Miami Beach nightclubs come in and out of vogue at a rate that can only be compared to that of pre-Beatles rock bands – it's like on *The Jetsons* when the daughter tells her father 'No, Daddy, that band was groovy *last* week!' Indeed, in the course of just three months, four very popular and very fashionable nightspots here went bust and disappeared. Celebrities move in and out of the scene – like that what's-his-name guy who changed his name to an unpronounceable symbol, Madonna, Madonna's brother, Madonna's hair stylists, Madonna's...well *you* know. Hell, even Mickey Rourke had a club that he ran when he wasn't outside punching people. Clubs here rise meteorically and fall like the Moscow stock market. The information in this section is the most volatile in the book.

Nightclubs in South Beach are generally a healthy mix of gay, lesbian and straight, though several are more exclusively gay. In this chapter, we list the ones that are mixed with the ones that are straight, as the lines are very blurry. If a place is predominantly gay, it will probably put up a polite sign: 'Welcome to the Warsaw Ballroom. This is a gay nightclub.'

Taking, buying or selling illegal drugs in Miami Beach nightclubs is a really bad idea: the Miami Beach police send undercover agents around the clubs and periodically carry out raids.

Straight & Mixed One of the best spots in Little Havana is **Cafe Nostalgia** (☎ 305-541-2631, 2212 Calle Ocho), with real Cuban music and a small dance floor in a totally great atmosphere of authentic Cuban memorabilia. They also play vintage Cuban music videos and film clips. The house band is complemented with musicians who stop in just to jam.

MIAMI

Don't You *Know* Who I Am?!?

For reasons best left to psychology, the more offensively, awfully and breathtakingly rude a doorman and the more ruthlessly exclusive a club, the larger the clamoring hordes of short-skirted women and big-tipping men trying to gain entry.

'If you're not dressed to the nines and walking with an attitude that says you totally fuckin' belong here, forget it, baby,' counsels Melanie Morningstar, longtime Beach Fabuloso and former nightlife columnist. Morningstar helpfully added that she's seen people successfully get in by offering bribes of up to $100 and even sexual favors to doormen at nightclubs.

Why anyone would pay $100 (the average cover charge on the Beach is about $10 – except when it's free, as is often the case) or risk death by blowing some lanky little thug to get into a place where drinks cost $8 a pop is beyond us, but there it is. Clearly, to get into some of the more popular clubs, you'll have more luck if:

You're Polite – Don't be meek, but don't act as if you're Sean Penn (unless you happen to be Mr Penn, in which case…Hey look! A photographer!).

You've Got Attitude – You're a lean, mean, partying machine, and don't let no one mess with you. Oh yeah, you're gorgeous, too.

You're Cool – When the competition is as fierce as it is here (it's about equivalent to the atmosphere in a department store three days before Christmas), a second's hesitation is enough to keep you milling about on a crowded sidewalk filled with wanna-bes.

You're Dressed Properly – Standard nightclub garb here is as it is in New York, Paris or anywhere else: look expensive. Or at least interesting – drag queens, *Star Trek* characters and other Fabulously, outlandishly or outrageously dressed people get in as well.

You Know Someone – and/or

You Are Famous

None of the above? This is only a hint, but 'Hi, this is [*your name here*] with South Africa *Vogue*; I'm in town doing a piece on…'

The club ***Amnesia*** (☎ *305-531-5535, 136 Collins Ave*) was the home of South Beach's most famous Sunday tea dance (post-beach, pre-club), but Amnesia's not exclusively gay, and these days this place is just a fun free-for-all. There's also a dance floor out in the courtyard – dance all night under the stars.

Bash (☎ *305-538-2274, 655 Washington Ave*) is still among the hotter predominantly straight nightclubs on the Beach, with a good dance floor inside and another one in the courtyard outside.

Club Deep (☎ *305-532-1509, 621 Washington Ave*) is enjoying a wave of favorable publicity and good times these days. The club offers different theme nights, such as ladies' night on Wednesday and Latin night on Sunday.

Groove Jet (☎ 305-532-2002, 323 23rd St) is *the* after-hours spot in town on Thursday, Friday and Saturday. Celebrity DJ Mark Leventhal, live music on some nights and a host of special events throughout the week make this place one of Miami Beach's mainstays.

Liquid (☎ 305-532-9154, 1439 Washington Ave) is an impossibly exclusive place that people are clamoring to get into – and unless you're dressed pretty Fabulously, forget it.

Twist (☎ 305-538-9478, 1057 Washington Ave) is still going strong – there's a darkish mood (a few small lamps spread a dim light) with music videos and a very nice wooden bar. There's never a cover and always a groove, and it's a predominantly gay crowd.

What is the story with the Russian names of bars in this town – don't people know how horrible the nightlife is in Moscow? *Red Square* (☎ 305-672-0200, 411 Washington Ave) does From Russia With Love nights Friday and Saturday, and martini and caviar night Tuesday (now yer talkin'). Just up the street, *КГБ* (☎ 305-534-2420, 637 Washington Ave) is another. The Kremlin, though, has gone the way of the five-year plan.

Once a very intimate restaurant, *Starfish* (☎ 305-673-1717, 1427 West Ave) is now an intimate nightclub, with strictly salsa on Friday night.

Gay & Lesbian The gay night scene in South Beach, according to a famous local quip, can be summed up as men that 'look like Tarzan, walk like Jane and talk like Cheetah.'

The *Warsaw Ballroom* (☎ 305-531-4499, 1450 Collins Ave) is the longest-lasting (it's been around for at least eight years) and one of the hottest gay nightclubs on the Beach; it's one floor plus a balcony. It has always been innovative with foam parties and dick dancers. Downstairs is the *Warsaw Bar*, with an amazing carved wooden bar. Amateur strip night is Wednesday, and After Tea (party and disco) is on Sunday.

Loading Zone (☎ 305-531-5623), in the alley between West Ave and Alton Rd at 14th St, may be the answer to trendy South Beach-brand gay bars (where leather tends

to mean shoes), with dark corners and less attitude – trendy attitude that is.

Strip Joints Sex is a large part of Miami's allure: the city is packed with young, beautiful and half-naked people partying and posing through the sultry nights. Spoken or unspoken, Miami promises sex with a fine degree of sleaze as much as it promises beaches. Whether you're straight, gay or bi, there's a pervasive atmosphere of dangerous sensuality and untold passion. Most of this is interaction in clubs, bars and on the beach, but there are a couple of venues where sex – or just nakedness and suggestive dancing – is the featured attraction, and these clubs are wildly popular.

None of the clubs listed here offers actual sex acts, but they do all offer a particularly masochistic form of entertainment: a totally nude woman – or, in one case, a man, for the ladies ('finally, a strip joint we can both go to and enjoy, dear') – rubs her genitalia along a man's legs and presses her breasts in his face while neckless goons stand by waiting to see if you make a move to reciprocate, at which point you're thrown out. Whee! Friction dancing, we love it!

On the Beach, the absolutely classic strip joint is *Déjà Vu* (☎ 305-538-5526, 2004 Collins Ave), boasting '100 pretty girls and three ugly ones' and all-you-can-drink booze for $20. Couples enter free on Saturday, when the club also offers those male dancers. Wanna give it a shot yourself? Monday's amateur night, with a $300 prize.

Club Madonna (☎ 305-534-2000, 1527 Washington Ave) is the place the pop-star Madonna sued, not the one she goes to. It's open nightly 6 pm to 6 am; there's a $20 entry charge. On Monday and Tuesday, it hosts striptease contests.

The Doll House (☎ 305-948-3087, 16300 Collins Ave) offers 'private' friction dances.

Gallery Walks
There are gallery walks on the second Saturday of the month (except in August) along Lincoln Road Mall. These were all the rage with locals a few years ago, but since then the art scene in Miami has become more

and more exclusive and expensive and less guerrilla-style.

If you do go, make an evening of it, with dinner before and some clubbing afterward. There's no set way to go about it; you just show up and pop into whatever galleries are open.

Also of interest, though not such a event, is Opening Night in the Design District (listed earlier in the chapter), a gallery walk held the second Friday of each month.

Cinema

There's a standard, googolplex-type cinema at every major shopping mall. The AMC Aventura Mall 24 (☎ 305-466-0450, 19501 Biscayne Blvd, No 3001) shows first-run films daily: before 4 pm, matinees cost $5.25. 'Twilight shows' between 4 and 6 pm are just $4.25. After 6 pm, the cost is $7.50 for adults, $5.25 for seniors, $4.25 for kids two to 12.

The film series at the Wolfsonian Foundation (listed earlier) is often co-sponsored by the **Miami Beach Film Society** (MBFS; ☎ 305-673-4567), a fascinating organization that also runs series independent of the Wolfsonian. The idea is to use Miami Beach's venues to make viewing a film more fun, so events run the gamut from Inflatable Rubber Raft Drive-In at the Raleigh Pool for a screening of Skirts Ahoy to the annual Food in Film: Movies to Dine For series, which began in early 1996. That series was shown at a number of Miami Beach restaurants and co-sponsored by Gourmet magazine – which was so excited about the series' success that it announced it would expand the idea to run nationally. Tickets are $75 per person, including dinner and cocktail hour. Contact the MBFS to find out what's on during your visit.

The **Alliance Cinema** (☎ 305-531-8504, 305-534-7171, 927 Lincoln Rd), tucked into the recess just east of Books & Books, does independent films by lower-budget filmmakers who ordinarily wouldn't make it to Miami. It began as a projection screen in the window of Books & Books and finally has grown into its own permanent space here. Movies change generally on Friday, except when a title is held over due to

popular demand. Every six months or so, it holds an 'Anti-Film Festival,' featuring films (about half of them locally made) with a 'quirky, edgy' bent. The Alliance also shows films on Sunday at Bar-Cinema Vortex at 1663 Lenox Ave, in the tiny doorway opposite the SunBank ATM, and next to Common Space Exhibition, a small art gallery.

The Road's second Deco theater (after the Lincoln Theatre, see Classical Music below), the 1934 **Colony Theatre** (☎ 305-674-1026, 1040 Lincoln Rd) is a 465-seat venue with great acoustics, hosting some concerts (Melba Moore was here when we visited) and theater, and also showing independent and gay- and lesbian-oriented films.

Theater

The **Area Stage** (☎ 305-673-8002, 645 Lincoln Rd), between Meridian and Pennsylvania Aves, presents cutting-edge original works with a strong emphasis on local talent. Ticket prices are $17 for adults, $8 for students under 25 with ISIC, based on availability.

Another cutting-edge house, the **Edge Theater** (☎ 305-531-6083, 405 Española Way, on the 3rd floor) was staging Clothing Optional and Tiny Alice and Zoo Story by Edward Albee at press time. Tickets generally cost $15, or $12 for seniors and students.

Formerly known as the Florida Shakespeare Theatre, the **Gables Stage** at the Biltmore (☎ 305-445-1119, 1200 Anastasia Ave), at the Biltmore Hotel, now does contemporary performances in addition to the occasional Shakespearean production. As we went to press, the schedule of upcoming events included the South Florida premiere of David Harris' Skylight, Beautiful Dreamer with Sharon Gless and John Steinbeck's Of Mice and Men.

Located on the University of Miami's Coral Gables campus, the **Jerry Herman Ring Theatre** (☎ 305-284-3355, 1321 Miller Drive, www.miami.edu/tha) has planned a number of experimental and studio productions; details will be announced. Actors Sylvester Stallone, Steven Bauer, Saundra Santiago and Ray Liotta are alumni.

Originally built in 1951, the *Jackie Gleason Theater for the Performing Arts* (☎ 305-673-7300, *1700 Washington Ave)* was actually the home of *The Jackie Gleason Show.* This theater is the Beach's premiere showcase for Broadway shows, the Florida Philharmonic, the Miami City Ballet, the Concert Association of Florida and other big productions.

The Miami Broadway Series runs the gamut from David 'Presto – CUT!' Copperfield to The Who's *Tommy*; there's a children's Story Theater series with productions of kids' favorites; and there are musical concerts by the likes of Liza, Donna and Ray Conniff. Ticket prices change by performance but hover in the $30 to $50 range for Broadway shows and concerts.

The *Gusman Center for the Performing Arts* (☎ 305-374-2444, *174 E Flagler St)* is a renovated 1920s movie palace now home to a huge variety of performing arts, including the New World Symphony and the Florida Philharmonic. They hold traveling shows, so it's not easy to nail them down, but as we went to press, the offerings on tap were Broadway show revivals, a local theatrical and performance group, concerts, variety shows and the annual Miami Film Festival, an international festival held in February. Ticket prices change for each performance.

The *Coconut Grove Playhouse* (☎ 305-442-4000, *3500 Main Hwy)*, at the corner of Charles Ave, two blocks south of the CocoWalk Shopping Center, celebrated its 40th anniversary in 1996, but the facility has been here for 72 years. The Playhouse gained fame and attention when José Ferrer was appointed artistic director in 1982. It constantly swaps shows with Broadway in New York – the Playhouse sends some, and some of the more popular Broadway road shows stop here. There are two stages, the main Playhouse stage and the smaller Encore Room.

Tickets to the Playhouse cost $35 from Sunday to Thursday, $40 on Friday and Saturday. Students under 24 with ID can apply for tickets on the day of the performance; if any tickets are left, they're yours for $10. In the Encore Room, tickets are $22 Sunday to Thursday and matinees, and $27 on Friday and Saturday evenings.

For Spanish-language theater, check in the Spanish press, or contact *Teatro Las Mascaras* (☎ 305-642-0358), *Teatro de Bellas Artes* (☎ 305-325-0515) or *Teatro Martí* (☎ 305-545-7866).

Classical Music

Catch classical concerts by the Florida Philharmonic and visiting orchestras throughout the year at the Jackie Gleason Theater for the Performing Arts, the Gusman Center for the Performing Arts and Dade County Auditorium. For information about concerts throughout the city and state, contact the excellent *Florida Concert Association* (☎ 305-532-3491, *555 17th St)*.

The *New World Symphony* (☎ 305-673-3331, 800-597-3331, *info@nws.org)* performs from late September to early May in the Lincoln Theatre (see below).

Michael Tilson Thomas, the NWS's artistic director, still conducts 12 weeks of the year despite all his national fame and fortune. A host of guest conductors and artists also appear. Each season offers a Thursday night Gourmet series, two Saturday night series (Crescendo and Intermezzo) and three series on Sunday evenings (Masterpiece, Interludes and the Twilight Chamber Series). In addition, there is an open-rehearsal series on select Saturday mornings, a family series and free concert series including Musical Xchanges, Musicians' Forums, New Music and Ensemble.

About 30% of the performances are free, and in September there are pre-season free concerts as well. The NWS has recently received grant money to allow its musicians to hold a series of free concerts featuring music of their choice.

Ticket prices for the remainder of the concerts cost from $10 to $54, depending on performance and seating. Tickets can be bought at the Lincoln Theatre box office.

The Beach's theatrical jewel, the beautiful *Lincoln Theatre* (☎ 305-531-3442, *555 Lincoln Rd)* is more than just host to the New World Symphony: it offers a wide variety of performances including South

Beat Concerts, 'An Evening with Four Poets Laureate,' free Musicians' Forum concerts and performances by visiting artists.

Besides being the home of the Florida Grand Opera, **Dade County Auditorium** (☎ 305-547-5414, 2901 W Flagler St) also sees classical music concerts held by the Concert Association of Florida, the Miami Symphony Orchestra and the San Francisco Symphony. To get to the auditorium, go west on Hwy 836 to the 27th Ave exit, south on 27th Ave to Flagler St (the third light) and turn right. The auditorium is on the right.

Opera

The **Florida Grand Opera** and the **Greater Miami Opera Association** (☎ 305-854-1643), which runs a program of visiting artists, perform at the Dade County Auditorium (see above).

Jazz

There's live jazz at several spots on the Beach and in Coconut Grove; cover charges range from free to $10. **Caroline's** (☎ 305-604-0008, 214 Española Way) has jazz Thursday through Sunday. There's Dixieland and jazz regularly at **La Deux Fontaines** (see Places to Eat) and at **A Fish Called Avalon** (☎ 305-532-1727, 700 Ocean Drive) in the Avalon Hotel. There's jazz every night in the 2nd-floor lounge at the **Van Dyke Hotel** (☎ 305-534-3600, 846 Lincoln Rd).

Dance

There are performances by dozens of non-profit dance organizations all over the area and the state of Florida; the best resource for information on what's happening when you're in town is the **Florida Dance Association** (☎ 305-237-3413, 300 NE 2nd Ave), at the Miami-Dade Community College Wolfson Campus, Miami, FL 33132. If you let them know where you'll be and when, they'll send off a schedule of performances and events.

The **Miami City Ballet** (☎ 305-532-7713, 905 Lincoln Rd) regularly performs at the Jackie Gleason Theater, the Bailey Concert Hall in Davie, the Broward Center for the Performing Arts in Fort Lauderdale and the Raymond Kravis Center for the Performing Arts in West Palm Beach. They also give holiday performances of The Nutcracker at several venues. The company often goes on the road around the US and internationally.

Family Day at the Ballet is an introduction to the ballet for children by the company's dancers and artistic director Edward Villella. Before performances, the director gives a talk and children have the opportunity to meet ballerinas. Tickets for kids are $6 to $16. The Miami City Ballet also runs DanceTalks, a series of talks hosted by Villella before each new repertory program, touching on 20th-century dance and choreography.

Part of the Performing Arts Network (or PAN), the **Ballet Flamenco La Rosa** (☎ 305-672-0552, 555 17th St), behind the Jackie Gleason Theater, is a professional flamenco dance company that performs flamenco with live music. They run on a very loose schedule, so call for individual performance dates and prices. In general, when they perform at the Colony Theatre (about three times a year), tickets are $20 for adults at the door, $18 in advance and $15 for students and seniors. They also perform at local festivals and special events. They hold classes every day for children and adults ($10) in all forms of dance, including jazz, modern, creative movement, Latin, flamenco, ballet and yoga.

PAN provides rehearsal space in addition to holding performance series, lectures, demonstrations and workshops.

Gambling

For casino-style action, **Sea Kruz** (☎ 305-538-4002, 305-688-7529) runs lunch and dinner gambling cruises. It sails 3 miles into international waters, where its full casinos are legal, and then cruises up and down the coast. It's a buffet-style affair, and while there's live music, the real action is the casino, which has nine blackjack tables, craps, roulette, slot machines – and hey, don't worry if you blow all your cash – they thoughtfully provide you with ATMs on board the ship (you can also do Visa cash advances).

The cost of the cruises varies, and there are frequent specials (two-for-one admission, for example), but at the time of writing lunch was about $12, dinner $15. Cruises leave from the 5th St Marina just south of the MacArthur Causeway (on the southwest tip of Miami Beach) at 12:30 and 7:30 pm Sunday to Thursday, 1:30 and 7:30 pm Friday and Saturday. Lunch cruises last from four to five hours. Leave your nest egg in the RV.

SPECTATOR SPORTS
Pro Football
Attending an American football game may be one of the most intense experiences in spectator sports. Miamians get more than a little crazy when it comes to their Miami Dolphins (☎ 305-620-2578), a successful NFL team that was coached for what seems like a thousand years by Don Shula, who retired in 1995.

Pre-season games begin in August, and during the season (September to January), there are usually at least two home games a month at *Pro Player Stadium* (☎ 305-620-2578, 800-255-3094), a mile south of the Dade-Broward county line at 2269 NW 199th St. On game days, there's bus service between downtown Miami and the stadium. If you're a real football nut, you can watch the team practice at their training facility near Fort Lauderdale. Take I-95 or Florida's Turnpike to I-595 west, to the University Drive exit, turn left, to SW 30th St and make another left. The facility is half a mile down on the right-hand side of the road.

Pro Baseball
The Florida Marlins (☎ 305-626-7400) is a relatively new National League baseball team that loses quite often over at Pro Player Stadium during the season from May to September.

Pro Basketball
The Miami Heat play National Basketball Association (NBA) games at the *Miami Arena* (☎ 305-530-4444), one block east of the Overtown Metromover station, between November and April. Tickets cost $14 to $40 in the upper decks, $55 to $70 in the lower decks. Note that they plan to move across the street to new digs near Bayfront Park soon, so check when you're in town for details.

Pro Hockey
From October to April, the Florida Panthers play National Hockey League games at the *National Car Rental Center* (☎ 954-835-7000, 2555 Panther Pkwy) in Sunrise, west of Fort Lauderdale. Tickets to games range from $14 all the way up to $67, but you can get pretty good seats for $30. From Miami, take the Palmetto Expressway (SR 826) or Florida's Turnpike to I-75 north, to the Sawgrass Expressway (Toll Road 869). After the toll plaza, stay in the far-right lane and take exit 1B.

College Sports
The University of Miami dominates college sports in the area, and the Hurricanes, or Canes, football team dominates UM sports. You can see the Canes play football at the *Orange Bowl Stadium* (☎ 800-462-2637). Ticket prices are $16 for general admission, $23 for reserved seats. From downtown, take I-95 to Hwy 836 west. Take the first exit, NW 12th Ave, turn left and go across the bridge. Turn right on NW 7th, 6th, 5th or 4th Sts toward the stadium.

The Hurricanes play college baseball at Mark Light Stadium. Tickets cost $5 for adults, $3 for seniors and children under 17; the Florida and Florida State series cost $6/4.

Hurricane basketball takes place at the Miami Arena. Tickets cost $13 for sidecourt seats; in the endcourt, they're $9 for adults and $2 for children under 17.

Auto Racing
The *Metro-Dade Homestead Motorsports Complex* (☎ 305-230-7223, 1 Speedway Blvd), on the east side of Homestead, is a new $50 million racing center. The *New York Times* quipped that it's hard to imagine anyone in

Homestead wanting to see something coming at them at 200 mph after Hurricane Andrew, but the complex holds five major race weekends a year, and if Formula One racing comes here as well, there could be many more. It's run by Miami Motorsports, which ran the Miami Grand Prix – now held here at the complex.

Horse Racing

For horse racing, there's *Hialeah Race-track* (☎ 305-885-8000, 2200 E 4th Ave), in Hialeah, with a French-Mediterranean-style clubhouse that was built in 1925. Races are from March to May, though you can always come in to get a look at the park's grounds and flamingoes (they raise them). Admission is still $1 to the grandstand and $2 to the clubhouse. Metrorail stops right there.

Calder Race Course (☎ 305-625-1311, 21001 NW 27th Ave) is an indoor course with horse racing from late May to mid-January, and the Festival of the Sun Tropical Park Derby from November to January.

Tennis

The annual Lipton Championship (☎ 305-442-3367) is a 10-day tournament played at the *Tennis Center at Crandon Park*, on Key Biscayne. There are two tennis tournaments associated with the FedEx Orange Bowl football classic: the Rolex-Orange Bowl Tennis Tournament (☎ 305-361-6440) and the International Tournament for players under 14.

Jai Alai

This fascinating and dangerous Spanish game in which players hurl a *pelota* – a *very* hard ball – at more than 150 mph can be seen (and bet on) at *Miami Jai Alai* (☎ 305-633-6400, 3500 NW 37th Ave, near MIA). Admission is $1, $2 for reserved seats and $5 for Courtview Club seats. Matinees are on Monday, Friday and Saturday from 1 to 5 pm, evening games from 7 pm to midnight. From Omni International Mall, take bus No 36, which stops right in front of the arena.

SHOPPING

Shopping malls dominate the scene so totally that there's really no local shopping scene anywhere in South Beach. While Lincoln Rd, Washington Ave and Alton Rd are lined with galleries and little knickknack shops, if you want to buy something big, you're probably going to end up in a mall.

Aventura Mall
(☎ 305-935-1110, www.shopaventuramall.com)
19501 Biscayne Blvd in Aventura; includes a Macy's, Lord & Taylor, Burdines and a huge AMC 24 cinema

Bal Harbour Shops
(☎ 305-866-0311, www.balharbourshops.com)
9700 Collins Ave; has really expensive stuff from people like Chanel, Tiffany, Louis Vuitton, Hermés and Zhiguli

CocoWalk Shopping Center
(☎ 305-444-0777, www.cocowalk.com)
3015 Grand Ave in Coconut Grove; in the heart of a formerly charming neighborhood, with cafés, the Gap, Victoria's Secret, a cinema and one redeeming feature, the Cheesecake Factory

Dadeland Mall
(☎ 305-665-6226)
7535 N Kendall Drive in Kendall; contains Florida's largest Burdines department store and more than 150 other shops

Loehmann's Fashion Island
(☎ 305-932-0520)
2855 NE 187th St at Biscayne Blvd in Aventura; has small, mostly chain, shops

Omni International Mall
(☎ 305-374-6664)
1601 Biscayne Blvd in downtown Miami; undergoing renovation and will be open again in 2000

Streets of Mayfair
(☎ 305-448-1700, www.streetsofmayfair.com)
2911 Grand Ave in Coconut Grove; one of the newest entries, with loads of fashionable shops and several restaurants

Fashion

The casting directors of the movie *Beverly Hills Cop* must have drafted the guy who played Serge from the staff at Versace Jean Couture (☎ 305-532-5993), 755 Washington Ave, where discerning fashion plates can purchase Fabulous things such as a $430 bathrobe or, for those with more meager budgets, a pair of blue jeans for $155.

Not to be outdone, Armani has his own A-X Armani Exchange (☎ 305-531-5900), 760 Collins Ave, with similarly priced merchandise.

Betsey Johnson (☎ 305-673-0023), 805 Washington Ave, has a good shop on the Beach, selling hugely popular women's clothing.

The Gap (☎ 305-531-5358), 673 Collins Ave; Banana Republic (☎ 305-674-7079), 800 Collins Ave; Urban Outfitters (☎ 305-535-9726), 653 Collins; Laundry Industry (☎ 305-531-2277); and even Sunglass Hut and Watch Station (☎ 305-672-7788), 673 Collins Ave, have shops in the area as well.

The Beach is a great place to buy cheap used clothing. Try Recycled Blues (☎ 305-538-0656), 1507 Washington Ave, which has used Levi's jeans for $12, shorts for $8 and jackets at $20.

If you're female, Ball (☎ 305-532-4100), 233 12th St, is *the* place to get that ultimate SoBe outfit: glitzy plastic, piggy pink and polyester – it has it all.

Mars (☎ 305-673-8040), 1035 Washington Ave, sells contemporary American clothing. Colorful dresses are $40 to $140; men's shirts are around $60. It also sells sunglasses, backpacks and watches.

Miami Surf Style (☎ 305-532-6928), 421 Lincoln Rd, is great for cheap jeans, hats and T-shirts. Deco Denim (☎ 305-532-6986), 645 Collins Ave, has Levi's from $20, Ray-Bans for about $60.

Flowers & Gifts

Flora Flora (☎ 305-672-5075), 1520 Lenox Ave (behind Blockbuster Video), is an outdoor stand with reasonably priced large plants, flowers and pots. It's open Tuesday to Saturday 10 am to 6 pm.

Designs by Rodney (☎ 305-673-4233, 800-754-9598), 1623 Michigan Ave, has natural flower baskets and even does edible flower arrangements. It's open Monday to Thursday 10 am to 9:30 pm and Friday, Saturday and Sunday to 11 pm.

Flowers & Flowers (☎ 305-534-1633), 925 Lincoln Rd, has hands down the best selec-

tion of exotic flowers and does the best arrangements on the Beach. It's also by far the most expensive. But this is the place to buy flowers that will impress a date, and it's always nice to walk in and look, even if you're not buying.

Fabulous (☎ 305-532-1856), 1251 Washington Ave, has postcards, gifts, wrapping paper, picture frames and balloons; it's a nice place if the service doesn't get snooty.

Flea Markets

There's a small flea market from noon to 6 pm Sundays on Española Way just west of Washington Ave. A larger outdoor flea market is held in winter on the second and last Sunday of the month on Lenox Ave between 16th and 17th Sts. The Opa-Locka/Hialeah Flea Market (☎ 305-688-8080), 12705 NW 42nd Ave, runs daily from 5 am to 7 pm, and has about 1200 vendors.

Music

Y&T Music (☎ 305-534-8704), 1614 Alton Rd, has records, tapes and CDs; used CDs are $7.99.

Used CDs & Records (☎ 305-673-6464), 1622 Alton Rd, has those for $7.99 or less. Boom Records (☎ 305-531-2666), 1205 Washington Ave, has knowledgeable staff and a very good selection of new and used CDs.

Spec's Music (☎ 305-534-3667) has almost 20 record supershops around Miami and the Beach with a good selection of CDs and a smaller one of cassettes. Its superstore at 501 Collins Ave is enormous.

Power Records has two locations: 1419 Calle Ocho (☎ 305-285-2212) in Little Havana, and 1549 Washington Ave (☎ 305-531-1138) in South Beach. Both have great selections of Latin, salsa, rhumba, Cuban and South American music at decent prices. Do Re Mi Music Center (☎ 305-541-3374), 1829 Calle Ocho, has a good selection of Latin cassettes, records, CDs and musical instruments.

Borders Books & Music (☎ 305-935-0027), 19925 Biscayne Blvd in Aventura, has a good selection of pop, rock, jazz and classical music in this book superstore. There's also a café.

Piercing & Tattoos

Everyone and their dog in Miami Beach seems to have a tattoo, and while piercing isn't as popular here as it is in some other large cities, Beach piercers can put a pin through it with the best of them.

Tattoos by Lou (☎ 305-532-7300), 231 14th St, is probably the most famous place on the Beach for tattooing, and it's been here the longest. You have to be at least 18 (bring your ID). Art Attack (☎ 305-531-4556), 1344 Washington Ave, does tattoos and body piercing ($50 minimum). They're very friendly, seem to have experience (one rather dreads the word 'oops' during a clitoral piercing) and definitely have clean equipment.

GETTING THERE & AWAY
Air

Miami is served by two main airports: the Miami International Airport (MIA) and the Fort Lauderdale/Hollywood International Airport (FLL). See Getting Around for information about getting from the airports to downtown and Miami Beach.

Miami International Airport MIA (☎ 305-876-7000, 305-876-7770 for flight information, www.miami-airport.com) is one of the USA's busiest international airports and one of the most poorly laid out and badly signed airports in the country. Parking lots are a good hike from the terminals, which are spread out in an open horseshoe design that makes all areas inconvenient. The main airport terminal building is in Concourse E. Concourses B, C and D are to the north of it, and F, G and H to the south.

Fort Lauderdale/Hollywood International Airport FLL (☎ 305-359-1200) is about 30 miles north of Miami, just off I-95. It's a much smaller and friendlier airport than

MIA, but obviously there are fewer services. International flights arrive at Terminal 3.

Bus

Greyhound (☎ 800-231-2222) has three main terminals in Miami. The sleazy main downtown terminal is Bayside station (☎ 305-379-7403), at 700 Biscayne Blvd. Greyhound's airport station (☎ 305-871-1810) is at 4111 NW 27th St, about a $5 cab or $1.25 bus ride away from the terminals; see the Getting Around section below for specific information. The last is the North Miami station (☎ 305-945-0801) at 16560 NE 6th Ave.

See the Getting Around chapter for Greyhound fares between Miami and other Florida destinations.

Train

The southern terminus of Tri-Rail (☎ 800-874-7245, TDD 800-273-7545), the commuter rail system running between Dade, Broward and Palm Beach counties, is in Miami. See the Getting Around chapter for more information.

Amtrak (☎ 800-872-7245) connects the Miami Terminal (☎ 305-835-1222), 8303 NW 37th Ave, with cities all over the continental USA and Canada. However, it's totally inconvenient and expensive to use Amtrak within Florida.

Car & Motorcycle

Miami is at or near the terminus of several major roads: Florida's Turnpike, I-95, I-75 and the Tamiami Trail (US Hwy 41). Distances from Miami are as follows:

22 miles to Fort Lauderdale
39 miles to Boca Raton
64 miles to the Palm Beaches
141 miles to Fort Myers
155 miles to Key West
228 miles to Orlando
245 miles to Tampa
251 miles to Daytona Beach
302 miles to St Augustine
331 miles to Gainesville
649 miles to Pensacola

GETTING AROUND
To/From MIA

Miami International Airport is about 12 miles west of downtown, sandwiched between the Airport Expressway (Hwy 112) and the Dolphin Expressway (Hwy 836).

Bus Metrobus No 7 to Government Center (where you can catch a connecting bus to your final destination) leaves from the lower level of Concourse E, ostensibly every 40 minutes. The ride takes 35 minutes and costs $1.25 for adults, 60¢ for seniors. They run from 5:26 am to 9:11 pm. The J bus leaves from the same place ostensibly every 30 minutes and takes a circuitous route ending up in Miami Beach about an hour later, with service starting and ending about the same time.

Shuttle It is sometimes cheaper for two people (and always cheaper for three) to take a taxi from MIA to Miami and Miami Beach. Blue SuperShuttle (☎ 305-871-2000) vans prowl the lower level outside the baggage claim area frequently – just wave one down. Costs vary depending on destination, calculated by the zip code of where you're going. But another major factor is whether your destination is a hotel or a private residence: the cost from the airport to the Clay Hotel & International Hostel (or any other hotel) is $11 per person, but to a private residence in the same area (zip code 33139) it's $14 for the first person and $6 for each additional person. So if you're alone and staying with a friend in South Beach, you can save yourself $2 by walking there from the Clay. If you're two people staying at a hotel, it's cheaper to get dropped off at a street address near the hotel.

Car & Motorcycle All the major car-rental companies, as well as some little ones, have offices at MIA – see Rental later in the chapter. Note that there's always a traffic jam in front of the terminals.

The most direct route from MIA to downtown Miami is Hwy 112 to I-95 south (25¢ toll); follow the signs for downtown.

To South Beach, take 37th Ave to Hwy 836 east to I-395, which leads into the MacArthur Causeway.

For northern Miami Beach, take Hwy 112 to I-195, the Julia Tuttle Causeway.

Taxi There is a flat-fee scheme in place between MIA and the five zones into which Miami is divided.

In general, the flat fee to anywhere in Miami Beach between Government Cut and 63rd St (Zone 4, including all of South Beach) from MIA is $24; north of 63rd St to 87th Terrace (Zone 3) is $29; between 87th Terrace and Haulover Beach (Zone 2) is $34; and from Haulover Beach to the Broward County line (Zone 1) is $41. Zone 5 is the village of Key Biscayne, which is $31. There's also a flat rate of $16 between MIA and the Port of Miami. These rates are per carload, not per person and include tolls and a $1 surcharge. Taxis swarm the lower level roadway.

To/From FLL

Many deeply discounted tickets from the USA and Europe plop you down in the shimmering new terminal of Fort Lauderdale/Hollywood International Airport, about 30 miles north of Miami. It's a great airport: there are fewer crowds and a slower pace. Newer, cleaner and easier-to-use terminals speed you through.

Bus & Train Tri-Rail (☎ 800-874-7245) has a shuttle bus from the airport to the Fort Lauderdale Airport Tri-Rail station (you can also take Broward County Transit – BCt – bus Nos 3 or 6).

Trains head down to the Tri-Rail/Metrorail Transfer Station ($3) about once an hour during rush hours, once every two hours in midday, from about 5:50 am to 11:30 pm on weekdays, and with less frequent service on weekends.

From the Transfer Station, take Metrorail to Government Center, where you can transfer to a bus to your destination. The journey to Miami Beach will take about two to 2½ hours and cost about $4.25.

Shuttle Tri-County Transportation Airport Express (☎ 954-561-8886) runs private limos and shuttles. A shared shuttle bus from the airport to South Beach is $12 per person. A private limo (more of a car, really) is $48. Catch the shuttle outside the terminal baggage area.

SuperShuttle can take you to, but not from, Fort Lauderdale. From the Clay Hotel, the cost is $21; from a residence anywhere in the 33139 and 33141 zip codes, it's $28.

Car & Motorcycle There are almost as many car-rental companies here as there are in Miami. Driving is straightforward: I-95 south (there's an airport on-ramp) to I-195 east for northern Miami Beach; to I-395 for South Beach; and straight through to downtown Miami.

Taxi Yellow Cab Company (☎ 954-565-5400, 954-565-8400) is the official airport taxi in Fort Lauderdale; a trip from FLL to South Beach would run about $40 to $50.

The Wave

The Wave (☎ 305-843-9283) is a free electric shuttle bus running the length of Washington Ave and Lincoln Rd in South Beach. There are six vehicles running Monday to Wednesday from 8 am to 2 am, Thursday to Saturday to 4 am, Sunday and holidays from 10 am to 2 am. They're festooned with decorative public art, nonpolluting and handicapped friendly – they even have air conditioning and piped-in music. And it's all free.

The route is from Alton Rd at Lincoln Rd east to Washington, down to 5th St, and west to Alton and back again. Stops are well marked and many are sheltered.

Metrobus

Metro-Dade Transit's buses cover a healthy amount of the city. Call ☎ 305-770-3131 (TDD 305-638-7456) Monday to Friday 6 am to 10 pm, Saturday and Sunday 9 am to 5 pm for specific route information or for travel planning assistance. Bus fare is $1.25, transfers are 25¢.

Disabled travelers should contact Metro-Dade at least two weeks before a trip for Special Transportation Services (STS) information. For lost and found, call ☎ 305-375-3366 Monday to Friday 8:30 am to 4:30 pm.

Transit booths, where you can get maps, scheduling information and tokens, are at Government Center (☎ 305-375-5771), NW 1st St between NW 1st and 2nd Aves; at the corner of E Flagler and E 1st Aves; and at the Omni Metromover Terminal at Biscayne Blvd just south of NE 15th St.

The Omni Metromover and Government Center Terminals are main junction points for buses downtown.

The following are some major routes:

bus	route
C, K	Between Miami Beach and Government Center
S, M	Between Miami Beach and Omni Mall
S	From Omni Mall to South Beach, north on Alton Rd then east on 17th St and north on Collins Ave past the South Beach Library and Bass Museum, and up to the Aventura Mall
8	Between the downtown transit booth and Calle Ocho
6,17, 22	Between Government Center and Vizcaya Museum of Science & Space Transit Planetarium and Coconut Grove
B	Between the downtown transit booth and Seaquarium and Key Biscayne on the Rickenbacker Causeway
24	Between the downtown transit booth and Miracle Mile, Coral Gables

Metromover

Metromover is Miami's neat solution to downtown congestion: it's made up of one-to two-car, rubber-wheeled, computer-controlled vehicles (there's usually no driver on board), running on an elevated track. Also see the boxed text earlier in the chapter.

There are three lines on two 'loops.' The Outer Loop's two lines, the Omni and Brickell Loops, run between the School Board station west of Omni Mall, and the Brickell Financial District station at SE 14th St and Brickell Ave. The Omni Loop starts at School Board station, through the Omni, around downtown and Government Center then back north. The Brickell Loop starts at the Brickell Financial District station, north to Government Center and around downtown, then back south. The Outer Loop runs from about 5 am to 10:30 pm, and shuttle buses run on the Brickell Loop between 10:30 pm and midnight.

The fare is 25¢. You can change between Metrorail and Metromover at Government Center. Metromover information is available at the transit booths or by calling the telephone numbers above for Metrobus information.

Metrorail

This is a 21-mile-long heavy-rail system with one line, running from Hialeah, through downtown Miami and then south to Kendall, connecting with Tri-Rail at the Tri-Rail/Metrorail Transfer Center at 2567 E 11th Ave, Hialeah, and with Metromover and Metrobus at Government Center.

The fare is $1.25, or $1 with a Metromover transfer. Metrorail or Tri-Rail to Metromover transfer is free. The trains run every day from 6 am to midnight.

Water Taxi

The Water Taxi (☎ 954-467-0008, www .watertaxi.com) is a fleet of cute little boats that tootle around the local waterways. They have two major routes, both of which run from 10 am to about 11 pm daily. The first, between Bayside Marketplace and the 5th St Marina at the southwestern end of South Beach or the western end of Lincoln Rd (you need to phone in advance to be picked up) costs $7.50 one way, $14 roundtrip and $16 for an all-day pass.

The second line ($3.75/7/8) is a downtown water shuttle service between Bayside Marketplace and the following locations: Biscayne Marriott, Crown Plaza, Plaza Venetian, Omni, Watson Island (Pan Am Air Bridge), Port of Miami, Hard Rock Cafe, Hotel InterContinental, DuPont Plaza, Sheraton Biscayne, Brickell Key, Hyatt Regency, Holiday Inn downtown, José Martí Park, East Coast Fisheries and Fisher Island (with resident or guest ID). They ask that

you tip the driver. If the driver is nice, $1 for the shuttle or $2 for the Beach/Bayside trip is plenty; if he/she is not, giving nothing is perfectly appropriate. Water Taxi also operates a much more comprehensive network of routes in Fort Lauderdale.

Car & Motorcycle

The sprawl of the Miami area is such that most visitors will end up doing some driving. Miami drivers are generally civil, though see Dangers & Annoyances in the Facts for the Visitor chapter for tips on when they are not.

Major Thouroughfares Miami Beach is connected to the mainland by four causeways built on Biscayne Bay. They are, from south to north the MacArthur (which is also the extension of Hwys 41 and A1A), Venetian (50¢ toll), Julia Tuttle and John F Kennedy Causeways.

The most important highway in the area is I-95, which runs almost straight north-south until it ends at US Hwy 1, south of downtown. US Hwy 1, which runs from Key West all the way north to Maine, hugs the coastline and is called Dixie Hwy south of downtown and Biscayne Blvd from there north to (and somewhat past) the city limits. Hwy A1A is mainly Collins Ave on Miami Beach.

Besides the causeways to Miami Beach, the major east roads are Calle Ocho, Hwy 112 (the Airport Expressway) and Hwy 836, which connects to I-395 (both called the Dolphin Expressway), running from the Homestead Extension through northern downtown and connecting to the MacArthur Causeway.

Parking Except in Coral Gables, South Beach and downtown, parking is fairly straightforward: regulations are well signed and meters usually state the hours they are enforced.

Parking in downtown can be a nightmare, or at least expensive. A good plan is to park in the Cultural Center Garage at 50 NW 2nd Ave, just west of the Metro-Dade Cultural Center. If you visit one of the museums in that complex, or check out a book from the library, you can have your parking ticket validated and parking is $2. Otherwise, you're at the mercy of private lots or undiscounted public ones.

In Miami Beach, there is municipal parking at 13th St and Collins Ave, 12th St between Collins Ave and Ocean Drive, on the corner of Washington Ave below 10th St and just north of Lincoln Road Mall.

Parking fines are generally less than $20, but a tow could cost you up to $75. If you find your car gone, your first call should be to Beach Towing (☎ 305-534-2128). They'll tell you they have it or give you the number of another company that may have taken it, or they'll tell you to call the police.

If Miami Beach is tough on enforcement, Coral Gables is positively Orwellian: metered parking is everywhere that valet parking is not. If you are a second late, the meter-watcher's there and you're hit with varyingly outrageous fines. We got hit with three tickets in two days, once because we were two hours late (and they put the second ticket right on top of the first one!).

Rental All the big car-rental operators can be found in the Miami area, particularly at the airports, along with a host of smaller, local operators. Thrifty Car Rental (☎ 305-604-6040) is at 1119 Collins Ave in Miami Beach. Check in the yellow pages for other agencies.

American Road Collection (☎ 305-871-1040), 3970 NW 25th St, rents out Harley-Davidson motorcycles and has offices in Miami and Fort Lauderdale. Prices run from $109 to $189 a day depending on the model and day of the week.

CruiseAmerica (☎ 800-327-7799) has several area locations and rents Honda and Harley-Davidson motorcycles from $89 to $129 per day including unlimited mileage. It does not rent helmets (and there's a helmet law). Renters must be over 21, have a valid motorcycle license and a major credit card. Loss/damage-waiver and liability insurance are each $12 per day.

Taxi

Meter rates are $1.50 at flagfall, $2 per mile. Taxis here are in generally bad shape, but they'll get you where you're going. If you have a bad experience, make sure you get the driver's chauffeur license number, his name and, if you can, the car's license-plate number, and then contact the Taxi Complaints Line at ☎ 305-375-2460. These folks really do chase down offensive drivers.

There are taxi stands here and there, but the usual way of catching a taxi – outside MIA and the Port of Miami – is to phone for one. Companies include AAA Cab (☎ 305-999-9990), Central Cab (☎ 305-532-5555), Eights Cab (☎ 305-888-8888) and Sunshine Cab Co (☎ 305-445-3333).

Bicycle

Miami is as flat as a pancake and smooth as a baby's butt, so biking around the Beach makes a lot of sense. In fact, it makes so much sense that people who don't have bikes will try to steal yours so they, too, can enjoy it. Bring along a sturdy U-type bike lock, or even better, bring two. Chains and padlocks do not deter people in Miami Beach, where bike theft rates rival those of Amsterdam. Everyone we know in Miami Beach has had a bike stolen, so be careful.

Bicycles are not allowed on buses, Metrorail or Tri-Rail, but you can bike across the causeways.

The Everglades

The second-largest US national park (after Yellowstone) and largest subtropical wilderness in the continental USA, the Everglades is a unique and delicate ecosystem made up of swamps and marshes at the southern tip of the Florida peninsula.

It's also one of the most well known and poorly understood areas of the USA. Visitors to South Florida hear about tours and the Shark Valley Tram Tour, and of the eco-logical threat the area is faced with, but many aren't able to take the time to find out more, or are scared off by tales of renegade alligators and poisonous snakes that lurk in the muck, waiting for innocent tourists to happen by.

While vast tracts of the Everglades are inaccessible to the public, the remainder is one of the most accessible wilderness areas in the state, with developed canoeing and kayaking routes and hiking and biking trails, and a very good information infrastructure.

Whether you just visit for an afternoon at the Main Visitor Center west of Florida City, or take the Shark Valley Tram Tour, or take advantage of the canoeing and free camping possibilities in the 10,000 Islands and along the Wilderness Waterway, we can't urge you enough to come here.

Also in this region is the Big Cypress National Preserve, a protected area at the northern end of the Everglades that is also open to hikers and cars. There you'll find the new Ah-Tah-Thi-Ki Museum of Seminole life.

The Tamiami Trail (US Hwy 41) is the main artery running between Miami and the southwest Florida coast, and is the best place from which to access the parks.

At the western end of the Glades, Everglades City is a good base for trips out to the 10,000 Islands, including the fabulous beaches on Marco Island (the only inhabited island, a wealthy enclave off the state's southwestern coast).

There's camping throughout the region, and hotels in several places. A new hostel has opened in Florida City, and there's a good B&B in Everglades City.

Highlights

- Cross paths with alligators – look, but DON'T FEED!
- Explore the 10,000 Islands by canoe or kayak and camp (free) on secluded island 'chickees' (thatched huts)
- Visit the Ah-Tah-Thi-Ki Museum to learn about Seminole life
- Canoe and hike in Collier-Seminole State Park
- Watch for egrets, herons, spoonbills, ospreys, anhingas, eagles and other birds
- Hike or bike the 17-mile trail to the Shark Valley Observation Tower for a 50-foot-high overview of the prairie, or kick back and take the tram instead
- Send a postcard from the nation's smallest post office in Ochopee

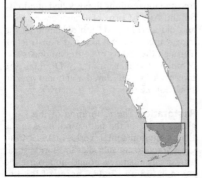

Everglades National Park

Though the threat to the Everglades is very real, it is an absolutely spectacular place to get into the real nature of South Florida. In the park, you'll see an amazing variety of flora and fauna. From the brackish waters of the mangrove and cypress swamps, to the hardwood hammocks, sawgrass flats, Dade County pinelands and marshes, to fascinating creatures such as crocodiles and alligators, bottle-nosed dolphins, manatees, snowy egrets, bald eagles and ospreys, there is simply no place in the entire world like the Everglades.

History & Ecology

The Calusa Indians called the area Pa-hay-okee, or grassy water. The late and much-missed Marjory Stoneman Douglas called it the River of Grass. In her book *The Everglades: River of Grass,* she said Gerard de Brahm (a surveyor) named them River Glades, which on later English maps became Ever Glades.

The Everglades is part of a sheet-flow ecosystem, beginning at the Kissimmee River, which empties into Lake Okeechobee at the south-center of the state, which, before humankind's meddling, overflowed and sent sheets of water through the Everglades and finally into the Gulf of Mexico. The resulting ecosystem was home to thousands of species of flora, and wildlife, including wading birds, amphibians, reptiles and mammals, flourished.

Enter business. Sugar growers, attracted by muck as they are, swarmed into the area and pressured the government to make the land available to them. In 1905, Florida Governor Napoleon Bonaparte Broward personally dug the first shovelful of dirt for what was to be

Marjory Stoneman Douglas

one of the largest and most singularly destructive diversions of water in the world. The Caloosahatchee River was diverted and connected to Lake Okeechobee; hundreds of canals were dug directly through the Everglades to the coastline in order to 'reclaim' land. The flow of water from the lake was then restricted by a series of dikes, and farmland began to sprout up in areas previously uninhabited by humans.

Unfortunately, the farming a) diverted the freshwater desperately needed by nature in the Everglades, and b) produced fertilizer-rich wastewater, which created explosions in growth of foliage, clogging waterways and further complicating matters.

More recently, with all the chemicals being poured into the Glades and local waters, the Florida Aquifer (the source of Florida's freshwater supply) is in great danger of being contaminated. Autopsies of local animals, including Florida panthers, have shown that mercury levels are extremely high. In addition, pollution running into the area from industry and farming in the north is killing foliage, and because of the diversion of the area's water, saltwater from the Gulf of Mexico is flowing deeper into the park than ever before. There are 16 endangered and five threatened species of animals within the park.

Efforts to save the Everglades were begun as early as the late 1920s, but they were put on the back burner by the Great Depression. In 1926 and 1928, two major hurricanes allowed Okeechobee to break free and the resulting floods killed hundreds. So, the Army Corps of Engineers came in and did a *really* good job of damming the lake – the Hoover Dike was constructed. Through the efforts of conservationists and prominent citizens, notably Douglas, the Everglades was declared a national park in 1947, but the threat is far from over.

Restoration The restoration of the Everglades is one of the hottest potatoes in the USA's environmental world. In 1995, Congress voted to cut subsidies to Florida sugar growers by a penny a pound, and to use the savings to buy 126,000 acres of land to restore a natural flow of water through South Florida, saying that about one-fifth of Florida land in sugar production would be purchased and allowed to revert to marsh-land. Additionally, the federal and state governments would spend $100 million to reroute and reconstruct South Florida's dikes, dams and levees, from northern Lake Okeechobee through the Glades.

The basic idea is to increase freshwater quantity within the Everglades, remove phosphorus upstream of water conservation areas, employ mitigation projects to enhance the Everglades with restoration objectives, and maintain a diverse habitat to meet the needs of wildlife. Gosh that sounds great, but it's easier said than done.

Thousands of scientists and environmentalists and scores of environmental and business groups are arguing about the best ways to meet the goals of restoration. The politics of it is highly divisive. The Everglades Coalition is the primary environmental group, comprised of 42 subgroups including the Conservancy (see the Naples section in the Southwest Florida chapter). The Conservancy and the Coalition call for restoration of the remaining Everglades lands to conditions prior to developmental impacts while maintaining flood protection and providing freshwater needs for the growing population of South Florida. The Coalition also calls for the continued restoration of the Kissimmee River Basin, the return of Lake Okeechobee to a more natural state, ongoing land acquisition to preserve and protect as much of the system as possible, and control of urban sprawl, which is spreading rapidly around the margins of the Everglades.

The Coalition has been working closely with local, state and federal officials on the 'Restudy' – the common name for the Central and Southern Florida Project Comprehensive Review Study (www.restudy .org). In October, 1998, a first draft of the Restudy was made public, to allow for debate and contributions. In July 1999, the final Restudy was to be delivered to the US Congress as a general blueprint for restoration. Once that passed (it was expected to) money and federal effort would be available for specific applications and processes.

Information

The main points of entry to the park all have visitors centers, where you can get maps, camping permits and information from rangers. Admission to the park at the Main Visitor Center entrance is $5 per carload, or $3 for pedestrians. The main gate is open 24 hours a day. Camping is $8 for tent sites and $10 for RVs and camper vans. (See Camping under Places to Stay for more information.)

Visitors Centers The Main Visitor Center (☎ 305-242-7700) and the Royal Palm Visitor Center (same ☎) are both off Hwy 9336 just inside the eastern border of the park, about 20 miles from Florida City. For advance tourist information, write to them at Information, Everglades National Park, 40001 State Rd 9336, Homestead, FL 33034-6733. The Main Visitor Center (also see the Activities section later in this chapter) is open 8 am to 4:30 pm daily; the Royal Palm Visitor Center is open 8 am to 4:15 pm daily.

The Gulf Coast Ranger Station (☎ 941-695-3311), on Hwy 29 in Everglades City (see Around the Everglades later in this chapter), is the northwesternmost ranger station, and provides access to the 10,000 Islands area. (You will also find the visitors center here.)

The Shark Valley Visitor Center (☎ 305-221-8776) is just off the Tamiami Trail (US Hwy 41).

The Flamingo Visitor Center (☎ 941-695-3094) is in Flamingo, at the park's southern coast.

Planning For gear and packing tips, see the Outdoor Activities chapter .

Books For all trips, you can work out specific itineraries with the assistance of a ranger and the *Backcountry Trip Planner*, a guide to the park published by the National Park Service (NPS). Dennis Kalma's *Boat & Canoe Camping in the Everglades Back-country and Ten Thousand Island Region*

THE EVERGLADES

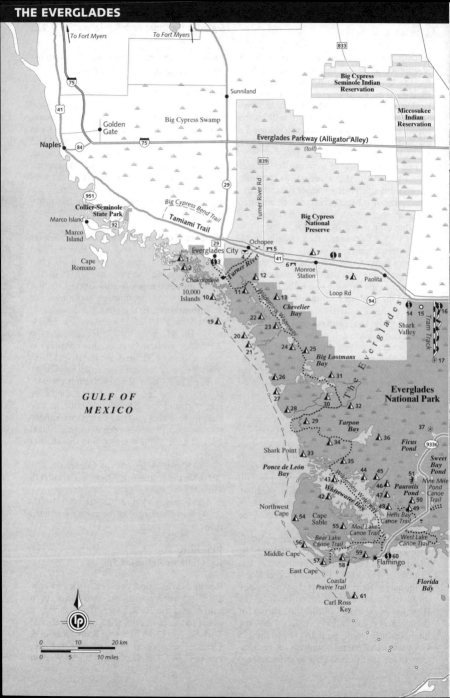

To Fort Myers

To Fort Myers

833

Big Cypress
Seminole Indian
Reservation

Sunniland

Miccosukee
Indian
Reservation

75

41

Golden
Gate

Big Cypress Swamp

Everglades Parkway (Alligator Alley)

Naples

84

(toll)

75

839

29

Turner River Rd

Big Cypress
National
Preserve

Big Cypress Bend Trail

Tamiami Trail

Collier-Seminole
State Park

951

Marco Island

92

Marco
Island

29

Ochopee

5

Cape
Romano

Everglades City

4

41

6

Monroe
Station

7

8

1

2

3

Turner River

12

Chokoloskee

9

Paolita

10,000
Islands

10

11

Wilderness Waterway

13

Loop Rd

94

Chevelier
Bay

The Everglades

14 15

16

19

22

23

Shark
Valley

17

Tram Track

20

21

24

25

Big Lostmans
Bay

26

31

GULF OF
MEXICO

27

30

32

Everglades
National Park

28

29

Tarpon
Bay

37

Shark Point

34

36

Ficus
Pond

33

9336

35

Sweet
Bay
Pond

Ponce de León
Bay

43

44

45

51

Nine Mile
Pond
Canoe
Trail

Wilderness Waterway

46

Paurotis
Pond

Northwest
Cape

42

47

50

54

Cape
Sable

55

48

49

Hells Bay
Canoe Trail

West Lake
Canoe Trail

Bear Lake
Canoe Trail

Mud Lake
Canoe Trail

Middle Cape

56

57

59

60

58

Flamingo

East Cape

Coastal
Prairie Trail

Florida
Bay

61

Carl Ross
Key

0   10   20 km

0   5   10 miles

(Florida Flair Books, Miami) is an excellent guide to trails.

For nature information and identification, the rangers themselves use *Florida's Fabulous Birds* by Winston Williams, *Florida's Fabulous Reptiles & Amphibians* by Peter Carmichael and Winston Williams, the National Geographic's *Field Guide to Birds of North America* and *Peterson Field Guide to the Birds* by Roger Tory Peterson.

Charts The Gulf Coast Ranger Station's gift shop sells the charts you will need while canoeing in the 10,000 Islands (National Oceanic & Atmospheric Administration's *Coast & Geodetic Survey*). Paper charts are $14, waterproof ones (we recommend these) are $16. You're looking for chart Nos 11430, 11432 and 11433. You can also order these charts directly from the Distribution Division N/CG33, National Ocean Service, 6501 Lafayette Ave, Riverdale, MD 30737.

Regulations All the park's resources are protected, including the plants, shells, artifacts and buildings. You can fish, *only* with a state fishing license; check at any ranger station for information. Free permits, available at ranger stations, are required for all overnight stays. In areas that do not have toilets, you'll need to dig a hole at least 6 inches deep for waste. Campfires are prohibited except at certain beach sites: use dead and down wood only, and build your fire below the high-tide line. Remove all your garbage from the park when you leave.

High Season & Aaarrgh! Season

The Everglades' seasons can be described as the dry season (roughly November to May) and the mosquito and no-see-um (so called because of their disturbing tininess in size but hugeness in biting power) season, which is the rest of the time. While the park is open year round, the best time to visit is in the dry season.

Dangers & Annoyances The main dangers you'll encounter will be weather and insects, though bad tides can be a real pain in the butt, not to mention in the blistered hands and sunburned face. See the Tide Charts boxed text for information and be certain you understand how to predict and use the tides to help you.

Weather Thunderstorms and lightning are more common in summer – but in summer the insects are so bad you won't want to be out here anyway. In emergency weather, rangers will go searching for registered campers. But note that in ordinary conditions, they won't do this unless they receive information that someone's missing. If camping, have a friend or family member ready to contact rangers if you do not report back by a certain day.

Biting Insects Mosquitoes are about half of the insect problem – and in summer the Everglades would appear to be the world's central mosquito-manufacturing plant. The other half is made up handily at dawn and dusk by the insidious no-see-ums: tiny (almost invisible) yet ferocious and really god-awful biting insects. Avon Skin-So-Soft or REI Jungle Juice are key equipment. But note that the insect problem in the dry season isn't so bad. Information on mosquito levels during summer is available at ☎ 305-242-7700.

Alligators & Crocodiles While alligators are common in the park, they are not very common in the area of the 10,000 Islands, as they tend to avoid saltwater. If you do see an alligator, it probably won't bother you, unless you do something overtly threatening or angle your boat between it and its young. If you hear an alligator making a loud hissing sound, you should get the hell out of Dodge – that's a call to other alligators when a young gator is in danger. Finally, never, ever, *ever* feed an alligator – it's stupid, selfish and illegal. Crocodiles are less common in the park, as they prefer coastal and saltwater habitats. They are more aggressive than alligators, however, and the

CHRISTIAN HEEB

Seminole exhibit at the Ah-Tah-Thi-Ki Museum, Big Cypress National Preserve

TED LEVIN

Roseate spoonbill in the Everglades

MAXINE CASS

CARL PURCELL

Bear Lake Canoe Trail in Flamingo

Strangler figs abound in the Everglades.

Sunset over Everglades National Park

Mangrove roots stabilizing the shore

The endangered Florida panther

same rules apply. See the Fauna section in the Facts about Florida chapter for more information.

Snakes There are four types of poisonous snakes in the Everglades: diamondback rattlesnake *(Crotalus adamanteus)*, pigmy rattlesnake *(Sistrurus miliarius)*, cottonmouth or water moccasin *(Agkistrodon piscivorus conanti)*, which swim along the surface of water, and the hugely colorful coral snake *(Micrurus fulvius)*. Wear long, thick socks and lace-up boots – and keep the hell away from them.

Critters Less dangerous but very annoying are raccoons and rats. They will tear through anything less than a solid and sealed plastic cooler to get to your food. Keep your food and food garbage inside a sealed cooler, and your water bottles sealed and inside your tent. (Open water can be smelled through your tent, and the last thing you want at 4 am is a raccoon slashing through your sleeping bag in search of a sip.)

10,000 ISLANDS

We think that the finest way to experience the serenity and unique beauty – which is somehow desolate yet lush, tropical yet foreboding – of the Everglades is by canoeing or kayaking through the excellent network of waterways that skirt the northwest portion of the park.

The 10,000 Islands are made up of a lot (but not really 10,000) of tiny islands and mangrove swamp that hug the point of the southwesternmost border of the Florida peninsula. On the habitable islands, the NPS allows free camping. These islands offer some amazing opportunities to enjoy the Everglades on an intimate basis.

Most of the islands are fringed by narrow beaches with sugar-white sand, though note that in most of the area, the water is brackish, not clear, and very shallow. It's not Tahiti, but it is a fascinating place. The best part is that you can get your own island for up to a week for nothing. That's right, free. (Contact the Gulf Coast Ranger Station for information.)

Tide Charts

Tide charts are as important to your journey as your ability to paddle – or lack thereof. They can be the difference between a fun trip and a nightmare of vast proportions. You can get National Oceanic & Atmospheric Administration (NOAA) charts from the ranger stations, at marinas or in local newspapers.

Tide charts list the date, the time and the height of low and high tide, but you'll need to calculate the correct tides for your location, as tide charts are set to a fixed point, such as Everglades City. For the most obvious examples (the ones printed on the ranger station charts), when it's high tide at Everglades City, you'll need to do the following:

- Add 1/2 hour at Sweetwater and Sunday Bay
- Add 11/2 hours at Plate Creek
- Subtract 1 hour at the Watson Place
- Subtract 11/2 hours at Tiger and Pavilion Keys
- Subtract 2 hours at South Lostman's

The **Wilderness Waterway**, a 99-mile path between Everglades City and Flamingo, is the longest canoe trail in the area; there are shorter canoe trails near Flamingo.

Near Everglades City at the park's northwest corner, you can take a downstream trip on the **Turner River** alone or with a group, and make it either an easy with-the-current drift to Chokoloskee Island, or add a bit of a challenge at the end and go upstream in the boating canal to the Gulf Coast Ranger Station. You can also canoe around the 10,000 Islands for any period of time you wish, and we highly recommend it!

Canoe & Kayak Itineraries

Note that despite what it says on Everglades National Park maps, Comer Key is permanently closed – it washed away in 1995. Getting around in the 10,000 Islands is pretty straightforward if you religiously adhere to NOAA tide charts, and rangers will help you develop an itinerary based on what you'd most like to see. For all these journeys, it is absolutely imperative that you have a nautical chart (see Charts under Planning earlier in the chapter) and a tide chart (see the Tide Charts boxed text). Going against the tides is the fastest way to make it a miserable trip.

For an easy day of paddling around the islands, just get a boat and cross the bay from the Gulf Coast Ranger Station and paddle out and around the mangroves to Sandfly Island or on the Chokoloskee Bay Loop.

For an easy overnight or two-night trip, you'll be wanting the islands closest to the ranger station: Tiger, Picnic, Rabbit, New Turkey, Turkey and Hog Keys, all with beach campsites.

For a nice few days (three to four) of canoeing, head south from the Gulf Coast Ranger Station, then past Chokoloskee and up the Lopez River, north near Sunday Bay, and then southeast to Sweetwater Bay, where there's a chickee at which you can spend the night. The next morning head out toward the Watson Place and southwest to Pavilion Key for an overnight stay at the beach campsite; then north to Rabbit Key for a final night on the beach. In the morning, head back north to the ranger station.

There are hundreds of other combinations; check with a ranger for more recommendations.

Organized Tours

Rangers lead free 5½-hour canoe trips (the tours are free, the canoes aren't) through the overhanging mangrove tunnels along the Turner River on many Saturdays during the dry season. They leave the Gulf Coast Ranger Station at 9 am. David Harraden's NACT (see Canoeing & Kayaking later) is the best outfit in the whole park for regular guided tours. For $50 per person you can get a guided canoe trip down the Turner River, including an excellent lunch. The daily tours start at 9 am and return at 3 pm (note that NACT is closed from May 1 to October 31).

Airboats & Swamp Buggies

Airboats are flat-bottomed boats that use powerful fans to propel themselves through water. While they are capable of traveling in very shallow water, they are very loud, and their environmental impact has not been determined. One thing is clear: while airboats in the hands of responsible operators, such as naturalists and geologists, have little impact on the surrounding wildlife, irresponsible operators can cause lots of direct and collateral damage.

Swamp buggies are enormous balloon-tired vehicles that can go through swamps. They definitely cause rutting and damage wildlife.

You'll be offered airboat and swamp buggy rides at stands all along US Hwy 41. Please assess the motive behind the operator's existence before just getting on a 'nature' tour: you may be helping to disturb the Everglades' delicate balance.

NACT also offers interesting day tours within the 10,000 Islands for approximately the same price.

For longer excursions it gets very expensive: a four-day, three-night camping journey through the islands is $450 per person.

The simplest is a boat tour from Everglades National Park Boat Tours (☎ 941-695-2591, 800-445-7724). Tours on the large pleasure boats leave from the dock at the Gulf Coast Ranger Station in Everglades City from December 20 to April 15 aboard the *Panther I* (at 9 and 11 am and 1 and 3 pm); *Panther II* (10 am, noon, 2 and 4 pm); *Manatee I* (9:30 and 11:30 am and 1:30 and 3:30 pm); and *Manatee II* (10:30 am, 12:30 and 2:30 pm, and a special two-hour sunset tour at 5 pm in December and early January). From April 15 to December 20, a boat leaves the dock every half hour between 9:30 am and 5 pm. Tours (except the special sunset tour) are 1³/₄ hours through the 10,000 Islands. The cost is $13 for adults, $6.50 for children six to 12. A Mangrove Wilderness tour costs $16/8. They claim these tours run at high tide only, but we've never seen one (a park employee said he saw it run three times in 1998).

Another option, and one recommended by many rangers, is the Majestic Everglades Excursion (☎ 941-695-2777), a six-passenger pontoon boat that tootles through the park on half-day trips for $60 for adults and $30 for kids, including lunch or a snack. You must call ahead and reserve tickets as it doesn't have a set schedule.

Getting There & Away

From the Tamiami Trail (US Hwy 41), turn south on Hwy 29; go until you're forced to turn right, which will bring you to the traffic circle. Turn left and follow the road and it will bring you straight to the Gulf Coast Ranger Station. The whole trip from Miami takes a little less than two hours on the Tamiami Trail, 3¹/₂ to four if you add a side trip on Loop Rd.

SHARK VALLEY

At the northern border of the park, just off the Tamiami Trail, the Shark Valley Visitor Center (☎ 305-221-8776) is a very popular way to get yourself easily and painlessly immersed in the middle of the Everglades prairie. You can bike or walk the 17-mile trail between the entrance and the 50-foot-high Shark Valley Observation Tower, which gives a pretty spectacular overview of the park. You will see a lot of flora and fauna: The last time we went, there was a 10-foot alligator in the main parking lot, lazily sunning himself with his mouth wide open. We gave him a wide berth.

Bicycle rentals (they're one-speeds but the ground is pretty flat), available from the cash desk at the entrance to the park, cost $3.25 per hour including tax. Another option is to take the Shark Valley Tram Tour, led by rangers or 'experienced tram drivers'; the journey over the paved 15-mile tram road takes two hours. The cost is $8 for adults,

$7.20 for seniors over 62 and $4 for children under 12. There's also a park entry fee of $4 per carload or $2 for pedestrians.

The trams leave every hour on the hour between 9 am and 4 pm in high season, and at 9:30 and 11 am and 1 and 3 pm in low season. Reservations are recommended in high season.

There's no public transportation to this point. Driving, it's about 18 miles from the western border of Miami, on the south side of the Tamiami Trail.

FLAMINGO

Flamingo, at the southernmost tip of the mainland of Everglades National Park, is more developed than the 10,000 Islands, and the least authentic Everglades experience you can get; with sightseeing and bay cruises, it's really geared toward holidaymakers. There are nature and bike paths, picnic tables, a bar, tourist trap…er…gift shops, tram tours, etc, as well as short canoe trails, including West Lake, a one-way, 7¹/₂-mile path; Nine Mile Pond, a 5¹/₂-mile circuit; Hells Bay, also a 5¹/₂-mile circuit; Mud Lake, a 5.8-mile loop and Bear Lake, 2 miles one way. Entry to Flamingo is through the Main Visitor Center road, Hwy 9336.

And in Flamingo, everything's more expensive, including canoe rentals (see Canoeing & Kayaking later).

From the Main Visitor Center, follow Hwy 9336 to the bitter end: welcome to Flamingo.

ACTIVITIES

The Main Visitor Center is the primary entrance to Everglades National Park (see Information earlier in this section). Just southwest of Homestead, a 30-minute drive from downtown Miami, it is packed with excellent information on everything in the park. A quick tour here is the fastest and easiest way to see the Everglades, or at least some of it.

Hiking

Very close to the entrance of the Main Visitor Center, the Royal Palm Visitor

Center is the entryway to the three-quarter-mile Gumbo-Limbo Trail, with gumbo-limbo and royal palm trees, orchids and lush vegetation, and the Anhinga Trail named for the odd anhinga birds (also called the snake bird, for the way it swims with its long neck and head above water), a half-mile route on which you'll probably run into alligators, turtles, waterfowl, lizards, snakes and, well, be prepared for anything.

You can drive the 30-odd-mile main road that runs between the center entrance and Flamingo. Along the way are the following trails: the Pinelands, a half-mile trail through Dade County pine forest – look for exposed limestone bedrock; Pa-hay-okee Overlook, a very short (quarter-mile) boardwalk trail with an observation tower; and Mahogany Hammock, a half-mile boardwalk that leads into totally lush and overgrown vegetation. The longest series of trails is at Long Pine Key, the starting point of a 15-mile series of walking trails where you may see many species indigenous to the Everglades. You may even get a chance, if you're very quiet and patient, to see a Florida panther.

Canoeing & Kayaking

See the 10,000 Islands section earlier in the chapter for more information on canoeing and kayaking opportunities in the Everglades.

There are rental outfits at Everglades City and Flamingo. In Everglades City, we recommend North American Canoe Tours (NACT), ☎ 941-695-3299) at the Ivey House Hotel, 107 Camellia St, which rents out first-rate canoes for $25 for the first day, $20 each additional day, or $20 for a half day; kayaks are $33 to $35 a day, and Sea Lion kayaks with rudders and upgraded paddles (which make going against the current a whole lot easier) go for $45 a day.

A good deal they have is a shuttle service for those willing to make the five- to 10-day trip between the Gulf Coast and Flamingo Visitor Center: for a $170 fee NACT will drive your car to Flamingo; when you arrive, turn in the canoe or kayak to the dockmaster, who will give you the keys to your car,

and you can drive away. It is possible to work out a shuttle schedule for a Flamingo to Everglades City trip, but you'll need to negotiate that with NACT.

Everglades National Park Boat Tours (☎ 941-695-2591), in the Gulf Coast Ranger Station, is the most expensive for overnights: it's $18 from 8:30 am to 5 pm or $36 for an overnight rental. They'll take your car to Flamingo for $150.

At the Flamingo Lodge Marina & Outpost Resort (☎ 941-695-3101) canoes rent for $22 for four hours, $32 for a full day and $40 overnight. They also rent kayaks – a single is $27/43/50, a double is $38/54/60, all with a $100 deposit. They rent bicycles as well for $3 an hour, $8 for four hours, $14 for eight and $17 overnight.

PLACES TO STAY

Also see the Everglades City and Marco Island sections for more options.

Camping

The following three types of campsites are available at no cost with a reservation from the Gulf Coast Ranger Station (above the visitors center; reserve in person only, no phone calls or faxes, and only within 36 hours of the intended stay): beach sites, on coastal shell beaches and in the 10,000 Islands; ground sites, which are basically mounds of dirt built up above the mangroves, along the interior bays and rivers; and 'chickees,' wooden platforms built above water on which you can pitch a free-standing (no spikes) tent.

Chickees, which have toilets, are the most civilized of the three, and certainly are unique: there's such serenity inherent in sleeping on what feels like a raft levitating above the water in the middle of a natural wonder. We found the beach sites to be the most comfortable, though in all three, biting insects, such as mosquitoes and no-see-ums, are rife, even in winter. The ground sites tend to be the most bug-infested of all.

Warning: if you're just paddling around and you see an island that looks perfectly pleasant for camping but it is not one of those designated campsites, beware – be very wary – as you may end up submerged when the tides change.

There is an additional Everglades campsite at Chekika, at the western end of Richmond Drive (SW 168th St), which is off Krome Ave about 20 miles south of the Tamiami Trail.

There are campsites along the Tamiami Trail (US Hwy 41); Big Cypress National Preserve manages those sites. See that section later in this chapter for more information.

You can camp at the Flamingo campground (see Flamingo above), run by the Flamingo Visitor Center (☎ 941-695-3101); sites with no hookups are $14.

Hostels

The new *Everglades International Hostel* (☎ 305-241-1122, www.members.xoom.com/gladeshostel/, 20 SW 2nd Ave) is a friendly hostel in a 1930s boarding house on a huge piece of property in Florida City. Owhnn (that's not a typo) makes sure everyone's happy, and hands out information on the Everglades, canoeing, kayaking, bicycling and on area attractions as well. She charges $12 for dorm rooms (six beds in a dorm), and $30 for double private rooms with shared bath.

Hotels

You can stay in the *Flamingo Lodge* (☎ 941-695-3101, 800-600-3813) for $65 in low season (May to October), $79 in fringe seasons (October to December and April) and $95 in high season. The rooms are all identical, and have two double beds, TV and air conditioning. The entry to Flamingo Lodge is just off the Main Visitor Center road, Hwy 9336.

Houseboats

Flamingo Lodge rents two types of houseboats which, if you're with five other people, can work out to be cheaper than you'd think: even with the top luxury model, it would end up being $47 per person per night. The boats, the luxury 37-foot Gibson Sport Series and the less luxurious and boxy, but somewhat larger, 40-foot pontoon boats,

all include refrigerator/freezer, a stove and oven, bathrooms with showers, propane, linen, pots and pans and flatware, life vests and charts. The Gibsons have air conditioning and diesel electric generators while the pontoon boats do not.

The pontoon boats, which can sleep six comfortably and eight not so comfortably, cost $275 plus tax for one night and $340 plus tax for two nights in summer; in winter there is a two-night minimum, and it costs $485 plus tax.

The Gibsons have a two-night minimum year round, and cost $525 plus tax for two nights in summer, $575 plus tax in winter. Expect to pay an extra $40 a day in fuel, and there's a $500 damage/fuel deposit required for all boats (cash or credit card). You don't need a special license; if you've never driven a boat before, cap'n, they'll give you an hour orientation course and set you free on the high seas with a $270,000 piece of maritime transport.

GETTING THERE & AWAY

The only sensible way to get here is by car. Take Florida's Turnpike Extension (toll) or US Hwy 1 to Florida City and take Hwy 9336 to the entrance of the park.

The only way to do this by public transport is idiotic: you can take Metrorail to Dadeland North ($1.25), then bus No 1 to the Cutler Ridge Mall ($1.25) and then No 35 or No 70 to Florida City (25¢ transfer). Greyhound no longer even serves Florida City.

Around the Everglades

ALONG THE TAMIAMI TRAIL

The Tamiami Trail, which blazes the way between Miami and Tampa, is, for the most part, straight as a die through monotonous swampland. But there are some points of interest along the way. There are also three rest stops with picnic areas along the trail; at the Oasis Visitor Center (see Big Cypress National Preserve below); Kirby Sorter

THE EVERGLADES

Roadside Park, with tables, grills and a small interpretive trail; and HP Williams Roadside Park, with picnic tables, just east of the entrance to the Turner River Rd.

Miccosukee Cultural Center

For a far more friendly and accessible introduction to Native American traditions and customs see Seminole Indians in the Big Cypress section below. The Miccosukee Cultural Center is a collection of tourist shops and pointless, inhumane alligator wrestling displays ($5). There is expensive gasoline at the filling station, and the gentleman running the restaurant – its air redolent with the scent of elderly frying oil – wouldn't let us write down prices in our notebooks: 'You want to buy something, fine, otherwise get out,' he said from behind his sunglasses. Nothing like that down-home Southern hospitality to gear up the ol' taste buds for deep-fried 'gator nuggets, eh? Our advice: fill up the tank and grab a bite before you get here.

Ochopee

Driving through the tiny hamlet of Ochopee (population about 115)…no…wait…turn around, you've missed it. That's right, kids, break out the cameras: Ochopee's claim to fame is the USA's smallest official post office! In a former toolshed, a charming and friendly female postal worker patiently poses for snapshots. For the cost of a stamp, you can send a postcard or letter from here, though be certain that she cancels the stamp nicely – some of ours were as smudged as a Russian visa stamp. The office is in the little shack on the south side of the Tamiami Trail.

BIG CYPRESS NATIONAL PRESERVE

Big Cypress National Preserve is a 1139-sq-mile federally protected area that is the result of a compromise between environmentalists, cattle ranchers and oil and gas explorers. It's a method of protecting the land while allowing pre-existing development to proceed to a certain extent. The area is a major player in the Everglades' ecosystem; the rains that flood the prairies and wetlands here slowly filter down through the Glades.

The preserve comprises about 45% of the total area of the cypress swamp, which, by the way, is not a swamp at all but a group of mangrove islands, hardwood hammocks, islands of slash pine, prairie and marshes. It is not pristine – there is rutting, growth of new and abnormal vegetation and shifts in elevation.

The preserve's name comes from the sheer acreage – not the height – of the dwarf pond cypress trees that fill the area. The great bald cypress trees are nearly gone from the area, as lumber and other industry took its toll before the preserve's establishment. Animals in the preserve include alligators, snakes, wading birds including white ibis, wood stork, tri-color heron and several types of egret, and a variety of other animals including the Florida panther (rarely seen), wild turkey and red cockaded woodpecker.

Under the park's charter, the retention of ownership of private lands bought before the preserve's establishment was permitted, as are off-road-vehicle activity, hunting and fishing, oil and gas exploration and cattle grazing. The trick of it all is to maintain a threshold of activity low enough to protect the region's flora and fauna yet high enough to accommodate the nature-bashing yahoos with their guns and swamp buggies.

The preserve is also the southern terminus of the Florida National Scenic Trail (FNST; see the Outdoor Activities chapter).

Florida Panther

Information

The main visitors center here is the Oasis Visitor Center (☎ 941-695-4111) about 19 miles west of Shark Valley along the Tamiami Trail. The Big Cypress National Preserve Headquarters (☎ 941-695-2000) – which is not the same thing as the visitors center – is just east of Ochopee. For advance information write to Big Cypress National Preserve, HCR 61, Box 11, Ochopee, FL 33943.

Hiking

There are 31 miles of the FNST, maintained by the Florida Trail Association, within the Big Cypress National Preserve. The southern terminus is just north of Loop Rd, which can be accessed by car from either the Monroe Ranger Station in Monroe Station or the Tamiami Ranger Station. The trail runs 8.3 miles north to the Tamiami Trail, passing right by the Oasis Visitor Center before continuing on. There are two primitive campsites, with wells but nothing else, along the trail. Note that off-road vehicles are permitted to cross, but not operate on, the FNST – use caution.

For the less adventurous, there's the short Tree Snail Hammock Nature Trail, opposite the Loop Road Environmental Education Center (closed to the public) off Loop Rd.

Driving

The two main trails for on-road vehicles are Loop Rd, a potholed dirt road that runs between the Monroe and Tamiami Ranger Stations, and Turner River Rd, which shoots straight as an arrow north from the Tamiami Trail just west of the HP Williams Roadside Park. There are excellent wildlife-viewing opportunities along the entire stretch of Turner River Rd, especially in the Turner River Canal that runs along the east side of it. The road leads to the northern area of the preserve where off-road vehicles are permitted to rut and root their way through the land.

Seminole Museum & Tours

Ah-Tah-Thi-Ki Museum The best news in Everglades tourism in years is the advent of the Ah-Tah-Thi-Ki Museum (☎ 941-902-1113) in the Big Cypress Preserve. The museum contains exhibits on Seminole life, history and the tribe today, which are fascinating. The museum was founded using proceeds from Seminole gaming, a powerhouse economic activity that annually provides much of the Seminole tribe's $120 million operating budget.

The museum is open daily and at night for special programs. Admission is $6 for adults, $4 for seniors and students. From Naples, take I-75 south to exit 14 (past exit 14a!) turn left (look for the sign), and then go north 17 miles. From Miami, take Hwy 27 to I-75 west to exit 14 and turn right (again, follow the signs).

Organized Tours Never before have the Seminole opened so much to the public. Their Website (www.seminoletribe.com) gives heaps of information on the tribe, their history and their customs. Sure, it's good for business. But Lee Tiger, the Seminole Tribe's tourism coordinator, is truly dedicated to bringing visitors closer to understanding the Seminole and Miccosukee people (Tiger Miccosukee), and especially to enabling them to experience Seminole life.

It's not the wild wild Glades, but it's an absolute breakthrough in thinking for the tribe, which until recently kept pretty much to itself as far as tourism went. Sure, you could gamble in their gaming halls, but the life itself was a closed door.

Tiger and the Seminoles have worked out day and overnight Seminole Safari packages where you sleep in a chickee hut, and hiking, airboating and Indian meals are also available. Please check out Tiger's Website (www.semtribe.com) for package and tourist information. To give you an idea, you can spend the day, for $36 per person, touring the Big Cypress area on an air boat, including a narrated trip to the museum. For $97 you'll get that plus a night in a chickee hut and a campfire storytelling session. Some of the activities, like swamp buggy tours and 'wildlife shows' are activities that us hand-wringing types at LP don't recommend. But the package is truly a unique opportunity –

Just Win...

Last edition we railed against political incorrectness in the state of Florida, which has named its state university sports teams the Seminoles, and given the state university campgrounds the unbelievably insensitive moniker of The Seminole Reservation. PJ O'Rourke once compared such practices to naming a professional basketball team the New York Kikes or the Detroit Niggers.

Seminole Tribal Chairman James Billie recently put the entire issue of sports teams' names to rest. In a speech at a southwest Florida college he said, 'I am not offended by the use of "Seminoles" by FSU. As long as they win.'

if enough travelers express interest in the tours and disinterest in the environmentally harmful aspects of them, things will likely change. If you take one of these tours, please drop us a note – LP addresses are on the last page of the book – and let us know what you thought of it.

Places to Stay

Aside from the two sites on the FNST, there are a total of seven campgrounds on the preserve. The campsites are totally primitive, so be sure to bring your own water and food. See the Outdoor Activities chapter for how to pack food and water. Note that the Dona Drive campsite, on many maps, is no longer open to the public. Campsites in the preserve – Bear Island, Midway, Monument Lake, Loop Rd, Mitchell's Landing and Pinecrest – are free, and you needn't register. Note that Mitchell's Landing, Loop Rd and Pinecrest only accommodate tents, not RVs.

Getting There & Away

Again, there's no public transport to speak of. By car from either the east or the west, take the Tamiami Trail (US Hwy 41); the Oasis Visitor Center is about halfway between Everglades City and Shark Valley.

EVERGLADES CITY

Everglades City (population 400 in summer, 1500 in winter) is a tiny little town that survives from the trade of fishermen who pull into the marina and live in RVs at the camp-

ground, and people coming through to visit the Everglades. It's a perfectly pleasant little town, in a fisherman's paradise kind of way; it's a sensible place to spend the night to get an early start on canoe trips in the 10,000 Islands. The Gulf Coast Ranger Station is at the southern end of town.

Orientation & Information

Hwy 29 runs south and through the city. At the intersection of the Tamiami Trail and Hwy 29, there's the Carnestown Welcome Station, a source for many pamphlets and brochures. At the traffic circle in downtown Everglades City, in the beautiful little city hall building, there is the Everglades Area Chamber of Commerce (☎ 941-695-3941), which has very primitive maps of the city. The Gulf Coast Ranger Station (above the visitors center) has stacks and piles of information on the 10,000 Islands and the Everglades. Also in the city hall building is the city library.

Wash clothes at the coin laundry across the street from city hall, next to the Right Choice (only choice, actually), Supermarket.

Places to Stay & Eat

Glades Haven (☎ *941-695-3954, 800 SE Copeland Ave, Hwy 29*), the commercial campground across the street from the Gulf Coast Ranger Station, is geared more to RVs than to tents but tents are welcome. Tent sites are $17, RV sites are $24, all including water, sewer and electric. There are hot showers in the bathrooms.

Here's a neat one: spend the night in a former bank and have breakfast in the vault. **On the Banks of the Everglades** (☎ 941-695-3151, 888-431-1977, 201 W Broadway) is a B&B inside a renovated classic-revival-style bank building. They have boxy little singles ($50), larger doubles (from $65 to $88) and efficiencies ($90).

The Ivey House Hotel (☎ 941-695-3299, fax 941-695-4155, 107 Camellia St) at the northern end of town, behind the Circle K convenience store and the post office, is a lovely, if a bit institutional-feeling, place to stay for the service and the food. Formerly a recreation hall for laborers working on the Tamiami Trail, the family-run place offers good meals (there's not a deep fryer in sight) and the rooms, while simple (no TV or telephone, shared bathrooms), are comfortable and clean. They cost $50 from November 1 to December 14 and from March 16 to April 30, and $70 from December 15 to March 15, including breakfast and use of the bicycles on a first-come, first-served basis. (They rent bikes out for $3 a day to nonguests.) Dinner – for guests and nonguests – is $10 to $15. These folks also run NACT, which operates some of the best nature trips around; see Organized Tours in the 10,000 Islands section earlier in this chapter. The hotel and NACT are closed from May 1 to October 31.

The **Rod & Gun Club Lodge** (☎ 941-695-2101, 200 Riverside Drive), west of Hwy 29, is a swank place. It was built as a hunting lodge by Barron Collier (See Collier-Seminole State Park below) in the 1920s as a place to relax after watching people dig his Tamiami Trail. It's open as a guesthouse now, with rooms at $50 in summer, $65 to $80 in winter. Its restaurant has seafood that averages $8 at lunch, $15 at dinner; steaks and other meat dishes average $17 to $18.

The **Captain's Table** (☎ 941-695-4211, 800-741-6430), at the right jig in Hwy 29 east of the downtown traffic circle, has surprisingly clean and cheerful rooms and a very nice staff. The rooms run from $45 to $75 in summer, $75 to $95 in winter, and include a 10%-off coupon to the **Captain's Table Restaurant** (☎ 941-695-2727) next door. No

relation to the hotel, this is a very social-realist-looking restaurant that does good, but expensive, seafood dishes. At lunch, from 11 am to 5 pm, sandwiches run from $4.75 to $7.95 and fried seafood baskets from $5.95 to $8.95; at dinner, broiled, blackened, grilled or fried seafood dishes run from $13.95 (shrimp scampi) to $14.95 (bay scallops, Everglades alligator or snapper) to $22.95 (Captain's platter of fried shrimp, scallops, oysters, clam, grouper, conch fritters, crab cake and alligator).

Cheaper fare can be found at **Burger Express** (☎ 941-695-4210, on Hwy 29 next to the BP gas station), with burgers around $2.50, fish and barbecue pork sandwiches and other offerings for a little more. They do fried chicken and country fried steak at night for $4.95, with mashed potatoes and gravy, veggies and a roll.

At **Cheryl's Deli** (☎ 941-695-2746, at Glades Haven) they make good sandwiches for $4.25, including lots o' toppings, but it's an extra 30¢ for cheese or hot peppers. If you ask for a sandwich at breakfast time it takes forever: 'You ordered an unorthodox breakfast,' we were chided.

Almost everything on the menu at **Susie's Station** (☎ 941-695-2002) is fried: chicken strips are $5.95, fried shrimp with French fries is $8.95, but the atmosphere is pleasant enough. It's on the west side of the traffic circle.

For groceries – especially if you're going camping for more than a day and need supplies – it's best to stock up before you come, as the Right Choice Supermarket just east of the traffic circle has some stuff, but it's about 25% more expensive than any Publix.

Getting There & Away

From the Tamiami Trail, turn south on Hwy 29; go until you're forced to turn right (you'll see the Captain's Table hotel and restaurant in front of you), which will bring you to the traffic circle. From there, turn left and follow the road and it will bring you straight to the Gulf Coast Ranger Station. The whole trip from Miami takes a little less than two hours on the Tamiami Trail, 3½ to four if you add a side trip on Loop Rd.

COLLIER-SEMINOLE STATE PARK

Perhaps the only memorial that celebrates man's conquering of the Everglades, outside of sugar plant offices, this state park and wilderness preserve (☎ 941-394-3397) is named after Barron Gift Collier, one of the main developers of the Tamiami Trail. You can see the Bay City Walking Dredge that was used to dig away the muck from the limestone base of the highway in the 1920s on permanent display just past the entrance on the right-hand side of the road.

The preserve is a 4070-acre section of the park where freshwater and saltwater meet. The area is made up of red, black and white mangrove and buttonwood. Inside, you'll see manatees (especially in winter), white ibis, snowy egrets, alligators, over 40 species of trees and three species of lizard – the five-lined skink, the brown anole and the chameleon-like Carolina anole.

There's a 13-mile canoe trail along the Blackwater River; you can rent canoes from the concession stand at the marina, just south of the entrance station: they cost $3.18 an hour, or $31.80 for 24 hours. There are ranger-led canoe trips at 9 am on Sunday. You can also canoe, with reservations, down to the primitive campsites at Grocery Place ($3/2 for adults/kids) or pay for developed camping in one of two sites, both with full bathrooms and water and electric hookups, within the state park (not the preserve) section. The cost is $11/9 with/without electricity.

There's a 6^1/$_2$-mile hiking trail through the reserve that winds through pine flatwood and cypress swamp, and an interpretive center near the main campsites. There are campfire programs on Saturday nights in January, at the campfire ring at the west end of the campsite.

Check the rangers' mosquito chart at the entrance.

Admission to the park and preserve is $3.25 per carload or $1 for pedestrians and cyclists. They're open every day of the year from 8 am to sunset. The park entrance is about 15 miles northwest of the intersection of Hwy 29 and the Tamiami Trail.

MARCO ISLAND

The only inhabited island in the 10,000 Islands, Marco Island (population 12,000 in summer, 35,000 in winter), has a gorgeous Gulf Coast beach, but it's highly developed by resorts and not really a budget traveler's destination. Nonetheless, the island is now becoming hugely popular with overseas visitors – especially English and German – and if you have the cash and like resort life, this is a pretty awesome place to kick back on a dazzling white-sand beach and have a nice rest.

Orientation & Information

The island is at the very southwestern end of the state. San Marco Drive cuts straight west to Collier Blvd, which shoots up the Gulf Coast and becomes Hwy 951, crossing East Marco Bay and reconnecting with the Tamiami Trail. The main resorts – the Hilton, Radisson and Marriott – are at the southwestern end of the island on S Collier Blvd.

Get tourist information and excellent free maps at the Marco Island Convention & Visitors Bureau/Chamber of Commerce (☎ 941-394-7549, 800-788-6272) at 1102 N Collier Blvd. You can wash clothes at Cathy's Laundry of Marco (☎ 941-642-6635) at 277 N Collier Blvd.

Beaches

There are two official public beaches. One is Marco South, at the southernmost end of S Collier Blvd before it cuts east, and the other is Tigertail Beach, the more developed of the two. At Tigertail, about three-quarters of the way up the western side of the island, there are public toilets and showers and a snack bar.

Organized Tours

The Marco Island Trolley (☎ 941-394-1600) tootles around the island on several loops. It runs from 10 am to 5 pm every day of the year. The fare is $10 and you can get on and off as many times as you like. To use it as an orientation tour, just stay on for one complete loop, which will take about 1^1/$_2$ hours, with narration.

Places to Stay

Camping There's one place to camp, and that's with the friendly folks at *Mar-Good RV Park (☎ 941-394-6383)*, where tent sites are $20 a night year round. The site has bathrooms with hot showers, a convenience store and a tiki bar. It's at 321 Pear Tree Ave in Goodland; take San Marco Drive to Goodland Drive, a right turn just before the Goodland Bridge back to the Tamiami Trail, down to Goodland Drive West, and left on Pear Tree Ave.

Resorts & Condos The other options are resorts, of which we'll cover the big three, and condo rentals, which we'll leave in the capable hands of the chamber of commerce (see Orientation & Information above). They will send you a brochure entitled *Marco Island & the Everglades*, with listings of 32 (count 'em!) realtors, all of whom we're just certain would be happy to help.

The following three resorts are all enormous places that are complete holiday destinations in and of themselves. They have health clubs, swimming pools, great beach access with cabanas, wave runner, bicycle and other sports equipment and rentals, and, of course, kids' activities, nightclubs and restaurants – from top end to Pizza Hut and convenience stores. As with any resort, note that these prices are the standard rack rates for those who question nothing, except 'Where do I sign?' You can always get better deals through a travel agent.

The *Radisson Suites Beach Resort (☎ 941-394-4100, 800-333-3333, 600 S Collier Blvd)*, the southernmost of the big three, has the best prices and very good services. Though it's not as blow-out swank as the Hilton or the Marriott, it's awfully respectable, with friendly and attentive staff, an enormous pool and a beach that's every bit as good as that of their more expensive neighbors to the north. Ask about their seasons and special offers: they run a year-round supersaver deal for $109 a room without breakfast, but this could change at any second and isn't always available. Otherwise, rooms run from $129 to $359 in summer, $239 to $759 in winter.

The *Marriott Marco Island Resort (☎ 941-394-2511, 800-438-4373, 400 S Collier Blvd)* has 735 rooms, 16 tennis courts and four swimming pools. Rooms range from $189 to $239 in summer, $289 to $349 in winter, suites from $329 to $479 in winter, tower suites $619 in summer, $959 in winter.

The *Marco Island Hilton Beach Resort (☎ 941-394-5000, 800-443-4550, 560 S Collier Ave)* is also expensive, with rooms running from $119 to $169 in summer, $239 to $349 in winter, and suites from $219 to $800 in summer and $389 to $1200 in winter.

Places to Eat

For quick snacks, hit the *Empire Bagel Factory (☎ 941-642-4141, 277 N Collier Ave)*, next to the laundry, with good bagels and sandwiches.

We were thrilled with the cheap and good food and the service at *Taste of Chicago (☎ 941-394-1368, 297 S Collier Ave)*, a family-run place with great breakfasts. Pasta dishes are priced from $6.50 to $8.95, chili is $2.95 ($4.95 with cheddar cheese and a side of spaghetti), and on Wednesday from 11 am to closing, beer-batter fish fry with either grouper or shrimp is served for $8.95, or a combination platter with salad, fries and bread for $10.95.

A good deal is the Sunday brunch at Marriott's *Voyager Restaurant*, from 10 am to 2 pm, with all-you-can-eat everything – omelets to seafood chowder to pancakes to sweets from the ice cream and dessert bar – for $16.95/$8.95 for adults/kids, or $20.95 with champagne.

Vito's Ristorante (☎ 941-394-7722, 1079 Bald Eagle Drive) is a pricey but well-regarded Italian place with fish dishes from $16.95 to $19.95 and pasta from $10.95 to $14.95.

The *Olde Marco Inn (☎ 941-394-3131, 100 Palm St)*, built as the home for the family of Captain William D Collier (not Barron Gift Collier), was the island's first hotel. It's now open as a restaurant, and every visitor to the island comes here at least once. Appetizers range from gulf shrimp to Marco Island stone crab claws or escargot for $8.95. Main courses specialize in seafood: sautéed snapper or grouper is $18.95, and a baked seafood combination of scallops, lobster, shrimp and fish is $25.95. Meat dishes include roast prime rib for $19.95. They also have a huge selection of boozy coffees – Irish to Swiss to Mexican.

Also, all the resorts have at least one restaurant.

Getting There & Away
There's no public transport, so you'll have to drive. It's about 30 miles west of Everglades City, via Hwy 92 off the Tamiami Trail, across the Goodland Bridge over Goodland Bay and up to San Marco Drive. From I-75, take the last Naples exit, and then Hwy 951 west to the island.

Florida Keys

• population 78,000

The string of islands to the south of Miami have held a fascination for visitors since the original Spanish landings in the early 16th century. But where most people head is Key West. About 90 miles north of Havana, Cuba, Key West is the legendary land of Hemingway, sunset celebrations, Jimmy Buffet's *Margaritaville* and Key lime pie.

While divers will have a good time here, and visitors won't regret the trip to Key West, the Florida Keys' reputation as a romantic, untouched, steamy paradise is quite simply slanderous and libelous bilge.

After Juan Ponce de León first sailed around the Keys in 1513 ('key' is the Anglicized version of the Spanish *cayo*, or cay), he was attacked by fierce Calusa Indians at the southwest corner of the state. Today, tourists making their way down the Keys will be attacked with as much vim and vigor by hawkers of everything from T-shirts to sponges, seashells to wind chimes, dive trips to stuff of the 'someone-went-to-blank-and-all-I-got-was-this-lousy-blank' caliber. Keys residents are cynical and weary from watching more than 5 million tourists a year drive too fast, wreck the coral and litter. Outside Key West there aren't a lot of concentrated 'attractions,' and you may have to drive many miles between places of interest. Mostly you'll see billboards and innumerable islands.

But if you gear your expectations realistically, and take the time to unearth what you're after, finding the romantic, quirky and, yes, even sultry side of the Keys is very possible. Key lime pie *is* awesome; Jimmy Buffet *does* serve up a mean margarita; Ernest Hemingway *did* live, work and drink here; and while it's under duress, the coral reef off the Keys is one of the most beautiful and ecologically diverse in the world.

Nowhere else in the world can you wake up in an underwater hotel, snorkel along spectacular reef, see the adorable but endangered Key deer, watch the juggling and acrobatic nonsense of the sunset celebration and finish

Highlights

- Swim with bottle-nosed dolphins
- Have a bowl of conch chowder and a slice of Key lime pie
- Watch the sunset, then spend the night barhopping in Key West
- Spend a night underwater at the unique Jules' Undersea Lodge in Key Largo
- Scuba dive or snorkel around colorful coral reefs and sunken Spanish galleons
- Stand at the southernmost point of the continental USA in Key West
- See rare loggerhead, leatherback and green sea turtles in the Dry Tortugas archipelago
- Help save the coral reef by volunteering with Reef Relief, Key West

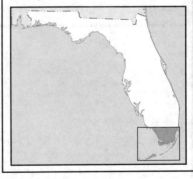

off the evening with a Hemingway Hammer at Sloppy Joe's Bar. And while Conchs – native Key West residents – can be cynical, they're also some of the most fun-loving, quirky, radical reactionary, friendly and downright interesting people you'll come across. Even if they *are* wearing Naugahyde sandals.

Early settlers in the Keys farmed limes, tamarind and breadfruit. The lower Keys saw pineapple farming, and over on Big Pine

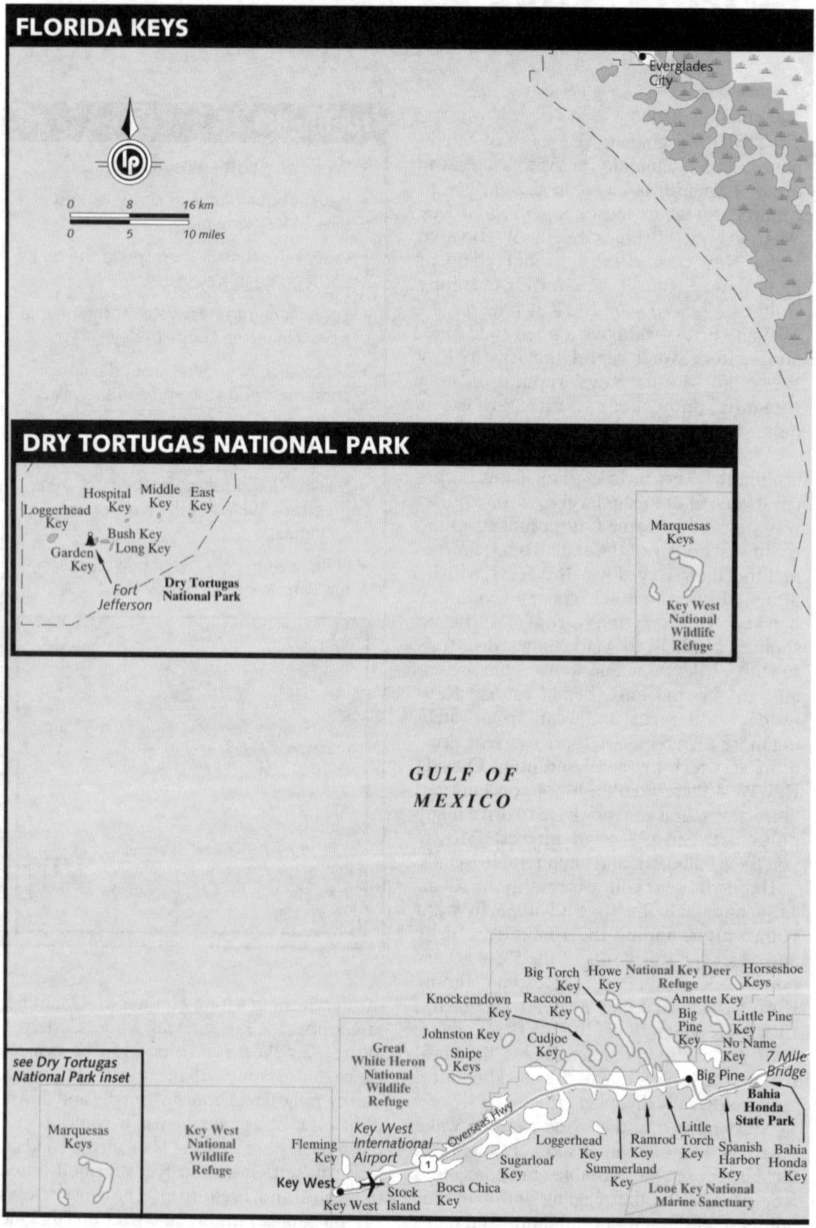

FLORIDA KEYS
Everglades City
0 8 16 km
0 5 10 miles
DRY TORTUGAS NATIONAL PARK
Hospital Key
Middle Key
East Key
Loggerhead Key
Bush Key
Long Key
Garden Key
Fort Jefferson
Dry Tortugas National Park
Marquesas Keys
Key West National Wildlife Refuge
GULF OF MEXICO
Big Torch Key
Howe Key
National Key Deer Refuge
Horseshoe Keys
Knockemdown Key
Raccoon Key
Annette Key
Big Pine Key
Little Pine Key
Johnston Key
Cudjoe Key
No Name Key
Great White Heron National Wildlife Refuge
Snipe Keys
Big Pine
7 Mile Bridge
Bahia Honda State Park
see Dry Tortugas National Park inset
Marquesas Keys
Key West National Wildlife Refuge
Overseas Hwy
1
Key West International Airport
Fleming Key
Loggerhead Key
Ramrod Key
Little Torch Key
Spanish Harbor Key
Bahia Honda Key
Sugarloaf Key
Summerland Key
Key West
Stock Island
Boca Chica Key
Key West
Looe Key National Marine Sanctuary

FLORIDA KEYS

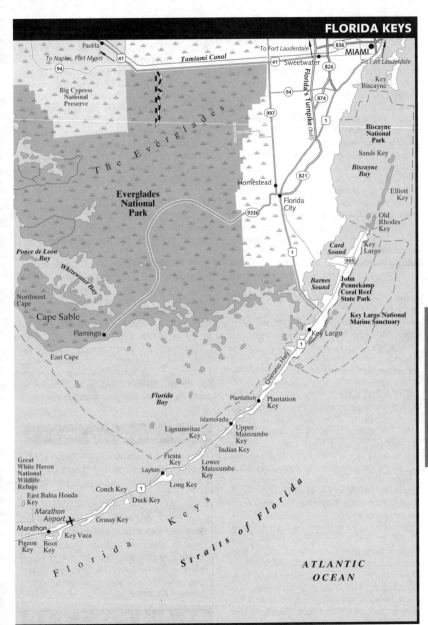

FLORIDA KEYS

Paolita

To Naples, Fort Myers

Tamiami Canal

To Fort Lauderdale

MIAMI

836

To Fort Lauderdale

41

94

Sweetwater

826

Florida's Turnpike (toll)

94

874

Key Biscayne

Big Cypress National Preserve

1

997

Biscayne National Park

Sands Key

Biscayne Bay

Elliott Key

The Everglades

821

Homestead

Everglades National Park

9336

Florida City

1

Old Rhodes Key

Card Sound

Key Largo

905

Ponce de León Bay

Whitewater Bay

Barnes Sound

John Pennekamp Coral Reef State Park

Northwest Cape

Cape Sable

Flamingo

Key Largo National Marine Sanctuary

1

Key Largo

East Cape

Overseas Hwy

Florida Bay

Plantation

Plantation Key

Islamorada

Lignumvitae Key

Upper Matecumbe Key

Indian Key

Fiesta Key

Lower Matecumbe Key

Great White Heron National Wildlife Refuge

Layton

Long Key

East Bahia Honda Key

1

Conch Key

Duck Key

Florida   Keys

Marathon Airport

Grassy Key

Marathon

Pigeon Key

Boot Key

Key Vaca

Straits of Florida

Florida   Keys

ATLANTIC OCEAN

FLORIDA KEYS

Key, locals caught and skinned sharks, salted the hides and prepared them for processing into shagreen leather.

In Key West and Islamorada, the non-farming population found a rather unique way of supporting themselves: they became 'wreckers,' salvaging goods from sinking or sunken ships. But they weren't pirates – they were federally licensed workers who would scavenge wrecks, bringing the cargo into Key West for auction.

Key West also saw sponging, or diving for natural sponges. Today you can still buy them in Mallory Square for a lot of money, but the main sponging industry moved north to Tarpon Springs, now a horrendous tourist trap in its own right, about half an hour north of Clearwater Beach (see the Southwest Florida chapter). However, tourism – especially after Flagler extended his FEC Railway to Key West in the late 19th century (see the History section in the Facts about Florida chapter) – became the Keys' main moneymaker, and remains such to this day.

The keys were battered in 1998 by Hurricanes Mitch and Georges; many campsites and some hotels were demolished. A number of places will not be rebuilt, while others are undergoing the long process now.

ORIENTATION

At the southern tip of the Florida peninsula, the keys sprawl from northeast to southwest, beginning with Key Largo. They're connected by US Hwy 1, also called the Overseas Hwy – a combination of highway and causeways built on the foundations and pilings of the FEC Railway, which was destroyed in 1935. US Hwy 1 is the main road through the Keys, and in many areas the only road.

The Keys are made up of hundreds of tiny islands, of which only about 45 are populated. From north to south, populated keys include Key Largo, Plantation Key, Upper Matecumbe Key, Fiesta Key, Long Key, Conch Key, Duck Key, Grassy Key, Key Vaca, Bahia Honda Key, No Name Key, Big Pine Key, Summerland Key, Sugarloaf Key, Boca Chica Key and Key West.

Addresses in the Keys work on a system of mile markers (MM), which are located along the Overseas Hwy: mile 0 is in Key West at the corner of Fleming and Whitehead Sts, and the final marker, MM 126, is 1 mile south of Florida City. The markers are small green signs at the side of the road, and sometimes addresses are further pinpointed by a 'bayside' (north) or 'oceanside' (south) appendix. While some businesses will give an exact address (a product of a local street number or Overseas Hwy address, as in many other Florida cities), most everyone just quotes and refers to an MM.

DIVING & SNORKELING

The diving and snorkeling opportunities along the Keys are amazing, offering sights ranging from the fantastically colorful fish and coral on the Florida reef to artificial reefs – sunken boats and planes that have been placed off the Florida reef to attract sea life – to actual wrecked ships on the ocean floor. The delicate Florida reef can be damaged by even touching it; see the Fauna section in the Facts about Florida chapter for more information.

There are dive shops on every Key; we list some that have been recommended to us, but there is such a high level of competition for diving business that you'll have no problem finding out your options once you

---

Underwater Camera Rentals

Tropic Isle Dive (☎ 305-289-0303) at MM 52.9 in Marathon rents Nikonos underwater cameras, which range in cost from $25 to $45 per day based on how much stuff you get. They also rent Sony underwater VHS and Hi-8 video cameras for $35 and $45 a day, respectively. You'll need to give them a credit card or cash deposit for the full value of the equipment – the Hi-8 and housing, the most expensive piece of gear available to rent, is worth $1000.

arrive. The reefs are all about 5 miles offshore. In general, you can count on an average of $50 for a two-tank dive including tanks and weights; expect an extra $20 for BC and regulator. Tank rentals themselves cost about $6 to $7 each. Dive shops will negotiate for lower prices in off-seasons, but it's a seller's market at peak times.

Wrecks & Ships

There are a number of popular shipwrecks and boats sunk as part of an artificial reef program. Some of the ships sunk were confiscated drug boats, others include obsolete Coast Guard cutters and commercial vessels. And some of the wrecks include Spanish galleons or their remains. In all cases, any loot that may have been inside has long since been picked clean; doubloons and bags of dope are best sought on dry land.

From south to north, wrecks and ships include the *Thunderbolt* (1986, 115 feet) off Grassy Key; portions of the remains of a Spanish galleon (1733) off Indian Key; the enormous four-decked *Eagle* (1985, 110 feet) on Alligator Reef off Islamorada; and the US Coast Guard cutters *Duane* and *Bibb* (1987, 100 feet and 90 feet – the *Duane* stands upright, the *Bibb* on its side) and the remains of the *Bentwood*, sunk during WWII, all off Key Largo.

Jules' Undersea Lodge (see the Key Largo section later in this chapter) is in the process of constructing the Sunken Temple of Atlantis, a replica of an old Grecian temple, with pottery, a fountain, colonnades (some standing, some tipped over) – you get the idea.

ACCOMMODATIONS

The main concern of anyone coming to the Keys is accommodations; while there are hundreds of hotels, they book up far in advance in peak seasons. Especially in Key West, reservations are essential at all types of accommodations. There are booking agencies throughout the Keys, both chambers of commerce and privately owned booths or concessions. But even at peak periods, accommodation agencies can book you into something, usually at about the

Beaches

The beaches along the Keys are usually very narrow ribbons of white sand lapped by calm waters. Beaches tend to be narrower in winter, due to the tide. There are sandflies on some, and the water is usually very shallow close to shore. We list several of the larger public beaches in the text, but some are noteworthy. The following are good public beaches, most with picnic tables, some with grills and all with toilets:

destination	mile marker
Harry Harris County Park	92.5
Lower Matecumbe Beach	73.5
Anne's Beach	73
Long Key	67.5
Sombrero Beach	50
Little Duck Key Beach	38
Bahia Honda State Park	37

price you ask them for, and while peak-season competition is fierce enough that most places will not lower their quoted price, shop around; some of the agencies will do their best to book you into rooms just a little more expensive than you'd wanted.

State park campgrounds in the Keys accept reservations a year in advance, but even if they tell you on the phone that they're all booked, it pays to check in person, as they always keep a percentage of sites open for walk-up trade.

Prices at practically all Keys accommodations change radically between peak and off-peak periods, and each hotel has its own definition of 'peak.' The difference in price can be literally 100%.

Essentially, in winter you'll pay as much as places can possibly squeeze out of you along the Keys, one of the world's great seller's markets. But for some reason, early winter – up to the third week in December – is still considered off-peak, or at least 'fringe,' at many accommodations. And there are pockets of peak and off-peak periods throughout the year. Expect to pay

FLORIDA KEYS

more from December 20 to March 30, the most expensive period, and the least from August to September. Also, weekday accommodations, especially in Key West, are generally cheaper than weekends. 'Weekends' in the Keys are Thursday to Saturday.

FOOD & DRINK
Drinking is a Keys tradition, and unfortunately, eating takes a back seat to it. Obviously, the big favorite is seafood, and it's available absolutely everywhere; it varies in quality from inedible deep-fried gook to splendid taste sensations. Almost every restaurant in the Keys has a bar attached or outside, and except for Key West, most drinking is done in these – or at resorts and campsites – as opposed to in dedicated bars.

GETTING THERE & AWAY
See the Key West Getting There & Away section for information on the Key West airport. The Keys' other commercial airport, used mainly by business travelers, general aviation and cargo planes, is at Marathon (☎ 305-743-2155), served by US Airways and American Airlines. But it's expensive to fly to Marathon, which is about a two-hour drive from Miami, so most people drive.

By car, there are two options: from Miami take I-95 south to US Hwy 1 and follow that until you can't go any farther – that'd be Key West. A shorter route is to take Florida's Turnpike Extension (toll) south and then pick up US Hwy 1 south at Florida City. See the Key West Getting There & Away section for specific Greyhound buses, shuttle service and air service to/from Key West and the Keys.

GETTING AROUND
Getting around is pretty idiot-proof in the Keys: there's one main road to everything and public transportation options are limited to Greyhound and two airports, of which only one is really used by travelers.

Unless you're staying in one place the entire time you're here, you'll need a car or motorcycle to get around the Keys. Greyhound runs the entire length of US Hwy 1 from Key West to Key Largo three times a

day, but outside of that and the local Key West city buses, there's no public transport, and distances are too far to make bicycling a real option for anyone except experienced riders. You can rent bicycles in most larger Keys, and both bicycles and scooters in Key West. Most major rental companies have offices in Key West, Marathon and Key Largo; see the Getting Around chapter for more information.

KEY WEST
• population 25,000
The capital of the Conch Republic, Key West has a well-earned reputation as a tropical paradise with gorgeous sunsets and sultry nightlife. It's gotten overrun by tourists and its Conchs have become cynical over the years, but if you look carefully, you'll find fleeting images of the Key West of the past: walking through the narrow side streets away from the action along Truman or Duval, you'll see lovely Keys architecture and get a sense of how the locals live – those who aren't there to sell you a T-shirt or book you on a glass-bottom boat ride.

History
The first European settlers in the area were the Spanish, who upon finding the bones unearthed from Indian burial sites named the place *Cayo Hueso* (pronounced 'kah-ya WAY-so') – Bone Island, a name that was later Anglicized into Key West. Bought from a Spaniard by John Simonton in 1821, Key West first saw development as a naval base in 1822, and it was the base for David Porter's Anti-Pirate Squadron, which by 1826 had substantially reduced pirate activity in the region. From then on, Key West's times of boom and bust were closely tied to the military presence here.

The construction of forts at Key West and on the Dry Tortugas brought in men and money, and the island's proximity to the busy and treacherous shipping lanes that had attracted the pirates in the first place created an industry in wrecking – salvaging goods from downed ships.

In the late 1800s, the area became the focus of mass immigration and political activity for Cubans, who were fleeing oppressive conditions under Spanish rule and trying to raise the money and men to form a revolutionary army. Along with them came cigar manufacturers, who turned Key West into the USA's cigar manufacturing center. That would end when workers' demands in Key West became enough to convince several large manufacturers, notably Vicénte Martínez Ybor and Ignacio Haya, to move their operations up to Tampa, in southwest Florida (see the Tampa section in the Southwest Florida chapter for a more complete history).

During the Spanish-American War, Key West may have been the most important staging point for US troops, and the military buildup lasted through WWI. And all of the Keys began to boom when Henry Flagler's Overseas Highway – running over a series of causeways from the mainland to Key West – underwent construction.

In the late 1910s, Key West became a bootlegging center, as people stocked up on booze for the rainy day that Prohibition was to bring.

While the Great Depression, which bankrupted the city, and a hurricane in 1935 ended most people's enthusiasm about Key West (though writer Ernest Hemingway resided here between 1931 and 1940), WWII breathed new life into the place when the naval base once again became an important staging area. And everyone in Washington was happy about that when the Bay of Pigs crisis happened in 1962 (see the History section in the Facts about Florida chapter).

Key West has always been a place where people buck trends. A large society of artists and craftspeople were drawn to the area at the end of the Great Depression by cheap real estate, and that community continues to grow. Gay men have long been welcomed – but the gay community in Key West began to pick up in earnest in the 1970s. Today it's one of the most famous in the country, and if not the largest, it's certainly one of the best organized.

The Conch Republic

Conchs are people who were born and raised in Key West. It's a difficult title to earn; even after seven years of living here you rise only to the rank of 'Freshwater Conch.' And by the way, it's pronounced 'conk' as in 'bonk,' not 'contsh' as in 'paunch.'

You will no doubt hear (and see the flag) of the Conch Republic, and therein lies an interesting tale.

In 1982, the US Border Patrol and US customs came up with a terrific, they thought, way of catching drug smugglers, illegal aliens and various riffraff. They erected a roadblock at Key Largo. As traffic jams and anger mounted, many tourists decided they'd just as soon take the Shark Valley Tram in the Everglades, thanks very much, and disappeared.

Enter a bunch of outraged Conchs, who came up with the brilliant idea of seceding from the USA. They formed the nation of the Conch Republic, whose first act was to secede from the USA, whose second act was to declare war on the USA and whose third act was to surrender and request $1 million in foreign aid.

Every February, Conchs celebrate the anniversary of those heady days with nonstop parties.

KEY WEST

PLACES TO STAY
2 Jabour's Trailer Court
6 Francis St Bottle Inn
18 Coconut Grove
19 Curry House Mansion
28 White St Inn
30 Holiday Inn La Concha
31 Marrero's
36 Pegasus Hotel
42 Big Ruby's Guesthouse
47 Tilton Hotel
48 Gardens Hotel
53 Mahogany House
54 Merlinn Inn
56 Chelsea House
57 Red Rooster
58 Key Lime Village
59 Sea Isle Resort
62 Wicker Guesthouse
64 Conch House Heritage Inn
71 Andrew's Inn
72 Key Lodge Motel
73 Duval Gardens
78 The Rainbow House
79 Spindrift Motel
80 Key West International
    Hostel
81 Marriott Casa Marina
82 Southernmost Point
    Guesthouse
84 Atlantic Shores Resort
85 Santa Maria Motel

PLACES TO EAT
4 Waterfront Market
5 BO's Fish Wagon
9 Planet Hollywood
20 5 Brothers Grocery
    & Sandwich Shop
22 Kelly's
24 Hard Rock Cafe
37 Alexander's Café
38 Island Wellness
41 Mo's Restaurant
44 Dim Sum
46 Le Café de Paris
49 Kyushu Japanese
    Restaurant
50 Camille's
52 Yo Saké
55 Siam House
65 The Deli
77 Banana Café
86 Louie's Backyard

OTHER
1 Conch Train Tour Tickets
3 Schooner Wharf Bar
4 Reef Relief
7 Chamber of Commerce
8 Billie's Bar
10 Key West Aquarium
11 Old Town Trolley Tours
12 Mel Fisher Museum
13 Audubon House
14 Captain Tony's Saloon
15 Rick's, Upstairs at Rick's,
    Durty Harry's
16 Sloppy Joe's Bar

17 Curry Mansion
21 Little White House
23 Jessie Porter's Heritage
    House Museum &
    Robert Frost Cottage
25 Wreckers' Museum/The
    Oldest House
26 Red Barn Theatre
27 Public Library
29 Post Office
32 Key West Business Guild
33 Margaritaville Café
34 Willie T's
35 Ripley's Believe It or Not!
39 Blue Heron Books
40 Bargain Books
43 NationsBank
45 Bourbon St
51 Smok'n Edna's
60 St Mary's Church
61 Donnie's Club 422
63 Momma's Laundry
64 Keys Moped & Scooter
66 Truman Medical Center
67 Moped Hospital
69 Key West Lighthouse
70 Hemingway House
74 Bonsai Diving
75 Treetop Bar at La Te Da
76 L Valladores & Son
83 Scooter Rentals in the
    Southernmost Motel
87 Southernmost Point

FLORIDA KEYS

Curry's
Dock

Gulf
Dock

Mallory
Square

Pier A

Pier B

*GULF OF
MEXICO*

*Submarine
Basin*

Truman
Annex

Front St

Duval St

Whitehead St

Simonton St

Eaton St

Caroline St

Greene St

Thomas St

Emma St

Geraldine St

Covington Ave

Fort St

DeKalb Ave

**Fort Zachary Taylor
State Historic Site**

*Harry S Truman
US Naval
Reservation*

Whitehead
Spit

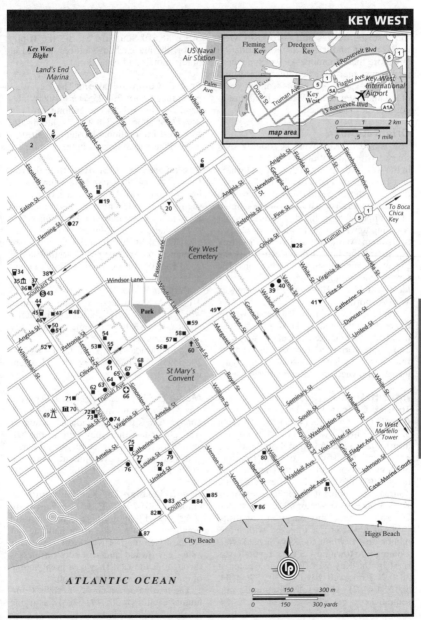

But while it's home to dozens of hotels and hundreds of restaurants and bars geared to all sexual desires and tastes, Key West isn't a resort, and it isn't a 'gay' destination any more than Miami is. 'All welcome' here means just that, and despite cynicism and tourist price gouging, visitors from all walks of life find a stay in Key West to be almost as good as they'd imagined.

Orientation

The island of Key West is roughly oval shaped, with most of the action taking place in the west end. The main drags are Duval St and Truman Ave (US Hwy 1). In the downtown area there's a grid street structure, with street numbers (which are usually painted on lampposts) in a hundred-block format counting upward from Front St (100) down to Truman Ave (900) and so on. Mallory Square, at the far northwestern tip, is the site of the nightly sunset celebrations. The Greyhound station (☎ 305-296-9072) is now located at 3535 S Roosevelt Blvd at the Key West Airport.

There are free tourist maps everywhere; the best is published by the Key West Business Guild (see Gay & Lesbian below), a gay-and-lesbian-oriented business association that has excellent information on gay/lesbian/bi-owned and -friendly businesses.

Information

Tourist Offices The Greater Key West Chamber of Commerce (☎ 305-294-2587, 800-527-8539, http://florida-keys.fl.us/keywcc .htm), 402 Wall St in Old Mallory Square, is an excellent source of information, brochures, maps and advice. They're open daily 8:30 am to 5 pm. The Monroe County Tourist Development Committee's Florida Keys & Key West Visitor's Bureau (☎ 305-296-1552) runs an excellent Website (www.fla-keys.com); it's packed with information on everything the Keys have to offer. Coming into town on US Hwy 1, you'll pass right by the Key West Welcome Center at 3840 N Roosevelt Blvd (☎ 305-296-4444, 800-284-4482), which sells discounted museum tickets.

Money NationsBank's main office is at 1010 Kennedy Drive; there's an Old Town office at 510 Southard St: dig the trippy decor. Private exchange offices abound at hotels, motels and attractions.

Post & Communications The Key West post office (☎ 305-294-2557) is at 400 Whitehead St. Buy prepaid telephone cards in dozens of shops and hotels, including the Key West International Hostel (see Hostels under Places to Stay, later in this section).

Bookstores & Libraries Blue Heron Books (☎ 305-296-3508), 1018 Truman Ave, has a small travel section, a gay studies section and a decent nature section, and they carry the Sunday *New York Times*.

L Valladores and Son (☎ 305-296-5032), 1200 Duval St, has paperbacks, a diverse foreign press and magazine section and a good Key West book section. They're open daily 8 am to 9 pm.

Bargain Books (☎ 305-294-7446), 1028 Truman Ave, is stocked from floor to ceiling with good, used travel guides, gay literature, erotica, tons of fiction, some pornography and magazines.

South Florida's first public library (☎ 305-292-3595), 700 Fleming St, was founded here in 1892.

Media The *Key West Citizen* and *Key West: The Newspaper* are the local rags of record. *Solares Hill* is the local radical newspaper (though far less than they were in the '60s and '70s), focusing on community interest and real estate development. National Public Radio (NPR) is at 91.3.

Gay & Lesbian The Key West Business Guild (☎ 305-294-4603, www.gaykeywestfl .com), 424 Fleming St, is a very helpful organization that, aside from handing out the best free map of Key West, represents many gay-owned and -friendly businesses throughout the city. They're a great source of information on lodging as well.

The newly opened Gay & Lesbian Community Center (☎ 305-292-3223) was trying to set up in a storefront downtown; call for details when you're here.

Smok'n Edna's (☎ 305-294-5995), 705 Duval St, sells smoking supplies along with handing out free and friendly information.

Laundry We went to Momma's Laundry (☎ 305-295-9022) at 517 Truman Ave. Also try Lee's Washhouse (☎ 305-294-3258) at 400 Truman Ave. M&M Coin Laundry at the corner of Virginia and White Sts is another option.

Toilets There are public toilets behind the chamber of commerce, at 402 Wall St. Throughout the rest of the city you're at the mercy of restaurants and hotels, though people are pretty happy to let you go about your business.

Medical Services In an emergency, Florida Keys Health Systems (☎ 305-294-5531, 800-233-3119), at 5900 College Rd on Stock Island, is the place to head; it has a 24-hour emergency room. Expect to pay at least $150 to $200 to be seen. For other illnesses, Truman Medical Center (☎ 305-296-4399), 540 Truman Ave between Simonton and Duval Sts, is a clinic open Monday to Friday 9 am to 4 pm, Saturday 9:30 to 11:30 am, closed Sunday.

Emergency The Key West Visitor Assistance Program (☎ 800-771-5397) is a 24-hour, multilingual switchboard that puts travelers in touch with the appropriate authorities in any kind of emergency – from passport loss to rape to hotel complaints.

Mallory Square

The site of Key West's famous nightly sunset celebrations, Mallory Square is a cobble-stoned area at the northwestern end of town. The celebration is unique and uniquely Key West, featuring jugglers, acrobats, bed-of-nails-lying-downers, and a generally carnival-like atmosphere designed, it would seem, to get as many people in the proximity of bars, restaurants, tourist-trinket shops and sidewalk stalls as possible.

But despite our obvious cynicism, the event *is* a fascinating thing – once. It takes place on Mallory Dock, on the other side of the parking lot by the water. Show up about an hour beforehand to get the full effect.

The saving graces of Mallory Dock's sunset celebration include Parrot Bill, whose well-trained and well-treated parrots delight young and old with tricks like flipping the bird (it's what it sounds like, but don't flip them back).

Mallory Square is also home to the excellent chamber of commerce, an aquarium and the Shipwreck Historeum (see Wreckers' Museums later).

Key West Aquarium

This aquarium (☎ 305-296-2051), on Mallory Square, 1 Whitehead St, has been here since 1932, and though its age shows, the friendly and helpful staff make up for it, and besides, kids always have fun in aquariums. They have touch tanks with starfish, conchs, sea cucumbers and other interesting things and lots of fish tanks filled with catfish, doctorfish, snappers, angelfish and more. Outside are the tanks for barracudas, sharks and sawfish; there are also turtles. They sometimes bring around live sharks for visitors to touch as part of their 'Pet a Shark' program. Signs are well done and staff members are happy to answer your questions. It's open daily 10 am to 6 pm, and there are tours at 11 am and 1, 3 and 4:30 pm. Tours take about 40 minutes and are included in the admission price, which is $8 for adults, $4 for kids four to 12. Tickets are valid for two days.

Hemingway House

This is, to us, one of Key West's great attractions. From 1931 to 1940, Hemingway lived in this lovely Spanish-Colonial house (☎ 305-294-1575) at 907 Whitehead St. It was here that he wrote *The Short Happy Life of Francis Macomber*, *A Farewell to Arms*, *Death in the Afternoon* and *To Have and Have Not*, and where he began *For Whom the Bell Tolls*. It was here, in the garden, that Hemingway installed Key West's first saltwater swimming pool: a

Ernest Hemingway

construction that set him back so much that he pressed 'my last penny' into the cement on the pool's deck. It's still there today.

Also note the Hemingway cats who rule the house and grounds – the brood features six toes.

Hemingway kept ownership of the house until his death in 1961. The house is open daily 9 am to 5 pm. Tours depart every 15 minutes and last about 30 minutes. Admission is $6.50 for adults, $5.50 for students, $4 for children.

Key West Cemetery
This is one of the more enjoyable cemeteries in the country for the odd characters buried here – tombstone epitaphs include 'I told you I was sick' and 'At least I know where he is sleeping tonight.' Guided tours are available on Saturday and Sunday at 10 am and 4 pm at the sexton's office (☎ 305-292-6829) at the Margaret St entrance; the cost of the tour is $5 for adults, $1 for children.

Curry Mansion
This 100-year-old Victorian mansion (☎ 305-294-5349), 511 Caroline St, was built by Milton Curry, one of Florida's first millionaires; it now functions as a guesthouse. On most days you can take a self-guided tour of the antique-packed rooms for $5 for adults,

$1 for children. If you're impressed enough by what you see to want to stay, rooms range from $125 to $225 a night in low season, $160 to $275 in high season. Note that the Curry Mansion is not the Curry House Mansion, Key West's oldest exclusively gay male guesthouse (see Places to Stay later in the chapter).

Wreckers' Museums
There are two museums dedicated to study of the wreckers. The **Wreckers' Museum/the Oldest House** (☎ 305-294-9502), 322 Duval St, was the home of Francis B Watlington. It's filled with period antiques and has enjoyable, volunteer-led tours. It's open daily 10 am to 4 pm (to 5 pm on Thursday); admission is $4 for adults, 50¢ for children.

More expensive and more interesting is the **Key West Shipwreck Historeum** (☎ 305-292-8990), 1 Whitehead St, which has a narrated film portraying the lives and times of the wreckers. Knowledgeable volunteers explain how Key West developed as a port. It's open daily 9:45 am to 4:45 pm; admission is $7 for adults, $3.50 for kids four to 12.

Ripley's Believe It or Not!
Ripley's Believe It or Not! is a chain of museums that has a good branch in Key West (☎ 305-293-9694), 527 Duval St. See the St Augustine section of the Northeast Florida chapter for a full description of Ripley's and Ripley himself. The 'believe it or not' part is up to you. Even if the answer's 'not,' it still may be worth the admission price, and you can easily spend an hour here. This one has a cool exhibit where you can see a mold of an actress' bum – we argued over whether it was Monroe or Mansfield. They totally do the place up to the nines during the month of October for Halloween. It's open daily 9 am to 11 pm; admission is $9.95 for adults, $6.95 for seniors and children five to 12 (under five are free).

Southernmost Point
This is, after all, the southernmost point in the continental USA, and there's a marker here at the corner of South and Whitehead

Sts, along with some street performers and many photo-seeking tourists. There's a shell salesman who sets up shop here.

Jessie Porter's Heritage House Museum & Robert Frost Cottage

A Caribbean-Colonial house, Jessie Porter's Heritage House Museum & Robert Frost Cottage (☎ 305-296-3573), 410 Caroline St, has the original furnishings and antiques of a Key West family who lived here. In the flower garden they play spoken-word recordings of Robert Frost's poetry. There are guided tours Monday to Saturday 10 am to 5 pm, Sunday 1 to 5 pm. Admission is $6 for adults, $5 for seniors, $3 for students and free for children under 12.

Key West Lighthouse

The Key West Lighthouse (☎ 305-294-0012) is a still-functioning lighthouse at 938 Whitehead St. Whitehead St? Yes. It may be farther inland than people might expect, but there are a couple of reasons for that. First, the navy filled in about 2000 yards between here and Fort Taylor. Second, the placement of the lighthouse isn't all that important when you consider that it's at the high point (10 feet above sea level) on a flat island in the middle of the ocean. Lighthouses are designed so that boats know that if they're lined up with the lighthouse's red lens, they're in trouble, so sometimes lighthouses end up in what may appear to be strange places.

The lighthouse has a third-order lens, but it also has a first-order lens that you can walk into (for an explanation of lighthouse lenses, see the Cape Florida Lighthouse section under Key Biscayne in the Miami chapter), and you can also climb the 88 steps to the top. Next door is the interesting lighthouse keeper's house. It's open daily 9:30 am to 4:30 pm; admission is $6 for adults, $2 for kids over seven.

Audubon House

This lovely house (☎ 305-294-2116), 205 Whitehead St, was built in the early 19th century by ship's carpenters for the Captain John H Geiger family, who lived here for about 120 years. In 1958 Colonel Mitchell Wolfson bought it and had it restored as a public museum (this was the first building to be restored in Key West). It was named after John James Audubon, who visited and painted in the garden in 1832 (the house hadn't yet been built).

You can wander through the house by yourself or, if you ask for it, get a free half-hour guided tour through the different rooms, which are filled with authentic 19th-century Key West furniture and many of Audubon's lithographs. The tropical gardens are especially nice, filled with many different kinds of beautiful flowers and other lush vegetation, such as birds of paradise, star fruit trees, fishtail fern and palms, hibiscus and jasmine (the list could go on and on). It's open daily 9:30 am to 5 pm; admission is $7.50 for adults, $3.50 for kids six to 12.

Mel Fisher Museum

The Mel Fisher Maritime Heritage Society Museum (☎ 305-294-2633), 200 Greene St, exhibits the galleon treasures of the Santa Margarita and the Atocha, discovered by the late Mel Fisher in 1980-85 (he started his search for these galleons in 1969). The various jewels, tools, coins and navigational pieces are displayed on the ground floor, along with a world map showing the routes of those ships and some hands-on stuff (touch an item that you can't see and figure out what it is). On the 2nd floor you'll find displays of modern diving techniques, an electrolysis tank and the like. Mel, whose motto was 'Today's the day,' could be seen walking through the museum until months before his death in 1998. It's open Wednesday to Monday 9:30 am to 5 pm and Tuesday 9 am to 5 pm; admission is $6.50 for adults, $4 for students and $2 for kids six to 12.

Little White House

This museum (☎ 305-294-9911) used to be the vacation house of President Harry S Truman. You can go through it only on a half-guided tour, not by yourself. You'll see Truman's piano, a lot of original furnishings and a 15-minute video about Truman's life. It's located in the Harry S Truman Annex (in which you can wander around by yourself) at 111 Front St, and it's open daily 9 am to 5 pm. Admission is $7 for adults, $3.50 for children.

East Martello Tower

The East Tower (☎ 305-296-3913), 3501 S Roosevelt Blvd (across from Key West Airport), houses an art gallery and an interesting museum of Key West history. You can climb the citadel in the central tower (all 48 steps) to a watchtower that affords a horrible view of the airport and a totally unimpressive view of the beach. But inside the tower are insane metal sculptures, which were originally stored here for lack of space elsewhere, that have turned into an attraction in and of themselves. Sure are better than the view. It's open daily, except Christmas, 9:30 am to 5 pm. Admission is $6 for adults, $2 for kids.

West Martello Tower

At Atlantic Blvd and White St, the West Martello Tower (☎ 305-294-3210) exhibits local plant life from the Key West Garden Club, which has its headquarters here. There are all sorts of tropical plants (sales are twice a year, usually in April and in the larger fair during November, call for details) and occasional flower shows. It's open to the public (admission free) 9:30 am to 3 pm Monday to Saturday – though the receptionist left after the last hurricane and it's staffed by volunteers, so the hours are a little shaky.

Fort Zachary Taylor State Historic Site

Fort Zachary Taylor (☎ 305-292-6713), at the southwestern end of the island, was in operation from 1845 to 1866. It defended against blockade-running Union ships during the Civil War. Today it's open as a state historic site and park, with showers and picnic tables and a beach – the deepest, clearest water on the island – great for swimming. It's open daily 9 am to 5 pm, with ranger-led tours at noon and 2 pm. Admission is $3.75 per vehicle, $1.50 for pedestrians.

Beaches

There are three city beaches on the southern side of the island; all of them are narrow, and the water is very calm and clear. **City Beach** is at the end of South and Duval Sts. **Higgs Beach**, at the end of Reynolds St and Casa Marina Court, has barbecue grills and picnic tables, and **Smathers Beach**, farther east off S Roosevelt Blvd, is more popular with the vroom crowd of jet skiers and parasailers. There is also an excellent beach at Fort Zachary Taylor State Historic Site (see above).

Diving & Snorkeling

The dive opportunities in Key West aren't as plentiful as in some of the more northern Keys, but they are definitely here. Because of pollution and activity, there's no snorkeling to speak of on Key West beaches. Most of the Key West dive companies take you west, to sites including Cottrell, Barracuda, Boca Grande, Woman, Sand, Rock and Marquesas Keys. In some of the dive sites – especially around the Marquesas – nondivers can go along and snorkel. Don't touch the coral.

The best opportunities for diving (and the skill levels required to dive them) include the following:

Cayman Salvage Master (advanced) – from 67 to 90 feet; a coral- and plant-covered fish farm

Eastern Dry Rocks (beginner) – 20 to 25 feet; there's snorkeling here too

Joe's Tug (intermediate) – a submerged tugboat, at a depth of about 65 feet

Western Dry Rocks (beginner) – massive coral and mounds of brain

Dive Companies Dive companies set up at kiosks around Mallory Square and other places in town, notably the corner of Truman and Duval Sts, to hawk to customers. Shop around carefully as prices vary greatly.

Captain Billy Dean's Diving (☎ 305-294-7177, 800-873-4837) is at MM 4.5. He's said to be the high-tech diving guru around here. Subtropic Dive Center (☎ 305-296-9914), 1605 N Roosevelt Blvd, specializes in reef dives. Bonsai Diving (☎ 305-294-2921, 305-296-6301), 1075 Duval St, and Dive Key

West (☎ 305-296-3823), 3128 N Roosevelt Blvd are other well-established dive shops here.

Reef Relief At the end of William St in the same building as the Waterfront Market (see Places to Eat later in this section), Reef Relief (☎ 305-294-3100, www.reefrelief .org), is a nonprofit organization that maintains a network of anchoring buoys along the Keys. The idea is that if boaters have an alternate anchoring spot, they won't lower their anchors onto the coral, thus damaging it. The buoys are free to all. Experienced divers who are interested in volunteering to clean the buoys, which is frequently necessary, should contact Reef Relief.

Inside Reef Relief's headquarters, you can see free exhibits on coral and the Florida reef system, and get detailed ecological information from the volunteers and staff.

Organized Tours
Old Town Trolley Tours (☎ 305-296-6688) narrated tram tours start at Mallory Square and make a large, lazy circle around the city with stops including Key West Handprint Fabrics, Angela St Depot, Trolley Barn, the Key West Welcome Center, East Martello Tower and the Southernmost Point. The cost is $16 for adults, $7 for children for one full circle from any point on the route (you can get off and back on, going in the same direction, for one rotation only), and it includes 50¢ per ticket off admission to the Hemingway House. The trolleys depart every half hour between 9:30 am and 6 pm.

The Conch Train Tour (☎ 305-294-5161) is pretty much the same thing, run by the same parent company as the Old Town Trolley Tours. Trams leave every 20 minutes in high season, every half hour in low season, between 9 am and 4:30 pm. The cost is $15 for adults, $7 for kids.

The friendly people at Mosquito Coast Island Outfitters & Kayak Guides (☎ 305-294-7178), 1107 Duval St, offer four- to five-hour near-shore natural history tours to Geiger and Sugarloaf Keys. You show up at their office at 8:45 am and they drive you to either Geiger or Sugarloaf, where you

paddle. The $45 cost includes snorkel equipment, snacks, bottled water and the guide – nice, friendly folks.

Also, Lloyd's Key West Nature Bike Tour (☎ 305-294-1882) runs several different island tours at a range of prices.

Places to Stay
Key West is packed with rooms of all sorts, and picking one can take a bit of planning. The basic categories are motels and hotels, B&B/guesthouses and gay/lesbian guesthouses. There is also the Key West International Hostel, and one campground in Key West itself. If you want the more authentic Key West experience, however, book a room in one of the city's dozens of B&Bs.

There are a number of exclusively gay and lesbian guesthouses, but traditionally all of the city's guesthouses are very welcoming to gay and lesbian couples – hey, it's Key West.

Except for the hostel, count on spending a rock bottom of $45 in low season and $60 in high season, despite what rack rates may be listed here. The room rates in all non-hostel accommodations are totally negotiable, and as changeable as the crowds on the day you arrive. One hotel booker told us that he pushes the price to the absolute limit of what the market will bear – a hotel room that rents for $120 on Saturday may be blown out for as low as $50 on Sunday. And as a rule, prices dip by at least 40% in summer.

Accommodation Agencies The chamber of commerce (as in some chambers on other Keys) has a booking desk. The agencies in the chambers are as honest as the day is long, though don't expect them to go out of their way to find hotels that are not chamber members. The chamber will try to book a room in your price range, but if you've ever told a real estate agent that your absolute limit is X, you know how quickly X can become Y.

Agencies in booths on street corners advertise great bargains that may or may not exist. As in any city, when dealing with an agency, try not to pay until you've seen the room.

Camping Just outside Key West, *Boyd's Key West Campground* (☎ 305-294-1465, 6401 Maloney Ave) on Stock Island (turn south at MM 5), has tent sites for $36, plus an additional $10 for electricity and water; waterfront sites are $43. Prices drop $5 in summer. There's a bus stop right there.

Just past Boca Chica Key and also accessible by bus is the *Geiger Key Marina* with sites for $30 in winter, 'less' in summer. It's at MM 10.5 and finding it is a little tricky: turn east past the Circle K onto Hwy 941 and left onto Geiger Rd.

Jabour's Trailer Court (☎ 305-294-5723, 223 Elizabeth St), just east of the Key West Bight at the northern end of Elizabeth St, is the only campground actually in Key West; they have tent sites in summer/winter from $35 to $40/$40 to $48. They also rent rooms, with TV and air conditioning but no telephones, and some with shared bathrooms, in summer/winter for $60 to $75/$90 to $105; mobile homes that sleep four to six people cost $100 to $150/$140 to $200.

Hostels The *Key West International Hostel* (☎ 305-296-5719, 718 South St) has dorm beds for $17/20 (tax and sheets included) for members/nonmembers; private rooms are $50 in low season, $75 to $100 in high season. They have a communal kitchen where you can cook your own food, or buy their $2 breakfasts or $2 to $3 dinners. Alcohol is prohibited. A taxi between here and the Greyhound station is $7 per person – so get off at the downtown Key West stop (at Caroline and Grinnell Sts) and then take a taxi for $3.50 per carload.

Motels & Hotels Chain hotels are represented by *Ramada* (☎ 305-294-5541), *Best Western* (two locations: ☎ 305-294-3763 and 305-296-3500), *Days Inn* (☎ 305-294-3742), *Econo Lodge* (☎ 305-294-5511), a rather dreary *Holiday Inn La Concha* (☎ 305-296-2991) and *Howard Johnson* (☎ 305-296-6595). *Marriott* (☎ 305-296-5700) also has a resort (see below).

Key Lime Village (☎ 305-294-6222, 800-201-6222, 727 Truman Ave) has friendly management and, before Georges, nice little

cottages with shared baths. They had been completely ripped apart and were being rebuilt when we visited – last time prices started at $32/$60 in summer/winter.

The *Tilton Hotel* (☎ 305-294-8697, 511 Angela St) has air conditioned rooms on the simple side, with shared bath and TV; some also have a small fridge. Room rates range from $55 to $90; weekly rentals are $225 and up. One of the rooms does have a private bath, but you need to reserve it specifically. There's a washer and dryer, a barbecue grill and free off-street parking.

The perfectly located and clean and friendly *Pegasus Hotel* (☎ 305-294-9323, 800-397-8148, 501 Southard St) has rooms in summer/winter for $79 to $119/$125 to $205; most rooms have only showers. There's a nice rooftop pool and Jacuzzi.

The *Spindrift Motel* (☎ 305-296-3432, 212 Simonton St), is a perfectly average motel with rooms in summer/winter from $59 to $89/$89 to $129.

The clean *Santa Maria Motel* (☎ 305-296-5678, 800-821-5397, 1401 Simonton St at South St) has a nice pool and was recently taken over by Marriott. Rooms run $59 to $69/$165 to $195 in summer/winter.

The *Key Lodge Motel* (☎ 305-296-9915, 800-458-1296, 1004 Duval St) has large, clean rooms, all with fridges, some with kitchens. In low season, they're from $75 to $93 on weekdays, $85 to $103 on weekends; in high season, they're $145 to $168 every day. There's a heated pool and free off-street parking. Coffee is served in the morning but not breakfast.

The *Marriott Casa Marina* (☎ 305-296-3535, 800-228 9290, 1500 Reynolds St), next to Higgs Beach, is a resort with the largest private beach on the island. As we went to press, prices in summer were $149 including a full American breakfast, but ownership as of October 1999 was to change to Windham Hotels and prices after that were unavailable. The place has two pools, a Jacuzzi, a sauna, a health club, three lighted tennis courts and two restaurants.

The *Gardens Hotel* (☎ 305-294-2661, 800-526-2664, 526 Angela St) is a pretty spectacular place: the house was formerly Key

West's largest private residence – and the walls around the hotel take up almost an entire city block in the historic district. The gardens are unbelievably lush and there's a kidney-shaped pool. In summer/winter, rooms run from $155 to $215/$245 to $335.

B&Bs The *Merlinn Inn* (☎ 305-296-3336, 811 Simonton St) is set in a beautiful green, secluded garden with a pool and wooden, slightly elevated walkways. The rooms are very airy, light and clean; everything is made from bamboo, rattan and wood. Rooms are $89 to $179, and the tree house (which isn't really in a tree, but is pretty high up) and the wheelchair-accessible tea house are $179 to $239.

Southernmost Point Guesthouse (☎ 305-294-0715, 1327 Duval St), opposite the blah Southernmost Motel, is a gorgeous Victorian house with a nice garden and porch area. Standard rooms are $55/120 in summer/winter, efficiencies are $75/145 and suites are $95/185; continental breakfast is included.

The friendly *Mahogany House* (☎ 305-293-9464, 800-336-0625, 812 Simonton St) is a guesthouse with an efficiency apartment at $69/129 in summer/winter and a one-bedroom apartment with a loft and two futon mattresses (it's large enough to sleep six) for $175/250. Both come with a full kitchen, it's clean and comfortable, and there is a Jacuzzi.

The *Wicker Guesthouse* (☎ 305-296-4275, 800-880-4275, 913 Duval St) is a lovely place – despite its location in the middle of everything – with an excellent pool and secluded garden. They have rooms with shared bath for $65/85 in summer/winter, studios for $95/155 and rooms with private bath for $79/125; they also have suites that sleep four for $95/155. There are tons of wicker and wood furniture, and the continental breakfast – a big one – is served buffet style out in the garden. There's a shared kitchen, and hey, don't stand under the palms when the wind's blowing, okay?

The *Conch House Heritage Inn* (☎ 305-293-0020, 625 Truman Ave) was built in 1875 and has been family owned since 1889. The place is very clean and the people are nice, and while it's gay and lesbian friendly, kids under 12 are a bit iffy. There's a small pool and a nice dining room, and continental breakfast is included. Rooms are $88 to $138 in summer and $128 to $178 in winter.

We really liked the *Frances St Bottle Inn* (☎ 305-294-8530, 800-294-8530, 535 Frances St). It is gay friendly and the staff make you feel at home. Rooms are $80 to $120/$135 to $155 in summer/winter, and they are very comfortable. The cheap rooms have the bath across the hall, and the private baths have shower only (no tub). There are antique bottles in every room (hence the place's name), and there is a huge porch. They also do a continental breakfast.

These next two defy categorization as either 'gay' or 'straight,' since the majority of guests on any given day may be gay or straight. Both are charming places, though the *Chelsea House* (☎ 305-296-2211, 800-845-8859, 707 Truman Ave), is the nicer of the two; it was built in 1870. Rooms, with TV, air conditioning, fridge and bath, cost $75 to $165 in summer, $95 to $205 in fringe seasons and $115 to $270 in winter. Breakfast includes fruit, cereal, muffins, bread and oranges (squeeze your own juice). The atmosphere is sort of like a college dorm in a Victorian mansion; there's lots of free parking, and cute brick paths lead to the small pool out back. It's an all-welcome place, with a clothing-optional sun deck, and Professor, the cat, reigns supreme over the paperback-book library.

Next door, the *Red Rooster* (☎ 305-296-6558, 800-845-0825, 709 Truman Ave) is a gay-staffed place with a very nice coffee bar downstairs and classical music piped throughout. It was more famous in its last incarnation – a notorious brothel whose wanton activities forced the nuns at St Mary's Church, across the street, to shade the windows to prevent students from peering across. It's been renovated and cleaned up, though a little of the former atmosphere remains. It has a very friendly staff, and a really nice side garden. Rooms are $69 to $109/$120 to $155 in summer/winter.

FLORIDA KEYS

Duval Gardens (☎ 305-292-3379, 800-867-1234, 1012 Duval St) has rooms with queen-size beds for $85/125 in summer/winter, efficiencies or a junior suite with living room and French doors for $99/149 and one-bedroom suites for $125/184. It has wicker and rattan furniture, a Jacuzzi and a sun deck. There's no pool but rates include a membership card for a private beach club with a pool and a health club. It's run by a very helpful couple, and breakfast is quite elaborate: it starts out with a buffet of pastries, fruit, coffee and juices, followed by different hot dishes, such as banana and syrup pancakes or toasted English muffins topped with tomato, bacon, egg and Hollandaise sauce. Parking is available, and there is a free cocktail hour around sunset.

White St Inn (☎ 305-295-9599, 800-207-9767, 905-907 White St) features beautiful gardens and a pool; rooms range from $85 to $120/ $130 to $200 in summer/winter. Continental breakfast is included. Try for a room not facing White St.

Andrew's Inn (☎ 305-294-7730, Zero Walton Lane) is another place with a beautiful backyard, a pool and a delightful tropical feel. Rooms with a queen-size bed are $115/165 in summer/winter; with king-size beds they are $125/175. Some have decks. Basically, each room has its own cat that hangs out, and a breakfast buffet is included, as are evening cocktails.

Gay Accommodations You will notice a dearth of women-only places – though there's a good one in the Rainbow House – but don't despair: many of the smaller gay guesthouses are lesbian friendly. When you arrive contact the Business Guild (☎ 305-294-4603) to see if any more have opened.

Coconut Grove (☎ 305-296-5107, 800-262-6055, 817 Fleming St) is a friendly gay place with rooms in summer/winter from $75 to $140/$99 to $210. They have a rooftop sun deck and a clothing-optional pool and Jacuzzi. All the rooms have fridges, and breakfast is a light continental affair – mainly cereal, fruit and coffee cake.

The very clean, Art Deco-ish *Atlantic Shores Resort* (☎ 305-296-2491, 800-526-3559,

510 South St) defies categorization: all are welcome. It's very popular with gay men, lesbians and Europeans and has a clothing-optional pool. Rooms range from $80 to $120/$120 to $180 in summer/winter. Apparently, lesbians like it here a lot.

The Rainbow House (☎ 305-292-1450, 800-749-6696, 525 United St) is exclusively for women – gay or straight. It's a very nice place with excellent staff, bleached wood furniture and two sundecks – one with a heated pool, the other with a hot tub. Rooms, including a continental breakfast, are $69 to $149 in summer, $109 to $229 in winter.

Key West's oldest exclusively gay male guesthouse, *Curry House Mansion* (☎ 305-294-6777, 800-633-7439, 806 Fleming St) – not to be confused with the Curry Mansion mentioned earlier – is in a cool 100-year-old, Victorian-style, three-story mansion. Rooms in summer/winter are $85 to $105/$130 to $160; some have shared bath. They do a full hot breakfast and have a happy hour daily 4 to 6 pm (except Sunday); there's a clothing-optional pool and Jacuzzi.

Big Ruby's Guesthouse (☎ 305-296-2323, 409 Appelrouth Lane), off Duval between Southard and Fleming, is a clean, slick place in an *Architectural Digest* sort of way; they have a nice tropical pool area. Rooms are $85 to $230 in summer, $145 to $320 in winter, $120 to $250 in fringe.

Marrero's (☎ 305-294-6977, 800-459-6212, 410 Fleming St) is an interesting place: it's in the (possibly haunted) mansion formerly owned by a cigar manufacturer. Some of the rooms are very large (if a little old) and some have kitchens; they range from $85 to $160 in summer, $100 to $180 in winter.

The *Sea Isle Resort* (☎ 305-294-5188, 800-995-4786, 915 Windsor Lane) is very clean and pleasant, with split rattan furniture, tiled floors and small fridges. Most of the rooms have showers only (three have bathtubs), and they always put a flower on your pillow in the evening. Rooms with queen-size beds are $85/140 in summer/winter, with king-size beds they are $95/150, with two queens (no pun intended) $100/140, poolside suites with kitchen $115/180; all rooms include continental breakfast. The entire place is clothing optional (a wood fence gives privacy), though you're asked to wear something at breakfast. An elevated wood deck overlooks the pool. Though it's 98% gay, it's not exclusively so.

Places to Eat
The cuisine of Key West has a good reputation that's undeserved – food has always taken a backseat to drink here, and there are only a few amazing culinary delights to be had without spending an awfully large sum of money. But most of the restaurants here offer reliably good food, fresh seafood and decent portions. It's not the best, but it's certainly not bad either. And it's interesting that a good percentage of the seafood comes from somewhere other than the Keys – that 'local' catch may be from the clear blue waters off Brooklyn.

Breakfast is an important meal here – probably as a hangover helper – and portions are large and full of grease. Lunch is an afterthought.

The problem, of course, is that many places cater to tourists, who can't really complain. The idea, therefore, is to find the few places left that cater to Conchs. It is in these eateries that Key West's charm, and that elusive Key West cuisine – spicy seafood, Italian- and Spanish-influenced cooking and tropical-themed side dishes and desserts – comes through loud and clear.

Don't miss Key lime pie, a sort of lime meringue made with Key limes, which are more lemony than standard-issue limes. There's such controversy over where the 'best' Key lime pie and conch chowder is to be found that we're copping out of it entirely: we have our favorites, but committing an opinion to paper about these sacred Conch subjects is dangerous – and we want to be alive to work on the next edition. OK, our favorite pie is at The Deli (see below), but that's all we're saying.

Breakfast The *Waterfront Market* (☎ 305-296-0778, 201 William St), next to Schooner Wharf Bar, isn't just a breakfast place – it's open most of the day and night – but it's a good spot for a bagel and coffee. It's also great for sandwiches, organic produce and health foods. They've got a juice bar and sell wine and beer. Outside the market is the Wyland Wall, a poor undersea mural.

Camille's (☎ 305-296-4811, 703½ Duval St) is an islander favorite that's been around forever; it does breakfast (eggs $2 to $6.95, omelets $3.75 to $6), lunch (specials from $7.95) and daily dinner specials that run the gamut from $7.95 to $15.95. There's good, friendly service here.

Banana Café (☎ 305-294-7227, 1211 Duval St) seems to know what it's doing: for breakfast, three scrambled eggs with vegetables, cheese and toast is $6.50; at lunch crêpes range from $4 to $7, and at dinner, steamed salmon is $19 and beef tenderloin is $20. There's live jazz on Thursday night.

Lunch & Snacks A local favorite, *5 Brothers Grocery & Sandwich Shop* (☎ 305-296-5205, 930 Southard St), is a Cuban market that does great sandwiches such as the 'midnite' ($2.55), Cuban ($2.80) and pork ($3.35). Hamburgers/cheeseburgers are $1.80/2.05, a large café con leche is $1.75, and on Friday they have conch chowder ($2.75).

If you can get past the criminally negligent service, *Baby's Place* (☎ 305-296-3739, 1111 Duval St) has lots of varieties of great premises-brewed coffee ($1.25), espresso and cappuccino ($2.25 to $2.75). They also have pastries and bagels and stuff, but we stormed out before getting the prices.

Le Café de Paris (629 Duval St) near Angela St, is a good sandwich stand. And vegetarians will appreciate *Island Wellness* (☎ 305-296-7353, 530 Simonton St), a kind of juice-bar-veggie-food-aromatherapy-holistic-massage-trapeze kind of place – *you* know. Anyway, they serve very good veggie and tofu-burger platters for $5 to $6.75, steamed veggie platters for $6.75 and black beans and brown rice for $5.25.

Alexander's Café (☎ 305-294-5777, 509 Southard St) is a very comfortable place with friendly service and reasonable prices. They've got a good range of Italian food including pizza ($11 for a 16-inch pie),

Key Lime Pie Recipe, or How to Start an Argument in the Conch Republic

No person who considers him- or herself a true Conch (Key West native) would ever give out their secret recipe for Key lime pie, but Kim Dyer went to an awful lot of trouble to compile *all* the recipes she could find and publish them (believe it or not) in a FAQ on an Internet newsgroup for Jimmy Buffet fans (alt.fan.jimmy-buffett; for information see the Website at www.geocities.com/TheTropics/Cabana/3239/index.htm). Thanks, Kim!

We've gone with simple, basic 'Key Lime Pie: Variant No 1.'

9-inch pie crust:

1 cup flour (Wondra if possible)
1/2 tsp salt
1/3 cup and 1 tbsp shortening
3 tbsp cold water

Combine flour, salt and shortening together, then, while still mixing, add water. Roll out dough onto a floured board and bake in a pie pan in a preheated 375°F oven for 10 minutes, or until lightly brown.

Filling:

1 1/2 cups sugar
Juice from 1 1/2 Key limes*
Grated skin of one lime
3 eggs
2 tbsp corn starch
2 tbsp flour
2 cups milk (yes, milk)
1 tbsp butter

Combine all this and then cook in a double boiler – not on direct heat or it will burn – and stir until thickened, about 20 to 25 minutes.

Meringue:

5 tbsp sugar
1 tbsp corn starch
1/2 cup water
3 egg whites
1/2 tsp cream of tartar

Combine 2 tbsp sugar, corn starch and water. Cook on direct heat until it thickens and becomes clear. Set aside. Combine the egg whites with the 3 tbsp sugar and 1/2 tsp cream of tartar and mix with an electric beater on high until smooth. Add the cooked sugar, water and corn starch and beat the entire mixture until fluffy.

Add filling to the pie crust, then pile on the meringue. Bake at 300°F for 10 minutes, then at 350°F until the meringue browns. Cool and serve.

*If you can't get Key limes, the next best option is to buy some Key lime juice through a company such as Key West Aloe (☎ 305-294-5592) – a 16oz bottle costs $4.20, two for $7.95 (add $5.95 shipping). Failing that, use a mixture that's half lemon juice and half lime juice.

Sunset fishing in the Keys

Nightly sunset celebration in Key West

Giant brain coral, Molasses Reef

Downtown Key West offers lovely architecture and a lively bar scene.

Dry Tortugas National Park, formerly known as Fort Jefferson

Spring Breakers at Smathers Beach in Key West

The historic Sloppy Joe's Bar, former haunt of Ernest Hemingway, is a Key West must-see.

spaghetti and meatballs and fettuccine Alfredo for $10.95.

BO's Fish Wagon (☎ 305-294-9272, 801 Caroline St) does a seriously good fried-fish sandwich for $6.50 or grilled for $8 – yumerooni, folks, and a cool atmosphere.

Don't forget Key West's obligatory **Hard Rock Cafe** (☎ 305-293-0230, 313 Duval St), with standard HRC offerings like good burgers under $10 and ribs for $14.99. Nearby, **Planet Hollywood** has the same offerings in a movie-trivia setting.

In the former home of Pan American Airways, **Kelly's** (☎ 305-293-8484), at the corner of Caroline and Whitehead Sts, is a very cool bar and grill with really nice outdoor tables. From here on October 27, 1927, the first Pan Am flight (001) departed to Havana, Cuba. They have their own brewery with several beers, and good lunch specials. It's owned by actress Kelly McGillis.

Dinner That fabled real local hangout with good food and not so many tourists is **Mo's Restaurant** (☎ 305-296-8955, 1116 White St), where inexpensive and great meals abound. Nothing but well-prepared, great food and good service. It's a little small (let's call it intimate) and you may have to wait a while for a table on weekends.

And speaking of excellent local hangouts, you gotta love **The Deli** (☎ 305-294-1464, 531 Truman Ave). Run by the same family since 1950, it's got really friendly service and extremely well-prepared food. Vegetarians can pile on side dishes such as mashed potatoes, rice and beans, zucchini, carrots and other veggies for $1.20 each, and others can hit the meaty dinner specials ($6.50 to $10.95), prime rib ($16), half a rack of ribs ($4.75) or fish and chips ($6.95). Sandwiches are from $2.25 to $7.50. No alcohol is sold.

We were on the verge of deciding that the **Siam House** (☎ 305-292-0302), at the corner of Simonton and Olivia Sts, wasn't worth a try when a customer told us it was a mistake to leave. He was right – and he didn't even mention the excellent and friendly service. Awesome Thai food, good spring rolls ($2.95), excellent fried rice and

ginger vegetables ($8.95), as well as shrimp dishes ($14.50 to $17.95) that set diners' mouths watering when they were carried out to some lucky patron's table. Only problem was the doughy tempura. It's open every day for dinner, and an all-you-can-eat buffet lunch ($6.95) is served Monday to Saturday 11 am to 3 pm.

The Pan-Asian food at **Dim Sum** (☎ 305-294-6230, 613½ Duval St), down the tiny alley that runs straight back to the Greyhound station, is fantastic, as is the atmosphere – very slick Japanese design, dark and intimate. It's very popular, very small and open only for dinner, so reserve. Try the Indian chicken curry ($16.95), vegetable Pad Thai ($12.95) and Thai whole fish at market price.

Yo Saké (☎ 305-294-2288, 722 Duval St) is our favorite Key West sushi place for its great service and better sushi – though it's on the pricey side (by the piece it's $3.50 to $4.50, rolls from $4.50). At lunch they have several specials with heaps of food for $8.95. The sushi bar seats are pretty uncomfortable; we prefer the traditional Japanese seating outside, off the romantic garden.

Kyushu Japanese Restaurant (☎ 305-294-2995, 921 Truman Ave) is still around, doing $1 a piece sushi from 5 to 8 pm.

Antonia's Restaurant (☎ 305-294-6565, 744 Windsor Lane) was recently gutted by fire, but they plan to reopen. Said to be an excellent restaurant treasured by the locals for birthday parties and other special events, it's a little expensive at about $20 an entree. Check when you're here.

Louie's Backyard (☎ 305-294-1061, 700 Waddell Ave) was started by a Conch in his house and has grown into one of Key West's most popular – if expensive – places. It's a great place for drinks on the deck, and the classic Key West food's not bad either, if you can afford it.

Entertainment
Theater The **Red Barn Theatre** (☎ 305-296-9911, 319 Duval St) is a tiny little playhouse that's been putting on a variety of plays for the past 16 years or so. The last season featured well-known and original shows.

FLORIDA KEYS

The Key West Players (☎ 305-292-3725), at the Waterfront Playhouse at Mallory Dock, is the community theater, putting on plays and musicals for adults and children.

Bars & Live Music More than a couple of people have been known to tip back a few in Key West – in fact, drinking is a Key West institution with a long and illustrious history of lushes from rumrunners (the people, not the drink) to Hemingway. And the tradition is immortalized in Jimmy Buffet's song *Margaritaville*.

Most bars in town have some sort of live music on most nights, and happy hours and drink specials happen all the time. Bars stay open until most people leave, at least until 2 am and sometimes later. The Pub Crawl is another institution here, and bars freaked out when police began enforcing the open-container laws that hindered customers from walking between bars carrying their drinks. Enforcement isn't as gung-ho now, but note that it is illegal to walk with an open container holding an alcoholic drink – even if it's a plastic cup.

For watering holes, most people head for one of a few of places. *Sloppy Joe's Bar* (☎ 305-294-5717, 201 Duval St) is the Hemingway hangout of record, with live entertainment every night; their Hemingway Hammer ($6.50) is made from 151-proof rum, banana and strawberry liqueur, blackberry brandy and a dash of white rum. Drinks and a 'cheeseburger in paradise' can be had at Jimmy Buffet's *Margaritaville Café* (☎ 305-292-1435, 500 Duval St). *Schooner Wharf Bar* (☎ 305-292-9520, 202 Williams St) is a pretty authentic-feeling sailor's bar and a real Conch hangout. It's on the water and a great place for drinks while watching the sunset or grabbing a cruise. Local musicians – playing everything from banjos to reggae – and local entertainers perform nightly.

Rick's (☎ 305-296-4890) – what a meat market! But people seem to really like it, and not just for their Wednesday and Thursday night specials: for $5 (low season) or $7 (high season) you get a wrist band allowing you to drink all you can from 9 to 11:30 pm

(make sure you bring your ID). Then, if you can maneuver the stairs, *Upstairs at Rick's* is a dance club. It all happens at (hic!) 202-208 Duval St.

Billie's Bar (☎ 305-294-9292, 407 Front St) has two bars, both open until 4 am. Their sunset happy hour has draft and domestic beers ($1 to $1.50) and well drinks ($2); they also serve sandwiches for $3.75 to $7 and entrees for $10 to $20.

Willie T's (☎ 305-296-5858, 525 Duval St) has an outdoor garden; inside, it's sort of hippy-ish, but not in an annoying kind of way. *Captain Tony's Saloon* (☎ 305-294-1838, 428 Greene St) has live music almost every night. *Durty Harry's* (☎ 305-296-4890, 208 Duval St) has five bars with live music every day.

Gay & Lesbian Bars Note that the 'straight' section of town begins at the waterfront at Mallory Square and continues to about the 500 block of Duval St. From that point on it's a good, healthy Key West mix of straight and gay.

Gay and lesbian bars change as often as they do in Miami Beach, so beware and check when you're here: publications like Key West Business Guild's map, *Gay West*, *Key West Columbia Fun Map* or *Crooz Control* are available at gay-owned and gay-friendly businesses throughout the city.

Atlantic Shores (☎ 305-296-2491, 510 South St) is a very popular local poolside spot for all-over sunning; there's a small snack bar and grill, the pool and, on Sunday, Tea by the Sea, the largest tea dance in Key West.

Donnie's Club 422 (☎ 305-296-9230, 900 Simonton St) is the only real lesbian club in town.

Bourbon St (☎ 305-296-1992, 730 Duval St) has a happy hour noon to 8 pm daily – the longest on the island – and all-you-can-drink beer 6 to 10 pm on Sunday. They do shows from jazz sax to drag throughout the week. It's a locals' hangout.

The beautifully named *Treetop Bar at La Te Da* (☎ 305-296-6706 x510, 1125 Duval St) also does lots of shows, and lots of locals show up for the happy hour. There are drag shows at midnight a couple of nights a week and live entertainment on weekends.

Shopping
The first order of business is to get yourself a pair of Kino sandals, the classic Key West footwear: Naugahyde sandals that are slippery when wet but cheap – expect to spend about $12 for a pair. There are many styles and colors, and they come in leather as well. If they ever break, bring them in and they'll be repaired.

There are so many opportunities to buy tourist stuff that you won't be able to avoid it. For a nice taste treat, look for Nelly & Joe's Key West Lime Juice salad dressings.

Getting There & Away
Air At the time of this writing – and prices change drastically – one could count on spending from $150 to $180 for a roundtrip flight between Miami and Key West. A direct flight between New York City and Key West can be as low as $284.

American Airlines (☎ 800-433-7300), Gulfstream Air (☎ 305-871-1200, 800-992-8532) and US Airways (☎ 800-428-4322) all have several flights a day (American has the most). Gulfstream, though, consistently has a better range of cheaper tickets than the others.

Flights on Cape Air (☎ 305-352-0714, www.flycapeair.com) run between Key West and Naples, Fort Myers and Fort Lauderdale, all between $90 and $100 each way.

For information on getting to Dry Tortugas National Park, see that section later in this chapter.

Key West International Airport is off S Roosevelt Blvd on the west side of the island.

Bus The Greyhound station (☎ 305-296-9072) is now located at 3535 S Roosevelt Blvd at the Key West Airport. A city bus runs between the airport and Duval and Eaton Sts every 40 minutes or so and costs 75¢. A taxi from the airport to the city will cost about $5.

Greyhound has four buses daily; rides cost $30 one way, $57 roundtrip, with a weekend fare (Friday to Sunday) of $32/60. Look into the buy-one-get-one-free ticket deal, which Greyhound runs occasionally (valid if you buy your ticket three days in advance).

Buses leave Miami's Bayside Station for the 4³/₄-hour trip at 7 am and 12:01 pm (both direct), 6:15 pm (change at the main Miami Airport terminal, arrive in Key West at 11:30 pm) and 11:40 pm (change at Miami Airport Terminal, get in at 5:30 am).

You can take the bus to any destination along the Florida Keys; there are official stops, but just tell the driver where you want to get off and they'll stop. If you're trying to get back to Miami from somewhere in the Keys, note that buses leave Key West at 6:15 am (arrive at 11:10 am, direct), 10 am (change at Miami Airport Terminal, arrive Bayside 3:45 pm), 12:30 pm (arrive Bayside 5:25 pm, direct) and 5:45 pm (arrive Bayside 10:40 pm, direct).

Stand anywhere on the Overseas Highway (US Hwy 1) and when you see the bus in the distance, signal firmly and visibly, using all methods at your disposal – up to and perhaps including a flare gun – and the bus will stop to pick you up. That is, if the driver sees you.

Fares and *approximate* travel times to other keys from Key West include the following (add $1 to all these prices on weekends):

destination	duration	price
Boca Chica	15 minutes	$6
Big Pine	40 minutes	$10
Marathon	1 hour	$12
Islamorada	1 hour 50 minutes	$19
Key Largo	2¹/₂ hours	$26

Shuttle Check with the Clay Hotel and International Hostel (see the Miami & Miami Beach chapter) for information on shuttle services that pop down to the Keys. SuperShuttle (☎ 305-871-2000) will take you from Miami to the Keys for $350 (maximum of 11 people). Your best bet is to put up a sign up at the Clay – if you can gather 11 people, you only pay $32 each.

Car & Motorcycle It's about 160 miles from Miami to Key West along US Hwy 1. Take Florida's Turnpike Extension (toll) south and then pick up US Hwy 1 south at Florida City. Don't be in a hurry; enjoy the view. There are keenly enforced speed limits at various places along the route, speeding fines are high, you'll probably get caught, and should you hit a Key deer while speeding (see the Key Deer boxed text, later in this chapter), penalties are stiff. Slow down.

Getting Around

The City Transit System (☎ 305-292-8200) is two buses that ply the same route. Outbound buses run from Mallory Square to Stock Island, inbound runs the reverse route, each stopping at the airport. Buses run every 15 minutes or so, from 6:05 am to 10:30 pm. You can get printed schedules right on the bus. The fare is 75¢ for adults, 35¢ for seniors and students, who need to get a reduced fare card ($1.50) from the Transportation Department office at 627 Palm Ave.

The best thing to do with a car in Key West is to sell it: parking is murder, parking tickets cost $10, they're quick to tow and traffic is restricted. The city is constructing a public parking lot on Caroline St, but until that's done you're at the mercy of private lots or hotel parking.

You can rent mopeds or scooters at several places on the island, and you don't need a motorcycle license; prices average $15 a day (8 am to 6 pm) or $25 for 24 hours. Try Keys Moped & Scooter (☎ 305-294-0399) at 523 Truman Ave; Scooter Rentals in the Southernmost Motel, 1319 Duval St; or Moped Hospital (☎ 305-296-3344) at 601 Truman Ave. The Key West International Hostel rents bicycles for $4 a day, $6 for 24 hours. Bicycle rentals are also available in lots of places; prices average $7 to $10 a day.

DRY TORTUGAS NATIONAL PARK

The Dry Tortugas (pronounced 'tor-TOO-guzz'), a tiny archipelago of seven islands about 69 miles southwest of Key West, was first 'developed' 300 years after its discovery by Juan Ponce de León. Today it's open as a national park, under the control of the Everglades National Park office (☎ 305-242-7700), and you can get there only by boat or plane.

Ponce de León named the area *Las Tortugas* – 'The Turtles' – for the hawksbill, green, leatherback and loggerhead turtles that roam around the islands, and sailors later changed that to Dry Tortugas for the obvious reason that there's no fresh water here.

The first development consisted of a lighthouse on Garden Key, to warn ships of the rocky shoals around the islands. In 1846, construction began on Fort Jefferson: the USA saw the wisdom in a fortification there to protect and control traffic into the Gulf of Mexico.

A federal garrison during the Civil War, Fort Jefferson was also a prison for Union deserters and for at least four people, among them Dr Samuel Mudd, arrested for complicity in the assassination of Abraham Lincoln.

In 1867, a yellow fever outbreak killed 38 people, and after a hurricane in 1873, the fort was abandoned. It was reopened in 1886 as a quarantine station for those with smallpox and cholera.

The fort was established as a national monument in 1935 by President Roosevelt, and in 1992, George Bush showed great character by signing legislation that changed the name from Fort Jefferson National Monument to Dry Tortugas National Park.

Today the park is open for day trips or overnight camping. On Garden Key you'll see Fort Jefferson, the site of the park's visitors center. There you can pick up information on the entire park, as well as walk around the seawall: information plaques on the seawall describe the wildlife you're likely to encounter both in the moat and in the water around the islands.

The fort's a fascinating place, and the sparkling water offers excellent snorkeling and diving opportunities. Sleeping over is a unique experience: so close to the hubbub of Key West, but blissfully peaceful.

1/1 Hst Frt w/Grt Vws, Trtls, Exc Snrkl & Dvg, No Wtr

How would you like to live in a historic fort on a deserted island? Members of the National Park Service (NPS) do. The nine full-time residents of Fort Jefferson live in apartments within the fort, using the ancient fort's catchment system (yeah, we believe that) and modern desalination devices to make fresh water; diesel-powered generators provide electricity for appliances, satellite dishes, TV/VCRs and stereos. It's a little like working in a far-off embassy to a country we're somewhat on the outs with except for one thing: it's *here*, in a tropical paradise where work is snorkeling and telling other people how to do it.

Competition for the positions – which usually last about two years – is fierce. So fierce, in fact, that the NPS actually gets away with charging the rangers rent to live out here.

The residents get four days shore leave for every four weeks worked, and they travel to and from the civilization of Key West aboard the *Activa*, an NPS boat.

The Islands

The park is made up of seven islands: Garden Key, on which the fort is located, is the only place you can stay overnight. Bush Key is closed to the public from March to September – it's reserved for nesting terns. The remaining keys – East, Middle, Hospital, Long and Loggerhead – are all closed from sunset to sunrise from May to September to protect nesting turtles.

Places to Stay

There are 10 free campsites on Garden Key. They are given out on a first-come, first-served basis, so reserve early by calling the Everglades National Park office (☎ 305-242-7700). Visitors are limited to 30 days per year here, no more than 14 days at a time. There are toilets but no freshwater showers or drinking water; bring everything you'll need (see the Outdoor Activities chapter for some packing suggestions).

Getting There & Away

If you have your own boat, the Dry Tortugas are covered under National Ocean Survey chart No 11438.

The *Yankee Freedom* (☎ 305-294-7009) is a fast ferry that runs between Garden Key and Land's End Marina at the foot of Margaret St in Key West. The roundtrip fare is $95 for adults, $85 for students, seniors and military, and $60 for children under 16.

They'll leave you out there overnight for $109 for adults and $79 for kids, including transport of 100lbs of your gear. Bring your own gear – Cayo Caribe Kayak Outfitters (☎ 305-296-4115, 305-296-3009) rents tents, coolers, cookers etc. The daily journey takes about 2½ hours. Board at the marina at 7:30 am (the ferry leaves at 8 am), and get back at 6:30 pm. Reservations are recommended. Continental breakfast, a picnic lunch, snorkel gear and a 45-minute tour of the fort are all included.

By airplane, Key West Seaplane Service (☎ 305-294-6978) will take you and up to nine other passengers (flight time 40 minutes each way). A four-hour trip is $159, an eight-hour trip is $275, and they'll fly you out there to camp for $299 per person, including snorkeling equipment. The plane will then pick you up at the beach in Key West; reserve at least a week in advance. Prices dip in summer.

THE LOWER KEYS

The main attraction in the Lower Keys is the National Key Deer Refuge, but there's skydiving and, of course, great diving and snorkeling as well, especially at Looe Key National Marine Sanctuary and Bahia Honda State Park. You can also arrange some wonderful kayak trips among the mangroves within the Great White Heron National Wildlife Refuge.

Orientation & Information

The Lower Keys stretch from Boca Chica to the Seven Mile Bridge just northeast of Bahia Honda Key. Get tourist information, accommodations and snorkel or dive information at the very helpful Lower Keys Chamber of Commerce (☎ 305-872-3580, 800-872-3722, 800-352-5397, http://florida-keys.fl.us/lwrkycc.htm) at MM 31 on Big Pine Key. You can get information on the National Key Deer Refuge and local flora and fauna at the refuge headquarters (☎ 305-872-2239) in the Big Pine Shopping Center, MM 30; the headquarters is open Monday to Friday 8 am to 5 pm.

Dive shops include Looe Key Reef Resort & Dive Center (☎ 305-872-2215, 800-446-5663), MM 27, and Reef Runner Dive Shop (☎ 305-745-1549), MM 25.

Change money at the NationsBank at MM 30.5. There's a coin laundry off Key Deer Blvd in Big Pine Key. A stop at the Big Pine Shopping Center, MM 30.5 (turn north on Key Deer Blvd, it's on the right), will take care of a lot of needs: it has a Winn-Dixie, the biggest food market in the area; Edie's Hallmark Shop, which has a small selection of books, mainly best-selling paperbacks; the Big Pine Key public library (☎ 305-289-6303); and the Big Pine Medical Complex (☎ 305-872-3735), a walk-in clinic.

Another Lower Keys walk-in clinic is the Big Pine Medical and Minor Emergency Clinic (☎ 305-872-3321) at MM 30 oceanside. For major emergencies, the closest hospital is Florida Keys Health Systems (☎ 305-294-5531, 800-233-3119), 5900 College Rd on Stock Island, a 24-hour emergency room.

National Key Deer Refuge

The National Key Deer Refuge (☎ 305-872-2239) is on large tracts of property that sprawl over several Keys, but the sections that are open to the public – such as Blue Hole, Watson's Hammock and Watson's Nature Trail – are on Big Pine and No Name Keys. Stop in at the Refuge Headquarters in the Big Pine Shopping Center, off MM 30, for information; it's open Monday to Friday 8 am to 5 pm.

The best times to see Key deer are in the early morning and late afternoon; ask at the refuge headquarters where the best places to see them are on the particular day you come.

Admission to the entire refuge is free. There are three established refuge areas, but all areas in the refuge marked with signs that read 'US Fish & Wildlife Service – Unauthorized Entry Prohibited' are open to the public from a half hour before sunrise to a half hour after sunset. Areas with a sign saying 'Closed Beyond This Point' are off-limits to visitors.

From MM 30.5, take Key Deer Blvd for 3¹/₂ miles. The first place you'll reach is Blue Hole; Watson's Nature Trail and Watson's Hammock are approximately a quarter mile farther on the same road.

Blue Hole The largest body of freshwater in the Keys, is in an old quarry, where you'll see very large alligators, turtles and fish in addition to a huge variety of wading birds. Please don't ignore the signs imploring you not to feed the wildlife – many tourists go right ahead and feed anything that wiggles, which is illegal and irresponsible.

Watson's Nature Trail This is a two-thirds-mile, self-guided walk through the Key deer's natural habitat. Guided walks are also available to groups and individuals. On weekends from December to March there are ranger-led three-hour guided walks through Watson's Hammock, a prime Key deer fawning area, but the hammock is closed completely to the public in April and May. Guided walks begin behind Blue Hole, but check with the rangers at the headquarters.

No Name Key There are fewer visitors here than in the Blue Hole or Watson's Nature Trail. No Name Key is a very good place to see Key deer in the early morning and late afternoon. Take Key Deer Blvd to Watson Blvd, turn right, go about 1¹/₂ miles to Wilder Blvd, turn left, follow it for 2 miles to Bogie Bridge, cross it and you'll be on No Name.

Key Deer

The tiny Key deer live primarily on Big Pine and No Name Keys. An endangered species, Key deer are classified as a subspecies of white tail deer. Once mainland-dwelling animals, the formation of the Keys stranded them on the islands, and evolutionary changes have resulted in a reduction in their overall size: since winter temperatures are higher here than on the mainland, they no longer require as much body mass to carry them through. Another major evolutionary change has been a reduction in the size of litters, from multiple to single births, to compensate for reduced grazing lands and scarce fresh water.

The biggest threat to the Key deer has been humans, who can't seem to stop feeding them. This has caused Key deer to fearlessly approach humans and, unfortunately, their vehicles. Key deer also have begun to change their natural behavior and travel in herds, which is against their solitary nature, in pursuit of handouts from people.

This lack of fear has lead to massive vehicular deaths – about 65% of which occur along US Hwy 1. In 1995, there were 94 Key deer deaths, of which 66 were positively confirmed to have been caused by deer getting hit by cars. Of the remaining 28 deaths, 15 to 18 are suspected to have been caused by vehicles.

Key deer are generally light to 'dead leaf' brown with black tails and a white rump. Fawns have white spots on their back and rib area for about the first month, after which they lose them. Some full-grown deer have a black mask over the eyes and the forehead.

Full-grown bucks normally weigh about 75lb to 80lb, does about 65lb. Bucks are from 28 to 32 inches high at the shoulders, does from 24 to 26 inches, and fawns weigh from 2lb to 3½lb at birth.

The rut, or mating season, is from September to December and the Key deer's gestation period is 204 days (fawning occurs in April and May).

Slow Down Speed limits are strictly enforced, and while there is no penalty for hitting a Key deer inadvertently, if you're speeding or intentionally trying to hit one, you're in violation of state and federal laws. If you are speeding, fines vary depending on the agency that catches you: state fines begin at $540 (reported to be dropping to $230) and federal fines at $230.

And Don't Feed Them Feeding Key deer is absolutely illegal, and if you're caught, fines can reach $25,000.

Great White Heron National Wildlife Refuge

This refuge (☎ 305-872-2239) is comprised of two large but little-visited wading bird nesting areas, where you can see herons, ibis, egrets, ospreys, hawks and even eagles, as well as fish, crabs, sponges, coral and mangroves. Kayaks and canoes are permitted within the preserve, since much of it is inaccessible except by boat, but there are no services.

For more information, contact the National Key Deer Refuge headquarters in the Big Pine Shopping Center (see above). See Kayak Nature Tours below for organized trips to the refuge.

Looe Key National Marine Sanctuary

Pronounced 'Loo,' this isn't a Key at all but a grove reef off Ramrod Key. The Key Largo (see Reefs & Attractions under John Pennekamp Coral Reef State Park later in this chapter) and Looe Key National Marine Sanctuaries were established in 1971 and 1981 to protect sensitive areas within the Keys, but they are actually a compromise between commercial activities and environmental protection. Looe Key is named for an English frigate that sank in the area in 1744. In 1998, the 210-foot *Adolphus Busch* – used in the film *Fire Down Below* – was sunk to create an artificial reef at 60 to 120 feet.

Activities that are permitted within the sanctuaries include sport and commercial fishing with hook and line and lobstering and crabbing within limits. But the sanctuaries protect against dredging, filling, excavating, building and removing or damaging natural features (which includes standing on, anchoring on or touching coral). Prices for dives to the wreck hadn't been set when we visited.

Diving & Snorkeling Within the sanctuary, snorkeling and diving are permitted, and thousands of varieties of hugely colorful tropical fish, coral and sea life abound. There are snorkeling trips to Looe Key aboard glass bottom boats from Strike Zone Charters (☎ 305-872-9863, 800-654-9560) at MM 29.5. Four-hour Looe Key snorkeling and diving trips at 9:30 am and 1:30 pm cost $25 per person and $5 for equipment for snorkeling, $40 plus $25 for equipment for diving.

Blue Water Tours (☎ 305-872-2896, 800-822-1386) has guided three-hour sea kayak tours and rentals as well.

The Looe Key Reef Resort (☎ 305-872-2215), MM 27.5 (see Hotels & Motels below), runs snorkeling and diving trips for $25/45 without the equipment; if you need to rent the gear, add $8 for snorkeling, $45 for diving. The trips last about four hours and hit two different locations on Looe Key Reef.

Bahia Honda State Park

One of the Keys' best beaches, Bahia Honda State Park (☎ 305-872-2353) – keep trying, it's always busy – at MM 36.5 at the foot of the Seven Mile Bridge, is a 524-acre park, including one small offshore island. It was battered during Georges. The beaches are sparkling white sand and very pretty, but in summer sandflies are rife. It's a very popular place – the 2½-mile expanse and the shape of the beach allow you to secrete yourself into little nooks and crannies for privacy, but despite listings in naturalist magazines, note that topless (women) or nude bathing is prohibited. Rangers will tell you once to put on clothes, after which you could be fined and ejected from the park.

Bahia Honda is the southernmost Key with exposed limestone, and along its nature trails you'll find silver palms, yellow satinwood and lily thorn (endangered). Admission is $3.75 per car, $1 for pedestrians or bicyclists, and tent sites and cabins are available (see Camping below).

Snorkeling The park concession (☎ 305-872-3210) rents snorkeling equipment ($4) and offers snorkel excursions every day at 10 am and 2 pm; the cost is $23 for adults and $19 for anyone under 18. In high season, reservations are a good idea; call and they'll put your name on the list. The concession also rents kayaks (singles/doubles are $10/15 an hour), and there's a restaurant and grocery store.

Bat Tower

The Bat Tower, on the National Register of Historic Places, is a wooden tower built in 1929 by Righter Clyde Perky. The idea was that the tower would attract bats, who would then eat the swarming masses of mosquitoes and make the Keys a wonderful place. The bats didn't come. The tower is off MM 17 on Lower Sugarloaf Key; if you're headed away from Key West, turn left, then go left on the little road off the parking lot.

SeaCamp

Newfound Harbor Marine Institute (☎ 305-872-2331, www.seacamp.org), 1300 Big Pine

Ave, Big Pine Key, is a nonprofit environmental education center that runs an educational camp. Between seven and eight thousand people a year take part in the SeaCamp programs, which run from three to 30 days, and while many are geared to children, there are some expanding adult programs as well.

In summer it's a full-blown coed summer camp with three 18-day sessions for campers 12 to 17 years old. The sessions (June 24 to July 11; July 14 to 31, and August 3 to 20) cost $2395 (about $130 a day), including housing, meals and programs (though scuba is an extra $350). There's photography, arts & crafts and, of course, lots of time in the water learning about the environment. Residential adult programs run from September to May and cost an average of $120 a day.

For more information, write to SeaCamp, 1300 Big Pine Ave, Big Pine Key, FL 33043.

Kayak Nature Tours

Nature photographer Bill Keogh at Lost World Adventures (☎ 305-872-8950, 305-395-0930, www.keys-kayak-canoe-tours.com) offers guided kayak journeys into both the Great White Heron and Key Deer Refuges. The trips are usually three to four hours and leave regularly in the morning and the afternoon, though two-hour sunset journeys also run, at $30. For the regular trips, you'll paddle along the red mangrove coastlines through the shallow habitat and check out what's what; the cost is $45 per person, and he usually takes no more than six people per guide to ensure that it's peaceful enough for all. Keogh also takes people out on his six-passenger catamaran; it's $200 for four hours or $250 for eight.

Tours leave from Jig's Fishing and Snorkeling Center at MM 30.2 bayside on Big Pine Key, where you can rent canoes and kayaks.

For the same prices as Lost World, Reflections Kayak Nature Tours (☎ 305-872-2896) will take you out on guided tours as well; they also offer kayak rentals. Tours leave from Palmer's Place Guesthouse (see Hotels & Motels later in this section), which is on Barry Ave off MM 28.5 on Little Torch Key

(which is 1 mile west of Big Pine Key). They'll deliver and pick up a kayak anywhere between Marathon and Sugarloaf Key for $20.

See Looe Key National Marine Sanctuary for information on snorkeling and kayaking there.

Skydiving & Air Tours

Sky Dive Key West (☎ 305-745-4386), right near the Bat Tower off MM 17, does tandem skydives for $219 (if you weigh more than 200lb, they charge $1 a pound more for each pound over 200), or $199 if you pay cash. Solo jumps (license and 300 jumps required) are $35, and you can save the whole thing for posterity on videotape for $99. At the same location, Fantasy Dan's (☎ 305-745-2217) does airplane tours from $20 to $50, depending on time in the air.

Places to Stay

Camping The *Big Pine Key Fishing Lodge* (☎ 305-872-2351, at MM 33) has tent sites for $24 and full hookup sites for $28 all year. They have an artificial beach, and while swimming in the ocean is not so great here, there is a pool. They also have motel efficiencies for $73 to $95 per night all year; there is a three-night minimum stay.

Sunshine Key Camping Resort & Marina (☎ 305-872-2217, 38801 Overseas Hwy, MM 39) was unfortunately leveled by Hurricane Georges, so we couldn't check it this time. Last time they had tent sites without hookups in summer/winter for $21.95/29.95; with water and electric it's $25/41; and waterfront sites with water and electric for $39/51.

There's camping at *Bahia Honda State Park* (☎ 305-872-2353, MM 37) – the phone is often busy; sites are $23.69 without electricity and $25.84 with. Waterfront sites (reserve far in advance or forget it) are an additional $2.30. Cabins, which sleep around eight people, are $96.85 from September 15 to December 14 and $124.60 the rest of the year.

Hotels & Motels *Palmer's Place Guesthouse* (☎ 305-872-2157, Barry Ave), off MM

FLORIDA KEYS

28.5 on Little Torch Key (call for directions), is a resort based around nature excursions run by its in-house nature tour company, Reflections Kayak Nature Tours (☎ 305-872-2896). Motel rooms range from $55 to $66. There are also efficiencies and cottages available; all prices include continental breakfast. Trips are additional (see Kayak Nature Tours earlier in this section).

Sugarloaf Lodge (☎ *305-745-3211, MM 17 in Lower Sugarloaf Key*) is something of a resort – not so huge, but not just a hotel. All waterfront rooms are from $80/120 in May to December/December to May.

Looe Key Reef Resort (☎ *305-872-2215, MM 27.5*) has motel rooms with two double beds, TV and phone for $70 to $135, depending on the season. They also rent snorkeling equipment ($8) and diving equipment ($25) and run snorkel/dive trips (see Looe Key National Marine Sanctuary above).

B&Bs There are three B&Bs on Big Pine Key, all oceanside. *Casa Grande* (☎ *305-872-2878, MM 33 oceanside*) has rooms for two with breakfast for $85 in summer, $110 in winter. Their Jacuzzi is hot in winter and cold in summer.

The Barnacle (☎ *305-872-3298, off MM 33 at Long Beach Drive*) is another choice, with rates from $95 to $125; $10 less in summer.

Deer Run B&B (☎ *305-872-2015*), also on Long Beach Drive, has rates ranging from $85 to $110.

Places to Eat

Good Food Conspiracy (☎ *305-872-3945, MM 30*) is a killer health food place with prepared foods as well as a juice bar, vitamins and the like. Orange juice is $1.55 to $1.80, smoothies $1.90 to $3.65.

Right next to the Big Pine Post Office at MM 30, the *Big Pine Coffee Shop & Restaurant* (☎ *305-872-2790*) is a trip into the past with breakfast specials from $2.30 to $6.95, a lunch-special cheeseburger with fixin's and fries for $3.80 and sandwiches from $3.45 to $5.50.

Island Reef Restaurant (☎ *305-872-2170, MM 31.5*) serves sandwiches for $4.95,

burgers for $4.50 to $5.95 and seafood salad for $7.95. Entrees such as meatloaf are $5.95, and fish and chips are $7.95. They are closed on Sunday.

Dip 'N' Deli (☎ *305-872-3030, MM 31*) has lots of subs and sandwiches for $2.75 to $4.60; their garden burger is $4.50. At dinner entrees range from $7.95 to $10.95, including steak, barbecue chicken, pork or ribs, fried chicken and meatloaf.

Mangrove Mama's (☎ *305-745-3030, MM 20*) is a very hip place, with live music (no cover charge) in their great bar on weekends and reggae on Sunday 8 to 11:30 pm. They do mainly Caribbean-inspired dishes and seafood; starters such as conch fritters and vegetable tempura are $4.25 to $8.95, salads $3 to $8, lunches (such as fried fish) $5.95 to $7.50 and burgers start at $5.75. Fish chowder is $1.95 to $2.50. Dinner is more expensive, such as catch of the day for $15 or coconut shrimp for $15.95; a surf-and-turf dinner is $21.95.

More Caribbean stuff is found at MM 30.2 on Big Pine Key at *Montego Bay* (☎ *305-872-3009*), with a Caribbean buffet for $12.95 with good jerk chicken in honey, served with a very *mon*-ish attitude.

MARATHON
• population 12,250

People come to Marathon to fish. That's not to say that nonfishers will be completely bored out of their minds; it's just that the area is really geared to fishing. But Marathon is also home to the Dolphin Research Center, where you – yes, you – can swim with dolphins in supervised programs.

The area is also home to Pigeon Key, in the middle of the Old Seven Mile Bridge, and a trip to this island is a very interesting look at the building of the very lifeline of the Florida Keys – the Overseas Hwy.

Orientation & Information

The Marathon area runs from the northeast end of the Seven Mile Bridge up through the Conch Keys.

Get a mother lode of information at the Marathon Visitors Center/Chamber of Commerce (☎ 305-743-5417, 800-262-7284, http://florida-keys.fl.us/marathon.htm) at MM 53.5. The chamber also sells Greyhound tickets; the Greyhound station in Marathon Key is between the FedEx building and the fire station between MM 51.5 and MM 52. The Marathon Airport is at MM 52.

Change money at the Republic Bank, 6090 Overseas Hwy, MM 50.5. Fisherman's Hospital (☎ 305-743-5533), MM 48.7, has a major emergency room.

Marathon Discount Book Center (☎ 305-289-2066), MM 48.5, has inexpensive close-out books and books on tape. Food for Thought (☎ 305-743-3297), at the Gulfside Village Shopping Center, MM 51 bayside, is a combination bookstore and health food shop – it carries newspapers, such as the *New York Times* and *Wall Street Journal*, some LP titles and other guidebooks, general fiction and literature, as well as vitamins, bulk products and frozen foods.

Do laundry at the Maytag Coin Laundry (☎ 305-743-3448), at about MM 53.5, for $2 per load; it's open Monday to Friday 7 am to 9 pm, Saturday and Sunday 7 am to 7 pm. Marathon Cleaners (☎ 305-743-5142) is at MM 51.5.

Tropic Isle Dive (☎ 305-289-0303), MM 52.9 oceanside, does one-hour photo developing starting at a little over $10.

Pigeon Key Museum

Pigeon Key is a 5-acre island about 2 miles west of Marathon over the Old Seven Mile Bridge. As Henry Flagler's FEC Railway progressed southward, the construction of the Seven Mile Bridge between Marathon and Bahia Honda Key (actually Little Duck Key) became an immense project. Pigeon Key was home, between 1908 and 1912, to about 400 workers.

After the completion of the bridge, Pigeon Key became home to maintenance workers. But after the hurricane that wiped out Flagler's railroad in 1935, the key once again became home to workers, this time converting the railroad to automobile bridges.

After a brief stint in the 1970s as a research facility leased by the University of Miami, the Pigeon Key Foundation formed

to preserve the island's buildings and to tell the story of the railroad and its workers.

Today the museum is open to the public, and you can see the old city, including the 'honeymoon cottage,' assistant bridge tender and bridge tender's houses, the section gang's quarters and several other buildings, including the 'negro quarters.'

Tours of the museum (☎ 305-289-0025, www.pigeonkey.org) run daily, and are $7.50. You can park at Knights Key, at the western end of Marathon (MM 47), and pick up a shuttle out to the island. Shuttles leave hourly from 10 am to 4 pm; the last shuttle returns to Knights Key at 5 pm. You can also ride or walk across the bridge.

Fishing Bridge

The Old Seven Mile Bridge is open as 'the World's Longest Fishing Bridge'; entry is free and it's right at the parking lot at the eastern foot of the bridge. If you've seen the movie *True Lies*, you will recognize the parking lot as the spot where the jarhead lost his Harrier.

Dolphin Research Center

The Dolphin Research Center (☎ 305-289-1121), MM 59 bayside on Grassy Key, is a nonprofit educational center in an open lagoon dedicated to spreading understanding about dolphins. In addition to programs that introduce dolphins to the mentally handicapped and use dolphins for physical therapy, they run half-day 'Dolph*insight*' programs three times a week, which include a guided tour of the facility and a workshop that explains dolphin physiology, training and conservation. The cost is $75. Not hands-on enough? You can join a full-day Dolphin Encounter program, in which you'll learn about and then swim with their dolphins for $110.

They also run educational walks at 10 and 11 am and 12:30, 2 and 3:30 pm; the charge is $12.50 for adults, $10 for seniors, $6 for kids four to 12. It's open daily 9 am to 4 pm.

Tropical Crane Point Hammock

This 63-acre museum (☎ 305-743-9100), MM 50 bayside, across from K-Mart, is a fun

Swimming with Dolphins

The idea of swimming with a dolphin is so romantic and mystical that some tourists don't stop to consider the effect it might have on the animals or themselves. The idea of just jumping in the water and swimming with wild dolphins is not altogether a good one – if you don't scare them away, they may just go ahead and treat you like a dolphin – and dolphins playing among themselves have a grand time body-slamming and biting each other.

Experts say 'structured' programs – in which staff accompany swimmers in controlled areas for swims with dolphins that are accustomed to human contact – are safer and more humane than 'unstructured' ones.

There are three swim with dolphins programs on the Keys; two – the Dolphin Research Center and the Theater of the Sea – offer structured programs only: swims are choreographed by staff who are there with you. The third, Dolphins Plus, also offers an unstructured program for those who are 'comfortable' in the water. While Dolphins Plus offers classroom training and orientation, unstructured programs may be riskier than structured ones. Dolphins Plus' structured program is offered on weekends and during some holiday periods. See the Marathon Key, Islamorada and Key Largo sections for full descriptions and prices.

place to stop. They have a geological and geographical history of the Keys, exhibits on pirates and wrecking, and a coral reef tunnel, which you can walk through, featuring underwater sounds. Also shown are tropical plants, mangroves and, best of all, a showcase with a cutaway sea turtle nest, allowing a rare glimpse. There are short but nice walking trails through the hammock, and the staff are very helpful and friendly. It's open Monday to Saturday 9 am to 5 pm,

Sunday noon to 5 pm. Admission is $7.50 for adults, $6 for seniors, $4 for students and kids under six are free.

Beaches & Wrecks

There is a public beach at the end of Sombrero Beach Rd, about 2 miles from US Hwy 1 at MM 50. There are public bathrooms, a picnic area, barbecue grills, a little playground and volleyball nets.

The wreck of the slave ship *Ivory Coast* (1853) is at Sombrero Reef; it's marked by a light tower, and there's an artificial reef built by Flagler to support the Overseas Highway.

Activities

Rent bicycles at the Blue Waters Motel, MM 48.5 (see Motels & Hotels below), or at Tilden's Pro Dive Shop (☎ 305-743-5422, 800-223-4563), MM 49.5. Tilden's also rents scuba equipment for about $40 a day; half-day snorkel/dive trips are $25/30. They go to 53 different locations of various depths; to get a full open-water certification is $275 for five days.

Places to Stay

Camping Some of the best camping is at Bahia Honda State Park, just on the other side of the Seven Mile Bridge (see Camping earlier in the chapter).

Jolly Rogers Trailer Park (☎ 305-289-0404, 800-995-1525, MM 59.5 bayside), has tent sites for $24 in summer, $25 to $30 in winter.

There's tent camping at the very friendly *Knights Key Campground* (☎ 305-743-4343, 800-348-2267, MM 47 oceanside). Sites without electricity or water are $22.95, sites with tent and table (water and electricity) are $27.95, inland sites with water and electricity are $42.95, shoreline sites $47.95 and marina sites $55.95. In off-peak times it's three days for the price of two. Take the last exit before the Seven Mile Bridge.

Motels & Hotels *Sea Cove* (☎ 305-289-0800, 800-653-0800, MM 54) is a neat family-owned place that used to have houseboat accommodations. Sadly, the boats all sank during Georges, and the owner is considering packing it all in. Currently she offers nice efficiency apartments (half cottages that sleep up to six in one large room) from $59 to $79. The people here are very friendly; off-season prices are very negotiable. All rooms have air conditioning and cable, and local calls are free.

The startlingly clean *Siesta Motel* (☎ 305-743-5671, 7425 US Hwy 1) has been here for 36 years and provides great service (speak clearly and slowly – the owners do). Singles/doubles are $50/60 in winter, $45/50 in summer.

The *Royal Hawaiian Motel Botel* (☎ 305-743-7500, MM 53) is a clean place with rooms that sleep four. In low/peak season they're $59 to $69/$95 to $105; all have a fridge and coffee-maker. There's a boat-dock/ramp and a pool.

Banana Bay Resort (☎ 305-743-3500, 800-226-2621, MM 49.5 bayside) is a fine option for the money, with very friendly and helpful staff and a really lush tropical setting. Depending on view, rates are $75 to $135 in summer, $85 to $195 in winter and $95 to $195 in peak times. A good breakfast buffet (coffee, juice, bagels, pastries, fruit) is included, and there is a nice pool. They also offer snorkeling and diving packages. No pets allowed.

Seahorse Motel (☎ 305-743-6571, 800-874-1115, 7196 Overseas Hwy) has medium everything – rooms in summer/winter are $49/69; efficiencies are $75 to $102/$95 to $122.

The *Blue Waters Motel* (☎ 305-743-4832, 800-222-4832, MM 48.5) is a very friendly and nice place. The rooms have very large bathrooms and cost $50 in September, $70 in summer and up to $110 in winter. There is a pool, docks and a boat ramp (no charge), and you can fish here; local calls are free and they rent bicycles for $5 per day, boats for $69 a half day, $99 a day.

Places to Eat

All of the following also have bars that get packed at night. The *Banana Cabana Restaurant* (☎ 305-289-1232, MM 49.5) at the Banana Bay Resort (see above) does good cheap lunches; burgers and sandwiches

are $5.25, salads are $5.95 to $7.95. The dinner menu changes daily (served from 6 to 10 pm) and offers dishes such as linguini in lobster sauce for $13.95 (delicious and huge) or a popular roasted duck for $12.95. The setting is quite tropical.

Shucker's (☎ 305-743-8686, 725 11th St) has sandwiches for $4.95 to $6.50 and Cajun chicken salad for $6.95. After 5 pm, grouper or shrimp (various preparations) is $16.95, filet mignon $19.95, and all entrees include salad, bread, potato or linguini or rice or fries. It's open daily 11:30 am to 10 pm.

Herbie's (☎ 305-743-6373, MM 50.5) is a very popular local place; burgers are $3.25, fried-fish sandwiches $4.25. Platters include fries, slaw and sauce and are $4.95 to $8.95, and their seafood combo platter is $11.95.

The extraordinary *7 Mile Grill* (☎ 305-743-4481, 1240 Overseas Hwy) is a very popular outdoor place, roofed with table and bar service. Shrimp bisque or magnificent Navy bean soup is $2.95, fish sandwiches are $4.95, a fish plate $8.95 and chicken wrap $4.75. They are open for breakfast 7 to 11 am, lunch and dinner are served 11:30 am to 8:30 pm. They are closed Wednesday (also on Thursday in summer).

ISLAMORADA
• population 1220

Home to some significant state historic sites, as well as to the cheesy-looking but fun Theater of the Sea, Islamorada (pronounced 'eye-luh-murr-AH-da') is probably worth a stop on the way through, even if you don't stay over.

Orientation & Information

The Islamorada area spans from Layton to Plantation Key. The Islamorada Chamber of Commerce (☎ 305-664-4503, 800-322-5397, http://florida-keys.fl.us/islacc.htm) is in an old caboose at MM 82.5 bayside. The main Greyhound station is at the Burger King at MM 82.5.

Change money at the NationsBank at MM 81.5. Islamorada Coin Laundry (☎ 305-664-4141) is at MM 82.2; it's open Monday to Saturday 8 am to 8 pm, Sunday 9 am to 5 pm.

The Islamorada Medical Clinic (☎ 305-664-9731) is at 82685 US Hwy 1, and the Mariners Hospital (☎ 305-852-4418) is on Plantation Key at MM 88.5.

Dive shops in the area include Cheeca Divers (☎ 305-664-2777, 800-934-8377) at the Cheeca Lodge (see Motels & Hotels later in this section), Holiday Isle Dive Center (☎ 305-664-4145, 800-327-7070), MM 84.5, Bud and Mary's Marina (☎ 305-664-2211) and Lady Cyana (☎ 305-664-8717).

Indian Key State Historic Site

Closed in 1998-99 for repair of hurricane damage, this historic site (☎ 305-664-4815) is a little island of only about 10 acres, but it has quite an interesting history. In 1831, renegade wrecker Jacob Housman bought the island after a falling out with wreckers in Key West and opened his own wrecker station on it. About 40 to 50 people lived permanently on the island, which Housman built up into a thriving little city, complete with warehouse, docks, streets and a hotel.

By 1836 Indian Key was the seat of Dade County. But Housman eventually lost his wrecker's license and the Second Seminole War was adding to his difficulties: in 1840 Housman lost the entire island after an Indian attack.

Today there's not much here, just the remains of the foundations of the original structures and some cisterns, Housman's grave and lots of plant life. But there is an observation tower and trails, and the free 1¹/₂- to 2-hour ranger-led tours (Thursday to Monday at 9 am and 1 pm) give a great history, not just of the wrecking operation but of the geological and natural history of the island. There's a catch, though: you need to have a boat or take a $15-per-person shuttle on the 10-minute ride from Robbie's Marina (see later in the section). The shuttles leave starting about an hour before the tours begin – it pays to show up early as the boat has room only for six people. If you've got your own boat, the island's open all the time, admission is free, but camping is not permitted.

Lignumvitae Key State Botanical Site

Lignumvitae Key State Botanical Site (pronounced 'lignum-VITE-ee'; ☎ 305-664-4815) is a 280-acre island of virgin tropical forest. The main attraction here is the Matheson House (1919), its windmill and cistern.

The forest here includes strangler fig, mastic, gumbo-limbo and poisonwood trees, as well as the native lignumvitae tree, known for its extremely hard wood. Bring mosquito repellent.

On the island, 1¹/₄- to 1¹/₂-hour ranger-guided walking tours are available Thursday to Monday at 10 am and 2 pm, but again, as with Indian Key, you can get here only by boat. From Robbie's Marina (see later in the section), tour boats leave on the 15-minute trip about a half hour before each tour – reservations are highly recommended. The cost is $15 per person.

Long Key State Recreation Area

Opened in 1969, Long Key State Recreation Area (☎ 305-664-4815), MM 68, is a 965-acre park. It, too, received hurricane damage in 1998, but it's open and under repair. Inside, you'll see gumbo-limbo trees, crabwood, poisonwood, and *lots* of wading birds in the mangroves (especially in winter). The park has sections on both the gulf and ocean, but their beach is small at low tide and gone at high tide.

The two nature trails, the 1¹/₄-mile Golden Orb and half-mile Layton Trail, head through several distinct plant communities. The hurricanes put the kibosh on ranger-led programs, but they should start again; last time they had winter ranger-led programs Wednesday to Friday, and a two-hour guided walk on the nature trails on Wednesday morning. On Friday evening they run campfire programs for the campers here.

The park also has a 1¹/₂-mile canoe trail through a saltwater tidal lagoon. Canoes cost $4 an hour or $10 per day.

Admission to the park is $3.25 per car, 50¢ per person, and there's camping here as well, see below.

Theater of the Sea

It looks very much like the cheesiest tourist attraction around, but the Theater of the Sea (☎ 305-664-2431), MM 84.5 bayside, has been here since 1946 and actually runs some very nice programs, including a structured dolphin swim (see the Swimming with Dolphins boxed text). Their sea shows, which run continuously from 9:30 am to 4 pm, include dolphins and sea lions; a marine exhibit has sharks, stingrays and tropical fish. Trainers feed the animals while describing their behavior and habitat. There's also a living shell exhibit, and a five-minute boat ride into their dolphin lagoon. Admission to the shows is $15.75 for adults, $9.25 for children three to 12. It's open daily.

Their structured dolphin swims and sea lion programs include a half hour of instruction and a half hour of supervised swim; the cost is $95/65 for the dolphin/sea lion programs. They're by reservation only; times are 9:30 am, noon and 2 pm.

Somewhere in Time

Somewhere in Time, the Museum of Spanish Shipwreck Treasures (☎ 305-664-9699), MM 82.8 oceanside, is a collection of artifacts, salvaged from shipwrecks along the Keys over many years, that were bought by owner Dick Holt. There are religious artifacts, bottles and coins on display. Holt, a jeweler, mounts coins and sells them as earrings, pendants, necklaces and so on. The museum is open daily 9 am to 5 pm; admission is free.

Robbie's Marina

Robbie's (☎ 305-664-9814), MM 77.5 bayside, rents boats; rates for a 15-foot boat start at $70 for half a day and, depending on boat size and number of people, rise quite briskly from there. You can also feed tarpons right from the dock here; admission is $1 per person and a bucket of fish is $2. The best time to show up for tarpon feeding is mid-morning. Robbie's pier is open 8 am to 6 pm.

Organized Tours Robbie's also does tours to Lignumvitae Key State Botanical Site (see earlier in the section) including the Matheson House and the gardens as well as the ranger-led tours. They run Thursday to Monday at 9:30 am and 1:30 pm and cost $15. Two-hour scenic sunset cruises out onto Florida Bay cost $125 for up to six adults.

Places to Stay

Camping The *Long Key State Recreation Area* (☎ *305-664-4815, MM 68*) has ocean-front campsites for $23.69 (no electricity or water, but there is a communal water faucet at every fifth site). Sites without/with electricity and water are $23.69/25.84, and there is a free dump station, though no sewer hookups.

KOA (☎ *305-664-4922, MM 70*), on Fiesta Key, has sites with no hookups for $35, sites with water for $39 and with water and electricity for $42 in winter, $27/30/33 in summer. They also have motel rooms from $130 to $150 with a kitchen ($95 to $115 in summer).

Motels & Hotels The simple rooms at the *Key Lantern* (☎ *305-664-4572, MM 82*) aren't oceanfront, but the staff members are friendly. Rooms include TV and fridge, but there's no pool. Rooms run $40 to $75.

The *Drop Anchor Motel* (☎ *305-664-4863, MM 85*) has rooms with refrigerators and coffee-makers; there are no phones in the rooms, but the motel has a pay phone. They have a pool and barbecue grills. From September to December, rooms run $50 to $125; from April to September the rooms are $60 to $150; from December to April they run $75 to $180.

The *Holiday Isle Resort* (☎ *305-664-2321, 800-327-7070, MM 84 oceanside*) is a city of hotels and restaurants, including *Holiday Isle, Harbor Lights* and *El Capitan Motel* and *Howard Johnson Resort*. There's also a Subway sandwich shop, a shopping mall, Jaws Raw Bar, a stage, a Tiki Bar and Rum Runner's, and Jose Cuervo Cantina and BBQ. They also have playgrounds, jungle gyms, volleyball and basketball and, on the weekend, live Polynesian and reggae bands. The activities are endless and based around partying, fishing, diving and parasailing;

FLORIDA KEYS

sort of a 'little Acapulco' (the atmosphere's the same, too).

Rates at these hotels are complex; these base prices are the least you can expect to pay, but you can spend a lot more: Harbor Lights has off-peak/peak rooms from $65 to $110/$85 to $145. Holiday Isle rooms are $85 to $375 off peak, $105 to $425 peak; El Capitan rooms are $90 to $200 off peak, $120 to $250 peak; and the Howard Johnson Resort costs $115 to $140 off peak, $140 to $175 peak. Guests at any of the above have the run of the resort.

The fabulously luxurious **Cheeca Lodge** (☎ *305-664-4651, 800-327-2888, MM 82 oceanside*) is a beaut of a resort if you like angling, croquet, golf and tennis – though they have most everything else you've ever desired as well. Their dive shop can arrange trips to Alligator Reef and to see *The Eagle* as well as to other destinations, or you can just walk on the lodge's own nature trails or sit by their pool or in the spa. Their Cheeca Van goes between the lodge and Miami International Airport ($150 for up to six people). Room rates range from $180 to $430 in off-peak seasons, $275 to $650 in peak seasons; suites are from $285 to $950 off peak, $375 to $1500 peak.

Places to Eat
Manny & Isa's Kitchen (☎ *305-664-5019, MM 81.6)* is a Spanish/American place with sandwiches from $2.50 to $4.50. 'Chopped sirloin' steak with grilled onions (which sounds suspiciously like a big hamburger) is $7.95, pork chops are $8.90 and broiled lamb chops $13.50. They have daily specials for about $7.95, and seafood dishes are $14 to $17.

There are about six restaurants at the Holiday Isle Resort (see above), including the **Horizon Restaurant** (☎ *305-664-2321 x600, MM 84)*, which does salads for $3.95 to $7.95, sandwiches for $4.25 to $7.95 and a soup-and-sandwich combination for $5.50. At dinner, main courses range from $12 to $20.

Whale Harbor (☎ *305-664-4959, MM 84)* does an all-you-can-eat seafood buffet; adults pay $19.95, kids $9.95 and children five and under $4. It's open Monday to Saturday 4 to 9 pm and Sunday noon to 9 pm.

The **Ocean Grill**, the more casual option at the Cheeca Lodge, has sandwiches and salads and entrees; lunch can run $6 to $15; at dinner main courses run $8 to $18, top end items like Florida Lobster or Strip steak are $25 to $29.

Their other restaurant, the **Atlantic's Edge** (☎ *305-664-4651)*, prepares the catch of the day any way you like; if you catch the fish they will cook it and serve it with vegetables, mixed grains and steamed creamer potatoes for $15.50 per person ($22 if it's their catch). Other entrees include their vegetarian medley for $15, baked mahi-mahi $20 or rack of lamb $36.

KEY LARGO
• population 13,000

Key Largo leapt into the public eye after the 1948 film of that name starring Bogart and Bacall, shot almost entirely on Hollywood, California, sound stages. Sensing that they'd better get their act together to capitalize on this but quick, the town, which had been known to that point as Rock Harbor, swiftly changed its name to Key Largo. Despite the presence of *The African Queen* in town, from the Bogart movie of *that* name, Bogie himself never came here to shoot anything; the boat was brought in as a tourist attraction.

Key Largo's biggest attraction is justifiably the underwater John Pennekamp Coral Reef State Park, the most accessible way to see the Florida reef, and divers looking for a unique experience will love Jules' Undersea Lodge, an underwater hotel.

Orientation & Information
The Key Largo area stretches from the northernmost section of the Keys down to Plantation Key. The very helpful Key Largo Chamber of Commerce (☎ 305-451-1414, 800-822-1088, http://florida-keys.fl.us/keylgcc.htm), MM 106 bayside, has tons of information on Key Largo and the rest of the Keys. The Key Largo Greyhound stop is at MM 102.

The Book Nook (☎ 305-451-1468), in the Waldorf Plaza shopping center at MM 99.5, sells tons of nature and travel books along

FLORIDA KEYS

with magazines, fiction and music; they have a big Florida book section and have been here more than 25 years. Cover to Cover Books (☎ 305-852-1415), in Tavernier at MM 90 oceanside, is another large general bookstore with good Florida and travel sections, as well as children's books and a coffee bar where you can sit and read their out-of-town and foreign newspapers. The Key Largo branch of the public library (☎ 305-451-2396) is in the Tradewinds Plaza shopping center at MM 101.5 – where there's also a Publix and K-Mart.

Change money at the NationsBank and wash clothes at the Waldorf Plaza Laundry in the Waldorf Plaza shopping center at MM 99.5. The biggest hospital in the area is Mariners Hospital (☎ 305-852-4418) at MM 88.5 on Plantation Key.

John Pennekamp
Coral Reef State Park

The first underwater park in the USA, John Pennekamp Coral Reef State Park (☎ 305-451-1202) has a public area of 75 sq miles of ocean, containing living coral reef, and 170 acres of land. It is by far the most user-friendly way to get out onto the Florida reef, with excellent ranger-led programs in winter, good information at the visitors center and a concession (☎ 305-451-1621) that rents anything you might need to get snorkeling or diving; it runs glass-bottom boat, snorkeling and diving trips every day. The park also has walking trails and a 3-mile network of canoe trails. The Wild Tamarind Nature Trail is home to air plants, gumbo-limbo, wild bamboo, Jamaica dogwood, crab-wood and, of course, wild tamarind. Other plant life along the trails includes white stopper bush (the skunky one), West Indian mahogany and strangler fig.

For snorkeling and diving, the best way to see the reef, you'll need transportation of some sort; you can rent sailboats, canoes, kayaks and motorboats, or hook up with organized snorkel and dive trips.

The entrance to Pennekamp is at MM 102.5, and the park is open every day 8 am to sunset. Admission is $2.50 for a car and driver, for more than one person in a car it's $5. Pedestrians and cyclists are $1.50 per person, mopeds and motorcycles are $2.50.

Visitors Center The Pennekamp visitors center is billed as 'the reef you can walk out to' – in case you don't have the time or inclination to don a bathing suit and jump in the water. The main feature in the center is their 30,000-gallon aquarium (along with several smaller ones) that showcases living coral and tropical fish and plant life. There's also a theater, where nature videos are shown continuously throughout the day.

Diving & Snorkeling Administratively speaking, diving and snorkeling along the reef isn't in the state park at all; it's out past the 3-mile limit in the federally managed Key Largo National Marine Sanctuary (☎ 305-451-1644), which extends for about 20 miles southwest along a line 3 miles off the Keys' Atlantic shore beginning at Broad Creek (see Looe Key National Marine Sanctuary, earlier in the chapter, for more information on the Key Largo National Marine Sanctuary). The areas are covered by NOAA Nautical Charts 11462 and 11451, available at dive shops along the Keys but not at Pennekamp.

Rangers and the concession are very helpful; ask about planning specific trips. The main snorkeling and diving areas within the sanctuary are, from north to south, Carysfort Reef, where you'll also find the 100-foot Carysfort Lighthouse (1852). Just south of the lighthouse is Carysfort South, the biggest shallow reef in the area, whose calm waters are perfect for snorkeling.

Elbow Reef, with three major wrecks, is a very popular dive site, but the most famous snorkel and dive site in the park is at Key

Largo Dry Rocks: the Christ of the Deep Statue. It's a 9-foot-high, 4000lb, algae-covered bronze statue of Christ built in Italy by Guido Galletti, installed as an underwater shrine to sailors and those who have lost loved ones to the sea.

Just southwest of the sanctuary are the sunken USCG cutters *Duane* and *Bibb*; see Wrecks & Ships, earlier in the chapter under Diving & Snorkeling.

You can rent a full scuba outfit – mask, two tanks, regulator, BC and weight belt – for $29 a day. Four-hour, two-dive trips leave at 9:30 am and 1:30 pm and cost $37; show up 45 minutes in advance. They also offer certification in resort diving ($150) open water ($450 private or $375 in a class), and advanced ($275/250).

The concession rents snorkel equipment for $10 a day, with a $35 deposit. They also operate 2½-hour snorkeling tours at 9 am, noon and 3 pm; adults/children under 18 are $24.95/19.95, $5 extra for equipment. A four-hour sailboat snorkel trip leaves at 9 am and 1:30 pm for $31.95/26.95.

Boating The park's 3 miles of canoe trails begin at the park marina; they are well-marked, easy trails through the mangroves. Paddleboats, canoes, kayaks and Hobie One sailboats and powerboats are available from the park concession. Canoes and kayaks cost $8 an hour, $28 for four hours, $48 for the day; paddleboats are $10 an hour; 12-foot Hobie One sailboats are $16 an hour, $48 for the day.

Organized Tours The 2½-hour glass-bottom boat tour (☎ 305-451-1621) goes out to Molasses Reef, at the southern end of the sanctuary, aboard the *San Jose*. Molasses Reef is part of a reef tract that extends from Fort Lauderdale through the Keys and on through the Dry Tortugas; it's named for a wrecked Jamaican ship that was carrying sugar cane molasses.

If this is the only chance you'll have to see the reef, you'll still come away amazed at the brilliant colors, the abundance of soft and hard coral and the tropical fish, stingrays, turtles, barracuda, angelfish, parrot fish,

Jewfish, grunts, grouper and snapper. The glass-bottom boat does not visit the Christ statue (see above). It leaves daily at 9:15 am and 12:15 and 3 pm, and costs $18 for adults, $10 for children under 12.

The *Key Largo Princess* is another glass-bottom boat that tours the area, leaving from the Holiday Inn Sun Spree (☎ 305-451-2121, 800-843-5397, see Hotels & Resorts later in this section) at 10 am and 1 and 4 pm. The cost is $17 for adults, $8.50 for children, and you cruise for about two hours.

In winter the park holds a wide variety of ranger-led programs that change regularly, including guided canoe trips, nature walks through the mangrove and hardwood hammocks, a campfire program, and a lecture series, usually held in January and February, with rangers and guest speakers holding talks on a range of environmentally related subjects, such as crocodiles, raising bananas, native versus non-native vegetation, area birds and wildlife.

Key Largo Undersea Park

This place is a trip. Key Largo Undersea Park (☎ 305-451-2353) is a sheltered natural mangrove lagoon area that's home to Jules' Undersea Lodge, an underwater hotel (see Places to Stay later in this section), which is reached only by diving. The 50-by-20-foot, steel-and-acrylic structure is permanently anchored 30 feet beneath the surface of the lagoon.

Originally, it was La Chalupa Laboratory, a research lab 110 feet underwater off the coast of Puerto Rico. The lab was home to aquanauts doing saturation dives to explore the continental shelf.

You can stay at the hotel or just visit it during the day (by reservation only). Divers can dive around the hotel with their own tanks (or rent equipment here; a one-tank dive is $25). If you want to actually enter the hotel, you can sign up for their three-hour mini-adventures ($60), which give you access to the hotel and use of its facilities as well as their three breathing hookahs – 120-foot-long air hoses that allow tankless diving.

Snorkelers can use the area as well for $10 including gear. It's not in a coral reef, but you will see some reef fish – such as angelfish, parrot fish, French angelfish and the like, lots of invertebrate growth and juvenile fish such as baby barracuda. You may get lucky and see some of their local snorkeling Elvises.

The entrance to the park is at MM 103.2; their office is open daily 9 am to 3 pm.

African Queen
At the Holiday Inn Sun Spree (☎ 305-451-2121, 800-843-5397), MM 100, you can take a ride on the *African Queen* – the one used in the movie with Hepburn and Bogart – when it's in port. It's an antique steam-engined vessel that can carry up to 15 people. Rides are $15 per person (at least two passengers), and you cruise the Port Largo Canal for about an hour. Reservations are a very good idea.

Dolphins Plus
This dolphin education center (☎ 305-451-1993, www.pennekamp.com/dolphins-plus) is off MM 99.5 bayside (but it's tricky to find; call for specific directions). Dolphins Plus specializes in swims with dolphins in recreational, educational and therapeutic programs. Their unstructured swims with dolphins (see the Swimming with Dolphins boxed text), which require a good deal of knowledge before embarking upon, are held twice daily, at 9 am and 1:30 pm. They include a classroom session and an hour in the water for $95. Longer swims are available as well. Their structured swims, which also include a classroom session, are offered only on some weekends and holidays (call for availability) and cost $125. If you're not swimming, admission is $8 for adults, $5 for students and children. Call for information on their in-water therapy sessions for special-needs children and adults.

Maritime Museum
The Maritime Museum of the Florida Keys (☎ 305-451-6444), MM 102.6, is a small but interesting museum. It is inside, of all places, a castle, and artifacts, treasures and other items from different fleets that sailed from the 1600s to 1700s are on display. They also show a 25-minute video on the Spanish Fleet of 1715. It's open daily 10 am to 5 pm. Admission is $5 for adults, seniors get a 10% discount, children under six are free.

Wild Bird Center
The Florida Keys Wild Bird Rehabilitation Center (☎ 305-852-4486), MM 93.6 bayside, is a nature center with a boardwalk and nature trail, and a bird rescue program – if you should spot an injured bird, call here. You can learn about the birds in the tiki hut educational center, which also, of course, sells T-shirts and such. There are sometimes guided tours, but usually it's a self-guided walk through the facility – bird habitats are well-signed. Expect to spend about 30 minutes to see the birds, which include herons, pelicans, hawks and ospreys. The center is open daily 8:30 am to 6 pm; admission is free (though they do depend on donations, they suggest $5 but you can give what you can afford).

Diving
Most dive shops are in the Pennekamp Park, and two others come well recommended – Capt Slade's Atlantis Dive Center (☎ 305-451-3020, 800-331-3483), MM 106.5, and Amy Slate's Amoray (☎ 305-451-3595), MM 104.2.

Organized Tours
Florida Bay Outfitters (☎ 305-451-3018), 104050 Overseas Hwy, rents kayaks for $10 to $15 an hour, $25 to $35 for four hours and $40 to $50 for eight hours. It also has canoes for $10 an hour to $25 a half day and $35 a day), and snorkeling, camping and boating equipment. From November to April (only in winter, simply because in summer there are too many bugs) they do half-day backcountry tours to seven-day wilderness trips into the Everglades National Park or two-day tours to Lignumvitae Key State Botanical Site and Indian Key Historic Site (see Islamorada earlier in this chapter).

Places to Stay
Camping Non-waterfront camping is available at *John Pennekamp Coral Reef State*

Park (☎ 305-451-1202). Campsites are $23.69 without electricity and $25.84 with; all sites have water hookups. There's a central dump station for RVs. If you've come by boat, there's overnight camping on the water within the park (you moor to the buoys) for $11, which includes use of the dump station and showers. You can reserve up to 60 days in advance.

The *Calusa Camp Resort* (☎ 305-451-0232, MM 101.5 bayside) was hit by a tornado after Hurricane Mitch. It's open but they're still cleaning up. Sites have water and electricity; they cost $22.30 for one or two people ($3 per extra person); full hookup sites (with sewer) are $33.45. It's not on the beach, but they do have a pool. While there are no grills provided and no open fires permitted, you can bring your own grill; no pets. The gates close at 6 pm, so watch it!

The friendly people at *America Outdoors Campground* (☎ 305-852-8054, MM 97.5 bayside) charge $40/33 in winter/summer for sites with water, electricity and cable; $45/38 for sites with sewer hookups; and $55/45 for waterfront sites. There are no grills, but you can bring your own. Pets (on a leash) are allowed in the campsites but not on the beach.

Hotels & Resorts Rooms at the clean *Bay Harbor Lodge* (☎ 305-852-5695, MM 97.7) are from $95 to $195 in winter and $65 to $155 in summer. Other Key Largo options are not very cheap and are mainly resorts. The *Holiday Inn Sun Spree* (☎ 305-451-2121, 800-843-5397, MM 100) is the largest in the Keys, and it's a city in and of itself, with restaurants, activities and, from the marina, casino cruises. Once again, rates vary wildly depending on the season (the staff giggle when you try to pin them down); count on $179 in winter and $109 to $129 in June.

The *Westin Beach Resort* (☎ 305-852-5553, 800-826-1006, MM 97) is another large resort. The prices here vary mainly on the view: 'nature trail'-view and island-view rooms are $290, bay views $350. Jacuzzi suites are $450; in low season those rooms would cost $250/300/400. All rooms have a balcony, and there are restaurants, bars, a pool, a hair salon and more.

Underwater Hotels Check out *Jules' Undersea Lodge* (☎ 305-451-2353, MM 103.2), an underwater hotel that can accommodate up to six people; it's permanently anchored 30 feet beneath the water's surface. The entrance is at Key Largo Undersea Park (see earlier in this section).

The first question everyone asks is whether it's safe. Well, consider that the safety systems here were designed for scientists living onboard for long periods of time. Even if all the backup generators and systems failed, there would still be about 12 hours of breathing time inside the hotel. During Hurricane Andrew, it remained completely online – when people on the surface were without power, the air conditioning still worked down there!

Your luggage is sent down separately. The rooms themselves are quite luxurious, complete with TV/VCRs and showers, and in the living room there's a microwave oven for popcorn. There are, of course, telephones and an intercom to the surface. You can even call for room service – there are staff members on duty 24 hours a day when guests are in the place.

If you're not a certified diver you can still stay here; they will get you a quick limited certificate for $75. There are several accommodation packages; the cheapest, the 'European-style' package, costs $225 per person, check-in at 5 pm, check-out at 9 am. The 'luxury aquanaut' package is $325 per person (if at least four people go, the price goes down to $275 per person). This package includes an aquanaut certificate, dinner and breakfast, and check-in at 1 pm, check-out at 11 am. And the 'ultimate romantic getaway' package is $1000 for two people per night – you get the place all to yourselves with flowers and caviar and other little extras. Reservations are required for all stays.

Advanced divers can also get an optional ($100) specialty 'underwater habitat' certificate, which includes learning how to transfer luggage and goods to the hotel without getting them wet and study of the history of underwater exploration – basically, it's something you can lord over your friends for the rest of your life. To stay here you must be at least 12 years old, and no alcohol, smoking or pets are permitted. They also have a whole lot of specialty diving courses, like diver propulsion vehicles, underwater archaeology and photography.

Places to Eat

Outside of the resorts and the restaurant at Pennekamp Park, try the **Crack'd Conch** (☎ 305-451-0732, MM 105), which is a fun seafood restaurant. Sandwiches (lunch only) are $5 to $8, dinners average $13 to $16, and steamed shrimp with salad and sides is $12.95. The most expensive thing on the menu is a platter with 'lots of different seafood' for $17.95.

At **Señor Frijoles** (☎ 305-451-1592, MM 104), a Mexican burger is $6.50, the burrito supreme is $7.95 and camarones rancheros are $12.95. But tequila takes center stage.

Treetops is the fine dining option in the Westin Beach Resort, doing seafood and steaks with good service; dinner with wine will run you $45 to $55 per person. **Sundowners** (☎ 305-451-4502, MM 104), next to Señor Frijoles, has an outside verandah and a glass-walled dining room. They do simple chicken and steaks from $12 to $24.

Southeast Florida

Between the hubbub of Miami and the Right Stuff on the Space Coast sit some of Florida's most famous – and infamous – beaches. In most of the places along this section of the Florida coast you'll run into opulence. From what is arguably the USA's yachting capital in Fort Lauderdale to the staggering (even swaggering) mansions at Palm Beach, this is a moneyed area.

But it's also very accessible. Even the most exclusive places are at least polite to travelers, and you can find ways to see the glamour without paying through the nose.

For example, you can have a great time window-shopping on Palm Beach's Worth Ave (looking at $600 pants!) and still manage to find a motel room for $30 to $40 in southern West Palm Beach or Lake Worth. You can get great Thai food for under $5 in West Palm Beach and loll on Fort Lauderdale's newly renovated beaches while spending no more than $14.40 (plus tax) for a bed.

The natural gem of the southeast coast is the area between Stuart and north Palm Beach, where pristine wilderness awaits in state parks and the Hobe Sound National Wildlife Refuge. The area is wide open for exploration and a wonderful way to get away from the golf courses, the developments and the highways. You can kayak around St Lucie Inlet State Park, canoe along the Loxahatchee River and camp in Jonathan Dickinson State Park, in either developed or totally primitive campsites.

And finally, Florida's southeast coast has a prize of such value, such eminence...well, it's obvious what we're saying is that on your way through you simply *must* snap a photograph of the world headquarters of the *National Enquirer* in Lantana.

FORT LAUDERDALE
- **population 150,000**

As recently as the mid-1980s the sand in Fort Lauderdale was sticky from beer. The streets were full of college students from all over storming about drinking cheap drafts till they passed out, celebrating that American university rite of passage: Spring Break. But since the late '80s, the town has managed to divest itself completely of this scene. They've renovated, groomed and trimmed the whole place, and done an exceedingly good job of it.

Today Fort Lauderdale is known more as an international yachting center than as a party spot. Ships owned round the world are repaired or built here; mind-bogglingly huge yachts make their winter home here; and some of the wealthiest European, Asian and American sailors can be seen here fussing over details with the city's countless support staff.

That's not to say it's not a partying town: it decidedly is. These days you can party at dozens of clubs, pubs and beach nightspots as long as you dress respectably and behave yourself. You can still party till you puke – if you like – but you'll puke in a sophisticated nightclub, in a toilet, and not out on the beach. Thank you very much.

Fort Lauderdale has some good cultural and historical sites, and lovely areas to walk through – notably the shopping district along E Las Olas Blvd and Riverwalk. Don't miss Hugh Taylor Birch State Recreation Area, and definitely take a water taxi or river cruise through Millionaire's Row – Fort Lauderdale by water is a unique look at an otherwise unseen display of the good life.

History

Small bands of Indians lived in this region for about 4000 years before the arrival of the Spanish in the 16th century. During the early period of Spanish control and the later occupation of Florida by the British, fighting between the Europeans and Indian groups on the west coast of Florida kept settlers at bay. But during the second era of Spanish rule, white settlers very slowly began to gain a foothold in the region. In 1821 the US took control of Florida (see History in the Facts about Florida chapter for more information), and by 1825, families – including the ill-fated Cooleys – had settled on the north banks of the New River.

In 1836, in the midst of the Second Seminole War, Seminoles attacked the Cooley residence, killing all but Mr Cooley, who was away. The Cooley Massacre, as it became known among white settlers, was a milestone in the city's history. In March 1838, Major William Lauderdale (for whom the city is named) and a force of troops from the Tennessee Volunteers established a fort and a stockade here. But white settlement remained stagnant for the next 30 years.

In the 1870s the area finally began to grow, and by the 1890s Fort Lauderdale was

SOUTHEAST FLORIDA

large enough to boast a post office, ferry and stagecoach services. Frank Stranahan established the first lodge in the city.

The real boom came with the advent of the Florida East Coast Railroad, which put Fort Lauderdale on the map – or at least on the route connecting the booming towns of Miami (to the south) and St Augustine (to the north) with the rest of the eastern seaboard. Immigrant groups, including large numbers of Danes and Swedes, as well as Japanese settlers in the north (see Delray Beach later this chapter) moved in. In 1925, the establishment of Port Everglades came just in time for the bust of the mid-1920s, and the hurricane of 1926 wiped out thousands of acres of lands and killed dozens in the area.

As with Miami, WWII provided just the boost Fort Lauderdale needed; and the public display of the captured German ship *Arauca* in Port Everglades served as a rallying point. German submarine activities in the area led to the establishment of military bases and training fields, which after the war brought in thousands of new settlers and lots of money.

The construction boom of the 1970s brought a new prosperity to the region, as well as hundreds of thousands of college kids, bent on getting plastered as cheaply as possible during Spring Break. The ritual was outlawed locally in the mid-1980s.

Orientation

The city is set in a grid wherever physically possible (it's hard with all the water), and it's divided into three distinct sections: the beach, on the east side of the Intracoastal Waterway; downtown, which is on the mainland; and Port Everglades, the cruise port on the south side of the city.

US Hwy 1, here called Federal Hwy, cuts through downtown, swooping under E Las Olas Blvd via the New River Tunnel. Hwy A1A runs along the ocean and is therefore appropriately named Atlantic Blvd (south of Sunrise Blvd) or Ocean Blvd (north of Sunrise). At its south end, Atlantic Blvd merges into Seabreeze Blvd (just south of Las Olas Blvd and the Swimming Hall of

Fame) and Seabreeze continues south until the curve where it becomes 17th St. The whole stretch is Hwy A1A.

Streets and addresses are prefixed N, S, E or W according to their relation to Broward Blvd and Andrews Ave; Broward Blvd is the north-south dividing line, and Andrews Ave, just west of Federal Hwy, is the east-west line.

The main arteries between downtown and the beach are Sunrise Blvd to the north (which runs from the beach at the east to the massive Sawgrass Mills Mall to the far west), E Las Olas Blvd in the center and 17th St/Seabreeze Blvd to the south (Seabreeze connects the beach to Port Everglades).

Between the beach and the mainland are almost two dozen small finger islands. Here, there's a mooring at every house and what seems like a boat and a half at every mooring – this is yacht country, maybe the yacht capital of North America. And along with yachts, of course, come the millionaires that putter around on them. If you're waterborne, you can cruise by Millionaire's Row on the New River, just west of the Intracoastal Waterway – that's south of E Las Olas Blvd, west of Las Olas Isles and east of downtown.

Of the two main free handout maps, the one published by the Las Olas Merchant Association is better on the whole than the one from the CVB. Dolph Map Company's *Map of Metropolitan Broward County* ($3) is available in gas stations.

Information

Tourist Offices The excellent Greater Fort Lauderdale Convention & Visitor's Bureau (☎ 954-765-4466, 800-227-8669, www.sunny .org) is at 1850 Eller Drive, Suite 303 in Port Everglades (from 17th St, take Eisenhower Blvd to Eller Drive, turn right and it's the first large building on the left). They run a fax-back information service at ☎ 800-227-8669. The City of Fort Lauderdale also runs a Website at info.ci.ftlaud.fl.us. Floyd's Crew House is a good local information source as well (see Places to Stay). There's a small tourist information booth on the beach side, on Atlantic just south of 5th St.

FORT LAUDERDALE AREA

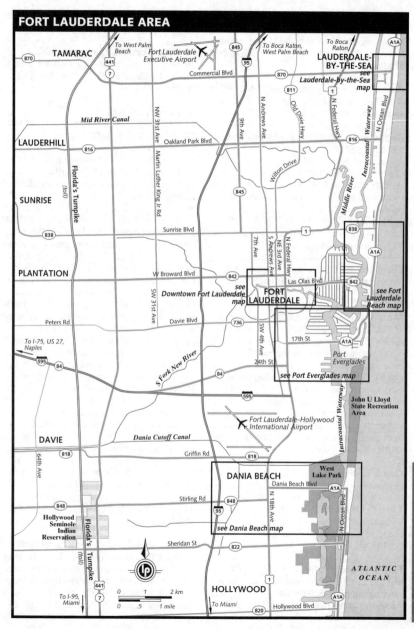

TAMARAC

870

441
7

To West Palm
Beach

Fort Lauderdale
Executive Airport

845

To Boca Raton,
West Palm Beach

95

To Boca
Raton

A1A

LAUDERDALE-
BY-THE-SEA

Commercial Blvd

870

811

1

*see
Lauderdale-by-the-Sea
map*

Mid River Canal

LAUDERHILL

816

NW 31st Ave

Oakland Park Blvd

9th Ave

N Andrews Ave

Old Dixie Hwy

N Federal Hwy

816

SUNRISE

838

Martin Luther King Jr Rd

Florida's Turnpike (toll)

845

Wilton Drive

Middle River

Intracoastal Waterway

N Ocean Blvd

Sunrise Blvd

1

838

A1A

PLANTATION

W Broward Blvd

842

SW 31st Ave

7th Ave

S Andrews Ave

NE 3rd Ave

N Federal Hwy

1

*see
Downtown Fort Lauderdale
map*

Downtown Fort Lauderdale

FORT
LAUDERDALE

Las Olas Blvd

842

*see Fort
Lauderdale
Beach map*

Peters Rd

Davie Blvd

736

To I-75, US 27,
Naples

595
84

S Fork New River

SW 4th Ave

17th St

A1A

Port
Everglades

24th St

84

595

see Port Everglades map

John U Lloyd
State Recreation
Area

Fort Lauderdale-Hollywood
International Airport

Intracoastal Waterway

DAVIE

818

64th Ave

Dania Cutoff Canal

Griffin Rd

818

West
Lake Park

DANIA BEACH

Dania Beach Blvd

A1A

848

Florida's Turnpike (toll)

Stirling Rd

848

95

N 18th Ave

N Ocean Blvd

Hollywood
Seminole
Indian
Reservation

see Dania Beach map

Sheridan St

822

ATLANTIC
OCEAN

441
7

To I-95,
Miami

0   1   2 km

0   .5   1 mile

HOLLYWOOD

To Miami

820

1

Hollywood Blvd

A1A

SOUTHEAST

Money NationsBank has branches at 1 E Broward Blvd (☎ 954-765-1502) and 2404B E Sunrise Blvd (☎ 954-561-5550). American Express (☎ 954-565-9481) is at 3312-14 NE 32nd St.

Post The main post office (☎ 954-527-2077) is at 1900 W Oakland Park Blvd; there's another at 330 SW 2nd St.

Bookstores Liberties Fine Books (☎ 954-522-6789), 888 E Las Olas Blvd, has a great selection of books and a small café. Clark's Out of Town News (☎ 954-467-1543), 303 S Andrews Ave at Las Olas Blvd, has out-of-town and foreign newspapers and travel books.

MacCarthy's (☎ 954-467-7410), 1400 E Las Olas Blvd, has some international newspapers and magazines.

Libraries Fort Lauderdale's main public library (☎ 954-357-7444) is at 100 S Andrews Ave.

Media The *Sun Sentinel* and the *Miami Herald* are the major dailies in the area. *City Link* (25¢) is a very well done local weekly covering music, clubs, restaurants, art and other entertainment; it covers all of southern Florida but has lots of information on Fort Lauderdale.

Hot Spots, *Scoop* and *David* are magazines that cover the gay and lesbian club scene; they are available at gay bars, clubs and guesthouses. National Public Radio (NPR) is at 91.3 FM.

Gay & Lesbian The helpful Gay & Lesbian Community Center of Greater Fort Lauderdale (☎ 954-563-9500, www.glccftl.org) is at 1164 E Oakland Park Blvd (2nd floor). Catalog X (☎ 954-524-5050), 850 NE 13th St, is one of the nation's largest gay and lesbian bookshops.

Film & Photography Hobby House (☎ 954-463-1522), 1201 E Las Olas Blvd, offers one-hour developing ($10 for 24 exposures) and passport photos ($9).

Laundry Try Las Olas Laundry (☎ 954-522-8197), 1206 E Las Olas Blvd.

Medical Services The largest public hospital in the area is the Broward General Medical Center (☎ 954-355-4400), 1600 S Andrews Ave.

Museum of Art

Fort Lauderdale's Museum of Art (☎ 954-525-5550), 1 E Las Olas Blvd, is one of Florida's best.

The impressive permanent collection (more than 5400 works) boasts pieces by such artists as Pablo Picasso, Henri Matisse, Henry Moore, Salvador Dali and Andy Warhol, as well as the core collection of works by William Glackens and by CoBrA artists Karel Appel, Carl-Henning Pedersen, Asger Jorn and Pierre Alechinsky (see the boxed text). You can't ever really know, though, what you're going to see on a particular visit, as the enormity of the collection far outpaces the available space – when we last visited they had photographs from Herb Ritts. Also not to be missed are the growing and equally impressive museum collections of Cuban and ethnographic art, including a large African and South American collection.

If you're here in the fall (from September to early October), keep an eye out for the Hortt Memorial Exhibition and Competition, Florida's oldest juried art show, which showcases the best of area artists.

Special openings for kids are held every month.

Parking is at the lot by the library. The museum is open Tuesday 11 am to 9 pm, Wednesday to Saturday 10 am to 5 pm and Sunday noon to 5 pm; it's closed Monday and federal holidays. Admission is $6 for adults, $5 for seniors, $3 for students, $1 for kids five to 18.

Museum of Discovery & Science

Fronted by the 52-foot-tall Great Gravity Clock, Florida's largest kinetic energy sculpture, the Museum of Discovery & Science (MODS; ☎ 954-467-6637), 401 SW 2nd St, is one of the best of its kind in the state and

Highlights of the Museum of Art

Be sure to check out the following works of art:

CoBrA The museum's CoBrA collection – CoBrA is an acronym for COpenhagen, BRussels and Amsterdam, the cities where the movement originated – is the largest in the US. It was donated by Meyer and Golda Marks, who fell in love with the work in the 1960s and began buying up all they could. The movement emerged just after WWII and was led by Karel Appel, Asger Jorn and Cornelis Van Beverloo (Cornielle). These artists, disenchanted with what they felt to be the restrictive art schools of the day – mainly Cubism, De Stijl and other geometric abstractionism – developed a fresh new style that shunned right angles and broke all the rules. What emerged was playful and childlike, colorful and violent.

Glackens The works of William Glackens (1870-1938) are the jewels in the museum's crown. The collection, much of it donated by the artist's son, Ira, is made up mainly of Glackens' late-19th- and early-20th-century works. Other works included in the bequest are by artists associated with Glackens, especially John Sloan, Ernest Lawson, Maurice Prendergast and George Luks.

African Art The theme of the African art collection is harmony, and many of the pieces are religious, ceremonial or spiritual. The mask collection is fascinating. The detailed explanations of the pieces are very good as well.

worth a visit by children and adults alike. The environmentally oriented museum is very visual and hands-on. It's open Monday to Saturday 10 am to 5 pm, Sunday noon to 6 pm. Museum admission is $6 for adults, $5 for children three to 12 and seniors over 65.

In the same building, **IMAX** movies are $9 for adults, $8 for children/seniors; a combination museum/film ticket is $12.50 for adults, $11.50 for seniors and $10.50 for children. In 1996, MODS became the fourth theater in the world to offer IMAX 3D films with a magic helmet. The helmet, which looks like a virtual-reality gizmo, includes several speakers for strategic sound placement, as well as high-tech 3D goggles (no more plastic glasses). Across the street, between the river and the museum, is a very cool parabolic display: two dishes face each other about 20 meters apart. Stand facing one dish and have a friend face the other. Whisper into the dish and your friend will hear you as if you're standing right next to them. Kids (and we) go nuts over it.

Fort Lauderdale Historical Society

This organization (☎ 954-463-4431) maintains a museum and a collection of historic buildings at 219 SW 2nd Ave, west of the railroad tracks, just near the start of Riverwalk. The museum holds exhibits on the history of Fort Lauderdale and Broward County, baseball and Seminole folk art. The historic buildings are the former **New River Inn** (1905), the **King-Cromartie House** (1907) and the **Philemon Bryan House** (1905). Walking tours around the houses are available by arrangement.

Museum hours are Tuesday to Friday 10 am to 4 pm; tours are $2 for adults, $1 for students, and free for children six and younger.

Riverwalk

A strip along the New River running west from Bubier Park to the Broward Center for the Performing Arts (see Entertainment later), Riverwalk is just a very pleasant bit of green and a lovely way to walk between the Museum of Art and MODS.

Las Olas Riverfront is a giant new shopping mall here, with stores, snacks and the dock for a river cruise (see Organized Tours later), as well as live music daily in the courtyard.

Stranahan House

One of Florida's oldest residences, a perfect example of Florida frontier design and a registered historic landmark, the Stranahan House (☎ 954-524-4736) is on the New River

at SE 4th St (behind the Hyde Park supermarket). It was built as the home and store for Ohio transplant Frank Stranahan, a trader who built up a small empire through dealings with the Seminole Indians. After losses in the real estate and stock market busts of the late 1920s and the collapse of his Fort Lauderdale Bank, Stranahan became despondent and ended up committing suicide by jumping into the New River.

Constructed from Dade County pine, the house has wide porches, exceptionally tall windows and a Victorian parlor, as well as

DOWNTOWN FORT LAUDERDALE

PLACES TO STAY
26 Riverside Hotel

PLACES TO EAT
4 Independence Brewery
5 Governmental Center Cafeteria
13 Marie's Sugar & Spice
14 Dicey Riley's
25 Zanzbar
27 Cheeburger! Cheeburger!
28 Japanese Village
29 China Yung Restaurant
30 O'Hara's Pub
31 Cafe Europa
32 Kilwin's
33 Mango's
34 Las Olas Cafe
35 Mark's
38 The Floridian

fine tropical gardens. You can see original furnishings, including fish dishes and hand-painted china given to the family.

The house is open Wednesday to Sunday 10 am to 5 pm; regularly scheduled tours run between 10 am and 4 pm. Admission is $5 for adults, $2 for children.

Bonnet House

The Bonnet House (☎ 954-563-5393) is a beautiful estate at 900 N Birch Rd (near the beach; enter through the west gate). The property's 35 acres are filled with native and imported tropical plants, including a vast orchid collection. However, you have to be on a tour to see the house and grounds, so you can't wander or bring a picnic. The tours, which last a little more than an hour, leave every hour on the half hour from 10:30 am to 1:30 pm Wednesday to Friday, and at 12:30, 1:15, 1:45 and 2:30 pm on Saturday and Sunday (show up 15 minutes prior to tour time). Admission is $9 for adults, $8 for senior citizens and $7 for students six to 17 and members of groups; children under six are free.

DOWNTOWN FORT LAUDERDALE

OTHER
1 Broward Central Terminal (Bus Station)
2 NationsBank
3 Chili Pepper
5 Governmental Center Building
6 Main Library
7 Broward Center for the Performing Arts
8 Museum of Discovery & Science, IMAX
9 Parabolic Display
10 Playground
11 Water Taxi Stop
12 Commuter Store
15 Fort Lauderdale Historical Society
16 The Philemon Bryan House
17 King-Cromartie House
18 New River Inn
19 Las Olas Riverfront Cruises
20 Clark's Out of Town News
21 Museum of Art
22 Squeeze
23 Downtowner Saloon
24 Stranahan House
36 Club Cathode Ray
37 Hobby House

P Parking

International Swimming Hall of Fame

If you know a competition pool holds 573,000 gallons you're enough of a swimming wonk to *really* enjoy the International Swimming Hall of Fame Museum (☎ 954-462-6536), 1 Hall of Fame Drive (SE 5th St), two blocks south of E Las Olas Blvd near the beach. Exhibits include thousands of photographs, medals, uniforms, paintings, sculptures – the list goes on and on.

The museum is open daily 9 am to 7 pm; admission is $3 per adult, $1 for students, seniors and military or a flat $5 per family.

Out back, the city-run Aquatic Complex is open to the public. Admission to swim is $3 a day, $16 a week; children under six cost $1.50 a day. Further discounts are available for students, Fort Lauderdale residents, military and senior citizens. Water aerobics classes are $3 a class. Entry is free for spectators except during some competitions – and there are a lot of those.

Radisson Bahia Mar Yacht Center

For fans of the hard-boiled yet lovable detective Travis McGee, the star of about 20 novels by the late, great John D McDonald, a visit to this yacht center (☎ 954-764-2233), just south of the Swimming Hall of Fame, is a pilgrimage. There's a plaque commemorating the fictional detective's digs here, where the *Busted Flush* moored at slip F-618. Entry is free; ask at the harbormaster's office for directions.

Hugh Taylor Birch State Recreation Area

Running north up the beach from E Sunrise Blvd, the Hugh Taylor Birch State Recreation Area (☎ 954-564-4521) contains one of the last significant maritime hammocks left in Broward County, as well as mangroves, a freshwater lagoon system and several endangered plant and animal species (including the gopher tortoise and golden leather fern).

Beach access is via a tunnel under Hwy A1A, and within the grounds you can fish, picnic, hike, bike or canoe (on their little half-mile trail; canoes cost about $6 an hour). Friendly rangers abound, and a video in the rangers' office describes what you'll see on your way through the park.

The park is open daily 8 am to 7:30 pm. Admission is $1 for pedestrians and bicyclists, $3 per vehicle with up to eight passengers, $1 for each additional passenger. Bus and group rates are available on request. Ranger-guided tours are given Friday at 10 am, weather permitting.

Activities

Diving Fort Lauderdale has tons of dive shops; try Lauderdale Undersea Adventures (☎ 954-527-0187, www.diverftlauderdale .com), which offers a week-long PADI openwater certificate class for $200, including books, equipment and four dives. It's at the east end of the 17th St Intracoastal bridge on the south side of the street. There's also an expensive dive shop at the Bahia Mar Yacht Center. In September, Ocean Fest, a dive trade show open to the public, is held in Lauderdale-by-the-Sea.

Water-skiing, Parasailing & Boating Water-skiing in Fort Lauderdale is possible on the ocean, but it's usually outrageously expensive; check on the piers below the bridge at Las Olas Blvd and look for flyers when you're in town. Jet skis are popular here, but we really wish you wouldn't use them. On the west side of the river near the Middle River bridge north of Sunrise Blvd, Bill's Sunrise Watersports Rentals (☎ 954-462-8962), 2025 E Sunrise Blvd, offers parasailing and also rents six-person 18-foot motorboats for $50 an hour, $85 for two

Fort Liquordale in earlier days

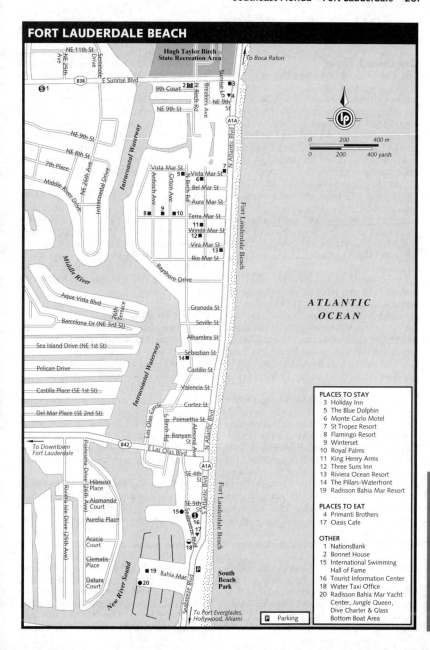

FORT LAUDERDALE BEACH

PLACES TO STAY
3 Holiday Inn
5 The Blue Dolphin
6 Monte Carlo Motel
7 St Tropez Resort
8 Flamingo Resort
9 Winterset
10 Royal Palms
11 King Henry Arms
12 Three Suns Inn
13 Riviera Ocean Resort
14 The Pillars-Waterfront
19 Radisson Bahia Mar Resort

PLACES TO EAT
4 Primanti Brothers
17 Oasis Cafe

OTHER
1 NationsBank
2 Bonnet House
15 International Swimming
Hall of Fame
16 Tourist Information Center
18 Water Taxi Office
20 Radisson Bahia Mar Yacht
Center, *Jungle Queen*,
Dive Charter & Glass
Bottom Boat Area

P Parking

SOUTHEAST

hours or $150 for four hours with a $200 deposit.

Organized Tours

The *Carrie B* (☎ 954-768-9920) is a 19th-century riverboat replica that offers sightseeing excursions down the New River and the Intracoastal Waterway to Port Everglades and back. Tours last about 1½ hours and depart from Riverwalk at SW 5th Ave and W Las Olas Blvd at 11 am, 1 and 3 pm daily; they cost $9.95 for adults, $4.95 for children under 12 (no other discounts).

Las Olas Riverfront Cruises (☎ 954-463-3372) runs 1½ hour cruises aboard the monstrous 85-foot *Anticipation* past Millionaire's Row and Port Everglades. The tours leave every two hours from 10:30 am to 8:30 pm.; tickets are $14 for adults and $8 for kids. Meet the boat at the Las Olas Riverfront mall.

Pro Diver II (☎ 954-467-6030) is a glass-bottom boat that lets you view underwater ocean wonders. The cost is $15 for adults, $10 for children under 12 (one child under five can get in free with one adult). If you really need to get closer, you can rent full snorkeling equipment for $5 extra. Excursions leave from the Bahia Mar Yacht Center (next to the *Jungle Queen*) Tuesday to Saturday at 9:30 am and Sunday at 2 pm.

The *Jungle Queen* BBQ & Shrimp Dinner Cruise (☎ 305-947-6597) is either a wondrous journey to a tropical island, a great meal and a funny vaudeville show, or the kitschiest, cheesiest romp into Borscht-belt glitz around. A Fort Lauderdale tradition, the *Jungle Queen* sails at 7 pm on the four-hour dinner tour ($25.50). On the way to the 'tropical' island where you dine, the narrator gives you all the dirt on the rich folks who own houses on Millionaire's Row, leads group participation in waving to the drawbridge attendants and offers trivia and local lore.

The barbecue dinner includes chicken (fine), ribs (good) and shrimp, which they make you peel – something they are not ashamed to tell you is done in order to slow you down. But you'll get full, for sure. Water, coffee and tea are included; soft drinks, beer and frozen drinks are extra ($2.50 to $3.95).

After dinner, you're ushered out to the theater, where you'll see a great Swedish juggler (did the Carson show), a 'singer,' and a comedian who's trapped in time ('Lady, I was *talking* to the duck!'). Your emcee tells about the glory days of vaudeville and sings ('You've gone for a cruise on a river/You've eaten a barbecue dinner…'). The audience seemed to love it. On the way back there's a sing-along, culminating in, of course, *God Bless America* as you return to port. The *Jungle Queen* also offers a three-hour afternoon tour ($11.50), sans meal and show.

The cruises leave from the dock at the Bahia Mar Yacht Center, just south of the Radisson Bahia Mar Resort at the southern end of town; parking is $5, but if you're smart you'll head to the municipal parking lot just south of the Oasis Cafe (☎ 954-463-3130) at 600 Seabreeze Blvd, a few blocks south of Las Olas Blvd, where it's $3 from 6 pm to midnight and a shorter walk to the boat.

Places to Stay

Fort Lauderdale's not exactly a budget traveler's dream, but dozens of little motels on the beach offer rates in the $35 to $50 range in high season, and a bit lower in low season when bottom-end motels have specials for around $25 to $30 for a double room.

On the lower end there are three youth hostels – though we recommend only one (see below) – with dorm beds from $11 to $14 including tax. And if you're here looking for work on a foreign-flag vessel, you have a choice of several crew houses, all at around $100 per week.

You'll find the highest concentration of hotels, motels and B&Bs is on the beach, in the '-mars' area – from Rio Mar St at the south to Vistamar St at the north, and from Hwy A1A at the east to Bayshore Drive. Wherever you go in town, be very careful about advertised rates – many are for singles, with huge jumps for additional people. If you've been ripped off or have complaints about a hotel, contact the Fort Lauderdale Division of Hotels and Restaurants (☎ 954-958-5520). On the flip side, hotels listed with the Superior Small Lodg-

Fort Lauderdale Beach is a favorite among skaters.

The Breakers hotel in Palm Beach is modeled after Rome's Villa Medici.

MAXINE CASS

MAXINE CASS

World-famous Florida oranges, in Kissimmee

Manatees in Blue Spring State Park

Florida souvenirs at SeaWorld Orlando

Walk underneath the Saturn V rocket exhibit at the Kennedy Space Center.

ings (SSL) association are generally of high standards all around.

Hostels The best deal on a cheap bed in town is at *Floyd's Youth Hostel and Crew House* (☎ 954-462-0631, fecreamer@aol .com), with clean dorm beds at $14.40 plus tax, cheaper if you book in advance. It's in the Port Everglades section of town, close to most of the crew placement agencies (see Getting There & Away later in the chapter), and a short bus ride to the beach. Staff are very friendly and protective of the property and of the guests and their belongings. Before you can stay here you'll be vetted on the telephone by Floyd; you must hold a valid passport regardless of your nationality, and there's zero tolerance for illegal drug use. Floyd's a very nice guy – he's just looking to keep things safe. And the many extras he provides – free local calls, use of his computer, incoming faxes, washer and dryer, tea, corn flakes, pasta, cocoa, rice, cooking oil and sugar, free barbecues (with beer) for guests every couple of weeks – make the place a spectacular value. He'll also pick you up free from the airport and the Greyhound and Amtrak stations.

Unfortunately, the hostels Sol y Mar and the International House are no longer recommended. The *International House* (☎ 954-568-1615, 3811 N Ocean Blvd) has gone from a fine option to a dire one. We've received lots of complaints from guests about cleanliness, roaches and nonstop parties, an unusable pool and other more serious infractions. At the very least, look at the rooms and speak to other guests before committing (ones we spoke with this time said it was fine but that the pool was dirty, so it may just go up and down). A universal complaint we've heard is that, after encouraging guests to pay in advance the cheaper weekly rate, management refused on at least two occasions we know of to give refunds to unsatisfied customers – even when HI headquarters was called. *Caveat emptor.* Beds here cost $13.08 for HI members, $16.35 for nonmembers.

Crew Houses These are not for the average backpacker, but rather for those seeking employment aboard yachts and ships moored nearby (see Sea in the Getting There & Away chapter). Generally these are the best places to pick up information on boat jobs, and all have listings of all the agencies in town. The first two places are near Port Everglades. In most cases, backpackers will not be admitted, so call first and make sure before showing up.

The exception to the no-backpackers rule is Floyd's Youth Hostel (see above), which is also a full-fledged crew house.

Joanne's Crew House (☎ 954-527-1636, 916 SE 12th St) is the best established in town and it's a beauty. In a sprawling and spotlessly clean ranch-style house, 20 people can await employment in true style. There is an enormous screened-in backyard, complete with pool and barbecue area on this one-acre property. In fact, everything – the kitchen, the rooms, the house – is huge, and the price is $120/week.

For the same price, the much smaller *Lynn Hawkin's Crew House* (☎ 954-779-7213, 1208 SE 6th St) has very nice and comfortable rooms, though it's a bit awkwardly located (far from port).

There are several apartments at *Camille's Crew House* (☎ 954-676-3569, 954-527-4653); weekly rentals (which hold four to eight people) are $100, which includes use of the washer and dryer and cable TV. Call for their address, which they don't print.

Sunshine Crew House (☎ 954-523-3043, 1200 S Miami), behind the Oasis Motel, has rooms at $120 a week.

Motels & Hotels Dozens of species of palm are planted all over the property of the *Winterset* (☎ 954-564-5614, 800-888-2639, fax 954-565-5790, 2801 Terra Mar St), which has two pools and very friendly management, though furniture is out of the 1970s (and not in a hip way, either). Rooms start at $35 per day, $225 per week in low season and go to $50 to $60 per day, $340 to $400 per week in high season.

Rooms at the *Monte Carlo Motel* (☎ 954-564-1311, fax 954-563-0436, 717 Breakers Ave at Vistamar St) have a good feel to them, with tiled floors (which makes it feel cooler)

SOUTHEAST

and very clean, nice kitchens. Room rates start at $39 in low season, $69 in high season.

Very best of luck to the seriously friendly Brazilian family who run **Three Suns Inn** (☎ 954-563-7926, 800-758-8884, 3016 Windamar St). It has large, spotless rooms from $49 in low season, $70 in high. There's a nice pool.

St Tropez Resort (☎ 954-564-8468, 725 N Atlantic Blvd) has very clean rooms and large bathrooms. It's a good deal in low season when, despite printed rates of $45 to $75, you can usually get a room for $40; prices rise to $85 to $110 in high season.

Riviera Ocean Resort (☎ 954-565-4443, 800-457-7770, fax 954-568-9118, 505 N Atlantic Blvd) is another totally reasonable option, with clean, tiled rooms and a nice pool area, a pool bar and tennis courts. For the price, it's not bad. Room rates start at $45 to $70 in low season, $75 to $95 in high season.

The Pillars-Waterfront (☎ 954-467-9639, 800-800-7666, fax 954-763-2845, 111 N Birch Rd) is a lovely resort at the end of Sebastian St on the Intracoastal Waterway. It has very large rooms, efficiencies and suites, a pool, barbecue area and tables lining its private pier. If you're going to spend $99 to $109 for rooms or $160 for a suite in winter, $59/room or $130/suite in fall and spring, and $59 to $69/room or $130/suite in summer, this is the place to spend it.

The grand **Riverside Hotel** (☎ 954-467-0671, 800-325-3280, 620 E Las Olas Blvd) is the oldest in Fort Lauderdale. Rooms are large, with fluffy carpets and Jacobean oak furnishings. Room rates are $119 to $189 April to May, $129 to $199 October to December and $179 to $299 December to April.

The **Holiday Inn** (☎ 954-563-5961, 999 N Atlantic) is a noisy property with rooms for up to four people at $189 December to February and from $69 the rest of the year.

Radisson Bahia Mar Resort (☎ 954-764-2233, 801 Seabreeze Blvd) is a standard top-end place with comfortable rooms, pool, tennis courts and health club. Service could be a lot better. It has around six seasonal rate changes but suffice it to say that rooms

run anywhere from $89 to $229 and average about $150.

The absolute hands-down luxury hotel winner in town is the **Hyatt Regency Pier 66** (☎ 954-525-6666, 2301 SE 17 St) at the Intracoastal Waterway. Rooms are wonderful, service is excellent, and nothing beats the view from the rotating rooftop cocktail lounge a gizillion feet up. The restaurants are pretty good, too. Rooms run the gamut from $169 to $379, and suites go up to basically 'how much you got?'

Gay Accommodations Several charming gay men-only guesthouses can be found in the -mars area. The one lesbian guesthouse closed.

The **King Henry Arms** (☎ 954-561-0039, 543 Breakers Ave) has large clean rooms for $64 to $81 in low season, $96 to $119 in high season. The rooms have safes and small kitchens. It's predominantly gay, but management says 'open-minded people of all orientations are always welcome.'

The Blue Dolphin (☎ 954-565-8437, 800-893-2583, fax 954-565-6015, 725 N Birch Rd) is a small, clean, newly renovated and very comfortable men-only place. Amenities include in-room coffee service, a clothing-optional pool and free parking. Rates are $65 to $129 in low season, $89 to $149 in high season. Wheelchair-accessible accommodations are available on advance notice. The staff speak fluent German and French.

Flamingo Resort (☎ 954-561-4658, 800-283-4786, fax 954-568-2688, 2727 Terra Mar St) has a calm garden, clean rooms ($68 in low season, $83 to $142 in high season), friendly staff and satisfied guests.

The premiere gay guesthouse on the beach is the lovely **Royal Palms** (☎ 954-564-6444, 800-237-7256, fax 954-564-6443, 2901 Terra Mar St). This exquisitely done place has spotless, large airy rooms (complete with CD/TV/VCR and library), a lush and constantly changing tropical garden, a very nice pool (with a waterfall) and lots of perks and extras. It's very isolated and serene, and if house policy didn't discriminate against women and heterosexuals, we'd recommend it as possibly the beach's finest place. Rooms

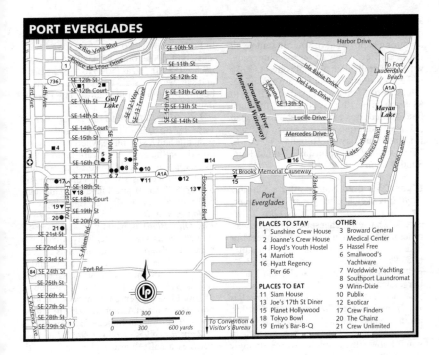

PORT EVERGLADES

PLACES TO STAY
1 Sunshine Crew House
2 Joanne's Crew House
4 Floyd's Youth Hostel
14 Marriott
16 Hyatt Regency
   Pier 66

PLACES TO EAT
11 Siam House
13 Joe's 17th St Diner
15 Planet Hollywood
18 Tokyo Bowl
19 Ernie's Bar-B-Q

OTHER
3 Broward General
   Medical Center
5 Hassel Free
6 Smallwood's
   Yachtware
7 Worldwide Yachting
8 Southport Laundromat
9 Winn-Dixie
10 Publix
12 Exoticar
17 Crew Finders
20 The Chainz
21 Crew Unlimited

are $105 to $175 in low season, $149 to $219 in high, with free parking and breakfast included. Clothing optional. Dig the towel sculptures on the beds.

Places to Eat

Downtown Who says fat-cat bureaucrats are unapproachable? If you're in the area and want to save a bit, why, pull up a bench and rub elbows with the best of them at the open-to-the-public *Governmental Center Cafeteria* (☎ 954-462-8368, 115 S Andrews Ave) in room 308 of the Governmental Center Building. Here you'll find the finest in administrative cuisine at taxpayer-subsidized prices: daily specials run $4.45 for a whole meal, like lasagna, salad and a roll or chicken Caesar. Also available are sandwiches ($3.17) and a breakfast special with two eggs, toast, bacon and coffee for $1.85 (served from 7:15 to 10:30 am). The cafeteria is open Monday to Friday 7 am to 3 pm.

You'll need to sign in with the security desk and get a pass to go upstairs. Another low-budget option is *Marie's Sugar & Spice* (☎ 954-524-2664, 304 SW 2nd St, which has good teas (foul coffee) and friendly service.

There's a lot of Irish going on at *Dicey Riley's* Irish restaurant and lounge (☎ 954-522-2202, fax 954-522-7176, 217 SW 2nd St). It's as close to an Irish pub as you'll get – draft Guinness, Bass and others, along with a full bar. A traditional Irish menu is supplemented by some foreign stuff, like fettuccine, but there's always the Sunday Carvery Smorgasbord: $8.95 gets you roast beef or turkey with stuffing, vegetables, Yorkshire pudding, gravy, potato, cranberry sauce and house salad. The bar is packed on weekends, and Irish traditional and contemporary tunes are played on Friday and Saturday.

Independence Brewery (☎ 954-524-1522, 111 NW 2nd Ave), a very nice restaurant/bar,

SOUTHEAST

also houses a microbrewery producing about a dozen kinds of beer ($3 a pint, 50¢ off during happy hours). You can sample all the beers free – they're on the bitter side, with a generally high alcohol content (3.8% to 7.5%). Appetizers at lunch are around $5, salads $4 to $7.50 and main dishes $5.95 to $8.95. At dinner, the appetizers are the same but main courses include beef shish kebab ($11.95) and fettuccine and penne ($10.95). It's open Tuesday to Thursday 11 am to 11 pm, Friday and Saturday 11 am to 1 am, Sunday noon to midnight.

E Las Olas Blvd Named after a *Saturday Night Live* sketch, **Cheeburger! Cheeburger!** (☎ *954-524-8824, 708 E Las Olas Blvd*) serves, what else, cheeseburgers (you can order a cheeseburger without the cheese 'for no extra charge'). A quarter-pound sampler is $3.95, a grilled cheese sandwich $3.25, grilled chicken sandwich $4.75, and Ham's burgersteak dinner is $7.95.

Kilwin's (☎ *954-523-8338, 809 E Las Olas Blvd*) makes tantalizing fudge, truffles, caramel, chocolate and ice cream. It's been in business since 1949, and when you walk in you'll know why: it smells overwhelmingly good and they make the fudge in front of you, $9.50 a pound (about two slices – and when you buy two slices, you get another one free).

Mango's (☎ *954-523-5001, 904 E Las Olas Blvd*) serves the yuppie business lunch crowd. It's got ferns, snappy service and lunch specials (served till 5 pm) like chicken and veggies for $6.50 and pastas up to $10.50; dinner entrees are $12.95 to $16.95.

The Floridian Restaurant (☎ *954-463-4041, 1410 E Las Olas Blvd*) is a 24-hour diner serving very good, if pricey, diner food. Skip the coleslaw, but try the Mess, a breakfast special ($6.75).

China Yung (☎ *954-761-3388, 720 E Las Olas Blvd*) is a classic American Chinese restaurant where the $5.50 to $6.50 lunch specials come with soup, egg roll and fried rice. Set dinners ($8.25 to $10.25) include ice cream.

O'Hara's Pub (☎ *954-524-1764, 954-524-2801 for information, 722 E Las Olas Blvd*)

features nightly jazz in a warm, comfortable atmosphere. During happy hour (Monday to Friday 5:30 to 7:30 pm), drinks are $1 off and a buffet is set out. On the menu are crab nachos ($8.50), pizzas ($6.25 to $6.75), salads and sandwiches ($5.25 to $6.75). Live music begins around 9 pm nightly (two-drink minimum).

Las Olas Café (☎ *954-524-4300, 922 E Las Olas Blvd*) is a little hidden and a truly romantic and lovely place, where you can sit outside on the green courtyard patio if you like. Appetizers are $5.25 to $7.25, walnut-crusted fresh fish is $16.95. It's open only for dinner, 5:30 to 10 pm Sunday to Thursday and 5:30 to 11 pm Friday and Saturday.

Japanese Village (☎ *954-763-8163, 716 E Las Olas Blvd*) is usually crowded, even though locals give it decidedly mixed reviews. It's also pricey: a spring roll is $5, à la carte sushi pieces run $1.25 to $3.50 and a sushi boat for three with soup, salad and rice is $48. The teriyaki combo entree is $13.50. Lunch is served Monday to Friday noon to 2 pm and dinner Monday to Thursday 5:30 to 10:30 pm, Sunday 5 to 10 pm.

Zanzbar (☎ *954-767-3377, 602 E Las Olas Blvd*) is a coffeehouse and wine bar with African and 'nature' influences (note the paw prints in the cement outside). The lunch and dinner menu consists mainly of quasi-exotic foods: appetizers are $6 to $11, unique mains include ostrich filet with mango, passion fruit and wild mushroom rice ($29.95) and almond- and mustard-crusted tuna ($20). Mmmm. A wide selection of South African wine is available.

Cafe Europa (☎ *954-763-6600, 726 E Las Olas Blvd*) has outdoor and indoor chairs and great pastries, decent sandwiches and espresso.

Mark's (☎ *954-463-1000, 1032 E Las Olas Blvd*) is a nice upscale place with pastas from $16 to $26, beef and fish dishes from $26 to $36 and fantastic service. At lunch it's marginally cheaper, with main courses running $12 to $18.

Fort Lauderdale Beach There's not a whole lot on the beach that's worth jumping up and down about. A great new offering is the **Primanti Brothers** (☎ 954-565-0605, fax 954-537-4882, 901 N Atlantic Blvd), which does great New York-style pizza (scientifically proven to be the best style of pizza available in the free world) in both Neapolitan ($1.75 a slice) and Sicilian ($2 a slice) versions. Large whole pies are $9.99 basic, and $14.99 with everything. They also do…um…interesting sandwiches, such as cheese, coleslaw and French fries on Italian bread for about $3.50.

Thai to Go (☎ 954-537-5375, fax 954-537-9001, 3414D N Ocean Blvd), on Hwy A1A near the HI Fort Lauderdale hostel, has decent Thai to go – the only seats in the restaurant are for waiting (smokers on the left, nonsmokers on the right). Lunch items start at $4.95 and dinners start at $6.95, with a few higher-priced specials. It's closed on Monday.

Port Everglades Crew-house dwellers will appreciate the large Publix and Winn-Dixie markets on the north side of 17th St just west of the Marriott; convenience stores can also be found along SE 17th St and on Federal Hwy. **Tokyo Bowl** (☎ 954-524-8200, 1720 S Federal Hwy) is a Japanese fast-food place with great cheap food; beef or chicken teriyaki for $3.79 and all you can eat sushi for $12.50.

More good Asian fare is available nearby at the **Siam House** (☎ 954-763-1701, 1392 SE 17th St Causeway), with great Thai specialties from $8.95 to $12.95 and seafood dishes up to $18.95.

Ernie's Bar-B-Q (☎ 954-523-8636, 1843 S Federal Hwy at SE 18th Court) is famous for its squalor and good, cheap food like enormous portions of conch chowder ($2.75/4.75 a cup/bowl) that comes with Bimini bread – basically challah with a sugary top. The soup itself can make a meal. Hours are 11 am to 11 pm or midnight daily.

The 24-hour **Joe's 17th St Diner** (☎ 954-527-5637, 1717 Eisenhower Blvd at SE 17th St), opposite Port Everglades and the Convention Center (the huge sign outside says Joe Bel Air's Diner), has way-cheap specials (breakfast $1.79, lunch $4.75 to $6.95, dinner $9.45 to $11.95). The inevitable **Planet**

Hollywood (☎ 954-462-7701, 1850 SE 17th St) is in this district as well.

At the Hyatt Regency Pier 66 (see Places to Stay), the **Mariner's Grille** has a great breakfast buffet for $9.50, good lunch specials and excellent food and service at dinner, when main courses run $15 to $20.

Entertainment

Performing Arts Diagonally opposite the MODS, the **Broward Center for the Performing Arts** (☎ 954-462-0222, 201 SW 5th Ave) is one of the state's largest and most important performing-arts complexes. The two venues here – the 2688-seat Au-Rene Theater and the 588-seat Amaturro – host a wide variety of first-rate concerts and theatrical productions. The Florida Grand Opera, Florida Philharmonic and Miami City Ballet all perform here regularly, and the PTG Broadway Series brings in major shows like *Rent, Les Miserables* and *A Chorus Line*. Depending on the seat and the performance, ticket prices can vary anywhere from $5 to a New York-esque $70.

The Broward Center's Family Fun Series of kid-oriented theater runs from October through April; tickets range $8 to $12. The box office is open Monday to Saturday 10 am to 6 pm, Sunday noon to 6 pm.

Parker Playhouse (☎ 954-763-8813, 707 NE 8th St) stages works for children during July and August as part of its Story Theatre program. From April to August, the **Fort Lauderdale Children's Theater** (☎ 954-763-6882, 640 N Andrews Ave) presents a wide range of performances for youngsters.

Clubs 'Fort Liquordale' is, if you hadn't noticed, a party town, and tons of clubs are available to suit a variety of tastes, persuasions, libidos and degrees of nuttiness. Cover charges vary incredibly and constantly, and coupons abound. Check in *City Link* for listings when you get to town, or check out the listings on their Website (www.clo-sfl.com). The following are but a few of the available options.

Baja Beach Club (☎ 954-561-4257, 3200 N Federal Hwy), at the northwest corner of Oakland Park Blvd and Federal Hwy, looks like an orgy at King Neptune's place. The enormous multilevel club features dance music, Spring Break parties, a Retro ('80s) Party on Thursday and dance parties on Saturday. Wednesday nights are ladies' nights (for women 18 and over and men 21 and over).

Club Soda (☎ 954-486-4010, 5460 N State Rd 7) features dancing for clean and sober folks (no alcohol). Fridays it's adults only; Saturdays all ages are welcome. Head west on Commercial Blvd, turn right on Hwy 441 (State Road 7), go half a mile north and you're there.

Nemesis (☎ 954-768-9228, 627 N Federal Hwy) is an alternative-music club set in a former funeral home (now *that's* alternative). It's naturally very popular with the People In Black. *Crash Club* (☎ 954-772-3611, 4915 NE 12th Ave), near Commercial Blvd and N Dixie Hwy, is another alternative place that does theme nights; some, like the painted lady and tattoo nights, are quite weird.

Chili Pepper (☎ 954-525-0094, 200 W Broward Blvd) is a staggeringly huge and pretty minimalistic dance warehouse with seven bars and outside patio and balcony areas (both with bars). Frequent live music features local and national bands. *Squeeze* (☎ 954-522-2151, 2 S New River Drive) is a progressive place showcasing local bands on Wednesday and Friday.

Near Squeeze, the *Downtowner Saloon* (☎ 954-463-9800, 10 S New River Drive) has live blues Thursday through Saturday in the blues room.

Gay & Lesbian Venues Almost 40 gay bars and clubs are scattered around Fort Lauderdale. Check in *Scoop* and *Hot Spots*, or ask around.

The Pier (☎ 954-630-8990, 3333 NE 32nd Ave) is a new complex comprising the Key West Cabana bar, a piano bar and a small munchies restaurant. With yacht parking on the Intracoastal and a clubby room with big overstuffed leather chairs, it's obviously oriented toward the more mature gay male. *The Copa* (☎ 954-463-1507, 2800 S Federal Hwy) has been around forever. It's a huge

disco with an outdoor deck. Drag shows take place several times a week. *The Saint* (☎ 954-525 7883, 1000 State Rd 84), just south and a little west of the Copa, is a large industrial music complex – expect 500 people minimum.

Club Electra (☎ 954-764-8447, 1600 SE 15th Ave) is a high-energy dance club with nights for men during the week and women on Friday to Sunday. It's off SE 17th St four blocks east of Federal Hwy; turn right (south) on 15th Ave and it's behind the Arby's. *Club Cathode Ray* (☎ 954-462-8611, 1105 E Las Olas Blvd) is kind of a Guppie hangout. Happy hour (two for one) is every day from 4 pm to 2 am; the place is open Sunday to Friday 2 pm to 2 am, and Saturday 2 pm to 3 am.

The Chainz (☎ 954-462-9165, 1931 S Federal Hwy) does a tea dance on Sunday evening.

The Whale and Porpoise (☎ 954-565-2750, 2750 E Oakland Park Blvd) is largely lesbian, and *The Omni* (☎ 954-565-5151, 1421 E Oakland Park Blvd) is another huge industrial place with a couple of bars, long two-for-one drink specials daily, lots of metal and chrome, drag shows on Thursday, and women only on Friday.

Spectator Sports

The *Florida Panthers* (☎ 954-835-8326) play NHL hockey at the National Car Rental Center, One Panther Parkway in Sunrise, and the *Fusion* (☎ 954-717-2200) play major league soccer at Lockhart Stadium, 5300 NW 12th Ave in Fort Lauderdale. Miami also has several pro sports teams (see Spectator Sports in the Miami & Miami Beach chapter). The Baltimore Orioles play their spring-training games at *Fort Lauderdale Stadium* (☎ 954-938-4980), 5301 NW 12th Ave (across from the Lockhart Stadium), and the NFL *Miami Dolphins* (☎ 305-620-2578) practice near Nora Southeastern University.

Shopping

The Swap Shop (☎ 954-791-7927), 3291 W Sunrise Blvd about a mile east of Sawgrass Mills, is an enormous circuslike flea market. We mean it – there's a real *circus* here every

19 Million People Can't Be Wrong

The biggest news in town is the largest factory outlet mall in the USA – the unbelievably enormous (it's more than 2 miles around the ring road), alligator-shaped Sawgrass Mills Factory Outlet Mall (☎ 954-846-2350). We're talkin' big: 19 *million* people came to this 2.35-million-sq-foot mall last year, making it a more popular draw than, say, Busch Gardens in Tampa. The prices, by the way, are the reason those millions of people came here: some items are as much as 80% off retail. Clothes and other goods are incredibly cheap, since they are often discontinued lines or slightly damaged or 'imperfect.'

'Only in America could a shopping mall become a tourist attraction,' many Europeans might think at this point. Well, Klaus and Juliette, consider that about 80% of those 19 million people were foreigners. (And while we're on the subject – McDonald's restaurants were not placed in Europe by the US State Department's cultural wing. There'd be fewer if people didn't clamor for them.)

The mall's main attraction is the 275-some-odd stores, including outlet stores of Saks Fifth Avenue, Neiman Marcus, Barneys New York, JC Penney, Spiegel (Chicago, 60609), Loehmann's, Mondi, Bernini, Levi's, Nine West, Kenneth Cole, MCM, Ann Taylor, Emanuel-Emanuel Ungaro, Ike Behar and Jones New York. Whew.

In addition to the shops, the mall features three food courts, two sit-down restaurants, daily entertainment programs, an 18-screen Cobb movie theater, a 900-member indoor fitness club with a 1 1/2-mile (yes, a mile and a half) indoor walking and running course, and a themed area that sounds spookily Disneyan in its description:

> …Cabana Court, which includes a beach scene and blue lagoon that houses a delightful animated alligator family and their singing flamingo and seagull friends.

Two staffed information booths give out good maps of the mall – you'll need one. Other helpful services include a foreign currency exchange center (bad rates) and three ATM machine areas. Wheelchairs are available at the information booths and 'smart carts' are at each entrance. Parking is no problem: there are 11,000 spaces.

The mall is at 12801 W Sunrise Blvd in the city of Sunrise, 9 miles west of Fort Lauderdale. By car, take the Sawgrass Expressway right to it (or take Sunrise Blvd, Hwy 838). Hours are Monday to Saturday 10 am to 9:30 pm, Sunday 11 am to 8 pm.

day in addition to movies, a tiny amusement park and lots of stuff to buy.

Getting There & Away

Air Fort Lauderdale/Hollywood International Airport (FLL; ☎ 954-359-1200) is served by more than 35 airlines, including some with nonstop flights from Europe. See the Getting There & Away chapter for more information.

Bus The Greyhound station (☎ 954-764-6551) is at 515 NE 3rd St at Federal Hwy,

about 4 1/2 blocks from Broward Central Terminal (see Getting Around later in the Fort Lauderdale section), the central transfer point for buses in the Fort Lauderdale area. Buses to Miami leave frequently ($5, about half an hour to an hour).

Train Tri-Rail (☎ 954-728-8445, 800-874-7245) trains run between Miami and Palm Beach via Fort Lauderdale; the trains also provide transportation to the Miami Arena (for basketball and hockey games), to Pro Player Stadium (for Miami Dolphins and

Florida Marlins games) and to several other tourist attractions. Daily tickets are $5. A wheelchair-access van service is available, as is a feeder system of buses at no extra charge. Free parking is provided at most stations. Call Tri-Rail for ticket and scheduling information. Amtrak (☎ 800-872-7245) passenger trains run on the same tracks as Tri-Rail.

The Fort Lauderdale station is at 200 SW 21st Terrace, just south of Broward Blvd and just west of I-95.

Car & Motorcycle Florida's Turnpike, the state's main toll road, runs north and south from Miami to Longwood. I-595, the major east-west artery, connects the western suburbs with Port Everglades, the airport and downtown Fort Lauderdale. It also connects with I-95, Florida's Turnpike and the Sawgrass Expressway, a north-south toll expressway that links western suburbs and also ties into I-95 and the Turnpike. The Sawgrass Expressway also connects to I-75, which runs to Florida's west coast.

All major car-rental companies have offices at Fort Lauderdale/Hollywood International Airport.

Boat Port Everglades Authority (☎ 954-523-3404) runs the enormous Port Everglades cruise port (second busiest in the world after Miami). From the port, walk to SE 17th St and take bus No 40 to the beach or to Broward Central Terminal. If you're coming here in your own boat (not unlikely here), head for Radisson Bahia Mar Yacht Center (☎ 954-764-2233).

Fort Lauderdale's premiere unofficial crew agency is the three-ring binder at Smallwood's Yachtware (☎ 954-523-2282), 1001 SE 17th St at 10th Ave. Owners come here, list their requirements in the book and wait for crew to get in touch. 'Official' agencies include Crew Unlimited (☎ 954-462-4624) at 2065 S Federal Hwy; Crew Finders (☎ 954-522-2739) at 4040 SE 17th St; the very friendly Hassle Free (☎ 954-763-1841) at 1635 S Miami Rd, No 8; and Worldwide Yachting (☎ 954-467-9777) at 1053 SE 17th St.

See Places to Stay, earlier in the chapter, and the Getting There & Away chapter for more information.

Getting Around
To/From the Airport Fort Lauderdale/ Hollywood International Airport (FLL), south of town off Federal Hwy or I-95, is about a 20-minute drive from E Las Olas Blvd. Broward County Transit's bus No 1 goes from the airport to Broward Central Terminal. Tri-Rail offers a shuttle connecting the airport terminal with the Fort Lauderdale Airport train station (you can also take BCt bus Nos 3 or 6); trains head from there up to the Fort Lauderdale station ($3) about once an hour at rush hours, once every two hours in midday. The trains run from about 5:50 am to 11:30 pm on weekdays, with less frequent service and more restricted hours on weekends.

The official airport taxi is Yellow Cab Co (☎ 954-565-5400, 954-565-8400; see Taxi later this section). Tri-County Transportation Airport Express (☎ 954-561-8886) runs private limos and shuttles. A private limo (more of a car, really) between the airport and Fort Lauderdale costs $24; a shared shuttle bus is $8. You need to reserve 24 hours in advance on the shuttle from Fort Lauderdale to the airport. For information on getting from the airport to Miami, see Getting Around in the Miami & Miami Beach chapter.

Bus TMAX (☎ 954-761-3543) is a free shuttle running every 15 minutes between all the downtown sites on weekdays and between the beach and downtown on weeknights and weekends.

Broward County Transit (BCt; ☎ 954-357-8400, TTY 954-357-8302) bus service runs between downtown and the beach, Port Everglades and surrounding towns and beaches. Broward Central Terminal is the main hub for buses in the area; it's at 200 W Broward Blvd, two blocks west of Andrews Ave on the north side of the street.

Fare is $1 for adults, 50¢ for seniors, disabled or youth; transfers are 15¢. Fare boxes onboard accept dollar bills.

From Broward Central Terminal, take bus No 11 to upper Fort Lauderdale Beach, bus No 1 to Floyd's Hostel, Joanne's Crew House and the Port Everglades area and bus No 40 to 17th St and Federal Hwy. From the Cyprus Creek Tri-Rail Station to HI Fort Lauderdale Hostel, take bus No 62; and from Oakland Park Blvd at around 36th St and Hwy A1A to the Sawgrass Mills Mall, take bus No 72.

The Commuter Store (☎ 954-761-3543), 310 SW 2nd St, is a one-stop shopping spot for anything transit related in the greater Fort Lauderdale area. It's open weekdays 9 am to 5 pm.

Car & Motorcycle Having a car or motorcycle is the easiest way to go, though parking is especially tight in high season and you usually have to pay for it. Pay lots are located north and south of Las Olas Blvd ($1 per hour), and all-day parking at the beach is available for $5 ($3 at night) at the municipal parking lot on Hwy A1A just south of SE 5th St, near the International Swimming Hall of Fame. Speed limits are enforced to such an extent that you may wonder if the cops get a commission – watch especially for flashing lights indicating school zones, in which the speed limit is 15 mph. Remove all valuables from your car when parking.

Taxi Meter rates are $2.45 flagfall, plus $1.75 per mile. Try Yellow Cab Company (☎ 954-565-5400, 954-565-8400).

Bicycle Fort Lauderdale's flatness makes it a great place to get around by bike. Floyd's Youth Hostel (see Places to Stay earlier) has bicycles for guest use – either free or $3 a day, depending on how things are. The St Tropez Resort (☎ 954-564-8468), 725 N Atlantic Blvd, rents bicycles for $4 an hour, $10 a day (8:30 am to 8 pm), $15 for 24 hours or $40 a week with a $50 to $100 deposit.

Water Taxi The Water Taxi (☎ 954-467-6677), 651 Seabreeze Blvd, is a full-fledged transportation option on the canals and waterways of Fort Lauderdale. It covers the

Gotta Ferrari?

Wanna Hummer? Or a Jag XJ6 to tool around in for the day? In Fort Lauderdale, the place to turn is Exoticar Rentals (☎ 954-467-1616), 1540 SE 17th St, where a slew of exotic and unbelievably expensive vehicles are available for rent. That Hummer, by the way, with air conditioning and tinted glass, will cost you a mere bag of shells – $299 a day plus an enormous deposit (this is another reason they make high-limit credit cards). The Jag goes for $295.

area bordered by 17th St to the south, Atlantic Blvd/Pompano Beach to the north, the New River to the west and the Atlantic Ocean to the east.

A $15 daily pass lets you ride as much as you'd like, though you're asked (or, rather, implored) to tip the driver each time. We say tip only if they're nice or helpful. Call from any commercial location downtown on the New River or along the Intracoastal Waterway (anyplace with a dock) and they'll swing by and pick you up.

AROUND FORT LAUDERDALE

The greater Fort Lauderdale area's division lines have been deliberately blurred by the CVB, which seeks to market the area's attractions as a package to entice more visitors. For this reason, many guidebooks and handout pamphlets list hotels, attractions and events in the entire region in a Fort Lauderdale context – for example, the Lauderdale-by-the-Sea Chamber of Commerce bills the Stranahan House as one of its attractions.

We've listed these towns and cities separately because they are indeed separate entities, but it should be noted that each one is within a 20-minute drive of the others. All are accessible by bus, and Tri-Rail serves Deerfield Beach, Pompano Beach and Hollywood. Many of the towns can also be accessed via the Intracoastal Waterway.

SOUTHEAST

Dania Beach
• **population 17,000**

Five miles south of Fort Lauderdale is Dania (pronounced 'DANE-ya') Beach, which has some nice beach (the town's just renamed itself Dania Beach though 98% of the town is inland), a fledgling antiques district, a peaceful state recreation area and the Graves Museum – the state's finest archaeological museum and collection. It's about a 10-minute drive or 15-minute bus ride from Broward Central Terminal to the museum. The town is also home to the immense West Lake Park, best enjoyed at the Anne Kolb Nature Center (see Hollywood later in this section).

Orientation & Information The antiques district goes two blocks north and south of Dania Beach Blvd along S Federal Hwy (US Hwy 1). Dania Beach Blvd runs between the beach/fishing pier and S Federal Hwy.

Change money at the NationsBank at 1991 Stirling Rd. A good landmark is the enormous Dania Jai Alai Palace (☎ 954-428-7766) at 301 E Dania Beach Blvd, with live action most days. The Dania Beach Library (☎ 954-926-2420) is at 485 S Federal Hwy.

Graves Museum of Archaeology & Natural History This wonderful nonprofit museum (☎ 954-925-7770), 481 S Federal Hwy, is staffed and run by volunteer members of the Broward County Archaeological Society, who contribute time, knowledge, money and artifacts to the outstanding collection. The museum, easily identified by its huge lizard skeleton on the facade fronting S Federal Hwy, has an extensive geology and paleontology collection, a very extensive pre-Columbian pottery collection, a unique pre-Columbian miniatures collection and museum-quality reproductions of objects discovered in the tomb of Tutankhamen.

DANIA BEACH

PLACES TO STAY
2 Motel 6
10 Paulie's Place

PLACES TO EAT
4 Bleep's Sub Shop
5 Penn Dutch Restaurant
6 King's Head Pub
7 Dania Beach Bar & Grill
8 Grampa's Bakery & Restaurant
9 Jaxson's Restaurant

OTHER
1 Dania Jai Alai
3 Toilets
11 Graves Museum of Archaeology & Natural History
12 Library

Its splendid gift shop has many artifacts brought back by staff from their travels and field trips to sites around the world. It is truly worth a visit, and kids will love it as well.

Free tours are available by appointment and can be tailored to your needs – students spend a great deal of time here. Casual visitors, however, can do the place in about an hour and a half. The museum is desperately struggling to pay its upkeep (like the $3000 per month air-conditioning bill), and donations (over and above the admission price) are appreciated.

Activities are available for kids on Saturday, and adult and children's classes are available year round. Call the museum for more information. Bus No 1 to/from Fort Lauderdale's Broward Central Terminal stops very close by.

The museum is open Tuesday to Saturday 10 am to 4 pm, Sunday 1 to 5 pm, closed Monday. Admission is $6 for adults, $4 for children four to 12. Tuesday is Senior Citizen Day, with a $3 admission for seniors.

Dania Fishing Pier The beach action is centered around this pier which stretches almost 900 feet out into the Atlantic. It's a must for fishers – we saw a nine-year-old boy walk off with a 2-foot barracuda! The pier and tackle shop are open 24 hours a day. Admission is $3 per person, $1 for spectators; fishing rod rental is $6 with a $30 deposit; bait runs $1.75 to $2.50. Aerated saltwater tanks along the pier keep your catch swimming while you hunt down their friends.

Antiques District 'District' is an overstatement. Tourist handouts hail this as the hottest antiques market around, though that's not saying much. Most of the shops are along the stretch of S Federal Hwy (US Hwy 1) running two blocks north and south of Dania Beach Blvd.

Places to Stay The beach is easy to reach from Fort Lauderdale, where cheaper accommodations are available, so you may want to consider day trips to Dania Beach. But local options are available.

About halfway between the beach and S Federal Hwy is a clean-as-usual *Motel 6* (☎ 954-921-5505, 825 E Dania Beach Blvd), with standard singles/doubles at $38/42; kids under 17 stay free. Bus No 7 stops directly in front.

The best deal on the beach is *Paulie's Place* (☎ 954-927-2010, 5611 N Ocean Blvd), which has spotless one-bedroom apartments complete with kitchens and dining rooms for $200 a week – negotiable in high season, when prices tend to edge up another $25 a week.

Places to Eat You can barbecue your own food and dine alfresco in one of the chickee huts near the Dania Beach Bar & Grill – grills are available right there.

For quick and cheap grindage on the beach, look to the *Dania Beach Bar & Grill* in the center of the main parking lot, near the pier, serving burgers, hot dogs and

DANIA BEACH

SOUTHEAST

Southeast Florida offers great fishing.

sandwiches. Nothing's more than $5, draft beer is $1.75 to $2.50. On the fishing pier, the *Patio Bar* has tiny pizzas ($2), hot dogs ($1.50) and burritos ($2), along with soft drinks and frozen cocktails.

At the smoky *Penn-Dutch Restaurant* (☎ 954-929-9220, 218 E Dania Beach Blvd) there are daily lunch specials for around $5. *Bleep's Sub Shop* (☎ 954-922-9522, 50 E Dania Beach Blvd) is an excellent '50s-type lunch counter serving up good 10-inch submarine-style sandwiches for cheap. For cheese or veggies it's $2.59, ham or salami and cheese, meatball or eggplant costs $4.25.

Just shy of being a real British pub (they don't overboil the vegetables or undercook the bacon), the *King's Head Pub* (☎ 954-922-5722, 500 E Dania Beach Blvd) makes very nice shepherd's pie ($8.50). It's a fun place with great friendly service and several regular expats, who keep their personal beer mugs hanging around. To find it, look for the original British phone box outside.

Bring the kids to *Jaxson's Restaurant* (☎ 954-923-4445, 128 S Federal Hwy) for a few minutes, but any longer gets expensive. The 40-year-old ice cream emporium is a wonderfully designed place – stuff hanging from the ceilings, license plates on the walls – and the ice cream is great. Banana

splits are $4.75/6.45 takeout/eat-in; hot fudge sundaes are $5.45 (eat-in only).

Grampa's Bakery & Restaurant (17 SW 1st St) is worth a look, though we *hated* the prune Danish. Breakfast specials like pancakes or waffles with fresh fruit and whipped cream are $2.25 to $3.99, sandwiches/subs $3.25 to $5.75, and burgers, chicken and fish dishes run $3.95 to $7.95.

Getting There & Away BCt bus No 1 runs from Broward Central Station to Dania Beach Blvd. An eastbound bus No 7 goes from there right to the beach every 20 minutes on weekdays, and every 30 to 40 minutes on weekends. If you're driving, turn east down Dania Beach Blvd and follow it to the end. Metered parking is available right at the beach for $1 per hour, quarters only. Unmetered spaces are for local residents only, and tow trucks prowl.

Hollywood
• population 125,000

Hollywood is directly below Dania Beach, but the only reasons to travel this far south are the beach, the 3-mile 'broadwalk' that lines it – swarming with in-line skaters and cute hunks of all nationalities – and the Anne Kolb Nature Center nearby. It's worth a day trip if you are in the area.

Orientation & Information The city is just north of the Dade County line and the Aventura Mall. Hollywood Blvd runs between the beach and the center of town, which are about 2 miles apart. Get tourist information at the Hollywood Chamber of Commerce (☎ 954-923-4000), 330 S Federal Hwy.

NationsBank has a branch at 1900 Tyler St and another on the beach at 3509 N Ocean Blvd. Hard Drive Cafe (☎ 954-929-3324), 1942 Hollywood Blvd, is an Internet café.

Hollywood Art & Culture Center This center (☎ 954-921-3274), 1650 Harrison St, is a museum featuring the works of local and regional artists. Special events take place here throughout the year – call for information when you're in the area.

Anne Kolb Nature Center This nature center (☎ 954-926-2481) in West Lake Park, a 1400-acre coastal mangrove wetland on the coast of the mainland at the Intracoastal Waterway, has a 65-foot observation tower, a lagoon, boardwalks and canoe, kayak, rowboat and bicycle trails. In the nature center are a 4000-gallon aquarium and two staff naturalists who explain the local flora and fauna. Canoe, kayak and rowboat rentals are $6.25 an hour, $13.25 for four hours and $25 for eight hours. Four paddling trails – the 1.2-mile Red Trail, the 1-mile White and Green Trails and the very short Blue Trail – all lead through the mangrove islands, not out on the Intracoastal.

Admission to the nature center is free; the exhibit area is $3 for adults and $1.50 for children. Staff offer a 40-minute boat tour through West Lake every hour on the hour; the cost is $8 for adults and $4 for children.

The park is open weekdays 9 am to sunset, Saturday and Sunday 8 am to 6 pm in winter, 8 am to 7:30 pm in summer. To get there, take Federal Hwy (US Hwy 1) to Sheridan St and go east for about 1¹/₂ miles; the marina is on the south side, the nature center on the north.

The Beach Packed with bikes and skaters – even Rollerblading cops – and lined with snack bars, souvenir shops and junky tourist trinket touts, the 'broadwalk' at Hollywood Beach is a scene. The sand itself is Okay, and the beach has enough character to make a day here interesting.

Places to Eat The open-air *French Green Market* in Young Circle Park South parking lot is an outdoor veggie market held on Wednesday and Sunday 9 am to 2 pm.

Now Art Gallery Café (☎ 954-922-0506, 1820 Hollywood Blvd) is a New Age (non-smoking) coffee/snack bar also offering a wide range of performances: live acoustic guitar on Wednesday and Saturday, various musicians on Thursday, classical guitar on Friday. Local artists' works are displayed.

Try My Thai (☎ 954-926-5585, 2003 Harrison St) serves excellent cheap Thai food,

with soups from $2 to $3.50, and main courses all around $10. It's open for dinner daily and for lunch Tuesday through Friday.

Entertainment Nearby, *O'Hara's Hollywood* (☎ 954-925-2555, 24-hour jazz hotline 954-524-2801, 1903 Hollywood Blvd) has live jazz, a fun atmosphere and swing dancing Sunday 2:30 to 6:30 pm.

Club M (☎ 954-925-8396, 2037 Hollywood Blvd) presents blues and acoustic music most days.

Getting There & Away Hollywood has two bus terminals: at Young Circle at US Hwy 1, and on Hollywood Blvd, further west at the center of the city. From Broward Central Terminal take BCt bus No 1 or 9 to Young Circle, then transfer to No 17 or 28 to Hollywood or to Hollywood Beach. The Greyhound station is on Tyler St, just off US Hwy 1 and Young Circle; about seven buses a day run to/from Miami ($4). By car, take US Hwy 1, Hwy A1A or I-95.

Davie
• population 50,000

If you've ever been to Dubbo, Australia, you'll get a familiar flash when you cross the Davie line. A sprawling, sparsely populated town that's slowly making the conversion from farmland to bedroom community, Davie's not a whole bunch of laughs – yeah, you'll see lots of people on horseback, but that only takes you so far. The classic piece of tourist information is that the McDonald's (☎ 954-791-6657) at 4101 SW 64th Ave has a corral and hitching post.

Whee.

But the town rodeo arena hosts national shows, and the Buehler Planetarium is interesting. Don't plan on spending a night here.

Orientation & Information Davie is southwest of downtown Fort Lauderdale. The downtown – don't blink – is a short strip of Davie Rd between Griffin Rd and about SW 39th St. There's a tourist information booth at the chamber of commerce office on Davie Rd at 42nd St, and a NationsBank at

6300 Stirling Rd. The folks at Army Navy Outdoors (☎ 954-584-7227), 4130 SW 64th Ave, opposite the McDonald's, are helpful and friendly if you need to know anything about rodeos coming to town.

Buehler Planetarium On Broward Community College's central campus, Buehler Planetarium (☎ 954-475-6680), 2501 Davie Rd, is a cool place to spend an hour or two. Using a very small Zeiss star machine, the college's astronomers project fascinating night sky displays while you sit in chairs that are so comfortable you may not want to leave. See constellations only visible from the North and South Poles. Show times and costs change, so call for information.

On Friday and Saturday at 8:45, 9:30, 10:45 pm and midnight, these sky-wonks let their hair down and produce intense laser shows that are set to rock music and projected against the backdrop of the moving night sky; $6 admission.

Matinees are a bit tamer, but much more educational. They're held on Friday at 7 pm, Saturday at 1:30 and 3 pm, and Sunday at 3 pm; tickets are $4 to $5.

Davie Rodeo Arena This arena (☎ 954-581-0790) is the place to see rodeos and the occasional folk art or crafts show. The arena hosts monthly, national five-star pro rodeo events, as well as the 10-day 'Florida Westfair' Western festival held in early February. No coolers, bottles, fireworks or firearms are allowed inside. Dang. It's one block west of Davie Rd just north of the canal, at the corner of SW 42nd St and 66th Ave.

Places to Eat Try *The Coffee Table* (☎ 954-424-3177, 7711 Nova Drive), serving gourmet coffees, as well as excellent desserts like cheesecakes and pies (about $2.50 to $5). All the art on the walls is by local artists, and entertainment here includes an open-mike night Thursday at 8 pm, poetry reading on the fourth Friday of the month at 7:30 pm, and live music on Thursday and Sunday nights. The *McDonald's* is in the 'heart' of 'downtown Davie' at Davie Rd just south of

SW 41st St. Stick around long enough and you may see someone riding through the drive-thru on horseback. The *Hitching Post Restaurant* (☎ 954-587-1400, 4483 SW 64th Ave) is a diner sort of affair.

If being here in the suburban east has you yearning for that country & western thing, head for *Davie Junction* (☎ 954-581-1132, 6311 SW 45th St), which doesn't exactly have a mechanical bull but does have two-stepping rowdies and a couple of pool tables (if you're rusty, they offer lessons on Sunday night).

Getting There & Away BCt bus No 9 runs between Broward Central Terminal and Davie Rd. By car, take I-95 south to I-595 west, to exit 7. Turn south and you'll run into downtown.

Lauderdale-by-the-Sea
• population 3000
Just north of Fort Lauderdale, this condo-clustered village is struggling to attract tourists but has too little bait. One good lure is the Ocean Fest dive trade show held in September. The only other bona fide attraction here is the fishing pier, where you can fish your heart out for a day ($3 adults, $2 kids under 12). Rod rentals and bait are available here, too, but we think the Dania pier is better. That said, this is a pleasant place to spend a morning or watch a sunset, and brunch at Murphy's Beach House is a nice experience.

Orientation & Information You can easily walk all of downtown. E Commercial Blvd is the town's main east-west artery, and Ocean Drive (Hwy A1A) is the main north-south route. The pier is at the end of Commercial Blvd at El Mar Drive, one block east of Ocean Drive. This is also the spot for most of the restaurants and touristy stuff. Get tourist information at the Chamber of Commerce (☎ 954-776-1000, 800-699-6764), in the middle of the triangle formed by the intersection of Ocean and Bougainvillea Drives. The chamber publishes *The Seaside Village of Lauderdale-by-the-Sea*, which is an

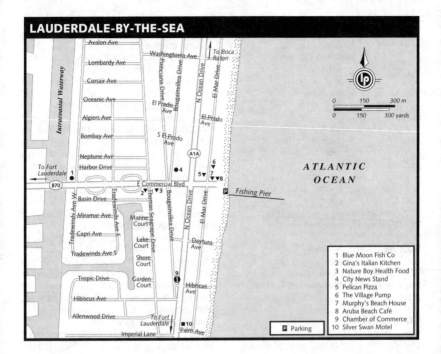

LAUDERDALE-BY-THE-SEA

ATLANTIC OCEAN

1 Blue Moon Fish Co
2 Gina's Italian Kitchen
3 Nature Boy Health Food
4 City News Stand
5 Pelican Pizza
6 The Village Pump
7 Murphy's Beach House
8 Aruba Beach Café
9 Chamber of Commerce
10 Silver Swan Motel

P Parking

advertiser-driven tourist information magazine with a good map of the city.

City News Stand, 4400 Bougainvillea Drive, carries out-of-town and foreign newspapers.

Places to Stay & Eat There is absolutely no advantage to staying here as opposed to in Fort Lauderdale. Prices for motels, hotels and apartments tend to be higher because the place is geared more to vacationing time-share and condo owners than to backpackers or travelers.

A good bet just south of the heart of town is the *Silver Swan Motel* (☎ 954-776-1765, fax 954-568-9547, 4208 N Ocean Drive), with nice, clean motel rooms from $31 in summer to $85 in winter. You can get a double room at the *Lauderdale by the Sea Motel* (☎ 954-776-1391, 4229 N Ocean Drive) for $50 in summer, $100 in winter, but service is less than warm and snuggly.

Pelican Pizza (☎ 954-351-0016, 4403 El Mar Drive) has excellent New York-style pizza for $2 a slice. Stop for a large garlic pie ($10), then get on Fort Lauderdale's *Jungle Queen* and talk real close to everyone.

Nature Boy Health Food (☎ 954-776-4696, 220 E Commercial Blvd) sells healthful salads and sandwiches starting at around $4 to $5. Just west is *Gina's Italian Kitchen* (☎ 954-491-2340, 226 E Commercial Blvd), which makes pizzas and lasagna-type dishes that looked and smelled great.

Murphy's Beach House (☎ 954-776-6708, 4400 El Mar Drive) does a great Sunday brunch for $7, and dinner specials like veal parmigiana or grilled chicken go for $9.95. At their takeout window you can get burgers ($5.95) and other fast food. Get sloshed next door at the *Village Pump* (☎ 954-491-9407, 4404 El Mar Drive), a fun and divey local bar and grill.

SOUTHEAST

Aruba Beach Cafe (☎ *954-776-0001, 1 E Commercial Blvd*) is a party place with sort of a Caribbean-beach atmosphere. It's pretty big and pretty loud, and everyone we spoke to liked it. A large window looks out over the ocean. Happy hour is weekdays 4 to 7 pm with $1 off all cocktails; on Sunday, a breakfast buffet is served 8 am to 1 pm and live music is presented 3 to 7 pm.

Blue Moon Fish Co (☎ *954-267-9888, 4405 West Tradewinds Ave)*, just off Commercial Blvd at the Intracoastal, offers seafood and a seriously eclectic menu in a spectacular waterside setting; heaps of glass and great service. Try the icky sticky caramel tart! Come for live jazz on Wednesday and Friday or a seriously cool gospel brunch on Sunday from 11:30 am to 3 pm.

Getting There & Away The city is just north of Fort Lauderdale on Ocean Drive. BCt bus No 11 from Fort Lauderdale Beach takes you right to Commercial Blvd at Hwy A1A.

BOCA RATON
• population 160,000

The affluent city of Boca Raton (the name in Spanish means, approximately and perhaps appropriately, 'mouth of the rat'), about 50 miles north of Miami, offers little in the way of activities unless you happen to take a keen interest in golf, shopping, tennis and pink buildings. The city is geared more for long-term residents and big-shot golfers than travelers – especially budget travelers.

Nevertheless, Boca can be a very pleasant place to spend some time. Its county parks are quite lovely, the beaches are clean, white and safe, and if you're up for some house-gawking, you've come to a city with ample opportunities.

Orientation
Boca is divided by the Intracoastal Waterway, with the majority of the city on the mainland. The town is a sprawler; residential neighborhoods stretch far west of I-95 and Florida's Turnpike.

Camino Real runs between the enormous grounds of the Boca Raton Resort & Club

and the Royal Palm Yacht Club and Golf Course. The main action, such as it is, is in the quadrant north of Camino Real Blvd, south of Spanish River Blvd (actually, while this is a convenient dividing point, you'll rarely need to go north of, say, 28th St) and east of NW 9th Ave.

As a constant reminder of the city's beginnings, the name Mizner (pronounced 'MIZE-ner'; see History in the Facts about Florida chapter) is given to as many things as possible. Mizner Blvd meanders through downtown in a roughly north-south direction, and Mizner Park, on N Federal Hwy near NE 2nd St, is a faux-village filled with chi-chi shops, a Liberties bookstore and some surprisingly inexpensive restaurants (for the area, that is).

The addressing system uses Palmetto Park Rd as the north-south divider, and Old Dixie Hwy (not to be confused with US Hwy 1, which here is called Federal Hwy) as the east-west divider. The most important county parks are between Palmetto Park Rd and Spanish River Blvd, between the Intracoastal and the ocean.

The most readily available commercial map of the city is Universal's Boca Raton map, available at area gas stations. The chamber of commerce sells Dolph's Boca Raton map for $3.

Information
The best starting point is in your hands; Boca has no tourist information offices as such, though hotels and many restaurants give away handouts on area attractions and disappointing maps. The marginally helpful chamber of commerce (☎ 561-395-4433, www.bocaratonchamber.com), 1800 N Dixie Hwy, hands out pamphlets, but they're closed on weekends (!). For information on Palm Beach County itself, contact the Palm Beach County CVB (☎ 561-471-3995), 1555 Palm Beach Lakes Blvd, Suite 204, West Palm Beach, FL 33401.

NationsBank has several offices in town, including ones at 1000 N Federal Hwy, 4000 N Federal Hwy and 2301 Glades Rd. American Express has a representative office in Adventure Travels of Boca Raton

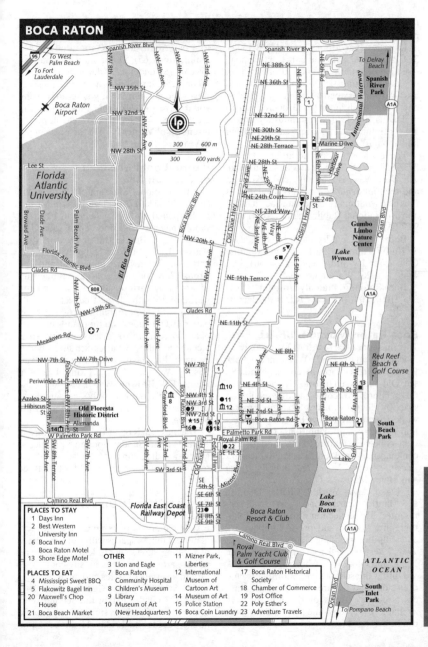

BOCA RATON

PLACES TO STAY
1 Days Inn
2 Best Western
  University Inn
6 Boca Inn/
  Boca Raton Motel
13 Shore Edge Motel

PLACES TO EAT
4 Mississippi Sweet BBQ
5 Flakowitz Bagel Inn
20 Maxwell's Chop
  House
21 Boca Beach Market

OTHER
3 Lion and Eagle
7 Boca Raton
  Community Hospital
8 Children's Museum
9 Library
10 Museum of Art
  (New Headquarters)
11 Mizner Park,
  Liberties
12 International
  Museum of
  Cartoon Art
14 Museum of Art
15 Police Station
16 Boca Coin Laundry

17 Boca Raton Historical
  Society
18 Chamber of Commerce
19 Post Office
22 Poly Esther's
23 Adventure Travels

SOUTHEAST

(☎ 561-395-5722), 30 SE 7th St. The main post office is at Mizner Blvd at NE 2nd St.

Liberties Fine Books (☎ 561-368-1300), 309 Plaza Real (Mizner Park), has a huge selection of Lonely Planet and other travel books and a fantastic Florida section. It also has a café and is open late: Sunday to Thursday 9 am to midnight (café open 8 am to midnight), and Friday and Saturday until 1 am (both the bookstore and café). You can mill about for hours.

The Boca Raton public library (☎ 561-393-7852) is at 200 NW Boca Raton Blvd. *The Boca News* is a locally produced daily, and the *Sun Sentinel* is readily available, as are the big nationals. Check at Liberties (see above). National Public Radio (NPR) is at 90.7 FM.

Boca Coin Laundry (☎ 561-368-7322) is at 101 W Palmetto Park Rd, and Camino Coin Laundry and Cleaners (☎ 561-395-4748) is at 261 W Camino Real.

Boca Raton Community Hospital (☎ 561-395-7100), 800 Meadows Rd, is the largest nearby.

Boca Raton Museum of Art

This museum of art (☎ 561-392-2500, www .bocamuseum.org), 801 W Palmetto Park Rd (the entrance faces lovely Alamanda St; see Old Floresta Historic District later in this section), overcomes its tiny exhibition space by filling it with a well-balanced mix of works from its impressive permanent collection and traveling exhibitions. The permanent collection features both modern and contemporary works, such as Pablo Picasso's *Beach Scene* and *Nude Figures on the Beach* and Henri Matisse's *Girl Playing Violin at the Piano*. Andy Warhol, Charles Demuth and Maurice Brazil Prendergast are all represented. The collection also includes photography, African and pre-Columbian art, and sculpture, including Henry Laurens' *The Two Sisters* as well as works by Etienne Hajdu and Giorgio de Chirico.

During the school year, Saturday is children's day and features tours and arts-and-crafts classes. Tours of the museum are available every day and specialized tours can be arranged free.

The museum's open Monday to Friday 10 am to 4 pm, Saturday and Sunday noon to 4 pm. Admission is $3 for adults, $2 for seniors (over 65), $1 for students and free for children under 12. Admission is free on Wednesday. Surprisingly, no public transport serves the museum, so if you're not driving you'll have to walk from downtown. The museum is planning to move to new digs just north of Mizner Park in the next couple of years.

International Museum of Cartoon Art

The International Museum of Cartoon Art (☎ 561-391-2200), 201 Plaza Real in Mizner Park, opened 1st-floor galleries in 1996 and should have its 2nd floor open soon. The brainchild of Beetle Bailey creator Mort Walker, the museum has had previous incarnations in Greenwich, Connecticut, and Rye Brook, New York. The collection is made up of works by cartoonists from around the world, and it's the largest collection of its kind anywhere: more than 160,000 works on paper, 10,000 books and thousands of hours of animated films. You'll see works by artists including Walker, Charles Schultz, Charles Addams, Jim Davis, Richard Outcault, Walt Disney, Winsor McCay, Frank Frazetta, Hérge, Dik Browne, Walt Kelly and Chic Young. Sadly there is only one sample of Bill Watterson's *Calvin & Hobbes*. *Eine Schande.*

The museum is open Tuesday to Saturday 11 am to 5 pm, Sunday noon to 5 pm, closed Monday. Admission is $6 for adults, $5 for seniors, $4 for students and $3 for kids three to 12.

Florida Atlantic University Galleries

FAU's galleries are commercial and academic exhibition spaces with a diverse range of rotating shows by students, faculty and visiting artists. The art is mostly contemporary, in a variety of styles and media.

The **Schmidt Center Gallery** (☎ 561-297-2966), 777 Glades Rd, in the Schmidt Performing Arts Center, is free and open to the public Tuesday to Friday 11 am to 4 pm,

Saturday noon to 4 pm, closed Sunday, Monday and holidays. Use parking lot 1 (visitors must use metered spaces), walk toward the enormous theater and turn left; it's down the hallway on the building's 'arm.'

The **Ritter Art Gallery** (☎ 561-297-2660), on the 2nd floor of the Schmidt Center, above the breezeway, is a teaching gallery that also features contemporary art – though more in the lines of public art, BFA candidate exhibits and some foreign student shows. The Ritter is free and open Tuesday to Friday 10 am to 3:30 pm, Saturday 11 am to 4 pm, closed Sunday, Monday and holidays. Also use parking lot 1 (visitors must use metered spaces), walk toward the enormous theater and turn right, go around the building and toward the outdoor tables of the Breezeway Café, enter the breezeway (ask anyone if you can't find it) and walk up the staircase in the middle of the corridor.

Mizner Park

This is an upscale shopping mall with free valet parking and plenty of chi-chi shops. Don't be put off: you'll also find a great bookstore, Liberties (see Information earlier in this section), some good deals on dinner, a Steve's Ice Cream shop, a high-tech AMC cinema and many interesting little stores. It's just north of NE 2nd St on the east side of N Federal Hwy.

Children's Museum

In a lovely little house that very much resembles a country kindergarten (it's one of the oldest houses in Florida), the Children's Museum (☎ 561-368-6875), 498 Crawford Blvd, features such wonders as an insect room and a child-size supermarket. The staff is lovely and the place is very entertaining for smaller children. The museum's open Tuesday to Saturday noon to 4 pm, closed holidays and the month of September. Admission is $1; children under two are free.

Boca Raton Historical Society

Come to the Boca Raton Historical Society (☎ 561-395-6766), 71 N Federal Hwy, even if only to see its headquarters, the Boca Raton

Town Hall (1927). Mizner had planned to build this gold-domed, Mediterranean-Revival building earlier, but the land bust intervened and architect William Alsmeyer scaled down the plans for the final building. It's nice to look at, especially its gold dome, hardwood and tile floors, and tall windows. The building was declared a historical landmark and turned over to the society in 1983.

The society gives lectures, city historical tours, slide shows and some classes, and also maintains and runs the Florida East Coast Railway Depot. Admission is free.

Florida East Coast Railway Depot

Built in the 1930s as a station serving the Boca Raton Club, this lovely Mediterranean-Revival-style train station on the west side of Old Dixie Hwy between SE 8th and 7th Sts has been restored (its official name is the Count deHoernle Pavilion) and now is used for meetings and conferences. Train buffs will probably be disappointed at the meager displays. On the north side of the depot are a somewhat dilapidated 1930 Baldwin steam locomotive and a 1964 Seaboard caboose, and on the south side are 1950s-era stainless-steel passenger cars (a dining car and a lounge car), all awaiting restoration.

The depot is open by appointment only; admission is free. Contact the Boca Raton Historical Society (see above) for details.

Old Floresta Historic District

Just north of Palmetto Park Rd around NW 8th and 9th Aves, the Old Floresta Historic District is one of the town's loveliest areas. It's a nice place for a stroll before or after visiting the Museum of Art (assuming the museum hasn't moved yet). Don't skip walking down Cardinal Ave between Periwinkle and Azalea Sts; it's canopied by trees, and the little houses tucked on either side are almost totally overgrown by foliage.

Some high points of the district are the following:

737 Hibiscus St – a very secluded pastel yellow corner house in a wild garden

800 Hibiscus St – shaded by palms, with a royal poinciana tree (overflowing with red flowers) and a gorgeous main entry door

801 Hibiscus St – china-colored medium-size house with arched windows and a lovely walled-in garden

Alamanda St, just behind the museum – a beautiful Spanish-style cottage almost completely overgrown by tropical plants, and, 30 feet west, a similar house

875 Alamanda St – a storybook, pastel yellow Spanish-colonial-style house with a grapefruit tree out front, charming ceramic tiles on its pillars and a Japanese-style garden fence

Gumbo Limbo Nature Center

A serene 17-acre nature reserve, the Gumbo Limbo Nature Center (☎ 561-338-1473, www.fau.edu/gumbo) is a wonderful place to walk and take in the undeveloped splendor of it all: the relatively undisturbed coastal hammock harbors egrets and other waterfowl, raccoons, and native and non-native trees. The unique microclimate between the ocean and lagoon is responsible for the presence of plant species ordinarily native only to tropical regions.

To see just how close, yet how far, you are from civilization, climb the 66 steps to the top of the 39-foot-tall observatory and gaze out over the trees to the ocean and, turning north, to the high-rise condos.

The park also features four saltwater tanks in which the friendly and extremely knowledgeable staff raise and care for threatened sea turtles. Center staff also patrol beaches during spawning seasons to protect loggerhead sea-turtle eggs as they wait to hatch. Inside the visitors center, see snakes, taxidermy of endangered species (either road kills or confiscations by the Department of Fish and Wildlife) and other educational displays. Staff also hold classes, show instructional videos and give tours and lectures.

The nature center is at 1801 N Ocean Blvd (Hwy A1A). It is easy to miss the entrance, as it's tucked away in foliage. It's open year round, Monday to Saturday 9 am to 4 pm, Sunday noon to 4 pm. Admission and parking are free, but donations are strongly encouraged.

Red Reef Beach & South Beach Park

Together, Red Reef Beach and South Beach Park (☎ 561-338-1473) take up 60-some acres just north and south of Palmetto Park Rd at the ocean. Highlights include lots of beach access, a small golf course, an artificial reef for snorkeling and picnic areas with barbecue grills and tables. Fishing is allowed outside marked swimming areas. No pets or alcoholic beverages allowed. The parks also offer nature walks in conjunction with Gumbo Limbo Nature Center and night excursions during sea-turtle mating seasons to watch females lay eggs in the sand. Hours for both parks are 8 am to 10 pm year round; parking is $8 on weekdays, $10 on weekends and holidays – no camping, camper vans or trailers allowed.

Spanish River Park

This park (☎ 561-393-7815), between the ocean and the Intracoastal just south of Spanish River Blvd, is the city's most landscaped park. It's a great place to walk through the wilds, though they don't have as much in the way of instruction or guided tours as Gumbo Limbo to the south. But this is the only park with camping facilities, though camping is limited to groups only (see Places to Stay below). The park is open by 8 am and closes at sundown year round. Parking is $8 on weekdays, $10 on weekends and holidays.

Organized Tours

The Boca Raton Historical Society (☎ 561-395-6766) leads a weekly city historical tour on Thursday at 9:30 am, leaving from Old Town Hall, at the northwest corner of Federal Hwy and Palmetto Park Rd. The cost is $10 per person.

Places to Stay

It seems as if we're prefacing a lot of this chapter with warnings, and this section is no different; this is not a budget location. Count on a rock bottom of $35 a day or $150 a week for a double in low season and $65 a day or $450 a week in high season, which stretches out longer here than in most

Florida cities. It may be well worth your while to stay outside Boca, like in, say, Delray Beach or Fort Lauderdale, where prices are somewhat cheaper.

Camping The only place to camp is at *Spanish River Park*, and camping here is limited to groups of 15 or more people from an accredited organization (like the Boy or Girl Scouts, religious groups or others that pass the vigilant eyes of the rangers). Camping must be arranged in advance by writing to Parks and Recreation Director, Boca Raton Parks and Recreation Department, 201 W Palmetto Park Rd, Boca Raton, FL 33432. Camping costs vary with group size.

Motels & Hotels The very friendly folks at the *Boca Inn/Boca Raton Motel* (☎ 561-395-7500, fax 561-391-0287, 1801 N Federal Hwy) have large and clean-enough doubles for $39 a day ($210 a week) in low season, $85 a day ($550 a week) in high season. This is probably the best deal in town in low season because of the size of the rooms and the cleanliness.

The *Shore Edge Motel* (☎ 561-395-4491, 425 N Ocean Blvd) has perfectly nice rooms for the day/week for $45/275. Efficiencies are $55/350 in low season and $95/675 in high season. There's a midseason as well.

The *Days Inn*'s (☎ 561-395-7172, 561-325-2525, 2899 N Federal Hwy) singles/doubles go for $39/45 in low season, and $79/89 high season. A 10% discount is given to AAA and AARP members.

Diagonally across the street is the *Best Western University Inn* (☎ 561-395-5225, fax 561-338-9180, 2700 N Federal Hwy), with singles/doubles for $46/49 a day in low season, $89/109 in high season. The price includes continental breakfast and a free shuttle to beaches, malls, Florida Atlantic University and the West Palm and Fort Lauderdale airports.

If you are really into treating yourself right, head for the enormous Spanish-Mediterranean *Boca Raton Resort & Club* (☎ 561-395-3000, 800-448-8355, 501 E Camino Real), a 963-room, 37-suite resort

Club Etiquette Camp

Think your kids are getting a little surly? Get even by sending them to Audrey Kardon and Rachelle Klein's Boca Raton Resort & Club Etiquette Camp (☎ 561-881-7733) for children seven to 16. The camp will indoctrinate...uh...teach your little darlings all they'll ever need to know about social courtesies, personal grooming, ballroom dancing (now more important than ever), French and, of course, magic and juggling.

At camp's end, semiformal graduation dinners are held for the happy and now far more polite campers and their parents. The camps run twice a year, and the price is a very considerate $798.

built by Flagler and Mizner that opened in 1926. Prices are insanely complicated. In winter, rooms and suites range from $305 to $550. In summer, they range from $135 to $250.

Places to Eat

Boca Raton's saving grace is its restaurants. For some reason, this town has gone Italian happy – dozens of Italian places dot the streets, and though we've only named a couple here, there are plenty more. Thai, Chinese and French cuisine are all available in town, as are bagels, steak, and seafood. Prices get stellar quickly, but you can get good eats cheap in several places (including some unexpected surprises). Fast-food and quasi-fast-food places abound, if you're so disposed.

We vote *Mississippi Sweet BBQ* (☎ 561-394-6779, 2399 N Federal Hwy) one of the top two reasons to visit Boca Raton (the other being the Gumbo Limbo Nature Center). This place has cheerful and friendly management, great service and killer barbecue. Try the hot Dixie wings ($4.75 to $7.95), ribs and wings basket ($5.95, or platter $10.95) or underspiced Choctaw Catfish

SOUTHEAST

($9.95). All platters come with choice of sides, including the best deep-fried sweet potato slices we've ever had in the States, homemade applesauce, crisscross fries or coleslaw. The chicken soup is excellent ($1.75 cup, $2.95 bowl), and a good selection of hot sauces from all over is available – try the Inner Beauty.

The **Boca Beach Market** *(1 N Ocean Blvd)* is a great source of snacks and some prepared meals and pizza as well. An old Boca standard is **Flakowitz Bagel Inn** *(☎ 561-368-0666, 1999 N Federal Hwy)*. The place is open only for breakfast and lunch, but whatta deal! You can get a variety of specials, good veggie, lox and other flavored cream cheeses, and bagels by the baker's dozen (13) can be had for $4.95 to $7.95. It's open daily 7 am to 3 pm; lines form outside for the take-away window.

Max's Coffee Shop & Grill *(☎ 561-392-0454, 404 Plaza Real)* in Mizner Park is the cheaper cousin of **Max's Grille** *(☎ 561-368-0080)* next door. The former has excellent comfort food like meatloaf and rich, thick soups, as well as good, greasy breakfasts for around $5. The latter is an upscale and expensive bistro. Neither is any relation to **Maxwell's Chop House** *(☎ 561-347-7077, 501 E Palmetto Park Rd),* which is an excellent upscale steak house.

Thai Boca *(☎ 561-367-0500, 887 E Palmetto Park Rd)* serves some of the most generous portions of Thai food we've seen in Florida, and the prices are pretty reasonable as well. Lunch combos for $5.50 include soup, spring roll and fried rice! And their $8.95 to $12.95 early-bird dinner (5 to 6:30 pm, cash only) includes soup, appetizer, main course and dessert. Regular dinner entrees run from $7.95 (pad Thai) to $14.95 (excellent Panang duckling in a coconut curry sauce).

Of the six main dining rooms and 10 restaurants at the Boca Raton Resort & Club, the two best are **Top of the Tower**, on the 27th floor of the tower, and **Nick's Fish Market**, on the beachfront. Both are elegant pan-European restaurants (obviously with seafood the specialty at Nick's, and Italian the focus at Top of the Tower) with à la carte

menus that will run you $40 per person without wine. The restaurants are both open to the public, but reservations are essential in winter.

Entertainment

Theater The city's most concerted effort at bringing in legitimate theater is the **Caldwell Theatre Co** *(☎ 561-241-7432, 561-930-6400, 7873 N Federal Hwy),* at Levitz Plaza, about half a mile south of the Boca/Delray county line. Tickets are $30 to $40. Students (those with a valid ID or ISIC) can get in for $5 if any seats are available in the half hour before curtain. Performances are Tuesday to Saturday at 8 pm, Sunday at 7 pm, including matinee performances Wednesday and Sunday at 2 pm as well as certain Saturdays throughout the year.

If you like dinner theater (and you know who you are), the **Royal Palm Dinner Theater** *(☎ 561-392-3755, 800-841-6765, 303 Mizner Blvd)* has good shows. Tickets are quite expensive: $47 to $49 for dinner and a performance (no shows Monday). Slightly cheaper ($41) matinee performances are offered on Saturday and Wednesday. The theater also hosts **Comics Anonymous** on Saturday at 10:45 pm. Cost is $6 and there's a two-drink minimum. Also here is the **Little Palm Theater for Young People**, a nonprofit regional theater troupe presenting classic children's stories and fairy tales on Saturday mornings at 9:30 am.

Live Music A 75-member orchestra (including the 18-piece Boca Pops Big Band), the venerable **Boca Symphonic Pops** *(☎ 561-393-7677)* ranks among the top in the nation. It plays primarily in the Florida Atlantic University Center Auditorium, but also at the Boca Raton Resort & Club, the Olympic Height high school and other venues. Tickets range $20 to $40.

Clubs Put those dance shoes away, for this is not a toddlin' town. If you want to boogie, you're much better off heading up to Delray Beach or down to Fort Lauderdale. If you're determined, try **Poly Esther's** *(☎ 561-447-8955, 99 SE 1st St),* with retro ('70s) music and lots of contests, promotions, games of Twister, costume nights and so on.

Bars Boca has at least two British pubs. The *Lion and Eagle (☎ 561-394-3190, 2401 N Federal Hwy)* is cozy and very, well, British. On one night we heard several instances of such phrases as 'there goes my bleeper,' 'filthy sod,' 'bollocks' and 'bleedin ell.' Pints of draft Guinness, Fullers ESB, Bass and Harp, though, are quite dear – $4, in fact. Live entertainment is offered on some nights, and the pub fare here includes excellent chicken curry and chips, ploughman's lunch platters ($5.50) and other main courses from $7.50 to $9.50.

Up the road a bit at the *Ugly Duckling (☎ 561-997-5929, 5903 N Federal Hwy)*, the staff is livelier and the atmosphere more upscale. The menu is more extensive as well. Live entertainment is supplemented by some disco nights and Sunday karaoke (from 8 pm to midnight).

Both of these pubs are run by Brits and are relatively authentic. And in both places you're likely to run into some raunchy but fun-loving journos from the nearby offices of the *National Enquirer.*

Getting There & Away

The closest international air service to the area is at Palm Beach International Airport (PBI, ☎ 561-471-7420), about a half-hour drive to the north on I-95, 3 miles west of West Palm Beach on either Southern Blvd or Belvedere Rd. See Getting Around below for information on getting from PBI to Boca Raton. Ground transportation is downstairs at level 1. Ignore the 'helpful' volunteers at the information counters.

The Greyhound stop (they couldn't actually put one of those ugly *station* things here) is at the corner of N Federal Hwy at NE 20th St at the city bus stop (across from McDonald's). For service detail see the Getting Around chapter.

The Tri-Rail station is at 601 NW 53rd St (the Yamato exit from I-95). Amtrak stops at Deerfield Beach, 5 miles south.

Boca Raton is between I-95 and US Hwys 1 and A1A. It's about a 40-minute

drive from Miami, or a 25-minute drive from Fort Lauderdale.

Getting Around

To reach PBI by bus, take Palm Tran (☎ 561-233-1111) bus No 1S from downtown Boca Raton to the downtown West Palm Beach terminal ($1), and transfer (20¢) to bus No 4S to PBI.

Tri-Rail has service between PBI and Boca Raton; the tickets are $4 one way, $6.25 roundtrip. From PBI, get a shuttle from the airport to the West Palm Beach Tri-Rail station, and another shuttle in Boca between the Tri-Rail station and the Boca Raton police station, 100 NW 2nd St. From the airport, shuttle service begins at 5:34 am weekdays with service about once an hour until 11:48 am, and then hourly from 2 to 10:21 pm. From Boca to PBI, the shuttle runs from the police station to the Boca Raton Tri-Rail station on approximately the same schedule, though the last one goes out at 8:02 pm. A taxi from PBI to Boca Raton will cost about $25.

Palm Tran (☎ 561-233-1111) runs buses all over the county. Regular bus fare is $1; seniors, students and people with physical disabilities pay 50¢. Transfers are 20¢. Bus No 1S goes from Mizner Park to the beach, the Museum of Art and Spanish River Park (at Federal Hwy). Bus No 8 goes out to the Morikami Gardens in Delray Beach.

Free parking is everywhere, and there's really nothing special to be aware of except that the entire city is one giant speed trap – obey every sign and nobody'll get hurt (or ticketed).

Taxi rates are $1.25 flagfall and $1.75 each additional mile. The biggest taxi company in the area is Yellow Cab (☎ 561-395-3221).

DELRAY BEACH
• population 49,000

Delray Beach is a lively town with an interesting history. It's far more welcoming than its neighbor to the south and more affordable, too, so we'd recommend staying here and going back into Boca only if you have to.

Originally populated by Seminole Indians, the land on which the town sits was

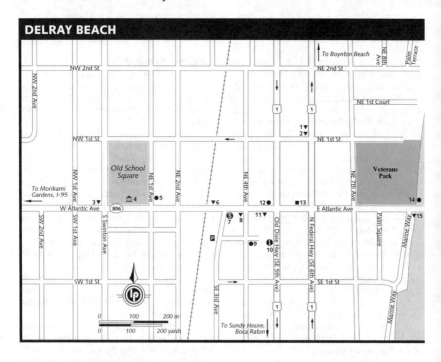

DELRAY BEACH

bought from the government in 1868 by Captain George Gleason for $1.25 an acre (Gleason was the son of William Gleason, the Lieutenant Governor from 1868 to 1873). The area was first settled by people from Michigan (Delray's named after a suburb of Detroit) and primarily blacks from the Florida Panhandle. Henry Flagler then acquired the land when it went into receivership after the freeze of 1895.

The Florida East Coast Railway also brought in about a hundred Japanese farmers from the city of Miyazu, Japan, to work farms in a settlement southwest of the city called Yamato. The Japanese workers planted a number of crops, but chiefly they were here to farm pineapples – an endeavor that failed to reach expectations and, with added competition from Cuban fruit companies, soon dried up. But the FEC railroad was coming through regularly, and businesses sprang up to support the traffic it produced.

Today Delray Beach is a small but very pleasant resort town. It's energetic but not full of itself, and there are pleasant restaurants, awesome chocolates, good beaches and fine museums here. One of the museums, the Morikami Gardens, is dedicated to the lives of the Japanese settlers at Yamato. With a mix of art and nature, it's a lovely and serene place where you can easily spend a couple of hours.

Orientation & Information

Downtown's main drag is Atlantic Ave, running east-west between I-95 and the Atlantic Ocean. US Hwy 1 is split through downtown: 6th Ave is US Hwy 1 north, 5th Ave is US Hwy 1 south. Most of the hotels are on the east side of the Intracoastal Waterway. Two public beaches span $1\frac{1}{2}$ miles north and south of Atlantic Ave, and a paved boardwalk on N Ocean Blvd runs north of Atlantic Ave.

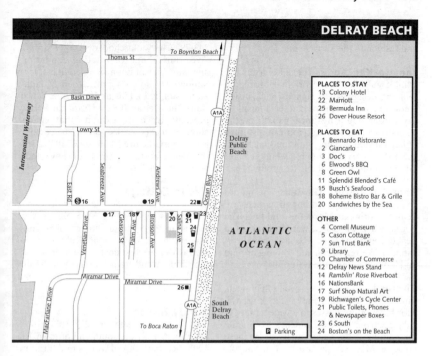

DELRAY BEACH

To Boynton Beach

Thomas St

Basin Drive

A1A

Lowry St

Delray
Public
Beach

Intracoastal Waterway

Seabreeze Ave

Andrews Ave

Ocean Blvd

East Rd

🏧 16

● 19

22 ■

● 17

18 ▼

20 ▼

🛈 ▽ 23
21

Venetian Drive

Gleason St

Palm Ave

Bronson Ave

Salina Ave

24

25

ATLANTIC
OCEAN

Miramar Drive

MacFarlane Drive

Miramar Drive

26 ■

A1A

South
Delray
Beach

To Boca Raton

P Parking

PLACES TO STAY
13 Colony Hotel
22 Marriott
25 Bermuda Inn
26 Dover House Resort

PLACES TO EAT
1 Bennardo Ristorante
2 Giancarlo
3 Doc's
6 Elwood's BBQ
8 Green Owl
11 Splendid Blended's Café
15 Busch's Seafood
18 Boheme Bistro Bar & Grille
20 Sandwiches by the Sea

OTHER
4 Cornell Museum
5 Cason Cottage
7 Sun Trust Bank
9 Library
10 Chamber of Commerce
12 Delray News Stand
14 *Ramblin' Rose* Riverboat
16 NationsBank
17 Surf Shop Natural Art
19 Richwagen's Cycle Center
21 Public Toilets, Phones
     & Newspaper Boxes
23 6 South
24 Boston's on the Beach

The helpful chamber of commerce (☎ 561-278-0424, www.delraybeach.com), is at 64 SE 5th Ave. The Delray News Stand (☎ 561-278-3399), 429 E Atlantic Ave, sells local, US and international papers. The library (☎ 561-276-6462) is at 29 SE 4th Ave. There are toilets along the public beach.

Morikami Gardens

George Morikami was one of the settlers brought over in 1905 to work in the Yamato settlement. When everyone else left, he stayed on in southern Florida and eventually struck it rich enough to buy several hundred acres of land in the area. He bequeathed 200 of them to Palm Beach County to build a museum in memory of the settlement, and the Morikami Gardens (☎ 561-495-0233, www.morikami.org) is it. Southwest of downtown Delray Beach at 4000 Morikami Park Rd, the Morikami is a splendid little piece of Japan, with a theater, several galleries, an authentic Seishin-An teahouse, a wonderful nature trail and a somewhat disappointing bonsai garden.

The museum is open Tuesday to Sunday 10 am to 5 pm, closed Monday. Admission is $4.25 for adults, $3.75 for seniors over 65, $2 for kids six to 18.

Galleries Tea ceremonies are held in the teahouse from October to June on the third Saturday of each month at noon, 1, 2 and 3 pm. The two gallery areas inside the exhibition hall house rotating exhibitions of artworks from both the permanent collection and private collections – historic photography, valuable artifacts, Japanese folk art and modern works of art by Japanese artists. On our visit we saw two typically excellent exhibitions: *The Exotic Self – Satsuma Ware of the late 19th and early 20th centuries,* featuring hugely colorful and incredibly valuable pottery; and *Showa*

SOUTHEAST

Threads – Kimono Tradition from the 1930s to 1960s, showing changes in kimono culture and fashion in the Showa era.

Yamato-Kan Across the lake from the exhibit galleries is the original Morikami building, designed as a Japanese villa. Inside (remove your shoes) you can see a Japanese dry garden and a historical exhibit on the Yamato-kan colony, and you can also play fibber's forum, a game with unusual Japanese objects – try to figure out what they are! Guided tours are available for groups.

Bonsai & Nature Gardens The nature trail, goldfish pond and bonsai gardens are near the original Morikami building. The bonsai when we visited were looking a tad peaked, but to be fair it was in the middle of summer. We really enjoyed walking around and looking at the little waterfall.

Classes In addition to a totally high-tech, interactive computer area for kids, the Morikami offers classes in a wide variety of subjects, from Nihongo Japanese to Sumi-e ink painting, from haiku poetry to Japanese cooking. Most classes are held during the winter months only.

Café Back in the main building, on the patio, the museum's Cornell Café serves darn good home-style Japanese food like cold *soba* noodles and teriyaki chicken ($5.95), sushi rolls ($4) and sesame noodles ($4.95). During winter arrive before 12:30 pm or you'll have an hour's wait or longer.

Getting There & Away The museum is 4 miles east of I-95. From Delray Beach, take Atlantic Ave west to Carter Rd and turn south (it becomes Jog Rd); the museum drive will be about three quarters of a mile down on the right-hand side of the road. From Boca Raton, take Yamato or Glades Rds west to Jog Rd and turn right; the museum is about 2 miles farther down on the left

Old School Square
The four acres of a former high school have been converted to the Old School Square

arts and entertainment complex. In it, the Cornell Museum of Art & History (☎ 561-243-7922, www.oldschool.org), 51 N Swinton Ave, runs about 10 rotating exhibitions annually. The museum is open Tuesday to Sunday 11 am to 4 pm, closed Monday. Admission is $3, kids under 12 free. Downstairs, the Delray Beach Historical Society presents traveling exhibits that change about every six weeks. Also in the complex is the Crest Theatre (☎ 561-243-3183), a 363-seat venue hosting a variety of shows and a popular annual lecture series.

Cason Cottage
The vernacular-frame Florida-style Cason Cottage (☎ 561-243-0223), 5 NE 1st Ave (across the street from Old School Square), was the home of Dr John Robert Cason, Delray Beach's first doctor. Built circa 1915, the simple wood-frame cottage now houses the Delray Beach Historical Society and occasional exhibits.

Sundy House
The Sundy House (☎ 561-278-2163), 106 S Swinton Ave on the south end of town, is a 1902 Victorian packed with period furniture and embellished by a lush garden. Tea and lunch are served in the dining room. Admission is free.

Activities
Richwagens Cycle Center (☎ 561-243-2453), 1155 E Atlantic Ave, rents bikes (kids', race, tandem, single-speed, multispeed) for $6 to $12 an hour, $15 to $24 per eight-hour day and $20 to $35 for 24 hours. The shop also rents equipment such as helmets, baskets and so on.

Surf Shop Natural Art (☎ 561-588-7925, surf report 561-588-7953), 1030 E Atlantic Ave, rents surfboards by the hour/day for $8/25, Boogieboards for $5/15. The shop also sells surf clothes, bikinis and T-shirts.

Boat Tours
Narrated sightseeing and Millionaire's Row-gawking tours are available aboard the *Ramblin' Rose* Riverboat (☎ 561-243-0686). Prices depend on the tour and the day, so

call for specifics; for an idea, a 3¹/₂-hour Saturday sightseeing day tour is $15.95 for adults and $4.95 for children, and Saturday dinner cruises (three hours) are $29.95. The ticket office is just west of the bridge at 801 E Atlantic Ave.

Places to Stay

A friendly family runs both the *Sea View Motel* (☎ 561-276-5182, 5019 N Ocean Drive) and *Henri's Motel (same ☎, 1 Tropical Drive)* in Ocean Ridge. Both places are very clean and have nice pools. Happily, they're also the cheapest in town. Motel rooms are $35 to $55, efficiencies (by the week only) $190 in low season, $445 in high, and one bedrooms (same deal) $230/495.

The other cheaper options are uninspiring, but they won't kill ya': the *Budget Inn* (☎ 561-276-8961, 2500 N Federal Hwy) has standard singles/doubles for $39/49 in low season and $69/79 in high season. The *Carlson Motel* (☎ 561-243-0182, 1600 N Federal Hwy) has rooms for $55/66. Both are on the north side of town.

The *Sea Aire* (☎ 561-276-7491, 1715 S Ocean Blvd) has a beautiful garden with a shuffleboard court, and staff really care about their guests. Large efficiencies are $60 to $75 in summer and $140 to $179 in winter. Other amenities include beach access, barbecue grills and a library for guests.

The *Bermuda Inn* (☎ 561-276-5288, 64 S Ocean Blvd) has clean rooms and nice service. From May to November rooms are $79, efficiencies $85 and one bedrooms $95; from December to April the rates are $85 to $95, or $750 a week. The *Dover House Resort* (☎ 561-276-0309, 110 S Ocean Blvd) has a garden with fountains and rents nice, clean one-bedroom apartments with tiled floors for $80 to $150.

The excellent *Colony Hotel* (☎ 561-276-4123, 800-552-2363, 525 E Atlantic Ave) is only open November to April. In low season, small but spotless rooms are $89 to $99, two-room suites $119 to $139; in winter, the same rooms are $139 to $149, suites $169 to $189. The enormous lobby is furnished with white wicker, much the way it was when the hotel opened in 1926, and the porch bar is open nightly. A breakfast consisting of Starbucks coffee and homemade muffins is included and served from a cart on the front porch.

The flashy *Marriott* (☎ 561-274-3200, 10 N Ocean Blvd) is a newly renovated place that's pretty spectacular. Oceanfront rooms run $169 to $299 off-season and $179 to $249 high season; standard hotel rooms run $99 to $129 off-season and $139 to $149 high season.

Places to Eat

Green Owl (☎ 561-272-7766, 330 E Atlantic Ave) does breakfast and lunch. Omelets are $2.20 to $4.45; two eggs, home fries or grits, toast and jelly is $2.50; sandwiches and burgers are $3.45 to $5.45 and a grilled-chicken-breast platter with cottage cheese, lettuce, tomato and cucumber is $4.95.

Doc's (☎ 561-278-3627, 10 N Swinton Ave) is a classic American outdoor diner that's been here since 1951, and we definitely recommend it. Portions are enormous and delicious. The burger combo comes with fries and a drink for $3.75.

Sandwiches by the Sea (☎ 561-272-2212, 1214 E Atlantic Ave) offers very large and good sandwiches from $3.75 to $4.95. It's more of a takeout place; the only tables are around the corner in the back, in a small, pretty courtyard.

Ellie's '50's Diner (☎ 561-276-1570, 2410 N Federal Hwy) is fun, with its '50s decor and tableside jukeboxes, and you can get a pretty good meal as well – none of their prices have changed since last time! Breakfast runs $3 to $6, sandwiches $4 to $7.

We loved the *Boheme Bistro & Grille* (☎ 561-278-4899, 1118 E Atlantic Ave). Its falafel and hummus are excellent (both $6.95). Sandwiches go for $4.75 to $6.95; full meals, like crab cakes, chicken breast or pizza dishes are $11.95 to $15.95.

Giancarlo (☎ 561-274-2012, 102 N Federal Hwy) is in a lovely old building dating from 1932. It's very cozy inside, since it's not one big dining area but several separate rooms with three to five tables each. The dinner buffet offers soups, meats, fish, pasta, veggies and salads for $14; pizzas

($6.95 to $9.95) are baked in a brick oven. It's closed Sunday.

Elwood's BBQ (☎ *561-272-7427, 301 E Atlantic Ave*) is a very cool barbecue place in a converted filling station; the decor features old gas pumps and lots of paraphernalia – the bar in the patio dining area is an old hydraulic truck lift. Appetizers are $3 to $6, entrees $9 to $13, and it's cash only. Live music is scheduled regularly.

Splendid Blended's Café (☎ *561-265-0135, 432 E Atlantic Ave*) may be the best place in town for a date. It offers magnificent service, lunch pastas for $7.95 and sandwiches for $6.95 to $8.95. Dinner pastas with a house salad are $9.95 to $11.95, and phenomenal main courses, like grilled tuna with sautéed mushrooms and garlic, or a wonderful venison, are around $16.95.

Busch's Seafood (☎ *561-278-7600, 561-278-7609, 840 E Atlantic Ave*), just west of the Intracoastal, is a Delray Beach tradition (in town since 1942). It serves great seafood dishes for $12.95 from 4:30 to 6 pm (they cost much more after 6 pm). Behind the restaurant is a lovely patio with a walkway/dock on the Intracoastal.

Bennardo Ristorante (☎ *561-274-0051, 116 N Federal Hwy*) is in the historical Falcon House (1925). It's a top-end place with an elegant atmosphere and several separate dining rooms, which keep space between you and that cigar guy who just sat down. Each room is named after a different family member – this restaurant is run by the same family that runs Giancarlo (above).

Entertainment

For live entertainment, try Elwood's BBQ (see above) or the ever-popular ***Boston's on the Beach*** (☎ *561-278-3364, 40 S Ocean Blvd*), a mellow, dark wood and down-and-dirty watering hole. Monday is reggae night; happy hour is Monday to Friday 4 to 7 pm.

The slicker and more energetic ***6 South*** (☎ *561-278-7878, 6 S Ocean Blvd*) is a bar and restaurant that does burgers for $4.95, sushi for $2.75 to $7.95 and a Sunday brunch for $8.95. Live music offerings Friday to Monday include calypso, rock and reggae.

Getting There & Away

The Greyhound station (☎ 561-272-6447, 800-231-2222) is at 402 N Federal Hwy. Buses go to and from Miami ($7/11 one way/return) twice a day, Tampa ($50/99) three times a day and Orlando ($29/52) twice a day.

Tri-Rail stops here; the station is at 345 S Congress Ave (which is west of I-95, off Atlantic Ave). See the Getting Around chapter for service details.

For a taxi, call Metro Taxi (☎ 561-276-2230).

Delray Beach is just north of Boca Raton on I-95, US Hwy 1 and Hwy A1A. Watch out for the speed traps on N Ocean Blvd between about 15th and 20th Sts.

LAKE WORTH
• population 27,000

Lake Worth is a pleasant town that is cheaper than its nearby neighbors. For some reason it's full of Polish and Finnish tourists. Well, *dzien dobry* and *kiitos*. The town was established in 1913, and for a while in the Roaring '20s it was quite the suave place to be seen – the Lake Worth Casino was a rollicking joint, and people came from miles around to frolic in the casino's enormous saltwater swimming pool. But the town never quite recovered its glamour after the 1928 hurricane wreaked havoc on the area.

Today Lake Worth is a sleepy place with not a whole lot to do except sit on the beach, but it's a good base for seeing the sights of Palm Beach and West Palm Beach, if only for a day or so. The Holiday Inn Gulfstream has renovated the casino and is making a go of restoring the town to its former glory.

In a Kaliningrad-esque freak of geopolitical divisions, Lake Worth's beach actually cuts across the southern portion of Palm Beach – a fact that enrages property owners in the latter, though they'd never admit it.

Orientation

Downtown Lake Worth is on the mainland just south of the city of West Palm Beach and north of Lantana. Lake Worth's beautiful beach is on the barrier island east of the Intracoastal Waterway and separates Palm

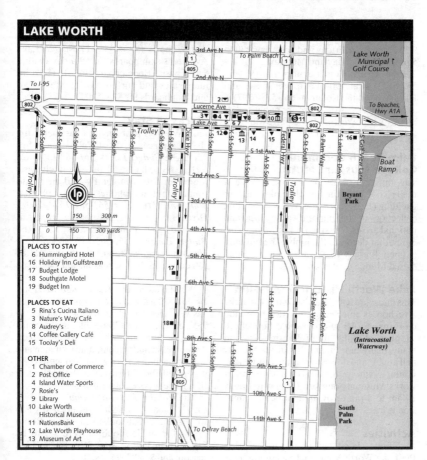

LAKE WORTH

PLACES TO STAY
6 Hummingbird Hotel
16 Holiday Inn Gulfstream
17 Budget Lodge
18 Southgate Motel
19 Budget Inn

PLACES TO EAT
5 Rina's Cucina Italiano
3 Nature's Way Café
8 Audrey's
14 Coffee Gallery Café
15 TooJay's Deli

OTHER
1 Chamber of Commerce
2 Post Office
4 Island Water Sports
7 Rosie's
9 Library
10 Lake Worth
Historical Museum
11 NationsBank
12 Lake Worth Playhouse
13 Museum of Art

Beach's southernmost section from the city of South Palm Beach.

The main drags downtown are both one way: Lake Ave for eastbound traffic, and Lucerne Ave for westbound. These two roads merge west of downtown to become Lake Worth Rd and east of downtown to become the Lake Worth Bridge leading to the beach.

US Hwy 1 is Dixie Hwy here, and north-south running streets in Lake Worth are lettered from west to east (Dixie Hwy was formerly called I St).

Information

The town has no tourist offices as such, but you can get area information at the public library or the Lake Worth Historical Museum (see below). Lake Worth's Polish-American Cultural Society of the Palm Beaches (☎ 561-640-2982) organizes Polish-American events and art shows.

Change money at the NationsBank at 14 N Federal Hwy. The main post office (☎ 561-964-1102) is at 4151 Lake Worth Rd. Main Street News (☎ 561-586-4356), 608 Lake Ave, has lots of international and US newspapers.

The public library (☎ 561-533-7354) is at 15 N M St. It's open Tuesday to Thursday 9:30 am to 8 pm, Friday and Saturday 9:30 to 5 pm, closed Sunday and Monday.

Palm Beach Coin Laundry Inc (☎ 561-582-6123) is at 1904 Lake Worth Rd, and Ring Around the Kollar (☎ 561-588-6797) is at 1404 Lucerne Ave. There are public toilets at the Lake Worth Municipal Swimming Pool (see Activities below).

Palm Beach Community College Museum of Art

This museum of art (☎ 561-582-0006) is a really cool place in the old Lake Theatre Building (1939), 601 Lake Ave, with rotating collections of contemporary art by local and national artists. Note the friezes, *Battle of the Sexes*, that decorate the lobby. The museum is open Tuesday to Sunday noon to 5 pm, closed Monday. Admission is $2.

Lake Worth Historical Museum

This museum (☎ 561-586-1700), 414 Lake Ave, houses an eclectic collection of period clothing, tools, photographs, household supplies, clothing, umbrellas, jewelry and many, many more items. It's inside the city hall annex, and downstairs is the Art League Gallery, where local artists show their works. Museum hours are Tuesday to Friday 10 am to 2 pm or by appointment. Admission is free.

Activities

A definite classic and great for the price, the Lake Worth Municipal Swimming Pool (☎ 561-533-7367), 10 S Ocean Blvd, is an Olympic-size pool that's open to the public. Admission is $2 for adults, $1 for children and seniors. It's great in summer but not heated in winter.

The Lake Worth Municipal Beach Fishing Pier (☎ 561-533-7367) charges $2 for adults, $1 for children and 50¢ for nonfishing spectators. You can rent rods for $5.30 per day, and bait costs $1 to $3. The pier is open Sunday to Thursday 7 am to midnight and Friday and Saturday 7 am to 2 am.

The best part of the beach for surfing, Boogieboarding, skimboarding and body-surfing is on the south side of the pier; for swimming, stay on the north side. Island Water Sports (☎ 561-588-1728), 728 Lake Ave, rents skimboards for $5 a day (with a $20 deposit), Boogieboards for $10 ($20), in-line skates and surfboards for $15 ($100) and longboards for $30 ($100).

Places to Stay

Lake Worth is probably the best bet if the cheaper places in West Palm Beach are filled. The *Budget Inn (☎ 561-582-1864, 828 S Dixie Hwy)* has small and absolutely basic rooms for $30. You get TV and air conditioning, but no phones or pay phones. *Southgate Motel (☎ 561-582-1544, 709 S Dixie Hwy)* has a small pool, a grapefruit tree and clean rooms from $32 to $53. The *Budget Lodge (☎ 561-582-1379, 521 S Dixie Hwy)* has regular rooms for $35 single or $40 double in the low season, and $45 single or $55 to $60 double in high season.

We stayed at the *Hummingbird Hotel (☎ 561-582-3224, 631 Lucerne Ave)*, which has very nice and clean rooms from $35 to $55 single, $45 to $75 double; most rooms share a bathroom with at least one other. Amenities include a community kitchen and laundry facilities. It's a good deal with (cook it yourself) breakfast included and the feel (if not the service) of a B&B.

The *Holiday Inn Gulfstream (☎ 561-540-6000, 1 Lake Ave)* hadn't yet opened when we visited, but it looked fantastic. Room prices for singles/doubles were set to be $109/119 in low season, $139/149 in high season, and $259/269 for suites.

Places to Eat

Run, don't walk, to *Rina's Cucina Italiano (☎ 561-547-2782, 701 Lucerne Ave)*, an unassuming little place that serves extraordinary desserts, a really nice lasagna ($6.95) and a good soup/sandwich combo ($5.99). The *Coffee Gallery Café (☎ 561-585-5911, 517 Lake Ave)* has lunch specials like quiche, salad, a soft drink and a cookie for $4.95, and lasagna or curry is $5.95. It's open daily 11 am to 11 pm.

TooJay's Original Gourmet Deli (☎ 561-582-8684, 419 Lake Ave) is a mediocre diner with a very large selection of sandwiches ($5.99 to $8.99). *Nature's Way Café (☎ 561-588-7004, 800 Lake Ave)* has nice fruit juices ($2.50 to $3.25) and whole wheat pita sandwiches ($3.75 to $5.40). *Benny's on the Beach*, a snack bar at the fishing pier, serves cheap burgers and cheap beer. *Audrey's Cookie Boutique & Cheesecake Company (☎ 561-586-0424, 7 N L St)* whips up a very good cheesecake.

Entertainment

The *Lake Worth Playhouse (☎ 561-586-6410, 713 Lake Ave)* seats about 300 people; tickets are about $15 for performances. The box office is open Tuesday to Friday 9 am to 1 pm and 1:30 to 4:30 pm, Saturday 10 am to 2 pm and one hour before the show. Right next door is the *Black Box Theater (☎ 561-586-6410)*, which puts on children's shows and stages avant garde performances; tickets are about $10.

Rosie's (612 Lake Ave) is a very cool and genial neighborhood bar with many different specials. It was under construction at press time but will reopen by 2000.

Getting There & Away

Greyhound (☎ 800-231-2222) has a flag stop on US Hwy 1. (If you are heading north, stand on the northbound side of the street and wave down the bus; heading south, stand on the southbound side.)

Lake Worth is south of Palm Beach on Hwy A1A, north of Boca Raton, Delray Beach and Lantana and south of West Palm Beach on US Hwy 1.

Getting Around

Three trolley lines serve Lake Worth, all of them originating from a trolley depot at the corner of Lake Ave and H St. The Red Trolley goes out to (among other places) a Finnish-American Rest Home, the Lantana Shopping Center and the Publix Town & Country Shopping Center; the Yellow Trolley runs directly to Lake Worth Beach; and the Blue Trolley heads to the northern end of the city and very indirectly to the beach. Trolleys run Monday to Saturday 9 am to 5 pm, Sunday until 3, 4 and 5 pm for red, yellow and blue, respectively. Fare is $1 for adults, 50¢ for those under 18, over 60 or handicapped.

Psychics, Blind Baton Twirlers & Miracle Diets

If you're driving past the town of Lantana, a pilgrimage to the headquarters of *National Enquirer* (☎ 561-586-1111) is almost a must – though, sad to say, tours aren't ordinarily given. The *Enquirer's* tasteless but (the industry grudgingly admits) accurate airing, er, reporting of the dirty laundry of celebrities – and its heroic tales of blind jugglers and miracle diets – have given it the largest circulation of any newspaper in the USA. The headquarters are at 600 SE Coast Ave in Lantana, but if you're traveling on US Hwy 1, you can't miss the enormous *National Enquirer* sign on the west side of the railroad tracks. If you call and ask for the marketing department and sound awfully convincing (we couldn't pull it off and we're *very* convincing when we try) they might bring you through on a VIP tour.

NICK SELBY

WEST PALM BEACH

• population 760,000

West Palm Beach is a large modern city pinned between extremes. To its east, across the Intracoastal Waterway, lies well-to-do Palm Beach, the famed land of moneyed excess. To the north, dangerous Riviera Beach lurks like a lit cigarette smoldering in West Palm's couch.

At first glance, the city seems to have all the usual urban problems with few of the advantages. But look further and West Palm's highlights positively shine: the Norton Museum of Art is perhaps the finest art museum in the southeast; the Kravis Center is one of the state's best performing arts centers; and Clematis St, downtown's main drag, is a chic, busy and vibrant center unrecognizable from just two years ago.

Orientation

West Palm Beach is on the west bank of Lake Worth (actually a wide stretch of the Intracoastal Waterway), which separates West Palm Beach from Palm Beach. With the exception of some winding, faux-British-named streets in the south (Marlborough, Argyle, Rugby...), the city is a straightforward grid with practical borders of Flagler Drive on the east, Palm Beach Lakes Blvd on the north, Southern Blvd on the south and Australian Ave on the west. Three main bridges connect West Palm Beach to Palm Beach: the Southern Blvd Bridge; the Royal Park Bridge, which connects Okeechobee Blvd with Royal Palm Way; and the Flagler Memorial Bridge, which connects Flagler Drive with Royal Poinciana Way. (The Flagler Bridge was closed for renovation when last we visited.)

Downtown is centered around the stretch of Clematis St between Olive and Tamarind Aves, with rough north and south borders of 3rd St and Okeechobee Blvd, respectively. Banyan Blvd is the more common name for 1st St. Many of the attractions in West Palm are far from the city center. See Palm Beach later this chapter for more area museums, sights and attractions.

It's difficult finding accurate and user-friendly free maps; the Convention & Visitors Bureau *Palm Beach County Map* is distorted – the system map put out by Palm Tran (see Getting Around later in the West Palm Beach section) actually tells you more about local streets. Dolph publishes a good area map.

Information

A tourist information booth in the Cuillo Center for the Arts (☎ 561-585-3433), 201 Clematis St, is open daily 9 am to 5 pm. The good Palm Beach County Convention & Visitors Bureau (☎ 561-471-3995, 800-833-5733, www.palmbeachfl.com) is at 1555 Palm Beach Lakes Blvd.

AAA (☎ 561-694-9090) has an office at 9123 N Military Trail, No 110. NationsBank has several branches in town; the main one is at 625 N Flagler Drive. The main post office is at 3200 Summit Blvd; the more convenient downtown station is at 640 Clematis St. The main library (☎ 561-659-8010) is at 100 Clematis St.

The *Palm Beach Post* is the local daily. *Broward New Times* (www.newtimesbpb.com), a freebie available in boxes throughout the city, is the best source for music, club, bar and restaurant information. National Public Radio (NPR) is at 90.7 FM.

Three good options for laundry are Rub-A-Dub, 526 Belvedere Rd; Wash Rite, 2601 Poinsettia Ave; and the Lavandería, 5900 S Dixie Hwy.

The three major hospitals in the city are Columbia Hospital (☎ 561-842-6141), 2201 45th St; St Mary's Hospital (☎ 561-844-6300), 901 45th St; and Palm Beach Regional (☎ 561-967-7800), 2829 10th Ave N. The Good Samaritan Medical Center (☎ 561-655-5511) is at 1300 N Flagler Drive.

Norton Museum of Art

Perhaps the best fine arts museum in the southeastern USA, the Norton Museum of Art (☎ 561-832-5196, www.norton.org), 1451 S Olive Ave, was founded in 1941 by steel industrialist Ralph Hubbard Norton (1875-1953). Its permanent collection of more than 4500 works is concentrated in three main fields: French Impressionist and Postimpressionist paintings, 20th-century American art

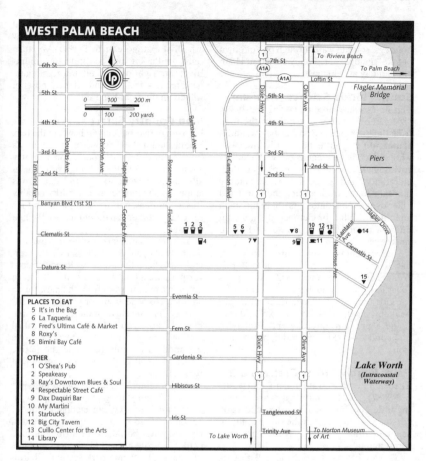

WEST PALM BEACH

PLACES TO EAT
5 It's in the Bag
6 La Taqueria
7 Fred's Ultima Café & Market
8 Roxy's
15 Bimini Bay Café

OTHER
1 O'Shea's Pub
2 Speakeasy
3 Ray's Downtown Blues & Soul
4 Respectable Street Café
9 Dax Daquiri Bar
10 My Martini
11 Starbucks
12 Big City Tavern
13 Cuillo Center for the Arts
14 Library

and Chinese art. Other areas of the collection include sculpture, the old masters, European and American modernism as well as 19th-century American art.

The museum's holdings include important works by de Chirico, Brancusi, Chagall, Cézanne, Matisse, Renoir, Gauguin, Braque, Degas, Stuart Davis, Hopper, Marin, Warhol, O'Keeffe and Duane Hanson. The Norton also hosts regular traveling exhibitions, and the caliber is usually stunning.

Free guided tours of the permanent collection run Tuesday to Friday 12:30 to 1:30

and 2:30 to 3:30 pm, weekends 2:30 to 3:30 pm. The museum is open Tuesday to Saturday 10 am to 5 pm, Sunday 1 to 5 pm, closed Monday and holidays. Admission is $5 for adults, $2 for students 13 to 21, and free to all on Wednesday 1:30 to 5 pm.

Mounts Botanical Gardens
This pleasant, free 15-acre botanical garden (☎ 561-233-1749), 531 N Military Trail, between Southern Blvd and Belvedere, holds tropical and subtropical plants, a tiny rain forest, hibiscus and rose gardens and an

herb garden. It's open Monday to Saturday 8:30 am to 5 pm, Sunday 1 to 5 pm, closed holidays. You can walk through on your own or take a guided tour, given Saturday at 11 am and Sunday at 2:30 pm.

South Florida Science Museum

This fine science museum (☎ 561-832-1988), 4801 Dreher Trail N, is just down the road from the Palm Beach Zoo (see below) and is a must-do if you're here with kids. The whole place is very hands-on, with exhibits covering sight, sound, holography, weather, electricity, and paleontology (including dinosaur fossils from around the world and killer dynamation dinosaurs). Skip the small aquarium exhibit. In October, the museum offers a great Haunted House – with live snakes yet!

The museum's open Saturday to Thursday 10 am to 5 pm, Friday 10 am to 10 pm. Admission is $5 for adults, $4.50 for seniors (over 62), $3 for students (13 to 21) and $2 for kids four to 12. Planetarium shows are held upstairs on weekdays at 2 pm, Friday at 7 and 8 pm and Saturday and Sunday at noon and 2 pm ($1.75 in addition to admission).

Palm Beach Zoo at Dreher Park

The Palm Beach Zoo at Dreher Park (☎ 561-533-0887), 1301 Summit Blvd, is an interesting little zoo, but even if you're not a zoo person, you should grab the opportunity to see the Florida panthers – North America's rarest animal.

The zoo has plenty of shade, and it's very well signed and user-friendly (though the cages are a bit on the small side). You can do the whole place in about an hour. Among the highlights are the American and bald eagles, rabbits, llamas and sheep, as well as the fire ants, waterfowl, reptiles and plants. There's a small lake, but skip the boat ride. We saw only two butterflies in the butterfly garden.

The zoo is open daily 9 am to 5 pm. Admission is $6, $5 for seniors, $4 for children three to 12. Wagons and double strollers are $4; a zoo map is 25¢ (skip it).

The easiest way to get there from central West Palm is to take I-95 south to the Southern Blvd exit, go east to Parker Ave, turn right on Parker and continue to Summit Blvd; turn right on Summit and right again on Dreher – the zoo and science museum will be on the right-hand side.

Lion Country Safari

It's a long drive, but definitely worth the trip. Established in 1967 as one of the country's first 'natural habitat' zoos, Lion Country Safari (☎ 561-793-1084) brings you unusually close to some exotic and dangerous animals – a feat other animal parks, notably Busch Gardens, fail to accomplish. And it's the cheapest theme park of the sort. We had a blast here.

You tour the safari section in your car, dutifully obeying about 400 signs admonishing you to keep the windows closed. No convertibles are allowed, but if that's all you've got, you can rent a van from the park for $6 an hour. No pedestrians or pets are permitted (see *Jurassic Park* for more information; kennels are available free). The safari section is broken into five areas, each one designed to roughly resemble the native African habitat of the animals kept in that particular area.

As you enter you'll pass bison and, just past them and staring longingly, a pride of lions. Watch for African elephants, lots of zebras, a rhino or two, some giraffes and chimps, water buffalo, Watusi (long-horned cattle), weirdly horned blackbucks and lots of others. The theme park section is harmless enough but is no comparison to the animals. Bring a picnic and some insect repellent.

The park is open daily 9:30 am to 5:30 pm; the last vehicle is let in at 4:30 pm. Admission is $15.50 for adults, $10.50 for seniors and children three to nine.

To get there take Southern Blvd (US Hwy 98) due west until you run out of gas, or about 17 miles west of I-95. Turn right at the sign (it is clearly visible; you didn't miss it) and drive about another 2 miles. The KOA camping entrance (see Places to Stay below) is right before the park entrance. The trip from West Palm Beach will feel longer than it is – just remember that past Hwy 7 it's another 8 miles to the park turnoff.

Ann Norton Sculpture Garden

Not associated with the Norton Gallery of Art, the Ann Norton Sculpture Garden (☎ 561-832-5328), 253 Barcelona Rd at the western edge of Lake Worth, contains brick sculptures that are…unique, anyway, and set in a lovely garden. It's probably enough to hitch yourself over the brick wall and gaze, as we did. It's open Tuesday to Saturday 10 am to 4 pm.

Places to Stay

Staying in West Palm Beach is not all that much cheaper than staying in Palm Beach, though you have some choice for doubles down in the $30 to $40 range in low season, $40 to $60 range in high season.

Cheap lodging is best found at the southern end of town just north of the Lake Worth line, where several family-run mom & pop motels line S Dixie Hwy. Note though that many motels have changed hands and standards have fallen since our last edition, and that prices get better if you stay in Lake Worth proper (see Lake Worth earlier this chapter).

Camping The ubiquitous *KOA* (☎ 561-793-9797) has a campground at Lion Country Safari (see Lion Country Safari earlier in this section for directions), where tent sites for two people are $22, including electric and water hookups; each additional person is $3. RV sites are $25, including electric, water and sewer hookups. Kamping Kabins are $36 a night.

Motels The fastidiously scrubbed, security-conscious *Apollo Motor Lodge* (☎ 561-833-1222, 4201 S Dixie Hwy) is one block south of Southern Blvd. Here you'll find simple rooms with TV and telephone for $35 single or double ($40 with a small fridge) in summer, or $45 single, $55 double in winter. Weekly rates are negotiable.

Vali Motel (☎ 561-585-2633, 5515 S Dixie Hwy) has adequate, clean and standard singles/doubles (no telephones but basic cable) for $35/38 year round. It's half a block south of Bunker Rd; look for the red-and-white striped chairs and palm trees in front of each room.

Just north, the *Royal Palm Motor Lodge* (☎ 561-582-2501, 7000 S Dixie Hwy) has spotlessly clean rooms, all with fridges and phones. The motel has two sections; the one along S Dixie is cheaper, with doubles starting at $40 a day, or $200 a week, in summer; $45/280 in winter.

The cheerful *Mt Vernon Motor Lodge* (☎ 561-832-0094, 310 Belvedere Rd), east of S Dixie Hwy, has a better location and a pool. Standard rooms go for $35 a day, $175 a week in summer; $49 a day, $195 to $245 a week in winter.

An extra $20 or so could get you into one of the expensive chain hotels near the highways, but if you're willing to part with $50 in low season, $69 to $84 in high season, you may as well give your money to a nice, family-run place like the *Parkview Motor Lodge* (☎ 561-833-4644, 800-523-8978, 4710 S Dixie Hwy). The Parkview offers a 10% discount for AAA and AARP members, and they are a AAA-listed hotel with lots of repeat business – reserve as soon as you can.

Places to Eat

Good news: West Palm Beach has several cheap and even good eateries, and decent mid-range choices abound. As with places to stay, the best deals are found in the southern section of town. A growing number of restaurants are opening up on Clematis St.

Starbucks (☎ 561-733-4342, 226 Clematis St) offers the chain's usual bean scene. *La Taqueria* (☎ 561-655-5450, 419 Clematis St) has killer burritos for $3.50, taco salads for $5, nachos for $3 and tacos for $2, along with some good specials and kitschy decor. *It's in the Bag* (☎ 561-655-4505, 423 Clematis St) makes take-away sandwiches ($5 to $8) and breakfast burritos ($2.25). Lousy service.

Roxy's (☎ 561-833-2402, 309 Clematis St), now in new digs opposite the old ones, is a favorite of Palm Beach and West Palm Beach residents of all income brackets and walks of life. The Roxy burgers ($5.25) are the reason. You can get more expensive fare here – like seafood dinners for $12.95 – but people we spoke with stuck to the basics.

The testosterone levels at *Fred's Ultima Café & Market* (☎ 561-659-9877, 400A Clematis, enter on Dixie Hwy) are astounding, but Fred's makes awesome wraps ($5.25 to $6), veggie burgers ($5.25) and sensational juice. There is also a serious hot sauce collection there. Try the Dave's Insanity. We dare you.

The *Bimini Bay Café* (☎ 561-833-9554, 104 Clematis St) has a nice location at the eastern end of Clematis overlooking the water. But the main reason we'd stop here is for the free buffet at happy hour (Monday to Friday 5 to 7 pm), with two-for-one drink specials at the bar and lasagna and veggie dishes at the steam tables. If you stay (the patio is nice enough), you can get sandwiches and burgers for $5.95 to $8.95, soups $3.50 to $5.

Nicky's Donuts (☎ 561-582-4565, 7116 S Dixie Hwy), in a 1950s-era building, is very cheap for breakfast (99¢ for one egg, one slice of bacon and toast; $3.99 for two eggs, bacon, grits or home fries and toast) and makes incredible apple strudel (99¢), as well as donuts and coffee all day.

Some of the best Thai food outside Thailand is at *Oriental Food Market & Takeout* (☎ 561-588-4626, 561-588-4699, 4919 S Dixie Hwy) in Raintree Plaza, a tiny shopping mall. Here humongous, steaming-hot portions of *pad Thai* with mixed vegetables cost $5.25; excellent garlicky vegetable soup is $2; and sumptuous red curry Panang (veggies, bell peppers and peanuts in a coconut-curry sauce) is $5.75. Skip the spring rolls, though – they were disappointing and served with maple syrup. Specify degree of spiciness when ordering, and though you can eat here, it's really a takeout place. The only drawback is the Styrofoam plates. It's also a first-rate Asian food and spice market. Hours are Monday to Saturday 11 am to 8:30 pm (last order 8 pm).

Up the road a bit, *Havana* (☎ 561-547-9799, 6801 S Dixie Hwy) is a basic, decently priced Cuban place with a 24-hour takeout window. A Cuban sandwich is $4.25; other sandwiches are $3.75 to $5.35. Daily lunch specials are $5.45 to $6.99. The restaurant is open Sunday to Thursday 11 am to 11 pm, Friday and Saturday 11 am to 1 am. *El Galeon Restaurante* (☎ 561-964-7491, 7100 S Dixie Hwy) specializes in Ecuadorian and Colombian food. It offers $1.99 breakfasts, $4.50 lunch deals and $7.50 dinner specials.

Howley's Restaurant (☎ 561-833-5691, 4700 S Dixie Hwy) does good lunch specials ($3.95 to $6.95 from 11 am to 2 pm) and dinners at around $7, in addition to big burgers ($3 to $5) and sandwiches ($2 to $5). It's open daily 7 am to 10 pm year round and very popular.

A strange entry, and one that is a bit out of the way, is the *391st Bomb Group Headquarters* (☎ 561-683-3919, 3989 Southern Blvd), adjacent to the airport. You walk into what appears to be a WWII US Army Air Force base in France or England – the front yard is filled with Willys Jeeps, sandbags and artillery; you get the idea. Inside, service is very good and it's a nice place for a steak ($16.95 to $21.95). Pasta is too expensive, though, at $14.95 to $18.95. At lunch (weekdays 11:30 am to 3:30 pm) specials run $5.95 to $9.95, and entrees like shrimp and scallops with penne go for $10.95. There's a two-for-one happy hour in the comfortable bar on weekdays from 4 to 7 pm. Headphones in all the booths (not at all the tables though) allow you to listen to PBI Air Traffic Control. Could be fun.

Entertainment

Supremely useful is the Palm Beach County Cultural Council, which operates a 24-hour ArtsLine on cultural events within the entire county. Call them at ☎ 800-882-2787 – you'll get a recording at night but live humans during the day.

Clematis by Night (☎ 561-833-8873) is a free concert series at Centennial Square, at the eastern end of Clematis St. It takes place Thursday nights in winter.

Theater The *Raymond F Kravis Center for the Performing Arts* (☎ 561-833-8300, 701 Okeechobee Blvd) is beautiful and acoustically pleasing, architecturally cunning and blessed with enough bang for the PR buck to attract top-notch shows. It holds three venues: the Alexander Dreyfoos Concert Hall (that's the one with the neato Art Deco-meets-European-opera-house architecture); the black-box Marshall Rinker Playhouse; and the outdoor Gosman Amphitheatre.

You never know what you might see here; the center hosts performances by top-name touring acts and shows, as well as an excellent regional arts series featuring classical symphony orchestras and recitalists. Prices change depending on the performance and performer; classical concert tickets generally range from $15 (balcony) to $65 (orchestra).

The *Cuillo Center for the Arts* (☎ 561-585-3433, 201 Clematis St) hosts regional and national bands and orchestras. The Clematis Street Theatre, within the Cuillo Center, also holds mainstage productions.

For more imformation on legitimate theater in the area, see Palm Beach later this chapter.

Bars & Clubs Clematis St is the best option, with the most famous offering being *Roxy's* (see Places to Eat earlier). The *Bimini Bay Café* has a great happy hour and huge outdoor patio overlooking Lake Worth (see Places to Eat earlier in the West Palm Beach section).

Cool bars here include the swank *My Martini* (☎ 561-832-8333, 225 Clematis St), the cavernous *Big City Tavern* (☎ 561-659-1853, 224 Clematis St) and *Dax Daquiri Bar* (☎ 561-833-0449, 300 Clematis St).

O'Shea's Pub (☎ 561-833-3865, 531 Clematis St) is a great late-night drinking spot with live music Wednesday to Sunday at around 10 pm; there's no cover charge.

Other places that look worth a try include *Ray's Downtown Blues & Soul* (☎ 561-835-1577, 519 Clematis St), a bar and nightclub with live blues and soul Wednesday to

Sunday; *Respectable Street Café* (☎ 561-832-9999, 518 Clematis St), across the street; and the nearby *Speakeasy* (☎ 561-804-9393, 521 Clematis St), which is also the home of Cinema Refuge, a venue for film, theater, art and music.

Spectator Sports

West Palm Beach is the winter home of the *Atlanta Braves* and the *Montreal Expos*, who play at the stadium on Palm Beach Lakes Blvd. The teams rotate use of the field and take on other major-league baseball teams in exhibition season games, generally held during March; call ☎ 561-683-6100 for a schedule.

The *Palm Beach Polo & Country Club* (☎ 561-793-1440), 13240 S Shore Blvd, holds polo matches that are open to the public. The season runs January 7 to April 14, and matches are held on Sunday at 3 pm. The box office is open Monday to Friday (and some Saturdays) 9 am to 5:30 pm. Admission is $8 general, $20 to $26 for box seats. From downtown West Palm Beach, take I-95 north to the Forest Hill Blvd exit and go 12 miles west.

Getting There & Away

The Palm Beach International Airport (PBI; ☎ 561-471-7420) is about 3 miles west of I-95 on either Southern Blvd or Belvedere Rd. PBI is served by major airlines including American, Continental, Delta, Northwest and United.

See the Getting Around section, below, for information on getting from PBI to downtown. Ground transportation is downstairs at level 1.

The Greyhound station (☎ 561-833-9636) is adjacent to the downtown Tri-Rail/Amtrak station (see below). You can take Palm Tran buses (☎ 561-233-4287, option 1 for schedule information) from as far north as Tequesta and as far south as Boca Raton. From Boca Raton, take bus No 1S from Mizner Park to downtown West Palm Beach. From Tequesta city hall, take bus No 22 to Gardens Mall, then transfer to bus No 1C.

SOUTHEAST

Tri-Rail stations in town include the downtown station (which is also the Amtrak station), 201 S Tamarind Ave just north of Okeechobee Blvd; and the airport station, 2600 Mercer Ave near Belvedere Rd.

Getting Around

Monday to Friday the free Planes to Trains shuttle runs every 30 minutes or so between the airport, the Amtrak/Tri Rail/Greyhound station and Clematis St. Additionally, bus No 44 ($1) runs between the airport and downtown every half hour daily. A taxi from PBI to West Palm is about $12, and to Palm Beach it's about $18.

Palm Tran buses serve the entire county. Fare is $1; 20¢ for transfers. Bus No 4C runs through downtown West Palm Beach, over the Royal Park Bridge, past most of the main downtown sights on the island of Palm Beach and back west over the Flagler Bridge.

Parking is a snap, with unmetered parking available almost everywhere. And the city is bicycle friendly; the streets are expensively smooth and easy to ride on. See Palm Beach below for bike rental information.

Taxicab meter rates are $1.25 at flagfall and $1.75 a mile. The biggest companies are Yellow Cab (☎ 561-689-2222) and Checker Cab (☎ 561-820-8121).

PALM BEACH

Few playgrounds of the rich and famous in this country attract as much attention as Palm Beach (population 9500 in summer, 25,000 in winter). Known primarily for its stunning mansions, society events ('Which disease is it tonight, dear?') and exclusivity, this is one of the most elite and strangest enclaves in America. It's populated during the winter 'social season' (which everyone calls simply 'the Season') by a veritable *Who's Who* from a 1986 Jay MacInerney novel: people like Ron Pearlman and Rod 'I won't retire – I *won't*' Stewart, F Lee Bailey, Mary Lou Whitney, Celia Farris, Jimmy Buffett, the Kravises and Du Ponts. All these people, and many many more, have lollipop- and Candyland-colored houses on or near Ocean Blvd, on which you can drive and be dazzled. Cocktail parties are endless – if a

genie ever asks you what you want, say without hesitation, 'A liquor shop in Palm Beach.'

But surprisingly, the exclusivity doesn't quite slam down upon you like a fortress gate, and visits by backpackers will be tolerated in an amused sort of way. Unless you're looking to spend a whole bunch of money, it's best to make it a day trip.

Orientation

The long, narrow island of Palm Beach sits between Lake Worth (the Intracoastal Waterway) to the west, the Atlantic Ocean to the east and north, and the town of Lake Worth to the south – with a tiny piece of South Palm Beach just below Lake Worth. A grid system is in place even here; County Rd is the main north-south artery and runs approximately through the center of the island.

Downtown is concentrated in the area between Royal Palm Way to the south, Royal Poinciana Way to the north, S County Rd to the east and Lake Worth, though it could be argued that downtown really consists of the entire area between Worth Ave to the south and Seminole Ave to the north.

In the downtown area, another important north-south road is Cocoanut Row – not to be confused with the east-west running Cocoanut Walk connecting Cocoanut Row with S County Rd and the southern end of the Breakers hotel property.

While Worth Ave (see below) grabs most of the fame and glamour, don't miss Ocean Blvd (Hwy A1A), on which sit some of the most grandiose and luxurious houses in the USA. Farther north, you won't see much more than a long stone wall at the Kennedy Compound, the family estate of the Kennedy clan; this chi-chi address hit its height of notoriety in 1991, when a visiting, lesser Kennedy relative was arrested here, charged with rape and – prepare for a shocker – acquitted.

The best available street map of town also happens to be free; it's the chamber of commerce's *Indexed Street Map of Palm Beach*, available at the chamber (see below). Also see West Palm Beach earlier this chapter for other area maps.

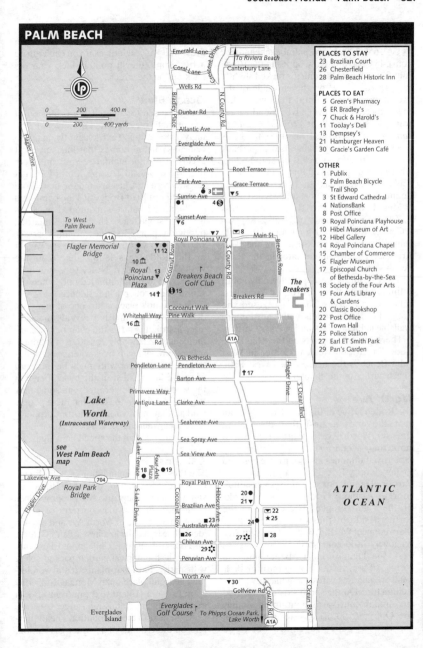

PALM BEACH

0 200 400 m
0 200 400 yards

To Riviera Beach

To West Palm Beach

Flagler Memorial Bridge

Lake Worth
(Intracoastal Waterway)

see West Palm Beach map

Royal Park Bridge

ATLANTIC OCEAN

Everglades Island

Everglades Golf Course → To Phipps Ocean Park, Lake Worth

PLACES TO STAY
23 Brazilian Court
26 Chesterfield
28 Palm Beach Historic Inn

PLACES TO EAT
5 Green's Pharmacy
6 ER Bradley's
7 Chuck & Harold's
11 TooJay's Deli
13 Dempsey's
21 Hamburger Heaven
30 Gracie's Garden Café

OTHER
1 Publix
2 Palm Beach Bicycle Trail Shop
3 St Edward Cathedral
4 NationsBank
8 Post Office
9 Royal Poinciana Playhouse
10 Hibel Museum of Art
12 Hibel Gallery
14 Royal Poinciana Chapel
15 Chamber of Commerce
16 Flagler Museum
17 Episcopal Church of Bethesda-by-the-Sea
18 Society of the Four Arts
19 Four Arts Library & Gardens
20 Classic Bookshop
22 Post Office
24 Town Hall
25 Police Station
27 Earl ET Smith Park
29 Pan's Garden

SOUTHEAST

Information

The Palm Beach Chamber of Commerce (☎ 561-655-3282, www.palmbeachchamber .com), 45 Cocoanut Row, opposite the Royal Poinciana Chapel (squint: it's tucked slightly beneath road level on the east side of the street), was more helpful than we would have expected, and even gives friendly local pointers. The excellent *Official Guide to Palm Beach* is posted on the chamber's Website and also available as a paperback book (it's free if you pick it up at the office, otherwise you pay $3.20 for postage).

NationsBank has an office at 140 N County Rd. The main post office is just north of Main St on S County Rd (you can't miss it). Classic Bookshop (☎ 561-655-2485), 310 S County Rd, is good for fiction. The only public library is at the Society of the Four Arts (see Entertainment later in the Palm Beach section).

Many businesses are quite friendly about letting you use their restrooms. Your best bets are the larger hotels (we used the Breakers). Public toilets with showers are available in Phipps Park and in Pan's Garden.

There are no hospitals on the island; the Good Samaritan Medical Center in West Palm Beach is the nearest (see West Palm Beach earlier in the chapter).

Worth Ave

The Rodeo Drive of the East Coast (we can hear the cries against that description already), Worth Ave is a little (and little) more than a quarter-mile of fantastically expensive boutiques and shops (we counted 15 jewelers before giving up), including Cartier, Daniel Foxx, Gallery Versailles, Giorgio Armani, Gucci, Chanel, Brooks Brothers and Frances Brewster. On the northern side of the western end, three alleys connect Worth Ave with Peruvian Ave via lovely little courtyards – from east to west, Via Demario, Via Mizner and Via Parigi. All are worth ducking into for their small art galleries, cafés and generally lovely architecture. On the south side of the street are similar courtyards containing similar fare. One crafty local suggested that you can pop into art gallery openings when you

stumble across them for free white wine, champagne or, more rarely, cocktails. But dress well – if you look as if you can't afford a free drink, they'll politely kick your ass back out on the street.

Ocean Blvd

One must see for oneself the profusion of staggeringly spectacular – nay, overwhelmingly ostentatious (extravagantly magnificent?) – palatial homes that line this most exclusive of thoroughfares. You can't help but notice Donald Trump's Mar-a-Largo at the southern end, just around the bend from the Southern Blvd Bridge; it's the coral- and sand-colored palace surrounded by a 15-foot-high stone fence. The manse is guarded by vividly painted statues of court jesters, who appear overburdened under the weight of the golden gas lamps that light the wrought-iron entry. Note, too, the light tower, said to be illuminated only when the squishy high-roller is in residence.

But Trump's place is just one of many – a drive along Ocean Blvd reveals mansion after mansion. And as the chamber of commerce understandably considers it inappropriate to reveal who lives where, you're left to gaze and wonder who might be the Lord of each Manor. Most of the beach beneath the seawall has been eroded, and some may take satisfaction in the fact that these people paid all that money for beachfront property in an area where no beach now exists.

Oh, and obey all the speed limit signs.

Gardens

The Preservation Foundation of Palm Beach (☎ 561-832-0731), 386 S County Rd, a privately funded group, runs two public gardens in downtown to act as barriers of green between the bustle of Worth Ave and the residential districts. The loveliest is **Pan's Garden**, on Hibiscus between Chilean and Peruvian Aves, a lush botanical garden packed solely with native Floridian plants. It's a wonderfully peaceful place open Monday to Friday 9 am to 5 pm (10 am to 2 pm from May to mid-November). Admission is free.

Right next to the Foundation's headquarters, on the grounds of a former gas station, is **Earl ET Smith Park**, at the corner of S County Rd and Chilean Ave. It's less green, but its centerpiece is a charming burbling fountain.

Behind the library at the Society of the Four Arts (see Entertainment later in the Palm Beach section) is the Philip Hulitar Sculpture Garden, in the Four Arts Gardens, open year round and maintained by the Garden Club of Palm Beach.

Phipps Ocean Park

One of the two public beaches on the island (the other is Midtown Beach, or the Palm Beach Municipal Beach), Phipps Ocean Park is almost halfway between Sloan's Curve (south of Southern Blvd) and the Lake Worth Bridge, just opposite the southern fire station and Ibis Way. It's about a quarter-mile of sand, and it's well patrolled by beach rescue. Metered parking is 25¢ for 15 minutes. Public showers and toilets are at the northern and southern ends of the park.

Both Phipps Ocean Park and Midtown Beach have bike paths, which are also found elsewhere on the island. Palm Beach Bicycle Trail Shop (☎ 561-659-4583), 223 Sunrise Ave, rents bikes for $7 an hour, $18 for an eight-hour day (9 am to 5 pm) and $24 for 24 hours.

Flagler Museum

In 1901, Henry Morrison Flagler, the industrialist who is almost single-handedly responsible for the creation of South Florida for the rich, gave Whitehall mansion to his bride, Mary Lily Kenan. Designed to be every bit as ostentatious as any mansion in Newport, Rhode Island, it succeeded – and how.

The house, which cost $2.5 million to build and $1.5 million to furnish (and that's in 1901 dollars) was in danger of being razed before Flagler's granddaughter, Jean Flagler Matthews, took the place over in 1959 and began raising money for its restoration.

Today it's open as a museum (☎ 561-655-2833), at Cocoanut Row and Whitehall Way (just south of Royal Poinciana Plaza), and its very pink ballroom is host to several balls, celebrations and school proms throughout the year.

Still, there's not much reason to pay the admission fee. The knowledgeable staff is appropriately reverent as they guide frequent tours throughout the palace, though the stories they tell simply reinforce a notion of a family of greedheads. Outside, you can look at Flagler's private railway car, the FEC Railway *Rambler*. The museum's open Tuesday to Saturday 10 am to 5 pm, Sunday noon to 5 pm, closed Monday. Admission is $7 for adults, $3 for children six to 12.

Hibel Museum of Art

This museum (☎ 561-833-6870), 150 Royal Poinciana Plaza, is entirely dedicated to the art of Edna Hibel (pronounced 'HIBB-ull'), who works in many media including rice paper, silk, shells, plaster, butcher paper and wood. Edna herself (in her 80s) stops in once a year to sign her works.

Follow her time in Mexico, beginning with *Mexican Beggar*. The model for this painting appears in many of her Mexican works, and he ends up a rich man in the last picture of the series. Also of note are her Breton series; her portraits of family, especially including her Russian *Grandmother* on aluminum; and paintings of her children at various stages of their lives.

The museum is open Tuesday to Saturday 10 am to 5 pm, Sunday 1 to 5 pm, closed Monday. Admission is free. Also on the plaza, in separate quarters, is the Hibel Gallery.

Episcopal Church of Bethesda-by-the-Sea

This historic landmark Gothic-style cathedral, 141 S County Rd, was built in 1926 to replace the city's original church (1889). It features somewhat impressive stained glass and the small but lovely Cluett Memorial Gardens out back. *Music at Bethesda*, a series of choral works (☎ 561-655-4554), usually runs the first Sunday of the month with additional performances throughout the year. Services are Sunday at 8, 9 and 11 am.

St Edward Cathedral

This Catholic church holds very crowded Sunday Mass at 7, 9 and 10:30 am and at noon; the rest of the week, services are held at 7:30 and 8:30 am daily.

The Breakers

The Breakers (☎ 561-655-6611), 1 S County Rd, is an extremely elegant hotel. It began as an 1896 beachfront addition to Henry Flagler's Royal Poinciana Hotel, which was so large that bellhops sometimes delivered messages by bicycle. The new addition, originally called the Palm Beach Inn, was intended to be a smaller, quieter version of the Royal Poinciana, with the same elegance. Guests liked it and began to request rooms 'over by the breakers,' which led to the hotel's rechristening.

In June 1903, the hotel burned down, but it reopened nine months later. What building material do you suppose they used right after a disastrous fire? In 1925, the newly built wood place burned again. The hotel was rebuilt yet again in 1926 – this Italian-Renaissance version of the Breakers is what stands today.

The hotel is modeled after the Villa Medici in Rome and features a 200-foot-long lobby with high arched ceilings. It is so vast Corinna almost couldn't find the toilets. The hotel offers golf, tennis, a fitness center, great children's programs, jogging trails and every other conceivable comfort (see Places to Stay later in the Palm Beach section for prices).

A free, one-hour guided tour runs through the public areas of the hotel on Wednesday at 3 pm, leaving from the south Logue. The best part of the tour is the banter from Mr Ponce, the hotel's long-standing historian. You'll hear local and hotel history and stories about the various rooms you'll pass – like the private dining rooms, where drinking and smoking parties took place during Prohibition and social status dictated the seating arrangements. Contact the hotel for more tour information.

Royal Poinciana Chapel

This charming wooden chapel opposite the chamber of commerce on Cocoanut Row, just south of Royal Poinciana Plaza, dates from 1895 and features vaulted ceilings and large, bright windows. Interdenominational services are held Sunday at 10:30 am.

Organized Tours

Seaside Activity Station (☎ 561-835-8922), 400A N Flagler Drive in West Palm Beach, offers two-hour water tours in the Intracoastal Waterway for $15 for adults, $8 for children. The guides point out large houses and relate Palm Beach historical tidbits. Tours run at noon on Monday and Wednesday to Saturday, and at 2 pm on Monday, Wednesday and Thursday in season. The company also offers two-hour bicycle tours on the island for $20/14 including rental; tours depart at noon on Wednesday, Friday and Saturday.

Places to Stay

Palm Beach ain't cheap. Unless you're completely committed to making the scene during 'the Season,' we'd suggest heading to one of the more inexpensive motels in nearby West Palm Beach or, even cheaper, Lake Worth.

Hotels The *Brazilian Court* (☎ 561-655-7740, 800-552-0335 fax 561-655-0801, 301 Australian Ave) is bright and cheerful and has friendly staff. Amenities include two large courtyards and rooms with enormous closets and lots of extras. Two of the hotel's more wonderfully quirky claims to fame are: a) Claude Millein, the executive chef, who worked in Teheran Palace and produced the very six-tiered birthday cake over which Marilyn Monroe serenaded President John F Kennedy; and b) the ultimate in decadence, a four item *pet* menu if you don't mind, with entrees from bowser burgers at $5.95 to chancellor chow (filet mignon) for $12.95, served with milk bone or tabby treat. Rooms range $95 to $150 in low season and $195 to $315 in high season. Suites go for $250 to $400 in low season and $525 to $850 in high season.

The Chesterfield (☎ 561-659-5800, 800-243-7871, fax 561-659-6707, 363 Cocoanut Row) does its best to achieve that chummy, old-boy, 'Tally-HO! chaps, Back to Blighty, what?' look, with a wood-paneled card/game room and traditional English tea served (by a traditional Nicaraguan) in the afternoons. Rooms are immaculate and luxurious indeed, with tons of amenities. Service is excellent, and staff is very friendly. In low season, room rates range $89 to $179, suites $239 to $399 and the penthouse is $499; in high season it's $229 to $399 for rooms, $569 to $899 for suites and $1099 for the penthouse.

Rooms at **The Breakers** (☎ 561-655-6611, 1 S County Rd) carry a grand price tag to match the opulence of the place. Rates vary widely, depending on the season and view. Traditional guestrooms are $180 to $360, deluxe rooms are $275 to $460 and ocean-front rooms are $350 to $570. Oceanfront suites run $650 to $930, but hey, live a little: imperial suites are just $1400 to $2300.

B&Bs The **Palm Beach Historic Inn** (☎ 561-832-4009, fax 561-832-6255, 365 S County Rd) is a charming, antique-filled Victorian with spotless rooms, fluffy carpets, lots of flowers and lace – it's very romantic, though a friend was disappointed with service last year. Breakfast (between continental and full) is served to you in your room anytime between 8 and 9:30 am. Room rates are low enough – if you're already in this bracket – to be considered reasonable. In low season, rooms range $75 to $95 and suites range $100 to $225; in high season it's $150 to $170 for the rooms, and $175 to $225 for the suites. Reserve early, as it's a popular place.

Places to Eat

There's a Publix Market on Bradley Place between Sunrise and Sunset Aves.

Gracie's Garden Café (☎ 561-820-8839, 240 Worth Ave), in the courtyard, is a really friendly little place with shakes (14 carrots for $3.95 and iced fruit cooler for $2.75), salads for $5 to $7, soup-and-half-sandwich combos for $5.75 and little pizzas for $6.

Green's Pharmacy (☎ 561-832-0304, 151 N County Rd) is a pretty classic pharmacy and lunch counter, with rough service. Breakfast, everything under $4, runs until

11:30 am. Burgers are $4.50 to $5.95, sandwiches $4.25 to $5.95.

Hamburger Heaven (☎ 561-655-5277, 314 S County Rd) is a standby with good and cheap fare, including great and cheap breakfasts, daily lunch specials for $5 and dinner specials for $11.95 (with soup and two side dishes). Dependably good burgers are $5, cheeseburgers are $5.95.

TooJay's Original Gourmet Deli (☎ 561-659-7232, 313 Royal Poinciana Plaza) is an overblown deli with good sandwiches from $5.99 to $8.99, grilled chicken dishes from $6.79, and good pastries and *rugelach* (a sticky, sweet pastry).

Dempsey's (☎ 561-835-0400, 50 Cocoanut Row) is a New York-Irish-pub kind of place, packed with booze hounds in the afternoon and younger crowds at night. Lunch specials are $6 to $8, sandwiches $5 to $7. At dinner, burgers are $9, veal or chicken dishes $13 to $18 and nightly specials $16 to $20. The Sunday brunch (make reservations) offers eggs, bacon, toast and coffee for $7.25 and omelets for $6.95.

Slick **Chuck & Harold's** (☎ 561-659-1440, 207 Royal Poinciana Way) does lunch with lighter food – tropical fruit salad, smoked chicken quesadilla and pastas are all under $14. Nightly dinner specials run $17 to $19, regular entrees including pasta are $15 to $26 and New York strip steak is $25.

Another Irish pub, **ER Bradley's** (☎ 561-833-3520, 111 Bradley Place) is not too shabby and not too expensive. It's famous for its hangover brunches – favorites like steak and eggs, corned beef hash and eggs and the Bradley's Benedict, all under $10. Dinners feature entrees like New York strip steak or jumbo baked shrimp for $16.95.

Amici Bar & Ristorante (☎ 561-832-0201, 288 S County Rd) specializes in good homemade pasta and Italian food. Appetizers run $5 to $12, and the pasta dishes might include tortellini stuffed with homemade cheese in a roasted pepper sauce ($16.50), or fettuccine with chicken, string beans, snow peas, leeks and sundried tomatoes ($17.50). Pizzas run $12 to $16, and meat and fish main courses range $19.50 to $28.

The Florentine Dining Room (☎ 561-655-6611, at The Breakers) isn't as expensive as you'd expect, but it's still right up there; count on $45 a person without wine.

Entertainment

Of course, the leagues of *National Enquirer* readers are here for just one thing: Au Bar, which, we're sorry to say, is gone. The best place to head, other than the legions of cocktail parties around town, is Dempsey's, or across the bridge.

The *Royal Poinciana Playhouse* (☎ 561-659-3310, 70A Royal Poinciana Plaza) is a legitimate stop-off for Broadway shows and productions despite its relatively small size (about 900 seats); most recently it housed *STOMP*, in its third season here.

Admission to all performances is $46.50 – except for opening nights and Friday and Saturday evenings, which are $49.

The *Society of the Four Arts* (☎ 561-655-2776, 2 Four Arts Plaza), at the western end of Royal Palm Way (just east of the Royal Park Bridge), throws its arms open to the public with concerts, films, lectures, recitals and documentaries through the high season and some of the summer. The complex includes a sculpture garden, library, garden and auditorium. The society's rotating art exhibitions are free, though a $3 donation is requested.

The film series is every Friday during the season at 3 and 8 pm; admission is $3 to $5. On Sunday free screenings are offered, usually of documentaries or historical films tied to current art exhibitions. Also offered in season: monthly concerts, usually on a Sunday at 3 pm and usually about $10; and lectures, usually Tuesday at 3 pm ($15), with speakers the caliber of John Updike, Dan Rather and Sir David Frost. The library is open for research year round.

Getting There & Away

No direct planes, trains or long-distance buses serve Palm Beach. If you're not driving, get to West Palm Beach and take Palm Tran bus No 4C. If you are driving, from the city of Lake Worth take the Lake Worth Bridge to Hwy A1A and turn north.

Getting Around

Palm Tran bus No 4C runs from Drexel Plaza shopping center at the west, down Okeechobee Blvd through downtown West Palm Beach, over the Royal Park Bridge, through most of the main downtown sights on the island of Palm Beach and back west over the Flagler Bridge.

Free one-hour parking is available along Worth Ave (it goes fast in high season, so be prepared to drive around the block a few times) and in lots to the north.

John D MacArthur State Park to Fort Pierce

By the time many travelers get to this neck of the woods, they've probably driven along I-95 and seen nothing but highway, development, cities and signs for golf condos. But the area between North Palm Beach and Stuart offers the greatest opportunities along the southeast coast to get out into Florida nature. North of the urban and suburban sprawl of the southern cities, the areas here along the barrier islands and the Intracoastal Waterway are largely undeveloped and protected.

The attractions of the nearby cities simply don't stand up to moonlight kayak paddles through St Lucie Inlet State Park, turtle watching at Hobe Sound National Wildlife Refuge or camping at Jonathan Dickinson State Park. John D MacArthur State Park has an excellent nature center, with ranger-led snorkeling trips. If the windswept sand dunes of these beaches aren't quite as dazzling as the beaches of the southwest coast, the peace and quiet here more than make up for it. And even if you're just driving through, stopping for a few hours will be a memorable rest.

For tourist information, contact the parks listed later in this section, the Stuart Chamber of Commerce (see Stuart, also later in the section) or the helpful people at Jupiter Outdoor Center.

The **Jupiter Outdoor Center** (☎ 561-747-9666), 18092 Coastal Hwy A1A in Jupiter, north of Palm Beach, is run by friendly and helpful people who will show you exactly what the area has to offer. Their territory is basically north of Palm Beach up to the St Lucie Inlet and west to Lake Okeechobee. The company offers kayak rentals and a wide range of guided tours and programs, such as a four-hour tour of St Lucie Inlet for $35. Those who would prefer to go off on their own can rent an entry-level, one-person, advanced single kayak for $15 for the first hour, $10 the second hour or $30 for four hours; canoes and two-person kayaks rent for $20/15/45.

GETTING THERE & AWAY
For much of the way north of Palm Beach to the town of Stuart, US Hwy 1 and Hwy A1A are the same road. But just north of Jonathan Dickinson State Park, Hwy A1A splits off and becomes Dixie Hwy, while US Hwy 1 becomes Federal Hwy. The two highways meet again in downtown Stuart.

Greyhound provides service only to Stuart; otherwise public transportation into this region is extremely inconvenient.

JOHN D MACARTHUR STATE PARK
While this state park (☎ 561-624-6950) is one of the smallest in the region, it runs excellent ranger-led interpretive walks and has one of the best turtle-watching programs around. Loggerhead, green and leatherback turtles nest along the beach here from May to August. The beach is reached by a 1600-foot boardwalk that runs from the nature center across Lake Worth Cove to the beach, where there are dune crossovers leading out to the shore.

You can't camp or go canoeing here (there are no boat launches), but if you've got a light kayak, you can bring it and paddle through Lake Worth Cove. No concessions operate in the park.

Interpretive Programs
The interpretive and nature center (☎ 561-624-6952), just south of the main parking lot, holds several aquariums and exhibits on baby sea turtles, snakes and other animals you may run into within the park. The center also screens a 15-minute video on the park's wildlife.

There are ranger-led trips to observe nesting turtles run on Monday and Thursday evenings during June and July – but you'll need to reserve a place; contact the nature center at least a month in advance – groups are limited. Also in summer, rangers lead snorkeling trips on the second and third Saturday of the month for advanced snorkelers with their own equipment. You'll see a 15-minute slide show of the area's sea life, then head off to explore the reef alongside the beach. And on weekends at 10 am, guided nature walks investigate all the park habitats, with rangers pointing out the various flora and fauna.

The nature center is open 8 am to sunset every day except Tuesday. The park is open every day (365 days) 8 am to sunset. Admission is $3.25 per carload, $1 for pedestrians and bicyclists.

Getting There & Away
The park is at the northern end of Singer Island. From the north, take PGA Blvd straight east to Hwy A1A; from the south, take Blue Heron Blvd to Hwy A1A. The entrance is just past the Blue Heron Bridge.

JONATHAN DICKINSON STATE PARK
Made up of almost 11,500 acres, this excellent state park (☎ 561-546-2771), between US Hwy 1 and the Loxahatchee River (just north of Tequesta), is a great stop – either for a day, overnight or longer. Hikers will love the East Loop and Kitching Creek hiking trails, and there's great canoeing along the river. Primitive and developed campsites and cabins offer a variety of overnight options, and for day-trippers looking for a lazy afternoon, a river cruise down to the Trapper Nelson Interpretive Site to see the former home of the Wild Man of Loxahatchee is nice.

There's no ocean access within the park, which from 1942 to 1944 was Camp Murphy, a US army radar-instruction facility. The park's attraction lies in its several habitats:

SOUTHEAST

pine flatwood, cypress stands, swamp and the 20% of it that is made up of 'globally imperiled' coastal sand pine scrub.

The park, open daily 8 am to sunset, is named for Jonathan Dickinson, a Quaker merchant who shipwrecked at Hobe Sound in 1696 on a journey from Jamaica to Philadelphia and was captured by Jobes Indians (see Books in the Facts for the Visitor chapter for information on *Jonathan Dickinson's Journal*). Admission is $3.25 per carload, $1 for pedestrians and bicyclists.

Observation Tower

You can drive out to the Hobe Mountain Observation Tower (Hobe 'Mountain' is a little hill) for an overview of the park. At the first stop sign after the park entrance, turn right and go about half a mile, turn right again and go about a quarter-mile. Look for the billboard telling you what's what. The tower is about 40 feet high, but 86 feet above sea level. There's no wheelchair access to the tower.

Canoeing & Kayaking

You can rent canoes from the concession stand (☎ 561-746-1466) at the boat launch on the Loxahatchee River; the cost is $6 per hour, $10 for two hours, $15 for four hours and $22 for eight hours. The concession is open daily 9 am to 5 pm.

Southern Exposure Sea Kayaks (☎ 561-575-4530) rents kayaks and offers tours of the area as well; call for prices.

Hiking & Biking

The park holds several short-loop hiking and bicycle trails, the most popular of which is the Kitching Creek Nature Trail (not to be confused with the Kitching Creek Hiking Trail, see below), just north of the boat landing; it can be walked in about 1½ hours. A two-mile bicycle trail begins very close to the park entrance and leads to the main park road.

Advanced hikers and backpackers will appreciate an excellent network of hiking trails (maintained by the Florida Trail Association) that lead to two primitive campsites.

From the ranger station, pick up the East Loop of the white-blazed Florida Trail, which leads to the Scrub Jay campsite, 5.6 miles from the ranger station. From about there, you can pick up the Kitching Creek Hiking Trail, which continues west-south-west toward the Kitching Creek campsite, 9.3 miles from the ranger station. The Kitching Creek campsite is about half a mile south of the Kitching Creek Return Trail, which heads back to the East Loop. See Camping below for more information.

The trail snakes its way in several directions, but it's well marked and blazed, and it offers no major physical challenges. Mosquitoes are rife and you can expect flooding and mud in summer. Get maps and instructions from the ranger station.

Interpretive Programs

The main interpretive program is the river cruise, but ranger-led nature walks take place every Sunday morning at 9 am and campfire programs are offered every Saturday night at 7 or 8 pm, depending on daylight saving time.

Organized Tours

The *Loxahatchee Queen II* offers a cruise downriver to the Trapper Nelson Interpretive Site. Nelson, the son of Polish immigrants, lived in this area for 38 years beginning in the 1930s. He created a zoo and nature sanctuary here; the zoo buildings are still standing, while the animals are long gone. The narrated tour gives you a good idea of the history. Boats leave four times a day on the two-hour cruise (45 minutes down the river, half an hour at the site and then back); the cost is $10 for adults and $5 for children.

Places to Stay

The park has three developed campgrounds (including one for youth groups only) with hot showers, two primitive campsites and, for the tentaphobic, cabins.

The Scrub Jay backpack campsite is at about the halfway point of the East Loop, and the Kitching Creek backpack campsite is at about the halfway point on the Kitching Creek Hiking Trail. Both are totally primitive but have water pumps. This water – which you should not depend on even working – must be chemically treated or, preferably, boiled. Bring along water, and make sure to seal the bottle and bring it inside your tent at night to protect it from raccoons. The cost for the primitive sites is $3 for adults and $2 for anyone under 18.

Tent or RV/van sites are $17 without electricity, $19 with electricity in December to April, $14/16 at other times; rates include up to four people (second vehicle is $3). There are no sewer hookups, but a dump station is available. The sites have grills, and you can make campfires if you bring your own wood (no gathering in the park, though you can buy wood from the concession for $5.50 a bundle).

The fully equipped cabins cost $65 to $85 per night (a two-night minimum stay is required on weekends).

HOBE SOUND NATIONAL WILDLIFE REFUGE

This refuge (☎ 561-546-6141) is a 968-acre federally protected nature sanctuary with two sections: a small slice on the mainland between Hobe Sound and US Hwy 1, opposite the Jonathan Dickinson State Park, and the main refuge grounds at the north end of Jupiter Island, accessed at the northern end of N Beach Rd.

The Jupiter Island section has 3 1/2 miles of beach (it's a favorite sea turtle nesting ground), mangroves and sand dunes, and the mainland section is a pine scrub forest. In June and July, turtle-watching walks take place on Tuesday and Thursday evenings (reservations are necessary), and birding trips can also be arranged through the Hobe Sound Nature Center.

The refuge is open to the public 8 am to sundown every day, and it can get crowded in winter. Admission is free, but donations are greatly appreciated. Vehicles (and this includes bicycles) are only allowed on the paved section of N Beach Rd, which extends as far into the park as the beach parking lot

(there's wheelchair access to the Jupiter Island beach from here).

Jupiter Island

The beach here is windswept dunes and is excellent for walking and swimming. There are no toilets or showers. Among the flora you may encounter are hand fern, milkweed and golden polypody, and fauna might include tortoises, snakes and bobcats as well as brown pelicans, ospreys, scrub jays and other songbirds. The campground on the island is for the exclusive use of Boy Scouts.

Blowing Rocks Preserve

This preserve encompasses a mile-long limestone outcropping riddled with holes, cracks and fissures; in heavy seas, water spews from the rock as if from a geyser. But while it's famous for its spewing water, it's also an area of four distinct plant communities: shifting dune, coastal strand, interior mangrove wetlands and tropical coastal hammock. The preserve is about 4 miles south of the Hwy 707 bridge on Jupiter Island.

Hobe Sound Nature Center

The nature center (same hours as the park), on the mainland strip just north of the entrance to Jonathan Dickinson State Park on the east side of US Hwy 1, has classrooms and a small area where incredibly friendly and knowledgeable rangers and volunteers will give you an up-close look at baby alligators, snakes and Terra – their Chilean rose-hair tarantula.

They'll also explain how the sand pine scrub forest is a fire-tolerant plant community: rangers manage the plant life through controlled burning of the forest, the heat causing the sand pine cones to release their seeds.

Getting There & Away

For the nature center, take US Hwy 1 to just north of Jonathan Dickinson State Park – the driveway is on the right. To reach the Jupiter Island section, continue north on US Hwy 1 until it forks, then bear right on

Hwy A1A. Take that to Hwy 707/708 east, across the bridge to Jupiter Island, and turn left (north) on N Beach Rd.

ST LUCIE INLET STATE PARK

Accessible only by boat, the main part of St Lucie Inlet State Park (☎ 561-744-7603) protects 6 sq miles of submerged limestone rock reef in the Atlantic Ocean just off Jupiter Island. Twelve species of hard and soft coral inhabit the reef, so you're urged to anchor only on sandy bottom. Snorkeling and scuba diving are permitted; Hobe Sound Nature Center (see above) sometimes offers snorkeling excursions.

The park borders also take in the northern tip of Jupiter Island, north of the Hobe Sound National Wildlife Refuge. Here you'll find excellent beaches, toilets and running water, piers, canoe trails and hiking trails. From the mainland at the eastern end of Cove Rd, a boardwalk runs from the dock opposite County Park to the beach.

STUART

• population 12,000

The old town of Stuart may not be the most exciting place in the world, but it's a very pleasant Florida pioneer town. It was established around 1880 by would-be pineapple growers. The pineapples never made anyone rich, but the crowds kept coming for the fishing along the St Lucie. And mariners who washed ashore here had a grand old time at Gilbert's Bar House of Refuge, a safe haven for shipwrecked sailors.

Orientation

Downtown Stuart is on a delta of the St Lucie River, where the river branches off to either the Atlantic or to Lake Okeechobee via the St Lucie Canal. The downtown area is bounded on the west by Dixie Hwy (Hwy A1A), which slashes through the city from southeast to northwest. The town's two main drags, Flagler Ave and Osceola St, are parallel to Dixie Hwy. E Ocean Blvd runs along the south of downtown, and Colorado Ave runs along the east. Colorado Ave becomes Kanner Hwy when it crosses US Hwy 1 south of downtown. By the way, in downtown, no matter what you do, you will get confused at the convergence of Colorado Ave, Flagler Ave, Dixie Hwy and E and W Ocean Blvd. Nothing you can do about it. Locals call it Confusion Corner; we called it 'driving around the block 10 times.'

E Ocean Blvd connects downtown to Stuart Beach, on Hutchinson Island, a barrier island east of the Intracoastal Waterway. Sewall's Point is a spit of land between Stuart and Hutchinson Island, separating the St Lucie River from the Intracoastal.

The chamber of commerce hands out their *Historic Walking Tour* pamphlet, which has a good street plan.

Information

The chamber of commerce (☎ 561-387-1088, www.goodnature.org) is at 1650 S Kanner Hwy, about three quarters of a mile south of downtown; take Colorado Ave south and it's on the right-hand side of the road after you pass US Hwy 1.

Change money at the NationsBank at either 900 S Federal Hwy or 3727 E Ocean Blvd on Sewall's Point. Island Hobby, 2401 SE Ocean Blvd, has out-of-town newspapers, including the *New York Times*, the *Times* of London, the *Daily Telegraph* and the *Village Voice* and *Miami Herald*.

Hutchinson Island

Stuart's **beaches** are excellent for walking, swimming and even some snorkeling.

We really liked the **Elliott Museum** (☎ 561-225-1961), 825 NE Ocean Blvd on Hutchinson Island. It is dedicated to inventor Harmon Elliott but contains an eclectic collection of exhibits. You'll see a fabulous miniature circus and re-creations of turn-of-the-century shops, such as an apothecary, barber shop and ice cream parlor. As you move through you'll also pass a Victorian parlor, a 1925 dining room and a typical 18th-century girl's bedroom, while another display shows off a hundred of Elliott's 118 patent certificates. There seems to be no rhyme or reason for the selection of the displays, but they're fun all the same. The museum is open daily 11 am to 5 pm; admission is $6 for adults, $2 for children six to 13.

Directly across the street, the Florida Oceanographic Society's **Coastal Science Center** (☎ 561-225-0505, www.fosusa.org), 890 NE Ocean Blvd, is absolutely great for kids, who spend more time in this tiny place than you'd think possible. Inside are four 300-gallon aquariums filled with tropical fish, an exhibit of a worm reef, and touch tanks with crabs, sea cucumber, starfish and other small yicky stuff. The Frances Langford fish collection is an entire wall of mounted fish. Oceans Below, an interactive computer game, simulates a scuba dive in any ocean in the world.

The center is open Monday to Saturday 10 am to 5 pm; admission is $3.50 for adults, $2 for children six to 12. The incredibly enthusiastic staff run guided nature walks on Wednesday and Saturday at 10 am. A boardwalk for self-guided tours was under construction when we visited.

South along the beach is **Gilbert's Bar House of Refuge** (☎ 561-225-1875), 301 SE MacArthur Blvd, which occupies the oldest house in Martin County (built in 1875). In more adventurous days it was one of 10 houses that the US Life-Saving Service established as safe havens for shipwrecked sailors, who would find food and shelter here if they washed ashore. Inside are exhibits of model ships and two aquariums, while the boathouse out back holds maritime exhibits and samples of turn-of-the-century lifesaving gear. Brr. Admission is $4 for adults, $2 for kids six to 13.

North of here in Jensen Beach is an interesting tourist attraction you'll just be bursting to get the kids to. **Energy Encounter** at the St Lucie Nuclear Plant (☎ 561-468-4111), on Hutchinson Island almost smack between Fort Pierce and Stuart (enter through gate B), is FPL's shimmering testament to the family values of nuclear power. The 30-plus interactive displays on the history of energy, all adroitly crafted propaganda, give you a snuggly feeling about the American nuclear industry. To be fair, the exhibits are really first rate, and the games are very clever, showing kids how we've come from campfires through wood and coal, electricity and finally, the pinnacle of

man's creativity, nuclear power. You'll note that all the employees are preternaturally cheerful. It's open Sunday to Friday 10 am to 4 pm, closed Saturdays. Admission is free. Isn't that nice?

Downtown Stuart

The main attraction downtown is the nicely renovated **Lyric Theatre** (☎ 561-220-1942), 59 SW Flagler Ave, a Mediterranean-Revival-style theater (1926) that is very active; see Entertainment later in the Stuart section. The **Heritage Museum** (☎ 561-220-4600), in the former George W Parks General Store at 161 Flagler Ave, isn't really worth the effort if you've been out to the Elliott Museum on Hutchinson Island – it's pretty much the same stuff, including turn-of-the-century antiques and way-of-life exhibits. But the building, a 19th-century wood-frame vernacular, is very nice. It's open Tuesday to Saturday 11 am to 3 pm.

There's an egregiously underpublicized art gallery over at the **Courthouse Cultural Center** (☎ 561-288-2542), inside the 1937 WPA-built Martin County Courthouse, 80 E Ocean Blvd. It's open Monday to Friday 9 am to 5 pm; admission is free. The gallery presents rotating exhibitions of works by local and regional artists.

Places to Stay

The Southwind Motel (☎ 561-287-0773, 603 S Federal Hwy) is a clean place with nice management. In summer, rooms are $35, efficiencies are $50; in winter they're $55/65 and cottages are $85. On weekends they have free barbecues.

The *Holiday Inn-Downtown* (☎ 561-287-6200, 1209 S Federal Hwy) has rooms for $89 in summer and $125 in winter. *Howard Johnson Lodge* (☎ 561-287-3171, 950 S Federal Hwy) has rooms for $65 in summer, $90 in winter.

The Homeplace (☎ 561-220-9148, 501 Akron Ave), in the historic district, is a romantic, antique-filled B&B with three bedrooms, all with private bath, at $110. A fourth room, with a private bath across the way, is $85. All include a full hot breakfast that changes daily – coffee, juice, fruit, homemade muffins or biscuits, cereal, an egg dish and a main dish like quiche or casserole. Other amenities include a pool, hot tub and evening wine and snacks.

At the **Harbor Front B&B** (☎ 561-288-7289, 310 Atlanta Ave), a Florida cracker-style home on two acres of land, rates range $85 to $175, including a full hot breakfast with a wide variety of good food.

Places to Eat

We liked **Alice's Family Restaurant** (☎ 561-286-9528, 2781 E Ocean Blvd), in the same shopping plaza as the Golden Peacock (see below). Food and service were good: breakfast is $2.45 to $4.25, steak and eggs are $6.45, sandwiches and burgers $3.25 to $4.95. Dinner specials (served Monday to Saturday 3 to 8 pm) include two side dishes and are $4.25 to $5.50.

Nature's Way Café (☎ 561-220-7306, 25 SW Osceola St) has nice fruit juices ($2.50 to $3.25) and whole wheat pita sandwiches ($3.75 to $5.40). They have another location in Lake Worth. **Osceola St Herbs Juice Bar** (☎ 561-221-1679, 26 SW Osceola St) is totally vegetarian. Salads are $2.50 to $4.95, sandwiches are $2.75 to $4.25, the veggie burger platter is $4 and smoothies are $2 to $4. **Edelweiss Deli** (☎ 561-283-6590, 40 SE Ocean Blvd), next to Groovy Movies A Go Go (see Entertainment below), has good subs and German beer.

Dine in the ambiance of a 1950s kung fu movie set at the **Golden Peacock Chinese Restaurant** (☎ 561-286-1661, 2389 SE Ocean Blvd), which serves excellent cashew chicken for $7.95, beef chow mein for $4.75, great vegetable dishes from $4 to $8.75 and seafood dishes from $7.95 to $11.50. Recommended!

The **Black Marlin** (☎ 561-286-3126, 53 SW Osceola St) is a very friendly neighborhood place, with pasta dishes from $8.95 to $11.95, pizza from $6.95 to $9.95 and sandwiches from $5.95 to $7.95. Appetizers like lobster ravioli with sundried tomatoes run $4.95, and dinner specials like Caribbean chicken are $10.95.

TA Vern's Bar & Grill (☎ 561-221-3333, 10 SW Osceola St, with another entrance at 7 SW Flagler Ave) is a fun neighborhood bar and grill with burgers from $5.95 to $6.95, Philly cheesesteak for $6.50 and a grilled chicken sandwich for $5.95. (Also see Entertainment below.)

Entertainment

The **Lyric Theatre** (☎ 561-220-1942, 59 SW Flagler Ave), a historic landmark theater built in 1926 and recently renovated, puts on a variety of shows, from performance art to classical concerts to rock concerts to opera. It's home to the Discovery Series, with daytime performances for schools and children. Call for information when you're in town.

The **Barn Theater** (☎ 561-287-4884, 2400 SE Ocean Blvd), between the shopping mall and the Chevron station, next to the Lutheran church, does mainly musicals; showtime's at 8 pm (doors open at 7:30 pm). Tickets are $14 to $18.

Groovy Movies A Go Go (☎ 561-221-0400, 28 SE Ocean Blvd), on the south side of Confusion Corner, is a very cool coffee-bar/video-screening place. The specialty here is foreign, independent, 'weird' and hard-to-find videos.

TA Vern's (7 SW Flagler Ave) presents live blues and jazz on Saturday nights and live music on Sunday afternoons right outside. Choose from about 70 different kinds of beer.

Getting There & Away

The Greyhound station (☎ 561-287-7777) is at 6545 SE Kanner Hwy. The closest Amtrak station to Stuart is in West Palm Beach. Avis, Dollar and Hertz have car-rental offices in Stuart; see the Getting Around chapter for more information. Unfortunately, there's no public transportation within or around the Stuart area, so you'll need a car to get around.

BARLEY BARBER SWAMP

This 400-acre freshwater cypress swamp preserve (☎ 800-257-9267) is one of the more admirable propaganda mechanisms and tax dodges of FPL (Florida Power & Lighting). The preserve, just off the southeastern edge of Lake Okeechobee and just north of the St Lucie Canal, offers a fascinating look at the area's wildlife. A 1-mile boardwalk loops through the entire place, which is just oozing with wildlife – specifics are available in the fantastic illustrated free guide to the preserve published by FPL, as well as on the FPL Website (www.fpl.com).

Admission to the preserve is free, and by appointment only. Call the preserve to make arrangements. You can also visit as part of a tour; several commercial operators in Palm Beach and West Palm Beach arrange them, as does the Audubon Society of the Everglades (☎ 561-588-6908), PO Box 16914, West Palm Beach, FL 33416.

Places to Stay
A friend highly recommended the *Seminole Country Inn* (☎ 561-597-3777, 888-394-3777, 15885 SW Warfield Blvd, Indiantown), about 5 miles from the preserve. It's an old-style B&B (they describe it as a nice room at your grandparents' house) with a lot of special programs, like the wild hog barbecue at the ranch. On this late-afternoon tour, you'll go out to their ranch, ride a hay wagon and eat a lunch of barbecued pork, potato salad, corn on the cob and cornbread muffins. After lunch, you'll take an hour-long tour of the ranch, then return to the campfire to roast marshmallows and listen to country music. Cost is $25 per person. The innkeepers also offer free tours of the Barley Barber Swamp preserve. Rooms run $75 to $95, $10 less in off-season. Call for directions.

FORT PIERCE
• population 38,000
A bit north of Hutchinson Island, the town of Fort Pierce is unprepossessing enough, but it contains some interesting museums; it's definitely worth a day trip.

The main downtown drag (such as it is) is Second St, which runs a block west from the Indian River. Here you'll find cafés and restaurants, the landmark Sunrise Theatre (1923), the Manatee Observation Center (see below) and Old City Hall. The town comes alive for the Fort Pierce Friday Fest, a

block party along Second St every Friday during winter months.

The St Lucie County Chamber of Commerce (☎ 561-595-9999), 2200 Virginia Ave, hands out tourist information Monday to Friday 8 am to 5 pm. A new tourist information booth is planned for the parking lot of the Manatee Observation Center – see below.

Manatee Observation Center
In winter you're almost guaranteed to see several manatees at the FPL-operated Manatee Observation Center (☎ 561-466-1600), 480 N Indian River Drive, just north of Moore's Creek. Look for the visitors center in the parking lot; inside are some really nice exhibits on Indian River life and manatees, and outside is an observation deck. Admission is free but a donation of about $1 a person is suggested. The gift shop is really nice, with tons of stuff on manatees and the environment – all the profits go to the center, which is mainly run by volunteers.

UDT-SEAL Museum
This museum (☎ 561-595-5845), 3300 North A1A, is a unique and very cool look at America's most decorated and secret combat troops, members of the US Navy's elite UDT (Underwater Demolition Team, also called frogmen) and SEALs. Pack some nails to eat as you learn of the SEALs' exploits from WWII through Somalia.

The museum is open Monday to Saturday 10 am to 4 pm, Sunday noon to 4 pm, closed Monday in summer. Admission is $4 for adults, $1.50 for kids.

Jim Backus Museum
Right behind the Manatee Observation Center will be a museum on the life and career of radio and television actor Jim Backus, best known as the voice of the original Mr Magoo and as Thurston Howell III on *Gilligan's Island*.

Harbor Branch Oceanographic Museum
One of the most respected ocean research institutes on earth, the Harbor Branch

Oceanographic Institution (☎ 561-465-2400, x428), 5600 US Hwy 1 N, north of the city, runs tours of its facilities and its museum. The museum holds life-size models of some of the institute's submarine research vessels, as well as 450,000 specimens of marine animals and plants from around the world. It's open Monday to Friday 9 am to 5 pm.

The museum's Harbor Branch Cajun Boat Tour cruise (☎ 561-465-2400, x688) is a saltwater ecology tour along the Indian River Lagoon in a motorboat. The tours run Tuesday to Saturday at 10 am, 1 and 3 pm, Saturday and Sunday at 1 and 3 pm only. Tickets are $16 for adults and $10 for kids. Kayak tours of the local waterways are also available here.

Getting There & Away

From Stuart, take I-95 or Hwy A1A north; it's about 25 miles. The Greyhound station (☎ 561-461-3299) is at 7005 Okeechobee Rd. Four buses daily ($6 one way/$12 roundtrip) connect Stuart and Fort Pierce.

Central Florida

From Disney World and the theme park madness of Orlando to the spiritualist outpost at Cassadaga; from canoeing in Ocala National Forest and at De Leon Springs to horseback riding and bicycling in Paynes Prairie State Preserve; from the fern capital of Pierson to the student nightlife in Gainesville, central Florida is a fascinating area. Though its reputation is built on costly, glitzy amusements (it has the densest concentration of theme parks in the world), there's much beyond the immediate Orlando area to tempt you away from the water-slides, movie studios, roller coasters, fairy-tale palaces and costumed characters.

Diving is exceptional in the natural springs that pop up here and there – don't miss Devil's Den, a spectacular underground spring southwest of Gainesville – and you haven't really lived until you have seen the manatees gathering at Blue Spring State Park, an oasis less than half an hour from downtown Orlando. Climbing down into some huge sinkholes and sleeping in a famous bordello are just a few of the cool draws of central Florida.

You'll need a car or a good bicycle to get anywhere off the beaten path, as public transport only works in the major cities and shuttle services are expensive.

Orlando

- **population 176,500**

If you're looking for Walt Disney World and you've opened to this section, think again: it's in its own section, where it belongs, as it's in the entirely separate city of Lake Buena Vista. Orlando is, believe it or not, a city in its own right whose locals would feel just fine, thank you very much, if all those ear-wearing yahoos would just get back in their cars and keep moving (except, of course, when they spend their money here).

HISTORY

At the end of the Second Seminole War, settlers and traders followed soldiers into the area. Originally named Jernigan (after settler Aaron Jernigan), the settlement here grew up around Fort Gatlin and became the Orange County seat in 1856. In 1857, the city was renamed Orlando for Orlando Reeves, a soldier killed by Indians at Lake Eola.

The city boomed several times; a railroad boom (which fueled a population boom), a real-estate boom and a citrus boom all

Highlights

- See Walt Disney World and Universal Studios Florida
- Make your own pancakes at the Old Spanish Sugar Mill
- Watch the manatees gather at Blue Spring State Park
- Take a glass-bottom-boat trip at Silver Springs, where the glass-bottom boat was invented
- Cave dive at Devil's Den
- Have your future (or your cards) read in Cassadaga, a township inhabited by spiritualists
- Spend the night at the Desert Inn Motel and bordello museum

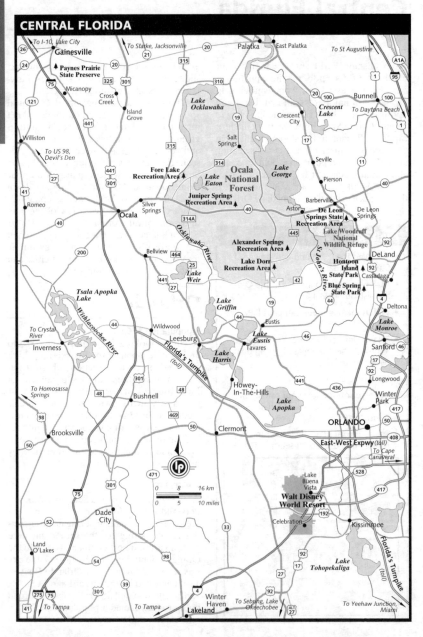

CENTRAL FLORIDA

helped bring prosperity to the area. And the late 1950s brought a boom that was to last: the Space Age. The Glenn L Martin Company (now Martin Marietta Defense Systems) began missile production, and the creation of Cape Canaveral and later Cape Kennedy Space Centers on Florida's east coast (see the Space Coast chapter) brought large infusions of cash and jobs to the area.

With the establishment of Walt Disney World in 1971, the area became theme park central worldwide. More than 35 million people came through here in 1997, making Orlando the fifth-ranking destination of overseas visitors, after San Francisco, Miami, Los Angeles and New York City. To get a better idea of the drawing power of the Mouse and others, consider that Honolulu is ranked sixth and Washington, DC is eighth.

But it's not just the theme parks doing all that attracting: while nobody was looking, Orlando established itself as the high-tech corridor – the Silicon Valley, if you will – of Florida. The specialty here is simulation technology, fueled by demand from NASA and the Kennedy Space Center, as well as by private industry.

ORIENTATION

Downtown Orlando is about 23 miles from Walt Disney World Resort, 20 from Kissimmee, 15 from SeaWorld Orlando and 9 from Universal Studios Florida. The downtown grid consists of an area roughly defined by South St to the south, Robinson St to the north, Garland Ave to the west and Rosalind Ave to the east.

Central Blvd is the north-south dividing line, and Orange Ave is the east-west dividing line. The main drags are Orange Ave and Church St, and downtown's most famous attraction is Church St Station, just between I-4 and the railroad tracks.

Just east of Rosalind Ave is Lake Eola (pronounced 'ee-YO-la'). The Lynx Bus Center (see Getting Around later in the chapter)

Getting Tickets

Discount tickets for most attractions, with the notable exception of Walt Disney World Resort, are available at ticket outlets throughout the city. While many of these are legitimate outlets, many more are decidedly not – they're scams, shams and shysters. The Orlando Police Department is unable to effectively control these outlets because they are so widespread and portable – many are in booths that can be moved if a complaint is ever lodged.

One common ploy is to offer free or deeply discounted tickets in exchange for your time and/or a commitment to buy something. The most common of this sort is run by time-share condominium or other property 'opportunities.' These can be fine if you're willing to give up a significant portion of your time listening to some salesperson extolling the benefits of the good life at Squeezy Acres, but before you do that be totally certain that you'll be under no obligation to buy or to commit to buy *anything* in exchange for the tickets – that all you have to do is listen to the pitch and the tickets are yours. If you don't see it in writing, move on. But even if that's the case, the deal can still blow – we received letters from people who tried and wished they hadn't. Also, if you're going to be driving to a place to listen to a sales pitch, find out if you can be reimbursed for your gas.

The best bet is to buy discounted tickets at the official ticket outlets run by the CVB, whose main outlet is at the Official Tourist Information Center (see the Orlando Information section)

Disney does not sell discounted tickets and will not honor tickets that were not officially purchased. Any discounted Disney tickets you will be offered are either false, dated, stolen or partially used and therefore invalid, worthless junk.

is between W Pine St and W Central Blvd one block west of Orange Ave.

The tourist quarter runs along International Drive, also called I-Drive, near Universal Studios Florida in the southwest part of the city. This area is served by regular Lynx bus service.

Universal Studios Florida theme park is near the intersection of I-4 and Florida's Turnpike; the main entrance is about half a mile north of I-4 on Kirkman Rd (Hwy 435).

SeaWorld Orlando is at the intersection of the Bee Line Expressway and I-4, about 15 miles south of downtown Orlando.

Maps

A good map is essential as the area is so sprawled out, and you'll have to spend some money to get anything with any sort of detail of the entire area. The CVB puts out the free *International Area Guide*, a guide to the whole city, in a variety of languages.

For the most detailed free map of the area contact the Orlando/Orange County Expressway Authority (☎ 407-825-8606) for its useful *Central Florida Express Map*. If you're going to pay, the cheapest, most readily available commercial map is Universal Map's *Greater Orlando, Orange County & Seminole County* for $2.50. Rand McNally and Dolph also publish maps to the area.

INFORMATION
Tourist Offices

Orlando's Official Tourist Information Center (☎ 407-363-5871, 800-551-0181, www .go2orlando.com), 8123 International Drive, Suite 101, Orlando, FL 32819, on the southeast corner of I-Drive and Austrian Row, sells discount attraction tickets and has a bizillion coupon books and handouts, such as the *Official Visitors Guide*, *Official Accommodations Guide* and *Official Attractions Guide*. The staff are all-around good eggs.

Orlando International Airport also has an Official Information Center (☎ 407-825-2352, TDD 407-825-4687), open daily 7 am to 11 pm.

The City of Orlando offers a helpful Website (www.ci.orlando.fl.us) that isn't flashy but is a great source of practical

ORLANDO

1 Charles Hosmer Morse Museum
2 Rollins College
3 Scenic Boat Tour
4 Albin Polasek Gallery
5 Orlando Science Center, Orange County Historical Museum, Museum of Art
6 Harry P Leu Gardens
7 Greyhound Bus Station
8 Gay, Lesbian & Bisexual Community Center
9 Little Saigon
10 Mystery Fun House
11 Belz Factory Outlet Stores
12 Shooting Sports
13 Wet 'n' Wild
14 Official Tourist Information Center
15 Ripley's Believe It or Not!
16 Sand Lake Hospital
17 Movie Rider

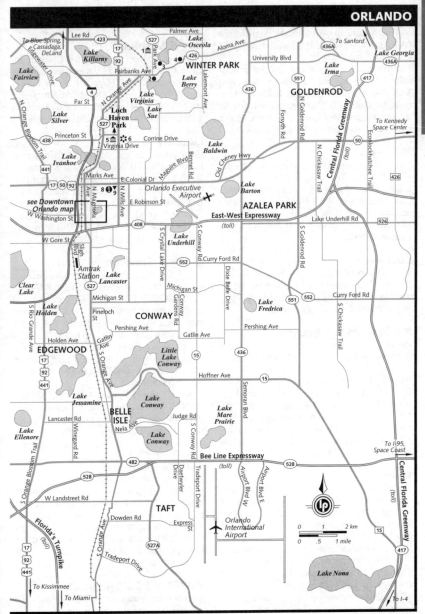

CENTRAL

ORLANDO

information, phone numbers, parking information and lots more.

The American Automobile Association (AAA; ☎ 407-894-3333) is located at 4300 E Colonial Drive.

Private information centers are practically everywhere and are usually associated with the infamous discount ticket brokers (see the Getting Tickets boxed text for an important caveat). Almost every hotel has a rack with leaflets from the usual suspects.

Money

NationsBank's main branch in town (☎ 407-420-2700) is at 390 N Orange Ave. American Express has a full-service office (☎ 407-843-0004) at the Sun Bank Center, 2 W Church St, Suite 1. Most of the theme parks and attractions have cash machines and foreign exchange desks.

Post

The main post office is on Magnolia Ave, between E Robinson and E Jefferson Sts. Its mailing address is General Delivery, 46 E Robinson St, Orlando, FL 32802.

Bookstores & Libraries

All the chains have shops in malls around the area: B Dalton (☎ 407-839-5809) has a shop at 55 W Church St; Barnes & Noble (☎ 407-856-7200) has a superstore with a café at 8358 S Orange Blossom Trail. In Winter Haven, The Booktraders (☎ 407-299-4904), 301 W Central Ave, has an enormous collection of used books, records and magazines. The main downtown library branch is at 100 E Central Blvd.

Media

The big daily is the *Orlando Sentinel*. Weekend pullout sections include special event and calendar listings. A few informative free handout papers in the area provide more timely information on bars, clubs, concerts, theater, comedy and other entertainment. Try *Where Orlando*, *Downtown Orlando Monthly* (www.downtownorlando.com), *Axis Orlando* or *UR – The University Reporter*, all available at bars and restaurants and in street boxes.

National Public Radio (NPR) is at 90.7 and 89.9 FM.

Gay & Lesbian

The Gay, Lesbian and Bisexual Community Center (☎ 407-425-4527, www.glcs.org), 714 E Colonial Drive (Hwy 50), has a library and resource center. Out & About Books (☎ 407-896-0204) at 930 N Mills Ave sells g/l/b literature and sells and rents videos.

Laundry

Coin laundries are scattered throughout town, and the HI/AYH Orlando/Kissimmee Resort (see Kissimmee under Around Orlando later this chapter) has laundry service available ($1 to wash and 75¢ to dry). Another good bet is Lake Eola Coin Laundry (☎ 407-841-2852), 807 E Washington Ave.

Medical Services

All of the larger theme parks have first aid stations. Main St Physicians (☎ 407-396-1195, 407-239-1195) is a walk-in clinic at 2901 Parkway Blvd, Suite A-3, in Kissimmee, open 8 am to 8 or 9 pm daily. A visit is $80, and you have to pay up front. They also offer a 24-hour service that sends doctors to most hotels in the area; the cost is $135 from 8 am to 10 pm and $175 from 10 pm to 8 am, plus medications.

Sand Lake Hospital (☎ 407-351-8550) is at 9400 Turkey Lake Rd. Check the telephone book under Pharmacies for listings of the several 24-hour pharmacies in the area.

Curfew

A curfew is in effect from midnight to 6 am in downtown Orlando for anyone under 18 years old. Offenders will be detained and, perhaps worse, their parents will be summoned to fetch them. It's not a joke – more than 3000 presumably insomniac youths have been arrested since the curfew's institution on June 1, 1993.

HARRY P LEU GARDENS

This 50-acre estate (☎ 407-246-2620, www.ci.orlando.fl.us/departments/leu_gardens/),

DOWNTOWN ORLANDO

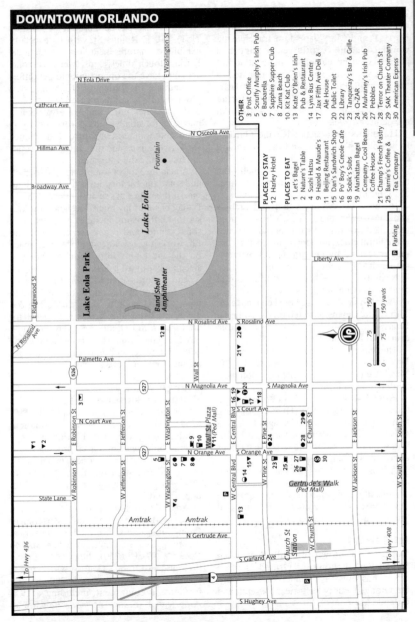

OTHER
3 Post Office
5 Scruffy Murphy's Irish Pub
6 Barbarella
7 Sapphire Supper Club
8 Zuma Beach
10 Kit Kat Club
13 Kate O'Brien's Irish
   Pub & Restaurant
14 Lynx Bus Center
17 Jax Fifth Ave Deli &
   Ale House
20 Public Toilet
22 Library
23 Tanqueray's Bar & Grille
24 O-ZAR
26 Mulvaney's Irish Pub
27 Pebbles
28 Terror on Church St
29 SAK Theater Company
30 American Express

PLACES TO STAY
12 Harley Hotel

PLACES TO EAT
1 Let's Bagel
2 Nature's Table
4 Sushi Hatsu
9 Harold & Maude's
11 Beijing Restaurant
15 Dan's Sandwich Shop
16 Po' Boy's Creole Cafe
18 Sobik's Subs
19 Manhattan Bagel
   Company, Cool Beans
   Coffee House
21 Champ's French Pastry
25 Barnie's Coffee &
   Tea Company

1920 N Forest Ave, is famous for its camellias (more than 2000 varieties) and roses. Harry P and Mary Jane Leu traveled the world collecting exotic seeds; they had planned to grow tea here on their estate, but it didn't work out. The land was donated to the city in 1961 to be used as a botanical garden and today it's a perfect place for an afternoon picnic or just a pleasant stroll. All the plants are well labeled.

Highlights include the Ravine Garden, the tropical plant area, and the North and South Woods, with oaks, pines and camellias (which have an absolutely lovely smell – the best time to experience it is from December to March).

In the Conservatory you'll find orchids and the Rose Garden, which boasts more than 1000 rose displays; one of our favorites is the floral clock, an enormous clock whose face is formed by delicate flower arrangements (it no longer tells the time, because kids climbed on the hands and tried to ride them, thus stripping the gears).

Twenty-minute tours of the **Leu House**, an 18th-century mansion listed on the National Register of Historic Places, are available every half hour until 3:30 pm.

The graves of the house's original owners, David and Angela Mizell, can be seen at the Mizell Cemetery – this is the only botanical garden in Florida with a cemetery.

From I-4, take exit 43 to Princeton St, follow that to Mills Ave (Hwy 17/92). Turn right, go to the second traffic light (Virginia Drive); go left onto Virginia for about 1 mile, following the curve to the left. The gardens are on the left side of the street.

Admission is $3 for adults and $1 for children six to 16. The gardens are open 9 am to 5 pm daily. The house/museum hours are Tuesday to Saturday 10 am to 4 pm and Sunday and Monday 1 to 4 pm.

MUSEUMS

North of downtown off Mills Ave, Loch Haven Park is home to Orlando's three major museums: the Orlando Science Center, Orange County Historical Museum and Orlando Museum of Art.

Orlando Science Center

Kids love this science museum (☎ 407-896-7151), 810 E Rollins St, with its excellent exhibits on nature, including a gator hole. During 'touch times,' kids (well, everyone, actually) have the opportunity to pet different animals. The Tunnel of Discovery holds physics stuff – exhibits on electricity, sound, optics, weather, etc – and Waterworks is a play area for smaller kids. A very cool overhead cinedome runs nature and science IMAX-type films, and the center hosts rotating traveling exhibits as well.

A neat idea to get some space for yourself and some fun for the kids is to send them to one of the museum's overnight camp-ins on Friday or Saturday night. Designed for kids six to 13, the camp includes a planetarium show, dinner and breakfast, excellent and fun workshop activities and sleeping space on the museum's floor (you provide the sleeping bag); cost is $20.

The center is open Monday to Thursday 9 am to 5 pm, Friday and Saturday 9 am to 9 pm, Sunday noon to 5 pm, closed Thanksgiving and Christmas. Admission is $9.50 for adults, $6.75 for children. Sunday to Thursday the planetarium show is included in the admission price; on Friday and Saturday it's an additional $6/4.50.

Orange County Historical Museum

The county's historical museum (☎ 407-897-6350), 812 E Rollins St, has permanent exhibits on prehistoric Florida, Orange County buildings and citrus production, as well as a re-creation of a newspaper pressroom and rotating exhibitions. A video of Orange County history screens in the 2nd-floor Grand Theater.

Adjacent (and included in the admission price) is the Orange County Museum of Firefighting, accessed through the historical museum. Kids especially love **Fire Station No 3** (☎ 407-897-6350), the oldest standing firehouse in Orange County, where inside you'll see late-19th- and early-20th-century firefighting equipment, including a 1911 American LaFrance *Metropolitan* horse-drawn steam pumper and the city's first motorized fire truck.

The museums are open Monday to Saturday 9 am to 5 pm, Sunday noon to 5 pm. Admission is $2 for adults, $1.50 for seniors and $1 for children six to 12; call ahead to find out about tours. Bus No 39 stops right in front.

Orlando Museum of Art

Founded in 1924, this museum (☎ 407-896-4231), 2416 N Mills Ave, has a permanent collection of pre-Columbian, African and 19th- and 20th-century American art. Exhibits include local, regional and international works, including African art from the Tishman Collection and Mayan archaeological finds from Caracol, Belize. All are on long-term loan to the museum.

The museum is open Tuesday to Saturday 9 am to 5 pm, Sunday noon to 5 pm, closed Monday and most major holidays. Admission is $4 for adults, $2 for children four to 11.

UNIVERSAL STUDIOS FLORIDA

As in Hollywood, California, this is a combination working movie studio and theme park that's a very entertaining way to spend a day. If you can do only one single theme park during your stay, we'd say choose Universal over any *single* Disney park.

The rides here are set to become even more gee-whiz roller-coastery than Busch Gardens. They're fun and can be scary. Waiting times are generally less than at Disney, though they can still get long. Approximate wait times are given at the end of each ride's entry below.

Orientation

Universal Studios Florida is near the intersection of I-4 and Florida's Turnpike; the main entrance is on Kirkman Rd (Hwy 435) about half a mile north of I-4 exit 3B. A second entrance is on Turkey Lake Rd. The park sprawls on a northeast slant from the main entrance and is divided into six distinct areas: the Front Lot, Production Central, Hollywood, New York, Expo Center and

San Francisco/Amity. New York, San Francisco and Amity are all cunningly realistic re-creations of those cities and are sometimes used as backdrops for films.

The most strollable areas in the park are New York and San Francisco, and you should take a half hour or so to explore the nooks and crannies and find storefronts and walls from movies. In New York, note Genco Imports *(The Godfather)* and Nazarman Pawn Broker *(The Pawnbroker)*. In San Francisco, the Fisherman's Wharf set would be much more realistic if the water it fronts were a bit colder, grayer and choppier, but that's nit-picking, isn't it? Hollywood is also worth some time.

Information

This is a highlights description – there's so much to see and do here, you should write or call before you go for an *Official Studio Guide* map and information packet: Universal Studios Florida (☎ 407-363-8000, www.usf.com), 1000 Universal Studios Plaza, Orlando, FL 32819. The Website is excellent and lets you download the entire studio guide in .pdf format, book tickets and vacation packages and lots more.

Get free maps to the park at the gate. Guest Services, which is also the lost and found and lost-kids area (families are usually reunited within 30 minutes of a park-wide alert, which you can order through any staff member), is to the right after you enter the gates, or in the window to the right before you enter. The park is open every day of the year. Hours of operation vary seasonally and with special events, but generally the park is open between 9 am and 6 pm year round.

Admission prices (including tax) for a one-day ticket are $44.50 for ages 10 and up, $36 for children three to nine; for a two-day ticket it's $66/55. Discount tickets are available at the city's Official Tourist Information Center, and discounts and specials like second-day-free programs are available from time to time, but ask, because no one will tell you. Parking is $6 for cars and motorcycles, $7 for RVs and campers.

Studio Tours (☎ 407-224-7750) have the benefit of getting you into the rides and shows without waiting in line. They cost $110 per person or $1500 for groups of up to 15 people.

You can change money at the First Union Bank just inside the main entrance; there's an ATM inside the park and one outside, both near Guest Services.

Most rides are wheelchair accessible. You can rent wheelchairs ($6), electric wheelchairs ($30 plus deposit) and single and double strollers ($6/12) at Guest Services.

For $5 you can place your animal in either indoor or outdoor kennels. Water is provided but food is not, though you can return during the day to walk and feed your pet.

Rides & Attractions

The Ride the Movies concept here puts you in 3D simulations based on the stories of movies. The technology is incredible, the effects are amazing and the rides are absolutely fantastic.

Terminator 2: 3D Housed in the Cyber-Dyne headquarters building along Hollywood Blvd, this is a killer three-screen, 3D, surround-sound and simulator experience. The film stars Arnold Schwarzenegger, Linda Hamilton and Robert Patrick. This is one of the first places many people head so as to cut down waiting time, don't come here until after midmorning.

Back to the Future This is hands-down the best flight-simulator ride in the state, maybe even in the country. Its 24 DeLorean-shaped simulators are stacked atop one another in a seven-story, 60-foot-high screening area filled with liquid-nitrogen fog. You start the ride in the 1950s and then blast into prehistoric times: through jagged mountains, down precipitous crevasses, in and around volcanoes – the special effects are phenomenal, and we'll be surprised if you don't 'feel' the Texaco sign. The film is said to be, if you calculate by the minute, the most expensive ever made, clocking in at a Costner-esque $16 million for 4½ minutes. Expect a half-hour wait.

ET Adventure This is a charming ride you take in little bicycle-like contraptions with an ET in the front basket. You're rescuing ET, taking part in the last minutes of the movie. You start to fly and skim the roof of a police car, then rise up over the city and through the sky to ET's home planet. On the way, you see ET babies and other weird spacey stuff, and at the end of the ride ET says good-bye to you by name! It's harmless stuff – great for kids but we loved it, too. It's about a 10-minute wait.

Earthquake – The Big One After being subjected to a film starring Charlton Heston which highlights the now dated and creaky but then spectacular special effects from the movie *Earthquake*, there's a brief and accurate demonstration of chroma-key and matte technology.

You then enter a really bitchin' replica of a San Francisco BART subway station and get into a pretty good BART subway train. Then the Big One (8.3 on the Richter scale) hits: the tracks buckle, the place crumbles, and you're nearly hit by an oncoming subway train and an 18-wheel truck that drops in…before, of course, the whole place catches on fire and floods. It's a 20-minute wait.

FUNtastic World of Hanna-Barbera This is a ride-through-cartoon – a flight simulator of sorts taking you through a computer-generated 3D toonscape of a spaceship. You emerge into the very entertaining world of Bedrock, which includes interactive video games; incredibly fun looping, SFX and dialog editors; and really cool digital samples of cartoon noises (at Yogi's Silly Sounds booth). It's about a 10-minute wait for the ride, none for the rest.

Jaws Here you board a tour boat in the town of Amity and start a little tootle around a lake before suddenly (!) coming under attack by gigantic rubber sharks. The explosions are terrific and it even gets a tad warm as flames burst forth from every which way and, in the end, fry the pesky beasts. Expect a half-hour wait.

Kongfrontation This takes place on New York City's Roosevelt Island Tram, with surprising – even for here – set detail (down to gum on the streets and authentic manhole covers). You start a ride to the peaceful island of thin-walled condos when suddenly (!) you come face-to-toe with the lady-lifter himself. Kong grabs hold of your tram and shakes it, and as he presses his rubbery Kong face in close you smell his Kong breath (which smells like…nah, we won't ruin it). You emerge – surprise, surprise – into the Kong shop, where you can buy Kong stuff

and, for $5, have your photo taken in the beast's hand. It's a half-hour wait.

Fievel's Playland Inspired by the cartoon *An American Tail* about a family of mice who immigrate to the US from Russia, this excellent area has giant-size sets (which make you mouse size) and a really fun waterslide. You wait about 15 minutes to board a little rubber raft and spiral down.

A Day in the Park with Barney If your kids like this repugnant purple dinosaur, this is the place to take them – personally we recommend telling your kids that Barney died in a horrible chipper-shredder accident, but hey, they're *your* kids, right? Twenty-minute shows start frequently throughout the day. Outside, an excellent Playland has lots of creative things for kids to bang on, push, climb and roll through and a very interesting whirlpool.

Shows
There's a range of stuff to be seen here, at a range of venues, and you probably won't be able to see everything in just one day unless you're a very good planner. Show times change frequently, but when you arrive you'll be handed a list of that day's shows, show times and venues.

Coolest Thing on Earth

Okay, we hated the movie *Twister,* despite the excellent special effects. But the best theme-park experience in Florida is at Universal's Twister, a 3D romp through a tornado.

We're not kidding, we mean they make a tornado – a five-story-high, 12-foot-wide actual twister fer Heaven's sake – that forms and dances around right in front of you, with rain and 35 mph winds, screams, howling noise…the works.

The experience starts with video shot specifically for the show starring Helen Hunt and Bill Paxton, your guides. You're led through some tame scenes, showing behind the scenes looks at the making of the movie and the special effects, and then into the main room, where, while you watch the scariest scene in the movie (they're cowering beneath the hut), the twister starts to kick in. Things start getting wet and the twister gets closer and closer, with the noise getting louder and louder until it's up to 110dB.

The effect is created with dozens of fans – 18 of which have 7-foot-long blades – that are positioned all around you. Unreal – and real.

Animal Actors Show Animals' rights activists may get upset with this one, but Nick thought it was fantastic. You'll see Babe the pig, Beethoven the dog, Mr Ed, Benji, an alligator named Chompers, a sea lion, Holly the stunt chimp and even a skunk.

Hitchcock 3D Theatre The Hitchcock 3D Theatre is just what it sounds like: a tribute to the films and filmmaking techniques of the portly master of suspense, including scenes from his movies, some of which become 3D.

Dynamite Nights Stuntacular This fun explode-o-rama has cops in speedboats and on jet skis chasing robbers in speedboats through dangerous fire rings. It's held every evening before closing on the main lake at the center of the park. If you love chase scenes you'll have a blast – or at least they will. Views are pretty good all around the lake, but they're probably best from the 2nd floor of Lombard's restaurant (though the 2nd floor isn't really open to the public, maybe you can sweet-talk your way upstairs like we did).

Wild, Wild, Wild West Stunt Show Better than you'd think, this fun stunt show stars a twinkly-eyed, fair-haired hero named Dusty or Randy or something, his dim-witted sidekick and a Ma Barker-inspired trio of bad guys, all of whom root, toot and shoot their way around the set for about 20 minutes. Some of the stunts are great – the fistfights, trick shooting, explosions and some from-the-rooftop and through-the-balcony falls – but the best part is staying around for a few minutes after the show and watching the set repair itself.

Gory Gruesome & Grotesque Horror Makeup Show This delivers what it promises, though if you're really into horror makeup it may be a little too short. But, as the press-kit gushes, the show annually goes through '365 straight-edge razors, 14,600 blanks, 912 quarts of stage blood and 547 gallons of our special blood and guts mixture,' so you won't feel cheated on gore! It's a discussion and demonstration – with volunteers – of basic horror makeup.

Nickelodeon Studios

About 85% of the original programming on the Nickelodeon cable television network is shot here, along with material for MTV and other Viacom-owned networks. You can tour the studios and look in on sets, though they may not be taping when you come (you'll always get the tour, and if they're not taping a real show you'll get to participate in a mock-up). Nickelodeon is, during the day, a children-oriented network, with such blockbusting hits as *Kenan and Kel*. At night, Nick at Nite runs classic TV reruns like *Taxi*, *Mary Tyler Moore* and *Bob Newhart*.

Nickelodeon offers a recorded taping schedule at ☎ 407-363-8586, so check before you come.

Studio Tour It's great fun, especially if you've never been in the magic world of TV. You'll see soundstages and, if you're lucky, whatever's being shot in them. If nothing is taping on that day, you'll head to a second control room and watch a videotape describing the various jobs around the studio, then move on to Stage 17, where you'll see either a game lab or just a mock-up of a game show complete with audience participation and, of course, GAK. You'll also pass through the classic TV memorabilia room, where you see Jeannie's original bottle and other classic TV artifacts. It's a 45-minute wait, but there's entertainment in the line.

Green Slime Geyser Nickelodeon will be remembered for the perfection of slime into their GAK product – a slimy gelatinlike substance that, in thickened form, is fun at home and in thinned form is used to dump on and throw at contestants on Nickelodeon programs. The Green Slime Geyser in front of the studios erupts every few minutes (on a random schedule), spewing forth GAK and splashing those standing within the clearly marked SPLAT ZONE.

Places to Eat

The park holds numerous fast-food and full-service restaurants. The fast-food places have meals and snacks in the $3 to $8 range, and the full-service places have appetizers from $5 to $9 and main courses from $8 to $20 (but averaging $14 to $16).

Stands sell quick snacks throughout the park, but bring your own bottled water or drinks, because who wants to spend $2.50 for a small bottle of water or $2 for a Pepsi? Vegetarian and kosher meals can be arranged through Guest Services (☎ 407-354-6356) one day in advance.

For quick sandwiches and salads, head for the *Boulangerie*. Or head for *Schwab's Pharmacy*, a pharmacy lunch counter with chili dogs, hot dogs and ice cream. *Mel's Drive-In* is a '50s diner with burgers and fries, chicken sandwiches and lots of vintage cars out front.

In New York, what looks like Louie's Restaurant, Giovanni's Fruit and Mamma Lugina's is all actually *Louie's Italian,* which does cafeteria-style Italian food – underwhelming at that. The linguine and clam sauce and the lasagna ($6.39) were decent.

On the pricier, sit-down side, *Finnegan's* is a New York-Irish-style bar and grill with sandwiches from $7.50 to $9.25, fish & chips for $10 and main courses like steaks for $12.95 to $16. From 5 to 7 pm there's a happy hour with half-price beer and wine.

The *Studio Star* has a lunch buffet for $9.95 ($4.95 for kids nine and under) until 4 pm, after which it's $12.95 for adults, $6.95 for kids.

Lombards at Fisherman's Wharf has similar prices and 'San Francisco' food, and there's always the *Hard Rock Cafe* at the highest end: memorabilia notwithstanding, we just don't pay that much for a sandwich and coffee.

Entertainment

Opened after we researched, *City Walk* is Universal's answer to Disney's Pleasure Island (which was itself an answer to Orlando's Church St Station) – a 30-acre park with restaurants, clubs, music venues and more. Once again Universal has outshined Disney with the quality of its offerings, which here include some huge names: *Jimmy Buffett's Margaritaville*, *Bob Marley – A Tribute to Freedom* (an exact replica of Marley's place in Jamaica), *Emeril's Restaurant*, the *Hard Rock Cafe* and *Hard Rock Live*, *NBA City*, the *NASCAR Cafe*, *City Jazz* and a 20-screen *Universal Cineplex*. The whole thing will be up and running in late 1999.

ISLANDS OF ADVENTURE

This newish park (☎ 407-363-8000, www.uescape.com/islands), also in association with Universal Studios Florida, has thrill coasters, restaurants and fast food, exhibits and interactive themed areas: Toon Lagoon, featuring Popeye; Seuss Landing, showcasing Dr Seuss stories and characters; Marvel Super Hero Island, with Spiderman, the Hulk and others; The Lost Continent; and *Jurassic Park*.

Opened in May 1999, it's next to Universal Studios Florida. Hours and pricing are similar: the park opens at 9 am and closing hours vary depending on the season. General daily admission is $44 for adults, $35 for kids three to nine (kids under three get in free). Call or check out the Website for more information, including package deals.

WET 'N' WILD

Wet 'n' Wild (☎ 407-351-1800, 800-992-9453, www.wetnwild.com), 6200 International Drive, is one of Florida's first water parks, and it's a very good one. The star of the show is Der Stuka, a six-story speed slide. The park was bought recently by Universal Studios, but it's still to be called Wet 'n' Wild.

Located right at the heart of International Drive, it's easy to get to, and lines here are far shorter than those at Disney. The park is well done, clean and safe, definitely family oriented and the rides are pretty cool, too.

At the center of the park is a tide pool; to the left are Raging Rapids and Mach 5, to the right Der Stuka and Bomb Bay; straight ahead are Blue Niagara, Wild One and Knee Ski. The park is surrounded by Lazy River, a swiftly flowing channel on which you can float aimlessly on a raft. Raging Rapids and Mach 5 are mat slides. On Mach 5 you're given a choice of routes: B is the shortest with the quickest turns, C is the longest and slowest. Bomb Bay and Der Stuka are speed slides; for Bomb Bay you step inside a capsule which is moved forward over the slide, at which point the floor drops out from under you.

Parking ($3 for cars, $5 for campers and buses) is across the street from the park. A Sunbank ATM is at the entrance, and lockers are to the right as you enter. You can bring a picnic with you to save money on food; there's a covered picnic area behind Bubble Up, the enormous climbable beach ball. In winter, the pools are heated to 85°F.

Admission is $26.95 for adults, $13.48 for seniors (over 55), $21.95 for kids three to nine. A second-day pass is $11.50. An annual family pass is $75. There's an extra $3 fee for the Wild One, where you're pulled around the lake on a bouncy tube by a jet ski. Tube, towel, locker and life vest package is $9, with a $4 deposit.

The park is open daily year round, but hours vary widely by season. The longest hours (9 am to 11 pm) are from June 14 through August 6; the shortest (10 am to 5 pm) are from November 1 to January 1.

SEAWORLD ORLANDO

We visited SeaWorld Orlando on a day marred by torrential rains and still managed to have a good time, though we think the admission prices are more than a little out of line (it costs more than a Disney park!). But some of that money does go to very good causes – the SeaWorld Orlando Animal Rescue Team is one of the best in the country – and if you're the sort of person who likes leaping dolphins, sliding sea lions and crashing whales, you're going to have an incredible time.

Orientation & Information

SeaWorld Orlando (☎ 407-351-3600, www .seaworld.com), 7007 SeaWorld Orlando

Drive, is near the intersection of I-4 and the Bee Line Expressway.

The park is oval-shaped, with the main entrance, Guest Services and the lost and found center at its northwest curve. Get a map with your ticket. It's open year round, but hours change often; generally it's open from around 9 am to around 7 pm, later in summer.

The admission cost pre-tax is $42 for adults and $34 for children three to nine. Parking is $5 for cars, $7 for vans and buses. Admission to the utterly unexciting Sky Tower is an extra $3 plus tax.

Change money at Guest Relations from 10 am to 3 pm. There's an ATM at the main gate and pay lockers ($1) near the main entrance. All attractions are wheelchair accessible. Stroller and wheelchair rentals are $5; double strollers are $10; electric wheelchairs are $25. Air-conditioned kennel service is $4 per day (bring your own food).

Toilets are well-signed and clean. Diaper-changing areas are available outside all women's toilets and outside the men's toilets near Shamu Emporium. Unisex diaper-changing areas are found near Wild Arctic and at the Hospitality Center. Nursing mothers have their own area (imagine the scandal, the dis*grace*, of actually nursing a human child in public!) near the women's toilet at the Friends of the Wild.

Things to See & Do

Other than the new Journey to Atlantis and Wild Arctic, the main attractions here are not rides but shows and displays. These high-lights are listed roughly in counter-clockwise order (with a couple of zigs and zags) from the entrance at the ticket plaza.

Stingray Lagoon Rays, the docile animals related to sharks, glide through the water with a grace and beauty all their own. This section of the park features a whole lot of them, including cownose, southern diamond and bat rays and the shovel-nosed guitarfish (actually a skate). You can feed the flappy fellers with stingray food ($1) of smelt, shrimp, clam and squid, available from the very friendly staff.

Whale & Dolphin Stadium This is the home of SeaWorld Orlando's false-killer whale and dolphin shows, starring some of the 40 dolphins that have been born at the park. Atlantic bottle-nosed dolphins boogie to sampler-driven Caribbean music, performing synchronized leaps from the water as the vet rides on the backs of Cindy and Dolly, the stars of the show.

Manatees: the Last Generation? Endangered manatees, whose population took even more of a pounding from a mysterious disease in early 1996, are the focus of this excellent exhibit. The heroic SeaWorld Orlando Animal Rescue Team rescues injured and sick manatees every year; in 1996 it was one of the major players in the race to discover what was killing the manatees off the southwestern coast of Florida.

Outside you'll see alligators, crocodiles and turtles. Inside, to the sounds of crickets and frogs, you'll see a four-minute film about the life of manatees, and you'll learn how human behavior is so devastating to this species that has no other natural enemies. See Fauna in the Facts about Florida chapter for more information about manatees and how they're threatened.

Penguin Encounter We had a blast here, as people movers carried us past penguin tanks with manufactured snow, the sounds of penguin calls barely audible over the hilarious and appropriate *oom-pah-pah* music. Dig the wild rockhopper penguins, which look very much like mid-1980s Rod Stewart.

A learning center here features a puffin area and touch-screen instructional videos on each type of bird included in the exhibit.

Sea Lion & Otter Stadium This is home to *Clyde and Seamore Take Pirate Island*, a 'funny' show starring sea lion, otter and walrus 'comedians.' It's an excellent show for kids, who do find it screamingly funny.

Terrors of the Deep With the exception of Wild Arctic, this is probably the most popular exhibit in the park (well, okay, after

the itty-bitty glasses of free beer at the Anheuser-Busch Hospitality Center). The sharks, rays, barracuda, lion fish and skates in this exhibition are swimming all around the Plexiglas tube you're carried through on a conveyor belt. It's absolutely fascinating to be this close to the enormous sharks, and kids love it when rays and skates glide over the surface of the tube eating little pieces of algae.

Anheuser-Busch Hospitality Center Anheuser-Busch, America's largest brewing company (it makes more than a billion cases of 20-some varieties of beer annually, as well as a host of other products including those little roasted-nut packs you get on airplanes), owns SeaWorld Orlando. At the hospitality center you can taste free samples of the company's beers, meted out in little 10oz cups (two per person over 21). But it's actually a very interesting attraction without the beer: you can learn a lot about recycling (A-B has its own recycling subsidiary), printing (yeah, they have a printing subsidiary, too) and other A-B endeavors. And out back, the **Clydesdale Hamlet** is home to a stable of Clydesdale draft horses, which are the trademark of Budweiser beer.

Shamu's Happy Harbor This is a wonderful kids' recreation area with probably the best climbing nets on earth (all ages), an air-bounce for kids up to 48 inches (122cm), very cool waterslides for kids under 42 inches (107cm) and a great sandbox. Other fun includes a small arcade and some neato but expensive radio-controlled boats and cars (it's an additional $1 for 2¼ minutes with the boats and $1 for 2 minutes with a truck).

Shamu Stadium Killer whales doing stunts, splashing the crowd. Some choreographed to rock music.

Wild Arctic This begins with an excellent flight-simulator ride. You're traveling in an incredibly high-powered helicopter to a remote Arctic station as a bad storm front moves in (they say they'll do their best to get you there safely). The helicopter is being flown by a nature-loving pilot who brings you very close to some polar bears before setting down on thin ice. Of course, after hearing an awful rumbling sound, you fall through the ice and it's touch and go there for a while, but...

Once you reach Base Station Wild Arctic, you'll see a fascinating Arctic exhibit featuring harbor seals, a beluga whale, polar bears, walruses and fish. Touch-screen interactive displays teach you more about the Arctic, and the very helpful and informed staff can answer any questions. Finally you emerge from your Arctic adventure in...the Wild Arctic gift shop.

Journey to Atlantis Other than playing a recording of David Hasselhoff singing *Fallin' in Love* as part of the Baywatch at SeaWorld Orlando show, the park hadn't been in the terror side of the entertainment business. But they're starting to change, and this waterflume/coaster ride is the first step. You ride in a raft and at the top, after a delayed hanging over the edge, you plunge 60 feet nearly vertically. Cool.

RIPLEY'S BELIEVE IT OR NOT!
The Orlando Ripley's Believe It or Not! (☎ 407-363-4418), 8201 International Drive, two blocks south of Sand Lake Rd (take I-4 to exit 29), is in a building cleverly designed to appear as if it were collapsing into a sinkhole.

Inside are the classic Ripley draws: shrunken heads, double-pupil wax figures and the holographic image of Robert Ripley, as well as interactive exhibits and films. It's fully wheelchair accessible and open 9 am to midnight daily. Admission is $10.95 for adults and $7.95 for children four to 12.

See St Augustine in the Northeast Florida chapter for general information on Robert Ripley.

MOVIE RIDER
This theater (☎ 407-352-0050), 8815 International Drive, is a flight simulator that shows two films daily, such as racing and plunging into a volcano. Admission (including both films) is $8.95 for adults, $6.95 for children.

TERROR ON CHURCH ST
This excellent spook show (☎ 407-649-3327), 135 S Orange Ave (northeast corner of Church St) in the center of downtown Orlando, is a walk through 23 different sets, all of them 'haunted' by actors in spooky costume, special effects, lights and sound. It's really fun to stand outside and watch the television monitors of victims walking through and getting the pants scared off them. If you're a horror movie or spookhouse fan, you can't do much better around here. Admission is $12 per person; kids under 10 are not admitted without a parent or guardian. It's open Tuesday to Thursday and Sunday 7 pm to midnight, Friday and Saturday 7 pm to 1 am.

MYSTERY FUN HOUSE
The Mystery Fun House (☎ 407-351-3355 for recorded information, 407-351-3359 for a human), 5767 Major Blvd, opposite the main gates of Universal Studios Florida, is a 15-room maze inside a large house. It's dimly lit, and you have to navigate your way through the creepy twists and turns. It's not a horror show: nothing comes out and grabs you or says 'boo.'

The other big draw here is **Destination Starbase Omega**, a souped-up laser-tag game. You're equipped with a vibrating shield and a laser gun, and you and other warriors enter a flight simulator that 'brings you' through an asteroid field and lands you on the starbase, where you proceed to leave the simulator and shoot the hell out of all the people who rode there with you.

Admission to the fun house (you can go through at your own pace) is $10.95 for all ages. The Starbase Omega bit (which lasts for a total of a half hour, the shooting part itself only 10 minutes) is $9.95, miniature golf is $4.95, and a combination ticket is $19.85. It's open 10 am to 11 pm daily.

Q-ZAR
More aggressive travelers might enjoy Q-ZAR (☎ 407-839-0002, 101 S Orange Ave), a laser-tag game in which you charge like a lunatic through various rooms, shooting at opponents with a laser-pistol and trying to

'capture' their 'base.' One game is $7, three are $18. You can get hit four times before you're 'out'; games last for 15 minutes or until everyone's dead.

SHOOTING SPORTS

Foreigners will be aghast at the ease at which this shooting range (☎ 407-363-9000), 6811-13 Visitors Circle opposite Wet 'n' Wild, rents handguns, shotguns, automatic and semiautomatic weapons out to anyone – *anyone* – over age 18 and able to behave in a non-insane manner. We're listing it because it's very popular and, okay, we did it, too. It works like this: you rent the piece (we chose a Glock 17) for an average of $37.50 including the gat, 50 bullets, eye protection, targets, lessons (if necessary) and range fees, and then head for the indoor range. Someone rented an *Uzi* when we were there. We left soon after. Blammedy Blam Blam! It's open daily 10 am to 10:30 pm.

PLACES TO STAY

Most of the places to stay in the area are not in downtown Orlando but along I-Drive, out by Disney and in Kissimmee, and most of the options are chain hotels that we won't bother describing. In the chains, package tours combining airfare, hotel, Disney ticket, etc are often the best way to go, and rates vary wildly from day to day. The greater Orlando area has the highest concentration of hotel rooms in the USA, so competition is fierce, rates are generally low and quality is acceptable.

It's usually cheaper to stay in Kissimmee (see Around Orlando later in this chapter), where multitudes of motels line Hwy 192 and rooms begin at $19.95 throughout the entire year. Kissimmee is also home to the HI/AYH Orlando/Kissimmee Resort, the only hostel around since the HI Orlando Hostel-Plantation Manor burned down (and won't be replaced).

Camping

The Orlando area is one of the few places in the state where camping is actually convenient and inexpensive. It's also relatively safe,

though make sure to leave valuables with management when you're away from the site.

KOA has two campgrounds in the area: one in the city of Orlando proper at 12343 Narcoossee Rd, 5 miles south of the Bee Line Expressway at exit 13 or 1 mile south of US Hwy 417 at exit 22 (☎ 407-277-5075, 800-562-3969), and another in Kissimmee (see Around Orlando later in this chapter). The Orlando KOA is at the southeastern end of the city and has tent sites for $20 and RV sites with full hookups for $30.

Raccoon Lake (☎ 407-239-4148, 800-776-9644, 9200 Turkey Lake Rd) in Orlando has tent sites for $15 to $18 year round. Full hookup sites are $25 in low season, $35 in high season, and cottages run $39 to $55.

Hotels & Motels

The downtown options are not altogether the best. The **Harley Hotel** (☎ 407-841-3220, 800-321-2323, 151 E Washington) is well located right on Lake Eola, but the rooms are somewhat aged and the whole thing is a little too expensive for what you get, with rooms from $89 to $109. **Travelodge** (☎ 407-423-1671, 800-578-7878, 409 N Magnolia Ave) has rooms for $65 to $85.

All of the motels and hotels along International Drive are chain places, and they're all about the same. Designed to accommodate package tourists from the USA and Europe, they each have pools, lounges, restaurants and are all convenient to fast-food places. They all offer shuttle services to the airport and the theme parks for about the same price. It's always cheaper to book these places through a travel agent as some sort of package as opposed to coming in and asking for the rack rates. Quoted prices on the telephone are often deceptive: you can always negotiate.

See Accommodations in the Facts for the Visitor chapter for more information on package tours and toll-free numbers for the larger chains.

Hotels along I-Drive include the following:

Best Western Plaza International
  (☎ 407-345-8195, No 8738) – somewhat but not entirely swank

Comfort Suites Orlando
(☎ 407-351-5050, No 5825) – usually very
comfortable with lots of perks, including free
breakfast

Continental Plaza Hotel
(☎ 407-352-8211, 6825 Visitors Circle) – a huge
place with a pool, opposite Wet 'n' Wild

Days Inn
(☎ 407-351-1200, No 7200) and (☎ 407-352-
8700, No 9990)

Hampton Inn
(☎ 407-345-1112, 7110 S Kirkman Rd) –
comfortable and reasonable

Holiday Inn Castle Hotel
(☎ 407-345-1511, No 8629)

Holiday Inn Express (☎ 407-351-4430, No 6323)

Holiday Inn International Drive Resort
(☎ 407-351-3500, No 6515) – one of the nicer
entries

Howard Johnson (☎ 407-351-2900, No 6603)

Howard Johnson Resort Hotel
(☎ 407-351-2100, No 5905) – nicer than the
previous Howard Johnson

Howard Johnson Universal Tower
(☎ 407-351-2100, No 5905)

Orlando Marriott (☎ 407-351-2420, No 8001)

Quality Suites
(☎ 407-351-1600, No 7600) and (☎ 407-345-
8585, No 9000) – the same kind of perks as
Comfort Suites but with large outdoor heated
pools, though no breakfast

Radisson Barcelo Hotel Orlando
(☎ 407-345-0505, No 8444) – a flashy place

Ramada Hotel Resort Florida Center
(☎ 407-351-4600, No 7400) – even flashier

PLACES TO EAT
Orlando has few outstanding restaurants
worth dressing up for, but there's a never-
ending supply of fast-food and chain restaurants, and there is some interesting
international cuisine that's very inexpensive.
You can't fire a pistol on I-Drive without
hitting a restaurant of some sort, and all the
steak houses and some of the other larger
places have all-you-can-eat breakfast buffets, which we found to be both crowded and
a rip-off. Theme dinner shows in Kissimmee
provide entertainment while you eat; see
Around Orlando later in this chapter.

The following restaurants are in downtown Orlando.

Restaurants & Cafés
Dan's Sandwich Shop (☎ 407-425-8881, 28 S
Orange Ave) is breakfast central. For $1.70
you'll get two eggs, potatoes or grits and
toast; omelets are $2.20 to $3.35. At lunch,
a turkey-melt platter with fries and coleslaw
is $4.50 and a tuna-melt platter with chips
and pickles is $3.45. It's open 7 am to 3 pm
Monday to Friday, closed Sunday.

Barnie's Coffee & Tea Company (☎ 407-
894-1416, 118 S Orange Ave) is a chi-chi
chain – not as chi-chi as Starbucks but chi-
chi nonetheless. It offers a wide variety of
flavored coffees and teas, as well as bagels,
pastries and cakes. One of those with coffee
is $1.75.

We loved the stuff at the tiny **Champ's
French Pastry** (132 E Central Blvd), where
cookies are 50¢, brownies and croissants are
$1 and cinnamon rolls are $1.35. It's open
Saturday noon to 6 pm , and Sunday and
Monday 7 am to 6 pm.

You won't go hungry at 50 E Central
Blvd, what with three different eateries on
the premises. The very friendly folks at **Po'
Boy's Creole Cafe** (☎ 407-839-5852) make
po' boys – sandwiches pressed in a grill like
a Cuban – in 6- and 12-inch lengths. They're
pretty awesome, and this is a very popular
lunch spot. Favorites include blackened
chicken $5/6, veggie $2.50/3.50, and crab-
meat omelet à la Creole $8. Next door is the
Manhattan Bagel Co (☎ 407-422-1987),
perfect for a quick snack like a pizza bagel,
or buy a dozen bagels for $4.99. Also at this
address is **Cool Beans Coffee House** (☎ 407-
481-2665).

Another good bagel place is **Let's Bagel-
Downtown** (☎ 407-425-2972, 345 N Orange
Ave). **Sobik's Subs** (☎ 407-425-0164, 55 E
Pine St) is a central-Florida chain offering
excellent, healthy and large sandwiches
from $2.75 to $5.50.

Beijing Restaurant (☎ 407-423-2522, 19
N Orange Ave) is a decent Chinese place
with lunch specials like beef or chicken stir-
fry served with egg roll and rice for $5, or
veggie versions for $3.75 to $5. At dinner,
prices for meat, chicken and fish dishes
range from $7 to $11, and vegetarian dishes
go for $5 to $7.

Planet Pizza (☎ 407-839-5998, 14 W Washington St) is the perfect foil for late-night club munchies, as it's right next door to Barbarella – see Entertainment later in the Orlando section. Sop up the booze with pizza (sold by the slice) or a calzone.

Several thumbs up for *Sushi Hatsu* (☎ 407-422-1551, 24 W Washington St), a Korean-Japanese (?) place that serves excellent kimchee (garlic and herb spicy marinated cabbage) for $3, great sushi by the piece from $1.75 to $3.50, and blow-out lunches ($5 to $7) and dinner specials ($8 to $15). We had a great meal here.

Nature's Table (☎ 407-872-7526, 25 E Church St and 331 N Orange Ave) special-izes in health-oriented sandwiches, though the shops are open only during the week and only for lunch, until 3 pm. The very good and overstuffed tuna sandwiches are $4.25, while vegetarian sandwiches run $3 to $4.

Over on N Mills Ave, on the way out to Leu Gardens, you'll find several good Viet-namese restaurants. *Little Saigon* (☎ 407-423-8539, 1106 E Colonial Drive), just off N Mills, has excellent service and food, lots of items for $4.50 to $7.50 and daily lunch and dinner specials, like shrimp paste on sugar cane, charbroiled beef and spring roll with rice vermicelli for $7.95.

Pebbles (☎ 407-839-0892, 17 W Church St) does good lunches; steak and seafood from $11 to $15. It's also a good bar; see Enter-tainment later in the Orlando section.

Self-Catering

Orlando is one of the great melting pots of Florida, and if you're staying in the hostel, a campsite or at a hotel with kitchen facilities you could do worse than stocking up on some interesting imported foodstuffs. All the local Publix and Winn-Dixies have expanded international food sections to accommodate the teeming hordes of foreign tourists; you won't find Vegemite, but chances are you will find Marmite and some other foods from Commonwealth countries there. There's a huge 24-hour Publix right across the street from the HI/AYH Orlando/Kissimmee Resort in Kissimmee.

For more exotic offerings, Orlando has several markets specializing in Asian, English and gourmet foods; many of them also sell prepared foods, cheeses, cold meats and desserts. The following are some inter-national markets:

Apna Bazaar – Middle Eastern & Pakistani
  (☎ 407-856-0238, 9432 S Orange Blossom Trail)
Bombay Bazaar – Indian
  (☎ 407-856-1780, 11301 S Orange Blossom Trail)
D&M West Indian & American Grocery
  (☎ 407-841-8933, 300 W Church St)
Dong-A – Vietnamese/Asian
  (☎ 407-898-9227, 816 N Mills Ave)
Pence & Pound House – British
  (☎ 407-628-4911, 630 S Maitland Ave)
  in Winter Park
Trung My – Vietnamese
  (☎ 407-894-4241, 720 N Mills Ave)

ENTERTAINMENT

Nightlife in the Orlando area is described either in breathless press releases from the major theme parks saying how great their nightspots are, or in grumbles from visitors who say there's nothing to do. They're both wrong: in and around Orlando you'll find a reasonably healthy club scene, and despite what you'll read elsewhere, there *is* more to area nightlife than Pleasure Island (see Entertainment under Walt Disney World Resort later in this chapter), City Walk (see Universal Studios Florida earlier in the Orlando section) and Church St Station.

See Kissimmee under Around Orlando later this chapter for the most popular dinner-theater venues.

Church St Station

Orlando's Church St Station (☎ 407-422-2434), on Church St between Garland Ave and the railroad tracks, east of I-4, is a col-lection of bars and nightclubs housed in beautifully renovated century-old buildings. The complex, done up in an Old South/Grand Ole Opry theme, takes up both sides of Church St. It may seem as fake as Plea-sure Island and City Walk, but the buildings and especially the railroad are real: if you see the Railroad Crossing warning light start flashing, get out of the way or risk being flattened by a mile-long flatbed hauler!

On the north side of the street are *Lili Marlene's*, a steak house; *Phineas Fogg's*, a dance club filled with airplanes and balloons (come for *really* cheap beer on Wednesday from 6:30 to 7:30 pm); and *Rosie O'Grady's*, which features Dixieland bands and can-can girls. And on the south side of the street, the *Cheyenne Saloon & Opera House* is guarded by an enormous grizzly bear at the entrance. Inside you'll find live music downstairs; a bar, steak house and barbecue restaurant on the 2nd floor; and a pseudo-casino where you can play blackjack, billiards and checkers (for fun only). *Crackers Seafood* is a seafood restaurant with a beautiful downstairs wine cellar that you can reserve for a private meal.

The complex is open 11 am to 2 am every day; admission is free until 5 pm, after which tickets cost $17.95 for adults, $11.95 for children (no one under 21 is admitted to Phineas Fogg's). The ticket buys you admission to all the shows (there are several per night), bars (which are not very cheap) and restaurants (ditto). The first shows start at 7:45 pm. One nice feature is an unsupervised playground on the 3rd floor of the north-side complex.

Bars & Pubs

Tanqueray's Bar & Grille (☎ 407-649-8540, 100 S Orange Ave) has live music Friday and Saturday nights. Happy hour is Monday to Friday 11 am to 7 pm, and lunch specials include dishes like chicken and rice with salad and soup for $3.95.

The best Irish place is *Scruffy Murphy's Irish Pub* (☎ 407-648-5460, 9 W Washington St), which has a great selection of Irish beers and a fun crowd.

Mulvaney's Irish Pub (☎ 407-872-3296, 27 W Church St) has Guinness, Murphy's Irish Stout, Newcastle Brown Ale, Samuel Adams and Killian's Red on draft. During happy hour, Monday to Friday 11 am to 7 pm, drafts are $2. It's open till 2 am.

The *Kit Kat Club* (☎ 407-422-6990, Wall Street Plaza) is a very cool place, with Roaring '20s atmosphere, pool tables, a serious jukebox, a huge array of beers and live jazz every second Saturday. Next door, *Harold & Maude's* (☎ 407-422-3322, 25 Wall Street Plaza) has a selection of espresso drinks, coffee and pastries.

Jax Fifth Ave Deli & Ale House (☎ 407-841-5322, 11 S Court Ave) has a comfy atmosphere and happy hour from 5 to 7 pm Monday to Friday. Food is available.

Kate O'Brien's Irish Pub & Restaurant (☎ 407-649-7646, 42 W Central Blvd) has live music on Friday and Saturday from 9:30 pm to 1:30 am (no cover), Newcastle Brown Ale, Guinness, Killian's and Samuel Adams on tap, and a buffet at its late-afternoon happy hour. Fish & chips are $6.95.

Pebbles (☎ 407-839-0892, 17 W Church St) has happy hour from 4 to 7 pm: margaritas, light pints and wine are $2.50 and well drinks are $1 off.

Howl at the Moon (☎ 407-841-4695, 55 W Church St) is a comedy piano bar where everyone we saw was having a great time singing along to kitschy show tunes and dodging the waitstaff. Get this: bring your own *food*. You must be at least 21 to get in.

The *Sapphire Supper Club* (☎ 407-246-1419, 54 N Orange Ave) is a chic bar with food and music – sometimes live jazz or alternative music.

Clubs

Nightclub cover charges in Orlando range from $4 to $8. The clubs here certainly aren't as exclusive as those in Miami Beach or Fort Lauderdale, but they can be fun. And you usually don't have to wait long to get in.

8 Seconds (☎ 407-839-4800, 100 W Livingston St) was once the Edge and one of the more popular discos in town, but it's gone country. Shoot.

Barbarella (☎ 407-839-0457, 68 N Orange Ave) is very crowded on Monday and Thursday nights, which are disco nights; it's great music and dancing, the male/female ratio is about equal and they have large-screen TVs with music videos.

Zuma Beach (☎ 407-648-8727, 46 N Orange Ave) is a meat market of epic proportions, with beach-garbed staff and a hot atmosphere.

Gay & Lesbian Venues

It's not Miami, but hey, at least there's something. The **Cactus Club** (☎ 407-894-3041, 1300 N Mills Ave) is a preppie hangout. **Southern Nights** (☎ 407-898-0424, 375 Bennet Rd), just north of the Orlando Executive Airport, attracts more of a mixed crowd.

Sadie's Tavern (☎ 407-628-4562, 415 S Orlando Ave) in Winter Park is a high-end lesbian bar with some quirky entertainment concepts. Another well-established lesbian bar is **Faces** (☎ 407-291-7571, 4910 Edgewater Drive), north of downtown on the west side of I-4.

Parliament House (☎ 407-425-7571, 410 N Orange Blossom Trail) is actually a motel with cruisey Western, piano and poolside bars, along with drag shows and other live entertainment. Next door at 500 N Orange Blossom Trail is a leather/Levi's place called the **Full Moon Saloon** (☎ 407-648-8725).

Lil' Orphan Andy's (☎ 407-299-7717, 5700 N Orange Blossom Trail) is the first gay bar in Rosemont and has a very mixed crowd of men and women.

Performing Arts

The two major performing arts centers in town are the **Bob Carr Performing Arts Centre** (☎ 407-849-2020, 401 W Livingston St) and the **Civic Theater of Central Florida** (☎ 407-896-7365, 1001 E Princeton St), both of which are host to performances of opera, classical music and theater.

The **SAK Theater Company** (☎ 407-648-0001, 45 E Church St), in the corner building, is a comedy/improvisation group that's been around for years. Their shows are always full on weekends, so you'll have to make reservations. Despite signs promising otherwise, no sushi is available anywhere in the building.

SPECTATOR SPORTS

The biggest news in town is the **NBA Orlando Magic** (☎ 407-896-2442), which plays home games at the Orlando Arena. Though Shaquille O'Neal no longer plays here, the Magic is still the most popular team in the state. The Arena (also called the 'O-rena') is at 1 Magic Place (600 W Amelia Ave – take I-4 north to the Amelia Ave exit). The **Orlando Miracle** (☎ 407-916-9622), a Women's National Basketball Association team, plays here as well.

SHOPPING

All the museums have gift shops, and all the theme parks have several (Disney has its own full-scale shopping mall in the Disney Village Marketplace). Orlando International Airport, in addition to its airportly duties, manages to be one of the city's biggest shopping malls as well: dozens of shops cater to last-minute souvenir purchases (the prices aren't bad at all), and a video arcade keeps the kids happy.

The area has several very popular shopping malls. Downtown at Church St Station is Church St Exchange (☎ 407-422-2434), 124 W Pine St. I-Drive is home to two major malls. At the southern end is the Mercade Mediterranean Village (☎ 407-345-9337) at No 8445, and at the north, the enormous Belz Factory Outlet Stores (☎ 407-352-7110) at No 4949 is so large it takes up football-field-size buildings on both sides of the street.

Out by Disney, the Crossroads Mall of Lake Buena Vista (☎ 407-827-7300), 8510 Palm Parkway, is a smaller affair than the others, but at night it's great fun to see the younger Disney staffers tearing loose and tossing back shot after shot at the mall's Baja Beach Club (the mall is very close to Disney staff housing; Stern magazine in Germany once called this bar the 'best place in Florida to get laid').

GETTING THERE & AWAY
Air

It is almost always cheaper to fly here as part of a package than to purchase airfare and everything else separately; see the Getting There & Away chapter for more information on charters, travel agents, packages and discount airlines. More packages are available to Orlando than to any other Florida city, and cross-marketing plans with the theme parks, hotels and airlines lower the final tally.

Orlando International Airport (MCO; ☎ 407-825-2001), in the far southeastern corner of the city, is the largest airport in central Florida. It's served by almost all major airlines, as well as charters and discount airlines.

Most of the really cheap charter airlines are now flying into Orlando Sanford Airport (SFB), the third busiest in the state, about 30 minutes northeast of the city. Getting from the airport to the city from SFB is about a $25 cab or limo ride; all the car-rental companies are represented here as well.

The following are some typical one-way airfares to/from other Florida cities: Miami $59, Tampa $45, Jacksonville $79 and Pensacola $149.

Bus

The Greyhound station (☎ 407-292-3424) is at 555 N John Young Parkway (Hwy 423). Routes to/from other cities are listed below (between six and 10 buses daily travel to/from each destination). Prices listed are one way/roundtrip:

destination	duration	price
Gainesville	2¹/₂ to 3¹/₂ hours	$21/41
Jacksonville	2¹/₂ to 4¹/₄ hours	$26/51
Miami	5¹/₂ to 11 hours	$32/63
Tallahassee	4¹/₂ to 8¹/₂ hours	$39/76
Tampa	1³/₄ to 3 hours	$17/31

Train

Amtrak (☎ 800-872-7245) provides service between New York City and Orlando on the *SilverMeteor* and *SilverStar* trains. Travel time from New York to Orlando is 22 hours. The *Sunset Limited* runs between Los Angeles and Miami via Orlando.

Fares depend on a wide variety of variables including day, month, number of passengers, whether you take a car or not, type of seating or cabin and, for all we know, how many socks the president of Amtrak has in the dryer when you call. See the Getting There & Away chapter for more Amtrak information and for a better grasp of the complex pricing system.

The Amtrak terminal (☎ 407-843-7611) is at 1400 Sligh Blvd, about 1 mile south of downtown and three blocks west of Orange Ave.

Car & Motorcycle

I-4 runs right through Orlando, connecting the city with Tampa to the southwest and Daytona Beach to the northeast. To/from anywhere on the southwest coast and anywhere north of Daytona on the East Coast, I-4 is the best bet.

From Miami, the fastest and most direct route to Orlando is via Florida's Turnpike (toll), about a 4¹/₂-hour drive. To avoid the tolls at the cost of about an hour, take I-95 to Hwy 50 south of Titusville, then go west to Winter Park and south to Orlando. You can also take I-95 to Hwy 528, the Bee Line Expressway, which speeds things up but involves another few bucks in toll. From the northwest, take I-75 south to Florida's Turnpike.

GETTING AROUND
To/From the Airport

Bus service is available between the airport and the downtown Lynx Bus Center. During the week, bus No 11 picks up at the first level of the airport in terminal A at 10 minutes and 40 minutes after the hour, beginning at 5:40 am and running through 7:40 pm; after that it's hourly between 8:40 and 11:40 pm. From the Lynx Bus Center to the airport, buses start running at 4:45 am and continue at 15 minutes and 45 minutes past every hour until 6:45 pm; then it's hourly from 7:45 till 10:45 pm. The fare is $1.

From Orlando International to the hostel by bus is pathetic and only recommended for serious pikers with lots of time: take bus No 42 east to the Florida Mall, then switch to the No 4 to Osceola Mall, *then* change for bus No 56 to the hostel.

Bus

Orlando is blessed with a highly efficient and inexpensive public transportation system. The Lynx System (☎ 407-841-8240, TDD 407-423-0787) operates 47 numbered routes, a 'FreeBee Downtown Circuit' and the Laser Shuttle connecting the University of Central Florida to routes 13 and 32, which leave from the Lynx Bus Center.

Fares are $1 per ride, 25¢ for seniors, 10¢ for transfers; a weekly pass is $10 and a monthly pass is $35. Bus stops are marked with a sign bearing a Lynx paw-print of sorts along with the number of the route(s) that stop there.

Getting to/from downtown Orlando will bring you through the highly efficient **Lynx Bus Center**, in the alley between W Pine St and W Central Blvd, one block west of Orange Ave. You can buy tickets and monthly passes and get system maps and specific route information from the information booth, which is open Monday to Friday 6:30 am to 8 pm, Saturday 7:30 am to 6 pm and Sunday 8 am to 6 pm. You can use the Lynx System to get to Winter Park (Nos 1 and 9, hourly), Kissimmee (Nos 4 and 18, hourly), Walt Disney World (No 50, every two hours), Universal Studios (No 21), and the youth hostel (No 50 to Disney then transfer to bus No 56, which stops right by the hostel; the last bus No 56 leaves Disney around 7 pm).

Shuttle & Limo Services
The biggest shuttle service in the area is Mears Transportation (☎ 407-423-5566), which runs vans between most major hotels, the youth hostel, campsites and the major theme parks. Expect to pay between $8 and $14 roundtrip for shuttle service unless your hotel or hostel has a special deal – many do.

Car & Motorcycle
The major car-rental companies all have offices in and around Orlando and at the airports. Several have desks at I-Drive hotels as well. See the Getting Around chapter for the toll-free numbers of the big companies.

Downtown Orlando has an infuriating one-way-street system that would seem to have been taken right out of either Kafka or Boston. Much of the eastern end of Church St is pedestrian only, and that which isn't mainly runs east only. Avoid the traffic circle around Lucerne Park to the south of Anderson St, where the southern area of down-

town is crossed by the East-West Expressway; if you're not careful you can go several times around Lake Lucerne before you get way over to the right and back into downtown.

Parking All downtown on-street parking is controlled by highly accurate digital parking meters, with highly accurate and seemingly digital parking enforcement personnel waiting to pounce with $10 tickets at the first second after meter expiration.

Parking for Church St Station is in the large public lot beneath I-4. Here a central meter system is in use. Remember your spot number and find the nearest central meter (a large yellow machine under a green umbrella). On the touch-tone key pad, enter your spot number, insert 75¢ per hour, then push the big button to the right for a receipt. Cops patrol constantly and possess an evil secret code that tells the central meter to tattle on scofflaws.

The City Parking Bureau (☎ 407-246-2154) also runs Central Blvd Garage at 53 W Central Blvd between Orange and Garland Aves; Library Garage at 112 E Central Blvd, opposite the Orlando Public Library; and Market Garage east of Church St Station (see Shopping earlier in this section); open 24 hours. Much more expensive private lots are also easily found.

Taxi
Fares are $3 for the first mile plus $1.50 for each additional mile. You need to call for a cab (as opposed to hailing one on the street). Major companies include Ace Metro Cab Co (☎ 407-855-1111), City Cab (☎ 407-422-5151) and Checker & Yellow Cab Co (☎ 407-699-9999).

AROUND ORLANDO
Winter Park
This pleasant college town just north of Orlando is a lovely place for a stroll or a boat ride (free on your birthday!), a cappuccino and some gallery- and museum-hopping. Park Ave is the main drag, where you'll find lots of cafés and trendy shops; like a mix of Miami Beach and Palm Beach,

CENTRAL

it's fashionable yet accessible, chic but not too expensive.

Get tourist information at the Winter Park Chamber of Commerce (☎ 407-644-8281), 150 N New York Ave.

Cornell Fine Arts Museum This well-respected museum (☎ 407-646-2526, www.rollins.edu/cfam), at 1000 Holt Ave on the Rollins College campus, presents rotating exhibits from its permanent collection year round, as well as traveling exhibitions in winter. It's open Tuesday to Friday 10 am to 5 pm and Saturday and Sunday 1 to 5 pm, closed Monday. Admission is free.

Charles Hosmer Morse Museum of American Art This pleasant and beautiful museum (☎ 407-645-5311), 445 Park Ave N, has a large Tiffany glass exhibit; we loved the exquisite *Magnolia Window*, made from drapery glass (which is heated and then folded to give it a three-dimensional look), and the *Butterfly Window*, which was made for Tiffany's New York house. Also on view are paintings and designs by Tiffany; late-19th- and 20th-century paintings and American art pottery. Admission is $2.50 for adults, $1 for children and students.

Albin Polasek Galleries The works of Czech sculptor Albin Polasek are shown here (☎ 407-674-6294), 633 Osceola Ave, in the serene lakeside gardens and interior of his last residence. As you enter the front garden you'll see the very impressive *Man Carving His Own Destiny* or *The Sower*. Inside, the house is a showcase exhibiting Polasek's sculpting tools and our favorite of his works, *Mother Crying Over World*. Enthusiastic and friendly volunteers will tell you more about the sculptor's life and

Fiction & Folklore: Zora Neale Hurston

Zora Neale Hurston (1901-60) was born in Eatonville, the first black incorporated town in the US, about 5 miles from Orlando. Her family broke apart when she was young, and she supported herself from the age of 14, working odd jobs and finding her way in 1919 to all-black Howard University in Washington, DC. In 1925 she moved to Harlem, the cultural capital of black America, and distinguished herself quickly as a bright young literary voice. Along with poet Langston Hughes and others, she rose to the forefront of what came to be known as the Harlem Renaissance, a flowering of black creative and intellectual achievement and a celebration of the African American experience.

Hurston came from a background of storytelling. As a child she'd listened to the men gathered on the porch of Joe Clark's store tell their 'big ol lies' to entertain one another. In later years, she became a good storyteller herself, which made her the life of every party in Harlem. Her interest in storytelling also led her to Barnard College, where she met Franz Boas – the father of modern American anthropology – and discovered the study of folklore. Under Boas' guidance, Zora won a research fellowship from Columbia University and headed back to the South to record the songs, tales, superstitions, games and traditions she'd grown up with.

In pursuit of folklore, she traveled from Florida to New Orleans and eventually into the rich culture of the Caribbean; she posed as a runaway bootlegger's moll, lived in the shanty towns of migrant turpentine workers and was poisoned nearly to death by a voodoo witch doctor in Haiti. But despite her travels and wild, far-flung adventures, Eatonville and the porch of Joe

CENTRAL

works. It's open Sunday 1 to 4 pm and Wednesday to Saturday 10 am to noon and 1 to 4 pm. Admission is free.

Scenic Boat Tours This company (☎ 407-644-4056) offers one-hour trips on 12 miles of the canals and lakes of the area, leaving from the eastern end of Morse Blvd. You'll pass by Rollins College, its Azalea Gardens, the small 'Isle of Sicily' and the Polasek Galleries, and you'll see local mansions and many birds. The tours leave every hour on the hour between 10 am and 4 pm daily, except Christmas. Admission is $7 for adults, $3 for children two to 11. Canoe and rowboat rentals are also available for $5 for the first hour, $1 for each additional hour.

Getting There & Away It's a snap to get from the Lynx Bus Center to Winter Park; bus Nos 1 and 9 make the trip hourly. By car,

head north on I-4 to exit 46, go east on Lee Rd and you'll hit downtown Winter Park.

Kissimmee

The area around Kissimmee (pronounced 'kih-SIH-mee') was once a peaceful landscape of swamps and green, but the extraordinary growth of theme parks has had a profound effect on the surroundings. Kissimmee's main strip, Hwy 192 (called Irlo Bronson Memorial Hwy and Vine Ave), is a horror of strip development – a depressing, sprawling ribbon of endless concrete, motels, shopping malls, fast-food and chain restaurants, wanna-be attractions, murderous traffic, blazing neon, tourist traps, oil-change joints and discount ticket stands of dubious reliability. It is also the area's cheapest place to bed down for the night.

For tourist information, contact the Kissimmee/St Cloud Convention & Visitors

Fiction & Folklore: Zora Neale Hurston

Clark's store would remain at the center of her work, appearing again and again in both her folklore and her fiction.

Mules and Men was published in 1935 and is considered by many the greatest work on black American folklore ever written. In Southern vernacular, it recounts tales of conjure men and hoodoo cures; Ol Massa and his favorite slave, John; Brer Rabbit and Brer Gator (like Disney has never seen them); and more. Before Hurston, white folklorists had portrayed black culture as the product of childish, silly and unsophisticated minds. Hurston instead revealed its wit, humor, imagination and complexity.

Her most famous novel, *Their Eyes Were Watching God*, was published in 1937. It is one of the earliest black feminist novels, telling the story of Janie Crawford, an independent black woman who loved who and how she wanted. The book was savaged by contemporaries like Richard Wright, author of *Black Boy* and *Native Son*, because it did not address race relations and black oppression but rather black community and black folk.

Hurston died in a welfare home in 1960 and was buried in an unmarked grave in the Garden of Heavenly Rest, in Fort Pierce. In the 1970s, a few dedicated black writers and scholars began the 'Hurston Renaissance' – her seven books were reissued, and Alice Walker made a pilgrimage to Fort Pierce to place a memorial stone on her grave. It reads:

Zora Neale Hurston
'A Genius of the South'
Novelist/Folklorist/Anthropologist
1901-1960

– Laini Taylor

CENTRAL

Bureau (☎ 407-847-5000, 800-327-9159) at 1925 W Hwy 192.

Splendid China This theme park (☎ 407-396-7111, 800-244-6226, www.floridasplendidchina.com), 3000 Splendid China Blvd, just off Hwy 192 west of I-4, does a tremendous job of simulating China: the crowds are thick and jostle you, and the staff, who barely speak English, are recalcitrant, heavily bureaucratic, loathe to part with specific details and generally uncooperative – almost exactly like in Beijing but without the spitting! At least, that's how it was when we were here.

Nevertheless, it *is* an interesting park with exquisite attention to detail and glorious landscaping (butterflies were everywhere when we visited). The exhibits are miniature replicas of famous Chinese sights, such as the Stone Forest, Great Wall, Temple of Confucius, Summer Palace, Imperial Palace/Forbidden City and Dr Sun Yat Sen's Mausoleum. If you follow the guides religiously you'll probably learn a lot about Chinese history.

We were fascinated by the **Terra Cotta Warriors** display, a replica of the tomb that Emperor Qinshijuang had built in order to have all his concubines, thousands of soldiers, his horses and vehicles buried with him (the original tomb was discovered in 1974).

To get information and background on a particular site, push the little button on the green box at the site or simply read the sign (they are identical). A free tram circles the park, hitting most sites. Guided tours are available for $5 and leave from Guest Services.

All kinds of performances (magicians, jugglers, etc) are held at different locations throughout the park; schedules are available at the ticket window. There are five restaurants within the park serving various regional Chinese dishes.

It's open 9:30 am to 7 pm daily. Admission is $26.99 for adults, $16.99 for kids five to 12, and $24.29 for AARP and AAA members.

A World of Orchids A lush display of hundreds of varieties of orchids in an indoor tropical jungle, A World of Orchids (☎ 407-396-1887, 407-396-1881), 2501 Old Lake Wilson Rd, jolts the senses on first sight. The effect of walking from the stark, concrete entry area through the giant metal doors into the gardens is a lot like walking into *Star Trek*'s Holodeck: you are suddenly immersed in a glorious land of windmill and areca palms, beautiful ferns, pineapple ginger, spider lilies and orchids galore, including *Dendrobium*, *Phalaenopsis*, *Vanda* and *Onicidium*. (Most of the plants you see here can be bought as well.)

Follow your nose from one luscious scent to the next – we found the back right quadrant to be the most fragrant when we visited. Or check out the goldfish pond, where the huge (and fat) goldfish are so used to being fed that if you hold your hand out over the water they'll scramble for food – whether you drop any or not. Guided tours are available, and an outside walking trail is planned for the near future.

Hours are Tuesday to Sunday 9:30 am to 4:30 pm, closed Monday, major holidays and the last two weeks of August. Admission is $4.50 per person, ages 16 and under are free.

Green Meadows Petting Farm This combination working farm/petting zoo (☎ 407-846-0770), on Poinciana Blvd (there's no street address) about 5 miles south of Hwy 192, is a pretty cool place for kids. They can run amok here, touching and petting cows, goats, donkeys, geese, ducks and chickens. They can also ride on horses and, if you take the tour, milk a cow! Tours (included with admission) leave regularly between 9:30 am and 4 pm. Admission is a little stiff at $15 per person (kids under two get in free), but you could make a day of it by bringing a picnic and hanging out among the creatures on the farm grounds.

Flying Tigers Warbird Air Museum A must for WWII nostalgia buffs, this museum (☎ 407-933-1942), 231 N Hoagland Blvd, in Hangar No 5 at Kissimmee Regional Airport, displays WWII fighter planes in various stages of restoration. Workers can take up to several years per plane, and some of the finished products can be seen for a fleeting period before they fly away to join air shows and air-tour-company fleets.

From the HI/AYH Orlando/Kissimmee Resort, go east on W Hwy 192 to the second light after the Medieval Times dinner theater and turn right; the entrance to the airport is about three quarters of a mile down on the left-hand side of the road. It's open Monday to Saturday 9 am to 5:30 pm, Sunday 9 am to 5 pm. Admission, including a guided tour, is $8 adults, $6 seniors over 60 and children five to 12, under five free.

Places to Stay There are plenty of accommodations in the area.

Camping The **KOA Kissimmee campground** (☎ 407-396-2400, 800-331-1453, 4771 W Hwy 192), just east of I-4, has tent sites for $25.95 and RV sites with full hookups for $39.95. Kamping Kabins run $49.95 to $59.95 for two adults.

Raccoon Lake Camp Resort (☎ 407-239-4148, 800-776-9644, 8555 W Hwy 192) is very close to the HI/AYH Orlando/Kissimmee Resort. Tent sites are $18 year round; sites with water and electricity are $23 in low season, $29 in high season; sites with full hookups are $25/32.

Hostels We have stayed at the **HI/AYH Orlando/Kissimmee Resort** (☎ 407-396-8282, reservations 800-909-4776, code 33, hi_orlandoresort@compuserve.com, 4840 W Hwy 192) twice and had fun both times. It looks more like a motel than a hostel, but it has a large common area and kitchen, a small swimming pool and a lake out back (though swimming in the lake is not allowed). Rooms (dorms and motel-style private rooms, some with kitchenettes) are clean and comfortable, and activities include weekly barbecues, swamp walks, trips to spring-training baseball games and games like Scrabble and Jenga in the common room.

Dorm beds cost $16 for HI/AYH members, $19 for nonmembers; private rooms run from $35 to $81 depending on the size, the season and whether you're an HI/AYH member. You *can* find motel rooms that are

cheaper than the cost of two dorm beds here. However, the hostel's rooms tend to be cleaner than those at most fleabag motels, the common areas and activities offer you a chance to meet other travelers and it's the safest option in town for women traveling alone.

It's inconvenient to get here without a car. From downtown, take Lynx bus No 50 to Disney and transfer to No 56, which stops right by the hostel. Also see Getting Around in the Orlando section earlier this chapter for information on getting here from the airport.

Motels & Hotels We have visited dozens and dozens of the more than 100 motels along Hwy 192 and found that with few exceptions they were virtually identical. All offer reasonably friendly service and reasonably clean, slightly rundown (but perfectly acceptable) rooms with brownish carpets and cable TV.

Rates tend to stay very low: typically, the cheaper motels run about $20/28 single/double most of the year, with bursts (they call them 'high season') during school holidays, when you should expect about a $15 to $20 increase. At Christmastime, the average double on the strip is between $44 and $55.

Of the cookie-cutter standard motels and hotels along the W Hwy 192 strip, the following are as good as any:

Buena Vista Motel
(☎ 407-396-2100, No 5200) – has an attached liquor store

Casa Rosa Motel
(☎ 407-396-2020, 800-432-0665, No 4600) – clean, with friendly service

Econo Lodge
(☎ 407-396-4343, 800-228-2027, No 4985)

Golden Link Motel
(☎ 407-396-0555, junction of Hwy 535)

Key Motel
(☎ 407-396-6200, No 4810) – very average; boasts that 'cold beer is available here'

Park Inn International
(☎ 407-396-1376, 800-327-0072, No 4960) – cleaner than most, with discounts for AAA members

CENTRAL

Ramada Limited
(☎ 407-424-2621, No 9200)

Residence Inn by Marriott
(☎ 407-396-2056, 800-228-9290, No 4786) – a nice, family-oriented place, with more expensive but absolutely superior rooms and suites. Prices here *are* negotiable, despite appearances: in high season it lists $109 for a studio (a suite with a queen-size bed and fold-out couch) and $189 for deluxe penthouses, but we were offered as low as $79 and $129 for the same rooms.

Sun Motel
(☎ 407-396-2673, No 5020) – a good deal and cleaner than average

Super 8 Motel
(☎ 407-396-1144, No 4880) – next to the HI Orlando/Kissimmee Resort; rooms include breakfast and HBO

Places to Eat Hwy 192 is lined with every conceivable fast-food and upscale fast-food place imaginable, including Red Lobster, the Outback Steakhouse, Shoney's, KFC, McDonald's and Denny's.

Restaurants & Cafés The always excellent **Taco Cabana** (☎ 407-846-1633, 910 W Hwy 192) has seriously good breakfast burritos for $1.59, bacon and eggs for 99¢ or a full breakfast for $2.99. Lots of combination plates are $3.50, the half-chicken platter with rice, beans, flour tortillas and lime is $5.29, a pitcher of frozen margaritas is $7.99 and three tacos and a soft drink cost $3.33.

The **Puerto Rico Café** (☎ 407-897-6399, 507 W Hwy 192) has meat dishes for $5 to $9 and seafood dishes for $10 to $15.

At **Havana's Cafe** (☎ 407-846-6771, 3628 W Hwy 192), lunch specials are $5 to $6, pepper steak $6.99, chicken filet skillet $8.95 and seafood dishes $12.95.

There's good French-influenced Thai food at **Basil's Restaurant** (☎ 407-846-1116, 1009 W Hwy 192), where appetizers range $4.50 to $8, and main courses like lime-grilled chicken with honey butter are $9.95; others go up to about $15.

Dinner Theater For some reason, Kissimmee is dinner-theater central, with three major offerings for those who like to watch, say, jousting while dining. The prices listed

below are for tickets at the door, undiscounted – *always* check in tourist rags and handout coupon books for discount tickets, which you'll always find and which could get you significant savings.

Medieval Times (☎ 407-396-1518, 800-327-4024, 4510 W Hwy 192) offers 'dinner and tournament' – mainly jousting and sword fighting (this is appetizing?) accompanied by a dinner of chicken and ribs, soup, a cocktail and two rounds of beer, wine or soda. The cost is $38.95 for adults, $23.95 for kids three to 12. Shows begin at 6 and/or 8:30 pm and last two hours.

The gaudy-neon **Arabian Nights** (☎ 407-239-9223, 800-553-6116, 6225 W Hwy 192), just east of I-4, promises a slew of performing horses, chariot races and the like. The two-hour dinner shows begin at 7:30 pm, and dinner includes either prime rib or veggie lasagna, along with salad, potatoes and lots of vegetables, dessert and unlimited Budweiser beer (this is appetizing?), soft drinks or wine. It's $36.95 for adults, $23.95 for children.

Capone's Dinner & Show (☎ 407-397-2378, 4740 W Hwy 192), a mile east of Hwy 535, is certainly the funniest dinner-theater in these parts. This gangland revue is set in a 'cabaret and speakeasy' in Prohibition-era Chicago (though half the cast members seem to have Long Island accents) and features 'mobsters, dames in hootchie kootchie outfits' – you get the drift. The unlimited buffet (take a deep breath) includes lasagna, ziti, sausage and peppers, chicken, ham, veggies, dessert, coffee, soft drinks, beer, sangria and rumrunners. It's $37 for adults, $24 for kids. (Note that there are *lots* of coupons out there for 50% off or buy-one-get-one-free, so search the tourist mags before paying.) The two-hour shows start at 7:30 pm.

Getting There & Away Kissimmee is about 25 miles southwest of downtown Orlando; take bus Nos 4 and 18 from the Lynx Bus Center. It's about a half-hour drive on I-4, or you can take the Orange Blossom Trail to where it intersects with Hwy 192 and turn west.

Yeehaw Junction
• population approximately 100

There's not much going on at Yeehaw Junction, about 60 miles south of Orlando, but the town has two die-hard tourist attractions that pack 'em in, as people make the journey from Miami to Orlando along Florida's Turnpike. One is pretty ho-hum: the Yeehaw Travel Center (☎ 407-436-1616), a discount ticket outlet open Sunday to Thursday 7 am to 9 pm, Friday and Saturday 7 am to 10 pm. The second attraction has charm, character and the dignity of having been placed on the National Register of Historic Places. We speak, of course, of the Desert Inn, one of central Florida's famous bordellos once operated to entertain workers on the Florida East Coast Railway and later I-95.

The *Desert Inn Motel* (☎ *407-436-1054, 5570 S Kenansville Rd*) has been completely renovated by owner Beverly Zicheck, who has created what is probably Florida's first Bordello Museum. You can even stay here, and though room service isn't what it used to be, the food itself is pretty rockin'. The inn charges $33.50 a night per room, slightly less if you're a truck driver. The museum, in several of the rooms, shows the bedrooms as they looked during the place's heyday from 1889 to 1953, complete with red satin bedspreads, hardwood floors, red-lined swings and saddles. Admission to the museum is $1.

The *restaurant* downstairs serves up awesome chili, and everything is homemade. Some people line up for the periodic roast beef dinners (Beverly starts with a 30lb piece of meat) that cost $7.95 and come with dressing, real mashed potatoes, coleslaw, Texas toast and a vegetable. Other more exotic offerings include gator burgers for $3.95, turtle, gator or frog dinners at $9.95 or a turtle/gator/frog combo at $11.95. At breakfast (the place opens at 7 am), the special is hash browns with onions topped with bell pepper, ham and eggs for $4.50. Any time of day, try a slice of homemade pie ($2.25 for meringue types, $2 for standard apple, peach, cherry or blueberry).

From January 18 to 21 the Desert Inn hosts the Bluegrass Festival and Chili Cook-off; contact Beverly for more information.

From Florida's Turnpike, take the Yeehaw Junction exit and head west at the traffic light for about half a mile – look for the sign that says 'Desert Inn Good Food Bar' – it's at the intersection of US Hwy 441 and Hwy 60.

Walt Disney World Resort

When Southern California's Disneyland attraction took off in a huge way, the concept of theme parks changed dramatically and permanently. Disneyland quickly became the standard for a family-oriented vacation resort, and parks everywhere found themselves scrambling to bring themselves up to the new scratch.

But something that especially caught Walt Disney's attention was that other hotels and concessions had begun building up around his property, in a manner that he (probably rightly) felt was entirely parasitic. So in the mid-1960s, under the *nom de guerre* Reedy Creek Development Company, Walt bought up thousands of acres of land in central Florida, with the revolutionary idea of creating a family-vacation 'city,' every aspect of which – hotels, resorts, restaurants, cafés, parks, parking and transport – he could control and profit from. The success of Disney's landgrab was perhaps topped only by its negotiating techniques with the state of Florida, which granted the company, among a lot of other things, the right to self-govern the municipality.

Walt Disney died in 1966 and his brother Roy took over responsibilities for guiding the project through to completion. The park opened in 1971 and in its first year saw more than 10 million visitors. When Disney World celebrated its 25th anniversary in October 1996, the park – and its 35,000 staff members – had hosted more than 500 million guests. That's about 23 million a year or 65,000 per *day*.

That should give you some idea of the staggering size of this operation. It is indeed its own city, complete with an elaborate

CENTRAL

WALT DISNEY WORLD RESORT

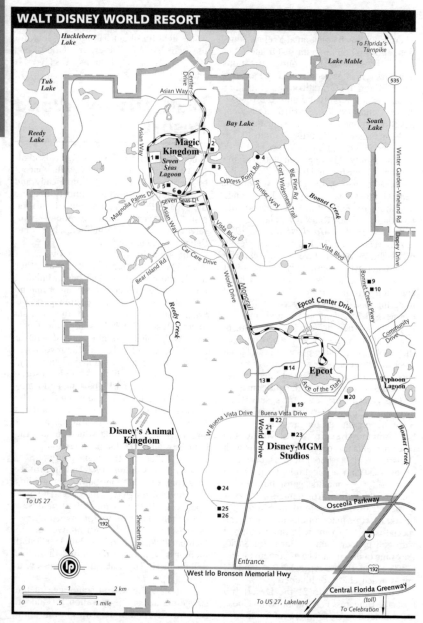

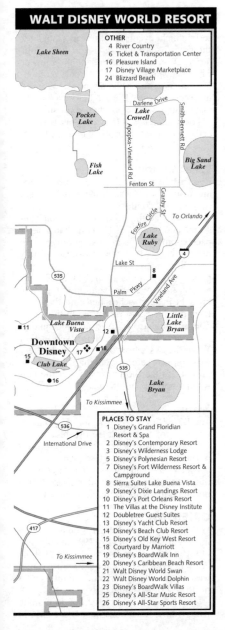

WALT DISNEY WORLD RESORT

OTHER
4   River Country
6   Ticket & Transportation Center
16 Pleasure Island
17 Disney Village Marketplace
24 Blizzard Beach

Lake Sheen

Pocket Lake

Lake Crowell

Darlene Drive

Apopka-Vineland Rd

Smith-Bennett Rd

Fish Lake

Big Sand Lake

Fenton St

Granby St

Foxfire Circle

To Orlando

Lake Ruby

4

Lake St

8

Palm Pkwy

Vineland Ave

535

Lake Buena Vista

Little Lake Bryan

11

Downtown Disney

12

15   Club Lake

17   18

535

16

Lake Bryan

To Kissimmee

536

International Drive

417

To Kissimmee

PLACES TO STAY
1   Disney's Grand Floridian Resort & Spa
2   Disney's Contemporary Resort
3   Disney's Wilderness Lodge
5   Disney's Polynesian Resort
7   Disney's Fort Wilderness Resort & Campground
8   Sierra Suites Lake Buena Vista
9   Disney's Dixie Landings Resort
10 Disney's Port Orleans Resort
11 The Villas at the Disney Institute
12 Doubletree Guest Suites
13 Disney's Yacht Club Resort
14 Disney's Beach Club Resort
15 Disney's Old Key West Resort
16 Courtyard by Marriott
19 Disney's BoardWalk Inn
20 Disney's Caribbean Beach Resort
21 Walt Disney World Swan
22 Walt Disney World Dolphin
23 Disney's BoardWalk Villas
25 Disney's All-Star Music Resort
26 Disney's All-Star Sports Resort

transportation system (featuring buses, trams, ferries, shuttles and a monorail) that is the envy of many US cities; full-fledged emergency services like a fire department, several medical centers, and an efficient and incorruptible police force; an energy plant; a *florist;* and an entire building dedicated to something called 'DOT compliance, RCID Environmental Permitting & Planning, Resort Design and Resort Displays.' The complex tunnel system beneath the Magic Kingdom park has *at least* 27 different entrances, which enables cast members to materialize as if by magic. All this is designed to make the theme park as isolated, self-sufficient and perfectly happy as it can be.

And just as Walt had envisioned, every penny you spend on anything goes to some Disney subsidiary or another. That's not to say it's unfair: it is not. While people can be shocked by the sticker price of a Disney vacation, we will say this: it is good value for the money, a truly family-oriented vacation spot that doesn't neglect the kids *or* the adults (it says a lot that more than 1000 couples get married here every year, and that the millennium week has been sold out since 1993) and offers a great feeling of fun and safety. While there are no bargains to be had, neither are there any rip-offs.

If it seems like we're kissing Mouse ass, you're wrong. The Disney Magic, we think, is the ability to suck at least $100 from every man, woman and child in the place per day. Over a three day visit in 1998 we dropped $200 a day in extra little charges.

We calls 'em like we sees 'em, and when we see a trap or something we don't like, we tell you about it. But we do say that if you're thinking about going, you'll probably have a great time. Now if we could just get all these screaming little kids out of here...

There's no way to cover all that Disney has to offer in this kind of format, so what follows is a highlights tour.

PLANNING
When to Go
As far as accommodations go, the cheapest time of year here is from the beginning of

372   Walt Disney World Resort – Orientation

CENTRAL

Not Without Seeing Minnie

Customer satisfaction is the name of the game at Walt Disney World Resort, and the staff has been trained to withstand with a smile onslaughts of abuse that would level mere mortals.

Staff (they're called 'cast members') are empowered to go to heroic lengths to ensure that a visitor (you are called a 'guest') is happy about everything. This covers things like giving an extra cinnamon roll to the family that's too hot and tired to have any more fun, to coordinating searches for missing kids.

During our visit, we watched in amazement as an angry mother told a cast member that she'd come all the way down from New York City and her daughter hadn't seen Minnie Mouse once. There was no way, by god, that she was leaving before her daughter saw Minnie.

The cast member found out that there were no Minnies around (there are, of course, several), and after looking at the guest again and seeing the determination in her eyes, the cast member went ahead and called a Character Zoo (there are, of course, several) and arranged for a Minnie to get into costume and haul her tail out there pronto.

It's something – the production of a French university student in an air-conditioned Muppet-fur suit in under an hour – we don't recommend you try at home. From angry start to Waving Minnie/Smiling Kid/Satisfied Mom finish, this transaction took seven minutes and 40 seconds.

That's cast dedication and a finely honed machine.

Have a nice day.

August to about December 18; it's very expensive around holidays. July and August are hot: temperatures average in the mid-90s (°F), and humidity levels hover at what feels to be 150%. Downpours occur frequently. For the best weather, come in early autumn,

but note that closing hours in autumn are earlier than at other times. Also note that certain night events like fireworks and laser shows are seasonal, so if you have your heart set on seeing the millennium show or whatever will come after it to replace Illumi-Nations (see the Millennium Show boxed text), check with Disney before going to make sure it will be on when you visit.

For reasons best left to sociologists, weekends tend to be less crowded than the beginning of the week.

What to Bring
Even when it's raining the temperatures are usually warm, so bring a lightweight rain poncho, comfortable clothing that you don't mind getting wet, a bathing suit, sunscreen and sunglasses. Carry it all in a backpack compact enough to keep on your lap during rides. Bring a two-liter, solidly resealing bottle of drinking water per person (water refills are free at any Disney restaurant). We saw that many people brought in sandwiches, but note that food from outside is not permitted in the parks. The grounds are sprayed and mosquitoes are generally not a problem, even in Fort Wilderness Campground (though there we'd play it safe). Speaking of spraying, bring a spritzer bottle to shoot at the kids when it gets too hot in line.

Maps
The *Walt Disney World Resort Map* has an overview of the whole resort, breakdown maps of the main parks, and a useful transportation network chart showing services between parks and resorts. You get free handout maps of each particular park. Transportation maps are available at the TTC.

ORIENTATION
Walt Disney World Resort is on a formerly marshy area north of Hwy 192, roughly west of I-4 and skirted on its east and some of the north by Hwy 535. It's about 23 miles southwest of the city of Orlando, about 4 miles northwest of Kissimmee.

The huge resort consists of four main parks (Magic Kingdom, Epcot, Disney-MGM

Studios and Disney's Animal Kingdom); two main water parks (Blizzard Beach and Typhoon Lagoon); numerous themed resort hotels; and areas for other activities, like Disney Village Marketplace.

Magic Kingdom is the northernmost park. The main Ticket & Transportation Center (TTC) is off of Seven Seas Drive, as are the main bus station and parking lots for Magic Kingdom.

Disney's answer to Orlando's Church St Station ('We have information that people are drinking elsewhere, sir') has the vaguely lewd name of Pleasure Island; it's at the eastern end of the property, just west of I-4.

INFORMATION

Getting information about Disney is one area where we feel that things could be a little easier – or at least cheaper: Disney does not even have a toll-free information or reservations telephone number. But unless you're actually staying at a Disney resort – and you don't have to – you really won't need to call Disney beforehand, anyway.

For reservations at Disney resorts, a slew of Disney-related information, and park prices and hours call ☎ 407-934-7639 weekdays 8 am to 10 pm, or Saturday and Sunday 8 am to 6 pm. The TDD number for hearing impaired guests is ☎ 407-939-7670. US military personnel and their families (who are given discounted admissions and hotel lodgings) should call Disney's Shades of Green Resort (☎ 407-824-3600) for information.

At peak times, you can expect a wait of about five to 10 minutes just to get to speak to an operator, and then another 10 to 15 minutes on the phone discussing options and making the reservation. The best time to call is early in the morning, as close to 8 am as possible. If you get tired of being on hold, you can enter your phone number and have Disney call you back – they promise to do so within two days (if you haven't heard from them by then, call back). Operators are, of course, preternaturally friendly.

For other information, call the main Disney operator at ☎ 407-824-4321. By mail, send requests for brochures or other information to Walt Disney Guest Communica-

tions, PO Box 10000, Lake Buena Vista, FL 32830-1000.

Disney on the Web is a very good option: start at www.disney.go.com/DisneyWorld. Also try Todd McCartney's fabulous site, www.disneycorner.com, with a zillion Disney links and heaps of information.

Money

There are cash machines in every park. You can change money at the Sun Bank in every park, from 9 am to 4 pm, and at Guest Relations after 4 pm, but we recommend bringing US money as exchange rates are generally poor. All Disney concessions accept traveler's checks, American Express cards and Visa and MasterCard (but not Discover) credit cards.

The Disney Dollar (D$) – a coupon traded on a 1:1 exchange rate with the US dollar – is a wonderful scam. While normal American money can be used anywhere in Disney, the powers that be would rather you use Disney Dollars, which are as good as cash in all Disney parks and concessions and at Disney stores around the USA. The reason for this is obvious: how many people spend every Disney Dollar they exchange? The answer, of course, is none, and Disney pockets the difference. If you want to buy a souvenir, you can get Disney Dollars at various places around the park. Mickey is on the D$1, Goofy on the D$5 and Minnie on the D$10.

Buy Tickets Early

With the exception of one-day passes, which must be bought at the gate, it's always a better idea to buy tickets in advance. Tickets should, if possible, be ordered three weeks in advance. If you're on the road, have them mailed to your hostel or hotel. Lines inside the park to buy tickets are long and slow. So, if you don't already have tickets, show up *early* – at least an hour before opening.

Admission Prices

Disney raises its prices every year, so these will be low when you go. It's best to buy your tickets before you get to the park – at a Disney store, or through the mail or Web – as lines to buy tickets can be very long.

Figuring out what type of ticket you need can get confusing, and you really need to pay attention to avoid the disappointment of being told that your ticket doesn't cover the attractions you want.

Children under three years are admitted free. Ticket prices given below (tax not included) apply for people 10 and up/three to nine:

One-Day One-Park
It's just that: one park only. You *can't* dash between parks, so be absolutely certain that the park you're entering is the one you want. These tickets are only available at the Disney gate and are only good on the day issued. $44/35.

Four-Day Park Hopper Pass
Unlimited admission to Magic Kingdom, Epcot, Disney's Animal Kingdom and Disney-MGM Studios for four days. You can visit any combination of those parks on any of the four days, but note that this *does not* include the water parks or any other attractions. It never expires; you can come back and use unused days whenever you want. $167/134.

Theme Park Annual Pass
One year unlimited admission to Magic Kingdom, Disney's Animal Kingdom, Epcot and Disney-MGM Studios. $309/259.

Five-Day Park Hopper Pass
This is a tricky one. It provides unlimited admission on *any* five days. You can come back, say, on another trip – even a year later – and reuse the ticket. You can visit any combination of those parks on any of the five days. Now here's the tricky part: this ticket also includes admission to Blizzard Beach, Typhoon Lagoon, River Country and Pleasure Island, but only for 'a period of seven days beginning with the first date stamped (first use).' So if you come back a year later you can still get into the theme parks, but you'll have to repurchase tickets to the water parks and Pleasure Island. $210/168.

Water Parks
A one-day pass for unlimited admission to Blizzard Beach, Typhoon Lagoon, River Country and Pleasure Island. $26.95/21.50.

Pleasure Island
Either a one day or annual pass for unlimited admission to Pleasure Island. Note the price of an annual pass is just a tad higher than two single admissions, so if you're going to go at least three times, the annual pass is probably worth it. Now ask yourself if you really want *three* nights of frozen blue drinks to make the annual pass worth your while (drinks, of course, cost extra). One-day $18.86, annual $54.95; no one under 18 admitted.

River Country One-Day Pass
$15.95/12.50

Discounts Florida residents are occasionally given hefty discounts on Disney admissions – there's no way to know when the specials are on without asking. During Spring Break periods students with an ISIC card can also get discounts. Be sure to ask if you qualify for a discount before you buy your ticket, as no one's going to come out and tell you.

Other than for Floridians, students and US military, no discount tickets for Disney attractions are available anywhere (not even for seniors, usually), so anyone who offers you one also may have a bridge to sell you in the New York area.

When you arrive at a turnstile, insert your pass into the slot at the front of the turnstile. The machine reads your card, decides whether you're worthy of admission and, if you are, unlocks the gate and gives you your ticket back.

Post & Communications

Mailboxes are available in all the Disney parks and hotels. Within the Disney property, you can dial ☎ *88 for reservations at Disney restaurants or resorts.

Books

Planning your daily itinerary within the parks will allow you to maximize time spent on rides, as opposed to walking through the parks, getting sidetracked by shows and parades, 'ooh! they're selling cinnamon rolls,' and other obstacles.

The most complete book to the resort is Birnbaum's propaganda-packed *Walt Disney World*, Disney's Official Guide.

A zealously pro-Disney college student named Todd D McCartney began compiling his self-published *Walt Disney World Made Simple* guidebook for some friends in England. Released initially only on the Internet, McCartney's book has now sold several thousand copies in print ($6.95) and should do very well indeed: it's good, and contains totally independent advice, though we think he gushes a wee bit sometimes. It's available at www.disneycorner.com/wdwms.

For the alternative view, check out Carl Hiaasen's *Team Rodent: How Disney Devours the World*.

Organized Tours
Nine different tours are currently available in the parks through the Disney tours department (☎ 407-560-6233). They range dramatically, from two-hour Saturday tours of the World Showcase's architecture, design and construction for $30; to the daily four-hour Keys to the Kingdom tour behind the scenes at Magic Kingdom (which includes a look at the Production Center and the tunnel system) for $50; to the Monday and Wednesday to Friday seven-hour Grand Backstage Magic tour through the main parks for $185.

Medical Services
The excellent nurse-staffed first-aid centers in each park hand out bandages, treat sunburn and can cope with more serious injury as well.

Disabled Travelers
The excellent *Guidebook for Guests with Disabilities* has maps and information on everything in the parks.

Disney has been outstanding in ensuring accessibility to disabled guests. Most attractions, shows and restaurants are wheelchair accessible. All the signs for rides carry information for disabled guests as to turbulence. Motorized wheelchairs are available for rental, but you can't use them on many rides; you'll have to switch to a nonmotorized wheelchair. On some rides you'll need to leave the chair entirely (staff will assist you if necessary).

Visitors with other disabilities will find assistance as well; braille and prerecorded tours are available. Check with Guest Relations for more information.

Personal Translator Units are available at Guest Relations. They're narration devices for the hearing impaired that offer tours in certain areas of Epcot in English, French, Spanish and German. The units cost $4 plus a $40 deposit that's refundable only if you return the unit on the same day.

Baby Centers & Sitters
There are baby centers in each park; see each park's handout map for specific locations, or check at Guest Relations. For private baby-sitting, call Kinder-Care (☎ 407-827-5444).

Lockers
Each park has a set of lockers for visitors' use. The cost is $3 a day, with a $2 deposit.

Kennels
Kennels are available at Magic Kingdom (☎ 407-824-6568), Epcot (☎ 407-560-6229), Disney-MGM Studios (☎ 407-560-4282) and Fort Wilderness Resort & Campground (☎ 407-824-2735). All cost $6 per day and $11 overnight, though there are no attendants at night.

Parking
The parking fee is $5 per car, $6 per camper/trailer, $10 per bus. The lots are enormous and go on forever (trams come by frequently). Pay close attention to the character and row number you're parked in. The reference marker is a Disney character: Pluto 44 will be in the Pluto Lot, row 44. A section of your parking permit is detachable and designed to have you write down your spot. If you do lose your car, after calling yourself a bonehead, find a uniformed attendant, who will mournfully arrange for a car to take you around until you figure it all out.

RIDES
Rides at Disney World are kind of tame. If you're looking for mad, swooping roller coasters or really terrifying stuff, head for

Busch Gardens in Tampa. The scariest exceptions to this rule include the amazing Tower of Terror (Disney-MGM Studios) and the final plunge at Splash Mountain (Magic Kingdom), which is as heart-in-throat as you'll really want.

Flight simulators are rooms that pivot, buck and rock in perfect time with a picture on a screen. So in Body Wars (Epcot), when you're placed in a miniaturized pod and injected into the human body, get set for a wild ride. There are several simulator rides here, and we include Honey I Shrunk the Audience (Epcot) in that category.

Lines

Crowds can get amazing, especially in high seasons. Disney provides in-line entertainment, ingeniously hiding the snake formation of a line so you can't tell how long it is, putting up signs that overestimate the actual waiting time to trick you into feeling like

you got away with something – but you're going to stand in line for 45 minutes to an hour to go down Splash Mountain. It could be a charming 45 minutes, but 45 minutes it is. Bring sunscreen.

Most rides have signs posting the approximate waiting time. If you want to test Disney security, try to cut in line – we saw two people try on two occasions and both were nabbed by very polite, suited and burly gentlemen who appeared seemingly out of nowhere.

The only strategy, unfortunately, is get there early and get in line for the most popular rides first. We found that in downpours – very common in the summer – people tend to seek shelter, and that's always a good time to nip into a line. And if you or your kids are not absolutely devoted to the idea of a parade, you're in luck: lines empty considerably while they're on.

Autograph Books & Passports

These things are very popular with kids; you can buy them here or bring your own. They are used to collect character autographs, and stamps in the passport from the different 'lands' in Epcot. Do the characters a favor and bring a large, thick pen – it's hard to grab a skinny little ballpoint in a 50lb rubber suit.

MAGIC KINGDOM

When most people think of Disney World, they are thinking of Magic Kingdom: its centerpiece, Cinderella's Castle, is the most recognizable of Disney's logos. The castle isn't really an attraction, it's just kinda there, though it holds a nice restaurant and some shops.

Walt Disney World Railroad, a steam-driven locomotive, circumnavigates the entire park, with stops at the main entrance, Frontierland and Mickey's Starland.

Main Street, USA

This is the first area of the park you'll see; it's a quaint replica of a good ol' American town. You can ride on a horse-drawn trolley (it's great to see the doo-doo cleanup person following the cart) or spend money in all the

Gay Day at Disney

Gay Day started in 1991 with a notice in a local gay computer bulletin board service saying, 'Hey, if you're into Disney let's show up.' Disney eventually put up disclaimers saying this was not an official event, but over the years it has grown into one of its biggest money-making days, and Disney (whose recent record of fair treatment to gay and lesbian employees has been exemplary, going so far as to extend health-care benefits to same-sex partners) now not only tolerates but assists in planning the event. Gay Day is still not an official Disney event, but in 1999 an estimated 70,000 gay and lesbian visitors descended on Cinderella's Castle on what is now a gay Florida tradition: Gay Day at Disney, the first weekend in June. For more information, get in touch with Good Times Tours at ☎ 305-864-9431, or check out the Gay Day Website (www.gayday.com).

Why Don't We Do It in the Moat?

Disney cast members, as chipper as they may be, are a little like New York City cops: they've seen it all. But admirable company loyalty makes them uncomfortable when asked about anything that may be construed as being 'against' Disney.

So when we asked around about the most outrageous thing that's happened at Disney, there were lots of tight-lipped smiles and not too much else.

But then: paydirt. A former cast member (and we won't tell you their nationality or sex) laughingly mentioned one incident in which a young couple smoked marijuana and then stripped naked and tried to have sex under a bridge on the banks of the moat surrounding Cinderella's Castle in Magic Kingdom. A couple of months later, we met a member of that very party and got more of the story.

It was a group of Floridians on holiday with their teenagers, and yes, the parents admit that their then-14-year-old son (let's call him 'James') met a teenage woman in the park, shared his marijuana with her, and, after a little discussion, the two agreed to have sex under the bridge.

They say that the teens were nabbed by undercover officers, posing as tourists, who popped up out of nowhere before any serious action had taken place, forced the naked teens to dress and then hauled them into custody. And as in Beverly Hills, the officers were forceful yet exceedingly polite. Disney won't really comment on its security forces, though it is generally believed that they have the power of arrest and that they operate as undercover agents who mingle with crowds, watching for pickpockets and other miscreants – including, apparently, copulating couples.

As for James, he says he was told by the Disney security that not only was he being ejected from the park – which is pretty much par for the course – he was also being declared *persona non grata* at all Disney property worldwide. Forever. If this is true, Disney may have succeeded where several noteworthy American politicians have failed: deportation of troublemakers.

Don't mess with the Mouse.

shops that line the street (the shops stay open for up to an hour after the park officially closes).

New Tomorrowland

With space and spacey stuff, this is the area that most kids head for first – especially with the drawing power of its two flagship rides: ExtraTERRORestrial Alien Encounter and Space Mountain.

Tomorrowland Transit Authority This is a mini-monorail ride above and around New Tomorrowland. It's a good way to get an orientation tour of the section, and you'll even pass through the Space Mountain ride, so

anyone in your party who may be getting cold feet can get a preview. Another good thing is that there's no waiting for this train ride.

ExtraTERRORestrial Alien Encounter This can scare the daylights out of younger kids, who will then ask to do it again. When you enter, an electronic steel scientist (whose voice will be instantly recognizable to anyone who knows the words to 'Time Warp') demonstrates an exciting molecular-transfer procedure in which a little alien is transported, *Star Trek*-style, from one tube to the next. You then take part in a similar experiment, but something, of course, goes wrong, and a ferocious alien is transported into your ship instead. Brrrr. It's about a 20-minute 'encounter' from start to finish. The waits were about 45 minutes in August, 1¼ hours in March.

Space Mountain This is a very popular 3½-minute roller coaster ride through, what else, space. You coast by earth as it would be seen from outer space, past astronauts working on the moon and swirl around the star-sprinkled galaxy. It's a fun little ride, but not as rough as we had expected, and despite the promises of total darkness we could still see the tracks throughout the entire ride. Waiting time for this one is about 45 minutes in August, 1¼ hours in March. (TV monitors entertain with the latest news from the galaxy and lots of FedEx ads.)

Star Command This is a great one for little kids: you're traveling through in a swivelable car and you've got a laser-firing cannon: aim for the Zs!

Grand Prix Raceway Another must for kids, who here can climb into gas-powered, grand-prix-style go-carts and streak around a track that circumnavigates the section.

Mickey's Starland
This is the area to head for with very small children. Most everything here is built to kid-size scale. Kids love to have their photos taken in front of the Daisy's Cafe, Duck County School and Duckburg News buildings.

Mickey's House All the rooms are roped off, so peek in to see Mickey's bedroom, living room, office and kitchen. Mickey's Starland Show out back is a stage show where you see Goofy, Minnie et al; the show runs every half hour 11 am to 2 pm and 4 to 6 pm. If you're worried that your kids won't get to see Mickey before they leave, this is the surefire place to catch him.

Grandma Duck's Farm The vegetable garden here grows everything Mickey and his friends like to eat. Some Disney restau-

rants actually use some of the vegetables grown here (yeah, right). Also here is a great petting area with goats, sheep and ducks.

Fantasyland
The name is pretty accurate for younger kids, who go wild here on sweet and relatively harmless rides like Cinderella's Golden Carousel, Dumbo the Flying Elephant, It's a Small World (from which you'll emerge with that song permanently emblazoned upon your psyche), the ever-popular Mad Tea Party teacup ride, and Snow White's Adventure.

Liberty Square
This is not the most exciting area of Disney World, but hey. Highlights include the following.

Haunted Mansion A glorified haunted house. A nice gimmick is the incredible expanding room as you enter – you can't tell if the ceiling's rising or you're sinking. Once in your cart, howling wolves and dogs pop in as you pass tombstones, hear lots of 'boo'-type sounds and see waltzing ghosts. Smaller kids may be scared by the 'ghost' that 'sits' in your cart on the way out. Eek.

Hall of Presidents Talk about ham-fisted propaganda! This is an audio animatronic (AA) show, starring every US president to date, narrated by Maya Angelou and extolling the virtues of the American system of government, life and culture in a sickeningly superior and self-congratulatory tone. The only lighter moments are provided by unintentional ironies; like the fact that the Ronald Reagan AA is more animated than the real president was. There are some neat aspects, such as the presidents mumbling among themselves during speeches. When we visited, Bill Clinton's AA gave a speech which Clinton himself recorded specifically for the attraction.

Frontierland
This is the most action/adventure-oriented section of Magic Kingdom, and lines for its rides are generally the longest during the

...But This One Takes the Cake

Disney's imagineers have come up with many compelling ways to separate you from your money. But with the Walk Around the World project, they've reached the height of unmitigated gall.

The Walk is a project to build a walkway, made of bricks bearing the name of sponsors, around Magic Kingdom. For $110, you, yes *you*, can immortalize your devotion to Disney by sponsoring the installation on the Walk of a 10-inch hexagonal brick tile embossed with your name and home state.

$110. For a brick.

And that $110 doesn't even *buy* you the brick! According to the Sponsorship Agreement:

Neither this agreement nor the installation of the brick entitles the Sponsor to any ownership interest in the brick...or free or discounted admission to Magic Kingdom or any other part of Walt Disney World Resort...Sponsor shall have no control over the design, format, material, appearance, construction, manufacture, installation, maintenance, repair, admission, or access to, or operation of the brick or the walkway.

You not only don't own it, you're not even allowed to *operate* it! People, of course, are buying the things up as fast as they can. So once again, Disney has convinced the visiting, *paying* public to not only cover their construction costs, but to turn the Walk into a profit center. We want to party with these guys.

day. It may pay to begin here, as opposed to in New Tomorrowland, especially if you're trying to get in more than one run on Big Thunder.

Splash Mountain Our favorite ride at Magic Kingdom. The sets are based on – and feature characters from – the Disney movie *Song of the South*.

You float through very amusing pathways and go down a couple of little drops (one in darkness) before you go through Brer Rabbit's laughing land (a welcome relaxation phase), which is filled with frogs, singing ducks and other happy creatures (dig the bees). Then, the third drop – the killer – sends you down more than 50 feet, at more than 40 mph.

If you think you winced during the big drop, you can find out: video cameras are strategically placed to catch your expression, and monitors on the way out show these images. You can get a color printout of your mug for $9.95.

Waiting times for this ride can get long: in August we waited almost a full hour, in March it was just under 1 1/2 hours. Kids have to be at least three years old and at least 44 inches tall to ride.

Big Thunder Mountain Railroad It's a toss-up whether this or Splash Mountain is the most popular ride in the park; waiting times are about equal. The ride is pretty wild, and the sets are excellent. You're on a mine-cart heading through an old mine, and if you ever wondered what it was like to be in a mine-shaft rail chase, this is the place to come.

Tom Sawyer Island To get your wits back and let the little ones burn off the energy they've stored up waiting in line and then freaking out on rides, take a short raft ride over to this little playground/island filled with rope bridges, caves and other things to climb in/on. The raft leaves from the dock between Big Thunder and Splash Mountain.

Adventureland

This is a jungly, safari-ish kind of place with great streetmosphere. We liked the following.

Pirates of the Caribbean We loved this water cruise almost as much as the kids with us did. You're on a riverboat, seeing first-hand how pirates lived, partied, robbed and burned down towns, but it's all in a very happy setting with lots of pirate songs. Yo ho ho. There are a couple of little sections of rapids, but for the most part it's pretty relaxing. Lines weren't very long when we went (about 20 minutes in August, 45 minutes in March), but can get up there.

Jungle Cruise It's exactly what it sounds like: a cruise through the Jungles of the World, with lots of very cute animals, AA figures and waterfalls. We liked it, but lines can be intolerable – best to show up early or during a parade or show.

Swiss Family Treehouse If you still have the energy, climb the long staircase here (no wheelchair access) and take in the view of Adventureland. The tree itself is pretty astounding.

DISNEY-MGM STUDIOS

This theme park's rides and attractions are absolutely first rate, but it is far less of a 'working studio' than they'd have you believe. And we were really disappointed with the alleged 'special effects' demonstration, which we thought was uninformative, patronizing and, worse, unimaginative. But great parades and shows take place here, and while the sets and street scenes may not be as impressive as those at Universal Studios Florida theme park, it's absolutely worth coming. If only to fall down an elevator shaft.

Shows & Characters

These change often. When we went, the following were offered.

Disney Character Parades
15-minute appearances throughout the day, on Mickey Ave

Indiana Jones Epic Stunt Spectacular
Booo. Bad stunts done too slowly and 'technical talk' that's dumb and just plain wrong (an actual quote: 'Let's shoot at 48 frames-per-second to give Cairo a really good look here, Bob.' Memo to writers: stationary objects like 'Cairo' don't look 'good' in slow motion, which is the result of shooting at 48 fps).

Mickey Mouse Autograph Sessions
On Sunset Blvd all day

Pocahontas: A Legend Comes to Life
Behind the scenes of the film; continuous showings in Walt Disney Theater

The Spirit of Pocahontas
25-minute stage show in the Backlot Theater

Toy Story Parade
This is the biggie, with all the *Toy Story* characters in a huge parade that snakes around the circle and down Hollywood Blvd; a 20-minute show; good time to get in line at the Tower of Terror

Rides & Attractions

Most of the 'rides' here are 3D, participatory or simulator based, with the notable exception of our first entry.

Twilight Zone Tower of Terror This may be the best and most terrifying ride in all of Disney World, and judging by the screams and the lines, a lot of people agree with us on that one.

It's in the imposing Hollywood Tower Hotel, which 'closed in 1939.' It's a beast of a Deco building that looks eerily gloomy even on sunny days, but what makes it really terrifying is that you can hear the muffled screams of riders from a quarter-mile away. AAAhhhhh!

The detail in the place is spectacular, and when you finally get to the entrance you'll see a setup video of the tale of the last guests to stay here before the place closed. You get into the elevator (sitting down and strapped in) and feel as if you're truly entering another dimension – it looks as if you're traveling in space, seeing stars and holograms float by. Though it only feels as if you've gone up a floor or two, in fact you've gone up 133 feet. The first falls are only a few feet each – the fall program is changed frequently, so yours may be different. But the big one is always 13 stories, which you descend in only 2.7 seconds: it's not a free-fall, but rather a forced fall, which is faster!

Jim Henson's Muppet Vision 3D This attraction is beautifully made and extremely funny; the 3D stuff is so real that kids actually try to reach for the characters. The theater is pretty much a replica of the one on the *Muppet Show*. Some of the Muppets stars appear 'live' (audio animatronics) – watch for the hecklers (who are sitting just where they should be) and the projectionist, who is none other than the Swedish Chef. You'll come out laughing. Waits can get long, but once you're in the main waiting area, a brilliant multiscreen Muppet show awaits – no chance escaping knowledge that the show is sponsored by Kodak.

Honey I Shrunk the Kids Movie Set Adventure Behind New York St, this is a fantastic playground area scaled to bring you down to sub-ant size. It's set in the back-yard from the movie, with oversize weeds, gigantic insects, huge Lego pieces, an over-size, water-sprinkling garden hose (oh, boy do kids like this one – there are triggers in the floor) and other enlarged items that make you feel decidedly shrunken. It is mainly for small children.

EPCOT

Epcot stands for Experimental Prototype Community of Tomorrow. Its trademark silver geodesic dome is visible throughout the park. Epcot is broken into two main sections: Future World and the World Show-case. While we went to the World Showcase with our Experienced World Traveler decoder rings held high, totally prepared to scoff, we were completely humbled by the extraordinary job that Disney has done in re-creating the very best of 11 countries. While Future World is definitely advertiser-driven, we enjoyed it (especially the Honey I Shrunk the Audience experience!).

Future World

This area is a combination amusement and educational park that can be very entertain-ing for older children and adults. Most of the rides are journeys that focus on the evolution of certain aspects of technology throughout history and offer bold predictions about the future.

While we did see a lot of people really enjoying themselves, we were a bit let down by the fact that this once glisteningly futuristic section has fallen a bit behind in its predictions. That said, Epcot still has plenty to offer, and when you take both Future World and World Showcase into account, you'll get your money's worth.

The area is broken up into sponsored pavilions, and there's no attempt to hide it. As the guide map gushes: 'Major corporations have combined their creative thinking with Walt Disney Imagineers to explore projections about the future.' Okay, so in the future we'll take photographs on Kodak film while eating Nestlé chocolate and making AT&T cell-phone calls – those are some of the major sponsors. These kooky guys and their far-fetched vision of the future!

Most of the rides in Epcot have short or at least fast-moving lines, as they operate on a conveyor-belt principle: the cars are constantly moving, and the entry and exit platforms are usually rotating at the same speed as the rides.

Highlights are listed below.

Spaceship Earth If anything, this is relaxing, as you spiral slowly up and down within the geosphere past displays of communication technology throughout history. It's not heavy-hitting technology, but it is interesting and some of the displays are very good.

Wonders of Life This amusing area is based around exploration of the human body. The main attraction is the flight-simulator ride **Body Wars** – essentially based on the movie *Inner Space* – in which a ship (with you inside) is miniaturized and injected into a human body. Something, once again, goes horribly wrong and you're in danger of being sucked into the heart, which as we all know would mean total destruction for your ship and the human host. Brrr.

Other attractions here include the laudable **Making of Me**, which shows the reproductive process from fertilization to birth (unfortunately they don't show any of the prefertilization events, but, well, this is Disney), and **Cranium Command**, a totally hilarious look at the command and control systems of a 12-year-old boy's brain and body.

Journey into Imagination The Journey into Imagination area includes the namesake ride as well as the magnificent Honey I Shrunk the Audience. Outside the buildings, smaller kids go absolutely wild with the jumping water fountains: they send little blups of water out of one hole, in an arc, down into another hole, and they're timed to make the water behave like a dolphin, swimming and jumping. Yay.

In Journey into Imagination – the ride – you sit in what looks like a huge recliner and, along with your AA host and his purple AA dragon, travel through an Imagine-Scape that's a lot like flying through a dream. It's a magical, smoky-foggy journey, and all the while the dragon is telling kids to use their imagination to help them be successful at life.

Upstairs there are tons of extremely neat techno toys.

To say **Honey I Shrunk the Audience** is a 3D film is kind of like saying that the space shuttle is a fancy airplane. It's a complete sensory experience, with a moving floor, audience-film character interaction and even dog-sneeze and mice. Absolutely a don't-miss. It's based on the Disney films *Honey I Shrunk the Kids* and *Honey I Blew Up the Kids*, and the original cast appears here.

We're not going to give it all away, but suffice it to say that you're truly in contact with many small things and it's hysterically funny, especially when people look in at the audience.

Living Seas We really enjoyed this look at underwater life. It's not so much a ride as an attraction, but some ride elements are involved. And though it's not SeaWorld

Orlando, Disney tries pretty hard with this pavilion, which includes one of the world's largest aquariums.

World Showcase

When we do our research, we're always on the lookout for something to make a joke about, and we thought that coming here would be the mother lode. How disappointing it was for us, then, when we saw just how well this section was done. For those who remain cynical, consider that a) all of the employees in a country's section are from that country, b) all of the country sections were designed and built with the cooperation of their own national tourist boards, and c) the reproductions are astounding.

All the country pavilions exhibit the absolute best that the real country boasts, and we're happy to report that, while it may be a little kitschy to make all the France employees wear berets, this place is absolutely fantastic.

The countries represented are (clockwise from the main park entrance, that is, from east to west): Mexico, Norway, China, Germany, Italy, America, Japan, Morocco, France, United Kingdom and Canada. For

Millennium Show

As we went to press, Disney let us know what they had in store beginning October 1, 1999. Their new millennium extravaganza, which will replace the IllumiNations fireworks shows, will run from then until January 1, 2001. Details were sketchy, but they plan to make the show far more interactive than any other Disney parade or celebration: think Brazilian Carnaval – where you're in the middle of a swirling, insane parade with characters, floats and 30-foot puppets – followed by a custom-built and even patented fireworks celebration. It all adds up to a good couple of hours every evening. It will be held in Epcot, around the lagoon.

the millennium show (see the boxed text) an extra pavilion will be built in Epcot celebrating technology of the future and highlighting an extra 25 nations.

Each country has restaurants and snack bars, shops and evening entertainment. See Places to Eat later in the Walt Disney World section for more information on the restaurants, and see Entertainment later in the section for information on the bars and evening entertainment.

All the countries are skirting the World Showcase Lagoon, around which the millennium show parade is held.

You can get a World Showcase Passport from any shop and have it stamped by the different country pavilions – there's a space for comments and signatures. It's a nice touch for kids.

DISNEY'S ANIMAL KINGDOM

Disney's Animal Kingdom is their newest theme park, and we spent an afternoon here on the last trip. We were slightly underwhelmed, though to be fair, not all of it was open when we visited.

Animal Kingdom centers around Safari Village, with the amazing **Tree of Life** – you can walk around the tree for hours and keep finding new animals carved into its trunk. Within the Tree of Life itself is **It's Tough to Be a Bug**, which is essentially a 20-minute 3D advertisement for the Disney/Pixar film, *It's a Bug's Life*. We haven't seen the film, but we still liked this attraction.

Dinoland USA offers dinosaur-themed attractions and the stage production of **Journey into Jungle Book**.

Conservation Station gives you a look at how they put the place together, an interactive area to learn about endangered animals and habitats around the world, and the Affection Section, a petting zoo. But with all the talk of conservation, the 'We Can Make a Difference' slogans and the Conservation Station brochures printed on recycled paper and extolling the virtues of recycling and reusing, we were shocked to see plastic doodads, nonrecyclable foam-rubber puzzles and games and toys for sale at the Conservation Station's gift shop.

The best part of the park is the **Africa** section, which features the Kilimanjaro Safari. In open-air safari cars you cruise through the jungle and see hundreds of animals walking and running 'in the wild.' The **Pangani Forest Exploration Trail** is basically a zoo.

The fun **Wildlife Express**, a 'steam'-powered train, runs between Africa and Conservation Station. African-themed gift shops are found throughout the park.

It will only get better as time goes on: Disney is quite pleased with the attendance figures and will no doubt put more into the park over the next few years. Plan on spending at least half a day here – it's worth a visit, but wasn't the highlight we thought it would be.

WATER PARKS

It's surprising, when you think about it, that Disney hadn't really pursued the water park concept until very recently, except for the 'swimmin hole' of River Country. With Blizzard Beach, Disney has one of the most exciting water playlands around; we went on a rainy day and had an absolute blast.

Blizzard Beach

This is the home of Summit Plummet, the world's tallest and fastest free-fall slide. Themed to look like a ski resort (and so much fun we'll forgive the execrable puns like the 'Avalunch' restaurant), Blizzard Beach features ski-ish things like a ski lift and snowcapped mountains, but mainly it's a slide and raft park that is a great way to spend at least half a day.

Lockers are available; the keys are on rubber wrist straps. You can also rent life preservers.

Slides & Rides Disney's main water attraction is **Summit Plummet** – a 120-foot waterslide on which riders reach speeds of 55 mph! Take it from us, you will want your arms crossed on your chest, your eyes closed and, especially, your nostrils pinched, because water flying up your nose at 55 mph is as much fun as a dental cleaning. You scootch off the top, pass through a tunnel (it's the one that looks like a ski-jump from the ground) and slide your buns off. It seems terrifying, but just go for it!

Slush Gusher is for those who don't feel quite up to the challenge of Summit Plummet. It's the same kind of slide and you go pretty fast, but it doesn't have the tunnel and it isn't as intense. You use mats for **Snow Stormers** and **Toboggan Racers**. The former is a twisty slalom course, and the latter shoots straight down. Both have sudden dips and are fast. Follow the safety instructions or risk friction burns. (Nick got one, but he *was* being an idiot at the time, and that's all he's got to say about that.)

Teamboat Springs is a really fun family-oriented white-water raft ride; rafts hold six people and streak down a 1200-foot course. **Cross Country Creek** is the standard slow-flowing moat around the park, in which you can lazily circumnavigate the area on a rubber inner tube. You'll pass through a waterfall on your way out of the tunnel beneath. **Tike's Peak** is the kiddie area at the base of Mt Gushmore; it is specifically designed for smaller children.

Typhoon Lagoon
This park has essentially the same slides and raft rides (though less radical) as Blizzard Beach, but with the major exceptions of Typhoon Lagoon, a bloody huge wave pool, and Shark Reef, a fish observatory. It's a place for relaxing at the 'beach'; you're allowed to bring coolers (but not alcoholic beverages or glass bottles).

You can't miss Typhoon Lagoon: it's the huge body of water as you enter that produces body-surfable waves every few minutes. It's pretty impressive, and those who don't like the waves can just hang out on shore. Several slide rides start from about the midpoint of Mt Mayday. Castaway Creek is pretty much the same as Blizzard Beach's Cross Country Creek.

River Country
Though aged, River Country is still a popular water park. Near Fort Wilderness, it offers small waterslides, ropes and tube rides, all built around an enormous swim-ming pool. Though a nice place for a picnic, as a water park it doesn't hold a candle to the other two.

OTHER ATTRACTIONS
Disney Institute
Created as an educational approach to holiday making, the Disney Institute (☎ 800-496-6337) offers its guests a total of 80 classes and programs in nine categories, including Entertainment Arts, Sports & Fitness, Culinary Arts, Lifestyles, Design Arts, Environment, Story Arts, Performing Arts and Youth. Programs to choose from include animation, photography, rock climbing, canoeing, cooking, self-discovery, storytelling, interior and agricultural design, landscaping and Florida wilderness, as well as dance, theater arts, music or spoken word. You get the idea. There's about a 15:1 student-teacher ratio. All classes are hosted by artists-in-residence or experts in a particular field.

The experts – or superstars, as the case may be – aren't constrained to work in the field for which they are best known. Excellent examples are: Grammy-award winning clarinetist Richard Stoltzman leading a class on bread baking, Bill Walton in a classical piano concert, and the collaboration of actor Andy Garcia and Mambo King Israel Lopez offering a Latin Music Festival. In the evening events such as live performances by artists-in-residence take place.

Lodging-and-program packages are available in all the areas of interest. Designed like a quaint, 1900s town, the institute offers lodging in either bungalows or townhouses (see Places to Stay below).

Disney Village Marketplace
Disney Village Marketplace today is a quaint shopping mall, but in the near future Disney plans to expand the boundaries of Pleasure Island to include the Disney Village Marketplace area. It will then hold an expanded movie theater and celebrity-owned restaurants (including one owned by Gloria and Emilio Estefan). See Places to Eat later in this section for information on the existing restaurants.

PLACES TO STAY

The best source for full descriptions of all the Disney places to stay is Birnbaum's *Walt Disney World*, which lists each resort's features and services. The prices we list here are the standard rack rates, and from the lowest to the highest, but they're just a guideline. You get much better deals by booking packages either through Disney or a travel agent.

Disney accommodations are designed with family stays in mind, so most of the rooms are large enough to accommodate groups of four or more. Suites are available in many of the resorts, and their price and capacity is very complicated; call Disney for information. Wheelchair-accessible rooms and practically any other special-needs rooms one could think of are available.

The main advantages of staying at the resorts, as opposed to in Kissimmee or Orlando, are convenience, preferential treatment at all Disney-owned attractions, the opportunity to enter the parks $1^1/2$ hours before the general public, and the excellent transportation network. Oh, yeah, and free Disney Channel in the rooms. The disadvantage is that you'll spend a whole lot more money here than you would staying at a hostel or motel in Kissimmee or Orlando.

To make reservations and get the rates for suites at any of the following places, call ☎ 407-934-7639, or go to the Website (www.disney.go.com/DisneyWorld), where you can also book some packages online. If you're calling on the day you want to stay, save yourself some hold time and contact the particular lodgings directly.

Camping

Disney's Fort Wilderness Resort & Campground (☎ 407-824-2900) is gorgeous and incredibly civilized; all 1192 tent and RV campsites have water and electricity ($35/59 low season/high season); some have sanitary disposal ($39/70) and some have all that plus cable-TV hookups ($49/74 – wait a minute, you *camp* with your TV?). The hookups are secreted within Disney trees. There are also 408 air-conditioned cabins (RVs, actually) with full kitchens ($179/275). These sleep up to six people.

The campground isn't plagued with mosquitoes, snakes, bugs, creeps or bothers, and it lets you get away to the great outdoors without all the fuss: roughing it, but very gently. You're treated as a Disney Resort guest, with all the attendant privileges like early park entry and preferred restaurant reservations. And there are organized activities like nightly sing-a-longs at the campfire and movies. You can rent bicycles and golf carts, and horseback riding is available.

Magic Kingdom Resorts

Disney's Wilderness Lodge (☎ 407-824-3200) has a Wild West atmosphere. Rooms are $180 to $390; character breakfasts are held daily at Artist Point.

Slightly hokey but fun all the same, *Disney's Polynesian Resort* (☎ 407-824-2000) has a lush and tropical setting. Rooms range from $274 to $530; Minnie's Menehune character breakfast is held daily in Ohana.

Socialistic-1970s-vision-of-the-future-looking *Disney's Contemporary Resort* (☎ 407-824-1000) has more than 1000 rooms; note that wheelchairs can't board the Monorail here. Rooms range $214 to $460; character breakfast buffets are held daily in the Contemporary Cafe.

Disney's Grand Floridian Resort & Spa (☎ 407-824-3000) is a very posh Victorian-style place at the Seven Seas Lagoon. It's best to walk into the immense lobby, listen to the grand piano tinkling, gawk at the giant birdcages, and then stay in Fort Wilderness! Rooms run $299 to $645. A character breakfast and dinner is held daily at 1900 Park Fare. On the Fourth of July, this is a good place to watch the fireworks at Magic Kingdom.

Epcot & Disney-MGM Studios Resorts

At *Disney's Dixie Landings* (☎ 407-934-6000), the rural South theme is reminiscent of Tara in *Gone With the Wind*. The 2084 rooms run $119 to $184 and sleep four. For the same price, *Disney's Port Orleans* (☎ 407-934-5000) does a fine job of reproducing the French Quarter in New Orleans (*avec* nightly Mardi Gras but *sans* filth and drunken creeps).

Disney's Caribbean Beach Resort (☎ *407-934-3400*) is made up of 'villages' modeled after Jamaica, Trinidad, Martinique, Barbados and Aruba. The 2000-plus rooms here sleep up to four people and are also priced from $119 to $184.

The enormous ***Walt Disney World Swan*** (☎ *407-934-3000, 800-248-7926*) features two gigantic (46-foot-tall) swans on the roof. Rooms range from $230 to $425. Character breakfasts are held on Wednesday and Saturday mornings at 8 am, and character dinners take place on Monday, Thursday and Friday at 6 pm. The similarly enormous ***Walt Disney World Dolphin*** (☎ *407-934-4000, 800-227-1500*) has a tropical setting and a 56-foot-high dolphin statue; rooms at the same rates.

Ahrr, matey: the very New England-style rooms at ***Disney's Yacht Club Resort*** (☎ *407-934-7000*) cost $264 to $540; 'concierge' rooms run $395 to $540. Rooms at ***Disney's Beach Club Resort*** (☎ *407-934-8000*) cost $264 to $535. The resort's Cape May Café has a daily character breakfast.

Disney's BoardWalk Villas (☎ *407-939-5100*) has an early-1900s' design. Studios (which sleep up to four) are $254 to $405; one-bedroom villas (which sleep four) are $315 to $450; two-bedroom villas (which sleep up to eight) are $440 to $685. ***Disney's BoardWalk Inn*** (☎ *407-939-5100*) has 532 cottages and 378 rooms. The complex pricing ranges from $254 to $770.

Modeled after Key West, the houses at ***Disney's Old Key West Resort*** (☎ *407-827-7700*) are available for rent *and* purchase. It's fantastically complicated, involving Disney's 'vacation ownership' (which the rest of us call 'timeshare condo'), so call for more information. Studios are $229, one-bedrooms $305, two-bedrooms $420 in low season and $284/365/550 in high season. Character breakfasts take place on Wednesday and Sunday.

Disney's Animal Kingdom Resorts

Disney's All-Star Sports Resort (☎ *407-939-5000*), ***Disney's All-Star Music Resort*** (☎ *407-939-6000*) and ***Disney's All-Star Movies Resort*** (☎ *407-939-7000*) are Disney's cheapest fully equipped hotels, designed to appeal to young travelers and sports, music and movie nuts. All have 1920 rooms, and all are themed: baseball, football, basketball, tennis, surfing, Broadway, calypso, jazz, rock & roll, country, cartoons and movies (101 Dalmations, Fantasia, etc). Rooms in the resorts are $74 to $104 all year, for up to four people.

Other Disney Resorts

The Disney Institute (see Other Attractions earlier in the section) replaced the Disney Village Resort. You can stay at ***The Villas at the Disney Institute*** (☎ *407-827-1100*) as part of a Disney Institute package, or just as a straight accommodation deal while visiting the Walt Disney World parks.

For accommodation only, the nightly cost is $204/275 for bungalows, $245/330 for one-bedroom townhouses, $335/430 for two-bedroom villas. Tree houses, which sleep six, are $365/475; eight-person fairway villas are $395/510; and Grand Vista homes, which sleep six to eight, are $1025/1475.

The packages include accommodation (minimum three-night stay) with various combinations of one-day passes to any one theme park, choice of programs, access to the fitness center, transportation and more. Call for information, as plans and prices change. Rates are around $540 to $765 with a bungalow; $595 to $860 with a one-bedroom townhouse; $730 to $1025 with a two-bedroom villa.

Non-Disney Properties

There are several non-Disney properties in the area and some of them are excellent.

Doubletree has two hotels in Lake Buena Vista; an attempt at a budget place is the ***Club Hotel by Doubletree*** (☎ *407-239-4646, 800-521-3297, 12490 Apopka-Vineland Rd*). It has rooms starting from an advertised $89, but it's more likely you'll pay the average prices of $119 to $149.

The outstanding ***Sierra Suites Lake Buena Vista*** (☎ *407-239-4300, 8100 Palm Parkway*) is a spanking new property very convenient to Downtown Disney, with spotless suites from an incredible $89, but averaging $129 to $299.

Immediately next to Downtown Disney, the *Courtyard by Marriott Downtown Disney Hotel* (☎ 407-828-8888, 800-223-9930, *1805 Hotel Plaza Blvd*) is a very good deal with standard hotel rooms from $99 to $169.

Right nearby is the *Doubletree Guest Suites Downtown Disney Resort* (☎ 407-934-1000, 800-222-8733, *2305 Hotel Plaza Blvd*), with suites from $138 to $279.

PLACES TO EAT

Prices and menus in the non-sit-down restaurants are about the same throughout the complex: burgers $3 to $6; hot dogs $1.75 to $3; pizza, Mexican and other fast food (excuse us, 'quick-service' food) $4 to $8 per person.

Character Dining

Kids absolutely love these places, where Disney characters prance around being generally charming while you eat. The schedule and variety of these events is so complicated, we're going to cop out and give you a couple of examples and then tell you to call Disney (☎ 407-939-3463) for more information and reservations.

If you're going to a character meal inside a Disney park, you'll need a valid ticket for that park – you can't go in just for the meal (nice try).

You can usually make reservations up to 60 days in advance. Reservations are almost always required, and if they're not, it's a good idea to make reservations anyway. Prices listed here are for ages 12 and older/three to 11.

One good bet is Once Upon a Time, at *Cinderella's Royal Table* in Cinderella's Castle, with Cinderella and others. It costs $15/8. The breakfasts are held from 8:30 to 10 am daily.

Mickey Mouse and his gang attend the *Garden Grill Character Experience*, which is open daily for breakfast, lunch and dinner (check times when you go). Breakfast costs $15/8; lunch and dinner $17/10.

Turkey Legs

Disney is constantly tempting guests with food throughout the parks: note the heavy smell of freshly baking cinnamon buns as you walk down Main St USA, which is purposely pumped out onto the street. One offering that proved irresistible to us – and we're for the most part vegetarian – was the smoked turkey legs. Smoked and then baked, the enormous legs (one's good enough for lunch) are good enough to make two vegetarians backslide. They're sold from the little stands near Frontierland and near Rockettower Plaza for $4.25 apiece.

Magic Kingdom

Main Street, USA If you're in the mood for Italian food, *Tony's Town Square Restaurant* serves breakfast, lunch and dinner. The *Plaza Restaurant* offers sandwiches and light entrees for lunch and dinner, and it also makes the largest ice cream sundaes in Magic Kingdom. Outside is the park's only cappuccino cart.

The Crystal Palace, a Buffet with Character is a cafeteria with chicken, pasta and salad dishes; character visits take place here. *Casey's Corner* is the place to grab a quick self-service hot dog or fries. Tables and bleacher seats are available, and the decor is decked out with cartoons.

Both the *Main Street Bake Shop* and *Plaza Ice Cream Parlor* are responsible for the overwhelmingly good smells that hit you as you enter into Magic Kingdom (baking exhaust is pumped out onto Main Street).

Adventureland This area has no full-service restaurants, but no worries: light snacks like tacos, nachos, tropical fruit and citrus yogurt (fitting to the theme) abound. And the best deal in the park is here, at the little cart selling gigantic, sumptuous smoked turkey drumsticks for $4.25. If you time it right you can waltz right up, but at peak lunch hours the line for these babies can be up to 20 minutes – they're *that* good.

Pecos Bill Cafe has burgers, smoked chicken and the like, and *Aunt Polly's Landing* does sandwiches, apple pie and cookies. *Sleepy Hollow* makes good cakes and pastries, and the outside patio has a great view of the castle.

Fantasyland At *Cinderella's Royal Table* (see Character Dining above), Cinderella is also around for lunch (11:30 am to 3 pm) and dinner (beginning at 4 pm). We recommend you make reservations for those meals as well, and *early*. The food here at dinner is big, beefy Henry VIII-style drumstick fare, with entrees from $18.95 to $23.95.

For burgers, sandwiches and salads, try *Pinocchio's Village House*, which also serves up wieners and other pseudo-German stuff and has an outside pretzel cart, or *Lumiere's Kitchen*, serving various fried nuggets and grilled-cheese sandwiches. Both are mainly for children, though there are some concessions to the grownups, too.

New Tomorrowland Here you'll find the very good *Cosmic Ray's Starlight Café*, with meat and vegetarian burgers, salads, soups and sandwiches, and *Plaza Pavilion*, which serves pizza and subs. Both places are cafeteria-style. And have we mentioned those awesome turkey legs? Well here is your second chance at Rockettower Plaza. (See the Turkey Legs boxed text.)

Liberty Square The *Columbia Harbor House* offers fried-fish and chicken baskets, but the big attraction here is the *Liberty Tree Tavern* (☎ 407-939-3463), a full service restaurant in Liberty Square with character dinners for $19.50 for adults, $9.95 for children; reservations necessary. Dishes include fish, ribs, chicken, oysters and clam chowder. It's open for (character-less) lunch as well.

Disney-MGM Studios
Of the four full-service restaurants in this park, the most expensive one is *Hollywood Brown Derby*, which offers seafood, steak, chicken and Cobb salad (tossed and served

tableside). *Mama Melrose's Ristorante Italiano* bakes its pizzas in a brick oven and serves all kinds of other Italian food.

Sci-Fi Dine-In Theater is a re-creation of a 1950s drive-in movie theater: tables are in vintage cars and as you eat your burger, pasta or sandwich ($6 to $10), you watch cheesy 1950s science-fiction movies.

Maybe we went to the *'50s Prime Time Café* on a bad day – we had a bad time, but everyone else we spoke with had a blast. It specializes in good old American cooking like meatloaf and pot roast.

Other places to eat within this park, like *Backlot Express*, *Min & Bill's Dockside Diner* and *Hollywood & Vine*, serve salads, burgers, sandwiches and other fairly simple and light things.

Epcot
While all the restaurants in Disney do a fine job, this is where they really shine. The international food is authentic and somewhat pricey. Note that we're only listing the flagship, or at least our favorite, restaurants at each of these countries – they all have more than these to offer.

Reservations, which are an exceptionally good idea, are given on a Disney-resort guest priority basis. When you call ☎ 407-939-3463, you're asked for your hotel and room number, but even if you're staying at one of the hundreds of anonymous campsites at Fort Wilderness you can still get resort-guest reservation status.

Canada Probably the least expensive option in the area, *Le Cellier* (no reservations required) has starters for $3.25 to $9.95 and main courses, like good prime rib, from $16.95 to $22.95. The excellent cold smoked beef brisket sandwich and other daily special sandwiches go for $7.50. Children's offerings include that old Canadian favorite, macaroni and cheese, or chicken and meatball stew for $3.99 with a drink and a cookie. Good deal, eh?

China Four major regional cooking styles of China are served up at the *Nine Dragons* restaurant. The Cantonese entrees include sweet-and-sour pork ($15.50) and Jade Tree beef ($19.95; stir fried with broccoli and oyster sauce). Among the Szechwan dishes are kang bao chicken ($16.75; stir-fried with peanuts and hot chili peppers) and the inevitable General Tso (or Chow or Tsau or Ting or...) chicken (also $16.75). For Mandarin flair, try Great Wall duck ($18.25) or mu shu pork (stir-fried shredded pork with vegetables, served in paper-thin pancakes with a rich, sweet brown sauce), and for Kiangche cuisine, try the saucy chicken ($15.45).

United Kingdom The *Rose & Crown Pub & Dining Room* has fish & chips for $13.25, bangers and mash for $15.98, traditional cottage pie at $11.75, and bubble and squeak for...just kidding. (On the last trip, Nick walked in, saw a guy dressed just like a lager lout at a football match and was about to comment on the realism of the Disney Streetmosphere when the lout beerily called out 'Oy! Tom!' and he and his real lager-lout friends walked out of the place with a sway in their step. Talk about authentic!) Prices rise slightly between lunch and dinner. A kids' menu runs $4.75 to $5.95.

The porch behind the beautifully done English pub is probably the best place to watch IllumiNations – if you can get out there (they don't accept reservations for seats out there, so you just have to show up early and try your luck). Also at the pub, Alice's Tea Party takes place on certain days; it's a free character 'tea' party (actually apple juice) with cookies, hosted by Alice and the White Rabbit. Ask when you're here.

France The best fun here is at the *Chefs du France*, which offers main courses from $17.95 to $24.95, very French (shall we say 'brisk') service and tuxedoed waiters and maitre d's serving Bermuda-shorted, flip-flop-shod tourists: 'Garkone...ah bay voo any more o' that kammenbare?'.

Au Petit Café comes up with creations like 'le suprême de volaille en croûte sauce au Porto' (herb-marinated chicken breast with julienne vegetables in puff pastry with

port-wine cream sauce) for $13.50 or just a simple quiche lorraine for $7.95.

Germany Walking into the *Biergarten* in Germany was almost scary for Corinna because it felt (and smelled) so real. The all-you-can-eat dinner buffet with roasted chicken, all kinds of sausages, sauerkraut, potatoes and more is $10.95 at lunch, $15.75 at dinner.

Italy When you order the fettuccine Alfredo ($16.50) at *Alfredo* (which is also known as *L'Originale Alfredo di Roma Ristorante*), you'll get to see their solid-gold serving spoon and fork (and hear the story of why, which brings us back to 1927, when Mary Pickford and Douglas Fairbanks...okay, okay, the somewhat interesting story is printed on the menu); antipasto is $9.95, roast chicken with rosemary and sage is $19.50. Look through the window at the front where you can see pasta being made fresh.

Japan Try *Mitsukoshi Teppanyaki*, where quick-handed chefs chop, dice, slice and sizzle right at your tabletop food such as *kaibashira* (scallops served with vegetables and rice; $11.75 at lunch, $20.25 at dinner). Among other offerings are lunch combinations for two and the dinner *san-kai,* which includes a shrimp appetizer, salad, soup, beef tenderloin, lobster tail, vegetables (with noodles), rice, dessert and tea for $59.90, also for two. There's a trendy tempura bar here as well.

Mexico Run by the same family that operates the branch in Mexico City, *Cantina de San Angel* serves *chilaquiles* (fried tortillas and shredded chicken with green tomatillo sauce, cheese, sour cream and onion, served with rice and refried beans; $10.25); *huachinango a la Veracruzana,* (red snapper filet poached in wine with onions, tomatoes, olives and peppers, served with rice, $19.50); and *plato tarasco* (grilled tenderloin beef topped with ranchero sauce, chili-pepper strips and cheese, with a chicken enchilada, cheese chile relleno, refried beans, guacamole and rice; $21.75).

Morocco The excellent *Marrakesh Restaurant* makes couscous – steamed and rolled semolina – in three varieties: vegetable ($15.50), chicken ($19.50) and lamb ($19.95). Other specialties include shish kebab ($20.95) and *diffa* (elaborate set meals for two; $27.95 per person). There's belly dancing (the dancer's, not yours) in the evenings.

Norway Modeled after a medieval Norwegian fortress, *Akershus* offers a spectacular *koldtbord* buffet for lunch ($11.95 for adults, $4.75 for children) and dinner ($18.50 for adults, $7.95 for children) with simply wonderful selections of salads, herrings and *lots* of other fish and seafood items, plus meatballs, lamb, vegetables and Norwegian-style breads.

Pleasure Island

Call ☎ 407-824-4321 for specific information when you come. Get snacks at the *Hill St Diner* and sweet stuff at *D-Zerts*. The *Portobello Yacht Club* serves Italian food like good pizzas (baked in a wood-burning pizza oven) and pasta dishes. *Pleasure Island Jazz Co* features a Mardi Gras all-you-can-eat Sunday brunch, and the $22 for adults includes readmission in the evening (it's $12 for kids under 12, who can't come in at night).

Planet Hollywood (see Places to Eat in the Miami & Miami Beach chapter for a fuller description of this chain) here used to be the highest-grossing restaurant in the *world*, raking in more than $50 million a year. At press time, the chain was in financial trouble.

ENTERTAINMENT
Pleasure Island is the Disney version of Church St Station, a theme-entertainment complex in downtown Orlando that was drawing guests away from the resorts here. It's basically an adult theme park (it serves liquor) within the Disney grounds. They've tried to accommodate all tastes here. Depending on your style, you can enjoy: comedy at the Comedy Warehouse; retro '70s tunes at 8traxx; rock & roll at the Rock 'n' Roll Beach Club; jazz at the Jazz Bar or the Pleasure Island Jazz Co; pop dance hits at Mannequins Dance Palace; live country & western at the Neon Armadillo Music Saloon; or a nightly New Year's Eve party at midnight. There's an AMC cinema nearby, as well.

Dinner shows at Fort Wilderness' *Pioneer Hall* feature an all-you-can-eat barbecue dinner and the Hoop-Dee-Doo musical revue ($36 for adults, $26.50 for ages 12 to 20, $18 for kids three to 11). Other dinner shows (at the same price or slightly less) include Mickey's Tropical Luau and the Polynesian Luau, both at the Polynesian Resort; and oom-pah-pah sounds at the Biergarten.

GETTING THERE & AWAY
It's either inconvenient or expensive to get to Disney by public transport or private shuttle services. From Orlando's Lynx Bus Center, in the alley between W Pine St and W Central Blvd, one block west of Orange Ave, you can catch buses to Kissimmee

Mouse, Shmouse...Where Can I Get a Drink?

Attention: there are no alcoholic beverages served in Magic Kingdom. Period. If you're there and you feel the urge for a brew, head for the nearby Contemporary Resort's bar.

Beer is served at the fast-food (excuse us, 'quick-service') restaurants at Disney-MGM Studios, and it's always fun to watch a father with screaming kids sucking down a Bud Light while waiting for the burgers to arrive.

But the place to go for good wine and beer or exotic liquor and liqueur is the World Showcase at Epcot, where you can sample stuff from around the world. The Rose & Crown Pub in the United Kingdom is a favorite.

(Nos 4 and 18, hourly) and the Disney parks (No 50, every two hours), but it's a long, ride.

Private shuttles from the HI/AYH hostel and area hotels are $8 to $10 per person and run every 15 minutes or so all day.

It's awful, but the whole place is designed to be accessed by car. From the Orlando Airport, take Hwy 417 to Hwy 536, which runs right through Disney. From downtown Orlando, take I-4 heading southwest; the exits are clearly marked. From Kissimmee take Hwy 192 to Hwy 535 and go north.

North from Orlando

Following Hwy 17 north from the Orlando area brings you into a charming rural region with several parks, recreation areas and notable small towns. Here you can try your luck at fishing in Ocala National Forest, watch endangered manatees at Blue Spring State Park, get a spiritual reading at Cassadaga, or check out America's fern capital (Pierson).

The area makes an easy day trip from Orlando or the major cities along Florida's east coast. If you come in spring or summer, you'll see all the free flowers you can pick sprouting up along the roadside in glorious carpets of purple, yellow and blue – they're part of a county beautification program. To be nice to the flowers, be careful not to remove the roots.

BLUE SPRING STATE PARK

Blue Spring State Park (☎ 904-775-3663) is the best place in the state to see manatees in their natural habitat. The best time to visit is between November and March, when the St John's River, to the north, gets cold enough to make the peaceful mammals seek the relative warmth of Blue Spring's 72°F spring run. During the peak season, an average of 25 to 50 manatees are here daily, but during exceptionally cold seasons (like 1996) the number is higher – the record in that year was 88.

Rangers count the manatees every morning and post their numbers at the entry gate. The manatees head right for the crystal-

Manatees cluster at Blue Spring State Park.

clear spring run, not the park's lagoon, and swimming is prohibited when manatees are present.

The park's other main attraction is the **Thursby House**, a three-story frame house built in 1872 (the third story was added by Thursby's son, John, in 1900). The house has been undergoing extensive renovation to restore its 1875-87 period appearance and hours may be limited; call ahead for the current operating schedule.

The park is off French Ave at the northern end of Orange City. The 5- by 10-foot sign is impossible to miss if you're looking. Park admission is $4 per car and $1 for pedestrians and bicyclists.

Places to Stay

Camping here is a great idea. Primitive sites are $3 for adults and $2 for anyone under 18;

tent sites without electricity are $16.65; sites with electric hookups (which also accommodate RVs and vans) are $18.77. All prices include tax. Reservations are a good idea and are accepted up to 60 days in advance.

Fully equipped two-bedroom cabins are also available for $55.50. The cabins have central heating and air conditioning, bathrooms, fireplaces and full kitchens. Demand is high – weekends are booked months in advance, and reservations are accepted up to one year in advance, so do it.

More camping opportunities exist at nearby **Hontoon Island State Park** (☎ 904-736-5309), northwest of Blue Spring. It's a lovely little island with an observation tower and playground. When you stand on the shores of the St John's River, at the edge of the parking lot, a ferry zips over and takes you on the one-minute ride to the island. The park is 6 miles southwest of DeLand, off Hwy 44.

CASSADAGA

About 20 minutes north of Winter Park, this sleepy little town is home to the Cassadaga (pronounced 'kassuh-DAY-guh') Spiritualist Camp, established in 1884 by George P Colby. Today it's a federally registered historic district. The camp houses a group of about 25 spiritualist-mediums who live and work in privately owned homes on church-owned land. The church, the Southern Cassadaga Spiritualist Camp Meeting Association (SCSCMA; ☎ 904-228-3171), believes in infinite intelligence, everlasting life on many planes of existence and the precepts of prophecy and healing.

For what it's worth, we believe that these folks genuinely believe in what they are doing and aren't charlatans. Their goal is to spread the word as opposed to line their pockets. They don't practice witchcraft or black magic; they don't condone hypnotism or promise to tell you your future; and they don't call themselves psychics but rather mediums.

Orientation & Information

The camp is mainly south of County Rd 4139, bordered roughly by Horseshoe Park to the west, by Lake St to the south, and by Marion St to the east. The Cassadaga Grocery & Sunflower Deli is on the north side of County Rd 4139 at Stevens St, diagonally opposite the Andrew Jackson Davis Building.

If you're a believer and/or you are looking for a reading, note that while dozens of psychics, hypnotists, faith healers and others have put out shingles in and around the compound, only SCSCMA-certified mediums are affiliated with the organization. Contact the SCSCMA for a list of certified mediums.

You can get more information in the Cassadaga Spiritualist Camp Bookstore & Information Center in the Andrew Jackson Davis Building, which also has public toilets and a bulletin board announcing services.

Readings & Healings

Church services and healings (laying-on-of-hands) are held at no cost at the **Caesar Formal Healing Center**, next to the **Colby Memorial Temple** at the intersection of Stevens and Marion Sts, Sunday at 10 am and Wednesday at 7 pm. Private sessions with mediums and healers vary in price from person to person, but generally speaking a one-hour reading costs in the neighborhood of $50.

Places to Stay & Eat

Camping is not allowed in this town. The **Cassadaga Hotel** (☎ 904-228-2323) is not affiliated with the camp but does offer spiritual readings and has a small restaurant. They've cleaned up a bit since last time, and rooms run $59.

The best food in the area is at the **Cassadaga Grocery & Sunflower Deli** (☎ 904-228-3797), on County Rd 4139 at Stevens St, which offers healthy vegetarian fare (at least one veggie meal a day like veggie chili, $2.75) and deli sandwiches ($3.80).

Getting There & Away

There's no public transport to Cassadaga. By car, take I-4 to exit 54, head to the light, go east on County Rd 4101 for a quarter-mile, then turn right onto County Rd 4139.

CENTRAL

LAKE WOODRUFF NATIONAL WILDLIFE REFUGE

This 19,000-acre protected refuge, just north of DeLand, is open to canoeists, anglers and, unfortunately, primitive-weapons hunters (those who use bow and arrow, blowguns or black-powder firearms – as if that's more humane than an AK-47). The majority of the park is made up of freshwater marshes, lakes and streams, and it's home to more than 200 species of birds, 42 species of mammals, 58 species of reptiles and 68 species of fish. You might see ospreys, ring-necked and wood ducks, alligators, bald eagles, manatees, swallow-tailed kites and blue-winged teal. But stay away from the place in September and October, when the 'refuge' is open to the primitive-weapons yahoos for indefensible deer and wild-hog hunts – on the theory that it's okay to murder animals as long as you're 'sporting' about it.

Admission and parking are free. Arrange group tours in writing through the office of the refuge manager, Lake Woodruff National Wildlife Refuge, PO Box 488, De Leon Springs, FL 32130. Camping is not permitted, and no picnic facilities are provided. To get here, take Hwy 17 to Retta St, go one block to Grand Ave and turn left. The office is about a quarter-mile down on your right. To reach the park, continue past the office to Mud Lake Rd, turn right and drive about 1 mile; the entrance is across the railroad tracks. Many of your co-nature-lovers will be teenage couples in large pick-up trucks – an appropriate vehicle, as this is a famous Lover's Lane.

DE LEON SPRINGS STATE RECREATION AREA

While the natural springs here are a year-round 72°F, it's a shame that the pool that was built around them is so ghastly – a Soviet-looking construction job that encased the quasi-oval-shaped gathering pool (☎ 904-985-4212) in cement. But hey, it's still a nice, large pool and except on weekends, it's usually pretty free of people. The concrete monstrosity metes out spring water into a creek that feeds into the Lake Woodruff National Wildlife Refuge, and you can (and

really should, if you have the chance) rent canoes and kayaks ($8.48 an hour, $18.55 for four hours and $25.45 for eight hours) from the little stand opposite the Old Spanish Grill (see below). Do *not* attempt to load a canoe on the boat launch – it's more slippery than a truckload of banana peels. Nick ended up butt down in the soup three times before he could get up, cut the sole of his foot in the process and was laughed at by both Corinna and the park rangers, who later made a peace offering of an iodine applicator and a bandage.

Why go through it? It is peaceful and pleasant and the water in the pool is wonderful (it's said to be a fountain of youth). Canoeing or kayaking through the area is a great opportunity to see wildlife, and best of all, afterwards you can have a meal at the *Old Spanish Grill & Griddle House* (☎ 904-985-5644). In a beautiful old sugar mill, they've installed electric griddles into the center of sturdy wooden tables. For $3.50 per person you make yourself all-you-can-eat pancakes in two flavors at the table, regular white flour or the excellent five-grain, all served with honey, molasses or maple syrup. We did something truly slick: ordered one fruit and cheese plate ($5.75) and one order of pancakes. Pour two large pancakes, flip them and put cheese and fruit on top of one, make a sandwich and flip the entire thing then cut and serve…yummers. At breakfast you can also cook your own eggs, bacon and sausage at the table. It's great fun.

Admission to the recreation area is $4 per vehicle, $1 for pedestrians and bicycles. Picnicking is okay, but camping is not. The entrance is just off Hwy 17 and is very well signed.

PIERSON

As the self-proclaimed 'Fern Capital of America,' Pierson is home to astounding greenhouses of the fuzzy green plants. You can't buy the ferns retail, but it's very interesting to see the copious quantities of ferns loaded onto 18-wheel trucks for transport to the northeastern USA, where they're a staple of city dwellings.

SEVILLE

We didn't see any barber shops in this little town, but on Hwy 17 at Bruce St, just north of the city, is a wonderful house whose yard is filled with fascinating whirligigs, wind-driven planes, sculptures and doodads that need to be seen to be believed. You can't go in (No Trespassing signs abound), but you can pull over and take a peek for as long as you'd like.

PALATKA

• population 3500

A lovely little town about 30 miles from St Augustine, Palatka (pronounced 'puhl-AT-kuh') has a heartbreaking history, a lovely state garden and the best onion rings in northern Florida.

At the close of the 19th century, it was a major steamship port, but bad news then came in *fours*: the local cypress mill closed, the boats stopped coming, the town caught fire and the freeze of the winter of 1895-96 hit with a clenched fist. The town managed to hold on to its status as something of a tourist destination until WWI, after which it faded in significance.

Today Palatka is struggling to fuel a resurgence. B&Bs are making their first tentative moves into the city, and visitors will find a lively art scene and two pleasant historic districts (Northside and Southside) filled with late-19th- and early-20th-century homes. The town faces an uphill struggle to draw visitors from the riches of nearby St Augustine, but overall, it's worth a stop.

The main drag is Hwy 17, in town called Reid St. Get tourist information at the chamber of commerce (☎ 904-328-1503), 1100 Reid St, just next to the Amtrak station (which is on 11th St just north of Reid).

David Browning Railroad Museum

This museum in the Amtrak station is run by the Palatka Railroad Preservation Society (☎ 904-325-7425; ask for Jerry Iser). Inside, you'll see railroad paraphernalia like schedules and maps of the railroads that came through Florida. But the star of the show is definitely the Railrodeo model train set.

Built by a reporter from Pennsylvania, this was the largest HO-scale transportable model railroad in the state. Highlights are its animated objects: lights, crossings, bridges, a little girl in a tire swing, kites, cranes and front-end loaders, and handmade circus wagons. The museum is open the first Sunday of the month from 1 to 4 pm. Admission is free, donations accepted.

Ravine State Gardens

This state park (☎ 904-329-3721) at the southeastern end of town was officially created as a WPA project in 1933. But the ravine itself was created over millions of years by water flowing from the St John's River. The 182-acre park has a 2-mile loop road and walking trails along the creek. In March and April, this is the home of the Palatka Azalea Festival.

The park is open 8 am to sundown all year; the loop drive is open to cars from 9 am to 4 pm. Admission is $4 per carload or $1 for pedestrians and bicyclists. No pets are allowed. To get here from the Larimer Arts Center (see below), drive west on Reid St to 9th St, turn left, follow the bend and continue after it becomes Crill Ave; turn left at Moseley Ave and left again at Twigg St. The park entrance is on the right-hand side of the road.

Other Attractions

In the third week of October, the Putnam County Tourist Development Council holds its annual tour of homes in the historic districts. But driving or walking through the districts on your own at any time of year is a pleasant way to spend an afternoon. You can get maps of the districts at the excellent Larimer Arts Center (☎ 904-328-8998), in the old library building at 260 Reid St. The center holds rotating exhibitions every month except July and August, and admission is free. When we visited they were showing photographs and paintings by local artists.

In the Northside Historic District, the 1884 Bronson-Mulholland House (☎ 904-329-0140), the former home of Judge Isaac

Bronson, is open as a historic museum on Tuesday, Thursday and Sunday from 2 to 5 pm. **St Mark's Episcopal Church** (☎ 904-328-1474) at 200 Main St, built in 1854, was the missionary center of the Episcopal Church in St John's Valley and a Federal troop barracks during the Civil War. It's open for services Sunday at 8 and 10:30 am.

In the Southside Historic District, the **Tilghman House** (1884-87), 324 River St, is now the gallery of the Palatka Art League. Hours are Thursday to Saturday 11 am to 4 pm. Admission is free.

Places to Stay & Eat
The *Azalea House* (904-325-4547, 220 Madison St) is a very nice B&B in a restored old home, with rooms from $79 to $109. On weekends you get a full gourmet breakfast; during the week it's expanded continental.

On the way out of town, don't neglect to stop into *Angel's Dining Car* (☎ 904-325-3927, 209 Reid St), an aluminum diner that claims to be the oldest in Florida. Maybe yes, maybe no, but the fusty place (the air stinks of old cigarette smoke) manages to serve up traditional diner food that we haven't seen anywhere else for a long time: cherry Coke ($1), delicious and enormous sweet-onion onion rings handmade from St Augustine onions (95¢ to $1.35), and Pusalow (pronounced 'PUSS-uh-loh'), which is chocolate milk with a little vanilla syrup and some crushed ice ($1).

Other dishes include huge, tasty cheeseburgers for $1.50 and sandwiches from $2 to $5. It's open Monday to Thursday 5 am to midnight, and round the clock from Friday at 5 am until Sunday at midnight.

OCALA NATIONAL FOREST
The Ocala National Forest is a 400,000-acre park about 10 miles east of Ocala and about 30 miles west of Daytona. Within its boundaries are several springs and lakes, and you can camp anywhere you please, though developed campsites are available as well. Ocala offers fantastic hiking, canoeing, fishing and swimming opportunities, and though it's not reachable by public trans-

portation, once you arrive the place is very accessible: good signs, helpful rangers and good facilities.

Orientation & Information
Two highways cross the park: Hwy 19 runs north-south and Hwy 40 runs east-west. The three major spring areas are Juniper Springs (basically right at the park's center), Salt Springs (in the northern area of the park) and Alexander Springs (in the southeast); all have camping facilities.

Other areas with campsites include Fore Lake (near the western border of the park, roughly where Hwy 40 connects with Hwy 314), Lake Eaton (around the center of 314), Clearwater Lake (at the southeastern border of the park) and Lake Dorr (in the south near Hwy 19).

The following are three visitors centers in and near the park:

Hwy 40 Visitor Center
(☎ 352-236-0288), 10863 E Hwy 40 (where Hwy 315 connects with Hwy 40) in Silver Springs

Salt Springs Visitor Center
(☎ 352-685-3070), 14100 N Hwy 19 (where Hwy 314 forks off Hwy 19) in Salt Springs

Pittman Visitor Center
(☎ 352-669-7495), 45621 State Rd 19 (where Hwy 445 forks off Hwy 19)

Juniper Springs Recreation Area
This is one of the most popular sites in the forest. Two incredibly clear and beautiful springs emerge here: Juniper Springs (swimming is permitted, $3 admission for noncampers) and Fern Hammock Springs (no swimming). Together they produce about 13 million gallons of water daily.

Three different camping areas are available; the Sandpine Loop (south) and the Tropical Loop (north) cost $13, and the tent area, near Fern Hammock, is $11. The campgrounds have no water or electricity hookups, but do have showers ($1 for noncampers) and a dump station ($5 per use by noncampers). The maximum stay is 14 consecutive days within a 30-day period. For more information on camping call ☎ 352-625-3147. Other facilities here include toilets, picnic areas, parking, telephones, a concession stand and an amphitheater.

A three-quarter-mile self-guided interpretive nature trail runs parallel to Juniper Creek, and a 66-mile section of the Florida National Scenic Trail runs right through this area.

You can canoe down Juniper Creek for about 7 miles; canoe rental (☎ 352-625-2808) costs $23 for two people or $26.25 for four people (plus a $20 deposit). The run takes about four to 4¹/₂ hours and the price includes pick-up and return shuttle at the bottom of the trail.

The park is open daily 8 am to 8 pm.

Salt Springs Recreation Area
This area features a 2-mile loop trail leading through hardwood hammocks, pine flatwoods and cypress forest. Campsites are $11 for primitive, $17 for full service. Showers ($1 for noncampers) and a dump station ($5 per use by noncampers) are available. For more information call ☎ 352-685-2048. The campground is open to noncampers from 8 am to 8 pm.

Canoe and boat rentals (☎ 352-685-2255) are available for the 5-mile Salt Springs Run down to Lake George and the St John's River; canoe rentals are $10 for four hours and $20 for eight hours; small power boats are $25/40; and pontoon boats are $65/100.

Alexander Springs Recreation Area
A 1-mile hiking trail loops through the forest here. Campsites without hookups but with hot showers and toilets are $13. Showers and a dump station ($2.50 per use by noncampers) are available. The campground is open to noncampers from 8 am to 8 pm; the day-use fee is $3 for swimming or $5 for scuba diving.

Canoe rentals are $16 for four hours and $23 for eight (plus a $20 deposit), including pick-up and shuttle. For more information call ☎ 352-669-3522.

Fore Lake Recreation Area
Camping is $5; there are no showers and no dump station. The area is open 8 am to 8 pm.

Lake Eaton & Lake Eaton Sinkhole
The Lake Eaton sinkhole, which is a little east of the Lake Eaton campground, is a huge one: 80 feet deep and about 450 feet in diameter. A 2.2-mile interpretive walking trail leads past it, a boardwalk runs around it, and a staircase leads down into it. Note how quickly the temperature changes as you descend, becoming even chilly at the bottom.

The primitive campground here (with no hookups, showers or dump station) costs $4 for one person, $6 for two.

Clearwater Lake & Lake Dorr Recreation Areas
Camping (showers and a dump station but no hookups) at both these areas is $8. Clearwater Lake is open to noncampers from 8 am to 8 pm; admission is $3 per vehicle. Lake Dorr's hours are 6 am to 10 pm; admission is $2.

Gainesville

• population 93,000

Gainesville is a college town, where most of the action focuses around the sprawling campus of the University of Florida (UF). In the last 10 years, the downtown has been totally overhauled, and people have been relocating here in droves since the city was voted Best Small Place to Live in the USA by *Money Magazine* in 1994.

ORIENTATION
The city is laid out on a grid system. Note that here, avenues run east-west and streets run north-south. University Ave is the main drag as well as the north-south divider; its intersection with Main St, the east-west divider, is considered the center of town. Downtown Gainesville is roughly bordered by 13th St to the west; 2nd St to the east, 2nd Ave to the north and 4th Ave to the south. The university is southwest of the center. Archer Rd between 34th and 43rd Sts is fast-food heaven, with about 36 options.

Addresses and streets are given a N, S, E, W or NE, SE, NW, SW prefix dependent on their relation to the intersection of Main and University. It's confusing, even to locals, whose trick is the mnemonic device APRIL (actually APRL) which means: Avenues, Places, Rds and Lanes run east-west while everything else runs north-south. Addresses denote cross streets – a No 7150 would be between 71st and 72nd.

Maps
The VCB (see below) sells copies of Rand McNally's *Gainesville City Map* and gives out some tourist maps and a map to the

Gainesville bikeway system (see Getting Around later in this section). Most buildings at the university that are open to the public hoard campus maps, which they reluctantly part with on request.

INFORMATION
Tourist Offices
The Alachua County Visitors & Convention Bureau (VCB; ☎ 352-374-5231, on the Web at www.co.alachua.fl.us/~acvacb) is at 30 E University Ave, just east of Main St. The VCB office stocks the usual tourist flyers

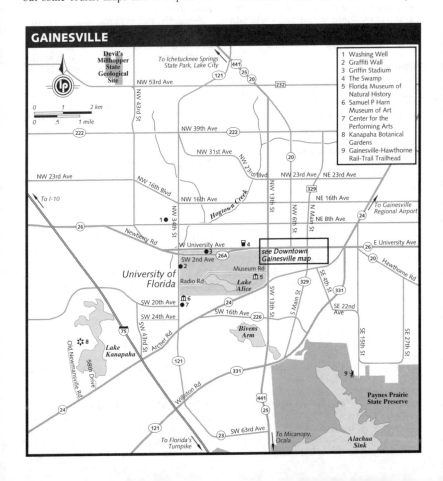

GAINESVILLE

1 Washing Well
2 Graffiti Wall
3 Griffin Stadium
4 The Swamp
5 Florida Museum of Natural History
6 Samuel P Harn Museum of Art
7 Center for the Performing Arts
8 Kanapaha Botanical Gardens
9 Gainesville-Hawthorne Rail-Trail Trailhead

Devil's Millhopper State Geological Site

To Ichetucknee Springs State Park, Lake City

NW 53rd Ave

NW 43rd St

NW 39th Ave

NW 31st Ave

NW 23rd Blvd

NW 23rd Ave

NE 23rd Ave

NW 16th Blvd

NW 23rd Ave

NW 16th Ave

NE 16th Ave

To I-10

Hogtown Creek

NW 13th St

N Main St

NE 8th Ave

To Gainesville Regional Airport

Newberry Rd

NW 34th St

W University Ave

E University Ave

SW 2nd Ave

Hawthorne Rd

University of Florida

Museum Rd

Radio Rd

Lake Alice

see Downtown Gainesville map

SW 20th Ave

SE 4th St

SW 24th Ave

SW 16th Ave

SE 22nd Ave

Bivens Arm

Old Newmansville Rd

Lake Kanapaha

Archer Rd

SW 13th St

S Main St

SE 15th St

SE 27th St

58th Drive

Williston Rd

Paynes Prairie State Preserve

To Florida's Turnpike

SW 63rd Ave

To Micanopy, Ocala

Alachua Sink

0   1   2 km
0   .5   1 mile

and literature. The Civic Media Center (CMC; ☎ 352-373-0010, www.afn.org/~cmc), 1021 W University Ave, has heaps of information on local culture, history, gay and lesbian resources, music and nightlife. It also hosts open-mike poetry readings and guitar concerts Thursday at 9 pm. Admission is $3 to $5 on a sliding scale depending on your income.

The old Hippodrome (☎ 352-375-4477, hipp.gator.net), at 25 SE 2nd Place just east of S Main St, is called 'the Hipp' by everyone in town and is a focus of Gainesville's cultural scene (see Entertainment later in the Gainesville section). It also has a fair amount of local information and a generally helpful staff. The AAA (☎ 352-373-7801) has an office at 1201 NW 13th St.

Money

NationsBank has branches at 1116 W University Ave and 1961 N Main St. An American Express representative is at House of Travel (☎ 352-378-1601), 3415 W University Ave.

Post & Communications

The downtown post office (☎ 352-371-6748) is at 401 SE 1st Ave. There's another one at 1401 N Main St (☎ 352-375-5665) and yet another at 1630 NW 1st Ave (☎ 352-377-2993). Socket 7 (☎ 352-373-8837), 1113 W University Ave, is an Internet café charging $7 an hour for terminal time.

Bookstores & Libraries

UF has several bookshops, including the main HUB (bookstore), the Collector's Shop at the Museum of Natural History and a Health Science Center bookstore.

Downtown you'll find several good used-book stores; see the friendly folks at Goerings' Book Center (☎ 352-378-0363), 3433 W University Ave, chock full o' Lonely Planet guides, or try University Ave Bookshop (☎ 352-371-0062), 804 W University Ave, or Omni Books (☎ 352-375-3755), located a bit inconveniently at the Westgate Publix Shopping Center, 99 SW 34th St (at University Ave). Wild Iris Books (☎ 352-375-7477), 802 W University Ave, right next door to University Ave Bookshop, sells feminist and women's studies books, as well as a good selection of gay and lesbian travel books and fiction.

The downtown library (☎ 352-334-3977) is at 401 E University Ave at the corner of SE 3rd St, just east of the courthouse.

Media

The big daily paper is the *Gainesville Sun* (www.sunone.com). The daily *Independent Florida Alligator* (www.alligator.org) is published by students at, but not officially associated with, UF. It's free and available all around town.

Other freebies available in vending boxes and at cafés, restaurants, clubs and bars include *UR* (University Reporter), a monthly entertainment guide; and the biweekly *Moon* (www.moonmag.com), that's heavier on arts and local news and politics. *Sleepless in Gainesville* is a down and dirty nightlife and music guide, and *Mea Culpa*, published by the CMC, is a monthly literary magazine.

National Public Radio (NPR) can be heard on 89.1 FM.

Gay & Lesbian

For gay and lesbian information and resources, call the Gay Switchboard (☎ 352-332-0700) or the LGB Union at UF (☎ 352-392-1665 x310).

Laundry

Most of the coin laundries are a bit out of the center. Coin Laundry, just before NW 17th St on the north side of University Ave is one; also try the Washing Well, at the corner of NW 34th St and University Ave. On SW 13th St, head for A-Best Coin Laundry, 2411 SW 13th St.

Medical Services

The largest hospital in the area is Alachua General Hospital (☎ 352-372-4321), at 801 SW 2nd Ave.

UNIVERSITY OF FLORIDA

The state's oldest university, UF (☎ 352-392-3261) was established in 1853 as the East Florida Seminary in Ocala and moved to Gainesville after the Civil War. It's one of the 10 largest universities in the country, with more than 40,000 students and a 2000-acre campus with more than 850 buildings, many of them historic landmarks in their own right. Near the Holland Law Center building, a historical marker notes the site of Native American burial mounds, and archaeologists have discovered artifacts from pre-Columbian settlements along Lake Alice, just east of the campus center.

The main reasons to visit the campus during your visit are the Florida Museum of Natural History, the Harn Museum of Art, the Center for Performing Arts and Griffin Stadium (also called Florida Field), where the people who made it so difficult for you to get a hotel room will be watching the Gators football team. Free campus maps are available at all campus museums.

Florida Museum of Natural History

We had a blast at this museum (☎ 352-392-1721), on the university campus on Museum Rd (park on the southeast corner of Museum Rd and Newell Drive). As you enter, a great sinkhole exhibit has caverns you can crawl into, good explanatory materials and even bats on the roof; kids love it. Walk past the mega-huge carcharodon megalodon, which makes Jaws look puny, and into the interactive computer room. Check out the temperate and tropical forest exhibit and the totally cheesy World of Maya exhibit.

A good Florida history timeline adorns the hallway leading to the Object Gallery, which is the best of them all. It's a room filled with…stuff…ots of stuff, neatly tucked away in stuff drawers, and you never know what you may discover. Check out the German surgical aids (drawer 199), bat skulls and skins (50), marine crustaceans (106), snake skeletons and bullfrogs (27), exotic birds (12 and 13) and common ones (1-11), and human (sadly, plastic) skulls (217). Near the main entrance, the satellite orbit demo is engrossing, until you realize that you won't get your coin back. The museum is open Monday to Saturday 10 am to 5 pm, Sunday and holidays 1 to 5 pm, closed Christmas. Admission is free.

Samuel P Harn Museum of Art

Another UF prize, the Harn (☎ 352-392-9826) presents rotating exhibits of fine art in all media, including works from both its permanent collection and traveling exhibitions. The permanent collection contains art from the Americas, Asia and Africa, as well as pre-Columbian sculpture and more than 150 pieces of art from Papua New Guinea. Schedules are erratic and exhibition length varies greatly throughout the year due to limited space (though the place is pretty big).

The museum also hosts lectures and artist talks; call when you're in town to see what's on. Guided tours are held Saturday and Sunday at 2 pm, and Wednesday at 12:30 pm, and 'family tours' are offered the second Sunday of the month at 1:45 pm. The museum is open Tuesday to Friday 11 am to 5 pm, Saturday 10 am to 5 pm and Sunday 1 to 5 pm. Admission is free.

University Gallery

This gallery (☎ 352-392-0201) offers rotating shows (six per year) dedicated to contemporary art by students and nationally known artists. In the spring, it presents works of faculty and MFA candidates. The gallery is in the Fine Arts Building complex on campus, in Building B. It's open Tuesday 10 am to 8 pm, Wednesday to Friday 10 am to 5 pm, Saturday 1 to 5 pm, closed Sunday and Monday.

Public displays of locally produced art also rotate through city hall, the Gainesville airport, the county administration building and the downtown library.

GRAFFITI WALL

Also called the 34th St Wall, this is one of the city's finest examples of right, and liberal, thinking. The long cement wall that runs along the east side of SW 34th St just south of SW 2nd Ave is a graffiti-permitted zone, whose management has been effectively turned over to the students and graffiti artists who paint on it. The main focus is a well-maintained memorial to the five UF students who were murdered in August 1990 by a serial killer – an event that continues to haunt the city's and university's residents.

CENTRAL

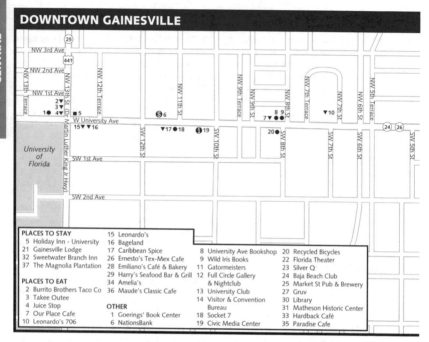

DOWNTOWN GAINESVILLE

PLACES TO STAY
5 Holiday Inn - University
21 Gainesville Lodge
32 Sweetwater Branch Inn
37 The Magnolia Plantation

PLACES TO EAT
2 Burrito Brothers Taco Co
3 Takee Outee
4 Juice Stop
7 Our Place Cafe
10 Leonardo's 706

15 Leonardo's
16 Bageland
17 Caribbean Spice
26 Ernesto's Tex-Mex Cafe
28 Emiliano's Café & Bakery
29 Harry's Seafood Bar & Grill
34 Amelia's
36 Maude's Classic Cafe

OTHER
1 Goerings' Book Center
6 NationsBank

8 University Ave Bookshop
9 Wild Iris Books
11 Gatormeisters
12 Full Circle Gallery
   & Nightclub
13 University Club
14 Visitor & Convention
   Bureau
18 Socket 7
19 Civic Media Center

20 Recycled Bicycles
22 Florida Theater
23 Silver Q
24 Baja Beach Club
25 Market St Pub & Brewery
27 Gruv
30 Library
31 Matheson Historic Center
33 Hardback Café
35 Paradise Cafe

With the exception of that memorial, the wall's an ever-changing exhibition of slogans, political manifestos, and thank-you notes to parents paying for students' education ('Thanks, Mom and Dad!'). While it's legal to tag here, it's considered bad form to paint over existing works or litter.

THOMAS CENTER

This historical museum (☎ 352-334-2197), 302 NE 6th Ave (in a building that now houses city offices), offers a small history exhibition and art galleries with rotating exhibitions. It's open Monday to Friday 9 am to 5 pm, Saturday and Sunday 1 to 4 pm. Admission is free.

DEVIL'S MILLHOPPER STATE GEOLOGICAL SITE

Welcome to one of Florida's most famous holes in the ground. It works like this: Limestone is susceptible to weak acids that are formed when rainwater mixes with decomposing plant matter. As these acids eat away at the limestone, caverns are formed. When the caverns get extensive enough, the whole limestone structure collapses on itself and presto! – it's a sinkhole. This one is more than 120 feet deep and 500 feet across. It's fascinating to walk down the 232-step wooden staircase into the hole, feeling the temperature decreasing with every step and looking at what amounts to a cutaway section of Florida's geological formation.

Even if you're not up for the hole, the 63-acre park is a pleasant enough place to spend an afternoon. There's an interpretive center without which we never could have written that paragraph; ranger-guided tours are held every Saturday morning at 10 am, and orienteering classes are given on the fourth Saturday of the month at 9 am.

The site (☎ 352-955-2008, 352-462-7905) is at 4732 Millhopper Rd, and is open 9 am to

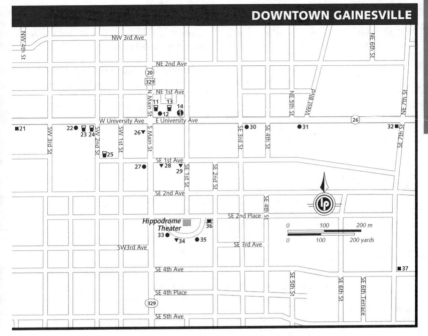

DOWNTOWN GAINESVILLE

5 pm daily. The admission of $2 per vehicle, $1 for pedestrians or bicyclists, is paid on an honor system: take an envelope from the kiosk near the entrance, place your money in it, keep the stub on you or put it on your dashboard if you're driving (rangers check). To get to the park, take University Ave west to NW 39th Rd, which becomes NW 43rd St; follow that to its intersection with Hwy 232, which is Millhopper Rd. The entrance is on the right.

KANAPAHA BOTANICAL GARDENS

The most wonderful thing about these 62-acre gardens (☎ 352-372-4981), aside from the volunteers, is its water garden: installed in 1994, the four waterfalls and the long babbling brook over newly landscaped hills and dales are courtesy of reclaimed wastewater from the regional utilities board. Apparently, when they tried to just, well, shove the water back into the ground, it wreaked havoc with the local pH balance. The gardens and the utility came up with this ingenious, environmentally friendly and lovely method of reintroducing the stuff into the ground slowly and gently. This is a very serene place to take a stroll any time of year. It also features a vinery, an herb garden and a butterfly garden – and there were still hummingbirds in the hummingbird garden when we visited in November!

The gardens are open Monday, Tuesday and Friday 9 am to 5 pm, and Wednesday, Saturday and Sunday 9 am to dusk, closed Thursday. Admission is $3 for adults, $2 for children five to 13, under five free.

To get here from downtown, take University Ave west to 13th St and turn left; continue to Archer Rd and turn right, following Archer 1 mile past I-75; the entrance is up the little dirt road on the right-hand side (look for the sign).

CENTRAL

PLACES TO STAY

Prices soar during special events such as football games or graduation, when people book months in advance and come from as far as California to see their little darlings. Check in newspapers or with the VCB to see if any such special events are planned during your stay, and, if so, call *well* in advance for reservations!

Rustic camping is available at *Paynes Prairie State Preserve* (☎ 352-466-3397), 10 miles south (see Around Gainesville later this chapter).

Hotels & Motels

SW 13th St Most of the cheap motels are on the outskirts of town, either at the southern end of SW 13th St or on approach roads. SW 13th St is the best bet. Chains include *Radisson Inn, Econo Lodge, Scottish Inn* and *Comfort Inn*.

The *Florida Motel* (☎ 352-376-3742, 2603 SW 13th St) has a classic motel sign and shoddy but acceptable rooms for $30/33 single or double, $70 per double during special events; local calls are 35¢.

Just next to the excellent Bahn Thai restaurant (see Places to Eat later in this section), the new *Super 8 Motel* (☎ 352-372-3654, 2000 SW 13th St) is a good deal, with clean rooms for $45 to $55, $90 during special events. The rooms have HBO.

Over at the *Bambi Motel* (☎ 352-376-2622, 800-342-2624, 2119 SW 13th St), the rooms, which are $30/32 single/ double, or $60/70 during special events, are nicer than the exterior would lead you to believe; they're large, with new TVs and HBO included. Beds were a bit soft for our taste, but they're OK.

Flashier is the *Days Inn University Motel* (☎ 352-376-2222, 1901 SW 13th St), the one with the large pool and big backyard, where clean singles/doubles with new TVs are $40 to $45, or $99 per room during special events. Some of the rooms have refrigerators.

The nice and very friendly *Cape Cod Inn* (☎ 352-371-2500, 3820 SW 13th St) has very clean rooms in a building that's a tad more romantic than the rest of its nearby compe-

tition, but it'll cost you: rooms are $43.95, $49.95 with whirlpool, $85 during special events, though a breakfast of muffins, juice and coffee is included.

W University Ave Over on the main drag of W University Ave is the *Gainesville Lodge* (☎ 352-376-1224, 413 W University Ave), with singles and doubles for $33/37, or $65/70 during special events.

The lax service and fusty rooms at the otherwise perfectly located *Holiday Inn-University* (☎ 352-376-1661, 1250 W University Ave) makes the standard rates of $82.50 per room, or $98.50 per room in the pathetically underappointed 'executive level' ($119.50 to $125 during special events), an absolute rip-off. Another Holiday Inn is out near I-75.

B&Bs

Of the several B&Bs in town, most are east of Main St. Check with the VCB for a complete list. We liked *Sweetwater Branch Inn* (☎ 352-373-6760, 625 E University Ave), with seven rooms, a cottage and a carriage house, all with claw-foot tubs, two with hot tubs, three with fireplaces; rooms range $72 to $90 on weekdays, $85 to $125 on weekends, more during special events.

We also liked *The Magnolia Plantation* (☎ 352-375-6653, 309 SE 7th St) for the free fridge filled with snacks and soft drinks, wine in the evening, and the pond out back. The parlor has a VCR and TV (no TV or telephones in the rooms), and the cats – Oliver, Whiner and blonde kitty. Rooms range $85 to $100 a night, higher during special events. They also have two cottages with Jacuzzis and fireplaces, $125 to $175.

Give the *Thomas Tourist Home* (835 W University Ave) a big swerve, especially if you're German: 'I don't mind telling you,' said the owner to Corinna – a German national – 'that I don't think much of Germans.' Yeah? Well, we don't much care for you, broccoli nose.

PLACES TO EAT

This is a fast-food-heaven college town, remember? Note that service in many places we list isn't what it could be; many servers have exams to cram for and 'Hey, dude, we're puttin' the *band* back together!' attitudes and are therefore far too busy to bring you your tuna salad.

Budget

The corner of W 13th St – both north and south – at University Ave is a great spot for cheap eats. For example, the burritos at *Burrito Brothers Taco Co (☎ 352-378-5948, www.burritobros.com, 16 NW 13th St)* are so good that crowds form. The amazing burritos are $1.90 to $2.60, tacos are $1 to $1.50 and enchiladas are $2 to $3. None of the beans or tortillas contain animal fat, and you can get your meal dairy-free on request. It also has excellent guacamole and chips ($2), and primo salsa. It's open until 10 pm daily.

Nearby, *Takee Outee (☎ 352-372-7907, 14 NW 13th St)* does Chinese takeout. Entrees range $3 to $5, combos $3.75 to $6; lunch specials are $3. On the corner, *Juice Stop* makes fresh squeezed juices.

On the south side of W University, excellent pizza is available at *Leonardo's (☎ 352-375-2007)*, which sells great slices for $1.50 to $3 and large 14-inch pies for $9 to $14. It's packed at lunchtime. Only a few feet east, *Bageland* serves up hearty and filling sandwiches on bagels. At breakfast, a bagel, orange juice and coffee is $2.29.

Caribbean Spice (☎ 352-377-2172, 1121 W University Ave) does great Caribbean takeout lunch specials of beef or veggie patty and a soda for $3.

Our Place Cafe (☎ 352-371-1172, 808 W University Ave) does a good breakfast special (two eggs, toast or biscuit, home fries or grits) is $2.95, sandwiches are $4.95 to $6.50, quiche $3.45 and Greek salad $4.25. Smoking is not permitted.

Across downtown, *Maude's Classic Cafe (☎ 352-336-9646, 101 SE 2nd Place)* serves good coffees and teas from $1 to $3.

Mid-Range & Top End

The Thai food is excellent at *Bahn Thai Restaurant (☎ 352-335-1204, 1902 SW 13th St)*, run by the second generation of the family that runs the one in Tallahassee. It's

an exceptionally good deal on weekdays from 11 am to 2:30 pm, when a 20-some-odd-entree lunch buffet goes for $6 per person. Dinner is pricier, with most entrees going for $8.95 and up, but the food is some of the best we've had in the state (and we like Thai food).

Ernesto's Tex-Mex Cafe (☎ 352-376-0750, 6 S Main St) has good service and food to match: the chicken mole and veggie specials ($8.95 to $13.95) are definitely worth the price. The menu also offers combo platters for $5.95 and some less expensive dishes.

Emiliano's Café & Bakery (☎ 352-375-7381, 7 SE 1st Ave) is a fine place to sit for lunch, either outside at a sidewalk table or inside (no smoking). The service is friendly, if overworked, and the cheap tapas bar lets you fill up on finger food and get out for $10 for a couple. Otherwise, lunch entrees are about $5.95 to $7, dinner twice that.

Harry's Seafood Bar & Grill (☎ 352-372-1555, 110 SE 1st St), in the old 1887 Opera House building, is another fine lunch place, with specials under $10. It also has a good happy hour, from 2 to 7 pm, with half-price well drinks, wings and oysters.

Mr Hans (☎ 352-331-6400, 6944 NW 10th Place) is an excellent Chinese restaurant just east of I-75 (exit 76). The fun thing is a formal attire requirement on some evenings for dinner. The great lunch specials include beef and chicken with Chinese vegetables in black bean sauce, or chicken and shrimp in orange sauce with hot-and-sour soup, egg roll and fried rice for $5.95. Dinner's more expensive; appetizers $4.50 to $8, main courses $8.95 to $14.

For a flashy evening, *Amelia's (☎ 352-373-1919, 235 S Main St)*, behind the Hipp, is a romantic spot with good Italian food and stellar bills. Antipasti range $5.95 to $9.95, fish $13.95 to $18.95 and pastas $8.95 to $12.95. Lunch is almost half price on everything.

Leonardo's 706 (☎ 352-378-2001, 706 W University Ave) may have the best food in town. It's fairly expensive ($10 to $24 for entrees) and is only open for dinner, but the Italian food here is said to be excellent, and served in enormous portions.

ENTERTAINMENT
Performing Arts
Formerly a federal building, later a post office, the **Hippodrome** building (1904-11) is one of Gainesville's most loved. Over the past 20 years, the Hipp (☎ 352-375-4477, hipp.gator.net, 25 SE 2nd Place) has been the city's main cultural center, hosting theatrical productions, an experimental cinema series, teen theater programs, kids' productions and more. It's worth visiting. Admissions vary.

UF's **Center for the Performing Arts** holds two theaters. The main, 1800-seat theater is home to concerts, theater and dance throughout the year. Tickets, available through the box office (☎ 352-392-2787) or through Ticketmaster, average $30 for professional road-show performances and around $5 to $10 for local performances, like those of Dance Alive!, a 33-year-old local dance troupe. Student discounts are almost always available. Downstairs is a smaller, 200-seat, 'black box' theater, home to UF Department of Theater (☎ 352-392-2038) productions, held usually once a semester. Call either venue and see what's on during your stay. The center is on the campus on Hull Rd, just next to the Harn Museum of Art.

Bars & Pubs
Have we mentioned that some college students live here in town? As one would imagine, their raging hormones and tough (ha!) work schedules demand a few outlets. Check in *UR*, *Moon*, *Sleepless in Gainesville* and *Mea Culpa* for listings.

The **Market St Pub & Brewery** (☎ 352-377-2929, 120 SW 1st Ave) looks and smells English. Beers brewed on the premises include, on any given day, four or five of a list of seven. Live acoustic and jazz music is presented on weekends.

Sports bars include **Silver Q** (225 W University Ave), which offers happy hour Monday to Saturday 4 to 8 pm and all day Sunday. Diversions include 12 pool tables and 20 TVs tuned to sports events.

Gatormeisters (☎ 352-377-6444, 15 N Main St) and **The Swamp** (1642 W University Ave)

are two very popular drinking spots. Frat boys will please head for **Baja Beach Club** (☎ 352-379-9953, 201 W University Ave).

Clubs & Live Music
One of the most popular clubs in town is the **Covered Dish** (☎ 352-377-3334, 210 SW 2nd Ave), which has original bands and a few cover-gigs. The **Florida Theatre** (☎ 352-375-7361, 233 W University Ave) is a disco/club that also has live local bands every Wednesday night ($3). On Friday and Saturday nights, their **High Note**, upstairs, does live jazz; 18 and over welcome. **Gruv** (☎ 352-371-4788, 104 S Main St) is another very popular disco.

The **Hardback Café** (☎ 352-372-6248, 232 SE 1st St), just opposite the Hipp, has live local alternative music, including punk and underground (some skinheads and dyke bands). Doors open at 10 pm; $3 to $4 cover.

Right behind the Hipp is **Paradise Cafe**, a combination record label, live music venue, disco and bar that was just opening when we researched. Looks like it will be a scene.

Full Circle Gallery & Nightclub (☎ 352-377-8080, 6 E University Ave) is an artsy, gay-friendly, all-welcome kind of place that plays old-wave, disco and acid jazz.

Gay & Lesbian Venues
The **University Club** (☎ 352-378-6814, 18 E University Ave) is predominantly gay, but it's open to everyone. The entrance is around the back at NE 1st Ave and up or down the stairs. **Melody Club & Ambush** (☎ 352-376-3772, 4130 NW 6th St) is a leather and Levi's place that also does drag shows.

In the middle of nowhere is **Oz** (☎ 352-332-2553, 7118 W University Ave), behind the Home Depot, two buildings down from the old Power Plant gym. It's a lesbian bar with a whole lot of activities, from male dancers and lesbian bands to cookouts.

SPECTATOR SPORTS
Griffin Stadium (also called Florida Field; ☎ 352-375-4683, 800-344-2867 within Florida) is the home of the UF Gators football team, which plays home games between September and December. Order tickets

early – they go very, very, very quickly and cost about $20 to $30 for a single game. The Gators have men's baseball and men's and women's basketball teams as well; call the above number for ticket information to all Gators athletic events.

GETTING THERE & AWAY

Gainesville Regional Airport (☎ 352-373-0249) is a midsize airport about 10 miles northeast of downtown with regular service from Air South. Most nonbusiness travelers don't usually fly to the area.

The Greyhound terminal (☎ 352-376-5252) is at 516 SW 4th Ave. Sample routes are listed below; prices are one way/roundtrip:

destination	duration	price
Jacksonville	1½ hrs	$15/29
Miami	11 hrs	$55/102
Orlando	3 hrs	$23/45
Tallahassee	3 hrs	$33/65

The nearest Amtrak station serving the Gainesville area is in Waldo (☎ 352-468-1403), 13 miles northeast. A taxi from the station to the center of Gainesville costs about $25.

Gainesville is in north-central Florida, about 3 miles east of I-75, about 150 miles southeast of Tallahassee via I-10 and I-75, about 108 miles northwest of Orlando, 62 miles southwest of Jacksonville, and 330 miles from Miami.

GETTING AROUND

No public transport is available between town and the airport. If you're slick you could jump a free hotel shuttle bus – we would suggest the downtown Holiday Inn's if we were to ever suggest such a thing. Cabs (see below) charge approximately $10 to $12 for the ride.

Gainesville Regional Transit System (RTS; ☎ 352-334-2600, www.go-rts.com) runs an excellent network of buses throughout the city. Fare is $1. Transfers and the UF campus shuttle are 25¢. An all-day pass is $2. All buses have bicycle racks (free). Bus Nos 1, 4, 5, 6, 7 and 10 cruise University Ave;

Nos 1, 3, 4 and 7 cover SE 4th Ave and Nos 1 and 13 cover SW 13th St.

The two big taxi companies in town are Gator Cab (☎ 352-375-0313) and City Cab (☎ 352-375-8294). Taxi rates in Gainesville are $2.80 for the first mile, $1.30 for each additional mile.

Gainesville has 77 miles of bike lanes painted onto roads; 19 miles of bike lanes separated from the roads by a curb; and many bike trails completely independent of city streets. In the city, bike lanes are marked with signs or with diamonds painted on the street. In rural areas, bike trails or rail trails are signed. The largest of these is the 17-mile Gainesville-Hawthorne Rail-Trail, which cuts across the northern end of Paynes Prairie State Preserve (see the Around Gainesville section below). But note that this trail is made of crushed lime-rock; wide tires are recommended.

Recycled Bicycles (☎ 352-372-4890) at 805 W University Ave doesn't really rent bikes, but you can buy a bike and sell it back to them the next day. They charge $10 per day (this is done for insurance). The shop is open Monday to Friday 9:30 am to 6 pm and Saturday 10 am to 5 pm.

AROUND GAINESVILLE
Paynes Prairie State Preserve

Made up of wet prairie, swamp, hammock and pine flatwoods, this wonderful and eerie preserve (☎ 352-466-3397) offers world-class birding (bald eagles, raptors, Florida wading birds and, in winter, sandhill cranes), a look at some unusual quadrupeds (one resident herd each of wild horses and bison), extensive hiking and mountain-biking (more than 34 trails) and good camping – all of which makes the park a worthy destination for a day trip or an overnight.

On weekends from November to April, free ranger-led tours of the prairie leave from the main visitors center at 8 am. And on the first weekend of each month during that period, ranger-led backpacking trips leave on overnight excursions; you'll hike 4 miles the first day and 2 on the second, with lots of stops for beginners and less mobile travelers. The trips cost an incredible $5.45

per person, with the park providing an outhouse, a ranger guide and a great campfire; you bring your own insect repellent, tent, food and marshmallows. It's fun for all but the most avid hikers.

The trails through the park are perfect for bicycling, and the 17-mile **Gainesville-Hawthorne Rail-Trail** is one of the hottest around. Rail-Trails, popular throughout central Florida, are built atop railbeds abandoned by the railroads. When the tracks are removed, hikers, bicyclists and equestrians have a perfect path. No mountain-bike (or canoe) rentals are available, so you will need to bring your own.

The park's *camping* options include drive-in family sites and walk-in tent sites (which are close to the parking lots). The cost per site is $12 with electric hookups, $10 without. You can reserve up to 60 days in advance, and because of football games in Gainesville, it's probably a good idea as the place gets booked out.

The preserve is between Gainesville and Micanopy on Hwy 441. It's open year round 8 am to sunset. Admission is $3.25 per car or $1 for pedestrians and bicyclists.

Rawlings Estate

Marjorie Kinnan Rawlings (1896-1953) was author of the Pulitzer-prize-winning novel *The Yearling*, a coming-of-age story set in what is now the Ocala National Forest, and *Cross Creek*, a book about her life at this estate (☎ 352-466-3672) just north of Orange Lake, off Hwy 325 between Island Grove and Micanopy.

Rawlings came to the area with her first husband in 1928, and she remained in the area after they divorced in 1933. She remarried in 1941 and continued to write at Cross Creek until her death.

The cracker-style house is open for guided tours only ($3 for adults, $2 for kids) Thursday to Sunday at 10 and 11 am and 1, 2, 3 and 4 pm. It's closed Monday to Wednesday and during August and September. Tour groups are limited to 10 people and are very popular, so expect a wait when you visit. The 8 acres of grounds are open year round 9 am to 5 pm. Admission is $3.25 per car or $1 for pedestrians and bicyclists.

Devil's Den

Devil's Den (☎ 352-528-3322) is an underground spring just outside the quaint town of Williston (known for its breeding of show horses; if you like horses, the area is nice to drive through just for a change of pace), about 18 miles southeast of Gainesville.

Divers simply do not want to miss this fantastic cave-dive opportunity; we thought it was one of the most spectacularly odd and beautiful places in the state. Swimming ($9 a day) is also permitted unless too many divers are in the water. It's a fine spot for an overnighter – you can camp at the site.

The spring bubbles up at a constant 72°F, so you can swim comfortably year round. Divers used to lower themselves down to the springs on rope ladders, but now a staircase has been dug into the ground – it's a wonderful sensation to enter a hole in the ground, walk down through solid rock and emerge into something right out of the movie *The Abyss* (portions of which were actually filmed at nearby Silver Springs). The eerie blue water is illuminated by the sunlight that shines through the opening in the ground about 20 feet above the surface of the water. The park also has activities like volleyball and horseback riding (guided trail tours; $15 for a half hour, $25 an hour). No pets are permitted in the park.

Marjorie Kinnan Rawlings

Diving Certified divers can dive here for $27 a day, and a full line of rental equipment is available (you can even get certified here in four days for $275 for one person, $500 for two). A basic rental package (not including flashlight, booties or hood) is $62 per day including admission to the park. The spring has a maximum depth of 56 feet and numerous tunnels to explore. You'll see six species of fish in the spring, as well as prehistoric fossils embedded in the cave walls and floor.

The spring is open Monday to Thursday 9 am to 5 pm, Friday to Sunday 8 am to 5 pm; sunset dives on Saturday cost an additional $10 if you've been there all day, or $15 if you show up just before sunset. Night dives can be arranged for groups of six or more.

Places to Stay & Eat Tent *camping* costs $7 per diver; $9 per nondiver; children under six $1. Campfires are permitted, but they must be in a fire circle and you must have an extinguishing material (such as sand or a lot of people drinking beer). Hot showers and barbecue grills are available. Cabins with kitchens are $85 to $95 a night and sleep up to four people.

Buy food and supplies at the Winn-Dixie supermarket on the corner of 727 W Noble Ave at Hwy 27 in downtown Williston. Also in Williston, the ***Ivy House*** *(☎ 352-528-5410, 106 NW Main St)* serves lunch Tuesday to Saturday, with meals like chicken supreme with yellow rice and salad ($5.95), and desserts like pumpkin roll or chocolate fudge pie ($1.50). Turkey and prime rib dinners ($12.95) are offered on the first Saturday of the month. No smoking.

Getting There & Away No public transport is available. To get here by car from Gainesville take I-75 then Hwy 121 south for 15 miles to the junction of US Hwy 27, which will bring you into downtown Williston. Turn west on Hwy 27A (toward the town of Bronson), turn at the sign and drive past Stonehedge Ranch; the Den is on the right-hand side of the road (look for the dive flag), up the dirt road past the fenced-off horse grazing fields – follow the signs. From Orlando, take Florida's Turnpike north to

I-75 north, to exit 70, and then take Hwy 27 north to Williston.

Silver Springs

One of the few saving graces of the otherwise debilitatingly boring city of Ocala is Silver Springs (☎ 352-236-2121, 800-234-7458), a theme park built around seven natural springs and the resultant stunningly clear Silver River. The park says that glass-bottomed boats were invented here in 1878, and if that's not enough of a claim, try this one: *Tarzan* movies and portions of *The Abyss* were shot here as well.

Things to See & Do The park has a sufficient number of fascinating attractions to justify the admission prices of $29.95 for adults, $10.95 for children (10% discount for seniors, AAA members, active military and the disabled). Parking is $3.

The glass-bottom boat ride is spectacular. As you slowly cruise over the eel grass, you'll pass over six small spring formations before the grand finale: a pass over Mammoth Spring, the world's largest artesian limestone spring.

Other attractions include our favorite, Doolittle Petting Area, where we met the sweetest camel on the planet: baby, you ain't lived till you been kissed by a camel. This one's got incredibly soft skin, smells clean and loves to be petted. But Corinna was in the middle of saying how cute he was when he reared back and – *KABOOM*! – let loose a camel sneeze with a concussive jolt and a shower of camel snot. *(Gesundheit.)* Other animals in the petting area include giraffes, goats, sheep, deer, buffalo, llamas and pigs.

Lost River Voyage is a boat ride through dense jungle, as is the Jungle Cruise, featuring animals from six continents including zebras, emus and giraffes; Jeep Safari offers a trailer ride through a 35-acre jungle and a look at the alligator pit.

Shows include Reptiles of the World, with demonstrations using live reptiles like alligators, snakes and lizards; and Creature Feature, a live and videotaped presentation on creepy things like scorpions, spiders, hissing cockroaches and bats.

Must-sees are the new Gator Lagoon, featuring 30 of Florida's largest alligators; Panther Prowl, with a Florida panther and a cougar; and the World of Bears – the largest bear exhibit in the world, with four species of bears in a 2-acre habitat.

Twin Oaks Mansion is a concert venue that has music throughout the year and the occasional superstar performer – Kenny Rogers, Willie Nelson and Ray Charles are regulars. The concerts are included in the cost of admission.

The park is open 9 am to 5:30 pm daily. For information, contact the Ocala/Marion County Chamber of Commerce (☎ 352-629-8051) at 110 E Silver Springs Blvd.

Getting There & Away The Greyhound station (☎ 352-732-2677) is at 512 N Magnolia Ave at the corner of NW 5th St in Ocala. The company offers 12 buses a day from Gainesville ($8 one way, $15 round-trip); the trip takes 45 to 75 minutes. Seven buses a day go to/from Orlando ($15/30; 1½ to 2½ hours).

By car, Ocala is 37 miles south of Gainesville and 72 miles northwest of Orlando. From Gainesville, take either I-75 or Hwy 301 south to Silver Springs Blvd (Hwy 40) and go east to get to Silver Springs. From Orlando, take Florida's Turnpike to I-75, and that to Silver Springs Blvd.

Space Coast

The major attractions along the stretch of coast between Fort Pierce and Daytona Beach are the galactic activities at the Kennedy Space Center – the western hemisphere's only manned spaceport. But the region is also noted for its well-preserved natural environment. Bird watchers have a field day at Merritt Island National Wildlife Refuge and Canaveral National Seashore, as do families and nature lovers. Whales have been spotted off Canaveral National Seashore, and some of the state's best sea turtle observation programs are run here (you need to reserve early!). And the strip between Sebastian Inlet and Cocoa Beach has Florida's best surfing.

You'll need your own transportation: public transport is spotty and shuttles and taxis are expensive.

Despite the abundance of inexpensive and even free camping opportunities, many of the affordable lodging options are motels that are packed to the rafters during launches and are generally on the run-down and sometimes spooky side. Unless you're camping, we highly recommend visiting the area from Orlando or somewhere inland as opposed to seeking shelter in the immediate vicinity.

KENNEDY SPACE CENTER

The Kennedy Space Center is among the most popular attractions in Florida, drawing more than two million people a year. As the only site in the western hemisphere from which humans have been launched into space, the place is a fascinating excursion for the average visitor and the mother lode to space junkies – and there are far more of those than you'd think. You can easily spend a full day here taking the bus tour, watching the IMAX films and walking through the exhibits.

History

Early Rocket Science Modern rocketry dates to the turn of the 20th century, when

Highlights

- Watch a space shuttle launch at the Kennedy Space Center

- Attend Space Camp to learn rocket science and go on a simulated shuttle mission – or offload the kids for a week while you soak in the sun on the nearby beaches

- See birds and wildlife at the Merritt Island National Wildlife Refuge, home to more endangered and protected species than any other refuge in the country

- Watch sea turtles lay their eggs at Canaveral National Seashore

Russian scientist Konstantin Tsiolkovsky proposed abandoning the use of solid fuel – that'd be gunpowder – as a rocket propellant in favor of multiple engines powered by liquid hydrogen and oxygen. The multistage rocket design is necessary to support the weight of the enormous amounts of fuel needed to propel an object free of the Earth's atmosphere. As each individually powered engine exhausts its fuel, it is jettisoned, allowing the remaining engines to boost the vehicle farther into space.

In 1926, American scientist Robert Goddard launched what is considered to be the

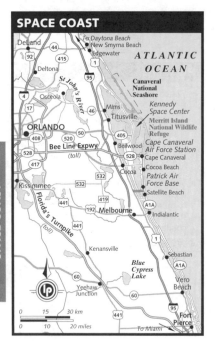

SPACE COAST

DeLand
To Daytona Beach
New Smyrna Beach
Edgewater
ATLANTIC
OCEAN
Deltona
Canaveral
National
Seashore
Osceola
St John's River
Mims
Titusville
Kennedy
Space Center
ORLANDO
Merritt Island
National Wildlife
Refuge
Bee Line Expwy
(toll)
Bellwood
Cape Canaveral
Air Force Station
Cape Canaveral
Cocoa Beach
Cocoa
Patrick Air
Force Base
Kissimmee
Florida's Turnpike
(toll)
Satellite Beach
Melbourne
Indialantic
Kenansville
Sebastian
Blue
Cypress
Lake
Vero
Beach
Yeehaw
Junction
Fort
Pierce
To Miami

0   15   30 km
0   10   20 miles

SPACE COAST

first successful guided rocket. But rocketry didn't gain military significance until just before WWII, when German scientists led by Wernher von Braun began to experiment with rockets as a weapon-delivery system. In 1942, Germany perfected the infamous V2 rocket, which could carry a payload of bombs at an altitude of 50 miles.

At the end of the war, American war spoils included von Braun (actually, he defected) and about 100 V2s. For their part, the Soviets managed to clean out substantial sections of the German's bomb-making archives and large numbers of German scientists to boot.

The Making of NASA When the Soviets announced on October 4, 1957, that they had successfully launched the unmanned satellite *Sputnik,* the Americans found themselves beaten in a race they'd thought they had covered hands down. The USA

launched its first unmanned satellite into Earth orbit in January 1958.

Fueled by propaganda campaigns and predictions of doom by American politicians, who envisioned Soviet flyboys over US airspace dropping atomic bombs at will, the National Aeronautics & Space Administration (NASA) established Project Mercury on October 7, 1958, and the race for manned space flight had begun. The central-eastern Florida coast was chosen for its weather, its proximity to the ocean for splashdowns and the huge and unpopulated tracts of land available to the government for testing.

Mercury Seven In recruiting the first seven astronauts – the word astronaut is derived from the Greek words *astro* (star) and *nautes* (sailor, navigator) – the government looked to a talent pool consisting of test pilots and fighter pilots from the various branches of the military. The requirements called for a jet-qualified, test-pilot-school graduate who had logged over 1500 hours of flight time in jets, held at least an undergraduate university degree, was a US citizen, and was less than 40 years old and under 5 feet, 11 inches tall (determined by the restrictive size of the capsule). There were 110 qualified applicants.

The testing and weeding-out procedure is well documented and in hindsight would seem to have been overkill in the extreme. In an effort to ensure a team of unshakable men, NASA subjected applicants to deprivations of sleep, light and other sensory input, as well as to humiliation and psychological stress bordering on cruelty. The candidates were forced to endure odd physical challenges such as electric shocks and plunges into ice water, and in one instance they were made to walk through a public hospital with their intestines filled to bursting with barium while holding the plug that prevented it from flushing out in an explosive rush. Scientists studied the applicants' sperm, stools, blood, tissue, urine and anything else they could think of to test.

The US plan was to begin with a series of cannonball-like, suborbital 'lobs,' in which the capsule would be fired into outer space and fall directly back to Earth. They then planned to graduate to full orbital flight after systems had been tested in the environment of outer space.

When the Mercury astronauts – Gus Grissom, Deke Slayton, John Glenn, Wally Schirra, Alan Shepard, Scott Carpenter and Gordon Cooper – were introduced to the media in 1959, the nation treated them with nothing less than hero worship. And that worship continued despite the abject failure of one of the primary goals of the program: putting the first man in space.

First Humans in Space On April 12, 1961, the Soviet Union announced that the first manned spacecraft had been placed in Earth orbit. The cosmonaut who piloted the craft was announced to have been Yuri Gagarin, the first of 20 Soviet pilots selected for the Soviet space program.

Secrecy has left many space-race-related questions unanswered to this day, and Gagarin's single Earth orbit may not have been the first. In his book *Heroes in Space: From Gagarin to Challenger,* Peter Bond says that there was speculation in the British press that Sergei Ilyushin had in fact completed three Earth orbits days before Gagarin's flight, but had become ill.

But the Soviets beat the USA into manned orbital flight. The US had, after a series of almost comical and widely publicized mishaps during testing of launch vehicles, launched a chimpanzee into suborbital flight by this time. Stops were pulled and after multiple delays, on May 5, 1961, a Redstone rocket carried Alan Shepard into a 15-minute suborbital flight. A couple of amusing incidents took place during the flight: the need for a human waste removal system became apparent after Shepard (who had been sitting in the capsule waiting to be launched for several hours) finally resorted to urinating in his spacesuit. Shepard had also forgotten to remove a gray filter from his cockpit periscope (the first Mercury capsule had no window), so the first American in space saw the world below in black and white.

On May 25, 1961, President John F Kennedy announced that the US intended to land a man on the moon by the end of the decade.

Titov & the Rest of Mercury Gus Grissom's Mercury flight, the second manned US suborbital mission (marred by the loss of the capsule after landing in the ocean) on July 21, 1961, came about a month before the biggest blow yet to the Americans: on August 6, 1961, the Soviets launched *Vostok 2,* piloted by cosmonaut German Titov who orbited the Earth 17 times in 25 hours.

While launches continued to leave from the Cape, Mission Control and the astronaut training program were moved to the Manned Space Flight Center (which is now the Johnson Space Center) near Houston, Texas, where they remain today.

Four other Mercury launches took place before the end of the Mercury program, including John Glenn's, when he became the first American to orbit the Earth, and Gordon Cooper's. Cooper, the last of the Mercury Seven to fly, orbited the Earth $22\frac{1}{2}$ times in 34 hours and released the first satellite from a spacecraft. He was also the last American to fly alone in space. (The seventh astronaut, Deke Slayton, had been grounded due to a heart condition and though he became Director of Astronaut Activities, he would not fly in space until 1975.)

Gemini The Soviets continued to beat the Americans in space firsts: first woman in space, first dual flight (two spacecraft in orbit together), first two- and three-person crew, and so on. The US Gemini program, successor to the Mercury Project, was designed to work out the bugs and procedures for two-man crews, as well as for testing flight endurance and docking procedures that would be used for the Apollo missions to the moon.

The accomplishments of the Gemini crews were as astounding as they were (and are) unheralded. They involved true piloting of spacecraft in ways the Mercury

SPACE COAST

astronauts never had, using the first onboard computers, space walks, space docking and more than 1000 hours of space flight on ships that left Earth at a rate of two a month. But their accomplishments were, at least in the media, simply overshadowed by the more spectacular nature of the Apollo missions to the moon.

Apollo During training tests before the first Apollo flights, Gus Grissom, Edward White and Roger Chaffee were killed when fire swept through the capsule as it sat atop a Saturn V rocket at the cape. The Apollo capsules had been designed with an inward-opening hatch (the ones on Mercury and Gemini opened outward) that required a minimum of 1^1/$_2$ minutes to open under optimal conditions.

Modifications to that door assembly delayed the first Apollo space flight until October 11, 1968. The deaths of the astronauts were the last until the *Challenger* disaster in January 1986.

Apollo 7 through *10* were preliminary flights spent perfecting the procedures:

Apollo 8
the first manned spacecraft to leave Earth's orbit and orbit the moon; December 21 to 27, 1968

Apollo 9
the first space test of the lunar module and orbital rendezvous and docking techniques; March 3 to 13, 1969

Apollo 10
dress rehearsal for the lunar landing and survey of the landing site at the Sea of Tranquility; May 18 to 26, 1969

Apollo 11 left Earth on July 16, 1969. On July 20, *Eagle*, the landing module, landed on the surface of the moon. As the world watched on television, Neil Armstrong delivered two of the best lines ever:

Houston, Tranquility Base here…Eagle has landed.

and

That's one small step for [a] man, one giant leap for mankind.

By the time the initial program was completed on December 19, 1972, six Apollo expeditions had landed, and 12 humans had walked on the moon.

Skylab & Apollo-Soyuz With the moon behind it, NASA turned its attention to creating a space station: a space platform on which astronauts would live and work for weeks and months at a time. Skylab's initial deployment was marred when the meteorite shield/sunshade broke loose; astronauts repaired the glitch 10 days later and over the next nine months, three crews lived on board the station. After 513 man-days in orbit, Skylab was abandoned, and on July 11, 1979, five years later, it fell through the atmosphere and disintegrated. National headlines screamed 'Skylab is Falling!'

By 1975, politics had thawed enough to allow the Soviets and the Americans to form a joint space venture: the Apollo-Soyuz Test Project, a link-up in space. The *Soyuz 19* and *Apollo* spacecraft launched on July 15; on July 17, they linked up and the world saw the first international handshake in space – the link up (not the handshake) lasted 44 minutes. Apollo-Soyuz also marked the first space voyage for Deke Slayton, who had been grounded during the Mercury program.

Shuttle Program The problem with all this high-falutin' space flight stuff was that it was obscenely expensive to send disposable billion-dollar buggies into space. In 1972, NASA began a program to develop reusable spacecraft.

Part airplane, part spacecraft, the space shuttle changed the way humans traveled to space after Apollo-Soyuz, and even resulted in some changes to the role of onboard personnel. Orbiters, NASA-ese for space shuttles, resemble chubby, short-winged airplanes: they're 122 feet long, 57 feet high and have wingspans of about 78 feet. They weigh, at liftoff, about 4.5 million pounds (of which 1.7 million is the external fuel tank), and their cargo bays, which are the whole point of the thing,

'Request Permission to Relieve Bladder'

With those words, astronaut Alan Shepard, forgive us, shepherded in the need for a whole new line of space-flight technology. Designers hadn't considered nature's calling on an astronaut during a 15-minute flight, but after sitting on the launch pad for several hours, the man had to go. Mission Control told him just to do it in his suit. On later flights, a sort of long condom was used, and, even later, baggies and other 'containment devices' were used for solid waste, while overboard urine dumps dealt with liquid.

That condom method would have been tricky indeed for female astronauts, so today, with extended flights on the space shuttle, NASA provides astronauts with the king of porta-potties: the Waste Containment System.

It looks and operates very much like a toilet on Earth would, with two exceptions. Thigh restraints keep the astronaut properly poised. And unlike on Earth, where gravity pulls waste matter away from the body, in the microgravity atmosphere of the orbiter an 'air flow system' much like a vacuum cleaner is used. The fecal matter remains on board, but the temperature of space freeze-dries it and it is then brought back to Earth with the orbiter.

For liquid waste, a central hose is provided, and astronauts each have their own personal urine collector cup that attaches to the hose. The cup is customized for men and women (both can urinate sitting or standing) and urine is vented into space.

Since you asked, they take sponge baths on the shuttle, not showers.

really, are 60 feet long and 15 feet wide. The orbiters' heat shields are made up of thousands of heat-resistant tiles.

Shuttles carry everything from military and commercial satellites to scientific experiments, and they're staffed by astronauts, scientists, technicians and specialists from many fields.

The orbiter is powered by three Space Shuttle Main Engines (SSMEs) – which are fed a mixture of liquid hydrogen fuel and liquid oxygen oxidizer contained in an external fuel tank (made up in turn of several smaller tanks) – and two solid booster packs that provide most of the thrust for liftoff. About two minutes into a flight, the spent solid rocket boosters are jettisoned and later recovered for reuse.

About eight minutes into the flight, the SSMEs are turned off and the external tank is jettisoned. The external tank disintegrates in reentry to the Earth's atmosphere. During shuttle flights, the orbiter maintains altitude control with jets of hydrogen and oxygen. On reentry, the orbiter is essentially

a huge and exquisitely expensive (about $2.1 billion) glider.

Shuttles fly at an altitude of anywhere from 190 to 350 miles above sea level at speeds of about 17,500 mph.

By 1977, the space shuttle *Enterprise*, a nonorbiting prototype, had been launched four times from atop a modified 747 jet airplane. The first orbital shuttle flight was by the *Columbia* on April 12, 1981. Over the next few years, manned space flight became routine almost to the point that no one paid attention any more: 23 flights were made between the *Columbia* launch and the *Challenger* disaster, which meant that the shuttle was going up almost six times a year for four years. *Challenger* introduced the dangers of space exploration to the public for the first time since *Apollo 13*.

Challenger About 73 seconds into the flight of STS-51-L – the space shuttle *Challenger* – on January 28, 1986, a leak in one of the two solid rocket boosters ignited the external fuel tank and caused an explosion that killed all aboard. As the takeoff was televised, the event was telecast worldwide.

The *Challenger* flight had been promoted by NASA as one highlighting its dedication to equal opportunities for minority crews. Lost were commander Dick Scobee, pilot Michael Smith and mission specialists Judith Resnik (one of the first female astronauts), Ronald McNair (one of NASA's first three black astronauts) and Ellison Onizuka (a Japanese-American). The two non-NASA personnel were Gregory Jarvis, a payload specialist for Hughes Aircraft, and most famous of all, Sharon Christa McAuliffe, a teacher at Concord High School in New Hampshire.

The press went wild over the telegenic and personable teacher when she was chosen from more than 11,000 applicants in 1984 to be the first teacher in space: she simply exuded traditional American family values. The attention that was paid her throughout her year-long training period added to the impact of the disaster: while Americans hold all astronauts very dear to their hearts, Christa, as everyone called her, was familiar enough to make her loss seem like that of a personal friend.

The loss set the shuttle program back three years, as investigations into the cause of the explosion, and subsequent redesign of

Shuttle launch at Kennedy Space Center

the solid fuel components and installation of new safety devices were carried out.

But the impact of the explosion is permanently etched on the minds of all who watched it. And as this final excerpt from the flight transcript reveals, it caught the crew as much by surprise as those on the ground:

T+1:05:
    Commander: 'Reading four eighty six on mine.'
T+1:07:
    Pilot: 'Yep, that's what I've got, too.'
T+1:10:
    Commander: 'Roger, go at throttle up.'
T+1:13:
    Pilot: 'Uh oh.'

Challenger's mission had been manifold: to launch a tracking data relay satellite; to fly a free-flying module designed to observe Halley's comet; to conduct a fluid dynamics experiment and three Shuttle Student Involvement Program experiments; and to complete a set of lessons for the Teacher in Space Project.

John Glenn In 1998, Senator John Glenn returned to space and became the oldest man ever to do so. At age 77, Senator Glenn's mission was to collect data on how space affects the aging process and to conduct other experiments. Critics called it the most expensive retirement gift ever, but anyone who thinks Glenn had a sightseeing tour is a cheesehead.

International Links & the Space Station From Skylab through the entire space shuttle program, links between NASA and other nations' space agencies have been consistently increasing. From the first flight carrying a non-US citizen (shuttle launch STS-9, November 28 to December 8, 1983, which carried West German physicist Ulf Merbold), to international cooperation in design of equipment and implementation of experiments, space exploration today is truly a global effort.

The NASA/International Space Station (ISS), officially under development since 1984, is a joint venture between six space

Close Calls

While only a few major disasters have marred the US space program, it's had its share of close calls. The first came when the explosive-bolt-driven escape hatch on *Liberty Bell 7*, Gus Grissom's Mercury craft, opened before the retrieval helicopter had hooked on to the capsule. Grissom jumped from the capsule, which filled with water and sank. Grissom's space suit also filled with water, and he nearly went under while waiting to be rescued. Debate continues to this day as to whether it was pilot error or technical malfunction.

John Glenn's *Friendship 7* Mercury craft sent back what turned out to be an erroneous message saying that his landing bag had deployed, making everyone on the ground panic that his heat shield had cracked – which would have led to his incineration upon reentry. Glenn used up all his fuel trying to stop the capsule's bucking during reentry but landed safely.

Scott Carpenter used up almost all his fuel doing what Tom Wolfe described as 'having a picnic,' Jim Lovell called 'monkeying around' and Carpenter himself called an 'error in yaw.' What he was doing was swinging the capsule this way and that, taking photos and having a blast until he realized how low his fuel was. Carpenter misaligned his retro rockets and over-shot the splash down target by 249 miles (402km).

And then of course, the biggie: *Apollo 13*, in which Jim Lovell, Fred Haise and Jack Swigert experienced a hair-raising explosion and loss of power that required them to use their lunar module as a life raft to get home. The story's too well known now that the movie *Apollo 13* has been such a success, but if you haven't seen it or if you have and wonder how accurate it is on technical details, consider the words of a retired Mission Control technician we met: 'I hardly ever recommend movies, but *Apollo 13*'s different. Like it or not, that's what happened.'

agencies comprised of 13 nations: Belgium, Canada, Denmark, Germany, France, Italy, Japan, Netherlands, Norway, Russia, Spain, the UK and the USA.

The ISS will be an orbiting platform designed to accommodate astronauts and spacecraft. This 'spacedock' could be used in a number of ways, including orbital construction and launch of spacecraft. The first pieces of the ISS were launched in late 1998, and the first residents could be in place there as early as 2003.

Probably the biggest partner with the USA has been Russia, which has been sharing information and technology aboard Russia's beleaguered and aged *Mir* space station. *Mir* has frequently been visited by shuttle crews and has been home to US astronauts along with Russian cosmonauts. The first stage of the ISS is expected to be put into operation around 2002.

Life on Mars In August 1996, NASA scientists announced the discovery of what appeared to be fossilized bacterialike life forms in a chunk of a meteorite they say originated on Mars. The meteorite had been discovered in the early 1980s by scientists in Antarctica. The findings of the NASA scientists were controversial and have faced scrutiny by the worldwide scientific community.

The world watched breathlessly as the first live video to be sent back from Mars arrived from NASA's *Pathfinder*, which landed (ever so conveniently, according to conspiracy theorists) on July 4, 1997.

The Future of Space With the break-throughs that have occurred since the Mercury and Sputnik/Vostok launches, and considering the way in which NASA has emerged from budget slashes, internal

SPACE COAST

So You Wanna Be an Astronaut...

Think you've got the right stuff? NASA picks new astronauts about every two years, and US citizens have first priority. You'll need at the very least a degree in biology, physics or mathematics and three years of related professional experience. Pilot astronaut applicants must have logged at least 1000 hours of pilot-in-command time on jet aircraft and must be able to pass a NASA Class 1 space physical. Mission specialists must pass a Class 2 space physical.

Wanna try? Download the appropriate forms at www.jsc.nasa.gov/ah/jscjobs/aso/astroapp.htm (there are actually HTML-based forms you can complete online, as well), fill them out and send them in to the Astronaut Selection Office, Mail Code AHX, Johnson Space Center, 2101 NASA Rd One, Houston, TX 77058.

May the force be with you.

shakeups and disasters, it's no longer so snickerable that NASA is studying projects that include a lunar base in the next century and a manned mission to Mars. They're not planning them yet, but they have established an Office of Exploration to study advances required to make those projects a reality. With seven to 10 shuttle missions a year, plus unmanned missions to Mars and Venus, NASA's got its hands quite full for the time being.

Orientation

The Kennedy Space Center (KSC) is on Merritt Island, on the east side of the Intracoastal Waterway (here called Indian River). The Banana River separates the main Kennedy Space Center complex from Cape Canaveral, which is also the site of the first launches of the US Space Program. The Cape Canaveral Air Force Station is now the site of the Air Force Space Museum and facilities for unmanned launches that put commercial and government payloads into orbit atop Delta, Titan and Atlas/Centaur rockets.

The space shuttle launch facilities are at Launch Complex 39, pads A and B. B is northeast of A.

The Kennedy Space Center Visitor Center is on Merritt Island, off the NASA Causeway, which begins at the junction of Hwy 405 and US Hwy 1. You can also enter the facilities by taking Hwy 528 (the Bee Line Expressway) to the intersection of Kennedy Parkway and turning north.

The handout maps at the visitor center are colorful but not too useful, though for the purposes of visiting they'll do just fine. For a much, much better idea of the lay of the land, get the Florida Official Transportation Map (see Maps in the Facts for the Visitor chapter).

Information

Tourist Offices The visitor center (☎ 407-452-2121) is the best source of information on the facilities. It's closed during all launches; everything is shut during shuttle launches and Cape Canaveral is closed to visitors during launches.

Information Central inside the visitor center complex has multilingual staff, and sign language and visual interpreters/guides are available on advance notice. Public TDD and free wheelchairs are also available.

Shuttle Launch Information You can get recorded information on shuttle launches at ☎ 407-867-4636. During countdown, recorded launch status is available at ☎ 407-867-2314. On the Internet, check out the shuttle homepage for information on upcoming and past launches and links to gezillions of other NASA sites (see the boxed text NASA Internet Addresses).

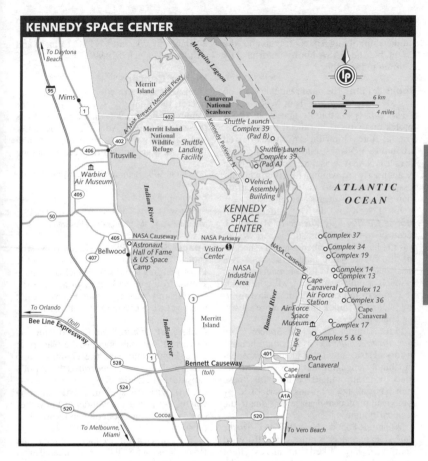

KENNEDY SPACE CENTER

Bus tours take visitors out to NASA's 6-mile viewing site; they leave the visitor center three hours before the launch. Tickets ($7 for adults and $4 for children) go on sale seven days prior to a launch, and they're necessary. You can reserve by phone (☎ 407-452-2121, ask for group sales), but you must pick up your tickets five days before the launch or you will not be admitted on launch day.

If you've got a car, you can get a free car pass by mail to view a launch from within Kennedy Space Center. Send a postcard with your name, address and the mission number of the launch you'd like to see to Car Passes, PA-PASS, Kennedy Space Center, FL 32899. The pass will be mailed to you about a month before the launch; if you'll be on the road, leave an address in Florida (like your hotel) to which NASA can mail the pass.

Not as prime for launch viewing are locations around Brevard County like along the Indian River on Hwy 1 in Titusville, along the Banana River on Hwy 528 (the Bee Line Expressway) and on Cocoa Beach.

Bookstore & Library The Gift Gantry at the visitor center sells quite a few books on subjects involving space travel and the center, but the NASA library unfortunately is closed to the public.

Books & Films The most readable work on the Mercury program, Tom Wolfe's *The Right Stuff*, is so accurate that even NASA quotes and cites it in official publications. The at-times hilarious, no-holds-barred account of 1950s test piloting and the early days of NASA was later made into an Academy Award-winning film that, while far less technically and historically accurate than the book, is always a great watch.

Jim Lovell and Jeffrey Kluger's *Lost Moon: The Perilous Voyage of Apollo 13*, recently re-released as simply *Apollo 13*, was the basis for the phenomenally successful film of the same name. The book is a great read (written in third person) and has as much *oomph!* as the film, with the bonus of details from Lovell's flight aboard *Apollo 8*, a glossary, index and a far more satisfying epilogue.

Peter Bond's *Heroes in Space: From Gagarin to Challenger* is a comprehensive history of space flight that includes excellent and highly engaging details of the Soviet space program and its cosmonauts: these men have all been heroes, overlooked by American readers and space fans due to the political climate.

William R Pogue's *How Do You Go to the Bathroom in Space?* is more straightforward than we'd have liked but an excellent resource for kids, as are *A Day in Space* by Suzanne Lord and Julie Epstein, based on interviews with shuttle astronaut Jeff Hoffman, and *My Life as an Astronaut* by Alan Bean, fourth man to walk on the moon.

Man's Greatest Adventure is a coffee-table book on the Apollo missions available at the KSC Gift Gantry, as are *Space Shuttle*, a technically detailed book on the development of the orbiter, and *Apollo to the Moon*, which describes each Apollo mission. Also available at the Gift Gantry upstairs are heaps of videos, including *America in Space, the First 40 Years, Destiny in Space,* and the

Patrick Stewart-narrated *Nine Worlds,* an online trip through the universe. All are available in PAL and NTSC formats and cost from $19.99 to $29.99.

Visitor Center

Operated as an attraction by a NASA contractor, the Kennedy Space Center Visitor Center opened in 1966, then expanded to its present size in 1967. Admission to the center and parking is free, but the bus tour and IMAX films are extra. Prices are as follows:

IMAX only – $7.50 for adults, $5.50 for children three to 11

Bus tour only – $14/10

Crew pass (1 IMAX film and bus tour) – $19/15

Mission pass (2 IMAX films and bus tour) – $26/20

Space Shuttle Plaza Hands down the coolest area of the visitor center, Shuttle Plaza features a full-size model of a space shuttle. You can walk through and see the cockpit and the cargo bay, but you can't really get close enough to touch anything.

Gallery of Spaceflight Packed with real spacecraft and scale models, the Gallery of Spaceflight's stars are the *Gemini 9* and the Apollo-Soyuz spacecraft (the Apollo capsule is real, the Soyuz is a full-scale model), with transparent plastic allowing you to peer inside and wonder just how they could stand being cooped up in those things for so long.

You can see a full-size model of the Lunar Rover, looking for all the world like a Tinker Toy, and a collection of moon rocks and Apollo patches.

Galaxy Center & IMAX Theater The five-story-high screens of the Galaxy Center's IMAX theater currently offer three films; ticket prices are $7.50 for adults, $5.50 for children three to 11. The films, all propaganda shorts produced by government contractors to make you feel one with the space program, are all so fantastically made and totally dramatic they actually manage to make you feel one with the space program. Just don't expect to see anything about the downsides, or especially the troubles on the *Mir* station.

Film schedules are subject to change, check when you arrive. *The Dream Is Alive*, narrated by Walter Cronkite, is a compelling look at life aboard a space shuttle; our favorite bits were watching everyday housekeeping tasks and the astronauts asleep (they look as if they're surrendering). The riveting *Mission to Mir* follows several American astronauts on their journey to Moscow and finally aboard the shuttle for the trip to Mir.

L5: First City in Space is a fabulously rendered 3D film of the first settlers to live on board the International Space Station – Corinna loved the 3D effects.

Air Force Space Museum

Complex 26, which launched the US's first satellite in 1958, houses a museum containing an absolutely fascinating collection of equipment, mementos and space paraphernalia you won't find anywhere else. It's staffed by a group of volunteers. Unfortunately, due to security and launch considerations, the museum was closed indefinitely. Call ☎ 407-853-9171 to see if it's reopened when you visit – if it has, we highly recommend a visit.

Organized Tours

Tour buses make a giant loop of the Kennedy Space Center complex, making three stops along the way. Between stops, the ride offers a recorded narration by astronauts Sally Ride (the first American woman in space) and Jim Lovell, as well as two KSC contractor employees. Drivers point out any wildlife – such as alligators – you pass on the way (see Merritt Island National Wildlife Refuge under Around Kennedy Space Center later this chapter).

The tour buses leave from the visitor center and proceed first past the unbelievably enormous Vehicle Assembly Building (VAB), where…well, vehicles are assembled. You'll also see the two crawler-transporters (tank-treaded platforms with a maximum carrying capacity of 14½ million pounds) that take six to eight hours to carry

---

NASA Internet Addresses

NASA's got a huge presence on the World Wide Web, and you can easily get lost clicking through hyperlinks to ever more fascinating subsites including shuttle photography, movies and audio clips, launch schedules, technical specifications, flight transcripts, space station information, a searchable historical archive and Hubble telescope images – and that's just scratching the surface. To get started, the best place to go is www.shuttle.nasa.gov, the NASA Human Space Flight page. It offers links to tons of topics, including the shuttle program, ISS, Mars exploration and more. For a broader view, try NASA's main homepage, www.nasa.gov.

The Website for the Kennedy Space Center is www.kennedyspacecenter.com.

---

the completed space shuttle stacks the 3½ miles from the VAB to the launch pad.

The first stop is the LC 39 Observation Gantry, halfway between pads 39A and B (where shuttle launches take place). This center screens a film on shuttle launches and has a history gallery. Next stop is the Apollo/Saturn V Center near the VIP launch-viewing site at Banana Creek. Here you can walk underneath a 363-foot-tall Saturn V rocket in a 100,000-sq-foot building dedicated to the Apollo era. The last stop is an exhibition where you can see pieces of the International Space Station being assembled and prepared for launch. Buses run between the sites every 10 minutes or so, so you can stay as long as you like at each attraction.

Places to Eat

Food here is a little pricey but still a pretty good value. Don't miss Space Dots ice cream sold in several stands; it's supercold ball-bearing sized nuggets of ice cream ($2.75) that'll give you an excellent chocolate brain freeze. The *Lunch Pad* and *Orbit* cafeterias, in the visitor center, both offer burgers ($4), fries ($2), good salads ($5.60) and soft drinks. The Orbit also offers hot meals like lasagna ($7).

Flee the institutional feel at *Mila's Roadhouse,* a sit-down place behind the Orbit with main courses from $6 to $9. The *Moon Rock Café* at the Apollo/Saturn center allows you to dine among the moon rocks.

Getting There & Away

From I-95, Hwy A1A or US Hwy 1, it is almost impossible to miss. From Orlando, take Hwy 528 (the Bee Line Expressway) straight east to the entrance.

Getting here without a car is totally inconvenient. Greyhound only has service as close as Cocoa and Titusville; buses leave Orlando at 7:30 and 10 am and the last bus returns at 7:45 pm from Cocoa. The price is $8/15, though that doesn't include the taxi (about $10 to $13) from Cocoa to the KSC. Busy Traveler Transportation (☎ 800-496-7433) charters cars for up to four people for $65 one way between KSC and downtown Orlando. Mears Transportation (☎ 407-423-5566, 407-759-5219, www.mears-net.com) goes to/from the HI Orlando Resort on Monday, Wednesday and Friday only, at a cost of $17 per person roundtrip.

AROUND KENNEDY SPACE CENTER

The area around the Space Center ranges from pristine nature to strip malls and surfer beach. You can camp free on Klondike Beach and, if you've got a canoe or kayak, on several islands within the Canaveral National Seashore. And an HI hostel is on the beach at Indialantic.

Great information about the area is available on the Web at www.space-coast.com.

Merritt Island National Wildlife Refuge

NASA uses only about 5% of its total landholdings for making things that go boom. In 1963, NASA turned management of its unused land over to the US Fish & Wildlife Service (USFWS), who then established the Merritt Island National Wildlife Refuge (☎ 407-861-0667).

The refuge is notable because it contains, in its mangrove swamps, marshes and hardwood hammocks, more endangered and threatened species than any other refuge in the continental USA. Along with Canaveral National Seashore, the area is one of the best birding spots in the country. Located on the Atlantic Flyway, this is migratory bird central, as birds migrate between the northern USA and South America in September and October and back in the spring. Birders will be able to spot practically the table of contents of any ornithological guide, from bald eagles and the entire heron family to spoonbills, black-necked stilts, terns and other seabirds and migratory birds.

Other species in the refuge include manatees, alligators, loggerhead and leatherback turtles, wild pigs, bobcats, gopher tortoises and deer.

Our first question was about the impact of the launches on the wildlife in the refuge, but rangers say that launches have but a short-term impact, mainly due to noise and commotion. Exhaust and its cumulative effects are monitored and the impact of a launch is surprisingly concentrated in a small area around the pads.

The best time to visit is from October to May, as that's the height of migratory bird season and also when the climate is most comfortable. From March to September, thousands of wading birds can be seen in spectacular breeding plumage within the park. Animal activity is highest between October and March, in the early morning and late afternoon.

Note that the refuge closes to the public two days before any launch, as NASA expands its security area. But if you're planning to visit right after a launch, be aware that more often than not launch dates are deferred due to technical problems or bad weather, and days can easily slip by with the refuge keeping its gates shut.

Admission to the refuge is free. To get to the main visitors center, take Hwy 1 to Hwy 406/402, turn east into the refuge and bear right when the road forks (the left fork will take you to Black Point Wildlife Drive, see Visitors Center below).

Visitors Center The center has excellent free information packages, including the main park brochure which offers a self-guided tour around the refuge's most popular and easily accessible attraction: the Black Point Wildlife Drive, a 6-mile loop. November to April, the center is open Monday to Friday 8 am to 4:30 pm, Saturday and Sunday 9 am to 5 pm. It's closed on Sunday from May to October and on all holidays.

Hiking For a quick immersion into the area's nature, you can take a quick walk on the refuge's quarter-mile, universally accessible **Boardwalk Trail**, directly behind the visitors center.

Three other hiking trails are about 1½ miles east (parking about a mile east) of the main visitors center: the half-mile **Oak Hammock Trail**; the 2-mile **Palm Hammock Trail**, which winds through hardwood forest and has boardwalks above the open marsh; and the 5-mile **Cruickshank Trail**, which begins at stop 8 along the Black Point Wildlife Drive and runs around a shallow marsh to a 12-foot-high observation tower.

Canoeing & Kayaking You can canoe and kayak in certain areas here, notably in **Mosquito Lagoon**, through the open waters and in the marshes. Note, however, that winds can get very strong and the waters are shallow. See Canaveral National Seashore below for kayak-tour information.

Canaveral National Seashore

Maintained by the National Park Service, the 25 miles of windswept and mainly pristine beach that make up the Canaveral National Seashore are a favorite haunt of surfers (at the southern end), vacationing families (at the north) and campers and nature lovers (on Klondike Beach, a 12-mile stretch in the center). Admission is $5 per carload, $1 for bicyclists and pedestrians. Parking lots 6 and 7 are nearest to the best surfing.

Besides the beach itself, a couple of other sights here are of interest. At the northern end of the Seashore, actually in Volusia County, is historically significant Apollo Park, in which Timucuan Indian remains have been found. And also within the park is the State House, a museum about life in the failed city of Eldora (1877 to 1900), which was founded on the old (before dredging) intracoastal waterway here. Admission to the museum is free.

You can get to the park through the city of New Smyrna Beach; to reach the North District Visitors Center and Apollo Beach, take Hwy 44 east to Hwy A1A and then turn south – it runs right into the parking areas (there are five convenient to beach access). The visitors center is about a quarter-mile past the lots; you can pick up free camping registration forms there (see below).

North District Visitors Centers All of the park's visitor programs and information services are handled by the North District Visitors Center (☎ 904-428-3384), which shows an excellent 12-minute video of the park's facilities, camping sites and trails. They also offer activities every month, from beach walks to demonstrations of cast netting, studies of evidence of Timucuan Indian life in the area (like Turtle Mound Archaeological Site, a shell mound) and walking lectures on local fish and wildlife. All children attending park programs are eligible to become junior rangers. Activity schedules are printed monthly and are available at the visitors center.

The park also maintains a South District office (☎ 407-267-1110).

Beaches Apollo Beach, to the north, is favored by families because it has calmer surf than beaches to the south, but note that rip tides occur now and then; see Dangers & Annoyances in the Facts for the Visitor chapter for what to do if you're caught in one (as if you'll be thumbing through this book while being carried out to sea: 'Hmm, Getting There & Away? No...Facts about Florida? glub glub').

Klondike Beach, the 12-mile coastal beach between Apollo and Playlinda Beaches, is as pristine as it can possibly be. Though some dune erosion has taken place, no trails exist and native plants are abundant. It's great for walking and biking on the hard-packed sand. Klondike Beach has the only free-permit beach camping at the Seashore; see Places to Stay below.

Playlinda Beach, at the southern end, is the surfer headquarters with decent (for Florida) breaks and lots of guys named Dude.

Turtle Watching This stretch of beach is prime turtle-nesting grounds; two crews of conservationists and rangers patrol the beaches at night, screening the nests of loggerhead, leatherback and green sea turtles.

Unparalleled turtle-watching opportunities are available, but only with a guide; about 4000 visitors a year take part in the Turtle Watch Program, governed by the Department of Environmental Protection. The program leads small groups (a strict maximum of 20 people) along the beach between June and July starting at about 10:30 to 11 pm. If you're lucky (and you usually are during nesting season) you'll find a female, watch her dig a hole, lay her eggs and return to the sea.

Demand for the tours is astounding and reservations must be made *months* in advance. You have to call the North District Visitors Center on May 15th or June 15th, starting at 8 am – the tours fill up quickly.

Canoeing & Kayaking You can canoe through Mosquito Lagoon (see Merritt Island National Wildlife Refuge earlier in the Around Kennedy Space Center section) and camp on various islands here free (see below). The staff at Osprey Outfitters (☎ 407-267-3535, www.nbbd.com/osprey) are excellent nature guides and know the entire region like the back of their hands; they lead half-day guided kayak trips through the area for $35 per person including rental and snacks; full-day adventures cost $60.

Places to Stay Camping in the National Seashore, on Klondike Beach or on the islands that fill the north end of Mosquito Lagoon (including Orange, Shipyard, Headwinds, Government Cut, North Dredge,

Middle Dredge, South Dredge, and Bissett Bay Islands), costs $5 for up to six people. Note that you're locked in to the park at 6 pm in winter, 8 pm in summer. No showers are available, though you'll find toilets in all the parking lots. Fresh water and more camping information are available at the North District Visitors Center (☎ 904-428-3384).

In the nearby city of Cape Canaveral, *Jetty Park Campground (☎ 407-783-7111, 400 E Jetty Rd)* has basic tent sites for $14.85 a night, as well as tent and RV sites with water and electricity for $18.43.

Up in the town of Mims, just north of Titusville, is the *KOA Cape Kennedy Campground (☎ 407-269-7361, 800-848-4562, 4513 W Main St).* Tent sites are $19, or $21 with electricity and water; RV sites with full hookups are $21 and Kamping Kabins are $30.

Titusville & Around

Titusville is the main gateway to both the Kennedy Space Center and the wildlife refuge, and it has excellent vantage points for watching a shuttle launch.

Space Walk of Fame The US Space Walk of Fame fronts the western bank of the Indian River. The memorial to Project Mercury includes a 20-foot sculpture of the astronomical symbol of the planet Mercury, which was used as the Mercury logo.

The base of the monument bears the handprints of the five surviving Mercury astronauts: Glenn, Carpenter, Schirra, Cooper and Shepard.

Astronaut Hall of Fame This museum (☎ 407-269-6100), 6225 Vectorspace Blvd, about 7 miles west of the Space Center off Hwy 405, has displays on the minutiae of the astronaut's lives, along with films and way-cool exhibits like a shuttle-landing simulator ride, a G-force trainer and a virtual-reality weightlessness gizmo that puts your video image aboard the shuttle. The gift shop rules – grab a pack of Asteroids: low-moisture cherries and raspberries ($3). It's open every day (except Christmas) 9 am to

6 pm, later in summer. Admission is $13.95 for adults, $9.95 for children.

US Space Camp One of the most innovative ideas in a summer camp is the US Space Camp (☎ 407-267-3184, 800-637-7223) on the grounds of the Astronaut Hall of Fame. Wernher von Braun (see History under Kennedy Space Center earlier this chapter) came up with the idea, envisioning the camp as a way of encouraging kids to study math and science. The original space camp opened in Huntsville, Alabama, in 1982, and this one opened in 1988. Since then, more than 30,000 kids have attended a program here.

The courses teach space science and rocket propulsion and simulate shuttle missions and astronaut training from different eras of the space program. Along the way, participants perform experiments in physics, chemistry and space science.

Corporations are also lining up to take part in the Space Camp corporate programs, which simulate launches and improve communications between departments by forcing them to be concise and stay focused.

Programs include the following:

Corporate Team Programs
Half-day, one- and three-day programs, in which your team designs a space station and works on a simulated shuttle launch; from $50 to $300 per person, limited availability

Parent-Child Program
For parents and their children seven to 11; $600 includes tuition, room, board and supplies for one adult and one child for three days

Space Academy
Five-day space camp for kids 12 to 14; $550 (summer) to $675 (winter); includes room, board and supplies

Space Camp
Five-day sleep-over program for kids nine to 12, year round; same price

Teachers Space Camp
Five-day program for teachers offered in conjunction with NASA and the Astronaut Memorial Foundation. Participating teachers may apply for continuing education credit through their individual school districts; $750

Warbird Air Museum In the TICO (pronounced 'TItusville-COcoa') Space Center Airport, this museum (☎ 407-268-1941) offers exhibits of historic war aircraft from WWI, WWII, Korea and Vietnam. The star here is a functioning C-47, built in October 1942, that's a veteran of the Normandy invasion, Operation Market Garden and the Battle of the Bulge. In 1995, the plane was used to ship 5000 pounds of toys to Cuban refugee children at Guantanamo Bay. Other highlights include an F-14 Tomcat, AT-28 Trainer, an L-19, and a US Navy A-6 and A-7, both Vietnam veterans.

Each year, the museum holds an air show as a fund-raiser for itself and its aviation scholarship program; it's held the second week of March, and more than 100 warbirds take part.

The museum is open 10 am to 6 pm every day except Thanksgiving, Christmas and New Year's Day. Admission is $6 for adults, $4 for children under 12. From I-95, take exit 79 to Hwy 405 east; the airport's on the right.

Places to Stay & Eat Just south of Titusville at 7275 S US Hwy 1 in Bellwood, lush and lovely Manatee Hammock Park (☎ 407-264-5083) is a super camping option that will get you close enough to the hubbub of the Space Coast with a lot less noise and for a lot less money. Run by Brevard County Parks & Recreation, this family-oriented campground has laundry facilities, a pool, recreation hall and a nature trail running straight through the place. Tent sites here are $12.10 (no water or electricity) or $16.23 (with water and electricity); full-hookup RV sites are $16.75.

The *KSC Ramada Inn & Suites* (☎ 407-269-5510, 3500 Cheney Hwy), at exit 79 from I-95, has rooms for as low as $66 in low season and fantastically complicated rates throughout the rest of the year, but it's a good option, with a pool, gym and sauna.

For a flesh-fest of epic proportions, hit *Fat Boy's Barbeque* (☎ 407-267-3468, 4280 S Washington Ave), where you can get stuff to go (baby-back ribs $5 for half a pound, $9.25 for a pound; half/whole chicken $4/8). But eat-in may be the best deal: a large rib dinner is $10.95 with potato, garlic bread and coleslaw; chicken dinners are $7.95.

The best-known restaurant in town is *Dixie Crossroads* (☎ 407-268-5000, 1475 Garden St), off I-95 exit 80 (turn east, it's on the right), a massive place offering rock shrimp, which the family that owns the restaurant introduced to the eating public. The shrimp are sweet and good. Also on the grounds is a botanic garden with tons of exotic plants. The place looks touristy but is worth a meal.

Getting There & Away Greyhound serves Titusville, but it's as inconvenient to get to the Space Center from here as it is from anywhere on the Space Coast. The station's at 100 S Hopkins Ave (☎ 407-267-8760).

Cocoa

This town is mainly an inconvenient Greyhound gateway, and not many people stop long enough to smell the flowers. (The Greyhound station – ☎ 407-636-6531 – is at 302 Main St.) But Cocoa has some claim to fame in its **Historic Cocoa Village**, a collection of 14 sites dating from between 1880 to 1925, gathered along Brevard and Delannoy Aves between King and Church Sts. The Brevard Museum of History & Natural Science (see Melbourne later in the chapter) hands out walking tour maps of the historic area, whose highlights include the still-functioning **Cocoa Village Playhouse** (1924), the **Porcher Warehouse & Home** (1883) and the **Victor Theater** (1924).

Astronaut Memorial Planetarium & Observatory This excellent planetarium and observatory (☎ 407-634-3732) houses Florida's largest public-access telescope. It's open Tuesday, Thursday and Friday evenings, and about once a month there's a *Mir* space station window – when the Russian station is visible through the telescope. Planetarium shows start at 7 pm, and show off what's billed as the world's only tandem team of Digistar planetarium projectors and America's only Minolta Infinium star projector. Afterwards, at 8 pm, films are shown in the three-story-high IWERKS (it's

like IMAX, but smaller) theater. Admission to both is $7 for adults, $5 for seniors and students and $4 for children; admission to either single show is $4/3/2. The planetarium and observatory are on the Broward Community College (BCC) campus, off Clearlake Rd between Michigan Ave and Rosetine St; from US Hwy 1 take Dixon Blvd west to Clearlake and turn north; the campus is on the left.

Places to Stay & Eat The *Dixie Motel* (☎ 407-632-1600, 301 Forest Ave) has curt service but clean rooms for $50 to $55 a night, $240 a week, higher during launches. Another good bet is the *Econo Lodge* (☎ 407-632-4561, 3220 N Cocoa Blvd), on US Hwy 1, with absolutely standard chain-motel rooms for $55 in low season, $70 during high season and launches.

The *Dutch Kitchen* (☎ 407-639-1270, 1312 Dixon Blvd) serves great breakfast specials like two eggs, toast, home fries and grits for $1.98, or with bacon or sausage for $2.50. It also offers Pennsylvania Dutch scrapple, a mélange of pork products in loaf form; 95¢ a slice. Daily lunch specials include items like hot beef sandwiches, Philly cheesesteak, and rib eye with potato and vegetable from $3.25 to $4.25.

The slickest place to eat in town is *Café Margaux* (☎ 407-639-8343, 222 Brevard Ave), in the Arcade, right in the center of the historic district. It's a French place, naturally, and it's far cheaper at lunch than at dinner. At lunch, a good range of menu items falls in the $6 to $8 range. Dinner runs $18 to $26, with items like braised Long Island duckling with mango-ginger relish, or seafood baked in puff pastry on steamed leeks with lobster cream.

Cocoa Beach

Snuggled between Cape Canaveral and Patrick Air Force Base, the optimistically named city of Cocoa Beach, despite what you may have seen on *I Dream of Jeannie*, is a desolate place with a hard-packed sand beach filled with partyers and surfers. While the town's motels and the beach get swamped during shuttle launches, there's not much to see or do here unless you're one of the above. The PR agency in charge of the Space Coast lists Ron Jon Surf Shop (☎ 407-799-8888) as one of exactly two tourist attractions in the area; the shop rents boards and Boogieboards and sells T-shirts, hoohahs, doodads and surfing accoutrements. Interested? It's at the corner of Hwy 520 and US Hwy A1A at 4151 N Atlantic Ave. Look for the ridiculous building on the east side of the street. There's surfing right near the pier (see below).

Cocoa Beach Pier The other attraction, justifiably famous as a great spot from which to watch shuttle launches, is the Cocoa Beach Pier, an 800-foot-long pier with some restaurants and bars. Parking is $3. The pier is free on the first Tuesday of the month, the first week in November and on Veterans' Day, Christmas and New Year's Day. At other times, it's 50¢ for spectators, $3.50 for adults and $3 for children and seniors; you can rent a rod and reel for $9.50 and buy bait for $3.

A booth just south of the pier offers hourly rentals of bicycles ($3), volleyballs ($2), Boogieboards, beach umbrellas and chairs ($3, $8 or $10 each, respectively, for four hours); or go for the Broiler Special – a day's worth of beach umbrella and two chairs for $14 in low season and $15 in high.

Another stand, Rosenberry, rents surfboards: foam boards or long boards are $5 an hour, $10 a half day or $15 a day; Boogieboards are $3/8/10.

Places to Stay The *Sand Dollar Oceanfront* (☎ 407-783-8628, 1465 S Atlantic Ave) has efficiency apartments (with very interesting carpets) from $65 to $75 a night, five-night minimum, or $350 to $500 a week; negotiable seasonal and monthly rates are available as well.

The *Cocoa Beach Oceanside Inn* (☎ 407-799-0883, 800-874-7958, 1 Hendry Ave) is a boxy modern place with large rooms that try for a resort feel. Rooms are $59 to $99 for pool view, $69 to $109 on the top floors, $79 to $119 for direct ocean-view rooms; higher rates in high season and during launches.

Talk about making lemonade from lemons: the *Silver Sands Motel* (☎ 407-783-2415, 225 N Atlantic Ave) actually *boasts* that it's 'styled for an earlier decade and weathered by an ocean breeze…we don't have a swimming pool, luxurious furniture or a restaurant on site.' Okay, but they do win when it comes to the clean rooms, friendly service and beachfront location. Motel rooms are $49 a night, $270 a week, and efficiencies are $59/325.

Places to Eat Open 5 am to 10 pm, *Marlin's* restaurant has cheapish breakfasts and seafood entrees from $7 to $12. Downstairs at the base of the pier is *Oh Shucks*, with happy hour Monday to Friday 4 to 7 pm: $1 off drafts. At other times, steamed shrimp are $5.95 a dozen, and clams and oysters are $3.95 for six.

Flaminia's Italian Kitchen (☎ 407-783-9908, 3210 S Atlantic Blvd), at the southern end of town, serves standard Italian fare. Pasta dinners with bread sticks and salad range $5.95 to $8; dinner specials average $9.

Cedar's of Lebanon (☎ 407-784-9005, 110 N Brevard Ave) specializes in Middle Eastern and Lebanese food. Appetizers like hummus and stuffed grape leaves are $2.95, *baba ghanouj* $3.95, and main courses like beef and chicken kebob and vegetarian Saba's Special (grape leaves, spinach pie and salad or tabouli) are $8.95.

Melbourne

Melbourne's a good base for turtle watchers and for more affluent surfers sick of battling the crowds at Cocoa Beach. For the latter, it's well located between the breaks at Patrick Air Force Base and Sebastian Inlet. Most of the Melbourne area's life is centered along the beach – on the east side of the Intracoastal Waterway – and in the towns of Melbourne Beach, Indialantic and Melbourne.

The Melbourne Chamber of Commerce (☎ 407-724-5400, 800-771-9922), 1005 E Hwy 192, has the usual pamphlets, as well as area maps for $1.60. It's open Monday to Friday 9 am to 5 pm, Saturday 10 am to 3 pm. The Greyhound station (☎ 407-723-4329) is at 460 S Harbor.

The **Historic Downtown** area, along E New Haven Ave right behind the chamber, is a pleasant-enough, antique-shop-lined street, but the antiques are about all the history you'll find here. A much better way to spend your time is a visit to **Crane Creek**, just two blocks west of the chamber of commerce, where you'll definitely see lots of river turtles and catfish (who'll swim to where you're standing, thinking you'll have bread – so maybe bring some) and, if you're lucky, manatees (we saw two happily playing in the water after just 10 minutes).

The **King Performance Center** (☎ 407-242-2219), 3865 N Wickham Rd, is home to performances by the Brevard Symphony Orchestra. It's also a good resource for children's performances in spring and fall. Take I-95 south to exit 73, and Wickham Rd east for 7 miles to Post Rd, then continue east to the center.

The **Brevard Museum of History & Natural Science** (☎ 407-632-1830), at 2201 Michigan Ave, has a permanent collection including local historical artifacts, archaeological items including Indian artifacts more than 7000 years old and exhibits on area wildlife. It also holds special exhibits on subjects as diverse as arachnids, powder horns and early-20th-century weaponry. Regular admission is $3 for adults, $1.50 for children; special exhibits are $5/3. It's open Tuesday to Saturday 10 am to 4 pm, Sunday 1 to 4 pm, closed Monday.

The **Brevard Zoo** (☎ 407-254-9453), 8225 N Wickham Rd, remodeled largely by volunteer labor, focuses on Latin American jungles and has good exhibits on sloths, spider monkeys and jaguars. Admission is $4 for adults, $3 for seniors over 60 and $2.50 for children two to 12.

For **surfing** information, call ☎ 407-953-0392 for a recorded announcement. The recording also usually features an ad for the Longboard House (☎ 407-951-0730), 101 5th Ave in Indialantic, which sells a huge selection of new and used surfboards and rents longboards for $20 a day.

The best breaks in the area are 18 miles south of Indialantic at Sebastian Inlet, which has strong currents and, on good days (as in, when storms brew in the Atlantic), 10-foot breaks. In Indialantic, surf is good behind the Comfort Suites Hotel, and on Patrick Air Force Base to the north, good waves can generally be found behind the Officer's Club.

Places to Stay & Eat HI's slightly fusty 12-bed *HI-Melbourne Beach* (☎ 407-951-0004, 1135 N Hwy A1A) hostel is right on the beach at Indialantic, convenient to a Winn-Dixie supermarket. Beds are $15.50 for HI members, nonmembers are $18.50; private rooms are $39 for efficiencies and $59 for one-bedroom apartments.

At the *Melbourne Quality Suites Hotel* (☎ 407-723-4222, 800-876-4222, 1665 N Hwy A1A) there are seriously nice two-room oceanfront (yes, all of them) suites with balconies for $89/99 single/double in low season, $119/129 in high season, including a good breakfast.

The fabulous *Cantina Dos Amigos* (☎ 407-724-2183, 990 N Hwy A1A) offers magnificent, authentic Mexican food. The place is cheap, cheerful, and the staff is friendly, but the food is the star; we thought we'd gone to heaven with the *pollo borracho* ($7.95) – chicken chunks in a nicely spicy tequila tomatilla sauce with garlic, tomatoes and black olives over a tortilla, smothered with melted cheese *and* served with rice, beans, a wonderful chicken-based tortilla soup and (the only drawback) oily *churros*. Corinna had the very tasty Rosarita Fajitas ($7.95), sizzling veggies in flour tortillas. With so much to eat, we had to take half of everything home, but our bill was $19.70 including dinner, a frozen margarita and an orange juice. Do it.

Northeast Florida

Many people get their first impression of Florida while driving south and arriving in Jacksonville, and that's too bad. Because as they flee the urban sprawl, they might miss out on some of the lovely areas close by, notably Amelia Island and especially St Augustine, the oldest city in the USA.

St Augustine's charming cobblestone streets and old Spanish- and English-built buildings (old not just by US standards but even by those of chilly, damp countries in which people drive on the left: many buildings here date to the late 1700s) make it an irresistible stop for those plying the endless ribbon of concrete that is I-95, and with its cheap camping, youth hostel and relatively inexpensive motels, there's just no reason why you shouldn't spend at least a day there, possibly more.

Northeast Florida is also home to the Birthplace of Speed: Daytona Beach. At various times of the year, it is jammed with racing fans (there to see the Daytona 500), swarming with motorcycle clubs (congregating for the madness of Bike Week) or seething with Spring Breakers (for whom Daytona is the last friendly port of call on the east coast of Florida).

DAYTONA BEACH
• **population 62,000**

What began in 1902, with men and their very expensive and very fast cars racing along the hard-packed sand, has culminated in a city dedicated to the pursuit of speed – in cars, motorbikes, whatever.

Ransom Olds and Louis Chevrolet began the craze, and were joined by wealthy wintering industrialists who either drove or financially backed race cars. By 1904, the event was called the Winter Speed Carnival, and over the next 30 years or so, Daytona Beach was to drivers what Edwards Air Force Base was to test pilots in the '50s: the place where records were made and smashed. The record for speed on the beach, set in 1935, is almost 277 mph.

Highlights

- Get to the heart of Florida's history in lovely St Augustine, the USA's first settlement, where you can take a tour of the country's alleged oldest house, drugstore, school, jail and more

- View the impressive collection at the Cummer Museum of Art in Jacksonville

- Check out the fast cars in Daytona Beach

- Pick your own strawberries by the quart at Tommy Howle's Vegetable Bin & Garden in Elkton

- Visit American Beach, an important site on the Black Heritage Trail

- Indulge in an amazing Southern meal, including ribs, collard greens, mashed potatoes and fried chicken at Fernandina Beach's Florida House Inn

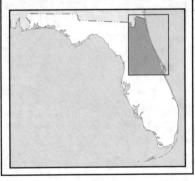

Stock-car racing became the new rush, and between 1935 and 1958 the beach was still the site for races. But in 1959, the Daytona Speedway opened, and made official what Daytona's tourist board had been claiming for years: Daytona Beach was the Birthplace of Speed.

Today, Daytona Beach is a town that thrives on racing and party-based tourism: it has one of the last Atlantic-coast Spring

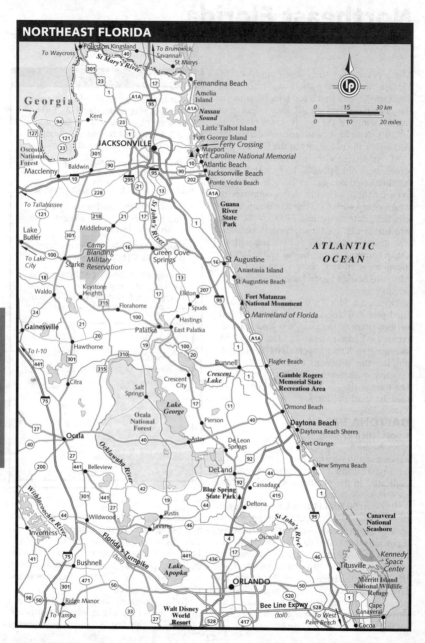

NORTHEAST FLORIDA

Breaks (arrests, hookers, drunk kids, fire engines) and, during Bike Week, the town goes absolutely insane, as hordes of Harleys – and their remarkably well-behaved owners – roar into town. The people coming to see that, along with the other races, carry the region financially through the entire year. Prices during special events are stellar, to pay for the long months of relative solitude. But Daytona is never really empty – revelers line the beach and pack the bars year round.

There is a great museum and some interesting attractions, but the atmosphere of the city is so geared to race fans that you may feel left out if you're not one of them.

Orientation

Daytona Beach spans from I-95 all the way across the Intracoastal Waterway to the Atlantic Ocean. The Daytona Speedway and the Daytona Airport are both at the western end of town, near I-95.

The main east-west drag is US Hwy 92, International Speedway Blvd. Hwy A1A is Atlantic Ave here, US Hwy 1 is called Ridgewood Ave. Main St is the north-south divider. 'Downtown' Daytona is Beach St, running north-south along the west end of the Intracoastal Waterway.

Information

The excellent Daytona Beach Convention & Visitor's Bureau (CVB; ☎ 904-255-0415, 800-544-0415, www.daytonabeach-tourism .com) is at 126 E Orange Ave. AAA (☎ 904-252-0531) is at 2525 International Speedway Blvd.

NationsBank's downtown branch is at 200 S Palmetto Ave. American Express is represented by Atlantic Travel Agency Inc (☎ 904-255-0070), 2430 S Atlantic Ave. The main post office (☎ 904-274-3500) is at 500 Bill France Blvd. The downtown office (☎ 904-253-5166) is at 220 N Beach St.

Mandala Books (☎ 904-255-6728), 204 W International Speedway Blvd, has a huge selection and good women's studies and sci-fi sections. Barnes & Noble has a superstore (☎ 904-238-1118) at 1900 W International Speedway Blvd, and there is Books-A-Million (☎ 904-255-5588) at 90 N Nova Rd

in the Daytona Mall. Atlantic News (☎ 904-677-1510), 2500 N Atlantic Ave in the Bellair Shopping Plaza, has national and international newspapers.

The main library (☎ 904-257-6036) is on City Island, in the Intracoastal Waterway just south of Hwy 92. The Daytona News-Journal is the biggie in town. National Public Radio (NPR) is at both 90.7 and 89.9 FM.

Volusia Laundraclean (☎ 904-255-3580) is at 1464 International Speedway Blvd. Snow White Laundromat & Dry Cleaners (☎ 904-677-8445) is at 2413 N Atlantic Ave.

There are two clinics, the Peninsula Medical Center (☎ 904-672-4161), 264 S Atlantic Ave, and the Halifax Medical Center (☎ 904-254-4000), 303 N Clyde Morris Blvd. Memorial Hospital (☎ 904-676-6000) is at 875 Sterthaus Ave.

Daytona International Speedway

The most famous raceway in the USA after Indianapolis, the Daytona International Speedway (☎ 904-947-6782) is certainly big. And loud. And when there aren't races going on, you can take a tour of the entire complex that's worth the $5, if only to get a sense of the amazing scope of the place.

In the main entrance, ticket booths are to the left, and there is a huge gift shop to the right (selling tasteful items such as Daytona International Speedway placemats – makes a great Christmas gift for that special race fan in your life). Above the shop, on a catwalk balcony, is the Gallery of Legends, an interesting history of Daytona racing from Olds vs Winston in 1902 on.

On the **Western Auto Pars America Speedway Tour**, you'll take a 30-minute tram ride through the garage areas, and drive on Pit Rd, while the narrator tells of the incredible feats of pit crews who, in 20 seconds or so, can change four tires, jam 22 gallons of 110-octane racing fuel into a car, and perform chassis adjustments and other fussing during races. The speed limit during races on Pit Rd is a relatively quaint 65 mph. The tour continues on a loop of the $2^{1}/_{2}$-mile track, with the narrator pointing out that on Turn 1, the monstrous $31°$ bank requires cars to travel at least 70 mph or slide off the road.

NORTHEAST

Be Richard Petty

Legendary stock-car racer Richard Petty has cut a deal with the Daytona International Speedway that will have avid race fans experiencing, to put it politely, soiled undergarments.

The Richard Petty Driving Experience (☎ 800-237-3889, or 800-BE-PETTY, www.1800bepetty.com) offers everything from the chance to experience racing from the passenger seat of a stock car, up through the ultimate thrill of tearing ass round the Daytona Speedway on an 80-lap solo program.

The cheapest option ($100 including admission to Daytona USA) puts you in the passenger seat of a two-seater stock car driven by a professional racer at speeds up to 160 mph (258 km/h).

The Rookie Experience ($330) is a three-hour course culminating in your getting into the driver's seat and hauling ass 'round the speedway for eight laps by yourself. The Winston Experience ($700) doubles your laps at more than double the price.

If you're ready to spend some serious time, effort and money really learning to drive a race car, the more advanced courses may not be of great value; you may be much better off in smaller and less flashy digs – say a local racetrack at home or even a mid-sized speedway somewhere else (this is like getting your pilot's license in a MiG as opposed to a Cessna 150). But advanced classes are held here as well. First, you'll need to take the Experience of a Lifetime ($1100), three 10-lap sessions, or the Racing Experience ($2200), an 80-lap course over two days.

Finally, passing one or both of those satisfactorily, you're ready for the $2500 Advanced Racing Experience, which is an intensive 40-lap polishing program.

All you need is money, a valid driver's license and the ability to drive a standard-shift car.

Back at the starting point, you can go into the stands and listen to a surround-sound demonstration of loud cars screeching by. Or, if you're lucky (as we were last time), you'll see actual race cars on practice laps.

The National Association for Stock Car Auto Racing (NASCAR) sanctions the Daytona 500 and Pepsi 400 at the Speedway (see below), as well as Goody's 300 Busch Grand National and the Daytona USA Motorsports Attraction 200, Goody's Dash Series event.

Races at Daytona include the following:

Bike Week
 Ten days of motorcycle racing, supercross, amateur motorcross, the Daytona 200 by Arai Motorcycle Classic and Vintage Motorcycle Racing; first week in March.

Classic Cars
 Daytona Beach Classic Car Speedway Spectacular with antiques, classics, sports cars and vintage race cars; late March.

Pepsi 400
 Meet NASCAR drivers and view show cars; Fourth of July weekend.

Speed Weeks
 Sponsored races include things such as the Busch Clash (a car race sponsored by a beer company called a 'clash'?) and the Rolex 24 – the only round-the-clock endurance race in North America (an American LeMans so to speak) – culminating with the Daytona 500 NASCAR Winston Cup; late January, early February.

Turkey Run
 Street rods and muscle cars, more of a car show than a race; Thanksgiving week.

Ticket prices to the Daytona 500 range from $40 to $150 depending on where you're sitting, and sell out several months in advance. Tickets to other events vary widely in price; call the box office (☎ 904-253-7223) for pricing information.

Daytona USA

Outside the Speedway is Daytona USA (☎ 904-947-6800, www.nascar.com), 1801 W International Speedway Blvd, a racing theme park with racing exhibits: Sir Malcolm Campbell's original Bluebird V, a car that set the world land-speed record in

Daytona Beach in 1935, and a full-scale replica of the Daytona Beach gas station that 'Big Bill' France once owned. Interactive displays let you announce a race (well – gives you a microphone and lets you try, anyway – we were hopeless), design and test a race car and try (go ahead!) to take part in a pit-stop maintenance session. This is great fun and worth every penny if you're a serious race fan, and 'are-we-there-yet?' boring if you're not.

It's open daily 9 am to 7 pm. Admission is $12 for adults, $10 for seniors, $6 for kids six to 12 (under six free).

Klassix Auto Museum
This museum (☎ 904-252-0940), 2909 W International Speedway Blvd, is dedicated to classic cars, and has every Corvette model from 1953 to 1994 (with an explanation of why there was no '83 'Vette) along with other cars and motorcycles including an excellent Harley-Davidson collection, a 1932 Deusenberg, a '55 Messerschmidt, a '57 Chevy Black Widow, Richard Petty's '77 Monte Carlo and Mello Yello, No 51 from the film *Days of Thunder*. Exit, of course, into the gift shop.

The museum is open daily 9 am to 6 pm. Admission is $11 for adults, $7 for children seven to 12.

Museum of Arts & Science
This great museum (☎ 904-255-0285), 1040 Museum Blvd off Nova Rd, is an incredible surprise: there's an excellent permanent collection of American, African and Cuban art, as well as rotating exhibitions, a planetarium and a nature and science center. About 20,000 school kids tromp through here each year.

The **Dow Gallery of American Art** has silver, glass, samplers and some noteworthy antique furniture.

Africa: Life & Ritual is an impressive collection, with items such as carved-wood commemorative posts, spears, *Asen* iron staffs representing plants, humans and animals, and a statue of the Yoruba god of mischief and chaos.

The **Cuban Museum**, the bulk of which was donated to the city by Fulgencio Batista (Batista lived in Daytona Beach after he was ousted from power in Cuba), features paintings by Cuban artists.

In the **science center**, the museum's prize display is the complete 13-foot-tall skeleton of a giant ground sloth, found 3 miles from the museum in South Daytona. While the bone condition was original, not mineralized, the head on the giant mammal is a reproduction (the real skull is in the case opposite the skeleton display, too delicate to be mounted on the larger exhibit).

Its excellent 96-seat planetarium offers shows Tuesday to Friday at 2 pm, and free films every Saturday.

Museum admission is $5 for adults, $2 for students and children. Planetarium admission is $3, though some astrological events are free.

Gamble Place
The 150-acre winter retreat of James Gamble (of Proctor & Gamble fame) at Spruce Creek Nature Preserve has an exact replica of Snow White's house, but unfortunately, it's closed indefinitely; check with the Museum of Arts & Science to see if the house has reopened when you visit – if so, it's worth a trip.

The Beach
Shops, miniature golf, arcades, cafés and fast-food places line the beach along the boardwalk amusement area. During the day, you can drive along the 18 miles of hard-packed sand on the beach; the cost is $5 in high season and during special events, otherwise it's free. The speed limit (strictly enforced) is 10 mph. Enter the beach at one of almost a dozen clearly marked driveways.

NORTHEAST

At the eastern end of Main St, at the ocean, the Daytona Beach Pier extends about a quarter-mile.

Surfers are better off heading down to New Smyrna Beach for surfing and surf shops; call ☎ 904-239-7873 for a surf report.

Real surfers will think the local surf-shop offerings are merely T-shirt shops, and they're not far off; Salty Dog has three locations on the beach: at 2429 N Atlantic Ave (☎ 904-673-5277), 100 S Atlantic Ave (☎ 904-253-2755) and 700 E International Speedway Blvd (☎ 904-258-0457). For foam BZ surfboards it's $25 a day; Boogieboards and skimboards are $15 a day plus a deposit.

Daytona Iceplex

Set to open after we researched, the Daytona Iceplex (☎ 904-334-7465), 2400 Ridgewood Ave (US Hwy 1) in Daytona Beach Shores, will have an NHL-size ice surface, open skate sessions and organized skate classes. Call for information.

Southeast Museum of Photography

This museum (☎ 904-254-4475), 1200 International Speedway Drive on the campus of Daytona Beach Community College, Bldg 37, holds fascinating rotating exhibitions of photography from around Florida and the USA, as well as lectures and children's programs. It's open 10 am to 3 pm and 5 to 7 pm Tuesday, 10 am to 3 pm Wednesday to Friday, 1 to 4 pm Saturday and Sunday, closed Monday. Admission is free.

Jackie Robinson Ballpark

Off Beach St on City Island, opposite the CVB, Jackie Robinson Ballpark is the place where Robinson, the first black baseball player to play in the major leagues, played his first game. The Class A Chicago Cubs farm team plays here (☎ 904-257-3172).

Halifax Historical Museum

This museum (☎ 904-255-6976), 252 S Beach St, exhibits Indian and Spanish artifacts, newspaper files dating back to 1883, a carved-wood replica of the Ormond Hotel and memorabilia from earlier beach days.

Art League of Daytona Beach

The Art League (☎ 904-258-3856), 433 S Palmetto Ave, has changing exhibits of state and national artists every three weeks between August and June.

Adventure Landing

This theme park (☎ 904-249-1044, www.adventurelanding.com), 601 Earl St, opposite the Adam's Mark Resort, is the newest in the area. It's a waterpark/mini-golf playland with innertube rides, a huge waterslide, go-carts and other kitsch.

Palms Gallery

This community arts gallery (☎ 904-322-7988), 128 S Beach St in downtown Daytona, is attempting to establish itself as a leading force in regional and local arts, with studios, galleries and special events. They're also planning to have a 24-hour café on the premises.

Ponce de León Inlet Lighthouse Museum

This lighthouse museum (☎ 904-761-1821), 4931 S Peninsula Drive, Ponce Inlet, about 5 miles south of Daytona, was rebuilt in 1982. It's an interesting place to spend an afternoon – and climbing the 203 steps to the top results in a splendid view of the entire area. (The lighthouse gets hit frequently by lightning, though, so don't climb it in storms.) It no longer has a Fresnel lens, but now has a modern strobe.

On the porch in front of Bldg 2, you'll see Cuban rafts that were found on Ormond Beach on September 6, 1994. Also on display here are nautical navigation tools and photos of lighthouses from all over the USA. There is a glassed-off re-creation of an 1890s lighthouse keeper's house. The lens exhibit building has first- to sixth-order lenses (see the Cape Florida Lighthouse section in the Miami chapter for more information on lenses), in various stages of restoration. The lenses are fascinating, and craftspeople are usually there to answer questions about them.

The museum is open 10 am to 7 pm daily. It costs $5 for adults, $1 for kids under 11.

Little Chapel by the Sea

Photo op: one of our favorite area attractions, the Little Chapel by the Sea, 3140 S Atlantic Ave, on the west side of the street, is a drive-in Christian church. That's right, you drive in and they put one of those things in your car window and you hear a sermon. It's worth a stop on your way to the Ponce Inlet Lighthouse. Services are 8:30 to 10 am daily. There's inside seating for the 9:45 am Sunday morning service. Admission is free, though they have a donation box.

Organized Tours

A Tiny Cruise Line (☎ 904-226-2343, www.visitdaytona.com/tinycruise), 401 S Beach St, runs one-hour cruises up the Halifax River at varying times and at sunset daily; at lunchtime, a two-hour cruise costs $12.95 for adults, $7 for kids.

Places to Stay

Motel and hotel prices in Daytona Beach are very low except during special events, when prices quadruple and rooms book up months in advance. The motels and hotels on Daytona Beach (there are about 400 of them) are absolutely alike – either small, semi-clean, mom & pop operations or big chains.

The **Streamline Hotel** (☎ 904-258-6937, 140 S Atlantic Ave), aka the Daytona Hostel, is one of the worst we've ever seen in any country; nasty staff, dirty rooms, old mattresses and a depressing atmosphere. Dorm beds (six to a room) are $15 per person, with a $5 key deposit. During Bike Week, the prices get even higher. We don't recommend it ever.

Motels & Hotels The clean, sterile **Beachside Budget Inn** (☎ 904-258-6238, 1717 N Atlantic Ave) has singles/doubles for $22/25; during car races, prices are $75 and during Bike Week, $85 to $95. The rooms have TVs.

Thunderbird Beach Motel (☎ 904-253-2562, 500 N Atlantic Ave) has large, very clean rooms with two double beds for $25 (single) and $27 to $32 (double, depending on the view) from August to January, and $35 to $55 from February to July. At special events, those rooms are $80 to $175.

The **Royal Arms** (☎ 904-253-0558, 800-329-7316, 801 S Atlantic Ave) has clean double rooms for $22 to $27 in low season. Prices in high season seem to be hard to pinpoint; we got an estimate of $27 to $35 during Bike Week and during special events, they charge 'over $100.'

Esquire Beach Motel (☎ 904-255-3601, 422 N Atlantic Ave) has rooms for $26 to $35 from September to February and $30 to $45 at other times. Rooms during Bike Week are $100.

The friendly **Sun & Surf Motel** (☎ 904-252-8412, 726 N Atlantic Ave) has free HBO, refrigerators and coffee-makers in the rooms, and a heated pool. Rooms are $42 to $44, efficiencies $45 to $48 and one bedrooms $68 to $71.

The **Ocean Villa Motel** (☎ 904-252-4644, 800-225-3691, 828 N Atlantic Ave) has rooms and efficiencies for $41 to $118 and two bedrooms for $72 to $184. They have two heated pools and a kiddie pool, a 60-foot waterslide, a game room and a shuffleboard court.

The **Radisson Resort Daytona Beach** (☎ 904-239-9800, 640 N Atlantic Ave) has very luxurious rooms and good service, a good pool and a nice, well-maintained beach section right outside; rooms run the gamut from $70 to $300 year round.

The **Adam's Mark Resort** (☎ 904-254-8200, 800-444-2326, fax 904-253-8841, 100 N Atlantic Ave) is a fabulously luxurious resort, with heaps of amenities and a beach that's all but private, what with their patrols and activities. Rack rates start at $119 per night for rooms.

B&Bs The **Coquina Inn B&B** (☎ 904-254-4969, www.coquinainn.com, 544 S Palmetto Ave) has four rooms from $69 to $105. Some rooms have fireplaces, and there's a lush garden patio and a Jacuzzi. Bicycles are available.

The Villa (☎ 904-248-2020, 801 N Peninsula Drive) is another B&B with four rooms, ranging from $65 to $145 in what they call the 'value season,' $90 to $170 in winter – call for special events prices, which, we take it, are as high as the market will bear. It's in a Spanish-style mansion filled with antiques;

there is a pool in the flower garden, and continental breakfast is included.

And finally, our friend at the CVB recommended highly the *Live Oak Inn B&B* (☎ *904-252-4667, 800-881-4664, fax 904-239-0068, 444-448 S Beach St)*, with 14 rooms, some with Jacuzzi and all with TV and VCR; rooms cost 'under $100.'

Places to Eat
Fast food is pretty much the order of the day. *Steak & Shake* (☎ *904-253-5283, 1000 International Speedway Blvd)* has double hamburgers for $3, a turkey club sandwich for $4.25 and fried-chicken dinner for $5.50. It's open 24 hours.

Lighthouse Landing (☎ *904-761-9271, 4940 S Peninsula Drive)*, near the Ponce Inlet Lighthouse, is an excellent and fun place that does veggie burgers for $3.25, shark kebabs for $4.95, and fish & chips and seafood for $9 to $12. It's open 11:30 am to 10 pm daily.

Anna's Italian Trattoria (☎ *904-239-9624, 304 Seabreeze Blvd)* is a very friendly place at the corner of Peninsula Drive. Tortellini alle panna is $10, penne alla vodka $12, risotto $12 to $14 and early-bird specials (served from 5 to 6:30 pm) are $5 to $8.

The *Dancing Avocado Kitchen* (☎ *904-947-2022, 110 S Beach St)*, in downtown Daytona, has absolutely stellar vegetarian food; the veggie breakfast burrito is $3.50, and the rest of the day salads run $4 to $6. There are some meat options as well, and good shakes.

Downtown on the Halifax River, the *Chart House* (☎ *904-255-9022, 1100 Marina Point Drive)* has seriously good high-end beef dishes and an awesome prime rib; main courses run $14 to $22. Another top-end place is *Sophie Kay's Waterfall Restaurant* (☎ *904-756-4444, 3516 S Atlantic Ave)*, in Daytona Beach Shores, with good Italian and European food; main courses are from $14 to $20.

Entertainment
Performing Arts The *Ocean Center* (☎ *904-254-4500, 101 N Atlantic Ave)* is a multipurpose facility, staging country and rock concerts, ice-hockey matches, wrestling and art shows, etc.

The *Seaside Music Theater* (☎ *904-252-6200, 1200 W International Speedway Blvd)* stages professional musicals at the Daytona Beach Community College.

The *Peabody Auditorium* (☎ *904-255-1314, 600 Auditorium Blvd)* holds mainly classical, but also pop concerts. Daytona Beach Civic Ballet performances are staged here and the London Symphony Orchestra performs here every other year (and has for 25 years).

There are constantly changing concerts at the *Oceanfront Bandshell* (☎ *904-258-3169, 206 B Moore Ave)*. In May, the Daytona Beach Music Festival is held here.

The *Daytona Playhouse* (☎ *904-255-2431, 100 Jessamine Blvd)* puts on local productions of musicals throughout the year. The box office hours are 1 to 3 pm Monday to Friday.

Bars & Clubs You can't swing a cat in this town without hitting some sort of bar. Most have happy hours, and all have them during big events.

Razzles (☎ *904-257-6236, 611 Seabreeze Blvd)* is a high-energy dance club.

The *Love Bar* (☎ *904-252-7600, 124 N Beach St)* is a gothic-kitsch-themed meat market that's definitely fun if you're single. In the same complex is *The Groove Bar* (*same ☎ and address)*, another kitschy place with a shag (the material, not the British verb) bar.

Ocean Deck (☎ *904-253-5224, 127 S Ocean Ave)* is a fun place right on the beach with a family-appropriate restaurant. There's a 30ish crowd upstairs and a fun-loving beach crowd downstairs listening to live music on weekends.

Bank and Blues (☎ *904-257-9272, 9 S Wild Olive Ave)* has lots of good blues throughout the year.

Shopping
A farmer's market is held every Saturday morning on City Island behind Jackie Robinson Ballpark (see Jackie Robinson Ballpark earlier in this section).

Tobacco Exotica (☎ 904-255-3782), 749 International Speedway Blvd, has everything tobacco: cigars, clove cigarettes, head-shop items, etc.

GI Jeff's (☎ 904-255-4000), 936 International Speedway Blvd, sells new and used military clothing and equipment, leather and the like.

Getting There & Away
Daytona Beach International Airport (☎ 904-248-8030) is just east of the Speedway. It's served by many major and some regional airlines.

The Greyhound station (☎ 904-255-7076) is at 138 S Ridgewood Ave. Daytona is a major stop on Greyhound's east-coast route and there are seven buses a day to/from Miami (6¹/₂ to 14 hours).

Amtrak (☎ 800-872-7245) does not go to Daytona; the nearest stop is DeLand, inland off US Hwy 92. There's connecting Amtrak bus service from the DeLand station, but it will cost about the same as a taxi, around $20.

Daytona is between I-95 and US Hwy 1 and Hwy A1A. It's about 53 miles to Orlando (west) or St Augustine (north), about 139 to Tampa and 251 to Miami. All major car-rental companies have desks at the airport. See the Getting Around chapter for a list of the major car-rental companies in Florida.

Getting Around
There is no public transportation from Daytona Beach International Airport. A taxi from there to downtown will cost about $10 to $12, to the beach about $16, or to Ormond Beach or Ponce Inlet about $18 to $21.

Votran (☎ 904-761-7700, www.velusia .org/votran/) runs buses and trolleys in town. Bus and trolley fares are $1 for adults and 50¢ for children and seniors, under six free; exact change is required. The trolley runs along Hwy A1A from Granada Ave in Ormond to Dunlawton Ave in Daytona Beach Shores from mid-January to Labor Day, every day, every 45 minutes from noon to midnight.

Taxi rates in Daytona are $2.40 flagfall, $1.20 a mile, $1 extra per person. The biggies

are Yellow Cab Co (☎ 904-255-5555) and Southern Comfort Taxi (☎ 904-253-9292).

Parking is free and easy in most places, but, in downtown, watch out for meter agents – use store-provided lots when you can. Do not speed, especially if you're driving on the beach where the strictly enforced speed limit is 10 mph. During major events, the speed limits in this speed capital are steady-as-she-goes or she-goes-to-jail.

AROUND DAYTONA BEACH
Flagler Beach
Thirty miles north of Daytona Beach is the charming and isolated town of Flagler Beach, a 6-mile-long protected island on the Intracoastal Waterway that's closed to vehicular traffic. The draws here are the beaches themselves, and a very nice state recreation area (see below).

At the southern end of town is the **Flagler Beach Pier**, a fishing pier that's great fun to walk out on ($1 to look, $3 to fish).

The only way to get to the Flagler Beach area is by car; take exit 91 off I-95 and then go east for 6 miles, or take Hwy A1A directly north from Daytona or south from St Augustine.

Gamble Rogers Memorial State Recreation Area
Three miles south of Flagler Beach on Hwy A1A sits Gamble Rogers Memorial State Recreation Area (☎ 904-517-2086), 3100 South A1A, a 144-acre park with swimming, hiking and biking trails and a **campground** (sites are around $19/21 a day, without/with electric). From May to September, you can go with a group to watch endangered and threatened loggerhead, green and, very occasionally, leatherback sea turtles crawl up the beach to nest – see the Fauna section in the Facts about Florida chapter for more information.

Washington Oaks State Gardens
Washington Oaks State Gardens (☎ 904-446-6780), 6400 N Oceanshore Blvd, Palm Coast, Florida 32137, has perhaps the most interesting beach on Florida's east coast. It's

littered with enormous boulders that are part of an outcropping of the Anastasia formation, which runs about 250 miles along the coast, but pops up above ground here. The Spanish used the area as the source for much of the *coquina* (see Architecture in the St Augustine section below) used in the construction of St Augustine.

The park has 5 miles of hiking trails, picnic areas and ranger-led walks on Saturday and Sunday. Admission is $3.25 per carload for the whole park, or $2 per carload for just the beach; take Hwy A1A south about 5 miles from Flagler Beach.

ST AUGUSTINE
• population 15,000

The nation's oldest city, St Augustine was settled by the Spanish in 1565. One of the earliest planned cities in the New World, St Augustine is a charming mix of narrow, cobblestone streets, European architecture and a Spanish-colonial flair that makes it an irresistible destination for at least a few days. (We liked it so much, we moved here to complete the first edition of this book!) There is simply a *lot* to do here.

Through the 144-block National Historic Landmark District clop horse-drawn carriages, and throngs of pedestrians gawk at the architecture and fill sidewalks lined with crafts shops, cafés, restaurants and pubs.

It's Europe by Disney without the admission fees; an American city with, at least in the downtown area, more cobblestone than asphalt, more coquina than cement, and more time and patience for the pleasures of living than one generally runs across.

And the city government can be lauded for using its noodle and coming up with creative ways to save, as opposed to bull-dozing, buildings by shrewdly recycling abandoned real estate. In that way, one deserted hotel became a college, another a city administration office and yet another a courthouse (and the courthouse has become, finally, once again, a luxury hotel; see Casa Monica Hotel, later in this section). It all adds up to a living time capsule that's a pleasure to visit.

On a sad note, in late 1998 the city administration voted to tear down and replace the Bridge of Lions. Details were sketchy as we wrote, but this landmark beauty will be relegated to the scrap heap of history in the near future.

History

St Augustine was settled by Spanish explorer Don Pedro Menéndez de Avilés. By the time Florida was ceded to the US by Spain in 1821, St Augustine had been sacked, looted, burned and occupied by Spanish, British, Georgian and South Carolinian forces.

Menéndez arrived at Cape Canaveral (see the Space Coast chapter) with about 1500 soldiers and settlers who made their way north and established St Augustine on September 4, 1565. It's named for the day on which they arrived on the Florida coast, August 28, the Feast Day of St Augustine, Bishop of Hippo.

Menéndez was here to battle French forces and Huguenot settlers who had established Fort Caroline, near present-day Jacksonville, but the French fleet did him the favor of getting caught in a hurricane; the few troops that survived it were butchered by Menéndez's men, giving the name to the bay near St Augustine: *matanzas* (slaughter).

The next attack came from the British, who occupied and burned the city in 1586 under the command of Sir Francis Drake. After another British attack in 1668, the Spanish decided that stone would suit their needs a bit better than wood, and they began work on the Castillo de San Marcos fort in 1672. Now the oldest masonry fort in North America, it has never fallen to attack, though it has been at various times under command of Spanish, British, US and Confederate troops.

In 1702, the British again burned the city; the fort held, unscathed. In 1740, British, Georgian and South Carolinian troops attacked again, this time from the south at Matanzas inlet. Though the city was set on fire during the retreat, the attack failed. But the attack showed the Spanish that the area

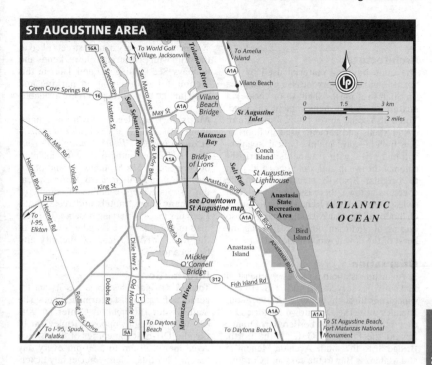

ST AUGUSTINE AREA

to the south of the city was as inviting to invaders as a large welcome mat, so they constructed tiny Fort Matanzas in 1742.

Beaten finally by fighting elsewhere in the French & Indian War, the Spanish ceded Florida in 1763 to Great Britain in a swap for Cuba. The British would hold the fort through the American Revolution, though as part of the Treaty of Paris ending that war, the fort was ceded back to Spain in 1783.

The British had remained in town for 20 years, and left their mark in many ways. Under their rule, residents of the failed New Smyrna Beach colony (south of present-day Daytona Beach) came to settle in the area, and many of their descendants remain to this day. The colony, established in 1768 by London physician Andrew Turnbull, had brought about 1500 Greek, Italian and Minorcan laborers to Florida to work an indigo plantation but failed after disease-carrying mosquitoes killed off hundreds of settlers. (New Smyrna Beach was reestablished by the late 1800s.)

The Spanish ceded Florida to the US in 1821. In the late 1880s, Henry Flagler brought his railroad through town, and created a boom in building, especially luxury hotels, gambling halls and restaurants. But as the railroad headed south, interest in the town by the rich northerners fell greatly, and the town was left in a condition similar to London's Docklands today: lots of very expensive, very luxurious and very empty buildings.

Today, the city retains much of its European flair – in fact, it reminds many of cities such as Prague, Kraków and Regensburg. The coquina and tabby buildings (see Architecture below) lend a faded, pastel but somewhat magical quality to the narrow streets, and the city's long and colorful history is palpable.

Architecture

The main building material used by the Spanish, and then everyone else, was coquina (in Spanish it means shellfish or cockle): a mixture of broken shells, cement and sand. You'll also come across tabby, a mixture of oyster shells and cement, used in flooring. The buildings are mainly typical Spanish-colonial style, with fragments of British-colonial thrown in and sometimes added on to original Spanish structures. Of the churches in town, there is a hodgepodge of styles, from Venetian Renaissance to Greek Orthodox to Spanish Mission. There are also dozens of Victorian buildings fringing the heart of the downtown historic district.

Orientation

St Augustine is about 35 miles southeast of Jacksonville, served by both US Hwy 1, which runs through the city, and I-95, about 10 miles west. The Downtown Historic District is the area roughly bordered by Orange St and the Old City Gate to the north, Bridge St to the south, Avenida Menendez and Matanzas Bay to the east, and Cordova St to the west. North of downtown, past the Castillo de San Marcos fort, Avenida Menendez becomes San Marco Ave, which intersects with US Hwy 1. The other main connecting artery to US Hwy 1 is King St, running east-west across the San Sebastian River then almost to Matanzas River. Near the end of King St is the Bridge of Lions, which becomes Anastasia Blvd on the east side of the river, connecting downtown with Anastasia State Recreation Area and Hwy A1A, which heads south to St Augustine Beach.

At the southern end of the city, Hwy 312 crosses the river on the Mickler O'Connell Bridge, and runs near the KOA campsite before joining with Hwy A1A and heading to the beach.

Downtown is best seen on foot. St George St is a pedestrian-only zone from Cathedral Place at the south to Orange St at the north.

If you're driving in downtown, beware that there's a somewhat tricky one-way system as well as very narrow streets filled to the brim with pedestrians on weekends and holidays. See Getting Around, later in this section, for information on parking and what limited transport options are available.

Maps Pick up decent downtown maps, along with ad rags such as *Visitor's Guide to St Augustine & St John's County* and *Your Place in History* (published by the chamber of commerce), *See St Augustine* and *Sight-seeing Map of St Augustine & Its Beaches*, at the visitors centers, chamber of commerce and many shops, motels and restaurants. Each has maps of varying decency. The best map of the area is the chamber's edition of the *Rand McNally* map of the city and beaches, for $3.

Information

Tourist Offices This place has its act together as far as tourist information goes. The main Visitor Information Center (☎ 904-825-1000) is roughly opposite Ripley's at 10 Castillo Drive, at the corner of San Marco Ave, open 8:30 am to 5:30 pm every day except Christmas. Here you can buy tickets for the sightseeing train, trolley and horse-drawn carriages (see Organized Tours later in this section). They also show a 52-minute film on the history of the city ($3/2 for adults/children), and a free 16-minute orientation video.

There's a smaller tourist information booth at San Marco Ave near Charlotte St.

Staff at the St Augustine Hostel are helpful and know the town well, and they have a pretty good bulletin board and collection of pamphlets.

Money NationsBank has a branch at the corner of King and Cordova Sts.

Post & Communications The main post office (☎ 904-829-8716) is at 99 King St. Send and receive faxes across the street at St John's Printing & Office Supply (☎ 904-834-1496, fax 904-825-0994). Pre-paid phone cards can be bought at a number of shops in town.

DOWNTOWN ST AUGUSTINE

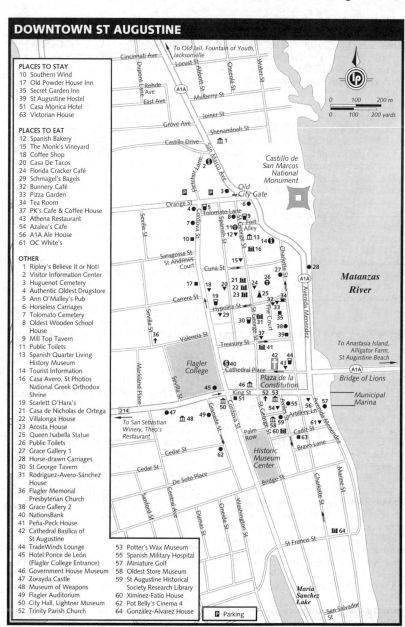

PLACES TO STAY
10 Southern Wind
17 Old Powder House Inn
35 Secret Garden Inn
39 St Augustine Hostel
51 Casa Monica Hotel
63 Victorian House

PLACES TO EAT
12 Spanish Bakery
15 The Monk's Vineyard
18 Coffee Shop
20 Casa De Tacos
24 Florida Cracker Café
29 Schmagel's Bagels
32 Bunnery Café
33 Pizza Garden
34 Tea Room
37 PK's Cafe & Coffee House
43 Athena Restaurant
54 Azalea's Cafe
56 A1A Ale House
61 OC White's

OTHER
1 Ripley's Believe It or Not!
2 Visitor Information Center
3 Huguenot Cemetery
4 Authentic Oldest Drugstore
5 Ann O'Malley's Pub
6 Horseless Carriages
7 Tolomato Cemetery
8 Oldest Wooden School House
9 Mill Top Tavern
11 Public Toilets
13 Spanish Quarter Living History Museum
14 Tourist Information
16 Casa Avero, St Photios National Greek Orthodox Shrine
19 Scarlett O'Hara's
21 Casa de Nicholas de Ortega
22 Villalonga House
23 Acosta House
25 Queen Isabella Statue
26 Public Toilets
27 Grace Gallery 1
28 Horse-drawn Carriages
30 St George Tavern
31 Rodriguez-Avero-Sánchez House
36 Flagler Memorial Presbyterian Church
38 Grace Gallery 2
40 NationsBank
41 Peña-Peck House
42 Cathedral Basilica of St Augustine
44 TradeWinds Lounge
45 Hotel Ponce de León (Flagler College Entrance)
46 Government House Museum
47 Zorayda Castle
48 Museum of Weapons
49 Flagler Auditorium
50 City Hall, Lightner Museum
52 Trinity Parish Church
53 Potter's Wax Museum
55 Spanish Military Hospital
57 Miniature Golf
58 Oldest Store Museum
59 St Augustine Historical Society Research Library
60 Ximínez-Fatio House
62 Pot Belly's Cinema 4
64 González-Alvarez House

P Parking

NORTHEAST

Bookstores & Libraries St Augustine is a haven for used-book lovers, with about a dozen used-book stores. The most well known are Avenue Books (☎ 904-829-9744), 142 King St, specializing in art books, and Wolf's Head Books (☎ 904-824-9357), 48-50 San Marco Ave, specializing in antiquarian books, ephemera, searches, etc. There's a small but very friendly little place called Second Read Books (☎ 904-829-0334), 51 Cordova St, which sells used general and children's fiction and has a good new and used selection of women's studies books.

The main St Augustine branch of the St John's County public library system (☎ 904-823-2650), 1960 N Ponce de León Blvd (US Hwy 1), is open Monday to Wednesday 10 am to 9 pm, Thursday and Friday 10 am to 6 pm, Saturday 10 am to 5 pm, closed Sunday.

Delve into the rich history of the area at the St Augustine Historical Society Research Library (☎ 904-825-2333), in the Sequì-Kirby Smith House, 6 Artillery Lane at Aviles St, open Tuesday to Friday 9 am to 4:30 pm.

Media The paper of record is the *St Augustine Record*. The best what's-on guide is the excellent *Folio Weekly*, a free paper with club dates, restaurant reviews and listings, clubs, pubs and concert listings and good local scandals. Also see free paper listings under Maps, above. National Public Radio (NPR) is at 89.9 FM. The Flagler College radio station at 88.5 FM is hands-down the best in the state, with a terrific variety of new music, jazz and pop. It's especially great on weekends when they run world-music programs.

Universities Flagler College's main building is the former Hotel Ponce de León. Once a posh getaway for the wealthy patrons of Flagler's railroad, the place has since been restored: it looks like a palace but smells like a four-year liberal-arts college. It's worth a look, and tours are available; see Hotel Ponce de León later in this section.

Laundry Coin laundries are inconveniently located; if you are staying at the hostel, you can wash and dry for $3. Otherwise, your best bets are the St Augustine Laundromat (☎ 904-824-3487), 179 W King St, at US Hwy 1, and the Laundry Room (☎ 904-824-4262), 405 Anastasia Blvd, about a mile east of the Bridge of Lions.

Toilets There are clean and free public toilets in several locations: behind the Florida Cracker Café on St George St between Cuna and Hypolita Sts, behind A1A Ale House, in the Government House and at the main visitor center.

Medical Services Flagler Hospital has two large facilities south of the city; the Main Campus (☎ 904-829-5155) is at 400 Health Park Blvd, and the West Campus (☎ 904-826-4700) is across the street at 1955 US Hwy 1.

Museums & Historic Buildings
Spanish Quarter Living History Museum
This museum (☎ 904-825-6830), at the northern end of St George St, is a re-creation of Spanish-colonial St Augustine in the year 1740 – the year the British attacked and subsequently burned the city. It's walled off from the street, and once you've paid your admission, you're free to wander through everything on your own except the de Mesa House, for which you'll need to be on a guided tour – they run at 10 am and noon, 2 and 5 pm. The de Mesa House is probably the most interesting on the property, especially if you like antiques, and if only to learn the origin of the term 'at loggerheads':

A loggerhead was a ping-pong-size ball of iron at the end of a staff that cowboys would use to heat drinks, by placing the ball in the fire, blowing off the ashes and then placing it in their drink. But the term comes from the drunken cowboys' tendency to brawl and try to crown each other with the devices.

Costumed employees go about the business of life in 1740 St Augustine – they're not re-enactors: they'll speak to you as a 20th-century person explaining an 18th-century procedure.

Many of the following sights are staffed: the Gómez House (a store in a private home), de Hita House, de Burgo-Pellicer House, a *taberna* (tavern), and a working woodshop and blacksmith. The Gallegos House, formerly the home of an army sergeant, is now host to cooking demonstrations.

Admission to the complex, which is open 9 am to 6 pm daily, is $6 for adults, $5 for seniors (over 62), $3.75 for students six to 18 or $12 per family of four.

City Hall & Lightner Museum One of the grandest government office complexes you'll ever come across, St Augustine's City Hall at 75 King St, opposite Flagler College, is in the former Hotel Alcazar (1888), a resort which in its heyday featured the country's largest indoor swimming pool, a health club and oodles of luxury.

Restored, and currently home to a local government dedicated to raising already outrageous local water-usage bills, the building is also home to the Lightner Museum (☎ 904-824-2874), primarily featuring 19th-century fine and decorative arts, early Americana and fine collections of European art including pieces from Tsarist Russia, decorative and applied art and loud classical music. It's worth a trip, and plan on spending between one and two hours here.

On the 2nd floor, we loved the story behind the Florentine painting *Cimon and Pera*, of a prisoner kept alive by his daughter's breast milk while his captors tried to starve him to death. There's also 19th-century glass vases and bowls, Tiffany, European, American and Bohemian glass, and German, French, Russian and English porcelain dated between 1700 and 1900. The museum's open 9 am to 5 pm daily. Admission is $6 for adults, $2 for students and children over 12, under 12 free. There are musical-instrument demonstrations daily at 11 am and 2 pm.

Government House Museum This is an interesting, if unspectacular, collection of the history of the settlement of the city, featuring a neat historical timeline and exhibits on Spanish explorers (including coins and artifacts from galleons), the British period, some archaeological finds, early plans of the

city, and military architecture. The museum (☎ 904-825-5033), 48 King St, at the west end of Government House Square, is open 9 am to 6 pm daily except Christmas. Admission is $3 for adults, $1.50 for students and children six to 18. There's a nice new Mediterranean-style sidewalk café out front.

Potter's Wax Museum If you're really into wax museums, or if you're with children, this museum (☎ 904-829-9056, 800-584-4781), 17 King St (great location), with Rambo and Jim Carrey in the window, may be worth it. Check out Cleopatra (a hot one, with a snake), Julius Caesar, Marc Antony, Edward the Black Prince and a concession to local history in the form of Juan Ponce de León, Pedro Menéndez de Avilés and Sir Francis Drake. If you're gonna go, you gotta see the 'tyrant room': Nixon, Hitler, Mussolini, Harry Truman (?) and others. It's open daily 9 am to 5 pm in winter, 9 am to 9 pm in summer, closed Thanksgiving and Christmas. Admission is $5.95 for adults, $4.95 for seniors (55 and older), $2.75 for children six to 12, under six free.

Oldest Wooden School House This museum (☎ 904-824-0192, 800-428-0222), 14 St George St, billed as America's oldest wooden school house, was built around the 1750s. It's a little house that was bought by Juan Genoply who conducted classes here. Later, it was used as a guardhouse and shelter during the Seminole Wars (1834-41). It has a very nice garden, and you'll learn a lot about 18th-century life and education – and a fair amount about carpentry: much of the wood used to construct the building was from old ships, and there's an anchor-chain surrounding the building. It's open 9 am to 5 pm daily. Admission is $2 for adults, $1.50 for seniors (over 55) and $1 for children six to 12.

Spanish Military Hospital This hospital (☎ 904-825-6808), 3 Aviles St, is small, and doesn't appear to be much, but the volunteers are wonderful: if you get a good one, plan on spending an hour hearing history, tales of Spanish explorers and perhaps the origin of the term 'sleep tight.' The building is a reconstruction of a military hospital that stood on the site during the second Spanish-colonial period (1784-1821) – the Spanish had, er, liberated the building from an Eng-lishman, William Watson, who had con-verted it from a stable to a residence. It's a fascinating, if small, collection of beds (note the length – the average height at the time was about 5 feet), medicines, medical equip-ment and an herbal apothecary. It's open 10 am to 4 pm daily; admission is free, but they request a donation of $1.

González-Alvarez House Alleged to be the oldest in America, this house (☎ 904-824-2872), 14 St Francis St, is said to have provable continuous occupancy from the early 1600s to today. True or not (and there are some very persuasive arguments, like the designated National Historic Landmark status and the fact that it's run by the St Augustine Historical Society), if you're going to visit just one 'oldest' site, the González-Alvarez House (and grounds) is perhaps the best. It has some lovely gardens, and exhibits on the residents and evolution of the house, and the British sacking of the city. It's open daily 9 am to 5 pm; tours leave every 30 minutes. Admission is $5 for adults, $4.50 for seniors, $3 for students or $12 for a family of four. The price includes parking.

Oldest Store Museum If you're in the neighborhood, it *may* be worth stopping by this re-creation of a general store from the 1800s. The museum (☎ 904-829-9729), at 4 Artillery Lane, is complete with wood-burning stove, hats, shoes, grinders, a dentist's chair, cloth bolts, etc. Open Monday to Saturday 9 am to 5 pm, Sunday noon to 5 pm, it's $5 for adults, $4.50 for seniors and $1.50 for children.

Museum of Weapons Though it'd rather call itself a museum of American history from 1500 to 1900, this is just what the heading says: a room full of guns. The museum (☎ 904-829-3727), 81-C King St, does, however, have a few added attractions.

Labeling is quite good, and our favorite was the 1⁵/₁₆-inch-long, 2 mm Pinfire Pistol from Austria. Made for ladies, it fires teeny, weeny bullets, designed to be fired into the ear canals of victims. *Charming.* You can also see a Bible that stopped a bullet during the Civil War – a period covered quite well indeed, in terms of weaponry, equipment, Confederate money, etc.

It's open 9:30 am to 5 pm every day but Christmas. Admission is $4 for adults, $1 for children six to 12, under six free.

Authentic Oldest Drugstore This old wooden house (☎ 904-824-2269, 800-332-9893), 31 Orange St, at the corner of Cor-dova St, includes an authentic pharmacy (complete with wax model remote-con-trolled pharmacist and optometrist) and an overpriced gift shop. It's open 9:30 am to 6 pm daily except Christmas, Thanksgiving and Easter.

Old Jail The former town prison and resi-dence of the town's first sheriff, Charles Joseph 'the Terror' Perry (who stood 6 feet 6 inches tall, weighed more than 300 pounds and was a shotgun, rifle and handgun marks-man), is now open as a museum (☎ 904-829-3800, 800-397-4071), 167 San Marco Ave. Built in 1892, the simple (but strong) struc-ture housed up to 64 of the riffraff of the day, at a time. Upstairs, there's a firearms collection on the walls, and you can see some rather barbaric and cramped general-population cells – complete with an Alca-traz-style main door-opening system. Downstairs, you'll see women's cells, solitary confinement and the kitchen.

Narration makes it more interesting than it sounds, such as the explanation of the area out back beneath the 'bird cage,' where locals used to picnic while harassing the unhappy occupant of the man-sized cage suspended above the lawn. Nice. Hear also of the hangings and, if you're lucky, the per-sonal opinions of your tour guide regarding the death penalty. The museum is open daily 8:30 am to 5 pm. Admission is $4.25 for adults, $3.25 for children six to 12.

St Augustine Lighthouse The lighthouse (☎ 904-829-0745) is on Anastasia Island off Anastasia Blvd at the corner of Lighthouse Ave, sometimes called Old Beach Rd, and tiny Ocean Vista Ave. Three hundred yards northeast of its original location (it was rebuilt because the old one was being gradually washed away by the sea), the black-and-white-striped St Augustine Lighthouse is a great place to bring kids over seven and over 4 feet tall (none younger or shorter are allowed). Originally equipped with a 4th-order lens, it currently uses a beefy 1st, which can be seen for miles at night – look east while in downtown and you'll see it slashing through the night sky.

The lighthouse tower (219 steps) is open to the public. The museum at the foot of the lighthouse contains things nautical. In winter, the museum's open 9:30 am to 7 pm, and the lighthouse tower 9:30 am to 4:30 pm. In summer, the museum's open 9:30 am to 6 pm, the tower 9:30 am to 6:30 pm. Admission for the tower and museum is $5 for adults, $3.50 for seniors (over 55), $2.50 for children seven to 11 (at least 4 feet tall). For the museum only, it's $2.50 for adults, $1.75 for seniors, kids are free.

Historic Museum Center The St Augustine Historic Museum Center is a collection of eight houses on a city block bounded by Palm Row at the north, St George on the east, Cordova on the west and Bridge St at the south. The highlight here is the **Prince Murat House** at 250 St George St at the corner of Bridge St. It's a pink coquina cottage, circa 1790, and named for Napoleon Bonaparte's nephew, Prince Achille Murat, who came to St Augustine in 1824 and lived in the house for only two months. Murat later moved to Tallahassee and married George Washington's grandniece, but on a return trip to St Augustine, he met Ralph Waldo Emerson, who later also lived in the house. The list of celebrities is long. In any of the houses on the route, or at the visitors centers, you can pick up a very detailed pamphlet entitled, not surprisingly, *St Augustine Historic Museum Center*, which

has detailed histories of all the houses. The following are the other houses:

Rose House	244 St George St
William Dean Howells House	246 St George St
Spear Carriage House	143 Cordova St
Worcester House	145 Cordova St
Star General Store	149 Cordova St
Dow House	42 Bridge St
Canova House	43 Bridge St

Peña-Peck House This house (☎ 904-829-5064), 143 St George St, a National Historic Landmark, was closed for repairs when we visited in 1998. Built in the 1740s as the home of the Spanish royal treasurer, Juan Estaban de Peña, it was later the home of Dr Seth Peck, who renovated it, gutted a wing and set up his office here. The building remained in the Peck family until the 1930s, when it was given to the Women's Exchange, which operates it today. Of the 12 rooms, only nine are open to the public. Doting volunteers guide you through the antique-filled rooms for $2.50 for adults, $2 for seniors, $1.50 for children and students ages 12 to 18, under 12 free.

Ximínez-Fatio House This house (☎ 904-829-3575), 20 Aviles St, is one of the few remaining structures from the second Spanish period. A coquina block house built in 1797 or 1798 (different sources give different dates), it was the general store and home of Andres Ximínez (pronounced 'yah-MIN-is'), a merchant from Ronda, Spain. Later the house was an inn, owned by Louisa Fatio (pronounced 'FAY-shee-oh'). Free guided tours are available October through August, Thursday to Monday 11 am to 4 pm (Sunday 1 to 4 pm), closed Tuesday and Wednesday.

St George St Of all the historic buildings on St George St, there are several outside the Spanish Quarter Living History Museum that are noteworthy. Though there are shops in them now, explanatory plaques outside the buildings give some further

NORTHEAST

background. From north to south along St George, they include the following:

Casa Avero
   built 1762; now home to St Photios National Greek Shrine, memorializing the Greek workers at the New Smyrna Beach colony – see Churches & Shrines later in this section

Casa de Nicholas de Ortega
   built circa 1740, reconstructed 1967; home of the gun-running Ortega family

Villalonga House
   built between 1815 and 1820; also reconstructed 1976) home of another Corsican, Bartolomu Villalonga

Acosta House
   built between 1803 and 1812, reconstructed 1976; home of Corsican George Acosta (1764-1812)

Rodriguez-Avero-Sánchez House
   built circa 1762; home of Francis Xavier Sánchez

Oliveros House
   built circa 1798; home of Corsican mariner Sebastian Oliveros and now home to Infiesta Cigars

Hotel Ponce de León Henry Flagler was a visionary, but if he ever envisioned 175 college students chowing down on sloppy joes and fish sticks in his flagship luxury hotel's dining room – the one with all the Tiffany glass and the ornate 35-foot vaulted ceiling – he certainly never said so in his memoirs. The hotel, which was completed in May 1887, and saw its first official guests on January 12, 1888, quickly became the most exclusive winter resort in the USA. Flagler College, which took over the property and has extensively renovated it, offers free tours in the main building from May to August every hour on the hour between 10 am and 4 pm daily. The tours take about 15 to 20 minutes, and meet in the rotunda just inside the building's main entrance.

The main rotunda is open to the public. When you enter, look up, and past the banners wishing happy birthday to students and announcing parties, to see if you can spot the astrologically themed designs. The best stained glass, surprisingly, is not within the awesome dining room itself but on the first landing of the staircases that rise to the

left and right of the dining room entrance. Outside in the courtyard is the turtles and frogs fountain and, in front of the gates, a statue of Flagler.

During the school year, you can arrange for a group tour with advance notice through the office of college relations (☎ 904-829-6481). Do try and see the Flagler Room, which makes the dining room look positively common. It's the site of some classes, concerts, poetry readings and the local community orchestra – check in *The Record* or *Folio Weekly* for ads of events here during your stay. Also check for concerts that may be going on across the street at the **Flagler Auditorium** (☎ 904-824-2874 x217), behind and to the west of the Lightner Museum, often home to classical music and jazz shows.

Casa Monica Hotel Tucked into a recess at the corner of Cordova and King Sts, the Casa Monica Hotel is to be housed in Flagler's former Cordova Hotel (circa 1880). The building was closed in the early 1930s, and re-opened as the St John's County Courthouse in the 1960s. Now Grand Theme Hotels has taken it over and it was scheduled to reopen as the Casa Monica in summer 1999 with 138 rooms, one of the world's coolest swimming pools, and four tower suites – should be a blast. For information, call Grand Theme Hotels (☎ 888-472-6312, www.grandthemehotels.com).

Can you believe we didn't make any Monica Lewinsky jokes?

Historic Remains
Old City Gate This gate, at the northern end of St George St, was built in 1739 to defend the northern St Augustine line from attacks by the British. The coquina pillars at the gate were built in 1808. Today, hardly anyone notices they're walking through something historic, and many people stuff litter into the small chambers inside the pillars.

Rosario Defense Wall Opposite the Tolomato Cemetery is a re-creation of a section of the Rosario Defense Wall, an earth barrier constructed by the Spaniards in the early 1700s to fend off British attack. The wall, which today appears very small, stopped the Brits not just by making them climb a bit, but also with natural defenses on the top: hard and spiky yucca plants and prickly-pear cacti.

British Slave Market In the Plaza de la Constitution, opposite the Bridge of Lions in the heart of downtown, the remains of the old town market run by the British still stand. This was the central market for food and for slaves during the British reign in the city.

An interesting historical note on the market: When St Augustine was ruled by the Spanish, many slaves from Georgia and the Carolinas would escape to St Augustine, where treatment was far better than in British-run colonies. While the Spanish had slavery, they believed that even slaves had human rights – it was, for example, illegal when selling a slave to break up a family. To tweak the Brits further, the Spanish ruled that any slave escaping from a British colony was granted freedom on arrival. When the British traded Cuba for Florida, many black slaves accompanied the Spanish there.

Churches & Shrines
Cathedral Basilica of St Augustine This magnificent 1797 Spanish Mission-style Catholic cathedral (☎ 904-824-2806), on Cathedral Place, near the Plaza de la Constitution on the northeast corner of St George and King Sts, is worth a look, whether simply to view the Rambusch stained glass or to take the free guided tours.

While most of the cathedral was destroyed by fire in 1887, many walls were left intact; the section south of the transepts is essentially original, while the roof and chancel wall were rebuilt. What stands today is an expansion and reconstruction, and the church was refurbished for the 400th anniversary of the city in 1965, when most of the dark wood-paneled ceiling was removed and the Chapel of the Blessed Sacrament added.

The courtyard is usually the site of some activity during city celebrations. There is a

weekday mass at 8 or 8:15 am and Sunday mass at 7, 9 and 11 am and 6 pm. The free guided tours run Monday to Friday from around noon to around 3 pm, Saturday noon to 3 pm and Sunday 1 to 4 pm in Spanish and 1:30 to 5 pm in English.

Trinity Parish Church The stained glass at the cathedral basilica is thoroughly outshined by that at this building (1821). The church (☎ 904-824-2876), 215 St George St, directly south across Plaza de la Constitution, was the first Protestant church in Florida. The glass here was mainly designed and constructed either by Tiffany personally or by his company; note the window in St Peter's Chapel, in the main building, signed by Tiffany himself. It's open 9 am to 4 pm daily. Services are held on Sunday at 7:45, 9 and 11:15 am, and Wednesday at 10 am. Tours by volunteer guides are available most every afternoon, though they don't adhere to a schedule, so call first. Groups are welcome on advance notice, and all tours are free.

Flagler Memorial Presbyterian Church This church (☎ 904-829-6431), 36 Sevilla St, at the corner of Valencia St, on which you enter, is our favorite in town and is definitely worth seeing. Built by Henry Flagler as a memorial to his daughter, Jennie, who died at birth, it's a spectacular Venetian-Renaissance church (1889-90), with its trademark dome beautifully illuminated at night. Each tile on the floors is imported Sienna marble, all the wood is Santo Domingo mahogany, and the 90-rank organ is the original, dating to 1890 and refurbished in 1970. The 105-foot-high dome contains a crown of thorns, which contains a triangle, which in turn contains three white dots, representing the Father, the Son and the Holy Spirit.

To the left as you face the church is the entrance to the gardens, also open to the public, though unspectacular. Services are held Sunday at 8:30 and 10:55 am. It's open for tours Monday to Friday 9 am to 4:30 pm, Saturday 9 am to 4 pm, and Sunday noon to 4:30 pm. There is no admission charge, but you can leave donations.

NORTHEAST

St Photios National Greek Orthodox Shrine In memory of the Greek laborers who worked at an indigo plantation at New Smyrna Beach (there were also Minorcan and Italian workers; see History earlier in this section), this shrine and museum (☎ 904-829-8205), 41 St George St, in Casa Avero, features a history of the development of the area, with old maps, mementos and diaries of settlers. You can light candles and make an offering in the shrine, which is in a lovely vaulted room that has piped-in chanting.

Back in the lobby, you can watch an 18-minute video of the history of the colony. Admission is free, and it's important to remember that this is indeed a shrine, and not a standard museum: while shorts and T-shirts are allowed, food and drink are not, and you should ask permission before taking photographs.

Our Lady of La Leche Shrine Built on the site of the first mass in St Augustine, at Mission of Nombre de Dios, the Shrine to Our Lady of La Leche (☎ 904-824-2809) is a 208-foot-tall stainless-steel cross, visible from many parts of downtown. Also on the grounds, the absolutely charming Prince of Peace Church holds services Monday to Friday at 8:30 am, Saturday at 6 pm and Sunday at 8 am, and the Chapel of Our Lady of La Leche is open to the public as well. The mission is at the corner of San Marco Ave and Ocean St. It's hard to miss – look for the towering cross.

Cemeteries
Huguenot Cemetery During a yellow-fever epidemic in 1821, half an acre of land just north of the Old City Gate (see Historic Remains earlier in this section) was set aside as a public cemetery. Owned since 1832 by the Presbyterian Church, interments were discontinued in 1884. Many of the gravesites of Protestant pioneers buried here are not marked. You can walk through the cemetery when the gates are unlocked.

The most prestigious graves are at the southwest end of the cemetery, including those of the Dr Peck Family. Directly behind the Burt family gravestones within the fence, Charles, Alice and Lucy Peck, antecedents of the owners of the Alligator Farm, are buried. Farther west, the center of the three crypts at the cemetery's western end is that of Ann Drysdale, notable in that, on the top of the crypt, her eulogy is engraved as spoken by an Episcopal minister. Leave a donation in the box within the right-hand gate pillar on the way out; there's no telephone.

Tolomato Cemetery On Cordova St, between Orange and Saragossa Sts, this cemetery sits on the site of what was, prior to 1763, a Native American village. Among the luminaries buried here is the first bishop of St Augustine, Augustine Verot, buried in the mortuary chapel at the rear of the cemetery. The last burial was in 1892. Note the tree to the north of the cemetery, in front of No 6 Cordova St – it's a palm tree growing from the trunk of a live oak!

Parks & Monuments
Anastasia State Recreation Area This recreation area (☎ 904-461-2033), on Anastasia Island (the entrance is on Anastasia Blvd), is a very nice state park with beach access at its eastern end, nature and hiking trails and a campground (see Places to Stay later). Admission is $3.25 per carload, $1 for pedestrians and bicyclists.

Castillo de San Marcos National Monument In 1672, after the British had burned the city down around them one time too many, the Spanish began work on this coquina fort (☎ 904-829-6506). It was

Castillo de San Marcos National Monument

completed 23 years later, and is now the oldest masonry fort in the continental US, and a national monument. You can explore the shot furnace, powder room, chapel and bastions. It's on the east site of San Marco Ave opposite the Old City Gate, and is open to visitors 8:45 am to 4:45 pm daily. There is a second fort in the area, Fort Matanzas; see the Around St Augustine section, later in this chapter, for more information.

Bridge of Lions One of the city's most distinctive features, the Bridge of Lions – with its trademark Mediterranean-Revival-style towers – was built in 1926 to connect the city with Anastasia Island. The bridge is named for the two lion statues at its west end, sculpted by an Italian named Romanelli, which were donated to the city by Dr Andrew Anderson. In its wisdom, the city (Republican) council voted to decimate this bridge – stay tuned.

Queen Isabella Statue At the northeast corner of Hypolita and St George Sts, in the little park, is a sweet little statue of Queen Isabella I, by Anna Hyatt Huntington. This is a very popular hang-out for Flagler students, hippies and other guitar-wielding people, a fun place to come.

Plaza de la Constitution This is the grassy area at the east end of King St between the Bridge of Lions and the Government House Museum. At the western end, two cannons point northwest and southwest. A monument to the Spanish Plaza de la Constitución is near the center, as is a gazebo. Another statue is just east of this, a memorial to Confederate soldiers who died in the Civil War. At the east end, a historical marker tells the story of this spot, where a British guardhouse and watchtower once stood, as well as the town's central market (see British Slave Market earlier in this section).

Other Attractions

Ripley's Believe It or Not! It's kitschy. It appeals to the base instincts. And we loved it. One of three of its kind in the state (the others are in Orlando and Key West), this museum (☎ 904-824-1606), 19 San Marco Ave, just up the street from the visitors center, offers pretty much what you'll find in all of the Ripley's museums.

The Believe It or Not part is up to you. Even if the answer is 'not,' it still may be worth the admission price of $9.95 for adults, $6.95 for seniors and children five to 12 (under five free). Just past the entrance, note the genuine two-headed calf; at the stairs to the right, Ripley's original cartoon. Also see tallest, heaviest and skinniest men exhibits and the World's Greatest Fake (PT Barnum's mermaid). Upstairs, try your luck at twisting your tongue (many people can't). There's a mirror handy. And when you turn the corner, be sure and look through the little window. The museum is open 9 am to 10 pm daily.

Fountain of Youth It's a nice walk through a pretty park and gardens, and it does have some perfectly fine background on the area and the Timucuan Indians, but to call this a Fountain of Youth is pushing the bounds of what even the most resolute tourist will believe. Okay, okay – allegedly, when Ponce de León was heading to Florida, he was searching for the fountain of youth, and it's said that he thought this might be it. It's a spring – granted, the water is high in calcium and iron and sulfur, but it's a spring.

The park (☎ 904-829-3168), 11 Magnolia Ave, one block east of the Old Jail, also has a planetarium show and a model of a Spanish galleon. It's open 9 am to 6 pm (last tickets sold at 5 pm) daily, except Christmas. Admission costs $5.50 for adults, $4.50 for seniors, $2.50 for students and children six to 12, and includes a sample of the magic water. The gift shop sells bottled water from the spring: $1 for small bottles, $2 for bigger ones.

San Sebastian Winery Northeast Florida's only winery is San Sebastian (☎ 904-826-1594), 157 King St. It's open for free tours and wine tasting, and they show an eight-minute video on the history of winemaking in Florida (it goes back a ways: the first wine in North America was made here by the

Robert Ripley

Many travelers scoff at 'tourist attractions,' but Ripley's museums are different. As a friend of ours (who spends about half his life in Asia as a buyer for his own business) says, 'Going into Ripley's gives you a sense of just what an amazing traveler and adventurer that guy was.'

That guy was Robert Ripley (1893-1949), a writer and traveler extraordinaire, who for more than 40 years traveled to 198 countries around the world in search of the strange, the amazing and the bizarre.

He began as a cartoonist for the *San Francisco Chronicle*, and eventually became a syndicated cartoonist with King Features. Later in his career, Ripley became a traveling broadcaster, and was the first man to do a live radio broadcast from Australia to New York. And he never stopped traveling until his death.

His taste certainly leaned to the weird: shrunken heads, six-legged and double-headed cows, pinhead sculpture (the Lord's Prayer, all 297 letters of it, etched into a pin head by a Sing Sing prisoner in the tank for forgery), miniature match-stick replicas, three-eyed men (he didn't actually *collect* that one), African human skin masks and photographs and stories of a huge collection of freaks from around the world.

The St Augustine Ripley's Believe It or Not! was the first in a series. The building in which Ripley's now stands, Castle Warden, was built in 1887 by William Warden, a partner of Flagler and Rockefeller, and in 1941 it was turned into a hotel by none other than Norton Baskin and his wife Marjorie Kinnan Rawlings, author of *Cross Creek* and *The Yearling* (see the Central Florida chapter for information on Rawlings' estate), and Ripley himself was a guest at the hotel several times.

Today, the castle is open as the prototype Ripley's, and while some of the exhibits may seem hokey and contrived, others are the genuine article. Say what you will, but Ripley simply *was* one of the trailblazers of modern travel information dissemination. Figuring out what's genuine and what's balderdash is simply a matter of whether you believe it or not.

Spanish in the 16th century). The winery's open 10 am to 6 pm daily, except from 11 am Sunday.

Zorayda Castle Moor fans will love this one-tenth-scale replica of the Alhambra, a 12th-century Moorish palace in Granada, Spain. Franklin Smith, a man who some say had more money than sense, was so impressed with the palace on a trip to Spain that in 1883 he built an exact (though seriously scaled down) replica of one of its wings. The castle (☎ 904-824-3097), 83 King St, filled with imported palatial appointments, is a neat place, and kids will love it.

There's a prayer room, and, on the center of the ground floor, a sultan's divan for lounging and entertaining, and silk rugs more than 300 years old. Upstairs, the Sultan's Den features a gaming table and settee, inlaid with thousands of pieces of sandalwood, rosewood, satinwood, mother of pearl and ivory that took five men nine years to complete. You can also see the Tower Alcove, where, in the original, King Mohammed el Hazare placed his three daughters, lest men be able to see into their rooms (two escaped and eloped with Spaniards, while the third died in the tower as a spinster).

Jacksonville by night

Historic St George St, in St Augustine

Daytona International Speedway

St Augustine's Castillo de San Marcos, the oldest masonry fort in North America

Flagler College, formerly Hotel Ponce de León

Ponce de León Inlet Lighthouse Museum

Beautiful pottery, sold in St Augustine's Spanish Quarter

There's also an Egyptian room with a 2300-year-old rug woven from cat hair and said to be cursed. During Prohibition, the castle was turned into a speakeasy (the Zorayda Grill Club) for men. At the side end of the staircase on the ground floor is a pull-switch which could have been used to ring the alarm when the fuzz dropped in. The whole place, by the way, is riddled with secret passageways.

It's open 9 am to 5 pm daily. Admission is $5 for adults, $4 for seniors (55 and older) and military, $1.50 for children six to 15.

3D World This 3D-theme place (☎ 904-829-9849), 28 San Marco Ave, is one of the cheesiest 3D-movie theater/rides we've ever been in. We caught *Titanic*, a 16-minute 3D documentary that should have been fascinating but was in fact annoying, and *The Castle of Doom* and *The Curse of King Tut*, both computer animated 3D rides. Booo. All three are $9, or $5 each. Our opinion? Save your cash.

Alligator Farm The Alligator Farm (☎ 904-824-3377), on Anastasia Blvd about a mile east of the bay, is something we recommend highly; alligators are very misunderstood, and here's a great chance to learn a lot about them from a knowledgeable staff. It's very fun, and unlike its nemesis in Kissimmee, this is not an alligator-breeding farm but a legitimate zoological park. There are pits teeming with the creatures – about 900 alligators and 200 crocodiles – and cages for their gator zoo: we saw a Siamese crocodile (extinct in the wild), and a small Chinese alligator on loan from a New York zoo.

There's a talk, starring a couple of baby beasties, and staff demonstrate how gators chomp down on objects that move into their mouths by reflex. Alligator shows are at the Reptile Theater hourly. Admission to the farm is $12 for adults, $8 for children three to 10. And hey, no pets, okay?

J&S Carousel This little trip to yesteryear is a lovely diversion, especially during Illuminations in December-January, when it's bordered by white lights and sports a waving Santa Claus. It's a small, old-fashioned carousel – complete with organ music – in Davenport Park, at the corner of San Marco Ave and May St (Hwy A1A) one block east of the library across the grass, which also has a small playground with picnic tables. Kids love it. It's open from around noon to around 9 pm, a bit later on weekends. Rides are $1.

Miniature Golf Next to the city marina is a small mini-golf course, open daily 9 am to 10 pm. Adults are $3 and kids $2.

Organized Tours
An orientation tour is not a bad idea here, and the locals who run these services are generally pretty knowledgeable and funny, in a hokey, touristy kind of way, if you go for that sort of thing.

Walking Tours The very friendly and knowledgeable Roland Loveless, bedecked in full early-1700s Spanish costume, runs 1¹/₂-hour walking tours through downtown daily for $7. Get information and make reservations directly at ☎ 904-797-9733.

Ghostly Walking Tours (☎ 904-461-1009, 888-461-1009) offer 1¹/₂-hour walking tours through the town and the cemeteries telling stories and legends about ghosts and the supernatural in St Augustine. The cost is $6.

Horse-Drawn & Bicycle Carriage Tours For a more expensive trip around the district, you can use either of the two horse-drawn carriage tour firms in town – though animal lovers would rather you didn't as there are very few regulations in place in the city to protect the horses, which are often subjected to long working hours. There are Colee's Carriage Tours (☎ 904-829-2818) and Sightseeing Carriage Tours – Gamsey Carriage Co (☎ 904-829-2391); both leave from Avenida Menendez just south of the fort, both charge $10 for anyone 12 and over, $5 for children five to 11 (under five free) or $35 minimum for a carriage. Both trips are about 2¹/₂ miles.

A far greener (and fresher smelling, if you use deodorant) option in good weather

NORTHEAST

Dat'l Do It

Be sure and try the fiery and flavorful locally grown datil (rhymes with that'll) peppers, available in mustard, vinegar (for splashing on collard greens) and sauces like Dat'l Do It and Dixie Datil (motto: ain't killed no one yet). All are available at Publix and some other local markets.

only is St Augustine Horseless Carriage Company (no ☎), which rents four-person bicycle-driven carriages for $10 per hour. It's at the lot at the corner of Orange and Castillo Sts, just south of the Old City Gate.

Train & Trolley Tours There's a nasty, cut-throat side of St Augustine life: the tourist choo-choo train market. There are two companies in the business here that loathe each other, and they're not too happy about customers that patronize the competition, either.

The companies, in *alphabetical order* to avoid even a hint of favoritism on our part, are St Augustine Historical Tours (☎ 904-829-3800), and St Augustine Sightseeing Trains (☎ 904-829-6545). Both companies offer essentially identical product (though Sightseeing Trains has a few more stops on their route) for the same price: a narrated journey through the historic district aboard either a red-and-blue 'train' (Sightseeing Trains) or a green-and-white 'trolley' (Historical Tours).

Narration is as you'd expect, though you do get some good historical background and, if the narrator's not made of wood, some humor as well. Tickets for both, which are good for two days, are $12 for adults, $5 for children six to 12 and free for children under six. There is no senior citizen discount. You can get on and off your company's trolley as often as you'd like, but remember to wear your admission sticker (red for Sightseeing Trains, and green for Historical Tours) at all times.

Sightseeing Trains offers free parking at 170 San Marco Ave or the Sugar Mill at the corner of Hwy 16 and San Marco Ave, north of downtown. Historical Tours has free parking at the lot in front of the Old Jail on San Marco Ave. Trolleys from both companies run about every 20 minutes; the first trolleys leave at around 8:30 am; the last trolley from Historical Tours is at 4:30 pm, Sightseeing Tours at 5 pm.

Boat Tours You can take a 1¼-hour cruise along the waterfront from Victory III Scenic Cruises (☎ 904-824-1806, 800-542-8316). The cruises leave from the Municipal Marina, just south of the Bridge of Lions, at 11 am, 1, 2:45 and 4:30 pm daily. There are additional cruises at 6:15 pm from April 1 to May 21, and at 6:15 and 8:30 pm from May 22 to Labor Day. The cost is $9.50 for adults, $8 for seniors, $6.50 for children 13 to 18 and $4.50 for children under 13.

Air Tours Flights over the city and area are available in private planes from the small municipal airport (☎ 904-824-1995) at the northern end of the city on US Hwy 1. There are lots of options but a great one is with Florida Aviation Courier Training (☎ 904-824-9401), which has one-hour air tours in a Cessna 172 for three passengers for $99 (total, not per person). You'll fly over downtown, and either down the coast of Flagler Beach or north toward Jacksonville. For far, far more expensive trips, North American Top-Gun (☎ 904-823-3505, 800-257-1636, www.natg.com), offers flights in warbirds.

Places to Stay

St Augustine is not a totally cheap place, though you can definitely get a motel room for $35 to $50 for a double. There's a youth hostel, as well as a few camping possibilities, and the city is teeming with B&Bs.

Camping Camping is inconvenient without a car. Surprise, surprise. Camping at the *Anastasia State Recreation Area* (☎ 904-461-2033, see Parks & Monuments earlier in this section) is the cheapest in town in winter if you use their rustic sites, but never if you use sites with electricity. In that case you should see Indian Forest Campground, below, which we think is a better value if you're not set on sleeping in a state park. Tent sites at Anastasia are $12 a night from October 1 to February 28, $15 from March 1 to September 30. Florida-resident senior citizens pay half price. Electricity is $2 a day. Campers are given the combination to the gate to gain access after the park closes at sundown.

The friendliest privately owned place in town for tent camping isn't really in town; it's *Indian Forest Campground* (☎ 904-824-3574, 1555 Hwy 207), about 2 miles east of I-95 (exit 94). Tent sites are $14 a day or $84 per week, and each has a fire ring and water and electric hookups. RV sites are $17/102, including electric, sewer and water and $19/112 with all that plus cable TV.

Another option is *State Park Campground of America* (☎ 904-824-4016, 1425 State Rd 16), and they're pretty laissez faire about the way they run things: when we visited there was a sign on the door saying 'just pick a site,' and a sign saying they're $19 year round. They have hot showers, picnic tables at each site, laundry facilities and a little store.

KOA has two locations near town; the closest is at 525 W Pope Rd (☎ 904-471-3113, 800-992-5622), at the intersection of Hwy 3, just across the Mickler O'Connell Bridge on Anastasia Island. It's more expensive, but they run a handy daily shuttle between the campground and the Plaza de la Constitution: it leaves KOA at 10 am and picks up at the Plaza at 4 pm. The cost is $4 per person roundtrip. Tent sites are $19.95 for two people including water and electric and a cooking grill. RV/van sites are $23 a night with water and electric or $25 with water, electric, sewer and cable TV. Kamping Kabins are $32 a night.

The second KOA (☎ 904-824-8309), 12 miles north of the city on Hwy 210 just off I-95 exit 96, is a bit cheaper but doesn't have shuttle service: rustic (no services) campsites are $18 a night, tent sites with water and electricity are $21; RV/van sites are $24, Kamping Kabins are $29 for one room, $33 for two rooms. The seventh night is free at all sites.

Hostels The *St Augustine Hostel* (☎ 904-808-1999, 32 Treasury St) couldn't be better located: two blocks north of King St near the corner of Charlotte St. Rooms are very clean and comfortable, and cost $12 per person in a dorm, with private rooms from $28 to $35. There's a good kitchen, usually packed with travelers, a library/common room with books, board games and an organ (no television) and a large terrace on the 2nd floor with a barbecue grill. Smoking is prohibited inside the building, but allowed on the terrace.

The hostel also rents bikes ($5 a day), is a great source of local information, and provides some lockers for valuables. There is only one telephone; local calls are 35¢ but use your calling card or call collect for long distance. Check in is 8 to 11 am and 5 to 10 pm; no lock out, but there's a combination lock on the front door, which is locked between 11 am and 5 pm and after 10 pm – you get the combo when you check in.

Motels There are plenty of choices in motels in town that run the gamut from as sleazy as you'd imagine to as nice as you'd want. The better ones are in the center, the cheaper ones along San Marco Ave and Anastasia Blvd.

Motels and chain hotels line San Marco Ave, and the area near where it meets US Hwy 1; chains include a very clean and friendly *Scottish Inns* (☎ 904-824-2871, 110 San Marco Ave) that doesn't appear to be run by a Scot and has rooms for $35/50 weekdays/weekends for a double in winter, $45/65 in summer; and *Comfort Inn Historic Area* (☎ 904-824-5554, 800-221-2222, 1111 Ponce de León Blvd), with rooms for $79.95 year round. The *Economy Inn* (☎ 904-824-4406, 94 San Marco Ave) is a perfectly reasonable place, with doubles for $35/45 weekdays/weekends in winter, $45/55 in summer.

Perhaps the nicest view in town is at the *Edgewater Inn* (☎ 904-825-2697, 2 St Augustine Blvd), just off Anastasia Blvd at the eastern foot of the Bridge of Lions. There is very friendly service and spotless rooms here, some which have large bay windows looking across the bay right at downtown. Rooms are $49 for a poolside view and $59 for a water view in low season, $55 for the pool and $69 for the water in high season, and rooms with bay windows are always $6 extra. Some rooms have baths, some showers. Price includes basic cable, as well as juice, muffins and coffee in the morning. You can also dock at their private marina – 75¢ per foot, 15-foot minimum.

Right across the street at the **Anchorage Motor Inn** (☎ 904-829-9041), rooms are nice and clean, and also have great views of the city, but service, when we visited, wasn't as happy (may be worth trying when you're here). Rooms are $40/47 per weekday/weekend in winter, $48/55 in summer, based on double occupancy; extra guests over 12 are $5 each.

B&Bs There are *at least* 25 B&Bs in the city and we've yet to hear complaints about any, so just because we don't list one here, or if we list one higher up on the list than another, it's really because it's a difficult field to narrow down and we had to just bite the bullet and pick a few. If you're planning a lengthy stay in a B&B here, you should contact Historic Inns of St Augustine, PO Box 5268, St Augustine, FL 32084-5268, for their free pamphlet, which has descriptions of 23 B&Bs in town, their phone numbers, and a good locator map but, alas, no prices. Be sure to find out about parking near the inn (it can be difficult), and ask if the price includes museum admissions or other perks (some do).

Our favorites in town – and again, this does not detract from the others – are the following:

At the **Victorian House** (☎ 904-824-5214, 11 Cadiz St), breakfast is usually a hot egg dish plus homemade granola, pastries and breads, fruit, juice, tea and coffee; rooms range from $80 to $115. This is in one of the loveliest parts of town, to the south of King St. Some (not much) parking is available.

The **Southern Wind** (☎ 904-825-3623) is actually two B&Bs; the first is at 18 Cordova St, the second is at 34 Saragossa St. Rooms in both of these lovely properties range from $70 to $155, including free wine in the afternoon, and free champagne on honeymoons and anniversaries. Breakfast is usually granola, fruit, pastries, quiche, a toast bar, juices, coffee and tea.

The **Old Powder House Inn** (☎ 904-824-4149, 800-447-4149, 38 Cordova St) is one of the best values in town – with a Jacuzzi, tandem or regular bicycles, free coffee and tea all day, and free wine and hors d'oeuvres in the evening. Breakfast is a little elaborate, with more than 30 rotating entrees (such as egg soufflé, baked apple and pecan pancakes, and strawberry crepes), homemade granola, fruit, muffins, juice, yadda yadda yadda. Rooms range from $79 to $169 on weekends, $15 to $20 less Monday to Thursday. Free parking is available.

The **Secret Garden Inn** (☎ 904-829-3678, 56½ Charlotte St), tucked way back in the alley, is a very romantic place with only three suites. Breakfast is usually pastries and breads, fruit, juice, tea and coffee. Rooms range from $105 to $125 for a double (extra person $10). Parking is available.

Places to Eat
There's plenty to keep you full, and cheaply. And cheap doesn't mean bad: case in point, excellent weekend lunches at Gypsy Cab Co, a St Augustine gem.

Snacks, Pizza & Fast Food The bulk of the fast-food chains are on US Hwy 1, stretching a bit north, and a couple of miles south, off King St. There's a **Pizza Hut** downtown on King St, but otherwise it's old-fashioned small businesses.

The most original snack spot is the **Spanish Bakery** (no ☎, 47½ St George St), where the aroma of freshly baking empanadas ($2), mini bread (50¢) and smoked-sausage rolls begins wafting out onto the street with the first oven-load of the day at 11 am. The lunch special of soup, mini bread and a soft drink is $3. It's open daily 9:30 am to 3 pm.

Some of the best cinnamon rolls (but not the best, see Theo's below) and pecan buns in the state are available at the **Bunnery Café** (☎ 904-829-6166, 35 Hypolita St). The smells wafting out onto the street here are nothing compared to sinking your teeth into one of these babies, which are $1.

We argue about the best pizza in town – it's between two. First is the **Pizza Garden** (☎ 904-825-4877, 21 Hypolita St), which does pretty downright awesome slices ($1.55 thin crust, $1.99 thick) and calzones ($4.50). Try the Stromboli with spinach, mushrooms, black olives and seasoning for $4.95, which is a meal. Beer and cappuccino are also served. It's open daily 11 am to 9 pm, Friday and Saturday until 10 pm. The other contender loses lots of points for being inconvenient as hell to downtown, but it's excellent: the **De León Pizzeria** (☎ 904-794-1917), at the Ponce de León Mall, where succulent New York-style slices are $1.50. The mall is on US Hwy 1, south of the intersection of Hwy 301.

If you're at the Old Jail or the Fountain of Youth, don't miss saying hello to Jim at **Jim's Lemonade & Fruit Shakes**, a tropical little place just across the street from the main entrance to the Fountain of Youth, at the corner of Magnolia and Williams Sts, with a ping-pong table and great fruit drinks for $1 to $3, and daily specials.

Schmagel's Bagels (☎ 904-824-4444, 69 Hypolita St) turns out some very good stuff; hot-pepper cream cheese (or about a dozen other varieties of cream cheese) on a bagel is $1.75, sandwiches are $3.50, and veggie burgers are $3.95. There are lovely courtyard tables.

Casa de Tacos (on Spanish St south of Cuna) is a taco stand from heaven; wonderful, fantastic burritos, tacos and other Mexican snacks for very cheap – humongous burritos are $2.50.

Restaurants & Cafés There's a good range of places in the under $10 category in town, but you can also find things on the more expensive side.

Our favorite place for breakfast is **Theo's Restaurant** (☎ 904-824-5022, US Hwy 1 at King St), a family-run Greek place that bakes all its own bread and cinnamon buns daily, and serves up excellent Greek and American for cheap. Their cinnamon buns are the best in the state of Florida. For lunch, they do sandwiches, burgers and salads, all in the $5 to $8 range.

Azalea's Cafe (☎ 904-824-6465, 4 Aviles St) does breakfast and lunch. They have quite a variety of sandwiches and salads and some pasta dishes all in the $5 to $7 range.

The **Manatee Café** (☎ 904-826-0210, 179A San Marco Ave), at the corner of May St (across from the carousel), does excellent and healthful sandwiches (veggie burger $4.50, hummus pita $3.95, veggie burrito $3.95 to $4.25) and absolutely astounding mixed-veggie juice ($3.30 to $3.95). They serve killer veggie burgers and tabouli, but we skipped the chocolate tofu pie ($2.50).

Of the two British tea rooms in town, we recommend only this one: for a great treat and a good value, one or two people can have afternoon tea at the **Tea Room** (☎ 904-808-8395, 15 Hypolita St) for $7.45, which includes 'dainty' sandwiches (your choice of filling), homemade scones and shortbread and a pot of tea. Too bad the cream's whipped and not clotted Devonshire double, but hey.

The best tzatziki in the state can be found at the **Athena Restaurant** (☎ 904-823-9076,

---

NORTHEAST

Secret Dressing

One of the most highly guarded culinary secrets in St Augustine is the recipe for the house dressing at **Gypsy Cab Co**. Locals and visitors go nuts over this yeasty, garlicky taste sensation that defies description – to the extent that they buy up dozens of 10oz bottles of the stuff for $7 a piece. That's right, $7 (though it doesn't cost extra when you have it with the salad in the restaurant – ask for some extra dressing). Once you try it, you'll probably agree that taking a bottle home is worth the expense. We, of course, were lucky enough to snare a copy of the complex recipe: for yours, send $750 to Nick & Corinna, Ruppertstrasse 20, 80337 Munich, Germany. Allow 16 to 26 weeks for delivery.

14 Cathedral Place), a classic Greek diner doing excellent breakfasts ($2.65 to $3.75), good burgers ($2.30 to $3.50), great salads (and only somewhat disappointing grilled fish when we visited). People line up outside for tables at dinnertime during special events and on some weekends.

PK's Cafe & Coffee House (☎ 904-825-4065, 135 St George St), at the corner of Treasury, is a local favorite – a diner with a few tables spilling out onto St George St. Stuffed baked potatoes are $3.95, chili $3.25, lasagna $4.95, and there are some cheap breakfast specials. Newspaper machines outside sell out-of-town and local papers. Relax.

Out by the lighthouse in Lighthouse Park, the very comfortable and friendly *Lighthouse Park Restaurant (☎ 904-826-4003)* has lunch main courses from $4.95 to $8.95, burgers from $4.50 to $5.50 (including an excellent veggie burger), and dinners a bit higher from $9.95 to $12.95 – with entrees such as coconut fried shrimp, south-of-the-border chicken and chicken Creole.

For about 25 years, *The Monk's Vineyard (☎ 904-824-5888, 56 St George St)* has been doing reliably good pub food; entrees average $8 to $10. They've got a huge wine list, a very pleasant (if narrow) front courtyard and good service.

Forget about service, though, at *OC White's (☎ 904-824-0808, 118 Avenida Menendez)*, where the only reason to go is the pasta and some of the seafood entrees. The pastas – such as seafood marinara and shrimp and scallop scampi, are very good ($12.95 to $14.95), and the fish dishes are fine, averaging $9.95 to $14.95. Skip the early-bird dinners, which are skimpy. It's a really nice place to sit, either in the large courtyard or on one of two floors (non-smoking is upstairs).

Riki Japanese Steak & Seafood (☎ 904-825-0520) in the Shoppes of Northtowne shopping mall at the northern end of town on the west side of US Hwy 1, is an excellent Japanese place with hibachi tables complete with food-acrobat chefs who slice and dice as fast as in those Ginsu knife ads. The sushi

bar is a good one, with rolls for around $3 and sushi by the piece from $1.50 to $2. Dinners average $8 to $10. It features friendly management, and slow but earnest service.

The *Rosenhof Restaurant (☎ 904-471-4340)*, at the intersection of Hwy A1A and Anastasia Blvd, is a very nice German place that has good food and service; German pancakes are $6.95, Hungarian goulash is $10.50, and their roast pork with bread dumpling and sauerkraut is $12.50.

The *Gypsy Cab Co (☎ 904-824-8244, 828 Anastasia Blvd)* is absolutely worth the trip to the east side of town for the excellent and cheap lunches. And the house dressing is superb (see the Secret Dressing boxed text). The lunch menu is about the same as the dinner menu with one big difference: you can get a full meal for $5.95 to $7.95. At dinner, entrees range from $13 to $17, including Cayman Island pork or gypsy chicken at $13, and Angus NY strip steak, salmon pesada or pepper-seared grouper with dijon cream sauce for $16. Desserts are excellent as well, with offerings such as raspberry cheesecake, tiramisu, coconut cream or Key lime pie for $3. Lunch is served Saturday and Sunday 11 am to 3 pm, dinner is served nightly. They have a second location at 11 S Dixie Hwy, for takeout and catering only.

The *Raintree (☎ 904-824-7211, 102 San Marco Ave)* is a fine choice for a big night out, with excellent service and food that's cheaper than you'd expect. The atmosphere in the charming old, yellow house is very relaxed, and entrees run from $8.95 to $20.95, including chicken breast and shiitake mushrooms in clear champagne sauce for $12.95, brandy pepper steak at $18.50, shrimp and scallop moutarde for $14.50 and rack of lamb for $19.95. Early dinner specials, served 5 to 6 pm, are from $8.95 to $10.95. It's open 5 to 10 pm daily.

Entertainment
Theater & Cinema Other than student productions at Flagler Auditorium, the biggest news around town is the annual

production of ***The Cross & Sword*** *(☎ 904-471-1965)*, the official Florida state play. It tells the highly romantic story, through *Pocahantas*-caliber rose-colored glasses, of the settlement of Florida, the befriending of the Indians and the various governments that led to the greatest…well, you know. The show runs from late June to early September every year at the St Augustine Amphitheatre *(☎ 904-471-1965)*, about half a mile east of the entrance to the Anastasia State Recreation Area on Anastasia Blvd. Admission is $13 for adults, $12 for seniors, $6 for children three to 12. There are other performances at the amphitheatre during the year that change annually, such as an annual Easter Passion Play in late March or early April. Call the amphitheatre for details of what's on when you're here.

Pot Belly's Cinema 4 Plus *(☎ 904-829-3101, 31 Granada St)* shows first-run movies for $3.50 at all times. But wait – there's more: you watch these movies from the comfort and luxury of a reclining easy-chair, while waitstaff bring you soft drinks, beer or wine, pizzas, sandwiches and other deli snacks and *smoking is allowed*. If you smoke, it's like watching a movie on a giant screen in your own living room. Okay, it's not as flash as the big places (the film melted at the most crucial moment in *Apollo 13*, leaving all of us on the edge of our recliners while they spliced it back together), but hey, it's a great deal. There's another more modern and expensive cinema in the Ponce de León Mall.

Bars & Clubs The classic St Augustine local bar is the ***TradeWinds Lounge*** *(☎ 904-829-9336, 124 Charlotte St)*, under the same management for about 50 years. It's got live music every night by many local and regional musicians and their mainstay band, Matanzas (though we're a little sick of the 'Chicken Shit' song), and cheap drinks and a fun atmosphere. Great happy hours are in the evening.

You can try to avoid it, but at the end of the day you'll end up at ***Scarlett O'Hara's*** *(☎ 904-824-6535, 70 Hypolita St)* at least

---

Rotagilla

Last edition, the best $14 we spent on our entire research trip was at the TradeWinds Lounge to see one of the rare performances of Rotagilla (pronounced 'rota-GEE-ya'), a collection of guys from around the region (including a journalist and a member of the Orlando Symphony Orchestra) who say that they stopped doing drugs in the 1970s and are therefore no longer funny.

They're wrong.

They have a band made up of fiddle, mandolin, guitar, drums, whistles, washboard, bass and banjo: if you have no idea what happens annually in Galax, Virginia, then this is the best bluegrass hybrid you'll come across.

They do spoofs on popular songs – *Swiss Mountain Breakdown*, *Volga Mountain Breakdown* – with drag hula dancers, and vying for the highlight: an a cappella version of the classic song *Wipeout*, and a series of songs concerning 'If the US Went Metric,' including such classic hits as *805 Kilometers away from Home*.

Half bar-band, half play, Rotagilla is some of the very best of Southern American humor, but they never lose sight of the music, which is excellent. Sadly, they've cut back their performance schedules and only perform annually: Labor Day weekend at the Elk's Club. If you're in town then, stop by the club (opposite the TradeWinds) for tickets.

---

once during your stay, and why not – it's a friendly neighborhood bar with great drinks (but poor food) and a good raw bar/liquor bar outside. Happy hour is 4 to 7 pm Monday to Friday.

The ***St George Tavern*** *(☎ 904-824-4204, 116 St George St)* is a rowdy local bar, with cheap drinks and a fun atmosphere – lots of Flagler students. It has daily $1.75 margarita specials and happy hours 11 am to 1 pm and 4 to 7 pm, sometimes three-for-one drinks. Just down the street, there's live acoustic folk and rock music at the *Mill Top Tavern* (☎ 904-829-2329, 10½ St George St), in the old millhouse near the Old City Gate, which serves up its own microbrewed Gristmill Amber Lager and Rosebud Pail Tail in a Weissbier glass for $3.25.

Ann O'Malley's Pub (☎ 904-825-4040, 23 Orange St), a block west of the Old City Gate, is a nice little Irish pub run by a nice little Irish lass serving Guinness, Harp and Murphy's (and half-and-half Guinness and Harp), as well as a bunch of bottled domestic and imported stuff. No live music, but there's a jukebox.

The other microbrewery in town, *A1A Ale House* (☎ 904-829-2977, 1 King St), on the south corner, has seven varieties of their microbrewed stuff from $3 a pint to $6 for a taste of all of them. They do ragtime and other live music, and have an expensive restaurant upstairs.

There's also live music at *OC White's* (see Places to Eat earlier) every night.

About 3 miles north of the northern city boundary, on the east side of US Hwy 1, the *King's Head Pub* (☎ 904-823-9787, 6460 US Hwy 1 N) is said to be an extremely authentic British pub – we've driven by but haven't gone in. Everyone we speak with says it's a hoot: look for the double-decker bus out front.

Shopping

This is an artsy town. Souvenirs are best found along St George St, and there are no surprises in availability. The wonderful people at Grace Gallery at 82 Charlotte St (☎ 904-826-1536) and 32 Charlotte St (☎ 904-826-1669) carry a great line of authentic Indonesian, Thai, Nepali, Guatemalan and Mexican handicrafts, as well as that from local artists, at really good prices. They themselves do all their buying in the countries the works are from, and they're great travelers, so it's a nice place to stop for conversation as well.

More local art can be found at other galleries including The Forest (☎ 904-824-4815),

39 Cordova St, and Moultrie Creek Pottery (☎ 904-829-2142), 218 Charlotte St.

Antique shops are scattered all around the downtown area; for a list, contact the Antique Dealers Association of St Augustine, 60 Cuna St, St Augustine, FL 32084.

For discounted clothing, cookware and a bunch of other stuff, try the St Augustine Factory Outlet, at the intersection of Hwy 16 and I-95.

Getting There & Away

St Augustine's municipal airport (☎ 904-824-1995) accommodates only private planes and charters, so the nearest commercial airport is Jacksonville International Airport, about 50 miles from town and served by American, United and Air South. If you've got a lot of time, you can take Greyhound to Jacksonville for $10, and then get a taxi from downtown Jacksonville to the airport and it will work out cheaper than a taxi from here (see Taxi below).

The Greyhound station (☎ 904-829-6401) is at 100 Malaga St, one block north of King St, just east of the bridge over the San Sebastian River. It's a quick walk down King St east, over to the heart of downtown, or you can use the hostel's shuttle ($1.50) by calling them in advance. (See Hostels under Places to Stay earlier in this section.)

Amtrak, infuriatingly, does not serve St Augustine but rather the thoroughly inconvenient town of Palatka, 25 miles west (see the Central Florida chapter). Taxis from Palatka to St Augustine run about $25 to $30. The hostel runs a shuttle between it and the Amtrak station that costs $25 a person.

From the north by car, take I-95 south to exit 95 and turn left (east), past US Hwy 1 to San Marcos Ave; turn right and you'll end up at the Old City Gate, just past the fort. Alternately, you can take Hwy A1A along the beach, which intersects with San Marco Ave; or US Hwy 1 south from Jacksonville. From the south, take I-95 to exit 94, Hwy 207 east; make a left when it dead ends into US Hwy 1, and a right on King St to get to downtown. Exit 93, US Hwy 1, takes longer and is slower.

Getting Around

There's no public transport in town. You can rent bicycles at the St Augustine Hostel for $5 per day.

Car & Motorcycle For the downtown area, a car is a gorilla on your back – several pedestrian-only streets, a complex one-way system and parking from hell are a few reasons why. But for day trips, camping, shopping at a real supermarket or to head to Fort Matanzas or the beaches, a car is key. Most of downtown has a 25 mph speed limit, and you must stop at every corner, especially in the center. There's an Avis office at the St Augustine Airport, and Budget (☎ 904-794-0708) has an office at Jack Wilson Chevrolet, on US Hwy 1 south of the city.

Parking is metered almost everywhere, meters are in effect every day and spaces are scarce. Meter agents diligently comb the streets and alleys looking for scofflaw offenders, and have hearts of stone when it comes to ticketing. Fortunately, tickets cost only $7.50. You can park for $3 a day in front of the main visitors center, and in front of the Old Jail. On weekends only, head early to the lot on Treasury St between Cordova and Spanish Sts (adjacent to 78 Spanish St, the three-story pink Victorian that we used to live in), where free parking is available in the NationsBank employee parking lot, but act fast. There's parking for hostel guests right out front (but it's limited, speak to the management).

Taxi Rates are set by each company, though the first two of these are actually owned by the same parent company. Ancient City Cabs (☎ 904-824-8161) charges $1.75 per person in downtown, $4.50 and up to St Augustine Beach, and $49 per carload to Jacksonville International Airport. The same trips from Baas LH Cab Co (☎ 904-829-3454) are $1.50 a person downtown, $4 to St Augustine Beach ($1.50 each additional person) and $65 per carload to the airport. And probably the worst option (because of often unsavory drivers and rattly, broken-down old jalopies), Comfort Cab Co (☎ 904-824-8240) charges $1.75 around downtown,

$4.25 to St Augustine Beach ($1.50 each additional person), and $55 per carload to the airport.

AROUND ST AUGUSTINE

There are some lovely areas and little towns to the west of St Augustine, including Palatka and, farther south, Pierson, Blue Spring State Park and Cassadaga; see the Central Florida chapter for information on those.

St Augustine Beach

The 7-mile stretch of St Augustine Beach is a nice, wide one, and other than a couple of barbecue places and surfer hangouts and the fishing pier, there's not much to do but hang out for a while. Take Anastasia Blvd to Hwy A1A right out to the beach; there's a visitors information booth right at the foot of the pier.

World Golf Village

Do you *really* like golf? We hate it to the extent that we left it out of this book completely, but there are so many who disagree with us that it justified the construction of this unbelievably huge testament to golf throughout history. About, if we were to guess, as large as Scotland itself, the World Golf Village (☎ 904-240-4200, www.wgv.com), between St Augustine and Jacksonville on US Hwy 1, is just opening as we write. It's a pleasure-drome for golf nuts, with world class and miniature courses, putting courses, an IMAX cinema and, of course, the official Golf Hall of Fame. Call for more information, or check with tourist offices in St Augustine or Jacksonville when you're here.

Berry Picking

About 13 miles west of I-95 on Hwy 207, the town of Elkton offers peace and quiet and the chance to pick your own strawberries for $2 a quart at Tommy Howle's Vegetable Bin & Garden, on the right-hand side of the road on the eastern end of town. The farm and market, which also sells excellent fresh vegetables and fruits including Augustine (sweet) onions and they-pick-'em

NORTHEAST

strawberries for $2.50 a quart, is just east of the St John's County Fairgrounds, home to various festivals throughout the year such as the annual Cracker Day (which is celebrated in October, *of course!*).

Spuds

While potatoes are the primary crop (and 'thing to see & do') in this sleepy little farming village just west of Elkton, it's not the Potato Capital of Florida. That honor goes to Hastings – the next town to the west, where potato chip stands abound (well, abound in a rural Florida kind of way – there are maybe four). But we've included Spuds because we just really wanted to see the town's name in print. Spuds, Spuds, Spuds. There's a college out there as well: Bethune Cookman College – Spuds Campus (☎ 904-692-1001).

Fort Matanzas National Monument

The area's second fort, Fort Matanzas (☎ 904-471-0116), was built in 1742 to secure the city from naval blockades, which had occurred on several occasions: during one attack, the early city was spared only by weather, which forced a British retreat that allowed Spanish supply ships to make their way back to the city from Cuba. But this tiny stone fort never saw action in a full-on war. Used until 1821, it's now a national monument. Admission and the short ferry ride aboard the *Matanzas Queen* from the entrance park on Anastasia Island, 14 miles south of the city, is free. There is, unfortunately, no public transport down to the park. By car, cross the Bridge of Lions and take Anastasia Ave to Hwy A1A south; the entrance to the park is on the right. The main park, which has a half-mile nature trail, a movie on the history of the fort, and beaches, is a lovely place to have a picnic. The ferry runs daily except Christmas (and during turbulent waters) 9 am to 4:30 pm.

JACKSONVILLE
• population 980,000

We slammed Jacksonville in the last edition, and while it's still not our favorite place, it is,

we must say, a whole lot better than we let on last time. Jacksonville – the largest city in America in terms of square mileage – probably has more square feet of concrete and asphalt than we've ever seen in one place. Its downtown is dodgy at night and you need a car to get anywhere (though there's now a shuttle bus from the airport to downtown).

There are, however, several noteworthy attractions, including one of the southeast's best art collections.

Orientation

The city of Jacksonville is trisected in a very rough T by the St John's River – which runs north-south, with a little east and then north jig, through the city and then banks almost due east – and the Trout River, which joins the St John's from the west. Downtown Jacksonville is on the west side of the St John's River on the little jig.

I-95 comes in straight from the north to a junction just south of downtown with I-10. I-295 breaks off from I-95 and forms a half circle around the western edges of the city.

One of the city's more charming neighborhoods is Riverside, better known as Five Points, at the intersection of Lomax, Park and Margaret Sts, home to the Cummer Museum of Art. Five points is home to several appealing restaurants, nightclubs and coffeehouses.

The Jacksonville beaches – from Ponte Vedra Beach at the south to Atlantic Beach at the north – are about a 40-minute drive east of the city.

Maps The best map of the area is probably HM Gousha's *Street Map of Jacksonville* ($2.25), available at gas stations and bookstores everywhere in the city. We say it's best because it's the clearest of the maps we looked at and also has a useful blowup of downtown. AAA, Rand McNally and Dolph also have maps to the area.

Information

The Jacksonville & the Beaches Convention & Visitors Bureau (☎ 904-798-9111, 800-733-2668, www.jaxcvb.com), 201 E Adams St, has useful tourist pamphlets, discount coupon

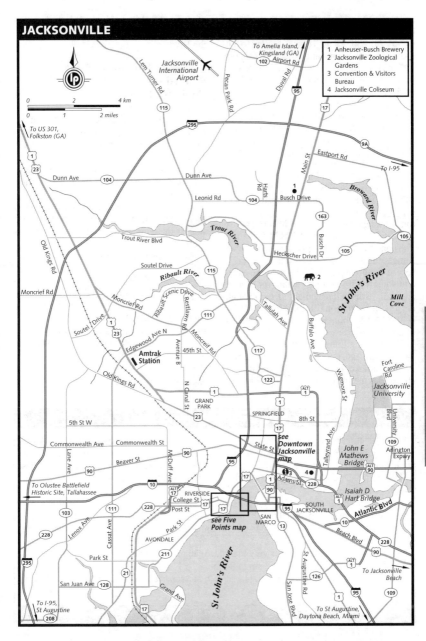

JACKSONVILLE

1 Anheuser-Busch Brewery
2 Jacksonville Zoological Gardens
3 Convention & Visitors Bureau
4 Jacksonville Coliseum

0   2   4 km
0   1   2 miles

To Amelia Island, Kingsland (GA)
Jacksonville International Airport
To US 301, Folkston (GA)

NORTHEAST

books and bus maps. There's also a visitors information center in Jacksonville Landing (☎ 904-791-4305), a mall open Monday to Saturday 10 am to 8 pm, Sunday 12:30 to 5:30 pm.

NationsBank has more than 25 branches in the city of Jacksonville; the main office is at 50 N Laura St, downtown near Jacksonville Landing. American Express has three offices; one at 9908 Baymeadows Rd (☎ 904-642-1701); and at two locations of Akra Travel: 841 Prudential Drive (☎ 904-391-7289) and 3216 Hendricks Ave (☎ 904-396-3388). The downtown post office is at the corner of Julia and Duval Sts.

Five Points News Center (☎ 904-354-4470), 1060 Park St, has out-of-town, US, some UK and European newspapers and tons of magazines. The main library (☎ 904-630-2665) downtown is at 122 N Ocean St. The conservative *Florida Times-Union* (www.times-union.com) is the daily paper of record around here. *Folio Weekly* is an excellent weekly with politics, restaurant reviews and club listings; it's available free throughout the area. National Public Radio (NPR) is at 89.9 FM, but on the air they refer to themselves as Stereo 90.

Dunn Coin Laundry (☎ 904-751-0186), 1403 Dunn Ave, is open every day 7 am to 10 pm; other coin laundries in the area include Baymeadows Maytag (☎ 904-730-3610), 5111 Baymeadows Rd, and Jean's Coin Laundry (☎ 904-389-8698) 1842 Blanding Blvd.

Cummer Museum of Art & Gardens

Northeast Florida's best collection of Western art is housed here (☎ 904-356-6857, www.cummer.org), 829 Riverside Ave, in the Five Points area, just southwest of downtown, in a building that looks more like a bank than a museum. Galleries are named and numbered, and straddle the courtyard. The formal gardens are behind the main building.

From the entrance, the rooms progress in numerical order from 1 to 5 on the left-hand side of the courtyard, and from 6 to 11 and the Tudor Room on the right.

Rooms include the following:

Room 1	Medieval to early Renaissance
Room 2	Renaissance works including Raphael's *Colonna Madonna*
Room 3	Late Renaissance works
Room 4	Baroque – a vaulted gallery, featuring Rubens' *The Entombment of Christ* and French tapestry
Rooms 5 & 6	temporary exhibitions
Room 7	porcelain

'Oh, Mom, Can't I Go to See Dr Jeremiah?'

Feeling ill in Jacksonville can be more fun than in most places. Welcome to Arlington Acute Care Center (☎ 904-743-2466), 1021 Cesery Blvd, just north of the Arlington Expressway, and Lakewood Acute Care Center (☎ 904-737-8686), 5978 Powers Ave, just west of Philips Hwy. Run by Dr Clifford Jeremiah, both these centers are full medical-treatment facilities that also feature museums.

Museums?! Museums. Keeps the kids occupied, keeps the parents happy. At Arlington, there are exhibits of mammal fossils, and an ocean series of sea-displays and shark replicas, while Lakewood offers exhibits on the Cretaceous period: life-size dinosaurs. In the waiting room.

It's a cool idea and the staff is very friendly. Arlington is open daily 8 am to 10 pm; Lakewood is open Monday to Friday 8 am to 8 pm.

Other, more conventional, medical facilities in Jacksonville include Saint Vincent's Medical Center (☎ 904-387-7300), 1800 Barrs St.

Rooms 8 to 10	19th-century paintings including Thomas Sully's *Portrait of a Young Lady*, Gainsborough landscapes, Winslow Homer's *Waiting for a Bite* and Bougereau's splendid *Return from the Harvest*
Room 11	Modern Impressionist paintings
Concourse Gallery	A hodgepodge of antiquities – don't miss the unbelievably intricate *Comic Mosaic Mask*

In the **formal gardens**, designed in the early 1900s and built in the 1920s, there's a spectacular live oak tree. The gardens are designed in the style of both English and Italian gardens. With your back to the museum, to the right is the English section, with ivy-covered benches, lovely shrubs and a view out over the St John's River, and, to the left, the Italian section, with Italian fountains, arches and pools.

In the **Art Education Center**, at the end of the Concourse Gallery, there are hands-on art exhibits for kids, and PCs running things such as Paintshop and less-complicated drawing and illustration software.

The museum is open Tuesday and Thursday 10 am to 9 pm (free admission 4 to 9 pm), Wednesday, Friday and Saturday 10 am to 5 pm, Sunday noon to 5 pm; closed Monday. Admission is $5 for adults, $3 for seniors and military, $1 for students and children.

Museum of Science & History

We had a blast in this museum (☎ 904-396-7062, www.jacksonvillemuseum.com), 1025 Museum Circle, across the river from Jacksonville Landing. Downstairs are balance, weight, sound, flexibility, etc, test machines, and a good geology exhibit, as well as manatees exhibits and a 'Native Wildlife of St John's County' showcase (note the detail in the background painting, even the power plant is included).

Upstairs are traveling exhibits (changed about every three months). We saw 'Criminology & Detectives,' where kids could dust a crime scene for prints, examine (we swear) bloody gloves and feel like a real detective, hot on the trail.

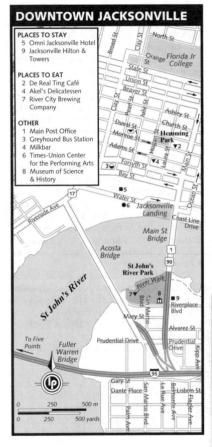

DOWNTOWN JACKSONVILLE

PLACES TO STAY
5 Omni Jacksonville Hotel
9 Jacksonville Hilton & Towers

PLACES TO EAT
2 De Real Ting Café
4 Akel's Delicatessen
7 River City Brewing Company

OTHER
1 Main Post Office
3 Greyhound Bus Station
4 Milkbar
6 Times-Union Center for the Performing Arts
8 Museum of Science & History

There are shows in the planetarium (we caught *Where in the Universe is Carmen Sandiego*) Monday to Friday at 2 pm, Saturday and Sunday at 1:30 and 3:30 pm.

The museum is open Monday to Friday 10 am to 5 pm, Saturday 10 am to 6 pm, Sunday 1 to 6 pm. The staff is very friendly. Admission is $6 for adults, $5 for seniors and military, $4 for children.

Jacksonville Zoological Gardens

Still in the (long) process of an incredible renovation and expansion, the Jacksonville

Zoological Gardens (☎ 904-757-4462), 8605 Zoo Rd (exit 124A from I-95), like New York City, will be a wonderful place if it ever gets finished.

Northeast Florida's only major zoo, which opened in 1914 with a collection comprised of one deer, has kept several of its excellent exhibitions open during their $17 million expansion. Most famous for its two Florida panthers and three white rhinos, the exhibits open at the time of writing included the **Main Camp Safari Lodge**, a huge thatched-roof area with the nuts and bolts of the park: café, first aid, wheelchair and stroller-rental stands, etc; **Okavango Village**, where board-walks lead from the aviary to exhibits and petting areas that have animals including black-cheek love birds, a dwarf zebu, goats and miniature horses; and areas featuring Transvaal lions, naked mole rats, elephants, alligators, jaguars, cape buffalo, giraffes, zebras and leopards.

Shows include Radical Reptiles, daily at 10:30 am; Raptor Rap, Monday to Thursday at noon; Elephant Encounter, Monday to Friday at 11:30 am, Saturday and Sunday at noon and 2:30 pm; and alligator feedings, Saturday at 2 pm.

There's a train ride around the zoo's 73 acres as well.

It's open daily 9 am to 5 pm, closed Thanksgiving, Christmas and New Year's Day. Admission is $6.50 for adults, $4.50 for seniors over 65, $4 for children three to 12. The train ride is an additional $3/2/1.50. Admission is free on Monday 9 to 11 am.

Anheuser-Busch Brewery

Very close to the zoo, the newly renovated Anheuser-Busch Brewery (☎ 904-751-8118), 111 Busch Drive (take I-95 north to the Busch Drive exit and follow the enor-mous billboards), offers free tours and, if you're over 21, they'll hand you 10oz samples of their beers. See the SeaWorld listing in the Central Florida chapter for an idea of what to expect – though here there's an additional display on the history of Bud-weiser advertising. It's open Monday to Saturday 9 am to 4 pm; tours depart on the hour.

Brest Museum

The Alexander Brest Museum and Gallery (☎ 904-744-3950 x3371), 2800 University Blvd N, in the Philips Fine Arts building on the campus of Jacksonville University, has a small and interesting collection of decora-tive arts including collections of works by Steuben and Tiffany, Asian and European ivory from the 17th to 19th centuries, pre-Columbian artifacts from Mexico and Central America from 3000 BC to 1500 AD, and Chinese porcelain and cloisonné from the 18th to 20th centuries. From downtown, take the Mathews Bridge east to Hwy 109 north, which becomes University Blvd. The museum is open Monday to Friday 9 am to 4:30 pm, Saturday noon to 5 pm; admission is free.

Fort Caroline National Memorial

Part of the Timucuan Ecological & Historic Preserve, a federally run reserve of land making up most of the northeast section of Jacksonville, up to and including the Kings-ley Plantation (see later in this chapter), the Fort Caroline National Memorial (☎ 904-641-7155), 12713 Fort Caroline Rd, is an approximately two-thirds scale model of the original fort founded here by French Huguenots in 1562. (See the St Augustine section to find out what happened to them.) Today, the re-creation, made from earth and wood, is on the site where it is believed that the original fort stood.

The park also features several hundred acres of pristine wilderness along the St John's River, and wildlife you'll likely run into include painted buntings (songbirds), woodstorks, red fox, raccoons, osprey, alliga-tors, wading birds, and occasionally river otters, bald eagles and bobcats.

Ranger-led programs have been drastically reduced thanks to when Newt was in Con-gress with his cronies, but the ones that are left are on Saturday: at 1 pm, there's a half-hour guided walk to the fort, and at 2:30 pm, a 1½-hour guided walk through the Preserve's Roosevelt area, a 550-acre section of nature walks and interpretive information on the area's shell mounds. The shell mounds them-selves have created an alkaline condition that has produced some very interesting flora; ask the rangers how best to see it.

About half a mile east of the main visitors center is a monument, on the bluff 75 feet above the St John's River, that reproduces the original column left here by Jean Ribault, who first landed at the inlet. In the visitors center, 10- to 12-minute videos on the Fort Caroline story and the preserve run continually throughout the day.

To get to the main visitors center from downtown, take the Mathews Bridge to the Atlantic Blvd Expressway (Hwy 10 east) and then turn left onto Monument Rd; follow that to Fort Caroline Rd and turn right. The entrance is about half a mile ahead. From the north, take I-95 to Hwy 9A (essentially the eastern extension of I-295) and follow that to Merrill Rd (there are big signs all the way). Turn left on Merrill, which becomes Fort Caroline Rd.

The fort is open daily 9 am to 5 pm. Admission is free.

Museum of Contemporary Art

The Jacksonville Museum of Contemporary Art had rotating exhibitions of contemporary arts and a smaller pre-Columbian exhibition (from 600 AD on). This museum was in a state of flux when we visited and may be out of business or have moved to new digs; check with the Convention & Visitors Bureau for more information.

Jacksonville Landing

This is a seriously popular shopping mall (☎ 904-353-1188), on the river in the heart of downtown, packed with shops, a food court, restaurants and coffee bars, and live entertainment; call to see what's on during your visit. It's on the north side of the St John's River, at the northwestern foot of the Main St Bridge.

Riverwalk

This 1.2-mile boardwalk on the south side of the St John's River opposite downtown and Jacksonville Landing is a somewhat pleasant city park, and there's a water taxi (see Getting Around later in this section) between here and the landing.

Beaches

The beaches, approximately 15 miles east of downtown (but 40 minutes' drive due to Jacksonville's snarled traffic), are about 25 miles of white sand from Ponte Vedra Beach at the south to Atlantic Beach at the north. There's not a whole lot to do out on the beaches except broil yourself, and prices at the beach resorts here are higher than you'd expect.

Adventure Landing

This new waterpark (☎ 904-246-4386, www.adventurelanding.com), 1944 Beach Blvd in Jacksonville Beach, is one of a chain of parks across the country. Adventure Landing has go-carts, laser tag, bumper boats, miniature golf, a video arcade and a waterpark with an 18,000-sq-foot wavepool, waterslides and a lazy river.

Organized Tours

Walk on the Weird Side (☎ 904-278-9409) does guided walking tours around the entire area; you can get one for as low as $6 if you're with a group, or personal orientation tours for an afternoon for about $80. They also do ghost- and unusual story-themed tours.

You can take 15- to 20-mile chugs up the St John's River aboard the *Lady St Johns* or the *Annibelle Lee*, both run by River Cruises Inc (☎ 904-398-0797), 917 Dante Place, which runs both lunch and dinner buffet cruises.

The Jacksonville Hilton and Towers (see Motels & Hotels below) runs the *Jacksonville Princess* (☎ 904-398-8800), a 149-passenger yacht that runs Sunday brunch, sunset cocktail party and romantic dinner cruises throughout the year. The *Jacksonville Princess* also does dockside lunches on weekdays.

Places to Stay

There are no hostels or camping in the immediate area; see the St Augustine, Amelia Island and Little Talbot & Fort George Islands sections for information on nearby options for hostels, camping and more hotels. The KOA just *north* of the

Georgia border, that calls itself the *Jacksonville North/Kingsland KOA* (☎ 904-729-3232, 800-562-5220), is just misleading: if Georgia is 'Jacksonville North,' so is Raleigh, North Carolina.

Motels & Hotels Jacksonville's accommodation scene is pretty institutional: except for a couple of B&Bs, it's all chains and all average in everything.

Check along I-95 and I-10, where chains congregate. Among them are the following: *Super 8 Motel* (☎ *904-751-3888, 800-800-8000, 10901 Harts Rd*); *Best Western* (☎ *904-751-5600, 800-528-1234, 10888 Harts Rd*); *Holiday Inn* (☎ *904-737-1700, 9150 Baymeadows Rd*); *Travelodge* (☎ *904-731-7317, 8765 Baymeadows Rd*); and *Quality Inn* (☎ *904-281-0900, 800-842-1348, 4660 Salisbury Rd*). Baymeadows Rd (Hwy 152) is about 30 miles south of downtown off I-95; Harts Rd is north, off Hwy 104 on the opposite side of I-95 from the Anheuser-Busch Brewery.

The biggest news downtown is the *Jacksonville Hilton & Towers* (☎ *904-398-8800, 800-445-8667, www.hilton.com, 1201 Riverplace Blvd*) right in the heart of the city. Rooms run from $75 to $154 and suites $119 to $350, though they frequently run special deals through the Convention & Visitors Bureau – check ahead to see if they're running one when you're in town. The Elvis Room, a bedroom within the hotel's presidential suite, was slept in by Elvis himself six times between 1955 and 1976. We couldn't get in, but the hotel says that it is 'tastefully' furnished.

The city's other biggie is the sparkling, 350-room *Omni Jacksonville Hotel* (☎ *904-355-6664, 800-843-6664, 245 Water St)*, with rooms averaging $149.

Out on Jacksonville Beach, staff at the *Hillsmoore Oceanfront Motel* (☎ *904-246-2837, 982 1st St)* are very helpful and friendly. That fact and their prices take the sting of not having a pool out of it (they do have a Jacuzzi): efficiencies, which sleep up to four, run from $25 to $79. They have a restaurant, gift shop, bar, etc, so 'you don't have to leave' the place.

The *Surf Side Motel* (☎ *904-246-1583, 1236 1st St)* has surly staff, but rooms, which are Okay, are $39.99 to $49.99 during the week, $69.99 on weekends and $79.99 on holidays. It has a pool.

The *Atlantis Motel* (☎ *904-249-5006, 731 1st St)* has rooms for $53 to $68 for singles and $58 to $70 for doubles, depending on the season.

Comfort Inn Oceanfront (☎ *904-241-2311, 1515 N 1st St)* has nice and large rooms from $69 to $109, pool-view rooms from $79 to $119 and oceanfront rooms from $89 to $129. They have a huge pool with waterfalls, a tiki bar that's packed with partyers, and the price includes a breakfast of cereal and muffins on Styrofoam plates.

The *Seabreeze Motel* (☎ *904-249-9981, 117 1st Ave N)* looks cool; it's in a '50s-style house next to the Beach Bakery.

B&Bs There are two B&Bs in the Riverside section of town. The *House on Cherry Street* (☎ *904-384-1999, 1844 Cherry St)* is a B&B with rates from $70 to $90, including tax, a full hot breakfast and wine in the evenings. Take Riverside Ave past St Vincent's Hospital, two streets beyond King St make a left onto Cherry; it's the last house on the right.

Another B&B is the 1914 prairie-style *Cleary-Dickert House* (☎ *904-387-4762, 1804 Copeland St)*, just off the river. From downtown, take Riverside Ave and turn left onto Copeland; it's at the corner of St John's. The house has singles/doubles at $80/90, and their honeymoon suite is $100; all prices are year round. Free wine and snacks in the afternoon and a full hot breakfast each morning are included. The owners are very friendly and Betty bakes all the bread and biscuits herself (she loves to cook).

On Jacksonville Beach, the *Ruby Inn* (☎ *904-241-5551, 802 2nd St South)* is a lovely old Nantucket-style place right near the ocean, with excellent rooms from $75 to $125 and garden rooms with courtyards.

Places to Eat

Downtown Check out *Akel's Delicatessen* (☎ *904-356-5628, 130 N Hogan St)*, a very popular downtown lunch spot with very big sandwiches for $3 to $5, decent pasta salad, but repugnant knishes. Service is very friendly and we walked out with lunch and soft drinks for two for under $6. It's open 7 am to 4 pm, breakfast runs from $1 to $5.

De Real Ting Café (☎ *904-633-9738, 45 W Monroe St)* is a killer Jamaican and Caribbean place with good deals: at lunch, main courses and specials average $5; at dinner, they go up to only $6 to $10.

At Jacksonville Landing *(☎ 904-353-1188),* there are several choices, and most people in downtown Jacksonville end up heading here for lunch or dinner. Fast-food places include an *Arthur Treacher's Fish & Chips*, *Bains Deli*, *Boardwalk Fries* (a sort of chi-chi fry place), *Chinese Combo King* (guess), *Johnny Rockets* (a '50s hamburger stand), and a *Sbarro* (overpriced pizza joint). There are several restaurants here as well, none notably noteworthy, including a *Fat Tuesday* and *Silver Spoon*.

On the south side of the St John's, *River City Brewing Company* (☎ *904-398-2299, 835 Museum Circle)* is a chic microbrewery that makes several kinds of beer – four are usually on hand at any time, with a fifth sea-sonal offering on tap as well. The restaurant certainly smells good enough: try their sausage sampler (beer, duck and Chinese smoked sausage) for $7.95; lunch dishes average $5 to $8, dinner from $10 to $16 and more creative main courses, such as nut-crusted pork tenderloin, average $14.95.

Five Points The best area we found for food was out of downtown in the Five Points area: *Heartworks Gallery Café* (☎ *904-355-6210, 820 Lomax St)* is a very cool gallery/café with exhibits of works by local artists. The exhibits change about every six weeks.

Gorgi's Derby House (☎ *904-356-0227, 1068 Park St)* has good breakfast specials, sandwiches and burgers for $2 to $4. Dinner specials, which come with two sides and bread, are $4 to $5, and include baked chicken, meat loaf and Polish sausage.

Five Points Cafe & Sweets (☎ *904-356-8380, 1005 Park St)* is good for coffee and cakes.

Jacksonville Beach Out on Jacksonville Beach, the *Bread & Pasta Shop* (☎ *904-246-1905, 1128 N 3rd St)* was a lifesaver for their

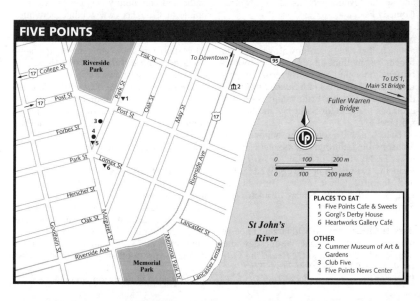

FIVE POINTS

St John's River

Memorial Park

Riverside Park

PLACES TO EAT
1 Five Points Cafe & Sweets
5 Gorgi's Derby House
6 Heartworks Gallery Café

OTHER
2 Cummer Museum of Art & Gardens
3 Club Five
4 Five Points News Center

0   100   200 m
0   100   200 yards

To Downtown

To US 1, Main St Bridge

Fuller Warren Bridge

fresh and healthy offerings, such as prepared pre-packaged pastas and excellent sand-wiches. The *First Street Grille* (☎ *904-246-6555, 807 N 1st St*) is a great outdoor place which shoots toward New Orleans food; you can fill up on small main courses for $6 to $8. They also do more expensive seafood dishes and a Caribbean steel-drum band plinks away at night.

Old Siam (☎ *904-247-7763, 1716 N 3rd St*) is a family-run Thai place with main courses from $8 to $12.

Entertainment

Music & Theater The *Jacksonville Symphony Orchestra* (☎ *904-354-5547, 300 Water St*), having played at a wide range of halls over the years, finally settled in at Times-Union Center for Performing Arts in Jacoby Symphony Hall.

The *Florida Theater* (☎ *904-355-2787, 1128 E Forsyth St*) – say thee-yator – is home to an eclectic mix of plays (from *Jesus Christ Superstar* to *Will Rogers' Follies*), music (from Seven Mary Three to some perform-ances of the Jacksonville Symphony Orches-tra to the WJCT Jacksonville Jazz Festival) and special events such as the Budweiser Comedy Fest.

The *Alhambra Dinner Theater* (☎ *904-641-1212, 800-688-7469, 12000 Beach Blvd*), about halfway between downtown and the beach, is something of a JAX institution: a buffet dinner and show. The cost for per-formances is about $35 for Sunday to Thurs-day shows, $38 on Friday and Saturday evenings, and $30 for Saturday and Sunday matinees.

There's usually something happening at Jacksonville Landing: live acoustic music every Friday and Saturday at *The Mill*, local band the Cosmic Pimps every Wednesday, and Jennifer Chase every Thursday at *Huey's*, which also holds a jazz brunch every Sunday 11 am to 2 pm.

Bars & Clubs They do acid jazz and poetry readings Tuesday, reggae Wednesday and Jamaican Friday night at *De Real Ting Café* (☎ *904-633-9738, 45 W Monroe St*) – see Places to Eat earlier in this section.

Milkbar (☎ *904-356-6455, 128 W Adams St*) has cheap drinks and lots of local and national bands throughout the week – it's a very popular place, if only for the music (there are DJs on nights when there are no concerts) and specials: old wave and hip-hop Monday (with $1 beers), ladies' night Wednesday (women get in and drink free), house and break-beat Thursday, Latin Friday, and break-beat, house and trance on Saturday.

Club Five (☎ *904-356-5555, 1028 Park St*), in a former theater at Five Points, does house, top 40 and hip-hop; Thursday to Sat-urday there's a $5 cover. Thursday is ladies' night, with free admission and drinks for women.

The *Comedy Zone* (☎ *904-292-4242*) at the Ramada Inn Mandarin, I-295 at San Jose Blvd (Hwy 13) south of the city, does shows Tuesday to Thursday at 8:30 pm, Friday at 9 pm, and Saturday at 8 and 10 pm. There's more weekend comedy at *Def Comedy Jam* at Club Carousel (☎ *904-725-2582, 8550 Arlington Expressway*).

Gay & Lesbian Venues A good resource for gay and lesbian listings of clubs, bars, baths and community services is available online at Club Jax (www.clubjax.com/info/gay.htm). *Bo's Coral Reef* (☎ *904-246-9874, 201 5th Ave*) has been around for more than 30 years. Thursday is amateur night – any-thing goes, no cover; Saturday there are cabaret and drag shows.

Metro (☎ *904-388-8719, 800-380-8719, 2929 Plum St*), with four enormous bars, calls itself a gay-entertainment complex, complete with disco, cruise bar, piano bar and leathery boiler room. For special events, there are drag shows and cabaret.

Spectator Sports

The *Jacksonville Jaguars* (☎ *904-633-6000, www.jaguarsnfl.com*) is an NFL expansion team that qualified for the playoffs twice in its first three seasons. Locals, therefore, are positively deranged about backing them. They play at 73,000-seat AllTel Stadium during the pro-football season from August to January – but get this: all season tickets are sold out and many individual tickets sell out as well, so plan ahead. The Jaguars are the area's only major-league professional team, but the *Jacksonville Lizard Kings* (☎ *904-358-7825, www.lizardkings.com*) are an East Coast Hockey League team and hope to be NHL soon; they play at the Jacksonville Coliseum, 1000 W Bay St.

The *Jacksonville Suns* (☎ *904-358-2846, www.jaxsuns.com*) are a minor-league baseball team that plays from April to September in Sam W Wolfson Park, 1201 E Duval St.

The *Toyota Gator Bowl* (☎ *904-798-1700, www.gatorbowl.com*) is a 50-plus-year-old NCAA Division I post-season college football match between the number two teams from the Atlantic Coast Conference and Big East Conference on New Year's Day. Buy tickets well in advance; it's at the Gator Bowl, at the eastern end of Adams St.

Getting There & Away

The Jacksonville International Airport (JAX; ☎ 904-741-4902) is one of the city's best offerings: a sparkling new terminal that's sensibly laid out and served by several major and some regional airlines. All major car-rental companies have offices at JAX (see Car Rental in the Getting Around chapter for information).

A one-way flight to/from Miami ranges from $40 to $100, depending on the airline (American is the most expensive), to/from Orlando $80, to/from Pensacola $150 to $175 and to/from Tampa $60 to $70.

The Greyhound station (☎ 904-356-9976) is at 10 Pearl St, at the western end of downtown. Jacksonville is a major Greyhound hub, with service heading south down I-95 up to 10 times a day (see the Getting Around chapter). West out I-10 to Pensacola, there are five buses a day; the trip takes from 8$\frac{1}{4}$ to 9$\frac{1}{2}$ hours and costs $57 one way, $110 roundtrip.

The Amtrak station (☎ 904-766-5110) is in the middle of nowhere, about 5 miles northwest of downtown, at 3570 Clifford Lane. JTA (see below) bus No NS4 runs between here and downtown, or you can do a $10 taxi in a quarter of the time.

By car, Jacksonville is about 36 miles south of the Georgia border, about 39 miles north of St Augustine and about 340 miles north of Miami, all right along I-95. Take I-10 east from anywhere in the Panhandle.

Getting Around

To/From the Airport There's no public transport to or from JAX. There are flat taxi fees to most destinations in town; the average fare is between $20 and $25, $30 to the beaches and $60 to St Augustine. The taxi stand is in the center island outside the main airport exit. Taxis at the airport are usually very clean and drivers know the area well.

Bus Jacksonville Transportation Authority (JTA; ☎ 904-630-3100, www.jtaonthemove.com) runs the local bus service in town (bus fare 75¢) and to the beaches ($1.35). The main downtown transfer center is at 201 State St opposite the FCCJ main building. From the downtown transfer center, take Northside bus No 10 – Panama to the Anheuser-Busch Brewery and the Jacksonville Zoological Gardens, weekends only to both; Westside bus No 4 or 2 to the Cummer Museum of Art; and Beaches bus Nos 1, 2 or 3 to the beach.

Monorail The Automated Skyway Express is a monorail that makes a simple loop over downtown for 35¢. Pick it up at the main station at Myrtle Ave at Jefferson.

Car & Motorcycle Face it: you're going to get lost at least once, probably trying to find Riverwalk. Traffic is frightful, drivers reptilian, especially during rush hours, which are always. Tune to NPR (89.9 FM) for rush-hour traffic information during 'All Things Considered' in the afternoon, which usually features the sentence, 'We have a multicar accident on the Mathews Bridge...'

That infamous Mathews Bridge, along with the Hart and Warren Bridges, is the main east-west connector between downtown and the beach. The Hart Bridge leads, confusingly, to Beach Blvd (US Hwy 90), out to the beach; the Warren Bridge, which is I-95, has an exit on J Turner Butler Blvd, also a hateful beach connector.

Parking is generally less of a problem than navigating.

Taxi & Water Taxi Metered taxi rates in Jacksonville are $1.35 flagfall, $1.35 a mile. The biggest company is Yellow Cab (☎ 904-260-1111).

The water taxi runs between the Riverwalk and Jacksonville Landing; fares are $2/3 one way/roundtrip for adults, $1/2 for seniors and children.

OLUSTEE BATTLEFIELD

About a half-hour's drive west of Jacksonville on I-10, the Olustee Battlefield Historic Site (☎ 904-758-0400) is a small interpretive center on the site of the Battle of Olustee, the largest Civil War battle to take place in Florida. The battle, on February 20, 1864, involved about 10,000 troops, and was significant as it denied Union troops the opportunity to cut off Confederate supply lines of food coming from Florida. But it was very short, lasting only an afternoon, after which the Union troops retreated to Jacksonville.

Though it is very pleasant and the visitors center museum contains some interesting exhibits on period uniforms, money and the like, unless you're here during the annual February 20 re-enactment (when thousands of Civil War nuts gather in full battle gear to re-create the Battle of Olustee), the most interesting attractions in the area are the two enormous nearby correctional facilities (that's 'jail' to you): the shiny **Baker Correctional Institution** is a nice place to start, right across the street. Also nearby is the **Columbia Correctional Institution** (☎ 904-758-8090), a bit farther away on US Hwy 90 East in Lake City.

The interpretive center at the battlefield is open Thursday to Monday 8 am to 5 pm, the museum opens at 9 am, and everything is closed on holidays from November to April. The site is off US Hwy 90 about 5 miles south of I-10's exit 45. Note that if you're coming from the east, there's an exit, but no entrance, to I-10 at exit 45, so you'll have to loop back east and then turn around if you want to continue heading west.

AMELIA ISLAND
• population 16,000

This richly historic area is one of northern Florida's greatest destinations. It's home to Fernandina Beach, a small city with a hugely intricate history, and to American Beach, the first resort for blacks in Florida (a must-see on the Black Heritage Trail, a guide to which is available at Florida bookstores or through Florida tourist information centers). It's also got three resorts and miles of shark-tooth-filled coastline, and we highly recommend a stop here, even if it's just for the day. Just to the south, on Little Talbot Island and Fort George Island, are two excellent state parks, and beyond those, the ferry to Mayport and Jacksonville.

History

The French first landed on an island off the coast of present-day South Carolina in 1562. Two years later, they moved south and established a settlement in the St John's River delta and began building Fort Caroline in Spanish-claimed territory. Upon arriving in St Augustine to defend the Spanish claim, Don Pedro Menéndez de Avilés launched two attacks against the French, and the second one led to the slaughter of 600 French settlers (see the St Augustine History section earlier in this chapter).

During the early years of the second Spanish period, Amelia Island's strategic location became key. In 1807, President Jefferson established his Embargo Act and, in 1808, a prohibition on slavery importation, and (to the delight of the chamber of commerce, which is thrilled to have something so scandalous in the area's past) Amelia Island became black-market central: pirates, cutthroats and smugglers traded slaves and rum, and prostitutes roamed freely.

In 1812, a group of rebels financed and backed by the US took over the island and turned over control to the US the next day. But after the Spaniards hit the roof, the US conceded that it really had no right to keep the place. Then in 1817, Sir Gregor MacGregor, a Scottish mercenary with revolutionary experience in Venezuela and the financial support of businessmen in Savannah and Charleston, hired on a force that took over the island from the Spanish on June 29. When the money ran out, so did MacGregor, who left two lieutenants in command. But wait…there's more!

The two left holding the bag, Lieutenants Ruggles Hubbard and Jared Irwin, formed a joint venture with a Mexico-based French pirate named Louis Aury (who was permitted to fly the Mexican flag anywhere he wanted, so long as he kicked back a percentage of his plunders to the Mexican government), and these three managed to turn the place into an even *more* scandalous town – it's said that there were more bars than street corners, and even more brothels.

Perhaps using moral outrage as an excuse to nab some nifty real estate, US troops moved in and took over in December 1819. In a face-saving compromise, Spain officially turned Florida over to the US in 1821 in exchange for US promises to pay claims of Spanish subjects (none of which, by the way, were ever paid).

Confederates took over the town for one year during the Civil War, after which the US regained control.

In the mid-1850s, a keen US Senator, David Yulee (the US Senate's first Jewish member), began work on his Ralph Kramden-esque dream of a trans-Florida railroad, which he completed in March 1861. In the one month during which it operated, the railroad ran freight between the island and Cedar Key on the Gulf coast, with stops at Baldwin, Gainesville and Bronson. Confiscated at the beginning of the war, the railroad was dismantled and the rails were diverted by the Confederate government to run north into Georgia. After the war, the railroad was rebuilt, but Yulee was by that time in prison in the north for treason.

During the boom years after the Civil War, hotels popped up like mad, and resorts (separate ones for whites and blacks) rose up on the beach. In 1897, the island became a major staging area for the US forces in Cuba. But the boom was killed when Flagler's railroad started sucking more and more northern tourists directly to the resorts

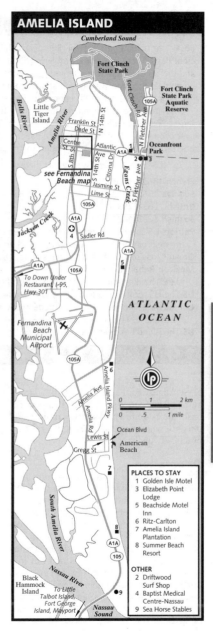

AMELIA ISLAND

Cumberland Sound

Fort Clinch State Park

Fort Clinch State Park Aquatic Reserve

Bells River

Little Tiger Island

Amelia River

Franklin St
Dade St
Centre St
S 8th St

see Fernandina Beach map

14th St
Atlantic Ave
Citrona Dr
Jasmine St
Lime St

N Fletcher Ave
Fort Clinch Rd

Egans Creek

S Fletcher Ave

Oceanfront Park

105A

A1A

105A

A1A

Jackson Creek

Sadler Rd

A1A

A1A

105A

To Down Under Restaurant, I-95, Hwy 301

Fernandina Beach Municipal Airport

ATLANTIC OCEAN

105A

Amelia Island Pkwy

Amelia Ave

Amelia Rd

Ocean Blvd

Lewis St

American Beach

Gregg St

South Amelia River

A1A

105

Nassau River

Black Hammock Island

To Little Talbot Island, Fort George Island, Mayport

Nassau Sound

0 ___ 1 ___ 2 km
0 ___ .5 ___ 1 mile

PLACES TO STAY
1 Golden Isle Motel
3 Elizabeth Point Lodge
5 Beachside Motel Inn
6 Ritz-Carlton
7 Amelia Island Plantation
8 Summer Beach Resort

OTHER
2 Driftwood Surf Shop
4 Baptist Medical Centre-Nassau
9 Sea Horse Stables

10 Flags

Local lore holds that since the Europeans showed up, Amelia Island has been ruled under eight flags. There are several problems with that, though, because of interrupted Spanish rule and the US Civil War. If you're going to count Spain twice in the beginning, as several tourist pamphlets do, then we say you should count the US twice in the end, as the US rule was indeed interrupted for a full year by the Confederates, who decidedly had a flag of their own.

And then there's argument about flags themselves: 'There's no documentation,' says James Perry, formerly the curator of the Amelia Island Museum of History, 'that the French ever even flew a flag.' And what is a flag, anyway – the Patriots flew one, while representing not a sovereign nation but a group of mercenaries and hot heads.

To settle the argument, we say that there were eight different flags flown at 10 different times:

French 1562-1565
Spanish 1565-1763
British 1763-1783
Spanish 1783-1821
Patriots US spy-backed rebels, who captured the island on March 17, 1812, gave it to the US the next day, who promptly gave it back to Spain
Green Cross of Florida MacGregor's gang, 1817
Mexican Rebel Flag Also in 1817, Aury and the boys. The US moved in and took over the island, holding it in trust for Spain, which finally ceded Florida to the US in 1821
US The US took over officially in 1821, and happily ran things until the Civil War
Confederate The secessionist Confederate Army took over in 1861. They managed to hold the island for a year, but on March 3, 1862, the US took over once again
US The island has been under continuous US rule since 1862

at St Augustine, Palm Beach and Miami – and it all happened so fast. In a Pompeii-like flash, the boomtown was frozen in time, and much of what you'll see here today remains practically unchanged.

Orientation

Amelia Island is Florida's northernmost barrier island, located just south of the Georgia coast and 30 miles northeast of Jacksonville. It's about 13½ miles long. The main activity is centered around the Downtown Historic District, at the northern end of the island in the tiny city of Fernandina Beach. The historic district is laid out in a grid, with east-west streets given names and north-south streets numbers. Centre St is the main street in this area, and is the north-south divider; it becomes Atlantic Ave east of 8th St.

The Ritz-Carlton, the Summer Beach Resort and the Amelia Island Plantation are all on the eastern coast of the island. Nestled valuably between these opulent resorts is American Beach (population: about 30 families), featured on the Black Heritage Trail as the first (and only) African American beach community in Florida.

The best free map for downtown is on the rate sheet for the Florida House Inn (see Places to Stay later in this section). *Amelia Now* is an advertiser-driven free guide to the city that contains a somewhat helpful map and a hodgepodge of features, ads, coupons, etc. It's available everywhere.

Information

The Amelia Island/Fernandina Beach/Yulee Chamber of Commerce (☎ 904-261-3248, 800-226-3542, www.ameliaisland.com), in the old railroad depot at the west end of Centre St in Fernandina Beach, has helpful staff, but, unbelievably, it's closed on weekends. Each of the bejillion B&Bs in town offer local information and restaurant recommendations.

NationsBank has a branch at the corner of 5th and Centre Sts. The main post office (☎ 904-261-4848) is at the corner of 4th and Centre Sts. Our favorite bookstore, for both conversation and selection, is the Book Loft (☎ 904-261-8991), 214 Centre St. The main library is at 25 N 4th St (☎ 904-277-7365).

The *Florida Times-Union* (www.times-union.com) is the daily of note, though you'll find *The New York Times* and the *Miami Herald*. National Public Radio (NPR) is at 89.9 FM from Jacksonville.

Try Maytag Laundry (☎ 904-277-3730), 913 S 14th St on Hwy A1A. There are spotless 'comfort stations' (toilets) behind the tourist information center in downtown Fernandina Beach.

Baptist Medical Center – Nassau (☎ 904-261-3627), is at 1250 S 18th St at Lime St. There's a medical clinic in the Wal-Mart plaza at the corner of US Hwy A1A and Sadler Rd as well. Nassau City Health Center (☎ 904-277-7280), 30 S 4th St, is a clinic open 8 am to 5 pm Monday to Friday.

Fort Clinch State Park
The US Government began construction of Fort Clinch (☎ 904-277-7274) in 1847. It has never been completed, and rangers can point out where different construction phases are visible in the masonry. It was occupied by both sides during the Civil War, but never saw any real fighting. Today, it's a state park, and re-enactors (whom most call authentic and others call nuts) hold openhouse garrison weekends, candlelight viewings and candlelight tours at least once a month, often times more, featuring demonstrations of the weaponry and fireplace cooking, and the fully equipped Civil War infirmary and the jail. The fort by candlelight is beautiful, and the re-enactors – who sleep in the fort during the garrison weekends to help stay in character – are a treat, whether

they're playing Union or Confederate troops (they do both).

Fort Clinch Rd is just west of the beach off Atlantic Ave, but if you're bicycling or walking to the fort from downtown, there's a quicker way: take Centre St to 14th St, go left to the end of the road and over the bridge; there you'll see a fence – you can slip your bike through and hop over. This is a time-saver only: slipping through the fence is not exactly a kosher move, and you still must pay the $1 admission fee for pedestrians and bicyclists at the Ranger's office. Admission for cars is $4.

Fernandina Beach
Most of the action on the island takes place in this small city that's just crawling with characters – stop by the Ship's Lantern, a souvenir shop on the main drag, and say hello to Bob Lannon, self-proclaimed Town Genius, who pokes fun at Northerners in a long, south Georgian drawl (Mr Lannon, it is believed, is from New Jersey).

Fernandina Beach residents, who refer to the rest of the world as being 'off-island,' eat well in very good restaurants, live well in lovely Victorian houses, and guests can stay well in any of the many spectacular B&Bs. The only drawback is the paper mill just upwind of the city, which sends whiffs of production aroma townward.

Amelia Island Museum of History
Florida's only oral-history museum (☎ 904-261-7378), 233 S 3rd St, in the former city jail (1879-1975), offers docent-led tours. The excellent exhibits are secondary to the oral history from the volunteers.

Don't miss the Galleon Room, dedicated to Spanish explorers and gold ships, with not much treasure but heaps of artifacts. Upstairs, wander freely and look at the old drugstore soda fountain. Tours are Monday to Saturday at 11 am and 2 pm. Admission is $2.50 for adults, $1 for students.

The museum also conducts two-hour walking tours of the Downtown Historic District, by appointment ($10 adults, $5 students). On Thursday and Friday at 3 pm, they also hold a Centre St Stroll ($5/2.50).

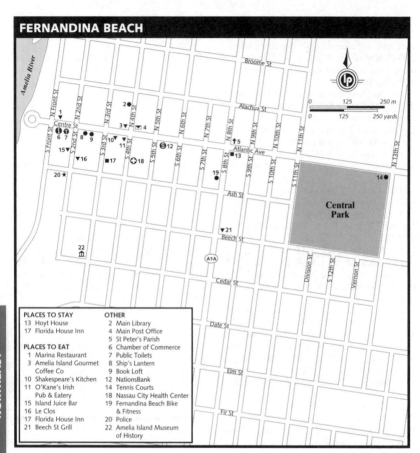

FERNANDINA BEACH

PLACES TO STAY
13 Hoyt House
17 Florida House Inn

PLACES TO EAT
1 Marina Restaurant
3 Amelia Island Gourmet
Coffee Co
10 Shakespeare's Kitchen
11 O'Kane's Irish
Pub & Eatery
15 Island Juice Bar
16 Le Clos
17 Florida House Inn
21 Beech St Grill

OTHER
2 Main Library
4 Main Post Office
5 St Peter's Parish
6 Chamber of Commerce
7 Public Toilets
8 Ship's Lantern
9 Book Loft
12 NationsBank
14 Tennis Courts
18 Nassau City Health Center
19 Fernandina Beach Bike
& Fitness
20 Police
22 Amelia Island Museum
of History

St Peter's Parish This neo-Gothic Episcopal church (1881-84; ☎ 904-261-4293), at the corner of 8th St and Atlantic Ave, features impressive stained-glass windows and a magnificent Harrison organ. Services are held Sunday at 7:30, 9 and 11 am and Tuesday at 7 pm.

American Beach

In 1901, AL Lewis (1865-1947) opened Florida's first insurance company, and it catered to black people. The Jacksonville company became very successful, and in

1935 Lewis, an African American, bought up land on Amelia Island and founded American Beach: the first black beach along Florida's segregated shores.

At its heyday, American Beach catered to throngs of Northern blacks, who boarded buses that would arrive 40 and 50 at a time, disgorging the masses into a resort owned and operated by black businesspeople. Blacks also owned the motel, the restaurants and the nightclubs. Black entertainers who performed at clubs in Jacksonville like the Two Spot would head up to American

Beach after their sets and play the rest of the night at the Ocean Rendezvous, then the resort's largest nightclub. That club also saw concerts by Ray Charles, Count Basie, Duke Ellington and a host of stars of the day.

After desegregation, the beach became less attractive than beaches closer to home, and the business dried out. Today, while the resort is still open, it is a ghost of its former glory. And surrounded by big business in the form of the Amelia Island Plantation, a multi-million-dollar resort complex, local residents worry that some of the 35 families that call American Beach home will sell out to the golf-course developers. The plan is to build a five-hole, 36-acre course and between 50 to 60 single-family houses on the area between Ocean St and Hwy A1A, from Burney Blvd to south of Lewis St.

Local resident, great-granddaughter of Lewis and 'unofficial mayor,' MaVynee Betsch (pronounced 'may-VEEN bech') has been leading the fight to get the beach listed on the National Register of Historic Places to protect it from further development. And despite increasing media attention, at the time of this writing things were looking bleak – there's a plot of about 40 acres just to the south, slotted for a golf course and some luxury housing.

Today, American Beach still operates as a summer resort, primarily for blacks but people of all races are welcome, and you can visit for a tour anytime. Ms Betsch is always happy to guide tours personally, and she operates the **American Beach Museum** out of her small mobile home, parked at the corner of Gregg and Lewis Sts.

On your own, the main sight other than the beach itself, with its long boardwalk, is **Nana**, a 55-foot sand dune – the tallest on the island, just south of the corner of Lewis St and Ocean Blvd. A tour is a far better idea, because it will cover aspects of the city and the resort that you'd never find out on your own. For tour or any other information, contact MaVynee at the trailer when you get here, or write her at MaVynee Betsch, American Beach Museum, Gregg St, American Beach, FL 32034.

Beaches
The main beaches are accessible by heading straight east on Atlantic Ave to the ocean. There are some fast-food places, as well as some accommodation options here (see Places to Stay later in this section). Two hours before and after a tide, run to the shore and look for the shark's teeth and fossils that are washed in.

Activities
There are free (unlit) municipal **tennis** courts at the corner of Atlantic Ave and 13th St in Fernandina Beach. In the unlikely event that the gate is locked, you can get the key ($5 deposit) at the Atlantic Ave Recreation Center, 2500 Atlantic Ave, open Monday to Friday 8 am to 8 pm, Saturday noon to 8 pm, and Sunday 2 to 4:30 pm.

Sea Horse Stables (☎ 904-261-4878), down the path that's the last left turn at the southern tip of the island before you reach the bridge over Nassau Sound, runs 5-mile, $1\frac{1}{4}$-hour **horseback riding** tours along the beach – at a walk only – every day for $45 per person. Reservations are recommended on weekends and holidays.

Longboarders are almost always well set for **surfing** here (though it can get a little mushy), but there're quite often some good waves for everyone. No surf rentals are available because of liability, but you can buy a board and then sell it back later (for about $20 less than you bought it for, get it?) from Driftwood Surf Shop (☎ 904-321-2188), 31 S Fletcher Ave.

The friendly folks at Kayak Amelia (☎ 904-321-0697, 888-305-2925, www.kayakamelia.com) do half-day and full-day **kayaking** trips ($50/85) through the tidal creeks and rivers around the island, or wonderful theme paddles, such as ones to Kingsley Plantation ($60; see later in this chapter) and the tai-chi paddle ($65), where you'll paddle to a beach and get tai-chi instruction.

If you're interested in **sailing**, Voyager Ventures (☎ 904-321-1244) runs sunset cruises aboard the *Voyager*, a replica of a 19th-century schooner, for $28 per person ($24 for seniors, $16 for kids under 12), as well as heaps of other options including overnight charters. They leave from the Fernandina Harbor Marina opposite the Chamber of Commerce.

Air Tours

Island Aerial Tours (☎ 904-321-0904) at Fernandina Beach Municipal Airport (take Hwy A1A to Parkway to Airport Rd and then follow the signs to the yellow hangar) offers short (six minute) 'round-the-island rides in their classic WACO open-cockpit biplane for $40 for two. They do longer 15-minute rides for $70 for two, and a half-hour tour of the entire region plus a lazy eight on request (Okay, since you asked and I happen to be a pilot: you fly in the shape of a figure eight, at the top and bottom of which you pull back to maximum pitch up attitude, twist around the outside arc of the '8' and end up in maximum pitch down attitude, then do it again on the other side. If you're looking to get that roller-coaster feeling, this is one expensive way to get it) for $100 a couple.

Places to Stay

Most places to stay are in Fernandina Beach. If you want to stay in American Beach, the oldest black-owned oceanfront motel in America is *American Beach Villas* (☎ 904-261-0840), open only from October to March. Also, several homes can be rented out by the day, week or month. For information on rentals, contact MaVynee Betsch (see American Beach above).

Camping Tent camping is free on American Beach, but you're allowed to do it only on weekends. Primitive and improved campsites are available at *Fort Clinch State Park* (☎ 904-277-7274; see earlier in this section). Sites are $18.50/20.50 without/with electricity. There are sites along the river and at the beach behind the dune system. Fires are in grills only, and you'll need to bring your own firewood as gathering it in the park is *verboten*; many Publix and Winn-Dixie supermarkets sell bundles. No pets allowed. There's a dump station and a bath house.

There's other camping nearby, at Little Talbot Island State Park – see later in this chapter.

Motels & Hotels Most of the motels are on the beach side of town. The *Golden Isle Motel* (☎ 904-261-6795, 2811 Atlantic Ave) has calm and friendly staff, and clean-looking singles and doubles with kitchen for $40, or $100 during special events.

The friendly and polite people at the *Beachside Motel Inn* (☎ 904-261-4236, 3172 S Fletcher Ave) offer double rooms for $48 to $120 on weekdays (more on weekends) and $222 to $600 a week. No pets. For that, we'd take a B&B.

The *Elizabeth Pointe Lodge* (☎ 904-277-4851, 98 S Fletcher Ave) is a flashy, frilly kind of place, designed to look a lot older than it is (it's actually just a couple of years old!) and the service is good enough to make it seem like a B&B even though it's more of a hotel (but the price does include a hot breakfast). Rooms have great ocean views, all have large tubs and nine have Jacuzzis; the decor is also très nautical. Prices range from $105 to $185.

B&Bs Selecting a B&B from all those available in town is a daunting task, best left to individual tastes. We went into all of them, and with the exception of one place, we were charmed and delighted by all the offerings. In the interest of space, we've had to leave lots out, and listed only our favorites. If you're lucky, you'll show up in time for the annual Christmas tour of the B&Bs, the first weekend in December – contact the chamber of commerce for a complete list, or check the island's Website (www.ameliaisland.com) for more information. The others are easy to find – their pamphlets are in racks at the chamber of commerce and in some restaurants.

The *Florida House Inn* (☎ 904-261-3300, 800-258-3301, www.floridahouseinn.com, 20 and 22 S 3rd St) is Florida's oldest hotel (1857), and in its heyday was host to luminaries including Ulysses S Grant, Cuban freedom-fighter José Martí and Rockefellers and Carnegies. It had a pretty rough patch this century, when it devolved into a flophouse, but Bob and Karen Warner came through like a white tornado and restored the place to what may be better than original condition. Many of the rooms have fireplaces, all are beautiful and decorated with obviously loving touches. Some have showers, others claw-foot tubs, two have Jacuzzis. Check out their new Tree House Row – these rooms are really, really nice. All rooms have telephone, air conditioning and TV. Breakfast includes homemade granola and varying hot entrees. The huge porches and garden area are wonderful. There's a very friendly pub downstairs, and their restaurant serves up remarkably good Southern cooking (see the Two Bests in One Town boxed text). Prices range from $75 to $140 for a double and reservations are a very good idea.

The irresistible warmth of the *Hoyt House* (☎ *904-277-4300, 800-432-2085, www .hoythouse.com, 804 Atlantic Ave*) – its owners, Rita and John, and their welcoming kitchen – drew us back again and again during our visit. Another fabulously renovated house, this one Victorian (1905), the Hoyt House opened in 1993 with nine rooms, all with telephone, air conditioning and TV. Each room is unique. There are little touches from Rita and John throughout the day, like homemade cookies, scones and biscuits, free wine in the afternoons, and lots of good food. Stop by the kitchen and say hello. Rooms range from $95 to $144, though you can bargain a bit during the week.

The *Fairbanks House* (☎ *904-277-0500, 800-261-4838, 227 S 7th St*) is another very nice property, with huge spacious rooms and very friendly service. Rooms here run from $125 to $225. There's no smoking anywhere on the property.

Resorts The rooms at the *Summer Beach Resort* (☎ *904-277-0905, 800-862-9297*), condominiums whose owners let them out to guests, are a fantastic deal. They have hotel-style rooms from $100 a night and $650 a week, ocean-view two-bedroom townhouses for $200/1300, and heaps of other configurations up to three-bedroom corner townhouses for $330/2150. They are at the southern end of the island.

The *Ritz-Carlton* (☎ *904-277-1100, 800-241-3333, 4750 Amelia Island Pkwy*) has the immaculate service one would expect from a Ritz anywhere, and holds very creative special programs, from cooking classes to skydivers arriving with the Beaujolais Nouveau. There's 24-hour room service, marble bathrooms with plush robes and countless other amenities. The hotel is on 13 acres of beachfront property; there is (of course) an 18-hole golf course, tennis courts, a spa and indoor and outdoor pools. Rates for standard-category rooms range from $123 to $195, deluxe ocean-view rooms from $173 to $245, club-level rooms from $248 to $320, and club suites from $323 to $395.

Amelia Island Plantation (☎ *904-261-6161, 800-874-6878*) is a 550-room resort primarily based around their golf courses, designed by Pete Dye and Tom Fazio. Room rates in low season (winter) are $158 for rooms, $194 for one-bedroom suites; in high season, it's $224/292. It's off Amelia Island Parkway south of American Beach – follow the signs.

Places to Eat
For snacks and an upscale jolt of caffeine, hit the *Amelia Island Gourmet Coffee Co*, on 4th St opposite the post office, where the local yuppies and politicos hang out, drinking good coffee (about $1 to $3 a cup) and eating great pastries, such as Plantation pecan pie ($3.75) and fruit-of-the-forest pie ($3.25).

KP Bola's (☎ *904-261-6251, 2124 Sadler Rd*), at the Sadler Square shopping center, is

NORTHEAST

Cooking at the Ritz

The Ritz's cooking school is a fine institution. Classes take place on Tuesday and Wednesday and will have you dicing and slicing with the best of them. Classes are themed on a particular style of cuisine, and the members cook all day and then eat the fruits of their labor family-style. The cost is $695 per couple including classes, supplies and accommodations.

a local favorite, and the closest you'll come to a vegetarian place in town. Great food, great prices and very popular.

Island Juice Bar (☎ *904-277-8800, 12C S 2nd St*) does great juices, smoothies and bagels. They're next door to ***Joe's 2nd St Bistro*** (☎ *904-321-2558, 14 S 2nd St*), which has great service and seafood, plus steak and poultry, a lovely courtyard and a huge wine list. Reservations are recommended. They also do vegetarian stuff.

Shakespeare's Kitchen (☎ *904-277-2076, 316 Centre St, 2nd floor*) serves generous portions of healthy, light sandwiches: blackened chicken and avocado for $6, veggie for $5, and a ploughman's special (fruit with mixed cheeses, fresh greens and bread) for $6.95. Weekdays they're open only for lunch, but on Friday and Saturday they also serve dinner 6:30 to 11 pm.

Larry's Charcoal Grille (☎ *904-261-2225, 1515 Sadler Rd*) has terrific sandwiches.

Elizabeth Pointe Lodge (☎ *904-277-4851, 98 S Fletcher Ave*), at the hotel of the same name, is a nice place for lunch. A ham-and-cheese melt, or soup with salad and bread is $5.95; club sandwich and soup is $7.90.

O'Kane's Irish Pub & Eatery (☎ *904-261-1000, 318 Centre St*) does serviceable Irish specialties but stay away from anything creative or vaguely Continental, which they're not as good at. Service is friendly. At lunch, try the chicken stew pie for $5.25 or quiche for $5.95, and at dinner definitely do the Irish stew ($8.50) and any Irish specials ($12.95 to $15.95). The portions are large, but what we had was a little oily (though it would make a good base for drinking, and there's plenty of that in the attached Irish pub).

The ***Beech St Grill*** (☎ *904-277-3662, 801 Beech St*) has exquisite seafood. While they are *not* cheap, you get what you pay for: grilled New York strip for $18.95, veal piccata for $17.95, roasted duck or roasted salmon filet for $16.95, daily fresh seafood specials for about the same price (some a bit cheaper) and fine service. (They were even polite when our credit card came up tilt on our splurge evening out – dinner for the two of us, with a bottle of wine and dessert, was

Two Bests in One Town

The ***Florida House Inn*** (☎ 904-261-3300, 20 and 22 S 3rd St) is, for food, service, atmosphere and price, Florida's best dining value. It's a boarding house-style restaurant (all the food is brought out in big bowls and everyone helps themselves), with brilliantly cooked traditional Southern dishes: delicious collard greens, great mashed potatoes and assorted other vegetables, awesome crabcakes, ribs, roast beef and real Southern fried chicken, as much as you can eat (we took that to be a personal challenge) for $5.95 (!!!) at lunch, $9.95 at dinner. Lunch is Monday to Saturday 11:30 am to 2:30 pm, and dinner Tuesday to Saturday 5:30 to 8:30 pm. Sunday brunch is $7.95. And don't forget to take up your dirty dishes when you're done (really). The boarding-house theme, which is a restoration of the original inn's dining room, is a really nice way to meet fellow travelers and locals – we had a great time and highly recommend it.

And the other best is Best Clam Chowder, the title held by the ***Marina Restaurant*** (☎ 904-261-5310, 101 Centre St). This place is also very popular, and serves simply the most exquisite New England (the creamy one) clam chowder we've ever had anywhere. Locals and visitors alike line up for lunch specials such as chicken croquettes, pepper steak or breaded veal, all with three vegetables, for $5.50 on weekdays and $6 on weekends. Prices double at dinner.

$60.) Reservations are recommended, and they are open for dinner 6 to 10 pm daily.

Les Clos (☎ *904-261-8100, 20 S 2nd St*) is a very intimate high-end French place with excellent food and an extensive (and expensive) wine list.

The Grill at the Ritz-Carlton resort (see above) is the best on the island; dinner for two will run you at least $150 with wine.

There are dozens of dessert offerings – it's awesome, and if you're looking to splurge, this is the place to do it.

Also at the Ritz is *The Café*. Breakfast specials run from $5 to $13, lunch from $8 to $17 and at dinnertime expect to pay $6 to $9 for starters, $15 to $22 for main courses. Macrobiotic foods are also available. The *Ocean Bar & Grill* serves lighter fare outside.

Another great bet is the *Down Under Restaurant* (☎ 904-261-1001), on the west side of the Intracoastal Waterway at Hwy A1A, under the bridge. Their main courses range from $13.95 for boiled shrimp to $17.95 for grilled dijon tuna, and $15.95 for 14-ounce rib-eye steaks.

Entertainment
It's not exactly a swingin' town, but there are some nice options for a drink or six. The *pub* downstairs at the Florida House Inn is a wonderful place with great service, good martinis, a hundred or so types of beer and a great old-fashioned bar.

The most jumping place in town is the landmark *Palace Saloon* (☎ 904-261-6320, 113-117 Centre St), where the atmosphere is gun-running free-spiritedness – perhaps because of the quantities of their trademark Pirate's Punch (it's a mix of red wine and what seems like the bottom nine rows of the bar – packs a wallop) being imbibed. It's a scene.

The *Amelia Community Theatre* (☎ 904-261-6749, 209 Cedar St) is a lovely little community theater now in its 18th season. On average, they perform eight plays a year, sometimes with dinner theater productions, and tickets start as low as $3; call when you're in town to see if anything's on.

Getting There & Away
There's no public transportation between the mainland and the island, so you'll need a car, bicycle or a very expensive taxi.

Jacksonville International Airport (JAX) is the closest airport. If you've got a private plane, you can land at Fernandina Beach Municipal Airport (☎ 904-261-7890), with a grass strip just about in the center of the west side of the island.

By car, take exit 129 from I-95 to Hwy A1A east; follow this straight out to the island, about 15 miles. If coming from the west, take I-10 to the Baldwin exit, stay on Hwy 301 through Baldwin to Callahan and take Hwy A1A for about 40 miles.

From the south, take Hwy A1A north to the little town of Mayport, where you can catch the **St John's River Ferry** (☎ 904-251-3331), also called the Mayport Ferry, which runs between the northern end of Mayport (follow the signs – it's unmissable) to Fort George Island, leaving every half hour from about 6 am to about 10:15 pm daily. You can drive, motorbike, bike or walk on; cars, motorcycles and scooters are $2.50, pedestrians and bicycles are 50¢. Pee first – there are no toilets onboard. The ferry drops you on Fort George Island about a quarter-mile south of the turnoff for the Kingsley Plantation (see below). To Amelia Island, continue up Hwy A1A – there's no public transportation; you'll have to drive.

Getting Around
For Fernandina Beach, walking is the best bet, but cars are necessary to get around the greater island. Parking is a snap, and it's free.

It's a great biking town and island – very flat and no major distances. Rent bikes at Fernandina Beach Bike & Fitness (☎ 904-277-3227), 115 8th St just behind the BP station, for $3 an hour, $11 a day or $40 a week, closed Tuesday and Sunday. Reserve early. Bikes should also be available at Driftwood Surf Shop (☎ 904-321-2188), 31 S Fletcher Ave, Fernandina Beach, for $10 per day and $40 per week.

LITTLE TALBOT & FORT GEORGE ISLANDS
Just to the south of Amelia Island, these two islands contain a very interesting state park and a historic site.

Little Talbot Island State Park
This treasure of an island (☎ 904-251-2320), about 9 miles south of American Beach across Nassau Sound, is a 2500-acre park with fishing, and nature and hiking trails, 5 miles of beaches, canoeing ($3 an hour, $12 a

day), camping and a picnic area. The maritime forest is made of Southern magnolia, live oak and American holly; Spanish moss is everywhere. Canoeing permission is granted depending on the tides.

There's **camping** here; it costs $15.75 year round for sites without electricity, $18 with electric hookups. All sites have water hookups.

The park entrance is on the east side of Hwy A1A. It's open 8 am to sundown every day; admission is $4 per car, $1 per bicycle or pedestrian. See St John's River Ferry, under Getting There & Away, above.

Kingsley Plantation

Zephaniah Kingsley and his Senegalese wife (whom he had originally purchased as a slave) established a cotton, sugarcane, corn and citrus plantation here on Fort George Island in 1814. Today, the plantation (☎ 904-251-3537), kitchen house, garden, barn and the remains of the 23 slave cabins are open as part of the Timucuan Ecological & Historic Preserve, and are a wonderful place to spend an afternoon with or without a picnic. The cabins are chilling, for their tiny size and their jail-like arrangement. There's printed information on the lives of the slaves, their task system and the slave community, but the rangers' oral history is far more compelling.

In the small garden outside, you can see Sea Island cotton growing – with its beautiful yellow flowers. Ranger-guided tours are given at 1 pm daily; the park is open Monday to Friday 9 am to 5 pm, Saturday and Sunday 1 to 3 pm. Admission is free; donations are appreciated. There's drinking water in the bathrooms.

Getting There & Away From Fernandina Beach, take Hwy A1A straight south to Fort George Island. The access road is on the west side of Hwy A1A; at the fork in the road, the left route is more direct; the right, through gorgeous canopied forest, is longer (about 3 miles) but far prettier. On either fork, watch out for pot holes the size of hall closets.

From the south, take the St John's River Ferry (see Getting There & Away under Amelia Island above) across to Fort George Island; it will drop you off about a quarter-mile south of the turnoff for the Kingsley Plantation.

Southwest Florida

With the warm, calm waters of the Gulf of Mexico lapping its white-sand beaches, southwest Florida is perhaps the state's most beautiful region, and contains possibly America's finest beaches – yes, including Hawaii. It also offers some of the best opportunities in the state for getting out into nature.

The area was developed at the end of the 19th century, when Henry B Plant, Florida's west-coast version of Henry Flagler, built a railroad line connecting the area with the northeast and ran a steamship line between Tampa and Havana, which brought in the tobacco that made Tampa America's cigar-making capital.

Henry Ford, Thomas Edison, John Ringling (who was as serious about art as he was about circuses) and a fascinating religious commune all set down roots here, and the region is rich with cultural attractions. You can tour Edison's rubber laboratories and winter home (along with Ford's winter home) and gawk at the fantastic collections of European, American, Asian and pre-Columbian art at the St Petersburg Museum of Fine Arts, maybe the state's best. And you can still watch cigars being hand rolled in Tampa's historic Ybor City district.

For exploring nature, there are the splendors of the Gulf barrier islands, from Naples to Clearwater Beach, where enticing swimming, canoeing, kayaking, hiking and biking opportunities abound. The Lee County Parks Department, in the Fort Myers area, runs some of the best programs around, and, even in a place as developed as Fort Myers Beach, you're never more than a half hour from total immersion in wilderness. Fantastic souvenirs and sightseeing are found right along the coast: from the mounds of shark's teeth that wash up on Venice's beaches to the unparalleled shelling at Sanibel, Captiva and Pine Islands and the area near Clearwater Beach.

The Tampa-St Petersburg area is becoming one of the hottest tourist draws in the

Highlights

- Hunt for shark's teeth in Venice
- Gather seashells from the 160 varieties on Sanibel and Captiva Islands (but if you take any live ones you could spend 60 days in jail! – see the Sanibel Stoop boxed text for more information)
- Shop for cigars in Ybor City, one-time cigar capital of the US
- Enjoy the St Petersburg museum circuit, home to some of the state's most impressive art collections
- See African wildlife and ride the terrifying roller coasters Kumba and Montu at Busch Gardens
- Spot manatees, alligators, crocodiles, otters and other critters at Homosassa Springs State Park
- Kayak among the pristine barrier islands of Matlacha Pass Aquatic Preserve

southern section of Florida. St Petersburg has three excellent museums that together rival any others the state has to offer. St Pete Beach and especially Clearwater Beach offer sunny, white-sand beaches that are great for relaxing and shelling; the Gulf islands around Clearwater Beach make for superb kayaking

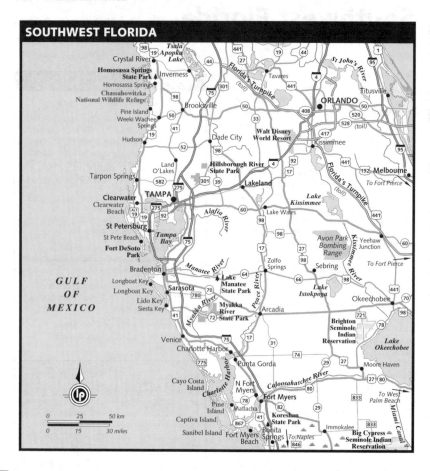

SOUTHWEST FLORIDA

and canoeing. Tampa also has several high-quality museums and attractions, with the revitalization of the historic – and now very hip – Ybor City district at its heart.

The area's two theme parks are also definitely worth a visit: Busch Gardens has the best roller coasters in the southeastern USA, and Weeki Wachee Springs is famous for its weirdly campy underwater mermaid shows.

Visit Homosassa Springs State Park for a close-up look at some of Florida's wildlife. The tourist trap of Tarpon Springs is less than an hour away, but we consider a visit there a waste of time: a once-quaint town now entirely made up of tourist shops, junk stands, expensive parking lots and exhibits on the sponge industry that are cheesy and overpriced – as is everything else here.

Hotels and motels in the region are priced a little higher than in other areas of the state, but there's inexpensive camping in several of the state parks and historic sites (best on some of the barrier islands west of Fort Myers) and youth hostels in Clearwater Beach and St Petersburg.

Gator crossing on Sanibel Island

MAXINE CASS

Cà d'Zan, Ringling home in Sarasota

MARESA PRYOR

Drop in at Busch Gardens, Tampa.

CARL PURCELL

Florida Aquarium in Tampa

MARESA PRYOR

Don CeSar Beach Resort in St Pete Beach

NIK WHEELER

Corkscrew Swamp Sanctuary

GAVRIEL JECAN

Sponges on sale in Tarpon Springs

Pelicans at Suncoast Seabird Sanctuary

Blue Angels preparing for a show in Pensacola

St Joseph Peninsula State Park, with 2500 acres of spectacular beaches and trails

But the best part is that there's less development here than on the east coast. Much of the coastline is protected, and the residents on the barrier islands and beach communities are quite content to leave the screaming hordes of Spring Breakers and the gaggles of fashionplates where they are, about 150 miles east of their serene coastline.

NAPLES
• population 198,000

We left Naples out of the first edition, and everyone – from travelers to curmudgeonly *Miami Herald* travel writers – wrote in to tell us we were wrong, so we went back.

We were wrong. Affluent Naples (see The Everglades map, earlier in the book) is worth a look, for great beaches and restaurants, and a superb nature center.

Orientation

Downtown Naples has a grid-based street system, with streets running north and south and avenues running east and west. One main shopping street, 5th Ave S, is home to the visitors center and an Internet café. Old Naples (bounded by 10th Ave S at the north, 14th Ave S at the south, the Gulf of Mexico at the west and the Gordon River at the east) is the center of town.

Information

The Naples Area Chamber Visitors Center (☎ 941-263-1858), at the northwest corner of 5th Ave S and Hwy 41, is open Monday to Friday 9 am to 5 pm but inexplicably and unforgivably closed on Saturday after 3 pm and all day Sunday. Better luck can be had at the outdoor concierge desk, on 3rd St S between Broad Ave and 12th Ave S, which is staffed in winter by very friendly people who hand out information and will make hotel reservations for you. In other seasons, the desk is kept supplied with pamphlets and brochures.

NationsBank has a branch at 796 5th Ave S.

The Lighthouse Bookstore (☎ 941-261-6619), 505 5th Ave S, sells a great collection of esoteric titles. Barnes & Noble (☎ 941-598-5200) is at 5377 Tamiami Trail N.

There's a branch post office (☎ 941-435-2100) at 1200 Goodlette Road N. Check email and surf the Web ($2 per 15 minutes) at Java Java (☎ 941-435-1190), 866 5th Ave S, but skip their egregiously awful coffee.

Wash clothes at the laundromat at 287 9th St S.

Things to See & Do

The Conservancy of Southwest Florida is a nonprofit environmental organization that lobbies for nature and ecological causes in Florida. It runs fabulous nature centers, including the **Naples Nature Center** (☎ 941-262-0304, www.conservancy.org), 14th Ave N, off Goodlette-Frank Rd, containing a museum of natural history, a wildlife rehabilitation center and a half-mile boardwalk that takes you through five ecosystems. There are also naturalist-led hiking and boat tours. You can rent canoes or kayaks ($13 for two hours), or take their boat trip ($6 adults, $2 kids). We urge you to visit.

The main action downtown is in Old Naples and along 5th Ave S, where a collection of shops, restaurants and cafés lie in wait. You can pick up guides for self-guided walking tours of Old Naples at the visitors center and concierge desk.

Naples' **beaches** are wonderful. Because construction was forbidden close to the water, that all-too-familiar Florida condo cluster along the seashore doesn't exist here. Maintained by the Registry Resort, Clam Pass County Park (☎ 941-353-0404) has a 3/4-mile boardwalk through a mangrove forest leading out to the beach. There's a free electric tram from the parking lot, and boat and kayak rentals and a concession stand, run by the Registry, right near the beach. The downtown's beach is the finest city beach in Florida – spotless, white sand and very popular. Right at the western end of 12th Ave S is **The Pier**, a fishing pier that's a center of activity, especially on weekends. It's a great place to watch the pelicans.

Right near The Pier is the late-19th-century **Palm Cottage** (☎ 941-261-8164), 137 12th Ave S, now home to the Collier County Historic Society, which holds tours at varying times during winter.

Tin City is a shopping mall that surrounds the **city docks** at the eastern end of 12th Ave S on the Gordon River. The boats make for a nice backdrop.

The **Caribbean Gardens** (☎ 941-262-5409), 1590 Goodlette-Frank Rd, is a botanical gardens and petting zoo that's great for kids, who love to watch the alligator feeding. Admission is $13.95 for adults, $8.95 for kids.

And if you're a teddy bear nut, you'll like the **Teddy Bear Museum** (☎ 941-598-2271), currently at 2511 Pine Ridge Rd but planning a move 'soon' and featuring teddy bears from around the world in a bizarre setting; there is, though, a good teddy bear gift shop here. Admission is $6 for adults, $4 for seniors, $2 for kids.

Organized Tours

The **Venetian Gondola** (☎ 941-262-5665), leaving from the dock in front of the Comfort Inn at 1221 5th Ave S, does a range of tours from aboard a gondola, starting with tours of Tin City for $10 a person ($25 minimum, six people maximum).

Naples Trolley Tours (☎ 941-262-7300) runs buses – painted up as trolleys – on a circuit through the city, stopping at almost every hotel and resort on the way. But because you can ride all day and get on and off as often as you'd like, and the ride's narrated with history and anecdotes about the city, it's definitely worth the $12 for adults and $5 for kids.

Places to Stay

Prices skyrocket in winter (approximately November to March), are high in summer and lower in spring and autumn. The **Seashell Motel** (☎ 941-262-5127, 82 9th St N) has squeaky-clean queen-size double rooms for around $39 in low season and as high as $89 in high season. The desk clerk didn't laugh when we asked if the manager, one O'Malley O'Ryan, was Polish.

The nicely isolated **Flamingo Apartment Hotel** (☎ 941-261-7017, fax 941-261-7769, 383 6th Ave S) has lived-in but clean efficiencies for $55 (seventh night free) in low season and $135 in high season. There's a small pool, and the place gets a lot of return business.

The fabulous **Lemon Tree Inn** (☎ 941-262-1414, 250 9th St S) has friendly staff, free lemonade in the lobby and spotless, well-appointed rooms for $49 to $95 in low season, $95 to $165 in high season, including a continental breakfast served outside in their gazebo. They rent bikes for $5 a day to guests.

Of the several area resorts, the best (if money's no object) is the **Registry Resort** (☎ 941-597-3232, 800-247-9810, 475 Seagate Drive), with large rooms, stunningly friendly staff and the city's best restaurants (see below). It's on Clam Pass Beach, and the resort manages the county park's concessions, including canoe and kayak rentals. Now the bad news: rooms run $250 to $390 and enormous suites $375 to $975. If you've got the cash, this is the place to be, hands down.

Places to Eat

There's a good **Cheeburger Cheeburger!** (☎ 941-435-9796, 505 5th Ave) with fantastic onion rings ($2.20) and great cheeseburgers from $3.95 to $4.95.

Annabelle's Café (☎ 941-261-4275, 495 5th Ave S) has great salads and lunch specials, such as huge sandwiches for $8 and chicken and veggie stir fry for $9; at dinner main courses run $13 to $23.

There's very nice pizza as usual at **California Pizza Kitchen** (☎ 941-566-1900, 5555 Tamiami Trail) in the Waterside Shops mall; pizzas run $8 to $11.

The best high-end splurge in the state is at the Registry Resort's (see above) two restaurants – both exquisite and expensive but seriously worth it: the **Brass Pelican**'s (☎ 941-597-3232) so-called quaint Florida menu is stunningly fresh seafood and wonderful steaks, all served up with a decidedly Asian influence. Across the lobby, **Lafite** (same ☎) is amazing for French and everything else, and very much a formal affair. Try – but don't fill up on – appetizers, such as pirouettes of lobster with blue-crab claws and snow pea sprouts ($13.75) or baked Vidalia onion with andouille sausage and crab meat ($12.75). Pacing is everything!

Leave room for main courses, from $28 to $37.50, include offerings such as roasted rack of lamb with caramelized onion-garlic herb crust, wild oregano-spiced veal chop with port wine figs and the highly recommended Lafite sampler: roasted lamb, roasted Asian-spiced duckling and tamarind-sugarcane grilled tiger prawn. There's an excellent wine list in both restaurants.

Getting There & Away
The Greyhound station (☎ 941-774-5660) is at 2669 Davis Blvd. Sample fares (one way/roundtrip) are listed below:

destination	duration	price
Miami	3¹/₂ hours	$19/38
Orlando	5³/₄	$43/86
Tampa	4¹/₂ to 6 hours	$31/62

Naples is at the southwestern end of the Tamiami Trail (Hwy 41), just northwest of Marco Island and the Everglades.

FORT MYERS
• population 46,500
Dubbed the City of Palms for the 2000 royal palm trees that line McGregor Blvd, Fort Myers was a sleepy resort town in 1885 when Thomas Alva Edison decided to build a winter home and laboratory here.

It was Edison who began planting the palms: he made a deal that he would plant them if the city agreed to maintain them after his death. He planted 543 as seedlings, and he imported another 270 from the Everglades, which lined the first mile of the avenue. Today McGregor is lined with palms for 14 miles.

Edison moved to the area in 1886 and expanded his estate over the years. In 1914, Henry Ford visited him and liked the place so much that he bought the house next door.

Today, both houses are open as museums, yet Fort Myers is known more for its beach life and excellent county and state parks than for Edison's grand experiments.

But a grand experiment is in the works today: the Buquebus, a high-speed ferry linking Fort Myers and Key West. If successful, this could be a major boost for tourism in southwest Florida – see the Getting There & Away section later for more information.

Orientation
The sprawling greater Fort Myers area is at the southwest corner of Florida, northwest of Naples, the Everglades and the 10,000 Islands. Fort Myers sits on the southern banks of the Caloosahatchee River; on the north bank is North Fort Myers and Cape Coral is to the west. To the southwest are San Carlos and the Estero Islands; the city of Fort Myers Beach is on the latter.

The downtown area is broken up by two intersecting grid sections. The core of the downtown historic district is comprised of a network of streets that are at a 45° angle to the standard north-south, east-west grid system that makes up the rest of the city. The 45° section is bounded on the south by ML King Jr Blvd, on the east by Evans Ave and on the west by Cleveland Ave (US Hwy 41, the Tamiami Trail), which runs into the Caloosahatchee Bridge and on to North Fort Myers.

There's not really a main drag in downtown, but what action there is (which is to say not much) is concentrated in the area bounded by Edwards Drive at the north, Fowler St at the east, ML King Jr Blvd at the south and Monroe Ave at the west. A little pedestrian mall called Patio de León is bounded by Main, 1st and Hendry Sts and Broadway.

Maps The best downtown map is right in this book, but you can find copies of downtown maps in *Downtown & Around Town Fort Myers Digest* (see Information below) and sometimes on the tram tour (see Organized Tours later in this section). Dolph Map Co's *Map of Fort Myers and Vicinity* is probably the best commercially produced map, with a good insert blowup of downtown; the Fort Myers Chamber of Commerce sells an imprinted edition of this map for $2. AAA's *Map of Fort Myers* is pretty good, and for the beach, their *Map of Cape Coral* features an inset of Fort Myers Beach and other areas, including Sanibel, Captiva and Pine Islands.

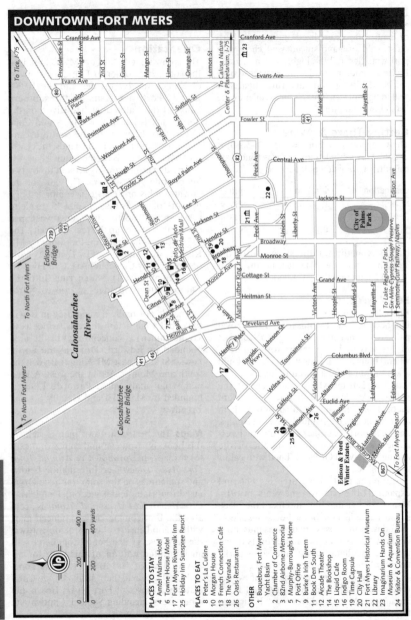

DOWNTOWN FORT MYERS

PLACES TO STAY
4 Amtel Marina Hotel
6 Towne House Motel
17 Fort Myers Riverwalk Inn
25 Holiday Inn Sunspree Resort

PLACES TO EAT
8 Peter's La Cuisine
10 Morgan House
13 French Connection Café
18 The Veranda
26 Oasis Restaurant

OTHER
1 Buquebus, Fort Myers
   Yacht Basin
2 Chamber of Commerce
3 82nd Airborne Memorial
5 Murphy-Burroughs Home
7 Post Office
9 Burke's Irish Tavern
11 Book Den South
12 Arcade Theater
14 The Bookshop
15 Liquid Cafe
16 Indigo Room
19 Time Capsule
20 City Hall
21 Fort Myers Historical Museum
22 Library
23 Imaginarium Hands On
   Museum & Aquarium
24 Visitor & Convention Bureau

SOUTHWEST

How Far?

Distances in the Fort Myers area are incredible: the Lee County Parks Department told us that the Lee County Manatee Park, which is 8 miles northeast of downtown, was 'pretty much downtown Fort Myers.' Anywhere you'll want to go outside of your immediate vicinity is bound to be at least 40 minutes away by car. And traffic, by the way, is murderous, so take that into account when you're planning your trip. To stay at Fort Myers Beach is great if you're after sun and surf, but if you're looking to canoe around the Matlacha Pass Aquatic Preserve (see Pine Island & Matlacha Pass later in this chapter) or to hit the Edison and Ford Estates, you're in for a long drive.

And another thing. The streets, they be strange, here, mon. At one point we found ourselves at the intersection of McGregor Blvd and McGregor Blvd.

Information

The Lee Island Coast Visitor & Convention Bureau (☎ 941-338-3500, 800-237-6444, www.leeislandcoast.com), 2180 W 1st St, Suite 100, has some very helpful planners and information kits. Among them, *Lee Island Coast – Vacationer's Guide*, an all-around orientation and information pamphlet; *A Nature Guide to the Lee Island Coast*, which is just that; and the excellent *Access Ability Guide* for handicapped visitors, listing ADA information on most major sights in the county.

Right downtown, the Greater Fort Myers Chamber of Commerce (☎ 941-332-3624), at the corner of Lee St and Edwards Drive, has the usual array of pamphlets and tourist brochures and the *Downtown & Around Town Fort Myers Digest*.

The enormous local AAA office (☎ 941-939-6500) is at 2516 Colonial Blvd. You can get to Colonial, which is a major connector, by taking Cleveland Ave (US Hwy 41) south.

NationsBank has several branches in the city, including one at 2400 1st St (☎ 941-335-1225). There is an American Express representative office at Ship 'n' Shore Cruises (☎ 941-433-0013), 15250 S US Hwy 41.

The main downtown post office is at the corner of Bay St and Monroe Ave. The area code for Fort Myers and around changed from ☎ 813 to ☎ 941 in May 1995, but many businesses still list 813 on pamphlets – use ☎ 941.

The biggest bookshop in town is the Books a Million (☎ 941-936-8871), 4125 Cleveland Ave, in the Edison Mall shopping center. Downtown, the Book Den South (☎ 941-332-2333), 2249 1st St, has high-quality used books, paperbacks and a travel section that's more literature than guides. Close by, The Bookshop (☎ 941-334-0141) in Patio de León has more paperbacks and a book search service. Barnes and Noble (☎ 941-437-0654) is at 13751 S Tamiami Trail.

The main library (☎ 941-338-3155), 2050 Lee St, is next to the Fort Myers Historical Museum. The main daily newspaper is the *News-Press*. For freebies, get the very good *Route 41*, with local politics and club information. National Public Radio (NPR) is at 90.1 FM; astronomical (not astrological) forecasts are broadcast Monday at 7:58 am.

SOUTHWEST

There are public toilets outside the entrance to the Edison Estate & Laboratory.

For laundry, we used the U-Turn Laundromat (☎ 941-334-7111), 2412 Cortez Blvd, near the Edison Estate.

The largest public hospital in the area is Lee Memorial Hospital (☎ 941-332-1111), 2776 Cleveland Ave.

Edison & Ford Winter Estates

The town's primary tourist attraction, the **Edison Estate & Laboratory** (☎ 941-334-7419) was the winter home of Thomas Edison, one of America's most prolific inventors. The grounds are absolutely lovely – Edison was an avid botanist – with more than 1000 varieties of plants. We liked the Dynamite Tree, which spreads its seeds through pods that, well, explode! The other Edison Estate landmark is the unbelievably enormous banyan tree just outside the entrance. Remember to stay on the paths as you walk through – the grass is infested with fire ants.

Edison's laboratory here was devoted mainly to his attempts to cross-breed an American rubber tree at the behest of car and tire makers Ford and Firestone, who wanted to establish a reliable domestic supply. After experimenting with thousands of plants, Edison successfully created a hybrid goldenrod plant that grew to a height of almost 12 feet in a season and contained 12% rubber – an unprecedented quantity. But the production process was too expensive and nothing commercial came of it.

The laboratory is a remarkable place, and it's been kept pretty much as Edison left it – the array of hoo-has and gizmos is amazing. Note the Hayfever Room at the far right-hand corner where goldenrod was thrashed and cut by unfortunate employees.

Adjacent to the laboratory is the Edison Museum, a fascinating collection of hundreds of Edison's inventions and possessions, such as his 1908 four-cylinder Cadillac coupe, tons of office equipment, movie projectors and kinescopes, Edison light bulbs, phonographs and the first three-wire generator system behind a very Stalinesque bust.

There are guided tours through the estate, which include a visit to the adjacent **Henry Ford's winter home**, the automaker/sometime philanderer. There are more specialized tours as well: on Monday, Wednesday and Saturday at 10 am and 2 pm, there are in-depth historical tours ($15 for adults and $7.50 for seniors, kids and students) and botanical tours of the grounds can be taken with a minimum of three people by appointment ($16/8).

Thomas Alva Edison

Thomas Edison (1847-1931) was a tireless and entirely commercially minded inventor who has a total of 1093 patents to his name (17 of which were co-patents with another inventor).

In Robert Conot's *A Streak of Luck*, Edison is quoted as having said, 'Anything that won't sell I don't want to invent. Its sale is proof of utility, and utility is success.'

And utilitarian Edison most certainly was: his patents include 389 under the category of 'Electric Light and Power,' 195 for phonographs, 150 for the telegraph, 141 for batteries, 62 for ore separators, 40 for cement, 34 for railroads, nine for motion pictures, eight for automobiles, five for 'electric pen' and mimeograph, three for typewriters, one for vacuum preservation, three for chemicals, an autogiro (a cross between a helicopter and an airplane), three for military projectiles, two for radio and one for rubber.

To get an idea of his energy, consider that he patented at least one gizmo a year for 65 consecutive years: he was issued 34 patents in 1872, 75 in 1882, 23 in 1907, and in 1931, the year of his death, he was issued two. But even death was not enough to completely sap his relentless pursuit: four patents were issued to him posthumously.

(Source: Historical Division, Edison and Ford Winter Estates)

The estate straddles McGregor Blvd at Larchmont Ave, south of downtown: the main entrance for both homes, the ticket office, Edison Museum and Laboratory and parking lots are on the east side of the street; the Ford home and garage, Edison home and guesthouse, memory garden and swimming pool are on the west.

The museum and estate are open Monday to Saturday 9 am to 4 pm, Sunday noon to 4 pm. The cost is $11 for adults, $5.50 for children six to 12.

Fort Myers Historical Museum

This museum (☎ 941-332-5955), 2300 Peck Ave, is a hit with kids if only to tour the *Esperanza*, a private railroad car. Permanent exhibits tell the story of the city's history and include Calusa and Seminole artifacts, models of the local military bases and a display on Colonel Myers – the man for whom the city is named. (Though he never actually visited his namesake fort, just as General Robert E Lee never set foot in his namesake county!) Other exhibits include a Spanish cannon, a complete saber-toothed cat *(Smilodon)* skeleton and an exhibit on Fort Myers' two WWII training bases, which trained British, American, Canadian, Russian and Yugoslavian pilots and gunners.

There are always traveling exhibits as well: when we visited it was Cooper glass, dime-store soldiers and war games. The museum's open Tuesday to Friday 9 am to 4 pm, Saturday 10 am to 4 pm, closed Sunday and Monday. Admission is $4 for adults, $2 for children.

Imaginarium Hands On Museum & Aquarium

The Imaginarium (☎ 941-337-3332), 2000 Cranford Ave off ML King Jr Blvd, just past the *News-Press* and *USA Today* plant – look for the big water tower – is a hands-on science museum that kids will go crazy over. We loved the hot-air balloon exhibition and the golf-ball-driven model of the human digestive system. Take a spin in the chemical-abuse simulator jeep on the electronic obstacle course to test your reflexes after a couple of virtual snoots.

In the Tiny Town area downstairs, there's a really cool bubble gadget – kids stand in the center of a circle and pull a string, which raises a hula hoop from a tray of soapy water at their feet and surrounds them with an enormous, cylindrical bubble. Upstairs, a television station exhibit called WIMG puts your kid against a matte and in front of a TV camera; through weather-forecasting technology, kids can then see themselves in the center of a hurricane video. There are also excellent exhibits on ozone depletion and weather – touching a cloud is neat – and a tornado machine. If their computer hasn't crashed, you can surf the Internet and play interactive CD-ROM games.

Outside, there's a touch tank with a stingray (he was sick when we visited) and crabs, horseshoe crabs, living shells, starfish and more. The new freshwater lagoon, according to a press release, will have '1200 pounds of freshwater fish' (sounding more like a place for fishmongers than an aquarium) and Florida aquaculture.

There's a 3D theater downstairs that has different shows every half-hour or so.

The museum is open Monday to Saturday 10 am to 5 pm, and Sunday noon to 5 pm, closed Christmas and Thanksgiving. Admission is $6 for adults, $3 for children three to 12. There's no senior discount.

Murphy-Burroughs Home

Call them hokey, but the 'living history' tours at this historic landmark home (☎ 941-332-6125), 2505 1st St, by the river, are still popular: you're led through the house by volunteers in the costumes and characters of Jettie and Mona Burroughs, daughters of Nelson Burroughs. A businessman (but not the electronics giant of the same name), Burroughs bought the house from a Texas cattleman named Murphy in 1918, and the house remained in the family until it was donated to the city in 1983. Tours run Tuesday to Friday 11 am to 3 pm, every hour on the hour. On Saturday, they host special events such as weddings and meetings. Admission is $3 for adults, $1 for students; parking is available at the nearby Amtel Marina Hotel.

Other Downtown Attractions

At the corner of Lee St and Edwards Drive, near the chamber of commerce, is the **82nd Airborne Memorial**, a monument to the Gulf Coast chapter of the Army's 82nd Airborne Division. Nearby is the **Fort Myers Yacht Basin**.

In 1976, the town elders got together and made a **time capsule** of items readily available during that year, to be opened on July 4, 2076. The capsule is at the front corner of the city hall property, on the corner of 2nd St and Broadway.

And every Thursday, from 7 am to 3 pm, there's a **farmers' market** under the entrance to the Caloosahatchee River Bridge. It's kind of colorful. This is not to be confused with the **State Farmers' Market** (☎ 941-332-6910), 2744 Edison Ave, which is more a restaurant and hotel buyers' hangout than a public attraction.

Calusa Nature Center & Planetarium

This nature center (☎ 941-275-3435) has a series of boardwalks through a cypress swamp, an Audubon aviary and a faux Seminole village. Inside, there are permanent and rotating exhibitions on the history and formation of southwestern Florida. But what the kids are really here to see is the live poisonous-snake exhibition, with snake and alligator demonstrations at 10:30 am and 1:30 pm daily. There are also snake feedings weekly (in May, they were on Sunday at 11:45 am, but call first) and nature hikes around the grounds.

The planetarium (☎ 941-275-2183) features shows on the southwest Florida night sky and films such as *Firstlight*, which tracks the development of the telescope from a clunky mirror in a tube to a misshapen mirror aboard a billion-dollar spacecraft.

There are astronomy shows in the afternoon, and on Friday and Saturday nights, laser shows with rock music that's surprisingly current.

It's open Monday to Saturday 9 am to 5 pm, Sunday 11 am to 5 pm. Admission to the museum and trails is $4 for adults, $2.50 for kids under 12; a combination museum, trails and planetarium ticket is $5/3. But they give out coupons left and right, so try showing them this listing to get $1 off a combination ticket. Go ahead: it's not like they said it's okay or anything, but it never hurts to try, right? Astronomy shows are $3/2, and laser shows are $5 per person. The complex is at 3450 Ortiz Ave, north of the intersection of Ortiz Ave, Colonial Blvd and Six Mile Cypress Parkway.

Lakes Regional Park

This innovative park is home to two very original creations: the Fragrance Garden (☎ 941-369-2003) and a miniature train village (☎ 941-275-3000). The Fragrance Garden was created in 1991 by Ed and Sylvia Blue to be a place where visually impaired and wheelchair-bound visitors could smell, feel and even eat herbs and flowers. It's fully wheelchair accessible, and signs are in print and braille, but the park is open to everyone and it's a nice place for a picnic (tables are provided). The gardens were built up by volunteers from the Master Gardeners Club, Boy and Girl Scouts and students in the RISK program – those at high risk of quitting school – at nearby Cypress Lakes High School. The garden is open 8 am to 6 pm every day except Christmas.

There is also a miniature train ($7^{1}/_{2}$-inch gauge) in the park, where kids and adults can take a little tootle around the $1^{1}/_{4}$-mile track. It runs every 15 minutes Tuesday to Friday 10 am to 2 pm, Saturday 10 am to 4 pm and Sunday noon to 4 pm. The cost is $2.50, kids under three are 50¢. Some of the admission fees will go to the project to restore the locomotive you'll see there, Atlantic Coast Line No 143, a 0-6-0 in horrendous shape. The rail line is closest to parking lot three.

You can rent boats here as well; Lakeside Marina (☎ 941-432-2017) rents paddleboats and canoes ($8 an hour) and canoes with electric trawling motors ($13 an hour) between 10 am and 4 pm Monday to Friday and 9 am to 5 pm Saturday and Sunday. There are alligators in the lake and on the small islands – ask at the marina where the best areas to see them are. See the Alligator Attacks boxed text in the Facts about Florida chapter for safety tips.

The park is at 7330 Gladiolus Drive in South Fort Myers. From downtown, take US Hwy 41 south to Gladiolus Drive; it's on the right-hand side of the road. Parking is 75¢ an hour, or a maximum of $3 a day.

Six Mile Cypress Slough Preserve

This preserve (☎ 941-338-3300) is a 2000-acre wetland that acts as a filter, or drainage way, collecting run-off water during heavy rains. Before making its way out to the Estero Bay Aquatic Preserve, the water is filtered by the slough, where sediment and pollutants settle or are absorbed by the plants. It's an eerie place to visit during the wet season (from June to October), when water up to 3 feet deep flows through the area.

The preserve has a mile-long boardwalk trail lined with benches, a picnic area and an amphitheater used for interpretive meetings (speeches interpreting the local flora and fauna). Admission to the preserve is $3 per carload; bicycles and pedestrians are free. From downtown Fort Myers, take Cleveland Ave south to Colonial Blvd (Hwy 884) east, to Ortiz Ave and turn south. This road will become Six Mile Cypress Parkway; the preserve entrance is on the left, north of Daniels Parkway (Hwy 876).

Seminole-Gulf Railway

Founded in 1888, the Seminole-Gulf Railway (☎ 941-275-8487) was a short line running between Arcadia and Naples with a second line running between Bradenton, Sarasota and Venice. Today, they run excursions and dinner tours on the line's restored trains. There are three-hour Sunday twilight dinner rides ($29.95 for adults; $19.95 for children) and Thursday evening Jazz Trains ($10), with a cash bar and light snacks. They also operate murder-mystery rides, two- and three-day packages and special events throughout the year; call for more information.

The station is near the intersection of Colonial Blvd and Metro Pkwy; from downtown, take Cleveland Ave south to Colonial

Blvd east until you think you'll run out of gas; the terminal is on the left.

Organized Tours

There's a 'tram' tour (☎ 941-334-7419) that runs a circle around the Murphy-Burroughs Home, Fort Myers Historical Museum, the Imaginarium and its depot at the Ford and Edison Estates. The tours run Tuesday to Saturday 10 am to 4 pm; no tours Sunday or Monday. Tickets are $3 for adults, $2 for children, and include unlimited rides for the day and discounts to the above attractions. They leave from the main entrance to the Edison Estate (see earlier in this section).

The Edison Estate itself is set to begin Caloosahatchee River tours aboard a replica of Edison's very own *Reliance*, an electric launch. It will run between the Fort Myers Yacht Basin and the Edison Estate. Call the estate for more information.

The Lee County Parks & Recreation Department runs four-night, five-day, guided eco-tours (☎ 941-432-2004, 800-733-7935 x10), with local accommodations at hotels and resorts included, in areas throughout southwest Florida and the Everglades. They're very expensive (about $650 per person, double occupancy), though perhaps you can find financial solace in knowing that the money goes to fund nature classes for children and adults at all the Lee County parks. Contact Parks & Recreation for more information.

Page Field, off of Cleveland Ave, just south of downtown Fort Myers, is flight-tour central: Classic Air Ventures (☎ 888-852-9226) operates a restored 1940 WACO UPF-7 open-cockpit biplane (that's right, goggles, leather helmet and all!). They have six different flights from six to 45 minutes in length, and prices range from $50 to $200 for two people. They're open November to April, Thursday to Saturday 10 am to 5 pm.

Classic Flight (☎ 941-824-9464) does similar tours of the area in their 1990-built, 1935-designed, WACO YMF-5 open-cockpit biplane. Their two main rides are a half-hour, 15-mile trip for $50 each and an extended 50-minute, 25-mile flight over the barrier islands for $85 each.

Float above Fort Myers.

And if you're obscenely wealthy or want to act as if you are, take a Balloon Odyssey (☎ 941-458-5750) over the city: a champagne picnic breakfast is $125 per person. Launch locations vary based on weather, so call first.

Special Events

The annual **Edison Festival of Light** (☎ 941-334-2999) takes place in the two weeks preceding Edison's birthday on February 11. There are dozens of mostly free events, block parties with live music and tons of food, high school band concerts, hymn sings, fashion shows and the Thomas A Edison Regional Science and Inventor's Fair, which features more than 400 student finalists from within the southwest Florida school systems. Could be a blast – especially considering how Thomas himself blew up his railroad car/laboratory as a child. The fair culminates in the enormous Parade of Light, the last major nighttime parade in the USA, drawing up to 400,000 spectators. For information, call or write the Edison Festival of Light, 2210 Bay St, Fort Myers, FL 33901.

Another fun event is the Fort Myers Beach annual Sandsculpting Festival, held the first week in November, when sand sculptors from around the country compete for a $3500 prize.

Places to Stay

Most people stay on Fort Myers Beach (see Around Fort Myers later in this chapter), but businesspeople tend to gravitate toward the courthouse-filled downtown area, where there are chain business hotels. There are three Holiday Inns (☎ 800-465-4329), including the ***Holiday Inn Sunspree Resort*** *(☎ 941-334-3434, 2220 W 1st St),* near the Edison and Ford Estates, and at the ***Holiday Inn Select Fort Myers*** *(☎ 941-482-2900, 13501 Bell Tower Drive)* at the airport. The ***Amtel Marina Hotel*** *(☎ 941-337-0300, 800-833-1620, fax 941-334-6835, 2500 Edwards Drive),* near the Murphy-Burroughs Home, and the ***Radisson*** *(☎ 941-936-4300, 800-333-3333, 12635 Cleveland Ave)* are here, too.

There's also a small cluster of motels downtown.

We liked the ***Towne House Motel*** *(☎ 941-334-3743, 2568 1st St),* a few blocks from the Murphy-Burroughs Home. It's got friendly staff and a small pool, and the rooms are pretty clean; singles/doubles are $28/30 in low season, $40/45 in high season.

But the king of downtown motels is ***Ta Ki Ki Motel*** *(☎ 941-334-2135, fax 941-332-1879, 2631 1st St),* right on the river, with a great pool and double rooms with fridge for $67 from December to mid-April, $40 the rest of the year.

There's a very nice new offering between the VCB and downtown. ***Fort Myers Riverwalk Inn*** *(☎ 941-334-2284, 2038 W 1st St)* has pleasant, clean rooms and friendly management; prices for singles/doubles are $39/69 in low season, $89/109 in high season.

Craig and Claire Poe run ***Li-Inn Sleeps B&B*** *(☎ 941-332-2651, fax 941-332-8922, 2135 McGregor Blvd),* a small (five room) smoke-free B&B in a house dating to 1912. It has friendly staff and doubles for $85 from mid-April to February, $95 other times.

Along Cleveland Ave (US Hwy 41), there are some more, somewhat seedier motels.

The *Fort Myers Inn Motel* (☎ 941-936-1959, 3511 Cleveland Ave) has not unfriendly staff and doubles from $39.

Places to Eat

A local favorite, in the Edison-Ford Square shopping center, is the *Oasis Restaurant* (☎ 941-334-1566, 2222 McGregor Blvd), very close to the Edison and Ford Estates. They do a very good breakfast special for $2.50, including eggs, bacon or sausage, homefries, toast and coffee. At lunch, they serve great burgers ($4 to $6), chicken pasta salad ($5.95) and sandwiches ($4 to $6.50).

Downtown Fort Myers has a couple of good, inexpensive restaurants, and some flashier entries.

The *French Connection Café* (☎ 941-332-4443, 2282 1st St) has great service and excellent salads including pasta, Caesar and Greek from $2.20 to $4.50. Big sandwiches or burgers are from $4.75 to $6.95. A killer French onion soup and daily soup specials are $2.35 (with a sandwich or salad it's $6/6.50). Takeout is available.

The *Morgan House* (☎ 941-337-3377, 2207 1st St) is the next step up with weekly specials such as prime rib Wednesdays for $10 or crab cake Thursdays for $9.75, otherwise, main courses run from $12 to $15.

The Veranda (☎ 941-332-2065, 2122 2nd St) wins for ambiance: it's in two beautiful houses that date to 1902 and have such intricate histories, they practically tell the entire story of southwest Florida (see the back of the menu). And considering the quality, it's also a wonderful bargain at lunch (Monday to Friday 11 am to 2:30 pm), with most of the offerings from their dinner menu reduced to main courses under $10. Dinner (Monday to Saturday 5:30 to 10 pm) is a far more serious and formal affair, and it's touted as 'Southwest Florida's most award-winning.' Main courses average $20 to $27, and it does smell wonderful (we didn't eat at those prices!).

We finagled a dinner, though, at *Peter's La Cuisine* (☎ 941-332-2228, 2224 Bay St), the other flashy place, very well known for its excellent continental food and its cool jazz upstairs (see Bars & Clubs below). At lunch, the menu's on the blackboard and the

deals are pretty good: $9.95 gets you a three-course lunch of soup, salad and an entree. But, at dinner, you'd better bring along Weimar Republic quantities of cash and put aside any vegetarian tendencies: among the appetizers is crisp sautéed foie gras with broiled mango and sauce balsamic ($23.95); carpaccio of lamb loin with a chiffonade of mixed greens and toast ($13.95); and grilled quail with angel hair pasta, roasted garlic and Grand Marnier beurre blanc ($13.95). Main courses include Dover sole à la meunière, completed table side (price set daily), roast rack of lamb in a rosemary sauce ($28.95), grilled filet mignon in an eggless bernaise ($26.95), and roasted salmon seasoned with pesto and served in a frothy garlic cream sauce ($24.95). Isn't this why they invented credit cards?

Entertainment

Theater The biggest player in the area is the *Barbara B Mann Performance Hall* (☎ 941-481-4849, 800-440-7469) on the Edison Community College campus, just northwest of the intersection of Summerlin Rd and Cypress Lake Drive. It's host to visiting Broadway productions such as *Grease*, visiting companies such as the St Petersburg (this is by *no* means the Kirov) Ballet, and artists such as James Taylor, Frank Sinatra Jr, and Art Garfunkel. It's also home to classical and pops series from the Southwest Florida Symphony, and there's a Community Concert Series with a diverse range of performances. Tickets are available at the box office or through Ticketmaster.

Right downtown, the beautifully renovated *Arcade Theater* (☎ 941-332-6120, 2267 1st St) is host to ever-increasing numbers of local productions.

The *Foulds Theater* (☎ 941-939-2787), on Royal Palm Square Blvd, south of Colonial Blvd between Summerlin Rd and McGregor Blvd, is home to Theatre Conspiracy, a troupe that bills itself as going 'from the classics to the cutting edge.' Performances look interesting. Shows have included *Goodnight Desdemona, Good Morning Juliet*, which tells the story of a young woman transported back to a combination of *Othello* and

Romeo and Juliet, making a farce of both, and Terrence McNally's *Frankie and Johnny at the Clair de Lune*. Prices vary.

Guess what's playing about a block away at the **Broadway Palm Dinner Theatre** (☎ *941-278-4422, 1380 Colonial Blvd*) at Royal Palm Square? Yup. Shows like *Nunsense, Cabaret* and *Forever Plaid*. Evening performances are Wednesday to Saturday at 8 pm and Sunday at 7 pm; matinees are Wednesday and Sunday at 1:45 pm. They do a buffet-style food service two hours before showtime (6 pm dinner, 11:45 am matinees, 5:30 pm Sunday dinner). Collared shirts and long pants are required for men (women, apparently, can wear what they like). Just a show costs $18; a meal and show combined is $29 for matinees, $31 on Wednesday to Friday and Sunday, and $34 on Saturday.

Bars & Clubs Downtown, the coolest place is the **Liquid Cafe** (☎ *941-461-0444, 2236 1st St*), with a chic setting, good (believe it or not) pies and coffee, and heaps of special events: live music every Saturday and on many a Friday, Verbal Art (poetry, music, etc) on Tuesday at 8:30 pm, cigar-rolling demonstrations, male wet-shorts contests and lots more.

Peter's La Cuisine (☎ *941-332-2228, 2224 Bay St*) does jazz nightly in its upstairs lounge (see Places to Eat above). There's no cover for the house band, the Mambo Blues Brothers, but varying covers when national acts visit. The **Arcade Theater** is about a block away, and you can hit its downstairs bar for pre- and post-theater cocktails.

Check out **Burke's Irish Tavern** (*1420 Dean St*), which is a very popular watering hole; next door is **Pulse** (*1414 Dean St*), which apparently has seen better days.

The **Indigo Room** (☎ *941-332-0014, 2219 Main St*), in Patio de León, is seriously popular and fun. For the local version of an after-hours club, where you BYO booze and pay small 'set up' fees, hit **Hollywood Underground** (☎ *941-433-1313*), way down on US Hwy 41, just south of Gladiolus Drive.

Check out the **Bottom Line Lounge** (☎ *941-337-7292, 3090 Evans Ave*), just north of Winkler Rd; all are welcome, but it's pre-dominantly gay and healthily lesbian. There are bartop dancers every night but Thursday, which is the traditional Sink or Swim night: unlimited draft beer ($5) or well drinks ($10) from 9 pm to closing. Sunday night there are guest strippers, and drag shows take place on Friday.

Spectator Sports

City of Palms Park, 2201 Edison Ave, is the spring-training home of baseball's **Boston Red Sox** (☎ *941-334-4700*). Games are played here during March. The **Minnesota Twins** (☎ *941-768-4270*) play at Lee County Sports Complex; it's just southwest of the intersection of Daniels Parkway and Six Mile Cyprus Parkway. During the regular season, the Fort Myers Miracle play here, which is the Minnesota Twins minor-league-baseball farm team.

Getting There & Away

Air Southwest Florida International Airport (☎ *941-768-1000*) is on Daniels Parkway, east of I-75. It's becoming more important as the southwest section of the state experiences growth, and is currently served by airlines including America West, American (seasonal service), American Trans Air, Canada 3000, Canadian Air, Carnival, Continental, Delta, LTU, Northwest/KLM, TWA, United and US Airways/British Airways.

Bus The Greyhound station (☎ *941-334-1011*) is at 2275 Cleveland Ave. Sample fares (one way/roundtrip) are listed below:

destination	duration	price
Miami	4 to 4½ hours	$20/40
Orlando	5½ to 7½ hours	$28/55
Tampa	2½ to 4½ hours	$20/39

Train Amtrak (☎ *800-872-7245*) has stops throughout the city for daily shuttle buses between Tampa and Fort Myers that pretend to be continuing rail service.

Car & Motorcycle Fort Myers is between I-75 and US Hwy 41 (the Tamiami Trail). It's about 140 miles from Miami and 123 miles from Tampa. Most major car-rental companies have offices at the airport; see the Getting Around chapter for more information.

Buquebus The Buquebus is a proposed high-speed link between the Florida Keys and Fort Myers. As we went to press, it had not started and information was hard to come by. But this promises to be an exciting development as it will significantly reduce the travel time between this area and the Keys, and therefore probably increase visitors from the latter to the former.

Getting Around
Because of the sadistic distances between everything you'll want to see, a car is key. But there is a decent public transport system that can get you around, if slowly. Within downtown and around the main Fort Myers sights, there's a trolley from Tuesday to Saturday (see Organized Tours earlier in this section).

Bus LeeTran (☎ 941-275-8726) buses run throughout Lee County, though not to Sanibel or Captiva Islands, and they take a while (like an hour and a half from downtown Fort Myers to Fort Myers Beach). The main downtown transfer center is at the corner of Monroe Ave and ML King Jr Blvd. Buses are divided by color, and fare is $1, transfers 15¢. From the transfer center, take orange bus No 140 south to Bell Tower (every 20 minutes), where you change for orange bus No 50 (every 45 minutes) to Fort Myers Beach; green bus No 20 runs between the transfer center and the Edison and Ford Estates.

Car & Motorcycle Downtown Fort Myers is about a 40-minute drive from Fort Myers Beach; the main connecting artery is Summerlin Rd (Hwy 869), which dead-ends into Colonial Blvd, an east-west running street. Another main connector between downtown and the beach is McGregor Blvd (Hwy 867), which forks away from Summerlin as it heads into downtown Fort Myers and becomes ML King Jr Blvd after it passes beneath US Hwy 41. Both Summerlin Rd

and McGregor Blvd intersect with San Carlos Blvd, which continues to Fort Myers Beach and south.

Taxi In Fort Myers, taxis cost $2.75 for the first mile, $1.50 for each additional mile. Companies include Yellow Cab (☎ 941-332-1055), Bluebird Taxi (☎ 941-275-8294) and Admiralty Taxi (☎ 941-275-7000).

AROUND FORT MYERS
The natural attractions in the Fort Myers area are some of the best the state has to offer. From the excellent county parks, to shelling on Sanibel and Captiva Islands, to the area's gem – the undeveloped splendor of Cayo Costa Island off Pine Island and the Matlacha Pass Aquatic Preserve – you can spend days in nature, kayaking or canoeing, watching the alligators, dolphins and manatees and really getting away from it all. On Estero Island, Fort Myers Beach manages to be both a party town (at its Times Square section) and a quiet beach resort (farther south near the Outrigger). Many people make this their base for exploring the area.

Lee County Manatee Park
This is the newest Lee County park (☎ 941-432-2004), with a manatee-viewing platform, picnic shelters, guided viewing programs and an 'Eco-Torium' with manatee displays and information. The park is along the Orange River, off of Hwy 80, about 8 miles east of downtown Fort Myers and about 1½ miles east of I-75 exit 25.

The park's hours are 8 am to 5 pm in winter and 8 am to 8 pm in summer. Admission is free, but there's a parking fee of 75¢ per hour to a maximum of $3 daily.

Corkscrew Swamp Sanctuary
Run by the National Audubon Society, Corkscrew Swamp Sanctuary (☎ 941-348-9151) is teeming with wildlife, including alligator, deer and more than 200 species of birds. The swamp is the world's largest subtropical-growth bald-cypress forest, and there's a 2-mile-long boardwalk trail through the center of the action. The preserve is northeast of the city of Bonita

Springs; take I-75 to exit 17 (south of Bonita Springs) and go east on Hwy 846; follow the signs and the jig to the left. It's remote, so bring a lunch.

The sanctuary is open daily: December through April from 7 am to 5 pm, May through November 8 am to 5 pm. Admission is $7 for adults, $5.50 for students, $3.50 for children six to 18. Get a copy of their excellent *Corkscrew Swamp Sanctuary – a Companion Field Guide* ($2), which has trail maps and color illustrations of flora and fauna you'll likely encounter.

Fort Myers Beach

Except for the beach (which is seriously nice), a ton of hotels and condos and a few energetic bars, there isn't much here. But anyone who thinks that the sunsets at Key West are the bee's knees should get a gander at these. A great sunset celebration, and one far more genuine than the circus in Key West, is at the tiki bar at the Outrigger Beach Resort (see Places to Stay below), where the giant horn is blown by a different lounge lizard each night at the moment the sun disappears.

If you want turmoil, head to the **Times Square** area, a party area surrounding the Estero Island side of the Sky Bridge, which connects it to San Carlos Island and the mainland. Otherwise, prepare for broiling yourself in the sun, drinking, parasailing and scootering around.

Orientation & Information Estero Island is about a 40-minute drive southwest from downtown Fort Myers. It's a 7-mile-long sliver of an island; the main drag – actually the *only* drag – is Estero Blvd. Estero Blvd eventually leads across a bridge to Lover's Key State Recreation Area (see Lover's Key later in this section), Bonita Beach and US Hwy 41 – the Tamiami Trail.

The Greater Fort Myers Beach Chamber of Commerce (☎ 941-454-7500, 800-782-9283), 17200 San Carlos Blvd (about a mile north of the Sky Bridge to the beach), has a decent collection of pamphlets, handouts and menus. They can also help with hotel

reservations and provide you with a voluminous list of time-share and rental condos along the beach.

If you need to do laundry, the Mid-Island Laundry and Car Wash (☎ 941-463-7452) is near the Outrigger Beach Resort (see Places to Stay below). The little automatic car wash is right outside the laundry.

Places to Stay Note that there's camping not far south of here at the Koreshan State Historic Site and at Woodsmoke (see Koreshan later in this section). The only campground that's on the beach proper is the friendly *Red Coconut RV Resort & Campground* (☎ 941-463-7200, 3001 Estero Blvd), between Lovers Lane and Donora Blvd. It has sites in four rows on the beach itself, and many more on the 'park' side, across Estero Blvd. Parkside tent sites are $30/44 in low/high season; beach sites are $41 to $52/$47 to $58.

There are some other friendly folks at *San Carlos RV Park* (☎ 941-466-3133, 18701 San Carlos Blvd), right before the bridge between the mainland and San Carlos Island. They have tent and RV/van sites with electricity and water for $23/28 in low/high season. They also rent mobile homes by the week: they're $335/460.

There are hundreds of practically identical small motels in the $30 to $50 range; we stayed at the *Outrigger Beach Resort* (☎ 941-463-3131, 6200 Estero Blvd) to recuperate from a long, long journey and thought it worth the extra expense. Efficiencies in low/high season are $95/120 to $140, deluxe and gulf-front efficiencies are $115/120 to $180. Their beachfront tiki bar has great sunset celebrations.

The *Caribe Beach Resort* (☎ 941-472-1166, 2669 West Gulf Drive) is more secluded and has a small pool and rooms from $64 in low season, $83 in shoulder and $153 in high season.

Several chains are here as well, including the *Best Western Pink Shell Resort* (☎ 941-463-6181, 275 Estero Blvd), which isn't bad at all, *Ramada Beachfront Resort* (☎ 941-463-6158, 1160 Estero Blvd), *Holiday Inn*

Fort Myers Beach (☎ 941-463-5711, 6890 Estero Blvd), and the recently remodeled *Grandview All-Suite Resort (☎ 941-765-4499, 8701 Estero Blvd)*.

Places to Eat There are fewer choices when it comes to food. Off the beach, about a mile and a half back toward Fort Myers, the *Split Rail (☎ 941-466-3400, 17943 San Carlos Blvd)* is a dependable source for breakfast and a weird mix of good Greek, Mexican and American food.

Just by the Sky Bridge, *Düsseldorf's on the Beach (☎ 941-463-5251, 1113 Estero Blvd)* is known more for its beer – more than 100 varieties – and oom-pah-pah atmosphere than for its food. The meals are cheap (for the area) and good: a German sausage sampler or the Kassler Rippchen (smoked pork chop either fried or boiled in sauerkraut), both served with German potato salad, kraut and German bread, are $7.50.

Locals say great things about *Snug Harbor Seafood Restaurant (☎ 941-463-4343)*, also right at the foot of the Sky Bridge, which does main courses such as crab cakes or broiled chicken breast from $11 to $15.

Getting There & Away If you're driving from downtown Fort Myers, take McGregor Blvd to San Carlos Blvd and follow that over the Sky Bridge. From the south on US Hwy 41, turn west on Bonita Beach Rd at the southern end of Bonita Springs.

By bus, take orange bus No 140 south to Bell Tower (every 20 minutes), where you change for orange No 50 (every 45 minutes). The fare is $1, the transfer is 15¢.

Getting Around A tram (25¢, every half hour from around 7 am to around 9 pm) runs between the pier (opposite the Sky Bridge) and Bowditch Point Regional Park at the northwestern end of the island, all the way southeast to Villa Santini Plaza at the 7000 block of Estero Blvd. At Villa Santini Plaza, you can catch a second tram that runs south between Fort Myers Beach and Bonita Beach, past Lover's Key.

Lover's Key State Recreation Area
Lover's Key (☎ 941-597-6196) is a state recreation area between Fort Myers Beach and Bonita Beach that's just emerged from a $5.5 million renovation. There's a wooden walkway and bridge from the parking area across Inner Key out to the Gulf beach at Lover's Key itself. It's quieter than Fort Myers Beach to the north, but that's about it. It's open sunrise to sunset. Admission is $3.25 per carload, $1 for pedestrians and bicyclists. Follow Estero Blvd straight south; the park's on the right. Canoe and kayak rentals are available.

Koreshan State Park
The settlement of the Koreshan Movement is now a state historic site (☎ 941-992-0311) in Koreshan State Park, on the corner of US Hwy 41 at Corkscrew Rd, Estero, with access to the Estero River Canoe Trail. The Koreshans, led by Cyrus R Teed, were a religio-scientific movement that settled in the area in 1893 to build a New Jerusalem (see The Koreshans boxed text).

In 1961, the last four Koreshans donated the group's 305 acres of land to the state of Florida in exchange for a promise to maintain the buildings of the settlement in perpetuity. The last Koreshan died in 1982.

Inside the park stand the remains of the settlement, including the members' cottage, machine shops and the art hall. In winter, rangers conduct campfire programs around the campfire ring, and there are slide programs every week.

The park is open 8 am to sunset every day; admission is $3.25 per carload or $1 for bicyclists and pedestrians.

Mound Key If you're canoeing the Estero River, Mound Key is an interesting destination; it's a mile into Estero Bay from the junction of the river (about 4¼ miles from the Koreshan site). Surrounded by forests of mangroves, the island is almost totally made of mounds of discarded oyster shells left by Calusa Indians who lived in the area. These folks ate a *lot* of oysters: many of the mounds that make up the key (which supported at least a thousand homes) are more than 30 feet high! The area is now a state archaeological site.

On the largest of the mounds was the town of Calos, which researchers think was the capital of the Calusa Indians' region. In 1567, Jesuit missionaries founded the San Antonío de Carlos mission on one of the mounds – the Calusa were not amused and the mission failed.

You can paddle to Mound Key from the Koreshan site; tides are generally calm enough, but check with rangers before you make the trip. Note that it's illegal to remove any of the shells, as this is a working archaeological site.

Koreshan Unity Foundation, Inc Across the street from the Koreshan State Historic Site, the Koreshan Unity Foundation, Inc (☎ 941-992-2184), 8661 Corkscrew Rd (at the corner of US Hwy 41), is a continuation of the original colony preservation society. The foundation no longer offers lectures, but it holds two festivals a year. The first is in April; it's a lunar festival held on the weekend closest to the 11th, the birthday of Annie Ordway, the first president of the Koreshan Unity (1903). The second festival is in October, on the weekend closest to the 18th, the birthdate of Cyrus Teed. The celebrations include musical events and guest speakers on men's and women's roles in society today and at the turn of the 19th century, communitarianism and other topics.

They've recently built a theater on their grounds and are planning concerts and activities in the future; call for what's on when you visit.

Canoeing The Estero River Canoe Trail passes through the northern end of the park, and you can rent canoes here for around $3 an hour or $16 for five or more hours. The canoe trail is about 1½ miles upriver and 1¾ miles downriver to its junction with Estero Bay.

Places to Stay There are 60 tent and RV sites (back-in, not pull-through) in the Koreshan site's *Scrub Oak Camping Area*. There is thick vegetation between the sites for privacy, and each has a picnic table, ground fire ring and hookups for water and electric-

The Koreshans

Inspired by a vision, Cyrus R Teed changed his name to Koresh (Hebrew for Cyrus, 'the anointed of God,' and with no connection to the ill-fated movement led by David Koresh near Waco, Texas). The Koreshans believed, among other things, that while the earth was indeed round, it was concave, not convex; humankind lived inside the earth and viewed the solar system within it. Under this theory (they never argued with the belief that the earth was 25,000 miles in circumference), that would have placed the sun – at the center of the earth – about 4000 miles from the inner crust on which people lived.

While a lot of pseudo-scientific mumbo-jumbo involving the use of a 'Pullman-built rectilineator' was used to explain this theory, the Koreshan Unity Foundation, Inc (see description in text) explains that the religious foundation for the theory was that the universe was God's greatest creation: talk in scientific circles of a 'limitless universe' disturbed the group.

Their religion was based (as is the Shakers') around a God of male and female essences, and adherents practiced community of goods and effort and a restricted form of celibacy. If simply joining the cooperative effort, members could maintain a family; to join the advanced ecclesia, and be allowed to live within the confines of the settlement, members had to impart their personal property and live a celibate life.

ity. Sites are $19.50 with hookups in winter, cheaper in summer. There are hot showers and a washer and dryer ($1 each). If you are camping here, you're allowed unlimited access to the park; day-use guests must leave at sunset. If you plan to arrive after sunset to camp, call the ranger station (see Koreshan State Historic site above) between 8 am and 5 pm to make a reservation. Reservations (accepted up to 11 months in advance with a Visa or MasterCard) are also essential on holiday weekends or when there are scout troops staying.

If they're full up at Koreshan, the nearest commercial camping in the area is *Woodsmoke Camping Resort* (☎ 941-267-3456), but they now take only RVs and pop-ups, for 'about' $35. It's just south of San Carlos Park, about 2 miles north of Estero and 9 miles south of Fort Myers at 19551 S US Hwy 41 (Tamiami Trail).

Getting There & Away The site is on the west side of US Hwy 41 (Tamiami Trail); from I-75, take exit 19, which becomes Corkscrew Rd. Go west 2 miles; the park entrance is on your right – if you hit a fence at the end of the road, you're at a gated subdivision and not the park entrance, so turn around; you've missed it. From Fort Myers Beach, take Estero Blvd south past Bonita Beach and over to US Hwy 41; go north to Corkscrew Rd, then west.

Sanibel & Captiva Islands

The southernmost Gulf barrier islands, Sanibel and Captiva are excellent day trips, though staying in the luxury resorts out here is prohibitively expensive. Everyone's here for the beaches, which are both glorious and one of the western hemisphere's best spots for shelling – as in shelling so good and so diverse that they've even got an enormous shell museum.

Sanibel's also got an eccentric, isolated and very clique-prone populace that can sometimes be haughty toward tourists. But if you can manage to get acquainted with some locals, you'll have an absolutely amazing time – that very eccentricity and clique-ishness make for very interesting conversations if you get into the right circles.

There's also good kayaking and canoeing around the islands and in the JN 'Ding' Darling National Wildlife Refuge.

Orientation & Information Unless you're coming by boat, small plane (there are only two small grass airstrips, both privately owned) or helicopter, there's only one way to get here: the Sanibel Causeway (Hwy 867), which has a $3 toll for cars, $1 for motorcycles. At the end of the causeway, follow Periwinkle Way to its end, at Tarpon Bay Rd (look for the post office), turn right, and then left onto Sanibel-Captiva Rd; the shell museum will be on the left-hand side, and the entrance to 'Ding' Darling Refuge on the right. It seems to take forever and you'll think you've missed it, but you haven't.

The Sanibel Island Chamber of Commerce (☎ 941-472-6374), 1159 Causeway Blvd, hands out pamphlets and information; they also operate a trolley on the island, which runs between the chamber and the South Seas Plantation from December to April.

Bailey Matthews Shell Museum This museum (☎ 941-395-2233, www.coconet.com/ sanibel-captiva/bm_shell.html), 3075 Sanibel-Captiva Rd, is dedicated to just what the name says. It's a serious effort: upstairs is a library (with everything from a *Seashore Coloring Book* to *Synopsis Omnium Methodica Molluscorum Generum*) and a computerized research center with an enormous conchological data bank and a 35-mm slide collection. Downstairs, the main exhibition halls have a huge range of exhibits, including displays on the edible scallops of the world, on the medicinal – and poisonous – properties of mollusks, on shells from around the world – including the Pacific Northwest, Japan, Saudi Arabia and South Africa – and on shells in tribal art. There's also a very neat sculpture – made from shells, of course – called *Horse Racing at a State Fair* by Rolland McMurphy. At the front desk is a basket of shells collected from the island – grab a few on your way out.

SOUTHWEST

The museum's open Tuesday to Sunday 10 am to 4 pm, closed Monday. Admission is $5 for adults, $3 for children eight to 16.

JN 'Ding' Darling National Wildlife Refuge Named for cartoonist Jay Norwood 'Ding' Darling, an environmentalist who helped establish more than 300 sanctuaries across the USA, this wildlife refuge (☎ 941-472-1100, www.iline.com/ddws/ding.htm) is a fascinating area at the northern end of Sanibel Island. Home to a huge variety of fish and wildlife, including alligators, green-backed and night herons, red-shouldered hawks, spotted sandpipers, roseate spoon-bills, pelicans and anhinga, the JN 'Ding' Darling Refuge has canoe trails, a 5-mile wildlife drive (on which you can take a naturalist-narrated tram tour), alligator observation platforms and walking trails. Note that shelling is prohibited here. The best time to visit is low tide, when birds are feeding.

The Wildlife Drive tram tours (☎ 941-472-8900) leave from the parking lot at the visitors center Monday to Thursday, and on Saturday at 10:30 am and 2 pm. On Sunday they leave at 2 pm.

Get interpretive materials at the visitors center, open Saturday to Thursday 9 am to 4 pm, closed Friday. The Wildlife Drive is open to bicycles and pedestrians Saturday to Thursday from sunrise to sunset. Cars are allowed in from 7:30 am. Admission is $5 per carload, $1 per family walking or bicycling.

Canoeing & Kayaking On Captiva Island, just north of the refuge, the 'Tween Waters Marina (☎ 941-472-5161) at the 'Tween Waters Inn rents canoes for $20 for up to two hours and $5 each additional hour, no reservations necessary. It's close enough to the refuge to paddle down from the marina, but ask if you'll be fighting heavy winds or tides, or check the *News-Press* weather section. Even if you stay around the resort, you can zip right across to Buck Key, where there are two canoe trails. They also offer 3½-hour guided kayak tours at Buck Key for $35. The resort is at the southern end of Captiva Island – huge signs are everywhere, you can't miss it.

On the grounds of the refuge, Tarpon Bay Recreation (☎ 941-472-8900), 900 Tarpon Bay Rd on Sanibel Island, rents canoes and kayaks for $20 for two hours, $5 for each

The Sanibel Stoop

There are about 160 varieties of shells on the beaches of Sanibel Island, and though it's so corny it's embarrassing, people around here really *do* refer to the act of bending over to pick them up as the 'Sanibel Stoop.'

We gave it a shot this time, figuring it a good way to get a whole bunch of Christmas presents cheap.

Low tide when we were here was at around 4:30 am, and like troopers, Corinna and I slogged our way out of bed at 3:45 and oozed our way out to the car. We went to the north-westernmost section of Sanibel, at Blind Pass (in our haste, of course, we forgot two rather key components: a flashlight and insect repellent). There's metered parking at the northern end of the bridge, in the lot on the west side of the road.

There were only two other people when we arrived, and as soon as we could see farther than the hands in front of our faces, we stumbled down the rocks and out into the channel.

The first half hour or so was a curse-fest of the 'I can't be*lieve* we listened to these island-tourist-trap-*idiots* telling us to get up in the *middle* of the night because there are *shells* here' variety. But as dawn broke, we started to get luckier. Or maybe it was that we could see. In

additional hour. They offer group trips through the refuge for $20 for adults, $10 for children under 12, or private tours for $35 per person.

Beaches & Shelling The main beaches are Bowman's Beach ($3 parking), Sanibel Lighthouse (75¢ an hour), Turner Beach (free but limited parking) and Gulfside Park (75¢ an hour). You can't go into the wooden **Sanibel Island Lighthouse**, but there's a fishing pier there and parking lots. The East, Middle and West Gulf Drives are the Gulf beach accesses.

Places to Stay Near the lighthouse, *Seahorse Cottages (☎ 941-472-4262, fax 941-395-7606, 1223 Buttonwood Lane)* is a perfectly reasonable option, with a small pool and pleasant rooms from $55 to $125 in summer, $90 to $185 in winter. There's a washer-dryer.

The *Sundial Sanibel Beach Resort (☎ 941-481-3636, 800-237-4184, fax 941-481-4947)*, has condominium apartments right on the beach and seriously good package rates throughout the year, such as three-night family-value vacations from $153 to $345 in summer and $206 to $395 in winter.

The *Captiva Island Inn (☎ 941-395-0882, reservations 941-472-4104, fax 941-472-6804, 11509 Andy Rosse Lane, Captiva)* has cottages in a wonderful setting; one-bedroom cottages are $150/230 in summer/winter, two-bedroom cottages $170/250.

Places to Eat Service in restaurants is universally appalling, and food is okay – just keep it simple – the grilled steak is always better than the bourbon-glazed whatever over pan-fried yadda yadda served with something en papillote.

Loco's Island Grill & Cantina (☎ 941-395-0245, 975 Rabbit Rd) has Mexican food, and live bands stop in now and then. Happy hours are Tuesday to Sunday 4 to 7 pm, and appetizers such as nachos and chili with cheese are $6 to $8, and main courses average about $10. Next door is the *Sanibel Island Comedy Club (☎ 941-472-8833)*, which if you stick around can definitely be worth it. Admission ranges from $10 to $20.

The *Bubble Room (☎ 941-472-5558, 15001 Captiva Drive)* is completely bizarre: packed with memorabilia from the 1930s and '40s, flashing lights, movie photos, bric-a-brac and hoo-has. It's worth a stop even if

The Sanibel Stoop

any event, we came up with boatloads of conch shells, cat's paws, slippers – more shells than we could carry – and felt mildly guilty about the verbal assault we'd imposed on the island's knowledgeable and helpful residents.

The best time to go out for shells is at low tide, preferably low tide in winter, and the best time of all is low tide in winter after a storm. There will invariably be other people out there looking with you, and locals, while sometimes standoffish in restaurants and bars, will cheerfully offer advice and counsel on shell-gathering strategy.

Anything that's dead is yours for the taking, but make certain that nothing's living inside your shell – taking live shells or sand dollars, sea stars or sea urchins is grounds for a $500 fine *and* up to 60 days in jail for the *first offense*. That same penalty applies to any shells taken from the 'Ding' Darling Refuge, where shelling is prohibited. These people are incredibly serious about enforcement, so use your head.

If you're really interested in shelling, the Bailey Shell Museum has tons of pamphlets, and they may still have copies of Joan Scribner's *Shelling Basics*, which describes all the varieties of shells and techniques for collecting, cleaning, preserving and showing them.

SOUTHWEST

you just have a drink – it's totally insane, as is the service. Appetizers ($5 to $8) include she-crab soup (crab and cream) and four large Gulf shrimp in garlic butter; main courses average from $15 to $25. But fill up on appetizers and have a drink or two.

A casual option is *The Lazy Flamingo* (☎ *941-472-6939*), which has a great raw oyster bar – $3.95 a half dozen, $6.95 a bakers' dozen (13). They also have good smoked fish ($4.95) and sandwiches such as mesquite-grilled grouper ($7.95) and grilled chicken breast ($5.95). They have two locations: on Sanibel at 1036 Periwinkle Way and on Captiva at 6520C Pine Ave.

We had a steak at the *Sanibel Steakhouse* (☎ *941-472-5700, 1473 Periwinkle Way*) which was overpriced but good (and here's one place service tried harder). Their sister restaurant *The Jacaranda* (☎ *941-472-1771, 1223 Periwinkle Way*) works hard at being a chic option, with appetizers from $5 to $8.50, meat main courses from $14.95 to $21.95 and seafood averaging $18.

Pine Island & Matlacha

Just north of Captiva Island, the gorgeous barrier islands that surround the pristine Matlacha (pronounced 'mat-la-SHAY') Pass Aquatic Preserve can be explored by kayak and canoe. The preserve, along with the Pine Island Sound Aquatic Preserve, covers 90 sq miles and more than 70 miles of coastline, and it's made up of islands, mangrove swamps, lagoons and bays.

Pine Island, at 17 miles long, is the largest in the area, and while it's officially broken up into several communities, everyone calls the whole thing Pine Island. It's been spared development by its location and by Florida state height and density zoning limits.

The communities include the tiny fishing village of Matlacha, with a permanent population of between 300 and 600; Bokeelia (pronounced 'bow-KEEL-ya'), at the northern tip of Pine Island, which is the commercial fishing center and home of the *Tropic Star* (see Getting There & Away under Cayo Costa State Park, later in this section); and Pine Island Center, the commercial district at the center of the island.

The island was inhabited by Calusa Indians from 300 AD to 1513 AD, when Ponce de León landed here – after which the Indians who weren't killed by soldiers were killed by disease.

Orientation & Information Pine Island is due west of North Fort Myers, and there's no public transportation out to the area. By car, take either US Hwy 41 north to Pine Island Rd (Hwy 78) or I-75 north to exit 26 (Bayshore Rd, which becomes Pine Island Rd). Follow Pine Island Rd west until you get there; you'll pass Matlacha and Little Pine Island.

The volunteers at the Greater Pine Island Chamber of Commerce (☎ 941-283-0888), on Pine Island Rd just east of Matlacha, hand out pamphlets and tourist information Monday to Saturday 10 am to 4 pm. There's a coin laundry next to the Burger Hut (see Places to Eat later in this section).

The Griffin Run strictly on 'island time' (meaning they're open roughly…well, whenever the hell they feel like it), The Griffin (☎ 941-283-0680) is a combination art gallery and restaurant that's a great source of local information. Run by art columnist and serial letter writer John Casey, the gallery shows works by local and regional artists, and the restaurant, run by Maureen, does great lunches for cheap Wednesday to Sunday and dinner by reservation. Even these hours are flexible, so call before you come (Maureen hates surprises) or risk an empty place. If you do call, you can work out a menu and price (dinner for two under $20) with Maureen directly. The gallery is open Wednesday to Sunday noon to 5 pm. Sort of.

Kayaking The absolute best way to see the entire area is through the very friendly folks at Gulf Coast Kayak (☎ 941-283-1125, mgreen@olsusa.com), 4882 NW Pine Island Rd on Little Palm Island, Matlacha. They offer several different tours year round as well as kayak and canoe rentals for self-guided trips. There are lots of trips and special events throughout the year, so call for information.

Canoe and single kayak rentals are $25 for a day; double kayaks are $35. You can take these boats for several days at a time if you want; it's great for camping trips to Cayo Costa State Park (see Cayo Costa Island later in this section). Reservations are recommended.

Places to Stay There are two camping options in the area; *Fort Myers/Pine Island KOA* (☎ 941-283-2415, 800-992-7202) has tent sites for $22.95/27.95 in summer/winter; RV and van sites with full hookups are $27.95/31.95. Kamping Kabins are $39.95 for a one room, $49.95 for a two room, year round. From I-75, take exit 26 and go west on Hwy 78 to the first four-way stop and turn left; the KOA is 5 miles down Stringfellow Rd on the left-hand side.

The other option is at Cayo Costa (see below), but there are also a few motels – some, more on the water than others: The *Bridge Water Inn* (☎ 941-283-2423, 4331 Pine Island Rd) is a way-cool, family-run place in a building built directly on a pier. It has motel rooms and five large efficiencies; the two corner efficiencies have huge sliding-glass doors that look out directly onto the aquatic preserve and the waterfront, and dolphins and manatees swim by regularly. It is as close to a perfect Florida experience as you'll get. Rooms run from $39 to $89 in summer, $49 to $115 in winter, and there's a sandwich shop on the property.

Knolls Court (☎ 941-283-0616, 4755 Pine Island Rd) has efficiencies in summer for $40/50 on the roadside/waterside, in winter for $60/70. All rentals are weekly by arrangement. The heavenly *Beachhouse Motel* (☎ 941-283-4303, 800-348-6306, 7202 Bocilla Lane) has very nice doubles for $70 and its own private pier.

Places to Eat There are a bunch of restaurants within walking distance of the motels, all along Pine Island Rd NW: they are mom & pop operations in Florida cracker decor, with a low tourist tolerance and consistently reliable seafood and burgers.

A stop at *Burger Hut* (☎ 941-283-3993, 4590 Pine Island Rd) should be mandatory if only for the experience: it's a '50s-style diner, with burgers made from meat that's ground fresh every day. It's open daily year round 7:30 am to midnight – Burger Jim, the owner, who cooks and cleans everything personally, hasn't had a day off in 18 years. A quarter-pound hamburger is $2.50; $2.70 with cheese.

The *Matlacha Oyster House* (☎ 941-283-2544, 3930 Pine Island Rd) does seafood specials for lunch and dinner every day: at lunch, grouper fingers are $7.50 and seafood-stuffed flounder is $7.95; at dinner, poached salmon is $13.50 and seafood strudel is $14.50.

Sandy Hook Fish & Rib House (☎ 941-283-0113, 4875 Pine Island Rd) is as good as its name: baby back ribs are $9.50, and combination platters such as grouper and baby back ribs run around $13.95. It has excellent views of the water.

And for entertainment, the best pool table and biggest local hangout is *Mulletville* (☎ 941-283-5151, 4597 Pine Island Rd).

Cayo Costa Island

West of Pine Island and north of Captiva Island, Cayo Costa Island is home to Cayo Costa State Park (☎ 941-964-0375), one of the largest completely undeveloped barrier islands in Florida.

The park offers incredible shelling, swimming, kayaking and canoeing opportunities, and Atlantic bottle-nosed dolphins live in the area and frolic just offshore. This is probably one of the best deals in the state in terms of getting down to the sun and fun of Florida beach life: white sand, sabal palms, gumbo-limbo hammocks, clear water and cheap accommodations.

Bottle-nosed dolphin

The only problems (if you could in any way call them that) are that you have to bring your own food (though cooking and picnic facilities are available) and there are no telephones or hot water in the cabins. Tent camping is $13 per night (no reservations are required), and cabins (reservations required), which have six bunk beds, cost $20 a night for four people, $5 for each additional person. Bring your own linen, utensils and, definitely, insect repellent.

Getting There & Away The island is reachable only by boat. The main dock is on the bay side; rangers run a tram between the island dock and the camping area, or you can walk – it's about a mile from the dock area. Gulf Coast Kayak (☎ 941-283-1125) rents kayaks (see Gulf Coast Kayak earlier in this section) as well as tents and other camping equipment, and they also run guided tours for groups of six or more to the park, which include everything you'll need except a toothbrush and sleeping bag; prices vary depending on length of stay.

The *Tropic Star* (☎ 941-283-0015, fax 941-283-7255) leaves from Knight's Landing in Bokeelia (at the northern tip of Pine Island) every day at 9:30 am for a cruise of the area, including a stop at Cayo Costa (where you can get off and camp) and Cabbage Key Inn (see below). The cruise (or the ferry ride, if that's what you're using it for) costs $25 for adults, $15 for children under 12, roundtrip; if you get off at Cayo Costa and camp, the $25/15 includes your return whenever you get around to coming back. A straight ferry ride to Cayo Costa is $20/12. The pickup at Cayo Costa is at 3 pm, and the boat returns to Knight's Landing at 4 pm.

The other option is a private water taxi; these also leave from Knight's Landing, and boats hold about six people. The cost is generally $15 per person one way, $25 roundtrip, with a minimum of $50 each way; Island Charters (☎ 941-283-2008) runs water taxis right to the Cabbage Key Inn (see below; about 15 minutes) for $15 to $20 per person, or ask the marina for a list of all available boats.

Cabbage Key
Supposedly, Jimmy Buffet's song 'Cheeseburger in Paradise' was inspired by this 100-acre key. The most notable sight here is the main hotel and restaurant.

The long list of luminaries who have stayed at the Cabbage Key Inn (☎ 941-283-2278) is diverse to the point of weirdness; it ranges from Julia Roberts to JFK Jr to Carson-sidekick Ed McMahon to Ernest Hemingway. Built on a Calusa shell-mound, southeast of Cayo Costa, the home was built by writer Mary Rinehart in 1938. The atmosphere is rich-goofy in a '21 Club' sort of way: lots of stuff hanging everywhere and twenty to thirty thousand $1 bills festoon the walls.

The story of the bills – the hotel says – goes like this: in the 1940s, commercial fishermen used to eat here, and when they were feeling fat, they autographed a dollar and stuck it to the wall. When they felt broke, they could always yank one down from the wall and buy themselves a bowl of chowder. Today, many guests do the same (yeah, right).

The *Tropic Star* (see Cayo Costa Island earlier in this section) stops here for lunch on its daily cruise.

The Cabbage Key Inn's menu at lunch is darn reasonable – black beans and rice for $3.95, homemade soup of the day $3.25, burgers $5.75 to $5.95, large salads are $6.95 to $8.95 and the unbelievably popular homemade smoked-salmon appetizer is $5.95 at lunch and at dinner. For a wonderful, romantic dinner, count on spending $100 including wine, appetizers, dinner, dessert and tip. If you're not staying here, you'll have to add in the cost of a water taxi (see Cayo Costa Island).

At dinner, appetizers include marinated char-grilled shrimp, shrimp cocktail ($5.95) or local stone crab for two (market price). Main courses start at $16.95 for Gulf shrimp on angel-hair pasta with scampi sauce, and include blackened grouper or mahi mahi ($18.95) or New York strip steak ($18.95). Key lime pie is $3.95, and they have a whole bunch of specialty drinks at around $5.

Spending a night here, in one of their six rooms or six cottages, is cheaper than we would have thought, but reserve early: rooms are $65, two-bedroom cottages are $145 and a three-bedroom suite is $200. On weekends and holidays, there's a two-night minimum stay required.

Organized Tours
Offering swamp-buggy rides billed as eco-tours (see the Air Boats & Swamp Buggies boxed text in the Everglades chapter for information on swamp buggies and their effect on the environment), Babcock Wilderness Adventures (☎ 941-637-0551, 800-500-5583, www.babcockwilderness.com) runs very popular nature tours through the enormous Crescent B Ranch on the Telegraph Cypress Swamp. Naturalist guides narrate the 90-minute tours, which promise alligators, panther, deer, wild turkey and boar. Reservations are required; the cost is $17.95 for adults, $9.95 for children. The ranch is northeast of North Fort Myers; take I-75 to exit 26 and take Hwy 78 east, then take Hwy 31 north for 6 miles.

SARASOTA
• population 55,000
The largest city between Fort Myers and Tampa-St Petersburg, Sarasota is an affluent but welcoming place with some first-rate attractions, great beaches, good restaurants, lots of live music and one of the best bookstores in the South. It's also circus central: John Ringling made this the winter home of his famous circus, and the Flying Wallendas and the Sarasota Sailor Circus, not to mention the National Circus School of the Performing Arts, are based here today.

Many travelers skip it because it looks too expensive, but appearances can be deceptive. While you can pay as much as you want for luxury around here, you can stay in the area pretty cheaply without too much inconvenience, and there are heaps of restaurants doing great and inexpensive food. The Mote Aquarium is a must-see tourist attraction, as is the Ringling home

and museum – John Ringling's circus may have made him famous, but he also gathered one heckuva fine art collection. And Lido Beach and Longboat Key offer some primo broiling territory along some of the country's finest beaches.

We were wondering why everyone was being so nice to us here: 'Yes, Mr Selby, right away.' 'No, Mrs Selby, but I'd be happy to help you find it.' And then we noticed the signs everywhere: 'Selby Library,' 'Selby Gardens,' 'Selby Gallery,' 'Selby Park.' Sarasota is indeed Selbyville, and we were, for the first time in months, in our element (well, okay, the element of the wealthy Selby family – to which we're not related – that to this day commits random acts of philanthropy throughout the area).

Orientation
The Tamiami Trail (US Hwy 41) zooms north straight as a die from Venice to the southern end of Sarasota, then it zips left near Wood St, follows the southwest curve of downtown and skirts Bay Front Park along the east coast of Sarasota Bay, then slashes northwest toward Tampa. Within town, it's called N Tamiami Trail north of Gulf Stream Ave and S Tamiami Trail south of Bay Front Drive.

Downtown Sarasota is a standard grid layout: streets and roads run east-west, avenues and boulevards run north-south. Downtown is bordered on the north by 10th St, on the south by S Tamiami Trail, on the west by N Tamiami Trail, and on the east by N Washington Blvd (Hwy 301). The main drag downtown is Main St, which runs northeast from Bay Front Park, then due east from Central Ave.

The Ringling Estate, Cars & Music of Yesterday and the airport are north of downtown; Myakka River State Park is southeast of downtown (see Around Sarasota later in this chapter). The beach, St Armand's Key, Mote Marine Laboratory and Pelican Man's Bird Sanctuary are on Lido Key, west of downtown.

The CVB sells copies of the House of Maps' *Street Map of Sarasota* ($2.50).

DOWNTOWN SARASOTA

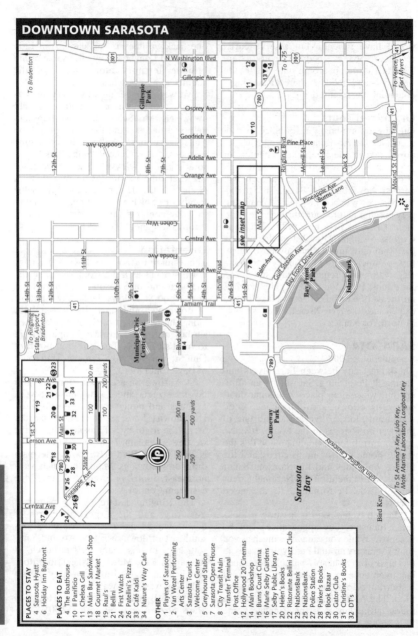

see inset map

PLACES TO STAY
4 Sarasota Hyatt
6 Holiday Inn Bayfront

PLACES TO EAT
10 Il Panificio
13 Chelsea Grill
18 Main Bar Sandwich Shop
19 Gourmet Market
21 Raul's
24 Bellini
26 First Watch
33 Patellini's Pizza
34 Café Kaldi
   Nature's Way Cafe

OTHER
1 Players of Sarasota
2 Van Wezel Performing
   Arts Center
3 Sarasota Tourist
   Welcome Center
5 Greyhound Station
7 Sarasota Opera House
8 City Transit Main
   Transfer Terminal
9 Post Office
12 Hollywood 20 Cinemas
14 Main Bookshop
15 Burns Court Cinema
16 Marie Selby Gardens
17 Selby Public Library
20 Helen's Books
22 Ristorante Bellini Jazz Club
23 NationsBank
25 NationsBank
27 Police Station
28 Parker's Books
29 Book Bazaar
30 Gator Club
31 Christine's Books
32 DT's

SOUTHWEST

Information

Tourist Offices The Sarasota Convention & Visitors Bureau (☎ 941-957-1877, 800-522-9799, www.cvb.sarasota.fl.us) has a Tourist Welcome Center at 655 N Tamiami Trail, and the Sarasota Chamber of Commerce (☎ 941-955-8187) is at 1551 2nd St. Both hand out reams of pamphlets and information on the area's attractions, including *See Sarasota*, which has a slew of hotel and motel coupons and more. For recorded information on music, jazz and film festivals, call the Sarasota ArtsLine (☎ 941-953-4636 x6000).

Money NationsBank has about 10 locations in town; the main office is at 240 S Pineapple Ave, and there are branches at St Armand's, 30 N Blvd of Presidents; and Siesta Key, 1237 Stickney Point Rd. American Express has two offices: one is at Around the World Travel (☎ 941-923-7579), 8383 S US Hwy 41, and the other at Key Travel (☎ 941-388-3975), 540 Ringling Blvd.

Post The main post office is at the corner of Ringling Blvd at Pine Place.

Bookstores Sarasota is good book-hunting country, with several shops on Main St. The Main Bookshop (☎ 941-366-7653), 1962 Main St, is a fantastic place – one of the best in the state – with four floors of new, remaindered and used books, an enormous selection of maps and LP titles, the LP newsletter and a first-rate Florida section. The fourth floor is the bargain section. Have a cup of free coffee and enjoy the very cool atmosphere. There are free poetry readings every Wednesday at 8 pm. It's open every day 9 am to 11 pm.

Other bookstores along Main St include Book Bazaar (☎ 941-366-1373), 1488 Main St, with used and out-of-print books, Christine's Books (☎ 941-365-0586), 1502 Main St, Parker's Books (☎ 941-366-2898, 800-247-2321), 1448 Main St, and Helen's Books & Comic Books Shoppe (☎ 941-955-2989), 1531 Main St.

Libraries The unbelievably fantastic Selby Public Library (☎ 941-316-1181) is in new digs at Five Points Park, 1331 1st St. They've got dozens of free computer terminals hooked into a T-1 Internet connection, very helpful staff and lots of programs for adults and children.

Media The main daily is the *Sarasota Herald-Tribune*, which is owned by the New York Times. *Elipse* has entertainment information. National Public Radio (NPR) is at 89.7 FM from Tampa, but you can still get it at 90.1 FM from Fort Myers here.

Gay & Lesbian We didn't find a community center, but the *Gay & Lesbian Information Line – Sarasota* (☎ 941-923-4636) has information on several matters of interest to gay, lesbian and bisexual travelers. The Sun Coast Cathedral Metropolitan Community Church (☎ 941-484-7068), 3276 E Venice Ave in Venice, holds all-welcome services every Sunday at 11 am.

Laundry We liked the people at the Colonial Laundry Center (☎ 941-366-5852), 290 N Lime Ave. Also try Violet Ray Laundry (☎ 941-954-1348), 2287 Lime Ave.

Toilets All the beaches have public toilets, and there's one at the Main Book Shop (see Bookstores above).

Medical Services The biggest hospital in the area is the Sarasota Memorial Hospital (☎ 941-917-9000), 1700 S Tamiami Trail.

Ringling Estate

The former winter estate of railroad, real estate and circus baron John Ringling and his wife, Mable, is now open as a museum (☎ 941-351-1660, www.ringling.org) at 5401 Bayshore Rd. Ringling and his wife traveled extensively and apparently never came home empty handed: they were avid art collectors, and over the years they built up a collection of works by artists including Cranach, Rubens, Poussin, Hals, Van Dyck and others. Ringling began work on a fine-arts museum in the early 1920s, and it was donated to the state of Florida after his death. You can also take a tour of Ringling's home, Cà d'Zan, and the enormous Circus Museum that was built in Ringling's former garage.

The museum and grounds are open every day except Thanksgiving, Christmas and New Year's Day 10 am to 5:30 pm. Admission to the grounds (including access to the museums and Cà d'Zan) is $9 for adults, $8 for seniors over age 55, Florida students and kids 12 and under free. Admission to the art museum only (not the Circus Museum or Cà d'Zan) is free on Saturday.

John & Mable Ringling Museum of Art

In an enormous and imposing Venetian-Gothic and Italian-Renaissance building, the John & Mable Ringling Museum of Art (1929) has a first-rate collection of 17th-century, late-medieval and Renaissance French, Dutch, Spanish and Baroque paintings, sculptures and tapestries.

The Ringlings opened the museum to the public in 1930 and bequeathed it to the state of Florida in 1936.

It's a wonderful place, and for once we weren't the only people frantically scribbling: dozens of art students make the rounds here regularly. Leave at least two hours to walk through the galleries and the sculpture garden properly.

The 22 galleries run in a horseshoe shape, and the sculpture garden courtyard is in the center. Highlights include several Rubens, including *The Departure of Lot and his family from Sodom* and the massive *The Four Evangelists*; a late-medieval room with several wacky and weird pieces; 16th- and 17th-century Italian rooms, with works by Francesco da Ponte, Bernardo Strozzi and Giovanni Francesco Barbieri's unmissable *The Annunciation*; the 17th-century French room, with Nicolas Poussin's lovely *Ecstasy of St Paul* and Claude Jaquet's pretty intense *Harpsichord* (1652); the large tapestries of the 17th-century Flemish room, especially Justus van Egmont's (designer) and Guillam van Leefdael's (weaver) *The Defeated Pompey Flees from Caesar*; and the Astor rooms, which contain decorative arts, including fans, frames, a Flemish cabinet with scenes from the Old Testament and vases.

There are also rotating exhibits of modern art and the **Asolo Theater**, a horseshoe-shaped, 300-seat theater that was originally built in the castle of Asolo, Italy, in 1798. In 1930, the theater was dismantled piece by piece to clear the way for a movie theater, and it was bought by the museum from a Venetian antique dealer in 1950. Today, it's open only for concerts, films and special events; contact the museum before you come to see if any are on during your visit.

Cà d'Zan Said to be 'House of John' in Venetian dialect, Cà d'Zan (1924-26) was the grand winter home of John and Mable Ringling. It was under renovation when we visited this time. Fronting Sarasota Bay, it's a pretty spectacular combination of Italian and French Renaissance, Baroque, Venetian-Gothic and modern architecture. It's unbelievably lavish; there's a catwalk around the 30-foot-high court, or living room, with very fine tapestries throughout. The house has a ballroom, dining room, and taproom (with vaulted ceilings and stained-glass panels); the ballroom and playroom had their ceilings painted by Willy Pogany, a set designer for the Ziegfeld Follies. Upstairs, following the stairs to your left as you enter the house, is John's bedroom, with an enormous ceiling painting, *Dawn Driving Away the Darkness* by Jacob de Wit. The bathroom contains such necessities as a bathtub hewn from a solid block of Siena marble, which also covers the walls.

You can tour most of the house, but the playroom is closed to the public.

Circus Museum We loved the Circus Museum, which contains the fascinating Barlow Animated Miniature Circus, original circus wagons, the cannon used to blast the Flying Zacchinis into low orbit, and dozens of circus posters and lots of paraphernalia. Narration near the miniature circus is full of interesting tidbits (though the narrator's voice is like a router). Circus fans will be pleased to know that the spirit of the circus is still alive and kicking in this city, though it is no longer the winter home of Ringling

Bros Circus (see Entertainment later in this section).

Selby Gallery

This gallery (☎ 941-351-4614) is at the Ringling School of Art Design (on ML King Jr Way, just east of 2700 N Tamiami Trail), and it runs rotating exhibitions on contemporary and historical art and design-related works. It is open Monday to Saturday 10 am to 4 pm when exhibitions are being held (call to see what's on during your stay), closed Sunday and holidays. Admission is free.

Marie Selby Gardens

The Marie Selby Gardens (☎ 941-366-5730, www.selby.org), 811 S Palm Ave, is an 11-acre botanical garden specializing in orchids (they have more than 6000) but with a wonderful selection of other botanical attractions. There's a hibiscus garden, an area dedicated to cacti and succulents, a tropical display house, cycad collections, a bromeliad display, a bamboo pavilion, a waterfall garden and, our favorite, the tropical food gardens, where everything's edible. There is a bay walk sanctuary here – a boardwalk over red, black and white mangrove (not to be confused with the Sarasota BayWalk, see later in this section).

The gardens are open every day except Christmas 10 am to 5 pm. Admission is $8 for adults, $4 for children six to 11. There are free wheelchairs and strollers available at the ticket office.

Mote Marine Laboratory

One of the USA's premiere organizations for shark study is the Mote Marine Laboratory (☎ 941-388-4441, 800-691-6683, www.mote.org), 1600 Ken Thompson Parkway, just east of the drawbridge between Lido and Longboat Keys. It operates the Mote Aquarium, an educational museum with programs for children and adults.

Volunteers expertly guide you through the museum, where you'll see sea turtles (along with photos of sea turtles hatching), Florida lobsters, skates, nurse sharks (and explanations of cancer research using sharks and skates – see Research at the Mote

---

Research at the Mote

The Mote's biomedical program concentrates primarily on researching the shark's immune system. The researchers are trying to understand the role that the immune system plays in conferring sharks and skates with a natural resistance to diseases, such as cancer, and they hope to use their findings to advance immunology research in humans. Since a shark's skeletal structure is made of cartilage, not bone, it has no bone marrow, which is the source of immune cells in mammals.

Since the program began in 1990, Mote scientists have established the existence of thymus glands in sharks, skates and rays as well as the existence of T-cells (thymus-derived lymphocytes); discoveries which have encouraged researchers looking for clues to human immune systems. Other research programs include work on coastal resources, fisheries and aquaculture, environmental assessment and enhancement, and marine mammals and sea turtles.

The Mote Aquarium is the outreach program run by the laboratory to get the public more involved in its work.

---

boxed text), a lot of shark jaws and a 135,000-gallon shark tank containing bull sharks, barracuda and grouper. There's also a 1000-gallon touch-tank filled with creepy things such as horseshoe crabs. The glass is minimizing – look at the tank from above and everything gets bigger. Other exhibits include cutaways of the Myakka River ecosystem, Florida reef systems and lots of other fish tanks, including sea horses, squid, octopi and fireworms. (Don't tap on the glass: it scares the squid and octopi and they ink, poisoning their water.)

If you're hungry, stop by the small café at the aquarium.

The aquarium is open daily 10 am to 5 pm, except on Easter, Thanksgiving and Christmas. Admission is $8 for adults, $6 for kids four to 17 and $3 for kids under four. There's regular bus service from downtown Sarasota (see Getting Around later in this section).

Goldstein Marine Mammal Center
Included in the price of admission to the Mote is a visit to the Ann and Alfred Goldstein Marine Mammal Center, across the street from the museum just past the boat yard, which is dedicated to research and rehabilitation of marine mammals. In the visitors center, you can watch on the video screens as volunteers and staff work with injured dolphins. The screens also list the mammal's specific ailments and give an assessment of their progress.

Airport Mote Exhibit If you're flying out of the Sarasota-Bradenton airport, check out the fish tank in Airside B, just before the security gate; it contains spadefish, leopard shark, soldier fish and porkfish. It's an interesting diversion before you catch your plane.

Sarasota BayWalk
The Sarasota BayWalk is a series of shell paths and boardwalks circling a series of ponds and jutting against red, black and white mangroves. It's next to the Mote Marine Laboratory, next to the bridge between Lido and Longboat Keys. Though interesting, it's not exactly naturally occurring: the lagoons were excavated by the Sarasota Bay Natural Estuary Program to different depths to attract different animals.

Pelican Man's Bird Sanctuary
The Pelican Man is Dale Shields, and he established this sanctuary (☎ 941-388-4444, www.pelicanman.com) to rehabilitate injured wildlife; it's just east of the Mote Marine Laboratory, on the south side of Ken Thompson Parkway. It's best known for pelicans (90% of all injured pelicans are hurt by fishing line) but all injured animals are helped. Since its inception in 1985 (with a pelican in Shields' bathtub), the sanctuary has grown to the point where it rehabilitates

4000 to 7000 animals a year. To date, they have rehabilitated more than 60,000 animals.

On display here are about 250 rehabilitated birds, including hawks, owls, storks, pelicans and other indigenous area wildlife; they are animals that have gone through the hospital process but for various reasons are non-releasable. The sanctuary has 24 paid staff members who are assisted by 300 volunteers, and the entire organization is run on donations. We urge you to visit; admission is by donation (we recommend $3 to $5 but please give as much as you can); 100% of donations go directly to helping injured animals.

The sanctuary is open every day except Christmas and New Year's 10 am to 5 pm.

St Armand's Circle
John Ringling bought this plot of land on St Armand's Key from Charles St Amand with the intention of developing it into exactly what it is today: an upscale shopping center surrounded by posh residences. Ringling employed circus elephants to help haul timber for the construction of the causeway between the mainland and the key, and the area was opened to the public in 1926. Today, St Armand's Circle (yes, they misspelled St Amand's name for posterity; ☎ 941-388-1554) is a shopping center built on a glorified traffic circle, packed with posh shops and cafés. It's a handy transfer point between buses that head off to the beach (bus No 4) and over to the Mote Aquarium and the Pelican Man's Bird Sanctuary (bus No 18).

Beaches
The area's excellent, white-sand beaches are located on barrier islands to the west of town, including Lido Key and Siesta Key. Beaches on Lido Key include Lido Beach and North and South Lido Beaches; on Siesta Key, there are Turtle, Siesta and Crescent Beaches. Longboat Key, a bit north, is exceptionally lovely. Parking is generally a snap; there are public lots, and there's public transport available from the mainland; see Getting Around, later in this

section, for bus information and driving directions.

Cars & Music of Yesterday

Just south of the airport, Cars & Music of Yesterday (☎ 941-355-6228), 5500 N Tamiami Trail, is an interesting place.

Cars here include a 1905 Rapid Depot Wagon, a '48 Jeepstar, a groovy '68 Volkswagen bus, an '81 DeLorean, a 1932 Auburn speedster and a tiny 1955 Metropolitan, and that most sought-after transporter, a 1976 Plymouth Voyager Van.

The music room opens on the hour and contains hundreds and hundreds of radios, turntables and other noisemakers. The guided tours looked painfully detailed. We watched as one poor victim had to take it alone! The game room is very fun if you're over 40 – these are the arcade games of your childhood, and anyone who's seen the movie *Big* will recognize the swami (25¢). Some games work, some don't, and no signs let you know not to put your quarter in.

The museum's open 9 am to 6 pm every day. Admission is $8.50 for adults, $7.65 for seniors, $5 for kids six to 12, and kids under six or adults over – we *swear* – 89 years are free; a family gets in for $6.75. You can't miss it as you drive north on US Hwy 41: look for the Flintstones' car outside.

Spanish Point

Spanish Point is a museum and archaeological site (☎ 941-966-5214) that crams about 4000 years of history into a 1½-hour, mile-long tour. The 31-acre site contains an Indian burial mound, two 1867 pioneer homesteads (with a reconstructed citrus packing plant), and five formal gardens created when the land was part of the winter estate of a Mrs Parker around 1913.

The new visitors center, at 500 N Tamiami Trail, is open Monday to Saturday 9 am to 5 pm, Sunday noon to 5 pm. The park itself is open Monday to Saturday 10 am to 4 pm (with guided tours at 10:30 am and 2:30 pm) and Sunday noon to 4 pm (guided tours at 12:30 and 2:30 pm). Admission is $5 for adults, $3 for children; on Monday, seniors

pay only $3. On Sunday afternoon there are historical reenactments.

Organized Tours

The Sarasota Bay Explorers (☎ 941-388-4200) operate a Sea Life Encounter Cruise that leaves from the Mote Aquarium daily at 11 am, 1:30 and 4 pm (and an additional tour Tuesday and Thursday at 8:30 am). You'll trawl and pick up and touch sea life such as sponges, sea horses, puffer and cow fish, all under the supervision of state-licensed educators. There's bird watching as well. The tour costs $24/20 for adults/children.

The Explorers also offer guided kayak tours from the Mote to Siesta Key for shelling, with lunch provided, for $65/50.

Places to Stay

It's always cheaper to stay in or just outside of downtown as opposed to on the beaches, but the beach options give good value for the money.

Downtown, the *Sarasota Hyatt* (☎ 941-953-1234, www.hyatt.com, 1000 Blvd of the Arts) has very nice Hyatt-esque rooms from $139 to $154, and great service, but steer clear of the Business Level rooms, which aren't worth the extra money. And right at the bridge with similar prices, the *Holiday Inn Bayfront* (☎ 941-365-1900, 1 Tamiami Trail) has reasonable rooms.

About halfway between the airport and downtown Sarasota on N Tamiami Trail is a spate of motels, including the *Super 8 Motel* (☎ 941-355-9326, 4309 N Tamiami Trail), with predictably Super 8-ish rooms for $39.95 year round.

The *Sunset Terrace Resort* (☎ 941-355-8489, 800-889-4776, 4644 N Tamiami Trail) has studio efficiencies for $34/$45 to $55 in summer/winter, two-room suites are $45/$55 to $65.

We thought the *Cadillac Motel* (☎ 941-355-7108, 4021 N Tamiami Trail) was a fine option, with doubles for $32 in low season, $41 in shoulder periods and $54 in high season; there's a decent pool, and rooms were very clean and smelled fresh.

The friendly, family-run **Sundial Motel** (☎ *941-351-4919, 4108 N Tamiami Trail*) is one of the best deals in town. Rooms run $27.95 in low season, $50 in high season. It's very clean and safe.

For a few dollars more, try the older, but still clean, **Best Western Golden Host Resort** (☎ *941-355-5141, 4675 N Tamiami Trail*), where the rooms are $49 to $54 in summer, $59 to $67 in December and January and $59 to $79 from February to April. Rates include donuts, juice and coffee in the morning. All the rooms have in-room safes, and some have fridges and coffee-makers.

The **Budget Inn** (☎ *941-355-8861, 8110 N Tamiami Trail*), north of the airport, still says that most of their rooms are $45 low, $59 high.

The **Express Inn** (☎ *941-365-0350, 811 S Tamiami Trail*) just south of downtown, seemed friendly enough, with efficiencies from $69 in summer, $89 in winter. There's a laundry room, and free coffee and donuts in the morning. It's popular with business-people.

The new **Wellesley Inn** (☎ *941-366-5128, 1803 N Tamiami Trail*) is nice and spotless, offering lots of amenities such as free local calls, HBO and continental breakfast. Singles/doubles go for $50/60 in low season, $100/110 in high season.

On Longboat Key, the **Sea Club I** (☎ *941-383-2438, 4141 Gulf of Mexico Drive*) is a spotless and very friendly place, with beach-front condos and nice pools. Efficiency apartments run $57 in low season, and up to $93 in high; one-bedrooms run $72 (low) to $109 (high) and villas are $93 to $114.

But the king of the hill in luxury around here is the **Resort at Longboat Key Club** (☎ *941-383-8821, 800-237-8821, fax 941-383-0359, www.longboatkeyclub.com, 301 Gulf of Mexico Drive*) at the southern end of Longboat Key. It's got stunningly deluxe hotel rooms and condos and tons of services. Guest rooms run $115 to $235 in low season, $230 to $370 in high season; club suites $155 to $285/$340 to $475, and there are several more expensive categories to choose from.

The enormous **Harrington House** (☎ *941-778-5444),* on Anna Maria Key, north of

Longboat Key (call for directions), is about what you'd expect from an excellent beach-side B&B: large rooms (some with fireplaces and Jacuzzi-type tubs), good beaches and lots of extras – including kayaks, canoes and bicycles. Many of the rooms have balconies overlooking the water. They have a full hot breakfast that changes daily. Room rates range from $129 in off-season weekdays to $179 to $239 at other times.

Places to Eat

For the most part, you need look no farther than a two-block stretch of Main St for a good place to eat. However, on your way to and from the Ringling Estate, a great place to use up your daily saturated-fat allowance is **Mel's Drive Through** (☎ *941-359-2586, 2030 N Tamiami Trail*). It's easy to spot – the place is shaped like a gigantic ice cream cone: hamburgers or cheeseburgers are $2, cheese fries $1.50, chili and nachos $1.50 and sundaes $2.25. It's open daily 11 am to 11 pm.

The **Gourmet Market** (☎ *941-953-9101, 1469 Main St*) has a great selection of froufrou food at decent prices.

We're thrilled **Patellini's Pizza** (☎ *941-957-6433, 1410 Main St*) is still going strong, with excellent New York-style slices ($1.50) and overstuffed calzones ($4 to $5). We thought this was some of the best pizza in the southwest.

Main Bar Sandwich Shop (☎ *941-955-8733, 1944 Main St*) has been here since 1958; they have a large selection of sand-wiches and salads from $3 to $6.

Raul and Bertha Boeras have been serving up Mexican and Cuban food since 1968 at **Raul's** (☎ *941-955-1844, 1544 1st St*). It's the kind of place in which a dominoes game doesn't look out of place. Very friendly staff and everything's under $9, such as *arroz con pollo*. Some dinner entrees, such as the Cuban-style roast pork, come with bread and salad or soup.

The very good **Il Panificio** (☎ *941-366-5570, 1703 Main St*) bakes *really* good bread. A large focaccia bread (10 to 12 inches) is $6, sandwiches range from $3 to $6 and excel-lent pastries are $2 to $3. Closed Monday.

Web surfing ($6/hour), coffee and pastry is at *Café Kaldi* (☎ 941-366-2326, 1568 Main St), which has a large selection of coffees ($1.50 to $3) and a cozy atmosphere.

C'est la Vie (☎ 941-906-9575, 1553 Main St) is a French bakery and café with really nice French pastries – the place is French yet friendly.

Nature's Way Cafe (☎ 941-954-3131, 1572 Main St) is yet another branch of this good health-food chain: sandwiches are $4.50 to $4.75, salads $2.75 to $5.75, vegetable pasta small/large $3.50/4.95, shakes $1.75 to $2.95.

First Watch (☎ 941-954-1395, 1395 Main St) is a great casual place for breakfast and brunch, with good omelettes from $4.95 to $6.25 and friendly service. It's popular and crowded.

The excellent *Chelsea Grill* (☎ 941-362-0808, 1991 Main St) is a good top-end offering on Main St, with great steaks and a very good wine list. Main courses hover in the mid-$20s.

The Sarasota Hyatt (see Places to Stay above) has a good restaurant and bar and *The Boathouse*, a suprisingly cheap and good snack bar out back.

Entertainment
Performing Arts On the Ringling Estate, the *FSU Center for the Performing Arts* (☎ 941-365-9629, 5555 N Tamiami Trail), is a regional arts theater with plays by their Asolo Theater Company as well as visiting companies. It is host to the annual Asolo Theatre Festival (☎ 941-351-8000), whose 1998 performances included *There's One in Every Marriage*, *Julius Caesar* and *The Sisters Rosenzweig*. Tickets run from $10 to $35 for matinees, $14 to $35 for performances from Tuesday to Thursday and $15 to $35 on Friday and Saturday. Students with ID who show up on the day of the performance may be able to get a $5 ticket. Tours of the center are available (when performances are scheduled) Wednesday to Saturday at 10, 10:30, 11 and 11:30 am.

The *Florida West Coast Symphony* (☎ 941-953-4252) performs classical concerts at two main venues in Sarasota and one in nearby Bradenton. Guest conductors include

David Wroe, Joel Revzen and Eduardo Diazmuñoz, and the orchestra also holds several series, including masterworks (with the full 60-piece orchestra), ensemble performances with the Florida String Quartet, and morning musicales, concerts featuring a variety of ensembles along with coffee and pastries. Tickets range from $8 to $30.

The *Players of Sarasota* (☎ 941-365-2494, 838 N Tamiami Trail), at 9th St, is a highly regarded, nonprofit local theater organization that puts on six performances of well-known plays each year. This year the list included *Carnival* and *Big River*, and *Love Songs at the Boardwalk Cafe*. Tickets run about $20.

The *Sarasota Opera* (☎ 941-953-7030, 61 N Pineapple Ave) has performed during its February to March season in the Sarasota Opera House for 40 years. Tickets run from $10 to $20.

The *Sarasota Concert Band* (☎ 941-955-6600, 777 N Tamiami Trail), with performances from big band to opera, classical to pops, makes its home in the city-run Van Wezel Performing Arts Center, which also hosts visiting theater, dance and musical companies.

Cinemas Check out *Hollywood 20 Cinemas* (☎ 941-365-2000, 1993 Main St), a 20-plex cinema at the eastern end of Main St.

The Sarasota Film Society holds the annual CINE-World Film Festival in November, which shows over 40 of the best international films of the year at the *Burns Court Cinema* (☎ 941-364-8662, www.filmsociety.org, 506 Burns Lane) between Palm and Pineapple Aves south of Ringling Blvd. Write them for a schedule of the upcoming films at the Asolo Center, 5555 N Tamiami Trail, Sarasota, FL 34243.

Circuses Under a big blue-and-white dome top, the *Sarasota Sailor Circus* (☎ 941-361-6350, 2075 Bahia Vista St), east off S Tamiami Trail, is nothing short of wonderful. It's made up of students, ages eight to 18, who attend school in Sarasota County. It's an extracurricular school activity, like after-school football, and you'll see high-flying, tumbling, clowning and a 95-piece band. The $250,000 arena was paid for through donations and gate receipts, and the circus performs during its regular season from late March to the end of school and then tours. It's been to Japan, Alaska and around the USA.

Rehearsals are free and open to the public; they're from October to March in the late afternoons, beginning at about 4:30 pm.

Bars & Live Music There's live music regularly at the *State Theatre* (☎ 727-895-3045, 687 Central Ave), a restored Art Deco theater (1927). There's 'old wave' music on Thursday night.

Ristorante Bellini Jazz Club (☎ 941-365-7380, 1551 Main St) does jazz until midnight and blues after midnight on Monday, Friday and Saturday, and various live acts on Thursday. There's usually no cover. The restaurant is pretty expensive; most people go just for the music.

There's live music every night at the *Gator Club* (☎ 941-366-5969, 1490 Main St). Rhythm & blues happens Monday to Saturday at 9:30 pm and jazz is heard on Sunday at 8 pm. No cover for any of the shows.

DT's (☎ 941-330-1387, 1528 Main St) is a sports bar cum hole in the wall that's good for a boisterous evening.

Café Kaldi (☎ 941-366-2326, 1568 Main St) is an Internet café that occasionally has acoustic guitar (see Places to Eat above).

Getting There & Away

Air The Sarasota-Bradenton International Airport (SRQ; ☎ 941-359-2770) is served by American, Canadian Airlines International, Continental, Delta, Northwest, TWA and US Airways. It's located at 6000 Airport Circle; take N Tamiami Trail north to University Ave (near the Ringling Estate), and then turn right.

Bus The Greyhound station (☎ 941-955-5735) is at 575 N Washington Blvd at 6th St. Sample routes are listed below (prices are one way/roundtrip):

destination	duration	price
Fort Myers	2 hours	$8/16
Miami	7 hours	$34/55
Tampa	2 hours	$13/26

Car & Motorcycle Sarasota is 60 miles south of Tampa and about 75 miles north of Fort Myers. The main roads into town are the Tamiami Trail (US Hwy 41) and I-75. The most direct route from I-75 is exit 39 to Hwy 780 west for about 8 miles; Hwy 780 turns into Fruitville Rd.

The usual suspects rent cars at the airport terminal.

Getting Around

To/From the Airport If you're driving from the airport, take University Pkwy west to US Hwy 41, then south straight into downtown. Bus No 10 runs between the airport and downtown via the Ringling Estate; buses are once an hour Monday to Saturday 6:50 am to 5:50 pm, no service Sunday or major holidays. From the downtown transfer point, buses leave on the same days once an hour 6:15 am to 6:15 pm. By taxi, count on spending about $10 between the airport and downtown, $17 to the beaches.

Bus Sarasota County Area Transit (SCAT; ☎ 941-316-1234) runs buses around the area; the fare is 50¢, no transfers and no service on Sunday. From the main transfer terminal downtown at Fruitville Rd and Lemon Ave, bus Nos 4 and 18 go to St Armand's Key; bus No 4 then goes to south Lido Key and the beach, and bus No 18 goes north on City Island Rd, near the Mote Marine Lab and Pelican Man's Bird Sanctuary, and up to Longboat Key. Bus No 4 leaves downtown at 15 minutes past the hour, bus No 18 at 45 minutes past. Note that the last bus back from the beach leaves south Lido Key at 6:30 pm. Bus No 10 goes between downtown and the Ringling Estate (past Cars & Music of Yesterday) at 15 minutes past the hour – it stops right at the entrance to the Ringling Estate.

Car & Motorcycle Parking's a snap, driving's a breeze, the streets are pretty safe and it's a happy situation for drivers. To get to the beaches, take the John Ringling Causeway (Hwy 789) in front of Golden Gate Point and Bay Front Park west, around St Armand's Circle and then follow Ben Franklin Drive. For the Mote Marine Laboratory and Pelican Sanctuary, turn right off the circle and right again just before the drawbridge to Longboat Key.

Taxi To get a cab, call either Diplomat Taxi (☎ 941-355-5155), Green Cab Taxi (☎ 941-922-6666) or Yellow Cab of Sarasota (☎ 941-955-3341).

AROUND SARASOTA
Myakka River State Park
This state park (☎ 941-361-6511) is a 47-sq-mile wildlife preserve of dense woodlands and prairies about 14 miles from Sarasota. The big draw here is the 70-person airboat ride (rangers say that the airboat, which stays in the upper lake area of the park, does not damage wildlife, but it sure is loud) and a nature tram tour. The airboat rides leave at 10 and 11:30 am and 1 and 2:30 pm (no 2:30 pm tour in summer), and the wildlife tram leaves at 1 and 2:30 pm. The cost for the tours is $7 for adults, $3 for kids five to 12.

There are ranger-led interpretive programs from Thanksgiving to Easter, including courses in beginning birding on Saturday morning, campfire programs Saturday night, and Sunday morning nature walks. You can also canoe along the Myakka River; the park rents canoes for $10 for two hours, $18 for four and $25 for eight.

If you would like to camp, tent and RV/van sites are $16.50/18.64 without/with electricity, and cabins with kitchens and linens are $60.50.

Admission to the park is $2 for one person, $4 for two or more up to eight. To get here from downtown Sarasota, take US Hwy 41 south to Hwy 72 (Clark Rd) and head east for about 14 miles; the park is on the left-hand side of the road, 9 miles east of I-75.

Crowsley Nature Center
Just outside the back gate of the Myakka River State Park, the Crowsley Nature Center (☎ 941-322-1000) is on the grounds of an old Florida homestead. The center offers nature walks, and there are environmentalists on hand to speak about native flora and fauna. You must be on a tour to see the grounds; tours are given at 10 am on Saturday and Sunday only. From Sarasota, take Fruitville Rd east from the interstate for about 11 miles; turn right at the stop sign and in 2½ miles the entrance is on the left-hand side of the road.

VENICE
A quiet, lovely stretch of white sand along the Gulf Coast, Venice happens to be the shark's tooth capital of the state. Shark's teeth have washed up on the shores for centuries due to coastal contours, and finding them is as easy as stepping into the water up to your ankles, reaching over and grabbing a handful of sand after a wave rushes in. If you don't have at least one tooth after 10 minutes, people, even the lifeguards, will make fun of your incompetence as a shark's tooth hunter – they're that plentiful. We found three in 10 minutes but had to leave; on the way out, we saw a kid with a *bag*ful.

In August, the annual Shark's Tooth and Seafood Festival is a beachside party with lots of food, games and tooth hunting. If you're really lazy, you can buy bags of teeth at a bunch of roadside stands and in some tourist shops.

Most people come to the beach for day trips only, but there are some decent motel deals to be had if you decide to stick around for the night. And if you're driving through and like old-fashioned root beer, don't miss stopping at The Frosted Mug (see Places to Eat below).

Air Tours
The Florida Flight Training Center (☎ 941-484-3771), 150 E Airport Ave, offers air tours of the area. Their excellent instructors will take you up for a half-hour flight in a C-152 two-seater or C-172 four-seater for a

bird's-eye view of the area for about $50. If you've got the stomach for it, for $100 you can go up with their aerobatics instructor, who'll flip you silly and safely. And if you really fall for it, an orientation flight in which you take the controls is $50. They're good people – Nick got his pilot's license here.

Places to Stay

The best deal in town – still – is the clinically spotless yet comfortable and welcoming *Gondolier Inn* (☎ 941-488-4417, 340 S Tamiami Trail) – note that this is Business 41, not Hwy 41. Run by a registered nurse with a yen for clean comfort, the place has all new mattresses, separate smoking and nonsmoking buildings (the nonsmoking rooms are nicer) *and* lower prices than the competition: singles/doubles are $36 to $42 in summer, $68 to $78 in winter. Breakfast (two kinds of bagels, three of cereal, juice, coffee, tea and cocoa) is included, and the seventh day is always free. We highly recommend it.

The Gulf Tide Motel (☎ 941-484-9709, 708 Granada Ave) also has very clean rooms, with fridge, stove, coffee machines and cable TV, for $49 to $89 in summer, $89 to $139 in winter.

The Banyan House (☎ 941-484-1385, vnc@gte.net, 519 Harbor Drive S) is a highly pleasant B&B in a spectacular, sprawling old house (1926), with Venice's first swimming pool and the best climbing tree in Florida in its shaded courtyard. Rooms run $89 to $110 depending on the season, and breakfast is 'continental plus' – there's always one main hot dish plus fruit, pastries and whatever Susan's got in store for that morning, all served on china. All rooms have private baths, most have balconies, and there are TVs. There's a common phone downstairs.

Places to Eat

Check out *Uncle B's Coney Dogs* (☎ 941-484-7243, 602 S Tamiami Trail), offering a good breakfast from $1.45 to $4.25. At lunch and dinner, burgers and sandwiches are $2 to $4, and large hot dogs are $1 to $2.

A seriously great bargain is *Mrs Chan's* (☎ 941-483-3737, 391 S Tamiami Trail/Business 41), opposite the Gondolier Inn, which

has a great hot Chinese buffet with about 15 different main courses for $4.89 at lunch and $6.89 at dinner. You can also order from the menu (the food's then a little better) with main courses from $7 to $11.

Sharky's on the Pier (☎ 941-488-1456, 1600 Harbor Dr S), at the Venice Fishing Pier, has a killer location and a fun crowd; their seafood isn't going to rock your world, but it's fresh and there are good burgers. It's a good place for drinks at sunset.

Althea's (☎ 941-484-5187, 220 W Miami Ave) does good salads from $2.25 to $5.75, and has rotating dinner specials from $10 to $12 – their stuffed-mushroom appetizer ($5) is awesome. Vegetable side dishes are always overcooked and yucky but vegetarian main courses, and the service, are good and the atmosphere intimate.

South of Venice, on the way out of town, stop off at the roadside root beer stand, *The Frosted Mug* (☎ 941-497-1611, 1856 S Tamiami Trail). It's been here since 1957 and serves real frosted-mug root beer ($1), and even root beer floats ($2). For the uninitiated, a float is a mug of root beer with a scoop of vanilla ice cream floating on top, and root beer is a traditional American soda that some love and some say tastes like carbonated toothpaste – there's no accounting for taste. Even if you hate root beer, they do an excellent fish sandwich for $4 and a very good veggie burger for $3, along with the standard burgers, fries and dogs. Definitely worth a stop, if just for the ambiance.

Getting There & Away

By car, take US Hwy 41 south from Sarasota for about 25 miles and turn west to the beach (bear right) and Business 41. Parking at the lots there is free. Greyhound has three buses a day between Sarasota and Venice (35 minutes, $7 one way, $13 roundtrip).

TAMPA
• **population 285,000**

Tampa is a city on the rise. At the center of its revitalization is Ybor City, the historic heart of the old cigar industry, which once dominated this town. But Busch Gardens is undeniably a strong draw, as it combines an excellent zoo with some of the best roller coasters you'll ever encounter. Tampa also offers a great hands-on science museum, a wonderful and interesting new aquarium, several high-quality art museums, one of the largest performing-arts centers on the East Coast and the elegant but haunted Tampa Theatre.

History
An Indian fishing village when Hernando de Soto arrived in 1539, Tampa wasn't really settled by Europeans (who drove off and killed – by war or disease – most of the natives) until the late 18th century, and it didn't become a city of consequence until 1855, when Fort Brooke was established here.

Around the turn-of-the-19th century, Cuban cigar makers moved into the area en masse, and over the next 50 years, the city would be known as the Cigar Capital of America. The two men who put Tampa on the cigar-making map were Vicénte Martínez Ybor and Ignacio Haya. In 1885, they moved their considerable cigar factories – Principe de Gales (Prince of Wales) and La Flor de la Sanchez y Haya, respectively – to present-day Ybor City, a section of Tampa. Haya's factory actually opened first, in February 1886, and Ybor's soon after. (Ybor's opening had been delayed due to a strike by factory workers.) The move from Key West – which had until then been the cigar-making capital of the USA for its proximity to Cuba – was precipitated by the strong organization of workers there: the cigar barons decided that moving was the only way to break the union's grip on their factories.

Workers were imported to the new (and un-unionized) factories from Key West and directly from Havana. And as if to send a message to Key West that its cigar-making days were over, a fire broke out there on April 1, 1886, that destroyed several cigar factories, including Ybor's Principe de Gales Key West branch. Ybor City became the largest functioning production facility, and the cigar business never looked back.

Cuban Influx & Martí As the factories drew thousands and thousands of workers – such as cutters and support staff like packers and shipping personnel – Ybor City grew to have the largest concentration of Cubans outside Cuba. These Cubans began organizing into leagues and clubs – notably El Liceo Cubano and La Liga Patriotica Cubana (the Cuban Lyceum and the Cuban Patriotic League). These organizations, and later others like the Ignacio Agramonte Cuban Revolutionary Club, formed the backbone of revolutionary organization through fundraising and propaganda.

José Martí (see José Martí boxed text) became a member of the Patriotic League (there is a statue of him across the street from the Ybor Cigar Factory building today), and stayed in Tampa when not traveling around Florida. In mid-November 1892, agents of the Spanish government attempted to assassinate Martí by poisoning him.

Immigrants & Health Insurance The prosperity of the area was making it attractive to other immigrant groups, and Italians were chief among them. Blacklisted from working in the Cuban factories, the Italians founded their own 'buckeye' factories, in which they manufactured cheap cigars known as cheroots (see any Clint Eastwood film made prior to 1976 for more information).

These Italians, along with Cubans and Spaniards, created mutual aid societies here to provide health care for the workers. In the earliest example of cooperative social health care in the USA, several societies – among them *El Porvenir, El Circulo Cubano* and *L'unione Italiana* – provided medicine and hospitalization to their members.

Other large immigrant groups that migrated to the area included Spanish, Germans and Jews from various countries.

Wars in Cuba & Decline During the Cuban Revolution and the Spanish-American War, Tampa was an important staging area for revolutionaries and troops to Havana, since it had the most developed communication with the island due to the well-established steamship routes that had evolved to supply the area with Cuban tobacco.

Ybor City remained America's cigar-making capital until the Castro Revolution

TAMPA-ST PETERSBURG

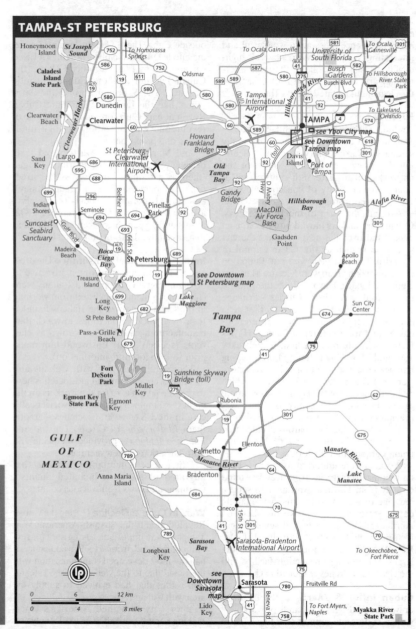

SOUTHWEST

José Martí

Born in Havana, José Martí (1853-95) was exiled to Spain in 1870 for 'opposition to colonial rule.' Eventually, Martí would travel and write extensively in North and South America. His anti-racist writings were vast, and he relentlessly pursued his vision of a free Cuba, stirring up anti-Spanish sentiment wherever he could.

Martí traveled throughout Florida, and while he was allowed to return in 1878 to Cuba, he was quickly booted out again by angry Spanish authorities. In 1895, Martí returned to Cuba to take part in the war for Cuban independence, and was one of the first to die in the conflict.

Martí is considered to be one of Cuba's leading writers and a hero of its independence. The Friends of Martí Park (see later in this section) in Ybor City commemorates the assassination attempt that took place here in 1892.

in 1959 and the resulting US embargo of Cuban products. Over the next three decades, Ybor City and the entire city of Tampa hit the skids; crime increased and the abandoned factories and housing became dangerous and dilapidated.

Tampa Today Tampa's resurgence of late is due in large part to the renovation, rehabilitation and gentrification of historic Ybor City, which was named a National Historic Landmark District in December 1990. More and more residents are pouring into the little community (especially since the Miami area has become so overcrowded), and it currently has a population of about 3000. Ybor City is now the center of Tampa nightlife. But additionally, the presence of Tampa's excellent museums and Busch Gardens, and the popularity of nearby beaches along the Gulf, are turning southwest Florida's oldest city into a prime tourist destination once again.

Orientation

Tampa is criss-crossed by major highways and interstates; US Hwy 41 (the Tamiami Trail) flies straight north through the center of the city. Northeast of Tampa, I-275 breaks off from I-75 as it goes south into downtown, running parallel to US Hwy 41, until it meets up with I-4 – this intersection is lovingly referred to by local motorists as Malfunction Junction. I-4 runs east and then northeast to Orlando and on to meet I-95 on Florida's east coast. I-275 runs west, across the Howard Frankland Bridge over Tampa Bay, south through St Petersburg and on to Sarasota.

The Hillsborough River runs through the western side of the city before cutting across to the east; it runs roughly north-south through downtown.

Downtown Tampa is bordered by I-275 at the north, the Hillsborough River at the west, Garrison Channel at the south and Meridian Ave at the east. Franklin St, in the center of downtown, is a pedestrian zone. Between 6 am and 7 pm, Marion St is closed to all vehicular traffic except buses.

Davis Island, home of Tampa General Hospital, and Harbour Island are situated in Hillsborough Bay, south of downtown.

The best map of the area is the cheapest one you can find, as they're all about the same. Check with the CVB's visitors center (see below) for handout maps, which you can also get at car-rental companies at the airport.

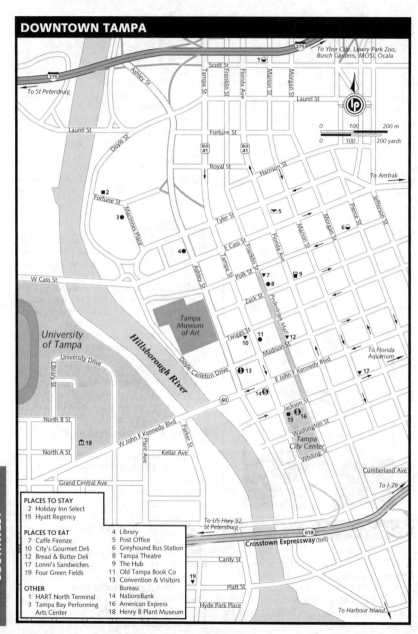

DOWNTOWN TAMPA

PLACES TO STAY
2 Holiday Inn Select
15 Hyatt Regency

PLACES TO EAT
7 Caffe Firenze
10 City's Gourmet Deli
12 Bread & Butter Deli
17 Lonni's Sandwiches
19 Four Green Fields

OTHER
1 HART North Terminal
3 Tampa Bay Performing
   Arts Center
4 Library
5 Post Office
6 Greyhound Bus Station
8 Tampa Theatre
9 The Hub
11 Old Tampa Book Co
13 Convention & Visitors
   Bureau
14 NationsBank
16 American Express
18 Henry B Plant Museum

Information

Tourist Offices Tampa/Hillsborough Convention & Visitors Bureau (☎ 813-223-1111, 800-224-1733, www.gotampa.com), 400 N Tampa Street, Suite 1010, has a wonderful visitors center. The Ybor City Chamber of Commerce (☎ 813-248-3712, www.ybor.org), 1800 E 9th Ave, is a good source of information for the Ybor City historic district.

To find out the weather, call ☎ 813-645-2506.

Money NationsBank has tons of offices, call ☎ 800-299-2265 for the branch nearest you in Tampa; their main office is at 101 E JF Kennedy Blvd. In Ybor City, there's a branch at 1701 E 7th Ave. American Express (☎ 813-273-0310) is at One Tampa City Center.

Post The downtown post office (☎ 813-288-4000) is at 925 N Florida Ave. There's a post office in Ybor City at 1900 E 12th Ave.

Bookstores Old Tampa Book Co (☎ 813-209-2151), 507 N Tampa St, downtown, has a huge selection of used books, with a much smaller collection of remainders. Books for Thought (☎ 813-988-6363), 10910 N 56th St at Whiteway (two blocks south of Fowler Ave), specializes in books by or about African Americans. Tomes and Treasures (☎ 813-251-9368), 408 S Howard Ave, is a gay and lesbian bookstore.

Libraries Tampa's main downtown library (☎ 813-273-3652) is at 900 N Ashley St. In Ybor City, there's a branch library (☎ 813-272-5547) at 1505 Nebraska Ave.

Media The major daily is the *Tampa Tribune*, though the *St Petersburg Times* and the *Miami Herald* are available everywhere as well. Get local news and club/pub/going-out and dining listings in *Weekly Planet*. National Public Radio (NPR) is at 89.7 FM.

Gay & Lesbian The gay and lesbian scene in Tampa is enormous but hard to pin down. The editor of the area's biggest gay news-magazine said things are in a constant state of flux, and we found that many phone numbers even a few years old had been disconnected.

M/C Film Festival (☎ 813-870-6233), 3601 W JF Kennedy Blvd, between Himes Ave and Dale Mabry Hwy is a seriously great resource. On Thursday during spring and summer, they show selections from the Pride Film Festival. They have a 35-foot-long bulletin board with local events and happenings, as well as a coffee and juice bar. There's a bus stop right in front; any bus going west on JF Kennedy Blvd stops here – look for the pink triangles and rainbow signs out front.

There are three main periodicals available around the city: *The Gazette* – a monthly with the most up-to-date and solidly reliable listings of gay, lesbian and bisexual community groups and resource centers – and *Watermark*. *Womyn's Words* is a monthly lesbian newsletter available at M/C Film Festival.

The International Gay & Lesbian Film Festival is held here in the first week of October at the Tampa Theatre (see later in this section).

Laundry We used the Busch Laundromat (☎ 813-932-8145), 1216 Busch Blvd E. But check this one out: Laundromat Express (☎ 813-837-9100) is a coin laundry at Phar Mor Plaza, 4306 Dale Mabry Hwy S, that's open 7 am to midnight and has pool tables (50¢), snacks and beer.

In Ybor City, there's a coin laundry at the corner of 7th Ave and 25th St.

Medical Services The biggest hospital in the area is Tampa General Hospital (☎ 813-251-7000), south of downtown on Davis Island. University Community Hospital is at 3100 E Fletcher Ave.

Museum of Science & Industry (MOSI)

Tampa's absolutely enormous Museum of Science & Industry (☎ 813-987-6000), 4801 E Fowler Ave, is one of the biggest draws around, and it's definitely in contention for the best hands-on science museum in the state.

Downstairs, there are traveling exhibits, a good gift shop and a very cool hot-air balloon exhibit: push the button and hot air fills the little balloon, which zooms skyward on its guidewire.

Upstairs, there are exhibits on electricity and power, and also, one of our favorites, the Energy Pinball machine: turn the giant screw to lift a giant steel ball to the top and send it on its journey through a wire pipe, which sends it through several different routes, each one demonstrating potential, trajectory, momentum or energy transfer. Which is a fancy way of saying that the ball makes an awful racket and resembles a giant Rube Goldberg contraption.

There are exhibitions on the human body and Florida, and, one of Corinna's favorites, one that shows the amount of garbage the average American generates every year.

MOSIMAX is the museum's IMAX cinema.

The museum's open Sunday to Thursday 9 am to 5 pm, Friday and Saturday 9 am to 9 pm. Admission to the museum, which includes admission to one IMAX film, is $13 for adults, $11 for seniors, students and kids 13 to 18, $9 for children two to 12. Admission to MOSIMAX is $7/6/5.

Tampa Museum of Art

This museum (☎ 813-274-8130), 600 N Ashley St, has rotating exhibitions throughout most of its enormous new building, and shows span a wide range – from avant garde to old masters, to sculpture, photography and works by emerging Florida artists.

Their permanent exhibition in the Barbara and Costas Lemonopoulos Gallery has antiques from Greece and Rome, including *Grave Altar of L Caltilius Diadumenus* (circa 160-170 AD), a very impressive collection including miniature vessels, Levantine oil lamps, a large collection of southern Italian vases and theater artifacts, and the ceramic amphora trophy, given to winners of horse races around 540 BC.

The glassed-in Terrace Gallery, overlooking the Hillsborough River, is an incredible backdrop for sculptures, including the chromed steel, metal and glass *Multiple Faces* by Richard Stankiewicz and a very funky and *Untitled* aluminum work by Carol K Brown.

The museum shop is excellent, with a good selection of books, colorful ties, jewelry and T-shirts.

The museum's open Monday to Saturday 10 am to 5 pm (to 9 pm Wednesday), Sunday 1 to 5 pm. Admission is $5 for adults, $4 for seniors and students, $3 for children six to 18. Admission is free Wednesday between 5 and 9 pm and Sunday.

Florida Aquarium

The phenomenal Florida Aquarium (☎ 813-273-4020), at 701 Channelside Drive, has exhibits over three floors that trace how water travels from its source to the open sea.

Take the elevator to the top to start at the beginning, Florida Wetlands, which has some very neat mist-covered water, itty-bitty fish, cool turtles, a limestone cavern and a canopied tree area. You'll see alligator hatchlings in the marshes, and there's a great Wetlands Lab where you can look at small animals. There's a mangrove forest here as well.

In Bays & Beaches, the beach (which is indoors) is complete with dunes, waves, sea oats and live seabirds.

The best is the coral reef, which is in a 500,000-gallon tank with 12-inch-thick walls. It's teeming with colorful coral and thousands of fish, and divers jump in and speak to the open-mouthed crowds via intercom several times a day from 11 am to 3 pm. It's interactive: the audience asks questions of the diver, who swims around pointing out the answers, grabbing sharks and so on – kids love it. There's also an exhibit on ocean drifters, such as moon jellyfish, and plankton under a microscope.

Channelside Drive is northwest of downtown between downtown and Ybor City. From I-4, get off at exit 1 and follow the signs. From downtown, signage is plentiful. Jackson St, heading east, is the quickest route to Channelside Drive. From either starting point, there are large blue and accurate signs pointing the way. The aquarium is open daily 9 am to 5 pm. Prices have come down since last edition, thank you! Admission is $10.95 for adults, $9.95 for seniors and kids 13 to 18, $5.95 for children three to 12; parking is $3. You could rent an audio guide for $1, but we say the exhibits are self-explanatory. They rent wheelchairs and strollers for $2.

Tampa Theatre

The Tampa Theatre (☎ 813-274-8286), 711 Franklin St Mall, is an extremely beautiful, atmospheric movie palace. It was built in 1926 by John Eberson – 1996 was their 70th anniversary – and it was placed on the National Register of Historic Places in 1978. Today it shows independent and classic films, but it also holds concerts and other special events. It's the place that locals bring their out-of-town friends to show off historic Tampa.

There are stars painted onto the ceiling (though no star formations), some of which ('wishing stars') twinkle. All the furniture in the 1446-seat theater is original, and, oh yes, the place is haunted by one Hank Fink, a projectionist here for 25 years who died in the late 1960s. People claim to have seen apparitions, and one story says that a projectionist quit because he heard strange noises in the booth; other staff members have heard creepy things such as keys rattling.

Come early to hear the mighty Wurlitzer organ, which is played before every movie by central Florida theater organ society volunteers; it features sirens, boat horns, cymbals, sleigh bells and other kooky sounds.

The old intercom unit in the back of the theater is neat, as is the Columbus statue on the left side of the stage. Other statues include figures from Greek and Roman mythology.

Admission prices are still the cheapest in town: $5.75 for adults and $3.75 for children, seniors and students.

Henry B Plant Museum

Railroad magnate Henry Plant's Tampa Bay Hotel, which opened in 1891, was one of the most luxurious places imaginable in the early days of the city, when Tampa was about as remote a place as was Miami at the southern tip of the state. All the rooms had private baths and electricity, and the hotel was furnished as extravagantly as possible, with items that included the furniture, sculptures and mirrors Plant's wife had collected during their travels.

After the hotel failed in the early part of the 20th century, the city of Tampa took it over, and today the National Historic Landmark building is open as the Henry B Plant Museum (☎ 813-254-1891), at 401 W JF Kennedy Blvd, across the river from downtown on the University of Tampa campus. You can gawk at the luxury and tour the hotel's grand salon, guest room, solarium and lobby, among others. The museum is open Tuesday to Saturday 10 am to 4 pm, Sunday noon to 4 pm; closed Monday. Admission is $3 donation from adults, $1 from children 12 and under.

The annual Victoria Christmas Stroll takes place from December 1 to 21, and it includes dramatizations of fairy tales by actors in period costume in different rooms of the hotel. Tickets are $6 for adults, $3 for children three to 12.

Lowry Park Zoo

The best exhibit at the Lowry Park Zoo (☎ 813-932-0245, www.lowryparkzoo.com), 7530 North Blvd, is the manatee and aquatic center; when we last visited, they had a 960lb manatee called 'New Bob,' though he may have been set free by now. There's an exhibit on panthers (Corrie and Butch), and alligators and bison can be seen in the Florida wildlife center.

In the Asian domain, you'll see one of only 2000 remaining Indian rhinoceros. There's an 18,000-sq-foot, free-flight aviary and, of course, a petting area in the children's village. The strangest exhibit is that of the naked mole rats – the only mammal known to live in a social structure similar to that of ants and termites (one queen and a few breeding males). They live underground and are native to northeast Africa.

The zoo is open daily 9:30 am to 5 pm. Admission is $7.50 for adults, $6.50 for seniors, $5.50 for children three to 11. Every year around Christmas they hold Illuminations, a night festival; admission is $4 per person, children under two are free. To get to the zoo from downtown, take I-4 west to

I-275 north to exit 31; go west on Fly Ave to North Blvd, turn right, and the entrance is about 200 feet ahead on the left.

Children's Museum of Tampa

This children's museum (☎ 813-935-8441), 7550 North Blvd in Lowry Park (next to the zoo), has rotating, hands-on interactive displays and, outside, a very slick, permanent, 45,000-sq-foot exhibition that kids love: child-size replicas of 24 downtown Tampa buildings. Peddle cars cost $1 every 15 minutes, and Lowry Park has picnic tables.

It's open Monday to Friday 9 am to 4 pm, Saturday 10 am to 5 pm and Sunday 1 to 5 pm. Admission is $4, children under two are free.

Contemporary Art Museum

The University of South Florida's Contemporary Art Museum (☎ 813-974-2849), on the USF campus at 4202 E Fowler Ave, runs six to eight exhibitions of works by university students and alumni. The museum is open Monday to Friday 10 am to 5 pm, Saturday 1 to 4 pm. Admission is free.

Ybor City

Once a dangerous and scary ghost town, Ybor City (pronounced 'EE-bore') is in the middle of a renaissance that rivals that of south Miami Beach. The area is a must-see for its energy and its history (see History earlier in this section).

Ybor City is in the northeast section of Tampa. The main drag is 7th Ave (La Septima), which is closed to vehicles on Friday and Saturday 9 pm to 4 am. The area is roughly bordered by 23rd St at the east, 13th St at the west, Palm Ave (between 10th and 11th Aves) at the north and the railroad tracks along 6th Ave at the south. 14th St is also called Avenida República de Cuba.

Ybor City State Museum Taking up about half a city block, the Ybor City State Museum (☎ 813-247-6323), 1818 9th Ave, is located in the former Ferlita Bakery building. The museum grounds include three reconstructed cigar workers' houses, the original brick ovens from the bakery, and nearby, La Casita, a separate historical museum, 1804 9th Ave.

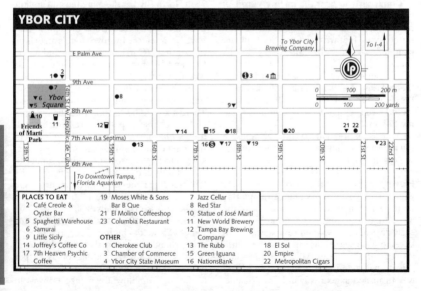

YBOR CITY

PLACES TO EAT
2 Café Creole & Oyster Bar
5 Spaghetti Warehouse
6 Samurai
9 Little Sicily
14 Joffrey's Coffee Co
17 7th Heaven Psychic Coffee
19 Moses White & Sons Bar B Que
21 El Molino Coffeeshop
23 Columbia Restaurant

OTHER
1 Cherokee Club
3 Chamber of Commerce
4 Ybor City State Museum
7 Jazz Cellar
8 Red Star
10 Statue of José Martí
11 New World Brewery
12 Tampa Bay Brewing Company
13 The Rubb
15 Green Iguana
16 NationsBank
18 El Sol
20 Empire
22 Metropolitan Cigars

The Ybor City State Museum has displays of the city's history, including fascinating photographs of the cigar factories and of turn-of-the-19th-century Ybor City. Tours of La Casita (you need a guide to get in) leave every 30 minutes from 10 am to 2:30 pm. The museum is open Tuesday to Saturday 9 am to 5 pm; La Casita is open 10 am to 3 pm. Admission is $1, including the tour.

Ybor Square Between 13th and 14th Sts and 8th and 9th Aves, the Ybor Square (☎ 813-247-4497) is in the former headquarters of the Ybor Martínez Cigar Factory. Today, it's a shopping mall and drinking spot, though with competition from nearby nightclubs, cafés, bars and restaurants, its heyday seems to be passing. You'll see the warehouse (home today to an Italian restaurant), stemmery house and factory. There's a statue of Queen Isabella of Spain on the 2nd floor of the mall to the left of the tour office; the statue was made in the 1880s by Ybor himself, and he dragged it around the world as an advertisement for his Principe de Gales cigars.

Friends of Martí Park The *Parque Amigos de José Martí*, across the street from Ybor Square, contains a white (and not very good) monument to Martí that was dedicated by Martí's son, actor Cesar Romero. This park is at the site of the house of Paulina Pedroso, where Martí stayed after the Spanish government attempted to assassinate him in 1892.

Cigar Shops In this former cigar capital of America, the best cigar shop is Metropolitan (☎ 813-248-3304, 800-607-3304), 2103 E 7th Ave, one of the few in the country to be set up like this: the entire shop is a humidor. They sell Arturo Fuente and Cuesta Rey cigars. Get some excellent cafe Cubano next door at El Molino Coffeeshop – see Places to Eat later in this section.

There's only one place where you can watch cigars being made; Tampa Rico Cigar Co (☎ 813-247-6738, 800-892-3760), in Ybor Square, carries Honduran and Dominican-

Cigar enthusiasts will enjoy Ybor City.

made cigars, and it offers cigar-making demonstrations 11 am to 3 pm daily. The oldest cigar store in Ybor City is El Sol (☎ 813-248-5905), 1728 E 7th Ave, which has been around since 1929. They sell Floridian, Honduran and Dominican cigars.

The most well-known of the Tampa brands is Havatampa, whose mass-marketed Tampa Sweets are available in supermarkets and tobacco shops throughout the state and the country. Their factory is outside Tampa, and they discontinued tours several years ago.

Ybor City Brewing Company Within the former cigar factory of Seidenberg & Co (1894), the Ybor City Brewing Company (☎ 813-242-9222), 2205 N 20th St, is a microbrewery that produces 6000 barrels of beer every year, including their Ybor Gold, Ybor Calusa Wheat, Ybor Brown Ale and Gaspar's Ale. The brews are available throughout Ybor City as well as throughout Florida.

Thirty-minute tours of the brewery (which does not have a restaurant or bar) are given Tuesday to Saturday 11 am to 3 pm on the hour, and they include a look at the brewing and bottling process, a history of the building and a beer tasting (it's not enough to get you drunk). Tours cost $2, $1 of which is donated to restoration projects within Ybor City.

Busch Gardens

The area's biggest theme park, the 335-acre Busch Gardens (☎ 813-987-5171, recorded information 813-987-5082), 10000 McKinley Drive, is an African-themed thrill park with the best roller coasters in the state and one of the state's best zoos, with about 2800 animals – though we wish it was possible to get a little closer, especially to the more exotic ones in the Serengeti Plain. Still, a day at Busch Gardens is, we think, worth the price of admission, though it's more worth it if you get a combination ticket to Busch Gardens/Adventure Island (see later in this section).

The park is open 9:30 am to 6 pm daily. Admission prices are $43.70 for adults, $37.30 for children three to nine; children two and under are free. It's accessible from both I-75 and I-275, both of which have Busch Blvd exits. From I-75 head west at the exit; from I-275 head east. The entrance to the park is on McKinley Drive, which juts north from Busch Blvd.

Orientation & Information The park sprawls northward from the main entrance, which leads to the Moroccan Palace theater. There are about nine main areas, and they are described below in rough walking or transport order. See individual listings below for the easiest way to get to adjacent regions.

Just past the main entrance in Morocco, Guest Relations is to the left, as are toilets and telephones. You'll find toilets throughout the park (they're well signed). If you need baby services, most of the toilets have diaper-changing tables, and there's a nursing area in the Land of the Dragons (see Bird Gardens later in this section). Stroller rentals ($2 to $5) are just to the right of the entrance.

As far as handicapped services, wheelchair rentals ($8, $35 for electric) are also to the right of the entrance, and most rides are ADA compliant – although wheelchairs aren't allowed on some, and they're not allowed on the Skyride. Check with Guest Relations for a brochure describing all the park's restrictions.

First aid is available in the infirmary, next to Das Festhaus in Timbuktu.

Several of the rides have height restrictions, which vary from 42 to 56 inches, and these are noted with the individual rides below. You'll find that lines at Busch Gardens are far, far shorter than at Orlando parks; on a high-season summer day, the wait for Kumba, currently the most popular ride at the park, was about 10 minutes.

As far as getting around the park, in addition to the monorail and Skyride, described under Crown Colony below, there's a train that circles around the Serengeti Plain, across the north of the park, south around Stanleyville, and around Timbuktu with stations at Nairobi, Congo (disembark only) and Stanleyville.

And, of course, you'll never be at a loss for a gift shop, and cafés are dotted around. There's even a bakery in Morocco.

Crown Colony Northeast of Morocco is the Crown Colony, from where you board the monorail, a circular ride over the Serengeti Plain, and the Skyride – a ride across the western edge of Serengeti, past Timbuktu, to the border between Stanleyville and Congo and back. You can use it as an orientation tour or get off at either end.

The Crown Colony House Restaurant is in a Victorian-style building overlooking the Serengeti Plain. In here, you'll also find the highly welcoming Hospitality Center, where you can get a 10oz cup of Anheuser-Busch beer (limit two per person per day, 21 and older). In the Clydesdale Hamlet, you can see the trademark Budweiser Clydesdale horses.

Egypt Adjacent to Crown Colony is Egypt. The star of the show may well be the new star of the park: Montu, the southeast USA's largest inverted steel roller coaster. This is the most unbelievably killer roller coaster we've ever ridden. It's a three-minute ride featuring an 'Immelman,' or inverse, loop – a 104-foot vertical loop that is the world's largest on an inverted coaster. But there are also two more vertical loops at a 45¹/₄° angle. Speeds on the coaster reach 60 mph, and the G-force hits a maximum of 3.85 (minimum height 54 inches).

The other big draw is the pushing-the-bounds-of-political-incorrectness simulator-ride, featuring Martin Short as an Egyptian tour guide. Okay, we thought it was a hoot, as did the Egyptian couple sitting next to us, so we figure it's okay.

Other attractions in Egypt include a replica of King Tutankhamen's tomb, a gigantic wall inscribed with hieroglyphics, and a Sand Dig area, where children can discover Egyptian antiques in the sand.

There are, of course, shopping bazaars and Egyptian-costumed characters roaming around.

Myombe Reserve Also called the Great Ape Domain, this is a 3-acre area landscaped to resemble the western lowlands, where the six gorillas and seven chimpanzees are from. It feels very tropical, complete with waterfalls and piped-in tropical fog. From here a pathway takes you north into Nairobi.

Nairobi This is home to the Animal Nursery, the petting zoo and the Nocturnal Mountain exhibit, which kids adore: noctur-nal animals can be viewed. Other exhibits here include the Show Jumping Hall of Fame, Reptiles, a tortoise display (six Aldabre tortoises) and an elephant display. The Kenya Kanteen serves ice cream and snacks.

Timbuktu This area is home to Scorpion – a 50-mph ride with a 360° loop and 62-foot drop (minimum height 42 inches) – as well as Phoenix, a boat-swing ride (minimum height 48 inches). There are also kiddie rides in this area, as well as – parent alert! – a video-game arcade. The Dolphin Theater stages live entertainment, and Das Festhaus (in Timbuktu?) is an oom-pah-pah restau-rant and entertainment complex, with a shopping bazaar. The infirmary is adjacent to Das Festhaus.

Serengeti Plain The Serengeti Plain lies north of Crown Colony, east of Nairobi and Timbuktu. It's an 80-acre habitat, populated by about 500 animals which can be seen best from the monorail and pretty well from the Skyride and the steam locomotive. But pro-tecting the animals, which include zebras, giraffes, kudus, hippos, lions, camels and buffalo, by giving them free range makes viewing them like this very difficult. The bumpy monorail ride lasts about 15 to 20 minutes. We liked the Skyride much better – it's more peaceful, you can hear the wind and animal sounds, and it's much more natural and relaxed.

Edge of Africa This new attraction allows you to get very up close with animals, some-times nose-to-nose with lions, hyenas, ostrich, zebras, hippos, giraffes, etc. The viewing is similar to that of Myombe Reserve, with glass between the visitor and the animal habitat.

Congo Everyone is trying to get here, to the northwest corner of Busch Gardens, for one reason: Kumba, which is the star of the Congo area and one of the best roller coast-ers you'll find. It's a crazy ride, featuring a diving loop that plunges from a height of 110 feet, a camelback loop (spiraling 360° and creating three seconds of weightlessness) and a 108-foot vertical loop. In addition, there are ducks, dips and swirls around pedestrian walkways and a generally terrify-ing vibe (minimum height 54 inches).

The other roller coaster ride here is the relatively tame (ha!) Python, a double spiral corkscrew that hits speeds of 50 mph (minimum height 48 inches). Rafts take you down the Congo River Rapids (height restriction 39 inches, or at least two years old), but note you *will* get wet: if not from the current splashing against the raft, from the water cannons that line the route. People actually *pay* to shoot water at innocent rafters as they float by.

Claw Island is home to absolutely heart-breakingly beautiful white and yellow Bengal tigers – there are feeding times posted near the fence, and it's gruesomely fascinating to watch these fluffy, elegant creatures ripping into lunch. There are more kiddie rides here, the Ubanga-Banga Bumper Cars and the seasonal (winter) Vivi Restaurant.

Stanleyville South of the Congo and west of Timbuktu lies Stanleyville. It's an African village featuring the Tanganyika Tidal Wave – a boat ride that plunges riders over a 55-foot waterfall (minimum height 48 inches). There's also Stanley Falls, a log-flume ride with a 40-foot drop (46 inches or with guardian).

Shows are presented in the Zambezi Pavilion and the Stanleyville Theater. You can walk through the Orchid Canyon, where there are orangutans and warthogs, the Stanleyville Smokehouse and the Bazaar Café.

Bird Gardens Originally, the park began here at Bird Gardens, which was a minor detour from the main action at the Anheuser-Busch Brewery tour: you'd guzzle some free beer and walk outside to see the birds. It was from this area that the attraction grew into what it is today. The brewery got shut down and was destroyed a few years ago. Built on the old brewery site is Gwazi, a double, wooden roller coaster that's the largest in the southeast – it opened in June, 1999.

The first area you enter is Land of the Dragons, an interactive children's area. It's an enchanted forest filled with colorful dragons, starring one called Dumphrey who romps around with the kids. There is a three-story-tall tree house to climb around in, slides, a Ferris wheel, a flume ride and a waterfall and dragon carousel (kids' rides have 56-inch height restriction). There's a nursing area here as well.

Other attractions within Bird Gardens include exotic birds and birds of prey, which can be seen in the lush, walk-through aviary. Bird shows are staged at the Bird Show Theater, and flamingos and pelicans abound. The koala habitat has Australian animals, including Queensland koalas.

Shows & Performances There are themed shows and performances several times daily, and these change often; check at Guest Relations or the ticket window for the day's shows and activities. Craft demonstrations and live entertainment take place in the Marrakesh Theater, the Tangiers Theater and the Moroccan Palace. Various animal acts occur all over, including shows starring alligators (Morocco), elephants and tortoises (Nairobi), orangutans and warthogs (Stanleyville) and tigers (Congo).

Adventure Island

Adventure Island (☎ 813-987-5600), 10001 McKinley Drive, is a water park that's also run by Anheuser-Busch. This 36-acre complex has 17 areas, and it's adjacent to Busch Gardens (see Busch Gardens, earlier in this section, for directions).

The newest attraction is Key West Rapids, on which rafters go down a six-story twist, ending in a 60-foot-long pool. Other slide rides include the Aruba Tuba (portions are in total darkness, others in daylight) and Rambling Bayou, where you go through weather 'effect' areas (parts are foggy, others have heavy rain). There's also a 9000-sq-foot swimming pool with waterfalls, diving platforms and translucent tube slides. And don't forget the 76-foot, free-fall body slide, Tampa Typhoon.

Admission is $18.95 for adults, $16.95 for children three to nine. Parking is $2. A combination ticket of Busch Gardens and Adventure Island is $48.50 for adults and $42.50 for children; you get one day at each park.

Activities

Canoeing The least-expensive canoeing in the area is at Clearwater Beach, where hostel guests can do it free, but closest to Tampa there's great and inexpensive canoeing at Hillsborough River State Park (see Around Tampa later in this chapter).

Bicycling Call Tampa Bay Bicycle Sport (☎ 813-938-5691) or the University of South Florida Bicycle Shop (☎ 813-974-3193) for information on events, meets, races or riding groups during your stay. Many Tampa Bay city buses have bicycle racks (see Getting Around later in this section).

Ice-Skating Town and Country Skateworld (☎ 813-884-7688), 7510 Paula Drive, one block north of Hillsborough Ave, is open year round and has afternoon and evening sessions from Tuesday to Saturday (call for specific times, as the schedule is a bit bizarre). Admission is $4 for afternoon sessions, $8 for evening sessions. Rental is included, unless you want speed skates ($2.50). From downtown, take I-275 south to the Veteran's Expressway (Tampa International Airport exit off the interstate). Take the Veteran's to Hillsborough Ave. Head west on Hillsborough to Hanley Rd (about 2 miles). Turn right on Hanley Rd; the rink is one block down on Hanley on the left side of the street.

Paintball Wanna shoot your traveling companion? Thunderbay Paintball (☎ 813-538-9946) has a field open Saturday and Sunday 9 am to 4 pm where you can blast away at each other with paint-shooting pellet rifles and handguns. You wear goggles, pads and splat suits, and sign waivers – prices change, call for information and directions to the field.

Cruises Carnival Cruise Lines (☎ 800-438-6744) runs cruises from the Port of Tampa aboard the *Sensation* to New Orleans, the Caribbean and Cozumel, Mexico, leaving every Sunday. Their *Tropicale* sails on four- and five-day cruises to Key West, the western Caribbean and Grand Cayman Islands, Cozumel and other destinations.

Holland America Cruise Line (☎ 206-281-3535) runs the *Noordham* from the Port of Tampa to Key West, Playa del Carmen, Georgetown, Ocho Rios, Cozumel and the western Caribbean every Saturday.

Organized Tours
The Big Red Balloon (☎ 813-969-1518), 16302 E Course Drive, in the city of Northdale, does one-hour balloon tours at sunrise – every day, weather permitting – for

$150 per person, with a champagne brunch after the flight. The central meeting point is at Dale Mabry Hwy and N Dale Blvd. Reserve about a week ahead on weekends, about a day or two ahead on weekdays.

First Class Gray Lines (☎ 813-535-0208) does trips from Tampa to Walt Disney World, SeaWorld, and other locations in Florida; rates are impossible to summarize (but generally not bad deals if you don't have a car), so call for more information.

Ybor City Ghost Walk (☎ 813-242-9255) runs scheduled tours throughout the city, hosted by an actor in period costume, and telling the tales of Ybor City past. They leave from Joffrey's Coffee Co (see Places to Eat later) Thursday to Saturday at 7 pm and Sunday at 4 pm. Reservations are recommended (the tours can be canceled for lack of interest). The price is $12.50 for adults, $7.50 per child (though you can get a $2 discount for reserving early).

Places to Stay
Unfortunately, there are no hostels in Tampa proper, but there's a great one in Clearwater Beach and a somewhat creepy one in St Petersburg – see those sections for information. Both are easily accessible by car.

There's a surprising lack of mid-range hotels in Tampa other than the chains, all of which are represented; most of the more inexpensive options are near Busch Gardens. There are no hotels in Ybor City yet, though the chamber of commerce is trying.

Camping There's cheap and good camping at Hillsborough River State Park (see Around Tampa later in this chapter).

The enormous *Tampa East Green Acres RV Travel Park* (☎ 813-659-0002, 800-454-7336, www.gogreenacres.com, 12720 Hwy 92) is a superstore RV park campground, with three properties. Tent sites (at *Tampa East Green Acres Campground*) are $23 year round; cottages, with a double bed and two bunk beds but no sheets are $41.

Green Acres Travel Park RV sites are $23/31 without/with full hookups in high season, $19/26 in low season.

All these mostly cater to the tourist traveling along I-4 and winter snowbirds. From I-75, take the I-4 exit east 3 miles to exit 9 (McIntosh Rd), turn right (south) and drive 1/8 mile to the entrance of the Travel Park, or continue south to Hwy 92, turn right and drive for about a quarter-mile to the campground entrance.

Hotels There are really two main choices downtown: the enormous *Hyatt Regency Tampa* (☎ *813-225-1234, 800-233-1234, 2 Tampa City Center*) with rooms running $169 to $185, and the *Holiday Inn Select Downtown Tampa* (☎ *813-223-1351, 800-275-8258, 111 W Fortune St*) behind the Tampa Bay Performing Arts Center, with rooms from $105.

Economy Inn Express (☎ *813-253-0851, 830 W JF Kennedy Blvd*), close to the University of Tampa and the Henry B Plant museum, is very clean, and rooms in low/

high season are $40 to $45/$45 to $50. HBO is free.

Near the airport, and all offering courtesy shuttle buses to the airport, are *Amerisuites Airport* (☎ *813-282-1037, 800-833-1516, 4811 W Main St*), with suites from $79 to $109; *Embassy Suites Tampa Airport/Westshore* (☎ *813-875-1555, 555 N Westshore Blvd*), with suites from $99 to $179; *Double Tree Hotel Airport/Westshore* (☎ *813-879-4800, 800-222-8733, 4500 W Cypress St*), with rooms from $79 to $179; *Tampa Airport Marriott* (☎ *813-879-5151, 800-228-9290*) right in the airport itself, with rooms from $79 to $225; *Ramada Inn Airport & Conference Center* (☎ *813-289-1950, 800-353-9536, 5303 W JF Kennedy Blvd*); and *Crown Plaza Tampa Westshore* (☎ *813-289-8200, 700 N Westshore Blvd*), with rooms from $89 to $189.

Near Busch Gardens and the University of South Florida, you'll find the most options (see the Family Value boxed text). Hotels here include *Holiday Inn* (☎ *813-971-4710, 2701 E Fowler Ave*), with rooms at $79 to $100; a nicely renovated *Motel 6 Busch Gardens* (☎ *813-932-4948, 333 E Fowler Ave*), with standard Motel 6 singles/doubles at $40/44; and *Scottish Inn* (☎ *813-933-7831, 11414 N Central Ave*) – along with a bunch of chain restaurants such as Red Lobster, Chili's and TGI Fridays, and chain stores such as Sports Authority, Circuit City and Pier 1 Imports.

Along Busch Blvd (Hwy 580), you'll find a slew of cheap but decent options. The clean and nice *Friendship Inn* (☎ *813-933-3958, 2500 E Busch Blvd*) has singles/doubles for $35/45 in low season, $45/55 in high season; during special events rooms are $75. There's a pool, laundry and free coffee.

The *Red Roof Inn Tampa Busch* (☎ *813-932-0073, 2307 Busch Blvd*) has singles and doubles for $39; during high season, they're $65.99. It has a pool and free coffee, local phone calls and *USA Today* daily.

The newly renovated *Budget Inn* (☎ *813-932-3997, 2001 E Busch Blvd*) has rooms for $35 during the week and $45 on weekends (single or double); during special events and in high season, the rate goes up to $55.

Family Value

Five or so cheers for the *Quality Suites USF Busch Gardens* (☎ *813-971-8930, 800-786-7446, 3001 University Center Drive*), which has excellent rooms, a nice pool, friendly, helpful and attentive staff and enough perks to make staying in a hotel fun even for the most grizzled of families or business travelers and the most cranky of guidebook writers. Everyone we spoke with here was happy, and why not? Rooms range from $109 to $139 depending on when you come, and all have at the very least two TVs, a refrigerator, a microwave, VCR, a boom box, and a bedroom and living room. Breakfast is an all-you-can-eat hot buffet that includes eggs, hash browns, grits, biscuits, bacon, sausage, muffins, cereal, juices, coffee and tea. They also give out free beer and wine from 4 to 7 pm every day – and that's not a typo! It's at 30th St and Bougainvillea (less than a mile from Busch Gardens).

Efficiencies are $5 more. Breakfast of coffee, juice and donuts is free, and they have a pool.

Places to Eat

Ybor City is really the place to head if you want an interesting meal. If you're downtown, you'll find more standard lunch places. But if you want a meal to remember, reserve a table at Bern's Steak House (see boxed text). For culinary festivals and special events, check out *Weekly Planet*.

In Ybor City, a good branch of *Joffrey's Coffee Co* (☎ 813-248-5282, 1616 E 7th Ave), has good croissant and bagel sandwiches ($4) and lots of coffee and tea, cakes and pastry. It's a nonsmoking place.

Keep your hands and feet clear of your mouths as you attempt to shovel in heroic quantities of the best barbecue sauce in the state at *Moses White & Sons Bar B Que* (☎ 813-247-7544, 1815 E 7th Ave), with a real oak-fired pit and platters (half a chicken or ribs) with two side orders for $6.75, and a half slab o' ribs for $9.75.

Also good is *Ybor City's B-Man's BBQ* (☎ 813-247-1966, 1604 N 17th Street), in the shack. Grab a chicken dinner with two sides and bread for $4.50 (!!); a ribs dinner is $7, half a slab of ribs is $8, a full slab $16. They have draft beer for $2.

Little Sicily (☎ 813-248-2940, 1724 E 8th Ave), is a great Italian-style deli with a few small outside tables. Huge sandwiches are from $2.89 to $5.79, good calzone is $3.99, ziti is $2.99, and, again, very friendly service.

El Molino Coffeeshop (☎ 813-248-2521, 2012 E 7th Ave) is a serious Cuban coffee place, none of that yuppie pansy stuff, just pure zoom juice, and $1 knock-yer-socks-off café con leche.

We asked the folks at *7th Heaven Psychic Coffee* (☎ 812-242-0400, 1725 E 7th St) why we wanted their prices and they couldn't tell us. Now that doesn't mean their readings ($20) are anything but on the up and up, but you can also play cards here or try your own hand at tarot – it's a fun place.

Cephas Gilbert, who showed up in America in 1982 with $37 in his pocket, now runs *Cephas* (☎ 813-247-9022, 1701 E 4th Ave), a piece of Jamaica in Ybor City. It may look a little rundown when you enter, but check out the back garden: it's lush, jungly and very Jamaican. Service is very friendly – note the sign outside that says 'respect due whether you're black or white' – and a huge plate of jerk chicken wings, curry goat chicken, brown stew, fish or vegetables (which Cephas says he grows himself) is $7.75. They also serve Red Stripe and Royal Stout beers ($2.50).

Spaghetti Warehouse (☎ 813-248-1720, 1911 N 13th St) has serviceable Italian, with everything under $10. Cool atmosphere in the renovated warehouse behind Ybor Square, with tables inside and outside.

Opposite, *Samurai* (☎ 813-248-5829, 1901 N 13th St) does great and cheap lunch specials: their Samurai Lunch includes hibachi chicken and sukiyaki ($6.95). Prices go up at dinner, but they have good sushi.

Said to be the oldest restaurant in Florida, the *Columbia Restaurant* (☎ 813-248-4961, 2117 E 7th Ave) is a gaudy, glitzy place that most people peg right away as a tourist trap. That aside, the interior is gorgeous, with a fountain at the center, but we were unimpressed with the lunch we had (set prices from $5.95 to $8.95 for dishes such as quesadillas, grouper and sautéed shrimp), though the salads were excellent. To be fair, we didn't come back for dinner, which is said to be better.

Probably the nicest place to eat in Ybor City in terms of atmosphere, *Café Creole & Oyster Bar* (☎ 813-247-6283, 1330 E 9th Ave), in the renovated El Pasaje Plaza, is a very chic and yuppified place with good beef and chicken dishes, though we were totally disappointed by the fish dishes, which we felt were disastrous. Service was very good, and they have an impressive wine list and desserts. Expect to pay about $7 to $10 for lunch and $25 per person at dinner with a drink and tip. It has live jazz on Friday and Saturday nights.

In downtown Tampa, there are three great sandwich places. *City's Gourmet Deli* (☎ 813-229-7400, 514 Tampa St) is incredibly good, with dozens of choices and the ability to mix and match; all their sandwiches are $4 to $6 and heaped with stuff.

SOUTHWEST

Bern's Steak House

This steak house (☎ 813-251-2421, 1208 S Howard Ave) is Tampa's landmark restaurant if ever there was one. The clever owner figured that allowing guests to linger after their meal over dessert and coffee meant keeping other warm (paying) bodies waiting outside, so he came up with the ingenious idea of forcing diners to get up and *move* to a separate room upstairs for dessert – and that's even touted as a special feature! Bern says he also wanted guests to be able to enjoy a cigar over dessert and coffee without provoking gunplay. Both the cigar-friendly dessert room and the main dining room are very slick places, and the steaks, as they say, are some of the best east of the west and north of the south.

Downstairs the atmosphere is heavy on red velvet, gold leaf and statuary; upstairs the dessert tables are made from redwood wine casks.

Their wine list has more than 7000 labels and 1800 dessert wines, and their cellars hold between half a million and a million bottles of wine from all over the world – predominantly American, French and Italian, but with a good representation of South American, Aussie and Chilean. But, if you're broke, there's always the Romanian section (blech).

Bern's weekly wine tasting from noon to 3 pm on Sunday has become a mecca for wine lovers; the cost is $5, which can go toward any purchase, and all the wines you taste that day are 10% off. Smashing. Can't pronounce Shiraz? Bern's sommelier, Ken Collura, holds wine tasting and appreciation classes Monday 6:30 to 8:30 pm at Side Bern's (see Places to Eat) for $20 – for more information, call ☎ 813-250-9463.

Steaks start from $20 and go right on up to a 60oz strip sirloin that serves six for $175.

The restaurant is open for dinner only. Reserve in advance – especially on weekends – as sometimes it's so full that they can't accommodate walk-ins in the dessert room (you can, by the way, come here just for dessert), where dinner guests have priority on seating.

Upstairs in the dessert room, prices range from a $3 scoop of vanilla ice cream to $17 flaming desserts such as cherries jubilee, baked Alaska, and bananas Foster.

Howard Ave is in the Hyde Park area of Tampa. It runs parallel to Armenia St, but each runs one way, so take Bayshore Blvd from downtown to Howard Ave, and then turn right on Howard. Bern's will be on your right.

The second is **Lonni's Sandwiches** (☎ 813-223-2333, 513 E Jackson St), swarming with workers from the county center building across the street, who are here for enormous, cheap and creative sandwiches, with Cuban, American and sometimes Asian blends.

And the third great place is the **Bread & Butter Deli** (☎ 813-301-0505, 507 N Franklin St), a Greek-run deli with amazing homemade soups and huge sandwiches.

Four Green Fields (☎ 813-254-4444, 205 W Platt St), on the edge of downtown, looks like a traditional Irish cottage (with, yes, a thatched roof), and it has Irish cooking, Irish music and, of course, Irish drinks including 30-weight Guinness. Mmmm. Guinness makes you fat.

The Italian-owned **Caffe Firenze** (☎ 813-228-9200, 719 N Franklin St), right near the Tampa Theatre, does very nice and chic Italian lunches and dinners. Lunch for two will run $25; at dinner, count on $25 a person with wine.

Side Bern's (☎ 813-258-2233, 1002 S Howard Ave) is the Bern's Steak House (see boxed text) spin-off, with desserts straight from the dessert room at Bern's and also featuring snacks and light meals, such as Bern's steak sandwich. The place is basically a cigar-wine-dessert bar to handle the overflow from the main restaurant.

In the Busch Gardens area, serious hot dogs abound at *Mel's Hot Dogs* (☎ *813-985-8000, 4136 E Busch Blvd*), all made by the Chicago Vienna Beef Company – the mainstay is the Mighty Mel Hot Dog ($2.39), a flabbergastingly large dog with relish, mustard and pickles on a poppy-seed bun.

Ruzik's Roost (☎ *941-971-8930, 3001 University Center Drive*), at 30th St and Bougainvillea, inside the Quality Suites USF Busch Gardens, is an interesting place, with (un)healthy portions of ribs, burgers and fries, all under $10. It's mainly for guests of the hotel, but some locals have been stopping in lately too. Maybe to look at all those weird plaques.

Taj (☎ *813-971-8483, 2734-B E Fowler Ave*) serves good Indian food. It has an all-you-can-eat $6.95 buffet Tuesday to Friday 11:30 am to 2:30 pm, Saturday and Sunday till 3 pm. Dinner is 5 to 10 pm. They have a fairly large vegetarian selection from $6.50 to $9.50; other dishes range from $9.95 to $15.95. It can get very crowded.

Nearby, *Lucy Ho's* (☎ *813-977-2783, 2740 E Fowler Ave*) serves good Asian/Chinese food, and even with a smile; Friday and Saturday, its all-you-can-eat lunch buffet is $5.95, and dinner specials are $10.95. At other times, main vegetarian courses are $5.75 to $6.95, and meat dishes range from $7.95 to $8.95. There are lots of chicken dishes; try the garlic chicken ($7.95) or Phoenix and Dragon ($8.95) – chicken breast with shrimp, garlic, ginger, green onion and sautéed vegetables.

CK's (☎ *813-878-6500*) is a neat place: a revolving restaurant at the top of the Marriott Hotel at the airport. It's open for dinner only, from 5 pm, and main courses – European and American – run $15 to $28. This is a great place for Sunday brunch, an enormous smorgasbord for $17.95 per person; add $1 and you get unlimited champagne after 1 pm. The brunch is served from 10:30 am to 2:30 pm.

In south Tampa, try *Bean There Traveler's Coffee House* (☎ *813-837-7022, 3203 Bay-to-Bay Blvd*). They serve coffee, espresso and cappuccino. There are maps and globes throughout, some travel books (including Lonely Planet) and the big 'Where You Bean' bulletin board where guests put up photos, postcards and other travel mementos. Take Bayshore Blvd from downtown to Bay-to-Bay Blvd and turn right; it's on the right side of the road, past MacDill Ave.

Entertainment

For cultural events, call the arts hotline run by the Hillsborough River Arts Council of Hillsborough County (☎ 813-229-2787).

Performing Arts The largest performing-arts center south of the Kennedy Center in Washington, DC, the *Tampa Bay Performing Arts Center* (☎ *813-229-7827, 800-955-1045, 1010 N MacInnes Place*) is home to major concerts, plays, the Tampa Ballet and special events. There are four theaters in the complex: the Fest Hall (a 2500-seat venue where mainstay Broadway shows and headliners perform), the Playhouse (1000 seats), the three-floor Cabaret and the 100-seat Off Center Theatre, a 'black box' venue that's home to cutting-edge performances by local and national artists and groups.

There are free guided tours (☎ *813-222-1000*) of the backstage area Wednesday and Saturday at 10 am by appointment. Ticket prices range from $10 to $50 depending on the venue, the performance, the night and the seat.

The *UT Falk Theater* (☎ *813-253-3333, 428 W JF Kennedy Blvd*) is a 900-seat theater operated by the University of Tampa.

The 90-piece *Florida Orchestra* (☎ *813-286-2403, 800-662-7286*) plays at the Performing Arts Center as well as in free park concerts.

USF School of Music (☎ *813-974-2311*), on the USF campus on Fowler Ave (accessible from Fowler Ave exits on I-275 and I-75), does a variety of concerts and recitals. Tickets are $3 per person, $2 for students and seniors; concerts at USF Theater 1 and 2 are $4 per person and $3 for students and seniors. The USF Theater also performs at both those theaters.

Also on the USF campus, the **Sun Dome** (☎ *813-974-3111, 4202 E Fowler Ave*) hosts rock, jazz, pop and other concerts.

Raymond James Stadium (☎ *813-872-7977, 4201 N Dale Mabry Hwy*) often presents concerts as well.

Bars & Clubs Ybor City is Tampa nightlife central. On weekends, expect intense crowds and partyers reveling into the wee hours – locals say that the best bet is to show up really early, get your hand stamped and then come back later and push through the crowds like a celebrity. Check flyers on walls and lampposts – they're the most reliable source of up-to-date party, concert and nightclub information.

There's a huge scene at the **Tampa Bay Brewing Company** (☎ *813-247-1422, 1812 N 15th St*), with live music, microbrewed beers and lots of themed night parties. Similarly, **New World Brewery** (☎ *813-248-4869, 1313 E 8th Ave*) is a bar and disco with a great jukebox and a hugely lubricated crowd and great dance music.

Red Star (☎ *813-248-4443, 1909 E 15th St*) is a far swankier establishment. The **Green Iguana** (☎ *813-248-9555, 1708 E 7th Ave*) is a cool bar and restaurant, with live music Sunday to Thursday and $1 drinks on Wednesday.

The **Castle Bar** (☎ *813-247-7547, 2004 16th St at 9th Ave*) has stayed popular for years; it gets an artsy and interesting mix of people. There's no cover.

The **Rubb** (☎ *813-247-4225, E 1507 7th Ave*) gets an older crowd; it's an eclectic rock, jazz, blues club with live bands on weekends.

The **Jazz Cellar** (☎ *813-876-3459, 1916 14th St*) has decent jazz every night. There's a $3 per person cover, but no minimum. It's behind the Ybor Square on 14th St, but the basement entrance is on 9th Ave between 13th and 14th Sts.

The **Empire** (☎ *813-247-2582, 1902 E 7th Ave*) is alternative to industrial, with a diverse straight and gay crowd.

Luna (☎ *813-248-3460, 1802 E 7th Ave*), sort of a lounge club sans piano player and martinis, is a dark ambient kind of place that's mixed gay and straight.

With irony both heavy and satisfying, the **Cherokee Club** (☎ *813-247-9966, 1320 E 9th Ave*), upstairs from Café Creole & Oyster Bar, is a predominantly lesbian (but now gay as well) club that was once a 'gentlemen only' club. It has dancing and, infrequently, live music, and it's open Friday and Saturday 8 pm to 3 am. Note the finger in the blue oval sign out front: it's a holdover from the old days in which it was the Chi Chi Club, and the gentlemen who frequented it included such luminaries as José Martí, Winston Churchill and Teddy Roosevelt. Bully, ladies!

Outside Ybor City, there are some other good nightspots, such as **The Hub** (☎ *813-229-1553, 701 N Florida Ave*), at Zack St near the Tampa Theatre, a fun local hangout that serves up cheap drinks – maybe the cheapest in town. Looks like a hole in the wall, but this bar gets packed on weekends.

Hyde Park Cafe (☎ *813-254-2233, 1806 W Platt St*) is packed on Tuesday night for eclectic music and on the weekends for straight-up disco. **Tampa Eagle** (☎ *813-223-2780, 302 S Nebraska Ave/Hwy 45*), between Channelside and Whiting, is a gay leather-and-Levi's place with intense dance music.

Spectator Sports

Football For NFL football, the **Tampa Bay Buccaneers** (☎ *813-870-2700*) play at Raymond James Stadium, at 4201 N Dale Mabry Hwy. Take I-275 to the Himes Ave, Howard/Armenia Ave or Dr Martin Luther King Jr Blvd exits. Games are played from August (pre-season) to December; single-ticket prices range from $20 to $50.

The **Outback Bowl** (☎ *813-874-2695*) is an NCAA (National College Athletic Association) football game on New Year's Day at Raymond James Stadium. If you've never seen an American college football game, this shouldn't be missed.

The **USF Bulls** (☎ *813-974-2125*) are a Division I-AA football team that started intercollegiate play in 1997. They play at Tampa Stadium; tickets run about $15.

Baseball The *New York Yankees* (☎ 813-875-7753, www.yankees.com) practice during spring training games at Legends Field, 3802 ML King Jr Blvd at Dale Mabry Hwy. It's a 10,000-seat stadium modeled after the House that Ruth Built, or Yankee Stadium, which is in the Bronx, New York (until Steinbrenner moves everything to New Jersey – the man is in talks to buy the NJ Nets basketball team as we write). Admission is free.

The Yankees' minor-league team, the Tampa Yankees, play at Legends Field as well, from April to September. Tickets are $3 for adults and $2 for kids.

Soccer The *Tampa Bay Mutiny* (☎ 813-289-6811, 888-289-6811) are in the Division I League of major-league soccer. They play at Raymond James Stadium (see Football above) from April to September; ticket prices are $7 to $30.

Watch the *Tampa Bay Cyclones* (☎ 813-985-5050), the US Inter-regional Soccer League's Southeast Pro Division team, play at the USF Soccer Stadium (from April to August). Tickets are $3 to $7.

Hockey The Tampa Bay Lightning play at the *Ice Palace* (☎ 813-229-8800), an entertainment complex that's host to NHL hockey games, basketball games, concerts and ice shows. The stadium is in the Channel District near the Florida Aquarium.

Getting There & Away

Air Tampa International Airport (☎ 813-870-8700, www.tampaairport.com) is about 13 miles west of downtown, off of Hwy 589. It's the major airport in the region, and most flights to the Tampa area land here – as opposed to at St Petersburg-Clearwater International Airport, the area's other big player. Tampa is served by more than a dozen major carriers including Air Aruba, Air Canada, Air South, America West, American, British Airways, Carnival, Continental, Delta, LTU International Airways, Midway, Midwest Express, Northwest, Southwest, TWA, United and US Airways.

Bus Tampa's Greyhound station (☎ 813-229-2112) is at 610 Polk St. Sample fares (one way/roundtrip) are listed below:

destination	duration	price
Gainesville	3 to 4 hours	$18/35
Miami	6½ to 9 hours	$34/56
Orlando	2 to 4 hours	$16/29
Sarasota	2 hours	$12/24
St Petersburg	½ to 1 hour	$6/12

Train The Amtrak terminal (☎ 813-221-7600) is at 601 N Nebraska Ave. Amtrak shuttle buses run between Tampa and Orlando several times daily.

Car & Motorcycle Tampa is 245 miles northwest of Miami, 135 miles southwest of the Space Coast and 85 miles south of Orlando. Between Tampa and Orlando, take I-4. Between Tampa and Miami, the fastest way is to take I-75 south to Fort Lauderdale and then I-95 south, though the more scenic route is US Hwy 41 (Tamiami Trail) south to Everglades City and due east to Calle Ocho in Miami. Major car-rental agencies are located at the airport.

Getting Around

To/From the Airport HART bus No 30 picks up and drops off at the Red Arrival Desk on the lower level. From the airport, buses run to the downtown North Terminal (see Bus below) about every half hour from 5:51 am to 8:35 pm. The trip takes about 40 minutes. From the North Terminal to the airport, buses run about every half hour from 5:45 am to 7 pm. Shuttle services ply the road outside the arrival areas; they generally cost from $11 to $15 to areas in Tampa.

All major rental agencies have desks at the airport. By car, take I-275 to Ashley St, turn right and you're in downtown. A taxi from the airport to Busch Gardens should cost about $25, to downtown about $12, to St Petersburg about $35 to $45.

Bus HART (Hillsborough Area Regional Transit; ☎ 813-254-4278, www.hartline.com)

buses converge on the downtown North Terminal at 1414 N Marion St, under I-275 at Scott St. Buses cost $1.15 and transfers 10¢. To take your bike on the bus, you'll need to go to the North Terminal and buy a photo ID card ($2). From that moment on, you can bring bikes aboard HART buses at no extra charge. Listed below are some popular destinations by bus (all leave from the North Terminal):

destination	bus no	departs
Ybor City	8, 46	half-hourly
Busch Gardens & USF	5	half-hourly
Lowry Park Zoo	7	half-hourly
Henry B Plant Museum	30	half-hourly
	17	hourly
MOSI	6 to University Transit Center*	hourly

*Note there are two routes on bus No 6, so check the destination.

There are also commuter buses during rush hours between Tampa and the coast: bus No 100x goes to St Petersburg and bus No 200x to Clearwater.

Trolley The Tampa-Ybor Trolley (☎ 813-254-4278) runs daily 7:30 am to 5:30 pm, several times an hour. Fare is 25¢ for adults, children under four and seniors ride free. The trolley route is as follows:

From the Marion St Transit Parkway at Fort Brooke Station, it goes west on Whiting St, north on Ashley St, east on Jackson St, then south down Franklin St, across the Garrison Channel, east on Knight's Run, north back across the channel, past the Florida Aquarium and north to Ybor City. In Ybor City, it runs east along 7th Ave from 12th St to 22nd, then west along 8th Ave and reverses the circuit.

Taxi Meter rates are 95¢ flagfall, and $1.50 per mile. Companies include Yellow Cab (☎ 813-253-0121), the Tampa Bay Cab Co (☎ 813-251-5555) and United Cab (☎ 813-253-2424). All offer senior discounts, but you'll have to ask.

AROUND TAMPA
Hillsborough River State Park
This 3400-acre state park (☎ 813-987-6771), 15402 N Hwy 301, is a spectacular bit of greenery, and canoeing around here is a noble way to spend an afternoon or an overnight, as there's inexpensive camping here as well.

The park (admission free) is open daily 8 am to sunset, and there are picnic facilities (grills and tables), nature and hiking trails and a new swimming pool ($1 admission). The pool is open Friday to Sunday in summer, daily in winter, 10 am to 5 pm.

Ranger-led nature walks are offered through the park on advance request and, during the busy camping season in winter, there are campfire programs on Friday and Saturday evenings, such as slide presentations or wildlife demonstrations. In winter, there are also sometimes guided canoe trips.

To get here from downtown Tampa, take Fowler Ave east to Hwy 301, and go north for 9 miles. There's no public transportation out here.

Fort Foster Also in the park is the Fort Foster Historical Site, a reconstruction of a fort that was originally built in 1836-37 as a bridge defense during the Second Seminole War, as the area was on a supply trail that ran from Fort Brooke in Tampa to Fort King in present-day Ocala. There were skirmishes here, but no major battles, and over the years the original fort deteriorated and was vandalized.

The fort's on the east side of Hwy 301. Access is an additional $1, payable on the honor system: put your money in an envelope, place the receipt in your car windshield and the envelope in the box. The fort's open for self-guided tours (weather permitting) on weekdays, 10 am to 3 pm, and on some (not all) weekends there are guided tours.

Canoeing The river's current is not at all challenging at this area, and you can rent canoes for $5 an hour (valid driver's license or a $10 deposit required). The current is highest from July to September, and when the river's high, they don't rent canoes. Along the river, you can see lots of wildlife, including, possibly, bobcats, white-tail deer, opossum, raccoons, gray foxes, red-tail hawks, osprey, lots of armadillos and water birds, and alligators – the best time to see them is early in the morning or in the evening.

The biggest commercial canoe-rental company is Canoe Escapes! (☎ 813-986-2067), near the Hillsborough River in Thonotosassa at 9335 E Fowler Ave, a half-mile east of I-75. They rent canoes in two sizes, which can hold up to two adults and two children for two-, four- or six-hour tours. These are easy, self-guided adventures downstream along the Hillsborough River, and the tours have stops along the way where there are picnic facilities (bring a cooler).

They give you river maps and, if necessary, paddling instructions. The cost for two adults is $28 per canoe for the two-hour, and $34 for four- or six-hour tours, including transport to the river and back to their offices. It's open daily except Thanksgiving, Christmas Eve and Christmas. The first boat out on Monday to Friday is at 9 am, last out is 2 pm, last pick up from the river is 5 pm; on Saturday and Sunday, they start an hour earlier, at 8 am, but last out and pick up are the same.

Places to Stay Camping for tents, vans or RVs is $14.50 per night with water only, $16.63 with water and electric (including tax). There are no sewage hookups, but there is a dump station, and there are hot and cold showers. You can make a campfire, but you're not allowed to gather wood in the park. Bring your own or buy it ($4) from the ranger station.

ST PETERSBURG
• population 238,629

St Petersburg is in the middle of a rejuvenation, at the center of which is a collection of museums that together form what may be the state's cultural powerhouse. The St Petersburg Fine Arts Museum has one of the finest collections in the state; the Dalí Museum is the largest collection of that artist's works outside Spain; and the Florida International Museum's blockbuster rotating exhibitions have brought national attention to St Petersburg with groundbreaking international shows such as Treasures of the Tsars, Splendors of Egypt, Alexander the Great and Treasures of the Titanic. And St Petersburg is one of two places in the USA where you can tour a real Russian missile sub.

Orientation

St Petersburg is a typically sprawling southwest Florida town. Though it's not as spread out as Fort Myers, it's still a good 20-minute to half-hour drive to the beach in the best of traffic. St Petersburg is about 20 miles southwest of Tampa across Old Tampa Bay; St Pete Beach is about 10 miles southwest of downtown St Petersburg.

The city is oriented on the ever-familiar grid: avenues run east-west and streets and boulevards run north-south. The north-south dividing line is Central Ave, and 34th St (Hwy 19) is the east-west divider, though people usually ignore the east-west designation. The directional indicator is placed after the street. Avenues count upward away from Central Ave, so 1st Ave N is one block north of Central, and 1st Ave S is one block south.

Downtown St Petersburg is the area roughly bordered by the bay at the east, ML King Jr Blvd (9th St) at the west, 10th Ave N at the north and 17th Ave S at the south.

AAA, Dolph and Rand McNally all print maps to the area, and the St Petersburg Chamber of Commerce gives out a Dolph map that's excellent.

Information
Tourist Offices The best source for advance information is St Petersburg/Clearwater Area Convention & Visitors Bureau (☎ 727-582-7892, www.stpete-clearwater.com), though their location in Tropicana Field, 1 Stadium Drive, is a little inconvenient for dropping in. They run a visitors line (☎ 800-345-6710), where you can get area information, order a visitors guide, make hotel reservations and more.

The best place for pamphlets, city maps and coupon magazines is the St Petersburg Area Chamber of Commerce (☎ 727-821-4715),

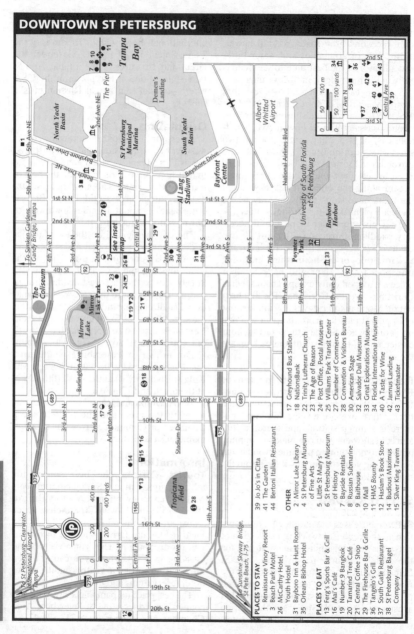

DOWNTOWN ST PETERSBURG

PLACES TO STAY
1 Renaissance Vinoy Resort
3 Beach Park Motel
26 McCarthy Hotel,
   Youth Hostel
31 Bayboro Inn & Hunt Room
35 Orleans Bishop Hotel

PLACES TO EAT
13 Ferg's Sports Bar & Grill
16 Mai's Café
19 Number 9 Bangkok
20 Tamarind Tree Café
21 Central Coffee Shop
29 The Firehouse Bar & Grille
36 Tangelo's Grill
37 South Gate Restaurant
38 St Petersburg Bagel
   Company

39 Jo Jo's in Citta
41 The Garden
44 Bertoni Italian Restaurant

OTHER
2 Mirror Lake Library
4 St Petersburg Museum
   of Fine Arts
5 Little St Mary's
6 St Petersburg Museum
   of History
7 Bayside Rentals
8 Russian Submarine
9 Baithouse
10 Mall
11 HMS Bounty
12 Haslam's Book Store
14 Budious Maximus
15 Silver King Tavern

17 Greyhound Bus Station
18 NationsBank
22 Trinity Lutheran Church
23 The Age of Reason
24 Post Office, Postal Museum
25 Williams Park Transit Center
27 Chamber of Commerce
28 Convention & Visitors Bureau
30 American Stage
32 Salvador Dali Museum
33 Great Explorations Museum
34 Florida International Museum
40 A Taste for Wine
42 Jannus Landing
43 Ticketmaster

SOUTHWEST

100 2nd Ave N. It also has information booths at The Pier (see later in this section) and at 2001 Ulmerton Rd.

Money NationsBank has branches downtown at 3100 Central Ave and 6201 Central Ave. The open-air post office (☎ 727-323-6516), 76 4th St N, is the most convenient in downtown (see Postal Museum later in this section). The main post office is at 3135 1st Ave N.

Bookstores The incredible Haslam's Book Store (☎ 727-822-8616), 2025 Central Ave, has a good Florida section, LP books and new and remaindered books in addition to their core used-book selection. Attic Bookshop (☎ 727-344-2398), 6601 1st Ave S, has books, sheet music and comics. Lighthouse Books (☎ 727-822-3278), 1735 1st Ave N, has sections on Florida and the Caribbean as well as rare and unusual books, maps and prints.

The Age of Reason (☎ 727-821-0892), 401 1st Ave N, opposite the open-air post office, has a good selection of used books (including Lonely Planet) and friendly service. The Oriental Book Shelf (☎ 727-867-7978), 6940 9th St S, has books on Japan and Asia.

Libraries The main library (☎ 727-893-7724) is at 3745 9th Ave N. Downtown, the Mirror Lake Branch (☎ 727-893-7268) is at 5th St and 3rd Ave N.

Media The major daily is the excellent *St Petersburg Times*, which runs a very good Website (www.sptimes.com) that has photographs, walking tours and information on major exhibits at the area's museums. National Public Radio (NPR) is at 89.7 FM.

Gay & Lesbian Affinity Books (☎ 727-823-3662), 2435 9th St N, is a gay and lesbian bookstore with books, videos, cards and music. Ask them about Healthy Lifestyles, a coming-out support group for adults 21 and over. The Line (☎ 727-586-4297) is an information and crisis hotline. For up-to-date club, bar and social organization information, pick up a copy of *Encounter* and

Womyn's Word (a lesbian newsletter). Both of these are available at Affinity.

Laundry Try the Snowhite Laundry (☎ 727-822-9021), 1117 4th St N (about nine blocks north of downtown).

Medical Services All Children's Hospital (☎ 727-898-7451), 33 6th St S, is the largest in the area. There's also Bayfront Medical Center (☎ 727-823-1234), 701 6th St S.

Salvador Dalí Museum

One of St Petersburg's star attractions – with the largest collection of works by Salvador Dalí outside Spain – is the Salvador Dalí Museum (☎ 727-823-3767, www.webcoast .com/Dali/), 1000 3rd St S.

While many of the galleries in the museum contain rotating exhibitions, there is always a permanent retrospective of Dalí's works on display from the museum's large collection.

Dalí is best known for his surrealist works, but the museum's collection covers the entire range of the artist's work: from his early works (1914 to 1927, which included Impressionism, Cubism, still lifes and landscapes) and his transitional period (1928) through Surrealism (1929 to 1940) and back to classical works from 1943 to 1989 and a collection of masterworks – 18 major oil paintings produced between 1948 and 1970.

You never know what will be up when you visit, though we were lucky enough to catch *Dalí Under the Sun: World Premiere of the Florida Collection*, which displayed all of the museum's 94 oil paintings.

Guided tours ($5 for adults, $2 for students) are given between five and nine times a day; ask at the ticket counter for more information. Photography is not allowed in the galleries, and you must check cameras and unbagged video cameras.

The museum's Master Gallery has four excellent oil on canvas paintings: *The Discovery of America by Christopher Columbus* (1958-59); *The Ecumenical Council* (1960); *Galacidalacidesoxiribunucleicacid* (1962-63); and (our favorite) *The Hallucinogenic Toreador* (1969-70).

SOUTHWEST

We thought their gift shop was fantastic – a museum gift shop with style – and prices are reasonable.

The museum is open Monday to Saturday 9:30 am to 5:30 pm, Sunday noon to 5:30 pm, closed Thanksgiving and Christmas. Admission is $9 for adults, $7 for seniors, $5 for students and military with ID; children under 10 admitted free.

Great Explorations Museum
If the kids get squirmy being led through the Dalí Museum, the best next stop is the nearby Great Explorations Museum (☎ 727-821-8992), 1120 4th St S. This is a really fun, hands-on science museum that gets kids down and dirty. The Touch Tunnel, an 8-foot-long, pitch-black maze, is (probably a poor idea for claustrophobics but) a really creepy and fun way for kids seven and older to spend five minutes. You enter the tube and crawl over different textured floors as it twists and turns, making you feel as if you're going much farther than you actually are.

The museum also offers interactive computer games, and everyone had fun with the safe-cracking display – kids line up to guess a three- and four-digit combination to open a locked door (we're still trying to work out exactly what skills this demonstration is trying to instill in the future of America).

Other features are a reptile room, a hurricane room (which simulates a condensed version of a category-3 hurricane, complete with a hysterical Channel 10 weatherperson), slapping pipes and, coolest of all, the cone pyramid: put your finger in the hole and your pulse drives a cloud maker.

The museum's open Monday to Saturday 10 am to 5 pm, Sunday noon to 5 pm. Admission is $6 for adults, $5.50 for seniors, $5 for children four to 17; children under three are free.

Florida International Museum
This enormous exhibition space (☎ 727-822-3693, www.floridamuseum.org), 100 2nd St N, is home to some of the most spectacular temporary exhibits in the country. And for all of you who think that guidebook writers get to experience it all, consider that once again our research schedule plopped us down in the city at a time when we could see none of it! In the last few years, they've put on Treasures of the Tsars, seen by more than 600,000 visitors and run in conjunction with the Kremlin Museum in Moscow; Splendors of Ancient Egypt, run in conjunction with the Roemer-und Pelizaeus-Museum in Hildesheim, Germany; Alexander the Great; and Treasures of the Titanic. And as we go to press, they're beginning their new show, Empires of Mystery, with gold, ceramics, textiles and other exhibits from empires throughout the world.

The museum hours and admission prices change with each exhibition, and there are several exhibitions a year, so call for more information.

St Petersburg Museum of Fine Arts
One of the best fine-arts museums in the state, the St Petersburg Museum of Fine Arts (☎ 727-896-2667, fax 727-894-4638), 255 Beach Drive NE (near The Pier), has an enormous permanent collection with works that as a whole make up a very well-rounded art history of diverse cultures. The collection is made up of Asian, Indian and African art, pre-Columbian sculpture, photographic works from superstars such as Jerry Uelsmann, Cycladic sculpture of the third-century BC and American and European paintings and sculpture.

Rotating exhibits are held in Galleries 17 through 20 and 22; when there are no temporary exhibits, these rooms contain contemporary art and photography exhibits from the museum's collection. The **Morgan Membership Garden** and the **Stuart Memorial Garden** host various events such as teas, and the **Marly Room** is home to concerts, plays and films: contact the museum to see what's happening in these areas during your visit.

The exhibitions are all on the main floor. While signs in the museum are very clear, the room numbering is somewhat confusing: pick up a floor plan and catalogs of rotating exhibitions at the ticket desk. Tours of the galleries are included in the price of admission and run Tuesday to Friday at 10 and 11 am and 1, 2 and 3 pm. On Saturday, tours are at 11 am and 2 pm, and on Sunday at 1 and 2 pm.

The museum is open Tuesday to Saturday 10 am to 5 pm, Sunday 1 to 5 pm; closed Monday, Thanksgiving, Christmas and New Year's Day. On the third Thursday of each month, it stays open until 9 pm. Admission is $5 for adults, $2 for students, $3 for seniors and groups of 10 or more, children under six are free. Admission is free to all on Sunday.

St Petersburg Museum of History

At the foot of The Pier, the St Petersburg Museum of History (☎ 727-894-1052), 335 2nd Ave NE, has a great display on the early days of aviation – St Petersburg was the take-off site for America's first scheduled airline flight on January 1, 1914. The plane used for that flight, the Benoist Airboat (restored in 1984), now hangs in the Flight One Gallery, which also has some very interesting early aviation artifacts.

The museum's open Monday to Saturday 10 am to 5 pm, Sunday 1 to 5 pm. Admission is $5 for adults, $4 for seniors, $2 for children seven to 17 and children under six are free.

Florida Holocaust Memorial

The Florida Holocaust Memorial (☎ 727-820-0100), 55 5th St S, the fourth largest in the USA, is in wonderful new digs downtown and worth a visit. There are rotating and permanent exhibitions not just of the Holocaust but of Jewish life throughout the world, with rotating exhibits on a number of subjects on several floors.

On the Road to Joy is a workshop for Holocaust survivors and their families. They also run a film series during the month of February.

The museum is open Monday to Friday 10 am to 4 pm and Sunday noon to 4 pm. Admission is $6 for adults, $5 for senior citizens, students and children free.

The Pier

A focal point of downtown, The Pier (☎ 727-821-6164), 800 2nd Ave NE, is something of a tourist trap. It's, well, a long pier, with a square fishing platform at the end, in the center of which is a five-story shopping mall with shops and restaurants. There's an aquarium on the 2nd floor.

At the baithouse, you can feed the pelicans, who are standing around waiting for you: four fish are $2, 16 are $5. Lazier pelicans you'll never see. You can also rent a fishing rod here for $10 a day with a $20 deposit; the rental price includes bait.

Bayside Rentals (☎ 727-363-0000) rents bicycles for $5 an hour, $10 for a half day and $15 for a full day.

The Pier is open Monday to Saturday from 10 am to about 9 pm, Sunday from about 11 am to 9 pm. Pier parking is $2, and there's a shuttle tram that runs between the parking lots and the action. Valet parking is $5; valets work from 11 am till the last car is gone.

Russian Submarine At the northeastern end of The Pier is, of all things, a Russian Juliett class submarine (☎ 727-821-6164), with missile launchers fore and aft of the conning tower. It was built at Krasnoye Sormovo, in Gorky, Russia, in 1968 and decommissioned in 1993, then bought by a Finnish businessman who turned the sub into a restaurant, and finally it was dragged here to be opened as a tourist attraction. Attraction it is. Admission is $8 for adults, $7 for seniors and $4 for children.

HMS *Bounty* The very same 18th-century tall ship used in the 1962 film *Mutiny on the Bounty* parks at The Pier for the winter; its summer home is in Fall River, Massachusetts (see Lonely Planet's *New England*). You can tour the boat, which has sailed more than 70,000 miles (including a one-year trip to Tahiti where the film was shot), Tuesday to Saturday every half hour from noon to 5:30 pm, Sunday noon to 6 pm. Guided tours (the only way to get onboard) cost $5 for adults, $4 for seniors, $3 for children over five. The ship is here from around October 30th to early May.

Little St Mary's This is perhaps the only toilet in the state of Florida that is also a historic landmark. Our story begins when Henry Taylor was stiffed on payment for his work as the designer of St Mary's Church, 515 4th St S. Taylor built the Romanesque-revival toilet as a miniature of the church, and dubbed it Little St Mary's. It's at the western end of The Pier.

Demen's Landing Facing The Pier to its south is Demen's Landing, Bayshore Drive SE at 1st Ave S, a waterfront park with picnic facilities. Each spring the American Stage in the Park (☎ 727-822-8814) presents its Shakespeare Festival here.

Postal Museum
It's a little much to call the itty-bitty display case at the rear of the downtown St Petersburg post office (☎ 727-323-6516), 76 4th St N, a 'museum,' but these postal types are a shameless lot. However, the Mediterranean-revival building it's in was the nation's first open-air post office, and it's a glorious thing, with a keystone-arched open front. The 'museum' contains postal paraphernalia such as stamps, inkwells and a numbering device. There used to be a large postal museum on the 2nd floor, but it was closed when we visited: the brochure promised that it 'contains artifacts of postal memorabilia of the St Petersburg area which is sure to delight young and old.' OK. It's still a fully functioning post office.

Feeling philatelic? No worries: the St Petersburg Stamp Club meets monthly at Trinity Lutheran Church (☎ 727-822-3307), 401 5th St N.

First United Methodist Church
Built in 1925 and located in the heart of downtown, this Gothic-revival church (☎ 727-894-4661), 212 3rd St N, is listed in the National Register of Historic Places. There are some pretty nice Tiffany-style stained-glass windows. Sunday services are held at 8:30, 9:45 and 11 am.

Sunken Gardens
Opened in 1935, Sunken Gardens (☎ 727-896-3186), 1825 4th St N, is a 5-acre tropical garden with a walk-through aviary that's home to colorful birds, lots of exotic flowers and other flora and fauna. Recently, the original owners sold the gardens to the city of St Petersburg, which plans to revamp the site. For now, Sunken Gardens is open daily 9:30 am to 5 pm; admission is $12 for adults, $6 for children three to 11.

Gizella Kopsick Palm Arboretum
This arboretum (☎ 727-893-7335), at N Shore Drive and 10th Ave NE, contains about 200 different palms and cycads representing about 45 species from all over the world. Examples include such wildly diverse entries as the jelly palm, the windmill palm, the triangle palm and, of course, your garden variety gru gru palm. Guided tours take place about once a month; call to see if one's on during your visit.

Organized Tours
Biplane Rides (☎ 727-895-6266), at Albert Whitted Airport near Bayfront Center, offers round the patch downtown air tours in a 1933 WACO biplane originally owned by William Randolph Hearst, for $35. Other tours are available as well.

Pierside Sight Seeing (☎ 727-363-0000), 800 2nd Ave NE, runs three two-hour tours of historic St Petersburg daily.

Gray Line Sightseeing Tours (☎ 727-535-0208, 800-282-4051) does one-, two- and three-day tours to such places as Walt Disney World, Busch Gardens, SeaWorld, Cypress Gardens and the Kennedy Space Center. Call for prices (which are more complicated than writing this book) and reservations.

Places to Stay
Camping Try the *Fort DeSoto Park Campground (☎ 727-582-2267, 3500 Pinellas Bayway S)*, with 235 campsites for $20.90 per night (tents or RVs), electric and water included. Reservations may be made, within 30 days of your stay, in person only at the Camp Office, at their Clearwater office (631 Chestnut St), or their St Petersburg office (150 5th St N, Room 125). They take only cash or traveler's checks – no credit cards. Also see the park description in Around St Petersburg.

There's also a big **KOA St Petersburg/ Madeira Beach** near Madeira Beach. See Places to Stay under St Pete Beach, later in this chapter, for more details.

Hostels The non-HI/AYH (no matter what they tell you) *St Petersburg International Youth Hostel* (☎ 727-822-4141, 326 1st Ave N) is in the McCarthy Hotel, three blocks from The Pier. Dorm as well as semiprivate rooms are available, as is a kitchen, common room and laundry facilities. Dorm rooms, which are clean enough but not the cheeriest in the world, are $15 for HI/AYH members, $20 for nonmembers; linen hire for those without a sleep sack is $2. Hostel rooms have no air conditioning or cable TV, but you can rent a TV from the desk.

Hotels & Motels The *McCarthy Hotel* (☎ 727-822-4141, 326 1st Ave N), home of the St Petersburg International Youth Hostel (see above), has decently renovated rooms and very nice staff. The rooms are spartan but basically clean, and many have a view of adjacent brick walls. The newly renovated wings on the higher floors are much cheerier. It's on the National Register of Historic Places, but it still has some of the best prices in downtown: singles and doubles are $43/49 including tax; weekly rates are, they say, $95 to $145.

The *Beach Park Motel* (☎ 727-898-6325, 300 Beach Drive NE) has older but spotless rooms with fridges, coffee-makers and other nice amenities, all $65 year round.

The *Renaissance Vinoy Resort* (☎ 727-894-1000, fax 727-822-2785, 501 5th Ave NE) is a large pink hotel on the bay and the most flashy offering in downtown. It has opulent dining and entertainment areas, and rooms include three telephones, a stocked 'refreshment center,' bathrobes and two televisions. Rooms with very nice views of the bay go for just $159 to $179 in low season, $229 to $289 in mid-seasons and $259 to $319 in high season.

St Petersburg Bayfront Hilton (☎ 727-894-5000, 800-774-1500, 333 1st St S) has Hilton-ish rooms from $119 to $189. It's got

a great location downtown, and restaurants and bars inside, as you'd expect.

B&Bs Check out the *Bay Shore Manor* (☎ 727-822-3438, 635 12th Ave NE), certainly the least-expensive B&B in town. They do a German-style breakfast (coffee, tea, milk, orange juice, bread and rolls, cold cuts, cheese, eggs, cereal), and each room has a TV, coffee-maker, microwave and mini-refrigerator. Singles/doubles are $79 for the first night, $59 or $69 each additional night depending on season.

Rooms at the very New Orleans-looking *Orleans Bishop Hotel* (☎ 727-894-4312, 800-676-4848, 256 1st Ave N) are very nice: all have clawfoot bathtubs and are tastefully decorated. All size beds (twin through king-size) are the same price, but the place has both B&B and standard hotel rooms. B&B rooms are $75 to $85 a night, or $500 a week; breakfast is on their great terrace. Efficiencies cost $55 Sunday to Thursday and $65 Friday and Saturday, or $210/265 weekly for singles/doubles.

Bayboro House (☎ 727-823-4955, 1719 Beach Drive SE) is a very nice Old South-themed place. Free wine is served in the parlor each evening; there's a new pool and a spa, each room has a private bath, VCR/TV and free movies, and includes beach chairs, beach towels and a morning newspaper. No children or smoking. Two-day minimum during holidays and special events. Rooms are $95 Sunday to Thursday and $105 Friday and Saturday in low season, $110/120 in high season.

Bayboro Inn & Hunt Room (☎ 727-823-0498, 357 3rd St S) is a historic house with theme rooms, such as Renaissance, Egyptian and Key West. No smoking, no pets; free wine in the evenings. Rooms are $75 to $135.

Places to Eat
St Petersburg Bagel Co (☎ 727-822-4092, 249 Central Ave) has great bagels for 50¢, sandwiches from $2 to $5, salads 75¢ to $3.50.

City's Gourmet Deli (727-577-6766, 11024 4th St N) in the Winn-Dixie shopping center at Bay View Plaza, is an exceptionally good sandwich place. Like their branch in Tampa, the sandwiches are piled high and around $4 to $6.

The city's best hot dog is at **Bill's** (☎ 727-328-1883, 2623 Central Ave), where you can get a dog with mustard, ketchup, spicy peppers, onions, relish, kosher pickle and celery salt for $1.95.

There's cheap breakfast all day at the friendly **South Gate Restaurant** (☎ 727-823-7071, 29 3rd St N). Dinner's from 4 to 9 pm daily, and during the day they do sandwiches for $2.95, a good Greek salad or chicken gyro for $4.25.

Central Coffee Shop (☎ 727-821-1125, 530 Central Ave) does breakfast and lunch Monday through Friday 6 am to 1:45 pm, Saturday 6 am to 11 am. Said to be excellent and cheap.

Tangelo's Grill (☎ 727-894-1695, 226 1st Ave N) does Cuban-style sandwiches such as roast pork on grilled Cuban bread ($3.75) or Spanish grouper ($4.75).

Vegetarians will like the **Tamarind Tree Café** (☎ 727-898-2115, 537 Central Ave). It serves about seven kinds of salads from $5 to $8, (such as Greek or their salad sampler of three with pita bread) as well as Mediterranean offerings such as hummus and falafel, vegetarian chili and sandwiches ($3.50 to $6.50).

A great Vietnamese place is the bare but friendly **Mai's Café** (☎ 727-894-2427, 1100 Central Ave) that's been serving up monstrously good food for 13 years; you can't go wrong with their soups ($5 to $7.95) and their bun (vermicelli with various extra ingredients, from $5.50 to $6.50).

Number 9 Bangkok (☎ 727-894-5990, 571 Central Ave) has good Thai food. Eleven choices for lunch include yellow curry with beef, chicken and pork for $5. Dinners are $6, house specials $8.

The **Fourth Street Shrimp Store** (☎ 727-822-0325, 1006 4th St N) is good for quick dinners from $5; fresh grouper dinner is $10.

The **Firehouse Bar & Grille** (☎ 727-895-4716, 260 1st Ave S) does soups, salads and sandwiches for around $5. They do live blues and jazz on Friday and Saturday night.

One of our favorite places was **The Garden** (☎ 727-896-3800, 217 Central Ave). At lunch, they do an excellent pesto pasta ($4.95) and Lebanese sampler ($5.75), and daily lunch specials are $5.25. At dinner, dishes include grilled lamb chops at $9.75 or wild mushroom pasta for $10.50; dinner pastas range from $8.75 to $11.95, seafood dishes from $9.95 to $13.95. It also has 'theme nights' and hosts live jazz (see Entertainment below).

Ted Peter's Famous Smoked Fish (☎ 727-381-7931, 1350 Pasadena Ave), on the way out to St Pete Beach, has been smoking fish for something like 3500 years (well, for 45 at least). They do absolutely succulent freshly smoked salmon ($12 per pound), mackerel ($7) and mullet ($6) in the little smokehouse, where you can get takeout; next door is a restaurant where they serve seafood specials and people drink lots of beer by the fireplace. A smoked-fish dinner (salmon is $15, mackerel $11, mullet $10) includes German potato salad, rye bread and butter, pickles, onion, lemon and coleslaw. It's goooood.

Jo Jo's in Citta (☎ 727-894-0075, 200 Central Ave) has good if somewhat pricey Italian food; main courses hover in the $10 to $16 range, such as baked pasta and veal piccata. They also do much cheaper subs.

For more expensive Italian in a very comfortable and beautiful setting, head for **Bertoni Italian Restaurant** (☎ 727-822-5503, 16 2nd St N), with great service, a nice bar and main courses from $12 to $20.

Entertainment

The St Petersburg entertainment scene is less exciting than that of its Russian counterpart, and that says a lot. For recorded information on upcoming events, call the St Petersburg Downtown Hotline (☎ 727-825-3333).

Theater The **American Stage** (☎ 727-822-8814, 211 3rd St S) is the oldest professional theater ensemble in the Tampa Bay area. It stages American classics and Broadway shows.

The *St Petersburg Little Theater* (☎ 727-866-1973, 4025 31st St S) is a community theater that puts on plays and musicals.

Bayfront Center (☎ 727-892-5767, 400 1st St S) houses both the Times Arena and the Mahaffey Theater. The complex holds Broadway shows, ice-skating performances, concerts and some sports events.

Live Music The *Coliseum* (☎ 727-892-5202, 535 4th Ave N), also called the Palace of Pleasure, opened in 1924 and, over the years, big bands, classical orchestras and rock bands have played here. It's been host to indoor-tennis matches, and in 1985, it made its film debut in *Cocoon* – that incredible ballroom scene. If you're here on a Wednesday, definitely hit the big band dance sessions; they begin at 12:30 pm. Most events are BYOB (and hey, coolers are welcome).

Tropicana Field (see Spectator Sports below) also hosts concerts; call for information while you're here.

Bars & Clubs An outdoor courtyard behind the Bertoni Italian Restaurant (see Places to Eat above), *Jannus Landing* (☎ 727-896-1244, 16 2nd St N) offers several concerts of local and national bands every week. It's very casual – shorts, T-shirts and jeans. There is a full cash bar, and all ages are admitted – but you'll be proofed to the gills if you look under 30 and try to buy alcohol. They also serve burgers, hot dogs and such. Tickets are generally under $15, and often about $10. You can get tickets from Ticketmaster.

The Big Catch (☎ 727-821-6444, 9 1st St NE) has been around forever. It has live bands, usually modern rock, on Friday and Saturday with a $3 cover and no minimum. It's open Thursday to Saturday 8:30 pm to 2 am.

A Taste for Wine (☎ 727-895-1623, 241 Central Ave), upstairs, is a very fun place, with wine tasting, wines by the glass and a very nice atmosphere.

The Garden (☎ 727-896-3800, 217 Central Ave) does Get Togethers – set-price dinner and wine-tasting evenings – with themes such as belly dancing, Spanish night with

tapas and a show – for $39.50. It also has live jazz outside with the Buster Cooper Jazz Trio every Friday and Saturday 8:30 pm to 1:30 am. Also see Places to Eat above.

Ferg's Sports Bar & Grill (☎ 727-822-4562, 1320 Central Ave) is a friendly neighborhood place with an outdoor bar area that's a huge scene, especially at gametime. Across the street, the *Silver King Tavern* (☎ 727-821-6740, 1114 Central Ave) seemed a little rowdier, if equally jolly. It has happy hour daily 4 to 8 pm, and it's open 11:30 am to 2:30 am.

Budious Maximus (☎ 727-898-8525, 1111 Central Ave) is a very popular disco, with reggae, Friday Funktion and afro-dub Thursdays.

Another disco is *Tamiami* (☎ 727-827-1518, 242 1st Ave N), with standard disco and hip-hop on most days and swing dance lessons Tuesday at 8 pm for $5.

Spectator Sports
Tropicana Field (☎ 727-893-9500 x106), 1 Stadium Drive, is home to the Devil Rays, one of major-league-baseball's newest expansion teams. It also hosts concerts, car races and other events. Parking is at 10th St and 4th Ave S.

Al Lang Stadium (for tickets ☎ 727-822-3384), 230 1st St S, is home to minor-league-baseball's St Petersburg Cardinals, a St Louis Cardinals farm team.

Shopping
Antique stores litter downtown St Petersburg, especially on the north side of Central Ave between 6th and 11th Sts, and along 4th St: Antique Alley Mall (☎ 727-823-5700), 1535 4th St N, has several sorts of antique places.

The big shopping mall in the area is Tyrone Square (☎ 727-345-0126), 66th St and 22nd Ave N, with 155 stores, including Burdines, Dillard's, JC Penney, Sears, and Kookla Fran & Ollie.

Getting There & Away
Air St Petersburg-Clearwater International Airport (☎ 727-535-7600) is served by several major carriers as well as charters,

and the occasional low-flying Lonely Planet author. It's at the intersection of Roosevelt Blvd and Hwy 686 in Clearwater. However, if you're flying into the region, you're more likely to land in Tampa; see the Tampa Getting There & Away section earlier in the chapter.

Bus The Greyhound station (☎ 727-898-1496) is at 180 9th St N. There's regular service here from all over Florida; sample routes are listed below (prices are one way/roundtrip):

destination	duration	price
Miami	7 to 8 hours	$34/56
Orlando	3½ to 4¾ hours	$16/29
Tampa	½ to 1 hour	$6/12

Train There's an Amtrak (☎ 800-872-7245) continuing rail shuttle-bus link between Tampa and St Petersburg; it'll drop you at the Pinellas Square Mall at 7200 Hwy 19 N.

Car & Motorcycle Several major car-rental companies have offices at the airport. It's 289 miles to Miami, 84 miles to Orlando. From Tampa, the best route is I-275 south, which runs right through downtown St Petersburg and continues across the Sunshine Skyway Bridge; it connects with I-75 and US Hwy 41 (the Tamiami Trail) on the south side of Tampa Bay. From Sarasota, take I-75 north to I-275 across the Sunshine Skyway. From Orlando, take I-4 south to I-75 to I-275.

Getting Around

To/From the Airport There's no local bus service directly to the airport; the closest you can get to it is about a half-mile away, at the corner of 49th St and Roosevelt Blvd, served by bus Nos 52 or 79. By car to downtown, take Roosevelt Blvd (Hwy 686) south, across the jig on Ulmerton Rd, to I-275 south. To Clearwater, take Roosevelt Blvd north to the Bayside (49th St) Bridge and go west on Gulf-to-Bay Blvd. Taxi fares from the airport to St Petersburg run between $15 and $20.

Bus Pinellas Suncoast Transit Authority (PSTA; ☎ 727-530-9911) has a downtown transit service center at Williams Park, on 2nd Ave N between 3rd and 4th Sts; it's open Monday to Saturday 7 am to 5:45 pm, Sunday 8 to 11:30 am and 12:30 to 4 pm. They sell daily/monthly unlimited-ride Go Cards ($2.50/40) and give transit information.

While there is public bus service between St Petersburg and places such as Clearwater and Tarpon Springs, there is no PSTA service between St Petersburg and St Pete Beach – you'll have to take bus No 35 to Pasadena (25 minutes) and then transfer for a BATS bus to St Pete Beach. The trip takes about an hour total; bus No 35 leaves the Williams Park station once an hour. Regular bus fare is $1, bills accepted.

Trolley The five major museums in town – the Dalí, Fine Arts, Historic, International and Great Explorations – along with a couple of hotels and The Pier have teamed up to provide a free (and pink) trolley service called The Looper, which loops around downtown, including all the museums, the retail district of downtown and The Pier. Just wave it down; the service runs every day between 11 am and 5 pm.

Car & Motorcycle Getting around and parking in St Petersburg is a cinch. To get to St Pete Beach, take I-275 to Hwy 682, which connects to the Pinellas County Parkway and west to the beach, or take Central Ave due west to either the Treasure Island Causeway or turn south on 66th St to the Corey Causeway.

Bicycle It's flat, but everything is very, very far apart. Lock your bike tightly and note that drivers are not used to people like you. Bikes can be rented at The Pier.

AROUND ST PETERSBURG
Boyd Hill Nature Park
This park (☎ 727-893-7326), 1101 Country Club Way S on Lake Maggiore, is 245 acres on Lake Maggiore with more than 3 miles of nature trails and boardwalks. There's a picnic area with grills and sheltered tables and a

playground northeast of the nature center. Bicycles are permitted, but not pets, in-line skates or skateboards.

There are six primary trails within the park: on the Willow Marsh Trail, you'll likely hear young alligators squeaking, but there are many more animals, including pig frogs, bald eagles, snowy egrets, box turtles and opossums, which can be found among the live oaks, cypress trees and ferns.

The friendly rangers here offer night hikes, bird walks, wildflower walks and ecology walks; daily tram tours take off at 1 pm. Night hikes take place at 8:30 pm on the second Monday night of the month, from April to October, at 7:30 pm during other months. Hikes take about one to 1¹/₂ hours; you'll explore the nature trails while rangers point out the different habitats and nocturnal animals that populate the place. Other walks are available; call for more information.

The park is open 9 am to 5 pm; from April to October, they stay open till 8 pm on Tuesday and Thursday. Admission is $1 for adults, 50¢ for children three to 17, and all activities in the park are included in the price. To get to the park, from downtown take I-275 to exit 4, turn east onto 54th Ave S to ML King Jr Blvd S, then north to the first traffic signal (Country Club Way S) and turn left (west) to get to the park entrance. Parking is free.

Fort DeSoto Park

This 900-acre county park (☎ 727-866-2484), on Mullet Key south of downtown, has self-guided nature and recreational trails for biking, blading, walking and hiking, and about 3 miles of swimming beach. The fort was built during the Spanish-American War, and if you tire yourself out after a day of fun in the sun, you can camp here as well (see Places to Stay earlier in this section). To get here, take I-275 south to exit 4 and follow the signs; it's at 3500 Pinellas Bayway S. There is a 85¢ toll on the approach road, but park entry is free; it closes at dusk.

Sunshine Skyway Bridge

Okay, it's not exactly an attraction, but it's impressive nonetheless: the 4-mile-long Sun-shine Skyway Bridge spans Tampa Bay south of St Petersburg. It's the continuation of I-275, which meets up with I-75 on the south side of the bay. The toll is $1 to drive across. Built to replace the old span, which was destroyed in 1980 when a ship, the *Summit Venture*, rammed into its base, the Sunshine Skyway is a shimmering modern bridge – and each of its supports are surrounded by 'dolphins': gigantic shock absorbers that are capable of withstanding the force of an 87,000-ton vessel traveling at 10 knots (talk about shutting the barn door after the…ah, never mind). The *Summit Venture* weighed 34,500 tons and was traveling at 8 knots when it struck the old bridge.

Much of the old bridge still stands, and the plan is to convert it into the world's largest fishing pier. When completed (parts of it are already open to the public), it will span almost 2 miles.

ST PETE BEACH
• population 9200

With a great white-sand beach and clear, blue water, St Pete Beach (they officially changed the name a couple of years back) makes a great day or overnight trip from St Petersburg or Clearwater. But unless you're camping, you'll do much better to stay in the Clearwater Hostel (actually the beach is better there anyway) and do day trips from there – hotels on St Pete Beach are either expensive or not worth the money they charge.

See the St Petersburg Getting Around section for information on how to get here by bus and car. BATS buses ply Gulf Blvd with frequent service.

Orientation & Information

St Pete Beach is on Long Key, about 10 miles west of downtown St Petersburg across the Corey Causeway or the Pinellas County Bayway. The island is long and narrow, and the main (and only) artery is Gulf Blvd (Hwy 699).

The St Pete Beach Welcome Center (☎ 727-360-6957), 6990 Gulf Blvd, hands out tons of pamphlets and discount coupons. It's open Monday to Friday 9 am to 5 pm.

Change money at one of NationsBank's two locations on the beach: at 4105 Gulf Blvd and 7500 Gulf Blvd.

Wash clothes at the Washboard Coin Laundry (☎ 727-360-0674) at 6350 Gulf Blvd.

Check email and surf the Web for $2 per 15 minutes at Internet Outpost (☎ 727-360-7806), 7400 Gulf Blvd at Corey Ave.

Don CeSar Beach Resort

This resort (☎ 727-360-1883) is probably the first thing you'll notice when you pull into St Pete Beach: built in 1928, this monster of a hotel was a hot spot for such characters as F Scott Fitzgerald, Clarence Darrow, Lou Gehrig and Al Capone. The enormous pink building was bought by the US Army in 1942 and turned into a hospital and conva-lescent center for army personnel. Stripped of all its splendor, the building was aban-doned in 1967 by the Veterans Administra-tion, which had taken it over after the war. It was reopened in 1973, and from 1985 to 1989 it was completely restored. Today, it's open as a resort hotel: in low season rooms run $169 to $239, and in high season they go up to $289 to $359.

Gulf Beaches Historical Museum

This new museum (☎ 727-360-2491), 115 10th Ave at Pass-a-Grille Beach (about 2 miles south of the Don CeSar Hotel), is located in the building that housed the Pass-a-Grille Church (1917) – the first to be built on a west coast barrier island. The museum has a large collection of photographs and artifacts from the beaches, dating from the early 1800s, and a good selection of interest-ing old postcards and church memorabilia as well. As yet they've got no Indian artifacts, but they're working on it. It's open Thursday and Saturday 10 am to 4 pm and Sunday 1 to 4 pm, closed Monday to Wednesday and Friday. Admission is free, but donations are accepted. Take Gulf Blvd south past the Don CeSar; the road becomes Pass-a-Grille Blvd, which runs into 10th Ave.

Organized Tours

The very friendly people at Dolphin Land-ings Charter Boat Center (☎ 727-367-4488, 727-360-7411, www.dolphinlandings.com), 4737 Gulf Blvd, offer several tours of the region, including their daily two-hour dolphin-watching trips at 9:30 am, noon and 2:45 pm ($25 for adults, $15 for kids under 11), an islands excursion for shelling ($35/25) and sunset sails from 7 to 9 pm ($25 per person). All of the above prices include free soft drinks (and a cooler, so you can BYO beer), and reservations are required.

Places to Stay

The *KOA St Petersburg/Madeira Beach* (☎ 727-392-2233, 800-848-1094, 5400 95th St N) is about 2 miles from Madeira Beach, which is north of St Pete Beach. It has tent and RV sites for $37.69, or $46.57 with water and electric, including tax. One-room Kamping Kabins are $55.45, two rooms $66.55. To get there from downtown St Petersburg, take I-275 north and get off at 38th Ave N, go west for 5½ miles and take a left onto 66th St, take a right onto Tyrone Blvd, and go 1½ miles to 95th St. Turn right and it's about a half-mile ahead.

The motel and hotel chains found along the beach include *Howard Johnson Lodge* (☎ 727-360-7041, 6100 Gulf Blvd), *Best Western* (☎ 727-367-2771, 5390 Gulf Blvd) and *Holiday Inn* (☎ 727-360-1811, 5250 Gulf Blvd).

The *Florida Dolphin* (☎ 727-360-7233, 6801 Sunset Way) is clean enough but unspectacular; rates range from $45 to $65, depending on the month.

The *Osiris Motel* (☎ 727-360-6052, 620 68th Ave) and the *Gulf Tides Motel* (☎ 727-367-2979, 600 68th Ave) are both pretty much exactly like The Florida Dolphin.

Travel Lodge of St Pete Beach (☎ 727-367-2711, 800-237-8918, 6300 Gulf Blvd) has very nice rooms from $75 in low season and $99 in high season.

A step up from all this, The *Alden Resort* (☎ 727-360-7081, 800-237-2530, fax 941-360-5957, 5900 Gulf Blvd) is one of the nicer places to stay on the beach, with two pools, Jacuzzi, tennis courts, a bar and barbecue area and good service; rooms start in low season from $77 for a hotel room, $99 to

$130 for suites; in high season, it's $111 for hotel rooms, $153 to $206 for suites.

Also good is the **Coral Reef Beach Resort** (☎ 727-360-0821 fax 727-367-2597, 5800 Gulf Blvd); rates start at about $110 for a king-size room, $120 for a room with two double beds and $150 for a suite. They also have a time-share condo on the premises for longer stays.

Places to Eat

The **Sea Dragon Restaurant** (☎ 727-360-0992, 7390 Gulf Blvd) is a Chinese place that does a lunch buffet from 11:30 am to 3 pm for $5.95 and a dinner buffet from 5 to 9 pm for $8 (including a soup and salad bar). Early-bird specials ($6) are available from 4 to 6 pm. Regular dinner dishes from the menu run $6 to $10.

Aunt Heidi's Italian Restaurant (☎ 727-367-3448, 6340 Gulf Blvd) is good for a quick bite; hoagies are $3.75, a baked ziti dinner $6.50, and they also have pizza and beer and wine.

Sunset Beach Cafe (☎ 727-367-3359, 9701 1st St E) serves reliable seafood, pizza and salads.

Bruno's (☎ 727-367-4420, 432 75th Ave) is a well-spoken-of Italian place open daily for lunch and dinner. Main courses ($11 to $16) include fettuccine primavera, veal rollatini and chicken cacciatore.

We were very pleasantly surprised at **PJ's Oyster Bar and Seafood Restaurant** (☎ 727-367-3309, 7500 Gulf Blvd). It has generous portions of seafood and friendly service. Appetizers – such as a half-dozen oysters or clams – are around $5, and main courses such as baked grouper are from $11 to $15. It's open for lunch and dinner.

Fetishes (☎ 727-363-3700, 6690 Gulf Blvd) is less expensive than you'd think but it can still get up there: we hear good things about their coq au vin, $12.95. Curried lobster Lorraine appetizer is $6.95.

The **Maritana Grille** (☎ 727-360-1882, 3400 Gulf Blvd) is expensive but good; main courses from $18 include Atlantic salmon with a horseradish crust, shrimp fricassee and lobster beurre blanc ($24). Prix-fixe dinner for two is $46.50.

CLEARWATER BEACH
• population 7000

Home to incredible white-sand beaches, one of southwest Florida's largest fishing fleets, and near enough to both Tampa and St Petersburg to be a base for either, Clearwater Beach is struggling to make a comeback to the powerhouse resort status it had up until about five years ago. And it's home to Florida's newest HI/AYH-member hostel, which is a superb, friendly source of local information and assistance.

The area's a great spot for canoeing and kayaking, shelling, bicycling and broiling yourself on the beach – which just about sums up the local 'tourist attractions.'

Backpackers will appreciate the scale of the island; unlike many Florida towns, it's only 3½ miles long, and it's easy to get around by foot or bicycle.

Orientation & Information

Clearwater Beach is on a barrier island about 2 miles west of downtown Clearwater (a separate city on the mainland) over the Memorial Causeway (Hwy 60), which to the east becomes Gulf-to-Bay Blvd. Roughly, there's a T-junction when the Gulf-to-Bay route hits the coastline; the road south is S Gulfview Blvd and north is Mandalay Ave, Clearwater Beach's main drag. Pier 60 is right at the T-junction. From St Petersburg, it's about a half-hour drive or a 1½-hour bus ride.

The Clearwater Visitor Information Center (☎ 727-462-6531) is on the south side of Causeway Blvd just east of the T-junction, behind the Beach Diner (see Places to Eat later in this section). This and the Clearwater Beach International Youth Hostel (see Places to Stay) are the best sources of local information.

Change money at the NationsBank at 423 Mandalay Ave.

The Clearwater Beach Medical Clinic (☎ 727-461-4464) is at 37 Baymont St.

Clearwater Marine Aquarium

This aquarium (☎ 727-447-0980), at 249 Windward Passage, is a nonprofit organization dedicated to educating the public and to

SOUTHWEST

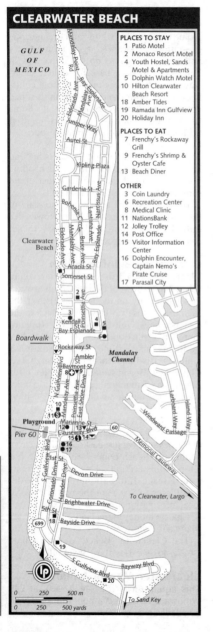

CLEARWATER BEACH

GULF
OF
MEXICO

Clearwater
Beach

Boardwalk

Mandalay
Channel

Playground

Pier 60

To Clearwater, Largo

To Sand Key

0   250   500 m
0   250   500 yards

PLACES TO STAY
1 Patio Motel
2 Monaco Resort Motel
4 Youth Hostel, Sands
   Motel & Apartments
5 Dolphin Watch Motel
10 Hilton Clearwater
   Beach Resort
18 Amber Tides
19 Ramada Inn Gulfview
20 Holiday Inn

PLACES TO EAT
7 Frenchy's Rockaway
   Grill
9 Frenchy's Shrimp &
   Oyster Cafe
13 Beach Diner

OTHER
3 Coin Laundry
6 Recreation Center
8 Medical Clinic
11 NationsBank
12 Jolley Trolley
14 Post Office
15 Visitor Information
   Center
16 Dolphin Encounter,
   Captain Nemo's
   Pirate Cruise
17 Parasail City

rescuing and rehabilitating marine animals. Currently, they are caring for two dolphins (named Sunset Sam and Halona), turtles (including loggerheads, Kemp's ripley and hawksbill), a huge variety of fish, sea otters and others. Presentations are run every half hour throughout the day.

It's open Monday to Friday 9 am to 5 pm, Saturday 9 am to 4 pm and Sunday 11 am to 4 pm; admission is $6.75 for adults and $4.25 for children (under three free). It's between Clearwater and Clearwater Beach, off the Memorial Causeway (Hwy 60), on Island Estates. The Jolley Trolley stops here, as does bus No 80.

Pier 60

Sunset at Pier 60 is Clearwater Beach's version of the sunset celebration begun at Key West's Mallory Square. It features jugglers and magicians, and craftspeople and artists set up stalls. It takes place on the pier from Thursday to Monday, two hours before and after sunset, and in winter there are free concerts on Friday and Saturday 7 to 10 pm and Sunday 5 to 8 pm.

Activities

The bay side of the beach is filled with mangrove islands, and it's great for **canoeing**. The calm waters of the Gulf also make it easy to paddle up to Caladesi Island (see below), which is a beautiful retreat.

The hostel has free canoes for its guests. You can rent kayaks at Aqua Azul Kayak Tours (☎ 727-530-7555), 17952 Alt US Hwy 19 N, on the east side of the Memorial Causeway. They rent solo or tandem sea kayaks, with paddling instructions, for $12 an hour, or $35 a day for a solo, $45 a day for a tandem. They also provide 4½-hour guided kayak tours for $42. There is a discount for hostel guests.

Parasail City (☎ 727-449-0566) runs **parasail** boats right opposite Pier 60. They'll take you 600 feet up for $35, 800 feet up for $45 or even 1000 feet up for $55, though there are $5 off coupons everywhere, even at the desk (if not, show them this book and tell them they said the listing was good for that same $5 discount).

You can **bike** along the beach or along the Pinellas Trail, a 47-mile bicycle path (see Around Clearwater Beach later in this chapter). The hostel rents out bicycles for $5 per day.

The city recreation center, right near the hostel, is open to the public and has **tennis** and other activities.

Organized Tours

See Resorts below for the historical tour of the Belleview Biltmore hotel.

It's Our Nature (☎ 727-441-2599, www .itsournature.com) runs guided nature walks in several areas, including Caladesi Island State Park, Honeymoon Island and Lettuce Lake Park in Tampa, from $10 to $20 per person.

Dolphin Encounter (☎ 727-442-7433), opposite Pier 60, runs daily 1½- to two-hour dolphin-watching cruises out to the Gulf of Mexico for $10.75 for adults, $6.75 for kids. April through October, they also run a sunset cruise for the same price, leaving at 6 pm.

Captain Nemo's Pirate Cruise (☎ 727-446-2587), right next to Dolphin Encounter, runs two-hour cruises aboard the *Pirate's Ransom*, a replica pirate ship, for $27 for adults, $20 for seniors and $17 for kids – but for the first two categories that includes free beer and wine.

Places to Stay

Hostels The HI/AYH-member *Clearwater Beach International Youth Hostel* (☎ 727-443-1211, 606 Bay Esplanade) is a resort-style hostel with dorm rooms at $12 for members and $13 for nonmembers; rooms are $75/84 weekly. Private rooms are available at their adjacent *Sands Motel & Apts*, where one-bedroom apartments are $41/56 for singles/doubles. There's a swimming pool surrounded by lush gardens, a picnic area and tiki huts, and it's only a three-minute walk to the beautiful beach.

The hostel has kitchen and laundry facilities ($1.50 each). You need at least a bottom sheet; they rent linens ($2 for a full set), and the whole place is air-conditioned. They have canoes available for free use (with a $50 deposit); there is table tennis, shuffle-board and a barbecue. Map and reference materials are available, and you can play a game of tennis nearby, as well as basketball and volleyball.

Motels & Hotels Chains along the beach include *Hilton Clearwater Beach Resort* (☎ 727-461-3222, 400 Mandalay Ave); *Ramada Inn Gulfview* (☎ 727-447-6461, 521 S Gulfview Blvd); *Holiday Inn* (☎ 727-447-9566, 715 S Gulfview Blvd); and *Days Inn* (☎ 727-447-8444, 100 Coronado Drive). On the mainland, there is a *Best Western* (☎ 727-442-6171, 25 Belleview Blvd).

The *Monaco Resort Motel* (☎ 727-443-6954, 648 Poinsettia Ave), a block from the beach, has motel rooms for $30 in summer, $35 from December 1 to January 31, and $55 from February 1 to April 30; efficiencies, with fully stocked kitchens, are $36/40/65. There is a pool.

Amber Tides Motel & Apartments (☎ 727-446-0438, 420 Hamden Drive) is a nice, quiet place off the main drag. They have a tiny pool. Room prices change by the month: the lowest prices, in June, are $40 for motel rooms and $38 for small efficiencies; the highest, in March, are $58/75.

The friendly folks at the *Patio Motel* (☎ 727-442-1862, 15 Somerset St) have a clean motel room ($36 in summer, $46 in winter), efficiencies and one- and two-bedroom apartments ($41 to $72 in summer, $54 to $85 in winter). There's no pool, but it's right on the water (many rooms look right out to the Gulf) and has a private beach.

A friendly Swiss-German couple runs the *Dolphin Watch Motel* (☎ 727-449-9039, 607 Bay Esplanade). It's right on the bay and has a heated pool, a spa, a private dock and barbecue facilities. Efficiencies are $49/59 for singles/doubles, larger one-to-four-person rooms are $65/85.

Resorts The *Belleview Biltmore Resort & Spa* (☎ 727-442-6171, 800-237-8947, 25 Belleview Blvd), off Hwy 60 and Fort Harrison Ave, in Belleair, near Clearwater (on the mainland), was built in the 1890s as a retreat for wealthy northeasterners. In the 1950s, the Duke of Windsor, his dogs and

SOUTHWEST

possibly Mrs Simpson stayed here, and he even wrote part of his memoirs here while dancing with the bandleader's wife and all the staff – he was apparently a hit at costume balls. As was, we assume, Lady Thatcher, who stayed here. It's not exactly a backpacker's hangout: while the pool and spa may be charming, room rates average $150 to $200 (though go much higher) but they have great package deals such as their romance package, with champagne, a full candlelight dinner and breakfast in bed for $189 per couple.

If that's too rich for your blood, take a tour instead; there's one every day at 11 am for $5, or $15 including a buffet lunch at their restaurant. You will see the tunnels underneath the hotel, a museum and a section devoted to the Army Air Corps, which was stationed here during WWII. The spa is open to the public; it's $15 a day for the gym, whirlpool and sauna.

Places to Eat

The *Beach Diner* (☎ 727-446-4747, 56 Causeway Blvd) is a '50s- and '60s-style diner. Its free juke box is filled with '50s beach music. Saturday is Dime Day noon to 3 pm, when they have 10¢ draft beers; raw or steamed oysters or clam or shrimp chowder are 10¢ as well – and there's no limit! There's a classic car show on the first and third Friday of the month. Been fishing? They'll cook up your catch (fried, grilled or blackened) and serve it to you with salad and potatoes or rice for $3.95. Burgers are $4.50, and their sublime milkshakes (made with Breyer's ice cream) are $1.99. And if you or your kids get bored, they have Legos on the tables.

Golden Treasure (☎ 727-448-0372, 432 Poinsettia Ave) has excellent Chinese food at decent prices. Combinations of soup, egg roll and an entree, such as kung pao chicken or Hunan beef, start at $4.50, and try their $3 hot and sour soup.

Frenchy's Rockaway Grill (☎ 727-446-4844, 7 Rockaway St) serves salads, burgers, seafood and Mexican food from $6 to $15. They make a great chimichanga, and we

hear the she-crab soup is to die for. There is live music on Thursday to Sunday nights, pool tables and a happy hour.

Frenchy's Saltwater Cafe (☎ 727-461-6295, 416 E Shore Drive) is a seafood restaurant that's popular with locals. It's said to have a great grouper sandwich and mussels marinara.

Frenchy's Shrimp & Oyster Cafe (☎ 727-446-3607, 41 Baymont) is 'the original hole in the wall.' It's a tiny place with picnic benches that's a great local hangout; specials include gumbo by the cup/bowl for $2.95/3.75 and crabby shrimp sandwiches for $5.35.

The hostel folks say that *Los Mariachis* (☎ 727-448-0372, 1200 Cleveland St), on the mainland, is one of their favorites, with great margaritas, excellent fajitas and chimichangas. The portions are huge, they make their own tortilla chips, guacamole and salsa, and on weekends a mariachi band plays. Entrees run from $6.95 to $15.

Entertainment

Shephards (☎ 727-441-6875, 601 S Gulfview Blvd) has reggae on Saturday and Sunday afternoons, and a beachfront tiki bar.

In Largo, south of Clearwater, *Storman's* (☎ 727-571-2202, 2675 Ulmerton Rd) does a Friday night party from 5 to 8 pm, with two-for-one drinks and $3, 32-ounce draught beers and a free buffet from 6 to 8 pm.

Old New York New York (☎ 727-539-7441, 18573 US Hwy 19) is where singles mingle on Friday and Saturday nights.

Getting There & Away

Bus The Clearwater Greyhound station (☎ 727-796-7315) is at 2811 Gulf-to-Bay Blvd at Hampton Rd. There are six buses a day making the half-hour trip from Tampa ($7 one way, $14 roundtrip).

From Clearwater, take Dart (☎ 727-531-0415) bus No 60 from the stop across Gulf-to-Bay Blvd westbound to the Park St Bus Depot, and change there to bus No 80 to Clearwater Beach. Get off at the tennis courts at the corner of Mandalay Ave and Bay Esplanade, and it's about a two-minute walk to the hostel.

From the Tampa Amtrak station, take the courtesy bus to Pinellas Park and change for PSTA bus No 18, which you take to the Park St Bus Depot, where you catch bus No 80 to Clearwater Beach (☎ 727-530-9911 for schedule information).

Getting to Busch Gardens by public transportation is the closest thing to hell on earth; a much better idea is to take the Gray Line (☎ 800-282-4051). It costs about $50, which includes the admission to Busch Gardens. If you consider that the admission is $36.45, Gray Line is essentially an $8.85 shuttle bus.

Car & Motorcycle From Tampa, take Hwy 60, the Courtney Campbell Causeway through Clearwater and west out to the beach. From St Petersburg, take Hwy 19 (34th St N) north to Hwy 60 and go west. From St Pete Beach, take Gulf Blvd north.

Getting Around
The red Jolley Trolley (☎ 727-445-1200) runs all around Clearwater Beach from north to south and onward to Sand Key; you just wave it down. Fare is 50¢, 25¢ for seniors. The beach route runs daily: Sunday to Thursday from 10 am to 10 pm, and Friday and Saturday 10 am to midnight. A second Jolley Trolley runs between the beach and Clearwater's Park St Station; this route runs every half hour 10 am to 10 pm.

AROUND CLEARWATER BEACH
Heritage Park
Just south of the city of Clearwater, Heritage Park (☎ 727-582-2123), 11909 125th St in Largo, is a 21-acre historical park and open-air museum. It has 22 structures, including the oldest house in the county, two Victorian houses, a schoolhouse, store, doctor's office, a mill, barn and a church. It's open Tuesday to Saturday 10 am to 4 pm and Sunday 1 to 4 pm; admission is free. By car or bike (it's about 10 miles), take Alt Hwy 19 south to Ulmerton Rd, turn right, and left on 125th St. From Clearwater Beach, take bus No 80 to Park St Station and then change for bus No 52 or 61 to the stop at

Walsingham and 125th St; the entrance is very close by.

Pinellas Trail
The Pinellas Trail is a paved, 47-mile county-run bicycle trail built on the track bed of the CSX railway. The path's very smooth – smooth enough for in-line skates or roller skates as well as bicycles – and it runs from St Petersburg to Tarpon Springs, though there is a gap at the north and south of Clearwater.

There are lots of stops along the way, with cafés, pubs, bike shops, skate shops, and fast-food places. As it's on the route of the old railway, the path cuts through widely varied terrain: sometimes you're in the middle of downtown (as in Dunedin), sometimes among orange groves (near Pinellas Park) and sometimes you're riding practically through people's backyards in bedroom communities.

To get there from the Clearwater Beach International Youth Hostel, which rents bikes (see Hostels in the Clearwater Beach section, earlier in this chapter), head down Gulf-to-Bay Blvd and over the causeway, and ride north on Fort Harrison Ave and east on Jones St for about three blocks. You'll pick up the southern end of the Clearwater to Tarpon Springs section of the path. It's 13.2 miles from Jones St to Tarpon Ave.

Contact the Pinellas County Planning Department (☎ 727-464-4751) for a copy of their free *Guidebook to the Pinellas Trail*, which lists rest stops and local attractions and has a mileage chart. It's the best guide to the trail. Also check with Rob at the Clearwater Beach hostel, who rides the trail all the time.

Sand Key
Sand Key Beach is a 65-acre park at the northern end of a long barrier island on the Gulf of Mexico, and it's a great spot for dolphin watching, especially on the channel side. There's pretty good shelling here as well (best at low tide, especially during new and full moons and after storms). The beach is about a half-mile long and the widest in

SOUTHWEST

the area. It's off the southern end of Clearwater Beach, connected by the Clearwater Pass Bridge. The Jolley Trolley (see Getting Around later in this section) goes here, or you can get here by bicycle.

The **Suncoast Seabird Sanctuary** (☎ 727-391-6211, www.gulfside.com/seabird/), 18328 Gulf Blvd (south of Indian Shores), is the largest wild-bird hospital in North America (1¹/₂ acres), founded by Ralph Heath Jr in 1971. About 40 different species of crippled birds have found a home here, and there are usually between 400 to 600 sea and land birds being treated and recuperating. Whenever possible, the birds are released back into the wild.

The sanctuary is open daily 9 am to dusk. Guided tours take place Wednesday and Sunday at 2 pm. Admission is free, but please leave a donation.

Honeymoon & Caladesi Islands

Honeymoon Island State Recreation Area (☎ 727-469-5942), 1 Dunedin Causeway, began its life as a grand prize in a 1940s contest held by Paramount newsreels and *Life* magazine. They were giving away all-expense-paid honeymoons on the island to newlyweds, who would come and stay in the 50 or so thatched huts that lined the beach. During the war, Honeymoon Island was a rest and relaxation site for exhausted war factory workers, and the place was never a honeymoon spot again. The road connecting the island to the mainland was built in 1964, and the state bought the land in the early 1970s.

Today, the park offers birding, swimming and great shelling. Coastal plant communities found on the island include mangrove swamps, virgin slash pine, strand and salt marshes. There are nature trails and bird observation areas here, as well as a ferry to Caladesi Island. Park admission is $4 per carload or $1 for pedestrians. To get here, take Hwy Alt 19 north to the city of Dunedin (pronounced 'dun-EDEN') and go west on Curlew Rd (Hwy 586), the Dunedin Causeway, which leads to the island.

Caledesi Island State Park (☎ 727-469-5918) is just south of Honeymoon Island.

You can actually walk there from Clearwater Beach (a 1921 hurricane and a 1985 storm filled in the gap between north Clearwater Beach and the island), canoe there or take a ferry from Honeymoon Island. There are picnic pavilions, a concession stand and you can swim, shell and walk along nature trails or on the secluded, palm-lined 3-mile beach. Wildlife you might see around here includes armadillos, raccoons, snakes, turtles, pelicans, ibis, osprey, cormorants and others.

The Caledesi Connection (☎ 727-734-5263) is at the western end of Curlew Creek Rd (Hwy 586) in Honeymoon Island State Recreation Area. It runs ferries to Caledesi every hour on the hour on weekdays, and every half hour on weekends, starting at 10 am; the last departure from Caledesi is around 4:30 pm. The fare is $6 for adults, $3.50 for children, and free for those under age four (no credit cards).

TARPON SPRINGS

About 15 miles north of Clearwater sits the tidy little tourist trap of Tarpon Springs. Touted as an authentic Greek sponging village, it's actually a collection of tourist attractions, touristy restaurants and crap-a-rooni stands. The seven-block Tarpon Springs Downtown Historic District, however, is a charming 19th-century area, with brick streets and the fabulous **St Nicholas Church**. The Greek-Orthodox church, built with 60 tons of Greek marble and featuring Czech stained glass, is the focal point of the annual Epiphany Day celebration on January 6th.

The city was indeed a sponging center, and attracted the Greek immigrants who made up so much of the town's culture from the early 1900s until the sponge died off in the 1940s. New sponge beds were discovered in the 1980s and today the sponge docks are again bustling, though we found everything here to be overpriced and cynical.

If you've never tried them, it may be interesting to sample Greek appetizers at the dozens of Greek restaurants around the docks. We left quickly.

From Clearwater, Hwy Alt 19 heads straight north to Tarpon Springs.

WEEKI WACHEE SPRINGS

• population 15

'The City of Mermaids,' Weeki Wachee Springs (☎ 800-678-9335, www.weekiwachee.com) is about 30 miles north of Clearwater, 80 miles northwest of Orlando and 70 west of Ocala. Most people come here as a day trip from the Clearwater/Tampa area, but there's a Holiday Inn across the street from the park entrance. As are other attractions in Florida, such as Marineland and Walt Disney World, Weeki Wachee Springs is now incorporated into its own city.

Hold it. Mermaids? Yup. Since 1947, families and celebrities, such as Esther Williams, Danny Thomas and Elvis Presley, have been coming here to see the star attraction at this 200-acre theme park: the underwater show starring long-haired women in mermaid costumes who swim in the natural spring (there are also mermen).

The spring has a constant temperature of 72°F, measures about 100 feet across and produces about 170 million gallons of water a day; it's the headwater of the Weeki Wachee River. The mermaids perform in the spring, alongside fish, turtles, otters, snakes and eels.

The shows here are the height of kitsch, a trip straight back to the 1950s. You watch the mermaids, about 20 of them, perform their mainstay show, *The Little Mermaid,* in an underwater theater – the audience watches through glass panels, making this the world's only underwater artesian spring theater. The theater was built in 1946 by Newton Perry, an ex-Navy frogman. Remarkably, the mermaids flail and swim about with what appears to be the greatest of ease.

Don't be fooled. Performing underwater requires incredible stamina, and the breathing apparatus is tricky. There are submerged air hoses on the sides of the theater: the mermaids swim over, grab some air, hold their breath while swimming around performing and then zip back for more air – for *half an hour* at a time! They train first on land and then in the water without the tail, practicing the moves of the 30-minute shows. It takes about six to eight months to get the whole thing to look as effortless as it does, and if it

looks easy, *you* try lip-synching to music underwater next time you're snorkeling!

The park also has a Wilderness River Cruise, a petting zoo with a pygmy goat, a fallow deer and a giraffe, and two bird shows: Birds of Prey – with eagles, hawks, owls and other raptors and Exotic Birds – with macaws and cockatoos. To see all the shows, expect to spend at least five hours here. The Mermaid Galley sells burgers, hot dogs and the like.

The park's open 10 am to 5:30 pm daily, a little later in summer and on holidays (note the totally campy and yet social-realist statue of two mermaids thrusting their arms skyward at the entrance). Admission is $16.95 for adults, $12.95 for children three to 10; parking is free.

To get there, drive north on Hwy 19 to the intersection of Hwy 50, about a half hour north of Clearwater; from I-75, take exit 61 and go west about 20 miles.

HOMOSASSA SPRINGS

Homosassa Springs (☎ 904-628-2311) is another spring to the north; this one, the headwater of the Homosassa River, is home to the Homosassa Springs State Wildlife Park, which amounts to the state's largest all-natural theme park.

The 168-acre park (actually it's 180, but some of it's submerged) does showcases and educational demonstrations about its diverse wildlife, which include manatees, black bears, bobcats, white-tailed deer, alligators, American crocodiles and river otters. The area is made up of wetlands, hydric hammock and spring-run streams that bubble out of the 45-foot-deep Homosassa Spring. Staff here also rehabilitate injured manatees.

The area was formerly a for-profit theme park (Homosassa Springs Attraction), and the old owners had installed a floating underwater observatory – launched on ways of banana peels as opposed to grease to protect the fish. Today, the Fish Bowl observatory is still used to watch manatees and fish.

As you enter, you get on pontoon boats that take you on an orientation tour of the park, after which you're free to wander on the nature trails. There's a snack bar, and picnic tables are available. Plan on spending about three to four hours in the park.

There are a bunch of interpretive programs held every day, including two each of alligator and crocodile demonstrations, animal encounter programs on snakes or birds of prey, and manatees.

Daily educational programs include the manatee, at 10:45 am and 3:45 pm, the animal encounter, at 11:30 am and 1:45 pm, and the alligator, at 12:45 and 2:30 pm.

The park is open daily from 9 am to 5:30 pm, ticket sales end at 4 pm. Admission is $7.95 for adults, $4.95 for children three to 12; there are AAA and AARP discounts and free kennels (no pets are allowed in the park). The park is about 60 miles north of Clearwater and 75 miles north of Tampa; take Hwy 19 north right to the entrance of the park.

Northwest Florida & the Panhandle

The Florida Panhandle, which stretches almost 200 miles from the Alabama border in the west and Tallahassee to the east, is known for three main features. First, its beaches are hands down the best in the continental USA; the Appalachian quartz sand along Panhandle beaches is so white it's literally dazzling, and it's so fine that it 'barks' when you walk on it. In various areas of the Panhandle, the warm waters of the Gulf of Mexico are brilliant turquoise and, astonishingly, emerald green, and they are always crystal clear.

Second, the Panhandle is known for Panama City Beach, called the Redneck Riviera for its popularity with visitors from nearby counties as well as nearby states like Alabama and Louisiana. Here, Spring Break never ends, and a huge selling point touted by tourism officials is that it's legal to drink beer on the beach.

And third, the Panhandle is known for its hurricanes, which seem to gravitate to the area like UFOs to Midwestern RV parks (or, actually, like UFOs to the Panhandle, which has more reported sightings of spaceships than any other area in the country).

But it's also home to incredibly pristine nature – from the Gulf Islands National Seashore to the dazzling beauty of Blackwater River State Park and Forest to the fascinating caverns at the Florida Caverns State Park in Marianna – as well as home to Apalachicola, the state's oyster capital.

Many of the areas in the Panhandle can be explored as day trips, using Pensacola, Panama City Beach, Tallahassee or Apalachicola as a base.

Pensacola's history predates even St Augustine's (in fact, the two cities argue over which is the nation's oldest settlement). The city has three gorgeous historic districts and some incredible beaches. You can also catch fantastic performances by the navy's Blue Angels precision-flying team, which makes the Pensacola Naval Air Station its winter home.

Highlights

- Enjoy the stunning beaches at Pensacola, Destin, Fort Walton Beach and Grayton Beach – known for their sugar-white sand, clear water and spectacular sunsets and moonrises

- Swim, hike and camp at St Andrews or Grayton Beach State Recreation Areas – both voted best beach in the USA by *Condé Nast Traveler*

- Stroll or drive along Tallahassee's lovely canopy roads

- Traipse through Florida Caverns State Park, among eerie stalactite and stalagmite formations

- Canoe on the Blackwater River, which, despite its name, is one of the clearest sand-bottom rivers in the world

- Relax in the peace and tranquillity of secluded St George Island

- Go innertubing at Ichetucknee Springs State Park

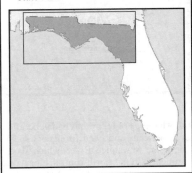

Tallahassee is the state's capital, though don't expect to see busy legislators running around cutting deals – the hard-working Florida legislature meets for only about 60 days of the year (and you thought guidebook writers had a good scam going). About 40 minutes east of the capital, you can find

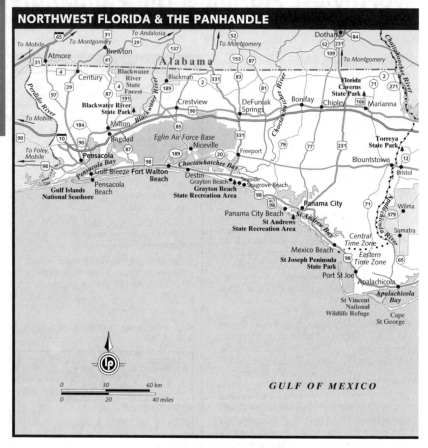

NORTHWEST FLORIDA & THE PANHANDLE

GULF OF MEXICO

out what type of fellow has had generations of Americans and even foreigners singing about the Suwannee River, which slashes through extreme north-central Florida before emptying into the Gulf of Mexico.

Even if you can't get out to the western stretches of the Florida Panhandle, don't miss the opportunity to explore the Nature Coast, the coastline that stretches along the 'big bend' of the state, where Steinhatchee Landing's superb restaurant and luxurious duplex cottages cost far less than they should.

PENSACOLA

• population 378,000; time zone CST

Pensacola is a surprisingly old city for the USA. Europeans originally tried settling in this area in 1559, but a hurricane and laziness resulted in them forfeiting the honor of first European settlement to St Augustine in 1565.

Pensacola was made a permanent settlement in 1568. Much of the downtown area today dates to the 1800s, though there are remnants of British and Spanish buildings dating to the late 1700s.

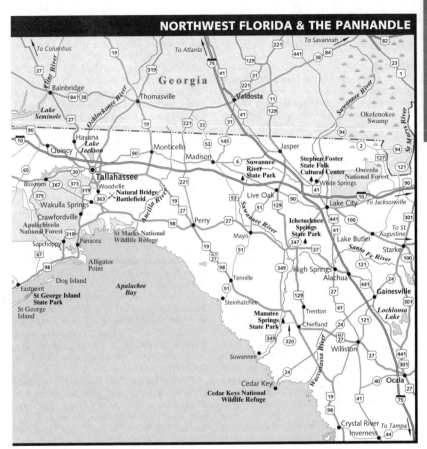

Today, Pensacola's main attraction – despite three historic districts that have undergone extensive reconstruction and renovation – is its beach, and unfortunately much of it was badly damaged in 1995 by Hurricane Opal. But even right after the hurricane, it was obvious what a treasure this beach is: gently sloped, sugar-white sand lapped by calm blue waters, and plenty of room for everyone to get comfortable. As we were researching this edition (in fact, the day we were to head to Pensacola) Hurricane Georges came through, and, though it

did far less damage than Opal, it closed down attractions and disrupted businesses once again. As we went to press, the cleanup was entering its final stages, and by the time you read this, the area should be back to normal.

Pensacola's also a naval city: the enormous Pensacola Naval Air Station is home to thousands of people as well as the Blue Angels, the navy's awesome precision-flying outfit. You can see them rehearsing here when they're in town, and the sight of the jets soaring up in tight formation and then breaking off and plummeting toward earth is something that even pacifists must admit is nothing short of spectacular.

History

The written record of the Indian population that made the area home for some ten thousand years is incredibly scant. Most historical accounts begin with the area's 'discovery' and exploration in the early 1540s by Hernando de Soto, and the attempt in 1559 by Spanish explorer Don Tristan de Luna to settle it. The settlement was a disaster: a hurricane wiped out much of it early on, and even though reinforcements arrived two years later, settlers opted to move on.

The relationship between the Spanish and the French, already testy, grew more openly hostile through the 17th century. The French had settlements at nearby Mobile, Alabama, and in 1719, the area was taken by the French and surrendered back to Spain four times.

During the period of British rule (1763-81), much of the planning of the city took place; remnants of British-built structures – including the government house and commanding officers' compound – can still be seen in the Seville Historic District, which the Brits laid out. When the Spanish took over again, the first thing they did was accept the street grids and change all the offensive names (any names involving the British Monarchy were nixed), thus the presence today of streets like Alcaniz, Palafox and Intendencia.

Andrew Jackson, the American general so keen on booting out Indians and colonial governments, swept unsanctioned into the area after the War of 1812 and simply took it. During the war, Spain had allowed British ships to dock at Pensacola – and the Brits had assisted in training and supplying the Creek Indians Jackson was fighting. The US initially gave it back ('Oh, okay...*here*'), but it was returned when the Spanish ceded Florida to the US in 1821. Andrew Jackson returned to Pensacola and became its first governor.

The city's deep harbor and geographical position were key factors in its development as a military city; construction of the first navy base was begun almost immediately after the US took control, and forts were built to defend Pensacola Bay from three sides.

Those forts would become a major focus of both Confederate and Federal troops during the Civil War, when fighting over them led to an enormous battle in the harbor, which ended in stalemate. After the war and an epidemic of yellow fever, which reduced the population, Pensacola went through a number of booms, probably the most important of which was based on lumber.

The navy, which had abandoned the Pensacola base in the early 1900s, reopened it as an air base in 1914 to train pilots for long-range flight and antisubmarine warfare. You can see the NC-4, the plane that made the first successful transatlantic flight (it wasn't nonstop, nor was it solo) at the National Museum of Naval Aviation here.

The area gained prominence again in WWII, when the US Navy's flight instruction school began working overtime, training thousands of American and foreign pilots. Pensacola Beach, connected to the mainland by a 3-mile-long bridge, became a popular tourist spot after the war.

Restoration of the historic districts began in the 1960s and '70s; North Hill was listed on the National Register of Historic Places in 1972. Today, Pensacola is a city with a strong military economy, filled with gawkers and sun worshipers. There's a vibrant

---

Time Zones

Get an extra hour of sleep free! The Panhandle is in two time zones: east of the Apalachicola River is on Eastern Standard Time (EST); west of the Apalachicola River is on Central Standard Time (CST). When it's 9 am in Apalachicola, it's 8 am in Panama City Beach and Pensacola. In this chapter, we list the city's time zone directly beneath its heading.

arts scene developing, and despite the devastating blows that Hurricanes Opal and Georges dealt to the city, it's coming back stronger than ever.

Orientation

The city is a typical Florida sprawler, and it's very difficult to get between places without a car unless you're walking in downtown, just north of the Port of Pensacola at the southeastern end of the city. Palafox St is the east-west divider, Garden St the north-south. Note that Palafox St is officially called

Palafox Place south of Garden St, and attempts are being made to register that section with the federal government as the Palafox Place Business District. But, confusingly, locals refer to it as Palafox, S Palafox Place, S Palafox St or just Palafox St straight through. And even worse, commercially bought and even locally obtained maps show different names for the street and several of the historic districts.

The North Hill Preservation District, about a mile northwest of downtown, is bordered by Palafox St to the east, Reus St to

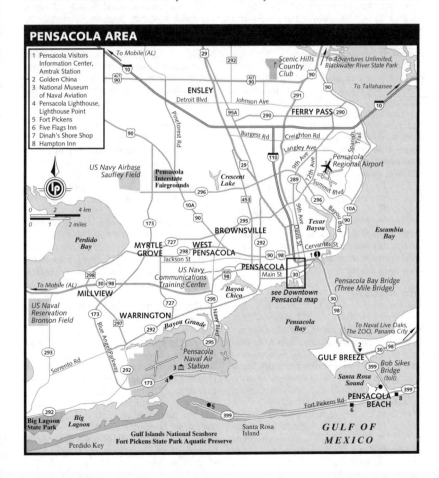

PENSACOLA AREA

1 Pensacola Visitors
  Information Center,
  Amtrak Station
2 Golden China
3 National Museum
  of Naval Aviation
4 Pensacola Lighthouse,
  Lighthouse Point
5 Fort Pickens
6 Five Flags Inn
7 Dinah's Shore Shop
8 Hampton Inn

the west, Blount (pronounced 'blunt') St to the north and the northern side of Wright St to the south.

Much of the southeast quadrant of downtown Pensacola is taken up by the Palafox Historic District, a collection of smaller districts that have been combined into one large and still growing preservation area bounded roughly by Cervantes St to the north, the waterfront to the south, Florida Blanca St to the east and Spring St to the west. Within the Palafox Historic District is Historic Pensacola Village, bordered by Government St to the north, Main St to the south, Jefferson St to the west and Alcaniz St to the east.

The Naval Air Station (NAS) is in the southwest quadrant of the city.

Pensacola Beach is on Santa Rosa Island, southeast of Pensacola and Gulf Breeze. Gulf Breeze is connected to Pensacola by the Pensacola Bay Bridge (everyone calls it the Three Mile Bridge) and to Pensacola Beach by the Bob Sikes Bridge ($1 toll). An older series of bridges that run adjacent to Three Mile Bridge on its eastern side are now open as fishing bridges and can be accessed by car only from the south side.

The Pensacola Visitors Information Center (see below) sells copies of Dolph's *Map of Pensacola* and gives out placemat-size free maps, which have the historic districts on one side and a simplified area map on the reverse. You can also find free handout maps of downtown at many downtown attractions.

Information

The excellent Pensacola Visitors Information Center (☎ 850-434-1234, 800-874-1234, www.visitpensacola.com), 1401 E Gregory St, at the foot of the Pensacola Bay Bridge, has a glorious bounty of tourist information, with volunteers and staff who really know the area. Other good sources of information are the Pensacola Beach Visitors Center/ Chamber of Commerce (☎ 850-932-1500, 800-635-4803), 735 Pensacola Beach Blvd, and the Pensacola Area Chamber of Commerce (☎ 850-438-4081, www.chamber .pensacola.fl.us), 117 W Garden St.

The Pensacola Historical Society Resource Center & Library (☎ 850-434-5455), 117 E Government St opposite Seville Quarter, is just what it sounds like. The Arts Council of Northwest Florida (☎ 850-432-9906) is of great help – see the Entertainment section for more information.

Change money at the downtown Nations-Bank, 100 W Garden St. American Express has a representative office at Fillette Green Travel Service (☎ 850-434-2543), 313 Palafox Place. The main downtown post office (☎ 850-434-3164) is at 101 Palafox Place.

The Arcade Newsstand (☎ 850-438-1796), 194 Palafox St, has magazines, newspapers, books, comics, and so on. Toni's Pipe Rack, $4^1/2$ Palafox Place, sells tobacco, books, the *New York Times*, *Wall Street Journal* and other out-of-town stuff. The main library (☎ 850-435-1760) is at 200 W Gregory St.

The *Pensacola News Journal* is the big daily; other papers include the *New American Press*, focusing on African American news, and the *Gulf Breeze Sentinel*. National Public Radio (NPR) is at 88.1 FM.

It's not easy finding a laundry in downtown Pensacola. On Santa Rosa Island, there's a coin laundry (☎ 850-932-3005) at 37 Via de Luna, and there's a gigantic one out toward the naval air station at 43 S Navy Blvd.

There are three hospitals in the area: Baptist Health Care (☎ 850-434-4011), 1000 W Moreno St (the closest to downtown); Sacred Heart (☎ 850-416-7000), 5151 N 9th Ave; and West Florida Regional Medical (☎ 850-474-8000), 8333 N Davis Hwy.

Historic Pensacola Village

This village (☎ 850-595-5985) is a collection of old homes and museums that are open to the public. One-hour guided walking tours of the area leave at 11:30 am and 1:30 pm from the main ticket office at the **Tivoli House**, 205 E Zaragoza St, and include a history of many of the buildings in the district, such as the **Lavalle House**, 205 E Church St, and the **Julee Cottage**, 210 E Zaragoza St, the former home of freed slave Julee Paton, which features an exhibit on black life in Florida. It also includes the TT Wentworth

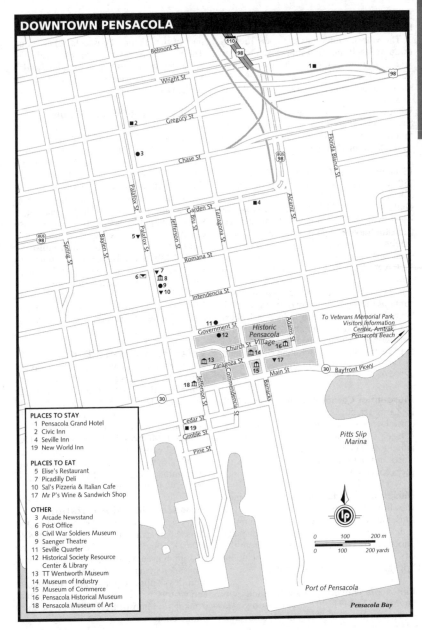

DOWNTOWN PENSACOLA

PLACES TO STAY
1 Pensacola Grand Hotel
2 Civic Inn
4 Seville Inn
19 New World Inn

PLACES TO EAT
5 Elise's Restaurant
7 Picadilly Deli
10 Sal's Pizzeria & Italian Cafe
17 Mr P's Wine & Sandwich Shop

OTHER
3 Arcade Newsstand
6 Post Office
8 Civil War Soldiers Museum
9 Saenger Theatre
11 Seville Quarter
12 Historical Society Resource
   Center & Library
13 TT Wentworth Museum
14 Museum of Industry
15 Museum of Commerce
16 Pensacola Historical Museum
18 Pensacola Museum of Art

Historic
Pensacola
Village

To Veterans Memorial Park,
Visitors Information
Center, Amtrak,
Pensacola Beach

Pitts Slip
Marina

Port of Pensacola

Pensacola Bay

Museum, the Museum of Commerce and the Museum of Industry.

The village's buildings are open Tuesday to Saturday 10 am to 4 pm, closed Sunday and Monday (unless otherwise noted below). Tours cost $6 for adults, $5 for seniors and military and $2.50 for children. Tickets for the tours are available at the TT Wentworth Museum. Note that you don't have to go on a tour to see the buildings, and that one admission ticket gains you entry to all the buildings in the village.

TT Wentworth Museum The Wentworth, 330 S Jefferson St, is made up of quirky exhibits. The 3rd floor holds the Discovery Gallery, where kids can play in Colonial Kidstown. The 2nd floor contains artifacts from the days of Spanish and British rule, exhibits on colonial life, a Coca-Cola room (don't ask) and some funky machines (like a 1960 Associated Press photofax receiver and power unit and a 1959 Philco Predictor TV). The 1st floor, though, is our favorite, as it contains the 'curiosities': two stuffed Kodiak bears looking very mean indeed, a Robert Wadlow's size-37 shoe, and – in a tie for most grizzly exhibit – the shrunken head of the 17-year-old son of an Indian chief (found in 1926) and a petrified cat, dead since the 1850s (found in 1966).

Museum of Commerce This museum, 201 E Zaragoza St, is a reconstructed 1890s period streetscape inside a brick warehouse. It has a horse-drawn buggy collection and, among others, a hardware store, a music store and a print shop (note the antique press collection).

Museum of Industry In the two joined warehouses across the street from the Museum of Commerce is the Museum of Industry, 200 E Zaragoza St, which displays photographs, equipment and tools from the city's different industrial booms, including brickmaking, railroad and lumber.

Pensacola Museum of Art This museum (☎ 850-432-6247), 407 S Jefferson St, is housed in the Old City Jail (1906-8) and holds about 18 different exhibitions a year; call for what's on when you're here. It's not part of the Historic Pensacola Village tour. The museum is open Tuesday to Friday 10 am to 5 pm, Saturday to 4 pm and Sunday 1 to 4 pm. Admission is $2 for adults, $1 for students and military.

Civil War Soldiers Museum

The small but interesting Civil War Soldiers Museum (☎ 850-469-1900), 108 Palafox Place, is definitely a worthwhile stop. Exhibits are in chronological order (begin on the wall to your left as you enter). Note the battlefield hospital, with its utterly charming bloody arms and legs lying a-round, and the photographs of field hospitals and amputation surgery. There are also exhibits on shelters (a re-creation of a soldier's campsite), projectiles, uniforms, alcohol, tobacco and drugs, and currency. It's very well labeled and easy to get through; a small bookstore is packed with offerings on local history and the Civil War. It's open Monday to Saturday 10 am to 4:30 pm, closed Sunday. Admission is $4 for adults, $2 for children six to 12.

Veterans Memorial Park

A moving monument to the veterans of all American wars, this 5½ acre park overlooks Pensacola Bay at Bayfront Pkwy and 9th Ave (take Main St east from downtown and look for the navy helicopter). At the southern end is the Wall South, a replica of the Vietnam Memorial in Washington, DC, engraved with the names of the more than 58,000 American soldiers who died in the war; among them are eight women, 'Angels on the Wall,' who were nurses.

Pensacola Naval Air Station

Every US WWII pilot was trained at the Pensacola Naval Air Station (NAS; ☎ 850-452-0111), and today it's host to one of the best air museums in the world, along with thousands of navy staff, their families and countless support personnel, contractors and visitors. In fact, the place is so huge that it takes up almost three pages in the local phone book.

Take Hwy 295 to the main entrance of the NAS, which is on the south side of the bridge at the end of Navy Blvd across the Bayou Grande. The checkpoint usually doesn't stop you from driving in. Once inside, Navy Blvd becomes Duncan Rd (which cuts through that most essential of military perks: the AC Reed Golf Course, chock-full of crew-cut men resplendent in their golfing best); take it to Taylor Rd and turn right, which will lead you toward the Advanced Redoubt ruins and Fort Barrancas (see Gulf Islands National Seashore later), the National Museum of Naval Aviation and the Pensacola Lighthouse.

National Museum of Naval Aviation
Maybe the best air-space museum around, the National Museum of Naval Aviation (☎ 850-453-2389, 800-327-5002, 1750 Radford Blvd, www.naval-air.org) is the largest of the navy's museums, and it's so good that it's Florida's most attended museum of *any* sort. More than a million people come here each year, and that's expected to double over the next 10 years. The first thing you'll notice (unless you happen, as we did, to show up during a Blue Angels rehearsal, see below) is the four A-4 Skyhawk jets that the Blue Angels retired when they upgraded to F/A-18s. You'll also see the new five-figured monument, *Spirit of the Naval Aviator*, with 9¹/₂-foot statues of naval aviators in WWI, WWII, Korea, Vietnam and Desert Storm uniforms. There's an IMAX cinema, featuring IMAX footage taken from the cockpit of Blue Angels jets running through maneuvers, landing and taking off on carriers and other ho-hum stuff. In the museum, there are also dozens of aircraft, from vintage warbirds to a Harrier jump-jet.

Volunteers – many of them retired navy flyers – enchant with war stories and demonstrations, and kids can suit up and enter the cockpit of their 'test plane.'

It's open daily 9 am to 5 pm; closed Thanksgiving, Christmas and New Year's Day. Guided tours (in five languages) are available on request. Admission to the museum is free. The IMAX movies cost $5 for adults, $4.50 for students, seniors and military.

How Close Is Close?

Looking from a plane once, we were alarmed to see an Alitalia jet about half a mile from our LOT Polish Airlines Tupolev. We thought that was cutting things pretty darned close. And then we spoke with the Blue Angels. During the Angels' Delta formation, the tops of the right and left wingmen's canopies (the door that covers the cockpit right over the pilot's head) are 36 inches below the chief's wingtips. Three feet (about the distance of cars in adjacent lanes on an interstate highway) and the skills of the pilots are all that stand between a glorious display of precision flying and several $30 million fireballs.

Blue Angels The Blue Angels (☎ 850-452-4784, www.blueangels.navy.mil/), who perform their spectacular air shows to about 15 million people a year, are a precision-flying team based at NAS Pensacola (they spend January to March at the Naval Air Facility in El Centro, California). The Angels were organized in 1946, when they flew Grumman F6F Hellcat jets. Today, the Angels are a navy publicity and recruiting tool, flying at about 35 show sites a year, during which four Boeing F/A-18 Hornet jet aircraft are flown in tight – *ooh* so tight – formation and perform rolls, loops and other precision maneuvers. Two other F/A-18s are used for solo flights, and the shows culminate with all six planes flying in their trademark Delta formation.

The Angels practice (quite a bit, actually – as you would if you were pulling stunts with $180 million worth of aircraft) generally on Tuesday and Wednesday mornings at 8 am when they're not out of town for shows. The viewing area is right behind the National Museum of Naval Aviation, and the pilots sign autographs after the flights. Call the Blue Angels' Duty Office (☎ 850-452-2466) on Monday for upcoming practice schedules.

Shows are usually an hour long and given on Saturday and Sunday at about 2 pm – if there's good visibility. With a 3500-foot cloud ceiling they perform a 'low show'; with a 1500-foot ceiling they give a 'flat' show, with some rolls and other maneuvers; above 8000 feet the Blue Angels perform the whole shebang.

To see if a show will be performed during your visit, contact the Blue Angels' events office at ☎ 850-452-2585. For an annual schedule, write to Blue Angels, Attn: Public Affairs, 390 San Carlos Rd, Suite A, Pensacola FL 32508.

Admission to the shows is free; park in the lot next to the chow hall across from the Angels' hangar, No 1854.

Pensacola Lighthouse Florida's second oldest lighthouse (it's on the site of the first) is now run by the US Coast Guard. You can visit the Pensacola Lighthouse – with 177 steps going up to its original crystal, first-order lens – only with a group of 10 or more, by arrangement with the US Coast Guard Auxiliary, on Sunday between noon and 5 pm. Admission is free.

The ZOO

One of the best areas in The ZOO (☎ 850-932-2229, www.the-zoo.com), 5701 Gulf Breeze Pkwy (Hwy 98, about 10 miles east of Gulf Breeze), is the Farm, a petting area where you can feed giraffes (you haven't lived until you've had a giraffe tongue slobbering on your arm). There are more than 700 great animals such as cougars, zebras, white tigers and snow leopards at The ZOO, and you can take a 10- to 15-minute choo-choo train ($1.75 extra) through its nature preserve. Animals – including llama, brown deer, addax, scimitar-horned oryx, fallow deer and sable antelope – think nothing of walking right up to the cars as you pass. A boardwalk has been added over the preserve, allowing you to see all the animals you'd see on the choo-choo, but free.

Colossus, the colossal gorilla, is on breeding loan to the Cincinnati Zoo for the foreseeable future (ol' Colossus has been trying to get it up since our last edition).

From the end of November through January 1 is the annual Holiday Lights festi-val, when The ZOO is beautifully lit at night; admission is $4 per person.

The ZOO is open daily, weather permitting, from 9 am to 5 pm in summer, to 4 pm in winter, closed Christmas and Thanksgiving. Call for Holiday Lights hours. Admission is $9.75 for adults, $8.75 for seniors, $5.75 for children three to 11.

Gulf Islands National Seashore

Covering many of the barrier islands for 150 miles between West Ship Island (Mississippi) and Santa Rosa Island, the Gulf Islands National Seashore (☎ 850-934-2600, 601-875-9057 in Mississippi) is a federally protected section of land with many natural and historical attractions. In Florida, it covers two sections of Santa Rosa Island and extends to the NAS across the Fort Pickens State Park Aquatic Preserve.

Much of the area was destroyed in Hurricane Opal – the entire western half of Santa Rosa Island, where Fort Pickens is located, was completely buried under sand by Opal's storm surge until summer 1996. Luckily, damage from Georges in 1998 was not as bad, and the entire park is open to visitors.

Fort Pickens This pentagonal-shape brick fort (☎ 850-934-2621) was built in 1829-34 and was the site of Geronimo's incarceration in 1886-87. Inside, you'll see the officers' quarters, a mine battery room, mine chambers, the powder magazine and Bastion D, which was destroyed in a magazine explosion on June 20, 1899. There's camping near the fort (see Places to Stay later).

Divers can get a close-up look at the **USS Massachusetts** remains at the Underwater Archaeological Preserve in the Fort Pickens State Park Aquatic Preserve. The ship is in 26 feet of water, $1\frac{1}{2}$ miles south-southwest of the Pensacola Pass at latitude 30,17'45"N and longitude 87,18'45"W.

The Fort Pickens area also offers swimming and nature and bike trails. Admission is $7 per carload, $3 for pedestrians and bicyclists. (The ticket, good for seven days' admission, also grants entry to other areas of the Seashore's property that charge admission, so save your receipt.) There are guided tours daily at 2 pm; on Saturday and Sunday there's a rifle firing demonstration in the fort parade. The rangers also offer programs daily at 10 am; the programming schedule changes annually.

Fort Barrancas Accessed through the NAS, this fort has been built, destroyed, remodeled and occupied by Spanish, French, British, Confederate and American forces – there's been some incarnation of Fort Barrancas on this site since 1698. The British built a second fort, the Advanced Redoubt, nearby. The fort is open daily 9:30 am to 5 pm. Admission is free, as are the ranger artillery demonstrations every morning. Guided tours leave from the visitors center daily at 2 pm. Advanced Redoubt is open Saturday and Sunday noon to 2 pm.

From the main NAS gates, take Duncan Rd to Taylor Rd and turn right; the visitors center is straight ahead.

Naval Live Oaks Native American shell mounds and burial sites have been found here at Naval Live Oaks (☎ 850-934-2600), about 6 miles east of Gulf Breeze. Americans found the area useful because of the super strong oak – ironwood – that grows here: it was the perfect material for the construction of warships. The park has several nature trails, and the helpful rangers at the visitors center will explain Indian artifacts and facts about the park and the region. They also run nature walks at various times of the year. If you're going to hike through the trails, bring a good insect repellent – the place is rife with bugs. There are picnic facilities, but camping is allowed for youth groups only. It's open 8:30 am to 5 pm; admission is free.

Pensacola Beach
The beach here is majestic, and if you're in the area, it would be a crime to miss a day, a sunset or a moonrise here. It's a gently curving, shimmering white-sand beach, with stunningly clear Gulf water. The sunsets are simply spectacular, though it's slightly disorienting to see a sunset to your right, as the beach faces almost due south. However,

beyond the very nice Hampton Inn and a couple of smaller places, there's not much else to see or do.

Pensacola Beach's streets have mainly Spanish names. The east-west drag running from Fort Pickens to the Bob Sikes Bridge is Fort Pickens Rd, which becomes Via de Luna heading east. Via de Luna is crossed by north-south-running avenidas, numbered up to 23.

The '50s-era neon sign welcoming one and all to the **'World's Whitest Beaches'** was originally constructed at the corner of Gregory and Palafox Sts, but it was moved to its present location at the entry to the Bob Sikes Bridge in the early 1960s. It's the height of kitsch – a 1950s sign of the future – and it's a beloved local landmark. That it survived Opal with nary a scratch should certainly be taken as an omen…of something or other.

Modeled after the sign, the **water tower** at Avenida 23 on Via de Luna is another beach landmark.

On Pensacola Beach, one of the buildings that made it through the hurricane with flying colors is the **UFO house**, 1304 Panferio Drive. It's a saucer-shaped thing right out of *It Came From Planet 9*, complete with a ramp leading to the entryway. We knocked, but no one was home, and gawking in, all we saw were some musical gizmotronics indicating a home-recording studio. Go to Rio Vista Drive, turn one block north to Panferio Drive and then go east.

Places to Stay
The cheapest camping in the Pensacola area is at Big Lagoon State Park and near the city of Milton at Adventures Unlimited; see Around Pensacola later in the chapter for both these listings.

Fort Pickens (☎ 850-934-2621), located on the western tip of Santa Rosa Island, has camping sites with picnic tables, grills, showers and water and electric hookups. Sites without/with electricity are $15/20.

Downtown chains include two *Motel 6*s: at 5829 Pensacola Blvd (☎ 850-477-7522) and 7226 Plantation Rd (☎ 850-474-1060); *Residence Inn by Marriott* (☎ 850-479-1000,

7230 Plantation Rd); two **Best Western**s, at 13585 Perdido Key Drive (☎ 850-492-2755) and 16 Via De Luna Drive (☎ 850-934-3300); **Red Roof Inn** (☎ 850-476-7960) at the intersection of I-10 and Hwy 291; and **La Quinta Inn** (☎ 850-474-0411, 7750 N Davis Hwy).

The **Civic Inn** (☎ 850-432-3441, 200 N Palafox St) is a fine option with typical motel-style singles/doubles for $36/44 on weekdays, $40/48 on weekends, year round.

The **Days Inn** (☎ 850-438-4922, 800-325-2525, 710 N Palafox St) has all the usual features of a chain place, with rooms at $49 to $99 in summer and $39 to $79 in winter.

The **Seville Inn** (☎ 850-433-8331, 800-277-7275, 223 E Garden St) is okay, with rooms from $44 to $75 in summer, $39 to $49 in winter, including donuts and coffee.

The upscale **New World Inn** (☎ 850-432-4111, 600 Palafox Place) has singles/doubles for $75/85 year round. It has a great location and clean rooms but somewhat snooty staff.

With many sections built back in 1912 as the L&N Railroad Depot, the **Pensacola Grand Hotel** (☎ 850-433-3336, 800-348-3336, pensacolagrandhotel.com, 200 E Gregory St) is certainly grand, and the prices reflect what you get: rooms are $80 to $90, and suites run $200 to $400 in winter; they are $90 to $110 and $220 to $450 in summer. There is a nice lounge and a restaurant downstairs.

A nice B&B just west of the heart of downtown, the **Yacht House** (☎ 850-433-3634, 1820 Cypress St) is across the street from the Pensacola Yacht Club. All rooms have a private bath and access to the screened-in porch. They do a 'Caribbean breakfast' – fresh tropical fruits, bagels, pastries, homemade jelly and English muffins and toast. Rooms range from $65 to $125 per night for a three-room suite with a private deck and hot tub.

In Pensacola Beach, the **Five Flags Inn** (☎ 850-932-3586, 299 Fort Pickens Rd) is an institutional-looking place with friendly service and beachfront rooms from $39 to $49 in winter and $75 to $85 in summer. To get there, turn right at the traffic light after the bridge and go west for a bit; the hotel's on the left.

Clarion Suites Resort & Convention Center (☎ 850-932-4300, 800-874-5303, 20 Via de Luna) is a newish place right on the beach. Rooms in summer are $115 to $166, and as low as $72 to $100 in winter. Rates include donuts, coffee and juice in the morning, and there's a pool.

The **Hampton Inn** (☎ 850-932-6800, 800-320-8108, 2 Via de Luna) is an excellent hotel, and it's cheap for what you get. Rooms range from $69 to $109 in winter and $109 to $159 in summer (higher during special events). The place has excellent service, and rooms are large and airy. If you get a beachfront room (the higher-priced ones), you get beautiful ocean views at sunrise and sunset. A good continental breakfast is included, and there's a pool out back. It's right past the first traffic light on the way to the beach from Sikes Bridge.

Places to Eat

Downtown, the cheerful and popular **Elise's Restaurant** (☎ 850-432-5100, 11 Palafox Place) does breakfast from $1.50 to $4, but it's famous for its great $5.98 lunch buffet – choose from two meats, four veggies, corn bread and salad bar. Lunch is served daily 11 am to 2:30 pm.

A very popular local place is **Mr P's Wine & Sandwich Shop** (☎ 850-433-0294, 221 E Zaragoza St). It's in the Moreno Cottage, which is home of the daughter of Francisco Moreno, who is considered by many to be the father of Pensacola (he had 27 kids). The small, cozy place serves lunch specials like quiche ($4.25 or $5.75 with soup and salad), sandwich platters ($5.25 to $5.75) and salads ($4.75 to $5.95).

Great sandwiches await at the **Picadilly Deli** (☎ 850-438-3354, 102 Palafox Place), including many vegetarian options from $2.75 and tuna sandwiches for $3.75. It has about 50 kinds of beer with which to wash them down.

Sal's Pizzeria & Italian Cafe (☎ 850-433-5385, 128 Palafox Place) sells slices for $1.70; spaghetti and chicken parmigiana is $5.75, served with salad and bread.

Founaris Bros Greek Restaurant (☎ 850-432-0629, 1015 N 9th Ave) is a friendly and good Greek and Italian place with a huge range of Greek pizzas from $5.15 to $17.75. Spanakopita, an elaborate spinach pie with feta cheese in phyllo dough, is a mere $2; Greek salads are $2.35 to $7, moussaka $7. It offers a whole bunch of sandwiches as well.

In Gulf Breeze, right near the north side of the Sikes Bridge, **Golden China** (☎ 850-932-2511, 830 Gulf Breeze Pkwy) has some of the best Chinese food we've had outside New York City, plus those great cardboard boxes for takeout. Staff are really nice, and the restaurant serves a $5.95 lunch buffet Sunday to Friday 11:30 am to 2:30 pm. Otherwise, from the menu, chicken, beef and pork dishes are $7.45, shrimp dishes $8.45, and *lo mein* (soft noodles and vegetables) $5.45.

Billy Bob's Barbecue Company (☎ 850-934-2999, 911 Gulf Breeze Pkwy) specializes in hand-pulled Carolina-style barbecue 'without the fat.' Daily specials include a rib lunch for $6.69; on Monday there's a Brunswick stew and a pork sandwich special for $4.95.

On the Pensacola Naval Air Station, right in front of the Pensacola Lighthouse, **Lighthouse Point** (☎ 850-452-3251) does an all-you-can-eat lunch buffet for $5.50 from 10:30 am to 2 pm – great for the grumbles if you're spending time in the aviation museum across the street.

In Pensacola Beach, across the street from the Hampton Inn, the **Sun Ray Restaurante & Cantina** (☎ 850-932-0118) is in the **Jubilee Restaurant & Entertainment Complex** (☎ 850-934-3108, 800-582-3208, 400 Quiet Water Beach Rd). It has $5.95 lunch specials daily from 11:30 am to 3:30 pm, such as shrimp and salad, quesadillas and mini-burritos. At dinner, burgers and sandwiches range from $5.95 to $7.50. Mexican dishes start cheaply with tacos for $1.95, but most mains run from $7.95 to $12.95. It's a very popular watering hole, serving Mexican specialty drinks for $4.

Tuesday is buffet night: buy a drink or two and there's free music and food. Wednesday features the White Sands Panhandle Bluegrass Band, Friday has eclectic rock and roll, and Saturday night is Latino night. The entertainment complex itself has jugglers, clowns and other live entertainment nightly.

Entertainment
Performing Arts The gorgeous Spanish-Baroque **Saenger Theatre** (pronounced 'SAYN-ger'; ☎ 850-444-7686, 118 Palafox Place) was reconstructed of bricks from the Pensacola Opera House, which was destroyed in a 1916 hurricane. It's home to Broadway road show productions as well as performances by the Northwest Florida Ballet and the Pensacola Symphony Orchestra and Pensacola Opera. Ticket prices vary by performance. The box office is open Monday to Friday 10 am to 5 pm in winter, to 4 pm in summer.

The **Pensacola Opera** (☎ 850-433-6737) performs two fully staged opera productions each year – featuring singers from all over the country – at the Saenger Theatre. Call the opera when you're in town to see what's on, or the Saenger Theatre for ticket information.

The 70-piece **Pensacola Symphony Orchestra** (☎ 850-435-2533) has been performing since 1926. The season runs September through April, with five concerts and a Christmas Holiday show, all held at the Saenger.

The **Jazz Society of Pensacola** (☎ 850-433-8382) is an appreciation society involved in a range of projects with local and national musicians. It holds an annual jazz picnic in June at the Pensacola Yacht Club and hosts events at Seville Quarter (see Bars & Clubs below), like Musical Gumbo on Friday night and Sunday afternoon at the Seville Historic District in the fall and winter.

Gallery Walks The Arts Council of Northwest Florida (☎ 850-432-9906, Seville Tower, 226 S Palafox, Suite 204) is in charge of **Gallery Nights**, held in March, July and November. Gallery Nights, which are walks between openings at the area's art galleries, have been going on since 1991 and are gaining popularity every year. The galleries are all in downtown Pensacola, including the following:

JD Hayward/Photography
  ☎ 850-438-0416, 122 Palafox Place

Jeweler's Trade Shop
  ☎ 850-432-4433, 26 Palafox Place

Schmidt's Gallery
  ☎ 850-433-7717, 8 Palafox Place

SOHO Gallery
  ☎ 850-435-7646, 23 Palafox Place

Bars & Clubs There will certainly be more options available, especially on the beach, when you get here. ***McGuire's Irish Pub*** *(☎ 850-433-6789, 600 E Gregory St)* is a local tradition. Happy hour is daily from 4 to 6 pm. It opens at 11 am, and live entertainment starts nightly at 9 pm.

  Seville Quarter *(☎ 850-434-6211, 130 E Government St)* is an entertainment and restaurant complex much like Orlando's Church St Station. It's home to numerous restaurants and bars, and is open daily at 11 am, with varying closing hours. Only people ages 21 and up are allowed in, except on Tuesday and Thursday when those 18 and older are welcome.

Getting There & Away

Air Pensacola Regional Airport (☎ 850-435-1746) is served by Continental, Delta, American and Northwest Airlines and US Airways. The airport is about 4 miles northeast of downtown, near the bay; the terminal is off 9th Ave on Airport Blvd.

Bus The Greyhound station (☎ 850-476-4800) is at 505 W Burgess Rd. Bus service includes several buses a day to/from each of the following destinations; fares are quoted one way/roundtrip:

destination	duration	price
Gainesville	7 to 8³/₄ hours	$63/126
Jacksonville	8¹/₄ to 9¹/₂ hours	$57/110
Miami	16¹/₄ to 20 hours	$83/168
Mobile	1 hour	$13/26
New Orleans	4 to 5³/₄ hour	$28/52
Panama City Beach	2¹/₂ hours	$21/42
Tallahassee	5 to 7 hours	$21/42

Train Pensacola is a stop for Amtrak's *Sunset Limited*, which pulls in at ungodly hours no matter which way you're going: from Los Angeles it arrives on Wednesday, Friday and Monday at 1:40 am; from Miami, it arrives on Monday, Wednesday and Saturday at 4:46 am. The Amtrak station (☎ 850-433-4966) is at 980 E Heinberg St at 15th Ave, just north of the visitors information center.

Car & Motorcycle To get to New Orleans, Louisiana or Mobile, Alabama, take I-10 west. To the rest of Florida and to the Panhandle, take either I-10 east or the coastal route (Hwy 98, through Gulf Breeze, Fort Walton Beach and Panama City Beach). From Pensacola, it's about 200 miles to New Orleans, 650 miles to Miami, 103 to Panama City Beach, 191 to Tallahassee and 355 miles to Jacksonville.

Getting Around

To/From the Airport From the airport, take ECAT bus No 2 to the downtown transfer station, and then bus No 16 to downtown Pensacola (see Bus below). A taxi should run from $11 to $13 to downtown, $18 to $20 to the beach. Driving, take Airport Blvd to 9th Ave or I-110 south, which go downtown and meet up with Hwy 98, which continues over the Three Mile Bridge to Gulf Breeze and Pensacola Beach.

Bus The Escambia County Transit (ECAT; ☎ 850-436-9383 x611, ADA x12) has limited bus service around Pensacola, but it's not very convenient between tourist destinations – it doesn't go to The ZOO or to the beach. Bus No 16 runs between Palafox St and the transfer station (also inconveniently located at the corner of Fairfield Drive/Hwy 295 and L St, northwest of downtown), from where you can catch bus No 2 to/from the airport or bus No 14 to the NAS. Fare is $1; transfers are 10¢.

Trolley The Tiki Trolley is a free weekend shuttle up and down Pensacola Beach that runs Friday and Saturday 10 am to 3 am, to midnight on Sunday. Stand by the trolley signs along Via de Luna and the trolley will pick you up.

Car & Motorcycle There are a few one-way streets downtown, but otherwise driving is straightforward and easy. It takes about 20 minutes to drive between Pensacola Beach and downtown. Several major car-rental companies are at the airport, though not Value or Alamo.

Taxi Rates in Pensacola are $1.50 flagfall, $1.20 each mile. Cab companies include Airport Express (☎ 850-572-5555), Yellow Cab (☎ 850-433-3333) and Green Cab (☎ 850-456-8294).

Bicycle On Pensacola Beach, Dinah's Shore Shop (☎ 850-934-0014), 715A Pensacola Beach Blvd, has bikes and skates for rent: bikes are $5 for two hours, $10 for eight hours; Rollerblades are $6 an hour, $15 for eight hours. It's just south of the tollbooth on the beach side of the Sikes Bridge.

AROUND PENSACOLA
Big Lagoon State Park & Perdido Key
A 700-acre state park on the Gulf Intra-coastal Waterway, Big Lagoon (☎ 850-492-1595), 12301 Gulf Beach Hwy, has nature trails, observation towers, a boat launch, camping and incredible spans of white-sand beaches. There are ranger-led interpretive programs on Saturday. The adjacent satellite park, Perdido Key, has what's considered to be the finest beach in the area; boardwalks lead down to it.

Admission to Big Lagoon is $3.25 per carload, $1 for pedestrians and bicyclists; admission to Perdido Key is $2.

Tent sites at Big Lagoon are $13.38/15.52 without/with electric including tax in high season and $11.15/13.30 in low season. The camping fee includes admission to both Big Lagoon and Perdido Key. It's about 12 miles southwest of Pensacola off Hwy 292.

Adventures Unlimited
A camping resort 12 miles north of the city of Milton, Adventures Unlimited (☎ 850-

623-6197, 800-239-6864) is on the Coldwater River, about 20 miles northeast of Pensacola. It offers a huge range of canoeing and tubing options, with hourly to three-day trips on the Coldwater and Blackwater Rivers and on Juniper Creek. The prices (including canoe, paddles and preservers) are reasonable: short trips are $14, day trips are $15, special 18-mile, five-hour trips are $17. For overnight trips, you can rent a canoe with tent, sleeping bags, stove, cooking kit (but not food) and lantern for $46 per person for one night, $62 per person for two nights.

The campground charges $15 for tents, or $39 in an air-conditioned camping 'tree house' (actually it's perched on stilts). Basic bunk cabins with air conditioning are $49, and fully equipped cabins (with kitchens and indoor bathrooms) are $69 to $109.

From Pensacola, take I-10 east to Avalon Blvd (exit 7) north to Hwy 90 east into Milton, turn left at the Burger King and go about 12 miles north – it's well signed. The mailing address is Route 6, Box 283, Milton, FL 32570.

Blackwater River State Park
There's incredible canoeing and camping at Blackwater River State Park (☎ 850-983-5363), one of the clearest (yet tinted with tannin, which gives tea its color) sand-bottom rivers in the world. The shallow ends are clear because of the white sand bottom. And the best part is if you're canoeing, you can camp anywhere along the riverbank – the only regulations are the obvious ones: don't cut live wood (only gather dead and down wood), bury human waste at least 6 inches deep, and take out what you brought in.

There are several nature trails throughout the park, and the rangers are trying to start some interpretive and/or campfire programs, but at the moment they're understaffed. They plan on doing programs in summer.

The park is located in the Blackwater River State Forest, the state's largest. The pristine forest runs south from the Alabama state line to just north of I-10, and the Blackwater River itself begins in the

Conecuh National Forest in Alabama. Its tributaries, the Sweetwater, Juniper and East Coldwater Creeks, run down through the Blackwater River State Park as well.

Canoeing Blackwater Canoe Rental and Outpost (☎ 850-623-0235, 800-967-6789) rents canoes for self-guided day trips along the Blackwater River for $15 per person and $20 overnight. You pay (get a receipt), they drive you upriver from 4 to 36 miles, and you paddle back downriver. For day trips, the canoe is yours until 30 minutes before sunset. They also do a three-night rental for $30 per person. For location, see Getting There & Away below.

Bob's Canoes (☎ 850-623-5457) offers canoe, kayak and tube trips on the Coldwater River. Day runs start at $14 per person; short trips (5 miles, about an hour and a half) are $13 a person. For canoe camping (you sleep on the riverbank), a 1¹/₂ day trip (from 2 pm to 6 pm the next day) is $19; full overnight trips (11 am to 6 pm) are $22 per person; two-night trips are $30 a person.

They also rent kayaks. One-person short trips are $17, two-person day trips are $17 per person, and two-person short trips are $15 per person. Innertube rentals are $9 – and for $5 you can also rent a tube for your cooler!

To reach Bob's Canoes from Pensacola, take I-10 east to exit 7 (Avalon/Milton), turn left (north) on Hwy 90 east, turn left at the Burger King (Hwy 87, Stewart St), drive for two traffic lights plus two blocks, and turn right on Munson Hwy (Hwy 191) for 7 miles.

Places to Stay Thirty sites are available within the state park itself; tent and RV sites are $8.52 plus tax without electricity, $10.81 with. All sites have water.

Getting There & Away To get to the entrance of the park as well as to Blackwater Canoe Rental from Pensacola, take I-10 east to exit 10 (Hwy 87), turn left, go north for 1 mile until you reach Hwy 90; turn right (east) and go 5¹/₂ miles until you see the canoe/state park sign. Take a left (north) and

drive 1¹/₂ miles; the Blackwater Canoe Rental and Outpost is on the right.

US Air Force Armament Museum

This museum (☎ 850-882-4062), outside the west gate of Eglin Air Force Base, will be of interest to weaponry buffs but not to many others. Outside, the place is surrounded by aircraft, including an A-10A Warthog, an F-16A, a much cooler B-17 Flying Fortress and the SR 71-A Blackbird reconnaissance plane that set the transcontinental speed record, flying coast to coast in 68 minutes and 17 seconds. Inside, there are tons of weapons, a Warthog simulator, a terrifying F-105 Thunderchief missile and this lovely entry:

The Sensor Fuzed Weapon (SFW), the first of a new class of smart munitions to enter production, provides multiple 'kills per pass' from a single weapon.

The gift shop has inflatable warplanes, lots of model airplanes, many 'Made in China' bullet key chains and, inexplicably, seashells and hand-painted electrical outlet and light switch plates with nautical themes. The museum is open daily 9:30 am to 4:30 pm; closed Thanksgiving, Christmas and New Year's Day. Admission is free.

To get here from Pensacola, take I-10 east to exit 12 (Crestview) and go south on Hwy 85 for a couple of miles to Hwy 123 (this bypasses Niceville). Take Hwy 123 for 5 miles until you pick up Hwy 85 again for a few miles and follow the signs.

FORT WALTON BEACH & DESTIN
• time zone CST

The resort region of Fort Walton Beach (population 21,471) and Destin (population 9500) stretches along the middle of the Panhandle, between Pensacola and Panama City Beach. The beaches are undeniably stunning, with perhaps the whitest Appalachian quartz sand on the Panhandle. But the area's development has been moving along at a jaunty clip, and while the region's tourism officials put forth a line of 'eco-friendly tourism,' the reality is increasing numbers of condominiums, teeming golf courses and ever larger tourist attractions.

But not all is lost: Indian Temple Mound Museum is a wonderful surprise. The beachfront between the two cities, owned by the US Air Force, is near pristine. The area just to the east has some of the world's best beaches, and the Grayton Beach State Recreation Area is absolutely stunning. You can use Destin and Fort Walton Beach as a base, but we suggest you move on quickly to the more natural splendors just 20 minutes down the road.

Orientation & Information

Fort Walton Beach is about 60 miles west of Panama City Beach, along Hwy 98/Alt 98. The beach is on Okoloosa Island, a barrier island at the southern end of Choctawhatchee Bay, separated from the downtown area to the north by the Santa Rosa River.

Destin, about 5 miles east along Miracle Strip Parkway (Hwy 98), is entirely contained on the barrier island.

The Emerald Coast Convention & Visitor's Bureau (☎ 850-651-7131 x227, 800-322-3319), 1540 Miracle Strip Pkwy, is open Monday to Friday 8 am to 5 pm, Saturday and Sunday 10 am to 4 pm. The South Walton Information Center (☎ 850-267-3511, 800-822-6877) is on Santa Rosa Beach at the corner of Hwy 98E and Hwy 331, open daily 8:30 am to 4:30 pm (in summer to 6 pm).

Change money at NationsBanks in Fort Walton Beach (☎ 850-729-4381), 189 Eglin Pkwy NE, on the mainland just north of the Santa Rosa River; or in Destin (☎ 850-837-3849), at 1014 Hwy 98E.

The Fort Walton Beach Medical Center (☎ 850-862-1111) is at 1000 Mar Walt Drive, on the mainland.

Things to See & Do

The Indian Temple Mound Museum (☎ 850-833-9595), at 139 Miracle Strip Pkwy, has a lovingly-put-together exhibit of Indian life including artifacts, tools and ceramics and a great display of Indian dwellings by region. Surrounding the museum is a small, well-marked nature trail. Admission is $2 for adults, $1 for children six to 17. From September to May, it's open Monday to Friday 11 am to 4 pm, Saturday 9 am to 4 pm, closed Sunday. In summer, it's open Monday to Saturday from 9 am to 4 pm, Sunday 12:30 to 4:30 pm.

It may bring in big tourist bucks, but we thought the **Gulfarium** (☎ 850-244-5169, 800-247-8575), 1010 Miracle Strip Pkwy, was rather depressing. Built in 1955 (and retaining attitudes toward animal rights from that period), the Gulfarium has fairly small pools with dolphins, seals and sharks, and a touch pool. If you must go, admission is $14.95 for adults, $12.95 for seniors and children.

Instead, consider bringing the kids to the **Focus Center** (☎ 850-664-1261), 139 Brooks St, with a computer room, physical science exhibits, a preschool adventure room and a make-a-4-foot-bubble exhibit. Admission is $2 per person. It's open 1 to 5 pm (daily June through August and on weekends September through May).

For a good view of the area and (unless you come right after a hurricane, as we did) great aerial photographs of the white sand and emerald waters, hop aboard **Penguin-Air Helicopter Rides** (☎ 850-664-5657), on the beach, charging $15 per person for a seven-minute minimum ride, $25 for 15 minutes and $50 to the Destin harbor (two-person minimum).

Henderson Beach State Recreation Area
This is a nice 208-acre park (☎ 904-837-7550), 17000 Emerald Coast Pkwy, Destin, with 1¼ miles of shoreline along the Gulf of Mexico. There are boardwalks, a picnic pavilion and outside showers. Admission is $3.25 per carload, or $1 per pedestrian or bicyclist.

Fred Gannon Rocky Bayou State Recreation Area
Twenty miles north of Fort Walton Beach in Niceville (really), this state recreation area (☎ 850-833-9144), 4281 SR 20, is sandpine forest with scrub vegetation overlooking Rocky Bayou, an arm of Choctawhatchee Bay, where you can view

Indian middens and artifacts. There's a fresh-water lake, packed with boaters, and you can camp here as well – see below.

Kayaking & Windsurfing In Fort Walton Beach, RogueWave Windsurfing (☎ 850-243-1962), 171 Brooks St on the mainland, rents kayaks ($15/40/60 for an hour/half day/full day) and windsurfing boards ($20/60/75).

In Destin, the cranky guy at The Kayak Experience (☎ 850-837-1577, 850-837-1579), 600 Hwy 98E, rents kayaks for $10/30/50/75 for one, four, eight and 24 hours. Guided tours of the river and harbor area are an extra $10 per person.

Diving & Snorkeling There's phenomenal diving in the Gulf of Mexico, where there are small sponge beds, natural and artificial reefs and wrecks, and a limestone ledge. There's 25- to 40-foot visibility in summer, and greater than 40 feet in winter. The nice people at Scuba Tech (☎ 850-837-2822), 301 Hwy 98E, know the entire area and arrange an array of dive trips. A four-hour, two-tank, 58-to-90-foot dive is $45 per person. If you need equipment, they rent a BC for $10, regulator for $15 and weight belt for $4. A complete package, including all that plus fins, mask and snorkel, is $45.

They also offer 2¹/₂-hour snorkel trips aboard the *Mongoose* for $20 a person including gear and a wetsuit if it's cold.

Places to Stay

Fred Gannon Rocky Bayou SRA (☎ 850-833-9144, 4281 SR 20) has campsites for $10.70 with electricity and water, $8.56 without.

Tiny (only about 10 sites) ***Holiday Travel Park*** (☎ 850-837-6334, 10005 W Emerald Coast Pkwy) has tent sites for $34.10 in summer, $26.40 in winter, with water and electric.

Crystal Beach Campground (☎ 850-837-6447, 2825 Scenic Hwy 98) has a nice pool, and RV sites only for $30 in summer, $21 in winter.

Howard Johnson (☎ 850-244-8663, 203 Miracle Strip Hwy) has, believe it or not, a very nice place near the air force base, with good service and rooms from $68 to $83 in summer and $42 to $53 in winter.

The ***Islander Condominium*** (☎ 850-837-1000, 502 Gulfshore Drive) is exactly the kind of place we were wailing about in the introduction to this section, but it has very nice apartments for $95/550 a day/week in winter, $190/1085 in summer.

Four Points Hotel by Sheraton (☎ 850-243-8116, 800-874-8104, 1325 Miracle Strip Pkwy) has nice, clean rooms with a fridge, microwave and coffee-maker for $76 to $150 and suites for $150 to $225, including a warm breakfast buffet. It has a pool and is right on the Gulf.

The swankest place here is the ***Sandestin Beach and Gulf Resort*** (☎ 850-267-8150, 800-277-0800, 9300 Hwy 98), a seriously luxurious resort with condos, penthouses and suites. But a mere hotel room here is actually cheaper than expected: $155 to $200 in summer, $85 to $105 in winter. Of course, you can spend much more: in summer the penthouses run $725 a night.

Places to Eat

There are more than 20 varieties of fish served at the multitudinous array of sea-food restaurants in the area. Unfortunately, many of those restaurants serve up the fish very poorly, or at least unimaginatively. At the **Old Bay Steamer** (☎ *850-664-2795, 1310 Hwy 98E*) the fish is done right. We ordered an awesome mushroom appetizer – steamed, stuffed with crab meat, topped with cheese and baked ($5.75). But the Old Bay Super Steamer ($41 for two) is tremendously good – Maine lobster (not those little Florida ones), three or four king crab legs, four white snow crabs and about 15 shrimp, plus corn, potatoes and salad. There was so much food, we couldn't possibly finish it – much as we wanted to. They do, however, give doggie bags!

Another good place is **Rick's Crab Trap** (☎ *850-664-0110, 104 S Miracle Strip Pkwy*), which does seafood and steak dishes. It offers a very yummy yellowfin tuna dip appetizer for $5.95, big enough for two to share, and entrees include crab cakes and broiled snapper for $10.95 and steamed shrimp and steak for $14.95.

In Destin, the **Donut Hole** (☎ *850-267-8824, 635 Hwy 98E*) does absolutely awesome donuts, large enough to warrant use of a knife and fork, and good coffee. It serves breakfast 24 hours a day, and dinner specials from $5.95 to $7.25. There are also excellent salads and omelets, and quarter-pound burgers, all $5.50.

Worth the trip east (but still in Destin city limits) is the phenomenal **Pig's Alley BBQ** (☎ *850-654-3911, 9848 Hwy 98E*), a shack seemingly on the verge of collapse but serving up real Southern barbecue – get a pork plate for $6.70, a half a slab of baby back ribs for $8.80 and hot dogs and hamburgers for $2.25/3.50.

The Veranda (☎ *850-654-0400, 2700 Scenic Beach Hwy or 98E*) does a good Sunday brunch 11:30 am to 2 pm for $12.95 and an all-you-can-eat lunch buffet the same time Monday to Saturday for $8.95, plus a soup and salad bar for $5.95.

Frangista (☎ *850-837-2515, 1820 Old Hwy 98*) is a more upscale seafood restaurant with appetizers like smoked salmon tartar ($9.75) and prosciutto-wrapped grilled asparagus ($7.95). Entrees include seafood manicotti and Gulf Coast seafood strudel for $18 to $29.

SEASIDE & GRAYTON BEACH
● time zone CST

The area between Destin and Panama City Beach is far less commercial than the Fort Walton Beach area, though it is home to the small, rather bizarre, planned city of Seaside. Grayton Beach is another absolutely sensational stretch of coastline.

Orientation & Information

Grayton Beach, Seaside and the little town of Seagrove Beach are 35 miles west of Panama City Beach along Hwy 98. There's a tourist information booth right at the eastern end of the Seaside Town Square, mainly there to hand out information on cottage rentals. The ranger booth at Grayton Beach SRA is also a good resource for local information.

Seaside

The original Stepford town, Seaside (www.seasidefl.com) is an entirely planned community begun in 1972 to evoke the traditional architectural styles of northwest Florida and provide a safe, secure and eminently walkable town life for its residents. The master plan called for a city of 80 acres, with houses all clustered around the central Town Square, the focal point of town life. The model has been lauded by architectural and mainstream press as nothing short of brilliant, and even Walt Disney imagineers sniffed around when planning *their* utopian community, Celebration. (Celebration, near Walt Disney World, is now the subject of lawsuits galore by disgruntled residents yelling their lungs out about Disney's control over every aspect of their lives, shoddy construction and poor public services. The residents of Seaside seem, like their setting, far more serene and content.)

And the overall effect is rather pleasant. The uniformity of the houses isn't jarring, and an individuality can still peep through the heavily restricted building codes. People are friendly, shops are cheery, restaurants pleasant, service peppy.

But it's a little sinister that even we – a hard-assed New Yorker and a skeptical *Munchener Kindl* were ever-so-peacefully lulled into accepting this obvious fraud, this *Pleasantville*ian perfection. We kept looking for hidden cameras and overpaid comedians á la *The Truman Show*, but this seemed to be the real McCoy.

There are plenty of little shops, and during wine festivals the place can be very fun. It's packed to the Laura Ashleyed valances on Fourth of July weekend and throughout the summer.

Grayton Beach State Recreation Area

One of the finest beaches on the planet is yours for the taking at Grayton Beach State Recreation Area (☎ 850-231-4210), 357 Main Park Rd, Santa Rosa Beach. It's a 1133-acre park along the Gulf. The Grayton Beach Nature Trail runs several miles from the east side of the parking lot through the dunes, pine flatwoods and finally a boardwalk. A second trail runs along the beach. A new bike trail runs for 9 miles along Scenic Hwy 98A (the moniker for the road between here and Seaside). Rent bicycles ($12 an hour or $20 a day) from Peepers & Timekeepers (☎ 850-231-4651), No 3 Market West in Seaside, on the beach side of the road opposite Town Square.

From Memorial Day to Labor Day, there are interactive campfire programs given by the rangers. Rent canoes here for $10 a half day or $20 a day, or just relax and hit the beach that Condé Nast called America's best in 1994.

Places to Stay

Tent sites are $20 at the *Grayton Beach State Recreation Area*.

Seagrove Beach RV Resort (☎ *850-231-3839, 4501 E County Hwy*) has tent sites for $21.80/131.80 per day/week.

The best place to get a motel room is the *Seagrove Villas and Motel* (☎ *850-837-4853, 3040 Scenic Hwy 30A or Hwy 98),* east of town, where wonderful staff offer large rooms for $63/441 per day/week in winter, $144/1008 in summer.

Josephine's (☎ *850-231-1940, 800-848-1840, 850-231-1939 for the restaurant, 101*

Seaside Ave) is a beautiful B&B in Seaside; all rooms have a bath, phone, TV/VCR, refrigerator, microwave and coffee-maker (and a little basket with cookies and coffee mugs you can keep). Most rooms have fireplaces and run for $130 to $190, suites $195 to $215. Bicycles are available. Smoking and pets are not allowed, and only 'well-behaved' children are permitted. They're so overwhelmed with people coming in that they won't show you a room but rather a photograph – we checked the rooms and the pictures don't lie.

Cottages are available from Seaside Reservations (☎ 800-277-8696), at the southeast end of Town Square. The rates are all published several times a year in the *Seaside Times*, a scrappy little propaganda rag put out, it would seem, by cottage owners. The rentals are by the week only.

Places to Eat

There are great sandwich wraps for $5 to $6.25 at *Roly Poly Wraps* (☎ *850-231-3799*), in Market West. The nearby *Cafe Spiazzia* (☎ *850-231-1297*) does big salads from $5.50 to $7.50, and pizzas for $3.50 a square.

Criolla's (☎ *850-267-1267, on scenic route 30A)*, a quarter-mile east of Hwy 283 and 2 miles west of Seaside, offers inventive tropical dishes like wood-grilled Yucatan grouper ($21.95), pan-seared salmon with skewered and fried soft-shell crawfish ($22.95) and dijon-crusted, bacon-wrapped tenderloin filet ($26.95). We haven't eaten here, but we liked the menu.

PANAMA CITY BEACH

• population 4400; time zone CST

The glorious Appalachian quartz sand beaches of Panama City Beach (also known as Party Central to generations of Southerners) were struck hard by Hurricane Opal, and then somewhat hard by Hurricane Georges.

We visited a week after Georges, and the impact of the storms was still visible at the western end of the beach, where the storms hit the hardest. But the beaches themselves, and those at St Andrews State Recreation

Area, have been cleaned and groomed – in fact, they look better now than they have for years!

Panama City Beach's nickname, the Redneck Riviera, may be cruel, but it's also fitting. Locals refer to the ordinance allowing open cans of beer on the beach as a 'highlight.' And in contrast to the resorts along the Atlantic coast – where citizens have demanded more and more cops to chase away the flock of college students visiting on Spring Break (for example, Fort Lauderdale, which pretty much outlawed the university ritual) – Panama City Beach doesn't just tolerate students partying on its beaches, it *recruits* them, as the Convention & Visitors Bureau boasts in an Internet release:

Perhaps the best thing about spending Spring Break on Panama City Beach is, believe it or not, the police. You can party on the beach and the local constabulary will not hassle you. In fact, the police here go out of their way to make you feel welcome – unlike other places on the Atlantic coast of Florida – and will not hassle students.

Isn't that nice?

But there's another side to the beach: it's home to a surprising number of religious – mainly Christian – retreats, and you'll find large groups of clean-cut, clean-living, upstanding citizens here, along with bookstores and shops selling religious items. And while nightlife here is definitely in the 'party with thousands' category, and fast-food places line the strip, there's some unspoiled nature here as well: St Andrews State Recreation Area at the island's eastern end was voted best beach in America by *Condé Nast Traveler* in 1995.

Orientation

Panama City Beach is located on a Gulf barrier island almost due west of the altogether separate city of Panama City, a military town based around the flygals and flyguys at Tyndall Air Force Base. Hwy 98, the main coastal road from the south, splits off at Panama City Beach and becomes Hwy 98 (at the north) and Hwy 98A at the south, along the beach, respectively known as Back Beach Rd and Front Beach Rd.

The island is about 27 miles long, from St Andrews State Recreation Area at the east to the Philips Inlet Bridge at the west. Hwy 98 connects Panama City Beach to Panama City on the Hathaway Bridge, which crosses St Andrew Bay. The split of Hwys 98 and 98A occurs at the northeastern end of the beach, just south of the bridge, and cuts almost due west at Thomas Drive. Hwy 392 runs along the coast between Front Beach Rd and St Andrews.

Front Beach Rd is more than a little like Hwy 192 in Kissimmee (see the Central Florida chapter): it's lined with fast-food joints, motels, hotels, miniature golf, cheesy amusement parks and everything one needs to sit on a beach drinking beer.

The visitors bureau gives away the most useful map of the area as part of a full-color brochure on general attractions. The most accurate map of the beach is available through the Bay County Chamber of Commerce (☎ 850-785-5206), or by writing to PO Box 1850, Panama City Beach, FL 32402.

Information

The Panama City Beach Convention & Visitors Bureau (☎ 850-233-6503, 800-722-3224, fax 850-233-5072), 12015 Front Beach Rd, has a very helpful visitors information center, which hands out pamphlets, dispenses good information and allows you to use the phone to make hotel and restaurant reservations. The modern building almost completely withstood the force of Opal, but look out the window at the pier, which didn't fare quite so well.

For money exchange, Bay Bank & Trust Co has two branches on the beach: at 7915 Back Beach Rd (☎ 850-235-3333) and at 17255 Hutchinson Rd (☎ 850-235-4078). There are several private exchange places along Front Beach Rd. American Express has a representative office in Panama City at Nervig Travel Service (☎ 850-763-2876), 569 Harrison Ave.

The biggest post office in the area is the General Mail Facility (☎ 850-747-4840), 1336 Sherman Ave in Panama City. The Panama City Beach post office (☎ 850-234-9101) is at

420 Churchwell Drive. The Book Warehouse (☎ 850-235-2950), 6646 W Hwy 98, has new and remaindered books, as well as some religious books. Panama City Beach Public Library (☎ 850-233-5055) is at 110 Arnold Rd.

The *News-Herald* is the largest regional daily. *Bay Arts & Entertainment* is a bimonthly with information on nightclubs and restaurants.

Beachside Laundry and Dry Cleaning (☎ 850-234-1601), 21902 Front Beach Rd, is open daily 8 am to 8 pm. Long Beach Coin Laundry is at 10444 Front Beach Rd.

The two largest medical facilities in the area are in Panama City: the Bay Medical Center (☎ 850-769-1511), 615 N Bonita Ave, and Bay Walk-In Clinic (☎ 850-763-9744), 2306 Hwy 77.

See the Facts for the Visitor chapter for general hurricane preparedness information and precautions.

Museum of Man in the Sea

The Museum of Man in the Sea (☎ 850-235-4101), 17314 Back Beach Rd, is a serious look at the history of diving. As you enter, there are some neat (if cheesy) experiments. Ever wonder how those hand-pumped diving systems work? You can crank up a Siebe hand pump here, used for dives down to 30 feet. You can climb into what seems to be a precariously perched Beaver Mark IV submersible and see models of Sealab III, an underwater laboratory. Though the place has seen better days (several of the exhibits are a little ratty), the staff seem to really care about the displays, and the museum is certainly less cynical than some other tourist attractions. And with admission prices of $4 for adults, $2 for children six to 16, and discounts for seniors, naval personnel and others – why not? It's open daily 9 am to 5 pm.

Zoo World Zoological & Botanical Park

This park (☎ 850-230-1243), 9008 Front Beach Rd, is home to more than 300 animals, including 20 endangered species. The zoo participates in the Species Survival Plan (SSP), which is governed by the American Zoological Association (though Zoo World is not yet a member). The plan brings together a network of zoos and parks to protect and breed endangered animals. Endangered animals here include jaguars, Sumatran orangutans, Bali myna, spectacled bears, siamangs (a large ape native to Borneo, Sumatra and Malaysia) and a golden lion tamarin – tamarins were one of the first species to be protected by the SSP.

Zoo World also has reptiles, chimpanzees and other primates, an aviary and a petting zoo that has a giraffe, a llama, goats, camels, deer, pot-bellied pigs and a gazelle (which you can pet only if you have food in your hand). There's a fun gift shop, too.

The zoo is open daily 9 am to dusk. Admission is $8.95 for adults, $7.50 for seniors, $6.50 for children three to 11.

Gulf World

This marine park (☎ 850-234-5271), 15412 Front Beach Rd, has the typical dolphins-jumping-through-hoops kind of stuff you'll see in a lot of places, including the Gulfarium in Fort Walton Beach. Shows run continuously from 9 am to 3 pm. Admission is $15.72 plus tax for adults, $9.71 for kids five to 12.

Coconut Creek Family Fun Park

We couldn't help ourselves, and started through the amazing and surprisingly fun Gran Maze at this park (☎ 850-234-2625), 9807 Front Beach Rd. Miniature golf and bumper boats are also available. Admission is $14 for unlimited access to the maze, golf and bumper boats, $6 for golf only, $6 for the maze only, $4 for bumper boat rides. You can find discount coupons all around town and at the visitors information center. Some kid claimed he did the whole maze in 16 minutes. Right.

St Andrews State Recreation Area

Once voted the best beach in the USA by *Condé Nast Traveler* – ahead of such shabby entries as the beaches on Oahu and Maui, Hawaii – St Andrews State Recreation Area (☎ 850-233-5140) is a 1260-acre park with nature trails, swimming, hiking and camping (see Places to Stay below). The recreation area has lots of wildlife, including deer, foxes, coyotes, snakes, alligators and all kinds of seabirds.

There is snorkeling available (rental prices were unavailable at press time), and every day from 10 am to 3 pm the *Shell Island Shuttle* leaves every half hour from the park's jetty area to Shell Island, where you can broil on the beach or snorkel. A roundtrip ferry ticket is $7.50 for adults, $5.50 for kids under 12.

The park is at the eastern end of the island; from Panama City cross the bridge and turn left on Hwy 3031, across the Grand Lagoon; the entrance is on the left. From the beach, take Front Beach Rd to Thomas Drive as far as you can go.

Diving & Snorkeling

Panama City Dive Center (☎ 850-235-3390, 800-832-4483), 4823 Thomas Drive, offers boat rentals and dive charters – you pay as little as $20 with gear, $15 if you bring your own. Boats leave daily at 10 am and 2 pm. It also offers a large range of dive trips.

Dixie Divers (☎ 850-914-9988), 109 B W 23rd St, runs three-day diving programs for $75 to $85, and an open-water certification plus five open-water dives (to get a PADI gold card) for $350, including equipment rental. Offshore, there are several shipwrecks, including a WWII liberty ship and a 220-foot tugboat, and 50 artificial reefs.

Organized Tours

The Glass Bottom Boat (☎ 850-234-8944) runs three trips a day from May to August at 9 am and 1 and 4:30 pm; in other months call for the schedule. The trips, which last from 3 to 3½ hours, give you a fantastic view of sea life through the clear water – you'll pass over sandy and grassy flats, and bottle-nosed dolphins will more than likely swim alongside and bark at you.

The boat makes a stop at Shell Island, with its stretches of white sand and windswept dunes (it's imperative that you bring sunscreen). On the way back, the crew lets out a shrimp net and identifies all the creatures they catch (don't worry: they throw

them all back), and you feed pelicans. It's a fun time on the water.

In summer, the excursions are $15 for adults, $11 for children up to 12, free to children under two; $1 less in winter. Note that you can get a $3-off coupon at the visitors information center. The boat leaves from the marina at 3605 Thomas Drive.

The best air tours on the Panhandle are given by Captain Dick Gregg of Bay Seaplanes (☎ 850-234-1532), 646 W Hwy 98, aboard his Cessna 180, which is parked in the marina at the Panama City side of the Hathaway Bridge. He'll take you up for a 10-, 20- or 50-mile trip (up to five people) for $18/30/60 per person, with a two-person minimum.

Places to Stay

Camping The *St Andrews State Recreation Area (☎ 850-233-5140)* has campsites for tents and RVs/vans in summer for $9 for a nonwaterfront site without electricity, $11 with electric; $11 for waterfront sites without electric and $13 with electric. In winter, the rates are $16/18/18/21, all including tax.

KOA (☎ 850-234-5731, 8800 Thomas Drive) has campsites for $20 with water only, and $23 with full hookups in summer, $13/20 in winter, with a 10% discount if you stay a week. Kamping Kabins are $40/23.

Hotels & Motels There are about a dozen chain places here, including Marriott, Holiday Inn and Howard Johnson.

There's a laid-back attitude about most things at the *Reef Motel (☎ 850-234-3396, 800-847-7286, 12011 Front Beach Rd)*, where rooms (all with two double beds) are $85/94 without/with a kitchen in summer, and $45/50 in winter.

The *Driftwood Lodge (☎ 850-234-6601, 15811 Front Beach Rd)* has perfectly pleasant motel rooms for $47 in winter, $57 in spring, $76 in summer; efficiencies are $52 to $65 in winter, $82 in summer.

We stayed at the *Palmetto Motel (☎ 850-234-2121, 17255 Front Beach Rd)*. Clean and very comfortable beachside rooms run from $60 to $135 in winter, $92 to $170 in summer. Across the street, rooms go for $36 to $48 in winter, $70 to $75 in summer. There is a nice indoor pool as well.

Quality Inn Beachfront Resort (☎ 850-234-6636, 800-874-7101, fax 850-235-4202, 15285 Front Beach Rd) has rooms from $100/ 139 single/double, efficiencies from $110/149 and penthouses from $199 to $279.

Largo Mar (☎ 850-234-5750, 800-645-2746, fax 850-233-0533, 5717 Thomas Drive) has nice clean suites with a three-night minimum rental during high season. Prices in summer are $120 ($710 a week) for one bedrooms, $155 ($930 a week) for two bedrooms and $270 ($1670 a week) for three bedrooms. In winter, rooms are $75 ($450 a week), $90 ($540 a week) and $145 ($870 a week).

Places to Eat

The food ain't great, but you won't starve. Seafood tends to be good – especially oysters, which are cheap and plentiful. Fast-food and chain places thrive here. Check with the visitors information center for up-to-date information on new restaurants; it also hands out a good selection of area restaurant menus.

Thomas Donut & Snack Shop (☎ 850-234-8039, 19210 Front Beach Rd) has 12-inch pizzas for $9; hot dogs and sandwiches are $2 to $4.50.

A great place for breakfast (skip the local Waffle House) is *Edgewater Waffle (☎ 850-235-1511, 536 Beckridge Rd)*, at the eastern end of the beach, with awesome waffles and breakfast specials under $5.

Shrimp City Seafood (☎ 850-235-4099, 3016 Thomas Drive) has fresh crab meat, oysters and fish. A snow crab platter is $5.99. *KoKomo's Oyster Bar & Grill (☎ 850-230-8411, 3901 Thomas Drive)* has a grilled fish sandwich for $4.25. It also offers steamed shrimp, crab, oysters and chicken wings. *Hamilton's (☎ 850-234-1255, at Thomas Drive and Grand Lagoon)* does seafood as well; stuffed shrimp and most other dishes go for $15. *Pier 77 (☎ 850-235-3080, 3016 Thomas Drive)* serves a broiled seafood platter for two for $14.

We wish *Panama City Brewery (☎ 850-230-2739, 11040 Hutchinson Blvd)* lots of luck – really nice food and good beers in a

chic setting. It's cheap at lunch, with specials from $7 to $11, and at dinner main courses (the nonfried kind) are $12.99 to $15.99. Try the beer sampler ($4.95) – a small glass of each of its five beers.

Entertainment

Along the beach, every restaurant with a bar does some sort of happy hour and drink specials, especially during Spring Break, when cheap beer flows freely. The two big nightclubs in town, *Spinnaker (☎ 850-234-7822, 8795 Thomas Drive)* and *Club La Vela (☎ 850-234-3866, 8813 Thomas Drive)*, adjacent to one another, are famous around the Panhandle for their jam-packed, meat-market, sleazy flesh-fests (including wet T-shirt competitions), strip shows and flirty pick-up-joint atmosphere.

Getting There & Away

The nearest airport is Panama City Bay County Airport (☎ 850-763-6751), 3173 Airport Rd in Panama City, served by ASA, Delta, Northwest Airlink and US Airways Express. There's no public transport from the airport to the beach; a taxi or rental car is your only choice.

Amtrak's *Sunset Limited* stops at Chipley (57 miles away) on Monday, Wednesday and Saturday at 2:08 am from Miami, and on Wednesday, Friday and Monday at 4:10 am from Los Angeles.

Greyhound has a flag stop in Panama City Beach at the stoplight at Hwy 98 and Hwy 79; the station in Panama City (☎ 850-785-6111) is at 917 Harrison Ave. Greyhound runs buses to/from the following destinations; fares are one way/roundtrip:

destination	duration	price
Gainesville	5$1/2$ to 9 hours	$54/108
Jacksonville	5$1/2$ to 6$1/2$ hours	$58/116
Miami	13$1/2$ to 14$1/2$ hours	$83/168
New Orleans	7 to 8$1/2$ hours	$28/52
Pensacola	2$1/2$ to 4 hours	$23/45
Tallahassee	3$1/2$ to 4$1/2$ hours	$13/26

By car, Panama City is 98 miles from Tallahassee; 287 miles from Atlanta, Georgia;

305 from New Orleans, Louisiana; 339 from Tampa; 340 from Orlando; 562 from Miami. From the south, take Hwy 98 right into town; from the east or west take I-10 to either Hwys 231 or 79, which run south to the beach.

Getting Around
The Bay Town Trolley (☎ 850-769-0557) runs up and down Front Beach Rd (50¢ a ride).

From the airport, a taxi will cost between $14 and $16. If you're driving, take Hwy 390 south to Hwy 98 west, straight to the beach.

Taxi meter rates are $1.50 at flagfall, $1.25 each mile. The biggest company is Yellow Cab (☎ 850-763-4691); others include Quality Transportation (☎ 850-267-7575) and Sea Coast (☎ 850-231-4050).

Affordable Limousine (☎ 850-233-0029) will pick up and drop off up to six people in a late-model luxury van or in a stretch limo anywhere along the beach – from bridge to bridge – for $10. Not a bad deal if there are a few of you. It's open and on call 24 hours.

The dudes at California Cycle Rentals (☎ 850-233-1391) rent bicycles for $10 a day; scooters are $9.95 an hour, or four hours for $25. They also rent motorcycles, but you must have a motorcycle license; prices start at $20 an hour. They have several offices on Front Beach Rd, at No 10025, No 10624, No 14932 (main office) and No 17280.

MARIANNA
- population 3500; time zone CST

Marianna's got more churches than street corners, and more cops – fat, donut-scarfing, coffee-swilling, car-ticketing cops – than churches. The reason you'd consider a visit to thuddingly boring Marianna is a visit to the fascinating caves inside **Florida Caverns State Park** (☎ 850-482-1228, 850-482-9598 for a recording), a 1300-acre park right on the Chipole River.

The park, 3 miles north of the little town on Hwy 166, is wondrous. The lighted caves contain eerie stalactites, stalagmites, flow-stones (the ones that look like rock waterfalls) and other formations that were made as calcite bubbled through the rocks. Only nine cavern rooms are open to the public,

but there are many more. The Florida Parks Service zealously protects and safeguards these delicate formations as well as the endangered gray bats that live in the caves. Unfortunately, the other caves in the park are open only to scientists, biologists and archaeologists.

A nice surprise is the Chipole River, which actually dips underground for a couple of hundred feet within the park. But there is also **camping, canoeing** and **riding** (if you brought your horse along – there are no livery stables).

The visitors center rents canoes year round for $10 per day (eight hours), $7 for half a day. To ride your horse along the trails costs $5 per person, or $12 for a family. To camp at one of the 35 sites within the park, it costs $8/10 without/with electricity from October to February, and $12/14 March to September.

There are also five archaeological sites near the cavern and the fish hatchery area, and four natural-stone Depression-era houses. Within the visitors center, there are archives and artifacts taken from archaeological digs in the park.

One-hour guided tours of the caves leave the main ranger visitors center every half hour from 9 am to 4:30 pm daily. The cave tours are limited to 25 people at a time, and they sell out fast; go to the ticket office at the cave as soon as you arrive. Tours cost $4 for adults, $2 for children three to 13. Admission to the park is $3.25 per carload, $1 for pedestrians and cyclists.

Places to Stay & Eat
The **Hinson House** (☎ 850-526-1500, 4338 Lafayette St), just west of downtown, is a comfortable place with large rooms, big (interesting) breakfasts and wine in the afternoons. Rooms run from $55 to $85. A bizarre gimmick is that it's decorated for Christmas year round.

Jin Jin No 16 (☎ 850-525-2294) does decent Chinese food, with main courses from $6 to $9. **Old Mexico** (☎ 850-482-5552, 4434 Lafayette St) has decent Mexican food, with a dinner special of burrito, taco and chalupa (stuffed tortilla) for $6.50.

NW & PANHANDLE

DEFUNIAK SPRINGS

- population 4000; time zone CST

Another wacky little northern Panhandle town is DeFuniak Springs, a diabolically depressing place whose dubious claim to fame (its self-appointed publicist said, beaming with pride) is that it's Florida's, and we quote, 'only perfectly round natural lake.' You gotta be kidding (it's not even perfectly round). It should be better known as the former home of the New York Chautaqua, a cultural and educational organization, from 1885 to 1922.

But DeFuniak Springs does have some wonderful old houses and buildings. **St Agatha's Episcopal Church** (1896) has some excellent stained-glass windows, and if you can catch the reverend, you'll get an earful about their history. The church is opposite the **Chautauqua Building** (1909), on the western shore of Lake DeFuniak. All around the lake are architecturally interesting houses, from Victorian and Queen Anne to traditional Florida vernacular. Pick up a brochure at the library within the Chautauqua Building or at the Hotel De Funiak (see below), published by the Walton County Heritage Association, with excellent descriptions and a map.

Well worth a visit if you happen to already be here is the **Chautauqua Vineyards & Winery** (☎ 850-892-5887), 1339 Freeport Rd (near I-10). It grows and presses its own grapes and other fruits for some interesting wines – including a drinkable *blueberry* wine. Honest. There are tours and free tastings available Monday to Saturday 9 am to 5 pm, Sunday noon to 5 pm.

The only place worth staying in town (avoid at all costs the Best Western near I-10) is the newly and wonderfully renovated *Hotel De Funiak* (☎ 850-892-4383, 877-333-8642, 400 Nelson Ave), in a Victorian building (1920) with eight rooms (singles/doubles $65/75) and four suites ($85/95). Downstairs is an excellent restaurant and an ice cream parlor.

APALACHICOLA

- population 2900; time zone EST

Florida's oyster capital, Apalachicola is a quaint old Southern town with the feel of a fishing village and, during its annual Seafood Festival in early November, the atmosphere of an old-fashioned carnival.

It's not really worth visiting for more than a day, but its proximity to St George Island and its peaceful streets make it a far more tempting base for excursions out there than, say, Panama City Beach would.

Apalachicola is also the former home of refrigeration pioneer Dr John Gorrie, who invented air conditioning here (he was granted the first US patent on mechanical refrigeration in 1851). Gorrie got around: he was also at various times the city's mayor, postmaster, treasurer, councilor, bank director and the founder of Trinity Episcopal Church. Today, Gorrie's house is open as a museum (albeit a mind-numbingly boring one).

Orientation & Information

Apalachicola is at the southern end of the Panhandle about halfway between Tallahassee and Panama City, south of the Apalachicola National Forest. Hwy 98 runs through the center of town and out toward St George Island (see later in the chapter) to the east and Panama City Beach to the west. Downtown Apalachicola, and the Apalachicola Historic District, is on the eastern end of the spit leading toward the Gorrie Bridge (Hwy 98), and its streets are in a grid that's on a 45° angle to compass points.

Market St is the primary southeast-northwest street; other streets west of Market St are numbered, beginning with 4th St. Streets are bisected by avenues, which are lettered beginning at Ave B, one block northwest of Bay Ave at the waterline. Ave E is the main drag, and the continuation of Hwy 98, running from Market St at the northeast all the way out of town and beyond to Panama City.

Get tourist information and city maps at the Apalachicola Bay Chamber of Commerce (☎ 850-653-9419), 99 Market St.

Things to See

The grand, columned and classic Southern-plantation-looking **Raney House** (1838), at Market St and Ave F, was originally the home of Harriet and David Raney, a two-time former mayor of the city. It's open for viewing Saturday 1 to 5 pm.

The **piers** at the waterfront are always interesting places to watch the boats coming in and out, and on the block between Aves D and F from Water St to Market St are two interesting sites, the **Sponge Exchange** (1840) and the **Cotton Warehouse** (1838). And just strolling in the downtown area is a very nice way to spend an hour or two.

Dr John Gorrie (1803-55) was one of the pioneers of refrigeration, which he developed to make conditions more comfortable for yellow fever patients. His house is now the **Gorrie House Museum** (☎ 850-653-9347), 46 6th St (one block south of Ave E). Inside, you can see and use a model of his condensing pumps. There are other displays on cotton and the cotton warehouses that used to be in the city and trade along the Apalachicola River, and very tiny exhibits of tools, pine resin samples and sea sponges. The museum is open Thursday to Sunday 9 am to 5 pm; closed Thanksgiving, Christmas and New Year's Day. Admission is $1 for adults, free to children under six and free during the annual Seafood Festival.

The **Trinity Episcopal Church**, at the corner of 6th St and Ave E, may make you think that you have closed your eyes and woken up in New England, with its columns and large windows. And you're not far off: the church was originally built in New York state. It was cut into sections and then sailed down the Atlantic coast, around the Keys and up to this spot, where the church was erected in 1836 (incorporated, with the help of Gorrie, in 1837). Services are held at noon on Wednesday and at 8 and 10 am on Sunday.

St Patrick Catholic Church is another interesting old (1929) church, close to the Gorrie House Museum, on Ave C and 6th St. It holds Mass Saturday at 5 pm and Sunday at 10 am.

The **First United Methodist Church** (1901), at the corner of Ave E and 5th St, replaced an even older church that had been at this location since 1846. It holds a Sunday service at 11 am.

Places to Stay

Apalachicola Bay Campground (☎ 850-670-8307, on Hwy 98 in Eastpoint), across the Gorrie Bridge from Apalachicola, has tent sites for $13; RV/van sites are $15; cable TV is $1. All sites have electricity and water; RV/van sites also have sewer hookups. (See St George Island later in the chapter for more camping options.)

The clean if shabby *Apalachicola Motel* (☎ 850-653-2116, 850-653-2117, on Hwy 98), just west of town, has singles/doubles for $49/55 in winter, $55/65 in summer.

The *Apalachicola River Inn* (☎ 850-653-8139, 123 Water St) has clean and comfy-looking beds, curtains and fabrics, but the baths and carpets are pretty worn. Rooms run from $69 to $79 in summer, $54 to $64 in winter.

An enormous downtown centerpiece, the 1907 *Gibson Inn* (☎ 850-653-2191, 51 Ave C) is a B&B with Victorian-style rooms year round from $70 to $80, $5 higher on weekends, including an American hot breakfast. There's a 10% discount for seniors and active military. Its restaurant is open all day; at dinner entrees are $14 to $24, and happy hour is on Friday from 5 to 7 pm.

The spotless rooms at the *Coombs House Inn* (☎ 850-653-9199, 80 6th St), close to the Gorrie House, are very comfortable and newly renovated. Rooms run from $79 to $139. There's a large verandah, wine and cheese are offered on Friday and Saturday nights, and breakfast is continental: pastries, fruit, juice, croissants, banana-nut muffins, coffee and so on. There's a second house one block east.

Places to Eat

Risa's Pizza (87 Market St) offers salads from $2 to $3.50, sandwiches from $2.50 to $3 and 16-inch cheese pizzas for $7. *Dolores' Sweet Shop* (17 Ave E) is a very cute and old-fashioned ice cream parlor in a crumbling brick building – look for the large sign with 'EAT.' It has very good pecan pie and decent coffee.

The very-comfortable *Apalachicola Grill* (☎ 850-653-9510, 100 Market St) has lunch specials, all under $6.99, including grilled chicken salad, a soup and sandwich combo and salmon salad.

A nice new addition is **That Place in Apalach** (☎ 850-653-9888, *15 Ave D*), formerly a nice, cozy Italian place and now a nice, cozy American/European place, with good service and food that's cheaper than it could be. Sandwiches, such as portabello mushrooms with smoked mozzarella and roasted peppers, are $7.25, crab cakes $5.95, chowder from $2.50 to $3.50. At dinner, main courses average $14 to $18.

Getting There & Away

There's no Greyhound service within 50 miles of here, so the only way to travel is by car, and taking Hwy 98 is a great way to really get into rural Florida. On our trip here from Tallahassee, official highway department road signs carried these messages: 'Slippy When Wet' and 'You BEST Slow Down' (the BEST, of course, was flashing!).

ST JOSEPH PENINSULA STATE PARK

This state park (☎ 850-227-1327) is a spectacular place. A 2500-acre park with 10 miles of wilderness trails, miles of beautiful beaches with dramatic dunes and canoeing and camping all make it worth a trip, if not an overnight trip.

Canoeing is very peaceful here; rent canoes from rangers for $3 an hour or $15 a day; overnight rentals are at the ranger's discretion.

Camping is $16.28/18.40 without/with electric in summer, $8/10 in winter, and there are furnished cabins for up to seven people costing $70/55 in summer/winter. There's a two-night minimum from October to February, and a five-night minimum from March to September.

The park is open daily 8:30 am to sunset. Admission is $3.25 per person, $1 for pedestrians and bicyclists. To get here from Apalachicola, take Hwy 98 west for about 5 miles and watch for a road veering off to the left (C-30) before you get to the city of Port St Joe (if you hit Port St Joe, you've missed it). Follow that road for about 10 miles.

There will be a sharp turn, in the middle of which will be another left-veering road; take that (there's a sign saying St Joseph Peninsula State Park) about 8 miles to the end and you're in the park.

ST GEORGE ISLAND
* **population 700**

Discovered by Europeans in the early 1500s, St George Island is a 28-mile-long barrier island that was, until Opal at least, one of the most paradisiacal islands in the Gulf of Mexico: secluded, away from the riffraff across a long bridge, flat as a pancake and fringed with blindingly white sand. Opal damaged many homes on the island, but it wreaked total havoc on St George Island State Park, which has since recovered.

Unless you're camping, St George Island isn't really a budget-traveler's destination – the cheapest room in the island's only motel is $50 in low season. But the camping, either in the state park or on Cape St George (the island that lies to the west of St George), is excellent, and the nature is spectacular.

Orientation & Information

The island is just south of the city of Eastpoint, across a 3-mile causeway. When you get to the beach, go straight until you can't anymore – this is known as Front Beach Drive, but also as Gulf Beach Drive. Yes, it's confusing.

St George Island State Park

This 1962-acre state park (☎ 850-927-2111) is at the northeast end of St George Island. There are hiking trails and boardwalks throughout the pine woods, marshes and live oak hammocks, and there's excellent swimming. At the campground here, tent sites are $12 without electricity, $14 with electricity. Admission to the park is $4 a carload, $1 for pedestrians and cyclists. The park, which took a serious beating after Opal, is pretty much back to normal now: they've relocated about 1½ miles of the park's roadway and removed about a quarter-mile of damaged or destroyed road.

Cape St George

If you're looking for peace and quiet, this is the place for you: there is free camping on the eastern and western ends of the Cape St George Reserve (also known as Little St George Island), an uninhabited island just west of St George Island across Sikes Cut. The area is absolutely idyllic, and the only sounds other than the occasional passing motorboat during the day are of the area's wildlife, which include snowy plover, least tern, black skimmer willet and osprey, along with the standard Florida-issue raccoons.

Though the camping is free, there are absolutely no facilities on the island – bring everything you'll need, including a gallon of water per person a day and food in a strong, sealable plastic (not Styrofoam) cooler. Take all your trash with you – leave nothing – and only set campfires (use downed and dead wood only) on the beach.

You don't need to reserve ahead, but the park rangers request that you let them know if you're going out there (call the Apalachicola National Estuarine Reserve at ☎ 850-653-8063) – they patrol for evil-doers and sometimes take out groups, so they like to know if they'll be running into someone.

But to get there, you'll need to get yourself a boat: try Jeannie's Journeys (☎ 850-927-3259), 139 E Gorrie Drive on St George Island. It rents sailboats (a 13-foot Alcon Puffer is $75 a day, $45 a half day; a 16-foot Prindle Cat goes for $125/75), kayaks ($20 a day) and canoes ($25 a day).

Places to Stay

The **Buccaneer Inn** (☎ 850-927-2585, 800-847-2091, 160 W Gorrie Drive) is the *only* motel on the island; rooms are $50 to $80 depending on the view and season; efficiencies are $70 to $100. The rooms are okay, though the kitchenettes have that Burger King feel to them. Pets are not allowed.

We recommend the luxurious **St George Inn** (☎ 850-927-2903, Franklin Blvd and Pine St), sort of a hunting lodge on stilts. It's a newly renovated B&B with singles/doubles for $70/90 year round. There's a restaurant here as well (see Places to Eat below).

Lots and lots of people stay here in condominium apartments, cottages and houses, which rent for an average of $500 per week in the winter, $650 a week in fall, $800 a week in spring and $1200 a week in summer. The people at **Anchor Vacation Properties** (☎ 850-927-2625, 800-824-0416, 212 Franklin Blvd) are very helpful. The biggest rental agents on the island for this type of accommodation are **Collins Vacation Rentals** (☎ 850-927-2900, 800-423-7418) and **Accommodations St George** (☎ 850-927-2666, 800-332-5196).

Places to Eat

The **Blue Parrot Oyster Bar & Grill** (☎ 850-927-2987, 216 W Gorrie Drive) is an oceanfront café and local hangout. A dozen raw oysters are $2.95, steamed $4.95. Sandwiches are $3.95 to $4.50, platters such as chicken tenders are $7.50 and the seafood combo is $12.95.

Paradise Cafe (☎ 850-927-3300, 65 W Gorrie Drive) is good for breakfast. It also has sandwiches for $4.50 to $7.50, burgers for $3.95 to $5.95 and entrees for $9.95 to $18.95. Happy hour is daily from 4 to 6 pm, and nightly specials (served after 5 pm) are $5.95 to $12.95.

The **Island Oasis** (☎ 850-927-2639, 29 E Gulf Beach Drive) has a daily happy hour from 4 to 6 pm: pitchers are $3.50, piña coladas and strawberry daiquiris $2.95. On Sunday from 11 am to 2 pm, it has a $5.95 brunch with $2.95 Bloody Marys and mimosas. Dinners run from $7.95 for smothered chicken breast to $14.95 for the seafood platter, including baked potato or French fries, salad and garlic bread.

The **St George Inn** (☎ 850-927-2903, Franklin Blvd and Pine St) also has a restaurant – a very good one indeed – doing 'southern-French-bistro-style with a Cajun twist.' In winter, dinner is served Wednesday to Sunday 6 to 9 pm; in spring, summer and fall it's served daily except Monday. Chicken Florentine is $12.95, crab-stuffed pork chops are $14.95, and oven-roasted grouper is $16.50. This place is very popular and crowded, so get here early.

NW & PANHANDLE

TALLAHASSEE

• population 135,000; time zone EST

When we think of capital cities, we tend to think of oppressively scaled places with enormously wide streets and belligerent politicians speeding by in limousines, or, worse, we think of Brussels. But Tallahassee is charming in its fierce opposition to anything that might spoil its natural beauty: its streets are so tree lined – many are completely canopied – that when viewed from the air it looks more like a small settlement in the middle of a lush green forest than a center of political might.

Perhaps that's because the legislature works so rarely (see Florida State Capitol later in the chapter). And yet, despite its unassuming appearance, this is a planned city – as most, perhaps, as Washington, DC – and a quick glance at a map reveals that 'all roads lead to Tallahassee': the capitol is at the hub of a loose network of roads that emanate in all directions.

Tallahassee was made the capital of the Florida territories in 1824, but not because of its own eminence. Tallahassee was a compromise between the two battling supercities of the time, St Augustine at the east and Pensacola at the west. In an 'Oh, okay, let's just put it in the middle' decision, a heavily forested and hilly little settlement became the center of the state's business.

'Tallahassee' is an Apalachee word that means 'old town.' The Apalachees, the original settlers of the area, were all killed off by disease or the Spaniards, who followed Hernando de Soto's arrival in 1539.

By the 19th century, the area was rich agriculturally, and it relied heavily on slaves to work the farms. During the Civil War, Tallahassee was the only Confederate city east of the Mississippi River that did not fall to Union troops – though there was a battle at nearby Natural Bridge (see History in the Facts about Florida chapter).

Today, Tallahassee is a surprisingly pleasant town, except during FSU football games, when tens of thousands of unbelievably avid football fans descend with great vigor on the area, filling all the hotels and restaurants and driving in cars festooned with the team's politically questionable flag and logo of a Seminole Indian warrior.

But as a stop for a day or two, Tallahassee is definitely rewarding. Despite the political intrigues at the capitol, the city has a slow pace that, at the end of the day, makes it a simply charming Southern city.

Orientation

The main drag is Monroe St, which runs north-south through downtown; it's the east-west dividing line for addresses. Tennessee St is the north-south divider. Tallahassee's downtown is pretty much in the center of the city, bounded by Tennessee St at the north, around Van Buren St at the south, the FSU campus at the west and Magnolia Drive at the east.

Thomasville Rd breaks off from Monroe St just north of Brevard St and runs northeast, up toward Maclay Gardens State Park.

The Civic Center is west of the Florida State Capitol and the Old Capitol. The Florida State University campus is about three-quarters of a mile west of Monroe St; Doak Campbell Stadium is at the southwest corner of the campus, on the south side of Pensacola St.

Florida Agricultural & Mechanical University is south of downtown, bordered by Orange Ave at the south, Canal St at the north, Adams St at the east and Perry St at the west.

There are somewhat useful tourist maps of the city at the Visitor Information Center (see below), and you can buy pretty much any map you will ever need at the Map & Globe Store (☎ 850-385-8869), 2029 N Monroe St in the North Monroe Shops Mall.

Information

Tourist Offices The Tallahassee Convention & Visitors Bureau (☎ 850-413-9200, 800-628-2866, fax 850-487-4621), 200 W College Ave, runs the excellent Visitor Information Center, which is inside the New Capitol building, just to the right inside the main entrance (west side, plaza level, off S Duval St).

To the left as you enter the lobby is the Florida Welcome Center (☎ 850-488-6167),

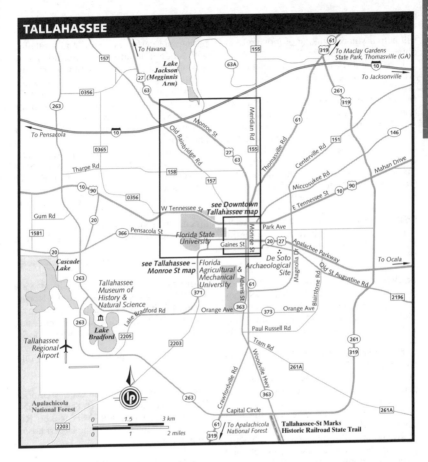

where Don Hardy – a nine-year veteran with a friendly drawl – dispenses information, pamphlets, coupons and flyers on attractions throughout the entire state. It's open Monday to Friday 8 am to 5 pm, Saturday and Sunday 9 am to 3 pm. The center also arranges free 30- to 40-minute guided tours of the capitol – you'll see the chambers and chapel and get a history of the building. There's a hotel reservation hotline – which might come in handy if you are showing up around the time of a FSU football game – at ☎ 850-488-2337.

The Visitor Information Center also hands out two very helpful brochures: *Touring Tallahassee*, a walking guide to the downtown district, and *Canopy Roads and Country Lanes*, a driving tour of the county. (See also Getting Around later in this section for a list of canopy roads.)

The Chamber of Commerce (☎ 850-224-8116), 100 N Duval St, is located in The Columns (circa 1830), Tallahassee's oldest surviving home. It's open Monday to Thursday 8 am to 5:30 pm, Friday to 5 pm. There's a (probably untrue) rumor that there is a nickel inside every brick. They no longer hand out general tourist information (but will help if you're thinking of moving to or doing business in the area).

Leon County has an excellent Tallahassee Website (www.co.leon.fl.us/visitors).

Money NationsBank has a downtown branch at 315 S Calhoun St, and branches at 2262 N Monroe St and 1321 W Jefferson St. American Express has three representative offices in the three branches of the Travel Center: at 703 N Monroe St (☎ 850-224-6464), FSU University Union, Room N-116 (☎ 850-561-9100) and at 1400 Village Square Blvd, No 11 (☎ 850-668-1360).

Post The main post office (☎ 850-216-4200) is at 2800 S Adams St; there's a more central location (☎ 850-385-4577) at 1845 Martin Luther King Jr Blvd.

Bookstores The Creative Book Exchange (☎ 850-222-5160), 1118 N Monroe St, has new and used books (which they buy and trade), a good kids' section, an unexciting travel section, good fiction and decent politics. It's open Monday to Saturday 10 am to 6 pm, Sunday noon to 5 pm. Black Cat News Exchange (☎ 850-222-1920), 115 S Monroe St, has Lonely Planet books and lots of mass print; they will order you anything they don't have. Bill's Bookstore has two locations: at the northeastern end of the FSU campus at 102 S Copeland St (☎ 850-224-3178) and at 1411 Tennessee St (☎ 850-561-1495), both selling new and used books and a lot of textbooks. Barnes & Noble (☎ 850-877-3878), 1480 Apalachee Pkwy, has a café.

Libraries The main library (☎ 850-487-2665) is at 200 W Park Ave.

Media The (what else?) *Tallahassee Democrat* (www.tallahassee.com) is the big daily paper of record. National Public Radio (NPR) is at 88.9 and 91.5 FM.

Universities Tallahassee is a major college town, with two universities. Florida State University (FSU; ☎ 850-644-2882) is a liberal arts school concentrating on sciences, computing and performing arts (and football), with undergraduate, graduate, advanced graduate and professional study programs. Total enrollment is almost 30,000 students. From September to April, there are free guided tours of the campus leaving from Visitor Services (☎ 850-644-3246), 100 S Woodward Ave, on Monday to Friday at 10 and 11 am and 1 and 3 pm.

The city's other university, Florida Agricultural & Mechanical University (☎ 850-599-3000) – also Florida A&M or FAMU (pronounced 'fam-you') – was founded in 1887 as the State Normal College for Colored Students, with 15 students and two instructors. Today, about 10,000 students of all races attend this university, which offers the must-see Black Archives Research Center & Museum (see later in the chapter).

Laundry Northwood Coin Laundry (☎ 850-385-9121), 1940 N Monroe St in the Northwood Mall, has tons of machines, a bunch of TVs and sassy service. Also try Plaza Laundromat (☎ 850-422-0262), 1911 N Monroe St.

Toilets There are public toilets in the Old and New Capitols.

Medical Services Tallahassee Memorial Regional Medical Center (☎ 850-681-1155), at Magnolia Drive and Miccosukee Rd, northeast of downtown, is the largest hospital in the area.

Florida State Capitol
Welcome to the ugliest building in modern America: the Florida State Capitol, also called the New Capitol (☎ 850-413-9200), at Pensacola and Duval Sts, is a 22-story monolithic slab of a monstrosity that's home to the ever-hardworking Florida legislature – which toils mercilessly for an entire 60 days a year, from March to May. If you're here at that time, you can get a glimpse of the pure grit of American politics as...wait a minute...just what are these folks doing for the other *nine* months of the year?

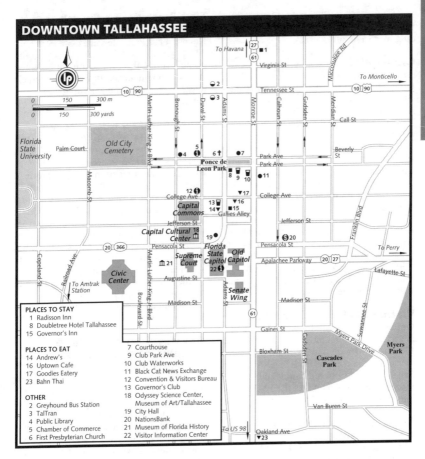

If the big swingers aren't here, at least take the free 45-minute tour. Tours leave every hour on the hour Monday to Friday from 9 to 11 am and 1 to 3 pm; Saturday, Sunday and holidays from 9 am to 3 pm.

Observation Deck You can see the view without the tour by taking the elevators up. The Observation Deck affords a panoramic view revealing just how much forest surrounds the city. You can easily make out landmarks like the Vietnam Veterans Memo-

rial and the First Presbyterian Church, and there is an art gallery with rotating exhibits here (as well as public toilets). Elevators 2 and 4 take you up all the way to the 22nd floor, and elevators 1 and 3 only take you to the 21st floor, from where you walk the last flight of stairs.

Heritage Chapel This chapel is an odd and somewhat eerie exhibit on the history of religion in Florida, which is told through writings on brass plaques. The chapel is in the lobby just south of the Observation Deck elevators. There are three or four weddings here a month.

Old Capitol

Originally built in 1845 and restored in 1902, *this* is a capitol. The Old Capitol (☎ 850-487-1902) is a grand structure, and it's now open as a museum, not just of Florida legislative history (you'll see the House and Senate Chambers, Supreme Court and Governor's Suite), but also of state history, with rotating art works and shows. There's a mastodon, a Civil War display, early Florida weaponry and logging tools, but the highlight is the stained-glass dome and red candy-striped awnings.

The building is adjacent to the New Capitol at the corner of S Monroe St and Apalachee Pkwy. It's open Monday to Friday 9 am to 4:30 pm, Saturday 10 am to 4:30 pm, Sunday and holidays noon to 4:30 pm; closed Thanksgiving and Christmas. Admission is free.

Vietnam Veterans Memorial

Opposite the Old Capitol on S Monroe St is a Vietnam War memorial honoring those Floridians who died, were injured or went missing in the conflict. It's a huge American flag suspended between twin granite towers inscribed with the names of the 1942 Floridians listed as killed and 83 missing in action.

Black Archives Research Center & Museum

This museum (☎ 850-599-3020), in the Carnegie Library on the FAMU campus, has one of the country's largest collections of African American and African artifacts, and it's a research center on black influence on US history and culture. There are exhibits on slavery and the treatment of slaves, a hands-on Underground Railroad exhibit for children, a 500-piece Ethiopian cross collection and a huge collection of papers, photographs, paintings and documents pertaining to black life in the USA. It's open Monday to Friday 9 am to 4 pm. Admission is free. It's at the corner of Martin Luther King Jr Blvd and Gamble St.

First Presbyterian Church

Tallahassee's oldest church, the Greek Revival First Presbyterian (1835-38; ☎ 850-222-4504), 102 N Adams St, is open to the public. During the 19th century, it accepted slaves as members, with or without their masters' consent, though seating was segregated.

Museum of Florida History

This museum (☎ 850-488-1673), 500 S Bronough St in the RA Gray Building (1976), isn't the state's most spectacular, but hey, it's free. Its star attraction is an American mastodon skeleton, but it also has collections of Indian artifacts, artifacts from the Spanish period and the Civil War (including a reconstructed Confederate campsite from 1861), farm equipment from different periods, quilts, cigar box labels, old clothes and more. This is also the home of the State Archives and State Library.

The hours are Monday to Friday 9 am to 4:30 pm, Saturday 10 am to 4:30 pm, Sunday and holidays noon to 4:30 pm; closed Thanksgiving and Christmas.

Odyssey Science Center & Museum of Art/Tallahassee

The Capital Cultural Center (☎ 850-671-5001), 350 S Duval St, in Kleman Plaza, houses the Odyssey Science Center on the 1st and 2nd floors and the Museum of Art/Tallahassee on the 3rd.

The Odyssey Science Center (☎ 850-576-6520, www.odysseysciencecenter.org) is a science museum with hands-on exhibits and Saturday morning science classes for children. Its permanent exhibits include a weather station and hydrogeology lab, and there are cool temporary exhibits – such as The Atoms Family. The museum is open Tuesday to Saturday 10 am to 5 pm, Sunday 1 to 5 pm, closed Monday. Admission is $5 for adults, $3.50 for seniors and children under 12.

The Museum of Art/Tallahassee (☎ 850-513-0700, moatallahassee.com) holds rotating exhibitions throughout the year. Parking is available in the garage under Kleman Plaza.

Cemeteries

There are two cemeteries downtown, open sunrise to sunset: the Old City Cemetery, which is bounded by Park Ave, Macomb and Call Sts and Martin Luther King Jr Blvd; and St John's Episcopal Cemetery (1840), at Call St and Martin Luther King Jr Blvd. There's a self-guided walking tour in the Old City Cemetery.

De Soto Archaeological Site

Just east of downtown and northeast of Myers Park, De Soto State Archaeological Site (☎ 850-922-6007) is said to be the site of the first encampment of Spanish explorer Hernando de Soto. In December, there are reenactments of the First Christmas in the New World, but the park was under renovation as we went to press. It's just south of Lafayette St, about 10 blocks east of Monroe St.

Knott House Museum

This museum (☎ 850-922-2459), 301 E Park Ave, is a restored Victorian house that was occupied during the Civil War by Confederate, and then Union, troops. On May 20, 1865, Union General Edward McCook read the Emancipation Proclamation from here; the date is still celebrated locally as Emancipation Day.

In 1928, William V Knott, a local politico, bought the house. It's called 'the house that rhymes,' because his wife, incorrigible teetotaler Luella Knott, wrote mainly insufferable temperance poetry that she attached to many of her furnishings, which are still here. Guided hour-long tours are given Wednesday to Friday 1 to 4 pm and Saturday 10 am to 4 pm. Admission is free.

Maclay Gardens State Park

A 20-minute drive north of downtown, the 1930s estate of financier Alfred B Maclay is now open as a state garden (☎ 850-487-4556), 3540 Thomasville Rd. During the peak blooming season from January to April, there are more than 200 varieties of flowers. The gardens are open year round (when we visited in the fall there was a huge group of seniors having a picnic here),

though the home is only open during the blooming season. There are nature trails and access to the lovely lake. Admission is free except during blooming season, when it's $3.25 per carload or $1 for pedestrians and bicyclists. From I-10, take exit 30 to Thomasville Rd north; follow the signs – the entrance is on your left.

Tallahassee Museum of History & Natural Science

This museum (☎ 850-576-1636, 850-575-8684, www.tallahasseemuseum.org), 3945 Museum Drive, about 4 miles southwest of downtown near Lake Bradford, is a history museum with hands-on nature displays and a working 1880s farmhouse with animals. There are also wildlife demonstrations and creative programs throughout the year – such as sing-alongs with singers from all over the Panhandle and shows like Spring Farm Days (which has demonstrations of late-19th-century farming techniques).

It's open Monday to Saturday 9 am to 5 pm, Sunday from 12:30 to 5 pm. Admission is $6 for adults, $5.50 for seniors, $4 for kids four to 15. To get there, take Gaines St to Lake Bradford Rd (Hwy 371), go south, and then bear right at the fork and follow Orange Ave to Rankin Rd, turn left and follow the signs.

Tallahassee Antique Car Museum

This museum showroom (☎ 850-942-0137, www.tacm.com), 3550-A Mahan Dr at Car Nations Plaza, has classic American cars, including a Ford Roadster, a 1931 Deusenberg and, of course, a DeLorean. It's open Monday to Saturday 10 am to 5 pm, Sunday noon to 5 pm. Admission is $7.50 for adults, $4 for kids six to 10.

Courthouse & Ponce de Leon Park

This WPA-built building (1936), at 110 W Park Ave, housed the US Courthouse and Post Office. Today, it's open to the public. You can walk in to look at the building's neoclassical columns and cupola, and the WPA murals. Just across the street is Ponce de Leon Park (circa 1880), a very pleasant bit of green with a fountain; it's the site of live jazz on Thursday night as well.

Tallahassee-St Marks Historic Railroad State Trail

This trail (☎ 850-922-6007) is a 16-mile paved trail for bicyclists and skaters; it's totally flat and well paved the entire length.

Bike rentals from About Bikes, at the head of the trail, are $4.50 per hour or $35 for 24 hours. In-line skates are $7 for one hour, $12 for two hours, $25 for 24 hours. The prices are discounted if you rent more than one bike or pair of skates. To get there from downtown Tallahassee, take Monroe St south, which becomes Woodville Hwy (Hwy 363), and take that across Capital Circle; the park is 100 yards ahead on the right-hand side of the road. It's open year round from 8 am to dark. Admission is free.

Organized Tours

A downtown walking tour ($6 for adults, $4 for students) leaves from Capital West Plaza Monday to Saturday at 10 am, 1 and 3 pm; check at the Visitor Information Center in the New Capitol for more information.

Horse-drawn carriage tours (☎ 850-509-4199, www.christopher.org/tallahassee/tours) run from Ponce de Leon Park on Saturday at 9 am and 2 pm, for $15 per person.

Tours With A Southern Accent (☎ 850-513-1000) runs self-guided cassette tours (you give a deposit for the Walkman) and guided tours of downtown for $20.

Places to Stay

Most of the hotels and motels in the area are clumped at exits along I-10 and are lined along Monroe St, between I-10 and downtown. Scour the Florida Welcome Center for discount coupons, which abound and can save you a lot of money on area accommodations, except during football games, when no coupon in the world can help you. Most places offer free local calls and will provide at least donuts and coffee in the morning.

About 10 minutes east of Tallahassee, the *Tallahassee RV Park* (☎ 850-878-7641, *6504 Mahan Drive/Hwy 90*) offers tents and RV/van sites with full hookups for $21.82. From I-10, take exit 31A and go west for a mile on Hwy 90.

About 15 miles farther east, there's a *Tallahassee East KOA* (☎ 850-997-3890) with tent sites for $14.50 with no hookups, $17.50 with water and electric, $19.50 for full hookups and $22.50 for Kamping Kabins; all prices are year round, even during games. Take I-10 to exit 33, turn south on Hwy 19 for half a mile, then west for 2 miles on the little access road (Hwy 158), which dead ends into Hwy 259, and then turn north again for half a mile. Can't miss it.

The *Florida State University Seminole Reservation* (☎ 850-644-6083, 850-644-6892, *3226 Flastacowo Rd*) is a 73-acre facility on Lake Bradford, but it no longer allows camping. 'The Rez' offers rustic cabins (kitchens, but no TV or telephone) on the lake for $35 per night for nonstudents, $25 for FSU students (though you can try and get that rate with an ISIC). It also has two large dormitory-style cabins, each with about 12 bunk beds; the cost is $60 per night or $6 per person, whichever is greater.

The best motel deal in town (we thought) was the spotless if bland *Executive Suites Motor Inn* (☎ 850-386-2121, 800-342-0090, *522 Scotty's Lane*). Rooms are $30 to $59, cheaper with coupons from the visitors centers, and all have Jacuzzis (!) in the bathrooms. They are clean and roomy; the price includes donuts, coffee and juice in the morning; and there's a pool.

The *Super 8 Motel* (☎ 850-386-8818, *2702 N Monroe St*) is a standard Super 8 in every respect, including price, which is $31/46 for singles/doubles.

We also liked the newly renovated and privately owned *American Inn* (☎ 850-386-5000, *2726 N Monroe St*), with doubles for $40 ($45 during graduation ceremonies and $55 during games). There's a pool, and you can rent a VCR and two movies for $5.

The *Best Inn* (☎ 850-562-2378, *2738 Graves Rd*) has double rooms for $41 to $65; add $10 during special events. It offers free cereal and milk at breakfast.

Ramada Limited (☎ 850-224-7116, 800-272-6232, *1308 W Brevard St*), at the corner

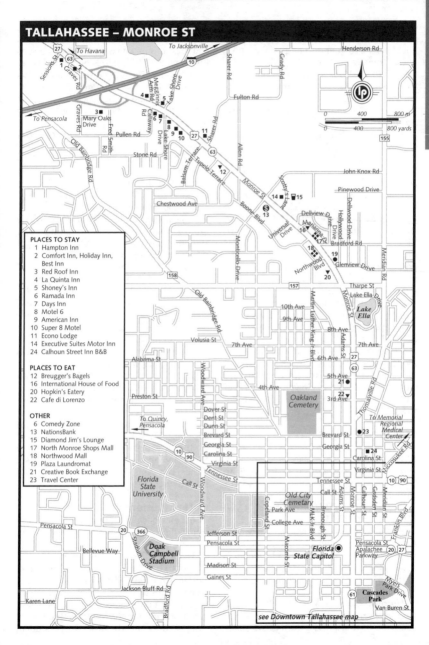

TALLAHASSEE – MONROE ST

PLACES TO STAY
1 Hampton Inn
2 Comfort Inn, Holiday Inn, Best Inn
3 Red Roof Inn
4 La Quinta Inn
5 Shoney's Inn
6 Ramada Inn
7 Days Inn
8 Motel 6
9 American Inn
10 Super 8 Motel
11 Econo Lodge
14 Executive Suites Motor Inn
24 Calhoun Street Inn B&B

PLACES TO EAT
12 Breugger's Bagels
16 International House of Food
20 Hopkin's Eatery
22 Cafe di Lorenzo

OTHER
6 Comedy Zone
13 NationsBank
15 Diamond Jim's Lounge
17 North Monroe Shops Mall
18 Northwood Mall
19 Plaza Laundromat
21 Creative Book Exchange
23 Travel Center

see Downtown Tallahassee map

of Tennessee St, has rooms for one to four people for $45 to $85, plus $6 each additional person (higher during special events).

La Quinta Inn (☎ *850-385-7172, 800-531-5900, 2905 N Monroe St*) has rooms from $60 to $76; during football games all rooms are $90, and at graduation $95.

Other chains in town include the *Radisson Inn* (☎ *850-224-6000, 800-333-3333, 415 N Monroe St*); *Shoney's Inn* (☎ *850-386-8286, 800-222-2222, 2801 N Monroe St*); *Best Western Seminole Inn* (☎ *850-656-2938, 800-996-6537, 6737 Mahan Drive*); and *Days Inn* (☎ *850-222-3219, 1350 W Tennessee St*).

There are two decent top-end options in the heart of downtown: The *Doubletree Hotel Tallahassee* (☎ *850-224-5000, 101 S Adams St*) offers good deals. Rack rates are $150 for standard rooms and $160 for premium rooms, but if you ask for the corporate rate, they plunge to a highly reasonable $79 to $149. The poshest place in town is the *Governor's Inn* (☎ *850-681-6855, 209 S Adams St*), with heaps of amenities (turndown service, bathrobe, free drinks and newspaper, etc) and rack rates from $120 to $220. Also see Entertainment.

Calhoun Street Inn Bed and Breakfast (☎ *850-425-5095, 525 N Calhoun St*) is a pleasant place on a tree-lined street very close to the center of downtown. A room with a double bed is $65, queen-size bed $75 to $95.

Places to Eat

Hopkin's Eatery (☎ *850-386-4252, 1840 N Monroe St*) is a terrific place with excellent garden sandwiches and salads for $3.50 to $6, and vegetarian primo platters for $5. It's closed Sunday.

The *International House of Food* (☎ *850-386-3433, 2013 N Monroe St*) is an East Asian/Middle Eastern food market with a deli counter. For about $2.50, you'll walk out with a sandwich. Platters are $3.99; dahl is $3.49. *Breugger's Bagels* (☎ *850-224-1409, 1216 N Monroe St*) has very good bagels for 49¢, or $4.99 a dozen.

Uptown Cafe (☎ *850-222-3253, 111 E College Ave*) is great for breakfast, and its soups are the toast of the town ($2.75 small,

$3.25 big) – soup usually sells out by noon. Sandwiches are good here ($3.20 to $4.75), and they also make very, very good cookies for about 85¢. It's open Monday to Friday 7 am to 3 pm. Fred, the owner, says he gets knockout Thai food at *Phen Thai*, in the strip mall behind Calico Jack's on Capital Circle NE, northeast of downtown – I wish we'd had time to check it out.

Diagonally across the street, *Goodies Eatery* (☎ *850-681-3888, 116 E College Ave*) isn't anywhere near as homey or comfortable, but it serves breakfast all day long and does sandwiches from $3.20 to $4.50; salads are $3.99 to $4.99. It's open Saturday 7:30 am to 4:30 pm.

Cafe di Lorenzo (☎ *850-681-3622, 1002 N Monroe St*) serves pasta, pizza and other Italian dishes for $8 to $11. If you get takeout, prices drop to about $3 to $5.50.

Chez Pierre (☎ *850-222-0936, 1215 Thomasville Rd*) is a cozy and not-yet-pretentious French place with a country setting. For what you get, it is very inexpensive. Lunch entrees include crepes poulet for $4.50, ratatouille Nicoise at $5.25 and boeuf stroganoff for $6.95. It offers homemade ice cream and sorbets daily. At dinner, prices are a bit higher, with entrees averaging $9.95 to $17.95. Lunch is served Monday to Saturday 11 am to 2:30 pm, dinner Tuesday to Saturday 6 to 9:30 pm (make reservations). Smoking is not allowed.

Lunch at the elegant *Andrew's* (☎ *850-222-3444, 228 S Adams St*) is very cheap for what you get and very good – soups are $2.25 and main courses (fish and pasta dishes) run from $5.95 to $6.95. Prices shoot up at dinner.

Entertainment

Theater Check the Friday Limelight section in the *Tallahassee Democrat* for theater listings.

The FSU Theatre Department (☎ 850-644-6500) has three venues. The *Richard G Fallon Mainstage Theater* in the Fine Arts Building, north of Call St on the campus, does large productions of plays and musicals. *The Studio*, in the Williams Building on campus, does mainly various free student

Bahn Thai

Three cheers for **Bahn Thai** (☎ *850-224-4765, 1319 S Monroe St*), south of the capitol, still one of the state's best Thai places. Monday to Friday from 11 am to 2:30 pm, there is a large all-you-can-eat buffet (15 entrees, soup, rice and fruit) for an incredible $4.85 per person, and regular entrees like *pad Thai* for $6.95 (very good), curry (which they actually make spicy) for $8.95 and chow mein for $5.75. Dinner prices are slightly higher. This is a Tallahassee institution, and many customers have been coming here for years – so often that the owner, Lamoi (Sue) Snyder, knows regular customers by their orders. She took one look at us and pointed to the table we sat at three years ago!

productions and MFA-candidate works. Off campus, at the corner of Lafayette and Copeland Sts, *The Lab* does a huge range of works from Shakespeare to *Grease* in its 150-seat thrust-stage setting.

The *Tallahassee Little Theater* (☎ 850-224-8474, 1861 Thomasville Rd) is a small community theater striving to break out of that mold; it offers several productions a year.

FAMU Essential Theater (☎ 850-599-3000), on the FAMU campus, is said to be excellent (even by the FSU Theatre Department). Its season is based around a 'Theater Unbound' schedule of shows; call for more information.

The *Capital Commons Amphitheatre* is host to the annual Spring Shakespeare Fest (☎ 850-671-0742) and the annual Caribbean Fest at Christmas.

Live Music The *Tallahassee Symphony Orchestra* (☎ 850-224-0461) performs at the FSU Ruby Diamond Auditorium at College Ave and Copeland St.

Most big-name concerts are held at the *Leon County Civic Center* (☎ 850-222-0400, 800-322-3602, 505 W Pensacola St), just west of Monroe St. There's live jazz on Thursday in Ponce de Leon Park (weather permitting) from 7:30 to 9 pm.

Bars & Clubs The cool *Club Waterworks* (☎ 850-224-1887, 104½ S Monroe St) has happy hour Monday to Friday from 4 to 7 pm with $1.75 Samuel Adams. There's jazz on Monday night (no cover) and on Satur-

day ($2 cover); Friday is cha-cha-cha night. It's dimly lit, there are couches here and there, and it has a good beer selection.

Diamond Jim's Lounge (☎ 850-386-9366, 531 Scotty's Lane) is surprisingly fun; it's in the Silver Slipper restaurant across the street from the Executive Suites Motor Inn. It's packed with locals and sometimes red-faced state legislators, and there's live country music Tuesday to Saturday.

Mustard Tree (☎ 850-893-8733, 1415 Timberlane Rd) is a yuppie dive with a two-for-one happy hour Monday to Friday from 5:30 to 7:30 pm.

The *Comedy Zone* (☎ 850-386-1027, 2900 N Monroe St), at the Ramada Inn, has comedians with two shows on Friday and Saturday; it's a bar at other times.

The Palace Saloon (☎ 850-575-3418, 1303 Jackson Bluff Rd) is a sports bar near Doak Campbell Stadium, with six satellite TVs, including a big-screen TV for NFL and FSU games. Live bands play Friday and Saturday (no cover).

Club Park Ave (☎ 850-599-9143, 115 E Park Ave), just west of Monroe St, is gay on Saturday night and Sunday night (when there are drag shows) and straight on Wednesday and Friday; it's closed the rest of the week. *Brothers* (☎ 850-386-2399, 926 W Tharpe St) is another gay and lesbian venue.

Across the street from the Governor's Inn is the hushed wood and brass elegance of the *Governor's Club* (☎ 850-224-0650, 202½ S Adams St), a bar associated with the hotel.

Spectator Sports

The FSU Seminoles play football games to packed houses at the more than 80,000-seat *Doak Campbell Stadium* on the FSU campus from September to November. Tickets (which sell out months in advance) are $25 no matter where you sit. FSU baseball happens in the spring at *Dick Howser Stadium*. For more FSU athletic information, call the athletic department (☎ 850-644-1830, 888-378-6653).

The FAMU Rattlers play football from August to November at *Bragg Memorial Stadium* (☎ 850-599-3141), on the FAMU campus.

Getting There & Away

Air Tallahassee Regional Airport (☎ 850-891-7800, 800-610-1995) is served by Delta, US Airways, American Eagle and several smaller airlines. It's about 5 miles southwest of downtown, off Hwy 263.

Bus The Greyhound station (☎ 850-222-4240) is at 112 W Tennessee, at the corner of Duval, opposite the downtown TalTran transfer center. Buses to/from Tallahassee include the following (there are approximately four a day for each); fares are one way/roundtrip:

destination	duration	price
Gainesville	3 to 3½ hours	$25/49
Jacksonville	3 to 4 hours	$29/55
Miami	12 to 15 hours	$60/115
Panama City	1 to 2 hours	$13/26
Pensacola	2¼ to 4 hours	$21/42

Train The Amtrak station (☎ 850-244-2779) is at 918½ Railroad Ave. The *Sunset Limited* arrives from Los Angeles on Wednesday, Friday and Monday at 10:25 am, and from Miami on Sunday, Tuesday and Friday at 11:44 pm.

Car & Motorcycle It's 98 miles to Panama City Beach, 163 to Jacksonville, 198 to Pensacola and 463 to Miami. The main access road is I-10 from the east and the west. To get to the Gulf Coast towns along the Panhandle, take Hwy 319 south to Hwy 98. From Gainesville, it's about 120 miles; take I-75 north to I-10 west.

Getting Around

To/From the Airport There's no public transport to and from the airport. Annett Airport Shuttle Service (☎ 850-878-3216, 800-328-6033) charges $10 per person between the airport and Tallahassee; they like to have 24 hours notice, but if you forget, their vans cruise by regularly. Tropic Transit (☎ 850-222-3375) is another shuttle service in town. A regular cab will also cost about $10 to $12. By car, take Capital Circle Rd (Hwy 263) to Lake Bradford Rd, north to downtown.

Bus TalTran (☎ 850-891-5200) has a main transfer point downtown on Tennessee St at Adams St. The fare is 75¢, and transfers are free. Some popular routes include the following:

Bus No 15 – Museum of History & Science

Bus No 1 – Monroe St to I-10

Bus Nos 3, 23, 26 – Doak Campbell Stadium

Bus No 22 – De Soto Park

FSU shuttle, bus Nos 14, 11, 5 – FAMU campus

Bus No 16 – north on Thomasville Rd to a half-mile south of Maclay Gardens State Park

Trolley The Old Town Trolley (☎ 850-891-5200) is a free shuttle service around downtown; it runs every 10 minutes Monday to Friday from 7 am to 6 pm. Look for the trolley signs. It runs as far north as Brevard St, then south to Madison St on Monroe St and around the Civic Center and back. Pick up route maps on the trolley or at the Visitor Information Center at the New Capitol.

Car & Motorcycle There are several canopy roads (those almost completely covered by foliage) in the area, and the best way to see them is by driving. They are along Old St Augustine Rd, Centerville Rd, Meridian Rd, Miccosukee Rd and Old Bainbridge Rd.

Parking is an absolute nightmare in downtown, and $10 tickets are handed out like bad advice in a cheap bar. There is a two-hour, metered public parking garage between Duval and Bronough Sts, across from the New Capitol. The one-way system is also a challenge, so be prepared for a frustrating experience and follow the signs.

Taxi Rates in Tallahassee are $1.20 at flagfall and $1.20 each mile. Companies include City Taxi (☎ 850-562-4222), Yellow Cab (☎ 850-580-8080) and Capital Taxi (☎ 850-942-1015).

AROUND TALLAHASSEE
Havana

The little town of Havana, about 12 miles north of I-10 on Hwy 27, is essentially a cute little antique mall. You'll find most of the shops along 7th Ave, off Main St (called Hwy 27 in town). Most shops are closed Monday and Tuesday.

The Historical Bookshelf (☎ 850-539-5040), 104 E 7th Ave, has a good selection of used books on history, aviation and political history, and a good Civil War section. Pepperhead Quarters, 1415 Timberlane Rd, has about 350 hot pepper products; taste your way through and chat for a while.

The big mall here is the Cannery (☎ 850-539-3800), 115 E 8th Ave, open Wednesday to Sunday 10 am to 6 pm. It's filled with antique shops and other stores.

Dolly's Expresso Café (☎ *850-539-6716, 206 1st St NW*) has awesome chocolate cheesecake, and sandwiches from $2.95 to $5. A latte will run you $2.

The *Willow Cafe* (☎ *850-539-9111, 211 1st St*) is always packed; it has quilts hanging on the walls and serves light lunches like spaghetti pie ($6.95) and paella, veggie salad, shrimp and corn chowder. It's open Thursday to Saturday 11:30 am to 2:30 pm and Sunday from noon to 3 pm.

If you feel like staying overnight, *Gaver's Bed & Breakfast* (☎ *850-539-5611, 301 E 6th Ave*) is a decent B&B with singles/doubles for $55/65 and $75 for a bigger room, including a full or continental breakfast. The house

was built in 1907. Credit cards, pets and kids under eight are not allowed.

Natural Bridge Battlefield

Fifteen miles southeast of Tallahassee, the Natural Bridge Battlefield State Historic Site (☎ 850-922-6007) is on the site where a ragtag group of Confederate soldiers prevented Union troops from reaching Tallahassee in 1865 (see Facts about Florida). The park is peaceful, and it's free: open daily from 8 am to sunset. Don't miss the annual battle re-enactment on March 6. From Tallahassee, take Hwy 363 south to Natural Bridge Rd in Woodville.

Wakulla Springs State Park

Edward Ball Wakulla Springs State Park (☎ 850-922-3633) is a 2860-acre park with a natural spring that covers about 3 acres and produces at peak times 1.2 billion gallons of water a day. Glass-bottom boat rides are available (when the water's clear) as well as a riverboat cruise. Both run daily 11 am to 3 pm and last about 30 minutes; the cost is $4.50 for adults, $2.25 for kids under 12. There's also swimming and a 6-mile hiking trail here. Some of the underwater scenes from the old Tarzan movies were filmed here, as well as scenes from *The Creature from the Black Lagoon* and *Airport '77*.

Scientist Sarah Smith discovered the bones of an ancient mastodon on the bottom of the spring here in 1850; since then the remains of at least nine other Ice Age mammals have been found – you may be able to see some of the excavation sites near the waterfront or on the glass-bottom boat tours.

Camping is not allowed, but if you want to stay in the park, check out the *Wakulla Springs Lodge* (☎ *850-224-5950),* an immense Spanish building dating from 1937 with a huge dining room and a walk-in fireplace. Rooms have private marble bathrooms; double room rates are $69 to $85.

The park is about 17 miles south of Tallahassee. Take Hwy 319 south to Hwy 61 south and follow the signs; the entrance is on

Hwy 267. Admission is $3.25 per carload, $1 for pedestrians and bicyclists.

APALACHICOLA NATIONAL FOREST

The largest of Florida's three national forests, the Apalachicola National Forest occupies almost 938 sq miles of the eastern Panhandle from just west of Tallahassee to the Apalachicola River. The forest is wet lowlands and slash pine and longleaf pine in the higher areas; other areas are made up of oak and cypress hammocks.

Nature within the forest is diverse, with dozens of species calling the area home, including mink, gray and red foxes, coyotes, eastern moles, six bat species, beavers, Florida black bears and possibly Florida panthers, though the Florida Game and Fresh Water Fish Commission says there aren't any left.

While access to the forest is free and there's free hiking, camping, boating and swimming throughout, note that it's also open to hunting.

Orientation & Information

Administratively, the park is dissected by the Ochlockonee River, which flows south right through the center of the park; the eastern half is controlled by the Wakulla Ranger District, the western half by the Apalachicola Ranger District.

The Apalachicola Ranger Station (☎ 850-643-2282) is just south of the city of Bristol, northwest of the park near the intersection of Hwys 12 and 20; the Wakulla Ranger Station (☎ 850-926-3561) is just north of Crawfordville on Hwy 319.

The forest's boundaries are Hwy 20 at the north, Hwy 319 at the east, the Franklin County line at the south and the Apalachicola River at the west.

Several highways transverse the park at various angles; the following are the major highways:

Hwy 65 – between Sumatra at the park's southwest border and Telogia, just north of the park's northern border

Hwy 267 – between Bloxham and Hwy 319

Hwy 12 – between Bristol and Wilma

Hwy 13 – east-west across the lower portion of the park between Crawfordville and Wilma

Hwy 67 – mainly north-south from just south of Bristol, at the northwest end of the park, down through Hitchcock Lake and Franklin County

Hwy 375 – from Bloxham to Sopchoppy

Get maps of the forest – key equipment – at the Visitor Information Center at the New Capitol in Tallahassee, or either ranger station, which also give out pamphlets and sell topographical maps. There are entrances to the park at the junctions of the above roads. Admission is free. Day-use areas are open 8 am to sunset year round.

Things to See & Do

The forest is filled with water and sinkholes, but the best place to see both is at the **Leon Sinks Geological Area**, with interpretive materials and rangers to help explain the sinkholes. It's at the eastern end of the park just east of Hwy 319, about 20 miles south of Tallahassee.

The huge forest offers almost untouched wilderness for hiking, horseback riding, walking and canoeing, though note that powerboats are permitted in the park. For information on canoe rentals, contact either ranger station.

On the western side of the forest, south of Tallahassee, is the **Munson Hills Loop**, a tough 7½-mile bicycle trail through the hilliest section of the forest in an area made up of hammock, dunes, hills and brush. If you run out of steam halfway, you can bail out; take the Tall Pine Shortcut out of the trail for a total distance of 4½ miles.

Swimming is available at Camel Lake, Wright Lake, Silver Lake and Lost Lake.

Places to Stay

All facilities are primitive, some with toilets, some not. With the exception of Silver Lake and Lost Lake, which charge $4, camping is free. There is camping available on the western (Apalachicola) side of the forest at Camel Lake (from Bristol, near the ranger station, take Hwy 12 south for 11 miles and turn east on Forest Rd 105 for 2 miles):

Cotton Landing (at the southwest part of the forest; from Sumatra take Hwy 379 northwest for 3 miles then turn left on Hwy 123 for 3 miles, then left again onto Hwy 123B for about half a mile); Hickory Landing (from Sumatra, take Hwy 65 south; turn right on Forest Rd 101 and left on 101B); Wright Lake, just northeast of Hickory Landing; and Hitchcock Lake, just west of the Ochlockonee River off Hwy 67.

In the eastern (Wakulla) section of the forest, there's camping at Silver Lake (from Hwy 20 take Hwy 260 south to Silver Lake), Lost Lake (northwest of Leon Sinks; take Hwy 20 to Hwy 373 and follow it to the Lost Lake turnoff) and, at the southeast section of the park, Mack Landing (from Sopchoppy, go northwest on Hwy 375) and Wood Lake (from Sopchoppy, take Hwy 375 to Hwy 22 west, to Hwy 340 south to Hwy 338).

TORREYA STATE PARK

Fifty miles west of Tallahassee, this lovely little park (☎ 850-643-2674) along the Apalachicola River, with its towering Torreya evergreen, elm and yew trees, is home to the Gregory House (a pre-Civil War plantation mansion) and a 7-mile hiking trail. Tours of the house are available daily at 10 am, Saturday and Sunday at 2 and 4 pm as well. The park is open daily 8 am to sunset. Admission is $2 per vehicle, $1 for pedestrians and cyclists. The Gregory House has a separate admission for the guided tour: $1 for adults, 50¢ for children.

Tent camping is cheap here: $3 for adults, $2 for students or kids under 17 years old if accompanied by an adult. RV camping is $8 per site, $2 extra for electricity.

The park is off Hwy 12, near Bristol. From Tallahassee, take Hwy 20 west, turn north on Hwy 12 and bear left at the fork, following the signs.

STEPHEN FOSTER STATE FOLK CULTURAL CENTER

• time zone EST

About 40 minutes east of Tallahassee off I-10, the Stephen Foster State Folk Cultural Center (☎ 904-397-2733) is a fine state park with exhibits and mementos honoring the composer of Florida's state song, 'Old Folks at Home,' Stephen C Foster (see boxed text), a man who never came near the area.

The center has a 5-mile-loop bicycle and hiking trail, an interpretive center, and a museum of Florida and Foster-related history. Free ranger-guided tours run frequently, sometimes with female rangers wearing antebellum dresses, and there are special events throughout the year, culminating in the Florida Folk Festival every Memorial Day weekend.

Other annual festivals are the Folk Life Days in November, celebrating 19th-century homestead life, and Stephen Foster Day in January, with musical programs, caroling and recitals of Foster selections. There are also several Elderhostel programs held here each year.

There's canoeing along the river, with canoe rentals available from American Canoe Adventures (☎ 904-397-1309). Tent camping is available for $8 per site (most have water hookups), and $2 extra for electricity.

Admission is $3.25 per carload, or $1 for pedestrians and bicyclists. From I-10, take Hwy 41 north just past the town of White Springs and follow the signs.

SUWANNEE RIVER STATE PARK

At the junction of the Suwannee and Withlacoochee Rivers, this 1800-acre state park (☎ 904-362-2746) offers a unique opportunity to see the confluence of rivers as well as bubbling springs. There's a scenic overlook, and you can still see the fortifications built by Confederates to protect the railroad bridge over the Suwannee, which they used to shuttle food supplies to the front (see History in the Facts about Florida chapter).

The park has canoe trails and rentals ($15 per day), and camping ($10 without electricity, $12 with). There are also interpretive nature signs along the Suwannee River Nature Trail through hardwood hammock, and the Sandhills Trail, which leads to the remains of the Columbus Cemetery and to the Old Stage Road, a major transport route between Pensacola and Jacksonville in the 18th and 19th centuries.

Stephen C Foster

While Stephen Collins Foster (1826-64) could be considered a true American legend (he was even born on the Fourth of July), his work in minstrel shows and his popularity at the height of slavery ensures that his legacy is tainted with, to say the very least, political incorrectness.

Yet his performances, and variations on slave songs of the era, are undeniably offset by his contribution to American culture. It was Foster who brought us 'Oh, Susanna!,' as familiar to listeners now as it was when released in 1846. And it was Foster who first brought the world's attention to the Suwannee River – a river Foster himself had never set eyes on.

The song is 'Old Folks at Home,' with lyrics penned in simulated 'Darkey' dialect: 'Way down upon the Swannee Ribber, far, far away/Dere's wha my heart is turning ebber/Dere's where the old folks stay.' Foster apparently chose the Suwannee on a whim: he was said to have been considering the Pedee and the Yazoo Rivers as well ('Way down upon the Yazoo River'?!?), but a misspelled map led to his selection of the 'Swannee,' which runs from north to south through extreme north-central Florida and empties into the Gulf of Mexico.

Despite its clearly racist tone and lyrics (a line from the chorus is 'Oh! darkeys how my heart grows weary/Far from de old folks at home'), its worldwide popularity was such that it was adopted by the state of Florida as the official state song.

Today, visitors to the Stephen Foster State Folk Cultural Center are treated to wildly disparate imagery: on one hand, the center is dedicated to the life and work of a man who spent most of his career writing 'plantation melodies.' On the other, the center itself is host to many fine programs that increase visitors' understanding of black and Indian culture and heritage.

In any event, it's interesting to note that here, in the most southern of southern states, this center is dedicated to the memory of a man who wrote a song of the South from his home in Allegheny, Pennsylvania. It could be worse – 'Oh Susanna!' was written in Cincinnati, Ohio.

The park is open daily 8 am to sunset. It's 15 miles from the town of Live Oak on Hwy 90. Admission is $2 per carload, $1 for pedestrians and cyclists.

ICHETUCKNEE SPRINGS STATE PARK

A day trip to the stunningly clear and blissfully refreshing waters of the hugely and justifiably popular Ichetucknee River should be considered mandatory for any visitor to central Florida (unless you're here on a weekend, when it's so crowded it's just not worth the effort). Ichetucknee Springs State Park (☎ 904-497-2511 for a recording, 904-497-4690 for actual humans) is one of the best places in the state to get out into nature effortlessly, and a good time is had by all, young and old alike.

The Ichetucknee (a name which means 'beaver pond') River is fed by the Ichetucknee Spring group, which consists of nine named springs (including Ichetucknee, Blue Hole, the three springs that make up Mission Springs, Grassy Hole Spring, Millpond Spring, Coffee Spring, and Devil's

Eye). Together these springs produce 233 *million* gallons of pure, sparkling clear water a day, which flow downstream at about 1¼ mph and maintain a constant temperature of 73°F.

The river in this state park is the finest place we know of to sit in an innertube, rubber raft or canoe and lazily float downstream. In addition to that, the opportunities for spotting wildlife here are fantastic – once as we put our tubes in, two river otters lazily flopped around several feet from us, and the whole way down we saw turtles, all kinds of birds, spectacular flora and lots of fish. There are alligators here too, but we didn't see any.

The spring has become so popular in recent years that the park now features regular trams bringing tubers to the river, as well as shuttle service between the north and south entrances to the park. But the Ichetucknee itself remains Florida's most pristine spring-fed river.

The park offers much more than just tubing and canoeing. You can go swimming, snorkeling and diving in some of the springs. And it's worth the trip, too, for the splendid hiking trails and ranger-led interpretive programs. While it is a stunningly diverse park, no camping is permitted on the grounds. But private campgrounds line the access roads leading to the entrances.

Because of the huge numbers of people coming here, and to protect the park's pristine conditions (as well as the sobriety of its guests), the park strictly forbids bringing in *any* alcohol, tobacco, pets, bottles, cans or disposable *anything*. Innertubes can be no larger than 5 feet in diameter. Rangers check bags as tubers board trams and they patrol occasionally; if you have any of the above you can be ejected from the park.

The park limits the number of tubers that can get on the river at the north entrance to 750 per day, though on weekend days it's not uncommon to see a total of 3000 people along the entire river.

Tubing

Floating down the river on a car tire's innertube is a wonderful occupation, but unfortunately it's not as comfortable as it looks. You use truck or very large car innertubes, which you can buy at auto parts stores for about $10 or rent from concessionaires along Hwys 238 and 47 for about $3 (the concessionaires also rent one/two person rafts for $5/10). If you rent the tubes, you needn't return them to the rental place but can leave them at the tube piles at the takeout point near the south entrance when you're finished – the vendors pick them up at the end of the day.

The longest ride possible here begins at the park's **north entrance** and ends at the south entrance. This run takes about three to 3½ hours, depending on how much you clown around on the way down. The north entrance is off the south side of Hwy 238. Drive in (admission for tubers for this run is $4.25 per person, kids under five free) and drop off your party at the upper tube launch. Then head out of the park and make the 7-mile journey to the south entrance. Turn left on Hwy 238, and head to the stop sign. Turn left again and head to the next stop sign. Turn left again and look for the south entrance sign on the left about half a mile past the bridge over the Ichetucknee River. The whole route is very twisty and turny and you'll think you've made a wrong turn but you probably haven't. At the south entrance, leave the car and catch the van shuttle back up to the north entrance to rejoin your party. The north entrance is open for tubing from Memorial Day weekend to Labor Day.

Two other shorter float options are available. Instead of starting from the north entrance, you can start farther downriver at the **Midpoint Tube Launch** (about a two-hour float down to the south entrance) or **Dampier's Landing** (about an hour). For either of these runs, park at the south entrance (which has lockers; free with your own lock or $1 to rent a lock) and either walk over to Dampier's or walk or take a tram to Midpoint (trams run Memorial Day weekend to Labor Day, otherwise it's a 12-minute walk). Admission for tubers at the south entrance is $3.25 for adults, children under five free. The south entrance is open for tubing all year, though it's darn cold in winter.

Canoeing

Canoes can be launched at the north entrance year round. They're available from private concessions around the park for around $20 a day. Ranger-led canoe trips are offered at sunset and sunrise from October to March; call the rangers for more information on specific times. The trips last about two hours and cost $10 per person, with a minimum of two people per canoe. Admission for canoers is $4.25 per person.

Swimming & Diving

For great swimming and spectacular diving, head for the park's designated swimming areas at the Ichetucknee Head Spring or Blue Hole, both reached via the north entrance. These natural pools have depths of from 1 to 20 feet. Admission at the north entrance for swimmers is $3.25 per carload, or $2 per carload if the honor system is in place (in which case you'll place your fee in one of the envelopes provided, slip it into the fee box and put the receipt in your car window).

You can go snorkeling along the river at the north entrance from Memorial Day weekend to Labor Day, and at the south entrance year round; admission prices are the same as for tubing. Certified cave divers are permitted to dive here from October 1 to March 31; the rangers hang onto your C-Card until you're finished with the dive. The cost is $5.35 per diver.

Hiking

The two small trails in the park are both well marked and feature informational signs along the way. The Trestle Point Trail, the smaller of the two and the closest to the trailhead, is a three-quarter-mile trail that passes several interesting sights, including Trestle Point (where trains loaded with phosphate used to cross the river) and an old phosphate mine pit. The longer Pine Ridge Trail, on the east side of Old Rd, is a 2-mile walk through hardwood hammock

that passes sinkholes and another old phosphate pit.

Both trails are accessed through the north entrance. Admission for hikers is $3.25 per carload, $2 when the honor system is in place.

Places to Stay & Eat

The concession at the south entrance offers hot dogs, pretzels, chips and soft drinks and, on weekends only for some reason, hamburgers. It's open the same hours as the park.

Several campgrounds along Hwy 238 all offer essentially the same thing: campsites, a bar/restaurant and quick access to tubing. *Fort Ichetucknee* (☎ 352-497-1928), just west of the intersection of Hwys 47 and 238, seemed as nice as any. The prices advertised were the same at all: $4 per person per night, or $7 per person for sites with water and electric hookups. Nearby on Hwy 27 just west of the intersection of Hwy 47 are a *Taco Bell*, a *pizza place* and a large convenience store; east of the intersection is *Burger Xpress*, with burgers, hot dogs and the like.

Getting There & Away

No public transport is available to or near the park, which is about 40 miles northwest of Gainesville. From downtown Gainesville, take NW 13th St straight north and pick up Hwy 441 (NW 13th becomes 441); take that straight up through High Springs, then take Hwy 27 to Hwy 47 north to Hwy 238 west to the park.

HIGH SPRINGS

Southeast of Ichetucknee Springs, Hwy 27 brings you through the center of the pleasant little town of High Springs, settled in 1883 when the Savannah, Florida and Western railroads ran from Live Oak to Gainesville. The town's **Historic Main St** is a good place to shop for antiques.

Bicycle Outfitters (☎ 904-454-2453), 10 N Main St, rents 21-speed bikes for an average of $20 a day and will arrange three-hour guided bike tours (for groups only) to Itchetucknee or to nearby **O'Leno State Park** for $30 per group plus the rentals. Staff can also help you plan and arrange overnight biking/camping trips throughout the region.

High Springs Campground (☎ 904-454-1688, 24004 NW Old Bellamy Rd) offers cheap camping, and at *Grady House B&B* (☎ 904-454-2206, 420 NW 1st Ave) you'll find nice rooms from $65 a night.

The Great Outdoors Trading Co & Cafe (☎ 904-454-2900, 65 N Main St) is a travel-gear shop and restaurant with offerings such as wonderful soups, couscous, pastas and serious desserts – we had the deep-dish apple pie ($3.50). Lunch specials are $5.95.

STEINHATCHEE
• population 800; time zone EST

This pristine, quiet little fishing village is about an hour southeast of Tallahassee along Florida's 'big bend' section, which is one of the state's most beautiful. Your best bet for seeing this area is to contact Dean Fowler, who runs the Steinhatchee Landing Resort (see below). This wonderful place has duplex cottages with tons of amenities and absolutely excellent service, and they can arrange any number of nature trips throughout the region.

We took a half-hour tootle on the Steinhatchee River with Dean, and on the way we saw hawks, herons, egrets, alligators, raccoons, ducks and pelicans. The glasslike river is incredibly tranquil and beautiful – the trees growing alongside are awesome, with washed-out roots reflecting the strangest shapes in the water. This place really makes you feel that you're getting away from it all.

But remember, this is the countryside, and not only does Steinhatchee look like a redneck haven, in some ways it is – but once you get on the river, nothing else matters.

Places to Stay & Eat
Cottages at the *Steinhatchee Landing Resort* (☎ 352-498-3513) all have screened-in porches, full kitchens, washer/dryers, dishwashers, TVs and VCRs, stereo systems, fireplaces and wood-burning stoves. One-bedroom, two-story houses are $120/135 in winter/summer, two-bedroom houses are $145/165, and three-bedroom houses go for

$235 to $245 in winter and $270 to $280 in summer. Weekly rates are available, and during holidays there is a three-night minimum stay.

On the property, there's badminton, a swimming pool, a playground, a jogging trail, free bicycle and canoe rentals, a spa, a fish pond, walking paths, volleyball, tennis, shuffleboard and archery. There is also a vegetable garden, and guests are welcome to pick anything in it. The resort is a little expensive, but we thought it was well worth the price. See Getting There & Away below for directions on how to get here.

The resort runs trips (with lunch) to Manatee Springs State Park (see below) on the Suwannee River, as well as Steinhatchee River tours and fishing trips.

Steinhatchee Landing Resort also runs a motel, the *Steinhatchee River Inn* (☎ 352-498-4049, 600 Riverside Drive), with rooms for $50 to $60 in low season and $60 to $70 in high season. All rooms have a TV, a coffee-maker and a fridge. There are no phones, but you can make local calls from the office and the pay phone. If someone calls for you long-distance, a staff member will bring you a cordless phone. The rooms upstairs all have full kitchens, and downstairs there are two suites that cost an extra $10 per person.

Sexton's Riverside Motel (☎ 352-498-5005, 301 1st Ave NW) is run by very friendly people who keep their place quite clean and nice. All rooms have full kitchens, cable TV and a queen-size and two single beds (if you need more, rollaways are available). Double rooms are $60.

At Linda Beem's *Lynn-Rich Restaurant* (☎ 352-488-0605, Hwy 51) they do awesome burgers ($5) and onion rings, and artery-clogging breakfasts from $2.50 to $5.

Steinhatchee Landing Restaurant (☎ 352-498-2345) is excellent. Appetizers are from $5.25 to $8.95, and entrees include chicken supreme for $12.95, seafood pasta Alfredo for $13.75 and serious steaks at $16 to $20.

Roy's (☎ 352-498-5000) has a great salad bar, and most seafood dinners are $10.75. It's about a mile west of the Landing.

Getting There & Away

You can only get here by car. From Tallahassee, take Hwy 19 (also called Hwy 19/27 and, later, Hwy 19/98) to the city of Tennille and go west on Hwy 51 for about 8 miles. Go past the horrific collections of mobile homes, and the Landing is on your left.

MANATEE SPRINGS STATE PARK

Every day, 117 million gallons of crystal-clear water gush from the springhead at Manatee Springs State Park (☎ 352-493-6072), 11650 NW 115th St. The spring, in which diving and swimming is permitted, flows through cypress, maple and ash trees before emptying into the Suwannee River and finally into the Gulf of Mexico, about 25 miles downstream. There's an 8½-mile hiking and biking trail, but the best part of this wonderful park is the viewing platform and boardwalk. When we visited, there was a family of manatees swimming just off the platform, and we saw an absolutely adorable baby alligator swimming across the spring run.

There's canoeing along the spring run; canoes are available from the concession for $5 for the first hour, $4 each additional hour (there are discounts if you're camping in the park). There's **camping** here: nice sites cost $10 without electricity, $12 with.

The park is open daily 8 am to sundown. Admission is $3.25 per carload, $1 for pedestrians and cyclists. It's at the end of Hwy 320, off Hwy 98, 6 miles west of Chiefland.

CEDAR KEY

- population 700; time zone EST

Once an important fishing port and the source of the wood for Eagle and Eberhard-Faber pencils – perhaps the most common brands in the USA – the town of Cedar Key was one of Florida's largest. At its heyday in the late 19th century, Cedar Key had the trade-oomph to become the western terminal of Florida's first trans-state railroad. (See the Amelia Island section in the Northeast Florida chapter for more information.)

But the town and port were demolished by a hurricane in 1896; the factory closed and the port never regained its luster. Today, Cedar Key is a pleasant, friendly small town (though it could be in danger of becoming a tourist trap at some point), with some great nearby beaches, good seafood and an impressive museum of local history. The town is not jumping, but it's certainly worth a visit.

Orientation & Information

The Cedar Keys area comprises 100 islands, 12 of which are the Cedar Keys National Wildlife Refuge. Cedar Key is at the southwestern end of Hwy 24, which is 25 miles southwest of Hwy 19/98. The town is very compact, and most of the action centers around the dock, at the southwest end of town. There are three noteworthy annual festivals: the Sidewalk Art Festival (April), the Fourth of July celebration and the October Seafood Festival.

The Cedar Key Chamber of Commerce (☎ 352-543-5600, http://cedarkey.org), on 2nd/Main St, is a good source of local information – though it's only open Monday, Wednesday and Friday 10 am to 1 pm. A better information source is the rangers at the Cedar Key State Museum (see below) or the friendly folks at the Yellow Door Coffeehouse (see Places to Eat).

The post office (☎ 352-543-5477) is at 518 2nd St, and the Cedar Key Bookstore is at 310 2nd St.

Cedar Key State Museum

The Cedar Key State Museum (☎ 352-543-5350), 12231 SW 166th St, is an excellent collection of local and regional historical displays and the collections of St Clair Whitman, who arrived in the area in 1882 at the age of 14 and seemed to collect everything he saw. Displays include insects, butterflies, glass, sea glass, bottles, and what's billed as the largest seashell collection in Florida (this last claim may be challenged by the Bailey Matthews Shell Museum in Sanibel; see the Southwest Florida chapter). The museum is open Thursday to Monday 9 am to 5 pm. Admission is $1 for adults, free for children under six.

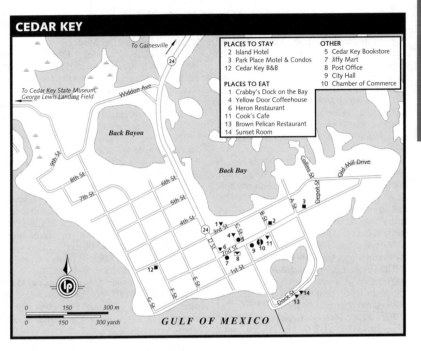

CEDAR KEY

To Gainesville

To Cedar Key State Museum,
George Lewis Landing Field

Widdon Ave

Back Bayou

Back Bay

Collins St

Old Mill Drive

Depot St

9th St.
8th St.
7th St.
6th St.
5th St.
4th St.
3rd St.
2nd St.
1st St.
A St.

12

GULF OF MEXICO

0   150   300 m
0   150   300 yards

PLACES TO STAY
2 Island Hotel
3 Park Place Motel & Condos
12 Cedar Key B&B

PLACES TO EAT
1 Crabby's Dock on the Bay
4 Yellow Door Coffeehouse
6 Heron Restaurant
11 Cook's Cafe
13 Brown Pelican Restaurant
14 Sunset Room

OTHER
5 Cedar Key Bookstore
7 Jiffy Mart
8 Post Office
9 City Hall
10 Chamber of Commerce

Cedar Keys National Wildlife Refuge

This wildlife refuge (☎ 352-493-0238) is on 12 islands in the Gulf of Mexico, about 5 miles from Cedar Key. Established as a breeding ground for colonial birds, today the refuge – which is home to 50,000 birds and 12 species of reptiles – is closed to the public except by advance arrangement by academics and researchers. Except for Seahorse Key, though, the refuge's beaches are open to the public during daylight hours. Seahorse Key, including a 300-foot buffer zone around the island, is closed to all public entry from March 1 to June 30.

The Cedar Key Lighthouse, which no longer functions, is on Seahorse Key. It's used extensively by the University of Florida for research and is generally closed to the public.

The keys can be accessed only by boat, and shallow water and mud flats make them tough to get to. You can contact the rangers' office or Wild Florida Adventures or Island Hopper (see below) for more information about exploring the area.

Organized Tours

We hear only good things about Wild Florida Adventures (☎ 850-352-2741, fax 850-528-2743), which conducts organized kayak tours of the entire area. Tour prices include the boat, paddles, life vests, drinking water and snacks for $45. The four-hour tours run twice a day from October 16 to May 14; there's also a morning trip from May 15 to October 15. You can request a brochure from Jeff and Renee Ripple, PO Box 142613, Gainesville, FL 32614-2613.

Island Hopper (☎ 352-543-5904) runs various pontoon boat trips throughout the region, and rents skiffs as well; call for price information.

Places to Stay

There is a very friendly campground in **Sunset Isle Park** (☎ *352-543-5375*), on Hwy 24 a mile west of the first bridge from the mainland on the north side of the street. Sites for two people in tent or RV are $12, including water and electric hookups.

The **Faraway Inn** (☎ *352-543-5330, at 3rd and G Sts*), on the site of the Eagle pencil mill, has double rooms from $40 to $75; the price includes use of bicycles, canoes and paddle boats.

The **Island Hotel** (☎ *352-543-5111, 224 2nd St at B St*) was once the best bet in town, but it's under new ownership. Rooms here range from $75 to $95 year round. At the restaurant, everything seemed a bit pricey, and when we asked to sit down we were curtly told in a low-rent English accent that we'd need to wait half an hour (even though the dining room was only half full).

The lovely **Cedar Key B&B** (☎ *352-543-9000, F and 3rd Sts*) is probably the best option in town: beautiful grounds, friendly owners and rooms from $65 to $115.

Park Place Motel & Condos (☎ *352-543-5737, 800-868-7963, 211 2nd St*) has motel rooms for $70 Sunday to Thursday and $75 to $85 on Friday and Saturday.

Places to Eat

The **Jiffy Mart** (*2nd St between D and C Sts*) is the town's convenience store, and most everything you'd want – if you're staying in a condo or motel room with kitchen – is at the Jiffy.

The friendly **Cook's Cafe**, next to the Chamber of Commerce, is very good at breakfast (lots of specials under $5).

Crabby's Dock on the Bay (*on Back Bay at 3rd and C Sts*) is a great seafood shack serving steamed crabs on newspaper – it's all local seafood, and plates run from $6 to $13. It's open December to May.

Other seafood is along Dock St: the **Brown Pelican Restaurant** (☎ *352-543-5428*) does a good soft-shell crab for $16.95. Nearby, the **Sunset Room** is – surprise, surprise – a good place to watch the sunset, and we liked its burgers. It also has very good soup and a nice bar.

The **Heron Restaurant** (☎ *352-543-5666, on 2nd St at D St*) is a pleasant bistro with live entertainment (like acoustic guitar on Friday and Saturday). Seafood jambalaya is $8.95, shrimp sautee $9.95.

We hear good things about the **Island Room** (☎ *352-543-6520*), on the ground level of the Cedar Cove Beach & Yacht Club, an upscale place that does main dishes like fettuccine Alfredo ($12.95), crab cakes and New York sirloin ($18.95). It also offers a Sunday brunch ($4.95 to $9.95).

The **Yellow Door Coffeehouse** (☎ *352-543-8008, 511 2nd St*) is run by some very nice and helpful folks, and they even make great coffee. Put a pin on the map showing where you're from.

Getting There & Away

There is no public transport to the area. Driving, take Hwy 19/98 or I-75 to Hwy 24 and follow it southwest to the bitter end. The area is very popular with private pilots, who land at George Lewis Landing Field, a grass strip on the island of Cedar Key with no aviation services (parking is free). Pilots: the local taxi driver, Lester Ridgeway, monitors CTAF (at press time it was 122.9, but check an air chart before arrival) and will pick you up. The five-minute ride from the airfield costs 'whatever you think is fair.'

Acknowledgments

Many thanks to the travelers who used the last edition and wrote to us with helpful hints, useful advice and anecdotes:

Wouter Adamse, Marco Akermann, John Allen, David Aronstein, Guy Berthiaume, Jette Borgstrøm, William Botts, SC Bradford, Jason Brome, JJ Bronson, Steve Brookwell, Lars Bruun Christensen & Krista Vanggaard, Jacob R Burger, Robin & Claire Caron, Phoebe Cartwright, Jon Casey, Victor Cerulli, Joel Charles, MJ Cheesbrough, Pamela Clapp, Melanie Copland, Carlos da Costa Coelho, Jay Davidson, A de Vries, Mitchell Denker, Andrew Dick, Ingo Dirnstorfer, G Dubin, Millie Ducker, Mark Foley, Shenandoah Gale, Geronimo Garcia, Lizette Gecel, Jan Gol Goldstein, Frank Gransee, DW Gray, Lori Green, Bob Grosse, Tanja Halme, Susan Henderson, Horst Hohenboeken, Gary Hudoff, Curt James, Karen Jensen, Glenn Joblin, Bob Kunst, Mary Latham, Terri Lituchy, Robert Magill, A McLaren, Leonardo Moraes Menezes, Tatiana Menezes, Debby Nieuwenhuizen, Eileen O Neill, David Pinder, Paul Quispel, Barbara Raleigh, Charles Roemer, Robert C Roney, Lisa Salvato, Marcel Sauer, Patrica Schubel, Margaret Sherman, Andrew V Smith, Pascal Sommacal, Philip Souham, Stefan Stoffels, John WP Storck, Ralf Südfeld, Margaret Terway, Madi Thomas, Adam David Trattles, Trond Ivar Hegge & Vnke Walberg, Nick Wayth, Matthias Wevelsiep, Nathan C Wheeler, Eric Wichems, Tanya Withers, Jalonda Woensdregt and Achim Zeilmann

Lonely Planet Guides by Region

L onely Planet is known worldwide for publishing practical, reliable and no-nonsense travel information in our guides and on our Web site. The Lonely Planet list covers just about every accessible part of the world. Currently there are 16 series: Travel guides, Shoestring guides, Condensed guides, Phrasebooks, Read This First, Healthy Travel, Walking guides, Cycling guides, Watching Wildlife guides, Pisces Diving & Snorkeling guides, City Maps, Road Atlases, Out to Eat, World Food, Journeys travel literature and Pictorials.

AFRICA Africa on a shoestring • Botswana • Cairo • Cairo City Map • Cape Town • Cape Town City Map • East Africa • Egypt • Egyptian Arabic phrasebook • Ethiopia, Eritrea & Djibouti • Ethiopian Amharic phrasebook • The Gambia & Senegal • Healthy Travel Africa • Kenya • Malawi • Morocco • Moroccan Arabic phrasebook • Mozambique • Namibia • Read This First: Africa • South Africa, Lesotho & Swaziland • Southern Africa • Southern Africa Road Atlas • Swahili phrasebook • Tanzania, Zanzibar & Pemba • Trekking in East Africa • Tunisia • Watching Wildlife East Africa • Watching Wildlife Southern Africa • West Africa • World Food Morocco • Zambia • Zimbabwe, Botswana & Namibia
Travel Literature: Mali Blues: Traveling to an African Beat • The Rainbird: A Central African Journey • Songs to an African Sunset: A Zimbabwean Story

AUSTRALIA & THE PACIFIC Aboriginal Australia & the Torres Strait Islands •Auckland • Australia • Australian phrasebook • Australia Road Atlas • Cycling Australia • Cycling New Zealand • Fiji • Fijian phrasebook • Healthy Travel Australia, NZ & the Pacific • Islands of Australia's Great Barrier Reef • Melbourne • Melbourne City Map • Micronesia • New Caledonia • New South Wales • New Zealand • Northern Territory • Outback Australia • Out to Eat – Melbourne • Out to Eat – Sydney • Papua New Guinea • Pidgin phrasebook • Queensland • Rarotonga & the Cook Islands • Samoa • Solomon Islands • South Australia • South Pacific • South Pacific phrasebook • Sydney • Sydney City Map • Sydney Condensed • Tahiti & French Polynesia • Tasmania • Tonga • Tramping in New Zealand • Vanuatu • Victoria • Walking in Australia • Watching Wildlife Australia • Western Australia
Travel Literature: Islands in the Clouds: Travels in the Highlands of New Guinea • Kiwi Tracks: A New Zealand Journey • Sean & David's Long Drive

CENTRAL AMERICA & THE CARIBBEAN Bahamas, Turks & Caicos • Baja California • Belize, Guatemala & Yucatán • Bermuda • Central America on a shoestring • Costa Rica • Costa Rica Spanish phrasebook • Cuba • Cycling Cuba • Dominican Republic & Haiti • Eastern Caribbean • Guatemala • Havana • Healthy Travel Central & South America • Jamaica • Mexico • Mexico City • Panama • Puerto Rico • Read This First: Central & South America • Virgin Islands • World Food Caribbean • World Food Mexico • Yucatán
Travel Literature: Green Dreams: Travels in Central America

EUROPE Amsterdam • Amsterdam City Map • Amsterdam Condensed • Andalucía • Athens • Austria • Baltic States phrasebook • Barcelona • Barcelona City Map • Belgium & Luxembourg • Berlin • Berlin City Map • Britain • British phrasebook • Brussels, Bruges & Antwerp • Brussels City Map • Budapest • Budapest City Map • Canary Islands • Catalunya & the Costa Brava • Central Europe • Central Europe phrasebook • Copenhagen • Corfu & the Ionians • Corsica • Crete • Crete Condensed • Croatia • Cycling Britain • Cycling France • Cyprus • Czech & Slovak Republics • Czech phrasebook • Denmark • Dublin • Dublin City Map • Dublin Condensed • Eastern Europe • Eastern Europe phrasebook • Edinburgh • Edinburgh City Map • England • Estonia, Latvia & Lithuania • Europe on a shoestring • Europe phrasebook • Finland • Florence • Florence City Map • France • Frankfurt City Map • Frankfurt Condensed • French phrasebook • Georgia, Armenia & Azerbaijan • Germany • German phrasebook • Greece • Greek Islands • Greek phrasebook • Hungary • Iceland, Greenland & the Faroe Islands • Ireland • Italian phrasebook • Italy • Kraków • Lisbon • The Loire • London • London City Map • London Condensed • Madrid • Madrid City Map • Malta • Mediterranean Europe • Milan, Turin & Genoa • Moscow • Munich • Netherlands • Normandy • Norway • Out to Eat – London • Out to Eat – Paris • Paris • Paris City Map • Paris Condensed • Poland • Polish phrasebook • Portugal • Portuguese phrasebook • Prague • Prague City Map • Provence & the Côte d'Azur • Read This First: Europe • Rhodes & the Dodecanese • Romania & Moldova • Rome • Rome City Map • Rome Condensed • Russia, Ukraine & Belarus • Russian phrasebook • Scandinavian & Baltic Europe • Scandinavian phrasebook • Scotland • Sicily • Slovenia • South-West France • Spain • Spanish phrasebook • Stockholm • St Petersburg • St Petersburg City Map • Sweden • Switzerland • Tuscany • Ukrainian phrasebook • Venice • Vienna • Wales • Walking in Britain • Walking in France • Walking in Ireland • Walking in Italy • Walking in Scotland • Walking in Spain • Walking in Switzerland • Western Europe • World Food France • World Food Greece • World Food Ireland • World Food Italy • World Food Spain **Travel Literature:** After Yugoslavia • Love and War in the Apennines • The Olive Grove: Travels in Greece • On the Shores of the Mediterranean • Round Ireland in Low Gear • A Small Place in Italy

Lonely Planet Mail Order

Lonely Planet products are distributed worldwide. They are also available by mail order from Lonely Planet, so if you have difficulty finding a title please write to us. North and South American residents should write to 150 Linden St, Oakland, CA 94607, USA; European and African residents should write to 10a Spring Place, London NW5 3BH, UK; and residents of other countries to Locked Bag 1, Footscray, Victoria 3011, Australia.

INDIAN SUBCONTINENT & THE INDIAN OCEAN Bangladesh • Bengali phrasebook • Bhutan • Delhi • Goa • Healthy Travel Asia & India • Hindi & Urdu phrasebook • India • India & Bangladesh City Map • Indian Himalaya • Karakoram Highway • Kathmandu City Map • Kerala • Madagascar • Maldives • Mauritius, Réunion & Seychelles • Mumbai (Bombay) • Nepal • Nepali phrasebook • North India • Pakistan • Rajasthan • Read This First: Asia & India • South India • Sri Lanka • Sri Lanka phrasebook • Tibet • Tibetan phrasebook • Trekking in the Indian Himalaya • Trekking in the Karakoram & Hindukush • Trekking in the Nepal Himalaya • World Food India **Travel Literature:** The Age of Kali: Indian Travels and Encounters • Hello Goodnight: A Life of Goa • In Rajasthan • Maverick in Madagascar • A Season in Heaven: True Tales from the Road to Kathmandu • Shopping for Buddhas • A Short Walk in the Hindu Kush • Slowly Down the Ganges

MIDDLE EAST & CENTRAL ASIA Bahrain, Kuwait & Qatar • Central Asia • Central Asia phrasebook • Dubai • Farsi (Persian) phrasebook • Hebrew phrasebook • Iran • Israel & the Palestinian Territories • Istanbul • Istanbul City Map • Istanbul to Cairo • Istanbul to Kathmandu • Jerusalem • Jerusalem City Map • Jordan • Lebanon • Middle East • Oman & the United Arab Emirates • Syria • Turkey • Turkish phrasebook • World Food Turkey • Yemen **Travel Literature:** Black on Black: Iran Revisited • Breaking Ranks: Turbulent Travels in the Promised Land • The Gates of Damascus • Kingdom of the Film Stars: Journey into Jordan

NORTH AMERICA Alaska • Boston • Boston City Map • Boston Condensed • British Columbia • California & Nevada • California Condensed • Canada • Chicago • Chicago City Map • Chicago Condensed • Florida • Georgia & the Carolinas • Great Lakes • Hawaii • Hiking in Alaska • Hiking in the USA • Honolulu & Oahu City Map • Las Vegas • Los Angeles • Los Angeles City Map • Louisiana & the Deep South • Miami • Miami City Map • Montreal • New England • New Orleans • New Orleans City Map • New York City • New York City City Map • New York City Condensed • New York, New Jersey & Pennsylvania • Oahu • Out to Eat – San Francisco • Pacific Northwest • Rocky Mountains • San Diego & Tijuana • San Francisco • San Francisco City Map • Seattle • Seattle City Map • Southwest • Texas • Toronto • USA • USA phrasebook • Vancouver • Vancouver City Map • Virginia & the Capital Region • Washington, DC • Washington, DC City Map • World Food New Orleans **Travel Literature:** Caught Inside: A Surfer's Year on the California Coast • Drive Thru America

NORTH-EAST ASIA Beijing • Beijing City Map • Cantonese phrasebook • China • Hiking in Japan • Hong Kong & Macau • Hong Kong City Map • Hong Kong Condensed • Japan • Japanese phrasebook • Korea • Korean phrasebook • Kyoto • Mandarin phrasebook • Mongolia • Mongolian phrasebook • Seoul • Shanghai • South-West China • Taiwan • Tokyo • Tokyo Condensed • World Food Hong Kong • World Food Japan **Travel Literature:** In Xanadu: A Quest • Lost Japan

SOUTH AMERICA Argentina, Uruguay & Paraguay • Bolivia • Brazil • Brazilian phrasebook • Buenos Aires • Buenos Aires City Map • Chile & Easter Island • Colombia • Ecuador & the Galapagos Islands • Healthy Travel Central & South America • Latin American Spanish phrasebook • Peru • Quechua phrasebook • Read This First: Central & South America • Rio de Janeiro • Rio de Janeiro City Map • Santiago de Chile • South America on a shoestring • Trekking in the Patagonian Andes • Venezuela **Travel Literature:** Full Circle: A South American Journey

SOUTH-EAST ASIA Bali & Lombok • Bangkok • Bangkok City Map • Burmese phrasebook • Cambodia • Cycling Vietnam, Laos & Cambodia • East Timor phrasebook • Hanoi • Healthy Travel Asia & India • Hill Tribes phrasebook • Ho Chi Minh City (Saigon) • Indonesia • Indonesian phrasebook • Indonesia's Eastern Islands • Java • Lao phrasebook • Laos • Malay phrasebook • Malaysia, Singapore & Brunei • Myanmar (Burma) • Philippines • Pilipino (Tagalog) phrasebook • Read This First: Asia & India • Singapore • Singapore City Map • South-East Asia on a shoestring • South-East Asia phrasebook • Thailand • Thailand's Islands & Beaches • Thailand, Vietnam, Laos & Cambodia Road Atlas • Thai phrasebook • Vietnam • Vietnamese phrasebook • World Food Indonesia • World Food Thailand • World Food Vietnam

ALSO AVAILABLE: Antarctica • The Arctic • The Blue Man: Tales of Travel, Love and Coffee • Brief Encounters: Stories of Love, Sex & Travel • Buddhist Stupas in Asia: The Shape of Perfection • Chasing Rickshaws • The Last Grain Race • Lonely Planet … On the Edge: Adventurous Escapades from Around the World • Lonely Planet Unpacked • Lonely Planet Unpacked Again • Not the Only Planet: Science Fiction Travel Stories • Ports of Call: A Journey by Sea • Sacred India • Travel Photography: A Guide to Taking Better Pictures • Travel with Children • Tuvalu: Portrait of an Island Nation

Index

Bold indicates maps.

Bold indicates maps.

Bold indicates maps.

Boxed Text

MAP LEGEND

BOUNDARIES

- International
- State
- County

HYDROGRAPHY

- Water
- Coastline
- Beach
- River, Waterfall
- Swamp, Spring

ROUTES & TRANSPORT

- Freeway
- Toll Freeway
- Primary Road
- Secondary Road
- Tertiary Road
- Unpaved Road
- Pedestrian Mall
- Trail
- Walking Tour
- Ferry Route
- Railway, Train Station
- Mass Transit Line & Station

ROUTE SHIELDS

- 95 Interstate Freeway
- 80 State Highway
- 1 US Highway
- 25 County Road

AREA FEATURES

- Building
- Cemetery
- Forest
- Golf Course
- Park
- Plaza
- Reservation

MAP SYMBOLS

- ✪ NATIONAL CAPITAL
- ◉ State, Provincial Capital
- ● LARGE CITY
- ● Medium City
- ● Small City
- ● Town, Village
- ○ Point of Interest
- ■ Place to Stay
- ▲ Campground
- ⛺ RV Park
- ▼ Place to Eat
- 🍺 Bar (Place to Drink)
- ☕ Café

- ✈ Airfield
- ✈ Airport
- ∴ Archaeological Site, Ruins
- 🏦 Bank
- ✕ Battlefield
- Beach
- ⋈ Border Crossing
- Bus Depot, Bus Stop
- Cathedral
- Cave
- ✝ Church
- Dive Site
- Embassy
- Fish Hatchery
- Footbridge
- Garden
- Gas Station
- Hospital, Clinic
- Information
- Lighthouse
- Lookout

- Monument
- Mosque
- ▲ Mountain
- 🏛 Museum
- Observatory
- ← One-Way Street
- ✦ Park
- P Parking
-) (Pass
- Picnic Area
- ★ Police Station
- Pool
- Post Office
- Public Toilet
- Shopping Mall
- Stately Home
- ✿ Synagogue
- Tomb
- Trailhead
- Winery
- Zoo

Note: Not all symbols displayed above appear in this book.

LONELY PLANET OFFICES

Australia
Locked Bag 1, Footscray, Victoria 3011
☎ 03 8379 8000 fax 03 8379 8111
email talk2us@lonelyplanet.com.au

USA
150 Linden Street, Oakland, California 94607
☎ 510 893 8555, TOLL FREE 800 275 8555
fax 510 893 8572
email info@lonelyplanet.com

UK
10A Spring Place, London NW5 3BH
☎ 020 7428 4800 fax 020 7428 4828
email go@lonelyplanet.co.uk

France
1 rue du Dahomey, 75011 Paris
☎ 01 55 25 33 00 fax 01 55 25 33 01
email: bip@lonelyplanet.com
www.lonelyplanet.fr

World Wide Web: www.lonelyplanet.com *or* AOL keyword: lp
Lonely Planet Images: lpi@lonelyplanet.com.au